THE OXFORD COMPANION TO JAZZ

THE OXFORD COMPANION TO

Jazz

EDITED BY

Bill Kirchner

OXFORD
UNIVERSITY PRESS

2000

OXFORD
UNIVERSITY PRESS

Oxford   New York
Athens   Auckland   Bangkok   Bogotá   Buenos Aires   Calcutta
Cape Town   Chennai   Dar es Salaam   Delhi   Florence   Hong Kong
Istanbul   Karachi   Kuala Lumpur   Madrid   Melbourne   Mexico
City   Mumbai   Nairobi   Paris   São Paulo   Shanghai   Singapore
Taipei   Tokyo   Toronto   Warsaw

and associated companies in
Berlin   Ibadan

Published by Oxford University Press, Inc.
198 Madison Avenue, New York, New York 10016

Oxford is a registered trademark of Oxford University Press

Library of Congress Cataloguing-in-Publication Data
The Oxford companion to jazz / [edited by] Bill Kirchner.
p. cm.
Includes bibliographical references (p.) and index.
ISBN 0-19-512510-X
1. Jazz—History and criticism. I. Kirchner, Bill.
ML3507.J32 2000   781.65'09—dc21   99-088598

9 8 7 6 5 4 3 2 1
Printed in the United States of America
on acid-free paper

Contents

Preface

My part in this book began in the fall of 1996, when Sheldon Meyer, then vice president of editorial at Oxford University Press, asked me to lunch. Sheldon, whose four-decade association with Oxford is legendary in the publishing field (he's one of the great editors and has been responsible for bringing a staggering number of outstanding jazz books, among others, into print), had an idea for a jazz volume different from any other. It would be an adjunct to the popular and influential *Oxford Companion* series, and it would contain specially commissioned essays on jazz—in all of its multifarious aspects—by a large number of the best authorities in the field. Sheldon had asked Dan Morgenstern, director of the Institute of Jazz Studies at Rutgers University and long respected as one of the finest writers on the subject, for a recommendation for someone to edit such a book. Dan had suggested me.

Gulp. I told Sheldon that I would think about his offer carefully— he knows great luncheon places, by the way—but my initial internal reaction was "No way." The responsibility of conceiving and supervising such a project was daunting, to say the least. But the more I thought about it, the more intriguing the prospect became. We agreed on terms, and off I went on a unique journey.

I began by compiling an extensive list of possible topics, and this became—after helpful suggestions from Sheldon, Dan, and author Gary Giddins—the basis of *The Oxford Companion to Jazz*. (The pieces here, by the way, are somewhat longer than is typical of other volumes in the *Companion* series.) Next, deciding on whom to ask to write the essays. I've been involved in jazz most of my life, and if I might flatter myself, I have a pretty good idea of who the movers and shakers in the field are: musicians, writers, producers, educators, broadcasters, record-industry people, and others. And when I don't know something, I generally know who can tell me what I need to learn. So the list of potential contributors came quite easily. I knew many of these persons already, and that made soliciting contributions less of a chore than it might otherwise have been. In a few cases, I asked Lewis Porter and Richard M. Sudhalter—both of whom have essays herein—for recommendations on writers, and they came through unfailingly.

I'm happy to report that surprisingly few folks whom I approached turned me down. In the almost two years it took to get these pieces delivered from all over the world, there were a handful of dropouts, and in all cases I was able to find replacements of comparable quality. My only regret is that I was not able to offer topics to all of the writers I wanted to include. If there are authors you think should be represented here who aren't, chances are good that either they declined to write a piece, or another equally qualified person got the nod for a particular topic. Such is life.

So, you may be wondering, what's it like to deal with fifty-nine experts with fifty-nine sets of work habits? Most interesting and varied, I reply diplomatically. Suffice it to say that I didn't, to the best of my knowledge, lose any friends in the course of this work, and I made quite a few new ones. My job encompassed a variety of roles: editor, friend, cheerleader, psychologist, and occasionally, pain-in-the-derrière. There were times when I internalized the late cartoonist-pundit Al Capp's self-description: an expert on nothing with opinions on everything. But I persevered.

Whether or not I triumphed is, of course, for you, the reader, to decide. But I feel satisfied that I did a job well worth doing to the best of my ability. Aside from all of the aforementioned gentlemen—most of all Sheldon Meyer, a consistent provider of sage counsel and encouragement—I'd like to thank Penelope Anderson, Joellyn Ausanka, and Susan Day of Oxford for their ceaseless expertise and good cheer; copy editor India Cooper and indexer Judith Hancock for their usual sterling work; and my wife Judy, whose support went well beyond the call of marital duty. And lest we forget, the inventor of e-mail, without whose invention this book would not have been possible.

This book is dedicated to the memory of William J. Kirchner (1923–1999).

THE OXFORD COMPANION TO JAZZ

Introduction

I think there are only three things that America will
be known for two thousand years from now: the
Constitution, jazz music, and baseball, the three
most beautifully designed things this country ever
produced.
  ••• *Gerald Early, author and cultural historian*

Jazz is not a "what," it's a "how," and if you do
things according to the "how" of jazz, it's jazz.
  ••• *Bill Evans, pianist and composer*

The word "jazz" means to me "no category."
  ••• *Wayne Shorter, saxophonist and composer*

he above quotes—the first from one of this volume's
fifty-nine contributors, and the others from two of the
most important jazz musicians of the past half century—
tell us a great deal about why this book exists, and what
makes jazz the unique and vitally important music that
it is.

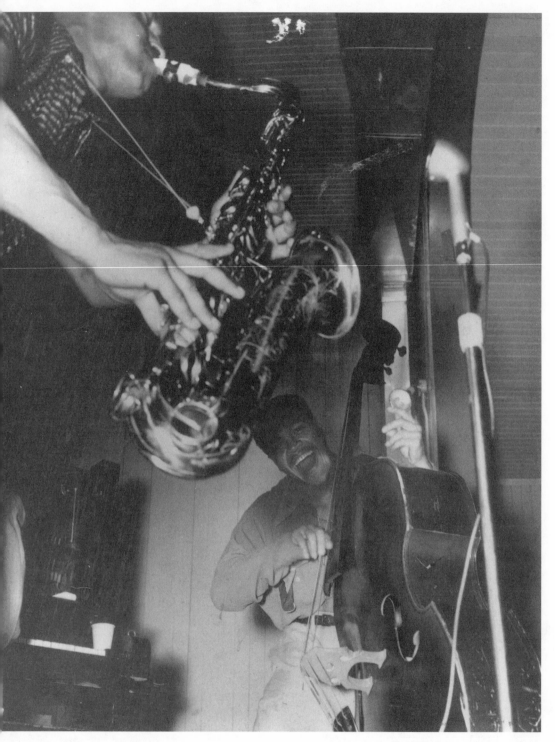

Photo: George P. Kahn.

Throughout the—roughly speaking—century-old history of jazz, there have been numerous attempts to "define" what the music is or isn't. None of these has ever proven successful or widely accepted, and invariably they tell us much more about the tastes, prejudices, and limitations of the formulators than they do about the music. You'll find no such attempts here.

Jazz has also been called "America's classical music"—a description that I disagree with. America's classical music is classical music: the works of Ives, Copland, Barber, Schuman, et al. Western classical music comes from an aesthetic with its own set of ground rules, and America's contributions to it have, for the most part, been created within that framework. One of the glories of jazz is that it has become an art music with its own rules and aesthetic, and as Wayne Shorter implies, even those rules are meant to be challenged, and often broken, rather than reverently adhered to. As is typical of the black American culture from which it emerged, jazz is a music of healthy defiance.

Jazz is also a music of inclusion, rather than exclusion. From its inception, jazz has been a melting pot of influences and techniques that have come from an immense variety of sources. Multicultural long before that term became fashionable, it has never been more so than now, played and listened to in most parts of the world. Though some might argue with Gerald Early's contention that jazz, the Constitution, and baseball are the only things for which America ultimately will be remembered, he does have an indisputable point about the vast influence of the three. Moreover, one could make a case that jazz has had a stronger worldwide impact than either the Constitution or baseball. Jazz is a force in numerous parts of the world where baseball is ignored, and as Mike Zwerin points out in his essay on European jazz, it often has endured in defiance—that term, once again—of totalitarian governments that were anything but sympathetic to the ideals of the U.S. Constitution.

If, as Bill Evans asserted, jazz is a "how" rather than a "what," then perhaps this book can be best described as a "book of hows." Specifically, how the music came into being, how it grew by leaps and bounds, how its greatest practitioners have made it what it is today, how it flourishes in a multiplicity of styles, how it has had a vital impact on other aspects of twentieth-century culture, how it continues to evolve, and more. That isn't to say that our contributors always agree on all of these issues. For example, you need examine only the first two essays to discover that two eminent scholars, Samuel

A. Floyd Jr. and William H. Youngren, have often differing viewpoints on the roots of the music. For me, such differences are part of the stimulation of this book.

About the contributors. As I mentioned, there are fifty-nine of them, and they are among the finest musicians, scholars, and critics in jazz at the end of the twentieth century. Fully half are musicians who are currently (or in a few cases, formerly) working professionals. Without in the least intending to slight the expertise of the non-musicians among our contributors, I view the high percentage of musician-authors here as a definite coup. It gives a "view from the inside" that makes this book all the more valuable. In fact, four of the essayists—Bill Crow, Dick Katz, Max Morath, and Randy Sandke—deserve to be mentioned in the pieces they wrote.

When I commissioned these essays, many of the writers asked, "Who is the intended audience for this book?" "Anyone," I replied, "from novices just coming to the music for the first time to seasoned listeners who know a great deal." This provided the authors with an additional challenge—aside from that of severely disciplining themselves in order to fit as much information as comfortably possible into a short format. A number complained mightily, and I was not unsympathetic, but I believe that all of our contributors have emerged triumphant from their ordeals. You, the reader, are the beneficiary. Whether you know a little or a lot about jazz, you'll know a great deal more after reading *The Oxford Companion to Jazz*. Read it from beginning to end, or dip into it at any point. But most of all, enjoy it. And the music.

African Roots of Jazz

Samuel A. Floyd Jr.

frican-American musical practices in the United States cannot be traced directly to specific populations in Africa with any degree of certainty. But it is possible to document certain general practices that are common to music in Africa and to black music in the United States and widespread in both. Thus we can draw reasonable conclusions about possible relationships between musical practices in Africa and those among jazz musicians in the United States. It can be hypothesized, for example, and determined to a high degree of certainty, that particular musical tendencies were brought with Africans to the New World, preserved within and outside the dancing ring of slave culture, and spread throughout African-derived populations in the United States, eventually becoming an integral part of the music we now know as jazz.

In traditional Africa, spiritual divinities were a part of the daily lives of entire societies. Known among the Yoruba as *orisha* and in other cultures variously as *abosom* (Ashanti), *vodun* (Fon), and *alose* (Ibo), these gods influenced the conduct of human affairs, arbitrarily created ill or good will, helped or hindered individuals and the group, informed or limited the knowledge of populations, and interacted

Calabash drummer at the court of Moro Naba, Ouagadougou, Upper Volta, c. 1950. Photo: Arthur S. Alberts. Courtesy of the Institute of Jazz Studies, Rutgers University.

with each other. Among the Yoruba's other numerous deities, for example, Olodumare was senior, known as God, creator of the universe; Orulna was the diviner and symbol of wisdom; Ochosi was the divine hunter; and Esu (also called Eshu, Legba, Esu-Elegbara, Eshu Elleguá) was an inveterate prankster who occasionally caused havoc in the lives of believers. For traditional Africans, these divinities dwelled in the material and the nonmaterial (or spirit) worlds and were an essential part of ritual in the societies that believed in them.

In sacred rituals, these deities mount and take charge of human hosts who dance to the songs and rhythms that the divinities are said to own, imitating their character and conduct. Thus, in highly stylized and controlled theatrics, the hosts become mediums who mime the character of their riders. (Africans say that it is not the hosts who do the dancing but the divinities themselves.) In these rituals, possession is brought on by drumming, chanting, singing, and persistent and energetic dance in the form of mass dancing, team dancing, small-group dancing (two, three, or four people), and ring dancing. In many African societies, this dancing took place in the dance ring—symbol of community, solidarity, affirmation, and catharsis—and also in formations that were linear, circular, semicircular, or serpentine.

A drawing in T. Edward Bowdich's book *Mission from Cape Coast Castle to Ashantee* shows a marching band in Africa in ritual ceremony, with the author explaining that the participants presented themselves to the king, formed and moved around a circle to the music of more than forty drums, and made salutes to umbrellas. Francis Bebey, in his *African Music: A People's Art*, discusses funeral processions in which the music could be celebratory, with sounding trumpets and drums showing vigorous respect for the deceased. In some of the burial ceremonies themselves, trickster tales are told; the dead, who are susceptible to humor and excitement, are said to like such stories. In at least one country, Suriname, versions of the Anansi trickster tale, for example, were told during burial ceremonies to amuse the spirit of the deceased.

The significance of these tales to a discussion of African influences on jazz music lies in the fact that they contain features that are shared with other African performance traditions: indirection, argument, and opposition, as well as "overlap, apart-playing, and interlock," as Roger Abrahams points out in his *African Folktales: Traditional Stories of the Black World*. These oral practices would come to be as effective in jazz music as they are in vocal narrative.

In processions and in the line and ring dances of African burial and other stationary ceremonies, the rhythms of the music were accompanied by shoulder and head movements, foot stamping, hand clapping, and vocal shouts that animated the performances. Among the Akan, young children imitated the steps and movements of adult dancers, moving "along the fringes of the ring and behind it," according to the musicologist J. H. Kwabena Nketia in his *Drumming in Akan Communities* (1963, 165–66). By observing and studying such activities, we have come to better understand the nature of "shouting" in African-American ring ritual and its derivatives. Shouting has implications for the origin of the second line of New Orleans jazz funerals and for the origin and nature of scat singing in early and later jazz music—for example, Louis Armstrong's vocal imitations of instrumental melodic improvisations, as in his "Heebie Jeebies" of 1926, and the riffing "calls" of Cab Calloway's *Hi-de-hi-de-hos*.

The rhythmic elements of African-American music were derived from African time-line practices in which the instruments of ensembles play multilinear rhythms that yield characteristic interlocking, cross-rhythmic (two or more contrasting rhythms played simultaneously), and polyrhythmic (two or more rhythms played simultaneously) musical configurations. Performed most frequently by a clapperless bell called the *gankogui*, steady asymmetrical (e.g., 3:2 rhythmic relationships) background rhythms are sounded continuously through dance performances. Gerhard Kubik, in his article entitled "Analogies and Differences in African-American Musical Culture Across the Hemisphere: Interpretive Models and Research," which appeared in volume 18 of *Black Music Research Journal*, has given examples of such background rhythms or time-lines (see page 11).

In African-American music, especially in jazz, time-lines became symmetrical (e.g., 2:2 rhythmic relationships) rather than asymmetrical (in the form of various underlying divisive pulses, riffs, and ostinati) and, in most cases, less persistent and less consistent. Nevertheless, the African time-line concept, in attenuated and modified form, virtually defines the rhythmic basis of African-American vernacular music and jazz. Together, the bell and the other instruments of African ensembles, with their resulting multilinear rhythms, comprise what Nketia, in *The Music of Africa*, has called "little tunes."

Regarding tunes in the form of singing, Alan Lomax, in his article entitled "Africanisms in New World Music" (which can be found in *The Haitian Potential*, edited by Vera Rubin and Richard P. Schaedel), demonstrated that across black Africa there exists an "extraor-

Cycle number	Pattern structure	Notation	Predominant geographical distribution
8	3+5	[x x • x • x x •]	universal
12	5+7	[x • x x • x • x • x x •]	Guinea coast, West Central Africa, Zambezi valley
16	7+9	[x • x • x x • x • x • x • x x •]	Central and West Central Africa
20	9+11	[x • x • x • x x • x • x • x • x • x x •]	(no data available)
24	11+13	[x • x • x • x • x x • x • x • x • x • x • x x •]	Pygmies of the Upper Sangha (Central African Republic, Congo)

dinary homogeneity of African song style" that, in part, is textually repetitious; slurred in enunciation; "lacking in embellishment and free rhythm; low on exclusive leadership; high on antiphony, chorally; especially high on overlapped antiphony; high on one-phrase melodies . . . ; and highest on polyrhythmic (or hot) accompaniments; and that African music generally is repetitious, cohesive, overlapping or interlocked, multi-leveled, and hot."

Despite the generalizations contained in Lomax's statement, to which exceptions may prevail depending on the specific locations in which Africans happen to reside, this song style, together with various African speech patterns, comprises the verbal basis of African melody and rhythm. Bebey has observed, for example, that in Africa the primary purpose of the instruments is to "reconstitute spoken language." According to Barbara Leigh Smith Bodichon, in her *American Diary, 1857–8*, many African peoples imitate instruments with their voices and add "peculiar . . . musical sounds at the end of the verses," a practice that probably grew out of some African peoples' propensity to *speak* the last words or syllables of musical phrases, which is probably related to their propensity toward elision and results from the tendency of these peoples to mirror in their singing the rises and falls of the pitches and pitch-inflections of their regular speech. Some of these practices are undoubtedly sources of the blue notes, elisions, and other melodic assets of African-American singing style. Other characteristics of traditional African music, ranging from the simple monophony of Watusi warriors to the complicated melodic polyphony (two or more melodies sounded simultaneously) of the pygmies of Central Africa, make use variously of melodic monophony (one melody without accompaniment), heterophony (a single melody sounded simultaneously in two voices or instruments, one, or each, containing modifications that depart from the original), and polyphony; parallel thirds; overlapping call-and-response events; and, Kebede points out, "tongue clicks, suction stops, explosive endings, throaty gurgles," and "hand-clapping with off-beat syncopation." In African "calls," says Bebey, communication is made effective by "the intonations and rhythmic onomatopoeia of speech," with African singers producing sonorities that are unusual and powerful through use of head and chest voice, stammers, inflections, and sonic characterizations that depict aspects of African life.

Nketia, in *The Music of Africa*, says that "although rhythm is the primary focus of drumming, some attention is paid to pitch level, for the aesthetic appeal of drumming lies in the rhythmic and melodic elements." Olly Wilson goes further, stating, in his article entitled "The Heterogeneous Sound Ideal in African-American Music" (in *New Perspectives on Music: Essays in Honor of Eileen Southern*, edited by Josephine Wright with Samuel A. Floyd Jr.), that the rhythm-motives of the drums and the pitches and contrasting timbres that produce them create "mosaics of tone color and pitch," which constitute a heterogeneous sound ideal. This sonic ideal results from the interaction that takes place among all the performing forces in an African ensemble—among, depending on cases, solo voice, chorus, hand clapping, and the rhythms of idiophones (hard-surface instruments played by striking), aerophones (wind instruments), and chordophones (stringed instruments). In the resulting "tonal mosaic," drum, rattle, bell, voice, and hand claps not only contrast but commingle in a sound complex that is unequivocally African. This African sound, which is reflected also in strictly vocal music, was brought to the Americas and came sonically to define the music of dance rings throughout the New World. In locations and situations in which enslaved Africans were denied use of the drum, and even outside such locations, they "patted juba," a practice that included among its various versions the hemiola of the hambone pat. Making use of the hands to drum upon thighs, chest, and other body parts, the juba pat was an extension and elaboration of simple hand clapping that evolved to become a complete and self-contained accompaniment to the dance.

The values of ancestor worship, trickster devices, and other symbolic practices of African culture, together with African time-line patterns and vocal and instrumental procedures, were preserved most effectively and shaped to the Africans' new circumstances in New World versions of the ring shout. It was from this cultural phenomenon that the elements of African-American music would emerge: calls, cries, and hollers; call-and-response devices; additive rhythms and polyrhythms; heterophony, pendular thirds (back-and-forth movement between notes two steps apart), blue notes, bent notes, and elisions; hums, moans, grunts, vocables (sung sounds and words devoid of meaning), and other rhythmic-oral declamations, interjections, and punctuations; offbeat melodic phrasings and parallel intervals and chords; constant repetition of rhythmic and melodic figures and phrases (from which riffs and vamps would be derived); timbral distortions of various kinds; musical individuality within collectivity; game rivalry; hand clapping, foot patting, and approximations thereof; apart-playing; and the metronomic pulse that underlies all African-American music—all coming to manifest themselves in the shuffling, angular, offbeat, additive, repetitive, and intensive, unflagging rhythms of jazz.

The most popular and ubiquitous instruments of slave culture—the banjo, flute, violin, triangle, drum, quills, and sticks (bones)—were well suited to the realization of the rhythmic and tonal stratifications of the heterogeneous sound ideal, as it would be made manifest in African and African-American music. This phenomenon played a critical role in determining the nature of jazz in the following ways. Melodically, this sound ideal is manifest in microtonal inflections in pentatonic and modally ambiguous contexts; in singing voices that are sometimes and variously rough, sandy, piercing, and falsetto; in wordless sounds that are sometimes used for their own value rather than for the communication of verbal meaning; in ease of movement between speaking and singing and speech-song; and in the use of ululations, grunts, hums, shouts, and melismas as integral and indispensable parts of the musical meaning. Rhythmically, this phenomenon manifests itself in hand clapping, foot patting, and patting juba, in the repetition of short rhythmic motives, cross-rhythms, accented and isolated second beats, and in "basing" (repetitive accompanying phrasings). Textually narratives, told in dialect and in call-and-response, are presented in metaphor, figure of speech, implication, indirection, and personification.

In jazz music, the African musical practices of heterophony, call-and-response, riffing time lines, cyclic structures, additive and cross-rhythms, intonations, and onomatopoeia became widespread, although transformed and somewhat attenuated. And given the African insistence on a heterogeneous sound blend, the specific instrumentation of the early jazz bands—clarinet, trumpet, trombone, tuba, banjo, and drums—may have been influenced as much by the preferences of transplanted Africans as by the instrumentation of European-derived band sections. African Americans used European musical instruments to syncretize a timbral mosaic that, together with other elements, came to be recognizable as the sound of jazz.

The call-and-response device is found in extended form in the twelve-bar blues of U.S. provenance, in which, for example, a two-measure instrumental "response" answers a pair of two-measure vocal "calls"—comprising a sonic mimicry that creates the illusion of speech or of narrative conversation—and in jazz, in call-and-response—style riffs. Thus jazz, like African music, possesses a "telling effect" that Albert Murray, in his *The Hero and the Blues*, says "asserts, alleges, quests, requests, and implies . . . mocks, groans, concurs, and signifies misgivings and suspicions," with the performance making use of what Dominique Zahan, in his book entitled *The Religion, Spirituality, and Thought of Traditional Africa*, refers to as "implication, euphemism, symbol, allegory." In jazz, as in African music, when dancers perform—with, in the African way, a bump here, a grind there, a nod and a dip elsewhere—they are responding to what the musicians play on their instruments; similarly, the musicians react to the movements, gestures, and urgings of the dancers.

In their dances, Africans pantomimed the poetry of African song. In this tradition, gestures are symbols, and artistic practice is judged according to aesthetic and ethical sensibilities that balance the good and the bad, the true and the false. Among the Yoruba specifically, according to Babatunde Lawal (in his article "Some Aspects of Yoruba Aesthetics," which appeared in volume 3 of the *British Journal of Aesthetics*), performing artistry is "judged by the quality of a presentation. A good singer or poet is judged not only by the quality of his voice but also by the quality of his composition," and, with drumming, "artistry in music is recognized in the individual's ability to 'talk' with the drum and in the over-all rhythm or melody of an orchestral performance." In Yoruba aesthetics, judgment is consensual, shared throughout the community. It is for these reasons, among others, that in performance settings jazz musicians and dancers react so effectively to one another and that jazz musicians rely so comfortably on their audiences for critical evaluation; it is also why jazz audiences communicate their approval and disapproval of artistic gestures and other realizations of aesthetic form through vocal encouragement, silence, or, sometimes, good-natured mocking.

Over the three centuries in which African musical practices and assumptions were transformed into new structures and ideas—molded in a process in which European instruments, forms, and practices were superimposed on a foundation of transplanted African cultural preferences and practices—black musicians performed on the violin, banjo, musical saw, reed flutes, drums (where and when they were not prohibited), sticks or bones, and rattles of various kinds; and they sang rhyme songs, songs of satire, derision, and mimicry, songs of nostalgia and nonsense, children's songs, lullabies, and songs of love, all with a humor that served as their armament in a struggle for life and liberty. Through it all, there was present the heterogeneous sound ideal, the contrasting conglomerate that is so well suited for the rhythmic, polyphonic, and tonal stratification of jazz.

In jazz, African musical practices such as time-lines, the song-style techniques described by Lomax, the calls, cries, and hollers, the game-rivalry, onomatopoeia, and all the rest are performed within a context that has been described by Thomas Brothers as "solo and cycle." In his article entitled "Solo and Cycle in African-American Jazz" (*Musical Quarterly*) Brothers offers a theoretical model for analyzing jazz along lines that echo the position that Richard Waterman took in his article entitled "African Influence on the Music of the Americas" (in *Acculturation in the Americas*, edited by Sol Tax), that is, that early Africans in the United States must have considered European musical ideas as source material to be explored within a "generalized" African musical context. Viewing Waterman's position as a hypothesis to prove, Brothers uses as a point of departure southern Ewe music, with its division of ensemble performance into two rhythmic groups: a variable group and a fixed group. He then identifies the harmonic "solo and cycle" in jazz performance as analogous to the "variable" group and "fixed" group in southern Ewe drumming. Brothers has discovered that although the harmonic cycle in jazz is organizationally slightly different than the Ewe rhythmic cycle, both produce and are dependent upon the same syntactical model. He cites Louis Armstrong's solo on "Big Butter and Egg Man" as an example of how pitch is used to articulate temporal relationships in a way that is similar to the "African model" and, scholar that he is, cites Lester Young's solo in "Lester Leaps In" and Coleman Hawkins's "Body and Soul" as examples that depart from that model. He indicates that these latter approaches are expansions of the approach founded by Armstrong, as they stretch "the connection between soloist and cycle without severing it." Brothers's purpose is to view pitch (which has been touted as the European contribution to jazz) and rhythm (touted as the African) as "complementary components of a consistent melodic idiom, rather than as independent parameters having distinct antecedents." He maintains that the solo-and-cycle approach to syntax eventually embraced by Armstrong and others came to jazz from earlier and simpler African-derived repertories and provided the basis for the later model.

This model, refined in various ways over the approximately seventy years of jazz's development, continues to embrace the many, diverse, and profound influences of African music on the formation of jazz. In melodies, as they are played by jazz musicians, for example, we hear microtonal inflections in pentatonic and modally ambiguous contexts, voices that are sometimes and variously rough, sandy, piercing, and falsetto, with vocal sounds that are sometimes used for their own value rather than for the communication of verbal meaning, and with ease of movement from speaking to singing. We hear also ululations, grunts, hums, shouts, and melisma as integral and indispensable parts of the musical meaning of jazz renditions. In rhythm, we hear the influences of African music making in hand clapping, foot patting, and patting juba, in the repetition of short rhythmic motives, in cross-rhythms, accented and isolated second beats, and the rhythmic oscillations and call-and-response patterns of riffs and phrasings. In song texts, we hear and experience the influences of tales and legends told in metaphor, figures of speech, implication, indirection, and personification in call-and-response fashion. In musical phrases, we hear the influence of Africa in the sounds of the blue notes, African-style elisions, and other melodic assets of African-American singing style that resulted from African Americans' use of the cultural, physical, and musical assets Africans brought with them to a new homeland in which jazz would be born.

European Roots of Jazz

William H. Youngren

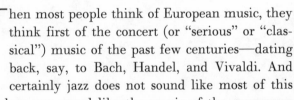

hen most people think of European music, they think first of the concert (or "serious" or "classical") music of the past few centuries—dating back, say, to Bach, Handel, and Vivaldi. And certainly jazz does not sound like most of this music. It especially does not sound like the music of the composers we most often hear today in the concert hall: Beethoven, Wagner, Brahms, Tchaikovsky, Mahler, Debussy. What distinguishes jazz most sharply from the music of these composers and their contemporaries is that jazz has a firm and steady beat, kept by the drums and the other rhythm instruments. Jazz, as we know, originated as dance music, and all dance music needs a secure rhythmic foundation to guide the dancers.

The concert music of the last few centuries, however, is not the only sort of European music. Europeans, like Americans, developed their own characteristic forms of dance music, and when they emigrated to this country, they brought their dance music with them. One type that has grown popular in recent years is Jewish klezmer music—which, everyone has noticed, sounds remarkably like jazz. Recordings made in Europe in the 1920s and even earlier show that

Sidney Bechet with the Wildcats in Columbia Studios, New York, 1947. Left to right: Johnny Glasel, cornet; Bob Mielke, trombone; Denny Strong, drums; Bechet, clarinet; Charlie Traeger, bass; Dick Wellstood, piano; Bob Wilber, clarinet. Courtesy of the Institute of Jazz Studies, Rutgers University.

it sounded that way before jazz could possibly have influenced it directly. Anyone who has ever attended an Italian or a Polish wedding will have heard other sorts of ethnic dance music that also sound rather like jazz. One reason these ethnic dance musics sound like jazz is that they too, being music for dancing, have a steady beat. But there is another, far more important, reason.

Jazz, the various sorts of dance music imported to this country from Europe, and the concert music of the last few centuries are all species of tonal music. That is, they are music written (or improvised) in a major or minor key, music organized according to the system of major-minor harmonic tonality that gradually developed, in ways that are still being debated, out of the modal music of the Middle Ages and the Renaissance and that became fully fixed in the early eighteenth century.

In the earliest jazz we can study closely, recorded jazz from 1917 on, the chord progressions that determine a melody's changing relation to the key of the piece are, roughly, those that were so used in the late eighteenth century, the time of Haydn and Mozart. Moreover, the phrases of the popular songs of the 1920s and earlier, which formed the basis for the vast majority of early recorded jazz performances, are similar in character to the phrases of late eighteenth-century music. They are mostly two or four bars long and are often arranged either in balanced pairs, each pair consisting of an "antecedent" and a "consequent" phrase, or else in sequences. The songs themselves are usually thirty-two bars long, and tend to fall into sections of eight or sixteen bars, though sections are often slightly extended, for effect—which was also a favorite trick of Haydn's. Except for waltzes and novelty numbers, the songs generally have four beats to the bar. A typical jazz performance of the 1920s will consist of a statement of the song by the full band, a series of solos improvised on the chord progressions of the song and perhaps (though not necessarily) making reference to its melody, and probably a concluding ensemble. Such performances may therefore be thought of as having a theme-and-variations form that is loosely (or not at all) structured melodically but strictly structured harmonically, a form similar to that of the baroque chaconne or passacaglia.

Thus the various interrelated elements of early jazz—harmony, melody, rhythm, and form—are very similar to those of late eighteenth-century music and are in fact derived more or less directly from them, by way of the American popular song literature. In 1919 the Swiss conductor Ernest Ansermet was in London with Sergi

Diaghilev's Ballets Russes. Ansermet chanced to hear the black jazz clarinetist (and, later, soprano saxophonist) Sidney Bechet, who was touring with Will Marion Cook's Southern Syncopated Orchestra, and he wrote an article about the experience. Ansermet described the form of the pieces he heard as "gripping, abrupt, harsh, with a brusque and pitiless ending like that of Bach's Second Brandenburg Concerto." Singling out Bechet as "an artist of genius," Ansermet compared him to "those figures to whom we owe the creation of our art as we know it today—those men of the seventeenth and eighteenth centuries, for example, who wrote the expressive works of dance airs which cleared the way for Haydn and Mozart."

Ansermet's comparison is not only apt but also, considering its early date, remarkably perceptive. That jazz was, from its beginnings, tonal music, and is therefore basically European or Western in nature, is so obvious that it should not need as labored a demonstration as I am giving here. The creators of jazz were, after all, men, most of them black but many of them white, who had been surrounded all their lives by tonal music—in church, in school, at parties, at celebrations on the village green. Moreover, the instruments they played—piano, violin, the various brass and woodwind instruments left over from Civil War bands—were constructed and tuned so as to produce the intervals and scales on which tonal music is based.

Yet as recently as 1968, Gunther Schuller, one of our finest writers on jazz, could emphatically declare, in the first chapter of his otherwise excellent book *Early Jazz*, that "*every* musical element—rhythm, harmony, melody, timbre, and the basic forms of jazz—is essentially African in background and derivation" (62). As I demonstrated at the time in my review of *Early Jazz* (*Hudson Review*, Autumn 1969), this sweeping statement is not only not proven by Schuller's argument; it also goes dead against what his principal source, A. M. Jones's *Studies in African Music* (1959), tells us about the ways in which the music of West Africa, ancestral home of most of the blacks imported to this country as slaves, is actually organized.

To say that jazz is basically European or Western in nature is of course not to imply that it could have originated in Europe—or indeed anywhere else than in the United States. Jazz is obviously a hybrid, containing both European and non-European elements, and it is only in this country that all of these elements could be found, coexisting and in the proper relation to one another. Jazz is European in the same sense in which English is a Germanic language. Like jazz, English too—thanks to William the Conqueror—is a hybrid. It has many more loanwords from French and other Romance languages than do any of the other languages that we classify as Germanic. Also, it has gradually lost most of the case-endings and other inflections still found in German. Yet English shares with the other Germanic languages the most basic underlying features of its syntax and phonology. Just so, jazz shares with other forms of European music the general harmonic and melodic characteristics that give it its firm basis in the Western tonal system.

These shared characteristics are of course not the ones that make jazz instantly recognizable as jazz—rather than as klezmer music or the Second Brandenburg Concerto. The characteristics that make jazz sound like jazz have usually, and probably correctly, been traced to the blues and to ragtime. From the blues came many melodic inflections, particularly ones involving the so-called blue notes—the flatted third, fifth, and seventh of the major scale. From ragtime came the syncopated figures found in both the melodies and the rhythmic background of early jazz. Many older jazz players have told of learning, anywhere from 1900 to around 1920, how to "rag" popular songs of the day by syncopating the melody, shifting accents, and so on. It was, as we know from ample written testimony, these bluesy inflections and syncopated rhythms that made jazz sound new and distinctive to its first listeners, and that made some love it while repelling others.

But what made jazz, at first hearing, relatively intelligible, to those who loved it and those who hated it, was the fact that it was tonal music, employing essentially the same melodic and harmonic language that the American popular song literature had employed at least since the Civil War. The melodic contours, the harmonic progressions, the ways in which phrases were formed and in which they responded to one another, the steady 4/4 rhythm—all these were familiar, even though tricked out in new dress. So the metaphor embodied in my title is most apt: the roots of a tree are out of sight, below ground level; just so, the roots of jazz, the traditional tonal language it inherited from the popular song literature, are below the surface of a casual listener's conscious attention. But just as with a tree, it is the European, tonal roots of jazz that first gave it life and that then enabled it to grow and thrive throughout its period of productive development.

The metaphor of roots is also applicable in another way to jazz. For as a tree grows, so too do its roots continue to grow—though remaining unseen. Just so, the specific uses that jazz made of the tonal language did not remain static but changed—often in ways parallel to the changes that had earlier taken place in concert music. As someone once said, jazz harmony went from the age of Mozart to the age of Mahler in about a quarter century.

Some of these changes came directly from concert music. Bill Challis, who arranged for Paul Whiteman's band in the late 1920s, was very fond of Debussy and Ravel, and we can hear their influence in his scores: in his frequent use of figures based on the whole-tone scale, of augmented triads, and of dominant ninth chords in parallel stepwise motion—as in Ravel's familiar *Pavane pour une infante défunte*. We can also hear it in the solos cornetist Bix Beiderbecke improvised on the Whiteman recordings of Challis scores and in Beiderbecke's piano piece "In a Mist," which he recorded—he was also a gifted pianist—in 1927.

The work that Challis and other arrangers did for Whiteman significantly influenced the later bands of Duke Ellington, Jimmie Lunceford, and Fletcher Henderson—for whom Challis wrote a few scores. In 1933 Henderson's tenor saxophonist Coleman Hawkins composed a wildly experimental piece, "Queer Notions," based mainly on whole-tone progressions, which the Henderson band recorded not once but twice.

Some of the changes in jazz harmony, however, seem to have been motivated internally, by changes taking place in popular songs. At the end of the 1920s, as slow ballads became popular—no doubt owing in part to the playing of jazz soloists such as Beiderbecke and Hawkins—lush romantic harmonies became more common in pop songs. Also, secondary dominant seventh chords began to be replaced, particularly in cadences, by minor seventh chords, creating a smoother harmonic flow, a more "sophisticated" sound appropriate to the ballads and the emotions they expressed. Finally, ordinary major and minor triads routinely had a sixth added to them. The joint effect of these and similar changes was to take the sharp edges off the chord progressions, to disguise slightly the dominant-tonic movement central to the operation of the tonal system.

The emergence of bebop, in the late 1930s and early 1940s, brought further harmonic changes that grew out of these earlier ones and that also had no direct parallel in concert music. The major triads that had had sixths added to them in the preceding decade now had major sevenths added instead, the major seventh producing a slight dissonant clash with the root of the chord. Dominant seventh chords picked up flatted fifths and flatted ninths. And, just as happened in concert music though in different ways, the increase in dissonance produced an increase in chromatic harmonic movement. Through a process called tritone substitution, cadences were formed from a series of chromatically descending seventh chords rather than by going through the dominant-tonic "circle of fifths."

From the late 1920s to the early 1940s there were also marked changes in melodic phrasing. The rather clipped, balanced phrases of the 1920s began, particularly in the work of Louis Armstrong between 1928 and 1933, to give way to longer, more lyrical lines and a romantic, rhapsodic style of improvisation that was, like the changes in harmony then taking place, well suited to slow romantic ballads. We can also see this change in the slightly later work of Hawkins and the other most important tenor saxophonist of the swing era, Lester Young. Each had a great influence on the boppers, and their two influences were complementary: Hawkins's long lines rigorously explored every possible implication of a tune's harmony, while Young's seemed to float, coolly ambivalent, above the chord changes—he was fond of landing, at the end of a phrase, on either the sixth or the ninth of the chord of the moment, two scale steps that are neither dissonant nor clearly consonant. We can also see these longer lines, though with a more traditional blues coloring, in the work of guitarist Charlie Christian.

These are only a few of the more important specific changes in the way jazz used the tonal system between the late 1920s and the early 1940s. Throughout this period and beyond, into the early 1960s, the general direction in which jazz moved was roughly similar to that taken by concert music after Wagner. Once jazz began to grow more complex harmonically, it necessarily became more dissonant, filled with extended and altered chords. Finally, in the 1960s and 1970s some players moved jazz out of tonality altogether, just as Schoenberg and other composers had done with concert music in the early years of this century.

Jazz is related to other European music not only at the deepest levels, by virtue of being based on the Western tonal system, but also in more superficial yet still important ways, through various stylistic borrowings. These borrowings are from three main sources: brass band music, which influenced jazz formally; Latin American music, which influenced it rhythmically, giving it what Jelly Roll Morton memorably called "the Spanish tinge"; and classical or concert music, especially opera and salon music, which influenced it melodically. There are of course other, less important sources—for example, klezmer music, which gave jazz the *fraylich* (or "Jewish wedding") trumpet playing of Paul Whiteman's Charlie Margulis and Benny Goodman's Ziggy Elman.

Brass bands were common in New Orleans from the Civil War on. It was from the marches played by the bands that rags, and such early jazz standards as "Fidgety Feet" and "Original Dixieland One-Step," derived their multistrain form, in which the key of the later strain (or strains) has one or more flats than that of the first strain. Also, the polyphonic structure of the early jazz ensemble—trumpet playing lead, clarinet elaborating an obbligato above, trombone providing a rhythmic foundation and occasional countermelodies—is taken from that of the marching band. Finally, certain famous bandsmen exerted a powerful influence on the development of jazz instrumental technique. Vic Dickenson, Miff Mole, and Trummy Young all declared their indebtedness to the records of Sousa's solo trombonist Arthur Pryor, from which they learned a *cantabile* trombone style that had no precedent in the European orchestral tradition.

When Morton spoke of "the Spanish tinge," he singled it out as one of the stylistic traits of jazz that distinguished it from (and made it superior to) ragtime. But John Storm Roberts has argued convincingly, in *The Latin Tinge* (1979), that the Latin American influence on American popular and dance music can be traced several decades before the first rags—in some mid-nineteenth-century piano pieces by Louis Moreau Gottschalk that have a Cuban habanera bass but that also anticipate ragtime in their phrasing. Far from being incidental, unrelated episodes, the tango craze of 1913, the rumba craze of the 1930s, and the subsequent development of Latin jazz have all been part of a long and steadily increasing Latin influence on American popular music. Recent research by Christopher Washburne (*Black Music Research Journal*, Spring 1997) shows that certain basic jazz rhythmic patterns are probably derived from Latin American music, and perhaps ultimately from Africa. The slave trade continued, though illicitly, in Cuba until the end of the nineteenth century, and Latin American slave owners were far more tolerant of their slaves' native music than were slave owners in this country. Therefore genuine survivals from African music are more likely to have been preserved in Latin America.

The three greatest early jazz musicians to have recorded extensively, Louis Armstrong, Sidney Bechet, and Jelly Roll Morton, have all testified to the influence of opera and, in Morton's case at least, other forms of concert music in the formation of their styles. As

Joshua Berrett has shown (*Musical Quarterly,* Summer 1992), it was from opera singers that Armstrong learned the high-flown bravura style that set him apart from the simpler and more straightforward New Orleans cornetists trained solely in the brass band tradition. Moreover, he interpolated in many of his recorded solos passages from favorite operatic arias and ensembles. Among the first records he acquired, as a teenager, were ones by Caruso, Tetrazzini, and Galli-Curci. Such slightly younger New Orleans cornetists as Sharkey Bonano, Wingy Manone, and Louis Prima have often been singled out as disciples of Armstrong—which they surely were. But it has been suggested that some of the similarities between their playing and his may be due to the fact that their Italian heritage gave them easy access to the same operatic music that influenced him, as well as to Neapolitan songs and salon music.

Bechet was a Creole, and his family was much better off than Armstrong's. As a child, he was often taken by his mother to New Orleans's French Opera House. His earliest recordings, like Armstrong's, are marked by a highly dramatic bravura style that clearly shows the influence of opera. He too bought Caruso's records, and in later years he liked to tell people that it was from Caruso that he got his pronounced and highly individual vibrato. The same influence operated on other New Orleans clarinetists as well—not only on the white players of Italian descent, such as Leon Roppolo and Charlie Cordilla, but also on the blacks: Omer Simeon, Jimmie Noone, Barney Bigard, Johnny Dodds. That Armstrong sensed he had a stronger affinity with the clarinetists than with his fellow cornetists is proven by his comment in a 1970 BBC interview: "I was like a clarinet player, like the guys run up and down the horn nowadays, boppin' and things."

In the recordings he made for the Library of Congress in 1938, Jelly Roll Morton fondly recalls his visits to the French Opera House: "I remember the old building very well, there on Royal Street." And he plays the "Miserere" from Verdi's *Il trovatore,* first straight and then as he "transformed" it to jazz. "Jazz music is strictly music," he insists at one point. "You have the finest ideas from the greatest operas, symphonies, and overtures in jazz music. There's nothing finer than jazz music because it comes from everything of the finest class music."

Morton certainly did not mean that jazz musicians should literally copy this or that classical piece—as some of them in fact were doing during the 1930s, when "swinging the classics" was all the rage. His stress on what he repeatedly called "transformation" and his proud claim that "I transformed every style to mine" suggest rather that jazz could benefit by borrowing, and adapting, techniques and turns of phrase from any worthy musical source. In the elaborately graceful melodic circumlocutions of both his published compositions and his improvised solos and backgrounds on his records, we can clearly hear the operatic airs and nineteenth-century salon pieces that lie behind them and that he undoubtedly played often during his early days, in the bordellos of Storyville. In the Library of Congress recordings he also claims to have "transformed" the different dances of an old quadrille into the successive strains of "Tiger Rag," and he plays the dances one after another: introduction, waltz, mazurka, "two-four time" (polka?), and so on. His claim was false: "Tiger Rag" was indeed based, at least in part, on an old quadrille, but it apparently had been worked out by a trombonist named Jack Carey. Nonetheless, Morton's mastery of the different dance forms, as well as their influence on his jazz playing and composition, is evident in his graceful, fluent performance.

In the eighteenth century, the German philospher Herder maintained that folksongs and folk poetry sprang spontaneously from the creative genius of an entire people. Historians have often represented jazz more as a product of the spirit of New Orleans blacks, the natural and inevitable expression of a particular *Volksgeist*, than as a musical style gradually and consciously developed by individual artists. From the beginning—or so the legend runs—jazz was collectively improvised, rather than composed and written down, because collective improvisation expressed the spontaneity and communal spirit that distinguished blacks from whites. The sensibility of the early jazz musician, the sort of figure long symbolized by the mysterious Buddy Bolden, was seen as having been shaped primarily by atavistic memories of African music and by direct experience of its American descendants: field hollers, country blues, work songs, and the like.

Yet the men who actually created jazz were not only surrounded from birth, as listeners, by Western tonal music; they also made their living by playing it. In the New Orleans of the 1890s, dance orchestras, both black and white, had to be able to play a variety of dances: waltzes, polkas, schottisches, mazurkas. As ragtime became popular, in the mid-1890s, these dances were joined by the two-step, which had become the dance that went with ragtime tunes, and which was itself edged out by the one-step in about 1912.

Of course the black musicians of the 1890s and early 1900s recognized the differences between their ragtime or jazz numbers and the other sorts of dance music they played. But there is no evidence that they regarded jazz as superior, or improvisation as more "natural" to them as black musicians. In fact, jazz seems not to have been improvised at first—at least in the city of New Orleans, as distinguished from outlying rural areas. The members of the pre-1890 dance and brass bands in the city were trained musicians who could read music and were proud of it. In the mid-1890s, when some bands began to take in players who could not read and so preferred to improvise, these bands were looked down on and their music was spoken of scornfully, by the older, trained players, both black and white, as "head music" or "ratty music."

The emphasis laid by many writers on jazz's African origins has taught us to think of it as a rare and delicate hothouse plant, different in kind from the hardy indigenous growth surrounding it. The borrowings from other types of music that we have been tracing have therefore been regarded by jazz historians with suspicion. They have often voiced the fear that jazz would be (or already had been) tainted or distorted by non-African, specifically European, elements. This view appears in its most extreme form in Rudi Blesh's *Shining Trumpets* (1946). "The dilution and deformation of jazz," writes Blesh, "took place from 1920 on because of the influences of commercialism, white playing, and sophistication of the Negroes themselves." By the mid-1940s, Blesh felt, this process had "advanced to the point where the music frequently ceases to be predominantly a Negro form, becoming a hybridized popular music rather than a fine-art form" (6).

Ever since jazz began to be taken seriously, the conviction that it either will be or already has been tainted or deformed has thus sent critics and historians off on a quest for the unadulterated archetype: absolutely pure black (which usually means New Orleans) jazz. Blesh rendered this goal by definition unattainable: since we have no black jazz recorded before 1920, all the jazz we can possibly know is already tainted. Other historians, less pessimistic, have claimed to find this perfectly pure black jazz in records by Armstrong or Morton or King Oliver. But it doesn't matter where they claimed to find it: it wasn't there. For the quest itself is misconceived, and its goal is a chimera, a logical construction devised to justify a particular sort of musical taste. The music we call jazz has always been "a hybridized popular music," developing in the midst of, borrowing from, and influencing other forms of popular music, including opera. Jazz also happens, however, to have quickly developed into "a fine-art form." For sometimes, though not very often, popular art really does, suddenly and mysteriously, attain the status of high art. Though the quest for the pure unsullied archetype has graced such august fields of inquiry as Homeric studies and the history of so-called Gregorian chant, it should simply be given up as a bad job.

Jazz's borrowings from other sorts of European music were the most natural thing in the world and should neither be wondered at nor deplored as signs of the dilution or deformation of a music once pure and perfect. Jazz was and is and always will be a hybrid, just as the music of Beethoven or Wagner or Stravinsky, at any and every stage of his career, is a hybrid. No one creates music (or anything else) in a vacuum, uninfluenced by the world around him. The task of the critic or historian lies not in unearthing (or simply positing) some pure and original form of the music that confronts him but rather in deciphering (so to speak) its genetic code. The fact that jazz was, from its beginnings, the particular hybrid that it was and is merely follows from, and further confirms, its status as a member of the large family of tonally based European musics.

Ragtime Then and Now

Max Morath

Ragtime's story is one of many chapters.

The opening chapter tracks this unruly American music as it coalesced in the late nineteenth century from undocumented folk origins. Early performers and composers left few fragments of their life and times, which have long since taken on a mythic quality. Urban tenderloins and a scruffy infant show business intersected a vigorous black culture, and a richly syncopated new music was spawned. Like other upheavals in popular music to come, it bubbled up from young people on hard times.

By chapter two ragtime had merged with commerce, and as the century turned, sheet music and piano rolls appeared, along with periodicals and trade papers, copyright files and primitive recordings. Research materials become accessible, although little historical scholarship was brought to bear at the time. Ragtime was scorned by the Establishment as ephemeral at best, trashy at worst.

The story of ragtime in chapter three is one of rise and fall. By 1910 or so ragtime had taken over the ballooning new industry called Popular Music. New styles of song and dance had usurped the name of ragtime, if not its musical imperatives. To public and publisher,

Painting of Scott Joplin. Courtesy of the Institute of Jazz Studies, Rutgers University.

ragtime had come to label the times as well as the music. Decades later the novelist E. L. Doctorow would wisely employ the seven-letter word to stamp the entire era in *Ragtime* (1974).

By chapter four ragtime had become a quaint and crotchety elder. After 1920 the best of the young musicians reveled in ragtime's off-spring, now labeled either "jazz," (James P. Johnson, Fats Waller, Earl Hines), or "novelty" (Zez Confrey, Pauline Alpert, Roy Bargy). Publishers seldom reprinted the great old rags, although attics and piano benches still bulged with original copies, to the delight of future collectors. A few kid piano players still assayed Scott Joplin's intimidating "Maple Leaf Rag" (1899), but ragtime was nostalgia—your daddy's derby, your mama's hobble skirt.

The current chapter of the ragtime story is, happily, open-ended. It began in mid-century as pianists, collectors, and scholars first revisited the earlier chapters. It climaxed in the early 1970s when the entire nation, it seemed, rose to embrace the life and work of one of the master figures, Scott Joplin.

Origins of the word *rag* are unclear. Most scholars agree it probably evolved in the argot of nineteenth-century black culture, referring derisively to tunes or songs outside the gospel canon. Itinerant pianists combined them—dance tunes, marches, a few blues—into multiphrase pieces called rags. The suffix *time* was added, as in "waltz time" or "march time." Sheet music from this early period discloses a rapid mutation: *Rag Time* became *Rag-Time*, then lower-case *ragtime*. The hyphen soon disappeared, and *ragtime* took over for good. The little noun *rag* lived on, of course, to identify, then as now, a specific piece of syncopated piano music.

As music for piano, a rag can be described rather precisely. It consists of three or four related sixteen-measure themes in duple time, the left hand maintaining a steady marchlike beat, the right hand layering syncopated figures above it. Today's perception of ragtime is generally thus defined, because the music has been viewed almost exclusively through the piano works of Scott Joplin. The rediscovery of this pioneer master has somehow deflected public and media interest in the larger story. Ragtime in its prime had abandoned strict musical parameters and became the term covering most of the popular music of its time. To revisit it solely as piano music is to ignore not only its other musical forms but its elusive role as a social force. If nothing else it represented a powerful vortex that swept black and white society and culture into a wary and often bitter partnership that enriched a century of American music.

Ragtime Piano

The piano takes center stage in both early and late chapters of the ragtime story, which have in common the respected figure of Scott Joplin (1868–1917). Joplin was born in northeastern Texas, near what is now Texarkana. His father was an ex-slave from North Carolina, his mother a freeborn woman from Kentucky. The Joplins, according to Edward A. Berlin's definitive biography *King of Ragtime* (1994), were a musical family and provided their son a rudimentary musical education. Joplin left home in his early teens to enter the rough world of show business as pianist, singer, and cornetist. He was probably among the young players at the Chicago World's Fair in 1892–93. In 1894 Joplin moved to Sedalia, Missouri, where he studied music at the new George R. Smith College, and where the semiretired music dealer John Stark published "Maple Leaf" (1899) and soon thereafter formed John Stark & Sons, the company that for years would set publication standards for piano ragtime. "Maple Leaf" was an immediate success, although it did not "sell a million copies the first year," as often claimed in Joplin blurbs. But whatever its initial sale, it was ragtime's first hit, and has remained so for a century. More than that, it established the matrix for hundreds of rags to come— the theme sequence AABBACCDD, which with some variation prevailed for years. Most composers in the vital Stark catalog conformed to it, including James Scott, Arthur Marshall, Artie Matthews, and Joseph Lamb, as did most composers with major midwestern and New York houses.

John Stark and Scott Joplin moved operations to St. Louis in 1901, inaugurating a creative period during which Joplin published over a dozen rags, plus collaborations with other Missouri composers, including Louis Chauvin, Arthur Marshall, and Scott Hayden. He also completed his first ragtime opera, *A Guest of Honor,* the score of which has been lost, although Edward Berlin's research has proven beyond question that the work existed and was performed frequently during 1903.

With "Maple Leaf" and other early works, Joplin brought a higher level of musicianship to published ragtime. His scores regularly indicated such basics as pedaling, dynamics, and phrasing (e.g., "Leola," 1905). Syncopation across the bar line, never scored in other early rags, was a Joplin staple, seen in "Maple Leaf" and even in his earlier "Original Rags," its final theme offering a profusion of syncopated figures both inside and across the bars. Here again Joplin influenced his peers, not only in the form of the rag but in techniques of composition, especially in subtle uses of syncopation. Kansas City's James

Scott (1886–1938), another mainstay of the Stark catalog, certainly followed Joplin's lead in form and style, although his highly pianistic rags, rampant with syncopation, are technically more demanding than Joplin's. James Scott brought his own innovations to the style; his rags offer frequent examples of the repeated treble figures that would soon, in jazz, become known as "riffs," as in the final theme of "Hilarity" (1910) and the trio of "Grace and Beauty" (1910).

In 1907 Scott Joplin moved to New York, where, with John Stark and other publishers, he introduced some of his finest works including "Fig Leaf Rag" (1908), "Solace—A Mexican Serenade" (1909), and "Euphonic Sounds" (1909). Joplin continued to pursue his dream of ragtime as a through-composed form of American piano music. Rags from his New York period stretch the then-accepted harmonic limits of popular music and expand the range of syncopated devices.

It is fatefully odd that Joplin's work, the guiding influence in ragtime's earliest days, did not enjoy continuing exposure. After the wild success of "Maple Leaf," Joplin composed a body of rags of increasing lyrical beauty and delicate syncopation, but except for "Maple Leaf" and a couple of others, these rags remained unheralded and obscure during his lifetime. Rags with simple syncopations and facile right-hand figures were the big hits—"Wild Cherries" (1908), "Spaghetti Rag" (1910), and the perennial "12th Street Rag" (1915). The average American played and heard few of Joplin's later rags but bought instead the more accessible rags of composers such as Charles L. Johnson, Henry Lodge, and Percy Wenrich. These composers and a hundred others learned from "Maple Leaf" and acknowledged its lead, but failed to enlarge upon it.

An exception was the Joplin protégé Joseph F. Lamb (1887–1960), first published by John Stark & Sons in 1915. Lamb composed rags all his life, and though his early output gained little attention, appearing as ragtime was already losing ground, his richly harmonized rags have played a major role in the ragtime revival.

Joplin meanwhile, remaining in New York, published his last rag, "Magnetic," in 1914. The last ten years of his life had been dominated by efforts to mount his second opera, *Treemonisha*. Except for a lackluster staged reading, probably in 1911, it was never produced during his lifetime. Scott Joplin died on April 1, 1917.

Ragtime in Song

It was natural that words would join music in the ardor of ragtime's youth. But the entry of its incessant syncopations into vocal music was long blighted by the racist nature of its first vehicle, the "coon" song, a descendant of the minstrel songs and jokes of the nineteenth century, in which African Americans are portrayed in degrading caricature. Coon songs, created by songwriters of both races, pose a difficult question: how could these songs, some quite wonderful at addressing universal themes of life and love, lampoon the very culture that inspired them? Are they worthy of our attention at all?

The answer seems to be that while coon songs themselves are quite properly collecting dust in the museums of popular culture, their endowment to American popular song was dramatic and demands consideration. Coon songs, after all, constituted *ragtime with words* and were every bit as popular in their time as instrumental rags for piano and band. While the social and emotional damage wreaked by these songs is inestimable, their impact on popular song must be gauged and is an essential chapter in the ragtime story.

The cover of 1897's "Syncopated Sandy" reveals an early glimpse of the word *ragtime*, then so new to print it was placed in quotation marks and hyphenated: "RAG-TIME." But ragtime's common presence in both vocal and piano music is clearly evidenced in this piece. The piano accompaniment is separated on two parallel systems, one "Straight," the other a modestly syncopated version labeled "RAG-TIME." The publishers boast that they have "succeeded in illustrating for the first time the absolute theory that the famous 'RAG-TIME' music . . . originated with the negroe [*sic*] and is characteristic of their people."

The words of the song, written for the famous (white) stage star May Irwin, typify the offensive nature of coon song lyrics: "There's a high-toned colored gent, a coon without a cent, his cash for clothes he spent, to outshine all coons he meant . . ." The accompanying parody is more hateful, referring to Sandy as "a bold bad nigger crook" who barely escapes "a lynchin' bee."

Ben Harney, a highly successful entertainer known in the trade as "the King of Ragtime," composed a hit coon song in 1896, "Mister Johnson, Turn Me Loose." It depicts activities supposedly stereotypical of black males—dice games and chicken stealing. But the lyrics are not as blatantly racist as those of other coon songs of the period. And their influence may be seen in a more positive light by noting Harney's innovative use of street language and idiom: "the boys was-a gamblin' with might and main, tho't I'd be a sport and be dead game"; "one fellow's point was a-Little Joe"; "don't take me to the calaboose." If a positive influence of the abrasive coon song lyrics may be said to exist, it is this role of introducing slang and the vernacular into popular song.

Several perennial survivors from the period were originally published as coon songs, including "Bill Bailey, Won't You Please Come Home" (1902), and "Ma Blushin' Rosie" (1900). *Ma* for *my* was a common code in coon song dialect, however mild the stereotypes therein might be. The delightful 1899 hit "Hellow, Ma Baby," long since rendered as "Hello, *My* Baby," was originally marketed as a coon song. A handful of coon songs survive intact, shorn of their racist tone. Most of them are the work of black writers and composers in the New York theater world of the period.

Syncopation, under the name of either ragtime or jazz, has been notoriously tardy in reaching the Broadway musical stage. But in its broad sense, as an energizing force affecting American musical culture at every level, its liberating spirit shines in the music and lyrics of early black musicals such as *In Dahomey* (Will Marion Cook, Alex Rogers, Bert Williams, George Walker, Jess Shipp), the first black musical to play a major Broadway theater (1903), *Rufus Rastus* (Ernest Hogan and Will Vodery, 1905), and *Shoo-Fly Regiment* (Bob Cole, Rosamond Johnson, and James Weldon Johnson, 1907). The songs from these shows may have been perceived as coon songs by their largely white audiences, but they were consistently free from vicious stereotype and mean language. Viewed almost a century later, having now cast off the mask of burnt cork, the best of these songs are still performed. They are songs rich in irony and humor that speak, as all good songs should, for everyone.

The Ragtime Dances

A new name usually attaches itself to popular music when the style, especially the *beat*, changes and a new dance craze results. Ragtime for years had been characterized by a steady beat in duple time, at a relatively relaxed "Slow March Tempo." Couples, if dancing at all, did the tiresome two-step or a timid cakewalk.

Then the breezy one-steps took over, first the turkey trot, then dozens of copycats—the bunny hug and camel walk, the snake dip and kangaroo hop. Tempo was upped, and the new dances offered couples an easy walk around step which was accomplished, shockingly, in prolonged embrace. Alas, no snappy generic name emerged, so these dances remained "ragtime," although tempo and texture had changed dramatically. This was surely the music that Irving Berlin's "Alexander's Ragtime Band" was playing in 1911, and the dance young Americans were flaunting in Berlin's other 1911 hit, "Everybody's Doin' It": "See that *ragtime* couple over there, watch them throw their shoulders in the air." The name adhered, but the up-tempo music, with little space for syncopation, was a distant cousin of the ragtime that preceded it—either the funky folk rags of the late nineteenth century or the graceful, deeply syncopated piano works of Scott Joplin and his peers.

The ragtime dance mania appears to have been a creature of Tin Pan Alley and white society, but its roots can be traced to black folk dances such as the eagle rock, the buzzard lope, and for that matter, a proto turkey trot, in evidence by that name at the Chicago World's Fair.

In 1914 the team of Vernon and Irene Castle became national celebrities as they undertook to refine and codify the one-step. They mellowed the dance toward a gentrified fox-trot, which then joined the waltz on the basic ballroom dance card for years. The Castles were closely linked to New York's ragtime community, relying on the eminent black conductor James Reese Europe and drawing heavily on material by leading black composers, including Luckey Roberts, Ford Dabney, and Chris Smith. They also tapped the already astonishing output of a young Irving Berlin, for decades to come the master of the American musical moment. It may be hard to find syncopation in Berlin's *music* at this stage, but he had become a wizard at devising *lyrics* in syncopated slang and internal rhyme. And in 1917, when a new label for American popular music finally surfaced, it was Berlin who led the pack with the neatly syncopating "Mr. Jazz Himself." Americans, after taking time out to fight in a European war, would now enter a new era named for its music. By 1920 the Ragtime Years had given way to the Jazz Age.

The Revival

The image of ragtime today reveals an odd contradiction. The allure of infant ragtime was the *beat.* The insistent, sometimes harsh syncopations against the beat were elating, almost subversive. Our renewed attraction to ragtime is *not* to its beat. Perhaps after years of pop music's energy we are surfeited; ours has been the Century of the Beat. So ragtime in its rediscovery—Joplin's ragtime—has instead charmed us with its grace and beauty. Joplin, unlike most other composers of piano ragtime, gave us melody. Most of his rags except the galloping "Maple Leaf" are actually songs—without words. They're still *rags,* of course. Insistent syncopations underpin his melodies and are *of* them, not appended to them. But the visceral excitement evoked by ragtime's two-beat is missing in the revival. We anoint Joplin and ignore his contemporaries, whose sturdy and stomping rags lack his felicity. We're somehow wary of the fun—the *rush* that ragtime's rampant rhythms offer. We still visit them, but mainly in the pizza parlor or the saloon. Only Joplin has made it to the concert hall and NPR.

Whatever the scope of the rediscovery of ragtime, it came as no surprise to the small cadre of devotees who kept watch during ragtime's fifty-year hibernation. Publication of *They All Played Ragtime* by Rudi Blesh and Harriet Janis (1950) signaled the first surge of rediscovery and has informed the movement ever since. In the 1950s a few reprint folios of the early rags began to appear. Bernard Kalban, a leading New York editor and one of the industry's few unswerving friends of ragtime, saw to it that rags in the old Mills Music catalog were made available, and also those of the pioneer New York firm of Edward B. Marks (formerly Joseph W. Stern & Co.). Audio recordings had been rare, generally issued on small, hard-to-find labels, although rags in honky-tonk style occasionally came along on major labels. Then the San Francisco pianist Wally Rose began recording some real gems of ragtime, and by the 1960s pianists of various disciplines were following suit. In the early 1970s Joshua Rifkin's all-Joplin LPs, in their scrupulous attention to notation and dynamics, brought a classical flavor to the rags. Moreover, since they were released on the prestigious Nonesuch label, these albums triggered a marketing breakthrough, and Joplin's ragtime finally found its way into the classical bins of the nation's record stores. Musicians of every stripe have since embraced Joplin, including André Previn, the Canadian Brass, James Levine, and the Boston Pops.

The Joplin boom—there is no other word for it—reverberated elsewhere in early 1972. The Joplin opera *Treemonisha* premiered in Atlanta, mounted by the superb team of Robert Shaw and Katherine Dunham, with orchestrations by the composer-musicologist T. J. Anderson, based on Joplin's piano score. *Treemonisha* was again staged by the Houston Grand Opera in May of 1975 and was brought to Broadway that October; the production undoubtedly contributed to Joplin's being posthumously awarded a special Pulitzer Prize in 1976 for his contribution to American music.

Other hit recordings had meanwhile appeared. Students of the New England Conservatory under Gunther Schuller revived stock orchestrations of Joplin pieces on *The Red Back Book of Rags* (1973). Similar settings were then employed by composer-arranger Marvin Hamlisch for the soundtrack of the hit movie *The Sting*, which won the Academy Award for Best Picture in 1974. Hamlisch accepted another Oscar for best score, after a gracious bow to the Joplin legacy. The film's main theme, an obscure Joplin rag called "The Entertainer," became a hit record and remains today a prime teaching piece for beginning piano students. With the Joplin renaissance leading the way, ragtime research and rediscovery burgeoned. Dozens of books, recordings, and reprint folios now provide access to a wide range of piano scores and ragtime lore; new ragtime compositions receive respect and performance on many levels; ragtime festivals dot the nation, drawing the faithful in ever-growing numbers.

Ragtime, then, has lived several lives under its own name. But its musical *essence* has pervaded a century of popular music. Ragtime, after all, meant syncopations against the beat. Always to sing or play *on* the beat was to be "square"—caught, as Webster's Second puts it, in "a markedly regular rhythmic form; as a *square* melody." *Square,* of course, came to mean out of style, quaint. To play or sing "square" implied the same thing—old-fashioned, tired, not *hip.*

Ragtime changed the rules. Musicians and singers, remaining always aware of the beat, began to sing and play around it. We take this freedom for granted today, but when we listen to singers and players recorded early in the century, we are amazed at how "square" their delivery is. They are *on* the beat. The ragtime kids took the notes off the page and off the beat and minted a new American way with music. The imperative? Keep the beat in your head or your hands or your heart, and do anything you please ahead of it or behind it, inside or outside it. Ragtime, then, viewed large, was the fountainhead of every rhythmic and stylistic upheaval that has followed, in a century of ever-evolving American popular music.

The Early Origins of Jazz

Jeff Taylor

I n March of 1917 the New York–based Victor Records released a single disc by the Original Dixieland Jass Band, a group of white musicians from New Orleans. The band had been in the city since January of that year, after a successful run in Chicago, and the two tunes they recorded, "Livery Stable Blues" and "Dixieland Jass Band One Step," are usually considered the first recordings of jazz. The record, joined by several more in the following months, created an international sensation and sold at least a quarter million copies. Just two years later, with jazz securely rooted in the national consciousness, the vocalist Creighton Thompson could exclaim: "Jazz, jazz, jazz, that's all I want to do; Play me a little jazz!"

Though the Original Dixieland Jass Band (or ODJB) recordings were, ironically, not made by the African Americans who had been jazz's primary creators, and though some scholars have claimed that the band's music lacked elements that define the tradition (improvisation and, to a large extent, the powerful but elusive rhythmic groove known as "swing feeling"), the issue of the discs was a watershed event in the music's history. They gave the public at large its first taste of this refreshing new music and inspired legions of younger musicians to explore the art. Yet if these performances

Sincerely Yours,
The "Original Dixieland Jazz Band"

The Original Dixieland Jazz Band, 1917. Left to right: Tony (Sbarbaro) Spargo, drums; Eddie Edwards, trombone; Nick LaRocca, cornet; Larry Shields, clarinet; Henry Ragas, piano. Courtesy Frank Driggs Collection.

provided the cornerstone of a rich body of recorded music, they also came at the end of an initial period of jazz's development; they represented the culmination of a musical story that had been unfolding for at least the previous three decades.

Unfortunately, investigating the evolution of this distinctively American musical language has proven a frustrating and treacherous path. Scholars and listeners are constantly faced with the vexing fact that jazz in its infancy was never recorded on disc; as a result, whatever is written or said about the actual *sound* of this early music must inevitably remain conjecture. The necessity of relying on the often conflicting testimony of musicians and listeners who were present during the birth of jazz, and the temptation to extrapolate features of early jazz from later recordings (such as those made in 1923 by King Oliver's Creole Jazz Band), have given rise to a variety of myths and rumors about the origins of the music. Though these myths often contain valuable insights, they have perpetuated an oversimplified view of jazz's early history.

In the most prevalent of these myths, jazz was created by mostly untrained musicians in New Orleans around the turn of the century. In 1917, after a period of gestation in New Orleans's red light district of Storyville, the music began to spread north, as jazz musicians were forced by stringent vice laws to seek employment elsewhere. Jazz then moved up the Mississippi to Chicago, and from there, in the late 1920s, to New York.

In the past twenty years, jazz scholars from a variety of disciplines have substantially revised this tale by reevaluating oral histories, studying related repertories, and examining largely uninvestigated sources (such as census records, newspapers, and documents related to the Works Project Administration). For one thing, though the primacy of New Orleans in the development of jazz is irrefutable, a variety of syncopated styles and repertories, ones related to but distinct from the ragtime and "country blues" traditions, are now known to have evolved in other regions of the country during jazz's formative years. In New York, Chicago, the Southwest, and even the West Coast, African-American popular music traditions both maintained a regional flavor and incorporated elements of the New Orleans style as it was disseminated in the first two decades of the twentieth century. As they did so, the effect may not have been so much one of "jazzing" a previously "nonjazz" repertory (as has been often suggested) but of fostering the creation of an entirely new idiom. The result was the bewildering variety of styles and ensembles heard on recordings of the 1920s, many of which have been long accepted as part of the jazz "canon."

The evocative tales of jazz's origins in brothels have been largely refuted as well, for though jazz has for a good part of its history maintained a relationship with prostitution and other illicit activities, most of the early jazz players found employment in social, civic, and cultural events outside the red light districts. Research into the musical repertories and styles that went into the making of jazz has also helped dismiss the idea that the music was created mainly by musically illiterate players. The evocative image of the "natural" jazz talent who plays entirely by ear was promoted early in the history of the music (by the members of the ODJB, among others) and was partly responsible for the music's immediate appeal. But many of the early players were, in fact, readers, and notated music in the form of written arrangements and lead sheets formed a fundamental part of the music's history.

One of the most important discoveries has concerned the early dissemination of the music. It is now known that New Orleans musicians were touring outside their home city even in the early formative years of jazz. Between 1907 and 1910, for example, pianist Jelly Roll Morton traveled extensively throughout the South and Midwest. By 1911 pianist Tony Jackson was having an important impact on Chicago's music scene, and scholar Lawrence Gushee has placed other New Orleans musicians in California as early as 1908. And, as Gushee points out, there is reason to believe other New Orleans musicians ventured far from home during the early days of jazz. Though there is no way to know precisely what style of music these players were performing, one suspects they both influenced the local musicians who heard them and picked up new ideas themselves along the way.

If recent scholars have refuted many of the established jazz myths, they have not yet replaced them with a cohesive story of their own. As jazz historiography continues to widen its scope, many more important discoveries will no doubt be made. In the meantime, the most one may do is to delve into the rich tapestry of social, economic, and musical factors that helped foster this art form, and hope to do justice to the hundreds of artists, many forgotten and unrecorded, who first gave jazz to the world.

The Word

It is not clear when the term *jazz* (or its early variants, *jaz* and *jass*) first came into existence, but its first known appearance in print was in a 1913 sports column of a San Francisco newspaper, with its application to a specific musical style coming two years later (in a reference to a white New Orleans group led by Tom Brown). A variety of theories have been suggested about the etymology of the term *jazz*: the word has variously been traced to earlier African and Creole terms and to the French verb *jaser* (to chatter). The word may also have roots in a verbal form (to "jazz something up" or to "jazz around") as a reference, perhaps, to the energetic styles of the early players and their tendency to deviate from a printed score or established musical routine. Most famously, it has been suggested that the word is a slang term for the sex act and related to the word *orgasm* or *gism* (semen). This last theory was certainly responsible for several musicians' steadfast avoidance of the term in describing their own music; yet such an origin has never been proven.

But even if scholars could definitively trace the origins of the word itself, there would still remain the problem of its application during the early days of the music, when there was no single repertory universally accepted by the general public as jazz (a quandary which has, to some extent, remained to the present day). Until the end of the 1920s (and perhaps even later) the term *jazz* was applied rather indiscriminately to any peppy, danceable repertory, from the songs of Irving Berlin to the raggy pyrotechnics of the "novelty" pianists. And after jazz became an international phenomenon in the late teens, the term was exploited (as was the term *blues*) as a potent advertising gimmick for the expanding recording and sheet music industries, one often applied to products whose connection to the jazz tradition was tenuous at best.

Nevertheless, for many *musicians* there was an important difference between jazz and other repertories, even in the earliest days of the music's dissemination. Though their stories conflict as to what made the tradition unique, performers such as pianist James P. Johnson, pianist, composer, and bandleader Ferdinand "Jelly Roll" Morton, and trumpeter Adolphus "Doc" Cheatham reserved the term *jazz* for a specific style, one distinct from the other popular musics being performed in the teens. Through imaginative research, Lawrence Gushee has supported the claim that what many musicians called *jazz* before around 1920 might more accurately be considered a type of instrumental ragtime from New Orleans, one with a distinctly regional flavor lent by that city's unique musical culture. Perhaps it would be more accurate to describe this music as not quite ragtime and not yet jazz; it was an elusive transitional music that would not begin to emerge as a cohesive tradition until great black jazz artists such as Morton, King Oliver, and Louis Armstrong began to record in the early 1920s.

Setting the Stage

If the sound of early jazz (or, perhaps more accurately, "prejazz") remains elusive, much may be learned about the creation of the music by placing it within the context of turn-of-the-century America. As historian Thomas Hennessey and others have shown, jazz was from its earliest days both a great art form and a commercial commodity. And like all musics, it directly reflected the complex social environment in which it was forged. The early history of jazz encompasses not just the development of a new musical idiom but the evolution of a society in which that idiom could flourish.

Given the sketchy nature of the evidence, beginning the story of jazz in a specific year (1890) may seem suspicious and arbitrary. But there are several excellent reasons for starting the tale here. For one thing, the last decade of the nineteenth century saw the beginning of a radical shift in population patterns in the United States, with the country moving from a rural to an urban culture. In 1890, only 35 percent of the U.S. population lived in cities, but over the following years the number increased dramatically. With the development of cities came the growth of the theatrical and music publishing industries.

On a more specific level, it was at the end of the nineteenth century that African Americans began to move into urban areas to find work and escape the oppressive racial policies of the South. The migration would reach epic proportions in the years around World War I, but even in this earlier period profound changes began to take place in the black communities of many cities. Enclaves of African Americans, which began to boast black-owned businesses and featured a well-defined class structure within the urban context as a whole, began to take shape. It was largely (though not exclusively) within these communities that the early black jazz musicians would find employment.

Related to America's changing demography were some radical shifts in social dancing, also taking place in the 1890s. The second half of the nineteenth century had seen a change from the "separate couple" dances of the quadrille, contradance, and cotillion to the "closed couple" dances of the waltz and polka. Near the end of the century, new closed couple dances began to emerge, ones inextricably linked to the popular music of the period (particularly ragtime), especially the two-step and turkey trot. Such developments set the stage for the intricate relationship between jazz and dance that would remain for the first fifty years of its history. Not only did playing for dancing provide the bread and butter of most early jazz musicians' careers, it exerted a dynamic influence on the music itself, as dance fads came and went and the demands of audiences changed. In addition, as dance halls, ballrooms, and cabarets competed more and more for the customer's dollar, a complex set of ties evolved between the club owners who hired the musicians and other levels of urban society—particularly organized crime.

Finally, the 1890s saw the development of mass marketing in the music industry. The explosive popularity of pieces such as Scott Joplin's "Maple Leaf Rag" (1899), and the emergence of the vastly lucrative businesses of New York's Tin Pan Alley, showed the viability of sheet music as a potent commercial product; piano rolls would follow, as would sound recordings. Without the influence of the music industry, jazz would have evolved in a much different way (if, indeed, it would have come into being at all); not only was the business responsible for bringing the music to international attention, but it created a method by which musicians could listen to and learn from each other. And the success of the music industry inspired black artists and entrepreneurs to build their own publishing and recording businesses; many of these companies, such as those led by W. C. Handy and Harry Pace, would play a significant part in the early dissemination of jazz. Some black businessmen also developed a role within the larger white-owned companies: Clarence Williams, for example, besides working as both a musician and publisher, became in the early 1920s an A&R representative for the OKeh company's race record series and was responsible for recruiting many of the artists who performed on that label.

New stylistic trends in urban African-American music at the end of the nineteenth century also helped set the stage for the creation of jazz. The most important musical traditions mined by the first generation of jazz musicians were undoubtedly ragtime and the blues. These traditions preceded jazz, but they also continued to coexist with it for much of its early history. Early jazz may, for example, be seen partly as an advanced branch of the ragtime tradition, but ragtime also maintained its own trajectory to some extent, with more "traditional" ragtime being performed and written well into the twenties. The blues, though it lent much to jazz, also continued as a discrete tradition, in both rural and urban incarnations. The creation of jazz was not so much a matter of a few brilliant musicians selecting elements of these and other repertories and combining them into a spicy new musical stew. Rather, jazz resulted from a complex and exciting period of cross-pollination between musicians and groups, with ragtime bands playing blues, blues musicians playing ragtime, and classically trained players exploring a host of popular music genres.

Still, specific features of ragtime and the blues may be identified in early jazz. The conceptual basis of ragtime—a heavily syncopated melodic line over a regularly accented bass rhythm—can be tied to the familiar arrangement of instruments in the early jazz ensemble, where the complex lines of the lead instruments are backed by the steady on-the-beat chording of a rhythm section. In addition, multi-strained ragtime pieces figured prominently in the repertory of most early jazz groups and continued to be a performance staple throughout the 1920s.

The blues lent jazz a specific twelve-bar form and, perhaps more important, a rich tradition of performance style that emphasized individual expression over "correct" instrumental technique. The fondness for bent pitches, for playing "between the cracks" of established Western tonality, and the variety of buzzes, growls, and scoops that are an indispensable feature of jazz's art arose mainly from the blues tradition. The blues may also have provided a conduit for the incorporation of Latin American elements into jazz, particularly in New Orleans. Some jazz scholars have suggested that the distinctive rhythmic components of Latin American music played a role in the development of jazz "swing" feeling, and several early jazz musicians, including Jelly Roll Morton and drummer Baby Dodds, recalled that in New Orleans the blues were played slowly and with a "Spanish" feel.

New Orleans

Typical features of the late nineteenth- and early twentieth-century urban landscape can be seen in New Orleans, where most of the great early jazz players were born. Yet in many ways the city was unique. Because of its status as an important port and its past ownership by both the French and the Spanish, the city boasted an ethnic diversity perhaps unmatched in any other city of its time; besides the strong European influence, the city had a distinctive Caribbean flavor. In addition, New Orleans was arguably the most musical city in the country, with a rich tradition of both classical and vernacular styles that stretched back to the eighteenth century.

New Orleans for most of its history maintained a distinctive racial climate. Slaves were allowed the freedom to maintain some of their African-based rituals, as well as the accompanying music, when many of these traditions had been strongly repressed in other areas of the South; indeed, slave celebrations in so-called Congo Square were known to continue well into the nineteenth century. In addition, New Orleans boasted an influential population of Creoles, American-born people of Spanish or French descent. A subset of this group—the so-called black Creoles or Creoles of color—played a pivotal role in the early development of jazz.

In New Orleans, as in other areas of the United States, sexual relationships frequently developed between slave owners and their female slaves, with children of mixed parentage a typical result. According to the city's Black Code of 1724, these slaves and their children could be freed and were allowed to own property. Some were given large bequests by their former owners. As a result, many of these Creoles ran plantations of their own or established prosperous urban businesses. Their children were often sent to France for education. By the mid-1800s, the Creoles of color represented a wealthy and influential class in New Orleans; because of their history and educational background they clung steadfastly to European-based customs and culture, establishing, among other institutions, a Negro Philharmonic Society in the 1830s. For most of the nineteenth century these Creoles, from whose ranks would come great early jazzmen such as Morton, reed player Sidney Bechet, and trombonist Edward "Kid" Ory, maintained both a social and a geographic distance from the poorer black residents who lived "uptown," and whose lives were steeped in more rural-based African-American folk traditions.

In the mid-1890s, as New Orleans's racial codes were revised, increased (and often reluctant) contact between the black Creoles and the "uptown" blacks began to take place. Oral histories suggest that these associations brought together the musical strands that contributed to jazz: from the Creoles came written traditions of classical music, European-style dances, and ragtime, and from the blacks the rich oral tradition of folk music and the blues. Certainly the truth was far less tidy; not all Creoles were grounded in European music (Sidney Bechet never learned to read music well, for example), and some "uptown" blacks did boast skill in written traditions. In addition, the role played by white musicians in New Orleans (such as bandleader "Papa" Jack Laine, who hired black musicians for his group) has been largely ignored, even though many natives of the city (the Sicilian-Americans who made up the ODJB, for example) were active on the popular music scene.

Many early jazz musicians have remarked, however, that as the musical styles of Creoles and blacks began to interact changes were felt in New Orleans's performing ensembles. Music was deeply integrated into the fabric of the city's life, and a variety of activities—social gatherings, political rallies, religious events—were accompanied by ensembles of different sizes and instrumentations, which provided work for musicians of many tastes and backgrounds. Several types of ensembles boasted a long history in the area, and their character and repertory were guided by their audiences and the context in which they played. They may be gathered into three general categories, though the boundaries between them remained somewhat fluid. The most informal ensembles were the combos that performed in the seedier cabarets and bars of the red light district; these were small groups that were often built around a pianist. Jelly Roll Morton, who frequently played in this context, recalls that the repertory of these groups consisted largely of slow blues and more up-tempo, rag-like stomps and "honky-tonk numbers." Better known were the brass marching bands, which would perform for public gatherings, picnics, funerals, and a variety of other events; these groups specialized in traditional marching music but also began to incorporate rags and blues into their performances during the early 1900s. The final category, loosely gathered under the heading of "dance bands," often included string instruments and played for dances, parties, and other social functions. The repertory varied widely, and clearly had to be adaptable to a variety of performance venues. The musically literate, high-class "society orchestra" led by violinist John Robichaux (a black Creole) specialized in written arrangements of popular dance music (especially waltzes, two-steps, cakewalks, and marches), while the rougher, less-trained group led by black cornetist Buddy Bolden specialized in the blues.

Though each of these ensemble types played a role in the gradual evolution of jazz in New Orleans, there is evidence that the dance bands provided the most fertile breeding ground for the new music. According to eyewitnesses, during the early 1900s many of these groups began to incorporate the looser, improvisatory, more blues-inflected "ratty" style of playing associated with "uptown" blacks, which, though not yet jazz, struck an exciting chord with many younger musicians. Bolden's group, in particular, requires comment in this regard, for the cornetist enjoyed wide celebrity during the formative years of jazz. Though Bolden's professional career was quite brief (he led his first group in the mid-1890s and by 1907 was forced by mental illness to stop performing) he had a profound effect on New Orleans musical life. His ensemble, which in 1901 included cornet, clarinet, valve trombone, guitar, bass, and drums, helped set a standard for New Orleans jazz instrumentation, while his powerful tone and passionate feel for the blues inspired a generation of younger New Orleans musicians. Perhaps more important, he is reported to have played with a distinctive and very personal rhythmic feel, perhaps prefiguring the infectious "swing" that would characterize the work of later jazz musicians. In addition, his talent for melodic decoration—though it fell short of true improvisation—encouraged younger musicians to develop a freer, more spontaneous approach to established repertory.

As noted earlier, there are no recordings of Bolden's group nor of any other New Orleans ensemble during the early history of jazz. But a few recordings provide hints to the general characteristics of their music and the rich cultural life from which it emerged. First there are the 1917 performances of the ODJB. The members of this group had been immersed from childhood in the exciting music scene of their hometown, and though they may have altered their performance style to fit the demands of the commercial marketplace (especially after their tours of Chicago and New York), their recordings do suggest some of the essential features of New Orleans jazz. In a performance such as "Livery Stable Blues," for example, one immediately notes the free (almost anarchic) approach to instrumental technique and tone color, as the musicians proceed through a catalog of bent notes, swoops, and vibratos (not to mention animal sounds) that would make a classical musician shudder. In addition, the densely polyphonic texture—cornet playing lead, trombone supplying a bass line, and clarinet embroidering above—captures at least the spirit of the collective improvisation common in the early New Orleans bands (even if a close listening shows that the ODJB's instrumental lines were clearly preplanned).

Another important recorded document comes from a decade after the first ODJB recordings. In 1927, in New Orleans, Columbia recorded eight performances by Sam Morgan's Jazz Band. Most of the members of this ensemble had never traveled outside of New Orleans and its environs and had remained relatively untouched by the constantly shifting musical trends of Chicago and New York. Therefore, the recordings may very well capture the sound of the early black New Orleans jazz bands. Though the group engages in a great deal of collective improvisation on these recordings, one is immediately struck by the relaxed, four-to-the-bar feel of the rhythm section and by the warm tone color of the featured instrumentalists, especially Sam and Ike Morgan on cornet. The effect provides a potent contrast to the frenetic tempos of the ODJB and may well signify a crucial element in early jazz: a passion and personal expressiveness brought on by a profound feeling for the blues.

Finally there remain the attempts made by several New Orleans musicians to re-create (often at a distance of several decades) the music they heard and played during the early days of jazz. Though some of these recordings (such as those made in the 1940s by trumpeter Bunk Johnson) have proved unreliable as historical documents, Jelly Roll Morton's 1938 recollections for Alan Lomax at the Library of Congress (now easily available on modern reissue) remain a rich lode of information. Morton's braggadocio was legendary, and his claims are occasionally contradicted by modern scholarship; nevertheless, his reminiscences (peppered throughout by sung passages and illustrations at the piano) vividly portray the sheer variety of music that captured the ears of the first generation of New Orleans jazz musicians, from rags and quadrilles to blues, popular songs, and operatic excerpts. And his attempts to re-create earlier styles in performance, though they are always laced with Morton's very personal musical voice, give glimpses of some of early twentieth-century New Orleans's most intriguing musical personalities.

Other Locales

New Orleans certainly gave a new musical idiom to the rest of the world and may have provided the catalyst for the creation of jazz. Yet other areas in the country, both urban and rural, played a crucial role in the early history of the music. New York had by the late nineteenth century become the center of America's entertainment industry. The city's thriving black theater scene, with its deft blending of blues, ragtime, operetta, and popular song, not only provided employment for many musicians who would later make their mark in jazz but established in its pit orchestras a musical tradition that was ripe for the incorporation of New Orleans music. In addition, James Reese Europe's group, though it performed social dance music and not jazz, set a standard for ensemble playing and was an important progenitor of the city's jazz orchestras of the twenties. Europe's Clef Club, a booking agency and social organization founded in 1910, also strengthened the role of black musicians on the New York scene. And though they specialized in a solo repertory, stride pianists such as James P. Johnson and Luckey Roberts were at the forefront of the music's transition from a rigidly syncopated ragtime idiom to a more fluid, blues-inflected jazz style. Unlike New Orleans, the rise of new popular styles in New York was documented, though in a rather haphazard way, on sound discs and piano rolls; though most of these recordings are peripheral to jazz, they do provide a much-needed glimpse into the city's prejazz music scene.

Chicago's role as a center of jazz in the 1920s is well known, but ragtime and syncopated dance music were being performed in the city some time before the important early New Orleans jazz musicians began to move north. Ragtime was heard at the 1893 World's Fair, which featured several important pianists (including Scott Joplin), and in the following years the city became an important center for ragtime publishing and the production of piano rolls. An all-black branch of the musician's union, Local 208, was founded in 1902 and served as a focal point for many musicians' working lives. Beginning with the establishment of the Pekin Theater in 1905, Chicago built a thriving entertainment district centered on South State Street; within just five years several important performance venues, including the Grand, Vendome, and Monogram theaters, were in operation. In addition, by 1910 several musicians who specialized in ragtime and syncopated dance music, including Dave Peyton, Glover Compton, and Clarence M. Jones, were well established in the city. By all accounts the New Orleans musicians who traveled to Chicago (especially after 1917) took the city by storm; yet as in New York the existing black popular music scene in the city also undoubtedly influenced the evolution of jazz there. Unfortunately, no recordings of early Chicago jazz and prejazz exist.

Finally, though long neglected, black music performed in the so-called territories during the early part of the century has now begun to be incorporated into jazz's story. In smaller cities and rural areas throughout the South, Southwest, and Midwest, popular musical styles steeped in black vernacular traditions reached audiences largely through traveling productions known as "tent shows." The brass bands that played for these shows (as well as for after-hours dances) were patterned after military groups and played marches, blues, and rags. These ensembles provided an important training ground for musicians who would later find their way to the important urban centers and make their mark in the jazz scene: W. C. Handy, for example, who moved to New York in 1918 and became a vital presence in the city's entertainment business, led a well-known touring brass band based in Memphis. In addition, solo pianists specializing in blues and ragtime built a performance tradition of their own throughout the territories, traveling from town to town playing in small cabarets and bars and accompanying silent films. Many of these players would later settle in Chicago and New York, where they came in contact with musicians from a variety of other backgrounds and lent their distinctive voices to an emerging music.

The story of jazz's early history will never be definitively recorded, for it is not a single narrative but many; a rich mosaic of musical voices, each with a tale to tell. Perhaps this is the music's greatest miracle: that it arose not from a single place or time but from a people, a country, and an era.

New York Roots: Black Broadway, James Reese Europe, Early Pianists

Thomas L. Riis

 New York's significance for jazz history lies in its open embrace of all things theatrical and seemingly all life forms with a dramatic or dramatizable element. Because the city possesses a long history of hospitality to the marginalized of the world—not merely twentieth-century immigrants arriving at Ellis Island, but Dutch sailors in the seventeenth century, English loyalists during the American Revolution, Atlantic pirates in search of safe haven, and all manner of scoundrels, scalawags, traders, and freebooters over the last several hundred years—its openness to unusual custom, indeed its flamboyant penchant for self-promotion, has conduced to the process of creating characters in costume, storytellers, and other citizens who work at being visible, striking, and larger than life.

Of course there was black music and drama in New York long before jazz. Musical interpolations were part and parcel of the African Grove Theatre productions in Five Points dating as far back as 1821. In the same decade free blacks "danced for eels" in Catherine Market. At the nearby Chatham Theatre such dance customs were immortalized in the landmark play *New York as It Is* twenty years later. Even before the blackface minstrel show African-American street-songs and

Lieutenant James Reese Europe's 369th Infantry Regiment Band, Hotel Tunis, Paris, 1919.
Courtesy Frank Driggs Collection.

dances were being appropriated, reshaped, and presented in a formal dramatic context.

By the turn of the century, before Harlem became the national center of African-American culture, New York supported more actors and professional musicians connected with the stage than any other American city. The theatricalization, so to speak, of black talent continued with the minstrel show itself in 1855 (when black performers added burnt-cork makeup to enhance the "authenticity" of variety shows), commercial imitations of the wildly successful Fisk Jubilee (choral spirituals) Singers in the 1870s, and pioneering traveling companies such as the Hyers Sisters that used the spirituals and newer songs by black composers Sam Lucas and James Bland in original plays designed as realistic comedies. Then in the 1890s ragtime came to town.

In the subsequent generation when the term *jazz* (or *jass*) began to be applied to music, its link to ragtime—an African-American product originating in the Midwest—was evident. Both implied spontaneity, looseness in many senses, rhythmic novelty, vitality, and black roots. The concentration of people, the high level of activity, and the relatively freewheeling social environment in New York allowed ragtime and stomp music to flourish there. Extensive numbers of performances took place, and recording was possible. A skilled freelance musician, especially a facile note-reader, could make good money in New York. Bands abounded. Social and theatrical events of every description needed music, first ragtime and later jazz, with the latter term driving out the older one by 1920.

Whereas most famous early jazz players specialized on instruments more portable than the piano, the presence of pianos in public venues everywhere by the turn of the century made them natural partners in any kind of small ensemble music taking place in even a moderate-size concert room, dance hall, or stage. Ragtime pianists came to New York from all over the country as the craze for the new syncopated style spread between 1896 and 1916. Ragtime songs, in the easily salable and thoroughly familiar format of piano/vocal score, rose high in popularity, then ebbed as recorded instrumental jazz and blues were adopted as natural heirs to rag.

Although early stage efforts to include ragtime did not all arise in New York, the growing and theatrically receptive cities of the eastern seaboard (especially New York) noticed, mimicked, and enlarged upon the broad outlines that characterized all musical comedies of the time: a flexible format, a mixture of song types always including the latest styles, a comic story or at least the presence of a star comedian, interpolated vernacular dances, and the avoidance of situations deemed to be inappropriate by white producers (such as a serious plot with romantic coupling, love songs, overtly tragic endings, and politically provocative dialogue) for shows with black actors.

While significant developments can be seen in such landmark shows as *Clorindy, or the Origin of the Cakewalk* (1898) and those produced by Sam T. Jack's Creole Burlesque companies (1890–97), John Isham's Octoroons (1895–99), and the Black Patti Troubadours (1896–1916), the crest of popularity for shows that properly can be deemed musical comedies spanned the decade from 1898 to 1908, coincident with the rise of piano ragtime in New York and elsewhere. These shows, though produced and financially controlled by white managers, were built almost solely with black talent: young cakewalk dancers, vaudevillians, composers, directors, choreographers, comics, scriptwriters, and instrumental musicians.

Both black and white ticket buyers flocked to the best of these productions: *A Trip to Coontown* (1898), *In Dahomey* (1902–3), *Abyssinia* (1906), *The Oyster Man* (1907), *Bandanna Land* (1908), and *The Red Moon* (1909). These shows and about two dozen others during the decade were formed around three distinct creative nuclei: the cakewalking team of Bert Williams and George Walker; Bob Cole and J. Rosamond Johnson; and Ernest Hogan, the singer-comedian advertised as "the Unbleached American" because he avoided the notorious makeup of minstrelsy. All of these performers and their companies, using original music, mounted fully staged and equipped, evening-long shows that began in New York, toured widely, and found large audiences and positive reviews. Most important, they stimulated an attitude indissolubly linked with jazz; they seemed to urge wild, spontaneous, sympathetic movement among singers, players, and audiences alike.

The most creative literate musicians whose efforts were realized in the black shows were J. Rosamond Johnson, known nowadays as the brother of intellectual James Weldon Johnson, with whom he coauthored *The Book[s] of American Negro Spirituals* (1925–26), and Will Marion Cook (1869–1944), a nearly forgotten pioneer whose assimilation of orchestral ragtime and syncopated song was crucial to the perception of his shows as distinctively modern and racial. (In *Music Is My Mistress* [1973] Duke Ellington hailed Cook as "His Majesty the King of Consonance," deftly capturing both his important influence and his conservatism from the jazz musician's point of view.)

The songs of Johnson and Cook generally avoid the sophisticated textures and persistent multiple syncopations of Scott Joplin and his fellow classic piano rag writers, but the presence of the basic offbeat emphasis of rag, plus an unmistakable bluesy quality in the melodies of the slower ballads, marks these as African-American precursors to jazz itself, long before Gershwin, Whiteman, and Grofé developed their more famous orchestral models. That Cook's music was known to the sweet bands of New Orleans is clear from the presence of band parts for his tune "On Emancipation Day" in the John Robichaux collection of the New Orleans Jazz Archive, Tulane University.

Johnson performed at the piano in his vaudeville act, and his arrangements of spirituals, as well as contemporary witnesses, indicate that he possessed formidable keyboard skills. Cook's main instrument was the violin, and he assumed the role of conductor and musical director for many shows.

James Reese Europe

One of the outstanding talents to emerge from a group of younger men who worked in the early all-black musical comedies was James Reese Europe (1881–1919). Hailing from Washington, D.C., he had grown up in the neighborhood of John Philip Sousa and studied violin and piano in a nurturing middle-class household. Forced by his father's death in 1899 to provide an income for his mother and sisters, he eventually joined his brother John, a pianist in New York, where his talents for music and leadership were quickly recognized.

He assisted with writing the music for songs to be interpolated by the Black Patti Troubadours' chief comedian, John Larkins, and had other tunes of his taken up by popular white vaudevillians. After playing in a groundbreaking concert of "syncopated" music—with Cook, he became one of the popularizers of this upscale term for ragtime—in 1905 with Ernest Hogan's Memphis Students (evidently one of the many commercial take-offs on the Fisk [Nashville students] Singers ensemble), he served as musical director in the Cole and Johnson brothers shows *The Shoo-Fly Regiment* (1906) and *The Red Moon* (1908). He also organized benefits and fund-raisers for the Colored Vaudeville Benevolent Association and was a member of their core leadership group known as the Frogs.

In 1910, seeing that black talent could be profitably employed in a variety of functions supported by rich socialites, Europe organized the Clef Club (and later the Tempo Club) and proceeded to develop an extraordinarily successful booking agency to supply well-outfitted and highly professional ensembles throughout the city. He himself conducted a group called the Society Orchestra.

By 1912 he had so successfully convinced a skeptical white public of the worth of new African-American music that he was able to organize two concerts in Carnegie Hall to showcase the latest works of European-trained composers like Cook and Will Tyers. Europe's bands in the Clef Club were note-readers and straight players, but individual soloists needed little encouragement to increase the momentum and intensity, and evidently Europe gave it to them.

The Castles

Europe's fame increased when his band was chosen in 1913 to accompany the young Anglo-American husband-and-wife dance team of Vernon and Irene Castle. This up-to-date, fun-loving, yet proper couple was precisely suited to the temper of the times, looking for thrills via the music of two-steps and a variety of "animal" dances (turkey trot, grizzly bear, bunny hug). Dances of the black folk—from farm, street, and dive—were transmuted and tamed through the ballroom slickness of the chic pair. Europe's polished ragtime played by bands of black performers in formal concert dress so perfectly managed to accompany these steps that they achieved an air of the mildly risqué, a naughty-but-nice novelty made to order for the white middle class aspiring to join the "smart set."

In 1914 Castle House was created as a venue in which the Castles could teach in a more intimate setting and demonstrate popular dance steps in versions made safe for genteel audience participation. This idea intensified an already phenomenal impact. Everything the couple did in the line of popular fashion was talked about and imitated. Castlemania reigned.

Their dance instruction booklet strictly forbade hopping, dipping, hip shaking, body twisting, and other suggestive or overexcited vernacular steps. But the Castles understood that the key to success was related to modern music. Fully crediting James Reese Europe with the invention of the music for the fox-trot—they liked the moderate tempo and unjerky syncopations he used in playing W. C. Handy's "Memphis Blues" for them—the Castles ultimately created this new dance as a box step with a few quick glides, skips, and kicks added. The swaying music in duple meter made the perfect substitute for all manner of tunes that had been used to accompany earlier, more ungainly steps.

Europe's fox-trots fueled the longest-lived dance craze of the first half of the century. The fox-trot phenomenon also influenced many subsequent dance fads and later orchestras, such as Paul Whiteman's, which were associated with jazz. More important, it represented the first time that a blues-inflected idiom entered the mainstream of American popular culture. As Europe's biographer Reid Badger has noted, "Without that diffusion [of the blues], much of what developed as characteristic American popular song and dance, or jazz for that matter, would be inconceivable" (1995, 116).

The sensation that the Castles created with Europe's music boosted his growing fame, but the frivolity all ended when World War I broke out and Vernon left America to join the Royal Air Force. Vernon Castle's example was not lost on Europe, and the latter's greatest musical triumph was still to come when he entered the military. Encouraged by New York friends and colleagues to believe that benefits would accrue to the black community in general only if its leaders aided the growing war effort, he enlisted in the army in September 1916 with the intention of joining a machine-gun company.

Within weeks, he was assigned the task of recruiting a band. He recognized that there existed a shortage of trained black woodwind players in the United States and recommended that his commanding officer, Colonel Hayward, look toward Puerto Rico. By May of 1917 Europe, through strong recruiting efforts and assisted by other experienced bandmen such as Noble Sissle (the future partner of Eubie Blake), Eugene Mikell, and E. E. Thompson, had assembled a band of some thirty players—it would later grow to fifty—for the Fifteenth Regiment band (centered in Harlem), which performed its first New York concert in June. An enthusiastic hometown audience turned out, but it would be another six months before any black combat units were allowed to set foot in France.

Once arrived "over there," however, Europe and his band found themselves in a surprisingly congenial setting. The French showered praise on their patriotism, musicianship, and esprit de corps. Redesignated as the 369th Infantry Regiment of the U.S. Army, and training with the French Sixteenth Division, the old New York Fifteenth Regiment was no more, and the Hellfighters band, as it came to be called, was on its way. Morale under the sympathetic French commanders was extremely good, and the French people's reception of the music of the 369th was tumultuous.

If one compares Europe's Society Orchestra recordings and the even more exuberant Hellfighters band performances with other renditions of popular songs at the time, it becomes clear what gave his groups the edge with listeners. Quick tempos coupled with onrushing energy immediately catch the ear. In performances by the large French group (with over four dozen players), which was constituted primarily of brass instruments, this sort of impetuosity was pleasantly shocking to its first hearers.

Even on the string-dominated Society Orchestra recordings, extra percussion (especially the drum solos of Buddy Gilmore in the "Castle House Rag" [1914, Victor]), typically called for in the final strains, heightened the volume, excitement, and rhythmic presence of Europe's arrangements and emphasized the (written-out) syncopations. "Too Much Mustard" (1913, Victor), "Down Home Rag" (1913, Victor), and "The Dancing Deacon" (1919, Pathé Frère) all exhibit this wildly ragged and intense quality of abandon.

Other bands playing the same songs sound polite, stiff, and monotonous. Europe's band, its members having been trained in the traditional manner, was perfectly capable of playing in the standard way. A Hellfighters recording of "How Ya Gonna Keep 'Em Down on the Farm?" (1919, Pathé Frère) with moderate tempos, correct intonation, and razor-sharp ensemble proves beyond a doubt that Europe was intentionally imparting a new verve within a big ensemble. In *Early Jazz* (1968) Gunther Schuller called the Hellfighters "the first big band."

Europe also paid attention to the contributions of his individual band members. He did not loose all restraints in encouraging improvisation—which would have been rather impractical in any case with such a large group—but dozens of admiring firsthand reports summon metaphorical images that range from tangy pineapples to rushing waterfalls (included in Badger's biography of Europe) to account for the completely unique sounds of his players.

Early Pianists Onstage

Even before Europe was spreading the fame of African-American instrumental music in France, a number of talented solo pianists back in New York, often natives of other eastern cities, were also making the transition from ragtime and stomp to jazz. Charles Luckeyeth "Luckey" Roberts, James P. Johnson, and Eubie Blake, who had been a member of Europe's Society Orchestra, were transforming popular Tin Pan Alley tunes and older rags, using their phenomenal technical abilities and new melodic and rhythmic methods. The steady left-hand oom-pahs of simpler rag pieces were deepened and made irregular with new stride bass patterns that went beyond simple broken octaves to add wider leaps and more chromatic chords in the lower register.

The combination of blues notes and rhythmic plasticity in the right hand, along with the frequent addition of elaborate arpeggios and operatic vocal figurations, pushed the younger generation of players to a realm which Scott Joplin (who died in 1917) would never know. With works like "Harlem Strut" and "Carolina Shout," Johnson not only created the model cutting-contest pieces of the day but began the tradition of popular pianists who thought in grander terms, who knew not only their fellow ragtimers' styles but the recordings of great classical players, artists such as Josef Hofmann and Vladimir de Pachmann.

Fats Waller, Art Tatum, Fletcher Henderson, Count Basie, and Duke Ellington are only the most famous performers who quickly absorbed the developments of the late 1910s. Other easterners involved in Johnson's Harlem circle included Willie "the Lion" Smith, Joe Turner, Cliff Jackson, and many lesser lights identified only by names or nicknames in a handful of sources: Carl Edwards, Alberta Simmons, Lippy Boyette, Willie Gant, Jack "the Bear" Wilson, "the Beetle," Willie Sewall, Willie Joseph, Corky Williams, Fred Tunstall, Bobby Lee, the sisters Gertie and Susie Monk, Dick Huff, Harold Gardner, Bob Hawkins, Russell Brooks, and Edgar Dowell.

The teenage players before the war learned from the older generation and picked up lessons from listening and imitating what went on in the saloons, dance halls, summer cafés, rent parties, and theaters. These slightly senior players, such as Luckey Roberts, Eubie Blake, and especially the legendary Abba Labba (Richard McLean), exemplified their own ear-learned neighborhood traditions and tended not to mimic the midwestern style of ragtime practiced by Scott Joplin and James Scott.

The East Coast style was special. In *Music on My Mind* (1964) Willie the Lion insisted that he heard boogie-woogie from an Atlantic City player before he'd heard the Chicago version of it from Pine Top Smith. In *Jazz From the Beginning* (1988) Garvin Bushell reported that Abba Labba "never took a steady job, . . . would come in and play for thirty minutes, cut everybody, and go out," flaunting both his skill and his independence. Abba Labba's technique reportedly was formidable (and included striding basses and melodic lines filled with chromatic experimentation), but not as elegant as James P. Johnson's.

In 1913–14 Johnson himself perfected his virtuosity in Harlem rent parties and the tough bars of the Jungles, the black club district formerly located between 60th and 63rd streets west of Ninth Avenue. In these working-class nightspots, many laborers newly arrived from the South habitually danced their leisure hours away to the accompaniment of solo piano players or pianists along with banjo, harmonica, or drum set. In such an environment, to take a strong, rhythmically clear and articulated approach was the only way for a pianist to be heard. Solid bass notes and high chords made a more resonant impression than notes clustered in the center of the keyboard, and that is exactly what Johnson's published music contains.

Of course endurance was prized, and treating a straightforward chord progression to an extended series of variations, in stomp fashion, was bound to catch the attention of the dancing listeners. By playing tremolos, cross-rhythms, and rolled chords (instead of the expected oom-pahs), with harmonic variety and persistent melodic inventiveness, the Harlem stride players became legends. Willie "the Lion" Smith's autobiography recounts in detail the numerous Newark and New York clubs that he and others worked in and depicts the trials and rewards of the business.

Luckey Roberts's and Eubie Blake's involvement in the New York theater scene once again reminds us of the Big Apple's historical enthusiasm for things associated with the stage. More than a neglible amount of Blake's subsequent influence and cachet came from his status as a composer and his acquaintance with Victor Herbert and Jerome Kern. His enduring fame came from his cocreation of the most important African-American musical comedy of the 1920s, *Shuffle Along* (1921).

The show gave ample opportunity for Blake to display his expert pianism; years later, when this early success had been almost forgotten, Blake enjoyed a revival in his personal popularity before he died at the age of 100 in 1983. His strength came also from his versatility as a composer; his written works ranged from early post–coon song rags to romantic ballads (such as "Love Will Find a Way"), novelty songs, dances ("That Charleston Dance"), and even political songs ("We Are Americans Too," "I'm Just Wild About Harry"), as well as jazz-named numbers ("Jazztime Baby").

Luckey Roberts contributed to a string of Harlem musical comedies beginning as early as 1912, when he had a small role in the early Darktown Follies hit *My Friend From Dixie*. He served as chief composer and musical director for three full musical shows before

1920: the musical comedies *My People* (1917) and *Baby Blues* (1919) and a revue called *This and That* (1919–20). A powerfully strong man with huge hands, Roberts was a commanding figure whose reach easily spanned tenths and even twelfths, enabling him to execute the most breathtaking strides on the keyboard. He continued to perform, work with other musicians, and compose for decades. He ultimately wrote more than a dozen musical comedies, published many rags that were popular with dance orchestras, became a prominent bandleader, and performed in Carnegie Hall in 1939.

The memoirs of Willie "the Lion" Smith, Eubie Blake, and James P. Johnson all confirm that a constellation of factors led to their success and the influence that they exerted on other pianists into the 1920s (James Reese Europe had died in 1919): their ability to read notes, to play in all keys, to spin out melodic improvisations with endless and flashy facility, and to hold their own socially in the rough-and-tumble world of New York nightlife. They listened to and absorbed the styles of other players. The frequency of their traveling to nearby towns also suggests that the best players were always learning and assimilating new skills while at the same time developing individual stamps or "signature chords," a highly desirable achievement for musicians who wanted steady employment.

The limits that these players placed on their own types of improvisation and their relative independence from many New Orleans– and Chicago-style ensembles has led to a never-ending discussion of the authenticity of their personal brands of jazz. But there can be no doubt that the technical flexibility, virtuosity, skill at transforming standard popular tunes, and showmanship that all exhibited redoubled their impact in the 1920s, 1930s, and 1940s. Their activities and commitment to the city of New York confirm that Broadway, Harlem, and their environs could lay claim to creating a dynamic part of jazz's early legacy.

The Blues in Jazz

Bob Porter

The blues is the music of black Americans. Originating in the South and first discovered in Mississippi, it is music that developed from field hollers, work songs, religious music, and folk melodies. Undergoing continuous change through the years, it has kept its characteristics throughout. The blues means different things to different people. Simultaneously a form and a feeling, it has provided inspiration for singers and musicians for over a century. Blues influence can be heard in each form of American popular music.

There is no trace of the blues before 1890. Many suggest that "Joe Turner Blues" may be the first blues to have found some recognition with a wide audience. This blues was originally named for Joe Turney, a man responsible for moving black prisoners from Memphis to the penitentiary in Nashville and brother to Pete Turney, former governor of Tennessee. Joe Turney was famous for his method of handcuffing eighty prisoners to forty links of chain. While the lyric of "Joe Turner" referred specifically to the area around Tennessee, the melody was known all over the South. Each locale had its own lyric. By the end of the first decade of this century, the term *the blues* was in general circulation among southern blacks.

The man who more than any other was responsible for the early popularization of the blues was William Christopher Handy. Handy was born in Florence, Alabama, in 1873 and became a professional musician just out of his teens. He worked the minstrel show circuit, slowly achieving a position of respect as a cornet soloist and bandmaster. In 1903 Handy was offered a position in Michigan to conduct a municipal band comprised of white musicians. It was a position of prestige with the prospect of greater opportunity and more money than anything Handy had previously had. Yet Handy turned it down in order to direct a black Knights of Pythias band in Clarksdale, Mississippi. Handy, in his autobiography, *Father of the Blues* (1941), could offer no logical reason for his decision. Seldom did such a decision have more important consequences in black music history.

Before the year was over, Handy knew the small towns of the Mississippi delta intimately. The fertile farmland of the delta stretched from Memphis south to Vicksburg, adjoining the river and at some points stretching many miles inland. His work required that the band be able to perform for all types of social functions. Handy had a remarkable memory for music. Snatches of melody, bits of rhythm, and folk tunes that he heard throughout his travels were the inspiration for many of his blues. Those songs, in turn, provided the foundation for a budding career as a songwriter. "Memphis Blues" was the first. Published in 1912, it was well known as a political song Handy wrote for E. H. Crump in his successful mayoral campaign of 1909. "St. Louis Blues," "Yellow Dog Blues," "Joe Turner Blues," "Beale Street Blues," "Aunt Hagar's Children," "Loveless Love," "Ole Miss," "Atlanta Blues," and more followed in quick succession.

The blues that Handy developed was twelve bars with the lyric and melody in AAB form, yet the lyric rarely utilized the full four bars. The space at the end of each line left room for fills, which allowed commentary on what had just been said or provided a setup for the next line. The fills could be vocal or instrumental. While there are many variations, chiefly eight- or sixteen-bar compositions, the space for fills is a constant.

What are known as blue notes are the flatted third, seventh, and (in later years) fifth notes in the scale. The twelve-measure blues chorus is, in its most basic form, based on only three chords: I7, IV7, and V, though there are seemingly unlimited permutations—many of them quite sophisticated. How a singer or instrumentalist deals with this harmonic pattern, the blue notes, and the fills between phrases determines his or her effectiveness as a blues performer.

Ma Rainey and her Georgia Jazz Band, 1925. Courtesy of the Institute of Jazz Studies, Rutgers University.

By 1918, W. C. Handy had moved his base of operations to New York, where he became a prominent music publisher. As much as Handy should be recognized as the man who codified the blues and shaped the music for its move into the popular mainstream, it should also be noted that his method of performing was not to last. Downriver, in New Orleans, musicians had been dealing with the blues for some time. There are no recordings of Buddy Bolden. His band had broken up by the middle of the century's first decade. Yet it seems likely that when Bolden and his band played "Make Me a Pallet on the Floor," "Careless Love," or "Funky Butt," blue notes, the distinctive characteristic of the blues, were a part of the performance.

Handy was most interested in sheet music sales, but the growing audience for phonograph records provided a second outlet for royalty income. The Original Dixieland Jazz Band recorded "Livery Stable Blues" (Victor) in 1917, and its release created a sensation. The band was a white band from New Orleans, and of the fifty-four titles released by the band during its earliest existence, more than 30 percent had *blues* as a part of the title. It was common at this time for songs without any structural connection to the blues to use the term in a title. The group recorded some of Handy's songs. Much the same could be said of the New Orleans Rhythm Kings, a Chicago-based white group, who came to prominence a bit later. While the white bands of the time learned much from listening to black music, they also had their own traditions. Still, the blues played a major part in their repertoire. If white jazz players, in general, relied less on blue notes for the substance of their solos, that didn't mean that players such as pianist Joe Sullivan or trombonist Jack Teagarden could not be impressive blues soloists, even specialists. The same is true for white jazz players in all styles.

With the recorded appearance of the great black bands of New Orleans, we get a different picture, and the contrast becomes apparent. King Oliver's Creole Jazz Band (1923 for Gennett, OKeh, and Paramount), Louis Armstrong's Hot Five and Seven (1925–28 for OKeh), and Jelly Roll Morton's Red Hot Peppers (1926–30 for Victor) were not only loaded with new ideas on the blues, but the soloists themselves were, to a man, outstanding interpreters of the blues. The key performers had to leave New Orleans in order to be heard since the Crescent City had no recording industry as such. Chicago was the initial destination, but eventually Oliver, Armstrong, and Morton all came to New York. Sidney Bechet, another New Orleanian, would not emerge as a leader on records until early 1932, yet his fame and virtuosity were well established in New York circles in the 1920s. It was one thing to use blues in repertoire; it was another thing to be a convincing blues soloist. Armstrong's 1928 version of "West End Blues" is an outstanding example of a great blues solo by a great jazz musician.

If the arrival of the great New Orleans musicians helped expose blues improvisation to an audience clearly thirsting for it, so did the advent of black vocal blues. Mamie Smith recorded "Crazy Blues" on August 10, 1920, for OKeh records, and still another milestone was reached. A huge best-seller, it launched countless other vocal blues recordings in its wake, and before long there was Clara Smith, Trixie Smith, and the Empress of the Blues, Bessie Smith. Sippie Wallace, Alberta Hunter, Ida Cox, and Victoria Spivey were among others in this field dominated by female singers, often referred to as vaudeville blues. The designation appears obscure today, but it is important to remember that these performers were professionals, with accompanists, managers, and all the incumbent trappings of show business.

Of the many prominent women in the blues field, Gertrude "Ma" Rainey stands out. She had performed in minstrel shows as a teenager in the early years of the century. There is some evidence that she heard and absorbed a primitive form of blues as early as 1905. By 1914 she and her husband were billed as "Rainey and Rainey, Assassinators of the Blues" in an act they performed for Tolliver's Circus and Musical Extravaganza. By all accounts she was an influence on most of the black singers of the era and was renowned for her ability to work an audience. Her recording career from 1923 to 1928 produced about one hundred songs. Ma Rainey introduced the blues standard "See See Rider" in her 1924 Paramount recording. Her attitude toward the music, toward her presentation, and especially toward men would continue to be passed down to future performers long after her retirement.

The kinship of blues and jazz was never stronger than in the 1920s. The rural black music that had inspired Handy had yet to fully emerge. By the end of the decade, it would arrive in the recordings of Blind Lemon Jefferson, Charlie Patton, Mississippi John Hurt, and Son House, among others. Called folk blues or country blues, it would distinguish itself from the vaudeville blues and create its own stream. This music would provide the basis of the modern blues business, which arrived with electric blues in the late 1940s and early 1950s, sparked by the great Texas guitar stylist T-Bone Walker, Muddy Waters, the father of modern Chicago blues, and the stand-alone brilliance of B. B. King.

With the success of "Crazy Blues," recordings became more important than sheet music sales. Hundreds of blues recordings were made in the 1920s, most of them in New York. Blues accompaniment has always been of interest to jazz fans. Clarinetists or saxophonists could slur or bend notes in a way that would enhance the blues line being sung. Brass players found ingenious uses for mutes, hats, or plungers. How the accompanist used the space allotted was often a key element. The placement of individual notes could provide a different feeling to a performance. A singing clarinet, moaning saxophone, or growling trumpet could emphasize or respond to a portion of the song in unique ways.

Pianists such as James P. Johnson and Sam Price were in great demand for recording sessions with blues singers. For an orchestra leader such as Fletcher Henderson, blues sessions became an important source of income. Henderson, who appears on hundreds of blues records, would utilize his own key soloists such as Louis Armstrong, Coleman Hawkins, or Buster Bailey on record dates. Henderson band members such as trumpeter Joe Smith and trombonist Charlie Green became known for their blues ability.

Another road to success for black bandleaders in the 1920s was the new medium of radio. When Duke Ellington began at the Cotton Club in Harlem in late 1927, he became a hero to his people not because they could gain entry to the whites-only establishment but because they could hear him on the radio. Because of the steady job, Ellington was able to keep some remarkable players: alto saxophonist Johnny Hodges, trumpeter Cootie Williams, and trombonist Tricky Sam Nanton among them. While Ellington preferred to wrap his orchestra in elegance and sophistication, at its heart, his was a great blues band. More than any other bandleader, he (and his soloists) had absorbed the language of the great New Orleans originators.

Ellington had begun recording in 1924 and Henderson even earlier. Radio and records were the twin methods of gaining publicity in the 1920s. By the end of the decade, each bandleader was well known in the black community of most major cities. In the Southwest, in Texas, Oklahoma, and nearby locales, the music was being shaped and molded in other hands. One could find the fine band of Ernie Fields in Tulsa, while in Houston the legendary band of Milton Larkin was a popular unit. Pianist-arranger Jesse Stone had a band headquartered in St. Joseph, Missouri. There were others in San Antonio, Dallas, and Omaha, but there were more of them in Kansas City than anywhere else.

Kansas City was a hub of big band activity. One of the reasons was that the mob had a solid operation there. Organized crime in America was fueled by the passage of the Volstead Act, which created Prohibition. Tom Pendergast ran the municipal government with the backing of local mobsters. The town was wide open for gambling, narcotics, and prostitution. There was so much money around that the Depression was scarcely felt in Kansas City. Under those circumstances it is not surprising that entertainers of all shapes and sizes flocked there.

Two bands stood above all others in Kansas City: the Blue Devils and the Bennie Moten Orchestra. The Blue Devils, under the leadership of bassist Walter Page, lasted from 1925 until 1933, while Moten, a stronger and more popular force, was a part of the scene from the early 1920s until his death in 1935. At that point, the best players from each organization came together under the leadership of a pianist who had played with both bands—William "Count" Basie.

Basie put together a group known as the Barons of Rhythm, which broadcast from its home base, the Reno Club. Among the members of the band were trumpeter Hot Lips Page and his replacement, Buck Clayton; tenor saxophonists Lester Young and Herschel Evans; alto saxophonist Buster Smith; guitarist and violinist Claude Williams; drummer Jo Jones; and singer Jimmy Rushing. This is a Hall of Fame lineup, and while there are no recordings of the Barons of Rhythm, we have plenty of recordings by Count Basie and His Orchestra beginning in 1937.

The Count Basie Orchestra recorded a song called "Swingin' the Blues" for Decca Records in 1938, and that title defines the Basie modus operandi. It was not an arranger's band like Fletcher Henderson's or one that emphasized the compositions of its leader such as Ellington's. The Basie band was built from the rhythm section and turned the spotlight on soloists. As such, the star soloists played a much greater role, especially the tenor saxophonists. Writer Albert Murray has dubbed this first Basie band the Old Testament band.

Of the key Basie performers, vocalist Jimmy Rushing stands out. Known as Mister Five by Five because of his height and girth, Rushing was equally at home with blues and pop songs. Several of his blues vocals became Basie standards: "Good Morning Blues" and "Sent for You Yesterday" on Decca as well as "Goin' To Chicago" and "Outskirts of Town" for OKeh-Columbia. An original member of the Count Basie band, Rushing stayed until 1949.

Apart from Rushing, there were major changes in the Basie band fairly quickly. Key substitutions on alto sax (Earle Warren), guitar (Freddie Greene), and trombone (Dicky Wells) made for a vast improvement in the strength of the orchestra. While the acceptance of the band by dancers and fans was immediate, those tenor sax chairs kept changing.

Evans and Young were distinctive stylists, and the contrast between them was important. Evans died in 1939, and his replacement was Buddy Tate. When Young left in 1940, a succession of players came and went—Don Byas, Lucky Thompson, Young again in 1944, and Illinois Jacquet. When Jacquet left in 1946, the transformation toward the New Testament band of the 1950s would begin.

Basie had to drop the big band for 1950 and much of 1951. When he re-formed, some major changes were undertaken. Band members such as Ernie Wilkins, Frank Foster, Thad Jones, and others were writing for a now formidable ensemble. Outside arrangers such as Neal Hefti and Quincy Jones were also important contributors to the repertoire. When singer Joe Williams and drummer Sonny Payne came aboard in 1955, the band soared. Basie kept his rhythm sound intact, and that was its distinguishing characteristic until the end. Long after the last vestiges of the Old Testament band had disappeared, the lessons of Kansas City were still being observed. Swing the blues.

After the departure from Kansas City of the Count Basie band, the focus turned to those who remained. Singer Joe Turner and pianist Pete Johnson were a formidable team at the Sunset Café. Turner was the archetypical blues shouter whose career lasted from the 1930s into the 1980s and was one of the few who made the transition to rhythm-and-blues, even rock-and-roll. A tall, heavy-set individual, Turner had a voice that displayed little subtlety and left even less to the imagination. Although he was functionally illiterate, Turner was capable of rocking the house and shouting the walls down. "Roll 'Em Pete" (1938, Vocalion) and "Piney Brown Blues" (1940, Decca) were among his best early recordings. Pete Johnson, who plays on both the Turner recordings, was one of the finest blues pianists in history. Promoter John Hammond brought him and Turner to New York. Within a short period of time they were involved in the boogie-woogie craze.

Boogie-woogie emerged as a blues piano style in Chicago. It first appeared on record, played by Pine Top Smith, in 1929 on Vocalion. In the hands of Johnson, Meade Lux Lewis, and particularly Albert Ammons, it enjoyed a huge burst of popularity in the late 1930s and

1940s. In boogie-woogie, jazz and blues elements came into close proximity again. As the fad faded, the music began to be more accepted in blues, where it proved easily adaptable to guitar and harmonica stylists. While boogie-woogie is rarely heard in jazz today, every blues band in America performs the style.

Despite the fact that many important musicians as well as entire orchestras had departed Kansas City by 1939, there was still enough talent to form one final ensemble of importance—the Jay McShann band. The band was built around McShann's own piano playing, the blues shouting of Walter Brown, and the alto sax of Charlie Parker. Like Andy Kirk and Count Basie before him, McShann was signed by Decca Records. Decca was a relative newcomer in the recording industry, having been formed in 1934 by Jack Kapp. Yet Decca was more active in recording the great black music of its day than either Columbia or the industry leader, Victor. Sometime after his big band recording dates of 1941 and 1942 for Decca, McShann expressed regrets that some of his more advanced arrangements had been shunted aside in favor of the blues. Yet the blues that the McShann group turned out were not only big sellers but also superb examples of Kansas City jazz. Among the best of those recordings were "Hootie Blues" from 1941 and "The Jumpin' Blues" from the following year. Jay McShann stands today as an artist who is revered in both jazz and blues circles.

Before World War II and the subsequent recording ban of 1942 and 1943, there seemed to be a continuous stream of young blues-oriented jazz bands arriving on the scene. Bands led by Earl Hines, Chick Webb, Cab Calloway, and Jimmie Lunceford were splendid orchestras playing great jazz, yet they were different in character from those of Erskine Hawkins, Lucky Millinder, Lionel Hampton, and Buddy Johnson, where the blues played a greater role. In each of these bands the beat began to change from ballroom swing to something with a little more backbeat, a heavier style.

The Hawkins band began as the Alabama State Collegians and had been recorded since 1936. Hit recordings came after the band switched to Victor, and songs such as "After Hours" and "Tuxedo Junction" were enormously popular with black audiences.

Lucky Millinder had been a front man for the Mills Blue Rhythm Band since 1933, but in 1941 his own band began to record for Decca. Several outstanding vocalists developed by Millinder included Annisteen Allen, Wynonie Harris, and Sister Rosetta Tharpe.

Lionel Hampton, one of the most famous black musicians in the country, was known for his association with Benny Goodman. Hampton, a recording leader for Victor since 1937, had recorded dozens of small-group titles with the very best jazz players of the time, but it was only when he switched to Decca in 1941 that his big band, formed in 1940, began to be heard. He managed to get two sessions cut before the August 1, 1942, start of the American Federation of Musicians recording ban. The honking, screaming tenor sax solo style that emerged from the Hampton band in players such as Illinois Jacquet and Arnett Cobb became an important part of all his subsequent bands. To get a harder, heavier rhythm feel, Hampton demanded that his drummer play with the butt end of the sticks. When auditioning a replacement for a departing soloist, Hampton would often decide to hire the man based on how well he played the blues.

Prior to the 1942 recording ban Buddy Johnson had been the pianist and leader of a smaller combo, yet his first big band, formed in 1944, was an instant success. Johnson's bluesy songs, the vocals of his sister Ella, and a hard-rocking ensemble were the principal ingredients of his Decca records.

These bands found virtually all of their following in the black community. Most of the white audience in what was still a segregated America had different tastes. A white band such as Woody Herman's (at one time billed as "The Band That Plays the Blues") had fans in the black community, yet Herman rarely performed for black people. The white press covered black bands in theaters or ballrooms, but mediocre white bands got more press than many of the bands mentioned above. In *The Big Bands* (4th ed. 1981), although there is a significant segment on Lionel Hampton, there is less than a column on Erskine Hawkins, one paragraph on Lucky Millinder, and no mention at all of Buddy Johnson.

While the big ballrooms of the East and Midwest were the touring venues for big bands, popular black groups in California tended not to travel so far nor appear in rooms as large. There were plenty of ballrooms in Los Angeles, yet it was music from smaller clubs that began to garner most of the attention.

Nat King Cole's trio vied with T-Bone Walker as the most popular group in the region, but there were others such as Roy Milton's Solid Senders and groups led by Joe Liggins and Johnny Otis. When Decca settled with the musicians' union in September 1943 and resumed recording, other labels were free to operate under the same terms. Columbia and Victor chose to hold out another fourteen months, but California experienced a sudden burst of small-label activity. Modern,

Aladdin, Black & White, Imperial, Specialty, Exclusive, Supreme, Jewell, Atomic, and Sunset were just some of them.

While many of these labels attempted to record a variety of music ranging from country to classical, the bedrock of their business was small-combo jazz and blues. Nat Cole's trio on Capitol begot Johnny Moore's Three Blazers (with Charles Brown)—first on Modern then Aladdin—which led to Ray Charles's Maxim trio on Swingtime, all with the same piano, guitar, and bass instrumentation. PeeWee Crayton followed T-Bone Walker (Capitol) on Modern, with Crayton clearly patterned on Walker. Combos such as Milton, Walker, and Amos Milburn featured mellow saxophone by Buddy Floyd, Bumps Myers, or Maxwell Davis. When Illinois Jacquet burst onto record with his more aggressive saxophone style (simultaneously on Apollo and Aladdin), he created a stir that would manifest itself in the playing of Big Jay McNeely and others. But it would take some time.

The problem here was marketing the music. All black music had been considered race music until Jerry Wexler coined the term *rhythm-and-blues* in 1949. The success of small combos on the West Coast was duplicated in the East and Midwest. Labels such as Mercury in Chicago and King in Cincinnati joined East Coast powerhouses Savoy, Atlantic, and Jubilee. None of these labels was in existence before World War II, yet each became a significant force in black music. Decca held sway among the big labels and maintained a solid roster of best-selling black artists. Columbia was nowhere in sight. After 1950, any R&B hits by the major labels would be a rare occurrence.

Decca artist Louis Jordan, the single most popular black artist of the entire decade, dominated the 1940s. His little jump band launched a thousand similar groups, and his brand of jump blues bridged the gap between swing and R&B. Once again we have an era where jazz and blues coincide. The popular combo leaders such as Jordan, Eddie "Cleanhead" Vinson, Bullmoose Jackson, and Nat King Cole were musicians. They were also adults.

The early 1950s were the great years of R&B. As the decade progressed, the vocalists became increasingly younger and attempts to spread R&B to a white audience meant that arrangers became more necessary to the recording process. Every big American city had at least one radio station where R&B was a part of the programming. If a record label could package young vocal talent with the right song in a catchy arrangement, concentrated airplay could create a hit record.

During the maturation of R&B, rhythm section players and tenor sax soloists became at least as important as the singers. Many of the key studio musicians who made R&B recordings came right out of the black big bands. As the specialists began to dominate the recording process, jazz and blues would grow apart once again. R&B vocalists would, more often than not, find themselves more comfortable in the blues field. The musicians were often drawn to soul jazz. Bebop or modern jazz had pretty much frozen them out.

Bebop is New York City music. Regardless of whether the music was in Charlie Parker's head while playing with Jay McShann or in Dizzy Gillespie's mind while working with Cab Calloway, it came together during World War II in New York City. Bebop was, in Parker's phrase, "a new conception." For the first time, blues feeling was not a necessary component for a successful soloist. Bebop tended to use the form for its own purposes, but there were many fine bebop players whose solo style placed little or no emphasis on blue notes. On the other hand, Charlie Parker was one of the finest blues saxophonists of all time. Dizzy Gillespie had great reverence for the blues, and his own bands made frequent use of the form and the feeling. White performers such as Barney Kessel and Zoot Sims were master blues soloists.

Older musicians who wished to keep their own way of playing frequently found refuge in soul jazz combos. Soul jazz groups could and did feature piano, yet the introduction of the Hammond organ in the late 1940s really brought the music into focus. Soul jazz should not be confused with soul music, the gospel-inspired secular black music so popular in the 1960s and early 1970s. Soul jazz had a customary combo size of three or four pieces, and rarely were more than five pieces included in a working group. Most clubs were very small, and the bandstand could frequently be found in the center of a circular bar. The organ was usually coupled with saxophone or guitar, and frequently both. Brass instruments, bass, or percussion were often added to the basic unit on record dates.

Many of the early organists were pianist-arrangers. Wild Bill Davis was the first, but Bill Doggett, Sir Charles Thompson, and Milt Buckner were others. The Wild Bill Davis Trio with guitarist Bill Jennings and drummer Chris Columbus served as the inspiration for the trios of Jimmy Smith and Groove Holmes, while Doggett's quartet with guitarist Billy Butler and saxophonist Clifford Scott served as a model for the organ-tenor group.

Jimmy Smith was the master of this idiom. He was technically gifted, and his work was imbued with deep blues feeling. His recordings, first for Blue Note but especially on Verve, were enormously successful. He was the best selling of all jazz artists in the 1960s. No fewer than ten of his albums reached the Top Forty pop charts!

Jack McDuff and Jimmy McGriff were blues masters in the Jimmy Smith mold, although each had his own distinctive style. On the other hand, Shirley Scott, Johnny Hammond Smith, and Groove Holmes were better known for playing standards and their own originals. But all organists knew how to use blues to rouse an audience. Saxophonists Willis Jackson, Lou Donaldson, Houston Person, and Gene Ammons often used organ accompaniment. Guitarists Wes Montgomery and Grant Green also used organ in working bands from time to time.

The important record labels were Blue Note, Riverside, Argo, and, above all, Prestige. Soul jazz tended to be music recorded for albums after the mid-1950s, although Bill Doggett was recorded for singles (his 1956 recording of "Honky Tonk" on King Records was a Number One hit) as well. Singles would be culled from the albums, often in edited form, for jukeboxes. The circuit for touring bands covered the eastern seaboard from Baltimore to Boston and throughout the Midwest all the way to Chicago. It was not uncommon to find organ bars featuring touring bands in the smaller cities of Ohio, Michigan, and Pennsylvania. By the late 1950s the music had reached the West Coast, and Los Angeles became a very strong hub of organ jazz activity. Modern jazz combos led by Cannonball Adderley or Horace Silver were every bit as popular as the soul jazz groups, largely because of original material, which utilized soulful harmony or danceable rhythms. Piano trios, such as the Three Sounds or those led by Les McCann or Ramsey Lewis, were very much a part of the scene. Popular vocalists on the circuit like Arthur Prysock, Etta Jones, or Little Jimmy Scott were not blues singers but artists whose specialties were blue ballads of the sort favored by musicians.

After the mid-1960s arrival of funk, exemplified by R&B groups such as the Meters and James Brown, virtuoso organists were less in demand than combos that could provide strong, danceable rhythms. The music began to wind down in the early 1970s as organists decided to add a variety of electric keyboards to their working groups. The distinctive touch that provided each organist with his own identity was completely obscured by electric pianos or synthesizers. And just as the end of a wartime economy had paved the way for the end of the big band era, so the rampant inflation, Arab oil boycotts, and increasing drug use in black neighborhoods made the soul jazz circuit a casualty of the mid-1970s. Within a decade it had completely disappeared.

By this time, fusion was a popular jazz form. Initially fusion was a producer's idiom, best exemplified by Creed Taylor and his CTI and Kudu imprints. Taylor moved the jazz soloist to what had been a singer's setting: orchestral accompaniment utilizing strings, brass, woodwinds, and a wide variety of percussion. (Fusion should not be confused with jazz/rock, which was small-group music adding jazz solos to rock rhythm and repertoire.) The use of blues by an arranger or blue notes by a soloist tended to be a sometime thing.

Blues and jazz stand as separate entities today. While their long-shared history no longer seems possible, the swing (actually, more jump-blues) revival of the 1990s has opened up an area of interest to each camp. The revival groups are mostly white, and their music emphasizes the rhythms and songs of the 1940s and early 1950s R&B. While black blues bands use a certain amount of jazz repertoire (usually from the soul jazz era), there is enough similar material from R&B groups to make it unnecessary. Blues fans and modern jazz fans are still suspicious of one another. However, that doesn't mean there isn't a player somewhere in America who will be able to unite form and feeling in a way that brings them together once again.

Bessie Smith

Chris Albertson

In the years after World War I, the burgeoning record industry's catalogs were dominated by operatic arias, warhorse overtures, Sousa marches, and "foreign language" series, a euphemism for ethnic music. Oddly enough—considering that they would become the dominant influence on American music—black people did not figure into record company marketing plans, neither as customers nor artists, until 1920. That's when Perry Bradford, a black songwriter, finally persuaded Fred Hager of OKeh Records to record a vaudeville singer named Mamie Smith. Her first release, "That Thing Called Love," sold well beyond Hager's expectations, so he authorized another session. Bradford had Ms. Smith sing "Harlem Blues," a tune from a 1918 revue, *Made in Harlem*, but changed the title to "Crazy Blues." It was an even bigger success, and it started the blues craze of the twenties.

By early 1923 the major labels were scouting for blues-singing ladies for their newly established "race" records divisions. Talent scouts tapped the vaudeville and minstrel shows and came up with singers who easily slipped into a blues repertoire. With few exceptions—most notably Gertrude "Ma" Rainey—these were not dedicated blues artists but rather so-called sweet singers, eager to jump on the bandwagon. Many of them exhibited minimal talent and are remembered today only for the high caliber of their recorded instrumental accompaniments. Others—Ida Cox and Clara Smith among them—made a natural transition to blues, but one singer towered above the rest: Bessie Smith's powerful voice and superbly timed delivery easily triumphed over the poorest of accompaniments.

Bessie was born on Charles Street at the foot of Cameron Hill in an area of Chattanooga, Tennessee, known as Blue Goose Hollow. The date was April 15, the year probably 1894, as noted on a 1923 marriage certificate. At first, she shared "a little ramshackle cabin" with her parents, two brothers, three sisters, and two nephews, but the children were orphaned while she was an infant, and the task of keeping the family afloat was left to Viola, the oldest sister, who took in laundry. Clarence, the oldest brother, helped out by performing odd jobs in the neighborhood, but his focus was elsewhere; extroverted and a comedian by nature, he had his sights set on show business.

Troupes of dancers, musicians, and comedians regularly crisscrossed the South, pitching their tents or renting storefronts from which to offer eager audiences momentary relief from daily drudgery. Like Clarence, many young African Americans saw in these itinerant productions a permanent escape—a stepping-stone to a better life. He seized such an opportunity in 1904 by taking to the road with a minstrel show. This left Viola to work things out in reduced circumstances, but Clarence vowed to improve them on his return. During her big brother's eight-year absence, Bessie—who shared his aspirations—began dancing and singing in the streets to the guitar accompaniments of another brother, Andrew. In 1974 Will Johnson, a friend of Andrew's, recalled seeing the sibling duo in front of the White Elephant, a saloon on the corner of Thirteenth and Elm streets, not far from the apartment to which Viola had moved the family. Now a spirited teenager, Bessie had a little act going; "whenever someone threw a fat coin her way," Johnson recalled, "she'd say something like 'That's right, Charlie, give to the church.' I always thought she had more talent as a performer—you know, dancing and clowning— than as a singer, at least in those days I don't remember being particularly impressed with her voice. She sure knew how to shake money loose from a pocket, though."

Bessie was ready to join Clarence in 1912, when he returned to Chattanooga with the Moses Stokes troupe. Much to Viola's chagrin, she auditioned successfully for the show's managers, Lonnie and Cora

Bessie Smith, 1928. Courtesy Frank Driggs Collection.

Fisher, who hired her as a dancer because they already had a singer, Gertrude "Ma" Rainey. For many years, it was thought that Rainey launched Bessie's career and taught her how to sing; one writer's vivid imagination included a kidnapping scenario wherein a kicking, screaming eleven-year-old Bessie is dumped at Rainey's feet in a burlap bag. But Bessie hardly needed to be taken out of Chattanooga by force.

By all accounts, Bessie was already an engaging singer when she left Chattanooga. Actor Leigh Whipper, who saw her perform in Atlanta in 1913, said that Ma Rainey "may have taught her a few dance steps, or showed her how to walk onstage, but Bessie was born with that voice and she had a style of her own . . . she obviously didn't know she was the artist she was. She didn't know how to dress, she just sang in her street clothes, but she was such a natural that she could wreck anybody's show." Thomas A. Dorsey, who was Ma Rainey's accompanist around that time, agreed that Bessie's singing talent was a self-developed natural gift; he pointed out that even after Bessie became a star, Rainey never took credit for helping her.

Between 1913 and 1921, Bessie successfully established herself with black audiences in the South, along the East Coast, and as far west as Muskogee, Oklahoma. With Atlanta's 81 Theater as her home base, she first toured as a lowly chorine with various companies, including Pete Werley's Florida Blossoms and the popular Silas Green shows. Eventually, her magnetic personality and commanding presence had her headlining her own shows at Atlanta's 91 Theater, which singer May Wright described as a "smaller and rougher theater." Details of Bessie's activities during this period are scant, but we do know that she and Hazel Green worked as a team at Baltimore's Douglas Gilmor Theater in 1918, advertised as the Hip Ha Hip Ha Girls. Unconfirmed rumors suggested that she was a widow, having married a soldier, Earl Love, who became a casualty in World War I.

By 1921 Bessie was living in Philadelphia, where she frequently enjoyed prominent billing at the Standard Theater. An ad in the September 14, 1921, issue of the *Philadelphia Tribune* contains the enigmatic line "Hits on Columbia Records and her 5 Jazzoway Dandies," but there is no tangible evidence of Bessie having recorded for any label before February 1923, when Frank Walker, the director of Columbia's new Race Division, sent for her. She had, however, previously made an unsuccessful audition for Thomas Edison, who noted "voice—NG" in his log, and for OKeh's Fred Hager, who had approved Mamie Smith's milestone session but deemed Bessie's voice "too rough." There was also a small item in the *Chicago Defender's* February 12, 1921, issue announcing that Bessie, "the greatest of all 'blues' singers," was presently "making records, with the aid of six jazz musicians, for the Emerson Record company" and that the initial release could be expected around March 10. Again, there is no proof of such recordings taking place, but it is interesting to note that Bessie was referred to as the "greatest" blues singer two years before making her known record debut with the Columbia coupling "Gulf Coast Blues" and "Downhearted Blues."

On June 7, 1923, as the record shipped to dealers, Bessie married Jack Gee, a Philadelphia night watchman whom she had met the year before. Their relationship soon became a case study in mutual spousal abuse. Jack was keenly interested in the money that show business generated, but he never accepted the lifestyle that accompanied it. "She was a strong woman with a beautiful strong constitution," recalled Jack's niece Ruby Walker, who toured with Bessie for fourteen years, "and she loved a good time." To Bessie, that usually meant high consumption of moonshine, heavy partying, and pleasures of the flesh. "Man or woman, she loved them young," said Ruby, "but I didn't let her get to my men, although she tried a couple of times." Bessie's ribald asides always took place on the road in Jack's absence and promptly ended with his return. "When Jack was around, you couldn't get Bessie to take a drink—she was no fun then, and she didn't want to hear about the good times we had when he was away."

When she initially hit the road as an "Exclusive Columbia Artist," Bessie's shows were modest presentations that mainly had her performing to piano accompaniments. That changed when "Down Hearted Blues" sold a staggering 780,000 copies in the first six months, and theater owners began reporting record ticket sales. Now Bessie's shows became ambitious productions with splashy costumes, elaborate headgear, a chorus line, comedians, props, and a full band. The press named her "Queen of the Blues," which Columbia upgraded to "Empress." A heavy show schedule had her spending a good part of each summer touring the South "under canvas" and the winter months headlining in theaters on the black-owned Theatre Owner's Booking Association (TOBA) circuit, whose contract for two thousand dollars per week eventually made her the highest-paid black entertainer of her day.

She was now regularly sending money to Viola, and Clarence joined the show as comedian, master of ceremonies, and business manager. In the latter capacity, he ordered a private railroad car custom-built for the troupe in 1925. It accommodated forty people in relative comfort, with room for the tent's long center pole, canvas, props, and souvenir merchandise. The car also served to lodge the cast in towns where hotels were for whites only. Ma Rainey had her own bus, but Bessie's railroad coach, with her name emblazoned in big letters on both sides, was a grander sign of "arrival."

Although sales of her subsequent releases never matched "Down Hearted Blues," Bessie continued to outsell most other artists, and Columbia renewed her contract each year. Throughout the twenties, she regularly took time out from her tours to record in New York. Her payment went from a flat fee of $125 to $200 per issued side, with no royalties, which meant that healthy record sales did not directly fatten Bessie's bank account, but they were valuable promotional tools that brought thousands of people to her live performances. A February 25, 1924, appearance at Cincinnati's Roosevelt Theater included "Twenty minutes in full ovation and bows," according to the *Chicago Defender;* three weeks later, when Smith fans caused a near riot outside of Pittsburgh's Lincoln Theater, the *Courier* reported: "Early in the evening, crowds started to gather, and by 7 o'clock in the evening the street car traffic was blocked. Thousands of people were turned away and those who did attend stormed the theater."

Bessie's majestic voice made most of her contemporaries sound gauzy by comparison, but there was more to her artistry than a powerful voice, for she rendered her songs with a mesmerizing honesty, which most people saw as a reflection of her offstage persona. "She sang from the heart," said Ruby; "she was very real—you knew that no matter what she sang about, she'd been there." She also had an innate aesthetic sense that dictated perfect timing and magnificent control. Others have noted her subtle movements—a slight shift of the hips, a raised eyebrow, a naughty smile. Recalling a 1925 Thanksgiving weekend performance in Newark, New Jersey, at the Orpheum Theater ("Memories of Bessie Smith," *Jazz Records,* September 1947), writer-photographer Carl Van Vechten, an ardent admirer, noted "the powerfully magnetic personality of this elemental conjure woman with her plangent African voice," recalled how the audience "burst into hysterical, semi-religious shrieks of sorrow and lamentations," and added that "Amens rent the air." Danny Barker and Zutty Singleton made similar observations, likening Bessie to a preacher whose audiences displayed churchlike emotions when she sang. Bandleader

Sy Oliver witnessed Bessie "hypnotize" and "walk" a fan during a Baltimore appearance.

Those who experienced her onstage have been quick to point out that Bessie was a versatile entertainer and that singing was but a part of her act, albeit the most memorable. Often, Bessie's songs were defiant declarations of independence that a feminist movement of a much later era could embrace. While her recordings do not capture Bessie's commanding stage presence and ability to interact with an audience, they give us a good idea of her vocal power, authoritative delivery, and ability to transcend woefully imperfect musical environments. Indeed, the woman who has been called the world's greatest blues singer sometimes suffered the world's worst accompaniments, but she also recorded with some of history's finest jazz musicians, including nine titles with Louis Armstrong and sixteen with James P. Johnson. On "St. Louis Blues" and "Reckless Blues," from a January 14, 1925, date, Armstrong's cornet becomes a second voice, perfectly interacting with Bessie's superbly paced, intensely personal delivery of the lyrics. Supporting these masterful duets is Fred Longshaw's plaintive harmonium, an unusual instrument in this context, but one that here seems perfectly natural. Of the eleven pianists with whom Bessie recorded, James P. Johnson was her favorite, the only one whose playing could match her vocal nuances. Like Armstrong, he went beyond mere accompaniment: weaving, rich musical texture into Bessie's words on a lusty number like "Lock and Key"; providing an impressionistic complement to her urgency on "Backwater Blues," her best-known composition. Another Smith favorite was trombonist "Big" Charlie Green, a Fletcher Henderson sideman who evidenced a remarkable rapport with Bessie on numerous sides, most strikingly on a 1928 two-part recording of "Empty Bed Blues." Bessie delivers this humorous tale with exquisite timing, savoring each double entendre as Green's jaunty trombone comments and turns the performance into a masterful interchange that effectively contrasts Porter Grainger's almost linear piano accompaniment.

As the twenties drew to an end, Bessie's married life was on a roller-coaster course; her binges became more frequent as Jack spent less time on the road with her. He now knew of his wife's bisexuality, having caught her in a compromising situation with a chorine, but Bessie calmed his rage by appealing to his materialism. She lavished him with expensive gifts, but none proved as effective as her naming him the manager of her show—a purely conciliatory gesture that eventually backfired.

By 1928 the blues craze that swept Bessie to stardom had ebbed, and the TOBA circuit was experiencing economic difficulties. Because Bessie's last show, *Mississippi Days,* had done quite well, the TOBA contacted Jack and—unaware that he was manager in name only—ordered two shows for the upcoming season. Delighted, Bessie agreed to give him three thousand dollars for production costs, although Clarence, the troupe's de facto manager, warned her against leaving such a task in Jack's inexperienced hands. "She should have listened to him," said Clarence's wife Maud in a 1971 interview, "but Bessie could be very stubborn, and back in those days she would do just about anything to keep Jack happy." It was actually too late, for Jack Gee was already involved in an amorous liaison with Gertrude Saunders, a glamorous-looking "sweet singer" who had starred in the original production of *Shuffle Along.* To boost that relationship, Jack split the three thousand dollars in half and produced a second show for Saunders. When Bessie found out that he had spent her money on another woman's show, she finally let the marriage go.

While 1929 was off to a bad start as far as Bessie's personal life was concerned, her career was still on track, but that, too, was about to change. Sales of blues records were down, but she seemed impervious to the pinch of shifting taste that was retiring many of her colleagues. The heyday of blues was clearly over, but Bessie's future looked good: Columbia renewed her contract for the sixth time, and on May 1, 1929, she was offered a featured spot in *Pansy,* a Broadway show produced by Maceo Pinkard and scheduled to open at the Belmont Theater on May 14. Although she would only sing two songs, Pinkard offered her star billing, heading an all-black cast of unknown performers; she saw it as a perfect opportunity to widen her performing horizon at a time when her past theatrical environment seemed imperiled. The eleventh-hour call should have served as a warning that all was not well—indeed, it wasn't.

Six principal cast members walked out at the last minute, replaced by recruits who had not attended the rehearsals, and the costumes were delivered after the curtain went up. New York's top theater critics were on hand, one observing that it was "as if the dancers were meeting each other for the first time on stage." Some were. Only Bessie received good notices, Richard Lockridge of the *Sun* calling her appearance "one momentary interlude of professionalism." In the *Evening Post,* Wilella Waldorf noted that that Bessie, "a rather weighty personage of great good humor, sang her song "over and over and over to wild applause, likewise executing sundry dance steps at intervals by way of variety." Two critics suggested that the audience kept Bessie singing in order to keep the rest of the cast from returning; Bessie finally announced that she was tired and "too fat for this sort of thing, anyhow." The show stumbled through three performances and closed.

The day after the disastrous opening of *Pansy*, Bessie made what is probably the definitive version of "Nobody Knows You When You're Down and Out," one of her most poignant recordings. Bessie made another career aside that summer when W. C. Handy recommended her to director Dudley Murphy for the starring role in *St. Louis Blues*, a seventeen-minute "talkie" that frames the title song in a thin plot. The only existing film footage of Bessie, it shows her acting and singing the classic blues tune with a large orchestra and chorus, a musical setting unlike any Columbia had given her. The film ran in black theaters but seemingly had no impact on Bessie's professional life, which had long since leveled off and now was in decline. Bessie's sagging professional life is commonly attributed to her drinking, but she was also a victim of shifting public taste, talking pictures, and the Depression.

On the Fourth of July weekend in 1930, Bessie was given bottom billing at Harlem's Apollo, then still a Yiddish burlesque theater looking for a new audience. Pinched by the Depression, Columbia now paid her only $125 per selection and, unlike in previous years, recorded no more than her contract called for. By the summer of 1931, the TOBA circuit had folded and Columbia was dropping Bessie from a dwindling roster of artists. On the other hand, her personal life took a turn for the better when she became romantically involved with an old friend, Richard Morgan, whose successful bootlegging operation had been wiped out by repeal of the Volstead Act. Richard, who was Lionel Hampton's uncle, now toured with Bessie, but the glitter days were over.

In 1933 John Hammond brought Bessie back into a recording studio to make four sides for OKeh with pianist Buck Washington and a formidable band that included trumpeter Frankie Newton and tenor saxophonist Chu Berry. This group, modern by the day's standards, obviously suited Bessie, who had just begun the process of bringing her act up to date. She was in rare form belting out "Gimme a Pigfoot and a Bottle of Beer," a rousing song that would become one of her best-known recordings. Barely perceptible in the background is Benny Goodman, who dropped in from an Ethel Waters date next door. It was Bessie's final recording session, and it ended with "Down in the

Dumps," but her career had reached its nadir, and things were beginning to look up.

As she stepped into the swing era, Bessie changed her repertoire to include such Tin Pan Alley material as "Smoke Gets in Your Eyes" and "Tea for Two." She also shed the wigs and feathers for the sleeker, more elegant look of satin evening gowns and swept-back hair. This is how she appeared at the Apollo, which now catered exclusively to black patrons. In 1936 Bessie found a new audience as a last-minute replacement for Billie Holiday at Connie's Inn, a Harlem club that had relocated to midtown Manhattan. She also made an impromptu appearance on 52nd Street, dropping in during a jam session at the Famous Door. "I feel as though I am on the brink of new successes," she told the *Chicago Defender*'s Allan McMillan in her seventh week at Connie's Inn. Indeed, her career appeared to be on the upswing; Lionel Hampton had plans to include her in his series of small-band swing recordings for Victor, John Hammond wanted her to cut some sides with members of the Basie band, and another film was planned. It was in this atmosphere of optimism that Bessie and Richard Morgan left to join Winsted's Broadway Rastus show in Memphis. On September 26, 1937, after a successful series of performances in the Memphis area, they headed for Clarksdale, Mississippi, planning to catch up with the show in Darling the following evening. Bessie's Packard headed south along Route 61 with Richard at the wheel and Bessie at his side. They had argued and now drove in silence down the dark road. Probably mesmerized by the long, straight stretch of road asphalt, Richard did not see a big truck until it was too late. In the ensuing collision, Bessie was thrown from the car, her right arm nearly severed, her body in shock from severe internal bleeding. She never regained consciousness but died at Clarksdale's Afro-American Hospital a few hours later.

Bessie Smith's artistry continues to inspire new generations of singers, extending her legacy well beyond her 160 or so recordings. She was cited as one of two major influences by Billie Holiday, whose recording debut by ironic coincidence took place only three days after Bessie's final session, in the very same studio. Several generations later, she became a source of inspiration for rock singer Janis Joplin, who in 1970 showed her gratitude by sharing with another Smith fan, Juanita Green, the cost of a stone for Bessie's unmarked grave. "She showed me the air and taught me how to fill it," said Joplin, who herself died two months later.

King Oliver, Jelly Roll Morton, and Sidney Bechet: Ménage à Trois, New Orleans Style

Bruce Boyd Raeburn

J elly Roll Morton once remarked that New Orleans musicians "had our own way of doing." Like many Crescent City jazz musicians, Morton preferred to work with "homeboys" whenever possible. In the early years when jazz was achieving initial idiomatic coherence, New Orleans players held a virtual monopoly on the syntax of collective improvisation, a musical give-and-take which resembled a street-corner conversation with everyone trying to get a word in edgewise. As talent began to transcend the strictures of format, however, elaboration of the idiom was refined into several discrete but not necessarily exclusive approaches— leadership of the ensemble, solo improvisation, and composition— each with its respective patron saint: Joe Oliver, Sidney Bechet, and Morton. Louis Armstrong's meteoric rise to stardom notwithstanding, the contributions of Oliver, Bechet, and Morton remain fundamental to an understanding of the rise and fall and resurrection of New Orleans jazz between the world wars, a process which brought the music to the forefront of American cultural achievement.

New Orleans in the nineteenth century was a city at odds with the American Way of Life: its colonial heritage was French, Spanish, and African; its religion was predominantly Catholic; and its demographics were racially ambiguous, especially evident in a Creole-of-color population that confounded Americanization. It was a city where music was regarded as a necessity rather than a luxury, which meant that musicians were plentiful and poor and that music was ubiquitous. An unrestrained vernacularism deriving from the colonial era had spawned a distinctive culture evident in language, food, architecture, and music, but by the end of the century American hegemony was a foregone conclusion. From 1880 to 1920 the Creole dialect gradually waned as a living tongue in New Orleans, so that even in Creole households it was heard only among the old folks when they wanted to keep something to themselves. Born into an Afro-French family on October 20, 1890, Ferdinand Joseph Lamothe was thus forced to learn the lessons of adaptation early, altering his stepfather's surname Mouton to Morton to avoid being called "Frenchy."

Morton learned his lessons well, and the nickname "Jelly Roll," a sexual metaphor which drew upon his early experiences in New Orleans brothels and black vaudeville, announced his unequivocal desire to succeed at becoming a player in the burgeoning field of American popular culture. Jazz was, after all, a new American music for a new century—a redirection of the New Orleans vernacular sensibility into "ear candy" for young people. The Victorian precept that "children should be seen and not heard" was one of the first casualties of an emerging Jazz Age which eschewed nineteenth-century formalism in favor of free expression. Ferd Morton was performing as a pianist at the Hilma Burt House in Storyville some time between the ages of fifteen and twenty, and he may have been active as a guitarist with string bands as early as 1897. Elder Creoles rejected jazz as American contamination: when "Papa" Louis Tio complained to young cornetist Natty Dominique about "those fools, just messing up good music," he probably already suspected that a new generation of "ear" musicians was deaf to such pronouncements. There was no doubt about where Jelly Roll stood on the issue: he neglected a formal musical education in favor of itinerant prospecting on the road. According to Lovie Austin, who worked for Morton as a transcriber in Chicago, the nation's first great jazz composer never did learn to read music well.

Sidney Bechet was another young Creole who turned his back on tradition. Born on May 14, 1897, he was the premier jazz prodigy, renowned for whittling his own reeds and making even the most dilapidated instrument sing. Violinist Peter Bocage recalled his facility with an E-flat clarinet: "He didn't know what key he was playing

Jelly Roll Morton and his Red Hot Peppers, Chicago, 1926. Left to right: Andrew Hilaire, drums; Kid Ory, trombone; George Mitchell, cornet; John Lindsay, bass; Morton, piano; Johnny St. Cyr, banjo; Omer Simeon, clarinet. Courtesy Frank Driggs Collection.

in, but you couldn't lose him." Driven by an intense ambition and a predilection for truancy, he sought an education in the streets of the city and the forbidden haunts of Storyville. His passion for jazz was already apparent at the beginning of his professional career as a thirteen-year-old clarinetist with the Silver Bells, and before long he was working his way through the best dance bands in town. Surrendering to an insatiable wanderlust in the fall of 1916, Sidney hit the Texas dime store circuit with Clarence Williams but was soon back home again when bookings dwindled. Next he joined the Bruce & Bruce Stock Company for a whirlwind tour of the South and Midwest, landing in Chicago in November 1917. Like Morton, Bechet left the verities of Creole culture to the old folks in New Orleans as he strove to position himself in the vanguard of an incipient jazz community. Recordings made by the Original Dixieland Jazz Band in New York in February 1917 had created a wave of excitement, demonstrating the power of jazz to stimulate not only youthful imaginations but also economic opportunities. Just as the Jazz Age was dawning in New York and Chicago, the implications of its significance for New Orleans musicians were being felt back home.

The most popular band in town was led by Edward Ory and Joe Oliver, whose scope of activity ranged from "subscription" dances for the children of the social elite at Tulane University to "midnight rambles" for a cross-section of the black and Creole communities at Economy Hall in the Treme. The response of the Ory-Oliver Band to the records of the Original Dixieland Jazz Band was revealing. The two "readers" in the band were Oliver and Manuel Manetta, a violinist who served as "straw boss," yet Manetta was fired because "Joe Oliver and Kid Ory wanted to follow the format of the Dixieland Jazz Band and use only five pieces." Clearly, Ory and Oliver were ready to respond to innovation wherever they found it. Ory went on to make the first jazz recording by a black New Orleans band: in June 1922 "Ory's Creole Trombone" was recorded for the Nordskog label in Santa Monica, but because of Nordskog's poor distribution, Joe Oliver's April 1923 Creole Jazz Band records were for many years thought to be the first.

Joseph Oliver was born in Abend, Louisiana, upriver from New Orleans, on May 11, 1885, the son of a Baptist preacher. He came to the city around 1900 following the death of his father and made ends meet by working for a Jewish family residing in the Irish Channel. By 1907 he was musically active as a cornetist with the Onward Brass Band and dance bands such as the Eagle and the Magnolia. From childhood he suffered from a disability—a blind eye resulting from a practical joke gone wrong—but it did not prevent him from earning a reputation for stamina and enthusiasm, two qualities essential to leadership. Oliver and Bechet came of age musically about the same time and frequently found themselves working together. In the spring of 1914 they joined the Olympia Band led by Armand Piron, a violinist who established the first black-owned music-publishing company in New Orleans with Clarence Williams in 1915. The Olympia became known as the "monocles" band at Tulane dances because of the protrusion of Oliver's bad eye when he hit high notes, a notoriety of sorts. In 1917 Oliver and Bechet renewed their collaboration briefly in Kid Ory's Jazz Band. Clarinetist John Casimir recalled that Ory had trouble keeping Sidney sober—"Bechet would blow them up, what I mean, you get drunk and don't come on the job"—so Oliver soon found himself in the company of Johnny Dodds instead. According to Ory, Oliver had begged the Kid for a chance to play in his band and, once hired, immediately began to contend for top billing. They appeared as the "Oliver-Ory" band at Milneburg, presumably because Joe had landed the job, and Ory decided not to contest it.

Observers who heard this band describe Oliver as hitting his creative stride with Ory, advancing the jazz vocabulary with the use of mutes and vocal effects. The crowds loved it, and so did Ory, but on June 19, 1918, the fun came to an abrupt halt. A police raid on the Winter Garden on Gravier Street put Oliver in jail for disturbing the peace, and, as his wife Stella recalled, "Joe thought it was awful that a man who was making an honest living could be taken to jail like that, so he went to Chicago." Oliver left in February 1919, in response to invitations from rival New Orleans bands in Chicago—Bill Johnson's band at the Royal Gardens and Lawrence Duhé's orchestra at the Dreamland Café. Sidney Bechet was with the Dreamland faction at the train station when Joe arrived and, like Oliver, found a way to join both bands as opportunity permitted. Given the shifting loyalties of New Orleans pickup bands, it was the normal thing to do.

Friendly competition and "cutting contests" were intrinsic to the New Orleans scene, keeping the musicians keen and alert to rising talents. Even before Oliver left, Kid Ory had been grooming Louis Armstrong to replace him, first in a cooperative venture with Pete Lala, and then at dances promoted on his own at Economy Hall. When Lala asked for a piece of the action and was refused, however, he sent fifty patrolmen to run Ory's customers away. As Ory put it,

Lala "had the power," and health reasons aside, such incidents explain his decision to move to Los Angeles in 1919. Like other expatriates, Ory assumed that economic and social conditions would improve once he left New Orleans. Had he maintained contact with Jelly Roll Morton, he might have thought twice about going, because Jelly was having similar difficulties in San Francisco.

Jelly Roll Morton's first professional sorties were to Biloxi, Mississippi, during the summer of 1907, familiar terrain because his godmother had a house there. Then he bounced between New Orleans and various Gulf Coast cities with black vaudeville stock companies such as William Benbow's, a connection which brought him to Washington, Philadelphia, and New York by 1911. Morton stayed in Texas between 1912 and 1914 but managed trips to Chicago, St. Louis, and Indianapolis. He returned to Chicago in August 1914 and published "The Jelly Roll Blues" in 1915. By the time he left for California in the summer of 1917, Jelly had sharpened his skills as a pianist, bandleader, and composer and was ready for stardom. After several band-building ventures in southern California and a brief sojourn in the Army, Morton opened the Jupiter in San Francisco with his lover, Anita Gonzales, in 1919. The combination of his predilection for firearms, a fast mouth, and a looming Prohibition, however, made confrontation with the authorities inevitable, and the police closed him down. For the next several years Morton played his way up and down the West Coast, from Vancouver to Tijuana, picking up bands, women, and inspiration for songs, but it all seemed to be taking him nowhere. Chicago was the place to be, so Jelly decided to crash the party, arriving in May 1923.

Oliver had seen Morton in Los Angeles in April 1922 on his way back to Chicago from his own San Francisco excursion set up by Kid Ory the year before, and they must have compared notes. Like Morton, Oliver had been struggling to maintain a stable roster of players. Paul Barbarin remembered the excitement of Joe's first night at the Royal Gardens in February 1919, when Oliver was crowned King. The coronation came at the hands of a West Indian master of ceremonies who placed a paper crown on Oliver's head after a particularly thrilling rendition of "I'm Not Rough," a blues showcase for "talking horn" perfected with Ory. Bechet was also on hand that night, but he would soon leave for New York and London, responding to an invitation from Will Marion Cook to join his Southern Syncopated Orchestra as a featured attraction. According to John Chilton, before he left Bechet had a falling-out with Oliver, but no details are provided, and Bechet fails to mention it in his autobiography. Most probably, Oliver had trouble with Sidney vying for the lead. In a New Orleans front line, the cornet predominates with clarinet relegated to a secondary, obbligato role—a position Bechet refused to accept. Among New Orleans cornetists Sidney Bechet was viewed as an occupational hazard, a situation which was exacerbated when he added soprano saxophone to his arsenal.

By October 1919 Oliver had replaced Duhé as the leader of the Dreamland band, and Johnny Dodds's arrival from New Orleans in January 1921 resulted from Duhé's resignation. During the trip to California, Joe hired Johnny's brother, drummer Warren "Baby" Dodds, for what was now known as King Oliver's Creole Band. While Oliver himself was not a Creole, he had learned to speak patois in New Orleans, and because many Americans associated the term *Creole* with a certain Old World éclat and elegance, it was a useful promotional tool. When Oliver returned to Chicago to open at the Lincoln Gardens in June 1922, Bill Johnson, trombonist Honoré Dutrey, and the Dodds brothers were with him, with Lil Hardin eventually to follow. In July he sent for Louis Armstrong, whose arrival from New Orleans on August 8, 1922, added the pièce de résistance to King Joe's band-building efforts.

The recordings made by King Oliver's Creole Jazz Band in 1923 are considered by many to be the definitive statement of a New Orleans ensemble, and they document the difficulty involved in balancing the predilections of individual personalities and those of the leader. As described by Baby Dodds, Oliver's leadership style was "not loud-spoken—he liked to kid and joke—he didn't say much unless he had something to say for the band." At first, he ran the band as a cooperative unit, but Dodds saw a change once the records started selling, at which point "our band" became "King Oliver's band" and the esprit de corps evaporated, along with some of the royalties. Oliver applied discipline when he thought it was necessary. Lil Hardin remembered that she was rarely assigned solos, and when she would "begin making runs" the boss would cut her off, saying, "We already got a clarinet in the band." For her, the band's success rested upon the painstaking organization that went into rehearsals, relying on "head" arrangements learned by rote.

Ultimately, it was the band's unity of feeling that came across in the recordings. The first Gennetts displayed a direct emotional appeal that captivated dancers and listeners alike. "Snake Rag" used stop-time breaks to dramatize the cornet interplay of Oliver and Armstrong, which was fused so tightly as to suggest a kind of musical telepathy. "Just Gone" was a portrait in polyphony with melodic variation, an object lesson in collectively improvised blending, while "Dippermouth Blues," a signature tune for Louis, demonstrated Oliver's amazing facility with wa-wa techniques in one of the earliest jazz solos ever recorded. The OKeh recordings made in June included a version of "High Society"—a perennial New Orleans parade favorite—complete with the obligatory piccolo solo popularized by Alphonse Picou. The Columbia recordings from October yielded "New Orleans Stomp," a piece which reveals the flair for Latin rhythms in the "out chorus" typical of New Orleans–style jazz, and the second OKeh session later in the month provided a preview of things to come in "Tears," a vehicle for some outstanding leads by Armstrong. By the end of 1923, the Creole Jazz Band had summarized the state of the art in jazz and suggested several possibilities for further development.

Whatever tore this band apart, the chemistry that brought it together was Joe Oliver's concoction, the culmination of years studying leadership among the Creoles. He observed the "Holy Trinity" of New Orleans style: a relaxed rhythmic verve with subtle dynamics for dancers; a melodic front line that was exciting, coherent, but also a little rough; and a dedication to joie de vivre in making music. Once the fun was forgotten, the band's days were numbered: the Dodds brothers went off on their own, and Lil set Louis up with Fletcher Henderson in New York, leaving Oliver feeling bewildered but resolute.

Jelly Roll Morton returned to Chicago on an advance from the Melrose Brothers for "Wolverine Blues" just in time to witness King Oliver's apogee. He started recording in June 1923 with a session for Paramount using a pickup band on his "Big Fat Ham" and "Muddy Water Blues." Next came a fortuitous collaboration for Gennett in July with the New Orleans Rhythm Kings, a white group composed primarily of musicians who had emerged from the ranks of Jack Laine's Reliance bands to make a name for themselves in Chicago. Significantly, the "homeboy" instinct prevalent among these musicians permitted an almost intuitive rapport to develop. "Milenburg Joys," co-composed on the spot with clarinetist Leon Roppolo and cornetist Paul Mares, became an instant classic. True to its name, the music recalls the relaxed ambience of the lakefront resort, where white and black bands played within earshot of each other on Sunday afternoons. Morton later admitted that his only real contribution to the piece had been the introduction, but not without adding, "Of course, the rest don't amount to much." Solo piano sides recorded at the session yielded several masterpieces, including the first recording of "King Porter Stomp." For the next three years, Morton tested the endurance of recording engineers and musicians throughout the Midwest, busily documenting his backlist of tunes with the help of such diverse talents as Natty Dominique, Boyd Senter, Zue Robertson, Lee Collins, Roy Palmer, and Voltaire de Faut—a veritable "rainbow coalition."

While he was attempting to create the ultimate band for himself, Morton paid close attention to Oliver's next project, the Dixie Syncopators, which began to take shape in the fall of 1924. Although he teased "Blondie" (his nickname for Joe) about the slow progress of the band, it was during this period that a close friendship developed between them. Oliver had a fondness for Morton's material, as a duet recorded for Autograph late in 1924 attests. "King Porter Stomp" and "Tom Cat Blues" were cut spontaneously, with Oliver hugging Jelly like a shadow on the former and then stretching out with some dazzling mute work and stop-chorus breaks in the latter. It was a mutual admiration society: Oliver recorded Morton's "London Blues" and "Froggie Moore" with the Creole Jazz Band and then "Dead Man Blues" with the Dixie Syncopators, while Jelly featured Oliver's "Doctor Jazz" and later wrote "Mr. Joe" in his honor. In October 1925 Ory made it a threesome when he arrived from California to work simultaneously with Armstrong's Hot Five, Oliver's Dixie Syncopators, and Morton's forthcoming studio band, the Red Hot Peppers. Chicago was still the place to be, but not for much longer. The New York scene had come alive with a vengeance, owing in large part to the exploits of Sidney Bechet, and the balance of power was shifting.

When the Swiss conductor Ernest Ansermet heard Sidney Bechet performing "Characteristic Blues" with Will Cook at London's Philharmonic Hall in 1919, he was unaware that it was typical New Orleans fare—a pastiche of blues effects and clarinet quotes taken from standards such as "Shake It and Break It." For him, that moment was all about "this artist of genius" who knew only that he must "follow his own way." Bechet's passion was mesmerizing, and he tended to attract the spotlight wherever he went. After his stint with Cook, he spent time in England and France with small groups, gaining exposure to life in Europe and testing his prowess as an improvisor. A return to New York in 1922 led to his recording debut with Clarence Williams's Blue Five in July 1923, the prelude to a series of sessions which paired Sidney and Louis Armstrong in late 1924 and early 1925. On the first sessions, Bechet's command of the soprano displays all the qualities one would expect from a mature soloist: "Wild Cat Blues" and "Kansas City Man Blues" are riveting performances, wedding a powerful vibrato with an imaginative exploration of blues motifs. The recordings with Armstrong were even more exciting, with "Texas Moaner Blues," "Cakewalking Babies From Home," and "Mandy, Make Up Your Mind" providing the arena for a musical battle that ranged from ingenious rhythmic flanking maneuvers and frontal assaults for the lead to the use of heavy artillery (a sarrusophone solo by Bechet!). On the second take of "Cakewalking Babies," the advantage shifted several times as Sidney and Louis grappled for supremacy, and it remains one of the earliest and most remarkable jazz duels on record. In July 1925 Sidney invested in a speakeasy scheme—the Club Basha in Harlem—but within a few months was looking for a way out and fled to France with *La Revue nègre*. Bechet embraced the Parisian lifestyle wholeheartedly and made trips to Germany and the Soviet Union—he met trumpeter Tommy Ladnier for the first time in Moscow—returning to Paris to work with Noble Sissle in the summer of 1928. On December 20 disaster struck: he was involved in a shooting with banjoist "Little Mike" McKendrick in Montmartre, three people were wounded, and Sidney spent eleven months in prison before being deported. Bechet returned to New York on December 22, 1930, to rejoin Sissle. Two nights later he and Ladnier were on the bandstand at the Rockland Palace when Jelly Roll Morton walked in and attempted to steal the pair for his band—an apt homecoming, indeed.

While Bechet was taking Europe by storm, Morton was contending with demons of his own back home. Shifts in popular taste and the acquisition of Victor Records by Radio Corporation of America had resulted in his expulsion from the label only months before, despite four years of very productive activity. The Red Hot Peppers recordings made in Chicago from September 1926 into June 1927 had raised the ante on New Orleans–style jazz, combining elements of ragtime, marches, vaudeville hokum, and blues to create an amalgam of unsurpassed beauty and variety, an artist's summation and clarification of New Orleans music by its most ardent theoretician. Unlike Oliver, Morton allowed his sidemen (including cornetist George Mitchell, clarinetist Omer Simeon, trombonist Kid Ory, and banjoist Johnny St. Cyr) a free hand on solos, and the Red Hot Peppers recordings benefit from the variegation this permitted within a composer's singular vision. "Black Bottom Stomp" showcases the composer's craft in its clever juxtaposition of riffs and breaks, the careful layering of tonal coloration, and a canny use of contrasting meters to intensify rhythmic thrust. "Dead Man Blues" reprises the dirge "Flee as a Bird" to replicate a New Orleans brass band funeral, gradually building tempo toward an aural epiphany. "Jungle Blues" ponders the riff, achieving density rather than effusion, while "Georgia Swing" (recorded in New York in 1928) is a freewheeling frolic, a steeplechase for the musicians, tempered by a subtle dynamic sensitivity. Morton's vision of New Orleans jazz was holistic: he gave it a brilliance and polish that had been lacking and achieved a coherence that was both personal and universal.

Yet as far as the public was concerned, he might as well have been bluffing. Karl Kramer, a booking agent with Music Corporation of America, remembered 1927 as the year of the "sweet" band. It was also when MCA signed Morton, who was viewed as a dubious commodity. The demand for "sweeter" orchestras was removing New Orleans players from the game, especially the ones that still maintained a devotion to collective improvisation. The Dixie Syncopators suffered a similar fate. Oliver relocated to New York in 1927, and Morton followed suit with a big bankroll a year later, hoping for a fresh deck and a chance to play an ace in the hole. Instead, they found themselves picked clean of their best players and ideas by the New York leaders and were forced to settle for scraps.

The Great Depression was unkind to jazz musicians—King Oliver lost his life savings in the bank failures following the Crash in 1929—but some were more successful at coping than others. Ellington's tenure at the Cotton Club from 1927 to 1931 provided the security and continuity required to assemble a truly superlative band. Ironically, Oliver had been offered the engagement first but refused it because the price was too low. Despite renewed activity for Victor as King Oliver and His Orchestra in 1929, Joe's fortunes continued to decline. His last recordings were made for Vocalion in early 1931, after which he embarked upon a relentless series of tours of the Midwest and South in a valiant attempt to recapture the public's fancy. Beginning in March 1931, trombonist Clyde Bernhardt spent eight months on the road with the band and recalled that 95 percent of their audiences were white; Oliver would play his "smooth, sweet numbers" for them, reserving the blues and jazz for black audiences. Musicians came and went, including star innovators such as Lester Young, and Oliver did his best to survive despite a downward cycle of worsening logistical problems, but by 1937 he had reached the nadir. In September of that year Louis Armstrong encountered him in Savannah, Georgia, selling produce on the street. The King talked about future tours, and Armstrong gave him a hundred-dollar bill. Oliver died on April 10, 1938, the victim of a cerebral hemorrhage and defeated expectations.

Oliver's death came at a time when the Fates were preparing a reversal of fortune for the pioneers of New Orleans jazz. Record collectors had begun to exercise their clout as a force in the market since the appearance of Charles Edward Smith's "Collecting Hot" in *Esquire* in 1934, and by the summer of 1938 Smith, William Russell, and Frederic Ramsey Jr. were working on *Jazzmen*, a history of jazz which apotheosized the early pioneers. In May, Jelly Roll Morton invaded the interview sessions being conducted at the Library of Congress by Alan Lomax, converted him, and then gave an epic account of his life in jazz. Jelly revealed himself in musical and emotional catharsis, providing details on his experiences as a Mardi Gras Indian, bawdy songster, aspiring gambler, and philosopher of jazz. Comparative New Orleans and St. Louis versions of "Maple Leaf Rag" spoke volumes on the distinctive features of New Orleans music, and the maestro offered his own theory of the French origins of "Tiger Rag." Living in obscurity, he had recorded only once after being dropped by Victor, a 1934 session with New Orleans trumpeter Wingy Manone which included Artie Shaw, Bud Freeman, and John Kirby. Although it was too late to do anything for Oliver except to eulogize him, the *Jazzmen* team and Lomax were in a position to rehabilitate Morton. Ramsey and Smith arranged sessions in September 1939 with RCA Victor to capitalize on the publication of their book: Jelly Roll Morton's New Orleans Jazzmen reunited "homeboys" Sidney Bechet, Albert Nicholas, Wellman Braud, and Zutty Singleton (Jelly had wanted Ory, too, but Ramsey failed to locate him until late in the second session), and according to Ramsey, Bechet's presence on the first session caused it to "soar." Smith and Lomax also persuaded Morton to record for General in December 1939 and January 1940, but the public's curiosity about "historical" recordings from a bygone era was insufficient to sustain the kind of return to glory that Jelly Roll had in mind. A trip to California in the winter of 1940 was to be his last. He died in Los Angeles from cardiac arrest on July 10, 1941. Kid Ory was a pallbearer at the funeral and purportedly overheard someone lamenting the lack of a brass band to send Morton off in style. His reply was "We'll do it next time."

Barely three months before Jelly's death, Sidney Bechet was in

New York making his One Man Band recordings, the logical conclusion, one suspects, of a cantankerous nature. His crucial role in the Jazzmen session had returned him to the RCA Victor fold after a lapse of eight years, following the New Orleans Feetwarmers recordings made with Tommy Ladnier in September 1932. The Feetwarmers was Sidney's favorite band, largely because of the affinity that existed between the two men, and their musical compatibility is evident on "I Found a New Baby" and an adventurous rendition of "Maple Leaf Rag." In "Shag" the changes to "I Got Rhythm" become the premise for an improvisational free-for-all which is startling in its audacity, but the records never caught on with the public, probably for that very reason. An affiliation with Noble Sissle kept Bechet working but not busy during the Depression, and at one point he and Tommy ran a tailor shop. On December 23, 1938, John Hammond revived the Feetwarmers for his Spirituals to Swing concert at Carnegie Hall, but Ladnier died six months later, on June 4, 1939. Bechet's rendition of "Summertime," recorded for Blue Note only four days after his friend's death, helped to launch the nascent label and comes across as an elegy to a lost friend. In March 1940 Stephen Smith of the Hot Record Society brought Sidney together with Muggsy Spanier, a trumpeter who greatly admired Ladnier, as the Bechet-Spanier Big Four. The musicians connected immediately, yielding an especially superb rendition of "China Boy" which played Bechet's dazzling artistry against Spanier's straightforward earnestness to very good effect. Following the death of Johnny Dodds on August 8, 1940, a date was arranged with pianist Earl Hines to record a tribute in Chicago: "Blues for You, Johnny" and "Blues in Thirds" matched the talents of the coleaders beautifully, despite some preliminary friction in the studio, and succeeded as a fitting eulogy for the departed clarinetist.

Thereafter, Sidney recorded prolifically but suffered from being typecast as a relic in a time of revolutionary change. The rise of bebop split the jazz audience during World War II, engendering a schism that ran deep. In 1949 Charles Delaunay hired Bechet for the first Paris Jazz Festival, pitting him against the leader of the bebop movement, Charlie Parker. Bechet stole the show and two years later relocated to France permanently, swept along by the momentum of his reception there. For a decade he enjoyed the benefits of mass celebrity, playing, teaching, living the good life, and marveling as adoring young fans fought pitched battles to get into his concerts. Yet time was catching up with him. When he recorded with the modernist Martial Solal in 1957 at the behest of Delaunay, his tone was thin and the results struck some as "cautious," a description which would have been impossible earlier. Eventually, even Sidney had to let go. When he died of cancer on May 14, 1959, the entire country mourned.

The music of King Oliver, Jelly Roll Morton, and Sidney Bechet accounts for the first flowering of jazz in America, the basic framework on which all subsequent development depended. Jelly, Sidney, and Joe took the communal music of their birthplace and transformed it into highly personal works of art, leaving a musical legacy that still brings enjoyment to jazz lovers the world over. Each, in his own way, was a perfectionist who chose a vagabond existence in pursuit of an elusive artistic vision, hoping for the triumphal return home that could never be. Yet, wherever they went, they took New Orleans with them, sharing much more than friendship. They gave their lives to jazz so that their spirit could live in it forever—three hearts for one music. It was their "own way of doing."

Louis Armstrong

Dan Morgenstern

In preparation for a fiftieth-birthday issue dedicated to Louis Armstrong, the editors of the magazine *The Record Changer* asked a number of musicians for tributes. The most succinct of these came from trombonist Benny Morton, who simply said: "What would we have done without Louis?"

Though he was never billed as the King of Jazz, Armstrong is the only legitimate claimant to that title. Without him there would of course have been the music called jazz, but how it might have developed is guesswork. This extraordinary trumpeter and singer was the key creator of the mature working language of jazz. Three decades after his death and more than three-quarters of a century since his influence first began to spread, not a single musician who has mastered that language fails to make daily use, knowingly or unknowingly, of something that was invented by Louis Armstrong. Or as Miles Davis put it: "You can't play anything on your horn that Louis hasn't played already."

Nor was his influence limited to jazz. Brass players in all branches of music expanded the range and expressive power of their instruments in the wake of Armstrong's unprecedented flexibility and range on the trumpet. He created a new kind of virtuosity. The creators of what is called "the Great American Songbook" made good use of the rhythmic and melodic inventions Armstrong fed into the mainstream of jazz. And popular singers, from Ethel Waters and Bing Crosby on, phrase and breathe in ways that stem from his liberating ways with words and music.

It may be difficult for those who knew Armstrong only as the genial entertainer with the instantly recognizable smile and gravelly voice—the image he presented in the final decades of his life, when he achieved his greatest international fame—to understand that this man was a truly revolutionary artist. It was his genius that transformed an interesting new dance music into a vehicle for an unprecedented freedom of individual expression within a uniquely balanced collective framework. In the words of Gunther Schuller, "through Louis Armstrong and his influence jazz became a truly twentieth-century language."

Born out of wedlock on August 4, 1901, in New Orleans, raised in the city's poorest, roughest quarter, out of school and working for a living before he'd finished fifth grade, Armstrong was not a likely candidate for world fame. But against all odds he not only survived but thrived. Sent to reform school at age twelve, he learned the fundamentals of music there (he'd already acquired a battered cornet and organized a quartet that sang and danced in the street for pennies) and by his mid-teens was able to supplement his income from work as a longshoreman or a day laborer by playing his cornet in the dives surrounding Storyville, the city's red light district.

Armstrong, who despite his limited schooling became an enthusiastic and prolific writer of letters, articles, and memoirs, describes one such joint, the Brick House, in his *Satchmo: My Life in New Orleans* quite vividly: "Levee workers would congregate every Saturday night. ... Those guys would drink and fight each other like circle saws. Bottles would come flying over the bandstand like crazy, and there was lots of just plain cutting and shooting. But somehow all that jive didn't faze me at all, I was so happy to have some place to blow my horn."

There wasn't much that ever fazed Armstrong. Blessed with a perfect physique for playing as demanding an instrument as his chosen horn and with a perfect disposition for making his way in the toughest of environments, "Little Louis" (the first of many nicknames he was known by) had a gift for making friends who could protect and defend him. He credited his "good sense and mother wit" with having carried him through his extraordinary life and giving him his ability

Louis Armstrong's Hot Five, Chicago, 1925. Left to right: Louis Armstrong, trumpet; Johnny St. Cyr, banjo; Johnny Dodds, clarinet and alto sax; Kid Ory, trombone; Lil Hardin Armstrong, piano. Courtesy Frank Driggs Collection.

to confront with equaniminity experiences he couldn't have imagined in his youth.

Musically, the New Orleans of that time was a very special place, and throughout his long career, Armstrong looked back on his apprenticeship years with great warmth and affection. But it is clear, not least from his own writings, that even early on his love of music and life was combined with a strong sense of responsibility, toward himself and his chosen profession. He soon noticed that musicians who were careless with their intake of alcohol on the job or inattentive to their health in other ways did not play well consistently, and he became a firm believer in the separation between work and play. Early and late in his career, he never indulged between sets, always warmed up before taking the stand, and reserved his pleasurable explorations for after working hours. Also early on, observation led him to decide that when he would front his own groups, he would let others handle business matters. This attitude was often misunderstood by commentators, but Armstrong explains it perfectly well in his autobiography. "I never cared to become a bandleader; there was too much quarreling over petty money matters. . . . I have always noticed that the bandleader not only had to satisfy the crowd but that he also had to worry about the box office."

Of course he did lead bands throughout most of his career, but he did not want the everyday banalities of the music business to take energy away from his playing. Making music was his full-time job, and he worked harder at it than most. He noted that his fourth and last marriage was successful because Lucille Armstrong understood "that the horn comes first," and he stated his modus vivendi as "The music—that's my living and my life."

Armstrong's key mentor in New Orleans was the cornetist and bandleader Joe "King" Oliver, who took the youngster under his wing, gave him pointers, and recommended him, early in 1919, to take his place with trombonist Kid Ory's band when he left for Chicago. "Little Louis" soon added another prestigious job, with Fate Marable's band on the Mississippi riverboats, which cruised as far north as Davenport, where young Bix Beiderbecke first encountered him. The Marable band was required to play the latest hits. This demanded reading music, and Armstrong's knowledge was rudimentary. Marable thought so well of the young man's playing that he hired him nonetheless, with the understanding that he would apply himself. Under the tutelage of an older band member, David Jones, Armstrong proved a quick study and soon learned to write as well as read music. Also in the band were such established players as the Dodds brothers (clarinetist Jimmy and drummer Baby), bassist Pops Foster, and guitarist and banjoist Johnny St. Cyr—all of whom would become Armstrong's sidemen.

We know little about Armstrong's playing at this time, but his only early peer, Sidney Bechet, who was four years older, recalled that the kid stunned him by playing the famous "High Society" clarinet solo on the cornet—something quite unheard of. This alone tells us that a very young Armstrong already had the technical facility to execute a passage that would have challenged the best cornetists of the day. About the time of his Marable association, Armstrong also demonstrated a gift for songwriting. He cooked up a number that he called "Get Off Katie's Head" and sold it outright for fifty dollars (a fair amount in 1920) to the Creole society bandleader A. J. Piron. The song became a big hit under the more respectable name of "I Wish I Could Shimmy Like My Sister Kate," thus teaching "Little Louis" another music business lesson.

He was well established in New Orleans by the summer of 1922, when King Oliver sent him a telegram asking him to join his now famous Creole Jazz Band in Chicago. In later years Armstrong would say that only Oliver could have lured him away from home, and it was with some trepidation that he heeded the King's call. When he arrived at the Lincoln Gardens and heard the band in full cry, he almost turned around to go back home, but before long the teamwork between himself and Oliver was the talk of musical Chicago.

Armstrong made his recording debut with the band on April 6, 1923, taking a solo on "Chimes Blues." It sticks close to the attractive melody, but in its sound, poise, phrasing, and relaxed swing it stands out from its plainer setting like a little gem. What the acoustic recording does not convey is Armstrong's true power; he was made to stand far back from the recording horn, much farther than Oliver. But according to Armstrong, not just he but also Oliver is underrepresented on the records. Their celebrated duet breaks, however, are indeed spectacular.

Armstrong also contributed to the band's repertory, co-composing "Dippermouth Blues" ("Dippermouth," sometimes shortened to "Dipper," was Armstrong's new nickname) and being solely responsible for "Weather Bird Rag," among others. The Oliver record on which Armstrong's work is the strongest precursor of his future is "Tears." The piece was a collaboration with his new bride, the band's pianist and most sophisticated musician, Lil Hardin, and features a stunning sequence of cornet breaks. It is certain that the Oliver records, quite aside from their technical shortcomings, do not accurately reflect the band's true range. For instance, Armstrong deposited for copyright with the Library of Congress on January 18, 1924—more than two years before he recorded it—the composition "Cornet Chop Suey." Is it not likely that he would have performed it with the band?

In any event, at the persistent urging of his wife, who was convinced that Oliver had hired Armstrong to keep him under wraps, the young man parted company with his mentor—reluctantly, but further prodded by the discovery that the King had been holding out money from his men. Armstrong soon received an offer from the prominent New York bandleader Fletcher Henderson, and Lil made sure that he accepted it.

The Henderson band, resident at Roseland, a popular ballroom in the center of Manhattan's theater district, was a very different musical proposition from Oliver's New Orleans–rooted ensemble. Made up of four brass, three reeds, and four rhythm, it performed from written arrangements. Some of these were stocks, but many others were the work of the band's musical director and lead saxophonist, Don Redman, a conservatory-trained multi-instrumentalist. Armstrong arrived during a rehearsal; the band was running through a medley of Irish waltzes. The newcomer found the right place in his part, but he played too loudly. Henderson stopped the music and asked the newcomer what the marking on that passage was. "*Pp*" was the answer. "Well," said the leader, "don't you know that means 'pianissimo?'" Armstrong apologized: "I thought it meant 'pound plenty.'" The quick Armstrong wit had broken the ice, and he was soon not just accepted but idolized by most of his new colleagues. The Henderson band was technically accomplished by the standards of September 1924, but its rhythm was stiff and unswinging, and the conception of the soloists—even of the tenor saxophone prodigy Coleman Hawkins—limited and frequently corny. The exception was Nebraska-born trombonist Charlie "Big" Green, an early master of the blues idiom.

Redman was quick to absorb many of Armstrong's lessons. His arrangements improved considerably during Armstrong's thirteen-month stay, as did the band's rhythm and phrasing, as well as the solo level. Hawkins in particular benefited from the association, and Armstrong also brought a former Oliver sideman, clarinetist Buster Bailey, into the band. As for the catalyst himself, he improved his reading and section-playing skills and gained confidence in his abilities, not least when such gifted young fellow instrumentalists as Rex Stewart would follow him around, attempt to copy his style, and even try to talk like him. And when Johnny Dunn, the much-recorded New York cornet star, challenged him in public, Armstrong responded in such definitive fashion that Dunn's stature was permanently diminished. He was not the last to learn that the usually amiable Armstrong could be a formidable antagonist.

But Armstrong's Henderson sojourn was not without its negative aspects. With the exception of "Sugarfoot Stomp" (Redman's retitling of "Dippermouth Blues"), on which Armstrong re-creates, in his own distinctive manner, Oliver's three-chorus solo, he was not extensively featured on the many records in which he participated. Occasionally, as on "Shanghai Shuffle," he would be allotted a full chorus, but mostly it was a matter of eight or sixteen bars, or some breaks. He makes his presence felt at every opportunity, but one feels that he is under wraps. And Henderson would not let him sing on records (a few half-spoken vocal breaks on one of the versions of "Everybody Loves My Baby" marks the first recorded appearance of that inimitable voice, but that was all), and rarely in person, though every time he did sing, the house would come down.

No doubt Armstrong's singing, then in its early bucolic stage, was too earthy for the college-educated Henderson, very much aware of performing for Roseland's white audience. Henderson's attitude, and the fact that he would give the band's two other cornetists almost as much solo space, still rankled Armstrong years later, and it is passing strange that he could have sat for more than a year in the Henderson band on Broadway without attracting the attention of the general public. Musicians, both black and white, of course took notice, and so did the audiences in Harlem, where the Henderson band often played on off-nights or at late-night dances.

Fortunately, New York offered Armstrong plenty of recording opportunities beyond the Henderson band. Some of these were in company with Henderson musicians, even the leader himself, in accompaniments to the then popular blues singers. We can hear Armstrong with Ma Rainey, with Maggie Jones (marvelous solos and obbligatos), and with the great Bessie Smith. There was also a series of dates under the aegis of the enterprising transplanted New Orleanian Clarence Williams, director of the OKeh label's prospering "race" catalog. Williams's Blue Five often backed his wife, singer Eva Taylor, but there was plenty of solo space, and also some entirely instrumental records. Best of all, Williams had the imagination to team Armstrong with Sidney Bechet, then on one of his relatively rare lengthy stays in the United States. Sparks fly when these two match wits. On two different sessions, they tackle the identical arrangement of "Cakewalking Babies From Home," soloing in turn and offering slashing breaks. On the version issued as by the Red Onion Jazz Babies, Bechet gets the best of Armstrong, but on the Blue Five disc the younger man gets his revenge.

It was when he returned to Chicago that Armstrong really found himself in demand. His wife was leading a band at the famous Dreamland Ballroom and had prepared a banner for his arrival welcoming "the World's Greatest Trumpet Player." Despite his entreaties, the banner stayed up for the duration of the engagement, and soon he was doubling in Erskine Tate's orchestra at the Vendome Theater, the South Side's most prestigious first-run movie palace, where the stage show included such semiclassical features for Armstrong as the "Intermezzo" from *Cavalleria rusticana*. This kind of "crossover" was no challenge for the trumpeter (Tate had made him switch to the more penetrating horn). As he recalled in 1966, reminiscing about his first phonograph, acquired in 1918: "Most of my records were the Original Dixieland Jazz Band—Larry Shields and his bunch. They were the first to record the music I played. I had Caruso records too, and Henry Burr, Galli-Curci, Tettrazini—they were all my favorites. Then there was the Irish tenor, [John] McCormack—beautiful phrasing." Many ingredients went into the making of Armstrong's musical imagination. Early jazz writers zeroed in on ragtime, spirituals, blues, marches, and dance music, but more recently musicologists have taken notice of the parallels between Armstrong's solo structure (including such elements as opening and closing cadenzas) and operatic arias.

The day after his return from New York, Armstrong was already in the studio, backing blues singer Bertha "Chippie" Hill. The pianist was Richard M. Jones, from New Orleans, who was Clarence Williams's counterpart with OKeh in Chicago. It was Jones who gave Armstrong his first record date as a leader, just three days after the Hill session. The band, a quintet billed as Louis Armstrong and His Hot Five, consisted of Lil Hardin Armstrong on piano, Armstrong's onetime New Orleans bandleader, Kid Ory, on trombone, and two riverboat colleagues, Johnny Dodds on clarinet and Johnny St. Cyr on banjo. All but Lil were New Orleanians, and all (including Lil, born in 1898) were the leader's seniors. With occasional substitutions and additions (a tuba player and drummer Baby Dodds made them the Hot Seven) the group recorded more than forty sides during the next two years. It was strictly a recording unit, performing just once in person, at a benefit concert.

These records made Armstrong famous. They were the first to consistently feature him in solo and ensemble lead and the first to showcase his singing. His own playing aside, the music is in an older style than his regular work in Chicago would reflect, as for instance with the Tate band, which recorded just once. Unlike the critics, who appear about a decade later, musicians at the time considered the other players old hat and listened only to Armstrong, and while it is possible to appreciate Dodds's warm tone and sincere blues playing and Ory's skillful deployment of his limited technical resources, only Armstrong's work remains undated.

Indeed, his solos on such pieces as "Big Butter and Egg Man," "Potato Head Blues," "Wild Man Blues," "King of the Zulus," and "Savoy Blues" remain peaks in the recorded history of jazz, while his vocal on "Heebie Jeebies" put scat singing on the map. His scatting on "Hotter Than That" is even more exciting. Like much of his singing, it rivals the playing in creativity. Eventually, Armstrong refined his approach to lyrics and became a master ballad singer. It has been said that he sings like he plays, and there are many trumpetlike aspects to the voice, such as, in the words of British critic Eric Thacker, his use of "dentals, labials and gutturals as he would use tonguing in a cornet solo, and enlivening the vowel colors with abrasive flutterings of the throat." Suffice it to say that nothing like Armstrong's singing had been heard before, and that it had a profound effect on the evolution of jazz and popular vocal styles.

A new Hot Five/Seven made its recording debut in June 1928. It was a closer reflection of Armstrong's day-to-day playing environment, since its members came from the ranks of the band, led by Carroll Dickerson and fronted by Armstrong, with which he was working at Chicago's Savoy Ballroom. And in pianist Earl Hines it paired Armstrong with his first peer on records since Sidney Bechet. Hines was a key representative of the new breed of players to whom Armstrong's vocabulary had become second nature, himself to become a great influence on pianists. Also on hand was Armstrong's close New Orleans friend drummer Zutty Singleton, a master of his craft. Don Redman was brought in for several sessions, playing and arranging. The eighteen sides that constituted the group's output are on a very high level, including such masterpieces as "Beau Koo Jack," "Basin Street Blues," and "Muggles," but the most famous (and perhaps the most famous of all jazz records) is "West End Blues," with its astonishing opening trumpet cadenza, a clarion call (Gunther Schuller's phrase) that put the world on notice that jazz was an art to contend with the highest forms of musical expression. But the entire performance is masterful. The composition, by the way, is by King Oliver, whose own recording of it is grotesque in comparison.

Musicologists Lewis Porter and Joshua Berrett have traced the cadenza's genealogy to a break on a November 1924 recording with an obscure singer, Margaret Johnson, "Changeable Daddy of Mine," showing that it was the result of years of refining an idea that was spectacular even in its comparatively embryonic form. Such findings—and Armstrong's subsequent use of elements from "West End Blues"—demonstrate the need to reconsider the nature of improvisation in jazz. That caveat also applies to the other great work from this period, the unique Armstrong-Hines duet on "Weather Bird" (the Armstrong piece from the Oliver days, now stripped of the "Rag" tag). The near-symbiotic rapport between trumpet and piano has been hailed as a triumph of "spontaneous creation," but it does seem more likely that the two musicians, inseparable friends at the time, had played through this three-strain piece before recording it. They certainly brought fresh ideas to the studio version, but knew where they were going—which doesn't in the slightest detract from their achievement.

The "second" Hot Five/Seven recordings ended in December 1928, closing a chapter in Armstrong's career. He visited New York the following March, making an impromptu early-morning record with an integrated group of musicians who'd been hanging out with him in Harlem, and later that day recording his first mainstream pop tune, an incredible instrumental and vocal rendition of "I Can't Give You Anything but Love." This was a breakthrough in terms of recorded repertory only, for Armstrong had long since been performing such material (and indeed had recorded it, in accompaniment to singer Lillie Delk Christian a few months earlier); the pianist Art Hodes recalled hearing Armstrong improvising for nearly half an hour on Noël Coward's "Poor Little Rich Girl." But even by the late 1920s, it was still uncommon for black artists to record show tunes; Ethel Waters was one of the few exceptions. Waters, however, rolled her r's and used other refined touches, while Armstrong's sound and approach were quintessentially African American.

A few months later Armstrong came to New York for good. He had been invited to try out for a new Vincent Youmans musical,

Great Day, but couldn't bear to leave his band behind. When he showed up with the band in tow, his manager hit the ceiling but was able to find him a job at Connie's Inn, a Harlem nightspot second only to the Cotton Club. It was a stroke of luck since *Great Day* (which became a costly flop) had no room for Armstrong. But the revue at Connie's Inn, *Hot Chocolates,* with a score by Fats Waller and Andy Razaf, turned out to be so good that it came to Broadway. There, at first, Armstrong performed the show's biggest hit song, "Ain't Misbehavin'," from the orchestra pit as an entr'acte, but the response was such that he soon found himself onstage; he also joined Waller and female lead Edith Wilson in a trio number that billed them as "A Thousand Pounds of Rhythm." After the show, Armstrong taxied up to Harlem to lead his band at Connie's Inn, and for a while was so popular that he also did a spot in the late show next door at the Lafayette Theater (the Apollo's predecessor). "Had to get my sleep coming through the park in a cab," he recalled years later. "Didn't exactly feel I had the world at my feet, but it was nice that everyone was picking up on the things I was doing."

Indeed everyone was. His recording of "Ain't Misbehavin'," backed with another song from *Hot Chocolates,* "Black and Blue," was his first real hit (issued by OKeh in both its race and regular series). Armstrong stripped "Black and Blue," a dark-skinned lady's lament about losing in love to lighter rivals, of the verse that could only be sung by a woman, and in the process transformed it into what has long been regarded as a protest song. As such, it and Armstrong are made emblematic of the hero's plight in Ralph Ellison's masterwork *Invisible Man.*

From 1930 to 1947 Armstrong would be at the helm of big bands, performing a repertory consisting mainly of popular songs but also of novelties and some of the jazz classics associated with him. On the road—and Armstrong's bands toured constantly—the band would play for dancing without the leader, who would do sets as a featured attraction, and for shows with Armstrong front and center. Critical opinion has generally not been kind to Armstrong's big bands, mainly because their unique role as a supporting entity for his playing and singing has not been fully appreciated. As such, they more frequently served him well than not. Essential was a good rhythm section, and Armstrong always made sure he had first-rate drummers (his favorite was the long-serving Sidney "Big Sid" Catlett). Arrangements were also important, and unfortunately not always the best. When they were of top caliber, the band could sound very good indeed, and it always had its share of capable soloists. But in the final analysis, Armstrong was the whole show, and thus the band had a thankless task, comparatively speaking. For musicians who did not aspire to solo, however, playing for Armstrong was a fulfilling task. And when he had a player of the quality of trombonist J. C. Higginbotham or altoist Charlie Holmes in the band, Armstrong made sure the man was featured.

Armstrong introduced or popularized an astonishing number of songs, among them many so-called evergreens and jazz standards. (Because sheet music, at least into the 1940s, was more important than records to the industry in terms of sales, he was often presented with new material to record at short notice, which was more of a problem to the band than to him; Armstrong was a famously quick study, who could make a song his own after a few runthroughs or even read it convincingly at first sight.) He enjoyed a particularly close relationship with Hoagy Carmichael, making the first record of "Rockin' Chair" (on which the two duetted), a memorable early "Star Dust," and remarkable interpretations of "Georgia on My Mind" and especially "Lazy River." Carmichael wrote "Jubilee" for Armstrong, and it debuted in one of the many feature films in which he appeared beginning in 1930; Armstrong also introduced "Eventide" and "Lying to Myself." In another film, he introduced "Jeepers Creepers," which won an Academy Award for Harry Warren and Johnny Mercer. He also had a special affinity for songs by Jimmy McHugh, starting with "I Can't Give You Anything but Love" and including "Exactly Like You" and especially "On the Sunny Side of the Street." His was the first recording by a jazz artist of "Body and Soul" and one of the first of "I Got Rhythm." The list could go on and on, to such late hits as "Hello, Dolly!" and "What a Wonderful World," which worked for no one else. And there was his theme song, "Sleepy Time Down South," from 1931 to the end.

Armstrong also wrote a goodly number of songs, some of which became quite well known. "Struttin' With Some Barbecue" is perhaps best known; the 1938 big band record is one of his all-time best, and the 1927 Hot Five is also remarkable. Others include "Swing That Music" (the title of his first autobiography, somewhat ghosted, but the first biography of a jazz musician to be published, in 1936), "Big Butter and Egg Man," "If We Never Meet Again," "Red Cap" (lyric by Ben Hecht), and "Pretty Little Missy," in addition to many of the Hot Five/Seven numbers.

As early as 1930, Armstrong pioneered in what would later become known as "crossovers." At the invitation of Jimmie Rodgers, the real father of country music, he and Lil joined the singer-guitarist in "Blue Yodel No. 9." In that same year, during a successful engagement in Culver City, where he became a favorite of the stars in nearby Hollywood, Armstrong also recorded the Cuban hit "The Peanut Vendor" and the Hawaiian "Song of the Islands." And years later but well before Fats Domino and Ray Charles, he tackled such country material as "Blueberry Hill" and "Your Cheatin' Heart."

The band Armstrong fronted in California included a young drummer named Lionel Hampton; when Armstrong heard him fooling around on the then-new vibraharp, he suggested that Hampton work out an introduction and accompaniment to "Memories of You," which thus became his debut recording on that instrument. In Chicago in early 1931, Armstrong put together his first big band proper—not a preexisting unit, but one especially formed for him. It consisted, not surprisingly, mostly of New Orleanians, but this time younger than himself. He later described it as the happiest band he ever led; it was a bit rough at the edges but had a great beat. His biggest hits with this group were the novelty "I'll Be Glad When You're Dead, You Rascal You" and the trumpet specialty on "Chinatown, My Chinatown" (in person, he might conclude this with as many as two hundred high C's, topped off by some F's for good measure). With this band, he made his first visit to New Orleans in almost a decade.

This was prompted not by sentiment but by an unwelcome visitation, in Chicago, from a notorious gangster carrying a message that he was to return promptly to New York. Apparently his new manager, an unsavory character named Johnny Collins, had welched on an agreement with Connie's Inn, but Armstrong did not know this and was loyal to Collins, who suggested that they swiftly embark on a southern tour, setting up dates as they moved along. This turned out well, since Armstrong was by now hugely popular with both black and white audiences. In New Orleans, he received a triumphant welcome, including a parade (an honor not commonly accorded black men in 1931), and a cigar was named for him. During his stay, he sponsored a baseball team, Armstrong's Secret Nine. On his opening night at a segregated nightspot on the banks of the Mississippi, some ten thousand blacks lined the levee to catch those golden trumpet sounds.

In 1932 Armstrong made his first foray abroad: a three-month tour of England. There had of course been many jazz-related American performers in Europe by then, starting with the Original Dixieland

Jazz Band and the Southern Syncopated Orchestra, featuring Sidney Bechet, both in 1919. And Bechet would spend most of the 1920s touring all over Europe with various bands. But Armstrong was the first jazz artist to appear as an individual star, not as a band member or leader. He did not bring his own accompanists but toured first with a band made up of black musicians of various nationalities, including some Americans, and then in another Armstrong first, at the helm of some of Britain's best white jazz players.

Reception ranged from unalloyed enthusiasm from jazz musicians and fans (there was a substantial number of the latter, nearly forty Armstrong performances being available on European record labels by 1932) to bewilderment and even booing. An amusing sidelight was a backstage visit from a delegation of musicians asking to examine Armstrong's trumpet and mouthpiece to ascertain that they had not been doctored in some fashion. His virtuosity was still not quite credible.

The visit made it clear to Armstrong that there were people of stature who took his music seriously (many came from the Continent to attend performances) and that (though London and the British hinterlands were hardly free from prejudice) there were places where racism was not a constant fact of life. A nonplaying visit to Paris topped off the trip. He would return soon, for a much longer stay.

Back home, Armstrong toured with a new (and lesser) *Hot Chocolates* and recorded under a new contract, with RCA Victor, the leading label. (Throughout the early Depression years, when the industry hit rock bottom, Armstrong continued to record consistently.) His 1933 band was among his best, with young Teddy Wilson making his recording debut and two first-rate soloists in the Johnson brothers, trombonist Keg and tenorist Budd. Armstrong's matchless sound was captured by Victor's engineers better than ever, and such masterpieces as "World on a String," "I've Got a Right to Sing the Blues," and a splendid new "Basin Street Blues" ensued.

By August, Armstrong was back in London. He was still managed by the unsavory Collins, but the man's rudeness soon caused Armstrong to fire him. In revenge, Collins took his client's passport (which was quickly replaced) and swore that Louis Armstrong would never work in his homeland again. Now booked by the British bandleader-entrepreneur Jack Hylton, the trumpeter toured Denmark, Sweden, Norway, Holland, and Belgium. His Copenhagen reception was particularly warm, with a crowd estimated by the unhyperbolic Danes at ten thousand on hand inside and outside the train station, a band (which never got to play), a motorcade, and a sea of flowers. Not until after World War II would comparable scenes be played out, and the young Armstrong was very moved; at first, he thought all those people were waiting for someone else, he said.

As luck would have it, the Danes were shooting a movie musical, and Armstrong was enlisted to perform in it. The three numbers thus preserved are the only audiovisual record of an unadorned vintage Armstrong performance, not something staged (and, more often than not, hoked up).

After some further performing in England, Armstrong (accompanied by Alpha Smith, his third-wife-to-be) took what was to be the longest vacation of his life, from April to October 1934. In an interview earlier that year, he pointed out that he'd had very little time off during the past ten years. He now rented an apartment in Paris and spent his time sightseeing and hanging out with the city's many resident and visiting musicians, including Django Reinhardt, who had been led to jazz by hearing an Armstrong record.

Armstrong then recorded in Paris, prior to a series of Salle Pleyel concerts; at the first, there were so many curtain calls that he had changed into his bathrobe by the final one. There were further concerts in Belgium, Switzerland, and Italy (unlike Hitler, Mussolini did not ban jazz), but then Armstrong abruptly decided to return home, arriving in New York in late January 1935. It was not a happy homecoming. Collins successfully blocked a prospective engagement, and to make matters worse, Lil sued for sizable back maintenance. Claiming lip problems as the reason for his inactivity, Armstrong searched for a solution to his troubles.

Recalling the good personal relationship he'd had with Joe Glaser, the manager of the Sunset Café in Chicago, where he was frequently featured in the 1920s, he sought him out. Glaser used his underworld connection to neutralize Collins, made a handshake agreement with Armstrong to become his personal manger, and set himself up with a desk in the Rockwell-O'Keefe booking agency office. (Tommy Rockwell had been with OKeh Records and had brought Armstrong to New York in 1929). Thus a unique relationship in the annals of show business began.

A new band was organized. Armstrong unveiled it in Indianapolis, on July 1, 1935, then returned to New Orleans for another welcoming parade and set attendance and salary records at Harlem's Apollo Theater. He also signed a contract with the recently formed Decca label and began to record prolifically, starting off with a startling solo on

"You Are My Lucky Star." With its use of double-timing and oblique harmonic approach, it presented a new phase of Armstrong's artistry, more controlled and sober, utterly relaxed (and, as always, the incarnation of swing), with sometimes majestic phraseology and a burnished and mellow tone. His singing, especially on ballads, also reached a new plateau of passion and maturity.

Amid the constant touring, interrupted by the occasional lengthy engagement or the making of films (during which Armstrong would usually appear with the band at night), there were highlights. Armstrong became the first black performer to host and star in a sponsored radio program when he and his band were signed as summer replacements for Rudy Vallee, a great Armstrong fan, on the *The Fleishmann Yeast Hour* in 1936. And the very frequent breaking of the color bar that resulted from his appearances onstage at movie palaces in the "downtowns" of cities all over the United States opened doors for other black artists.

It was not least due to such achievements that Armstrong was deeply wounded by what he branded "the modern malice"—the tendency of the younger black musicians involved in the rise of bebop after World War II to publicly brand Armstrong an Uncle Tom and his music as passé. During that war, he had spent more time than most bandleaders performing free of charge for members of the armed forces, often making lengthy detours to visit military bases, and throughout his working life he had been unstintingly generous in helping musicians and entertainers down on their luck—every week, he would obtain a fresh bankroll from Glaser purely for the purpose of handouts.

But he was caught in the sniping between two extreme but vociferous factions of the jazz world: the beboppers, or "progressives," and the traditionalists, or "moldy figs." This feud was fueled by the coincidentally contemporaneous rise of modern jazz and rediscovery of the music's past. One might have thought that Armstrong's position was such that he would be above the fray, spanning both poles, but once he was attacked, he gave as good as he got. Ironically, his own playing at this point in time actually reflected what was brewing in contemporary jazz, as can be heard in much of his recorded work between 1943 and 1949, which is to say the final big band years and the beginnings of the All Star period, and in his hiring and showcasing the young modern tenor saxophonist Dexter Gordon.

The All Stars were formed in 1947 as a result of the general decline in popularity of the big bands, on the one hand, and, on the other, the enthusiastic public and critical response to two New York concert appearances by Armstrong in a small-group setting, coinciding with his performing with a traditional group in the feature film *New Orleans*. Though loath to put his big band sidemen out of work, Armstrong applied himself to the new format with ferocious energy. He now had to do much more sustained playing than with the big band, and, being Armstrong, he never was stingy with those high-note climaxes that had become his musical signature. To be sure, there were showcase features for the sidemen, who in the first edition of the All Stars included such formidable contenders as trombonist-singer Jack Teagarden, drummer Big Sid Catlett, and clarinetist Barney Bigard (and, just a bit later on, old chum Earl Hines), but even on those, the trumpet took the lead on the last chorus. And of course Armstrong could always rest his embouchure by singing—but that was work, too.

The All Stars soon visited Europe, starring at the first international jazz festival, held in Nice in early 1948. By 1950 they had embarked on the busiest touring schedule of any band in the history of jazz—or any other music, for that matter. Armstrong's international popularity rose to its highest level; his numerous live performances were reinforced by frequent film and television appearances and a string of hit records, some made with studio bands rather than the All Stars, who were often captured in live recordings. The hits included such (on the surface) unlikely material as "Mack the Knife" from *The Threepenny Opera* and "La Vie en Rose," made famous by Edith Piaf, as well as the aforementioned "Blueberry Hill" and the South African song "Skokiaan." Armstrong could turn anything into jazz.

South Africa was one of the few countries the All Stars did not visit, but they made considerable impact elsewhere on that continent. Their first trip, in 1956, found them in Ghana, where the reception was spectacular—a crowd of some hundred thousand. Armstrong was delighted to meet a woman who reminded him of his mother. Highlights were captured on film and were incorporated in the documentary *Satchmo the Great*, narrated by Edward R. Murrow. On his next African venture, Armstrong toured the former Congo, where a civil war was in progress; a cease-fire was declared so both sides could enjoy an outdoor concert, en route to which the star was carried in state.

Another country not visited by Armstrong was the Soviet Union. He had been chosen as the first American jazz artist to perform there under the auspices of the State Department's Cultural Exchange Program. But the man who had been dubbed "Ambassador Satch" (short for "Satchmo," his most lasting nickname aside from "Pops") for his goodwill activities on behalf of his homeland had been watching and reading about the Little Rock, Arkansas, school crisis of 1957 when, while being interviewed, he was asked about visiting Russia. Angered at the treatment of black children and the federal government's reluctance to act on their behalf, Armstrong lashed out, not only at Governor Orville Faubus but also at President Dwight Eisenhower, and questioned how he could defend his country if asked by the Communists about civil rights. Glaser pressed him to modify his stand, but to no avail. (Some five years later Benny Goodman toured the USSR.)

With changes in personnel less frequent than their demanding schedule might imply (among the closest and longest associates were trombonist Trummy Young and pianist Billy Kyle), the All Stars honed and perfected what many jazz critics disparagingly labeled an "act." Perhaps it was (how could it be otherwise when the show had to go on, regardless of hours traveled and sleep missed), but it was a stirring act, perfectly paced and timed with Satchmo at the helm. And as those who attended countless performances can attest, not one encounter with Armstrong failed to include matchless artistry, the sound of that horn alone being something to marvel at.

In the recording studio, the All Stars could rise to the occasion and were captured at their best on two George Avakian–produced Columbia albums, *Louis Armstrong Plays W. C. Handy* and *Satch Plays Fats* (Waller, that is). There were also frequent encounters with peers, in the studio as on television and in films. Chief among these, perhaps, were the collaborations with singer Ella Fitzgerald, herself profoundly influenced by Armstrong. These began on a small scale for Decca in the late 1940s but culminated with the albums produced by Norman Granz for his Verve label in the following decade, presenting them in a repertory of great songs (many of them Armstrong "firsts") and a unique version of *Porgy and Bess*. (There were only a few encounters with Billie Holiday, who was even more inspired by Armstrong than Fitzgerald.) Another notable summit meeting was with longtime admirer Duke Ellington, done on the run, with no advance planning, using the All Stars with Ellington as pianist; the results, issued on Roulette, were nevertheless impressive. The two also worked together in the film *Paris Blues*, again without the Ellington band, though he managed to make an ad hoc assemblage of local and expatriate jazzmen in Paris sound very Duke-ish. Also notable was

The Real Ambassadors, a kind of jazz oratorio by Dave and Iola Brubeck, recorded for Columbia and performed at the Monterey Jazz Festival with Armstrong and the All Stars, Carmen McRae, and the vocal trio of Lambert, Hendricks and Ross. Armstrong was at home with the new material, especially the pretty "Summer Song."

But perhaps the most remarkable achievement of Armstrong's mature years, certainly from a trumpet perspective, was the musical autobiography of 1956–57, a three-LP project, lavishly produced for Decca by Milt Gabler, for which Armstrong revisited past triumphs from the King Oliver days to the early 1930s. Faced with such a challenge, Armstrong managed not only to frequently equal but on occasion even surpass his past masterpieces. One such instance was the landmark "I Can't Give You Anything but Love."

Nothing seemed capable of slowing Armstrong's pace. In 1959, while in Italy, he suffered what surely was a heart attack, though Glaser managed to pass it off as acute indigestion (Armstrong was indeed a champion eater—and an apostle of laxatives), but was back in harness within weeks. Five years later, he accomplished a near-impossible feat: a new record of his knocked the Beatles from the Number One spot on the Top Forty charts that they had occupied for months. Armstrong had almost forgotten that he had recorded the title song from a new Broadway show, *Hello, Dolly!* A ditty of no particular distinction that no one else—even Barbra Streisand, with whom he duetted in the film version—could do much with, it was transmuted by the Armstrong touch into the biggest hit of his long career, which gave the aging performer enormous satisfaction. He never tired of it, nor did his audiences. In 1968 he proved once more that he could work wonders with unpromising material, transforming a number of Walt Disney–related songs, including an oddly dark and ominous "Chim Chim Cheree."

But that iron constitution was weakening, and he was hospitalized several times in 1968; during his last stay, Glaser was taken ill and died in the same hospital. Armstrong bounced back, at first only singing, then taking up his beloved horn again. There were many tributes; now all musicians, even those who had once scorned him, sang his praises. His final trip abroad was to England, in late 1970; his last stand, in March of 1971 at the Waldorf-Astoria in New York City. After that engagement, he suffered a heart attack. He died in his sleep in his home on the morning of July 6, 1971—two days after celebrating what he believed to be his seventy-first birthday and telling visitors that he'd soon be on the road again.

Ten years later, a young trumpeter emerged from Armstrong's hometown and came to sudden fame with his combined jazz and classical skills. Wynton Marsalis often invoked the Armstrong name, and with reverence. He also performed Armstrong music, and while there had long since been younger trumpeters who idolized Satchmo, such as Ruby Braff and, a generation later, Warren Vaché Jr., they were white. Now, suddenly, there were young black trumpeters who could (and wanted to) evoke the Armstrong legacy, some, notably Nicholas Payton (also a New Orleanian), with surprising satisfying results. But the man himself had a surprise in store.

In 1989, in the film *Good Morning, Vietnam,* the hero, in his role as a disc jockey, plays many records, among them "What a Wonderful World," which had been a 1967 hit in England for Armstrong. In the film, his name is not mentioned, his face unseen. There is no trumpet—just that voice. On the strength of that unannounced performance, there was a sudden demand for the record, which was quickly reissued, stayed in the Top One Hundred for many weeks, and even reached the Number Thirty-three spot; the song has since become emblematic of Armstrong.

He would have been pleased—he didn't know he was immortal.

Bix Beiderbecke

Digby Fairweather

As the twenty-first century approaches, the days of the individual voice in jazz are largely gone. Players today draw luxuriously from the collected innovations of previous generations to produce highly trained, musically efficient composites which seldom sound truly new. But it wasn't always so. Back in the formative years of the music, styles were hewn in magnificence from the unshaped stone of jazz. And with Louis Armstrong, Bix Beiderbecke was the most striking of jazz's cornet (and, of course, trumpet) fathers; a player who first captivated his 1920s generation and after his premature death, founded a dynasty of distinguished followers beginning with Jimmy McPartland and moving on down from there.

Beyond his musical legacy, Beiderbecke became the first high-profile romantic hero of jazz music. He was the first "young man with a horn"; the prototype artist whose creative flair shone more brightly because of its premature self-destruction. The concept of self-abnegation for art's sake is a seductive one, and, just seven years after his death in 1931, Beiderbecke was the inspiration for Dorothy Baker's romanticized fantasy *Young Man With a Horn* (1938), filmed by Warner Bros. with stars Kirk Douglas, Lauren Bacall, Doris Day, and a central colleague of Beiderbecke's, Hoagy Carmichael, in 1950. Books about Bix—including the once-standard *Bugles for Beiderbecke* by Charles Wareing and George Garlick, published in 1958—similarly combined loving enthusiasm for their subject with disappointing lack of hard fact. And it wasn't until 1974 that records were set straight with the publication of *Bix: Man and Legend* by cornetist-author Richard M. Sudhalter with Philip R. Evans and William Dean-Myatt, a superbly researched and warmly presented biography which included—for the first time in jazz bibliography—a week-by-week diary of its subject's life.

What picture emerges of this youthful jazz genius of the cornet? To begin with, the image is of a quiet, single-minded, and serious young man; intelligent, sometimes humorous, but frequently—both on and off the stage—half hidden in a world of his own. With Beiderbecke, unquestionably, music was the preoccupation—and the only message. "He never had any show or display of ego," emphasized Hoagy Carmichael, "and he wasn't a show-off in any way! He never handled his horn like other horn-players do, you know, put it way up in the air and all that stuff when he's hitting a beautiful phrase! No! He kept it right down here where he liked it, and where he could hear it, and loved it! And he'd forget about whoever was listening, or anything else. And he was just Bix Beiderbecke, a great musician—and that soul showed right there at the end of that horn!" Many of Beiderbecke's contemporaries emphasize the pure-music concerns of their idol. And there's no doubt that what he produced from his earliest days was truly extraordinary. In jazz terms Beiderbecke may be viewed as what Gil Evans would later term a "sound-innovator"; in short, he put something there that wasn't there before—the greatest challenge to face any jazz musician.

Beiderbecke is sometimes conceived as the great contemporary "alternative" to Louis Armstrong, but his was no latecomer's qualification of Armstrong's musical genius. In fact Beiderbecke developed his style within the same historic time zone as Louis, and his first ground-breaking recordings (with the Wolverines) were made twenty-one months *before* Armstrong cut his first sides as a leader with the Hot Five. Both players were innovators who laid down separate routes along the jazz road. For sure, they shared qualities: superb (albeit different) tones, technical sufficiency for all their purposes, and total originality. But where Armstrong's playing was bravura, regularly optimistic, and openly emotional, Beiderbecke's conveyed a range of intellectual alternatives. Where Armstrong, at the head of an ensemble,

Bix Beiderbecke, 1928. Courtesy Frank Driggs Collection.

played it hard, straight, and true, Beiderbecke, like a shadowboxer, invented his own way of phrasing "around the lead." Where Armstrong's superior strength delighted in the sheer power of what a cornet could produce, Beiderbecke's cool approach invited rather than commanded you to listen. But the resonance of his plangent sound, his challengingly motivic improvisation, and above all his harmonic knowledge made him the most intellectually challenging musician of his era (as well as an audible forerunner of the "cool school") and every bit Armstrong's equal. "In those days," said Louis later, "there wasn't any finer notes come out of a horn! To me he was superior all the time—a born genius." It's indicative of Beiderbecke's artistic status that his work was equally feted by black and white jazz society of the time, and trumpeter Doc Cheatham confirms that had Bix not come along, jazz music of the period might have found itself in a creative rut. It was "beginning to hit a brick wall," explained Cheatham, talking of the music's formative 1920s years. "And [then] all of a sudden we started hearing the recordings of this guy Bix Beiderbecke, which opened up many roads for us to keep going. Because he brought forward so much melody and harmony in his solo work that it kind of opened our eyes to the fact that here was something we needed to do—to learn to play!"

This elusive innovative strand in Beiderbecke's work can certainly be traced back to his extraordinary gifts as a pianist from youth. There is plenty of evidence that piano training served numerous generations of jazz musicians well; fifteen years after Beiderbecke's death Dizzy Gillespie would similarly advise Miles Davis to master the piano as a means of expanding his harmonic/melodic concept. Beiderbecke himself was playing the piano by the age of two—"he stood on the floor and played it with his hands over his head," recalled his sister Mary Louise—and five years later the *Davenport Daily Democrat* headlined: "Seven-year-old boy musical wonder! Little Bickie Beiderbecke plays any selection he hears." From then on, despite his lifelong association with the cornet, piano would run like a strand through Beiderbecke's music, furnishing and illustrating in full the harmonic complexities which he wove into the single melodic lines of his cornet playing. His skipping piano fantasia "In a Mist" (also known as "Bixology," composed between 1925 and 1927 and published, after transcription by Bill Challis, by Jack Robbins in 1928) is the best known of them. But its precedent "Cloudy" (written in 1924 or earlier and first recorded by trumpeter Randy Sandke with symphony orchestra in 1997) as well as three more—"Candlelights"

(1930), "Flashes," and "In the Dark" (1931) (all recorded in full by Ralph Sutton in 1950)—are striking examples of contemporary piano impressionism, conveying the influence of Beiderbecke's preferred composers: Debussy, Ravel, and Stravinsky as well as Eastwood Lane, Cyril Scott, and Edward McDowell. Amid the magnificence of Beiderbecke's bell-toned cornet playing, his piano playing—partly, no doubt, because of its confinement to just one recording, "Bixology (In a Mist)," from September 9, 1927—is occasionally and regrettably underdiscussed. But: "I sometimes think he played piano better than he did the cornet," said Bing Crosby in his autobiography *Call Me Lucky* (1953). "He had a superb ear, an inimitable style, and was a serious student of avant-garde classical music. In that respect as a jazz artist he was years ahead of his time."

It would, however, be perverse to suggest that Bix Beiderbecke's true contribution to jazz has been instrumentally misplaced. He was above all a brilliant and innovative cornetist whose contribution to jazz enhanced and altered the music, as well as conferring star status on Beiderbecke himself for much of his short life. Time has mellowed the impact of his performance amid the more dramatic changes of bebop and beyond, but at the time Bix's music was strange, new, and infinitely seductive, earning the instant admiration of fans and appreciation from fellow players at the very highest and most youthfully competitive level. Matty Malneck—violinist with Paul Whiteman's A-team of musicians back in the 1920s—described how Whiteman's players would seldom show up for a nine A.M. rehearsal call, until Beiderbecke arrived in the orchestra's ranks and would pass the time while waiting for his peers playing cornet duets with pianist Roy Bargy. One by one Whiteman's musicians heard the word that extraordinary music was being made and began showing up on time for rehearsal "because," said Malneck, "we knew there was something going on. This was a special talent. Even Bing Crosby started coming early!"

Beiderbecke's move to cornet playing had been prompted originally by the Original Dixieland Jazz Band's recording of "Tiger Rag" and "Skeleton Jangle," brought to the Beiderbecke home by his elder brother Charles in 1918. Inspired by Nick LaRocca's lead, Bix first borrowed a cornet from neighbor Lee Ely and later bought one for himself from a friend and musical associate, Fritz Putzier, for thirty-five dollars. He made rapid progress, and after his first musical jobs around Davenport reluctantly attended Lake Forest Academy while making regular trips to Chicago to soak up and play amid that city's burgeoning jazz scene. These trips helped to seal his expulsion from Lake Forest on May 22, 1922.

Beiderbecke continued to play, commuting between Davenport and Chicago, until in 1924 he joined the Wolverines, a brilliant young Ohio-based ensemble who—between February and October that year—recorded fifteen sides for the Gennett Record Company. Beiderbecke's music on these sides belongs in classic discography. The band's repertoire harks back here and there to the Original Dixieland Jazz Band—six of their fifteen titles had already been recorded by the ODJB—but the results are years ahead from Bix's first on-record influence, and the Wolverines' recordings of "Big Boy" and "Tia Juana" in addition have band voicings that are both impressionistic and highly complex, suggesting the positive input of Beiderbecke's piano approaches. Above all, though, these fifteen titles reveal a tough and formed cornet talent, in charge of his surroundings. Bix's first solo on record—"Jazz Me Blues," from February 18, 1924—is an assured and correlated chorus, and over the ensuing fifteen sides most aspects of his solo style are to be heard fully formed and in place; the blue half-attack opening on "Copenhagen," fleet fingering of "Tiger Rag," and operatic opening motif of "Royal Garden Blues" are examples. It's also to be noted that by this time his lip had toughened up from earlier, more tentative years; on nine of the Wolverines' recorded titles he proceeds commandingly from lead to opening solo without any need for a respite from playing.

In September 1924, bandleader Jean Goldkette spotted Beiderbecke, who by this time was making headlines with the Wolverines at New York's Cinderella Ballroom, and head-hunted him for his prestigious orchestra, resident at the Graystone Ballroom in Detroit and recording for RCA Victor. At Beiderbecke's first recording session with the Goldkette orchestra on November 24, 1924, however, his solo choruses displeased RCA's influential executive Eddie King, and this combined with Bix's lack of reading ability prompted Goldkette to regretfully dismiss his new employee—at least for the moment. Beiderbecke's response was to enroll at the University of Iowa as an "unclassified student" in a dutiful attempt to readopt the conformist career hopes of his conservative family, but the attempt was to last just eighteen days; after a brawl on campus, Beiderbecke—already a regular drinker—was expelled.

In ensuing weeks he continued to play. He roomed for a time in New York with Red Nichols and, more important, formed a steady professional association with saxophonist Frank Trumbauer at the

Arcadia Ballroom in St. Louis. In Trumbauer, Beiderbecke found a worthy musical equal, and from spring 1926 the two of them were costars in Jean Goldkette's greatest orchestra, playing ballrooms, concerts, and college campuses as well as broadcasting and recording under Trumbauer's tight-ship direction. For Beiderbecke, at the peak of his powers, this was a triumphant return after his first-time failure, and his problems with music reading amid a trumpet section were quickly overcome. "At rehearsal he'd just listen," said Fred Bergin, Goldkette's longtime office manager, "and later, about the fourth time he would pick up the cornet and play [with the others]. And his ability to pick out odd notes like the 6th, 9th and 2nds made it so wonderful that the music would seem to bloom or explode. And he didn't have any notes in front of him at all—it all came right out of his head!"

These were golden days for the all-star Goldkette ensemble, with its brilliant arranger Bill Challis and fellow cornermen including Don Murray, Doc Ryker, Spiegle Wilcox, Howdie Quicksell, Steve Brown, and Chauncey Morehouse. In October 1926 they took part in a legendary battle of jazz at New York's Roseland Ballroom, easily besting the vastly experienced Fletcher Henderson and his orchestra, and recorded again (under the more benevolent supervision of Nat Shilkret and with correspondingly greater success) for RCA Victor in January and February 1927; titles included "My Pretty Girl," "Hoosier Sweetheart," and possibly Goldkette's greatest side, Fletcher Henderson's "Stampede," arranged by Don Redman. Trumbauer the organizer and Beiderbecke the visionary made ideal partners; their superbly complementary and compatible gifts at this period are framed in classic small-group recordings (now on Columbia) for Tommy Rockwell of OKeh Records. These include "Trumbology," "Clarinet Marmalade"—two more deserving milestones in jazz recording—"I'm Comin', Virginia" and "Way Down Yonder in New Orleans" (May 1927), and the side which in Sudhalter's phrase "marks the arrival of Bix Beiderbecke's name in the pantheon of immortal jazz soloists": "Singin' the Blues." With Charlie Parker's "Parker's Mood," Louis Armstrong's "Potato Head Blues," and a very few others, Beiderbecke's spun chorus of storytelling on "Singin' the Blues" has achieved immortality as well as the ultimate accolade of obligatory re-creation by any respectful cornetist or trumpeter from later generations. It was also among the first jazz solos to be treated to the compliment of "vocalese" re-creation, by Marion Harris in 1934.

In September 1927 (after one final recording session producing the

Bix-rich "Clementine") Goldkette was temporarily forced to disband his strong-spirited and superbly drilled team of musical athletes; all of them knew that their next stop would probably be with Paul Whiteman, America's supremo of dance and sometimes hot music. Already Whiteman had dropped in to conduct the band at Young's Million Dollar Pier in Atlantic City and offered Trumbauer, Challis, and Beiderbecke star places in his orchestra, but Trumbauer saw the chance to open for himself at the Club New Yorker, and did so— with Beiderbecke, Sylvester Ahola, Bill Rank, Frank Signorelli, and other peer-equals—until the new venue closed down in under a month. Within four more weeks, Beiderbecke and Trumbauer had flown to Indianapolis to join Whiteman at last, for the final great phase of Beiderbecke's career.

Paul Whiteman's role in jazz—and in Bix Beiderbecke's own story—is still occasionally misrepresented. Far from a hard-nosed commercial pillar of popular music, Whiteman was a lively minded, openhearted man with both sympathy and admiration for the superb players who found themselves under his baton. He was also an intelligent fan of jazz music and—like Stan Kenton later—an active supporter and promoter of worthy talent within his ranks. In his orchestra, Beiderbecke was at last framed in surroundings which, by popular definition, offered the maximum exposure for his talents: state-of-the-art orchestral jazz of the time, fashioned by Bill Challis and his arranging peers.

Bix's first recorded solo with Whiteman—whether by chance or design, Walter Donaldson's unique song "Changes," about a musician happy in any key and consequently "the talk of Dixieland"—features his challenging straight-muted cornet after Bing Crosby's vocal, in a solo which negotiates the difficult chord structure of this piece with sublime ease. From then until September 1929 there would be around half a hundred more recordings with Paul Whiteman's orchestra, many including premier Beiderbecke contributions. Among them were "Mary," "There Ain't No Sweet Man That's Worth the Salt of My Tears," "Back in Your Own Backyard," "Louisiana," "Coquette," "Dardanella," and "From Monday On"—altogether a cornucopia of Bix-riches. In between times he also recorded definitive sides with his "Gang"—a small group featuring Bill Rank, Adrian Rollini, Don Murray, Izzy Friedman, and others—which are one apotheosis of what is generally termed "white Dixieland."

It was now, however—amid the roller-coaster surround of Whiteman's schedule—that Beiderbecke's gradual personal descent gathered momentum. There were triumphs, including, in October 1928, a Carnegie Hall three-piano performance (with Roy Bargy and Lennie Hayton) of "In a Mist" which received a thunderous ovation. But the stresses of performance, constant travel on a band bus with drink as a substitute for food, and—gradually—Beiderbecke's exclusion from Whiteman's increasingly commercial show forced the cornetist into ever-heavier drinking and corresponding fits of aggravated bad temper, untypical of the pleasant man beneath. "Bix generally felt pretty rough," recalls Bing Crosby of the period, "so much so that if anybody asked him, 'How do you feel,' he answered, 'I don't ask you how you feel. Why do you ask me how I feel? You know I feel bad. Just leave me alone!' "

From November 1928 to March 1929, Beiderbecke was absent from Whiteman's aggregation, getting over pneumonia in Davenport; his leader replaced him temporarily with the young and gifted Andy Secrest. After his return to the orchestra, Beiderbecke—in Herb Wild's words—sat in the section in "a sort of stupor," walked with a cane for support (he was then twenty-six years old), and finally collapsed on the Whiteman recording session (ironically of Friday, September 13) which—after three fluffed takes—had at last produced a successful version of the (equally) ironically titled "Waiting at the End of the Road" complete with eight-bar Bix solo. This time Beiderbecke, in a very poor state, was admitted to the Keeley Institute for alcoholism in Dwight, Illinois, and stayed there for five weeks before rejoining his family in Davenport for Thanksgiving dinner 1929. He had been ordered onto the wagon for life.

In spring 1930 Beiderbecke returned to New York, but by this time he had been removed from Whiteman's payroll after reluctant personnel reductions by the leader following the collapse of Wall Street. Dance halls were closing amid the Depression, the recording industry was in a slump, and radio had taken over as quick, easy, and cheap entertainment. Session players who survived into radio studios had to be efficient sight-readers of music; Beiderbecke was not. Finally, however, at the behest of producer John Wiggin, he landed a regular spot on the new (and remarkably named) *Camel Pleasure Hour* for NBC, sponsored by Camel cigarettes and on the air Wednesday evenings at 9:30. In the large orchestra were many old friends from his Whiteman days; Nat Shilkret was in charge of hiring then, and music was arranged by Bill Challis. But Beiderbecke by now was beginning to play erratically; on occasion trumpeter Leo McConville had to take over his solo duties, and on the program of October 8, Bix blanked out as he rose to take an on-air solo. He returned to Davenport after this breakdown for the last time, for four and a half months. It was during this period, touchingly, that Paul Whiteman revisited Davenport too, and Beiderbecke—secure and recuperating in what appeared to be fine style at home—took the stage to blow a tune with the orchestra and receive his former leader's public accolade.

Finally, in late February 1931, the cornetist moved back to New York, first to his regular Manhattan hotel (where a string of visitors carrying bottles once again paraded to his room) and last of all to a quiet apartment in Queens. At this point Bix was contemplating marriage to Helen Weiss, but it was not to be: during the long hot summer of 1931 he contracted pneumonia and died on Thursday, August 6. The story was over; the legend was ready to begin.

It continues today, though time—and regular repetition of the tragedy of youthful artistic demise in both jazz and pop music—have mellowed the starkness of Beiderbecke's story. Two films have been produced about him; first and more important, *Bix*, a vivid and finely researched 1981 documentary by Brigitte Berman, which is the most sympathetically valuable portrait of its subject since *Bix: Man and Legend* was published seven years earlier. Rather less impressive— though decorated with fine re-creative music by Bob Wilber featuring cornetist Tom Pletcher in the (soundtrack) role of Bix—is director Pupi Avati's *Bix*, a fictionalized "interpretation of the legend" (in Avati's words). Enjoyable film though this is, the character of cornetist Andy Secrest is cast as Salieri to Beiderbecke's Mozart—an insulting imprecation which would certainly have deeply distressed Secrest had he not died in good time back in 1977.

The days are perhaps gone in which collectors search for uncredited Beiderbecke solos on record with the zeal that men of God once searched for the Holy Grail. But echoes of the mystique still ring forth; deep in the rock era of the 1980s in Britain, three productions for television—*The Beiderbecke Affair, The Beiderbecke Tapes*, and *The Beiderbecke Connection* (by Alan Plater, starring James Bolam and Barbara Flynn)—attracted mass audiences. In all three, Beiderbecke's soundtrack role was played by Kenny Baker. And regularly trumpeters and cornetists from Richard Sudhalter (whose early work in America and Britain celebrated Bix) to Tom Pletcher and most recently Randy Sandke have gone back to most eras of Beiderbecke's music to reexplore its beauteous subtleties. With such works, plus his own recorded legacy, the Beiderbecke legend moves more safely on now than ever it did in its creator's turbulent lifetime.

Duke Ellington

Mark Tucker

The career of composer, bandleader, and pianist Edward Kennedy "Duke" Ellington spanned many eras of American musical history. Born in Washington, D.C., in 1899, Ellington began performing professionally in the period between 1915 and 1918, just as the word *jazz* was gaining currency and the first recordings of this boisterous, syncopated music were going out to the public. He came of age in New York City during the 1920s, joining Louis Armstrong, Fletcher Henderson, Bessie Smith, George Gershwin, and other notable figures in producing music that embodied the brash spirit and blues-tinged optimism of the Jazz Age. In the 1930s and 1940s he reached artistic maturity, winning acclaim as both a distinctive composer and a popular exponent of big band swing. In later years Ellington absorbed influences from bebop, soul jazz, bossa nova, gospel, and rock, composed a series of sacred works, and looked outside the United States for inspiration in *The Far East Suite* (1964–66), *The Latin American Suite* (1968), and *The Afro-Eurasian Eclipse* (1970). By the time of his death in 1974, Ellington had witnessed the panoramic unfolding of jazz history from the orchestral ragtime of James Reese Europe to the electric fusion of Weather Report. Along the way he had played a key role in developing the music's potential as a medium for serious creative expression.

Evaluating Ellington's legacy poses challenges. One is coping with its massive dimensions. Over a fifty-year period he gave countless performances throughout the world, made hundreds of recordings, and wrote over a thousand compositions. Few can say they are familiar with all of Ellington's music. While a small group of pieces enjoys great popularity, others are championed primarily by critics or known only to aficionados and record collectors. The variety of Ellington's output is a second factor that complicates assessment. He wrote three-minute mood pieces and extended suites for the concert hall, innovative instrumentals and formulaic Tin Pan Alley ballads, dance numbers for nightclub acts and ballet productions, music for film, radio, theater, and television. What critical yardsticks can measure such a diverse body of work? Certainly the vague and inconsistent standards employed by jazz critics fall short of the task—which is one of the reasons Ellington consistently sought to distance himself from the "jazz" label and the narrow categorization it implied. Yet another problem in sizing up Ellington's achievement results from the nature of his artistic collaborations. For nearly thirty years Billy Strayhorn worked closely with Ellington as co-composer and arranger, writing individual pieces like "Take the 'A' Train" (1941), which became the band's signature theme, as well as sections of larger works. Trombonist Juan Tizol, clarinetist Jimmy Hamilton, and many other members of the orchestra added to the repertory, at times furnishing Ellington with melodies and motives that he integrated with material of his own. Given the fluid creative process operating within his ensemble, it is difficult to discuss Ellington's artistry apart from the sounds and styles of players who surrounded him. Finally, there is a tendency among writers to view Ellington chiefly as a composer, treating his other roles—as orchestra leader, pianist, arranger, and interpreter of African-American history and culture—as subsidiary. There is no evidence that Ellington saw himself this way. Rather, he strove to integrate and balance his varied activities, keeping in motion a complex music-making operation that required boundless creative energy and the involvement of many others—players, singers, arrangers, lyricists, copyists, managers, publicists, and record producers.

To understand what propelled Ellington toward a career so brilliant and idiosyncratic, we must look to his beginnings.

Duke Ellington and His Orchestra, Oriental Theatre, Chicago, 1940. Left to right: Juan Tizol, Joe "Tricky Sam" Nanton, Lawrence Brown, trombones; Johnny Hodges, Barney Bigard, Ben Webster, Otto Hardwick, Harry Carney, reeds; Sonny Greer, drums; Fred Guy, guitar; Ellington; Jimmy Blanton, bass; Wallace Jones, trumpet; Rex Stewart, cornet; Ray Nance, trumpet. Courtesy Frank Driggs Collection.

Early Years

Ellington grew up in the nation's capital, a racially segregated city that in the early 1900s had one of the largest and most diverse African-American communities in the nation. There, restricted by patterns of discrimination yet surrounded by examples of black achievement in education, professional trades, and the arts, he and his sister Ruth were encouraged by their parents, James Edward and Daisy Kennedy Ellington, to strive for excellence. Beyond taking rudimentary lessons in piano and harmony, Ellington acquired musical knowledge mostly on his own. As a teenager he listened closely to black pianists performing ragtime and popular tunes of the day and practiced hard to gain keyboard proficiency. This activity resulted in his first composition, a flashy piano solo titled "Soda Fountain Rag"; his second piece—and the only other dating from his Washington years—was a mildly risqué blues song, "What You Gonna Do When the Bed Breaks Down?" In time Ellington began playing with small groups for dances and parties, eventually leading and booking his own bands under the name of The Duke's Serenaders, which in 1919 advertised their services as "colored syncopaters" specializing in "irresistible jass." By the time he reached his early twenties, Ellington was a proficient pianist and a successful local bandleader. In 1923, though, he decided to head north and pursue his musical career in New York.

Settling in Harlem, Ellington initially worked as a sideman in a band called the Washingtonians led by banjo player Elmer Snowden. By 1924 he had taken over the group as it held forth nightly at the Hollywood, a midtown cabaret later renamed the Kentucky Club. Now Ellington began stretching his talents in different directions. Beyond entertaining as bandleader and pianist at the Hollywood, he composed and arranged new numbers for his group to play. He sought to break into the songwriting field, collaborating with lyricist Jo Trent to produce a half dozen titles between 1923 and 1926. Ellington also launched his recording career around this time. He recorded several of his own pieces in 1924, one a novelty song called "Choo Choo (I Gotta Hurry Home)" (Blu Disc/Classics) that revealed the Washingtonians as a competent mid-1920s dance band with an impressive "hot" trumpeter named James "Bubber" Miley.

Ellington built his group's musical identity around individual players. Miley's growling, muted trumpet—inspired by King Oliver—formed one of the main ingredients, giving the band an expressive solo voice at once mysterious and soulful. Ellington cast Miley in lead roles on compositions such as "East St. Louis Toodle-Oo" (Vocalion/Classics, 1926), "Black and Tan Fantasy" (Victor/Bluebird, 1927), and "Creole Love Call" (Victor/Bluebird, 1927). Other important instrumentalists were trombonist Joseph "Tricky Sam" Nanton (another muted-brass specialist), the sweet-toned saxophonist Otto Hardwick, the lyrical trumpeter Arthur Whetsol, and the extroverted drummer William "Sonny" Greer. On piano Ellington contributed solos in a full-bodied Harlem stride style that showed the influence of James P. Johnson and Fats Waller. Recordings made by Ellington's band after 1926 increasingly featured his own works, a mixture of "hot jazz" numbers and slower, blues-oriented pieces.

Ellington's pace accelerated late in 1927 when he and his orchestra began performing at Harlem's Cotton Club, where they remained in residence until early 1931. His productivity increased partly because the nightclub demanded a steady supply of fresh pieces for theatrical skits and dance routines, and also because regular radio broadcasts and a Victor recording contract offered outlets for introducing new works to the public. His ensemble expanded to twelve pieces—three reeds, five brass, and four in the rhythm section—and featured new primary colors in its tonal palette, notably saxophonist Johnny Hodges, clarinetist Barney Bigard, and plunger-muted trumpet specialist Charles "Cootie" Williams (who replaced Miley). Ellington's wider exposure at the Cotton Club, together with effective marketing on the part of his manager Irving Mills, led to important theatrical engagements (*Show Girl* with Maurice Chevalier [1928]) and film appearances (*Black and Tan* [1929], *Check and Double Check* [1930]). With the release of such recordings as "Mood Indigo" (Brunswick/Classics, 1930), "The Mystery Song" (Victor/Bluebird, 1931), and the two-part *Creole Rhapsody* (Victor/Bluebird, 1931), Ellington began drawing critical attention for his skills as composer.

On the Road

After leaving the Cotton Club in 1931, Ellington and his orchestra embarked on a busy schedule of touring that would remain characteristic for years to come. They played theater engagements and one-nighters across the United States and in Canada, making their first of many trips to Europe in 1933. As the swing craze took hold, Ellington responded with pieces designed for dancers ("Steppin' Into Swing Society" [Brunswick/Classics, 1938]), "Bouncing Buoyancy" [Columbia/Classics, 1939]), romantic ballads ("Solitude" [Victor/Classics, 1934], "I Never Felt This Way Before" [Victor/Bluebird,

1940]), and virtuosic flag-wavers for his orchestra ("Braggin' in Brass" [Brunswick/Classics, 1938], "The Giddybug Gallop" [Victor/Bluebird, 1941]). Following the example of "Creole Rhapsody," he experimented with longer forms in *Reminiscing in Tempo* (Brunswick/Classics, 1935), a meditative mood piece composed after the death of his mother, and *Diminuendo and Crescendo in Blue* (Brunswick/Classic Jazz, 1937), a study of textures and dynamics built on the twelve-bar blues. He devised vehicles to show off outstanding solo voices in his orchestra, among them "Clarinet Lament" for Barney Bigard (Brunswick/Classics, 1936), "Yearning for Love" (Brunswick/Classics, 1936) for trombonist Lawrence Brown, "Boy Meets Horn" (Brunswick/Classics, 1938) for cornetist Rex Stewart, and "Concerto for Cootie" (Victor/Bluebird, 1940) for trumpeter Cootie Williams. The arrival of bassist Jimmy Blanton in 1939 and tenor saxophonist Ben Webster the following year helped the Ellington orchestra develop into one of the most dynamic instrumental ensembles of the swing era. Ellington was quick to feature the talents of his new recruits: a Webster solo formed the centerpiece of "Cotton Tail" (Victor/Bluebird, 1940), while Blanton assumed a prominent role on "Jack the Bear" (Victor/Bluebird, 1940) and recorded a series of duets with Ellington at the piano. Another person who contributed significantly to the sound of the band was Billy Strayhorn, who joined the Ellington organization in 1939 as composer and arranger. Strayhorn's predilection for rich chromatic harmonies and lush textures fit in well with the Ellington aesthetic; pieces by Strayhorn like "Chelsea Bridge" and "Raincheck" (both Victor/Bluebird, 1941) displayed "Ellingtonian" characteristics without being derivative, while his suave arrangement of "Flamingo" (Victor/Bluebird, 1940) reinforced Ellington's image of urbane sophistication.

That image was magnified in the 1940s as Ellington took on large-scale projects that few of his bandleader contemporaries were attempting. In 1941 he joined a creative team in Los Angeles to produce *Jump for Joy*, a theatrical revue that sharply criticized stereotypical depictions of African Americans in music. Two years later he made his Carnegie Hall debut on January 23, 1943, with another work that directly confronted racial issues: *Black, Brown and Beige* (Prestige), a lengthy musical essay in three movements subtitled *A Tone Parallel to the History of the Negro in America*. By appearing at Carnegie Hall with an ambitious piece of symphonic dimensions, Ellington demanded to be judged as a serious artist—a right he had claimed since the early 1930s at the Cotton Club, but never before so adamantly.

Although critical response to *Black, Brown and Beige* was mixed, Ellington's bid for legitimacy succeeded. From then on he was viewed not just as a talented writer of songs and instrumental dance music but as a gifted composer who worked with American vernacular idioms. This newly won status was reflected in the title of Richard O. Boyer's lengthy 1944 profile of Ellington in the *New Yorker*: "The Hot Bach." Journalists repeatedly queried Ellington about the relationship between jazz and classical music, and between his work and that of established European composers. Meanwhile Ellington returned with his orchestra to Carnegie Hall nearly every year, premiering new extended compositions ranging from the quasi–piano concerto *New World A-Coming* (Ember, 1943) to multimovement offerings such as *The Perfume Suite* (Prestige, 1944), *The Deep South Suite* (Prima/Music Masters Jazz, 1946), and *The Liberian Suite* (Prestige, 1947). In the decades that followed, the suite remained Ellington's preferred form for large-scale works. But he also achieved impressive results with single-movement programmatic pieces built upon limited motivic material—a short rhythmic phrase in *The Tattooed Bride* (VJC, 1948), a minor-third interval in *Harlem* (Encore/Columbia Jazz Masterpieces, 1951).

While Ellington's reputation as a composer rose in the second half of the 1940s, his band suffered financially as swing waned in popularity and other styles—bebop, rhythm-and-blues, solo vocalists—caught the public's ear. His recording career was disrupted in 1946–47 as he searched for a new label affiliation, and it came to a halt in 1948 after a ban was imposed by the musicians' union. Nevertheless, the relentless touring continued, and Ellington succeeded in keeping his orchestra afloat during a time when other big bands were dissolving or downsizing. He lost some key players who had been with him for years—Joe Nanton died in 1946, and Johnny Hodges, Lawrence Brown, and Sonny Greer left in 1951—but quickly recruited new talent, such as the rhapsodic tenor saxophonist Paul Gonsalves (1950) and the witty, bebop-inflected trumpeter Clark Terry (1951). By 1955 Hodges had returned and a forceful drummer, Sam Woodyard, had joined the rhythm section. Yet despite a strong instrumental lineup and a distinguished track record as a composer, Ellington was forced in the mid-1950s to make even greater commercial concessions than in the past. He recorded kitsch like "Bunny Hop Mambo" and "Echo Tango" (Capitol, 1954) and accompanied an aquatics show in Flushing, Long Island, for six weeks the following summer.

Later Years

Ellington soon rebounded from this low point. In July 1956 the band gave a galvanizing performance at the Newport Jazz Festival, thrilling the assembled crowd with a powerful version of *Diminuendo and Crescendo in Blue* (Columbia, 1956) that let Gonsalves loose for a lengthy solo propelled by the rhythm of Woodyard's drums and Jimmy Woode's bass. Ellington's much-heralded Newport appearance and a *Time* magazine cover story on August 20 helped put him back in the limelight—though truly, he had never been far from its glare. A string of major projects followed: *A Drum Is a Woman* (Columbia, 1957), an hour-long television musical that attempted to trace the history of jazz from Africa to the present; *Such Sweet Thunder* (Columbia, 1957), a suite commissioned by the Shakespeare Festival in Stratford, Ontario; scores for two major Hollywood films, Otto Preminger's *Anatomy of a Murder* (1959) and Martin Ritt's *Paris Blues* (1961); *Suite Thursday* (Encore/Columbia Jazz Masterpieces, 1960), inspired by a John Steinbeck novel and premiered at the Monterey Jazz Festival; and *My People* (Flying Dutchman/Columbia, 1963), a theatrical production conceived for the Century of Negro Progress Exhibition in Chicago. During these years Ellington and his orchestra toured Europe several times and signed with Columbia, resuming an active recording schedule. Beyond the fees generated by performing and recording, Ellington's ASCAP residuals helped to subsidize his ensemble. The return of distinguished alumni established continuity with the past: Lawrence Brown rejoined in 1960, and Cootie Williams, who had left in 1940, came back in 1962. The Ellington orchestra of the late 1950s and early 1960s maintained high performing standards. Especially strong was the reed section of Johnny Hodges, Russell Procope, Jimmy Hamilton, Paul Gonsalves, and Harry Carney; each player was adept at both soloing and accompanying, and the five together achieved a richly variegated timbral blend.

In later years Ellington often tailored projects to the format of the long-playing record. He appeared as pianist in small-group settings on *Piano in the Foreground* (CBS, 1961) and *Money Jungle* (Solid State/Blue Note, 1962), the latter featuring bassist Charles Mingus and drummer Max Roach. Special guests were invited to record with Ellington and his orchestra, such as singers Ella Fitzgerald and Rosemary Clooney, saxophonists Coleman Hawkins and John Coltrane, and the Count Basie band. There were "concept" albums. *Recollections of the Big Band Era* (Atlantic, 1962–63) looked to the past, while *Afro-Bossa* (Discovery, 1962–63) explored moods and rhythms associated with contemporary bossa nova and Latin jazz trends. Commercial pressures occasionally led Ellington and Strayhorn to interrupt composing so they could arrange and record current pop material, such as numbers from Disney's film *Mary Poppins* in 1964 and songs by the Beatles the following year.

But Ellington, as usual, was following several agendas simultaneously. Amidst the swirl of recording projects, the daily production of new pieces and arrangements, and the steady travel—including trips to Europe, the Middle East, India, and Japan—he accepted a commission to write a liturgical work for San Francisco's newly completed Grace Cathedral. The resulting *Concert of Sacred Music* (RCA, 1965) combined sections from earlier works with newly composed material and brought together Ellington's orchestra with vocal soloists, choirs, and tap dancer Bunny Briggs. Ellington was not alone among jazz musicians in addressing religious themes. New Orleans players had long played hymns and spirituals, Mary Lou Williams and Dave Brubeck wrote large-scale liturgical works, and John Coltrane expressed his faith on such recordings as *A Love Supreme* (1964) and *Ascension* (1965). But the First Sacred Concert, as it came to be called, proved a landmark for Ellington, influencing his programming and public pronouncements in the years that followed and paving the way for two later works similar in size, structure, and character: the *Second Sacred Concert* (Prestige), premiered at New York's Cathedral of St. John the Divine in 1968, and the *Third Sacred Concert* (Victor), unveiled at London's Westminster Abbey in 1973. Theatrical, entertaining, didactic, and ranging in mood from quiet reverence to brassy bombast, the three Sacred Concerts count among Ellington's last major creative acts. Though much of the choral writing shows his relative inexperience as lyricist and composer for mixed voices, the orchestration has moments of inspired majesty, and at least two pieces—"Heaven" and "T.G.T.T.," sublimely performed by Swedish soprano Alice Babs in the Second Sacred Concert—achieve Ellington's goal of spiritual rapture.

Together with the Sacred Concerts, the suite form continued to focus Ellington's compositional energies in his final years. He and Strayhorn drew upon recent travel experiences with the orchestra to produce *The Far East Suite* (RCA/Bluebird), issued on disc in 1967. After Strayhorn's death that year, Ellington recorded *And His Mother Called Him Bill* (RCA, 1967), a tribute to his longtime composing and arranging partner. His music continued to celebrate specific places in *The Latin American Suite* (Fantasy, 1968), *The New Orleans*

Suite (Atlantic, 1970), *The Afro-Eurasian Eclipse* (Fantasy, 1970), *The Togo Brava Suite* (United Artists/Sequel Jazz, 1971), and *The Goutelas Suite* (Pablo, 1971). This attraction to geographically inspired program music also turned up in *The River* (Warner/LMR, 1970), a commission from the American Ballet Theater that was choreographed by Alvin Ailey. Though illness kept him from finishing his projected opera *Queenie Pie* and his suite *The Three Black Kings*, Ellington completed his memoirs, published as *Music Is My Mistress* in 1973, and stayed out on the road as long as he could. He gave his last public performance in March 1974 and died in New York on May 22, a few weeks after his seventy-fifth birthday.

Ellington enjoyed a long, full, and exceptionally productive life in music. He thrived on variety, assuming multiple roles as part of his daily creative routine. Keeping in mind his skill at integrating these different activities, it is also useful to consider them individually.

Composer, Arranger, Songwriter

Ellington was in his mid-twenties when he began producing new music for his band. Like many of his contemporaries in popular music who took up composing and arranging during the 1920s, Ellington lacked formal training in these areas. Instead he relied upon his keyboard knowledge and ensemble experience and listened closely to the work of others—especially to the musicians playing next to him on the bandstand. Recordings document Ellington's progress as a writer. After some rough early efforts, Ellington gained proficiency and polish during his stint at the Cotton Club. By the 1930s he had become so secure technically that he could follow his musical imagination wherever it led. Pieces like *Diminuendo and Crescendo in Blue* (1936), "Battle of Swing" (Brunswick/Classics, 1938), and "The Sergeant Was Shy" (Columbia/Classics, 1939), with their inventive orchestration and arresting effects, brim with joy and confidence. One senses a composer relishing the privilege of hearing his ideas realized with such skill, and the performer-composer partnership fueled Ellington's drive to compose. What began as a purely practical need—replenishing the repertory of a band playing nightly before the public—evolved into something of an obsession. In later years, when not performing or appearing at public functions, Ellington increasingly withdrew to be alone with his muse. To be sure, he was often working under deadline—a commission to fulfill, an album to make, a new work to premiere—but such pressure, accepted without complaint, seemed vital to Ellington's creative process. There were less stressful ways to organize a musical life, and he wanted no part of them.

One of the traits that set Ellington's music apart was its vivid pictorial quality. In his memoirs Ellington recalled the visual images evoked by some of his players, and as a composer he often seemed to be striving for a similar goal. Sometimes the titles suggested as much, as in "Sophisticated Lady," "Dusk," "Transblucency (A Blue Fog You Can See Through)," "Sunset and the Mockingbird," "Little African Flower," and "A Portrait of Mahalia Jackson." Ellington also described scenes, real or imagined, that his music aspired to illustrate, as in his evocative sensory account of "Harlem Air Shaft" or his claim that "East St. Louis Toodle-Oo" depicted an old man heading home after a hard day's labor in the field. Whether or not Ellington had these pictures in mind as he wrote does not matter. Like many other composers, he may have dreamed up titles and descriptions after the works were finished. More important is the strong impression Ellington's music gave that it was representing something else—a kind of painting with tones. Composers of Western European art music, of course, had been fascinated with pictorial techniques for centuries. But Ellington was largely unfamiliar with this tradition. Instead he discovered it from sources closer to home: pit orchestras supplying music for theatrical productions, pianists and organists improvising soundtracks for silent movies, bands accompanying acts in nightclubs.

At the Cotton Club, Ellington and his orchestra came to be identified with a style called "jungle music" that summoned up images of exotic, dangerous-seeming locales. Some listeners to "The Mooche" (Okeh/Classics, 1928) may have been transported to an imaginary Africa when they heard its eerily wailing clarinets, snarling brass, and "primitive"-sounding temple blocks. For white patrons at the Cotton Club, this music was a titillating reminder of their presence in the heart of a large and unfamiliar African-American community; still others heard "The Mooche" as parody—a cartoon jungle not to be taken seriously. With such pieces, Ellington honed his skills in musical portraiture. Long after leaving the Cotton Club he kept returning to elements of the "jungle style"—especially muted brass sonorities—and to the painterly training he had undergone there. In "Ko-Ko" (Victor/Bluebird, 1940), he drew upon "jungle" conventions to depict the dancing of African slaves in New Orleans's Place Congo. In "Bula" (Atlantic, 1963)—which Ellington called a "gutbucket bolero"—these same traits decorate a long, ostinato-driven, orchestral crescendo. In "The Shepherd (Who Watches Over the Night Flock)" (Fantasy, 1966), a tribute to Pastor John Gensel, Cootie Williams's bluesy plunger-muted lines allude to the troubled souls cared for by the minister.

Pieces depicting trains formed another pictorial genre favored by Ellington. These include the comic novelty song "Choo Choo" (Blu-Disc/Classics, 1924), the virtuosic showpiece "Daybreak Express" (Victor, 1933), the dissonant, bluesy "Happy-Go-Lucky Local" from *The Deep South Suite* (Musicraft, 1946), the modernistic "Track 360" (Columbia, 1958), and the rocking "Old Circus Train Turn-Around Blues" (Azure, 1966). Whistle effects and locomotive rhythms can be heard in a number of other works, too, such as "Harlem Air Shaft" (Victor/Bluebird, 1940) and Strayhorn's "Take the 'A' Train" (Victor/Bluebird, 1941).

Beyond sonic imagery, a rich vein of feeling runs through Ellington's music. Some pieces—like "Mood Indigo," "Solitude," "Frustration," "Melancholia"—explore individual states of being, others cover a range of emotions. The blues is a constant presence, either guiding the structure or flavoring the melodies and harmonies.

Ellington's interest in composing longer works in the jazz idiom has drawn considerable attention from critics and historians. His extended compositions from the 1930s and 1940s—such as *Creole Rhapsody*, *Reminiscing in Tempo*, and *Black, Brown and Beige*—sparked controversy at the time and have been hailed for their ostensibly innovative formal procedures. Yet Ellington's most skillful handling of form is found not in the long works but in compact statements three minutes in duration—roughly the length permitted by one side of a ten-inch, 78 rpm recording. Ellington's composing habits were shaped by writing for this medium. This can be seen in his tendency to construct longer works by joining together shorter, quasi-independent sections—as in the first two movements of *Black, Brown and Beige* and in all the suites. Rather than mapping out large-scale development strategies as a conservatory-trained composer might do, Ellington preferred working on the local level, at times proceeding chorus by chorus like an improvising soloist. Overall, Ellington seemed less concerned with aspects of musical structure than were his critics. He poured his creative energies into other areas—tone color, texture, harmony, emotional expression—which collectively account for his music's seductive appeal.

If Ellington's formal innovations have been overemphasized, his skills as an arranger have been unduly neglected. A few arranging projects have drawn acclaim—such as the adaptations he and Strayhorn made of Tchaikovsky's *Nutcracker Suite* and Grieg's *Peer Gynt Suite* (Columbia, 1960)—but generally his "original" works and composing activity have dominated the critical discourse. In Ellington's case, though, as with many other jazz musicians, the line between composing and arranging was frequently blurred. Recasting an existing piece—whether a pop song or a classical favorite—required producing new music, orchestrating, and making formal decisions. Ellington often went through the process with his own compositions, devising new settings for works that had been in his repertory for years. In "The New East St. Louis Toodle-Oo" (Master Records/Classics, 1937), for example, he retained the plunger-muted trumpet theme but wrote new lines for brass and reeds to thicken and darken the textures, resulting in a more integrated ensemble sound. Ellington's arrangements, like his compositions, consistently demonstrate an exceptional ear for orchestration. Strayhorn, too, viewed arranging as an opportunity for creative expression, not just a routine function. As the archival work-in-progress of musicologist Walter van de Leur and others helps clarify Strayhorn's contributions to the Ellington library, and as scores and transcriptions from recordings become more widely available, it will be possible to discuss the art of arranging for the Ellington orchestra with greater thoroughness and precision than before.

Ellington's songs, like his arrangements, have been given short shrift in the literature. One writer to focus on them briefly was Alec Wilder in *American Popular Song* (Oxford University Press, 1972). Wilder found aspects to praise in "Sophisticated Lady," "In a Sentimental Mood," and "Prelude to a Kiss," but pointed out (by way of criticism) that most of Ellington's songs began as instrumental pieces to which words were added later. Yet their "instrumental" character hardly seems to have limited their popularity among singers and listeners. Moreover, Wilder's claim is true for only a portion of Ellington's song output; many others were written explicitly for vocal performance, from his first copyrighted composition, "Blind Man's Buff" (1923), to numbers for shows like *Chocolate Kiddies* (1925), *Jump for Joy* (1941), *Beggar's Holiday* (1946), *A Drum Is a Woman* (1957), and the unfinished opera *Queenie Pie*. Ellington's songs include both his most familiar and least known works. An important area of creative activity for him, they deserve a comprehensive study that considers their musical and textual features, relationship to instrumental compositions, and reception by musicians and audiences.

Bandleader and Pianist

Ellington was one of the twentieth century's great performers. Traveling with his orchestra to different parts of the globe, he was greeted with outpourings of enthusiasm and affection. Onstage he cut an impressive figure with his dignified bearing, butter-smooth patter, and uncanny ability to draw inspired performances from his road-weary orchestra. Few American musicians remained so popular for so long.

One key to Ellington's appeal as a performer came from the distinctive musical identity he created for his orchestra and preserved for nearly half a century, despite changes in personnel and musical style. This derived in large part from the music he wrote for the orchestra, as well as from the lengthy tenures of individual musicians—like baritone saxophonist Harry Carney, who worked with Ellington from 1927 to 1974—which insured a certain consistency of sound. Another factor behind Ellington's success was his skill and charisma as a bandleader. Though no disciplinarian, Ellington commanded such respect for his musicianship that players responded by pushing themselves to the upper limits of their abilities. When fifteen talented instrumentalists joined together this way, united by a common purpose and uplifted by the collective sound they produced, the results could be electrifying.

Ellington presided over his orchestra from the keyboard. Like Count Basie, he used the piano as a conductor's baton, cuing with chords, setting tempos, making segues, and directing the general flow of musical events. His early apprenticeship with ragtime and Harlem stride served him well in the long run, giving him a solid technical base that he never lost—though again like Basie, he gradually dropped the left hand's time-keeping duties in favor of an elliptical style of interjections, fills, and decorative flourishes. Occasionally he devised pieces that featured his own talents, such as *New World A-Coming* and "The Clothed Woman" (Prestige, 1947), or took his turn soloing in the course of arrangements ("In a Sentimental Mood" [Victor/Bluebird, 1945]). He also performed and recorded in more intimate contexts that provided occasions for demonstrating his keyboard artistry. His incisive touch and penetrating tone can be heard on albums such as *Piano Reflections* (Capitol, 1953), *Piano in the Foreground* (CBS, 1961), and *Duke Ellington—The Pianist* (Fantasy, 1974). In small-group settings Ellington also adopted an intimate mode of address quite different from his extroverted playing with his orchestra.

As Gunther Schuller (1989) has noted, Ellington's most striking characteristic as a pianist was his sound—full, resonant, and impressively varied in its range of dynamics and tone colors. Whether cutting through dense orchestral textures or dominating in a trio, that sound instantly announced Ellington's presence. It also made an impact upon younger pianists who were forging their keyboard identities in the 1950s and 1960s, among them Randy Weston, Cecil Taylor, Abdullah Ibrahim (Dollar Brand), and Ran Blake.

The Ellington Legacy

Despite controversy over the extended works and reservations about some of the band's personnel in later years, Ellington sustained the admiration of critics and musicians throughout his career. Since Ellington's death in 1974, his reputation has continued to climb due to reissues of his recordings on compact disc, performances of his works by jazz repertory orchestras, and passionate advocacy by such musicians and writers as Stanley Dance, Martin Williams, Gunther Schuller, Albert Murray, Stanley Crouch, Kenny Burrell, and Wynton Marsalis. If earlier Ellington had won a secure position in the jazz pantheon, by the 1980s and 1990s it was not unusual to see him proclaimed as one of the twentieth century's greatest composers and creative artists.

Such recognition is well earned. But Ellington deserves more than fulsome praise and fervent tributes. He needs to be assessed for the broad range of his musical activities, not just canonized as a Great Composer. Musicians and the general public alike should become better acquainted with his recordings; they should know not only "Mood Indigo" and "In a Sentimental Mood" but "Blue Mood" (Columbia/Classics, 1932), "Indigo Echoes" (Columbia/Columbia Legacy, 1935), and "Mood to Be Woo'd" (Victor/Bluebird, 1945). Critical standards for evaluating the music must be developed that are both consistent and context-sensitive. Ellington's methods of collaboration—with Strayhorn, band members, choreographers, lyricists, and filmmakers—are just beginning to be explored.

Finally, the central position of race in Ellington's work must be acknowledged in seeking to understand the nature of his creative achievement. Together with Langston Hughes, Zora Neale Hurston, Aaron Douglas, and other black writers and intellectuals who emerged during the Harlem Renaissance of the 1920s, Ellington undertook the challenge of representing the African-American experience through art. He did this in short forms as well as long ones, in

"Sophisticated Lady" and "Harlem Speaks" as well as *Black, Brown and Beige* and *My People*. As he confidently stated in 1931, "I think that the music of my race is something which is going to live, something which posterity will honor in a higher sense than merely that of the music of the ballroom today."

The prediction has come true. Jazz has been proclaimed a "national treasure." Ellington has been showered with tributes. Streets and schools have been named after him, and statues honor his memory. Probing the full complexity of the man and uncovering the multiple layers of his artistry are challenges that lie ahead. Meanwhile, Ellington's music remains a vital part of contemporary life, delighting listeners and inspiring performers, building a bridge between the ever-receding past and that bold new world a-coming.

Hot Music in the 1920s: The "Jazz Age," Appearances and Realities

Richard M. Sudhalter

T he European "Great War" had raged for 977 slaughterous days when, on April 6, 1917, President Woodrow Wilson brought the United States in against Imperial Germany and the Central Powers. "We have no selfish ends to serve," he told Congress. "We desire no conquest, no dominion." Why, then, millions of Americans wondered, enter what is clearly a European conflict, sending men by the thousands to fight and perhaps die? Among the young, especially, bewilderment soon escalated to frustration, then to outright anger.

While Wilson agonized in Washington, a small but telling event was occurring in midtown Manhattan. A quintet of young white musicians from New Orleans, lured north by better job prospects, began a trial engagement at the Paradise Room of Reisenweber's, Eighth Avenue and 58th Street, hailed by the *New York Times* as the city's "newest, largest and best-equipped restaurant." The Original Dixieland Jass Band, as they styled themselves, had been a hit in Chicago, amid a growing fad for New Orleans novelty orchestras. Their publicity-minded cornetist Dominick James "Nick" LaRocca had then led them east in search of wider fame—and right into a burst of desperate public revelry.

The promise of the new century—a golden age fusing emergent technology, humanism, and the fruits of the industrial revolution—had quickly evaporated amid carnage on an unprecedented scale. The young, impaled between war fever and disenchantment, responded immediately: just as rock would underscore a future generation's uprising against the perceived moral excesses of an entrenched order, so it was with "jass." Night after night, Reisenweber's shook to frenzied merrymaking, with the Original Dixieland Jazz Band (the spelling had evolved) providing ever more fevered music. Their success was contagious, with dozens of other "Fives" springing up across the country.

In the semantics of the time, *jazz* quickly became synonymous in the American vocabulary with forced gaiety, abandon—and any music lively or loud enough to promote it. Popular "Jazz Age" images, lifted from early cinema and from the cartoons of John Held Jr., soon became those of flappers and sheiks, bootleg booze and nonstop whoopee, all to the accompaniment of "Margie" or "Ain't She Sweet," played clipped and too fast.

Yet the music later identified as "genuine" jazz was in fact a different, rather subtler, phenomenon—more a "how" than a "what," developing parallel to the public model. When it had a name at all, its practitioners and acolytes called it "hot music," or just plain "hot," a coherent blend of improvisation, rhythmic intensity, emotional involvement, and personalization of style and execution. It was an insiders' definition, its own kind of gnosis: a body of revealed understanding unperceived by the wider public; a sense of fraternity, even of embattlement. No serious professional of the '20s referred to himself as a "jazz musician": to fellow bandsmen he was the one in their midst who "played hot."

If the public drew any distinction at all between "jazz" and "hot music," it was casual, and usually racially based. Prevailing mythology held that life among Negroes was earthier, sexually freer, so why shouldn't that be true of the music? Some young whites (they were not yet a discrete socioeconomic entity identifiable as "teenagers") might know genuine "hot" when they heard it, but they weren't the ones who kept the heartland ballrooms in business. The "Jazz Age" went its roisterous way.

With this in mind, it's not inconsistent that much of the purest hot music (the quotation marks can now be discarded) of the 1920s was played on records, by bands formed specifically for the purpose. Louis Armstrong's Hot Five and Hot Seven, Jelly Roll Morton's Red

The Cotton Club, Harlem, 1929. Courtesy Frank Driggs Collection.

Hot Peppers, Bix Beiderbecke's Gang, and the numberless groups led in New York by cornetist Red Nichols had no life outside a recording studio. A 1925 gladiatorial encounter between Louis Armstrong and soprano saxophone pioneer Sidney Bechet on "Cakewalking Babies From Home" (OKeh) could only have occurred with a recording group, in this case pianist Clarence Williams's Blue Five. The gladiators earned their outside livings in musically far more prosaic ways.

True hot music was still a work-in-progress, groping its way toward a canon or codex of performance norms. The best way to discover what worked and what didn't was to experiment: with arrangement, instrumentation, texture, harmony, form, tempo—and, perhaps most telling of all, the emergent possibilities of individual solo styles. Everything seemed to be up for grabs.

Immigration from Europe, which had kept the industrial North supplied with cheap labor, fell off with the war. The resultant void, in turn, stepped up northward migration of southerners, most of them black. The South's cotton-based economy was moribund. Biloxi, Miami, and New York had undermined the preeminence of New Orleans as a seaport. When, in 1917, the black weekly *Chicago Defender* launched its "great northern drive," the hitherto steady flow became a flood, an estimated half million arriving before 1920. Chicago's industrial growth, importance as the major east-west transportation link, and now its exploding demographics, made it a key destination—and an excellent incubator for social entertainment: there seemed to be a theater on every block, surrounded by countless dance halls, ballrooms, cabarets, and small restaurants, each with some kind of band.

Late in 1921, Mike Fritzel, whose Arsonia Café of prewar days had featured ragtime bands, hired eight white musicians—four from New Orleans, four from the Midwest—to play for dancing at his Friars' Inn, a basement cabaret on Wabash Avenue in the Loop. They included trumpeter Paul Mares, trombonist George Brunies, bassist Steve Brown, and the brilliant, shadowed clarinetist Leon Roppolo.

Soon after their opening, Fred Wiggins, manager of the Starr Piano Company's South Wabash Avenue showroom, heard them and signed them to make records for the company's fledgling Gennett label as the Friars Society Orchestra (shortly to be renamed New Orleans Rhythm Kings). Such hot tunes as "Farewell Blues," "Discontented Blues," and "Tiger Rag" reveal a band more polished than the Original Dixielanders, with lilt and rhythmic buoyancy; Roppolo, moreover, played solos, melodic variations, with coherence and poise. His chorus on the haunting "Tin Roof Blues" establishes this sensitive, emotionally troubled man as the first significant jazz soloist on records.

New Orleans musicians had been a growing force in Chicago dance bands since before the war. Doc Cooke's orchestra at the Dreamland Café featured the stentorian trumpeter Freddie Keppard and graceful, fluid clarinetist Jimmie Noone. Tom Brown's white Band From Dixieland had drawn crowds to Lamb's Café in 1915. Such transplanted Louisianans as trombonists Honoré Dutrey and Edward "Kid" Ory, clarinetists Darnell Howard and Omer Simeon, and trumpeters Natty Dominique and Punch Miller formed a cadre of high-quality South Side journeymen.

But pride of place belonged to another octet, this one led by the veteran cornetist Joe "King" Oliver; it included fellow emigrés Johnny and Warren "Baby" Dodds (clarinet and drums, respectively) and introduced, on second cornet, Oliver's young protégé, Louis Armstrong. Throughout 1923 they recorded often, first for Gennett, then for Columbia, OKeh, and the Chicago-based Paramount label. What strikes the ear now is how consistently well they played together, Johnny Dodd's clarinet counterlines knitting the ensembles into a seamless fabric. The twinned cornets of Oliver and Armstrong highlight the opening of "London Café Blues" and step out for a much-imitated sequence of breaks on "Snake Rag" (both Gennett). If rougher in texture than the Rhythm Kings, the Oliver band also generated stronger rhythm. And in Armstrong, even at so early a stage, they had a soloist of commanding presence: his maiden solo effort, on "Chimes Blues," is a no-nonsense preview of coming attractions, opening vistas of possibility for any musician aspiring to play hot music.

Fortunately, hot ensembles also began recording in New Orleans in 1924, and continued throughout the decade. Those records show the degree to which the emigrés, black and white, were working within established stylistic traditions. Whether in the two-cornet lead of Oscar Celestin's Tuxedo Orchestra on "It's Jam Up" (Columbia) or the graceful clarinet of Sidney Arodin on "Panama," with Johnnie Miller's New Orleans Frolickers (Columbia), the shared background and line of descent are clear. Louis Armstrong, recording "Cornet Chop Suey" (OKeh) with his Hot Five up north in early 1926, is using his unfolding virtuosity to advance musical concepts he had learned at home. Jelly Roll Morton, doing "Black Bottom Stomp" and "The Pearls" (both Victor) with his Red Hot Peppers, also in Chicago, later that same year, is codifying and summing up, even while moving ahead.

Predictably, the South Side also lured young white musicians growing up in the tidily residential northern and western suburbs. Cornetists Jimmy McPartland and Francis "Muggsy" Spanier, clarinetists Frank Teschemacher and Bud Jacobson, saxophonist Bud Freeman, drummers Gene Krupa and Dave Tough, banjoist Eddie Condon, pianist Joe Sullivan, and other fervent youngsters were ringside regulars at the Friars' Inn and frequent visitors to such South Side venues as the Lincoln Gardens, the Plantation, and the Sunset Café. The degree to which they transformed what they heard into something completely their own became clear when, in late 1927, they began to make records. Vigorous, aggressive, bursting with nervous energy, their music crowds and jostles the beat. To hear them freewheeling through such songs as "Nobody's Sweetheart" is to hear the insistent accents of a northern big city—a city, in Nelson Algren's phrase, "on the make."

Both their reigning deities were cornetists: Armstrong, already an Olympian figure, supplanted Carroll Dickerson in 1927 as leader of the house band at the Sunset; his bravura flights (paired memorably and often with those of Pittsburgh-born pianist Earl Hines) were fast becoming the standard against which all hot playing was judged. Counterbalancing him was the wholly more introspective Leon Bix Beiderbecke. Born in Davenport, Iowa, Bix had made his initial impact with the Wolverines, a band of young midwesterners popular on the college campuses of Ohio, Illinois, and Indiana. If they lacked the elegance of the Friars' Inn band or the sheer firepower of Oliver's men, they compensated with an engagingly upbeat four-to-the-bar their fans called "sock-time." That, and Beiderbecke's fresh lyricism, carry them through thirteen titles recorded for Gennett in 1924, including the melodically fetching "I Need Some Pettin'" and Hoagy Carmichael's maiden composing effort, "Riverboat Shuffle."

Bix's work, fully mature by 1927, introduced a new sense of emotional complexity to hot music: subtle, layered, his solos were at once pensive and plaintive ("Krazy Kat"), spirited and solemn ("I'm Comin' Virginia"), shot through with melancholy even in their sunniest moments ("Sorry"—all OKeh). Even his personal manner, remote and preoccupied, made him seem enigmatic, older—though only three years separated him and his young devotees.

Mass migration from the South had also fed the rapid growth of Harlem, in uptown New York City, as a desirable black residential area; by the '20s, it was the locus of a cultural renaissance, with poets, artists, novelists, dancers, and musicians of all persuasions living and working in the neighborhoods north of West 110th Street. Community growth brought parallel expansion of nightlife: the Capitol Palace, Connie's Inn, Ed Smalls' Paradise, the Cotton Club and Lenox next door, the Nest, Pod's and Jerry's, and numerous smaller places featured bands, floor shows, comedians, solo pianists, and such singers as the "Empress of the Blues," Bessie Smith. While such all-black revues as *Shuffle Along* delighted Broadway audiences, their stars— singers Adelaide Hall and Baby Cox, dancer Bill "Bojangles" Robinson, and the tiny, beloved comedienne Florence Mills—often came "home" to the Lincoln or Lafayette theaters uptown, performing for friends and neighbors.

Pianists had been a key feature of Harlem social life since the war years. Their "Harlem stride" style, descended from ragtime, emphasized a rhythmic left hand, in a regular root-chord-root-chord "oompah" pattern, and a highly embellished, syncopated, often virtuosic right. James P. Johnson, Charles "Luckey" Roberts, Willie "the Lion" Smith, and others less known played in cabarets, theaters, vaudeville—and, perhaps most famously, at apartment rent parties. A small fee paid at the door granted admission to an evening of food, drink, music, and other refreshments, all to help residents raise a month's rent. Regular happenings, they provided a forum for ever-competitive piano "ticklers" eager to test their "stuff" against that of their peers. Among those who learned their craft at such affairs was James P. Johnson's young disciple, Thomas "Fats" Waller.

Pianist Charlie Johnson's popular house band at Smalls' Paradise included such talents as saxophonist-arranger Benny Carter, high-stepping trumpeter Sidney de Paris, trombonist Jimmy Harrison, expert drummer George Stafford, and—briefly—trumpeter Cladys "Jabbo" Smith, who struts handsomely through the band's 1927 record of "Don't You Leave Me Here" (Victor).

Georgia-born, Smith learned trumpet and trombone in an orphanage, and by 1926 was being talked up in Chicago and New York as competition for Louis Armstrong. His records with Johnson, Duke Ellington, and James P.—and, above all, nineteen extraordinary titles recorded for Brunswick under his own leadership in 1929 ("Jazz Battle," the first, is representative)—show the kind of nimble, daredevil style later epitomized by Roy Eldridge and, through him, Dizzy Gillespie. Regrettably, Jabbo's high living and personal unreliability cost him more than a few career-making opportunities.

Sidney Bechet, grand master of New Orleans reed players, turned up in New York in 1923, after triumphs and adventures in Europe, staying long enough to record with Armstrong and pianist Clarence Williams, open his own Club Basha (pronounced "Bash-*shay*" after his surname), and even work briefly with Duke Ellington before sailing again late in 1926.

Beyond dispute, the most prominent and versatile of the black New York bands was that of Georgia-born pianist Fletcher Henderson. From its 1923 debut at the Club Alabam on West 44th Street, it set a standard for up-to-date arrangements (mostly by saxophonist Don Redman) and soloists such as Coleman Hawkins on tenor sax, Harrison and Benny Morton on trombones, and several outstanding trumpeters, beginning with Armstrong's year-long stay in 1924–25, and including the fiery Bobby Stark, velvet-toned Joe Smith, New Orleans emigré Tommy Ladnier, and the volatile Rex Stewart. Redman's scores, drawing on principles of sectional division and interaction established by Ferde Grofé and others in the previous decade, brought small-band flexibility and texture to Henderson's eleven pieces. Harrison, especially, fused dexterity with the more vocalized inflections of the blues; Joe Smith's crooning lyricism balanced neatly with Ladnier's austerity; in Buster Bailey, Henderson gained a bright-toned, technically facile clarinet soloist.

Since mid-1924 Henderson's midtown headquarters had been Roseland, at the corner of Broadway and West 51st Street. The ballroom's all-white clientele soon spread the word about a miraculous black dance orchestra, able to serve up waltzes and South American specialties with the same aplomb that characterized its hot offerings. Musicians came, listened, admired, and even copied; rival bands challenged Henderson's in "Battles of Music" at their own risk.

At the end of 1927, Duke Ellington's orchestra moved from the Kentucky Club uptown to the more prestigious (also whites-only) Cotton Club, 644 Lenox Avenue at 142nd Street, drawing capacity crowds with a smorgasbord of "exotic" floor shows (songs by Jimmy McHugh and Dorothy Fields) and hot instrumentals. Regular radio broadcasts, high-voltage publicity, and a parade of celebrity guest stars helped maintain the club's prominence.

Visitors walking a few blocks down Lenox Avenue could find pianist Luis Russell leading another distinctive outfit at the Saratoga Club. Born in Panama but brought up in New Orleans, Russell stocked his band with emigrés: trumpeter Henry "Red" Allen, clarinetist Albert Nicholas, bassist George "Pops" Foster, and drummer

Paul Barbarin set the tone, supported by Bostonian Charlie Holmes on alto sax and, on trombone, the irrepressible Georgian J. C. Higginbotham. "Higgy" whoops and hollers through the Russell band's record of "Ease On Down" (Brunswick), driven hard by Foster and Barbarin, and contributes lustily to a 1929 "St. Louis Blues," on which Russell's men back fellow homeboy Louis Armstrong.

Don Redman, meanwhile, was off to Detroit, to assume direction of McKinney's Cotton Pickers, in residence at Jean Goldkette's sumptuous Graystone Ballroom. A polished orchestra, it boasted such hot soloists as Prince Robinson, whose emergence as a hot tenor sax soloist had preceded that of Coleman Hawkins; agile trombonist Claude Jones; the engaging singer-saxophonist George "Fathead" Thomas; and John Nesbitt, a skilled arranger whose trumpet style often reflected his admiration for (and friendship with) Bix Beiderbecke. Such records as "Nobody's Sweetheart," arranged by Redman, and Nesbitt's own "Stop Kidding," show an ensemble precision far exceeding that of Henderson's orchestra.

White musicians in New York, meanwhile, faced a somewhat different situation. Bix and the Wolverines might stimulate the Charleston-happy kids for a few weeks at the Cinderella Ballroom, 49th and Broadway, but only with Willie Creager's "straight" outfit keeping older patrons happy. Paul Specht might make a point of featuring his seven-piece Georgians, jazz history's first "band within a band," but conditions in the dance halls, and in hotels, restaurants, and theaters, were generally more restrictive.

The majority of significant white jazz activity seemed to take place on records, and careful listening yields the conclusion that racial separation also produced musical separation. Members of the fraternity might know one another, sometimes jamming together uptown after hours; but in general, white and black hot styles followed two distinct lines of development.

It is too easy by half to suppose that hot music erupted only in New Orleans, working its way north only to Chicago, thence to New York. A growing body of research traces vigorous activity in cities as otherwise unrelated as St. Louis, Indianapolis, Kansas City, Memphis, Houston, Cincinnati, and Minneapolis. "Territory bands," black and white, traveled complicated itineraries throughout Texas, Oklahoma, the plains states, and the Southwest, bringing hot music with them.

Records permitted hot musicians everywhere to listen to, and learn from, one another with a regularity not available on the job. A coolly delivered 1923 chorus by Illinois-born C-melody saxophonist Frank

Trumbauer on "I Never Miss the Sunshine" (Victor), recorded with the popular Benson Orchestra of Chicago, found avid reception among all colleagues, regardless of race. What Ted Gioia has termed an "artful balance of emotion and logic" in Trumbauer's and Beiderbecke's 1927 "Singin' the Blues" solos helped shape an entire generation, including the innovative Lester Young. Louis Armstrong's trumpet solos on such landmark discs as "Willie the Weeper" and "West End Blues" (OKeh) inspired equal wonder on both sides of the racial divide.

The Original Memphis Five, a respected white ensemble led by the trumpeter Phil Napoleon and featuring Miff Mole on trombone and clarinetist Jimmy Lytell, recorded their orderly stylings for dozens of labels, under dozens of pseudonyms, beginning in 1921. The ten-piece California Ramblers, dominated by bass saxophone virtuoso Adrian Rollini, broke down regularly into smaller "hot" units, recording as the Goofus Five (after one of Rollini's novelty instruments), Five Birmingham Babies, University Six, Varsity Eight, and more.

The practice reached its ultimate refinement in cornetist Ernest Loring "Red" Nichols. From the moment of his arrival, in 1924, he applied unerring business skills to cultivating and expanding a network of contacts among publishers, recording executives, bookers, theater managers, Broadway contractors, and other providers of work. Playing in Ross Gorman's pit orchestra for an *Earl Carroll's Vanities* revue in 1925, he found a musical kindred spirit in Irving Milfred "Miff" Mole. The first improvising trombonist to successfully forsake his instrument's old marching band role as a sometimes comical ground bass, Mole played cleanly and adroitly, his lines coherent and witty even at fast tempos. His effect on fellow trombonists is clear in such otherwise disparate soloists as Tommy Dorsey, Claude Jones, Benny Morton—and even occasionally in Jimmy Harrison.

Until the arrival of Jack Teagarden in late 1927, Miff dominated hot trombone playing in New York; his solos distinguish hundreds of records, whether under his own leadership, that of Nichols, or under more commercially minded leaders. Such was his stature that the words "trombone passages by Miff Mole" appear under the band credit on a pair of 1925 Brunswick titles by the otherwise anonymous Cotton Pickers.

As a team, Red and Miff were fast, ultrareliable, bringing polish and verve to whatever they tackled. If Nichols's hot cornet solos now and then sacrificed substance for style, the result was never less than pleasing. Countless fellow brassmen followed his example. Perhaps most significant, Nichols and Mole seem to have pioneered the idea that hot records could be made not just for dancing but for "the approval of your fellow musicians right there in the studio." This was new: black bands may have often swung more, with more relaxed interaction, but these collaborations, in their sheer perfection, offered what can be termed hot chamber music, the modern jazz of its times. Harmonically advanced, it seemed most inventive in matters of form and design, particularly in compositions by such insiders as clarinetist Fud Livingston and pianist Arthur Schutt. Livingston's well-named "Imagination" employs shifting tonal centers, irregular phrase lengths, unexpected settings for solos.

In the 1920s sense, hot solos were invariably melodic paraphrases, using harmonic variations, substitutions and chordal extensions as color elements to make a melodic line more exotic, poignant, or merely novel. Improvisation strictly on chord changes, so integral a part of later jazz forms, was rare: its first occurrence on record is surely "For No Reason At All in C" (OKeh), a series of melodic arabesques on the chords of the pop standard "I'd Climb the Highest Mountain," played by Trumbauer, Eddie Lang, and Beiderbecke (at the piano) in 1927.

Among the white New Yorkers' other hot music innovations: Jimmy Dorsey's bright, almost vibrato-less tone (admired at a distance by young Charlie Parker) and technical command; Vic Berton's flexible tuned tympani, rhythmic and melodic; and, perhaps best of all, the violin-guitar team of Joe Venuti and Eddie Lang. Close friends with a shared South Philadelphia childhood, they worked as a unit, sometimes independently, sometimes under such leaders as Jean Goldkette, Roger Wolfe Kahn, and Paul Whiteman. Venuti, a virtuoso violinist, was outspoken, volcanic of temperament, given to epic practical jokes; the quieter Lang, born Salvatore Massaro, was skilled equally in rhythm section, solo, and accompaniment, and could play the blues with conviction, as his recorded duets with guitarist Lonnie Johnson more than illustrate. Between 1926 and 1930 there seemed few bands of any consequence that did *not* use the team on one occasion or another—even if it meant just inserting them for half a chorus on some otherwise unrelated record.

Their OKeh and Victor dates together under Venuti's name, whether as a duo or with the Blue Four or Blue Five, often (as on "Beating the Dog" and "Ragging the Scale") incorporated Rollini's powerful bass sax; each selection is a fully realized, finely wrought musical miniature, harmonically and texturally rich—but with plenty of solo room. "Four-String Joe" draws on Venuti's ability to play four-voice chordal passages holding his bow upside down; "Doin' Things" expounds on a paraphrase of Debussy's *The Maid with the Flaxen Hair,* while "Running Ragged" mines the coloristic potential of Frank Trumbauer's skills as a bassoonist. Music, in other words, for both mind and heart. Eddie Lang's death, at age thirty-one, following what should have been a routine tonsillectomy, left Venuti bereft—and jazz history much the poorer.

Racial segregation in 1920s popular music worked its mischief in sometimes subtle ways. Record companies operated on the conviction that white customers preferred their "jazz" lively rather than sensuous, and not too intense. Those few who preferred the earthy couplets of a Bessie Smith or Ida Cox blues to the coy allure of Ruth Etting or Helen Kane could find them on discs in each label's separately numbered "race" series, generally sold in black neighborhoods.

Such marketing assumptions often contradicted reality: a great part of the hot music core audience was in fact among young whites, especially on the campuses; "sweet" dance music, by contrast, found widespread and lasting response among blacks, particularly in communities tied to family and church. It is relevant to note that the maximum attendance record at Harlem's "home of happy feet," the Savoy Ballroom, was long held by Guy Lombardo's orchestra.

Such label policies affected the ways in which white and black dance orchestras were used. No Victor or Columbia executive heeded Fletcher Henderson's pleas to record the waltz medleys in which he took such pride; for marketing purposes his was a hot band, and hot music was what his band would record. Detroit's Jean Goldkette Orchestra, with Bix, Trumbauer, clarinetist Don Murray, and bassist Steve Brown, bested Henderson's stars in a 1926 hot music "battle" at Roseland; but in Victor's studios it was just another white band, dispensing pop novelties for a musically conservative public. Little wonder that descriptions of Goldkette's as "a band like nothing you've ever heard," by its alumni and by such admiring witnesses as Artie Shaw, enjoy little currency among historians. The few records that show its hot side—"Clementine," "My Pretty Girl" (both Victor)—remain tantalizing, but lonely, hints.

Another record company casualty seems to have been the orchestra led by drummer Ben Pollack and featuring such stars-in-the-making as Benny Goodman, Jack Teagarden, and Chicagoan Jimmy

McPartland. Pollack records, like those of Goldkette, offer only appetizers: Goodman's soaring clarinet on "Bashful Baby"; Teagarden and McPartland darkening "My Kinda Love" (both Victor) with the inflections of the blues.

(Teagarden's late-1927 arrival from Texas had shaken up both white and black hot music circles. Here was a trombonist—and singer, it shortly transpired—whose agility matched that of Mole, but whose phrases were longer, more vocalized, and steeped in the blues. Pollack was quick to snap him up, and his solos turned dozens of records with Red Nichols and others into instant collector's items. Fletcher Henderson all but adopted him, showing him off like a son at after-hours jam sessions all over Harlem. Fellow trombonists as diverse as Tommy Dorsey and Jimmy Harrison were among his acolytes.)

Perhaps the most difficult white ensemble of the time to evaluate is that of Paul Whiteman. From 1920, the year of its first successes, this large group, as outsized as its leader, dominated the public face of the "Jazz Age"; its early records, if well arranged and played, seldom approached any hot music ideal. But Whiteman, a man of shrewd instincts, came to realize that a significant part of his "King of Jazz" image sooner or later would have to include the real thing. He made his first move in early 1927, attempting to sign up Red Nichols's Five Pennies entire; though Nichols, Jimmy Dorsey, and percussionist Vic Berton came aboard, only Dorsey was still present by autumn. Whiteman, undeterred, watched the Jean Goldkette Orchestra collapse, then snapped up Trumbauer, Beiderbecke, Brown, trombonist Bill Rank, and arranger Bill Challis.

Over the next two years Whiteman featured his new soloists in attractive and original settings. Such records as "Louisiana," "Lonely Melody," "From Monday On," and the masterly "Changes" (all Victor) occupy a niche unique in hot music annals; again and again, Bix and his confreres (including Bing Crosby's rhythmic, relaxed vocals) lift and illuminate. Through canny use of weight and texture, color and blend, Challis and the other arrangers, notably Tom Satterfield and violinist-songwriter Matty Malneck, often lend Whiteman's ensemble an alluring, lighter-than-air quality. Whiteman's may never have been a "jazz" band in the later, more accurate sense of that word—but it never claimed to be. A surefooted light music ensemble, it served its cadre of hot improvisers well, and Whiteman himself fostered the careers of such figures as Jack and Charles Teagarden, Bunny Berigan, Red Norvo, Mildred Bailey, Johnny Mercer, Hoagy Carmichael, and arranger-composer William Grant Still.

Toward decade's end, once rigid racial lines began to blur. "Mixed" record dates teamed Louis Armstrong with Jack Teagarden and Eddie Lang ("Knockin' a Jug"); Lang with blues guitarist Lonnie Johnson ("Two-Tone Stomp," OKeh); Fats Waller with Teagarden ("You Rascal You," Columbia) and Eddie Condon ("The Minor Drag," Victor); Coleman Hawkins with Pee Wee Russell ("One Hour," Victor) and Bud Freeman ("Girls Like You . . . ," Columbia, unissued). Ethel Waters, already admired as the first major singer to apply the inflections of the blues to a standard pop song repertoire, was recording often with such white jazzmen as Benny Goodman and Tommy and Jimmy Dorsey.

The once rhythmically foursquare "hot chamber music" of the white New Yorkers took on new, interactive elasticity as it assimilated musicians from Chicago, the Midwest, and the Southwest. Red Nichols, moving away from his association with Mole, was now recording regularly with Teagarden, Goodman, Gene Krupa, and other adoptive New Yorkers. Such Brunswick titles as "Dinah," "China Boy," and "Carolina in the Morning" (in a particularly imaginative Glenn Miller arrangement) are rhythmically intense, rich in blues feeling.

The stock market crash of October 29, 1929, added a kind of exclamation mark to the end of a decade that had already started to unwind, especially in the pop music industry. Harry Barris's 1934 song "Let's Spend an Evening at Home" summed it up admirably: why go out dancing and dining, spending precious dollars, when you could simply turn on the radio or Victrola? Even Whiteman, outsized symbol of a decade's extravagance, had to trim his personnel to eighteen pieces for an engagement at Manhattan's Roxy Theatre.

Nor was he alone. Louis Armstrong was playing on Broadway, making solo records backed by a Lombardo-like big band. The California Ramblers, once seemingly ubiquitous, were barely limping along. Benny Goodman, Tommy and Jimmy Dorsey, and other prominent hot music figures were most often occupied in radio and commercial recording bands. Fletcher Henderson's orchestra, dropped from the Vincent Youmans show *Great Day* in mid-1929, spent months on the road, and between then and October 1930 did not record at all. As work thinned out for Ben Pollack's band, Jack Teagarden and other sidemen found refuge in Broadway pit orchestras. Adrian Rollini, realizing that his bass sax no longer played a musically central role, began to polish his skills at the xylophone and vibraphone.

Bix Beiderbecke, icon and inspiration to a generation of young hot musicians, was by this time lost in illness, inner conflict, and the alcoholism it fed; his death in mid-1931 at age twenty-eight shocked and saddened the entire hot music fraternity. By mid-1932, trombonist Jimmy Harrison was dead at thirty-one, victim of stomach cancer; tuberculosis claimed James "Bubber" Miley, twenty-nine, whose plunger-muted trumpet solos had shaped Duke Ellington's band sound; Chicago clarinetist Frank Teschemacher, twenty-six was killed in an auto crash. All four had helped define hot music in the 1920s; all four took a major piece of the decade's musical ferment with them.

Many other young players who had emerged in the '20s were on their way to musical maturity; clarinetist Pee Wee Russell, at first affected by Bix's poised orderliness, had by 1930 deconstructed and reconfigured his style in an almost surrealistic amalgam of sounds and shapes. New Orleans trumpeter Henry "Red" Allen had done much the same thing, departing from the original Armstrong model. He and Russell dominate the Rhythmakers records of 1932, and the music they make together defines, embodies, a fusion of hitherto disparate hot music streams.

Alongside such individualism something like a hot jazz canon was emerging; for every Russell or Allen there were dozens more who seemed content to formulate solo styles out of the examples of Louis and Bix, Hawkins and Goodman, and other pacesetters. The first creative flowering was over, supplanted by a kind of unspoken consensus, inevitable beginnings of a stylistic orthodoxy. A new wave of arrangers—Benny Carter, Lyle "Spud" Murphy, brothers Fletcher and Horace Henderson, Glenn Miller, and arguably the most prophetic of all, the Casa Loma Orchestra's Gene Gifford—were evolving the patterns of band scoring that would shortly coalesce in swing.

Whatever it had or had not been, the "Jazz Age" was over.

Pianists of the 1920s and 1930s

Henry Martin

I n New York, the jazz pianist of the early 1920s was called a "tickler"—as in "tickle the ivories." Since jazz was part of popular culture, the audience expected to hear the hit songs of the day, stylized and personalized by their favorite players. Often hired to provide merriment as a one-man band, the tickler was a much-honored figure of the era. He was wary of departing too often or too radically from the melody, since this could alienate listeners. As recordings were relatively rare and not especially lifelike, the piano was the principal source of inexpensive fun—a self-contained party package for living rooms, restaurants, bars, and brothels.

The ticklers exploited the orchestral potential of the piano with call-and-response patterns between registers and a left-hand "rhythm section" consisting of bass notes alternating with midrange chords. This "striding" left hand lent its name to "stride piano," the principal style of the 1920s.

Stride developed during the second decade of the century as a high-energy by-product of ragtime, possibly in response to the mood of the country during and after the First World War. Mechanization (the car, the airplane, the telephone) led to a dramatically increased speed

Fats Waller, 1930s. Courtesy Frank Driggs Collection.

of life, which was reflected throughout modernist culture, in both the popular and fine arts.

Striking in its heightened speed and intensity, stride piano featured an aggressive interlock of the hands, a technique in which the right hand seemed to pull at the rhythmic comping of the left. The excitement was turned up another notch by an increased tempo, a faster harmonic rhythm (speed of the chord changes), and a more linear feeling of the beat. While the right-hand pivot figurations and multisection forms of ragtime were usually retained, a more directed, single-note melody became the norm. The stride artists also incorporated bluesy qualities into their playing, whereas the blues was rare in classic ragtime. These stylistic changes also resulted from competition among the pianists, as each tickler would try to come up with the most dazzling effects. They stole the best of these so-called tricks from each other for their own use and personalization.

The top stride players were easterners centered in New York; indeed, the style was often called "Harlem stride." James P. Johnson was its seminal figure, with Luckey Roberts, Eubie Blake, and Richard "Abba Labba" McLean as key predecessors. While Johnson's greatest importance was as a player and composer of stride piano works, he was also a leading popular musician of the time, as both songwriter ("Charleston," "Old Fashioned Love") and composer of Broadway musicals (*Runnin' Wild, Keep Shufflin'*). Later, he turned his attention to concert works, among them *Yamekraw*, a rhapsody for piano and orchestra.

While Johnson's piano rolls date from 1917, his first solo records, made in 1921, feature stride in its maturity, and they are superb: "The Harlem Strut" (Black Swan), "Keep Off the Grass" (OKeh-Columbia), and, most important, "Carolina Shout" (OKeh-Columbia). The latter became the signature composition of stride. Indeed, players coming to New York to test their skills with the best of the best often competed by performing "Carolina Shout" in "cutting contests," an early and intimidating form of jam session. Cutting contests often took place at the popular "rent parties," communal money-raising affairs to help the host avoid eviction.

One of the ways in which Johnson extended ragtime technique was in his treatment of the left hand, which in stride can be represented as 1-2-1-2 with 1 as bass note, 2 as midrange chord. Johnson often interrupted the two-bar 1-2-1-2 // 1-2-1-2 pattern with cross rhythms: 1-1-2-1 // 1-2-1-2 or even 1-1-2-1 // 1-1-2-1. Note in the latter pattern how each 2 falls "incorrectly" on the relatively strong third beat of the bar. This delightful cross-accent, which momentarily confuses the meter, added complexity and swing to his performances and was soon picked up by other players.

Most of us equate jazz with improvisation. Since Johnson was the pioneering New York jazz pianist of his time, let us examine "Carolina Shout" for a sense of its improvisational technique. The printed music shows the following form (each letter denoting a sixteen-bar section, or "strain"):

Intro (4) // AA'B C D E F G // Coda (7)
"Carolina Shout"—Sheet Music Format (1926)

The introduction is four bars, the coda seven. Sections D, F, and G have the same harmonic pattern, but each presents a different musical idea. The piece itself begins in G major then modulates to C major at section D.

The sheet music dates from 1926, but in the 1921 recording of the work Johnson did not play the piece as it was to be published. Instead, we hear the following:

Intro (4) // AA' B CC' (D) E G // Coda (4)
"Carolina Shout"—Johnson—OKeh Format (1921)

In fact, not a single bar of the OKeh recording was rendered precisely in the sheet music. Section C was performed twice, creating a parallel with section A. Section D was modified considerably from the published music, so it is in parentheses. Section F, the weakest in the sheet music, was omitted entirely. Finally, the ineffective coda was replaced by a much snappier ending. Further analysis would show that Johnson's piano roll performances of 1918 and 1921 also featured discrepancies with the published version and with each other. And even by that time, the work had undergone long development: Johnson wrote it around 1914!

Was Johnson improvising? A hard question; while the performances and the sheet music are all distinct, the main features of the piece remain intact. Johnson was in effect performing the melodic *essence* of each section of the piece—a *paraphrase*. There was improvisation, but on a larger scale: Johnson interpreted the work by omitting, rearranging, and reorganizing its previously worked-out sections.

This was an altogether different approach to improvisation as compared to later jazz. On the countless occasions Johnson performed

"Carolina Shout," similar paraphrase surely occurred. Most of the sections were played, but *how* they were played and their precise orderings were determined on the spot. Since, by and large, the piece remained "the same," we call such a work a "set piece" or "set composition." Its performance consists of paraphrase within each section and spontaneity in the overall design of the piece. Impromptu "blowing," as later understood in jazz, might occur on the harmonic pattern of a later section (often section C), but the players tended to use previously worked-out material. These works generally followed the multistrain form of classic ragtime, with a modulation to the subdominant (the "trio") after the opening sections.

The stride artists composed brilliant set pieces, which they could fall back upon as a "sure thing" whenever virtuoso display was necessary, but they also played more freely. As Duke Ellington once wrote about Johnson: "It was me, or maybe Fats [Waller], who sat down to warm up the piano. After that, James took over. Then you got real invention—magic, sheer magic."

As an example of Johnson's magical invention, consider his solo "Scouting Around" (1923, OKeh-Columbia). The work begins with five blues choruses. Though improvised, these choruses are meticulously planned, each with an associated four-bar break at the top of the chorus. We are led to expect a simple multichorus blues performance, but Johnson then introduces a modulation, and the piece finishes as a set composition! "Scouting Around" is a transitional form in jazz piano, a work merging chorus-by-chorus improvisation with set construction. Other works of Johnson feature similar felicities; "Snowy Morning Blues" (1927, Columbia), for example, has long been admired—not only for its superb melodic material but also for Johnson's ability to evoke a jazz band. Among Johnson's other fine stride compositions, "Riffs" (1929, OKeh-Columbia) and "Jingles" (1930, Brunswick-Columbia) are outstanding.

The stride pianist achieving greatest popular acclaim was Johnson's protégé, Thomas Wright "Fats" Waller. Like so many black jazz artists, Waller first learned music at church, his father being a Baptist lay preacher. With his background, Waller became the first jazz artist to record on pipe organ, although his fame as a pianist far eclipsed his work on the less common instrument. Already a working musician in his teens, Waller met Johnson, with whom he studied. Johnson helped with jobs and connections, leading to Waller's first recordings as a piano soloist in 1922 for OKeh-Columbia: "Muscle Shoals Blues" and "Birmingham Blues."

Like Johnson, Waller was a gifted songwriter, eventually penning his famous tunes "Squeeze Me," "Honeysuckle Rose," "Black and Blue," and "Ain't Misbehavin'." His ebullient personality led to a celebrity career as singer and entertainer, yet his songs, compositions, and stride playing are his finest achievements. Among his solo piano pieces recorded for Victor (BMG), those especially recommended include "Handful of Keys" (1929), "Numb Fumblin'" (1929), "Valentine Stomp" (1929), "Smashing Thirds" (1929), "African Ripples" (1934), "Clothes Line Ballet" (1934), "Alligator Crawl" (1934), and "Viper's Drag" (1934). "Valentine Stomp," for example, has ingenious harmonic surprises and a terrifically driving section as part of the trio. In addition to these set pieces, composed directly for solo piano performance, Waller recorded fine stride versions of popular material, including his own songs.

Although Waller's stride style is based directly on Johnson's, it is smoother and bouncier, less likely to include Johnson's rhythmic variations of the left-hand stride formula. This is how Waller tackles "Carolina Shout" in a recording from 1941:

Intro (8) // AA B (D) (E) G H! (as E′?) A+Coda
G major   C major   *G major!*
"Carolina Shout"—Waller—Victor, Take 2 Format (1941)

Waller's two A sections are virtually identical, omitting Johnson's A′ variant. He cuts section C, takes considerable liberties with sections D and E, then after section G, returns with entirely *new* melodic material (H)! (I place E′ in parentheses because H relates harmonically to E.) Finally, Waller alters the piece's overall design by returning to the opening A section in the original key. Thus, Waller's performance of "Carolina Shout" improvises its large-scale structure through sectional variants—even outright additions! Again, we see the Harlem stride approach to set pieces as centering more on composition than on improvisation.

Like Johnson, Waller was interested in more extended composition. On a tour of Europe in 1939, Waller, during a stopover in Britain, recorded the *London Suite* for solo piano (His Master's Voice), which included "Piccadilly," "Chelsea," "Soho," "Bond Street," "Limehouse," and "Whitechapel." Earlier stride pieces such as "African Ripple" and "Clothes Line Ballet" also showed Waller's interest in "crossover" jazz-classical work, rather like Gershwin's *Three Preludes*. Sadly, Waller's early death prevented him from further explorations in this area.

Among the other great Harlem stride pianists of the 1920s, there was Willie "the Lion" Smith, a good friend of Johnson's. He can be heard to excellent advantage on his solo piano compositions recorded for Commodore in 1939, including "Echoes of Spring," "Passionette," and the wildly virtuosic "Finger Buster." There was also much skill among the Harlem stride pianists less well established. Donald Lambert ("the Lamb") and Stephen Henderson ("the Beetle") were able to hold their own against all competition. Better known was Clarence Profit, a fine player and bandleader of the late 1930s.

The urban stride pianists of the East may be contrasted with the more informal "country" players, who specialized in blues and its subgenre known as "boogie-woogie." Sometimes called "western" pianists in order to distinguish them from the eastern stride school, these blues artists were important in the continuing development of jazz through the later 1920s and 1930s. The difference between the western and eastern players typifies a dichotomy observable throughout jazz history: many of the western pianists were casual musicians, mostly self-taught and working largely with grooves, riffs, and patterns; they were sometimes looked down upon by the polished eastern musicians who could read fluently, compose, and perhaps had studied more formally. Of course, there was not always a strict separation: many a pianist raised in one idiom learned to perform the style of the other.

The boogie-woogie pianists approached the blues with a driving left hand of continuous eighth notes sometimes called "eight to the bar." In particular, the rolling feel of boogie-woogie—and its raw power—paralleled the emerging swing style and the rhythmic momentum of the big bands. Compared to stride, the boogie-woogie left hand was easier to learn: a repeating bass riff from two to eight beats long remained stationary for the duration of a harmony. At a chord change, the left hand would shift up or down the keyboard and continue playing the "same" riff in the new harmonic area. Because these shifts came slowly—every two to four bars—the left hand could be placed on a kind of "automatic pilot," with the pianist able to focus attention on blues licks in the right hand. This independence enabled the best players to create startling cross-rhythms between the hands.

As James P. Johnson is the father of stride, we often look to Jimmy Yancey as the father of boogie-woogie. Unheralded, he worked most of his life as a groundskeeper at Comiskey Park, home of the Chicago White Sox. In later life, he drew attention largely because of the boogie-woogie craze of the late 1930s and the success of his student Lux Lewis. Finally recorded in 1939, his performances of "State Street Special" (1939, Victor-BMG) and "Bear Trap Blues" (1940, Vocalion) show sensitive, heartfelt blues sentiment without meretricious technical display. Note that Yancey deftly varies the boogie-woogie accompaniments within a performance so as to complement the character of each chorus. His simplicity recalls the folk roots of jazz, as does the vividness of his mood and feeling.

Meade "Lux" Lewis was the most famous of the boogie-woogie pianists. The cross-fertilization of eastern and western styles is evident in that he was influenced by both Jimmy Yancey and Fats Waller. He worked in Chicago before recording the famous "Honky Tonk Train Blues" (1927, Victor-BMG). In the later 1930s, Lewis was "discovered" by the jazz impresario John Hammond, which led to a major career. He became probably the best-known boogie-woogie pianist of the era, recording such important numbers as "Yancey Special" (1936, Decca-MCA), "Bear Cat Crawl" (1938, Vocalion), "Tell Your Story" (1940, Blue Note), and "Bass on Top" (1940, Blue Note).

"Honky Tonk Train Blues" is an undisputed masterpiece of the genre. The cross-rhythms that Lewis sets up between the hands are intricate and astonishingly independent; the right hand uses the left hand as a foundation but often seems to have a mind of its own. This performance is one of the most exciting depictions of the train motif commonly heard in jazz and blues.

Just as many blues and boogie-woogie pianists could play stride, the eastern stride players could play the blues. Further, as has been pointed out, stride in part developed from ragtime by incorporation of blues elements. Yet their specialties remained largely regional. Johnson and Waller, for example, recorded blues extensively, although they were far more at home in the cultured, postragtime world of New York.

Still, combinations of western blues (and boogie-woogie) and eastern stride helped propel the development of swing piano styles in the later 1920s and 1930s. Among the many players who combined aspects of both traditions were Count Basie, Benny Moten, Mary Lou Williams, and Jay McShann. As an excellent case study, consider the style of William "Count" Basie. Bill Basie's early pianism was in marked contrast to the blues-based, witty style he soon developed. A northeasterner from Red Bank, New Jersey, he participated early on in cutting contests with established stride artists, including Johnson, Smith, Lambert, and others. Although younger and less experienced, he apparently acquitted himself well. While his first lessons were with his mother, he also studied informally with Fats Waller.

Basie—like so many of the New York players, a well-rounded musician—became a musical director for touring vaudeville shows. In 1927, finding himself in Kansas City when the show he was playing closed, he remained in town, eventually joining Walter Page's Blue Devils and, in 1929, Bennie Moten's Kansas City Orchestra. Upon Moten's death, Basie became the leader of the group.

While Basie's earlier stride phase can be heard in recordings with Moten, his more familiar style is a blues-oriented minimalism—heavy on the right hand, with blues licks, simple riffs, and plenty of open space. The classic Basie style can be seen as a reaction against the dense, virtuosic stride school of his early professional experience. Further, the style fitted well with big band playing, where there was no need to provide a pulse.

In fact, rather than as a solo artist, Basie's strength was as anchor of the Count Basie Orchestra, with quiet, brief, laconic solos contrasting the heavier big band textures. As a rhythm section player, he developed a signature style, adding telling touches to the overall sound of the band. He also recorded effective solo features accompanied by rhythm section only. A fine example of his blues- and riff-based style with extreme economy of means can be heard in "Way Back Blues" (1942, Columbia).

The most important pianist in the transition from stride to swing was Earl "Fatha" Hines. From a musical family in Duquesne, Pennsylvania, Hines was playing professionally by age fifteen in the Pittsburgh area. He made his first records with vocalist Lois Deppe in 1923 and soon after moved to Chicago, where he became a key player in its thriving jazz scene. Eventually Hines teamed up with Louis Armstrong, who had been active in both Chicago and New York, to make some of the finest records of early jazz. Armstrong and Hines were well above the levels of most late-1920s musicians in terms of their technique and ideas, as can be heard in their superb duet recording of "Weather Bird" (1928, OKeh-Columbia).

Hines's first records with Deppe, recorded when Hines was nineteen, show that he had absorbed the basic elements of stride. As he matured through the 1920s, he simplified the stride "orchestral piano," eventually arriving at a prototypical swing style. The right hand no longer developed syncopated patterns around pivot notes (as in ragtime) or between-the-hands figuration (as in stride) but instead focused on a more directed melodic line, often doubled at the octave with phrase-ending tremolos. This line was called the "trumpet" right hand because of its markedly hornlike character, but in fact the general trend toward a more linear style can be traced back through stride and Jelly Roll Morton to late ragtime from 1915 to 1922.

The simplified right hand led Hines to a freer concept of improvisation. Abandoning the multisection set pieces of stride, Hines and others focused on popular songs with their thirty-two-bar structures. That is, jazz piano turned to the "chorus"; the primary structural form of a jazz performance became a series of variations, largely improvised. Further, while solo piano continued to be important in the 1930s, pianists such as Hines performed more often in bands. Hence the left hand gradually became less important for timekeeping; the pianist could play more spontaneously with the pulse taken for granted.

Even as a young lion, Hines was well known for his daring, flashy style, which recalled the exuberance of the stride musicians. He was a powerful player with a driving beat and a left hand that encompassed both stride and walking tenths. Hines would often interrupt the steady flow of the rhythm with audacious cross-rhythms and breaks, keeping the listener off balance and wondering if, when the rhythm resumed, Hines would land on his feet. These qualities can even be heard on Hines's very first recording, "Congaine" (1923, for Gennett, with Deppe's Serenaders), which contains a remarkable stride solo.

Although Hines recorded many outstanding solo records, he spent much of the 1920s and 1930s as a bandleader, fronting groups based in Chicago and New York. Among the finer Hines solo recordings of his own compositions are "A Monday Date" (1928, QRS), "57 Varieties" (1928, OKeh-Columbia), and his well-known tune "Rosetta" (1939, Bluebird-RCA). "57 Varieties"—titled from the pun on "Hines" with the "Heinz" soup company—owes considerably to the stride tradition, being a brilliant multisection set piece. Performances on "Rosetta" and other fine popular songs, such as "Body and Soul" (1940, Bluebird-RCA) and "On the Sunny Side of the Street" (1941, Victor-BMG), show Hines's imaginative chorus-by-chorus improvising. Hines also performed superbly with his bands, which were among the best of the era. Fine piano solos and imaginative arrangements can be heard in "Cavernism" (1933, Brunswick-Columbia), "Pianology" (1937, Vocalion), and "The Earl" (1941, Bluebird-RCA).

Another Pittsburgh native who enjoyed a distinguished career was Mary Lou Williams, one of the great composer-arrangers in jazz. She became especially well known as the pianist and arranger for the

Andy Kirk band, beginning in the late 1920s. A great deal of the band's sound derived from Williams's imaginative charts, although she was a tasteful, intelligent soloist as well. She later wrote outstanding arrangements for many of the major bandleaders, including Benny Goodman, Earl Hines, Tommy Dorsey, Duke Ellington, and Dizzy Gillespie, while leading her own groups.

Building on the Hines legacy from the 1920s, Williams brought together the major piano styles of the era. Her first solo piano recording, "Night Life" (1930, Brunswick-Columbia), shows mastery of stride. Nonetheless, she was equally at home in boogie-woogie, as can be heard from her assured performance of "Little Joe From Chicago" (1939, Columbia). Rooted in swing, Williams continued to expand musically, eventually befriending modernists Thelonious Monk and Bud Powell and absorbing aspects of bebop and other modern styles. But piano performance was only one facet of her excellent musicianship: she also wrote compositions that embraced European concert music, an early important work being the *Zodiac Suite* of 1945. Deeply religious, Williams converted to Catholicism and wrote a number of sacred works for a variety of media. In the latter part of her career, she taught at Duke University.

Theodore "Teddy" Wilson epitomized swing piano, as it emerged from the work of Hines. Although Wilson was not raised in the Northeast, but rather in Tuskegee, Alabama, he was a highly schooled player, having briefly studied music at Talladega College. In 1933 Wilson arrived in New York, where his exquisite musicianship eventually led to an invitation to join Benny Goodman's band in 1935. This was an important crossroads in jazz history—the first time a black instrumentalist became part of a major white group. In fact, Wilson became a featured soloist of the "band within a band," a trio with Goodman and drummer Gene Krupa that was later enlarged to a quartet with the addition of black vibraphonist Lionel Hampton.

In addition to his work with Goodman, Wilson recorded piano solos and often directed small-group recordings that are major documents of swing-era jazz. These sessions used both black and white musicians from the most well known ensembles of the time, including, for example, Benny Goodman, Chu Berry, Roy Eldridge, Benny Carter, Johnny Hodges, Ben Webster, Billie Holiday, Bobby Hackett, Lester Young, and Cozy Cole. The sessions resulted in numerous classic sides featuring Billie Holiday, such as "These Foolish Things" (1936, Brunswick-Columbia) and "More Than You Know" (1939, Brunswick-Columbia).

Wilson's style was less risky and aggressive than Hines's, but instead more controlled and refined. He exploited all registers of the piano, his striding bass line supporting elegant swing-style runs. His left hand featured a deft use of tenths that created a "tenor line" counterpoint in the piano's middle register. More removed from the stride style than Hines, he usually accented the four beats of the bar very evenly. Further, he focused on elegant and swinging chorus improvisation that fully supplanted the set pieces popular before the mid-1930s. He can be heard to excellent advantage in the Goodman Trio and Quartet recordings, including "After You've Gone" (1935, Victor-BMG) and "Moonglow" (1936, Victor-BMG). Among his most memorable solo piano recordings are "Rosetta" (1935, Brunswick-Columbia), "Between the Devil and the Deep Blue Sea" (1937, Brunswick-Columbia), and "Smoke Gets in Your Eyes" (1941, Columbia).

As possibly the best-known pianist of the swing era, Wilson can be seen as predecessor of several important players emerging in the 1930s. Among the best was Billy Kyle. Kyle, well known as the pianist and arranger of the John Kirby sextet, demonstrated a single-note style that combined aspects of Hines and Wilson. The Wilsonian elegance is evident in all his work, but he often experimented with the interruptions and rhythmic trickiness we associate with Hines. He can be heard to excellent advantage on a trio recording for Decca-MCA (1939), in which he plays "Finishing Up a Date" and "Between Sets."

Although swing as exemplified by Hines and Wilson dominated jazz piano in the late 1930s, the boogie-woogie craze helped a number of other pianists to achieve prominence, among them Bob Zurke. He was a member of the nationally recognized Bob Crosby band from 1936 until 1939, garnering *Down Beat*'s Best Pianist award in 1939. Like many sidemen with established celebrity, Zurke briefly tried his luck at leading a band in 1939, then worked largely as a solo pianist for the remainder of his short career.

Interestingly, the Crosby band, a white ensemble, was the first jazz band with a historical consciousness; that is, in addition to the hits and swing-based jazz of the time, they also played dixieland, paying homage to the 1920s. Their success owed much to Zurke's boogie-woogie "down home" energy and power. Crosby featured a band-within-a-band, known as the Bob Cats, in which Zurke was often featured. He was also accomplished as a stride stylist and can be heard to excellent effect on "Little Rock Getaway" (1937, Decca-MCA).

Like Zurke, Joe Sullivan achieved national prominence in the

Crosby band. Born in Chicago, he eventually developed a driving, swinging style reminiscent of Hines. His ability to integrate pianistic influences can be heard in his first New York solo recording, "Honeysuckle Rose" (1933, Columbia), in which broken tenths are contrasted with a striding left hand, boogie-woogie and blues choruses, and even a walking bass. The rhythmic density of Harlem stride is diminished, with a bluesier, more easygoing feel in its stead.

Another important pianist associated with both the Crosby band and Benny Goodman was Jess Stacy. Better known as an ensemble player than as a soloist, Stacy derived his style from elements of both Wilson and Hines but was an understated, thoughtful player. In a series of solo and trio recordings made in 1935 for Paramount, Stacy recorded Bix Beiderbecke's set pieces "Flashes" and "In the Dark." In the same session, Stacy recorded (with a trio) the fine and swinging "The World Is Waiting for Sunrise." Despite the trio setting, tenths and occasional stride-style left hand are in evidence. The right-hand runs are Wilson-esque, with phrase-ending tremolos reminiscent of Hines. Stacy's most famous career moment was a wonderfully gentle, inspired improvisation in the climactic "killer-diller" number, "Sing Sing Sing," from Goodman's 1938 concert at Carnegie Hall.

Although he was not the youngest of the pianists discussed here, Arthur "Art" Tatum rightfully finishes up our survey of the 1920s and 1930s, for he is the apotheosis of classic jazz piano—an intimidating, surpassing player in virtually every area. He combined the emerging swing style with the most virtuosic elements of stride and took each to another level. Almost blind, Tatum could read music only with difficulty. After an apprenticeship in Toledo (where he was born) and Cleveland, he eventually arrived in New York in 1932, where he began his recording career. A legendary cutting contest in which Tatum unveiled his hyperkinetic "Tea for Two" (later recorded for Brunswick-Columbia, 1933) established his dominance among the Harlem stride players.

Tatum's style was at once innovative—with extensive reharmonizations that inspired such bebop modernists as Charlie Parker and Charles Mingus—yet solidly based in the stride tradition. He was capable of playing with blinding speed, grabbing complex chords in his left hand to support decorative runs and elaborate passage work in his right. It was through such virtuoso "tricks" that Tatum recalled the great ticklers of the 1920s. However, there was an important difference: Tatum did not compose his own multistrain set pieces; instead, he worked almost entirely with popular songs, devising arrangements that are among the treasures of jazz piano. Still, Tatum's playing has inspired controversy: some critics feel that his awesome technical command actually diminished the creative content of his work.

We are fortunate that Tatum's playing has been documented with exceptional thoroughness. There are not only the piano solos from the 1930s and 1940s but also fine piano trio work with guitar and bass, beginning in 1943. In the 1950s Norman Granz produced hundreds of recordings of Tatum, both as a solo pianist and in small-group sessions with such players as Ben Webster, Buddy DeFranco, Roy Eldridge, and Benny Carter. These final recordings are a monumental tribute to the pianist and remain one of the great legacies by any jazz artist; the solo recordings alone contain numerous treasures.

Although Tatum recorded much superb work, "Aunt Hagar's Blues" (1949, Capitol) must be singled out. Not unlike James P. Johnson, Tatum was much more at home with popular songs and stride-based performance than with the blues. Yet this performance has it all: intricate pianism, unusual harmonic moves and voicings, and a remarkably rich blues feeling. A fine example of an exquisite set arrangement is "Get Happy" (1940, Decca-MCA), which incorporates an unusual left-hand trill that serves to store up potential energy, as in a coiled spring. When Tatum uncoils the spring with the up-tempo stride to follow, the music's rhythmic momentum, now unleashed, swings furiously.

As the swing era waned in the early 1940s, pianists began to search for other approaches. After Tatum's unprecedented virtuosity, where could jazz piano go? The times were ripe for a new paradigm, and it was provided by the beboppers. These jazz revolutionaries of the early 1940s played with far less rhythmic regularity in the basic underlying pulse and a more angular, unpredictable improvised line. The left-hand regularity of stride did not fit the directions of bop especially well, so jazz piano in the 1940s found a new way: far more reliance on the right hand with a bass player and drummer supplying the rhythmic pulse. The self-contained one-man band of stride now fully gave way to the piano trio of modern jazz.

Coleman Hawkins

Kenny Berger

oleman Hawkins occupies a unique position in the history of jazz. He was born at the dawn of the twentieth century, and thus at the dawn of jazz history. His professional career began at roughly the same time that the first jazz recordings were made and continued through the swing and bebop eras, ending in the late 1960s, by which time the jazz avant-garde was firmly established. Though many of Hawkins's contemporaries could boast equal or greater musical longevity, Coleman Hawkins was unique in that his musical style continuously evolved with the times. Though he was called the "father of the tenor saxophone," he was never content to rest on his laurels. In Hawkins's case, quite the opposite was true, for Coleman Hawkins was an artist who was obsessive about being on the cutting edge. He could not tolerate being thought of as old-fashioned, or past his prime, either as a musician or as a man, and found it impossible to grow old gracefully. The role of esteemed elder statesman, played with impeccable grace by contemporaries of his, such as Benny Carter and Doc Cheatham, was one which Coleman Hawkins couldn't allow himself to live long enough to play.

Coleman Randolph Hawkins was born in St. Joseph, Missouri, on

Coleman Hawkins, Kelly's Stable, New York, 1939. Courtesy Frank Driggs Collection.

November 21, 1904, the second child of William Hawkins and Cordelia Coleman Hawkins. He was an only child, however, since the Hawkinses' first child, a girl, had died at age two, a year before Coleman was born. His first exposure to music came from his mother, who played the organ at church services and the piano at various social functions. Hawkins received solid musical training beginning in early childhood. He began studying piano at the age of five and continued to play it throughout his life. He then began to play the cello and, at the age of nine, C-melody saxophone. His early studies included harmony, theory, and ear training, and he was quoted as saying that he could read music before he could read words.

This early grounding in the fundamentals of music, combined with his family's belief in the value of education, helped to shape Hawkins's approach to music throughout his life. He retained a lifelong love of the piano, playing it for his own pleasure, as well as for the purpose of learning and exploring new musical ideas and material. Because of this background, combined with his innate curiosity and intelligence, Hawkins was well equipped to enter the music profession as a teenager, with the skills of sight-reading, transposition, and improvisation already under his belt to a degree far in advance of others his age.

Though his mother wished him to continue his classical cello studies, young Coleman's fascination with the saxophone soon led to the cello being relegated to the role of a double (musicians' parlance for a secondary instrument). This was both a wise and bold decision on his part. It was wise in the sense that professional opportunities for African-American players in the classical field were practically non-existent when Hawkins entered the music profession, circa 1920, and would remain so for at least another forty years. It was bold in the sense that the saxophone was still considered a newcomer to jazz, and as a tenor soloist, Hawkins had few, if any, role models to guide or inspire his development.

It is astounding, in view of the instrument's popularity and importance throughout the history of jazz, to be reminded that when Coleman Hawkins first appeared on the scene, the tenor saxophone was considered to be purely a background instrument; its use as a vehicle for melodic lines, let alone as a solo voice, was considered unusual. The only saxophone soloists of note at the time, jazz or non-jazz, played either the alto, the soprano, or the soon-to-be-obsolete C-melody. The C-melody saxophone is pitched a whole tone higher than the tenor and resembles a slimmed-down tenor in appearance, though

C. G. Conn, a leading American instrument manufacturer, made a popular "goose-neck" model, which resembled an elongated alto. The C-melody enjoyed its greatest popularity among amateurs, due to the fact that it is pitched in the key of C, enabling a player to read off of a piano score without needing to transpose the notes. Though it is closest in range to the tenor, the majority of C-melody soloists, most notably Frank Trumbauer, an early influence on both Benny Carter and Lester Young, played it with a light, alto-like timbre.

Some of Hawkins's first jobs were in the in the vicinity of Atchison, Kansas, roughly forty-five miles from Topeka, where he was sent to continue his schooling at the Industrial and Educational Institute, an all-black school which his parents deemed preferable to the segregated schools in St. Joseph. During this time, Hawkins also worked in various theater orchestras in Kansas City, Missouri. This led to his first job with a name group and his first appearances on recordings.

In 1921 he was hired as an extra player for a Kansas City appearance by the singer Mamie Smith, who carried her own backup group, the Original Jazz Hounds. Mamie Smith was the first black artist to have a hit record, ("Crazy Blues," OKeh, 1920) and thus had a nationwide reputation. Hawkins became a regular member of the Jazz Hounds in April of 1922, and in May of that year he traveled to New York with them and made his first appearance on records, playing C-melody saxophone on "Mean Daddy Blues" (OKeh), in the choppy, slap-tongued style that was in vogue among saxophonists during the 1920s. He continued working with Mamie Smith until 1923, when, after a tour of the West Coast, he decided to settle in New York.

During 1922 Hawkins began to make the permanent switch from C-melody saxophone to tenor. Though he quit playing cello at this time, a case can be made for the instrument having much to do with shaping his approach to the tenor saxophone. His use of long, arpeggiated lines spanning the horn's entire range, and of call-and-response figures in contrasting registers, giving the illusion of counterpoint, can be traced to his background as a cellist. In addition, one of his personal favorites among his many recordings was a version of Schumann's "Träumerei," on *Hawk and the Hunter* (Sesac/Everest, 1965), a piece he used to play on the cello.

Hawkins jumped into the busy New York freelance music scene with both feet and soon became one of the players regularly called upon for recording work by a busy young pianist, arranger, and publisher named Fletcher Henderson. Most of these records were of pop tunes, many of them vocals. The material was selected by the various record companies who employed Henderson as leader, contractor, and producer, with most of the arranging chores being handled by Don Redman, a pioneer in the art of jazz arranging, who was in Henderson's employ.

Hawkins's first recorded tenor solo appears on Henderson's recording of "Dicty Blues" (Vocalion/Columbia), recorded on August 9, 1923. Though he still employs the popular slap-tongued style, Hawkins's solo displays a compelling assertiveness and good command of the horn's entire range. At this time, the Henderson band was mainly a studio ensemble, playing only occasional live gigs. In late 1923 Henderson accepted a steady job at the Club Alabam on West 44th Street, giving his band a chance to cohere as a unit, and giving Coleman Hawkins an excellent place in which to develop and showcase his talents.

While continuing to grow as a soloist, Hawkins returned to doubling at this time, playing clarinet and baritone and bass saxophones in section work, soloing on the latter on "Pensacola" and "Florida Stomp" (Columbia). He also recorded a pair of little-known C-melody solos with Henderson in 1924, on "War Horse Mama" (Brunswick) and "Naughty Man" (Columbia), on which, as historian J. R. Taylor points out, he sounds eerily like Trumbauer. By the mid-1920s, he gave up doubling to focus exclusively on the tenor.

The Henderson band continued to record frequently, with Hawkins by now well established as a featured soloist. In 1924 a young cornet player from New Orleans left King Oliver's Creole Jazz Band and joined the Henderson crew during an extended engagement at the Roseland Ballroom. The immediate and far-reaching impact that Louis Armstrong's playing had on the jazz world in the 1920s needs no retelling here, but suffice it to say that if the musicians who directly influenced Coleman Hawkins can be counted on the fingers of one hand, leaving a few digits left over, Louis Armstrong was one of them, though Hawkins was always loath to admit it. Armstrong's influence on Hawkins lay mainly in the area of swing feeling, which helped Hawkins to develop an escape route from the stiff rhythmic confines of the slap-tongued style. Hawkins's dilemma at this point was finding a smoother, more legato way of phrasing, without compromising his powerful rhythmic drive. By 1926 he had the situation well in hand, as his smoothly flowing yet hard-driving solo on "The Stampede" (Vocalion/Columbia) demonstrates.

It was at this time that Hawkins met the one musician whose influence on him was so profound that even his legendary sense of pride did not prevent him from openly acknowledging it. That musician was the pianist Art Tatum. The influence of Art Tatum on the evolution of jazz harmony cannot be overstated. Though he is widely credited with having been a huge influence on pianists, from Nat Cole to Cecil Taylor, his influence on both Coleman Hawkins and Charlie Parker is solid proof of his importance in other areas besides pure piano virtuosity.

When Hawkins first encountered Tatum, most jazz improvisers built their solos by embellishing the melody of the song at hand. The idea of basing a jazz solo primarily on the harmonic structure of a piece was still in its infancy. Pianists, with all the ingredients of harmony literally at their fingertips, possessed a decided advantage in this regard, as is obvious in the advanced nature of the harmonies employed by players like Tatum and Earl Hines. Hawkins, with his thorough knowledge of keyboard harmony and his continually evolving technical command of the tenor, combined with his natural inclination toward creative risk-taking, was the ideal player to adapt Tatum's concepts to a single-line instrument.

This change in approach did not bear fruit right away, as Hawkins struggled for some time to cram as many notes and ideas into his solos as this style required, without making them sound like mere arpeggios. This is a pitfall all harmonically oriented improvisers face, as John Coltrane found out thirty years later when he was accused of merely running scales. Hawkins resolved this problem by loosening the strict, on-the-beat rhythmic approach he had been using, starting and ending his phrases in rhythmically unexpected places. When this element of his style completely jelled, he became one of the rhythmically freest players in jazz. The rhythmic character of some of his best work resembles the "speech rhythms" used by avant-garde players such as Eric Dolphy. On one of Hawkins's last recordings with Henderson in 1934, "Hocus Pocus" (Bluebird), he builds his solo using languid quarter-note triplets, producing the sort of floating, laid-back feeling usually associated with his karmic opposite, Lester Young.

In 1929, with a pickup group called the Mound City Blue Blowers, Hawkins recorded a solo that presented a tantalizing preview of a harmonic and rhythmic approach that would revolutionize the art of jazz ballad playing. On James P. Johnson's "One Hour" (Victor), Hawkins produces a solo in which his rhythms at times seem to float above the surface of the underlying pulse in a sort of implied rubato, while maintaining an intense forward momentum. Rather than embellishing the song's melody, Hawkins bases his solo on its harmonic structure; his encyclopedic knowledge of harmony and voice-leading allowing him to probe these aspects of a song to depths previously unexplored by jazz soloists.

Prior to leaving the Henderson band in 1934, Hawkins revealed great potential as a composer and arranger, though he chose not to explore these aspects of music in depth, for the same reason he forsook doubling; namely, to devote all his time and energy to his tenor work. In August of 1933 the Henderson band recorded a remarkably "progressive" Hawkins composition titled "Queer Notions" (Vocalion/Columbia). Arranged by Fletcher Henderson's brother Horace, "Queer Notions" employs the whole-tone scale, which was the most commonly used device for sounding "far out" in 1920s and 1930s jazz, but in this case it is utilized with far more subtlety and sophistication than was the norm. Nearly every published reminiscence by a member of the Henderson band contains a reference to a legendary Hawkins arrangement of "Singin' in the Rain" that was, unfortunately, never recorded.

By 1934 a combination of the Depression economy and the leader's lax attitude toward business matters brought hard times to the Henderson band. At the suggestion of his friend bassist June Cole, Hawkins arranged a visit to Europe through the auspices of the prominent British bandleader and booking agent Jack Hylton. Hawkins was pleasantly surprised at the warmth of his reception and by the degree to which his reputation preceded him. Like every other black artist who visited Europe, he found the absence of constant, overt racism to be a refreshing change. Hawkins ended up staying in Europe for five years. The star treatment that he received was perfectly suited to his temperament and self-image. He appeared most often as a guest soloist, often playing only a couple of feature numbers, in the manner of a concerto soloist on a symphony orchestra program. He appeared throughout Europe with the Hylton orchestra and played several dates in England with a group led by Hylton's wife Ennis, billed as Mrs. Jack Hylton & Her Boys. In 1935 Hawkins and the Jack Hylton group played several dates in Holland, to be followed by a tour of Germany. German politics being what they were, Hawkins was refused permission to appear there. The Hylton band went without him—so much for Europe as a safe haven from racism. He then established a residence in The Hague and played concerts and made several recordings with a Dutch group, the Ramblers. Later that same year, he toured Scandinavia and considered making Copenhagen his home, but problems with visas and work permits prevented him from doing so.

By this time Hawkins had found an ideal balance between the

stiff, choppy rhythmic approach of his early style and the quasi-rubato feel of some of his late 1920s work. His playing now possessed a rhythmic self-sufficiency that allowed him to play with the same degree of power and drive regardless of the tempo and, more important when playing with European rhythm sections, regardless of the quality of his accompanists. On his recordings with both the Hylton band and the Ramblers, the accompaniments were rhythmically and harmonically tame, to say the least, but Hawkins's efforts are always worth hearing.

On April 28, 1937, Hawkins recorded four titles that stand as the crowning achievements of his European sojourn. For the first time since crossing the Atlantic, he found himself recording with a group of his peers, including Benny Carter, American drummer Tommy Benford, the great guitarist Django Reinhardt, and French violinist Stephane Grappelli, on piano. The group also included two of France's finest saxophonists, altoist André Ekyan and tenorist Alix Combelle. The best-known sides from this session, "Honeysuckle Rose" and "Crazy Rhythm," comprised the initial release by the French label Swing. Inspired by the quality of his cohorts, Carter in particular, Hawkins turns in some of his finest work.

In 1939 Willard Alexander, an agent with the William Morris Agency, suggested to Hawkins the idea of coming back to the States and forming his own big band. Though he took his time deciding, it was only a matter of time before Hawkins would grow restless with the comparative lack of stimulation and competition in Europe. With World War II fast approaching, he decided to return home.

Soon after returning to New York at the end of July 1939, Hawkins debuted his band at Kelly's Stable on West 51st Street. It was a nine-piece band plus a vocalist, and it consisted of young, mostly unknown players. The band had various weaknesses, the most glaring of which was its sparse instrumentation. With Hawkins featured most of the time, the combination of three brass, two alto saxes, and rhythm provided a skimpy underpinning for his sumptuous tone, which also tended to overpower the undermanned sax section in ensemble passages.

On October 11, 1939, Coleman Hawkins and His Orchestra made their only recordings for Bluebird, a subsidiary of RCA Victor. "Meet Doctor Foo" and "Fine Dinner" are undistinguished medium-tempo Hawkins originals, and "He's Funny That Way" features a pleasant vocal by Thelma Carpenter. Since these recordings were released as two-sided 78 rpm singles, a fourth number was needed, a fact undoubtedly known to the participants well in advance.

The story usually told is that the inclusion of "Body and Soul" was an unplanned, spur-of-the-moment decision. Historian Dan Morgenstern has suggested that, since Hawkins was playing "Body and Soul" every night at Kelly's, to considerable acclaim, the tale of its being tacked on as an afterthought was probably concocted by Hawkins to add to the record's mystique.

"Body and Soul" begins with a four-bar introduction by pianist Gene Rodgers, after which Hawkins proceeds to lay down a solo for the ages. Hawkins's solo is one of the finest examples of pure, spontaneous, creative artistry in the history of recorded jazz. He strikes a perfect balance of all the elements at his command, creating one memorable melodic phrase after another while probing the song's harmonies to previously unexplored depths. Hawkins hints at the song's melody during his first six bars, but he is improvising right from the start, never actually stating the theme. A truly remarkable aspect of this solo is the way it is built with a seemingly infallible sense of inner logic in terms of thematic development, dynamics, register, and rhythmic intensity, while possessing an emotional immediacy perceivable to all listeners, even those totally unaware of its technical merits.

"Body and Soul" was the first pure jazz recording to become a commercial hit, and nobody was more surprised by this than Hawkins himself. He was especially amazed that it caught on with the general public even though the song's melody was not stated. In addition, Hawkins's solo uses chord substitutions that were considered extremely advanced at the time. For many years "Body and Soul" was considered by musicians to be the exclusive property of Coleman Hawkins, and no other tenor saxophonist could play it without his or her version being compared unfavorably with Hawkins's. Hawkins himself, with his aversion to dwelling in the past, grew to resent being asked to play "Body and Soul" on nearly every gig in the wake of the recording's success and would amuse himself by playing it in different keys and changing key every eight bars. Unlike nearly every other artist who has had a hit, Hawkins never attempted to re-create this solo, either on live dates or on subsequent recordings.

Hawkins continued to lead his big band, which eventually expanded to include seven brass, four saxophones, and four rhythm. The band never realized its potential for several reasons, most having to do with Hawkins himself. Though the consensus view of nearly every sideman employed by Hawkins was that he was a relaxed, understanding leader who was easy to get along with, Hawkins was extremely lax in certain areas. He was notorious for being late to rehearsals and jobs and lacked the ability to be the kind of taskmaster needed to whip a band into shape. He also was a notoriously disorganized businessman who would sometimes vanish on pay nights, leaving his sidemen in the lurch.

He was known for his strong sense of personal dignity, which manifested itself in his impeccable manner of dress and his insistence on always being paid top dollar for his work. These admirable qualities helped speed the demise of his big band, as he was unable to make musical or personal compromises. He made no attempts to ingratiate himself with audiences by engaging in verbal patter, and he vehemently refused agents' and club owners' requests to play more commercial material. His social conscience impelled him to reject lucrative jobs when they involved playing for all-white audiences.

After some unsuccessful touring, Hawkins broke up his band in November of 1940, returning to Kelly's Stable with a small group. He worked in Chicago with a local big band and sextet, and then, in late 1942, moved back to New York. He took another small band into Kelly's for several months and participated in numerous recording sessions for independent labels, including Signature, Commodore, and Keynote.

After "Body and Soul," Hawkins became anxious to find a new musical direction. Always open to new ideas, he kept close tabs on developments among players of the new music being played uptown at Minton's and Monroe's and at various 52nd Street venues. His reaction to the work of Charlie Parker, Dizzy Gillespie, Thelonious Monk, and the other budding beboppers was positive from the start. He became a lifelong friend and champion of Monk's, playing his compositions and using him as a sideman.

In February of 1944 Hawkins led two sessions for the fledgling independent label Apollo, which, like most independent jazz labels at the time, originated out of a record store. These sides, by a twelve-piece band with arrangements by Budd Johnson featuring Hawkins and Dizzy Gillespie as soloists, are generally considered the first bebop recordings; however, as Scott DeVeaux (1997) has pointed out, the music of this tightly arranged twelve-piece unit bore little resemblance to the experiments being conducted at Minton's. Gillespie's composition, "Woody 'n' You," which eventually became a jazz standard, presents the most challenging harmonies on these sides. Hawkins sounds right at home, but Gillespie is, understandably, the more adventurous soloist. The Apollo recordings served to link Hawkins's name with the latest innovations in jazz. They also used his fame to help introduce Gillespie and his cohorts to a wider audience.

Hawkins then formed a small group in which his tenor was paired with that of Don Byas, eighteen years his junior and arguably the most advanced tenor player in jazz at the time. Many of the sidemen that Hawkins used in the mid- to late 1940s were associated with the new music. They included, at various times, trumpeters Miles Davis, Howard McGhee, Vic Coulsen, Benny Harris, and Fats Navarro, trombonist J. J. Johnson, bassist Oscar Pettiford, drummers Max Roach, Denzil Best, and Shelly Manne, arranger Tadd Dameron, and pianist Thelonious Monk, who made his recording debut with Hawkins, for the Joe Davis label in 1944.

The remainder of the 1940s found Hawkins dividing his time between extended gigs at 52nd Street clubs and tours with producer Norman Granz's Jazz at the Philharmonic, which presented a sort of stock company of musicians in staged jam sessions at various concert halls. He also traveled to the West Coast in 1945 with a bop-oriented group that included McGhee and Pettiford, recording several sides, among them "Rifftide" (actually Monk's "Hackensack"), "Stuffy," and "Hollywood Stampede" (Capitol/Classics).

Hawkins's next important recording, "Picasso" (Clef/Verve), is a milestone in the history of recorded jazz. A stunning unaccompanied saxophone solo, it was recorded for a 78 rpm boxed set titled *The Jazz Scene* for Granz's new Clef label, first issued in 1948. To this day, there is much controversy as to exactly when "Picasso" was recorded. Most discographies list 1948 with no exact date; others say 1945. It was recorded in New York at Asch Studios, owned by Moses Asch, who had been the distributor for all of Granz's productions until the two had a falling-out in 1947. This lends credence to J. R. Taylor's contention that "Picasso" was recorded sometime between June 1946 and January 1947, while Asch and Granz were still in business together. Hawkins laid the groundwork for "Picasso" in 1945, when he recorded two brief unaccompanied solos as a demonstration record for Selmer, the French manufacturer whose saxophones Hawkins played exclusively beginning in 1935. "Hawk's Variations Parts 1 & 2" (Selmer/Baronet/Classics), though boldly conceived, sounds more like an introspective warmup than a fully realized performance.

"Picasso" was recorded in two four-hour sessions in which Hawkins spent roughly equal amounts of time working things out at the piano and on his horn. It is possible that "Hawk's Variations" is a pair of out-takes from the first session. The finished performance is a marvel of thematic development and rhythmic mastery, alternating passages of nearly operatic drama with ones of irrepressible swing. Hawkins's background as a pianist and cellist is never more evident than on

"Picasso," where his playing sometimes suggests Tatum-esque harmonic flourishes as well as the implied polyphony of J. S. Bach's *Six Suites for Violoncello*. Hawkins had wanted to record an unaccompanied solo since 1944, citing Pablo Casals's performance of the Bach suites as an inspiration. Since "Picasso" was named for Granz's favorite painter, it could be said that Granz and Hawkins each had a different Pablo in mind.

By the 1950s Hawkins had attained the status of revered elder statesman, a designation that he hated. At this time he began to display the fear of old age that would haunt him the rest of his life. He started lying about his age to interviewers and once even did so on a passport application. He fought this demon most effectively by remaining open-minded and willing to take on new musical challenges. Though his personal record collection was almost entirely comprised of classical works, he always made a point of going to clubs to keep abreast of the latest developments in jazz and was known for encouraging promising musicians. During the last fifteen years of his life, Hawkins's own groups included such younger players as trumpeters Thad Jones and Booker Little, pianists Barry Harris, Wynton Kelly, and Eddie Costa, bassists Henry Grimes and Paul Chambers, and drummers Paul Motian and Andrew Cyrille.

Perhaps the best known of Hawkins's cross-generational encounters is his appearance alongside John Coltrane in a septet led by his old friend Thelonious Monk (*Monk's Music*/Riverside/OJC, 1957). The program is all Monk originals, and Hawkins shows no fear in tackling the difficult material. He also turns in a gorgeous rendering of the ballad "Ruby, My Dear." In 1959 Hawkins explored the music of another original pianist-composer, appearing on *Randy Weston Live at the Five Spot* (United Artists). Here he tears into several fine Weston originals, including "Hi-Fly" and the waltz-time "Beef Blues Stew," with the combination of sage wisdom and youthful abandon that was his trademark.

The sixties found Hawkins co-leading a quintet with trumpeter Roy Eldridge and working with a steady rhythm section of Tommy Flanagan on piano, Major Holley on bass, and Eddie Locke on drums, both with and without Eldridge. The quintet recorded for Verve, while Hawkins also made several albums for the Prestige and Impulse labels. The Prestige dates include *Night Hawk*, an excellent two-tenor session with Eddie "Lockjaw" Davis. The Impulse dates include the long-awaited pairing of Hawkins and Duke Ellington, with a small band rather than the full orchestra, and an updated version of the

1937 Paris sessions with Benny Carter, *Further Definitions*. The latter date features a four-saxophone front line, with Hawkins, Carter, Phil Woods, and Charlie Rouse all in top form, with a rhythm section of Dick Katz (piano), John Collins (guitar), Jimmy Garrison (bass), and Jo Jones (drums).

The early 1960s found Hawkins accepting one new musical challenge after another, always coming out on top. In 1960 he appeared as a guest soloist on one track, "Driva' Man," on Max Roach's *We Insist—Freedom Now Suite* (Candid). It is a blues in 5/4 on which he turns in a dramatic, emotionally charged solo containing a loud reed squeak, which the usually fastidious Hawkins insisted be left in, feeling that it fit the stark, anguished mood of the piece. The worldly, well-informed Hawkins was proud to perform music with a political message, which was the main focus of Roach's music at this crucial time for the civil rights movement. On February 22, 1961, Hawkins appeared on Abbey Lincoln's classic album *Straight Ahead* (Candid). With music by Roach, Lincoln, Monk, and Mal Waldron, and words by Lincoln, Langston Hughes, Billie Holiday, and James Weldon Johnson, it is one of the most emotionally intense jazz vocal albums ever recorded. Hawkins is featured on five of the seven tracks, and his playing is stunning throughout. He employs noticeably less vibrato than was his custom, and much of his playing here is thematic and motivic, rather than harmonic, especially on "Blue Monk."

The last of Hawkins's significant recordings is *Sonny Meets Hawk* (RCA Victor), a 1963 pairing of Hawkins and Sonny Rollins. The two feed off of each other constantly, with Rollins continually throwing his idol one musical curveball after another, and Hawkins sometimes taking up the challenge, other times bringing things back down to earth.

The ending of the Coleman Hawkins story is not a happy one. By the mid-1960s, he began feeling as though he had nothing left to accomplish and that the scene had passed him by. He was financially well off, having literally never been out of work, but the thought of being put out to pasture was unbearable to him. Never a teetotaler, he began to drink more and more heavily. Always known for his prodigious appetite, he would sometimes go without eating for days on end. He maintained this self-destructive pattern while continuing to travel and perform. A stocky, robust man, he began losing weight until he appeared shockingly thin and frail. Known for always being smartly dressed and groomed, the Hawkins of the late sixties appeared startlingly unkempt, with straggly hair, an unruly beard, and ill-fitting clothing. He was diagnosed with bronchial pneumonia while on tour in Europe in 1968 and died at his Manhattan apartment on May 19, 1969.

The legacy of Coleman Hawkins is widespread and multifaceted. In addition to virtually inventing the tenor saxophone as a jazz instrument, he took the art of the improvised solo beyond the limits of "jazzing" the melody and taught the jazz world how to explore its materials in depth. He was the most significant pre-bop figure (along with, arguably, Lester Young) in the transition from the swing era to the birth of bebop, and one of the few (others include Mary Lou Williams, Budd Johnson, and Pee Wee Russell) to follow this transition to its next stages. Though much is made of the natty attire and dignified deportment of conservative young jazzmen in recent years, Hawkins predated them in these areas by a good sixty years. One can only speculate as to how the relentlessly adventurous Hawkins would have reacted had he lived to hear their musical conservatism.

In Jean Bach's marvelous documentary film *A Great Day in Harlem*, Sonny Rollins states that as a youth he saw Hawkins as not just a musical influence but as a role model; thus, Coleman Hawkins was more than the father of the tenor saxophone. He was the prototype for the idea of the jazz musician as a serious, creative artist.

Lester Young

Loren Schoenberg

Lester Young introduced a new sensibility to jazz: one that was at once close to the swinging New Orleans roots of the music and yet malleable enough in its basic abstraction to appeal to any and all contemporary artists. With an arsenal of fresh and daring devices, Young created melodies and phrases that remain a vital part of the jazz language. His solos revealed an architectural perfection that contrasted with their seemingly effortless nature. For Young, it had to flow, and flow in a speechlike manner befitting his New Orleans–based patois, which he eventually transformed into a James Joyce–like double-talk based on all manner of veiled allusions, double entendres, and hoo-hah. His speaking voice was high for a man of his stature (over six feet) and at times bordered on the feminine; he was a master of the poetic potential of curse words, which he used with taste and with humor. Lester Young was above all a speechlike player. He reveled in sounds for their own sake. The actual notes sometimes took a back seat to the timbre and the shape. These sounds gave his playing a variety of emotional gradations equaled by few and surpassed by none. Young painted with sound, occasionally shooting out macabre utterances in rapid succession, but far more frequently airing them out in

Lester Young, 1939. Courtesy Frank Driggs Collection.

languorous space. He could be astonishingly articulate one moment, then suddenly babble humorously on just a few notes without losing coherence. Indeed, he would use these primarily rhythmic episodes as resting places on his way to yet another exciting climax a couple of choruses ahead. And it was his original sense of rhythm that made Young one of the most sophisticated musicians in the entirety of jazz history. Merging the swinging roots of his native Louisiana with the more even phrasing of Bix Beiderbecke and Frank Trumbauer, Young arrived at a rhythmic synthesis that could turn instantly from one rhythmic wave to another.

Born at his mother's family home in Woodville, Mississippi, on August 27, 1909, Lester Young came from a musical family based in and around New Orleans; parents, siblings, aunts, uncles, and cousins all played in the family band. His first instrument was the drums; he maintained that the reason he switched to the saxophone in early adolescence was that too many pretty girls were getting away while he packed them up! (Young must have still dabbled on the drums in later years, since Jo Jones insisted that Lester Young remained the best drummer he ever heard.) The highly developed sense of counterpoint that enveloped so much of the music young Lester heard was not lost on him. What note to play, when, and in what register called for split-second decision making, and Lester was nothing if not fast. On the all-too-few recordings where he got to engage in no-holds-barred polyphony, Lester played with prescience, wit, and, as always, beauty (the 1938 Kansas City Six, Glenn Hardman and his Hammond Five, Basie's Bad Boys, various Teddy Wilson/Billie Holiday sessions). He also exhibited a degree of extroversion that comes as quite a shock when juxtaposed with the almost exaggerated sense of relaxation for which he eventually became renowned. (In later years, Young favored a porkpie hat and a cape that became as much his signature as his playing in the jazz world.)

One of the basic threads in the development of the music has been the reaction to what have become the established norms of a particular instrument. Young himself was the product of just such an event. The cornetist Bix Beiderbecke was inspired to find his own voice after hearing Louis Armstrong. Whereas Armstrong's solos were invariably "heroic," Beiderbecke's music had a reflective air about it. This is not to say that both sensibilities were mutually exclusive; it's where the emphasis was placed. It was this air of detachment and humor that captivated the teenaged Young as he listened to Beiderbecke on record with the Jean Goldkette and Paul Whiteman orchestras. The

C-melody saxophonist Frank Trumbauer was also on those recordings. He kept his virtuosity way in the background most of time, preferring to croon melodies in a swooping style that masked the intonation problems that eventually drove his chosen instrument into obscurity.

As he grew through adolescence, Lester began to run away from the family band, sometimes for weeks at a stretch. He disliked the minstrelsy the entire family had to engage in, and when an extended southern tour approached, he left. This was on top of a very complicated relationship with his father, Billy Young, who was at once in awe of the young Lester and needed to control him. His overflowing musical talents and proficiency on the alto, tenor, and baritone saxophones made Lester a welcome addition to any band, and he floated in and out of several between 1928 and 1936. He spent quite a bit of time in Minneapolis, where he married for the first time. Young was married three times; his first two wives were white, and both of these brave unions created more than their share of tragedy. The best jazz bands were located in and around Kansas City, and that remained where Young gravitated throughout the early 1930s. There were stints with the famed Blue Devils, during and after Walter Page's tenure as leader, and six months with King Oliver in 1933. Indeed, this collaboration between Young and Armstrong's mentor facilitates many fascinating connections in the jazz lineage. Many musicians have shared the bandstand for a night or two in bands put together for special occasions, but to play for an extended period in a band led by a major player cannot help but be a significant influence.

The many links between the musicians that eventually formed the Count Basie band is illustrated by following Young after he left King Oliver. This was the tail end of Bennie Moten's reign as king of Kansas City jazz. In 1933, after many disastrous months on the road, the Moten band replaced George E. Lee's band at a new Kansas City nightspot, the Cherry Blossom. When Moten told the band that he intended to pull up stakes and hit the road again, they called a band meeting and, with Moten's approval, voted to stay in town and elected Count Basie the nominal leader. Bennie Moten, now without his road gig and his band, created a hybrid unit along with Lee to play across town, at the Club Harlem. Soon thereafter, the Texan saxophonist Herschel Evans (who would create the tenor battle as a jazz convention with Young a few years later) joined the new Basie band, and Young was hired by Moten and Lee. It was during this period that the legendary battle between Coleman Hawkins (on tour with Fletcher Henderson's band) and Young took place. Hawkins was late for the Henderson job, and Lester, in the audience for the express purpose of hearing Hawkins in person, sat in the great man's chair, played his saxophone and clarinet, and then ran back to his own sparsely attended job without ever hearing Hawkins play. When the Henderson band returned to Kansas City several days later, Hawkins lost no time in seeking out the "local" who had sat in for him. What ensued was one of the most fabled "cutting contests" in jazz history. For the first time in his career, Hawkins's legendary endurance and creativity were not only matched but surpassed in a session that lasted well after the sun had risen. Young actually seemed to grow stronger as the hours went by, and Hawkins (who, soaked with sweat while being bested for the first time, played the last part of the session in his undershirt—far from the norm for the sartorially splendid Hawkins) was nearly late for yet another night's gig.

When Basie landed an engagement at Sam Baker's hotel in Little Rock, Arkansas, early in 1934, Herschel Evans switched places with Young so he could stay in Kansas City. And it was during that engagement that Young received an offer from Henderson to take Hawkins's chair. Young played an active role in this. He gave a friend, George Dixon, from Earl Hines's New York–bound band, a letter for Henderson, stating his willingness to come to New York immediately if needed. Young's replacement in Little Rock was Buddy Tate, who was to inherit Evans's spot in the later Basie band. Most significant, it was during this period that Young began playing with Count Basie, Walter Page, and Jo Jones. The result of all those nights and the millions of quarter notes that passed between them would bear fruit when they finally recorded together on the legendary Jones-Smith recordings of November 1936. But Young's sudden entry into jazz's major leagues would have to transpire first.

Although all we can tangibly base our assessment of Young on is the recordings, they do not tell the whole story by a long shot. His influence clearly preceded his debut on disc. As Ralph Ellison noted in this excerpt from an essay he wrote about one of Young's main disciples, the guitarist Charlie Christian: "Perhaps the most stimulating influence upon Christian, and one with whom he was later to be identified, was that of a tall, intense young musician who arrived in Oklahoma City sometime in 1929 and who, with his heavy white sweater, blue stocking cap and up-and-outthrust silver saxophone, left absolutely no reed player and few players of any instrument unstirred by the wild, exciting original flights of his imagination. Who else but Lester Young, who with his battered horn upset the entire Negro section of the town? One of our friends gave up his valved instrument for the tenor saxophone and soon ran away from home to carry the new message to Baltimore, while a good part of the efforts of the rest was spent trying to absorb and transform the Youngian style." The profundity of Young's effect on Christian can be heard on the recordings they made together in 1939 and 1940.

When Hawkins decided to emigrate to Europe in the spring of 1934, Henderson called upon the unknown Young, not the established New York Hawkins-ite Chu Berry, to fill what was jazz's most prestigious tenor saxophone chair. What should have been an absolute triumph soon turned into something more akin to humiliation, Young's ultimately short tenure was made unbearable by his fellow bandsmen's taunts as they found him to be the anti-Hawk. And if that weren't enough, Young, boarding with Henderson, was woken up every morning by Mrs. Henderson playing Hawkins's recorded solos. One good thing did come out of this unhappy time, and that was the beginning of Young's friendship with Billie Holiday. Unable to bear one more Hawkins musicale at chez Henderson, Young found a room in Holiday's mother's flat. Not only was their musical partnership kindled, but Billie also introduced Lester to the ins and outs of life in New York.

The Henderson band left New York for an extended tour of the Midwest, and the musical ostracism and stress finally became too much to bear. He requested a discharge, along with a note stating that he hadn't been fired. Then it was back to Kansas City, where he joined Andy Kirk's band, at which point Kirk's tenorman, Ben Webster, one of Hawkins's finest disciples, came to New York and gave the Henderson band just what they wanted. For many musicians, this would have been the end of the story: going to New York to join the major leagues, and coming back a few months later, horn in hand. To make matters worse, Young didn't fit in the Kirk band either, and he was let go shortly thereafter. He flitted between Kansas City and Minneapolis over the next several months, working in a variety of bands, auditioning in vain for Earl Hines, and struggling to make ends meet. While in Minneapolis, he heard a broadcast of the Basie band and was so dissatisfied with the tenor player (one Slim Freeman), that he sent a telegram to his ex-leader asking for his job back. This set in motion a series of events that would have both of them on the stage of Carnegie Hall in less than two years' time.

John Hammond was a leading jazz critic who had championed Young during his brief Henderson stint two years earlier. Hammond was also closely associated with Benny Goodman (his future brother-in-law), who was winding up an extended engagement at Chicago's Congress Hotel. Ever on the prowl for a new band to proselytize, Hammond happened upon the Basie band broadcasting on a short-wave station from their nightly gig at Kansas City's Reno Club. Inquiries followed, and by Halloween of 1936 the Basie band was on their way to Chicago to prepare for their New York debut Christmas week. It was during this Chicago stay that the Jones-Smith recordings were made. They were so named because Basie had already signed with Decca Records, so the band made these four Vocalion sides ("Shoe Shine Boy," "Lady Be Good," "Evenin'," and "Boogie Woogie") under the names of the drummer and the trumpeter. Young's solos on them started a musical landslide that removed Coleman Hawkins from the position of primacy he had enjoyed for over a decade. Each title is chock full of innovations. Walter Page paces the band by playing four quarter notes to the bar, and sometimes two to the bar. On "Lady Be Good," he plays a different note on each quarter note behind the opening piano solo, then plays two repeated notes when Lester comes in, setting up an ascending and descending arc that Lester builds his solo over. This concern with spontaneous musical architecture was one of the many innovations that this rhythm section, with Page at the helm, wrought.

Young's two choruses were frequently cited by drummer Jo Jones as his best on disc. What one hears is nothing less than the redefinition of an instrument and a radical reworking of the jazz language. Subtle manipulations of the embouchure and the fingering of the horn produce sounds that give the solo a vocal aspect new to the music, and these timbres are then subtly woven into the solo's narrative function. A "sighing" sound centered around Young's middle D on the tenor, which keeps coming back, and a "shake" on his upper-register A refute the canard that somehow Young's sound was lacking in vibrato, volume, or other more overt emotional manifestations. Then there is the outrageous and fetching melodic phrase that opens the second chorus; saxophonists to this day marvel at it, for it is the sort of figure that would never fall naturally under the fingers, yet in Young's hands sounds so inevitable.

"Shoe Shine Boy" reveals another side of Young's virtuosity. He drums out two choruses with an on-the-beat swinging intensity that disappeared from his playing shortly thereafter, replaced by the languorous, behind-the-beat phrasing he became so famous for. The tempo is very fast, yet the ease with which he plays his two choruses belies the tremendous technique it took to pull it off. Peppered throughout these solos are many phrases that became part of jazz's lingua franca within a decade. There is an alternate take of "Shoe Shine Boy" that reveals Lester's creative way of varying what was already a "set" solo, and he catches the rhythm section off guard on more than one occasion with his subtle variations on the text. The influence of these recordings was immediate, but mostly for the radical redefinition of the rhythm section; Young's playing took a while to sink in to the musical community at large. The sixteen-year-old Charlie Parker learned to play chord changes and different keys by memorizing Lester's solos, and many aspects of Young remained in Parker's vocabulary. Some were verbatim phrases, but the more profound influence was in the realm of Lester's musical rhetoric. Hammond arranged jam sessions for the Basie-ites after they arrived in New York, and it was at one of them that Goodman and Young played together. Not only did they switch horns (Goodman eventually gave Lester a clarinet), but it was at that session that Basie and Walter Page first played with the guitarist Freddie Greene, who was in the house band led by drummer Kenny Clarke.

They were reunited a few weeks later at a Teddy Wilson recording session that inaugurated the legendary Young–Billie Holiday musical partnership ("This Year's Kisses," "He Ain't Got Rhythm," "I Must Have That Man"). Several weeks later, Holiday joined the Basie band, and the sheer amount of time she and Lester spent together making music contributed to the success of their collaborations. At the root of their conceptions was the ability to communicate sheer joy with none of the attendant hysteria that was mistaken in many quarters for "swing." Hear their duet on the last bridge of "Sailboat in the Moonlight" for its passion and understatement. In fact, the variety of songs and chord changes, and the unusual keys Young encountered on the Wilson-Holiday sessions, tell us more about the depth of his musicality than the more celebrated Basie recordings, where the keys and harmonic structures were quite limited. On many of the titles, Young plays while Holiday is singing, and what he creates is far from the traditional obbligato behind a vocalist. It is true counterpoint, and one can focus on either Young or Holiday with no loss of the melodic imperative that was one of the greatest legacies Armstrong bequeathed to them both. They even switch functions during the last bridge of "Who Wants Love": Young croons the melody while Holiday floats in and out around it, before they land in a perfect unison on the words "stories of castles in the air." Ironically, once their partnership attracted attention and her commercial potential increased, the format of the Holiday sessions became more standardized. There was now little room for the extended tenor sax/vocal conversations of the 1937 sessions, and they were replaced largely by more conventional written backgrounds. There were exceptions, the most intimate being the 1938 "You Can't Be Mine," where it sounds as if they are both only thinking their parts, so Zen-like and effortless is the communication.

The Kansas City Six recordings were made at the same time that fall and are similar to the Holiday series in that they reveal a subtler facet of Young's genius than we get on the Basie recordings. Organized by the Kansas City trombonist and innovative arranger-composer and electric guitarist Eddie Durham (who had just left the Basie band after a one-year stint as a de facto musical director), the session was played at a very low dynamic level. Jo Jones never has to go beyond whispering the beat with his brushes, yet the music that results is deeply felt, immensely swinging, and profoundly influenced by the blues—among the most prophetic and profound meditations on jazz ever recorded. On this session and the Glenn Hardman date done several months later, we get our best glimpses of Young's clarinet playing. It was so deceptively simple that no less a virtuoso than Artie Shaw exclaimed that "Lester played better clarinet than a lot of guys who played better clarinet than he did." His playing on "Pagin' the Devil" reveals much about the pure New Orleans roots of his blues conception, and the effervescent lyricism of "On the Sunny Side of the Street" makes one wish that he hadn't laid the instrument down until his last years, when he was too ill to play it—on recordings at least. Then there is the March 1939 session, which remained unissued until the mid-1970s, that produced "I Ain't Got Nobody," on which Lester solos on both clarinet and tenor and, unlike most musicians who "double," brings out the inherent qualities of each instrument. His playing over the ensemble riffs at the end of Jimmy Rushing's "Goin' to Chicago," which predates the more famous big band version, is a lesson in the true elegance of the jazz clarinet. The Hardman session, done at the same time, also has rare doses of Lester on both horns and is among the true treasures of his discography (hear also his Bix-like humorous breaks on "The Jazz-Me Blues").

But it was through the Basie records that Young had his greatest influence. It may have been the rhythm section and that entrancing combination of both the rural and the cosmopolitan in their blues that first drew listeners to Basie, but once they got there, Young's never-before-heard stylings were a major attraction. The Young solos on such Decca recordings as "One O'Clock Jump," "Jive at Five," "You Can Depend on Me," and "Every Tub" were memorized and repeated by an entire generation of players. Almost immediately, his influence spread to other players: Sam Donahue in Gene Krupa's band, Georgie Auld with Artie Shaw (who combined Young with Herschel Evans, as did Illinois Jacquet a couple of years later), and Budd Johnson (an old friend of Young's) with Earl Hines all played in the Young vein by 1939. Young was by leaps and bounds the most heavily featured sideman in the band, and as he entered his last year with Basie, he created one classic solo after another—"Tickle Toe" (his own composition), "Pound Cake," "Let Me See," "12th Street Rag," and "Clap Hands, Here Comes Charlie" being among the most influential. And within the Basie band itself, Young's willful harmonic contradictions ("Taxi War Dance," "Broadway") became a major part of trumpeter Harry Edison's vocabulary.

Big bands were the major component in popular music at the time, with all the attendant adulation and attention. Young had his share of admirers, including the more serious young musicians who, coming to maturity in the wake of Charlie Parker and Dizzy Gillespie, found in Young's approach a path through the complexity of what became known as bebop. But what these musicians heard Young play on all those nights spent in front of the Basie bandstand was never captured on disc. However, we get more than a glimpse of the free-flowing Young in full flight on a handful of broadcast recordings, most notably a 1939 *America Dances* broadcast to England. Young creates sounds and melodic phrases that do not show up anywhere else in his discography. Factor in all the testimony from the likes of Billie Holiday, Mary Lou Williams, and John Carisi that Young needed at least five choruses to warm up before he really began playing, and the value of these titles becomes clearer. On "Time Out" and "Swinging the Blues," Young imbues his tone with such a variety of hues and timbres that they become an equal partner with his already exalted melodic and rhythmic vocabularies. What results is a transcendence of the ordinary musical boundaries realized by only the greatest artists. The ascending swoops, hoarse hollers, keening cries, and bubbling laughter are all Young's own. It is at moments such as these that Young is truly reinventing his chosen instrument and expanding its emotional potential. His sense of abstraction matches that of Earl Hines or Art Tatum; the sheer level of swing and depth of blues feeling can be compared to the mature Armstrong and Parker.

Young's style continued to evolve throughout the Basie years. The full-toned declarative utterances of his 1937 work ("Honeysuckle Rose," "Yours and Mine") gave way to a svelte understatement, couched in a tone that the pianist-composer Mel Powell once described as "velvet" ("Five O'Clock Whistle," "Blow Top"). Young's sound was an integral element in the construction of his unique musical vision. Furthermore, Young constructed musical narratives that relied heavily on referring in abbreviated form to previously stated motifs. This also contributed to his masterly use of space. As with Thelonious Monk, the rests in Young's music became as significant as the notes. Young made his first recording of his signature theme, "Lester Leaps In," in 1939 with Basie's Kansas City Seven. While far from his most inspired playing, it is nonetheless a textbook example of many of his most famous devices. He is much more creative on the other tune recorded that day, "Dickie's Dream." The three extant takes reveal Young working over the same basic thematic material with a composer's patience. (Young's complete studio recordings with Basie from his first stint with the band are available in their entirety on a series issued by the French Classics label. The Basie airchecks cited have been issued on the VJC label, the Kansas City Six on Decca/GRP, and the Holiday titles on CBS/Sony.)

The untimely death of Herschel Evans in early 1939 set in motion a series of events that drove Young from the Basie band in late 1940. It was only natural that a player of his originality and untrammeled creativity would eventually become bored with the relatively limited solo opportunities of a big band, even if it was one of the best. The return of Coleman Hawkins to New York in mid-1939 and the success of his recording of "Body and Soul" must also have helped push Young along on the road to becoming a leader in his own right. It was also rumored that John Hammond, once Young's greatest booster, had advised Basie to refuse Young a raise, and Hammond's support—or, more precisely, its absence—was certainly a factor in Young's failure to establish himself as bandleader in 1941. But even more significant was Young's sensitive personality. In the cutthroat world of the music business, someone of his poetic nature didn't stand a chance. Young chose as his pianist Clyde Hart, whose musical sophistication and sense of the abstract were rare indeed. The band's only long-term engagement was three weeks at Kelly's Stable, opening on February 27, 1941, following Coleman Hawkins (whose pianist was Hart, at liberty given Young's lack of work). An altercation with a waiter—possibly having racial overtones—caused Young to literally walk out of the club, and that was the end of his bandleading career in New York. All that remains of the band is an aircheck ("Taxi War Dance," "Tickle Toe") and a session backing vocalist Una Mae Carlisle ("Blitzkrieg Baby," "Beautiful Eyes"). What makes this all the more tragic is that never again were all the facets of Young's art in such perfect concord; just the sound of Young playing a background at this time (Holiday's recording of "Romance in the Dark") is thrilling.

Before leaving for California to put together a band with his brother Lee, Young appeared on sessions with Billie Holiday ("All of Me," "Let's Do It") and Sammy Price ("Things About Coming My Way," "The Good Drag," "Just Jivin' Around") that are the last visions of this incarnation of Young. Lee Young was the antithesis of Lester—extroverted and highly motivated in the business end of music. Their band, with arrangements by Gerald Wilson and Billy Strayhorn, played around Los Angeles and had more than a modicum of success. The band never recorded, but one radio broadcast was preserved. Lester plays superbly on "Benny's Bugle," and his extended solo uses space in a fashion new even for him. The only studio recording he made during this time period supports the thesis that economy of means was preoccupying his musical thoughts. These four titles ("Tea for Two," "I Can't Get Started," "Indiana," and "Body and Soul") were made with pianist Nat Cole and bassist Red Callender, and they remain among the least known and most tantalizing items in his discography. The telepathy between Young and Cole reaches the same heights that his and Basie's had. In many ways, these sides presage the Apollonian elegance of Miles Davis's playing on "Kind of Blue": chord changes are replaced by an overarching lyricism that eschews the whole concept of "playing the changes."

On September 1, 1942, Lee and Lester Young's band opened at New York's Café Society Downtown, a club known for its enlightened racial policy. The band was a hit, their run was extended repeatedly, and Lester was finally achieving the stature he deserved as a leader. It all came to an abrupt end when Billy Young died in Los Angeles in early February 1943. After attending the funeral, Lee decided to stay on the West Coast. Lester returned to New York and failed to regain his professional footing. There was the occasional freelance work before he found a steady gig in the saxophone section of Al Sears's big band. There had already been overtures from the Basie band: Young's replacement, Don Byas, was giving the leader a hard time of it, and Lester was persuaded to fill in for a week at the Apollo Theater in October. After this came a truly astounding engagement at the Onyx Club on 52nd Street with a quintet co-led by Dizzy Gillespie and Oscar Pettiford. The drummer was Max Roach, and the original pianist was Thelonious Monk, replaced by George Wallington. Having to grapple with their unusual repertoire must have produced wonderful results, based on the way Young dealt with the new material thrown him on the Holiday sessions. (When left to his own devices, or while in the Basie band, there tended to be a great similarity in keys and chord progressions.)

As it turned out, Byas left Basie at the beginning of December, and he and Lester exchanged jobs. This must have been a traumatic event for Young—coming back to the very chair he had left three years earlier, headed for stardom. Albert Murray has identified in Young's style the sound of a soldier who has been through hell and has lived to tell the tale, and that sound creeps into Young's playing at this juncture. There also began to creep into his work a slight trace of ennui. His most outstanding work from this period comes from outside the band. The most well known was his debut session as a leader, done for Keynote in December 1943. Four titles were recorded, and there are two takes of each, which once again illustrates Lester's compositional approach toward improvisation. He takes a basic outline and bases his variations quite logically on it, hitting the major junctures at similar places in both takes but varying the route to them. The interplay with drummer Sid Catlett is a major component in the success of this session. Much of the up-tempo blues "Afternoon of a Basie-ite" is a joyful and humorous conversation in rhythms between the drums and the tenor. The heavy tone that many associate with Young's postwar work was really introduced on this session; indeed, at one junction during "I Never Knew," Young sounds uncharacteristically like Don Byas. But it was Young's laid-back reading of "Sometimes I'm Happy" that cast the largest shadow over the jazz world at the time. Though he turns the solo sections over to pianist Johnny Guarnieri and bassist Slam Stewart, it was Lester's coda that caught jazz's collective ear. His quote of an old song, "My Sweetie Went Away," became almost a mark of hipness when it was in turn quoted by legions of musicians who worshiped Young's playing. A few years later, Gerry Mulligan used it as the inspiration of his original "Jeru."

In August 1944, on the very Hollywood soundstage from which he would be taken by the Selective Service, Young, in the course of recording titles for possible use in the Warner Bros. short film *Jammin' the Blues*, made some of his best music of the period, most notably "If I Could Be With You" and "Sweet Georgia Brown," neither of which was used on the soundtrack. Young did go through hell during his fourteen months in the Army, winding up court-martialed and sentenced to the detention barracks. The routine physical and psychological testing recruits undergo before admission should have made it clear that Young was not military material. Nonetheless, he was inducted and not allowed to play in the camp band where he was stationed; things went rapidly downhill from there. The tragic ironies that mark his case remain an indictment of racism in the U.S. military.

Young went directly from the depths of his imprisonment to the greatest heights of his career within the space of six months in 1946. Behind it all was Norman Granz, a jazz entrepreneur who had be-friended Young in 1942 and had produced *Jammin' the Blues.* Through a canny manipulation of personal management and concerts that were recorded, Granz maintained a stable of jazz artists for over a decade; using his clout to fight for integration wherever his product was sold, he broke down many walls. Lester Young stayed in Granz's circle for the greater part of his thirteen remaining years. Work with his own band alternated with Jazz at the Philharmonic tours that took him to Europe on several occasions. His finest postwar moments in the recording studio took place mostly in the company of great pianists. A second trio with Nat Cole (this time with Buddy Rich) has Young outlining the harmonies in a much more obvious way than was his wont. There were also a poetic series of quartet dates with John Lewis in 1950–51, an invigorating 1952 session with Oscar Peterson, and a charming, almost nostalgic reunion with Teddy Wilson in 1956.

Once again, it is the live recordings that supply a more direct reading of Young's true abilities. His first tour after his discharge found him featured alongside Coleman Hawkins, and the 1946 Carnegie Hall versions of "Lady Be Good" and "Sweet Georgia Brown" recall the nimble-fingered glory days of the mid-1930s. A recently discovered 1947 Town Hall concert (which received reviews so dismal that Young himself rebutted them in print) has perhaps definitive versions of such Young staples as "These Foolish Things" and "Just You, Just Me." Then there is the justly celebrated 1949 Carnegie Hall JATP concert with Charlie Parker, and to hear the two of them on "Embraceable You" is as instructive as it is rare. Some of the frustration that Young might very well have felt on all those JATP concerts when he was forced to listen to lesser players get ovation after ovation using his own devices tastelessly seems to have come out on the 1952 "Jam Session Blues," where he piles one honking climax atop another, showing what he could have always done, if he had not had the taste not to.

But the most fascinating of all Young's postwar recordings was made in a German nightclub in 1956. Although one can only wish that something like this could have been recorded fifteen years earlier, we finally get to hear Young stretching out over several minutes on both the blues and on his longtime theme song, "Lester Leaps In." It is not just the length of the solos that makes these recordings so precious, it is the content. As in the 1939 *American Dances* broadcasts, we hear melodies and eccentric instrumental techniques that Young never used in the recording studio. Most interesting is the leisurely way the choruses are paced, with thematic references reaching across a sea of choruses; this is an element of Young's genius that was not lost on the young Sonny Rollins.

Young died on March 15, 1959; his final years were marked by a gradual descent into alcoholism that would also ensnare his great rival Coleman Hawkins a decade later. And although in some circles his life has been viewed, as was Billie Holiday's, as an unmitigated tragedy, there was certainly a lot more joy and love of life than we have been led to believe.

What remains is the music, and the question that Sonny Rollins once posed: exactly what planet did Lester Young come from?

Streamlining Jazz: Major Soloists of the 1930s and 1940s

John McDonough

In the '30s and '40s streamlining became the essence of a modern sensibility that found many expressions. It was a beauty born out of motion, not emotion. And because jazz itself was an expression of motion in rhythmic terms, it inevitably felt its influence. This essay is about that confluence and the work of a second generation of soloists who got jazz moving in the form of swing.

Ever since Louis Armstrong's lionhearted cadenza at the top of "West End Blues" or his three-chorus aria on "Tight Like This" (Okeh/Columbia) first sounded the call, the hero-soloist has been the spiritual essence of jazz: manifestly original, defiant, and the supreme symbol of the primacy of the individual over the group.

But heroes must have limits to conquer. Jazz in the '30s and '40s was a music challenging the limits of its origins. In its early days passion was inclined to count more than polish, and no one judged another's often self-taught intonation or attack too severely if the feeling was there. What changed in the '30s was that important soloists came to judge these matters very seriously indeed. In the struggle to outgrow its origins, jazz became caught up in an arms race of virtuosity that took the solo from folk art to popular art to the portals

206

of high art. Speed, range, accuracy, elegance of phrase, and harmonic daring became the battlefields.

But the real beneficiary was content. Conceptual advances were enabled by expanding perimeters of knowledge, technique, and rhythmic insight largely set by a succession of major soloists. Example: Red Allen began as an Armstrong clone on "Biff'ly Blues" and "Everybody Shout" (Victor). But he found his voice with Fletcher Henderson in such recordings as "Yeah Man!" and "Queer Notions" (Vocalion/Columbia) where he broke Armstrong's ideas into more intricate rhythmic sequences. This is because Armstrong thought in terms of the quarter note; Allen, the eighth note. Technique followed concept.

In the late '30s Harry James and Roy Eldridge then pushed the perimeter wider. Building on Armstrong, James replaced his mentor's sense of formal rhythmic symmetry with a broad, cocky lyricism, seasoned with quirky dissonances and startling, often ripping breaks in his phrasing. Framing these ingredients in a sleek, rolling flow of eighth notes, James could sustain solos of spectacular momentum and assurance that brought these contradictory elements into balance. Solos with the Benny Goodman orchestra on "Roll 'Em," "St. Louis Blues" (Columbia), and "Honeysuckle Rose" (Blu-Disc/Phontastic), or on "I Found a New Baby" (Brunswick/Columbia) and "Sheik of Araby" (Varsity/Savoy) with his own band, are prime examples, recorded before he deployed his talents to more commercial purposes.

Eldridge upped the ante in his own way by building on Red Allen's virtues, then sharpening his attack and range at fast tempos. Years later he would tell interviewers that he wanted to play the trumpet like the saxophone. This demanded an unprecedented precision and articulation that let him pack a whirling force of energy and movement into his solos and pace it all to peak and break at the crest of the tension. He often marked these crests with screech notes of fracturing force. But he seldom lingered over them, as if they were something stately and special. In early solos on "After You've Gone" and especially "Heckler's Hop" (Vocalion/Columbia), he blew them off with a sudden, explosive jolt and moved on. By the time Eldridge made his second "After You've Gone" with Gene Krupa's band in 1941 (Columbia), his breathtaking speed was consuming notes into long, strobing streaks of sound which the ear heard as wild, careening glissandos that defied all precedents of trumpet technique. By 1940 James, Eldridge, and others had led jazz to a new standard of musical technology that turned syncopation into swing with a looseness and

Red Norvo recording in wartime, New York, 1940s. Courtesy Frank Driggs Collection.

spontaneity it hadn't had before and that would one day take the music to the next round in the arms race, bebop.

Almost as soon as swing defined itself as jazz, the music faced its first real controversy. Was swing the real thing or some denatured commercial concentrate corrupting a music in which success was commonly viewed with suspicion? It was an argument that led to the first split in the jazz culture. Behind one barricade stood the Purists, armed with a belief that the only true jazz was traditional, hot, and small enough to fit on a very tiny bandstand. One Purist was Milt Gabler, whose Commodore Record Shop became a Manhattan safe house for those impatient with the adulterations of swing. In 1938 he launched Commodore Records and began recording worthy players in sessions typically (but not exclusively) organized according to the primary Commodore creed, dixieland.

Although history tends to condescend to dixie today, in the late '30s it was still a significant, free-spirited, and relatively contemporary alternative to what some saw as the regimentation of the big bands. Moreover, swing had made jazz conscious of its roots and inspired a desire to preserve them before it was too late. The ghost of Bix Beiderbecke was already feeding the fable that jazz musicians were sensitive souls likely to burn themselves out early. Commodore was the first to answer the call. A year later came Blue Note, which many forget built its reputation on hot traditional jazz long before it discovered Thelonious Monk and Miles Davis. At the same time, the major companies began looking more closely into their vaults for material to reissue. In 1938 Victor produced an album of twelve Beiderbecke pieces, mostly with Paul Whiteman's band. Then in 1940 the first continuing programs of album reissues were launched by George Avakian at Columbia and Dave Dexter at Decca.

What's interesting about this sudden focus on history, though, is that jazz was still very young. Most of the major soloists who personified its past were no older than those playing in the contemporary big bands. The struggle between past and present was less a matter of generation than of context.

Bud Freeman was a swing star with the Tommy Dorsey and Benny Goodman bands when he became house tenor saxophonist at Commodore in 1938. His wide vibrato would have been hot on any other instrument but sounds oddly dry and supple in his hands. Freeman was an original not owing too much to either Coleman Hawkins or Lester Young. He played in short, balanced phrases, though with the right rhythm section he could produce fluent, legato sprints that hinted at Young.

Another Commodore regular was Pee Wee Russell, whose roots went back to the '20s, when he played a relatively correct clarinet. But his sound and phrasing grew so eccentric in the '30s, he escaped classification. His eccentricities were sheltered and celebrated by the Purists, but not imitated. His sound quivered and shook in the upper register, croaked and growled in the lower, while his lines lurched in lumpy rhythmic cadences that seemed to tie themselves in little knots. For the nonconforming jazz fan, he was the ideal object of awe.

Freeman, Russell, Eddie Condon, Muggsy Spanier, Wild Bill Davison, George Brunies, Max Kaminsky, Joe Sullivan, Art Hodes, Jimmy McPartland, and other old Chicago hands were joined by rediscovered New Orleans veterans who saw their careers revived by swing: Sidney Bechet, Kid Ory, Jimmie Noone, and, briefly, even the Original Dixieland Jazz Band. Over it all Bix Beiderbecke persisted as a mythic figure.

Then in 1936 Boston writer George Frazier announced in *Down Beat* that he'd found the next Bix, a young guitarist-turned-cornetist named Bobby Hackett. Though Hackett insisted Armstrong was his model, his warm tone and smooth, easy attack had an affinity for the kind of soft-spoken melodic variations that had distinguished Beiderbecke—but which, alas, were now out of fashion in the '30s race to virtuosity. Yet Hackett managed to fill a historic gap without sounding historic. Even on a Bix staple such as "Singin' the Blues" (Vocalion), his notes were chosen with adroit discretion and fell into place with the precision of ball bearings. His style had an unforced, self-effacing polish that was, in its way, quite in tune with the modern polish of swing. Yet he traveled with the Purists and is remembered largely as a dixieland player, proving the ultimate power of context over content.

Another major soloist whose fate was influenced by context was Jack Teagarden. He might have been the preeminent trombonist of the swing era. But in 1934 he turned down offers from a still unknown Benny Goodman and instead sought shelter from the Depression in a five-year contract with Paul Whiteman. When Goodman went to the top, Teagarden was left sitting out the prime years of the swing era as a featured soloist in an out-of-fashion dance band. After forming his own band in 1939, he seemed to sink out of sight, at least if the polls of the time are to be believed. Yet his smooth, shock-proof phrasing, lyrical sound, and flawlessly integrated triplets put him among the most important trombone soloists. He sounds downright jaunty in 1940 with Ben Webster and Dave Tough on "Shine" and "The World Is Waiting for the Sunrise" (H.R.S.). These and his late-'40s work with Louis Armstrong's All Star group (caught in magnificent concert performances at Town Hall and Symphony Hall) helped provide the lifeline by which historians have salvaged his reputation.

But in the larger picture, the Purists' fundamentalism was a rearguard action, not a beachhead position. Wrapped in a second-generation notion of the one true jazz with its songbook of traditional blues and stomps, they had no way of seeing yet that there was no future in being the second anything, the next anybody. Critical mass was with the big bands. It was their soloists who would give the period its own original identity.

I would suggest that that identity not only evolved out of the music but was influenced by a larger cultural context as well. Jazz chugged into the '30s as a Model T and rode out a streamliner. The analogy is instructive because jazz, like art, architecture, and design, had always been an element of twentieth-century modernism. In the mid-'30s swing, with its long, flowing lines cruising over a dynamic and unbroken rhythmic flow, was a logical expression of a spirit of modernity that found beauty in notions of speed, progress, and aerodynamic technologies; in design principles that merged various subforms into a kind of dynamic continuum through smooth, rounded, transitional lines. Within a few short months during 1934–35 these principles of functional simplicity came together with remarkable suddenness and ubiquity: diesel streamliners, the Burlington Zephyr, the Chrysler Airflow, Flash Gordon, the biomorphic silhouette of Jean Harlow in satin, and that masterwork of streamlining, the DC-3.

As airplanes and actresses moved through space, swing moved through time: swiftly and smoothly. Melody was stripped and rounded into the "functional simplicity" of the riff. Bennie Moten's "Blue Room" (Victor) anticipated this in 1932. Layer by layer, the melodic formalities are peeled back until all that is left at the end is a single-note proxy. Swing evolved from the more formal syncopation of early jazz and became the natural matrix of a popular musical abstraction of the modern machine: clean, precise, and magnificently technocratic. The breakthrough of jazz to pop status jelled when its essential form, swing, came into alignment with a fundamental spirit of the times driven by a sense of forward motion and intellectual progress. It would seem more than coincidence that the first DC-3 took to the air as the airways sprang to life with the sound of Benny Goodman's clarinet and the long elegant lines of his theme, "Let's Dance."

Trains became a direct inspiration for Duke Ellington's 1933

"Daybreak Express" (RCA Victor) and Count Basie's less literal "Super Chief" and "9:20 Special" (both Okeh/Columbia). Though "Jumpin' at the Woodside" (Decca) is named for a hotel, it embodies an air-splitting sense of velocity that is far closer to the way one might imagine a Zephyr.

One of the early indicators of rhythmic streamlining came when the beat started its shift from the rigid framework of the press roll and began to glide on the steely, sustaining float of the hi-hat cymbal. The drummers who defined various aspects of swing rhythm are well known: Sid Catlett, Gene Krupa, Chick Webb, Buddy Rich, Dave Tough, and even, in a nonstandard kind of way, Sonny Greer. But if they are the Raymond Loewys and Norman Bel Geddeses of jazz rhythm, Walter Johnson may well be the Constantin Brancusi. With Fletcher Henderson in 1932–33 he pioneered the hi-hat's capacity to produce a subtle, elastic, more continuous beat on "New King Porter Stomp" and "Yeah Man" (Vocalion). Yet, of the five soloists we hear on "New King Porter Stomp," including Coleman Hawkins and Rex Stewart, only trombonist J. C. Higginbotham seems to move into Johnson's relaxed, pliant groove. Hawkins sounds almost resistant, playing against the flow with arching, out-of-tempo arpeggios.

If there is one person who personifies and objectifies the evolution of two-beat syncopation into the penetrating purity of four-four swing, it is the silvery, metallic motion machine that was drummer Jo Jones and the first Count Basie rhythm section. The Brancusi comparison may be closer to the mark with Jones. Just as his "Bird in Space" did not represent a bird but flight itself, Jones's hi-hat sound sculptures transcended "the beat" to time itself. Even when Basie ensembles chopped or doddled, the propulsive sizzle of Jones's shifting cymbal triplets, underpinned by the gentle cut of Walter Page (bass) and Freddie Green (guitar), gave them an aerodynamic thrust and became a force soloists could not ignore.

Of the major swing soloists, none moved in more perfect register with the new aerodynamic spirit than tenor saxophonist Lester Young. Someone once described his sound as hollow and tubular, an interesting literary image of a sound; one suggested, perhaps subliminally, by the rounded, legato geometries of his art deco rhythmic flow. It was a soft, unsentimental tone well suited to Young's unexpected phrasings. There is a 1940 "I Got Rhythm" broadcast (Jazz Archives) in which he sails in on nearly six bars of sheer rhythmic motion chewing on a single F. The music that follows is less remarkable for its content than for its explicitly gliding sense of movement. In a 1939 jam session on "Lady Be Good" (Vanguard), he launches a second chorus with a sudden jet stream of triplets. The smooth, continuous swerves and arching swoop that follow seem entirely consistent with other expressions of streamlining outside music: the natural curves of an Eero Saarinen or Charles Eames silhouette, or the long, gliding suspension cables over the Golden Gate Bridge.

Young was not the first soloist to address and amend the new rules of motion and shape in the '30s. Different soloists came to swing's evolving functional simplicity of rhythm in different ways. By its nature the trombone lent itself to smooth surfaces and long, seamless curves, a fact which made Tommy Dorsey and Lawrence Brown major influences by the sheer force of their mastery. But no one exploited the horn's capacities with more originality or whimsy than Dicky Wells. His freedom from formal tempo and oblique phrasing are evident, if a bit ill at ease, in conventional swing charts like "Harlem Twister" and "Marie" (Victor) with Teddy Hill. But they suddenly make sense with Young on "Dickie's [sic] Dream" (Vocalion), in which he and Young become mirror images of each other in their mutual affinity for the unexpected and their brief overlap of solos.

Among brass and reed players, most grew along lines set down in the late '20s by Louis Armstrong and Coleman Hawkins, who founded the basic dynasties by which (or against which) major soloists of the '30s and '40s would be classified. Though Armstrong was content to retire as an innovator by the mid-'30s and live largely off his musical interest, the innovations themselves would echo well into the '40s in the work of others, who would spend whole careers digesting, perfecting, and extending their implications. But of all the lights Armstrong lit, none was more prophetic than his spectacular sound and dramatic flair with high notes. Though not a trumpet virtuoso by formal standards, he gave an impression of virtuosity. And from that issued the march of jazz from its folk origins to greater options through technique.

The Armstrong-Allen-James-Eldridge-Gillespie progression has been noted. But other trumpets of the period also left lasting impressions. Ziggy Elman's boldness produced performances of astonishing spectacle on "Gin for Christmas" with Lionel Hampton and "Hawaiian War Chant" from a broadcast with Tommy Dorsey (Victor). The astringent lyricism of Harry "Sweets" Edison had a rhythmic drive and modern edge to it, but without the modern expedients of speed and harmonic surprise. And Oran "Hot Lips" Page and Taft

Jordan established identities for themselves that held close to the Armstrong model.

Then there was Charlie Shavers, virtually the only major soloist who made his reputation outside a big band. Shavers was a trumpeter unlike any other. His Olympian command gave him easy access to an unlimited musical vocabulary, which included trills, triple-tongued acrobatics, and a vibrato that strutted and pranced when he wanted it to. He folded them all into a stabbing attack of astonishing precision, power, and often playfulness. That precision was the backbone of the John Kirby Sextet, a sleekly structured, some might even say dainty, yet driving ensemble with a penchant for crystalizing even classical themes into biting little riffs. Shavers's cup-muted trumpet blended with Buster Bailey's clarinet and Russell Procope's alto to give the balance and illusion of a big band. But on "Royal Garden Blues" (Vocalion), he briefly unleashes his open horn and lets loose the kind of sharp, almost shrill intonation and fearsome audacity that kept challengers at a distance.

The audacity in Bunny Berigan's playing was less spectacular, but the spirit of Armstrong lay closer to its core. He played fluent solos in a warm tone seasoned with a hot vibrato and mapped often ingenious passages between upper and lower trumpet registers. Fans developed an ear for his work through fine choruses piggybacked onto Benny Goodman's "Sometimes I'm Happy" (Victor) and especially Tommy Dorsey's megasellers "Marie" and "Song of India" (Victor). They boosted his status to leader and led to his 1937 magnum opus, "I Can't Get Started," a tune on which he had already built a series of stately cadenzas and theme statements. It ran a perfectly paced gamut from somber reserve to cathartic triumph and back again in the most ascendent Armstrong manner. All that and an early death at the hands of his own weaknesses inflated his reputation to mythic proportions. Though this view has moderated, Berigan remains a leading voice of his time.

Not everyone competed in the virtuoso game. Buck Clayton played dozens of small-scale, finely honed solos with the early Basie band and on many small-band sessions with Teddy Wilson and Billie Holiday. His gentle precision is at its silkiest on "I Know That You Know" and "Way Down Yonder in New Orleans" from 1938 (Commodore). His open trumpet attack was delicate and laid-back, and it sang with a soft tangy vibrato well captured on "After Theater Jump" and "Six Cats and a Prince" (Keynote, 1944).

Cootie Williams and Rex Stewart were confirmed Ellingtonians with contrasting sounds but a common interest in unorthodox timbres. Williams joined a massive, majestic sound to the plunger mute, which served him as brilliantly with the Benny Goodman orchestra ("Superman," Columbia) and sextet ("Royal Garden Blues," "Benny's Bugle," "Breakfast Feud," all Columbia) as with Ellington. Stewart had a smaller, more tart tone and a brittle, punchy attack that suggested bottled-up intensity. He made artful use of freak half-value ("Boy Meets Horn," Brunswick) and subtone ("Menelik," Victor) effects that marked him as an interesting maverick. Williams and Stewart battled to a dazzling draw in "Tootin' Through the Roof" (Brunswick), a resplendent but neglected Ellington gem from 1939.

Outside of Bud Freeman and Lester Young, nearly every important tenor saxophonist through the mid-'40s was a subcategory of Coleman Hawkins, who had removed himself to Europe during the crucial 1934–39 period, as if to give his disciples space to grow on their own. But his big sound was a constant that marked a generation of tenors, many of whom literally followed in his footsteps. It was Ben Webster, for instance, who replaced him with Fletcher Henderson as Webster hopscotched through the '30s from Bennie Moten to Henderson to Cab Calloway to Teddy Wilson and finally to Ellington in 1940. His early solos with Moten and Henderson are fervent and overeager. A recognizable profile appears on "Sing You Sinners" and an unissued "Stealin' Apples" (Vocalion) with Henderson. When we pick him up in 1939 with Teddy Wilson ("71," "Exactly Like You," Vocalion) and Lionel Hampton ("Early Session Hop"), suddenly Webster's voice has acquired the three-day beard that would give it its edge. By the time he recorded with Sid Catlett's quartet in 1944 (Commodore), he had become a rhapsodic ballad player, whose smooth, rounded phrasings could take a song from soft pillow talk to erotic passion in one chorus.

If Webster followed Hawkins, the man who often followed Webster was Chu Berry, whose short but brilliant career was well documented before his death in 1941. He emerges early with Benny Carter's first band of 1933 and comes into his own in the mid-'30s with good, punchy solos on Henderson's "Stealin' Apples" and "Christopher Columbus" (Vocalion). If Roy Eldridge was a reflection of Hawkins transposed to trumpet, Berry was a refection of Eldridge transposed back to tenor. Both were speed players. On "Jangled Nerves" with Henderson and "Swing Is Here" with a Gene Krupa small group (both Victor), each keeps pace with the fastest tempos in galloping lines of glancing eighth notes that share a strikingly similar shape and intensity. Slowed down a bit and with vibrato throbbing, Berry comes on like a torrent on "Sweethearts on Parade," a sleek, churning juggernaut of swing tenor with Lionel Hampton (Victor) that may be his finest single record. Though he fielded a smaller tone than Hawkins or Webster, his ballads combined intimacy and breadth. He took on "Body and Soul" a year before Hawkins and gives "Star Dust," "Sunny Side of the Street" (all Commodore), and "Ghost of a Chance" with Cab Calloway (Columbia) solid romantic dimension.

Lester Young remained a one-man dynasty, much admired by critics but rarely adopted by musicians as a model. It would fall to the first wave of the bop generation (Wardell Gray, Stan Getz) to fully pick up his lead. The last important tenors to come out of swing in the '40s still favored the Hawkins lineage: Illinois Jacquet, who wrote the book on programmed pandemonium with Hampton; Don Byas, whose quick ear caught some early theoretical stirrings of bop; and Flip Phillips, who arrived last and tied everything together in a well-balanced summation of the Hawkins-Webster-Young era.

The swing era was a rare meritocracy. Most of the best big bands were actually led not by singers or comics but by their finest soloists: Benny Carter, Harry James, the Dorseys, Gene Krupa, and later Dizzy Gillespie. But Artie Shaw and Benny Goodman, both clarinetists, were the most famous brand names of their time and among the most brilliant soloists. It would be hard to hear the makings of stardom in Shaw's early work. But he forced himself to grow and mastered a sound of enormous dimension: big, round, poised in the middle register; a hard, brittle shell of perfection in the top that could quiver with a hair-raising vibrato. Less an improviser than an interpreter, he reconfigured melodies in variations punctuated by grace notes and pirouettes. The distance of his lines seemed to stretch for bars through phrases that appeared to duck through shadows as if unbroken by a breath, a remarkable signature of implication and illusion. His solo on "Star Dust" (RCA Victor) achieved a special immortality because of its popularity, but his variations on other standards such as his two versions of "It Had to Be You" (Victor) were no less sublime. Though not a hot player, he navigated riff pieces like "Everything's Jumpin'" and cyclones like "The Carioca" and "Traffic Jam" (Victor) with elegance and passion.

The soloist who set the pace in the Goodman band was, of course, Goodman, the first jazz musician to record Mozart. Yet the ghost and spirit of New Orleans and Chicago were all over every note he played, especially in the fervent pitch fluctuations that made his solos sear with a heat surpassed only by Edmond Hall. Like Norman Zapf, who in 1934 dropped a smooth steel skin over a Hudson locomotive to produce America's first streamlined steam engine, Goodman dropped a prodigious virtuosity over the work of his early mentors to produce an equally modern musical silhouette. Goodman and his immensely symbolic Carnegie Hall concert seemed proof of the technocratic notion that refined technique was not a barrier to passion but, as in classical music, a key to it. Not a crutch but a lamp.

This was certainly born out in the mid-'40s when bebop changed the basic grammar of the music for all instruments. What no one could have predicted, however, was that the bop revolution would spring from an alto saxophone. The alto was regarded as something of a section horn in prebop days. Though it gave us Tab Smith, Hilton Jefferson, Earle Warren, Willie Smith, Jimmy Dorsey, Russell Procope, and Pete Brown, only Johnny Hodges and Benny Carter achieved peerage among the major soloists. Hodges played with a relaxed, legato attack at faster tempos; but his real gift was his sound, a rich timbre ideal for finger painting in long, mournful smears of blue. Though he recorded a landmark version of "Sunny Side of the Street" in 1937 (Victor), one that forever changed the way musicians heard the song, his key work of the '30s and '40s was an aspect of the larger Ellington picture and is best considered in that context.

Carter was unique among the major soloists in that he was equally influential as an arranger-composer. But the arranger behind "Lonesome Nights," "I'm Comin', Virginia" (Swing), and "All of Me" (Victor) was only an ensemble projection of the soloist on "Crazy Rhythm" (Swing), "I Can't Believe That You're in Love With Me," and "Smack" (Commodore). Carter favored medium to fast tempos. The brilliant Commodores, especially the two vastly different takes of "I Can't Believe," give us a rich composite of his style elements: the jump cuts over wide intervals, the fast connecting slurs, the easy moves in and out of tempo, and the buoyant sound that lent itself so well to such shifting tensions.

Once when considering the conflicting pressures of art and commerce, Artie Shaw devised a compromise: "Three chords for beauty and one to pay the rent," that is, if the last chord pays enough, it can subsidize the first three. So to take refuge from market tyranny, Shaw and other leaders created safety zones where their best soloists could play in protected preserves. Woody Herman had the Woodchoppers, Basie the Kansas City Six, and Shaw the Gramercy Five. But no one was more influential than Goodman, whose quartet and sextet not only made remarkable music but brought the first electronic instruments into jazz, first Lionel Hampton on vibraphone, then Charlie Christian on electric guitar. Each symbolized the perfection possible when technology and art meet.

The vibes became a class-A jazz instrument in the hands of Hampton, who joined Goodman in 1936 and made ballads such as "Moonglow" (Victor) shimmer as convincingly as he made rhythm standards swing with torrential turbulence. In the rush of his solos, he nonchalantly threw off ideas that became staples in the Goodman repertoire: "Flying Home," "Dizzy Spells," "Opus 1/2," "Shivers," and "Til Tom Special." At the same time, he put together under his own name for Victor twenty-three ad hoc sessions that became a procession of the leading soloists of the time. He went on to lead a big band for more than half a century. But little he did after Goodman significantly raised his standing as a major soloist.

Red Norvo made his reputation on what Leonard Feather called a "dehydrated vibraphone," the xylophone. It had a fragile, glassy sound that seemed breakable and designed for fine detail, not Dionysian disinhibition. With no place to hide, Norvo crafted carefully phrased, creative solos that were in proportion to the astute and gentle arrangements Eddie Sauter fashioned for his band in the '30s. In 1944 Norvo joined Teddy Wilson in the Goodman Sextet and made the transition to vibes, though eschewing its motorized vibrato. The three make a vivid front line playing ensembles like "Slipped Disc" (Columbia) in thirds, and the vibes gave Norvo's solos a tensile strength not possible on the xylophone. In 1946 Norvo moved on to Woody Herman and became brain trust of the decade's most advanced band-within-a-band short of bop, the Woodchoppers.

If the small groups of the era were one safety zone for musicians, the ultimate retreat was the jam session. Here musicians could kick ideas around among the cognoscenti without threat of public accountability. Since most fans were denied access to these private sanctums, they acquired a certain mystique. By the mid-'40s, though, much of the jazz establishment was centralized on 52nd Street in New York, making possible occasional all-star concerts that featured staged jam sessions. None was more anticipated than the Esquire All-American Jazz Concert in 1944, where the history of jazz seemed to assemble at the Metropolitan Opera House for a few final hours of consensus before the arrival of bop: Armstrong, Eldridge, Norvo, Hampton, Hawkins, Teagarden, Tatum, and more. They all jammed on "Flying Home" and "I Got Rhythm."

Meanwhile, in Los Angeles, a young promoter named Norman

Granz was organizing jam sessions in a small network of L.A. clubs on their off-nights. They were drawing customers and attention. In July 1944 he rented L.A.'s Philharmonic Auditorium for $175 and booked a handpicked crew that included Nat Cole, Illinois Jacquet, and J. J. Johnson for what *Down Beat* called at the time "the city's first full-scale jazz concert." With that, the jam session became a stage show. By the turn of the decade Jazz at the Philharmonic had replaced the big bands as the biggest brand name in jazz.

In early concerts in Carnegie Hall, in 1938–39, jazz was on its best behavior. But JATP was less restrained. With plenty of seats and regular performances, the audiences were young, demonstrative, and perhaps the least culturally housebroken concertgoers ever to cross a philharmonic threshold. Critics derided their behavior and attacked Granz as a profiteer. But he had the loyalty of the musicians and saw to it that a lot of the profits ended up in their pockets.

JATP performed several historic functions. First, by mixing the best swing (Hawkins, Young, Eldridge, Webster, Carter) and bebop players (Parker, Gillespie, J. J. Johnson, Hank Jones), it erased the notion that bop was for the hip and the old-timers could take a walk. It drew the two generations together. More important were its marketing innovations. If Charlie Parker revolutionized the music, JATP revolutionized the way it was sold. Concerts and LPs "personally supervised by Norman Granz" made headliners out of sidemen, and live recordings presented jazz as a documentary made in performance, not studio limbo. Concerts leveraged records, records leveraged concerts, and Granz built the first vertically integrated jazz enterprise in history.

By the end of the '40s swing and popular music had gone their separate ways and new innovations were making jazz itself increasingly complex and categorized: trad, swing, bop, progressive, cool, hard bop, and the beginnings of an avant-garde with Lennie Tristano. There wasn't one style or two, as there had been before the war. There were many with more on the way, and all competing with each other for a shrinking base of young listeners.

Perhaps it wasn't so surprising that one of the last persons to have a major impact on the music as the '40s ended was not a musician but a salesman.

Jazz Singing: Between Blues and Bebop

Joel E. Siegel

Debates about what constitutes jazz singing, and which vocalists should be embraced by or excluded from the jazz community, have raged for decades. Earlier in the century such definitions and discriminations were of less consequence. From the mid-'20s through World War II, American music evolved and flourished in a myriad of overlapping styles—folk, gospel, blues, jazz, musical theater, swing, and Tin Pan Alley ballads and novelties. These two decades of artistic ferment and fusion were, arguably, the most fertile epoch in the development of our national popular music. In such a fecund era, there was little need or time for categories.

If Al Jolson, who derived his style from vaudeville and minstrel shows, could be celebrated as "the jazz singer," it's evident that the term has never been precisely defined. Some singers (Ethel Waters, Bing Crosby) began performing and recording with jazz accompaniment, then expanded their horizons (and downplayed the jazz elements) to conquer Broadway, Hollywood, and the Hit Parade. Others (Annette Hanshaw, Lee Wiley) grew increasingly influenced by jazz musicians as their careers evolved. Instrumentalists (Louis Armstrong, Jack Teagarden) doubled as inspired singers; the Boswell Sisters and the Mills Brothers imitated instrumental groups with startling accuracy.

The task of establishing criteria for jazz singing collapses under the weight of contradictions, ambiguities, and exceptions. If we insist that a jazz vocalist must improvise upon (rather than merely embellish) melodies, then we have to exclude Wiley and Ivie Anderson. If we only include singers who transform lyrics into personal statements, how do we classify Ella Fitzgerald and Maxine Sullivan, whose paramount impulses were melodic and rhythmic rather than emotionally expressive? Or Slim Gaillard, who invented his own language; or Leo Watson, who sometimes did away with language altogether?

Just as the short story can only be incontrovertibly defined as something briefer than other forms of prose fiction, the sine qua non of jazz vocalizing is musicianship: the ability to sing and swing authoritatively in a jazz context. Beyond this, acceptance by jazz musicians, reviewers, and fans is meted out on a case-by-case basis. A vocalist with faulty pitch, stiff time, and clumsy phrasing should not be encouraged to apply, yet one can name bona fide jazz singers with at least one of these technical problems. Better, finally, to forget about pigeonholing and examine the contributions of singers whose work has been influenced by, and in turn has inspired, other jazz artists.

Such a survey necessarily emphasizes female singers. With a few notable exceptions, women in this period were restrained from distinguishing themselves as jazz instrumentalists but readily accepted as vocalists. Unconstrained by codes of masculine behavior that discourage displays of emotion, women vocalists were free to express themselves more openly and spontaneously than their male counterparts. Largely for this reason—and there are others—singing was (and remains) the sole area of jazz primarily developed by women.

More than any other performer, Ethel Waters is responsible for fusing black and white musical traditions into the hybrid art of jazz singing and, beyond that, American popular song. The impoverished daughter of a thirteen-year-old rape victim, the young Waters fantasized escape from her oppressive surroundings by imitating black actors and music hall artistes. At her 1917 Baltimore stage debut, she sang "St. Louis Blues"; subsequently, billed as Sweet Mama Stringbean, she toured southern black theaters performing blues and risqué novelties.

Waters made her first recording in 1921. Lacking the raw power of Bessie Smith's majestic voice, Waters sang blues with optimistic vibrancy, an expression of her indomitable nature. She sails through

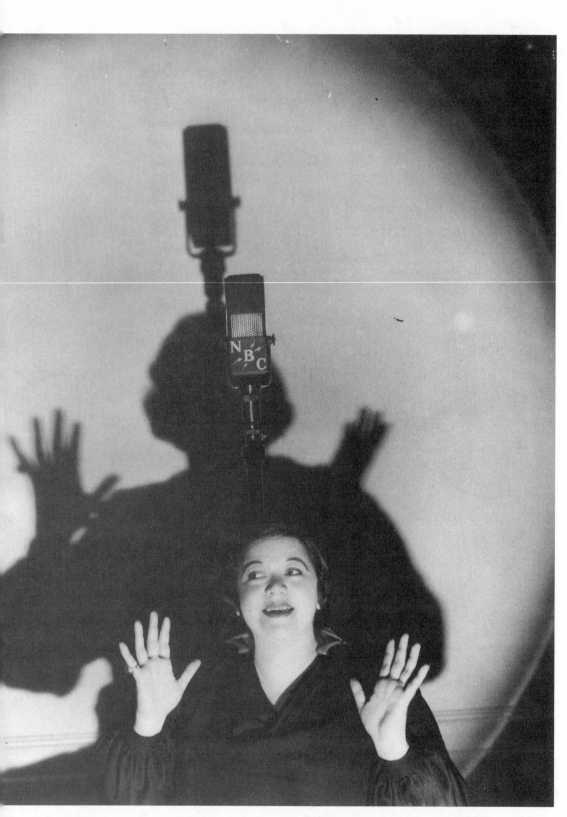

Mildred Bailey, NBC publicity photo. Courtesy of the Institute of Jazz Studies, Rutgers University.

the sixteen-bar choruses of 1923's "Ethel Sings 'Em," a precursor of Billie Holiday's "Fine and Mellow," without conceding that social, economic, or romantic adversity could possibly defeat her. In Waters's case, blues singing was merely a stepping-stone to a career that would transcend racial, artistic, and even national boundaries.

As ambitious as she was gifted, Waters sought to reach the more affluent white audience that supported Nora Bayes, Sophie Tucker, and other highly paid vaudeville headliners. A superb mimic with a quick ear, she welcomed the challenge of fresh repertoire. After touring with pianist Fletcher Henderson, in 1925 she replaced the legendary Florence Mills at the Plantation Club on Broadway, where she introduced (and promptly recorded) "Dinah," one of her signature pieces. Even this early, one notices the rolled *r*'s and other elocutionary refinements she borrowed from her white counterparts. These mannerisms sometimes hardened into affectations; her 1930 recording of "Memories of You" is more Palm Court than gin mill, and increasingly—a sign of her mainstream acceptance—she recorded with white musicians, among them Benny Goodman, Joe Venuti, Jack Teagarden, and the Dorsey brothers. But she never fully abandoned her blues and jazz roots. She recorded "West End Blues" two months after Louis Armstrong's classic 1928 recording and continued performing spirituals as well as new compositions by black songwriters J. C. Johnson and Andy Razaf.

There was no stopping her ascent into realms previously closed to black artists. She introduced "Am I Blue?" in the groundbreaking 1929 Hollywood musical *On With the Show*. Her 1933 Cotton Club interpretation of "Stormy Weather" backed by Duke Ellington attracted the attention of Irving Berlin, who showcased her that year in his Broadway musical revue *As Thousands Cheer*. Berlin wrote three classic numbers for her—the sultry "Heat Wave," "Harlem on My Mind" (a witty send-up of Josephine Baker), and, most memorably, "Supper Time," the heartrending lament of a southern woman whose husband has been lynched. Subsequently, she took on stage roles in nonmusicals including *Mamba's Daughters* (1939) and *The Member of the Wedding* (1950), for which she received the Best Actress Tony Award.

Waters's restless artistic quests and personal tribulations ultimately found resolution in religion, as detailed in her two autobiographies, *His Eye Is on the Sparrow* (1951) and *To Me It's Wonderful* (1972). From 1957 she devoted most of her energies to evangelicalism, traveling internationally with the Billy Graham Crusade. Her lyrical voice, supple time, and spirited delivery of lyrics influenced several generations of jazz singers (notably the trinity of Ella Fitzgerald, Billie Holiday, and Mildred Bailey) and cabaret artists (Adelaide Hall, Mabel Mercer). Although, at times, her high-hat affectations alienated the jazz community, and, overall, her work falls short of the inventiveness and emotional intensity of some of her successors, Waters is the seminal figure in the evolution of modern jazz singing. Classics, a French label, is in the process of reissuing her complete recordings on CD.

Annette Hanshaw is a significant but little-known transitional vocalist linking Waters with the great swing era singers. A Pathé record executive heard the vivacious fifteen-year-old performing at a 1926 New York party thrown by her wealthy father. She soon cut a demo with trumpeter Red Nichols and, before her sixteenth birthday, launched her recording career. Hanshaw signed a contract with Columbia two years later and made nearly a hundred sides for the label before she abandoned recording at age twenty-four and, four years later, gave up singing altogether. However, she maintained her interest in music by working as a booking agent and was a habitué of New York jazz clubs until her death in 1985.

Recording under her own name as well as an assortment of pseudonyms (Gay Ellis, Dot Dare, Patsy Young, Janet Shaw) for various Columbia labels, Hanshaw performed material ranging from show tunes and movie songs to peculiar novelties, including Helen Kane baby-talk imitations and ersatz-Hawaiian exotica. An anxious perfectionist, she concluded many of her disks with the exclamation "That's all!"—a trademark chirp of relief. In her finest work, backed by the Dorsey Brothers, Eddie Lang, Muggsy Spanier, and other jazzmen, Hanshaw bypassed the stiffness and theatricality of her contemporaries, incorporating blue notes and bent tones into a conversational style made possible by improved microphone technology. Two '90s CD reissues (Take Two and Living Era) of her late '20s and early '30s recordings—including "Big City Blues," "Am I Blue?" (which rivals Waters's celebrated version), the hard-swinging "I Have to Have You" with a go-for-broke Spanier solo, and "Moanin' Low" with the Dorseys—resurrect the legacy of this delightful singer.

The incomparable Boswell Sisters were, themselves, a self-contained instrumental ensemble. Initially, Connie (who played cello, saxophone, and trombone), Martha (piano), and Vet (violin and bass) performed exclusively classical repertoire. But black music of their native New Orleans, introduced by family servants, steered them toward jazz-inflected singing. Filled with complex harmonies and tricky syncopations, Connie's vocal arrangements for the trio set the standard for subsequent jazz singing groups including the Mills Brothers and the Spirits of Rhythm. Between their 1924 cabaret debut and 1936, when the trio disbanded, the Boswells appeared in vaudeville and on radio, recorded extensively (most memorably with the Dorsey Brothers), sang in Hollywood films, and participated in the first American public television transmission. Subsequently, Connie altered the spelling of her name to Connee and began a successful solo career, despite her confinement to a wheelchair, the consequence of a childhood accident. Her smooth, rich voice and refined musicianship appealed equally to the public and her peers; Ella Fitzgerald famously cited Connee as her main influence, singling out Boswell's natural, unpretentious delivery. Bing Crosby shared lively ad-lib duets with her on his radio broadcasts, and Bunny Berigan and other top-flight jazz players appeared on her recordings. By the time of her death, others had absorbed Boswell's innovations, and her singing seemed somewhat outdated, perhaps because she tended to stress musicianship at the expense of feeling.

Holiday, Fitzgerald, and Sarah Vaughan share a separate chapter of this volume, as befits their musical and cultural achievements. Were it not for a run of bad luck, Mildred Bailey would be acknowledged as their peer. Although celebrated in her heyday—in the early '40s, she had her own weekly CBS radio program—Bailey died too young to enjoy the retrospective reappraisals afforded other musicians with the appearance of the twelve-inch LP.

Born Mildred Rinker in Tekoa, Washington, Bailey (the surname retained from a brief early marriage) came from a musical family. Her mother, who was part Coeur d'Alene Indian, taught young Mildred tribal music and chants. Her father played violin, and her three brothers all chose music careers. (Al Rinker toured with Paul Whiteman's orchestra as one of the Rhythm Boys vocal trio.)

Bailey demonstrated sheet music and played piano accompaniment for silent movies in Seattle, then moved to Los Angeles, where she performed on radio and in a speakeasy. In 1929 Whiteman hired her to join his orchestra, making her the first female singer to be featured with a dance or jazz band. She toured with Whiteman and appeared on his radio broadcasts but did not record with his orchestra until 1931. By then, she had cut eight sides backed by Eddie Lang and Jimmie Noone pickup combos as well as the Casa Loma Orchestra.

On her October 1929 debut recording, "What Kind o' Man Is You?"

the basics of Bailey's style are apparent, notably her self-assurance and euphoric delight in singing. But her work betrays lingering vaudeville influences—a pronounced vibrato, theatrical glissandos on some sustained tones, an attempt to lower her naturally high voice—that she would quickly refine from her work. Only two years later, the up-tempo "Concentratin'" and the ballad "Georgia on My Mind" find the elements of her mature style in place: the sweet treble tones; the meticulous pitch; the unflagging sense of time; the seemingly effortless phrasing; the instinct for summoning the precise emotion to convey the mood of a lyric.

With the exception of Peggy Lee (who paid explicit tribute to Bailey on her 1959 recording of "All Too Soon"), no jazz-oriented singer has proved as adept as Bailey at interpreting such a wide assortment of material. Without resorting to Waters's chameleon-like persona shifts, Bailey performed show tunes, spirituals, jazz compositions, standards, comedy numbers, pop ephemera, and blues without sacrificing a shred of her ebullient individuality. (Interestingly, she recorded more authentic blues, including several numbers associated with Bessie Smith, than her African-American counterparts, Holiday and Fitzgerald.) Her mastery of rhythm is breathtaking. On the bobsled-paced "When Day Is Done" (1935), the redoubtable Teddy Wilson, Chu Berry, and her then-husband Red Norvo strain to keep pace with her. Three months later, a classic session with Wilson, Bunny Berigan, Johnny Hodges, and Grachan Moncur that yielded three Fats Waller tunes and a blues, featured no drummer, a detail that usually passes unnoticed because Bailey was such an indefatigable timekeeper.

Commentators often pay Bailey the backhanded compliment of praising her use of craft to compensate for an unremarkable vocal instrument. In truth, her voice possessed a delicate, bell-like purity, a sound so engagingly buoyant as to make her instantly recognizable. Too little has been said about her gift for improvisation, probably because her melodic and harmonic inventions seem as logical and shapely as the original melodies. On "You're Laughing at Me" (1937), Bailey never sings Irving Berlin's five-note title phrase as written. Her choice to replace the songwriter's ascending line with her own descending phrase shrewdly underscores the lyric's bitterness. Similarly, on a recently released alternate take of "I See Your Face Before Me" (1938), she does not duplicate Arthur Schwartz's melody until the song's B section. It's little wonder that instrumentalists otherwise predisposed to dismiss vocalists admired her work.

From the mid-'30s through the early '40s, Bailey's most productive period, she recorded extensively as a leader and with the band she and Norvo, billed as Mr. and Mrs. Swing, co-led. Recurrent illnesses slowed her career, and some of her later recordings proved to be less adventurous than her earlier work. Her death at forty-four was an irreparable loss. The French classics label has launched a complete, chronological Bailey CD reissue series to rescue her music from the oblivion into which it had fallen. The Old Masters label has issued two CDs documenting her earliest performances. Compilations of her best work appear on three import discs, from Living Era, Affinity, and Jazz Archives (the last appropriately titled *A Forgotten Lady*). Collections of Bailey's collaborations with Norvo, whose sparkling xylophone underscored her lilting voice as compatibly as Lester Young's cool saxophone cushioned Billie Holiday's disenchanted tones, are available on Columbia Legacy and Hep, the latter a three-CD series issued under Norvo's name collating his 1936–38 band recordings.

Some striking parallels link Bailey with her friend and admirer Lee Wiley. Oklahoma-born Wiley also had a mother of Indian descent (Cherokee, although her sister has disputed this), sang with an orchestra (Leo Reisman) early in her career, performed on her own radio show, and married a musician with whom she fronted a band. But Wiley's brief, bitter marital and musical union with pianist Jess Stacy was not as productive as the volatile but affectionate Bailey-Norvo partnership, and, in many other ways, the pair offer a study in contrasts. Unlike Bailey, a big woman self-conscious about her girth, the trim, glamorous Wiley was something of a femme fatale whose paramours included Bunny Berigan and Victor Young (both musical and recording collaborators as well) and the doomed aviator Wiley Post. Bailey leaped at every chance to perform and record, whereas Wiley was diffident about her career, walking away from opportunities that could have elevated her to stardom. Jazz was at the heart of Bailey's singing from the outset, but the jazz elements in Wiley's honeyed voice intensified as she progressed.

Less an improviser than a song stylist, Wiley relied on subtle ornamentations and a relaxed, almost lazy sense of swing to personalize her material. Seldom straying beyond medium tempos, she confidently sang behind the beat, frequently ending phrases with a distinctive vocal device technically known as an inverted mordent (singing a note, then briefly hitting the tone above it before returning to and sustaining the original note.) After nearly a decade as a professional singer, she cemented her reputation by recording a quartet of trend-setting albums devoted to contemporary songwriters—Gershwin (1939), Rodgers and Hart (1940), Porter (1940), and Arlen (1942). Seamlessly fusing cabaret and jazz, these collections (now paired on Audiophile CDs) showcased Wiley's gossamer contralto in loose small-group settings featuring, among others, Bud Freeman, Joe Bushkin, Pee Wee Russell, Fats Waller, and Bobby Hackett.

In the mid-'40s Wiley participated in Eddie Condon's nationally broadcast Town Hall concerts, but she did not make another album of her own until *Night in Manhattan* (1950), accompanied by Hackett, Bushkin, and a small string ensemble. The success of this project led to two additional songwriter collections (Irving Berlin and Vincent Youmans) the following year, which pitted her against Cy Walter and Stan Freeman's unyielding cocktailish duo-pianos. By the time she cut her masterpiece—1956's *West of the Moon* (RCA), a challenging selection of material brilliantly interpreted and enhanced by Ralph Burns's sensitive arrangements—audiences had come to favor newer, bebop-inflected vocal styles. After one more album, her career faded, only to resurrect briefly several years before her death, with a valedictory 1971 recording and two triumphant 1972 Carnegie Hall appearances. (Both have been issued as Audiophile CDs.)

Wiley absorbed the innovations of her peers, notably Waters and Bailey, and translated them into a style that subtly implied what her predecessors had made explicit. Nonchalant and somewhat aloof in her approach to time and lyric content, she charted a path for several generations of intimate singers, among them Peggy Lee, Jeri Southern, Blossom Dearie, Shirley Horn, and Audrey Morris, who understood how to imply more by doing less.

Within years of Bailey's trailblazing association with Paul Whiteman, nearly every jazz and dance band of consequence traveled with what was then called a girl singer. Some were mainly decorative, restricted to warbling the occasional chorus of straight melody and otherwise dressing up the bandstand. But touring with bands offered an invaluable musical education to those so inclined, and several of these songstresses made important contributions to orchestras and, subsequently, on their own. Among the most memorable: Helen Ward (with Benny Goodman 1934–36), Dolly Dawn (with George Hall 1935–41 and, as of this writing, still singing), and Helen Forrest (with Artie Shaw 1938, Benny Goodman 1939–41, and Harry James 1941–43). Still in her teens, Peggy Lee was hired to replace Forrest in Goodman's band on such short notice that she initially was forced to sing arrangements written in her predecessor's keys. Her 1942 crossover version of blues singer Lil Green's "race record" "Why Don't You Do Right?" became an international hit. A year later, she married Goodman guitarist Dave Barbour and left the band, briefly retiring to raise their daughter. Resuming her career in 1945, she recorded (and in some instances wrote) a string of Hit Parade singles that launched her as a solo artist. Like Waters and Crosby, she extended her talent beyond jazz to encompass acting (1955's *Pete Kelly's Blues*, for which she received an Academy Award nomination) and meticulously staged supper club performances. Ever alert to changing musical currents, Lee effortlessly negotiated the transition from swing to postwar singing, with a string of hits that extended to the Beatles-era "Is That All There Is?" (1969). MCA and Capitol have reissued multidisc anthologies of her work.

Helen Humes, who sang with Count Basie's band between 1938 and 1942, withdrew from music several times, only to be welcomed with increasing enthusiasm each time she returned. She was just thirteen when she made her precocious first blues recordings for the OKeh label. John Hammond was instrumental in convincing Basie to hire her. She shared vocal duties with Jimmy Rushing, who got the lion's share of the band's trademark blues material; Humes was largely relegated to ballads and swing numbers. After leaving Basie she had several influential mid-'40s rhythm-and-blues hits, the saucy "Million Dollar Secret," and a jump tune, "Be-Baba-Leba," then married and put her career on hold. In the early '60s she made three highly regarded Contemporary albums (all reissued as OJC CDs) with the inspiring participation of Ben Webster, Benny Carter, Art Pepper, Teddy Edwards, André Previn, and Barney Kessel, then withdrew again, supporting herself by working in a Kentucky munitions factory. She surfaced once more in the mid-'70s, this time to remain, with a Newport Jazz Festival appearance followed by a three-month Manhattan engagement accompanied by Ellis Larkins. Humes's high, clear voice, with its echoes of Waters and Bailey, retained its youthful zest until the end. She was not an innovator but a versatile, vivacious artist who, for over half a century, sang with warmth, confidence, and humor.

Unlike Basie, who employed Humes, Rushing, Joe Williams, and other compelling vocalists, Duke Ellington did not risk having his orchestra overshadowed by singers. His choices ran from pleasantly bland (Joya Sherrill, Ozzie Bailey) to downright grating (Al Hibbler). Ivie Anderson is generally conceded to be Ellington's finest vocalist, rivaled only by Betty Roché, who appeared with the band in the mid-'40s and again in the early '50s. Anderson toured with Ellington from 1931 through 1942, when chronic asthma forced her retirement from the rigors of life on the road. Praised for her onstage poise and dignity, Anderson, who always dressed in white, looked fragile, an appearance belied by her lively onstage banter with drummer Sonny Greer. In her first recording, she introduced Ellington's mantra "It Don't Mean a Thing" (1932), and subsequently she etched some of the leader's signature pieces: "I'm Checkin' Out Go'om Bye" (1939), "Solitude" (1940), and "Mood Indigo" (1942). Records (a CD of her Ellington singles is available on Jazz Archives) apparently fail to capture the charm that made her such a favorite with audiences. Her thin alto and straightforward delivery of lyrics never quite transcend the boundaries of band singing, which is probably as Ellington intended.

Like Humes, Maxine Sullivan abandoned music several times, then scored some of her greatest artistic triumphs in her final decades. Her second record, a 1937 swing version of the Scottish folk song "Loch Lomond" arranged by bandleader Claude Thornhill (who used horns to imitate bagpipes), made her an overnight star and, for a time, typecast her as a swinger of traditional folk airs including "Annie Laurie," "If I Had a Ribbon Bow," and "Molly Malone." The same year, she performed with and married John Kirby, leader of the chamber jazz sextet known as the "Biggest Little Band in the Land." She appeared with Louis Armstrong on Broadway (*Swingin' the Dream*) and in Hollywood's *Going Places* and as a single in cabarets and jazz clubs until the early '50s, when she remarried and devoted her energies to nursing and community work. After a brief comeback in the mid-'50s with two excellent recordings—one of songs by lyricist Andy Razaf and the other remakes of her early successes (both reissued as a Fresh Sound two-fer CD)—she again retired to raise a daughter. In the early '70s, she embarked upon the most prolific period of her career, during which she released nearly two dozen albums and toured extensively. Petite and perky, Sullivan sounded like she looked; her style was sweet, gently swinging, and lyrical. Early in her career, she floated above her material like a silvery bird, generating more light than warmth. In her final years, when age and illness made voice production more effortful, she dug deeper into the emotional content of her songs. Her album of compositions by Burton Lane (on Harbinger CD), cut two years before her passing, proved to be her finest achievement, her blithe, still-girlish voice miraculously intact yet tinged with mature wisdom, wit, and poignancy.

Thanks to compact discs, several talented but nearly forgotten swing era singers have been rediscovered. Louisiana-bred Teddy Grace recorded with Mal Hallett's and Bob Crosby's orchestras and cut her own small-group sessions, most memorably a five-disc 1938 blues album featuring Dave Barbour and Buster Bailey. A freewheeling, uninhibitedly rhythmic performer, she interpolated trombone growls and country yodels into her performances. During a World War II War Bond tour, Grace damaged her vocal chords, thus ending her musical career. Shortly before her death, David W. McCain, who annotated two '90s CD reissues of her work (Hep and Timeless), found Grace in a California nursing home, where she expressed astonishment that people still remembered her.

Not all of the era's creative vocalists graduated from swing bands. Fats Waller protégé Una Mae Carlisle launched her career in 1937 with a two-year stint in Europe. Hitler's ascent sped her homeward, where she signed with RCA and recorded a duet with Waller as a prelude to two solo sessions on which she sang to her own piano accompaniment with support from Waller's sidemen. On follow-up records, she performed exclusively as a vocalist, backed by pickup groups that included Benny Carter and Lester Young, then cut sixteen sides with John Kirby's sextet. (In clubs, however, she continued to accompany herself.) A sensitive, understated singer with careful diction and sound musical instincts, Carlisle also was a competent songwriter. (Peggy Lee recorded her "I See a Million People" during her tenure with Benny Goodman.) After World War II, health problems and unproductive affiliations with marginal record labels affected her popularity. She died at forty, with much of her potential unrealized.

Singer-trumpeter-dancer Valaida Snow was born in a trunk to a Tennessee vaudeville family and trained as an entertainer from the time she could speak and walk. At twenty-one, she appeared on Broadway in Noble Sissle and Eubie Blake's *Chocolate Dandies*, then toured Asia and Europe before returning to Broadway in 1931 to appear with Ethel Waters in *Rhapsody in Black*. Following a long engagement with her then-lover Earl Hines at Chicago's Grand Terrace, she relocated to England, where she recorded extensively for the Parlophone label. She continued to work in Europe, even after war was declared. While appearing in Denmark, she was imprisoned and brutally mistreated by Nazi occupation forces. Her health broken, she was released and repatriated in 1942. After a slow recuperation, she unsuccessfully attempted to revive her career. In the years preceding her death at fifty-two, she survived by performing at Catskills resorts. Hailed as a brilliant artist by Hines and Louis Armstrong and celebrated by royalty—Queen Wilhelmina of the Netherlands gave her a golden trumpet—Snow has begun to achieve a portion of overdue immortality through reissues of her recordings.

Several long-forgotten singers still await rediscovery and reevaluation. Jerry Kruger, a vivacious, high-spirited songstress, recorded in 1939 with Benny Carter and Ernie Powell and in the early '40s with Frankie Newton and with a Cootie Williams–led Ellington group. Although better known as cabaret artists, Bee Palmer and Marion Harris also sang and recorded with jazz musicians. Both anticipated the postwar "vocalese" vogue (King Pleasure, Eddie Jefferson, Lambert, Hendricks & Ross) of adding lyrics to instrumental improvisations by singing adaptations of Bix Beiderbecke's and Frank Trumbauer's celebrated "Singin' the Blues" solos—Palmer in 1929 and Harris in 1934.

The seminal male jazz singer is also the seminal jazz trumpeter, whose life and art are discussed at length in his own chapter of this volume. Louis Armstrong's vocals embody the essentials of jazz singing: an inimitable sound; the gifts of improvisational ability and swing; and a personal, interpretive approach to lyrics. His work opened a world of expressive possibilities from which his successors, female and male, had merely to pick and choose elements that suited their artistic inclinations and sensibilities.

Fats Waller, Henry "Red" Allen, Hot Lips Page, Bunny Berigan, Roy Eldridge, Wingy Manone, and many other instrumentalists followed Louis's example, expanding their performances and audience appeal by singing when the spirit moved them. Waller's vocal talents tend to be overshadowed by his achievements as a pianist and composer, but his uninhibited approach to popular song influenced a legion of singer-instrumentalists including Cleo Brown, Nat "King" Cole, Louis Jordan, Martha Davis, Rose Murphy, and Nellie Lutcher. Unlike Billie Holiday, who neutralized the bromidic, rose-colored lyrics of Tin Pan Alley ephemera with skepticism bordering on sarcasm, the irrepressible Waller addressed his material with a blending of rambunctious mockery and unexpected affection. On such recordings as "How Can You Face Me?" (1934) and "My Very Good Friend the Milkman" (1935), he simultaneously evokes both laughter and tenderness.

Perhaps the most memorable post-Armstrong singer-instrumentalist was Texas-born Jack Teagarden, whose grainy, unruffled drawl was an extension of his peerless trombone style as showcased in such signature pieces as "A Hundred Years From Today" (1933) and "Stars Fell on Alabama" (1934). Although his vocals were featured throughout his associations with Paul Whiteman and Louis as well as with his own groups, his crowning achievement as a singer came just two years before his death. *Think Well of Me*, a 1962 collection of songs by composer-lyricist Willard Robison, primarily showcases Teagarden as a vocalist backed by a string orchestra. Largely ignored when released, its 1998 Verve CD reissue drew praise for Teagarden's heartfelt delivery of lyrics and brief, gemlike trombone solos.

A number of singers, among them Cliff Edwards, Gene Austin, Smith Ballew, Red McKenzie, Putney Dandridge, Bob Howard, and the enigmatic Charlie Palloy, figured in the transition from the declamatory styles of male vaudeville performers. (Edwards's "I Don't Want Nobody but You" [1926], recorded two months after Armstrong's trailblazing "Heebie Jeebies," is a key early contribution to the evolution of scat vocalizing.) But it was Bing Crosby who transfigured popular singing. Buttressed by new electronic recording techniques, his crooning delivery, buttery baritone, relaxed diction, and easeful swing ended the dominance of piping tenors and thundering bassos. Although initially inspired by Al Jolson, the influences of Armstrong, Waters, and Bix Beiderbecke swayed him in the direction of jazz. As a member of the Rhythm Boys trio, he performed with Paul Whiteman's orchestra from 1926 to 1930, appearing on such memorable sides as 1928's "From Monday On." Branching out as a single, he recorded with Frankie Trumbauer ("Some of These Days") and Duke Ellington ("St. Louis Blues") in 1932 and, in the first decade of his solo career, headed small-group sessions featuring many of the musicians who backed Waters, Hanshaw, and Bailey: the Dorseys, Lang, Berigan, and Goodman. Crosby's enthusiasm for jazz is especially evident on "Moonburn" (1936), on which he is energized by and, in turn, encourages Joe Sullivan's rollicking piano. As he attained movie and radio stardom, Crosby began to favor more conventional orchestral backings, and his repertoire shifted from swing tunes and ardent ballads to commercial material with string and vocal-group settings, even Hawaiian, cowboy, Irish, and country-and-western songs. But he never fully severed his jazz roots, and intermittently collaborated on radio and records with Armstrong, Teagarden, and Lionel Hampton and duetted with Boswell and Wiley.

The antithesis of Crosby's mellow croon, Jimmy Rushing's husky tenor sparked the Basie band from 1935 to 1950, delivering the happiest, most propulsive urban blues ever swung. Striking out on his own in the '50s, Rushing fronted romping small-group blues sessions with former Basie-ites and revealed a long-suppressed penchant for tender love songs. His extraordinary 1971 valedictory album, *The You and Me That Used to Be* (RCA), contains only one blues, but his gruffly romantic versions of "More Than You Know" and the title tune make one regret that he was typecast so long as a blues shouter.

An antic tradition of jazz-based jive singers begins with Cab Calloway, the extroverted bandleader whose repertoire largely consisted of songs about sex and drugs. His effusive showmanship—the white tuxedo, the wild gyrations, the long, flaying black hair—overshadowed his abilities as a balladeer and scat singer and prefigured the performance styles of rock musicians. Calloway's theatrical presentation of novelty tunes—"Minnie the Moocher" (1931) and "Reefer Man" (1932)—served him well when he appeared as Sportin' Life in the 1952 revival of *Porgy and Bess* and the 1967 all-black Broadway company of *Hello, Dolly!*

Singer-guitarist-pianist Slim Gaillard took jive vocalizing several steps further by creating nonsense songs (1938's "The Flat Foot Floogie") and, by the mid-'40s, devising his own hipster lexicon. But the swing era's scat master was Leo Watson, whose staggeringly fertile improvisations and stream-of-consciousness wordplay were showcased on only thirty-eight recordings, notably sessions with Artie Shaw (1937) and Gene Krupa (1938). *The Original Scatman,* an Indigo CD, collects twenty-three of these, ending with Watson's surrealistic "Jingle Bells" from his final session in 1946.

By the early '40s, the first generation of jazz singers had largely run its course. World War II mobilization hastened the collapse of big bands, the training ground for so many vocalists. Dizzy Gillespie, Charlie Parker, Thelonious Monk, and Kenny Clarke were jamming in Harlem's after-hours clubs, developing a new music that, by the decade's midpoint, would redefine jazz. Young Sarah Vaughan absorbed their bebop inventions, challenging swing band singers Fitzgerald and Anita O'Day to update their own styles. Crosby increasingly devoted his energies to Hollywood, leaving Frank Sinatra, Billy Eckstine, and a host of followers to extend and refine his innovations. Dinah Washington and Kay Starr returned to blues and gospel roots, bringing jazz singing back to basics. And Peggy Lee, ever conscious of the contributions of her musical ancestors, fused these in a prescient style that crystallized the most enduring elements of the past and leapfrogged beyond bebop to foreshadow the "cool" vocalists (June Christy, Chris Connor, Helen Merrill, Julie London) of the 1950s.

Ella Fitzgerald, Sarah Vaughan, and Billie Holiday

Patricia Willard

Artistry should not be regarded comparatively. Ideally, each artist should be enjoyed on her own merits. Because they were contemporaries, Ella Fitzgerald, Sarah Vaughan, and Billie Holiday rarely escaped comparison. Periodicals pitted them against one another in polls. Critics and fans gulped the bait. Seemingly above the clamor yet energized by both the promotion and the adulation, these three African-American women dedicated their unparalleled talents to exploring and interpreting American music.

"Uses her voice like an instrument" emerges in written assessments all too frequently, neglecting or negating acceptance of the human voice as the original, organic musical device. Ella, Sarah, and Billie firmly established equalities in a genre historically dominated by a nonsinging brotherhood.

Each had unique, instantly recognizable gifts. All were jazz singers. They could hear and create their own rhythmic and melodic innovations. Each also chose, usually encouraged by managers and producers, to cross over into more financially rewarding popular music. Each, to varying degrees, realized commercial success. A tantalizing sampler of this triumvirate—plus another one-of-a-saucy-kind—is

Billie Holiday, Paramount Theatre, New York, February 1941. Photo: Leo Arsene. Courtesy
Frank Driggs Collection.

compiled on the CD *4 BY 4: Ella Fitzgerald, Billie Holiday, Sarah Vaughan, Dinah Washington* (Verve).

For all their professional accomplishments, recognition, economic gains, and envied orbits in the show business firmament, none enabled them to capture the ephemeral illusion of family life, children, or an enduring partnership with a mate. Emotional scar tissue from their impulsive, erratic, often disastrous, romantic entanglements informed the poignancy and profundity of their songs if not their spirits. Their personalities were as distinctively different as their voices, yet all yearned in vain to be birth mothers. Ella and Sarah developed loving relationships with their respective adopted son and daughter. Billie collected godchildren from Italy to Hollywood.

All emerged from humble origins. Only Sarah came from a somewhat stable, two-parent home, and only she had formal music training. Not one of these amazing achievers was a high school graduate. Neither Ella nor Billie ever got there, and Sarah quit in her junior year. Each acknowledged the invaluable lessons, pleasures, and hardships of education-by-big-bands.

Ella Jane Fitzgerald was born in Newport News, Virginia, April 25, 1917, according to her estate, although many references state the year as 1918. Not until intensive research by British author Stuart Nicholson for his 1993 Fitzgerald biography were accurate details of her early life known. Shy, reticent, and perennially uncomfortable with strangers, she granted few interviews and, on those rare occasions, volunteered no insights and little information beyond her great esteem for colleagues.

William Fitzgerald, a thirty-something wagon driver, was Ella's father. Her mother, Tempie Williams, a decade younger, was a laundress. Around 1921, Ella and her mother, with her new companion, Portuguese immigrant Joseph Da Silva, moved to Yonkers, New York. Ella's half-sister Frances Da Silva was born there in 1923.

Tall, gawky, and haphazardly dressed, the adolescent Ella was no harbinger of the elegant, mature gentlewoman she would become. She aspired to be a famous dancer. From the age of eight, she had danced in the streets with her peers, begging older children to teach her such tap steps as the fast-traveling "Shuffle Off to Buffalo" and novelty dances the rugcutters at the Savoy Ballroom were into. Occasionally, she sang as she danced, but the movement, the rhythmic moves—that was the excitement.

Orphaned in her mid-teens, she and Frances shuttled in and out of relatives' flats and Harlem foster homes. More than once Ella ran away from intolerable situations to fend for herself. Half a century before government took over the racket as a legal lottery, she was earning a daily commission as an uptown numbers runner. She also is said to have served as a lookout for a madam—that is, she watched for vice officers and warned the "working girls."

On November 21, 1934, within months of master of ceremonies Ralph Cooper's introduction of his "Amateur Night in Harlem," Ella sailed through dance auditions. At the crucial moment, intimidated by the competition, with absolutely no preparation, she came onto the stage of the Apollo Theater singing and totally captured that very tough, "show me" audience for first place. Although she apparently was paid the standard ten dollars for passing the audition, she was denied the coveted prize of a week at the popular 125th Street showhouse. Cooper cited her slovenly appearance as his reason for not honoring his commitment.

Benny Carter's band had backed her singing debut, and Carter, a multi-instrumentalist, composer, and occasional singer, was impressed with the very musical if ungainly young vocalist. He arranged an audition with bandleader Fletcher Henderson. Again, her looks did her in. Two months later, Ella won the nearby Harlem Opera House amateur contest and was awarded a week's engagement.

Admirers wangled her a tryout with drummer-bandleader Chick Webb. Reluctantly, he offered her two probationary weeks at no pay. She was a hit. Band members were so enthralled by her fresh, raw talent that they volunteered as surrogate family and advisers to the teenager they called "Sis." According to Nicholson, the frequently published tale that Webb and his wife legally adopted Ella was sanctioned by Webb for publicity purposes, but was not true.

Praise for Ella appeared in every issue of the music business's most important journals, *Down Beat* and *Metronome* and England's *Melody Maker*, bringing the deserving Webb band more press than it ever before had enjoyed. *Down Beat* dubbed her "First Lady of Swing," an identity that would undergo vocal revision.

Ella was an exuberant, natural extension of the Webb band. Their first recorded sides, cut for Brunswick, June 12, 1935, were "I'll Chase the Blues Away" and "Love and Kisses." That same year, she decided to sing a favorite traditional nursery rhyme and implored Al Feldman, an arranger who used to dance to Webb at the Savoy, to notate and arrange her outline for the tune. (Feldman became the successful orchestra leader Van Alexander.) The song was "A-Tisket, A-Tasket." Recorded May 2, 1938, it was Fitzgerald and Webb's only million-seller.

The three titles, plus forty more from her beginnings with Webb are in the double CD *Ella Fitzgerald: The Early Years—Part 1 With Chick Webb and His Orchestra (1935–1938)* (Decca). Their subsequent recordings, mostly popular standards, are on the CD *Chick Webb and His Orchestra Standing Tall With Ella Fitzgerald* (Drive Archive). When Webb died, she became the band's leader and toured nearly three years. Trumpeter John Birks "Dizzy" Gillespie was among her sidemen for four weeks in 1941. Her marriage that year to a fan, Ben Kornegay, lasted little longer.

Throughout her career, she acknowledged the pervasive influence on her singing of Connee Boswell and Louis Armstrong. Certainly, the Boswell sound is strong in Ella's Webb recordings. Her link to Armstrong is delightfully reciprocal on the CDs *Ella Fitzgerald and Louis Armstrong* (Verve) and *Best of Ella Fitzgerald and Louis Armstrong* (Verve).

Ella's voice alone could have earned her supremacy. Her intuitive rhythm and improvisations came from so deeply within that she could neither be imitated nor challenged. Above all, she translated notes, refrains, and even the pain of her early life, possibly through a musical mask, into joyousness for her listeners. Ella did not sing sad songs. Lyrics might lament an imperfect romance, but even the bitterest became delectable in her sunny, clear, warm caress. She did not originate but may have perfected scat, the often eloquent substitution of whimsical, extemporaneous, and occasionally onomatopoeic syllables for written melody and/or words or absence of words. Ella's scat thesaurus was an orchestra of instrumental timbres.

Her journey to Verve may be the most beatific in jazz. Norman Granz, less than a year Ella's junior, had a keen ear for music, an astute head for business, and a crusading passion for equality and justice. In the middle 1940s, he became convinced that Ella's refreshing songs and her enormous audience appeal were the perfect complement to his increasingly well attended Jazz at the Philharmonic concerts. Her excitingly improvised "How High the Moon," often called JATP's anthem, was first recorded in that context and is on *The Complete Jazz at the Philharmonic on Verve, 1944–1949.* The more she performed her mix of pop and jazz tunes on his shows, the stronger his determination became to assume total management of her career.

Under the guidance of the Gale, Inc., agency and Decca artists and repertoire executive Milt Gabler, she had recorded a number of popular songs, often "covering" already successful versions by other singers, as well as capturing in her own jazz language "Lady Be Good" and "Flying Home." Granz envisioned a more intense focus.

On December 10, 1947, Ella married Gillespie big band bassist Ray Brown in Youngstown, Ohio. Soon both were touring with the all-star JATP. As Ella's popularity soared, Brown, too, was earning adulation with the Oscar Peterson Trio. By August 28, 1953, continuously pulled apart by conflicting itineraries, Ella and Ray divorced. She retained custody of their adopted son, Ray Jr. By December, Granz was her personal manager, but two more years of maneuvering were necessary to wrest her from Decca to become the principal artist on his newly formed Verve.

Granz promptly inaugurated the *Song Book* series with *Ella Fitzgerald Sings the Cole Porter Song Book*. The concept was a perfect marriage. Her jazz following was delighted, and the vast audience devoted to the cherished composers of popular song was reintroduced to that music in the exhilarating Fitzgerald mode. *Song Books* of Richard Rodgers and Lorenz Hart, Duke Ellington, Irving Berlin, George and Ira Gershwin, Harold Arlen, Jerome Kern, and Johnny Mercer followed. This monumental project, recorded between early 1956 and late 1964 with small groups, big bands, and full orchestras, probably is the most intricately faceted of her career. The entire collection, including tracks never released on the individual *Song Books*, has been packaged on sixteen CDs as *The Complete Ella Fitzgerald Song Books* (Verve).

With Ellington there were triumphant touring and recording encores under the Granz aegis. These include a rehearsal and previously unissued tracks, preserved on *Ella Fitzgerald and Duke Ellington: Cote d'Azur Concerts* (Verve) and *Ella at Duke's Place* (Verve). As Ellington trumpeter Herbie Jones, who played on both, has observed, "Even when Ella forgot lyrics, she established a criterion. Not only did she score a hit with her 'How High the Moon is the name of this song, How High the Moon though the words may be wrong . . . ,' she did it again on Gerald Wilson and Billy Strayhorn's 'Imagine My Frustration' on the . . . *Duke's Place* session. When she sang 'belle of the wall' instead of 'ball,' she just laughed in tempo and went on singing. We thought we'd do another take but Norman went with that one, and it's great."

Television shows on which she starred, costarred, and guested have been preserved on video, and she can be heard on several American and Italian motion picture soundtracks, but her actual on-screen feature film appearances number only four: *Ride 'Em Cowboy*, 1941; *Pete Kelly's Blues*, 1955; *St. Louis Blues*, 1958; *Let No Man Write My Epitaph*, 1960. In all, she played a singer, usually named Ella.

She performed with symphony orchestras as well as with Count Basie's band, Oscar Peterson's Trio, and her own small groups led by pianists Tommy Flanagan, Jimmy Rowles, Jimmy Jones, Paul Smith, and Lou Levy. Benny Carter, Nelson Riddle, Gerald Wilson, Marty Paich, Buddy Bregman, Gordon Jenkins, Bill Holman, Neal Hefti, Bill Doggett, Frank Devol, Jim Hughart, Oliver Nelson, Jimmy Jones, and Russ Garcia were the principal arrangers of her superb big band charts. *Ella Sings Brightly With Nelson* (Verve) is among the recorded evidence.

Health problems related to severe diabetes plagued her later years. Shortly before she died on June 15, 1996, she donated her complete music library to the Library of Congress and artifacts from her career to the Smithsonian Institution in Washington, D.C.

"If Ella were a musical instrument," Frank Sinatra said a few years earlier, "she'd be the whole damn orchestra. Her pure and almost childlike voice is a melody unto itself. Never have such innocent sounds been set to music nor has such music sounded so effortless. Ella is musical perfection."

Sarah Lois Vaughan, the only child of Ada and Asbury "Jake" Vaughan, was born March 27, 1924, in Newark, New Jersey. He was a carpenter who played guitar nonprofessionally. His wife sang in Newark's First Mount Zion Baptist Church choir. By her early teens, Sarah was singing alongside her mother, rapidly advancing to soloist and playing the organ for services. She had private music lessons from the ages of seven through fifteen, shortly after which she began appearing in local nightclubs. Whenever she could, Sarah crossed the Hudson to Harlem and snuck into the basement of the Braddock Hotel to listen to Ella and the Webb band rehearse.

At eighteen, Sarah prevailed in the Apollo competition. The singer whose name was on the marquee that week was Ella Fitzgerald. According to legend, she praised and encouraged the newcomer. Barely a week after Sarah's nineteenth birthday, she was seated at a piano facing another piano player, bandleader Earl "Fatha" Hines, and sharing the vocal microphone with his bandsinger Billy Eckstine. Gillespie and Charlie Parker were among the young conceptualizing geniuses in the group. Later she would credit their presence with the "in tune" honing of her ear and and the notes she chose. "Horns always influenced me more than voices," she insisted, although she repeatedly expressed deep admiration for Fitzgerald, Holiday, Eckstine, Bob Eberly, Jack Leonard, Nat Cole, Mahalia Jackson, Marian Anderson, Doris Day, Jo Stafford, and Rosemary Clooney.

Within that freshman year with Hines, the innovators, Sarah included, matriculated to yet another bandstand with Eckstine as leader. Of all her learning experiences, the most concentrated and intense undoubtedly was the barrage of ideas, sounds, and road camaraderie experienced with these two aggregations. "East of the Sun," with Gillespie doubling on trumpet and piano, recorded New Year's Eve, 1944, is an intriguing sampling of Sarah at this stage on *Dynamic Duos: Memorable Meetings in Jazz* (Drive Archive). The CD also offers such significant couplings as Billie Holiday with Ellington, Billie with Stan Getz, Ella with Webb, and Louis Armstrong with Fats Waller.

Sarah's very personal contribution to the then-revolutionary harmonic and rhythmic progressions of bebop is clear on *Dizzy Gillespie, Sarah Vaughan, and Charlie Bird Parker—The Jazz Collector Edition* (Laserlight) containing her exquisite "Lover Man" of May 11, 1945, and "Mean to Me," both with Dizzy and Bird, and the latter including Max Roach. Almost exactly five years later, she improvised a new melody on "Mean to Me," freshly minted with Miles Davis, Budd Johnson, Benny Green, and Tony Scott as her companion horns, included with yet another "East of the Sun" on *Sarah Vaughan: Columbia Years, 1949–1953.*

She and Billy collaborated throughout their careers. In 1949, they recorded a series of duets for MGM, released on a thick, 33⅓ rpm, ten-inch disc, an ungainly forerunner of the larger, flexible LP. Eight years later, they came together again for *Sarah Vaughan and Billy Eckstine: The Irving Berlin Songbook* (Emarcy), arranged and conducted by Hal Mooney. And in 1972, their voices compatibily deepened, they shared a grand two weeks with Ellington at the glitzy Grove of the Los Angeles Ambassador Hotel.

An often told story, probably true, is that at Sarah's fourth opportunity to record, October 1, 1945, with violinist Leroy "Stuff" Smith's trio, Musicraft Records owner Albert Marx delayed the session to argue whether she was to be paid ten or fifteen dollars. He won.

As Sarah amassed a following, she built a reputation for mercurial temperament, walking out midway through recording sessions and club dates with Eckstine and John Kirby and even on her own solo engagement at the Spotlite on New York's 52nd Street. Lonely and in need of career direction, she assuaged both voids September 16, 1946, when she married her newly retained personal manager, trumpeter George Treadwell.

He became her musical director and conductor as well as her arbiter of fashion, negotiator of contracts, and designer of her new and improved image. On most levels he was quite effective; however, the souvenir program he supervised for her late 1940s concert tour nearly self-destructed in hyperbole. One page was headlined "And The Vaughan Came Up Like Thunder." The text proclaimed that she now was known as "The Royal Lady of Show Business" and that she was "the freshest, most inspired and most original sepia singer to come along since the day when Chick Webb featured a dusky girl of 'tisket-a-tasket' [*sic*] fame...Ella Fitzgerald." *Metronome* was quoted: "Not since...Billie Holiday has a singer hit other singers so hard." The lavishly illustrated keepsake was already in distribution when Tread-well hired a Southern California publicist couple who issued a blitz of press releases, all commencing "Sarah, that Vaughan-derful Girl..."

Sarah survived. Her gap-toothed smile was corrected dentally. She dressed in glamorous gowns, and she acquired her all-time favorite accompanist, pianist Jimmy Jones. Both were devotees of hanging out, jamming, and the occasional cutting contest; their rapport was such that, although many singers and bandleaders solicited Jones's arrangements, he and Sarah never used written music. "Sometimes she leads and I follow," Jones related, "and sometimes I lead and she'll follow any place I go."

Her voice had the richness, range, power, and control to project operatic arias, although jazz critics frequently observed that the parameters of such training would be a ruinous harnessing of her improvisational instrument. She longed for "a modern opera" to be written for her by Leonard Bernstein; she fantasized about asking him but never had the courage.

With Americans' proclivity for anointing their luminaries with titles and, in jazz, quirky nicknames, Sarah acquired an abundance. "Sassy" signified more than just a cute contraction of her given name, as did "Sass," dating to childhood. Her road language earned her the sobriquet of "Sailor." Radio host Dave Garroway began calling her "The Divine One," reminiscent of another Sarah (Bernhardt). Eventually, Sarah established an office in Beverly Hills, California, with the skewed name of "The Devine One" on the same Canon Drive as Fitzgerald's Salle (Ella's spelled backward) Productions.

Possibly Sarah's very best small-group performances were with her trio of Jones, the versatile bassist Joe Benjamin and drummer Roy Haynes. John Malachi temporarily spelled Jones during an illness, and Richard Davis succeeded Benjamin. All are on the CD *Swingin'*

Easy: Sarah Vaughan and Her Trio (EmArcy). She dazzles, swooping gracefully from soprano to contralto on ballads, offering a reprise of "Body and Soul," her good-luck song from the Apollo contest, scatting on "Shulie a Bop," which she and Treadwell composed, and impetuously having fun with the rhythm sections. On December 16, 1954, composer-arranger Ernie Wilkins augmented the Jones/Benjamin/Haynes triad with the lyrical young trumpet virtuoso Clifford Brown, Herbie Mann, and Paul Quinichette to record "Lullaby of Birdland," a masterpiece by all concerned with Sarah scatting multiregister syllables against each musician. The eight tunes from this group's two sessions are on *Sarah Vaughan* (EmArcy) and also included in *Complete Sarah Vaughan on Mercury, Vol. 1.*

Under George's guidance, Sarah signed lucrative contracts with prestigious promoters and recording companies. At a 1949 Just Jazz concert at the Los Angeles Shrine Auditorium, she had top billing over her idol, pianist Art Tatum. In 1951 she made the only appearance of her career on screen in a feature film, singing "Black Coffee" in the Allied Artists Production *Disc Jockey*, and in 1954 Mercury became her new label for more commercial repertoire with its subsidiary EmArcy as concurrent jazz base. *The Complete Sarah Vaughan on Mercury, Vol. 2, Sings Great American Songs, 1956–1957* is among four multi-CD collections from that alliance. *Vol. 2* encompasses the Eckstine duets and some but not all of the selections from *Sarah Vaughan Sings George Gershwin* (Verve). The latter double-CD package includes several compelling alternate and incomplete takes not on the "complete" Mercury. Jimmy Jones and Hal Mooney conducted the orchestras and arranged the music on most tracks.

Less than a decade after having to argue over a five-dollar increment for a recording session, she was enjoying her first million-selling record, "Broken Hearted Melody," collecting annual royalties in the hundreds of thousands, playing Carnegie Hall, fulfilling her eighteenth engagement at Birdland, guesting on the major network television shows, and touring Europe for the U.S. Department of State. She added a portable sewing machine to her road luggage. Other vestiges of domesticity eluded her. So did access to her bank balances.

By 1958, amid rumors that Treadwell had become physically abusive and was diverting her earnings, they divorced. Her several more marriages and liaisons—principally with businessman Clyde B. Atkins, lifelong friend John "Preacher" Wells, restaurateur Marshall Fisher, and trumpeter Waymon Reed—also were unsuccessful. In 1961, with Atkins, she adopted a baby girl, Debra Lois. Although—

or perhaps because—Fisher demonstrated selfless devotion and professional acumen, she apparently tired of him.

During her years with him, she was in demand by symphony orchestras and collaborated with Michael Tilson Thomas on an ambitious Gershwin project. Her spectacular voice sounded more glorious than ever. She sang at the Carter White House. *Sarah Vaughan: Send in the Clowns* (Columbia Jazz Masterworks/Legacy), produced by her longtime colleague Bobby Shad, originally for his Mainstream label, is from that interval.

For the final nine years of her life, Sarah restricted her relationships to music. She alternated concerts for which she was paid upwards of thirty-five thousand dollars with impromptu gratis performances in nightclubs on her nights off. She and good friend Carmen McRae often showed up unexpectedly on Southern California bandstands where pianist-composer-humorist Jimmy Rowles was playing. Usually Sarah would make sure her audience was aware that she was wearing an outfit she had designed and sewn that day on the machine she kept in her dining room even when she hosted parties.

Just in time, the National Academy of Recording Arts and Sciences awarded Sarah its Lifetime Achievement Grammy, February 22, 1989. Her final recording session was the introductory duet with Ella on Quincy Jones's all-star *Back on the Block* (Qwest) that year. On April 9, 1990, watching a television performance by Debby, who had become actress Paris Vaughan, her daughter by her side, Sarah succumbed to lung cancer.

Billie Holiday was born Elinore DeViese April 7, 1915, in Philadelphia, Pennsylvania, although all references prior to Stuart Nicholson's diligently researched 1995 Holiday biography state her birthplace as Baltimore, Maryland. She was known as Eleanora Fagan in Baltimore soon after birth. Her nineteen-year-old mother was Sadie Fagan, a Baltimorean who commuted to Philadelphia to work as a housekeeper. Guitarist Clarence Holiday acknowledged being the father. According to Nicholson, the name DeViese was a spelling variation on Frank DeVeazy, a waiter whom Sadie initially named on birth documents. Because Sadie was married to Philip Gough from 1920 to 1924, Eleanora's surname in some histories is listed with that stepfather's surname. The two dramatic opening sentences of Billie's 1956 autobiography *Lady Sings the Blues* ("Mom and Pop were just a couple of kids when they got married. He was eighteen, she was sixteen, and I was three.") were motivated either by her persistent desire to have a family history or by the provocative writing style of her collaborator William Dufty, a *New York Post* reporter.

Insecurity, abuse, and deprivation defined her childhood. Shunted among close, distant, and proxy relatives while her mother worked at menial jobs, Eleanora, as Elenore Gough, was committed to an institution for troubled adolescent "colored girls" at the age of nine and raped by a neighbor when she was ten. At eleven, she dropped out of fifth grade. Soon she was working for a Baltimore bordello, cleaning and running errands. It was there, listening to the house Victrola, that she became enchanted with Louis Armstrong and his Hot Five's recording of "West End Blues." Bessie Smith's blues and the styles of Ethel Waters and Sophie Tucker so moved the youngster that she decided she must become a singer with a name like the beautiful silent film actress she admired, Billie Dove.

By fourteen, Billie was working with her mother in a Harlem whorehouse. Arrested, Sadie got off. Her daughter, who gave her age as twenty-one, was sentenced to one hundred days. Billie was fifteen when Sadie got a job in the kitchen at Mexico's Harlem speakeasy, musicians' favorite gathering place for jam sessions and cutting contests. Billie started singing, table to table, for tips. Singer Marge Johnson, who was appearing with bandleader Charlie Johnson at Smalls' Paradise, set up an audition for Billie there. An excited Billie blew the opportunity by not knowing in what key she sang.

Soon she could be heard at all the uptown clubs, at some as the booked attraction, at others as a drop-in guest. She was subbing for Monette Moore at Covan's on West 132nd Street the serendipitous night John Hammond came in. Twenty-two-year-old Hammond was New York correspondent for the *Melody Maker*, scion of a wealthy and socially prominent family, a civil libertarian, staunch supporter of live, broadcast, and recorded jazz, and soon-to-be brother-in-law of Benny Goodman. He decided that Billie was "the best jazz singer I had ever heard," a conviction he maintained throughout his life.

On November 27, 1933, Hammond was responsible for Billie Holiday's initial recording, "Your Mother's Son-In-Law" with the Goodman Orchestra. Billie's almost frantic-sounding first date and rapidly developing confidence can be heard on *Billie Holiday: Lady Day's 25 Greatest, 1933–1944* (ASV Living Era). This CD also has "What a Little Moonlight Can Do" and "Miss Brown to You" from July 2, 1935, the wellspring of significant recordings with pianist Teddy Wilson, and a track from her first date with tenor saxophonist Lester Young, "I Must Have That Man," January 25, 1937, as well as several subsequent pairings.

Wilson, intrigued by what he termed her "internal metronome" that produced impeccable time no matter how idiosyncratically—and pithily—she might phrase, offered her both stimulating and symbiotic introductions and accompaniment. Attuned to her special aural affinity for the saxophone, he paired her with Young, Ben Webster, Johnny Hodges, and Harry Carney. The combined personnel of their recording orchestras embraced nearly the entire jazz aristocracy of New York.

"Me, Myself and I" on *Billie Holiday With Lester Young: Lady Day and Prez, 1937–1941* (Giants of Jazz) almost challenges the listener to decide if the duet is vocal or instrumental. On their "Mean to Me" and "Georgia on My Mind," she reconstructed the notes to her very personal vocabulary. Lester consistently asserted that he had to know the lyrics of a song before he could play it effectively. Billie said, "I don't think I'm singing. I feel like I'm playing a horn. I try to improvise like Les Young, like Louis Armstrong, or someone else I admire. What comes out is what I feel. I hate straight singing. I have to change a tune to my own way of doing it. That's all I know."

But because of the powerful and often profound message she had to communicate, she never eschewed words for scat syllables. She didn't have to. Within her limited vocal range she packed more musicality and unique ability to interpret lyrics than any other singer.

Holiday's musical couplings with Wilson and her tenures with the Basie band and at Barney Josephson's Café Society Downtown also resulted from Hammond's efforts, as did her cinema singing debut at nineteen in the Ellington short *Symphony in Black*. (She had been an extra in Paul Robeson's 1933 *The Emperor Jones*.) She did not appear on film again until the 1947 feature *New Orleans*, in which she portrayed a maid and girlfriend of her inspiration Louis Armstrong. In 1950 she made a two-reel short with the Count Basie Sextet. *Lady Sings the Blues*, a 1972 film purporting to be her biography, starring Diana Ross, was almost total fiction.

A stunningly tall woman whose weight seemed to fluctuate with her fortunes, she radiated a bittersweet beauty. An excruciating sadness shadowed even her happiest smile. Self-effacing about her talent and her looks, she carried herself proudly—thus the name "Lady." Young extended it to "Lady Day," and she reciprocated with her highest accolade, "Pres" for President.

Clarinetist Artie Shaw, with whose band she sang for several months, continued to praise her for sixty years: "She was always shooting toward tragedy, it was just a question of how and when . . . I never heard her hit a bad note that was off by even a sixteenth of

a tone. She had a remarkable ear . . . and a remarkable sense of time
. . . She had her own thumb-print, when she sang it was unmistakenly
her . . . [when] she sang something it came alive, I mean, that's what
jazz is about."

For some critics, Billie's unique style was an acquired taste. Her
small, clear, always in-tune voice was not spectacular. Her singing
was. For several years New York's *Amsterdam News* carried
noncommittal-to-lukewarm notices of her appearances as Billy Hal-
liday, echoing the Apollo advertisement for her first date there in
1934.

Aside from strong, spiritual bonds with Young and other warm,
lasting friendships, she was compulsively drawn to handsome, violent,
exploitive men. Reports vary on who introduced her to the heroin
which would ultimately destroy her health and her career, but many
blamed her first husband, Jimmy Monroe, brother of Monroe's Uptown House nightclub owner Clark Monroe. Jimmy, described as
sportsman, impresario, marijuana dealer, and/or pimp, and Billie
were married August 25, 1941. By the second year the liaison was
over, and she was claiming to be married to addicted trumpeter Joe
Guy. A former New York clubowner, John Levy (not the bass player
and personal manager), was next, and on March 28, 1957, Billie, as
Eleanora Fagan, married Louis McKay in Ciudad Juarez, Mexico.
Every one of these men had been involved in drug arrests, usually
with her. Some people speculated that the McKay ceremony was to
prevent their being forced to testify against one another since both
were under indictment in Philadelphia. She already had served a jail
sentence of a year and a day for a drug bust with Guy in 1947.
Consequently, she had since been ineligible for a New York Cabaret
Card permitting her to work in clubs there.

Billie's personal travails were integral to her music. She wrote
"Don't Explain" as catharsis for the pain of hearing Monroe fumble
excuses for coming home with lipstick on his collar. Two versions are
on the Grammy-winning double CD package *Billie Holiday: The
Complete Decca Recordings*, a 1944–50 collection of sessions originally
produced by Milt Gabler. This package contains her definitive "Lover
Man," "Good Morning Heartache," the first sessions with the string
section she long had craved, and a somewhat over-arranged version
of her original "God Bless the Child," along with perceptive notes by
reissue coproducer Steven Lasker. *Billie Holiday: The Complete Commodore Recordings* are Gabler's 1939–44 devotions to the Holiday
oeuvre on his own label and include two takes of the chilling "Strange

Fruit," Lewis Allan's (né Abel Meeropol) dirge to the then not un-common lynching of African Americans. Decca had refused to record the song. Radio stations banned it, as many did her "Gloomy Sunday," the latter on grounds that it inspired suicide.

Seventeen months before she died, she made *Billie Holiday: Lady in Satin* (Columbia), an album with strings and voices arranged and conducted by Ray Ellis that was one of her favorites. Her pervasive sincerity despite a deteriorating, often raspy voice renders it especially affecting.

Possibly the most comprehensive collection is *The Complete Billie Holiday on Verve, 1945–1959* (Verve), ten CDs documenting her free, sensitively produced sessions for Norman Granz including Jazz at the Philharmonic appearances, rehearsals, studio discussions, and alter-nate takes, all with superb instrumental artists of the era. Bobby Tucker, her accompanist from 1944 through most of 1948, is the pianist on several tracks and is heard again in their 1954 and 1955 reunions. According to their clarinetist friend Tony Scott, who rec-ommended Tucker to Billie, he refused job offers from Ella, Sarah, and Dinah Washington to wait for Billie while she was in jail. He left her to accompany Billy Eckstine in December 1948, not the sum-mer of 1949, as most references state. Rowles was her pianist from December 12, 1948.

On May 31, 1959, Billie was admitted to New York City's Metro-politan Hospital with what would be diagnosed as a liver ailment complicated by cardiac failure. No drugs were involved; however, twelve days later she was arrested in her bed for possession of heroin. Dufty and her night nurse were with her when she died at 3:10 A.M., July 17. Fifteen fifty-dollar bills, advance payment for a series of autobiographical articles, were taped to her body. Her bank account registered seventy cents.

Jazz and the American Song

Gene Lees

John Lewis, the composer, pianist, and music director of the Modern Jazz Quartet, has noted—indeed emphasized—that jazz evolved in a symbiotic relationship with the American popular song: "Jazz developed while the great popular music was being turned out. It was a golden age for songs. They had a classic quality in length and shape and form and flexibility of harmony. The jazz musicians were drawn to this music as a source of material. It gave an opportunity to players."

Lester Young not only knew the melody of every song he performed, he made it a point to know the lyrics as well and insisted that every jazz musician should do the same. In October 1939 Coleman Hawkins made a two-chorus recording of Johnny Green's "Body and Soul." It became something of a hit and established him as a major star among jazz fans. And it would be seen in retrospect as a precursor of bebop.

Trumpeter Bunny Berigan's biggest hit was his recording of the Vernon Duke–Ira Gershwin song "I Can't Get Started." Two of the major hits of the big band era were Artie Shaw's recordings of Cole Porter's "Begin the Beguine" and the Hoagy Carmichael–Mitchell Parish song "Star Dust."

Jazz musicians used popular songs from the earliest days. In New

Orleans, they played such songs as "Home Sweet Home," which has roots in opera, including Rossini's *Barber of Seville*. The New Orleans Rhythm Kings recorded "Angry," "Marguerite," and "Sobbin' Blues." The Original Dixieland Jazz Band, on its pioneering session in January 1917, recorded "(Back Home Again in) Indiana" and "At the Darktown Strutter's Ball." The Wolverines with Bix Beiderbecke did "Oh Baby," "Copenhagen," "Susie," and "I Need Some Pettin'," all pop material. Louis Armstrong by 1929 was performing "I Can't Give You Anything but Love" and "Ain't Misbehavin'."

At the same time, jazz was producing its own repertoire of "originals," among them some of the oldest tunes associated with jazz, such as "Tiger Rag," "Sensation Rag," and "Bugle Call Rag." Jelly Roll Morton, though by no means the first musician to record "originals," anticipated Duke Ellington, John Lewis, Thelonious Monk, Dave Brubeck, Horace Silver, and others by composing instrumental works for the groups he led, such as the Red Hot Peppers. Many of his pieces, including "King Porter Stomp," became standard fare for jazz groups and continued to be performed as the twentieth century ended. So too did many Kansas City compositions and the various pieces associated with the Count Basie band, such as "One O'Clock Jump."

Many of these instrumental compositions, with lyrics added, passed into the repertoires of singers, such as Monk's "'Round About Midnight," Lionel Hampton's "Midnight Sun," Erroll Garner's "Misty," Ralph Burns's "Early Autumn," and particularly Duke Ellington compositions such as "Don't Get Around Much Any More," "I Got It Bad and That Ain't Good," "Sophisticated Lady," "I'm Beginning to See the Light," "In a Sentimental Mood," and "Do Nothing Till You Hear From Me." Fats Waller contributed considerably to the "popular" song repertoire: "I've Got a Feeling I'm Falling," "Ain't Misbehavin'," "Black and Blue," "Keepin' Out of Mischief Now," and "Honeysuckle Rose." There is this difference: these Waller songs, many of them collaborations with lyricist Andy Razaf, were designed to be vocal material; the Ellington compositions began as instrumentals.

The hits of the day were familiar to a wide audience and thus gave the performer comparatively easy access to the listener. In later years, Dave Brubeck would say that he liked to open concerts with "St. Louis Blues" because it is known to audiences all over the world. Once an audience's attention is captured, he said, the judicious performer can lead listeners wherever he or she might want to go.

From the standpoint of the audience, the use of this repertoire had

78-rpm record of "Body and Soul" by Coleman Hawkins and His Orchestra. Courtesy of the Institute of Jazz Studies, Rutgers University.

two evident advantages: it was material with which the listener was already comfortable; and it provided a basis on which to assess and appreciate the performer's improvisations.

Jazz musicians have always shown a willingness to incorporate material from other idioms into their work. Witness the Afro-Cuban movement in the 1940s, the wholesale importation of Brazilian songs into jazz from the 1960s right into the present, and the widespread use of the French song "Autumn Leaves." Even grand opera made its contributions to jazz.

But the American song, as it evolved from about 1915 onward, was growing in elegance and sophistication.

In retrospect, the very term *popular music* seems something of a misnomer. Some time in the late 1960s or early 1970s I was introduced to Harold Arlen by Johnny Mercer. I asked him whether he and George Gershwin and Jerome Kern and the other important songwriters of their era were aware that what they were creating was actually art music. Arlen looked a little startled, as if no one had ever asked the question, and after a pensive pause said, "Yes."

The United States is enthralled by the legend of the boy-next-door who without training or the development of professional skills just lucks out and becomes a success: it is intrinsic to its land-of-opportunity mythology. A number of Hollywood song-and-dance movies glorified this legend. It is—or was, before the rock-and-roll era—inherently false, as one realizes on examining the backgrounds of some of the most important composers of classic "popular" music.

Despite the legend of humble origins endlessly repeated in the lay press, many of the major songwriters of the classic era were from the middle and upper middle class, not the poor, the best example of the last being Irving Berlin. The great lyricists of the period had comparable backgrounds, and for the most part they too came from the ranks of the privileged.

That jazz was created intuitively by a gifted but ignorant people in some sort of cultural vacuum is integral to its mystique. The idea is, by the way, certainly condescending and thus subtly racist. Harry "Sweets" Edison said, "Jazz is no folk music. It's too hard to play."

From its earliest days, the music was developed by people of education. Even Buddy Bolden was a high school graduate, and in the one authenticated photo of his group, taken about 1905, we see that his bassist Jimmy Johnson's left hand rests on the neck of his instrument with the middle and ring fingers close together in the correct position taught to (and by) symphony bassists.

Benny Carter recalls studying the Cecil Forsythe orchestration treatise toward the end of the 1920s. Claude Hopkins studied at the Washington Conservatory and had a bachelor's degree from Howard. Pianist Lou Hooper, a figure in Harlem jazz of the 1920s and later one of Oscar Peterson's teachers, was graduated from the Detroit Conservatory in 1916 and ended his career on the faculty of the University of Prince Edward Island. Jimmie Lunceford studied with Paul Whiteman's father, a Denver music educator, then went to Fisk University, graduating with a bachelor of music degree in 1926; he was a music teacher before becoming a bandleader. Lil Hardin Armstrong also studied at Fisk. Don Redman, the son of a music teacher, was a child prodigy who could play most instruments before he entered high school and graduated with a degree in music from Storer College at the age of twenty. Teddy Wilson studied violin for four years at Tuskegee and then was a music theory major at Talladega College. Earl Hines intended to be a concert pianist, and so did one of the pianists he inspired, Mel Powell; both were diverted into jazz, though Powell later returned to classical music as a composer. Milton Hinton aspired to a career as a symphony violinist but turned to jazz bass when it became obvious that such a career was closed to him.

Given the background of men like Carter, Redman, Hooper, Hopkins, and Lunceford, it is inconceivable that they were unaware of the revolutionary turn-of-the century developments in European music. By 1927 William Grant Still—who had a degree from Oberlin College—was studying with the avant-gardist Edgard Varèse and had previously studied with George W. Chadwick while Chadwick was director of the New England Conservatory. Another of Still's influences was Will Vodery. Educated as a scholarship student at the University of Pennsylvania, Vodery became one of the outstanding arrangers of the 1920s and 1930s. He orchestrated at least twelve theater musicals and from 1913 into the 1920s arranged music for the *Ziegfield Follies*. He was in heavy demand through the 1920s and worked as an arranger on the Kern-Hammerstein *Show Boat* before moving to Hollywood to be an arranger and musical director at Fox Films, the first black musician to penetrate that studio world.

In music, private teaching has always been at least as important as class instruction, and a great many of the early black musicians had solid training, whether they had degrees or not.

James Reese Europe, in 1913 and 1914 musical director for Vernon and Irene Castle—who launched the dance craze on which the big band era was built—had been trained on violin and piano in Washington, D.C. He was the first black bandleader to make records, and the first man to play something akin to jazz in Carnegie Hall, on May 5, 1912, February 12, 1913, and February 15, 1919. This was a quarter century before the famous From Spirituals to Swing concert in Carnegie. The Europe band used skilled and schooled musicians. Eubie Blake, who played piano in it, said, "That Europe gang were absolute reading sharks. They could read a moving snake, and if a fly lit on that paper, he got played."

Will Marion Cook, leader of the Southern Syncopators and one of the major influences on Duke Ellington, was a graduate of Oberlin College and studied composition with Dvořák and violin with Joachim. Scott Joplin studied composition and theory at George Smith College for Negroes. The stride pianist James P. Johnson had solid "classical" piano training.

It can be seen, then, that parallel developments were occurring in both jazz and the better kind of popular music: the makers of both were musically educated men, no matter what impression the public might have of them. An affinity of the one for the other seems only logical, even inevitable. The jazz musicians were drawn to the songs; the songwriters were drawn to jazz, particularly George Gershwin and Harold Arlen, who drank deep of jazz: its influence infuses their work.

The best of these popular composers gravitated to the Broadway musical theater and to Hollywood movies, because these media allowed scope for the musical imagination and more or less rapid exposure of the material. Even so-called Tin Pan Alley, the New York music-publishing complex of companies, was producing excellent songs. And this material had in turn more or less rapid exposure to a wide public through the medium of network radio.

Network radio developed toward the end of the 1920s. Four major networks covered the United States and could be heard well up into Canada: NBC, CBS, the Mutual Broadcasting System, and the NBC Blue Network (which evolved into ABC). In the depths of the Great Depression, when record sales fell so far that the recording industry almost collapsed, network radio became the primary source of musical entertainment in North America.

The men who developed these networks at first had no idea what to present on this burgeoning medium of entertainment and, willy-nilly, education. They seized what was available: symphony orchestras (NBC and CBS maintained their own full symphony orchestras on staff), Broadway show music, and the big dance bands, the best of which were heavily influenced by jazz. Some of them *were* jazz bands, like that of Duke Ellington, but even the jazz bands played ballads for dancers, and at this point it becomes an exercise in casuistry to argue whether they were at such times jazz or dance bands.

So powerful was network broadcasting that it could make a new song a national hit literally overnight. Mildred Bailey did this in 1933 with a new song by Johnny Mercer and Hoagy Carmichael: she sang "Lazy Bones" on her radio show and it soon was a hit, being performed by any number of other singers.

In the meantime, the networks had taken to making "remote" broadcasts of the big bands and were able to make huge and almost immediate successes of new groups, as witness the experiences of Benny Goodman and Glenn Miller. Network radio *made* them. And the bands in turn were drawing much of their repertoire from musical theater and the movies. The name bands became so big that many of them appeared as stars in the movies. This symbiotic relationship of network radio, Broadway musical theater, the movies, the big bands, and various emerging singers, such as Mildred Bailey and Bing Crosby, raised the level of American popular music to unprecedented heights.

One can go through the list of hits each year of the 1930s and find quantities of gems and even masterpieces among them. 1930 produced "Body and Soul," "Embraceable You," "Exactly Like You," "Fine and Dandy," "Get Happy," "I Got Rhythm," "I'm Confessin'," "Sunny Side of the Street," and "Them There Eyes," all of which became favorites of jazz musicians.

The year 1934 produced "All Through the Night," "Anything Goes," "As Long as I Live," "Autumn in New York," "Blow Gabriel Blow," "Blue Moon," "The Continental," "Deep Purple," "Flirtation Walk," "For All We Know," "I Get a Kick Out of You," "I Only Have Eyes for You," "If There Is Someone Lovelier Than You," "Let's Take a Walk Around the Block," "Love Is Just Around the Corner," "Miss Otis Regrets," "P.S. I Love You," "Solitude," "Stars Fell on Alabama," "Stay as Sweet as You Are," "Two Cigarettes in the Dark," "The Very Thought of You," "Winter Wonderland," "You and the Night and the Music," and "You're the Top."

The next year produced "Begin the Beguine," "Bess, You Is My Woman Now," "Broadway Rhythm," "Cheek to Cheek," "East of the Sun and West of the Moon," "I Can't Get Started," "I Feel a Song Coming On," "I Got Plenty o'Nuttin'," "I'm Gonna Sit Right Down and Write Myself a Letter," "I'm in the Mood for Love," "Isn't This a Lovely Day?," "It Ain't Necessarily So," "It's Easy to Remember,"

"Just One of Those Things," "Lovely to Look At," "Lullaby of Broadway," "Lulu's Back in Town," "Maybe," "Moon Over Miami," "My Romance," "Paris in the Spring," "The Piccolino," "Red Sails in the Sunset," "Soon," "Stairway to the Stars," "Summertime," "A Woman Is a Sometime Thing," and "You Are My Lucky Star."

It should not, of course, be forgotten that trivial songs were also popular. But no one tried to claim they were art, as the record company publicists would in the case of "folk" songs and rock in the 1960s. They were seen for what they were.

While it was indeed a big band era, the little independent labels were recording small-group jazz with musicians drawn from those bands (and from other origins as well, of course). Thus you find on the Commodore records such tunes as "Jada," "At Sundown," "You Took Advantage of Me," "Three Little Words," and "Memories of You" recorded by Bud Freeman, "I Know That You Know" and "Love Me or Leave Me" by the Kansas City Five, "My Blue Heaven" and "That Old Feeling" recorded by Teddy Wilson, and "I Surrender Dear" and "I Can't Believe That You're in Love With Me" by Coleman Hawkins.

The novel *Young Man With a Horn* by Dorothy Baker, later made into a melodramatic movie with Kirk Douglas, purported to be based on the life of Bix Beiderbecke, the drama built on the musician's torture at having to play "popular" music. By the testimony of those who knew him, Beiderbecke was proud of his presence in and work with the Paul Whiteman band. But more to the point, the jazz musicians didn't play the popular songs because they had to, they played them because they liked them. Every jazz musician was expected to know these songs: they were the lingua franca of the art form, and a rising young musician who didn't know them was likely to find himself politely (or not so politely) barred from the bandstand. When Oscar Peterson, Ray Brown, Edmund Thigpen, and colleagues operated the Advanced School of Contemporary Music in Toronto from 1960 to 1964, they insisted that their students know that repertoire, and know it accurately. All the older musicians, to this day, know that material thoroughly and can play it on request in any key (within reason; preferably the flat keys) at a moment's notice.

Jazz musicians took this dependency on the American song a step further: they began basing "originals"—their own compositions—on the chord structures of popular songs. The first recorded example is "For No Reason at All in C," recorded May 13, 1927, by Frank Trumbauer, Eddie Lang, and Bix Beiderbecke. It is based on the changes of "I'd Climb the Highest Mountain," which came out the previous year.

Duke Ellington's "Hot and Bothered," "Slippery Horn," and "Braggin' in Brass" use the chord changes of "Tiger Rag," first recorded in 1918 by the Original Dixieland Jazz Band, and his "In a Mellotone" comes from the 1917 Art Hickman song "Rose Room." "Donna Lee," attributed to both Miles Davis and Charlie Parker, is based on the 1917 song "(Back Home Again in) Indiana." Benny Harris and Charlie Parker built "Ornithology" on the chords of the 1940 song "How High the Moon," which itself, during the early days of the Jazz at the Philharmonic concerts and LPs, became so popular with musicians that it became known as the national anthem of jazz (John Coltrane would base "Satellite" on it). They liked its descending pattern of modulation and ran the song into the ground. (A similar quality attracted them to Bronislau Kaper's theme for the movie *On Green Dolphin Street*.) Billy Strayhorn derived "Take the 'A' Train" from "Exactly Like You" (and the Brazilian song "So Danço Samba" in turn derives from " 'A' Train"). Charlie Parker got "Yardbird Suite" from Earl Hines's "Rosetta." Juan Tizol's "Perdido" comes from the 1932 Earl Hines song "You Can Depend on Me," which also produced Lennie Tristano's "Wow." Thelonious Monk based "Evidence" on the 1929 song "Just You, Just Me," which was particularly popular with jazz musicians in the 1930s and 1940s. George Wallington's "Godchild" comes from Harold Arlen's 1931 "Between the Devil and the Deep Blue Sea." Kay Swift's "Fine and Dandy" yielded Gerry Mulligan's "Westwood Walk" and, with wry attribution, the Woody Herman number "Keen and Peachy," a joint work of Shorty Rogers and Ralph Burns. Interestingly, Burns's "Early Autumn"— which began life as an instrumental and became a song when Johnny Mercer put words to it—in turn yielded the Brazilian song "O Barquinho." Charlie Parker's "Koko" and Jimmy Raney's "Parker 51" both come from Ray Noble's "Cherokee." Cole Porter's "What Is This Thing Called Love" is the foundation for Tadd Dameron's "Hot House," Lee Konitz's "Subconscious Lee," Coltrane's "Fifth House," and Bill Evans's "These Things Called Changes."

Probably the most appropriated song in jazz history is George Gershwin's 1930 "I Got Rhythm": its offspring include Sidney Bechet's "Shag," Lester Young's "Lester Leaps In," Count Basie's "Jump for Me," Duke Ellington's "Cotton Tail" and "Love You Madly," George Wallington's "Lemon Drop," Dizzy Gillespie's "Dizzy Atmosphere," Monk's "Rhythm-a-ning," Miles Davis's "Swing Spring" and "The Theme," Sonny Rollins's "Oleo," and Parker's "Red Cross,"

"Dexterity," "Moose the Mooche," and "Steeplechase." "Good Bait" by Tadd Dameron and Count Basie and "Tuxedo Junction," attributed to Erskine Hawkins, William Johnson, and Julian Dash, belong in this group.

And that is by no means an exhaustive list, even of the "I Got Rhythm" tunes. Nor does it take into consideration all the jazz "originals" that combine harmonic elements of two or more other tunes. Gerry Mulligan's "Young Blood" combines the "I Got Rhythm" changes for the front strain with a bridge derived from that of "Honeysuckle Rose." (And the first eight bars of Waller's 1929 "Honeysuckle Rose," with II-V-I changes, are interchangeable with Victor Young's "Sweet Sue," which came out a year before it.)

Some years ago, one of the English jazz critics wrote a column decrying the practice of basing jazz compositions on the harmonic content of other songs, without, apparently, realizing how extensive it was and indeed how accepted. He said that something should be done about it. What? You cannot copyright a set of chord changes, and besides, certain changes are so common in popular music (and jazz) as to be a virtual underpinning: for example, the ubiquitous I-VI-II-V, often repeated in other keys in the course of a song.

Of late, a certain amount of revisionist argument has held that jazz *is* the blues. This is patently false, as any examination of the tremendous use of standard songs in jazz, and the basing of new tunes on the standards, makes clear. Art Tatum, one of the greatest of all jazz musicians, was not particularly interested in playing blues, and rarely did. Neither was Teddy Wilson. Indeed, not all the great jazz players even liked the blues. Ben Webster, one of the masters of the ballad, once said to me, "If I never have to play another blues, it's all right with me."

The "standards" formed by far the largest portion of the jazz repertoire, and any number of albums attested to this: the Miles Davis–Gil Evans recording of *Porgy and Bess,* the Bill Potts album (with soloists such as Zoot Sims and Bill Evans) titled *The Jazz Soul of Porgy and Bess,* recordings of the songs from that score by Ella Fitzgerald and Louis Armstrong, Norman Granz's *Song Book* series of albums by Fitzgerald dedicated to Gershwin, Porter, and the other great composers of "popular" music, similar songbook recordings by the Oscar Peterson Trio, a hugely successful recording by the Peterson group of the *West Side Story* music, a similarly successful André Previn album of the music from *My Fair Lady,* a Chet Baker album titled *Chet Baker Plays the Best of Lerner and Loewe,* and many more.

In his introduction to Alec Wilder's monumental book *American*

Popular Song: The Great Innovators, 1900–1950, music historian James T. Maher—in fact coauthor of the book—writes: "By 1950 the professional tradition in song writing was nearing its end.... Consumption patterns in popular music had changed rapidly in the post World War II years. Singers and singing groups enjoyed a new primacy in the ordering of the economic priorities in the pop market.... The rock era was about to begin." Alec Wilder, in private conversation, put it this way: "The amateurs took over."

The soldiers returning from World War II in and shortly after 1945 married the girls they used to take dancing to the big bands, and began families. An evening—or even afternoon—out required the hiring of a baby-sitter, among other complications. Not only did audiences for the big bands drop off in the late 1940s; so did attendance at baseball games and movies. Americans became accustomed to movie theaters converted into supermarkets, with the price of lamb chops displayed on marquees where the names of stars used to be. And soon there was a new medium of entertainment, one that acted further to keep the young families at home: television. Advertising agencies and their clients by 1950 were discovering the extraordinary power of TV to sell merchandise, and the big radio networks—the highway of communication for the big bands, Tin Pan Alley, and musical theater—redirected their energies from radio broadcasting to TV, at first only to local programs but in the 1950s to the nascent networks. In time CBS, NBC, and ABC ceased to produce radio network shows almost completely.

Radio became more and more a local affair, and the stations by 1955 were discovering what came to be known as the Top Forty (and in time even Top Twenty and Top Ten) format, playing the big hit songs over and over. Radio no longer carried live broadcasts of big bands, nor did it hire symphony orchestras or generate its own music: the local stations could play records all day, at negligible cost. The record companies, anxious to get their wares exposed, developed the practice of payola: the bribing of program managers and disc jockeys to expose their records. Despite repeated attempts by law enforcement agencies and the Federal Communications Commission, payola simply could not be extinguished.

And the radio stations and record companies jointly discovered something else: the lowest common denominator of public taste. Network radio had proved to be the most powerful medium of education the world had ever known. Nonnetwork radio proved to be its antithesis: a medium of diseducation, if we might coin a word. If one consults the hit lists of the 1950s and 1960s, one notices a steady rise in the number of bad songs, along with the concomitant decline of exposure to the great classic songs of the past and the development of new ones of that stature. With the proliferation of FM broadcasting in the 1950s, the corporations owning the stations disseminated a soothing rationale: tacitly admitting that what was heard on AM broadcasts was, increasingly, trash, they said that FM would be the medium of "good" music and higher culture. But they would abandon even that sophism, and FM soon began the transition to current pop and rock.

Something else was happening, little noted in the jazz world to this day. When the big bands declined and were dismantled, musicians just out of jobs, the inventive ones anyway, found fresh employment in nightclubs. So did the better singers, themselves products (for the most part) of the big bands. And the audiences who had come to see the major soloists of the bands as stars followed them into these nightclubs. By 1960 the rise of jazz festivals, at first in Newport, Rhode Island, then in Monterey, California, and soon in other cities as well, provided further employment. And there was still enough jazz heard on the radio to help build an audience of younger listeners. This too would change.

It was not uncommon, a few years ago, when one asked a younger person how he or she had acquired a taste for Irving Berlin or Cole Porter or for jazz to get this answer: "Well, my mother and father had a big record collection, and I listened to it." You will encounter that answer only rarely now. A fan of Elvis Presley who was fifteen in 1955, when Presley's career came to a seismic pinnacle, was turning sixty as the twentieth century ended. It is unlikely that he or she ever had a Rodgers and Hart collection.

Nor is anyone likely to be exposed to Porter and Berlin by listening to the radio: stations which play that kind of music have grown very rare in the United States. On December 27, 1998, WQEW, the last station in New York presenting that kind of music, changed format. Stephen Holden wrote in the *New York Times* of December 16, 1998, that "the thought of a New York climate in which the voices of Frank Sinatra, Ella Fitzgerald, Tony Bennett and a dozen others like them can't be heard regularly on the radio is almost unimaginable." He noted, "WQEW is not exactly a temple of enlightened nostalgia; but with its passing, a vital link to our cultural past is being severed."

Almost simultaneously, the city's most important cabaret, Rainbow and Stars, at the top of Rockefeller Center, was closed. A few cabarets still exist, but their ability to preserve and disseminate the major songs of the American repertoire is as nothing compared with that of the major radio networks in the past, when the songs could be heard by millions of persons day after day. Thus too the few—very few—radio stations that still present such music.

The severing of cultural ties to our history presents a new situation in jazz. First of all, not only do many (but by no means all, of course) of the younger musicians not know the "standards." The audience, for the most part, doesn't know them either. And little new popular music of quality is being produced. Or put it this way: the little that is produced gets scant exposure, since the singers who might record it sell few records and can't get their records played on the radio anyway.

The decline in the quality of music on Broadway to the level of *Cats* and *Phantom of the Opera* and their meandering banalities is yet another factor. The audiences who attend such shows grew up on music that is, in composer David Raksin's phrase, at the level of finger-painting and wouldn't know a good score if they heard it. The situation is no better in Hollywood, which used to give us Rodgers and Hart and Harry Warren. Watch the Golden Globe or Academy Awards broadcast, and if you are, as the French say, of a certain age, you will be appalled at the level to which film-score songwriting has fallen since the days of Johnny Mandel's music for *The Sandpiper* and *The Americanization of Emily,* among other films, and Henry Mancini's to any number of pictures.

If the audiences for jazz, in the shrinking number of jazz clubs and the diminishing number of jazz radio stations, don't know the standard songs, why should younger jazz musicians play them, even if they know them? One reason, of course, could be that they like them. But the body of great standard songs is no longer a given between musicians and listeners. So why should they perform and record them? Why not write and record "originals" and pocket the attendant royalties? In fact, many younger performers are doing exactly that. There are very few among them, however, of the compositional strength of Horace Silver, Dave Brubeck, John Lewis, Duke Ellington, Dizzy Gillespie, and Gerry Mulligan, all of whom, let us note, started out playing the standards and did so until they had built followers who came to appreciate them as composers. And most of them based many of their "originals" on standards.

As material for improvisation, "modern" popular music, including that derived from Broadway and the movies, not to mention Nashville, is pretty thin gruel. Can you conceive of a jazz album of the hits of Waylon Jennings? Tammy Wynette? Garth Brooks? Or the songs from *The Lion King*? Can you imagine anyone recording an album titled *The Jazz Soul of Andrew Lloyd Webber*?

This is not to say that all is lost. Younger instrumentalists and singers continue to record standards. There are still successful revivals of the classic Broadway shows that introduced much of this repertoire. And at this writing, Lincoln Center is inaugurating a concert series devoted to the American popular song. But these and other like developments have the feeling of a rearguard action; they amount to limited preservation of a great tradition, not a further evolution.

John Lewis is right. Jazz evolved in a very close relationship with popular music, a popular music of the highest quality and subtle intellectual appeal. That era is over.

Pre–Swing Era Big Bands and Jazz Composing and Arranging

James T. Maher and Jeffrey Sultanof

The American dance band has often mirrored its rich past while moving forward as a vital part of cross-cultural exchanges. In the post–World War I era its commonplace popular song repertoire was first reshaped by "symphonic" orchestrations, then was transformed by the creative scoring of young arrangers, black and white alike, audaciously probing the future. Immediately after the war it surfaced as a show business commodity with an underpinning of historical changes in dancing, broadcasting, recording, and filmmaking. Quickly, its publicity—pro and con—pushed it into the celebrity world, where it deployed its exciting and musically turbulent other self: jazz (which in after-hours jamming, and later in public performances, often subverted segregation, as the musician-writer Rex Stewart has observed).

In Europe in the early nineteenth century, the first celebrity dance orchestra emerged during the Congress of Vienna (1812–22). At that time violinist Joseph Lanner started a dance orchestra, creating a historic "book" of his own music. Soon, Lanner had four orchestras meeting the demand for his music in ballrooms, beer gardens, concert rooms, and private mansions. The first leader of a Lanner spin-off band was Johann Strauss I, who eventually toured as the first continental "name" band. Waltzes written by Strauss and his namesake son became the smash hits of the era and are still being played and recorded.

Nathaniel Gow, successor to his father, Niel, as a prominent Edinburgh leader, composer, teacher, and dance musician, led a band that played privately at Carlton House for the Prince Regent (crowned George IV, 1820) and then became the favorite of London's waltzing nobility at Almack's. He led "the most requested dance band of his time" in the British Isles.

In Philadelphia, Francis Johnson (1792–1844) was not only a peerless improvising black multi-instrumentalist, but also a composer whose work gave an "American" mint mark to the music of the new nation, a brass-band leader, a concert conductor, and the leader of the dance band of choice of the exclusive Assemblies of "Old Philadelphia" society and dancers summering at Saratoga Springs. He led the first American ensemble to perform in Europe (1837), met Johann Strauss I and Philippe Musard, brought Strauss's waltzes and Musard's concept of the "Promenade" concert, as well as the cotillion ball, back to America, and toured as far west as St. Louis, being saluted en route by the *Detroit Free Press* (1839) as "one of those men who by his own unaided exertions has found his own way ... to the topmost round of the ladder of fame, and it may be said of him without fear of contradiction, that as a composer or a musician, he stands without a rival in the United States." When he died in 1844, the *Philadelphia Ledger* observed that "Frank was one of the most celebrated personages" of the city, and "famous all over the union."

The four Dodworth brothers—Allen, Thomas, Harvey, Charles— born in London and brought to New York as youngsters in 1825 by their dancing-master father, organized ensembles for theater, chamber music, parades, and dancing. They were frequently in demand during the summer for popular Hudson River excursion boat *ad libitum* dances, and by the mid-1840s their dance band "dominated New York City winter balls," providing "unqualified satisfaction." Further, they helped form the New York Philharmonic, taught music, ran the city's leading dance school, introduced the saxophone into the American concert wind band, and ran the music store that may have imported the first saxophones from Paris.

Dance bands in general flourished in the United States after the Civil War. Historian-bandleader-educator Rick Benjamin has documented that the publishing company of Carl Fischer carried over five hundred dance and theater orchestra titles by the mid-1870s. These

Fletcher Henderson Band, Atlantic City, N.J., July, 1932. Left to right: Russell Procope, clarinet and alto sax; Coleman Hawkins, tenor sax; Edgar Sampson, alto sax and violin; Clarence Holiday (Billie Holiday's father), guitar; Walter Johnson, drums; John Kirby, bass; Henderson, piano and arranger; Russell Smith, first trumpet; Bobby Stark, second trumpet; Rex Stewart, cornet; J.C. Higginbotham, trombone; Sandy Williams, trombone. Courtesy Frank Driggs Collection.

were called stock arrangements, because they were "stocked" (cata-
logued) by music publishers, and marketed for ensembles in two sizes:
small orchestra (seven pieces) and full orchestra (ten pieces). Later
on, there were also quite a number of itinerant black circus sideshow
and tent show bands, about five pieces in size, moving across the
country. The great Ringling Bros. bandmaster Merle Evans recalled
how, by 1900, the younger circus bandsmen would gather enthusiastically between shows to listen to them. Syncopated dance music
was alive in many different places in those years, not just New
Orleans.

Dance orchestras of Afro-American musicians were commonly
found along the eastern seaboard from Washington to Boston playing
for high society balls as early as the 1880s. The years before World
War I in general were very good for black ensembles and entertainers.
Part of that demand was met by composer-arranger-organizer James
Reese Europe, who led the creation of the Clef and Tempo Clubs as
booking offices for dance ensembles large and small. Accepted and
championed by moneyed patrons, Europe further cemented his identification as *the* dance band man when he became the musical director
for Vernon and Irene Castle, the most popular dance team in the
country. Social dancing in general was becoming accepted in society,
due largely to the efforts of the Castles, who set up dancing schools
and social events and even opened their own club.

The first seeds of the new dance music were sown during the
second decade of the twentieth century. Ensembles from New Orleans
began playing in major cities across the country—Bill Johnson with
the Original Creole Orchestra, Tom Brown in Chicago with his Band
from Dixieland in 1915, and the Original Dixieland Jazz Band, which
opened at Reisenweber's Café in New York in 1917. In the cases of
Brown and the ODJB, audiences were initially bewildered with what
they heard, and it was the musicians themselves who showed patrons
how to dance to the new style of syncopated music, with its radical
ensemble improvisation. The music later known as *jass* or *jazz* virtually exploded in New York by the end of the decade.

Anticipating a "dance craze" after the war, ballrooms and dance
halls were built in nearly every major city in the country. At one
time, dance halls had quite an unsavory reputation; in the early nineteenth century, they were sometimes called "free-and-easies," and
even the classiest of them were little more than hiring halls for
prostitutes, another reason why public dancing was often shunned in
that era. With tougher state laws for the control of dance halls (and,

in some cases, regular police inspection), the newer ballrooms flourished. Some of the best remembered of those early spots were the Arcadia, the Cinderella, and, of course, Roseland in New York, the Graystone in Detroit, and the "million-dollar" Trianon in Chicago.

Art Hickman's band is generally considered the first important organized band in this period. Originally six pieces (trumpet, trombone, piano, two banjos, and drums), two more musicians were later added (violin and string bass). The group was organized in 1913 and played the summer season at the St. Francis Hotel in San Francisco. They were a star attraction at the San Francisco World's Fair in 1915. In 1919 Hickman added two saxophones, a proto-reed section.

One cannot stress too heavily the importance of the introduction of the saxophone into popular music at that time. Saxophone ensembles had been mainstays in brass bands, live shows, and vaudeville at the turn of the century (e.g., the Six Brown Brothers) and were generally regarded as novelty instruments. But it was the introduction of the instrument into Hickman's ensemble, as well as its becoming part of the theater and pit orchestrations by Frank Saddler for the Kern/Wodehouse/Bolton Princess Theater shows, that pointed the way to their acceptance in popular music ensembles. Saxophone parts were included in dance band stock arrangements as early as 1916; previously, sax players had to adapt cello parts. The saxophone made a string section sound larger, and two or three of them made a nice balanced contrast to brass sections of two or three instruments. At first, Hickman's saxophone "unit" played in counterpoint to, or in harmony with, the strings or brass. But a new concept in dance bands was emerging: the orchestra divided up into "choral" sections, much like a choir with its four "voices."

Hickman helped ensure his band's popularity by writing a song that eventually became a standard, "Rose Room." In 1919 Columbia Records brought the band to New York for two weeks of recording. Other bands that became big names later on were first organized in the late teens. King Oliver's Olympia band was first organized in New Orleans in 1916 and moved to Chicago in 1918; Paul Specht and Ted Lewis started their units in 1916. Meyer Davis became a leader in 1915. Isham Jones's first band was organized in 1917; by the early 1920s, he had what many considered the finest dance band in Chicago.

Paul Whiteman organized a dance band to appear at the Fairmont Hotel in San Francisco in 1918; within a year it had become a movie colony favorite in Los Angeles, thanks largely to Ferde Grofé's innovations in dance band orchestration. Grofé's concepts would not only give the Whiteman band its musical signature, but they were to become a historic landmark in arranging. Grofé, as biographer Jim Farrington has documented, was schooled in harmony and counterpoint and well trained as a multi-instrumentalist (violin, viola, alto horn, piano, portable organ, celeste). His long years of pre-Whiteman itinerancy included performing in medicine shows, dance halls, theaters, symphony orchestras, restaurants, and hotels and on silent movie lots (setting the mood for the actors). He had both played and arranged for Art Hickman, and he had even participated in after-hours jam sessions while a pianist and arranger with Art Guerin's Jazz Band in San Francisco. Grofé restructured commonplace "routines" and parts distributions of dance band scoring (e.g., his famous "harmony choruses" with soft harmonic reed voicings under a solo saxophone or trumpet melody line); in short, he brought a more formal "orchestral" sound to Whiteman's music. Upon hearing Whiteman's ensemble play at an Atlantic City hotel, a representative from the Victor Phonograph Company signed the ensemble to a contract. "Whispering" (Victor) became the first of many big recorded hits for Whiteman's band, reportedly selling over two million copies, and made him an international name.

Although it made appearances mostly at its own roadhouse near New York, the Ramblers Inn, the California Ramblers was a very influential group from its first recorded appearance in 1921. Managed by Ed Kirkeby, who often sang with the band, this organization may have been the first all-star jazz-oriented big band. At one time or another, sidemen included pianist Irving Brodsky, Tommy and Jimmy Dorsey, Red Nichols, bass saxophonist Adrian Rollini, and trumpeter Chelsea Quealey. The band's recordings were issued under a wide variety of names for a variety of labels, including some of the last recordings issued by Edison.

Ben Pollack had been the drummer with the New Orleans Rhythm Kings, although he was born and raised in Chicago. He eventually put together one of the most exciting orchestras of the day, which included Benny Goodman, Glenn Miller, Jack Teagarden, and Jimmy McPartland. The band only worked sporadically and made recordings which rarely showed what it could do, although "Waitin' for Katie," "Singapore Sorrows," and "My Kinda Love" (Victor) are still impressive today. Miller wrote a number of scores for the band, and the other chief arranger was Joseph "Fud" Livingston, who wrote some of the most melodically and harmonically challenging music of the time.

The Ben Bernie, Vincent Lopez, Ted Lewis, and Whiteman bands also played in motion picture theaters as part of live stage shows. Usually there were from three to five acts; the band was required to perform its own music, but sometimes also had to provide the music for the other acts on the bill. If the band was booked for a three-week stay, the musicians had to prepare three totally different presentations of music. Fred Waring became a master at this skill; his planning and pacing of live shows was legendary, often changing on the spot to adapt to audience reaction.

However, few musical departures of the Jazz Age had greater long-range impact than the scoring innovations of the leading black arrangers. Paradoxically, they combined the conservatory training of Don Redman, the inbred formality of Fletcher Henderson, and the unique timbral orchestrations of Duke Ellington, all with the formative legacy of plantation music and the consequent uninhibited, improvisational performance practices it generated in the playing of black musicians everywhere in the country.

Fletcher Henderson had been making dance recordings for Black Swan Records from its inception in 1921 and was organizing groups for club engagements by 1923. A job at the Club Alabam (formerly the Little Club) in 1924 was Henderson's "official" debut as a leader of his own orchestra. Louis Armstrong joined the orchestra that same year, and his tenure made a profound impression on soloists and jazz bands in general; almost every dance band in the country was encouraged to have at least one musician in its ranks who could play "hot" solos. Henderson's band during the 1920s was a veritable all-star unit; at one time or another, trumpeters Armstrong and Rex Stewart, trombonist Jimmy Harrison, and reedmen Don Redman, Coleman Hawkins, Benny Carter, and Buster Bailey were members. It became a house band at Roseland, and Henderson was cited in *Variety* as the "Ivy League prom king." Redman was Henderson's first important arranger, and such recordings as "Copenhagen," "Shanghai Shuffle," "TNT," and "Henderson Stomp" (all Columbia) show off his vision of jazz orchestra styling: an interplay of brass and reeds, often in a call-and-response manner. He also further developed the idea of backgrounds behind soloists, either chordal or riff-based lines that were jazz-oriented in contrast to Grofé's "harmony chorus" figures. Both Fletcher and his younger brother, Horace Henderson, continued along the same path beginning in 1931, long after Redman left to become the musical director of McKinney's Cotton Pickers.

The work of the Hendersons is thought by many historians to be leaner, less cluttered, and more swinging than Redman's work. It was said by Henderson's musicians that the music almost played itself with its relaxed swing; in fact, Rex Stewart later said that Fletcher often took improvised licks he heard his band members playing, organizing and harmonizing them into an arrangement. These qualities are evident in such Henderson classics as Fletcher's "Down South Camp Meeting" (Decca), "King Porter Stomp" (Columbia), and Horace's "Big John's Special" (Decca). Henderson arrangements were an important element in the success of the Benny Goodman orchestra, and both Hendersons' treatments of pop tunes were imitated by every major swing band of the era. Benny Carter also contributed important arrangements to the Henderson band, including "Keep a Song in Your Soul" (Columbia) and "Happy as the Day is Long" (Decca). Carter would score a series of his own compositions for his own band that were memorable for their block-chord voicings and sinuously flowing saxophone section passages, which also became "swing era" cornerstones ("Lonesome Nights," OKeh; "Symphony in Riffs," Columbia).

Charlie Johnson led an impressive big band at Smalls' Paradise in Harlem starting in 1925 and remained there for ten years. Luis Russell, a pianist-arranger born in Panama, led an excellent New Orleans–style big band; its members included Henry "Red" Allen, Pops Foster, J. C. Higginbotham, Paul Barbarin, and Albert Nicholas. Such recordings as "Feelin' the Spirit," "Jersey Lightning," and "Louisiana Swing" (all OKeh) show off the band at its best. Russell's band later became the accompanying group behind Louis Armstrong, sacrificing its individuality.

Duke Ellington's first important job was at the Hollywood Club beginning in the fall of 1923; in March of 1925, the name of the establishment was changed to the Kentucky Club, and the band broadcast locally every night after 2:00 A.M. Patronized by Broadway personalities, jazz musicians, racketeers, and the "in" crowd of that era, the Ellington band soon built a strong reputation playing for the featured revue and for dancing afterwards. Trumpeter Bubber Miley and trombonist "Tricky Sam" Nanton became important formative voices in the Ellington orchestra at this time. Publisher-promoter Irving Mills heard the band and eventually became Ellington's manager, getting him recording work and publishing his music. It was Mills who arranged for Ellington to open at the Cotton Club in Harlem on December 4, 1927. Ellington's broadcasts from the club were heard all over the country. The band was now ten pieces. Ellington widened his harmonic and melodic vocabulary, tailoring his music to that of his players, who now included Barney Bigard, Harry Carney, and, by 1928, Johnny Hodges. Such early recordings as "East St. Louis Toodle-Oo," "Black and Tan Fantasy," and "Creole Love Call" (with the wordless soprano of Adelaide Hall) (Victor and OKeh) signaled a unique, major voice in American music.

By 1924, according to *Variety*, there were more than nine hundred dance bands, representing steady work for about 7,200 musicians. Whiteman, Meyer Davis, Paul Specht, and Sam Lanin started their own agencies. There were sixty-eight Whiteman orchestras across the country playing music from the Whiteman library, eleven in New York alone. Meyer Davis built a society-band empire in Washington, D.C. Eventually nationwide booking agencies were set up to handle dance bands; one of the most important was founded in 1924 by Jules Stein and Billy Goodheart. Music Corporation of America became one of the biggest bookers of bands during the big band era, eventually representing such important leaders as Benny Goodman and Tommy Dorsey. Another large agency formed in the 1920s was Rockwell-O'Keefe, later called General Artists Corporation.

Recordings and radio helped to publicize and popularize bands. Victor released one or two Whiteman discs a month, as did Brunswick with its leading best-seller, Isham Jones. Fletcher Henderson, the California Ramblers, and Duke Ellington were also popular with record buyers. Such was the demand that some of these groups recorded for several labels under many names. By 1922 newspapers, department stores, and other organizations owned radio stations, and virtually anybody who walked into the studio could perform on the air. Vincent Lopez and Paul Specht both claimed to have made the first radio broadcast of a dance band (1920/1921); live broadcasts from clubs, dance halls, and restaurants became standard late-night radio fare by the late 1920s, and such unsponsored broadcasts created huge fan bases for bands led by Coon-Sanders, Duke Ellington, Fletcher Henderson, Jan Garber, and Anson Weeks, as many listeners could pick up broadcasts from hundreds of miles away.

Also active across the country were various dance and jazz ensembles later called territory bands. Basically, these bands played within a given booking "territory," although some ensembles made occasional tours to cities several hundred miles from their home base. Besides servicing the many ballrooms in large and small cities throughout the East, Midwest, South, and Southwest, many of these ensembles were training grounds for musicians who subsequently played in the popular orchestras of the big band era. On occasion, a territory band became a national attraction. Two such groups were house bands at Jean Goldkette's Graystone Ballroom in Detroit. Gold-kette managed one of the finest jazz/dance orchestras of the twenties, with such musicians as Bix Beiderbecke, Frank Trumbauer, Steve Brown, Don Murray, Joe Venuti, and Eddie Lang. Bill Challis's innovative scores of such songs as "My Pretty Girl, "Blue River," and "Clementine" (Victor) helped to make this ensemble a hard one to beat in a "battle" with another band, even topping Henderson's band at Roseland in 1926. Goldkette also managed McKinney's Cotton Pickers. Originally an ensemble from Ohio led by drummer William McKinney with trumpeter John Nesbitt as its chief arranger, the Cotton Pickers hired Don Redman as musical director in the summer of 1927. Recordings of Redman's arrangements of "Gee, Ain't I Good to You," "Miss Hannah," and "Wherever There's a Will, Baby," and of Nesbitt's scores of "Stop Kidding" and "Plain Dirt" (all Victor), show this group at its musical peak. The band never recovered from the departure of Redman in 1931. Nesbitt later freelanced until his untimely death in 1935.

Another memorable territory band was led by pianist Bennie Moten from his home base of Kansas City. The Moten band included such musicians as Jimmy Rushing, Count Basie, Eddie Barefield, Eddie Durham, and Oran "Hot Lips" Page. Many of these musicians had been members of Walter Page's Blue Devils, a rival band active until 1931, when Page was forced to disband for financial reasons. The Moten band's style was based on a relaxed swing feel and tunes which were riff- and blues-based, making it a precursor of the Count Basie band. Perhaps the band's best recordings were made in 1932 at its last recording session, which featured arrangements by Durham, Barefield, and Basie. "Moten Swing," "Milenberg Joys," and "Prince of Wails" (Victor) are considered classics in Kansas City big band swing. Other popular territory groups included Zach Whyte (Ohio; Sy Oliver, arranger), Alphonse Trent (Southwest), and Les Hite (West Coast).

By the mid-1920s, the average dance band was made up of ten pieces: two altos and one tenor saxophone doubling on other reed instruments and sometimes violin, two trumpets, one trombone, banjo/guitar, piano, string/brass bass, and drum set/percussion. If an additional instrument was added, it was usually a second trombone. The alto-tenor-alto lineup was formalized so that if a band had only two saxophones, the preference was for one alto and one tenor.

As early as 1922, Abel Green was writing in *Variety* of the importance of the arranger in preparing the music bands played, often setting the band's musical style along with the leader. Sometimes if the leader was a front man only, the arranger bore the entire responsibility of the band's "book." By that time, many of the techniques for writing for dance orchestras were so common that in 1925 leader-arranger Arthur Lange self-published the book *Arranging for the Modern Dance Orchestra*. This volume became the text for many up-and-coming arrangers; it is known that Glenn Miller studied it extensively.

Lange was also one of the key writers of stock arrangements of the period; other active arrangers at that time were Bob Haring, Jack Mason, Elmer Schoebel, Frank Skinner, Mel Stitzel, and Walter Paul. For many years, it was generally thought that most recording dance and jazz bands used their own arrangements. However, research by Vince Giordano has shown that even Fletcher Henderson's band used stock arrangements as starting points for many of its recordings and live gigs. Arranger Don Redman and/or other band members added instrumental parts, rewrote endings, added transitional sections, and opened up the arrangements for improvisation. Stocks were also used by bands to fulfill requests by dancers for pop hits. Publishers provided stock arrangements free of charge to professional bands so their songs could be played. It should also be noted that even the most jazz-oriented of bands, such as the Henderson, Goldkette, Moten, and Lunceford ensembles, played in any number of different dance styles, from fox-trots to waltzes to tangos. If ballroom patrons were not motivated to dance, the band was considered a failure and would be fired. Both Henderson and later Lunceford prided themselves on their playing of waltzes.

Paul Whiteman broke another barrier in the dance band world when he began giving formal concerts in 1924. He had discussed giving a jazz concert as early as 1922 when his band played in the pit of *George White's Scandals* (the same production that presented George Gershwin's proto-opera *Blue Monday*). Upon hearing that his rival Vincent Lopez was planning his own jazz concert, Whiteman rented Aeolian Hall and invited the most important classical music artists, critics, and members of the society world to the event. Gershwin was joltingly reminded through a newspaper item that he had agreed to write a composition for the concert, which was only about five weeks off. He became a national celebrity overnight when his composition *A Rhapsody in Blue* created a sensation. Over the years, Whiteman made many appearances with his orchestra performing newly commissioned concert music, always looking to find another Gershwin.

By the late 1920s, Whiteman was offering generous contracts to many top jazzmen of the day. Upon the dissolution of the Jean Goldkette Orchestra in 1927, Bix Beiderbecke, Frank Trumbauer, Steve Brown, and Bill Challis joined Whiteman's ensemble. His arranging staff included some of the great innovators of American music: Challis, Ferde Grofé, Tom Satterfield, Lennie Hayton, and Matty Malneck. Whiteman also pioneered the practice of white orchestras commissioning black musicians to write arrangements by hiring William Grant Still and Don Redman to contribute music to his band's book. "Changes," "Lonely Melody," and "San" (Victor) show how impressive this band was, and a reevaluation of Whiteman's place in the history of jazz is just beginning.

The Depression brought major changes to the band business. With widespread unemployment and former ballroom patrons now raising families and needing money for basic necessities, many of the jazz-oriented bands suddenly had no work and were forced to disband. The recording industry was extremely hard hit; with free music available on the radio, record sales plummeted. Several labels went bankrupt and were bought by others.

Radio audiences preferred the "sweet" bands of Guy Lombardo and Jan Garber. Yet some important jazz-oriented groups emerged in popularity during this era. The Casa Loma Orchestra was a big favorite among college and high school students for its exciting, driving instrumentals and the beauty of its ballad performances. Arranger Gene Gifford set the Casa Loma style with such instrumentals as "Casa Loma Stomp" and "Black Jazz" (Brunswick). Gifford's arrangements were admired and widely imitated; Gil Evans has said that the Casa Loma band was a great favorite of his. While some historians have questioned whether the band really "swung," others are convinced that the popularity of the Casa Loma Orchestra was the true beginning of the swing era. Certainly it was a pioneering all-around dance band and a precursor of things to come.

Tommy and Jimmy Dorsey's orchestra was also a favorite of the college crowd. A unique sound was created with an instrumentation of one trumpet, three trombones, three reeds, and a four-piece rhythm section. The melody was played in the middle to low register (tenor sax and trombones), almost in imitation of Bing Crosby's baritone voice (interestingly, Bing's brother Bob sang with the band). While the Dorsey Brothers band was also strong in the ballad department, its personnel was loaded with excellent improvisers, starting with the leaders themselves, and such Brunswick and Decca recordings as "Stop, Look and Listen," "Honeysuckle Rose," "I Can't Dance (I Got

Ants in My Pants)," "St. Louis Blues," and "By Heck" were filled with exciting, danceable big band jazz with hot solos. In 1935, however, Tommy and Jimmy got into a dispute during an engagement at the Glen Island Casino, and Tommy walked off the stand. Taking over most of the Joe Haymes Orchestra, Tommy was back in business soon after with a band that became, in the opinion of several writers, the best all-around ensemble of the big band era.

Among black bands, a European tour of the Ellington orchestra in 1933 was a major success. His music was treated with great respect and interest even by non–jazz enthusiasts. Jimmie Lunceford's band came into its own by the mid-1930s. Originally known as the Chickasaw Syncopators, the band was made up of his former high school students, and a Decca recording contract yielded "Stratosphere," "Swanee River," and "My Blue Heaven." Pianist Earl Hines had a new band that performed and broadcast in Chicago with Jimmy Mundy as arranger, recording for Brunswick.

An event which signaled the beginning of a new era in dance music was the Saturday night NBC radio series *Let's Dance*, debuting on December 1, 1934. Performances by the Kel Murray, Xavier Cugat, and Benny Goodman orchestras were rotated for each time zone during each weekly three-hour broadcast, providing most listeners their first exposure to the Benny Goodman Orchestra. The band's arrangements by Spud Murphy, Fletcher and Horace Henderson, Jimmy Mundy, Joe Lipman, Benny Carter, and others signaled a new kind of dance music. Goodman went on tour and scored his first big success at the Palomar Ballroom in Los Angeles in August of 1935. On March 3, 1937, the band opened at the Paramount Theater in New York and created a national sensation, and the brief swing era burst wide open.

Swing Era Big Bands and Jazz Composing and Arranging

Max Harrison

ollowing the Depression, the early 1930s seemed a bad time for jazz. Yet music's unfolding cannot be subsumed in cultural, still less social, history, and recordings—our sole reliable witnesses—prove that the language of jazz continued to develop. What happened in the 1930s was built on the 1920s, the achievements of that decade being consolidated and synthesized, then germinating further innovations. These became known as swing.

In the jazz of the 1930s there was no specifically "new movement." There seldom is; yet people prefer fantasy to fact, and hence various dates have been accepted as marking the start of this swing music. The most plausible remains August 21, 1935, the day of a spectacularly successful performance from Benny Goodman's dejected band at a ballroom in Los Angeles. Yet by then swing was almost old, and a less improbable candidate is the now-forgotten Casa Loma Orchestra, which from 1930 recorded in a style that seemed new to jazz. Played with extraordinary impetus, "Maniac's Ball" (Brunswick) is representative, and tension is increased relentlessly through each idea being slightly more propulsive than the last. Gene Gifford, the band's chief arranger, was preoccupied not with melody or color but with almost

Count Basie Band, Famous Door, 52nd Street, New York, 1938. Left to right: Jimmy Rushing (hidden), vocals; Walter Page, bass; Jo Jones, drums; Freddie Green, guitar; Basie, piano; Herschel Evans, Earle Warren, Jack Washington, Lester Young, reeds; Buck Clayton, Ed Lewis, Harry "Sweets" Edison, trumpets; Benny Morton, Dan Minor (hidden), Dicky Wells, trombones. Courtesy Frank Driggs Collection.

abstract lines, masses, opposing patterns. A precise interlocking of performance and arrangement explains the feeling of continuity which this music powerfully imposes, and through a paradox only possible in music such pieces sounded both strictly controlled and frantic.

As such they influenced bands of greater reputation, and recordings in a comparable manner, which sound flamboyantly offhand yet demanded much careful rehearsal, were set down by Fletcher Henderson, Jimmie Lunceford, Bennie Moten, Earl Hines, Goodman, Mills's Blue Rhythm Band, and others. But none of that marked the emergence of swing, and we must go further back to observe that some of the forces shaping 1930s swing were active in the 1920s. Consider Chick Webb, who by 1927 was leading a band in a Harlem ballroom, Andy Kirk, who began recording that same year, and Luis Russell, who started a year earlier. Benny Carter's first arrangement, with already characteristic saxophone writing, was recorded in 1928, this being "Charleston Is the Best Dance After All" (Victor) for Charlie Johnson, and among many other inventive scores he followed with "Six or Seven Times" (Victor) for McKinney's Cotton Pickers in 1929, "Somebody Loves Me" (Columbia) for Henderson in 1930, and "Heebie Jeebies" (Vocalion) for Webb in 1931.

Adapting New Orleans style to a larger group, Russell's band seemed backward-looking while being the opposite. Items like their 1929–30 "Jersey Lighting" and "Louisiana Swing" (both OKeh) embodied new ideas that owed little to established practice, and as late as 1934 their "Ghost of the Freaks," scored by Bingie Madison, had fresh ensemble thoughts, although Madison's "Primitive" (both Banner) admitted to the Casa Loma stamp. Another direction was taken by the Dorsey Brothers Orchestra, and this had some resemblance to Paul Whiteman's band without ever establishing a real identity. Good recordings by it survive, however, such as their 1933 "Shim Sham Shimmy" (Brunswick) with an excellent Bunny Berigan solo. Still another direction was taken by Mills's Blue Rhythm Band, and its "Feelin' Gay" (Melotone) starts with a sequence of perfectly timed and executed sectional flourishes before the soloists take over, steady the tempo, and drive the piece to its destination. Likewise from 1933 is their re-reading of "Drop Me Off at Harlem" (RCA), which is memorable precisely because it is so un-Ellingtonian.

It is not easy to define the musical differences between those last two pieces, still less to isolate divergences between Ellington's and the Blue Rhythm Band's accounts of "Drop Me Off at Harlem." The

Ellington performance (Brunswick), however, is by that rarity in jazz a *composer's* band: nearly all the music discussed in this chapter is by *arrangers'* bands.

Again, arranging emerged well ahead of swing. Once instrumentation significantly extended, somebody had to organize the music by writing much of it down, and Don Redman was early in this field. He worked for Henderson from 1923 to 1927, and although others were likewise active, he hammered out a method of orchestrating for large jazz ensembles that long remained influential. Although distinguished instances of the craft are mentioned below, this was a secondary activity because the arranger usually started with another man's ideas, the melodic line and harmonies of the piece the band was to play. Occasionally, however, the theme too originated with the arranger; specimens included Gifford's many titles for the Casa Loma, Will Hudson's "White Heat" and "Jazznocracy" (both Victor) for Lunceford, and Eddie Durham's "Toby" and "Lafayette" (both Victor) for Moten.

Such jazz-oriented pieces addressed the more awakened minds among listeners, whereas arrangers' energy was devoted mainly to current popular songs ranging in quality from excellent to—more often—abysmal; these songs are what swing bands chiefly played. The present book heavily emphasizes jazz as art, but this and certain other chapters necessarily deal with ensembles which mostly performed to audiences having no concern with jazz, still less with art, and who only wanted music for social dancing. Such bands were essentially touring entertainment troupes which spent much time not playing jazz. This fact, applying to all the groups mentioned below, is stated here once and for all.

It should be added that most of the best arrangers wrote for several of the leading outfits. This meant that it remains hard to locate the origins of any one ensemble's style. And yet the finest swing bands were strikingly different one from another. This was a matter of interpretation, depending on the bandleader's personality, musical and otherwise. Whatever the craft of the arranger, how was his score performed? What was the tempo? How was the ensemble balanced? Who took the solos? These and other questions were answered by the leader, and on them the character of his group depended. Of nobody was this more true than Goodman, and despite his vast output of performances and recordings, his chief qualities were his virtuosity as a clarinetist, which made him fiercely demanding of other players, and his musical curiosity. This latter was not only evident when, at the height of his popularity as a bandleader, he involved himself in the utterly different music of Mozart, Bartók, Copland, Hindemith, and others. It was apparent earlier.

Take his 1934 "Nitwit Serenade" (Columbia), intriguingly scored by Will Hudson so as to veer toward the Casa Loma's "Maniac's Ball" while rewriting King Oliver's "Dippermouth Blues" (Gennett/OKeh). Note also the same date's blistering long-unissued second take of "Bugle Call Rag" (Columbia) and the fleet "Music Hall Rag" (Columbia) with its brilliant clarinet solo. Repeatedly Goodman contributed masterful, aggressively leading phrases, and his regular working band, founded in 1935, was perhaps inevitable. Quickly identifiable, it was excellently rehearsed, with intelligent ensemble dynamics, but its book consisted primarily of formulaic Henderson scores which applied call-and-response patterns mechanically to countless popular ditties. These appealed to the dancing public, which did not mind the admirable solos from Goodman, Berigan, Jess Stacy, and others. Many others, nearly all more resourceful than Henderson, arranged for Goodman, including Buster Harding, Budd Johnson, Margie Gibson, and Benny Carter, whose score on "Limehouse Blues," from a 1935 airshot with a superb Berigan solo, should be noted. Indeed, airshots, taken from broadcasts of performances given to live audiences, are quite often preferable to many swing bands' studio recordings.

Because they were linked with his early success, Goodman retained affection for the Henderson scores, yet his band's output soon grew more ambitious, more in accord with his musical curiosity. Eddie Sauter was a composer as well as an arranger and had worked inventively for Red Norvo's exploratory band. From 1939 he produced sixty-odd scores for Goodman, and rather than setting one section against another in Hendersonian mode, he blended instrumental voices, suggesting attention to Ellington and to Bill Challis and others who wrote for Whiteman in the 1920s. Popular songs like "Moonlight on the Ganges" and "Coconut Grove" (both Columbia) were recomposed as tone poems for band so that one forgot their vernacular origins. This was real jazz orchestral writing, some of its detail covertly glancing toward bop. Sauter's particular vehicles for Goodman such as "Clarinet à la King" and "Benny Rides Again" (both Columbia) were virtually at the level of Ellington's miniature concertos. Many other Goodman records deserve comment, especially scores by Mel Powell like "The Count," "Clarinade," and "The Earl" (all Columbia). In his and Sauter's hands, and elsewhere, jazz arranging was turning into composition. And in the early 1940s Goodman's playing (of jazz) was at its finest.

Lunceford was like Goodman and Redman in that, having had

classical training, he insisted on thorough rehearsal and high levels of proficiency. The main architects of the Lunceford style were his pianist Edwin Wilcox, also classically trained, Willie Smith, among the great altoists of jazz, and Sy Oliver, an engaging trumpeter and a particularly original orchestrator. Early among Oliver's many remarkable scores for Lunceford were "Swingin' Uptown" and "Breakfast Ball" (both Victor), although still better is Lunceford's own 1934 "Stratosphere" (Decca), which anticipates the jazz of ten years later. A particularly fine Oliver piece is "Stomp It Off" (Decca), but its two-beat feeling was conservative for 1934. Perhaps *the* outstanding Lunceford recording is Oliver's 1936 recomposition of Hudson's "Organ Grinder's Swing" (Decca), a ne plus ultra of swing with its extreme yet perfectly managed textural contrasts. Note "For Dancers Only" and a magnificent "Annie Laurie" (both Decca). Others who contributed to Lunceford's library included Gerald Wilson with "Hi, Spook," Wilson and Roger Segure with "Yard Dog Mazurka," from which Kenton borrowed for "Intermission Riff," and Edgar Battle with "Strictly Instrumental," with its suggestions of Basie influence (all Decca). Hear also Durham's "Oh Boy" for its use of two baritone saxophones in the first chorus, in unison and harmony.

In 1939 Oliver left to write for Tommy Dorsey, whose bandleading, since he left Jimmy with the Dorsey Brothers Orchestra in 1935, had been rather aimless. He had employed outstanding musicians like Berigan, Max Kaminsky, and Dave Tough, and there had been enjoyable records such as "Weary Blues" (Victor), arranged by Spud Murphy in 1935, "Star Dust" (Victor), arranged by Paul Weston in '36, and several in '38 scored by Deane Kincaid like "Panama" and "Copenhagen" (both Victor). But Oliver focused the identity of what had become a highly efficient band. Performed with vehement precision were 1941–42's "Loose Lid Special," "Well, Git It!" and "Blue Blazes" (all Victor): very fast, vividly conceived for the ensemble, and with excellent solos.

Benny Carter made major contributions to jazz throughout an uncommonly sustained career. The structural clarity of his compositions, arrangements, and solos on alto, clarinet, and trumpet appeals to the head as well as to the heart. A great melodist, he developed his improvisations with a composer's sense of form while producing a lovely tone on the alto, quite different from Smith or Hodges. Fine specimens include "Blue Interlude" (Decca) and "Krazy Kapers" (OKeh) with the Chocolate Dandies in 1933, and his two choruses on take three of "Smack" (Commodore) in 1940 are one of the great alto solos in all recorded jazz. Carter's clarinet sound was independent too, as on "Dee Blues" (Columbia), again with the Chocolate Dandies, or "Never Swat a Fly" (Victor) with McKinney's, both in 1930. Outstanding instances of his trumpeting, lyrically elegant yet with that extra edge the instrument gives, include "Once Upon a Time" (OKeh) with the Dandies again in 1933, and especially "Star Dust" with Willie Lewis in Paris (Pathé). Carter's name must be added to Redman's as a pioneer of scoring for big swing bands. "Keep a Song in Your Soul" (Columbia) for Henderson in 1930 was a landmark, and "Symphony in Riffs" and "Lonesome Nights" (both Columbia) under his own leadership in 1933 marked a further stage. It is regrettable that Carter's European recordings, like those of Coleman Hawkins and Bill Coleman, have been ignored by American commentators, especially his August 1937 sessions at The Hague, Holland.

An addendum to Carter's countless recordings are those made with his band by Spike Hughes in 1933 with Henry Allen, Dicky Wells, and Coleman Hawkins added. Hughes's composing and bandleading followed on from Fred Elizalde's comparable work in London during the 1920s. There were other European jazz composers, such as the Belgian David Bee, several of whose scores were recorded by distinguished bands over a long period—for example, "High Tension" (OKeh) by Luis Russell in 1930 and "Obsession" (Decca) by Ted Heath in 1952. There is no space to deal with Hughes's London recordings, rewarding though some of them are, but the unusual character of the composing and orchestration of such pieces as "Nocturne," "Pastorale," "Donegal Cradle Song," and "Arabesque" (all Decca), quite distinct from even the best American practice, must be noted. Additionally, they prompted, as did "Fanfare" and "Sweet Sorrow Blues" (both Decca), particularly fine solos from Allen and Wells, and Hawkins's contributions to "Donegal Cradle Song" and "Arabesque" are among the most affecting solos he ever recorded.

Arrangers for Hines's band included Quinn Wilson, Jimmy Mundy, Henri Woode, Bingie Madison, Buster Harding, and Budd Johnson, and with so many pens it is unsurprising it took a while for any unified style to emerge. In 1933 Mundy's "Cavernism" (Brunswick) did suggest a style, albeit Redmanish; Mundy's 1934 "Fat Babes" (Decca) was in that tradition also. The following year's "Bubbling Over" (Decca), arranged by Lawrence Dixon, was in the manner of Moten's "Toby" (Victor), but none of this tamed the band's energy. From '33 "Harlem Lament" (Brunswick) was an imaginative Wilson score with brilliant Hines. He was incomparably his band's finest soloist, of course, and it is a pity that did not more positively affect what they played. After a bad period in the mid-1930s this outfit's best achievements came during 1939–41, this being largely due to Johnson. Yet it is to Hines's credit that he employed Parker, Gillespie, Wardell Gray, and others as the swing bands were turning toward modern orchestral jazz, in effect to bop and what came from it. So the ending of the swing era was as inconclusive as its start.

Although the loose, relaxed ensembles of the Basie account of a popular song like "Pennies From Heaven" (Decca) probably reflect the character of the best of the dancing for which this band played, his group achieved, on its earliest and best recordings, a massive yet classic simplicity that offered a viable alternative to Ellington's sophistication or the Lunceford outfit's virtuosity. Basie's music was descended from territory bands such as Page's Blue Devils but also from elsewhere. Thus his 1939 "Jive at Five" (Decca) closely resembles "Barrelhouse," a Tab Smith score recorded three years earlier by the Blue Rhythm Band (Columbia).

The simple outline of early pieces like "Roseland Shuffle" (Decca) seemed to derive, however, from the daring simplicity of piano solos such as the one Basie contributes to "Doggin' Around" (Decca). Equally striking are some keyboard passages of the quartet "Red Wagon" (Decca), with their rejection of melody and their use of silence and of musical space. "How Long Blues" (Decca) is minimalist jazz, subverting the predictable cadences of the blues with wry understatement, and a similar case is his second solo on "John's Idea" (Decca), with each phrase reduced to absolute essentials. Such tactics allow the plain yet forceful pulse generated by Basie, Green, Page, and Jones to assert itself to a hitherto unprecedented extent.

Indeed, the activities of Basie's team were highly influential and led directly into bop's subsequent revision of the rhythm section's function. Meanwhile it changed the relationships between solos and ensembles and this is observable on more than one level. Thus Young's characteristic utterance on "Jumpin' at the Woodside" (Decca), marking a brave departure from established norms, is answered by the extraordinary momentum of the closing ensemble, while Edison's amazing entry in "Swingin' the Blues" (Decca) seems to be born out of the ensemble riffs, later to be capped by massive phrases by the whole band. (Other Basie soloists included Buck Clayton, Vic Dickenson, Buddy Tate, and Don Byas.)

Despite such performances Basie raises acutely the question of what the swing bands played. One of his records, "Our Love Was Meant to Be" (Decca), arranged by Skip Martin, who also worked for Goodman, Barnet, and Miller, is an excellent instance of how a popular song could be transformed into jazz. There were plenty of others, such as Jerry Gray's version of the 108-bar "Begin the Beguine" (Bluebird) for Shaw and Oliver's unexpected speeding-up of "Lonesome Road" for Lunceford. Sauter's arrangements of such material for Goodman were sensitive also, as in his striking modulations during "The Man I Love" and "When the Sun Comes Out" (both Columbia) accompanying Helen Forrest or "How Deep Is the Ocean?" and especially "My Old Flame" (both Columbia) for Peggy Lee. Yet such material is ultimately facile in appeal, and its alliance with jazz thoroughly unfortunate. Even the advances of free jazz resulted in no divorce, and the bands' finest moments came when they turned completely away from the popular fare of Broadway and Hollywood.

That meant, as repeatedly hinted above, jazz composition, the writing of independent pieces, these receiving less public attention than the rest of swing's huge output. A brief list might start with Redman's "Chant of the Weed" (Brunswick—his initial recording); Coleman Hawkins's "Queer Notions" (Columbia) (orchestrated by Horace Henderson, recorded by Fletcher's band), a hapax legomenon of swing; Norvo's in parts virtually atonal "Dance of the Octopus" (Brunswick); Edgar Sampson's scores for Webb such as "Stompin' at the Savoy" (Columbia) and "Blue Lou" (Decca), later reworked for Goodman; items by Horace Henderson (Fletcher's younger, more gifted brother) like "Shufflin' Joe" and "Kitty on Toast" (both Vocalion); Sam Lowe pieces for Erskine Hawkins such as "Tuxedo Junction," "Rockin' Rollers' Jubilee" (both Bluebird); many items by Mary Lou Williams for Kirk starting with "Mess-a-Stomp" (Brunswick); numerous scores commissioned by Shaw including Ray Conniff's "Lucky Number," Buster Harding's "Bedford Drive," and Sauter's "Maid With the Flaccid Air" (all Victor); many pieces commissioned by Charlie Barnet like Andy Gibson's "Shady Lady" (Decca) and Billy May's two-part "Wings Over Manhattan" (Bluebird), passing through several moods and tempos. And there was a special category of miniature concertos, including Howard McGhee's "McGhee Special" (Decca) featuring himself with Kirk, and Ralph Burns's "The Moose" (Decca), a vehicle for the brilliant Dodo Marmarosa with Barnet. There were numerous others.

One jazz composer subjected to supercilious, misinformed comment was Reginald Foresythe. His father was in fact West African, his mother German, and he spent considerable time in America. Hines recorded his faintly Ellingtonian "Deep Forest" (Brunswick) in 1932, as did Whiteman, who also recorded several other Foresythe pieces. In 1931 he wrote the complete book for a fifteen-piece band led by Wild Bill Davison and including Frank Teschemacher; Davison later claimed that music was far ahead of its time. Foresythe was associated with Whiteman during his several visits to the States and in 1935 had four of his compositions recorded by a group including Goodman (Columbia).

His most representative recordings were cut in London, however. Selecting almost at random: "The Autocrat Before Breakfast" (Columbia) has, again, a little of Ellington, something of Delius, and a decidedly European ambience; not quite jazz, not really dance music, it is a cultural mixture, and melodious as Foresythe usually is. In "Landscape" (Decca) the reed scoring leans toward France rather than Harlem. For the rest one can do no more than list a few of his always absorbing compositions: "Aubade," "Lament for Congo," "Angry Jungle," "Duke Insists" (all Columbia), "Mead and Woad," "Garden of Weed," "Revolt of the Yes-Men," "Meditation in Porcelain."

A very different case was that of the charismatic drummer Chick Webb, who for years led a very popular band at Harlem's Savoy Ballroom. His 1929 "Dog Bottom" and slightly Ellingtonian "Jungle Mama" (both Brunswick—as by the Jungle Band) were somewhat ahead of their day and almost orchestral in approach. Carter, Hodges, Bobby Stark, and Jimmy Harrison were early members; later factors were Taft Jordan, Sandy Williams, Elmer Williams (tenor), and Ella Fitzgerald's singing. Carter aside ("Blues in My Heart," "Soft and Sweet"—both Brunswick), the best arrangements were Sampson's, such as "Let's Get Together," "Facts and Figures" (both Decca), etc. These often had flowing reed statements with staccato brass comments, sometimes with staccato intersectional counterpoint, as in "What a Shuffle." The band's appeal to dancers was obvious, as suggested by the controlled exaltation of "Clap Hands, Here Comes Charlie" and "Harlem Congo" (both Decca); the latter, scored by Charlie Dixon, has a fine solo by the underrated clarinetist Chauncey Haughton and great drumming.

Moving in quite another direction was Bob Crosby's outfit. A mildly attractive singer of the sentimental ballads that were a considerable part of his as of other bands' output, he was simply the front man. More unexpected was the repertoire of New Orleans and dixieland pieces and new themes in that idiom such as "South Rampart Street Parade" and "Dogtown Blues." The fusing of small traditional and large swing band textures was skillfully done, principally by Bob Haggart and Matty Matlock. Further, the spontaneity of New Orleans music was preserved, because the band's members, like Billy Butterfield, Floyd O'Brien, Irving Fazola, and Eddie Miller, thoroughly understood the older jazz. Besides being of great value in themselves, their performances of such items as "Muskrat Ramble," "Dixieland Shuffle," "Farewell Blues," "Panama," "Milenburg Joys," "Hindustan," and "Vultee Special" (all Decca) were a prelude to the New Orleans revival. At a time when swing bands were moving, at various speeds, toward modern jazz, it would be surprising if at least one did not look another way.

A different example of the variety of the swing bands' music was provided by Andy Kirk. As so often, an arranger and composer was the main force, and besides writing most of the book, Mary Lou Williams also was an admirable pianist whose horizons went far beyond swing. On the early records of 1929–30 the band had not arrived at a particular style, and "Travelin' That Rocky Road" (Brunswick) shows an obvious Redman influence, the opening saxophone chorus being a spin-off from the McKinney's version. However, Williams's solos are excellent, as in "Gettin' off a Mess" and "Cloudy" (the 1929 performance) (both Brunswick).

By 1936, when they began recording regularly, she had shaped the band in a more decisive way: Kirk had got his other main improviser, Dick Wilson, and his own tuba had been supplanted by Booker Collins's fine bass. And the band did not follow fashion, retaining lightness of touch and ease of movement. This is illustrated by "Lotta Sax Appeal" or "Steppin' Pretty" (both Decca). Other than Williams's playing and writing, the chief attraction was Wilson's tenor, as in "Scratchin' the Gravel" or "Corky" (both Decca). His linear distillations are so concentrated as almost to be aphoristic. Other worthy soloists included Harold Baker and Howard McGhee. Floyd Smith's electric guitar work has been described as "Hawaiian Gothic."

The most enigmatic figure mentioned in this chapter is Artie Shaw, whose autobiographical *The Trouble with Cinderella* (New York, 1952) at least confirms Talleyrand's idea that words were given men to conceal their thoughts. Seemingly not always interested in music, certainly not in jazz, he was probably repelled by the music *business*. Yet as the 1930s wore on Shaw became a surpassingly brilliant clarinetist with a particularly beautiful tone and extraordinary control of the top register, never sounding like Goodman. And he was creative, with abundant invention that was characterized by lyrical melody and rhythmic verve in long, highly mobile lines.

Shaw's first band, of 1936–37, emphasized strings, although their jazz use went back to Whiteman and they had more recently and relevantly been employed by Miller. That early band was not very swinging, nor did the arrangements compare with what Sauter was then writing for Norvo, or Oliver for Lunceford. His second band in 1937 had a standard fourteen-piece instrumentation and was much better, not least its rhythm section: Shaw would in turn employ Wettling, Rich, and Tough. The leader's prominently featured solos were now superior to those of any other jazz clarinetist, with the one exception, and the ensemble, while still imperfect, had improved internal balance. It was Jerry Gray, who had played first violin in the earlier string band, who began to set the band's style. This arose with scores like the 1937 "Blue Skies" (Brunswick) and the following year's "Begin the Beguine" (Bluebird) with its 108-bar chorus, although Shaw's contributions included "The Chant," "Nightmare," and the two-part "The Blues" (all Brunswick). Note also Luis Russell's "Call of the Freaks" and Carter's "Lost in the Shuffle," and "Symphony in Riffs," all best heard not in the studio recordings but in 1937 airshots (Swingdom).

A distinctive style was finally achieved by Gray with the 1939 "Lover, Come Back to Me" (Bluebird). The band was now swinging more, and the ensemble tone was more ample and the music more emotional, including the leader's playing. Another of his compositions, "Non-Stop Flight," is, again, far better in the 1939 airshot (Jazz Guild) than the previous year's studio version. Also to be heard are the excellently arranged "One Foot in the Groove," "Out of Nowhere," and "Traffic Jam" (all Bluebird).

In November 1939 Shaw disbanded, only to reappear a few months later with a new studio outfit of thirty-two pieces including thirteen strings—shades of Kenton's Innovations in Modern Music: This recorded in March 1940, including "Frenesi" (Victor) scored by William Grant Still. Later that year "Star Dust" (Victor), arranged by Lennie Hayton, was a classic performance by Shaw's twenty-three-piece touring band, with fine solos from Butterfield, the leader, and Jenney. Yet Shaw again disbanded in 1941 only to form another band with Allen, Higginbotham, Carter, twelve strings, and a harp. This recorded once before once again Shaw abandoned the project. By that time he had set down his "Concerto for Clarinet" (Victor), which sounds like a Hollywood producer's notion of what such a piece should be like and is a touchingly incompetent venture from one of Shaw's supposedly highbrow inclinations.

Certainly his progress as a bandleader had been erratic, but his thirty-two-piece Symphonic Swing, which toured in the latter half of 1941, initially seemed more purposeful with Hot Lips Page, Max Kaminsky, and in particular the trombonist and arranger Ray Conniff, who contributed such excellent pieces as "To a Broadway Rose" (Victor). This band also employed strings rather well, as in Conniff's "Just Kiddin' Around," Margie Gibson's "Deuces Wild," and Fred Norman's "Solid Sam" (all Victor). But Shaw disbanded yet again and in 1942 joined the Navy. He led a fine but unrecorded Navy band in 1942–43; his post-Navy bands are dealt with elsewhere in this volume.

Like Presley and the Beatles later, Glenn Miller was hugely popular with the worst judges, and his monstrous success from 1939 was more a fact of social than musical history. His first records of 1935 (Columbia), despite the presence of Berigan and Eddie Miller (and Tchaikovsky's help with "A Blues Serenade"—as later with "Moon Love"), had little character. A couple of years later pieces like his own "Community Swing" (Brunswick) were slightly better. Yet there have been thousands of Miller records and "rediscovered" broadcasts which the entertainment industry has heedlessly issued and reissued. This was, deliberately and calculatedly, music for a mass market that made few demands. But Miller programmed some rather good jazz-inclined scores early on; here, we can only list a few, mainly from 1939. They include Eddie Durham's "Glen Island Special" and "Slip Horn Jive," Joe Lipman's "Blue Evening," Bill Challis's "Guess I'll Go Back Home," Charlie Dixon's "We Can Live on Love," and "Rug-Cutter's Swing," composed by Horace Henderson and arranged by Bill Finegan (all Bluebird). Miller had notable soloists in Bobby Hackett, Ernie Caceres, and Al Klink, but he chose primarily to feature the low-temperatured inconsequentiality of Tex Beneke's echoes of Coleman Hawkins.

A little ahead of the main thrust of swing, Charlie Barnet started recording in 1933 and was soon concerned with emulating Basie and particularly Ellington. He also bought scores from Carter ("Nagasaki," "On a Holiday"—both Bluebird), Redman, Horace Henderson, even Ellington. Most of the Ellington pieces he programmed, however, were transcribed off discs by Andy Gibson, including "The Gal From Joe's," "Echoes of Harlem," "Ebony Rhapsody," and "Harlem Speaks" (all Bluebird). Barnet got as close to Ellington's style as anyone could. There might be occasional pieces like "Midweek Function" or "In a Mizz" (both Bluebird), which are mixups of several styles, yet normally he kept Ellington and Basie distinct: compare "The Duke's Idea" with "The Count's Idea" (both Bluebird).

Barnet was a better writer than player, as is suggested by his "Blue Juice," "Mother Fuzzy," or "Murder at Payton Hall" (all Bluebird). These are written in the Ellington style rather as Billy Strayhorn might have done. Naturally Barnet's outfit played the same populist dross as all the other bands, but he was the first considerable figure to perform a major jazz composer's work in quantity solely because of the inherent quality of the scores: the earliest repertoire band. Also present was that comparative rarity in jazz, genuine musical humor. Contrast "The Wrong Idea," deftly caricaturing 1930s Mickey Mouse bands, with Skip Martin's Basie-like "The Right Idea" (both Bluebird).

If Barnet had gone no further his would have been a respectable achievement. Yet if Gibson's "Smiles" (1942) is followed by "Gulf Coast Blues" (1944) (both Decca), we can hear Barnet's music aligning itself in gesture, instrumental texture, and harmony with the modern orchestral idiom. The latter piece, composed by Clarence Williams (!) and arranged by Gibson and Ralph Flanagan, even has some bitonal harmony. Note also the airshot of Ralph Burns's reworking of "Cotton Tail" (Swing Era), which quotes "Apple Honey," later recorded by Woody Herman. Barnet's, like Shaw's and several other swing bands, had arrived at modern jazz, and this should not surprise us. After all, Armstrong's solo on his 1935 "I've Got My Fingers Crossed" (Decca) was almost bop.

In one sense Cab Calloway's band ought to have appeared in this story much earlier. Their precipitate account of "Hot Toddy," composed by Benny Carter, perhaps scored by Walter "Foots" Thomas, was seen in a film, *The Big Broadcast of 1932*. Despite the embarrassing inanity of his singing—if you want to call it that—Calloway kept an excellent band with fine soloists and often imaginative arrangers. That band emerged from the rough, tough Missourians, and Thomas was its early arranger and music director. Certainly it was he who mainly set up the Calloway band's style, or refined it from what the Missourians had been doing, and the very fast "Some of These Days" (Brunswick) is a good example of his functional writing. Harry White's "Evenin'" (RCA), with its rich harmony, was quite advanced for its day; note also his "Zaz Zuh Zaz" and evocative "Harlem Camp Meeting" (both Victor), all from 1933.

Resourceful scoring by Andy Gibson appeared in the 1940s, as in "My Gal" (Columbia) and "I'll Be Around" (OKeh). In fact, along with Calloway's vocal grotesqueries there were excellent instrumental performances such as Carter's "Lonesome Nights" (OKeh), a vehicle for Chu Berry, "Willow Weep for Me" (OKeh) for Hilton Jefferson, and "Special Delivery" (OKeh) for Jonah Jones and Berry, both arranged by Gibson. "Cupid's Nightmare" was a striking Redman composition with very chromatic harmony (even if it glanced toward "Mood Indigo"); it is better judged in the slightly earlier Meadowbrook airshot (Jazz Panorama) than in the studio recording.

And Gillespie was soon making himself felt. He is rather in Eldridge's shadow during his solo on his own "Pickin' the Cabbage" (Vocalion) (in E-flat minor, be it noted) but sounds more personal in "Pluckin' the Bass" (Vocalion), a vehicle for Milt Hinton, and Buster Harding's "Bye Bye Blues" and "Boo-wah Boo-wah" (both OKeh). Several of these pieces, "Cupid's Nightmare" perhaps most of all, were, again, modern jazz in their thoughts and feeling. Soon to follow were Cootie Williams's recordings of Monk's "Epistrophy" (retitled "Fly Right") (Columbia) and "'Round About Midnight" (Hit/Majestic) (with Bud Powell at the piano). Such scores as Gil Fuller's "Things to Come" (Musicraft) for Gillespie's postswing band were not far over the horizon.

Yet perhaps at this later date the future is no longer quite what it was. E. C. Carr suggested, "The historian is an inveterate simplifier. He tidies up the infinite variety of events in order to make them intelligible" (*Times Literary Supplement*, June 3, 1977). And beyond any considerations of history one should admit that critical "conclusions" in the arts are only staging posts on the road to further inquiries.

The Advent of Bebop

Scott DeVeaux

"Bebop" was a label that certain journalists later gave it, but we never labeled the music. It was just modern music, we would call it. We wouldn't call it anything, really, just music.

••• *Kenny Clarke, quoted in Dizzy Gillespie,*
To Be or Not to Bop *(1979)*

The word *bebop* (or *rebop*) first surfaced in musicians' argot some time during the last two years of the Second World War. Originally, it was a scat syllable, an onomatopoeic shorthand for a certain kind of off-balance rhythmic gesture favored by musicians like drummer Kenny Clarke. Within a few years, however, it had become synonymous with a revolutionary new way of playing jazz associated with Dizzy Gillespie, Charlie Parker, and Thelonious Monk. Bebop was a brief, explosive moment in American culture, greeted in the mid- to late 1940s by as much controversy and misunderstanding as genuine acceptance. Only much later would it be clear how profoundly and irrevocably bebop had transformed the art of jazz improvisation. Indeed, it is safe to say that jazz as we know it today is shaped in bebop's image.

Like most styles of jazz, bebop is easier to describe than to define. The characteristic bebop ensemble is the small group, such as a quintet with saxophone and trumpet accompanied by piano, string bass, and drums. Soloists like trumpeter Dizzy Gillespie, alto saxophonist Charlie Parker, and pianist Bud Powell improvised with unprecedented agility and rhythmic flexibility, shifting gears smoothly between pithy, bluesy passages to phrases played so fast that individual notes could barely be distinguished. Their repertory consisted of twelve-bar blues and familiar thirty-two-bar pop tunes ingeniously disguised by substituting a rhythmically intricate melody (or "head") for the original.

The rhythm section in bebop was not, as in previous jazz styles, a relatively unchanging rhythmic foundation. The steady dance beat could be heard only in the bassist's "walking bass" pattern (four even quarter notes to the bar) and in the penetrating timbre of the drummer's ride cymbal. The rest of the rhythm section was left free to be more imaginative and interactive. Pianists accompanied soloists with unpredictable rhythmic patterns (a practice known as "comping"), typically altering the chord progressions with richer, more dissonant voicings. Following the lead of Kenny Clarke, drummers engaged soloists in an ongoing dialogue with improvised polyrhythms on the remainder of the drum kit.

Because its loose, improvisatory format offers an obvious point of contrast to the swing styles that preceded it, bebop is often represented by jazz historians as a conscious revolt against the tightly controlled commercial entertainment offered by the swing bands of the 1930s and 1940s. Yet it is not at all apparent that during the formative years of bebop its inventors felt alienated from the large swing bands. Parker, Gillespie, and many others continued to work with large dance orchestras during the war years; and from 1945 onward, Gillespie made it a point to present his music in big band format whenever feasible. It makes more sense to see bebop as deriving from a musical environment that was very much a part of the musical culture of the swing era, even if largely invisible to the casual fan: the jam session.

After the night's gig was over, swing era musicians headed out in search of places where they could relax and continue to improvise in more informal settings. The best known of these venues is Minton's Playhouse, an unpretentious club on 118th Street in Harlem now famous as the site where many of the innovations that came to characterize bebop took shape in the early 1940s. Another, equally

Town Hall jazz concert, New York, May 16, 1945. Left to right: Harold West, drums; Curley Russell, bass; Al Haig (hidden), piano; Charlie Parker, alto sax; Dizzy Gillespie, trumpet. Courtesy Frank Driggs Collection.

influential site was Monroe's Uptown House, located at the heart of the entertainment district in Harlem. But at any given time, jazz players had their choice of more than a dozen venues in New York City alone, ranging from well-established clubs to dingy basement dives to ad hoc sessions held in apartments or hotel rooms.

For all their apparent casualness, jam sessions were serious business. Then as now, jazz musicians needed to learn their craft by playing with others. In an era before formal jazz degree programs, they seized upon the open-ended music-making available night after night in congenial surroundings to work out new musical ideas and to push their creative powers to the limit. The jazz world was also sharply competitive. Jam sessions proved the ideal arena in which promising newcomers pitted themselves against the profession's best. Not for nothing were they also widely known as "cutting contests."

Still, the informal "all comers welcome" atmosphere of the jam session meant that anyone, including rank beginners and nervy incompetents, might walk up on the bandstand. To make them think twice about it, experienced musicians came up with the equivalent of a musical obstacle course: calling for tunes with difficult chord progressions at impossibly fast tempos and in unusual keys, perhaps modulating up a half step with every chorus in the bargain. The idea, of course, was not simply to harass the incompetent but to provide those at the top of their game with fresh challenges. The more ingenious among them devised more creative routines. Dizzy Gillespie worked out complicated chromatic substitutions to the usual standards like "I Got Rhythm" and rehearsed them ahead of time with his Cab Calloway bandmate, bassist Milt Hinton. At Minton's Playhouse, the house pianist, Thelonious Monk, challenged newcomers with the unorthodox harmonic syntax of his repertory of original compositions. Their sense of rhythmic independence, meanwhile, was severely tested by Kenny Clarke's habit of peppering his accompaniments with sharp bass-drum accents—a practice still known today by the wartime-inspired term "dropping bombs." Only the most resourceful and inventive of musicians thrived in such a bracing environment. As Miles Davis, who began frequenting the club in 1944, put it in *Miles: the Autobiography* (1989): "That was Minton's. You had to put up or shut up, there was no in between."

None of this was foreign to the spirit of the swing era, which was by its nature sharply competitive and open to artistic experimentation. In retrospect, the links between the innovations of bebop and certain swing era practices are obvious.

Many of the young musicians were noticeably influenced by the rhythmic sensibility of the extraordinary guitarist Charlie Christian, among the first to play with electric amplification and well known after 1939 as a soloist with Benny Goodman's Sextet. At a time when most jazz musicians divided the quarter-note beat into decidedly unequal pairs of eighths, Christian—possibly influenced by the string-band phrasing of the western swing bands he would have heard in his native Oklahoma—favored constructing lines of even eighth notes which, by shifting the accent back and forth from downbeat to offbeat, could be shaped and reshaped into a kaleidoscope of patterns. Christian was a regular at Minton's until illness forced him to retire in 1941 (he died of tuberculosis the following year); his unpredictable phrasing meshed beautifully with the densely polyrhythmic drum styles pioneered by Clarke and his followers. Rhythmic suppleness of a different kind was exemplified by tenor saxophonist Lester Young, whose laconic phrases, often coming to rest on the ambiguous intervals of a sixth or a ninth in relation to the harmonies, were a direct influence on Charlie Parker. Parker is said to have proved his competence as a teenager in the demanding world of Kansas City jam sessions by learning Young's 1936 solo on "Lady Be Good" (Vocalion).

Those drawn to unconventional chromatic harmony found other sources of inspiration. Many aspiring musicians were deeply impressed by the angular dissonances found in such Duke Ellington compositions as "Main Stem" (1942, Victor) and the complicated harmonic substitutions tossed off by pianist Art Tatum. (Among Tatum's young fans was Charlie Parker, who heard the pianist night after night while washing dishes at Jimmy's Chicken Shack in Harlem in 1939.) The soloing of tenor saxophonist Coleman Hawkins, as exemplified by his 1939 recording of "Body and Soul" (Bluebird), showed how this intricate harmonic idiom might be transferred to a single improvised line. But a fascination with harmony was not restricted to a handful of mavericks: a wide range of swing era musicians, from Benny Carter to Roy Eldridge to Artie Shaw to Mary Lou Williams, foregrounded chromatic dissonances in their playing and composing. And every instrumentalist of the time felt the pressure to match the technical standards for range, speed, and cleanness of execution set by these and other members of the top rank of swing era virtuosi.

By the early 1940s, then, a new approach to small-combo jazz playing was developing, characterized by a more flexible approach to rhythm, a more aggressive pursuit of instrumental virtuosity, and an increasingly adventurous harmonic language. We can hear some of this music today because Jerry Newman, a jazz enthusiast then attending Columbia University, happened to be on hand with portable recording equipment on a few occasions at Minton's and Monroe's. Among the most remarkable documents of early bebop is his acetate recording from Minton's in 1941 of "Topsy" (renamed "Swing to Bop" when issued on LP on Everest) featuring the electrifying interaction between Christian and Clarke. Another set of private recordings captures the informal ambience of a hotel room in Chicago where, on a February night in 1943, Parker and Gillespie, then on tour with the Earl Hines band, traded choruses on "Sweet Georgia Brown" (Stash).

At the time, however, such music-making was not meant for outsiders. For one thing, because only a handful of musicians actually drew a paycheck for playing in a house band, the remainder were technically in violation of union policy prohibiting playing without pay. While the American Federation of Musicians (AFM) put up with jamming in venues frequented primarily by fellow professionals, it threatened stiff penalties for those foolish or indiscreet enough to extend the practice to more openly commercial spheres. Since with few exceptions pursuing a career as a jazz musician meant playing with a large dance orchestra, there was little incentive to consider even the most artistically stimulating jam session as anything other than a backstage experiment.

Thus in the years before 1945, the musicians who would be in the forefront of bebop were known to the general public, and to their fellow musicians, as part of the up-and-coming generation of African-American swing soloists and arrangers. Dizzy Gillespie, who worked for more than a dozen different bands in the early 1940s, could be heard on recordings (as well as in live performance and on the radio) as an inventive arranger on Cab Calloway's 1940 "Pickin' the Cabbage" (Vocalion/OKeh) and as a blisteringly fast trumpet soloist on Les Hite's "Jersey Bounce" (Hit) and Lucky Millinder's "Little John Special" (Brunswick), both recorded in 1942. Charlie Parker's fluid, bluesy playing fit perfectly with the Kansas City sound of Jay McShann's band, as exemplified by his famous solo on the 1941 "Hootie Blues" (Decca). Parker's up-tempo solos, however, startled professional musicians into realizing that jazz playing had taken a quantum leap to a new level of intensity. Trumpeter Howard McGhee, who heard Parker take an extended solo on the challenging harmonic progression to "Cherokee" with McShann in 1942, recalled: "We all stood there with our mouths open because we hadn't heard anybody

play a horn like *that* . . . that *complete*" (interview with author). Together, Parker and Gillespie toured the country, first as sidemen with
the Earl Hines band, and later in 1944 as the main instrumental
attractions of a new band led by vocalist Billy Eckstine (see below).
Even the eccentric Thelonious Monk seemed to be finding his niche
in the world of swing by 1944 as the composer of the Cootie Williams
band's moody theme song, " 'Round Midnight" (Hit/Majestic).

What prompted these prodigies to pin their professional hopes not
on swing but on a new jam-session style of jazz? One crucial factor,
certainly, was a growing dissatisfaction with swing—not so much
with musical style per se as with the various obstacles that hindered
them from furthering their careers in music. Another crucial factor
was racism, which pervaded the daily lives of black musicians and
hindered them at every step.

Although the leaders of bebop were African Americans, it would
be a mistake to view the movement as inspired by racial separatism.
The general camaraderie among like-minded musicians in the jazz
community ensured that musical experimentation unfolded in environments as free from racial hostility as was possible in America of
the 1940s. Still, black musicians had a particular incentive to seek out
new musical and professional paths. With few exceptions, black bands
were denied access to commercial broadcasts and prestigious hotel
ballrooms, severely limiting their potential earnings. The ritual hu-
miliations of discrimination made life on the road, especially in the
Jim Crow South, an exhausting and often dangerous ordeal. A more
subtle, if no less pervasive, racism made it difficult for white Americans to accept black musicians as celebrities. As a 1940 report in
Down Beat put it bluntly, "The truth is that the public will absorb
only a very limited number of Negro bands." Small wonder that the
most talented and ambitious of the upcoming generation of black jazz
musicians began actively searching for alternatives.

But what alternatives were available? One necessary precondition
for bop was the gradual emergence of a commercial outlet for small-
combo jazz. The process had begun in the mid-1930s: with the end
of Prohibition in 1933, small clubs featuring lively music and alcohol
became suddenly profitable. In particular, New York, with its high
concentration of nightclubs occupying the converted brownstones lining 52nd Street, became a mecca for those seeking an intimate experience with "hot" music. By the early 1940s, "Swing Street," as
52nd Street was known, offered steady employment for those, like
Coleman Hawkins, Billie Holiday, or Art Tatum, in the top rank of

jazz performers. Further credit for the renaissance of small-group jazz must be given to a handful of determined jazz enthusiasts turned entrepreneurs, such as Commodore Records' Milt Gabler, who cultivated an earnest, respectful, and well-heeled audience willing to pay a modest admission fee for public jam sessions—and mollified the AFM by paying the musicians union scale.

In the mid-1940s, small-group jazz was suddenly more welcome in recording studios as well. The catalyst, ironically, was the ban on recording called by the musicians' union in August 1942. The idea behind the ban was to force concessions for musicians put out of work by the use of recordings in jukeboxes. Two of the large companies that dominated the market, Columbia and Victor, resisted the union's demands for more than two years; but when the third, Decca, gave up in late 1943, the door was opened for dozens of smaller companies, the so-called independents, to begin recording on the same terms to which Decca had agreed. A number of these record labels—Savoy, Keynote, Blue Note—specialized in jazz. With the market wide open, they set about building their catalogues with new recordings. Not surprisingly, their first clients were the well-established swing performers not already contracted to one of the major companies. But soon thereafter they began to search in earnest for new faces and new sounds.

It is in this context that the bebop generation made its move. First, some of the young musicians who frequented Minton's gained a foothold on 52nd Street. Dizzy Gillespie formed a quintet, often called the "first bop combo," with bassist Oscar Pettiford that made its debut at the Onyx Club in late 1943 with Max Roach on drums. (Charlie Parker was invited to join but apparently never received the word; the saxophone slot was filled first by Lester Young and later by Don Byas and Budd Johnson. In apparent affirmation of the priority of musical sensibility over racial considerations, the rhythm section was completed by white pianist George Wallington.) The group's repertory was a motley assortment of originals and unorthodox arrangements of jam-session standards. Among the tunes played at the Onyx were "A Night in Tunisia," a Latin-flavored tune originally written by Gillespie for the Earl Hines band (an aircheck of "Tunisia," with solos by Gillespie and Johnson, has recently been issued on CD); Monk's " 'Round Midnight"; "Salt Peanuts," "52nd Street Theme," and other thinly disguised versions or variants of George Gershwin's "I Got Rhythm"; and the breathtakingly fast Gillespie original "Be-Bop" (later reworked for Gillespie's big band as "Things to Come").

Much of the music that had been circulating informally for some time was now tightened up with an eye toward public consumption. As Gillespie later explained in his autobiography, *To Be or Not to Bop* (1978): "Jamming at Minton's and Monroe's we had our fun, but with the level of music which we'd developed by 1944, it wasn't very profitable, artistically or commercially. We needed to play to a wider audience and Fifty-second Street seemed ready to pay to hear someone playing something new."

The new music—still unnamed—was exciting enough to make a deep impression on many of those who heard it. As a result, some of the innovations began to spread. Coleman Hawkins in particular played a crucial role. The veteran tenor saxophonist, who had been performing on 52nd Street with his own small group, gathered a twelve-piece band featuring Gillespie, Roach, and others for a pair of recording sessions on the sixteenth and twenty-second of February of 1944 that included the blues "Disorder at the Border" and Gillespie's "Woody 'n' You" (Apollo). (Two years later, Gillespie's solo from "Disorder" was recycled as the opening riff chorus of "Cool Breeze," as recorded by Billy Eckstine in 1946.) In May, he made the debut recording of Gillespie's "Salt Peanuts" (Apollo). Inspired in large part by what he heard at the Onyx Club, Hawkins spent the remainder of the year leading quintets with many of the younger stars, including trumpeters "Little Benny" Harris and Howard McGhee, and Thelonious Monk, who made his first commercial recordings in October under Hawkins's leadership (Joe Davis). (Monk returned the favor a decade later, inviting Hawkins to play on the famous Riverside recordings with John Coltrane in 1957.)

The younger musicians, however, were still eager to establish their own reputations—not an easy task for those languishing in relative obscurity as one of several acts on the bill at the Onyx Club. Hoping to parlay some of the new musical ideas into mainstream entertainment, Gillespie took on the job of serving as music director of a new full-size dance orchestra to be led by vocalist Billy Eckstine. Starting up a band in 1944, well after the initial swing boom of the late 1930s had cooled off, was an expensive and risky proposition. But the band's backers, well aware that Eckstine's singing on the blues head arrangement "Jelly, Jelly," recorded with Earl Hines in 1940 (Bluebird), had sold exceptionally well with black audiences in the South, clearly hoped to score a similar success four years later. At the same time, however, Eckstine was an ardent fan of the new currents in jazz and was determined to make the band a showcase for arrangers and soloists. With Gillespie's help, he managed to staff his band with a remarkable roster of as yet little known musicians, including Charlie Parker, drummer Art Blakey, vocalist Sarah Vaughan, and tenor saxophonists Dexter Gordon and Lucky Thompson.

The Eckstine band embarked in the summer of 1944 on a grueling tour of black venues in the South and Midwest. Eyewitnesses—including the eighteen-year-old Miles Davis, who sat in with the band in St. Louis as a replacement for an ailing member of the trumpet section—vividly recall the impact of big band arrangements of such bebop classics as "A Night in Tunisia," "Blue 'n' Boogie," and "Salt Peanuts." And yet such enthusiastic reactions were in the minority. Because of the limited access black bands had to the mass media, none of the more challenging instrumental music could be heard on radio or recordings. Most of the audiences, having been attracted to dance halls and theaters by the few recordings made in May that featured Eckstine as a blues singer, such as "Good Jelly Blues" (DeLuxe), came away puzzled and disappointed by the experience. Subsequent recordings by Eckstine over the next few years, including "I Love the Rhythm in a Riff," "Second Balcony Jump," and "Oo Bop Sh'bam," offer some sense of the band's powerful ensemble sound and dynamic soloists—albeit absent the distinctive qualities of Gillespie or Parker, who left before the end of 1944.

In some ways, the dilemma faced by the Eckstine band reflected the coming rift between the mass black audience and jazz. The Second World War had drawn hundreds of thousands of black workers into the industrial economy for the first time, relocating them in urban centers such as Los Angeles and Detroit. Newly prosperous and eager for entertainment, this working-class audience asserted its taste for strongly rhythmic, bluesy music. Ultimately, that taste would be satisfied only by the revolution in black popular music that by the late 1940s came to be known as rhythm and blues. Eckstine's musicians found themselves in the uncomfortable position of having to try to "educate" their public (the word is the musicians' own) to appreciate a more self-consciously sophisticated and harmonically complex approach to black musical idioms.

Could bebop ever have succeeded as "commercial" entertainment in the swing mold? Not to judge from the experience of trumpet player Henry Jerome, who added a number of bebop-oriented arrangements to his band's book in late 1944 after being urged by some of his sidemen, including tenor saxophonist Al Cohn, drummer Tiny Kahn, and his saxophonist–band manager Leonard Garment (the future presidential adviser), to keep up with the "progressive" styles of Gillespie and Parker. "If we had done as much business as with the musicians who came down there to dig it," Jerome later recalled to Ira Gitler in *Swing to Bop* (1985), "we would have been rich. But no one dug it. The people didn't dig it because they couldn't dance to it."

But the involvement of white bandleader and clarinetist Woody Herman with the bebop sound in 1944–45 raises other, more intriguing possibilities. Several of Herman's recent hires, including bassist Chubby Jackson and trumpeter Neal Hefti, were fascinated by what they heard on 52nd Street and worked some of the new musical ideas into the band's head arrangments. The results can be heard on some of Herman's recordings, such as the 1945 "Caldonia" (Columbia), an up-tempo blues in which the trumpet section plays a brilliant unison passage clearly inspired by Gillespie's soloing. This version of the Herman band, later dubbed the "First Herd," appeared nationwide on prime-time radio programs and had its recordings distributed by Columbia, one of the major labels. It is hardly surprising that the Herman band emerged as the best-known "progressive" big band of its time while the Billy Eckstine band labored in obscurity. One could only imagine the impact a similar band featuring Parker and Gillespie as soloists might have made, had its music enjoyed similar publicity and exposure.

Instead, the bebop pioneers turned to less prestigious venues where their talents had a better chance of becoming recognized: jazz-oriented nightclubs and the recording studios of independent record companies. Parker dropped out of the Eckstine band in the summer of 1944 to eke out a precarious existence playing at clubs on 52nd Street and at Harlem jam sessions. By September, he had made his debut as a freelance recording artist, performing among other things a blues ("Tiny's Tempo") and an "I Got Rhythm" derivative ("Red Cross") with guitarist Tiny Grimes for Savoy. Gillespie joined him in New York at the beginning of 1945, and together they formed a quintet that would open at the Three Deuces on 52nd Street in April and at Billy Berg's nightclub in Los Angeles later in the year. To advertise the group, Gillespie began an ambitious and almost frenetic program of recording, at first for various new and obscure labels such as Guild, Continental, Black and White, and Manor.

The circumstances for recording were far from ideal. Some of the musicians that Gillespie would have liked to use were simply not available. The twenty-year-old Bud Powell had just suffered a severe head injury at the hands of the police. Max Roach was on the road with Benny Carter's big band, while Kenny Clarke was serving in the Army. Parker himself was in bad odor with the musicians' union, reportedly owing money to three different locals. Added to these logistical complications was the fact that recording companies employing Gillespie and his cohort did not see themselves as documenters of a new art-music idiom but as entrepreneurs competing for a share of the burgeoning market for "race records." Some now-forgotten recordings, such as "That's the Blues" (Continental), on which Gillespie and Parker play off-center riffs behind blues singer Rubberlegs Williams, show how bizarre the mixtures of progressive jazz and more old-fashioned black entertainment could be.

Other stylistic juxtapositions preserved on record proved more fruitful, or at least less jarring. Coleman Hawkins continued his commitment to mastering the new progressive sounds at the end of 1944 by forming a combo that included Oscar Pettiford and trumpet player Howard McGhee. This group was subsequently documented on recordings for Moe Asch's studio in New York and for the emergent industry giant, Capitol, in Los Angeles. Another striking conflation of old and new can be heard on a June 1945 recording led by Red Norvo: on "Congo Blues" (Comet), solos by Parker and Gillespie alternate with those of swing veterans Teddy Wilson, Flip Phillips, and Slam Stewart.

The crucial small-group recordings that came to define bebop as a genre also date from 1945. On recordings for Newark-based Savoy and Los Angeles–based Dial, a crucial shift in the way in which the nascent bebop idiom would be presented on records and in live performance came into focus. The format was still that of the public jam session: a straightforward presentation of a tune followed by improvised solos. Many early bop tunes, such "Blue 'n' Boogie" (Guild) and "Dizzy Atmosphere" (Musicraft), were built on riff patterns distinguishable from comparable swing era tunes primarily by their breakneck speed.

The asymmetric, convoluted, and rhythmically intricate writing that we associate today with bebop tended to emerge only toward the end of these early recordings, in what is usually known as the "outchorus." (The outchorus of Coleman Hawkins's "Hollywood Stampede" [Capitol, 1945], based on the chord progression to "Sweet Georgia Brown," quotes both Benny Harris's "Ornithology" and Gillespie's "Be-Bop.") Only when this more disorienting material was shifted to the *beginning* of the recording, as in "Shaw 'Nuff" and Tadd

Dameron's "Hot House" for Guild Records (the former based on "I Got Rhythm," the latter on Cole Porter's "What Is This Thing Called Love?"), were listeners faced with an aesthetic challenge that matched the in-your-face temperament of the music. In a frequently cited observation, drummer Dave Tough vividly recalled in the 1955 anthology *Hear Me Talkin' to Ya* what it was like to hear Parker and Gillespie's playing on 52nd Street: "As we walked in, see, these cats snatched up their horns and blew crazy stuff. One would stop all of a sudden and another would start for no reason at all. We never could tell when a solo was supposed to begin or end. Then they all quit at once and walked off the stand. It scared us."

If bebop scared some, it enthralled others. Making the most of the limited resources of the jam session–style combo, bebop offered both listeners and performers an artistic experience of unprecedented intensity. Much of this initial impact survives on the earliest commercial recordings, such as Charlie Parker's tour de force "KoKo" (Savoy), an updating of his brilliant routine on "Cherokee" with Jay McShann that is one of several bebop records from 1945 to be given a place of honor on the widely distributed anthology *The Smithsonian Collection of Classic Jazz*. But more to the point, the intensity and immediacy of bebop can be felt throughout the following half century of jazz practice. In the opening pages of his autobiography, Miles Davis perhaps summed it up best. Thinking back to the shock of first hearing the Billy Eckstine band, he reflected more than forty years later: "I've come close to matching the feeling of that night in 1944 in music, when I first heard Diz and Bird, but I've never quite got there. I've gotten close, but not all the way there. I'm always looking for it, listening and feeling for it, though, trying to always feel it in and through the music I play every day."

The New Orleans Revival

Richard Hadlock

The revival of New Orleans jazz probably began in 1917, when the first Victor records by the Original Dixieland Jazz Band, led by cornetist Nick LaRocca, were issued. As representatives of New Orleans polyphony—spontaneous improvised part-playing—the ODJB had profound influence, for several years, upon coming-of-age musicians. Clarinetist Benny Goodman and cornetist Bix Beiderbecke were but two youngsters who memorized entire passages recorded by LaRocca's quintet of seemingly "illiterate" instrumentalists. (Actually, trombonist Eddie Edwards could read music quite well.)

The ODJB enjoyed success in Chicago, New York, and London, inspiring countless new dixieland bands, all attempting to play improvised counterpoint according to New Orleans rules. "Original Fives" (not always very original) or "Hot Fives" (some not so hot) turned up on recordings frequently until 1928 or so. After that time dance orchestras prevailed, with radio broadcasts from ballrooms replacing records in many Depression-struck homes. Due in part to the brilliance of New Orleans trumpeter Louis Armstrong, jazz after the late twenties became a soloist's art, generally supported by sympathetic orchestral arrangers.

Muggsy Spanier's Ragtime Band, 1939. Left to right: Bob Casey, bass; Marty Greenberg, drums; Spanier, cornet; Rod Cless, clarinet; George Brunies, trombone. Photo: Duncan P. Schiedt. Courtesy of the Institute of Jazz Studies, Rutgers University.

Young Chicago jazz musicians who had been swept up by imported New Orleans music—King Oliver, the New Orleans Rhythm Kings, Louis Armstrong, Johnny Dodds, and Jimmie Noone—did not forget their mentors. Most of them earned their livings in dance bands, but they remained eager to participate in jam sessions, which allowed collective improvisation. Almost from its beginning, this talented Chicago fraternity had to cope with jazz evangelists who preached against "commercial" bands, calling for a return to "authentic" New Orleans—black New Orleans—music. One such was Milton "Mezz" Mezzrow, whose clarinet playing was not in the same league as that of local artists Benny Goodman and Frank Teschemacher but whose views had some effect on musicians and great influence upon pioneer French jazz writer Hugues Panassié.

In his second jazz history (*The Real Jazz*, 1942) Panassié pronounced the clarinet playing of Benny Goodman and Artie Shaw to be "like birds twittering in the trees," urging a return to "pure" New Orleans jazz. Mezz and Hugues seemed to agree, Rousseau-like, that white musicians (other than Mezzrow himself) had little chance of playing "real" jazz.

For some years after 1929 New Orleans jazz, although still performed in Louisiana, went into hiding. Echoes of it could be heard in Duke Ellington's orchestra, played by New Orleans natives Barney Bigard (clarinet) and Wellman Braud (bass). Armstrong was a conspicuous entertainer and always on the scene. Trumpeter Red Allen could be found with fellow New Orleans players in the ranks of Luis Russell's orchestra.

By 1933 bandleaders King Oliver and Jelly Roll Morton had virtually disappeared and Nick LaRocca had become a building contractor. Trombonist-bandleader Kid Ory, who had taken New Orleans jazz to California in 1919, went into chicken farming. Dixieland, it seemed, was quite dead.

It was during those awful years, however, that jazz record collecting came to life. College kids and professional types, including musicians, went on the hunt for rare copies of Oliver, Morton, or Bix Beiderbecke with the Wolverines. Campus gatherings to swap information led to "hot" clubs and jazz societies. By 1936 the first *Hot Discography* by French scholar Charles Delaunay and an English tome, *Rhythm on Record* (by Hilton R. Schleman), helped promote more jazz research and scholarship. All this activity set the stage for a true revival of dixieland.

In 1934 RCA Victor issued the first of many successful recordings by Fats Waller with a small, free-swinging band. Competitors struck back with New Orleans trumpeter-entertainer jazzmen Louis Prima and Wingy Manone, each fronting his own dixieland band. Excellent ensemble players such as trombonist George Brunis and clarinetists Pee Wee Russell and Joe Marsala were brought forth from relative obscurity to play in these sessions.

A dixieland band working on New York's 52nd Street, led by trumpeter Eddie Farley and trombonist Mike Riley, enjoyed a moment of national fame with its 1935 hit record, "The Music Goes 'Round and 'Round." The entertainment marketplace began to warm up to New Orleans–style jazz.

Collectors and purveyors of "real" jazz helped assemble a 1937 *March of Time* documentary film to commemorate the twentieth anniversary of the Original Dixieland Jazz Band's first records. Nick LaRocca came out of Louisiana to reassemble his old gang, even to cut some new records for RCA Victor. Although soon forgotten, this small revival led to larger revivals.

Big band leaders Tommy Dorsey and Bob Crosby introduced dixieland units into their ballroom, theater, or hotel presentations. Swing fans responded positively to the freewheeling ensembles, jazz solos, and contemporary rhythm sections of the Clambake Seven and the Crosby Bobcats. The Bobcats, half of them born in New Orleans, achieved an exquisite balance of swing, intelligent polyphony, and respect for the ODJB–Armstrong–Oliver–New Orleans Rhythm Kings music of the past. Saxophonist Eddie Miller and clarinetist Irving Fazola often revealed the mellow influence of New Orleans clarinetist Leon Roppolo.

All this dixieland activity inspired New York restaurateur Nick Rongetti to feature the band of New Orleans trumpeter Sharkey Bonano in his new Greenwich Village steak house. After Bonano returned home, guitarist Eddie Condon was usually to be found at Nick's, surrounded by dixieland-nurtured pals such as Bobby Hackett, Muggsy Spanier, and Max Kaminsky (trumpets), Joe Marsala, George Wettling (drums), and trombonist Brunis.

New Yorker Milt Gabler, whose Commodore Music Shop had become a jazz mecca in the thirties, launched his Commodore record label in 1938. His love of dixieland jazz, as expressed by the ex-Chicagoans and others in Condon's circle, led Gabler to recruit musicians from Nick's for his first sessions. After *Life* magazine covered an early Gabler studio date, players such as Pee Wee Russell, Hackett, and saxophonist Bud Freeman enjoyed wider recognition and began to get more calls for work.

Gabler's Commodore records had considerable impact upon a group of incipient revivalists in Australia. Pianist Graeme Bell and his brother Roger (cornet and drums) were ordering records from Commodore, adding to their understanding of traditional jazz, which had begun with record collecting around 1934. A gifted (though determinedly amateurish) multi-instrumentalist named Ade Monsbourgh became part of their group, as did collector-publisher Bill Miller. Miller's widespread activities, including starting a record company, helped spread the New Orleans–dixieland revival down under. By 1940 the Bells were ready to form a semiprofessional combo, and by 1947 they had become Australia's leading jazz players.

In California a similar evolution was taking place. Lu Watters, a reputable lead trumpeter and experienced bandsman-arranger (his first recording date was with Jack Danford in 1929), was compiling an impressive collection of hard-to-find first-class New Orleans jazz recordings—Morton, Oliver, and Armstrong. Logically, Watters recruited some collector-musician friends into a "hot" swing band, transmuted by 1940 into an outright revivalist octet.

With Bob Scobey (second trumpet), Turk Murphy (trombone), Ellis Horne (clarinet), and a banjo-tuba combination in the rhythm section, Lu's band offered up neat, if somewhat ponderous, versions of venerable blues, marches, and stomps. Pianist Wally Rose also soloed on vintage, nearly forgotten rags. With the issuing of its first records in 1942, Watters's Yerba Buena Jazz Band came to represent not just West Coast revival jazz but a worldwide musical movement toward an idealized past. A half century later Lu's music was still played by scores of trad bands in every part of the world.

By 1939 New Orleans jazz was making a solid comeback. RCA Victor underwrote a series of recordings supervised by Hugues Panassié which featured (along with Mezz Mezzrow, of course) Harlem pianist James P. Johnson and New Orleans trumpeter Tommy Ladnier. The towering figure in these sessions, however, was soprano saxophonist Sidney Bechet, whose majestic style had matured since the twenties, when he was already matching Armstrong in vigor, imagination, and swing. (Bechet, like the ODJB, had taken New Orleans music to Europe in 1919.)

The modest success of Panassié's half–New Orleans, half-swing dates prompted RCA to revive Jelly Roll Morton in a band that included Bechet and New Orleans clarinetist Albert Nicholas. In 1940 Bechet landed his own contract to produce small-band recordings for RCA.

Two other 1939–40 groups, though short-lived, made significant contributions to the dixieland revival. Muggsy Spanier's Ragtime Band adapted the music of the ODJB, the New Orleans Rhythm Kings, Armstrong, and Oliver to a 1939 swing rhythm section and produced a set of sixteen dixieland masterpieces. Brunis on trombone and Rod Cless on clarinet made the woven ensemble passages ring with authority and individuality.

Bud Freeman's Summa Cum Laude Orchestra combined Max Kaminsky's spare but firm lead, Pee Wee Russell's often startling filigrees, Freeman's sure rhythmic counterpoint on tenor sax, and valve trombonist Brad Gowan's rather conservative but knowledgeable part-playing—all supported by a rock-steady swing rhythm section. Freeman drew upon the music of Bix Beiderbecke and various Chicago associates as well as the ODJB and Armstrong for inspiration. (Gowans, Freeman's main arranger, was a devout ODJB fan and appeared in other settings on clarinet, playing in the 1917 style of Larry Shields.)

Eddie Condon went on from Freeman's rhythm section to create a role for himself as concert producer, recording director, nightclub front man, writer, and the sort of wise-cracking Manhattan personality journalists collect and acclaim. Like his old boss, Nick Rongetti, Condon kept the music in his Greenwich Village club hot and free, with as few traces of "modern" jazz (bebop) as possible.

Following the publication of the landmark book *Jazzmen* (1939), a score of jazz critics and theorists went into hardcover print. The "purists" lined up against the "progressives," then began squabbling among themselves. Panassié was battling Charles Delaunay for dominance in the French jazz scene. Even less moderate than the French was Rudi Blesh, whose *Shining Trumpets: A History of Jazz* (1946) reinforced Mezzrow and Panassié's Noble Savage views and condemned Charlie Parker and other modernists as non–jazz musicians.

During the forties and fifties a few critics parlayed skirmishes between bebop and traditional jazz into ideological warfare. Traditional or dixieland players were called "Mouldy Figs." Muggsy Spanier answered one such critic, Leonard Feather, with a composition called "Feather Brain Blues."

Some jazz writers became key movers in the ongoing revival of traditional jazz (the word *dixieland* was losing favor with fundamentalists and with many musicians). Ex–Ivy Leaguer George Avakian produced revival albums for Decca and Columbia. Rudi Blesh started a record company of his own (Circle), which issued the legendary 1938 Jelly Roll Morton Library of Congress recordings; Blesh also hosted a national radio show called *This Is Jazz*, exposing some forgotten jazzmen to a vast audience. He and Harriet Janis wrote *They All Played Ragtime* (1950), which helped make the world aware of composers such as Scott Joplin, Joseph Lamb, and James Scott.

Charles Edward Smith, Fred Ramsey, and Bill Russell, editors of and contributors to *Jazzmen*, unearthed a pioneer jazzman named William "Bunk" Johnson, still robust and willing, if fitted with teeth, to play again. The rehabilitation of Bunk took a couple of years, but the old man turned out to be a good trumpet player and a great talker. After several recording sessions and a stay with the San Francisco revivalists, Bunk captivated New York in 1945. His run at the Stuyvesant Casino was a curious parallel to the 1917 invasion by the Original Dixieland Jazz Band. The "primitive" New Orleans sounds of Bunk, clarinetist George Lewis, trombonist Jim Robinson, and drummer Baby Dodds (he of the great 1923 King Oliver band) brought jazz fans, college kids, curious musicians, and debutantes to Second Avenue. Bunk's face, handsomely framed by his snow-white hair, appeared in *Mademoiselle*, *Vogue*, and a gaggle of news or entertainment magazines.

In 1940, while Bunk was preparing for his Grand Entrance, a group of righteous enthusiasts recorded a band of New Orleans gaffers in their hometown. Among the nearly forgotten old men were a faltering Kid Rena (trumpet) and the legendary clarinetist Alphonse Picou, who ran through his famous, widely copied variations on "High Society." The old-timers also performed an ODJB piece, "Clarinet Marmalade."

About the same time, Decca Records issued a New Orleans jazz album with new performances by Armstrong, Bechet, clarinetists Jimmie Noone and Johnny Dodds, pianist Richard M. Jones, and others. The revival was on in earnest.

Now there began to be divisions within the young revival musicians. The formalists were as concerned with repertoire as with maintaining spontaneity and agreeable counterpoint; the naturalists leaned toward simple songs upon which they could build a rolling polyphonic ensemble, often reaching peaks of excitement without any solos at all.

Lu Watters and Turk Murphy were, by 1946, leaders of the formalists. Among their followers were Graeme Bell in Australia and George Webb in England. Turk Murphy cited Gershwin's "Lady Be Good" as the sort of trite jam session warhorse he wished to avoid. Instead, he and the Watters band found pleasure in multiple-strain pieces by Oliver, Morton, and other sophisticated early composers. The naturalists had no problem with "Lady Be Good." They would see it as a fine base for old-style collective improvisation. It was, in fact, recorded in the fifties by New Orleans marching bands.

At least two central figures in the revival of New Orleans jazz could move with ease from formalist to naturalist settings, seemingly at home in either camp. Bunk Johnson enjoyed playing unstructured blues and silly pop songs such as "Bell Bottom Trousers," yet he was anxious to record pieces from the challenging *Red Back Book* of ragtime band arrangements. Sidney Bechet spun magnificent improvisations on blues and simple songs such as "Summertime," but he had total recall when it came to routines on rags, cakewalks, and marches of old.

Bechet and Johnson recorded together in 1945 (Blue Note), in a naturalist mode. The results were quite engaging, but these two proud men were unable to get along while working a regular job. Bechet went on to influence the revival in several ways. He helped jazzmen such as trumpeter Wild Bill Davison and pianist Art Hodes learn old numbers they had never heard. He opened a school of jazz, which sent clarinetist Bob Wilber on his way to a long and impressive career in jazz. He introduced new talent, such as outstanding young trumpeter Johnny Windhurst.

After Bechet moved to Europe in the late forties, he worked with and taught young traditionalists such as Claude Luter, Michel Attenoux, and Claude Bolling (France), Humphrey Lyttleton and Wally Fawkes (England), and Peter Schilperoort (Holland). Sidney became something of a European superstar in the fifties, and he seemed to enjoy every moment of it.

Bob Wilber went on to form his Wildcats, a disciplined, rather formalist band that moved more toward swing than did the Watters or Murphy bands. Out of this period came the brilliant pianist Dick Wellstood and a talented second trumpeter, smitten by Bunk Johnson, named Jerry Blumberg. A later Wilber band sounded closer to the swing sessions recorded by Bechet in 1940 and 1941. Throughout his bright career Wilber has returned to Bechet repeatedly, even fronting a combo called the Bechet Legacy.

The success of Wilber's tightly organized band inspired another formalist revival group, led and rehearsed by trombonist Wilbur de Paris. The veteran bandsman featured his brother Sidney on trumpet and the ex-Morton New Orleans–born clarinetist Omer Simeon. His repertoire included original compositions, obscure pieces from the twenties, Morton classics, rags, and show tunes. The college crowd loved de Paris's New New Orleans Jazz Band and helped it to enjoy a long run at Jimmy Ryan's in New York. When illness forced Simeon's retirement, he was replaced by New Yorker Garvin Bushell, who had learned his first jazz licks from recordings of clarinetist Larry Shields with the Original Dixieland Jazz Band.

In England the revival of New Orleans jazz became a "trad fad." Art students and university people got it started to the music of trumpeters Humphrey Lyttelton (a graduate of Eton and George Webb's Dixielanders) and Mick Mulligan. The students disdained smooth swing and neatly clad professionals (the establishment), so most bands of the late forties and early fifties were deliberately amateurish and purposely indifferent to convention. Eventually Lyttelton and others encouraged their fans to dance and to accept reasonably trim arrangements and band attire.

Trombonist Chris Barber found success as a bandleader during the trad jazz craze, which lasted until a rock group called the Beatles ended the "Hit Parade" affluence of trad in 1962. Barber featured banjoist-vocalist Lonnie Donegan and clarinetist Monty Sunshine, whose uncomplicated, melodic style sold lots of records. (Bechet's "Petite Fleur" was a big hit for Chris and Monty.)

Barber's attempt to combine forces with trumpeter Ken Colyer failed, probably because Barber was more formalist than naturalist Colyer could accept. Colyer then led his own band, solidly grounded in the New Orleans ensemble styles of George Lewis and Bunk Johnson, to considerable popularity in Great Britain. His fans adored his integrity: he refused to consciously "market" his music.

After the war Lu Watters reorganized in San Francisco, returning to the Dawn Club in 1946. Replacing the talented but somewhat diffident clarinetist Ellis Horne was a more assertive master of part-playing, Bob Helm. In 1947 the band moved across the Bay to open its own restaurant, Hambone Kelly's. When Watters retired in 1950, Helm joined Turk Murphy, now on his own and still stressing repertoire as much as improvisation.

Others on the West Coast were adding to the revival. In Los Angeles Kid Ory got back into the band business around 1944. Pete Daily was making records in an updated ODJB style. Trumpeter Bob Scobey prospered with a band featuring vocalist Clancy Hayes. In Portland the Castle Jazz Band was joining the banjo-tuba brotherhood, declaring its faith with an original piece by banjoist Monty Ballou called "No Bop Hop Scop Blues."

In Southern California Les Koenig put out much of this traditional music on his Good Time Jazz label. He also released sessions by George Lewis and Bunk Johnson.

Back in New Orleans the ongoing revival was making life easier for many older musicians. Record producer Bill Russell had started preserving the music in the mid-forties on his American Music label. George Lewis and friends (trumpeters Kid Thomas and Percy Humphrey and trombonist Jim Robinson, among others) were now in demand all around the world, often leaving in their wake a cluster of zealous trad performers, as in Japan with Osaka's New Orleans Rascals.

The demand for Dixieland and New Orleans jazz from the late forties on was sufficient to grab the attention of notable swing soloists. Some, like Jimmy Dorsey, Louis Armstrong, Buster Bailey, Jack Teagarden, Red Allen, Barney Bigard, and Edmond Hall, drew upon their formative years recalling the New Orleans sounds of the twenties. Others, such as trombonists Vic Dickenson and Benny Morton and trumpeters Buck Clayton, Rex Stewart, and Pee Wee Erwin, had to teach themselves the old dixieland routines.

Former Bobcats and big band sidemen Yank Lawson (trumpet), Bob Haggart (bass), Lou McGarity (trombone), Matty Matlock (clarinet), and Billy Butterfield (trumpet) helped to keep dixieland going with many albums under various band names and record labels. Haggart went on playing and composing until his death at eighty-four in 1998.

Trad venues came and went over the decades. For a while there were ritualistic collegiate dances at New York's Central Plaza and Stuyvesant Casino. The 52nd Street jazz strip disappeared, replaced by a scattering of saloons and pizza joints around Manhattan. Turk Murphy ran a succession of clubs in San Francisco, most of them called Earthquake McGoon's.

In New Orleans some fans opened a low-rent concert room, Preservation Hall. There on any single evening one might have heard a couple of fumbling, over-the-hill musicians, one or two eager young disciples from up north or from Europe, and, with luck, a moving clarinet solo or two from such as Willie Humphrey, Raymond Burke, or perhaps George Lewis himself. The long-admired polyphonic skills of hometown players have tended to become routinized into brittle, predictable musical artifacts for tourists.

The revival rolls on, ever producing new musicians who will make a lifelong study of hot jazz ensemble part-playing. Just as star performers regularly emerged from traditional jazz over the decades—Australia's Bob Barnard (trumpet), England's Roy Williams (trombone), Scotland's Sandy Brown (clarinet), America's Bob Helm (clarinet), and Sweden's Bent Persson (trumpet) are a few—so the new century will have its creative luminaries. Californian multi-instrumentalist Clint Baker, a born jazz naturalist, is one such young, inventive player. So is Australian trumpeter-pianist Stephen Grant, who may lean more toward formalism as found in Jelly Roll Morton's music.

Alongside and sometimes mixed with the New Orleans revivalists are the repertory orchestras. These companies are transcribing many "hot dance," swing, and bebop recordings, then presenting them in concert or on compact disc with today's improved sound. Bob Wilber, New Orleans trumpeter Wynton Marsalis, historian Gunther Schuller, and British pianist Keith Nichols are a few who are producing thoughtful repertory music.

In the late years of the twentieth century, traditional jazz clubs and jazz bands have multiplied beyond all predictions. There are in the world hundreds of New Orleans dixieland–based bands and over one hundred festivals celebrating their music. A plethora of trad records, jazz cruises, and monthly concerts sponsored by local dixieland fan clubs continue to find support, but there is some concern that aging trad patrons are not being replaced by younger fans.

Perhaps, after all, there never was a manifest New Orleans jazz revival. Perhaps this multifaceted music simply refused to go away entirely, on leave occasionally but always reappearing and finally thriving throughout the century.

Charlie Parker

James Patrick

As if by immaculate conception, the first wave of modern jazz recordings appeared in late 1945 and early 1946. Granted the wisdom of hindsight, we know this startling music had been taking shape over the previous six or seven years, but much of its development had been hidden from the music public. In a dispute between the American Federation of Musicians and the three "majors" of the recording industry (Columbia, Decca, and Victor), most commercial recording was silenced from August 1942 to November 1944. Various wartime measures—the drafting of musicians, a shortage of shellac needed for the manufacture of phonograph discs, gasoline rationing, and transportation restrictions—further reduced opportunities for exposing new music. It should not be surprising, then, that when many people first heard bebop it sounded like a blurred image of the jazz past or, worse, seemed disturbingly disconnected to earlier jazz traditions. Woody Herman's drummer Dave Tough was no exception:

> As we walked in, see, these cats snatched up their horns and blew crazy stuff. One would stop all of a sudden and another would start for no reason at all. We never could tell when a solo

was supposed to begin or end. Then they all quit at once and walked off the stand. It scared us.

As it turned out, bebop was not merely the next new jazz style. Bebop would not only endure but become established as *the* preeminent jazz style—standing among all those that preceded it or those that developed after its first emergence as the lingua franca, the common practice idiom of the art of jazz. At the center of this is Charlie Parker, the legendary Bird.

Charles Parker Jr. was born on August 29, 1920, in Kansas City, Kansas, the only child of Addie and Charles Parker Sr., grew up in Kansas City, Missouri, and died on March 12, 1955, in the Manhattan apartment of the Rothschild baroness, Pannonica de Koenigswarter. Charlie Parker was one of the great transforming figures of twentieth-century music, and the history of jazz is inconceivable without him. Like Armstrong, Beethoven, or Schoenberg, Parker was one of those ultra-rare originals in which a tradition's past, present, and future merge. In a musical culture where creativity and individualism are aesthetic, indeed, ethical first principles, Parker was a landmark innovator. Bird is also one of jazz's most traditional musicians, and, like jazz itself, his music was a wondrous synthesis of diverse and seemingly irreconcilable elements. Parker appears to have liked—or found useful—almost any kind of music, and the raw material he refracted was a large and variegated mix. There was jazz, especially the great soloists Louis Armstrong, Benny Carter, Roy Eldridge, Coleman Hawkins, Johnny Hodges, and Lester Young, and, less probably, Jimmy Dorsey, Rudy Wiedoeft, and Rudy Vallee. There was popular music, including children's ditties, folk melodies, dance tunes, and Tin Pan Alley and Broadway songs. In his later years, Parker also developed a fondness for "classical" music and particular admiration for the modern composers Bartók, Hindemith, Schoenberg, Stravinsky, and Varèse. Foremost, however, was the blues and the robust milieu of black music in Kansas City during the 1930s.

No other jazz musician has so gripped the imagination of fellow artists and lay people alike. Parker's reputation was fueled not only by the brilliance of his music but also by the colorful and often lurid saga of his personal life. Parker's time on earth was brief and turbulent. The basic problem for the Parker biographer is that virtually any tale about the man could be true. We have an extensive anecdotal lore, which has been gathered from hundreds of informants, a large percentage of them credible. From these we know that Parker could

Charlie Parker, c. 1947. Courtesy of the Institute of Jazz Studies, Rutgers University.

be caring or self-absorbed, coarse or refined, generous or greedy, affable or withdrawn, and display any number of other polarities in behavior. Clearly Parker was a fundamentally troubled man who added the self-inflicted insults of heroin and alcoholic addiction to his burdens. Trumpeter Kenny Dorham succinctly explained, "He had to have a lot of everything." Probably the best composite portrait presents him as a supremely dazzling musician, witty, highly intelligent, articulate, reckless, and irresponsible. Bird was a suave manipulator who could charm even those people he had badly mistreated—*until* he went to the well once too often, which happened with several of his friends, most of his musical and business colleagues, and all of his four most serious relationships. In a rare moment of self-revelation, Parker rhetorically asked trumpeter Benny Harris, "What good is love if you can't take?" Many lives were and continue to be enriched by Charlie Parker, but as another musician laughingly put it, "To know Bird you got to pay your dues." Given Parker's complex and volatile personality, it is sometimes too easy to lose sight of the extraordinary power that music exerted on him. Until his late years—when the appetites and dark forces overcame him—the Parker story is, at its core, about the triumph of music as the dominant obsession in a perplexing array of contesting compulsions. The ultimate tragedy is that Charlie Parker's astonishing music could not save Charlie Parker from himself.

Parker's chaotic personal life and the transcendency of his mature playing might suggest that he was some kind of black Mozart for whom great art came quickly and easily. In fact, Charlie was a spoiled mama's boy who showed little interest in or aptitude for music until his middle teens. When he first became seriously committed to the life of a musician his progress was slow, and he was sometimes cruelly humiliated. In his own words:

> I had learned to play two tunes in a certain key . . . the first eight bars of "Lazy River" and I knew the complete tune of "Honeysuckle Rose." . . . So I took my horn out to this joint where . . . a bunch of fellows who I had seen around worked and the first thing they started playing was "Body and Soul" . . . So I go to playing my "Honeysuckle Rose" . . . They laughed me off the bandstand.
>
> Everybody fell out laughing. I went home and cried and didn't play again for three months.

Parker eventually responded, however, with a steely resolve to work hard and grow. He recalled this period near the end of his life:

> I put quite a bit of study into the horn.... In fact, the neighbors threatened to ask my mother to move once... they said I was driving 'em crazy with the horn. I used to put in at least eleven, eleven to fifteen hours a day.

Like most jazz musicians of his time, Parker learned the basic components of his craft in a concurrent fashion through practical experience. As he was learning his instrument, he was also acquiring improvising skills, basic harmony, and a repertory and studying older jazz masters firsthand or on recordings—each advance tested via a process of trial and error in the fiercely competitive Kansas City bands and jam sessions. At the age of fifteen Charlie quit school to become a full-time musician, married his childhood sweetheart, Rebecca Ruffin, and started using heroin. For the next four years Parker apprenticed in a number of local and regional bands. Parker's first major breakthrough occurred in 1937. During that summer he was employed at a resort in Eldon, Missouri, studied harmony with guitarist Efferge Ware, and memorized several of tenor saxophonist Lester Young's recorded solos. When he returned to Kansas City his playing was vastly improved, and he worked with alto saxophonist Buster Smith, who, along with Young, would become a central influence on his early style. Parker experienced his next major breakthrough at a jam session in New York, where he spent most of 1939. That famous epiphany is recalled in a 1949 interview for *Down Beat*:

> Charlie's horn first came alive in a chili house on Seventh Ave. between 139th St. and 140th St. In December, 1939. He was jamming there with a guitarist named Biddy Fleet. At the time, Charlie says, he was bored with the stereotyped changes being used then. "I kept thinking there's bound to be something else," he recalls. "I could hear it sometimes but I couldn't play it." Working over "Cherokee" with Fleet, Charlie suddenly found that by using higher intervals of a chord as a melody line and backing them with appropriately related changes, he could play this thing he had been "hearing."

Parker's personal behavior became increasingly reckless, but he was now convinced of his musical destiny, and his quest would not be restrained by any customary sense of responsibility. In 1940 Charlie asked Rebecca for a divorce and extracted a promise from his mother that she would care for his wife and two-year-old son, Leon. In Rebecca's words:

> He held my hand and he says, "Rebec, would you free me, please.... I believe I could become a great musician if I were free."... And that was all. He would never be back.

From 1940 to 1942 Parker played in Jay McShann's band, made his first recordings, and acquired his nickname Yardbird, eventually shortened to Bird. In December 1942 he was hired as a tenor saxophonist by Earl Hines, whose band included several other young modernists, Dizzy Gillespie among them. Parker remained with Hines until April 1943, returned to Kansas City, and in May 1944 was persuaded to rejoin Gillespie and other former Hines colleagues as the nucleus of Billy Eckstine's legendary band. By August 1944 Parker had left Eckstine, and in September he cut his first small-group recordings as featured soloist with guitarist Tiny Grimes. During this crucial 1940–44 period, Parker made only a small handful of commercial recordings. Before the Grimes date he is highlighted in only a few brief solos, most notably "Hootie Blues" (1941), "Swingmatism" (1941), and "The Jumpin' Blues" (1942) with McShann. It remains one of the profound laments in the history of jazz that, due to the AFM recording ban, neither the Hines nor Eckstine bands in which Parker worked are preserved in sound. On the other hand, approximately thirty privately made recordings ranging from 1940 to early 1944 have survived and preserve Parker in a diverse assortment of musical contexts: solo, unaccompanied alto saxophone; small McShann groups; the full McShann band; alto plus guitar; a Harlem jam session; and one item with Parker, Gillespie, and bassist Oscar Pettiford made in a Chicago hotel room in 1943.

The year 1945 was pivotal and decisive. In New York Parker led his own group for the first time and worked extensively with Gillespie in small ensembles. From January 4, 1945, to February 5, 1946, Parker and Gillespie made sixty-five seminal recordings together (including private recordings, airchecks, and alternate takes from studio sessions) with one or the other as leader or the two together working as sidemen. Several of these would define the new jazz and serve as a core canon for the modern era: "Dizzy Atmosphere," "Groovin' High," "Hot House," "KoKo," "Salt Peanuts," and "Shaw 'Nuff." By the time Bird made his first shocking and brilliant recordings as a leader on November 26, 1945, at the age of twenty-five he had been a professional musician and heroin addict for nearly ten years. The genius of Charlie Parker—as it was now fully revealed—owed less to the divine muses than it did to his hard work, study, broad experience, and the determined will to fulfill his destiny as a great musician.

Parker and Gillespie took their new music to Hollywood in December 1945 for an eight-week nightclub engagement. Gillespie returned to New York, and Bird remained in Los Angeles, recording and performing in concerts and nightclubs until a nervous breakdown and his chemical appetites led to a six-month confinement at Camarillo State Hospital. Parker was released in late January 1947 and returned to New York in early April. Throughout 1946 and early 1947 the jazz press had kept bebop insiders up to date about Parker's West Coast odyssey. The faithful were primed for Bird's return, and a reenergized, if not rehabilitated, Charlie Parker did not disappoint them. Parker formed his classic quintet with Miles Davis, trumpet, Duke Jordan, piano, Tommy Potter, bass, and Max Roach, drums— with Bud Powell, John Lewis, Tadd Dameron, or Al Haig sometimes on piano or Curley Russell on bass. This group remained intact for nineteen months (a period of relatively remarkable stability in Bird's volatile career), worked and traveled regularly, and from May 1947 to September 1948 recorded many of the finest specimens of Parker's music for the Dial and Savoy companies: "Donna Lee," "Chasin' the Bird," "Embraceable You," "Scrapple From the Apple," "Klactoveeseds-tene," "Another Hair Do," "Barbados," "Ah-Leu-Cha," "Parker's Mood," and "Marmaduke."

By 1950 Charlie Parker was not merely a cult hero worshiped by obeisant hipsters but also a star. He was now recording exclusively for the (eventual) Verve company and Norman Granz, who was determined that under his guidance Parker could receive mass appreciation if presented in "fresh dimensions." Granz insisted that Bird perform "pretty tunes written by good song writers" and recorded him with string ensembles, big jazz bands, Afro-Cuban outfits, woodwind and vocal groups, and other large and expensive conglomerations usually denied to jazz artists at the time. Much of this was poohpoohed by the jazz hard core, but there is no denying that such records as "Just Friends" and "April in Paris" (both 1949 and released together on *Charlie Parker With Strings*) had a tremendous effect on his career. The Verves contain very little of Parker's very best playing, but due to their broad distribution and constant availability for the past five decades they remain among his most well known recordings. Among these are the unalloyed small-group bebop items: "Laird Baird" (1953), "Confirmation" (1953), "Kim" (1953), "She Rote" (1951), and "Blues for Alice" (1951).

Parker had achieved critical and popular success. He performed at Carnegie Hall, visited Europe in 1949 and 1950, and headlined the Festivale Internationale de Jazz in Paris. He was the winner of magazine polls, received excellent reviews, was the subject of feature articles, and had a nightclub, Birdland, named in his honor. At the same time he began to unravel again. His marriage to Doris Sydnor dissolved, there was more heroin and alcohol, and his health deteriorated. He was arrested on a narcotics violation and, as a result, his New York City cabaret license was revoked, which banned him from nightclub employment. There was unprofessional and sometimes bizarre behavior on and off the bandstand; there were troubles with club owners, his booking agency, and the AFM. Sporadically employed and badly in debt, Parker twice attempted suicide in 1954 and was admitted to Bellevue Hospital in New York. Two remarkable medical documents summarize this last fragile and pathetic stage in Parker's life. They read in part:

> The [admitting] diagnosis was acute and chronic alcoholism and narcotic addiction . . . Evaluation by psychiatrists indicate [sic] a hostile, evasive personality with manifestations of primitive and sexual fantasies associated with hostility and gross evidence of paranoid thinking. Psychoanalytic diagnosis: "latent schizophrenia."

Additional medical tests were performed including a neurological examination, a spinal tap, and a blood Wasserman sample, which indicated that Parker had syphilis, but the disease had not yet attacked his central nervous system.

Parker's last public engagement was on March 5, 1955, at Birdland (where he had been barred as a performer and customer), and he died seven days later. The official cause of death given by the medical examiner was lobar pneumonia. The attending physician (who refused to sign the death certificate) attributed Parker's death to advanced cirrhosis of the liver and a heart attack and estimated his age to be around sixty. Bird was thirty-four.

The mature Parker style is complex, but also one of supreme clarity and coherence. Perhaps the three most immediately striking features are his sound, tempos, and rhythm. In contrast to the rich timbres of Johnny Hodges and Benny Carter, Parker developed a hard, penetrating tone with a slow, narrow vibrato, which was eminently suited to the aggressiveness of the new music. With regard to tempo, we should recall that a standard mechanical metronome of the time operated within a range of Largo at 40 quarter note beats per minute to Presto at 208. Several of Parker's recordings (especially a number of live performances) are totally off this tempo map and are true Prestissimos ("as fast as possible"), such as the hypersonic "KoKo" (1949 at 360), "Dizzy Atmosphere" (1947 at 375), and "Salt Peanuts" (1949 at 385). At the other end of the scale, some of Parker's most dazzling and ornate studio performances use very slow tempos, such as "Parker's Mood" (1948 at 80), "Funky Blues" (1952 at 65), and "Embraceable You" (1947 at 60). Parker's rhythm is a marvel of continuous variability. The tremendous drive of his line often owes relatively less to basic syncopation rather than to an enveloping irregularity at several different levels of musical time. The basic pulse is constantly broken into a succession of varied and discontinuous subdivisions. The length of phrases and the positioning of their beginnings and endings within the measure are highly irregular, while accentual bombs drop here and there. Dizzy Gillespie nailed it when he said: "Bird had a knack for getting from one note to another like nobody else."

Parker's solos avoid direct reference to the original melodies. Paraphrase—the use of ornamentation or other modest reshaping in which the original tune is perceivable in the variation—is usually reserved for opening or closing statements when a well-known popular song is serving as the theme. Typically Parker based his solos on the underlying chord structure, endlessly creating new melodies with no obvious resemblance to the originals. In doing so, Parker often used a process known to musicologists as centonization (from the Latin *cento*, patchwork) whereby new works are created out of short, preexisting melodic formulas. Thomas Owens has identified about one hundred of Parker's formulas and demonstrated in exhaustive detail how Parker's solos—never identical and never "formulaic" in the narrow sense—were in large part the result of his constant variation and redisposition of these melodic cells.

Identifying a core of "greatest hits" or hypothesizing a stash of indispensable recordings for the proverbial desert island has long been an entertaining parlor game for jazz aficionados. In the case of Charlie

Parker, the expert literature suggests that there is a commonly accepted handful of pieces that must be heard by anyone who wants to experience the full measure of Bird's music. A few of these are briefly discussed below. Fortunately, all are currently in print and available to listeners.

"KoKo," Savoy, November 26, 1945

Parker's "KoKo" solo provides a summary of his most exciting playing style and faultless instrumental technique at very fast tempos. The piece is based on the chord structure of "Cherokee," which had figured prominently in his second developmental breakthrough and was one of his featured numbers with the Jay McShann band. Yet other facts indicate that the "Cherokee"/"KoKo" concept held special significance for Parker. First, after 1945 he reserved the piece for use on special occasions such as radio broadcasts or important concerts at Carnegie Hall in New York. Second, he embedded into his performances a small collection of figures that function as a kind of melodic autobiographical sketch: an in-your-face accelerated quotation of the "Cherokee" melody; a quotation from the New Orleans standard "High Society"; a fast-moving sequential lick incorporating "Tea for Two," which was originally concocted as a mnemonic aid to the improvisational navigation of the difficult chord structure of the middle section of "Cherokee"; an isolated, sustained, and blues-inflected single note (F); and a long, descending figure reminiscent of pianists Fats Waller's and Art Tatum's recordings of "Tea for Two." Parker calls attention to these figures by their unusual degree of internal repetition and by positioning them at the most prominent places in the chorus—at the very beginning and end, or at the beginning of the B section of the AABA structure. What is most remarkable, however, is that given the formidable challenge of keeping his line moving and composing at very high speed, Parker produced a melody of great logical design.

"Lady Be Good," Clef, January 28, 1946

Lester Young's 1936 version of George and Ira Gershwin's "Lady Be Good" was one of the solos that Parker memorized in the summer of 1937. Bird's 1946 performance not only pays homage to his roots in Kansas City but also serves as a two-chorus history lesson as the solo evolves from the beginning swing era flavor into the full-fledged Parker style. In the opening section Parker employs implied call and response, answering his references to Gershwin's melody with repetitive riff phrases, and inserts figures recalling moments from the Young solo. In the second part the line is fast-moving and rhythmically and harmonically complex. Throughout the solo, however, the blues are never far away, and Parker's tone and declamation are unusually strident and intensely expressive—a distant remove from Ira Gershwin's coy words about a lonely guy in the big city. Near the end, Parker rounds things off with an aggressive, signifying blues lick and a variant of the opening idea to provide a brief recapitulation of what has transpired and how far we have traveled in two short choruses.

"Embraceable You" (Take 1), Dial, October 28, 1947

Parker frequently turned to another Gershwin song, "Embraceable You." In all, there are seventeen surviving versions from 1943 to 1953, but the classic slow ballad specimen is the first of two studio takes made in 1947. Parker's one-chorus solo has been discussed by several eminent jazz writers and has even served as the token jazz example in general books devoted to "serious" music. Despite the title, this recording is hardly a performance of the 1930 song since Parker almost entirely avoids direct contact with Gershwin's original melody. Instead of simply paraphrasing Gershwin's tune or linking together patchwork figures to fit with the underlying harmony, Parker builds much of his solo on a rapid six-note figure (C-G-F-E-D-E) presented at the very beginning. The writer Gary Giddins has identified this figure as a quotation from the opening of the 1939 pop song "A Table in a Corner." This improbable overlay, moreover, serves as a concise distillation of Gershwin's entire first phrase. What might have begun as a merely ingenious quotation unfolds as a tour de force of improvised motivic composition. The six-note idea is reiterated and variously repronounced (to borrow a well-chosen word from the great critic Martin Williams), transposed, ornamented, speeded up, slowed down, its contour broadened, and enveloped in long, fast-moving phrases—all this motivic wizardry projected against Parker's exquisite overall dramatic pacing and narrative design.

"Klact-oveeseds-tene" (Take 1), Dial, November 4, 1947

Parker's composition almost certainly was conceived at this studio date and consists of an assembly of three elements: the introduction and coda, which was borrowed from "The Chase," recorded earlier in 1947 for Dial by tenor saxophonists Dexter Gordan and Wardell Gray; a modest reworking of the AABA chord pattern of Juan Tizol's "Perdido" (1942); and a newly composed melody to be used only for the A sections, leaving the B section open for improvisation. The tempo is medium up. There are two takes, and each offers forty-eight measures of Parker improvising during the opening and closing themes and in his one-chorus solo. A comparison will show that the two have much in common with regard to Parker's deployment of several of his favorite figures, used pretty much in the same way and in the same places. Yet the first take is something very special. The general tendency toward rhythmic irregularity is taken to a dangerous extreme in the fragmented beginning. Three very short but progressively longer ideas of two notes, three notes, and six notes are punched out and isolated from each other by silence. As Parker develops these ideas by combining, transposing, and ornamenting them, the line becomes increasingly continuous and the fragmentation is resolved. What initially may have seemed absurdly reckless is quickly transformed into a statement of awe-inspiring, logical structure. As for the weird title, Parker was usually content to allow the record companies to name his pieces, but Bird himself supplied this one and let others ponder its meaning. One speculation has it that it is fractured German for *Klack* (an interjection denoting the noise "slap-bang!") and *wiedersehen* ("good-bye"). Another suggests that it refers to the call letters of KLAC, a radio station in Southern California where Parker spent 1946 and early 1947. Probably the most plausible explanation was provided by the amateur Parker recordist Dean Benedetti: "Why, man, it's just a sound." There is no evidence that Parker ever performed this piece again.

"Parker's Mood" (Take 2), Savoy, September 18, 1948

The entire compass of Parker's music—from the simple and direct to the complex and oblique—ranges within the basic framework of the twelve-measure blues. The blues offered two contrasting, but not irreconcilable, possibilities to Parker: a cherished heirloom through which tradition could be transmitted, and a familiar referential idea that could be elaborated upon in the modern jazz manner. "Parker's Mood" is Bird's slow blues masterpiece. The rhythmic subtlety is fantastic: the complexity of individual phrases; the staggered, not-quite-on-the-beat flow. At the same time, there is the singable/speakable naturalness of vocal/oral tradition in the varied inflection of repetitive figures. The net effect is a performance that, all at once, is progressive and traditional, astonishing and deeply moving. Jay McShann, Parker's early employer, once remarked:

Ask me what did he do, I tell them he played the blues...
anything that Bird played...Bird played the blues. Regardless
of how much technique he had. He played the blues....Bird
was one of the greatest blues musicians in the world.

Parker was above all a great improviser, and probably no other musician before the advent of free jazz was so committed to and trusting
in the principle of spontaneous creation. Bird's off-the-top approach
could be dangerous and exhilarating, with so little assured by pre-
meditation and so much riding on the reflexive moment. Tommy
Potter described the sometimes hectic atmosphere at the Dial and
Savoy studio sessions:

On record dates he could compose right on the spot. The A and
R [artists and repertoire] man would be griping, wanting us to
begin. Charlie would say, "It'll just take a minute," and he'd
write out eight bars, usually just for the trumpet. He could transpose it for his alto without a score. The channel [the B section
of thirty-two-measure AABA pieces] could be ad libbed. The
rhythm section was familiar with all the progressions of the
tunes which were usually the basis of originals.

In his autobiography, Miles Davis recalled the first public engagement of the classic quintet in 1947:

You had to be ready for anything....A week or so before opening night, Bird called for rehearsals....On the first day of rehearsal, everybody showed up but Bird...and I ended up rehearsing the band. Now opening night...we ain't seen Bird in
a week, but we'd been rehearsing....When it's time for the
band to hit, he asks, "What are we playing?"...He played like
a motherfucker....It was something. We were...amazed....
You came to expect it. And if he didn't do something incredible,
that's when you were surprised.

Parker once advised a young musician:

First you master your instrument, then you master the music;
then you forget about all that shit and just *play*.

He was telling this jazz apprentice that you needed to be prepared if you wanted to enter the magic zone of spontaneity.

A few observations about Parker's approach to musical form are instructive. The basic, overall shape of a typical Parker performance is utterly traditional and unremarkable. Parker relied on the time-honored theme and variations procedure, with the ubiquitous twelve-bar blues and thirty-two-measure $8+8+8+8$, AABA patterns as the most frequent designs for the initially stated themes and the subsequent solo choruses based on them. Still, Parker continuously came up with new ways to shake up this basic plan. He combined composed (preexisting) melody with improvised melody, tended to use only as much composed material as might be required to provide a sense of repetitive coherence, and, generally, enlarged the role of improvisation and thrust it into places where it did not normally "belong." A conventional performance would dictate that someone play the melody of the theme more or less as written while the rhythm section provided the basic harmony and pulse. This would be followed by individual solo choruses, new melodies based on the melody or harmony of the theme, and the performance concluded with a restatement of the theme. Parker, however, liked to mitigate the distinction between composed theme and improvised variation and, otherwise, challenge normative procedures. Parts of the theme's melody might be improvised:

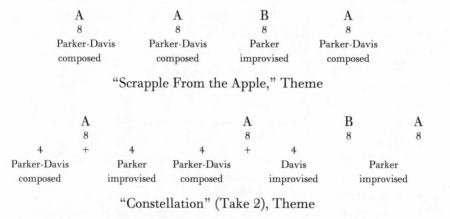

A	A	B	A
8	8	8	8
Parker-Davis composed	Parker-Davis composed	Parker improvised	Parker-Davis composed

"Scrapple From the Apple," Theme

A		A		B	A
8		8		8	8
4	+	4	4	+	4
Parker-Davis composed	Parker improvised	Parker-Davis composed	Davis improvised		Parker improvised

"Constellation" (Take 2), Theme

The internal choruses might be divided up between multiple soloists. Sometimes only part of the initially stated theme would return at the end, often replacing the last phrase of the final solo chorus. These two ideas are combined in "Ah-Leu-Cha":

A'	A''	B'	A	[ABA]
8	8	8	8	8 8 8
Parker		2+2+2+2	Parker-Davis	omitted
improvised		Russell-Roach	composed	
		improvised		

"Ah-Leu-Cha," Last Chorus

Sometimes composed themes would be omitted altogether and their normal function supplied by an elaborate introduction. Parker's "KoKo" solo is a variation on a theme (the song "Cherokee") that never appears:

Introduction   [Theme—Omitted]

				A	A	B	A
8	8	8	8	16	16	16	16
Parker-Gillespie	Gillespie	Parker	Parker-Gillespie				
composed	improvised	improvised	composed				

Variations	Drum Solo	[Theme—Omitted]	Coda
64 + 64	32		(same routine as introduction)
Parker	Roach		
improvised	improvised		

"KoKo" (1945), Complete Performance

Like all great music Parker's has the potential for any number of different strategies for its analysis. This is reflected in the divergent approaches taken in three excellent, large-scale studies: Thomas Owens's *Charlie Parker: Techniques of Improvisation* (1974), Lawrence Koch's *Yardbird Suite: A Compendium of the Life and Music of Charlie Parker* (1988), and Henry Martin's *Charlie Parker and Thematic Improvisation* (1996). Whereas Owens is chiefly concerned with the formulaic construction of Parker's melodic vocabulary and Koch with the harmonic relationships of melody to a given chord patterns, Martin focuses on motivic organization that is revealed by voice-leading analysis. In addition, Carl Woideck's *Charlie Parker: His Music and Life* (1996) is a first-rate general survey with especially strong treatments of Parker's 1940–43 apprenticeship and the tantalizing hints of new directions in the final years.

Parker was a genius, but his terrifying ability to produce sublime spontaneous composition was girded by a few elemental factors. First, superior instrumental technique whereby the musical idea could be transmitted instantaneously to musical performance. Second, a limited repertory and range of harmonic material with which he was intimately familiar. Third, a large, though necessarily limited fund of melodic figures—his musical vocabulary—which could be drawn on quickly. Fourth (and more mysteriously), the utter internalization of these things so that the process of improvised creation, assembly, and reassembly could be carried out spontaneously with great expressive freedom. Still, any earnest attempt to describe Parker's art ends with a shrug. Bird's music is so well made, his manipulation of melody, harmony, and rhythm so unified, and the emotional effect so profound that no single interpretation seems sufficient or even the best path to its understanding. Among the millions of words written about Charlie Parker, Bird's own explanation may be the most useful: "It's just music. It's playing clean and looking for the pretty notes."

Cool Jazz and West Coast Jazz

Ted Gioia

One of my teachers, the late Donald Davie, delighted in describing works of art with metaphors drawn from weather reports. *All* artistry, he suggested, tended to either the *cool* or the *hot*.

For Davie, the paragon of cool was found in sculpture. The sculptor, confronting the cold and unforgiving marble, practices an art requiring meticulous care, precision, and attention to even the smallest details. The hot artist, in contrast, neglects subtle gradations in a celebration of intensity, a mad abandonment to the creative force.

I learned much of my love of the cool in my classes with Davie, who made it clear which of the two extremes he preferred. One of his books was called, in fact, *The Poet as Sculptor*. And his description of lesser "hot" works—overblown efforts which he characterized as "warm," "moist," and "mushy"—had a decidedly pejorative edge.

Given my love of the cool, I often wonder why I ever gravitated to jazz. Jazz is not only a hot art form—it may well be the hottest. No other creative pursuit celebrates immediacy and intensity to such an extent. Not only does jazz abandon itself to the moment, it actually refuses to accept any longer time horizon. In the heated atmosphere of the jam session, there is little time to mull over finely etched nuances and subtle shadings.

Despite these obstacles, the cool aesthetic has always found a few lonely champions in the jazz arena—fascinating individuals who have provided an alternative to the dominant hot stylists. As such, they stand as double outsiders in the already counterculture world of jazz. Much of our fascination stems from the inner paradox at the core of cool jazz: namely, its ability to *keep* its cool . . . and even thrive in the hottest of art forms.

This symbolic and contradictory dimension of cool jazz was already evident in the life and times of its first major protagonist, Leon Bix Beiderbecke. The scion of a German-American family, Bix was born at the close of a cold Iowa winter in 1903 and confronted at adolescence by an even chillier family reception of his aspirations to become a jazz musician. Counterbalancing these cool ingredients are the hot ones: the cherubic boy's devil-may-care disregard for the niceties of a musical education (for that matter, any education); a temperament that gravitated to extremes, both in life and art; above all, a fascination with the new jazz sounds gravitating northward from the warm, moist environs of New Orleans. Bix understood the power of syncopated rhythms—which lay at the heart of the jazz revolution— but also knew how to soften their impact to maintain the melodic flow of his lines. In addition, he proved that a clear, sculpted tone could be as effective as the hot and dirty brass sounds of New Orleans. A beguiling, almost feminine quality infused his music. One is tempted to call it "prettiness," except for the fact that the term makes it sound all too simple. And Beiderbecke always reached for the complex—whether experimenting with whole-tone scales, unusual harmonies, or other progressive techniques.

Beiderbecke's frequent associate, saxophonist Frank Trumbauer, has been far less celebrated (and mythologized) by later jazz historians, yet his playing may ultimately have exerted an even greater influence than Bix's. For not only did Trumbauer attract many direct followers with his smooth and seemingly effortless saxophone work, but he exerted tremendous indirect impact on cool jazz through his most famous disciple, Lester Young. Young, more than anyone else, laid the groundwork for the later blossoming of the so-called cool school in the 1950s. One notes Young's light, fluid tone, his preference for *melodic* improvisation, and, above all, his refusal to mimic the standard "hot" phrases, harmonic deconstructions, and scalar patterns of his contemporaries. The rhythmic flow of his

Gerry Mulligan, 1983. Photo: Mitchell Seidel.

music is subtle, less tied to the ground rhythm than that of any previous jazz improviser.

These elements would all reappear in the postwar blossoming of cool jazz. The early stages of this new movement were every bit as quiet and unnoticed as one would expect from a *cool* revolution. Although Miles Davis's nonet sides from 1949 and 1950 are now routinely known as the "Birth of the Cool" recordings, this name was unknown at the time. In fact, the band itself was hardly known—despite a lineup of future Hall of Fame talent. Was this, really, the Birth of the Cool? True, there were predecessors—most notably the Claude Thornhill orchestra—but no ensemble would do more to legitimize the cool aesthetic as a distinctly *progressive* approach to modern jazz. Gil Evans and Gerry Mulligan had contributed arrangements to Thornhill, and Lee Konitz had been a sideman; now all three were part of the Davis nonet. Each would later develop different facets of the cool style—as would fellow band members pianist John Lewis (through his Modern Jazz Quartet) and Gunther Schuller (via his advocacy of so-called third stream mergings of classical and jazz idioms).

The Davis nonet turned the jazz idiom on its head. Previously large ensembles had built their music around the contrast between sections. Trumpets, trombones, reeds, and rhythm demonstrated what the pop psychologists call a "love-hate" relationship: they would embrace momentarily, but then split off into warring factions, repeating the process again and again. Fans didn't complain: this make-love-*and*-war complex created much of the visceral excitement of the big band sound. The Davis nonet, in contrast, offered a music of unity, a holistic sound. New Age gurus would applaud its exemplary togetherness. The model here was not a symphony orchestra or a jazz big band, rather a choir. Just as voices in a choir aim at a blending of sounds, so did the instrumentalists in the Davis nonet. The novelty of the textures was amplified by the unusual choice of instruments. The tenor sax, the heart of the jazz sound for most listeners, was conspicuously absent. Instead trumpet and trombone, alto and baritone sax, fused with less traditional jazz instruments French horn and tuba, supported by piano, bass, and drums.

The orchestral innovations of the new cool movement were matched by a different approach to the soloist's art. Davis was in the process of crafting an "antivirtuosity" of grand proportions, one built on tone, texture, and sensitivity to space. His trumpet would whisper, moan, caress, and occasionally exclaim. This was especially striking coming on the heels of the bebop revolution of the 1940s, in which rococo excess was the hippest style. Most of the members of the nonet had deep roots in the bop idiom. But in this new setting, they pared away at the long-winded excesses of that style. No modern jazz band had ever been so demure.

Yet there is some irony here. The Birth of the Cool ensemble, for all its importance, was a *flop* as a commercial entity. It gave few performances before disbanding. Virtually all of its influence came via a small body of recordings. You might be surprised to learn that, if you spent the few minutes necessary to listen to classic nonet sides such as "Boplicity," "Israel," "Jeru," "Move," "Moon Dreams," "Godchild," and "Venus de Milo," you would have heard about half of the band's legacy. Yet the very failure as a working unit may have spurred the nonet's longer-term importance. For the band members would come to exert far more impact on the jazz scene as individuals than they ever could have done as part of a single group.

Gerry Mulligan's stint in California in the early 1950s proved decisive for the emerging West Coast sound. Modern jazz in Los Angeles in the late 1940s was as hot as the asphalt under which the city was then being covered. It took as its primary model the bebop styles of the East Coast. Mulligan's L.A. quartet changed all of that, questioning the conventional wisdom about jazz music's rhythmic essence, its melodic impulses, its approach to composition, even its assumptions about instrumentation. In the process, the quartet revealed a whole new realm of possibilities. Mulligan's finely etched baritone sax lines entered into a ruminative counterpoint dialogue with Chet Baker's trumpet phrases. True, there had been counterpoint lines in jazz since its earliest days of New Orleans. But this was something *else*, different the way an intimate tête-à-tête between lovers differs from the boisterous banter of fraternity boys. Never before had the softer extremes of the dynamic spectrum been so finely explored by a jazz band— and in this regard Mulligan was ably assisted by drummer Chico Hamilton, who shimmered where others pounded. No piano or guitar cluttered the pristine harmonic textures of the band, and this imparted even greater clarity to the interlocking horn lines.

The quiet revolution was now making noise. *Time* magazine profiled the new band, and soon crowds were lining up around the block to hear the Mulligan Quartet. By the time the band broke up, both Mulligan and Baker were established as leaders of the new cool school. Even Hamilton, who left the quartet for an obscure sideman gig with Lena Horne, would later flourish as a prominent West Coast bandleader—building on the reputation earned while with Mulligan—in a stint noteworthy for his championing of the cello in jazz and for his discovery of altoist Eric Dolphy.

Mulligan went on to front memorable larger bands and to perform or record with other cool jazz players (valve trombonist Bob Brookmeyer, alto saxophonist Paul Desmond, tenor saxophonist Stan Getz, pianist Dave Brubeck), but also to venture into encounters with musicians of different temperaments, from pianist Thelonious Monk to Chicago-era traditionalists. His virtues as a soloist—basically smarts, sensitivity, and swing—made him a welcome contributor in almost any setting. Baker stayed equally loyal to the cool muse, playing the role of the world-weary romantic until the end of his life. His offstage behavior, marred by arrests and the seamier side of the addict's life, was at odds with the lover-boy part he played with his horn and as a vocalist. Yet his music never stopped sounding heartfelt and romantic, even when audiences had to close their eyes to block out the sad visage onstage. Then, with the horn at his lips, Baker seemingly was imbibing from the fountain of youth, evoking a sweetness of phrasing, a depth of feeling, and a luminosity one associates with the first impulses of love.

By the mid-1950s, the cool school on the West Coast had grown into a virtual university. Classes were in session almost every night at the Lighthouse, a club in Hermosa Beach where up-and-coming jazz musicians—trumpeter Shorty Rogers, drummer Shelly Manne, and reedplayers Jimmy Giuffre, Bud Shank, and Bob Cooper, among others—made waves before setting out as major bandleaders linked to the new style. At times these artists supported themselves with uninspired commercial projects, but the vast majority of their recordings from the 1950s contained jazz of the highest quality. Of course, there were critics who were hostile to this music—or perhaps merely envious of jazz players who could make a decent living in a sunny climate—and tried to brand it as formulaic and uninspired. But most of the recordings sound surprisingly fresh today.

The work of drummer Shelly Manne is a case in point. Manne recorded tonal and atonal works, in intimate duos or large orchestras, abstract experimental efforts alongside hard-swinging combo charts, extended compositions, casual jams, Afro-Cuban, Cole Porter . . . the list goes on and on. He was invariably pigeonholed by critics as "another West Coaster" (although few dared dismiss his extraordinary skills as a percussionist), yet no player of his era was less deserving of any pigeonhole. Giuffre and Rogers were equally wide-ranging and almost as frequently misunderstood. Their music encompassed everything from free jazz to rhythm-and-blues, with much else thrown into the mix—as evidenced by the many exceptional records made by these players during the 1950s, including Giuffre's *Tangents in Jazz, The Jimmy Giuffre Clarinet, The Jimmy Giuffre Three;* Shorty Rogers's *The Swinging Mr. Rogers* and *Big Band Express;* and Manne's *The West Coast Sound, The Gambit,* and *At the Blackhawk.* This was *liberating* music, from almost any perspective. How did its critics miss the point? One is almost forced to conclude that they rarely got around to listening to the records, but merely to each other.

Alto saxophonist Art Pepper may have been the most enigmatic of the West Coast players during this era. His early recordings as sideman with Stan Kenton and Shorty Rogers—"Over the Rainbow," "Art Pepper," "Bunny"—found him closely aligned to the cool school. His lines are almost too delicate, his tone almost overripe. During the 1950s a new, harder-edged sound was superimposed on this substrate. The sweet, soft side still predominated, but it coexisted with a feisty, hard-bop facet of Pepper. By the 1970s, when Pepper was attempting a triumphant comeback after years of incarceration and dissipation, the roles were reversed. A rhapsodic and turbulent style—drawing on the innovations of John Coltrane and Ornette Coleman—was now in the ascendancy, yet even here a gentler muse would occasionally surface. Indeed the two forces would often coexist in a single phrase, a caressing line ending with a harrowing cry. The interplay between these two forces—one is tempted to say, between these two Art Peppers—made this riveting, almost hypnotic music.

Dave Brubeck, who symbolically led the smaller cadre of modern jazz players in Northern California, represented a similarly complex musical heritage. His music was cool and melodic (so much so that he even enjoyed a hit single with "Take Five") but also impatiently experimental. It was the avant-garde side of Brubeck that made headlines—his studies under contemporary classical composer Darius Milhaud were an especially favorite theme with journalists looking for an angle—and this notoriety as a progressive made less noticeable his links to the cool school. Yet Brubeck's longtime colleague Paul Desmond more than made up for this oversight. Desmond was a lyrical player who, like Chet Baker (with whom he collaborated on a handful of brilliant recordings), never played two notes when one would suffice . . . and even that one was viewed with skepticism. Desmond was a romantic; and like all romantics, he knew that it never paid to be long-winded. But he also brought a witty, cerebral touch to his solo lines, with a bite of irony not found in Baker (or in many jazz musicians, for that matter).

Brubeck and Desmond were wonderfully prolific. For a number of years, they managed to release a new recording every three months or so. The "classic" Brubeck quartet, which included hard-swinging drummer Joe Morello and smooth-swinging bassist Eugene Wright, was a particular favorite with fans, who filled concert halls and bought the band's records in numbers seldom associated with modern jazz. Yet even when playing in an intimate duo (as they did all too rarely) or in other settings, Brubeck and Desmond made for compelling listening. They left behind an exceptional body of work, spanning over a quarter of a century, which represents one of the greatest jazz legacies from that era.

Equally prolific, even more long-lived, and almost as famous, the Modern Jazz Quartet offered a similar contrast between its two leading protagonists. John Lewis, who had served at the Birth of the Cool as pianist for the Davis band, played the role of calm, collected, and cerebral foil to vibraphonist Milt Jackson, a freewheeling improviser more suited by temperament to the hot. Yet the tension between the two stylists was a productive one—and points to a truism about cool jazz: at its best, it succeeds not by diminishing the intensity of jazz but by *channeling* it. One is reminded of the laser beam which, we are told, conveys far more energy and heat than a mere bonfire; but its force is overlooked by those who judge merely on the basis of smoke and flame. The Modern Jazz Quartet projected exactly that type of intensity: focused, clear, cutting to the quick.

If they compiled a record book for jazz bands, the MJQ would capture more than a few of the honors: over forty years as a working unit; thirty years without a personnel change (following Connie Kay's takeover on drums from Kenny Clarke); over twenty years of near-constant performing on the road. During this period, the MJQ successfully grappled with everything from fugue ("Concorde") and commedia del'arte (*The Comedy*) to jazzy workouts on the blues form ("Bags' Groove") and poignant ballads ("Django").

The MJQ offered ample testimony to the virtues of stability and decorum, maturity and experience. Their blending of sounds was seamless, but the individuality of each member was never lost, somehow standing out in the midst of the totality. One is tempted to conclude that the decades of playing together created this exceptional melding. Yet recordings from the early 1950s suggest that the band had "chemistry" virtually from the start. Truly, they differ little in ethos or temperament from the (fortunately) misnamed *Last Concert* recording from 1974. The latter would have been a fitting last will and testament, with its majestic command and noblesse-oblige ease ...*except* for the fact that the band refused to break up. Before long, the MJQ was performing and recording again, expanding a discography that was already of Proustian proportions.

No artist pushed the emotional distance of cool jazz to a farther extreme than Lee Konitz, another alumnus of the Birth of the Cool band—except perhaps his frequent colleagues, pianist and mentor Lennie Tristano and tenor saxophonist Warne Marsh. These three visionary artists proffered a music that would never gain the large audiences enjoyed by the MJQ or Brubeck, characterized by byzantine melodic lines, attenuated rhythms, and acerbic harmonies. Although Konitz for a time brandished a sweet tone reminiscent of Desmond's, his music with Tristano and Marsh exhibited a precocious quality designed to inspire awe more than endearment. One suspects that the admirers of this extraordinary body of work, much of it recorded for the Atlantic label in the 1950s (noteworthy projects include *Tristano, The New Tristano,* and *Lee Konitz and Warne Marsh*), were mostly other musicians, who marveled at its depth and complexity. The general public, casual fans who might be enticed to purchase a record by Brubeck or the MJQ, found little sustenance here. Let's be blunt: if the other players discussed here were, by definition, cool... well, Tristano and his school could be positively chilly. And though we are told that cold showers and morning swims in freezing waters have a salutary effect on our health, few are tempted to try them often enough to gauge the results.

Stan Getz stood at the opposite extreme of the emotional spectrum. No sense of aloofness or distance diluted his warm melodicism. With his first important recording, "Early Autumn" made with the Woody Herman band, Getz mesmerized listeners with an almost too limpid tone and an uncomplicated emotional relationship to his musical material. During the 1950s Getz mostly kept his distance from other cool players. Many of his finest records from the period find him working alongside beboppers or hard-boppers (Dizzy Gillespie, Sonny Stitt, Jimmy Raney, Horace Silver, J. J. Johnson). But even in the hottest surroundings, Getz espoused a set of musical principles that championed taste over bravura, melody over mindless scales. And his few collaborations with Mulligan, Baker, Manne, and other like-minded cool players were almost universally successful, inviting efforts as refreshing as the other side of the pillow on a hot summer night. And though he is remembered primarily as a stellar ballad player (hear his renditions of "Blood Count," "I Remember Clifford," "Lush Life") and advocate of bossa nova ("Desafinado," "The Girl From Ipanema"), he was also capable of persuasive experimental efforts, such as his 1961 *Focus* recording with sixteen strings.

Few later jazz players attempted to learn from Getz. Yet this neglect is as surprising as it is lamentable. No saxophonist of his generation reached a larger audience than Getz—a fact which should catch the attention of more ambitious hornplayers—and he achieved this without the compromises and bad artistic decisions which so many other jazz musicians have embraced in the pursuit of popularity. This is most evident in Getz's bossa nova recordings from the mid-1960s, which were major commercial successes, even challenging the Beatles on the *Billboard* charts, and yet also substantial artistic achievements.

These mid-sixties successes were misleading. By this time the era of cool jazz was all but ended. True, almost all earlier jazz styles were forced to take cover, caught between rock and the hard place the music business had become. But cool was especially out of favor in an age which favored intensity of experience—whether Coltrane or Ayler, Hendrix or Joplin—over subtler approaches. By the close of the decade, cool jazz was a historical phenomenon, not a vibrant idiom.

Yet cool jazz left a legacy. A host of later styles borrowed from it in varying measures. For example, the classically tinged jazz music which came to the fore in the 1970s, often associated with the ECM label, was a clear heir of the cool tradition. Although the ECM sound would never be confused with Miles or Mulligan, MJQ or Getz, its *values* are essentially the same: clarity of expression; subtlety of meaning; a willingness to depart from the standard rhythms of hot jazz and learn from other genres of music; a preference for emotion rather than mere emoting; progressive ambitions and a tendency to experiment; above all, a dislike for bombast.

But the ECM artists were merely the most prominent examples of the cool *ethos* surviving the demise of the cool school. Other performers in other idioms—New Age, minimalist, pop, classical, ethnic, folk—also showed that they had listened carefully to their cool antecedents. The cool school of the 1950s may have become part of history, but cool itself could never grow passé.

And this is true for a very good reason. As I mentioned at the start, coolness represents a body of timeless artistic values. The cool can no more disappear than can the hot. This spectrum is inescapable; it takes the temperature of art. And art-making. We only stop taking the temperature when the body is lifeless. And as long as the jazz body is still pulsating with vigor and energy, the cool will remain with us.

Jazz and Classical Music: To the Third Stream and Beyond

Terry Teachout

The relationship between jazz and classical music has often been close—at times surprisingly so—but is ultimately equivocal. Though the two musics employ the same harmonic system, they arise from different conceptions of rhythm and form, and attempts to amalgamate their characteristic features in a single coherent style have thus proved problematic.

Jazz Instrumentalists

Classic ragtime, jazz's immediate ancestor, was a fully notated piano music that demanded fluent reading skills. As a result, even the earliest jazz pianists typically studied with classically trained teachers and consequently knew more about the classical repertoire than other instrumentalists, most of whom were either self-taught or received informal lessons from other like-minded players. New Orleans, the earliest center of jazz, had an opera-based classical-music culture, and though only whites and (until the turn of the century) "Creoles of color" were admitted to public performances, some second-generation players, Sidney Bechet and Louis Armstrong in particular, were influenced by the expansive solo styles heard on the recordings of such

Modern Jazz Quartet. Left to right: John Lewis, piano; Percy Heath, bass; Milt Jackson, vibraphone; Connie Kay, drums. Courtesy of the Institute of Jazz Studies, Rutgers University.

opera singers as Enrico Caruso and John McCormack. Jelly Roll Morton went so far as to imply that the vocal ensembles of nineteenth-century Italian opera were precursors of the improvised ensemble style of New Orleans jazz.

By the '20s, it was not unusual for jazz musicians to be at least casually familiar with classical music. The Harlem stride pianists regularly interpolated classical themes into their compositions, and some had more far-reaching aspirations: James P. Johnson wrote symphonies and concertos (see below), while Willie "the Lion" Smith's original pieces for solo piano, including "Echoes of Spring" and "Passionette" (Commodore, 1939), suggest a fusion of late ragtime and the light classics. Such black players as Coleman Hawkins, Earl Hines, Teddy Wilson, and Fats Waller (who played Bach's organ music privately and is thought to have studied with the classical piano virtuoso Leopold Godowsky) might well have pursued classical careers under other circumstances, but racial segregation made this impossible, so they went into jazz instead, at the same time remaining conversant with classical music and being influenced by it.

Meanwhile, Bix Beiderbecke, Red Nichols, and many of the other white musicians associated with the Jean Goldkette and Paul Whiteman bands, particularly Eddie Lang, Joe Venuti, the arranger Bill Challis, and the saxophonist-composer Fud Livingston, were listening to the works of Claude Debussy, Maurice Ravel, Igor Stravinsky, and other early modernists (as well as the harmonically sophisticated piano solos of such "novelty pianists" of the early '20s as Zez Confrey) and incorporating harmonic devices gleaned from these scores into their own playing and writing. Beiderbecke, who played both cornet and piano, codified this influence in four "written" miniatures for solo piano transcribed by Challis from his playing, the best known of which is "In a Mist" (OKeh/Columbia, 1927), containing whole-tone progressions based on those heard in the music of Debussy. The harmonic vocabulary of the French impressionists eventually entered the basic language of jazz improvisation, in part because of the early example of Beiderbecke and his colleagues.

From the '30s onward, it became more common for musicians to take up jazz after having had reasonably extensive classical training, usually beginning in the public schools. (Miles Davis, for instance, learned the trumpet as a student in the public school system of East St. Louis, later studying briefly at New York's Juilliard School, America's leading classical conservatory.) Accordingly, their playing techniques tended to be more standardized than the idiosyncratic styles of such earlier soloists as Bechet and Beiderbecke, and they were likely to have heard a wider range of classical repertoire. Also starting in the '30s, players with jazz backgrounds began to work in radio and film-studio orchestras, alternating between popular and symphonic or quasi-symphonic engagements; some of them, including the trumpeter Manny Klein and the pianist-conductor-composer André Previn, performed both jazz and classical music.

Today's jazz instrumentalists, many of whom have academic degrees in music, are almost always at ease with "legitimate" techniques, and though most working musicians continue to specialize, others now move freely between the two musics. A few have even appeared publicly as classical-music soloists. The first of these, Benny Goodman, recorded the Mozart Clarinet Quintet with the Budapest String Quartet (Victor, 1938); thereafter, he played classical music frequently, performing with leading orchestras and commissioning several major works for clarinet, including Bela Bartók's *Contrasts* (1938) and the concertos of Paul Hindemith (1947) and Aaron Copland (1947–48). As a teenager in Chicago, Goodman had studied for two years with a classical clarinetist, Franz Schoepp, and in the late '40s he resumed formal study with the English clarinet virtuoso Reginald Kell.

Despite his long-standing interest in classical music, Goodman never succeeded in becoming a completely idiomatic classical player, and his example, perhaps for this reason, has not been widely pursued by noted jazz soloists. Keith Jarrett and Wynton Marsalis have devoted large parts of their solo careers to the performance of classical music, and George Shearing has also played it with some frequency; many other instrumentalists have appeared with "pops" orchestras, but they usually perform arrangements of popular songs and similar material. No important jazz vocalist has sung classical music publicly (though Cleo Laine performed and recorded the speaking role in Schoenberg's *Pierrot lunaire*).

Classical Composers and Performers

As early as the middle of the nineteenth century, the New Orleans–born Louis Moreau Gottschalk was composing piano pieces such as *La bamboula* (1847, subtitled "Danse des negres") and *Le banjo* (1854–55) whose syncopated melodies and repeated-note figurations reflected his firsthand knowledge of the vernacular instrumental music out of which ragtime developed. European composers began to encounter ragtime and related styles around the turn of the century, usually through published sheet music, and soon started to write pieces that made reference to its syncopated rhythmic patterns. Erik Satie's *Jack-in-the-Box* (1899), thought to be the first such work, was followed by Percy Grainger's *In Dahomey (Cakewalk Smasher)* (1903–9), Debussy's "Golliwog's Cakewalk" (from *Children's Corner Suite*, 1906–8), Stravinsky's *Ragtime* (1918), *L'Histoire du soldat* (1918), and *Piano Rag Music* (1919), Hindemith's *Suite "1922"* (1922), and various other works.

Shortly afterward, classical composers began to hear jazz on record and in performance, and many were inspired to compose music that either incorporated such elements of jazz as the lowered thirds and sevenths of the blues scale or sought in some other fashion to unambiguously evoke its spirit (often, to be sure, in a superficially comprehended manner). Among the most lastingly successful of these attempts were Darius Milhaud's ballet score *La Création du monde* (1923), orchestrated for an ensemble resembling the early dance bands in instrumentation; Copland's *Music for the Theater* (1925) and *Piano Concerto* (1926); Ravel's *Violin Sonata* (1923–27), whose slow movement is a Gallic-sounding "blues," and *Piano Concerto in G* (1929–31), modeled after the *Concerto in F* of George Gershwin (see below); Constant Lambert's *Rio Grande* (1927), *Piano Sonata* (1928–29), and *Concerto for Nine Instruments* (1930–31); Kurt Weill's *Mahagonny-Songspiel* (1927) and *Die Dreigroschenoper* (1928), in which the influence of European dance bands can also be heard; and Dmitri Shostakovich's *Suites for Jazz Orchestra* (1934 and 1938). Interestingly, few of these composers made any effort to write for working jazz ensembles; Stravinsky composed *Ebony Concerto* (1945) for the Woody Herman band (Columbia, 1946), but this piece, like *L'Histoire du soldat* before it, in fact owed little to jazz save its instrumentation and a modest amount of blues-derived melodic coloration.

The direct influence of jazz on classical music proved to be a passing phase of modernism, however, and was already dying out in the '30s, by which time Milhaud and Copland had explicitly repudiated jazz as a source of inspiration (though Copland briefly returned to it in the concerto he wrote for Benny Goodman). While a number of prominent classical composers have since shown some interest in jazz and popular music—Krzysztof Penderecki's *Actions* (1971), for example, was written for a fourteen-piece big band, while Sir Michael Tippett's *Third Symphony* (1970–72) contains a "blues" movement for soprano and orchestra—the only ones to have been specifically and significantly influenced by the language of jazz are Leonard Bernstein and Gunther Schuller (see below). The improvisatory elements in the music of such avant-garde composers as John Cage, Karlheinz Stockhausen, and Pierre Boulez are not jazz-based.

Several classical singers, among them the sopranos Eileen Farrell, Renée Fleming, and Sylvia McNair, have sung popular standards in a jazz-inflected style, often accompanied by jazz musicians, and some instrumentalists, most notably the violinist Itzhak Perlman and the clarinetist Richard Stoltzman, have experimented with jazz improvisation, usually within the context of pieces created specifically for them by jazz composers. Claude Bolling has composed "jazz suites" for such classical soloists as the flutist Jean-Pierre Rampal, the cellist Yo-Yo Ma, and the violinist Pinchas Zukerman, but the solo parts in these works do not involve improvisation.

"Symphonic Jazz"

In 1924 George Gershwin, a classically trained pianist and popular songwriter who was familiar with jazz, composed *Rhapsody in Blue*, a concerted work for piano and the twenty-three-piece "jazz band" of Paul Whiteman, then the most influential large dance band in America. The piece was scored by Ferde Grofé, Whiteman's pianist and chief orchestrator, who also had extensive classical training. *Rhapsody in Blue* was the first significant attempt by a popular musician to create a large-scale composition in which elements of classical music, popular song, jazz, and the blues were combined into a stylistically unified whole (Scott Joplin's opera *Treemonisha*, completed in 1911, was not staged until 1972).

Gershwin continued to pursue this elusive goal for the remainder of his short life in a series of increasingly sophisticated concert pieces, starting with the *Concerto in F* (1925) and the tone poem *An American in Paris* (1928) and culminating in the full-length opera *Porgy and Bess* (1935). These works, though they contain jazz- and blues-derived melodic patterns and instrumental effects, are not jazz—they employ classical forms and are fully notated, eschewing improvisation of any kind—but they are also not pure classical music, and it is only in recent years that classically trained orchestra players have become capable of executing them in an idiomatic manner. Partly because of this inherent ambiguity, Gershwin's "classical" scores fascinated contemporary listeners and critics and have remained popular to this day. No other songwriter of the interwar period had sufficient technique to create comparably ambitious scores, but Whiteman subsequently commissioned concert-style pieces from other composers, the best known of which is Grofé's *Grand Canyon Suite* (1931), and this body of work, together with Gershwin's concert music, came collectively to be known as "symphonic jazz," even though much of it had nothing to do with jazz per se.

In the late '30s, a few composers, foremost among them the songwriter Alec Wilder, began to produce fully written-out scores that incorporated jazz and classical techniques with an eye to performance by players with experience in both fields; Wilder continued to work in this vein, producing a lengthy series of jazz-flavored instrumental sonatas and octets for woodwinds and rhythm section. Not until the '40s, however, did another American composer achieve popular success comparable to that of Gershwin in straddling the worlds of classical music and jazz. Leonard Bernstein was classically trained (he studied informally with Copland and was heavily influenced by Stravinsky) but was also deeply involved with jazz and popular music, and he synthesized elements of all three musics into a unified, strongly personal style in the ballet score *Fancy Free* (1944). Though Bernstein's later concert works were not as explicitly jazzy as *Fancy Free* (except for *Prelude, Fugue and Riffs*, composed in 1949 for the Woody Herman band), his musical-comedy scores, particularly *On the Town* (1944) and *West Side Story* (1957), made effective use of jazz-derived techniques.

Jazz Composers and the Challenge of Form

Nearly all jazz is influenced to some degree by classical music, if only because it is normally organized according to the rules of functional tonality. Beyond this, it can be difficult to isolate specific cases of influence. Complex harmonies are not in and of themselves proof of classical influence, nor is the use of traditionally "classical" instruments; most jazz musicians identify stringed instruments with classical music, but few would claim that Harry James was influenced by it when he added four violins to his big band in 1941, or that the countless albums of popular standards recorded by jazz soloists "with strings" have any substantive relationship to classical music. By the same token, the mere fact that such big band compositions as Duke Ellington's "Concerto for Cootie" (Victor, 1940), Artie Shaw's "Concerto for Clarinet" (Victor, 1940), and Stan Kenton's "Concerto to End All Concertos" (Capitol, 1946) use the word *concerto* in their titles does not make them concertos, save in the limited sense that most of them are virtuoso showpieces.

A different problem is posed by the many jazz versions of classical compositions that achieved wide circulation in the '30s and '40s, such as Tommy Dorsey's "Song of India" (after Rimsky-Korsakov; Victor, 1937), the Eddie South–Stephane Grappelli–Django Reinhardt "Improvisation Swing du premier mouvement du Concerto en re mineur" (after Bach; Swing, 1937), the John Kirby Sextet's "Anitra's Dance" (Charlie Shavers, after Grieg; Vocalion/Columbia, 1939), Art Tatum's "Humoresque" (after Dvořák; Decca, 1940) and the King Cole Trio's "Prelude in C Sharp Minor" (after Rachmaninoff; Capitol, 1944). Some of these arrangements were banal, others ingenious, but nearly all trivialized the original material on which they were based (unless it was trivial to begin with), and in certain cases may also have reflected the desire of class-conscious jazz musicians to prove their "legitimacy" at a time when jazz was not regarded as an art music. The only arranger of the period who consistently succeeded in creatively "recomposing" classical music was Gil Evans, who displayed in such adaptations for the Claude Thornhill band as "Arab Dance" (after Tchaikovsky; Columbia, 1946) a command of orchestral color and texture that grew more pronounced throughout the middle years of his career, climaxing in the elaborate recompositions of pieces by Manuel de Falla and Joaquín Rodrigo that he created for Miles Davis's *Sketches of Spain* (Columbia, 1959–60).

The special case of Evans notwithstanding, the conversion of classical themes into thirty-two-bar repeated-chorus song form does not constitute a serious response to the classical challenge, which is above all formal. Jazz composition has been formally limited throughout its history—it exists chiefly to stimulate the imagination of the improviser—and exceptions from the first half century of jazz are rare. James P. Johnson was the first major jazz musician to work in the larger forms, but such works as *Yamekraw (A Negro Rhapsody)* (1928) and *Harlem Symphony* (1932) either went unperformed or were soon forgotten, and were in any case structurally naive; Duke Ellington also experimented with large-scale form in *Reminiscing in Tempo* (Brunswick/Columbia, 1935), *Black, Brown and Beige* (Victor, 1943), *The Tattooed Bride* (Columbia, 1950) and *A Tone Parallel to Harlem* (Columbia, 1951), but eventually abandoned it in favor of multimovement suites, many of them composed in collaboration with Billy Strayhorn, which make no attempt at extended musical development.

Instead of exploring organically larger forms, "advanced" composers and arrangers of the '30s concentrated on expanding the still-rudimentary harmonic language and instrumental palette of jazz. Coleman Hawkins's "Queer Notions" (Vocalion/Columbia, 1933), written for the Fletcher Henderson band, is an experimental composition in which the whole-tone-based chord progressions introduced to jazz by the Beiderbecke-Nichols group are used not for coloristic purposes but to create extended periods of tonal ambiguity; Red Norvo's "Dance of the Octopus" (Brunswick/Columbia, 1933), recorded three months later by an ensemble consisting of marimba, bass clarinet, guitar, and string bass, is the earliest known example of a jazz composition containing nontonal harmonic language. (Significantly, "Dance of the Octopus" was coupled on 78 with Norvo's arrangement for the same unorthodox instrumentation of Beiderbecke's "In a Mist.")

In 1940 Artie Shaw assembled a twenty-three-piece big band that included nine string players (and a pianist, Johnny Guarnieri, who doubled on harpsichord), and several other bandleaders, including James, Tommy Dorsey, and Glenn Miller, followed suit. The string sections in these bands were too small to counterbalance the standard big band instrumentation, so they were generally used to accompany ballad performances arranged in the commercial style of studio orchestras; a year later, though, Shaw launched a thirty-two-piece band with a fifteen-piece string section whose book contained several pieces, including Paul Jordan's "Evensong" and "Suite No. 8" (Victor, 1941), that employed compositional techniques derived from classical music.

Postwar Developments

By the mid-'40s, a growing number of musicians had begun to feel constrained by the convention-ridden musical language of late swing era jazz. The rise of bebop was one response to this sense of limitation, as was the increased frequency with which jazz composers and arrangers sought out such classical teachers as Mario Castelnuovo-Tedesco and Stefan Wolpe; around the same time, the big bands of Dizzy Gillespie, Woody Herman, and Stan Kenton, following the lead of Ellington and Shaw (and Whiteman before them), started to perform concert-style scores by jazz composers intended not for dancing but listening, including George Russell's "Cubana Be/Cubana Bop" (Gillespie; Victor, 1947), Pete Rugolo's "Elegy for Alto" and "Monotony" (Kenton; Capitol, 1947), and Ralph Burns's four-movement *Summer Sequence* (Herman; Columbia, 1946–48).

An important step in the transformation of the traditional dance band into a true "jazz orchestra" was taken by Kenton when he organized his forty-piece, seventeen-string Innovations in Modern Music band, a controversial, short-lived ensemble (1950–51) that played works ranging in style from the boppish jazz originals of Shorty Rogers to the atonal concert pieces of Bob Graettinger. Graettinger's four-movement *City of Glass* (Capitol, 1951), the most ambitious work performed by the Innovations band, was the first score by a jazz composer directly comparable in harmonic density to the avant-garde classical music of the '30s and '40s, as well as the longest through-composed piece for jazz ensemble (well over sixteen minutes) to have been recorded in its entirety since Ellington's thirteen-minute *Reminiscing in Tempo*.

Except for Graettinger and the more conservative Ralph Burns, jazz composers of the '40s continued to show little interest in extended form, remaining content to loosen the rigidly repeating song-form structures of jazz. This lack of interest is conspicuous in the otherwise advanced work of Edwin Finckel and George Handy, both of whom wrote for the Boyd Raeburn band, and Eddie Sauter, who wrote for the bands of Red Norvo, Benny Goodman, Artie Shaw, and Ray McKinley (and later for the influential Sauter-Finegan Orchestra, which he co-led with the composer Bill Finegan). Finckel's "Boyd Meets Stravinsky" (Raeburn; Jewell/Savoy, 1946), Handy's "Dalvatore Sally" (Raeburn; Jewell/Savoy, 1946), and Sauter's "Clarinet à la King" (Goodman; Columbia, 1941), "The Maid With the Flaccid Air" (Shaw; Victor, 1945), "Hangover Square" (McKinley; Majestic/Savoy, 1946), and "Idiot's Delight" (McKinley; Victor, 1947) all rank among the most innovative big band compositions of the '40s, but none exceeds the length of a single 78 side.

A more thoroughgoing attempt to integrate modern classical techniques into a jazz context was made by the West Coast–based composers of the '50s, most notably Lyle "Spud" Murphy, whose "Fourth Dimension" and "Poly-Doodle" (Contemporary, 1955) incorporate quartal harmony and polytonality, and Duane Tatro, who made extensive use of composed counterpoint and nonfunctional dissonance in the strikingly original instrumental miniatures heard on his album *Jazz for Moderns* (Contemporary/OJC, 1956). Several West Coast composers also wrote multimovement works intended for performance by small and medium-sized jazz groups, including Bill Holman's *Quartet* (Contemporary, 1956) and Charles Mariano's *The Gambit* (Contemporary, 1957), both composed for an ensemble led by Shelly Manne.

For the most part, West Coast instrumentalists seem to have found it difficult to develop playing styles fully consistent with such demanding settings. An exception was Dave Brubeck, who studied composition with Milhaud before forming a long-lasting jazz quartet with Paul Desmond in which the two men experimented with bitonality, improvised counterpoint, and irregular time signatures. The New York–based pianist Lennie Tristano also developed an improvisational method notable for its use of chords chromatically altered to the point of atonality, while Mel Powell, a swing era pianist and composer who later studied composition with Paul Hindemith, recorded a series of albums, including *Borderline* and *Thigamagig* (both Vanguard, 1954), in which he accompanied mainstream jazz musicians in a style characterized by the fluent use of postimpressionist harmony.

The innovations of Tristano, Powell, and the West Coast composers, though widely discussed by critics, were not taken up by other players and subsequently were relegated to obscurity. (Perhaps not coincidentally, Powell left jazz altogether not long after recording *Borderline* and *Thigamagig*.) In particular, the West Coast composers' use of larger forms proved of no interest to musicians working in small-group contexts; Thelonious Monk, the most admired jazz composer of the postwar era, wrote only single-chorus instrumental melodies, while the extended works of such later players as John Coltrane and Ornette Coleman are unrelated to the classical-music tradition.

The Third Stream and After

Starting in the mid-'50s, the Modern Jazz Quartet, a New York–based ensemble led by John Lewis, recorded a series of compositions by Lewis, including "Vendome" (Prestige, 1954) and "Concorde" (Prestige, 1955), that resembled the experimental works of the West Coast school in their attempt to import fugal techniques into a small-group jazz context. Around the same time, Lewis and the classical composer Gunther Schuller organized the Jazz and Classical Music Society (originally the Modern Jazz Society), a group devoted to the performance of music "written by composers in the jazz field who would not otherwise have an opportunity for their less-conventional work to be presented under concert conditions."

In 1956 a contingent from the Jazz and Classical Music Society recorded *Music for Brass* (Columbia, 1956), an album of compositions for brass ensemble by Lewis, Schuller, Jimmy Giuffre, and J. J. Johnson; the following year, a mixed ensemble of jazz and classical instrumentalists led by Schuller recorded *Modern Jazz Concert* (Columbia, 1957), a collection of six extended pieces by Schuller, Giuffre,

Charles Mingus, George Russell, and the classical composers Milton Babbitt and Harold Shapero, all commissioned by and premiered at the 1957 Brandeis University Festival of the Arts. (The contents of these two albums, minus the pieces by Babbitt and Shapero, are now available on the Columbia CD *The Birth of the Third Stream*.) Schuller contended in a lecture at the Brandeis Festival that these works represented a new synthesis of jazz and Western art music, which he dubbed "third stream music." *Modern Jazz Concert* and *Music for Brass* soon became the subject of intense debate in the jazz community, and numerous other composers, including Teo Macero, Friedrich Gulda, André Hodeir, Gary McFarland, Bill Russo, Eddie Sauter, and Lalo Schifrin, began to experiment with related compositional ideas.

Third stream music is typically (though not always) composed for mixed groups of jazz and classical instrumentalists. The standard jazz rhythm section is sometimes omitted—Russo's *An Image of Man* (Verve, 1958), for instance, is scored for alto saxophone, guitar and string quartet—and the regularly sounded beat of traditional jazz heard only intermittently. In most third stream works, fully written-out ensemble passages, often of considerable musical complexity, alternate with simpler improvised episodes involving one or more jazz soloists. The inherent tension between composition and improvisation may be emphasized, as in Sauter's *Focus* (Verve, 1961), a suite for tenor saxophone and strings in which Stan Getz's solo part is completely improvised from beginning to end; in other pieces, such as Schuller's *Transformation* (Columbia, 1957), the improvised sections are carefully integrated into the larger compositional scheme.

The extent to which the original third stream composers drew on classical techniques varied considerably. Mixed-media works such as Schuller's *Concertino for Jazz Quartet and Orchestra* (Atlantic, 1960), in which the Modern Jazz Quartet performs the function of the "concertino" ensemble in a concerto grosso, and Giuffre's *Piece for Clarinet and String Orchestra* (Verve, 1959), a through-composed work whose solo part, though fully notated, presupposes idiomatic jazz inflection, clearly seek to reconcile the disparate elements of jazz and classical music. By contrast, J. J. Johnson's *Poem for Brass* (included on *Music for Brass*) and George Russell's *All About Rosie* (included on *Modern Jazz Concert*), which are intended for performance by jazz instrumentalists and contain no distinctively "classical" features, conform to the third stream model only in the relative complexity of their harmonic language and formal structure.

The third stream movement continues to this day under the auspices of Schuller and Ran Blake, who chaired the third stream department of the New England Conservatory of Music from 1973, and many highly imaginative mixed-media pieces, including Michael Gibbs's *Seven Songs for Quartet and Chamber Orchestra* (Gary Burton; ECM, 1973), Claus Ogerman's *Symbiosis* (Bill Evans; MPS, 1974) and Keith Jarrett's *Arbour Zena* (ECM, 1975), continued to be premiered and recorded well into the '70s. Unfortunately, these compositions failed without exception to enter the working repertoires of established soloists and ensembles, and public performances of them are now rare. (Orchestra U.S.A., a third stream ensemble founded by John Lewis in 1962, disbanded three years later, and Stan Kenton's Los Angeles Neophonic Orchestra, a similar group founded in 1965, was equally short-lived.) Much the same has been true of pieces by jazz composers specifically written for performance by classical musicians, such as Dave Brubeck's oratorio *The Light in the Wilderness* (1968), Roger Kellaway's ballet score *PAMTGG* (1971), and Anthony Davis's operas *X* (1985) and *Amistad* (1997).

The latter failure reflects a practical problem of stylistic integration which is also common to third stream music: not only are most classical musicians unable to improvise, but they find it difficult to realize in performance the unwritten rhythmic nuances intrinsic to the jazz idiom. (In addition, works in which electronically amplified jazz instrumentalists are accompanied by unamplified classical ensembles pose near-insuperable problems of acoustical balance in live performance.) The larger failure of the third stream idea to engage the interest of more than a small number of major jazz soloists also suggests the possibility of an underlying incompatibility between jazz improvisation, with its spontaneous variations on regularly repeating harmonic patterns, and tightly organized classical structures such as sonata-allegro form, in which there is no room for discursive episodes that are freely improvised rather than organically developed.

For all these reasons, it may be that the future of attempts to synthesize jazz and classical music lies not in third stream works for traditional classical media or mixed groups but in substantially through-composed instrumental pieces written for large and medium-sized jazz ensembles. Many of George Russell's compositions, including *Jazz in the Space Age* (Decca, 1960) and *Living Time* (Bill Evans; Columbia, 1972), fit this description, as do such works as Lalo Schifrin's *The New Continent* (Dizzy Gillespie; Limelight, 1962), in which Dizzy Gillespie is accompanied by a big band, and Carla Bley's *A Genuine Tong Funeral* (Gary Burton; Victor, 1967), a "dark opera without words" performed by Bley, the Gary Burton Quartet, and a five-piece horn section. Of comparable interest are such recent extended compositions for jazz orchestra as Bob Brookmeyer's *Celebration* (1997), Bill Holman's *All About Thirds* (1998), and Maria Schneider's ballet score *The Hand That Mocked, the Heart That Fed* (1998), which aspire to more rigorous formal challenges, as well as a higher degree of harmonic and contrapuntal complexity, than the big band scores of the past.

Whether such a synthesis is possible within the less structured framework of small-group improvisation remains to be seen, however, and given the fact that jazz continues to be primarily an improvisationally based small-group music, it seems probable that at least for the present, jazz and classical music will continue for the most part to travel on related but independent stylistic tracks.

Pianists of the 1940s and 1950s

Dick Katz

n any art form, it is important to remember that as changes occur, there is much overlapping. Eras do not define themselves with precision. Significant changes tend to happen gradually, and even though stylistic breakthroughs seem initially revolutionary, the passage of time confirms the fact that true innovation is built solidly on the past.

The years between 1940 and 1960 saw jazz piano styles undergo an amazing transformation.

The three acknowledged masters in 1940 were Earl "Fatha" Hines, Teddy Wilson, and, of course, Art Tatum. Hines, it is agreed by most, is the true source of most "modern" jazz piano. Wilson, originally a Hines disciple, was probably the most popular and imitated pianist in the thirties and into the forties. Tatum is still considered by many the greatest of all time, truly in a class by himself.

These jazz icons continued to flourish at a high creative level well into the postbebop era. Their collective greatness transcended and endured all manner of trends and stylistic innovations, and they individually profoundly influenced the future masters of the music.

During the forties, prior to and during the bebop innovations of Bud Powell and others, there were a number of other important

Bud Powell. Courtesy Frank Driggs Collection.

pianists who functioned mainly as sidemen to the preeminent instrumentalists. They rarely if ever worked or recorded as leaders, and therefore were only known to real jazz aficionados. However, they in turn had their followers, making a fascinating stylistic kaleidoscope.

One of the most influential was Billy Kyle. He first attracted attention as a member of the popular John Kirby sextet, "the biggest little band in the land," as they were billed. Kyle was the perfect accompanist to the intricate, polished arrangements of trumpeter Charlie Shavers. His sparkling, light, but percussive solos were very rhythmic in a way that hinted at the future. Using features of Hines and Teddy Wilson, he forged his own style. His influence can be heard in pianists as different as Nat Cole, Bud Powell, and even Horace Silver.

Mel Powell was a teenage prodigy who became a star in Benny Goodman's 1941–42 band. Also a brilliant composer-arranger, he made many historic recordings with Goodman that featured his Hines-derived style. Originally an amalgam of Hines, Joe Bushkin, and Teddy Wilson, he eventually settled on Wilson as his main model, sounding uncannily like him in his later records with Goodman in 1945. However, Powell eventually abandoned jazz, studying with Hindemith at Yale and becoming a successful avant-garde composer and dean of music of the California Institute of the Arts. He died in 1998.

Joe Bushkin recorded with Bunny Berigan and many others before becoming a major pianistic presence with the legendary Tommy Dorsey Orchestra, which included dazzling talents like Buddy Rich and a very young Frank Sinatra. Bushkin's style was characterized by a crisp, incisive touch, rhythmic interest, and a very individual way with grace notes, which made him easy to identify.

Pianist Clyde Hart was an important transitional figure, mostly known only to musicians. Born in 1910, he died from tuberculosis in 1945. Originally a Teddy Wilson–inspired soloist, he was rapidly absorbing the elements of bebop before his illness cut short his promising career. Some of his best solos are on the Savoy recordings with guitarist Tiny Grimes's quintet, which featured Charlie Parker. These solos reveal a fertile imagination and an awareness of the then new harmonic language but retain a swing era left hand and rhythmic feel. He also was a fine arranger.

One of the most in-demand pianists of the 1940s was Johnny Guarnieri. Featured with both the Benny Goodman and Artie Shaw bands, he later became a mainstay in the radio studios. But between

1943 and 1947 he made countless jazz recordings with many of the greatest horn players, including the classic Lester Young sessions on the Keynote label. Guarnieri also played the harpsichord with Artie Shaw's Gramercy Five. His attractive style was a creative blend of Fats Waller, Teddy Wilson, Count Basie, and Earl Hines. He also could stride at supersonic speed. Later in life he cast much of his repertoire in 5/4 time, including "Maple Leaf Rag"!

In addition to Hines, Tatum, and Wilson, there are three pianists who are, in Duke Ellington's overused phrase, "beyond category": Duke, of course, Count Basie, and Mary Lou Williams.

Ellington was somewhat taken for granted as a pianist. His composing, public persona, and nonstop activity often obscured his keyboard prowess. Originally a stride disciple of Willie "the Lion" Smith and other Harlem masters, he crafted his own irresistible style that encompassed much of what later became contemporary piano playing. His ear for tonal color extended from the piano to his amazing orchestration. Also, he used the piano as another orchestral voice rather than just background accompaniment. (His composition "The Clothed Woman" is a good example of his imaginative and virtuosic piano art.)

Another underrated piano master was none other than Count Basie. Also a stride expert in his youth (he was a Fats Waller "pupil"), he, in concert with his legendary original rhythm section—Walter Page, Freddie Green, and Jo Jones—succeeded in liberating the accompaniment from the locked-in, sometimes overheavy rhythmic style of other bands of the period. Basie's use of space and imaginative "feeding" of soloists set the stage for bop piano "comping." Basie almost single-handedly invented and brilliantly demonstrated the adage "less is more." He affected pianists as diverse as Thelonious Monk and John Lewis, among others. This truly "royal" artist continued to charm musicians and audiences right up to his demise in 1984.

Clarence Profit is someone who should be mentioned. He died in 1944 at age thirty-two and was a musician's musician—a fine stride player who was very harmonically advanced for his time. He was a favorite of Art Tatum's, and their keyboard encounters were legendary.

Long before feminism was even a word, Mary Lou Williams proved to be a lasting and important force in jazz. From her days as a pioneering (woman) soloist with the Andy Kirk Orchestra in the early 1930s to her death in 1981, she defied categorization. A master of every style from ragtime and stride through swing and bebop right up to modal, she enthralled all who heard her. Williams also was a gifted composer-arranger and was a mentor to Bud Powell, Monk, and others. Her style embraced all the essential elements of jazz piano, and she was always uniquely herself. Fine examples of her early work with the Andy Kirk Orchestra are on the CD *Andy Kirk and Mary Lou Williams* (Decca Jazz). A later work, *The Zodiac Suite,* can be heard on the Jazz Classics label.

Another fine transitional piano figure was Ken Kersey. Replacing Mary Lou Williams with Andy Kirk's orchestra in 1942, he recorded a hit with Kirk called "Boogie Woogie Cocktail." Blessed with a fluid technique, he often reminded one of Teddy Wilson. He was one of the first pianists to play consecutive descending minor seventh turnarounds between eight-bar segments or preceding the V chord in the blues. However, he never became part of the bop movement and gradually lapsed into obscurity.

Eddie Heywood is probably not a well-remembered pianist, but in the 1950s he was a star who overcame partial paralysis in his hands in midcareer to achieve great commercial success with his hit "Canadian Sunset." However, his early (1944) recordings with Billie Holiday on Commodore and with Coleman Hawkins on Signature show his early brilliance as a first-class Hines-influenced soloist with a definite style of his own that touched many pianists of the period.

Also, in the 1940s, Lionel Hampton featured an innovative pianist named Milt Buckner. This ebullient musical sorcerer devised a style called "block chord." This is essentially an orchestral style that involves harmonizing each note of a melody with a closed-position four-note chord and doubling the melody an octave below. The technique entails moving both hands up and down the keyboard in tandem, a style sometimes called "locked hands." Many pianists popularized the style, including George Shearing, Oscar Peterson, Nat Cole, Billy Taylor, and others.

When Nat King Cole vacated the piano bench to concentrate on his singing, he interrupted one of the most impressive sagas in piano jazz annals. The transition from brilliant pianist to megastar pop singer was gradual; he had achieved several hits with his wonderful trio in the 1940s. He, like Teddy Wilson, had Earl Hines as a model. Cole eventually forged a style that artfully combined Hines, Wilson, Billy Kyle, and some of the harmonic savvy of Art Tatum into an individually expressive whole that was immensely appealing to musician and layman alike. The key element in Cole's style was rhythm. His playing (and singing) never dates because of his utterly relaxed way with the beat. He had thoroughly mastered the 12/8 feel (think 4/4 in triplets) of the Southwest blues players and boogie-woogie specialists. His skill with both quarter- and eighth-note triplets gave his playing a kind of timeless swing. Harmonically, he predated or coincided with the advent of bop, using II to V progressions and descending minor sevenths as substitutions when appropriate. Also, his singing, pearly touch enhanced everything he played. His trio was the model for many subsequent trios, including Art Tatum's, in the 1940s.

Cole's influence on pianists was immense. A list of post–World War II pianists whom he influenced would include Bud Powell, Al Haig, Hank Jones, Oscar Peterson, Ahmad Jamal, Tommy Flanagan, Bill Evans, and many others, including myself. Cole was born in 1917 (the same year as Thelonious Monk); he died of lung cancer in 1965, only forty-seven years old. Cole's best solos, including the famous "Body and Soul," are on the eighteen-CD set, *The Complete Capitol Recordings of the Nat King Cole Trio* (Mosaic). Another great solo is "Back to the Land" with Lester Young and Buddy Rich on *Lester Young Trio* (Verve).

About the time that Nat Cole was becoming popular with his trio—around 1945—bebop was beginning to thoroughly shake up the jazz world. Its most dazzling and creative innovative pianist was Earl "Bud" Powell. In a general way, Powell's innovations paralleled what Earl Hines had done over twenty years earlier: he translated the improvised lines of horn players—in this case Dizzy Gillespie and Charlie Parker—to the keyboard. Powell also responded to the complex requirements of the style by devising a new way to accompany rhythmically. He was among the first to change the function of the left hand. Leaving most of the bass line to the bass player, he reinforced the horn players' ensemble and solo playing with chordal punctuations in the "right" places. Also, the complexity of Powell's right-hand solo improvisations, even though they were obviously influenced by Gillespie and Parker, revealed a totally unique and original mind of his own. His solos had an almost Bach-like purity of line. However, his musical roots seemed planted in Tatum, Wilson, Billy Kyle, and Bach, which he played as a child. Like many great musical artists, his playing seemed to emanate directly from *him*, rather than from the instrument.

Naturally, Powell had many followers. Among the earliest to master the style was Al Haig, a pianist with a refined technique, who brought a cool, controlled approach to the idiom. Whereas Powell was torrential, Haig played shorter lines with a light touch and cool aplomb. His ballads showed his classical training to good advantage; his pedaling was exemplary. His best work, in the opinion of many, was with Parker, and also on the early records of Stan Getz on the Roost label. Bud Powell's best work as a leader can be found on the Verve and Mosaic (Blue Note) labels. "Tempus Fugit" on *The Complete Bud Powell on Verve* is a good example. Powell also inspired what has been loosely described as the "Detroit school" of pianists: Hank Jones, Barry Harris, Tommy Flanagan, and Roland Hanna, to name a few.

Hank Jones is now considered the dean of all the jazz pianists. Originally inspired by Fats Waller, Tatum, and Wilson, he evolved into a most satisfying and tasteful all-around compendium of what is best in the tradition, including bop. He has recorded prolifically and with every major jazz artist. Fortunately, he is well represented on many solo and trio CDs. His amazing Tatum-like harmonic imagination and his ability to create with both hands are still cherished around the world.

Before going on, keep in mind the other pianists who helped create so-called bop piano. Insiders were always aware of Elmo Hope, Walter Bishop Jr., and Walter Davis Jr. These pianists were close friends of Powell's when all were very young, and they often exchanged ideas, but it was Bud who emerged as the dominant musical force. Elmo Hope did not record much, but he was very highly regarded both as pianist and composer. Walter Bishop Jr. was an early associate of Charlie Parker and appears on many of the classic Parker masterpieces. He expanded his style to include a wider palette from bop and was a talented poet as well. Walter Davis Jr. captured Powell's elusive rhythmic attack and knew many of Bud's wonderful and complex compositions, which he plays definitively.

Of all the pianists who came under the magic spell of Powell, Barry Harris probably comes closest to his conception and overall spirit. He also has mastered the rhythmic subtleties that really are resistant to exact musical notation, like much other jazz. Harris, however, has grown into a charismatic, delightful, one-of-a-kind musical personality on his own. He has a large following and is a one-man jazz university with his teaching and vocal training.

Tommy Flanagan, a fellow Detroiter, is now one of the most esteemed pianists in the world. He played on some of the most historic records ever made, including Sonny Rollins's *Saxophone Colossus* (Prestige) and John Coltrane's *Giant Steps* (Atlantic). Tommy was definitely a Powell disciple, but he also listened closely to Nat Cole, Hank Jones, Al Haig, Tatum, and Wilson to forge his own wonderful musical personality. As with the other Detroit talents, this type of lyricism—"playing the pretty notes," as Charlie Parker was quoted as saying—is a salient feature of his playing.

Preceding Flanagan, Harris, and other aforementioned Powell disciples were Duke Jordan, George Wallington, and Dodo Marmarosa, three pianists who figured importantly in the early years of the then new music.

Duke Jordan brought a gentler lyricism to the idiom. He plays on many of Charlie Parker's classic records and is famous for the beautiful, inspired introductions he improvised; Parker's "Embraceable You" is a good example. He eschews the hard rhythmic attack of Powell and others, preferring to apply an almost Teddy Wilson–like elegance to his lines. Jordan also has composed many fine pieces, including "Jordu."

George Wallington was one of the first pianists, white or black, to grasp the intricacies of bop piano and his style owed much to Powell, but he was formidable, nevertheless, and he was the pianist in the very first bop band to appear on 52nd Street in 1943, the Oscar Pettiford–Dizzy Gillespie Quintet. He also composed catchy lines like "Godchild" and "Lemon Drop." Wallington gradually retired from music and eventually joined the family air-conditioning business.

While on the subject of Bud Powell's contemporaries in the forties, several other outstanding players should be mentioned. Argonne Thornton, a.k.a. Sadik Hakim, was an early bop stylist whose playing was characterized by eccentric nonlyrical lines and a Monk-like rhythmic style. He recorded with both Lester Young and Charlie Parker.

Another legendary early modernist was Joe Albany, who, after a very promising beginning in California, which included gigs with Charlie Parker and some solos on Lester Young records, lapsed into obscurity. He occasionally resurfaced in the fifties to play with Warne Marsh and others but, plagued with personal problems, he never fulfilled his great potential.

In the opinion of many, Dodo Marmarosa was the most gifted of all the pianists who figured in the bebop saga. Blessed with a beautiful legato touch and a fluid technique, he developed an original style, which, while not conventionally Powell-type bebop, blended perfectly with the bop idiom, as well as with earlier styles. He combined advanced chordal and scalar elements with graceful rhythmic phrasing. His style hints at diverse influences such as Nat King Cole, Lennie Tristano, and even Erroll Garner, his schoolmate in their native Pittsburgh. The reader is urged to seek out the records he made with Artie Shaw's Gramercy Five and, of course, the classic Dial Charlie Parker recordings. Unfortunately, illness cut short his brilliant career, and he has not recorded since 1962. His own "Mellow Mood" trio performance in the Smithsonian *Piano Jazz* set is truly memorable.

John Lewis is a pianist-composer whose keyboard artistry reflects a unique mix of European classical practices with the Afro-American blues tradition. He shares this combination with Art Tatum, among few others. However, Lewis's style, like Count Basie's, is deceptively simple. He avoids technical display in favor of the southwestern tradition of "telling a story," like, say, Lester Young. He knows how to imply ideas and use silence effectively. In his pre-MJQ days, he worked and recorded with Lester Young and Charlie Parker, appearing on many of their famous records.

Besides Nat King Cole, there are four other outstanding pianists who became household names beyond the jazz audience. They are Erroll Garner, George Shearing, Dave Brubeck, and Oscar Peterson. Their popularity is due to their individually unique ability to communicate with the uninitiated or casual jazz fan without compromising their musical ideals.

Unique is an inadequate word to describe Erroll Garner. He was a musical phenomenon unlike any other. One of the most appealing performers in jazz history, he influenced almost every pianist who played in his era, and even beyond. Self-taught, he could not read music, yet he did things that trained pianists could not play, or even imagine. Garner was a one-man swing band, and indeed often acknowledged that his main inspiration was the big bands of the thirties—Duke, Basie, Lunceford, et al. He developed a self-sufficient, extremely full style that was characterized by a rock-steady left hand that often sounded like a strumming rhythm guitar. Juxtaposed against this was a river of chordal and single-note ideas, frequently stated in a lagging, behind-the-beat way that generated terrific swing. The call-and-response style of the bands was also usually present. Garner's "Misty" is one of the most recorded songs of all time. His artistry touched the complete neophyte as well as the musical sophisticate. His colorful thirty-plus-year career ended with his passing in 1977. Garner's prolific recording saga included a masterpiece—the live 1955 *Concert by the Sea* (Columbia). Also, the 1947 recording of

"Fantasy on Frankie and Johnny" is Garner at his most creative. This rare gem is on the Smithsonian boxed set.

George Shearing reached a mass audience in a different fashion. Blind from birth, he arrived in the United States from England in the 1940s, already a well-established swing era stylist there. He quickly learned the complexities of modern jazz, and his grasp of bebop attracted musicians and fans alike. The early recordings of his quintet (piano, vibraphone, guitar, bass, and drums) proved a big success and set his musical course for many years to come. Shearing's group smoothed out the more jarring aspects of modern jazz and made the music accessible to millions. Shearing's eclecticism became an asset, and his virtuosic way with the block chord technique was one of his most identifiable features. He also excels at playing ballads, often using his beautiful, refined touch to cast the melodies in various classical styles. Many consider *The Complete Live George Shearing* (Mosaic) his best recorded work. (The annotation is by this writer.)

Oscar Peterson is probably the most famous jazz pianist in this book who is still performing. Originally from Montreal, he began mesmerizing audiences in 1949 at his Carnegie Hall debut. He is still doing just that at this writing in 1999. An awesome technician and performer, he matured into an instantly recognizable musical personality whose playing encompassed much of jazz piano history from stride through bop and beyond. Under producer and recording pioneer Norman Granz, he has probably recorded more albums than any other jazz artist, both on his own and with just about every other prominent instrumentalist. Originally inspired by Nat Cole and Art Tatum, he still retains much of their influence. Peterson's trio has become a model of small-group playing, as was Nat Cole's for countless other like units. In addition to a prodigious number of Verve recordings, there is the two-record set on Prestige featuring violinist Stephane Grappelli, and one called *My Favorite Instrument* on the MPS label.

Another widely respected name is Dave Brubeck. Although not a big influence on other pianists, he is undeniably a dominant presence in modern jazz history. As a pianist and composer, he pioneered in using meters like 5/4, 7/4, and 5/8. His quartet with the gifted alto saxophonist Paul Desmond recorded prolifically. Brubeck's compositions "In Your Own Sweet Way" and "The Duke" are favorites of musicians, and Desmond's "Take Five" (Columbia) is now a standard. Brubeck's style is noted for its harmonic richness, sometime reflecting his celebrated teacher, Darius Milhaud. Also, Brubeck's massive bombastic chordal improvising has often brought audiences to their feet.

The Brubeck quartet came to prominence in the mid-1950's. Brubeck even appeared on the cover of *Time*. His many recordings are on Fantasy/OJC, Columbia, and Telarc.

Ahmad Jamal never attained the level of celebrity that Garner, Peterson, Shearing, and Brubeck did, but for a relatively short period in the late fifties, his trio reached a mass listenership. His recordings of "Poinciana" and "But Not for Me" (Argo) were especially popular. He is a different kind of virtuoso who uses his prodigious technique sparingly and in unexpected places. His use of space and silence and his sense of form affected Miles Davis deeply, and Miles even instructed his pianist, Red Garland, to emulate Jamal's chordal voicings and Charleston-like left hand. Jamal later embraced Latin and other idioms for his trio.

Not all jazz pianists are high-energy "hot" players. Ellis Larkins, who came to attention in the forties, was initially a Wilson-influenced ensemble performer. But by the late fifties he had created his own sonic atmosphere. As a classical prodigy, he put his training to good use. His touch is the envy of many, and he skillfully uses all the resources of the instrument. He has a vast repertoire of the great song composers such as George Gershwin. Larkins rarely strays far from the melodies, but harmonically he has perfected voicings that have eluded many and influenced many others. Rhythmically, he reminds one of Erroll Garner, with laid-back right-hand phrasing. But unlike Garner, he is a master of understatement. He can be entirely persuasive at barely audible levels. Larkins has long been a coveted accompanist for many singers, including Ella Fitzgerald. He lays down a keyboard "carpet" that has never been duplicated.

A totally different aesthetic motivated the revolutionary Lennie Tristano. A blind virtuoso raised in Chicago, he focused on complex linear improvisation that utilized polyrhythmic and polytonal concepts. Using only a relatively few standard songs as a harmonic basis, he composed many striking pieces that sound like spontaneous solos. Sacrificing the conventional concept of the "swinging" rhythm section, he insisted on a near-metronomic, almost faceless bass and drum accompaniment. His 1949 recordings with saxophonists Lee Konitz and Warne Marsh have become classics and have had a far-reaching influence on artists such as Bill Evans, Herbie Hancock, and others. Tristano's group also recorded "Digression" and "Intuition," perhaps the first completely improvised "free" music still considered jazz.

Jimmy Jones was a gifted and polished artist who remained a musician's musician. His command of impressionist harmony was unequaled until Bill Evans appeared. He was Sarah Vaughan's accompanist for eight years and had a way of improvising with chords that was unique.

One of the most striking and original pianists in Europe is Martial Solal. He is revered abroad but has not achieved fame in the United States for a variety of reasons beyond his control. Solal takes elements of Tatum, Garner, Powell, and Monk and combines them with his personal advanced harmonic and rhythmic concepts to achieve an unusual virtuoso style. He has an acute sense of abstraction, and his work demands close attention to appreciate its nuances. Blazing speed is always at the service of real musical ideas, and he also knows how to use both hands creatively. Solal can generate remarkable swing, even though his rhythms can be very convoluted.

A different and very talented abstractionist was pianist-composer Herbie Nichols. A contemporary of Thelonious Monk, he was very much affected by that master, but he developed into a complete original. His piano playing drew on a large body of music, both European and American. Nichols's compositions are noted for their originality. His CDs on Blue Note have posthumously become classics. He died in 1963 at the age of forty-four. Each passing year sees his musical stature grow in importance. His neglect during his lifetime is an artistic tragedy.

Creating his own jazz universe became the successful mission of Horace Silver, one of the seminal jazz figures of the 1950s and 1960s. A terrifically exciting performer, he combined the complexities of bebop with a deep feeling for traditional blues to create an instantly identifiable way of expressing himself. He was one of the greatest influences on pianists after Bud Powell and before Bill Evans. He is a brilliant composer whose large output of original compositions helped define what became "hard bop." Silver's structured riff-like accompaniments gave his quintets an almost big band feel.

There are other influential pianists who deserve more space here. Wynton Kelly's "groove" and peerless "comping" inspired everyone who played with him or ever heard him. His style combined a sophisticated grasp of bebop with his West Indian feel for rhythm—an unbeatable combination. Sonny Clark, an almost underground figure who died young, had a beautiful, gentle, lyrical, linear style that owed much to Bud Powell. Musicians love him, and his small Blue Note output is much in demand by collectors. He also composed several attractive themes. And not to be overlooked is Dave McKenna, who is a living legend to many musicians. He is an elegant performer who fuses prebop idioms and sophisticated later elements with great panache. He works mostly as a soloist and is admired for his ability to sustain a single-note bass line at any tempo. Also a great ballad interpreter, he sometimes evokes the voicings of Ellis Larkins. Dick Hyman says, "McKenna is his own rhythm section. The left hand plays a four-four bass line, the right hand plays the melody, and there's that occasional 'strum' in between—like three hands."

Phineas Newborn's legendary reputation preceded his arrival in New York by several years. In 1956 he created a sensation with his Tatum-Powell-Garner style. He had a blinding technique, and his trademark was executing incredibly fast unison bebop lines with both hands, usually two octaves apart. Mental illness interrupted his brilliant career; after years in virtual obscurity, he resumed recording in the 1970s, but died in 1989.

A special favorite, especially among musicians, was Red Garland. As a member of Miles Davis's 1950s quintet, he left a great legacy on the Davis recordings. He had a very personal, understated conception of the bebop melodic vocabulary, which he articulated with a beautiful soft touch. He also had an individual block chord technique, inspired by Ahmad Jamal.

Ray Bryant is another fine artist who uses diverse influences to produce an infectious, attractive style. His beat, love of the blues idiom, and two-handed approach have established him as an important part of the jazz piano tradition.

Like Thelonious Monk's, Randy Weston's piano style defies outright imitation. He take elements of Monk, Ellington, and a little Bud Powell and ingeniously melds them with aspects of his own intense interest in African cultures, particularly those of Morocco, Tangier, and Nigeria. His compositions, like Monk's, are intrinsically bound to his playing style. In addition to many waltzes, his "Little Niles," "Hi-Fly," and "African Cookbook" are justly well known.

One of the most delightful and talented jazz personalities is the indefatigable Marian McPartland. Over the years she has grown into a superlative, sensitive performer, always bubbling with new ideas. Her acute harmonic sense and beautiful touch color everything she plays, and she is a daring, amazing improviser. She is also an educator, and her popular National Public Radio series has presented a wonderful cross-section of jazz pianists and other instrumentalists over the years (including myself).

Pianist-composer-spokesman-author-educator Billy Taylor has done as much as anyone in jazz history to promulgate an awareness, understanding, and appreciation of jazz to large audiences. His articulate presentation of established and new jazz talent on the CBS program *Sunday Morning* is an invaluable cultural resource. Because of his public persona, his brilliant piano playing has sometimes been underappreciated. Starting in the 1940s, he has performed with just about every jazz great, including Charlie Parker. The influence of his mentor, Art Tatum, is a prominent feature of his playing.

Almost unknown to the general public, Jimmy Rowles is justly famous and loved by innumerable pianists around the world. His individual touch, one-of-a-kind chord voicings, and fresh interpretive ideas have delighted listeners and musicians since the 1940s. His career encompassed working with almost all of the great instrumentalists, including many of the great singers like Billie Holiday and Peggy Lee. A good example of his work is his performance of his "The Peacocks" with Stan Getz on Columbia.

Another brilliant pianist was Hampton Hawes. Working mostly on the West Coast, he updated certain aspects of Bud Powell and was moving toward modal jazz at the time of his premature demise. Carl Perkins overcame a handicapped left hand to become a world-class pianist; he also was a California fixture on the jazz scene and died young. Russ Freeman was an important contributor to what was somewhat unfairly characterized as West Coast jazz. He was featured on many recordings with Shorty Rogers and others.

Fiery and *versatile* are words to describe Lou Levy, a pianist originally inspired by Bud Powell. He has performed outstandingly with Stan Getz and Peggy Lee and with Supersax, the five-saxophone group.

Two pianists who left the United States for Europe and made fine careers abroad are Kenny Drew, an important part of the bop scene who had recorded with John Coltrane, and Horace Parlan, a popular individualist in Europe. Another pianist with a personal style is Sir Charles Thompson. The composer of the hit instrumental "Robbins' Nest," he crafted a style that combines Count Basie's economy and certain harmonic and rhythmic features of bop.

Bebop record collectors will remember Gil Coggins and Wade Legge. Coggins was on some early Miles Davis Blue Note records, and Legge worked with Dizzy Gillespie and Charles Mingus. These are two largely forgotten, very talented pianists.

Not all pianists were Bud Powell spin-offs. The late Eddie Costa was an outstanding pianist and vibraphonist. He was considered very advanced and very adept at polyrhythms and was extremely flexible.

His promising career was tragically cut short by a fatal automobile accident.

Add the name of Dick Twardzik to those innovators like Herbie Nichols who did not live to see their work disseminated and accepted in their lifetimes. Twardzik was a legend in the Boston area and left one great trio recording for Pacific Jazz. His playing was abstract and innovative, and he was considered a near-genius.

As an example of how much diversity there is among jazz pianists, consider the wonderful Dick Wellstood. Long known as one of the finest stride players, he was much more. He had a great sense of humor, knew other styles, and even recorded John Coltrane's "Giant Steps" in stride.

Dick Hyman has long been respected as one of the most accomplished jazz pianists extant, capable of just about anything possible on the keyboards (piano, organ, and more). He is a kind of renaissance man, and his repertory work is invaluable. He plays all styles from Scott Joplin to Cecil Taylor.

Taylor has been the most successful of the so-called avant-garde pianists since the 1950s. He is also one of the most controversial, with a style that many do not even consider to be jazz. Long before Ornette Coleman, he was making "free" music atonally.

Space limitations in this chapter make it impossible to discuss the many fine pianists that contributed (and still do) to the infinite world of jazz piano, but here are a few who should not be overlooked. McCoy Tyner, before his modal innovations in the 1960s, was an accomplished bebop player who also was and is at home playing standards.

Sir Roland Hanna, who came to New York from Detroit about the same time as Tommy Flanagan and Barry Harris, is a versatile, classically oriented, very swinging pianist-composer who also came to prominence in the late fifties. He now is internationally renowned. Bobby Timmons, the composer of "Moanin'" and "Dat Dere," was a fine bop pianist who was a big contributor to the jazz-funk movement started by Art Blakey and Horace Silver.

Then there are Don Friedman, Steve Kuhn, John Bunch, and the very underrated Richard Wyands. They all deserve more space here. The two outstanding omissions here are, of course, Thelonious Monk and Bill Evans. They are covered elsewhere in this book.

Paul Bley is an often astonishing improviser. His advanced "free" style has enriched the music since his arrival from Canada in the early 1950s. Other fine pianists deserving much more space are Junior

Mance, a great blues artist and versatile mainstreamer; Cedar Walton, a living legend and a favorite of many pianists; the all-time great Jay McShann, a contemporary of Count Basie who has continued to swing through all eras; and the marvelous late Ram Ramirez, the composer of "Lover Man."

I would like to dedicate this chapter to a great talent—Jaki Byard—who lost his life tragically in February 1999. He was a jazz colossus who never fully got his due, a brilliant pianist-composer who knew and lived every facet of this great music called jazz. Like Erroll Garner, he was a musical magician and a great musical storyteller and wit, whether he was playing ragtime, stride, bop or "free" style.

These are just some of the fine jazz pianists who helped make what is a priceless musical tradition that is still growing. There are only eighty-eight keys on the piano, but there are an unlimited number of ways to enjoy the music of the pianists written about here.

Hard Bop

Gene Seymour

"I loved bebop for taking jazz further along. But as hip and as great as it was, there was a period when musicians had kinda ... not totally, but somewhat ... eliminated the blues, you know? They got so sophisticated that it seemed like they were afraid to play the blues, like it was demeaning to be funky. And I tried to bring that. I didn't do it consciously at first. But it started to happen."

••• *Horace Silver, author's interview, 1993*

The late David H. Rosenthal, in his 1992 history *Hard Bop: Jazz and Black Music, 1955–1965*, advanced the idea of hard bop as being far more than just a subgenre of jazz. He characterized it as a "new mainstream," able to absorb the accessible and exuberant sounds associated with black popular music while providing its more adventurous practitioners with a foundation for experiments. Instead of grasping for greater complexity, hard bop provided jazz music with an innovative way of keeping things simple. And of making simple things sound extraordinary.

The Jazz Messengers, 1959. Art Blakey, drums; Wayne Shorter, tenor sax. Photo: Charles Stewart. Courtesy of the Institute of Jazz Studies, Rutgers University.

Two Altos and the R&B Factor

During the 1940s, the synthesis of formal innovation and pure show-manship embodied by Louis Armstrong throughout the previous two decades of jazz history split into two tangents, both of which were personified by alto saxophonists. With Charlie Parker, the improvi-sational genius, went the part of Armstrong's legacy that emphasized virtuoso experimentation and formal innovation. The showmanship banner, meanwhile, was picked up and waved by Louis Jordan, an altoist as influential as Parker in the development of post–World War II American music. Like Parker, Jordan served his apprenticeship in swing bands, notably the Chick Webb orchestra, where, between 1936 and 1938, he developed a following for his broad, lusty alto playing and his comparably broad comedic sense. In 1938 Jordan formed his own combo, the Tympany Five, and throughout the succeeding de-cade, they recorded some of the signature hits of the early rhythm-and-blues era, including "Saturday Night Fish Fry," "Is You Is or Is You Ain't (Ma' Baby)," "Choo Choo Ch'Boogie," and "Caldonia (What Makes Your Big Head So Hard?)." Jordan did not "invent" R&B any more than Parker single-handedly invented bebop. Just as other mu-sicians in Parker's generation were discovering new ways of playing with chord changes and harmonic progressions, Jordan was part of a great wave of singers and instrumentalists making their own postwar sound. The R&B of the 1940s was both a culmination and extension of the hard-driving swing put forth by big bands led by Cab Calloway, Count Basie, Jay McShann, and Lionel Hampton, whose 1942 hit, "Flying Home," with its explosive tenor sax solo by Illinois Jacquet, epitomized the "jump music" of the early 1940s.

Historians are now inclined to place the development of modern jazz and rhythm-and-blues on separate trajectories. And it is true that most of the pop music beyond the 1940s can be traced directly to the Jordan and other hard-rocking R&B music, while Parker's long-term influence, as noted before, is beyond pop's direct reach. But in their emergent period, bebop and R&B were both part of the same heady musical atmosphere that invigorated black listeners in the predawn of the civil rights movement. Bands who specialized in dance-happy R&B carried in their personnel one or two horn players who were as inventive within the rhythmically tighter confines of the music. Not surprisingly, many of these same trumpeters and saxophones who worked with R&B would help write the history of 1950s modern jazz and beyond.

During the late 1940s, the peak years of bebop experimentalism, there were hints that a leaner, more muscular and aggressive variant of bop would make its presence known in the coming years. The strongest of these hints could be heard in the music of arranger-composer Tadd Dameron, whose best-known compositions, "Good Bait," "Our Delight," and "Hot House," became lasting bop standards. Yet even through the distorted harmonies of these and other Dameron tunes, a simple yet strong melodic flow is sustained, prefiguring the hard-bop sound of the succeeding decades.

In trumpeter Fats Navarro, a virtuoso player with a bright, diamond-hard sound, Dameron found a perfect vehicle for his densely textured melodies. The 1947–49 sessions of Dameron's band featuring Navarro, presently available on the two-disc set *Fats Navarro and Tadd Dameron: The Complete Blue Note and Capitol Recordings* (Blue Note), represented both a peak achievement of the bebop era and a harbinger of the brash, elemental sound of the hard bop to come.

The Pivotal Year

In 1954 pianist Horace Silver was present at several sessions that, taken together, could be viewed as the birth and baptism of hard bop. Two months into the year, he played with a quintet led by drummer Art Blakey at the Birdland jazz club. Bassist Curley Russell completed the rhythm section, while the front line consisted of trumpeter Clifford Brown and saxophonist Lou Donaldson. Their February 21, 1954, performance, captured on the two-volume *A Night at Birdland With the Art Blakey Quintet* (Blue Note), carried a great deal of portent for the future of modern jazz.

Silver's big break came four years before when tenor saxophonist Stan Getz spotted him performing in a Hartford nightclub. He toured with Getz for a year afterwards, by which time he had acquired enough confidence to move to New York and collect club and studio gigs. In 1952 he began recording with his own trio, which featured Blakey. Those 1952–53 sessions, collected under the title *Horace Silver Trio* (Blue Note), display Silver's percussive, dynamically straightforward approach to the piano as well as his affinity for strong, simple melodies.

Blakey was by then a veteran of bands led by Mary Lou Williams, Andy Kirk, Jimmie Lunceford, Fletcher Henderson, and Billy Eckstine. After leaving the latter's orchestra in 1947, he organized a rehearsal band called the Seventeen Messengers and an octet called the Messengers. At around the cusp of the 1950s, Blakey had performed and recorded with such diverse artists as Buddy DeFranco, Thelonious

Monk, Charlie Parker, Tadd Dameron, and Fats Navarro before forming the quintet that played at Birdland that February night.

On April 29, 1954, Silver was the pianist at a recording session led by trumpeter Miles Davis, who was at the time in the midst of a comeback from drug addiction. Silver and Blakey had recorded with Davis the month before. This time, bop veteran Kenny Clarke was on drums while Percy Heath was on bass and trombonist J. J. Johnson and saxophonist Lucky Thompson joined Davis in the front line. Critic-historian Dan Morgenstern has labeled this "all-star session" as being "among the key recordings in the history of modern jazz."

Only two tracks were cut that day. One was "Blue 'n' Boogie" a Dizzy Gillespie blues given an up-tempo treatment. The other track, "Walkin'," also a blues, moves at a more leisurely pace, just as its title implies. But it proved far more influential in its deployment of a soft, sweet, low-down blues backdrop to Davis's compelling play with time and space. Silver's own approach to the basic melody is just as delicately framed—and as deceptively simple—as Davis's melodic variations. *Walkin'* (Prestige/OJC), the album that includes this classic, is regarded as a touchstone not only for Davis's subsequent career but for hard bop.

By the end of 1954, Blakey and Silver organized another quintet with bassist Doug Watkins, trumpeter Kenny Dorham, and tenor saxophonist Hank Mobley. The recordings they made were released the following year under the title *Horace Silver and the Jazz Messengers* (Blue Note). As with the sessions recorded earlier that year at Birdland, the music on this album is melodically simple and rhythmically aggressive. The beat was large and heavy enough to support any tune and its myriad variations, propelling the "narrative" of the instrumental performance without yielding to unnecessary flash. Silver's compositions were likewise uncomplicated. In their simplicity, however, there was infectious energy and warmth similar to the satisfactions delivered by an earthy blues singer. The well-rounded, riff-inflected design of such Silver tunes as "Doodlin'" and "The Preacher" made them both accessible to pop audiences and admired by jazz aficionados. The tunes were easy to grasp, hard to forget.

Meanwhile, Clifford Brown, who was on the Birdland stage with Blakey's quintet on that memorable February 1954 session, was, six months later, in a recording studio with drummer Max Roach to begin one of the most potent collaborations in modern jazz. The trumpeter, whose effervescent style picked up where the dazzling Fats Navarro had left off, was twenty-three years old that summer and had already acquired a reputation as one of the most prodigious and gifted horn players of the decade. His meteoric rise had nearly been curbed at its beginning when, in June 1950, he had been injured in a car crash and spent a year recuperating. His first recordings, in 1952, were with a rhythm-and-blues band, Chris Powell and the Blue Flames. He had also worked briefly with Tadd Dameron in the summer of 1953 and recorded that same year with trombonist J. J. Johnson's sextet and with combos featuring saxophonists Gigi Gryce and Lou Donaldson, pianists Elmo Hope and John Lewis, and bassist Percy Heath. (Those latter sessions can be found on *Clifford Brown: The Complete Blue Note and Pacific Jazz Recordings* [Blue Note].) In the fall of 1953, Brown toured Europe with Lionel Hampton's band. His Paris recordings with both the Hampton band and a small French combo are collected on *The Complete Paris Sessions, Vols. 1–3* (Vogue).

Word of the fiery young trumpeter with the voluptuous tone and the fluent technique was spreading throughout the jazz world. Both Charlie Parker and Dizzy Gillespie were leading advocates for Brown. Gillespie had visited Brown during his convalescence, while Parker had convinced Blakey to add Brown to his band for the seminal Birdland gig. Such advocacy of Brown's talents had prompted Max Roach to beckon the trumpeter from the East Coast to the West to play in the drummer's newly formed quintet.

By that time, Roach, at thirty, had established himself, along with Blakey, as one of the busiest and most important percussionists in postwar jazz, having played with Parker, Gillespie, Miles Davis, and many others. The Brooklyn-born drummer had come to California in the fall of 1953 to replace Shelly Manne as drummer with Howard Rumsey's Lighthouse All-Stars. Though he had recorded as a leader with Debut, the short-lived label he founded with Charles Mingus, Roach had by 1954 been known primarily as a sideman with modern jazz's glamorous bands. From the beginning of their collaboration, Roach insisted that Brown share top billing with him. Between 1954 and 1956, the Clifford Brown–Max Roach Quintet, which included pianist Richie Powell, bassist George Morrow, and tenor saxophonist Harold Land, laid down some of the most breathtaking small-group jazz ever recorded, all of which can be heard on *Brownie: The Complete EmArcy Recordings of Clifford Brown* (EmArcy, ten discs).

Both Brown and Roach shared both a formidable command of their respective instruments and an innate sense of thematic logic that contributed to the riveting flow of their solos. Roach's mastery of the trap set's storytelling capabilities was unassailable. And rarely in jazz have raw ability, tonal clarity, and conceptual lucidity been found in one musician to the same high degree that they were realized in Brown. The group's August 1954 recording of "I Get a Kick Out of You," with its displays of Roach's rolling thunder and Brown's sky-scraping inventiveness, represents as pure a distillation of modern jazz as anything else produced during that important year.

Though much of the work in Brown's last two years was with Roach, he also made significant recordings with vocalists Sarah Vaughan, Dinah Washington, and Helen Merrill. Tenor saxophonist Sonny Rollins would assume Harold Land's spot in the quintet's front line for its last recordings in early 1956. In June of that same year, Brown was killed in another road accident. He was not yet twenty-six years old. In just four years, Brown had established a stylistic model for the next couple of generations of trumpeters. Most of these trumpeters would evoke his memory in their playing. None, it can be safely said, would come close to being his equal.

The Jazz Messengers: Standardizing Bop

The cooperative unit of Silver, Blakey, Mobley, Dorham, and Watkins that went by the name of the Jazz Messengers stayed together for another year, recording a two-night session, *At the Cafe Bohemia, Volume One* and *At the Cafe Bohemia, Volume Two* (Blue Note), in November 1955. Dorham, Silver, Mobley, and Watkins all went their separate ways in 1956. Blakey was allowed to keep the Jazz Messengers trademark, and for the next four decades the bands that carried the name "Art Blakey and the Jazz Messengers" would constitute a musical dynasty, a traning academy for composers and bandleaders, and a working model for ensembles that allowed individual expression within the parameters of the Blakey beat and the hard-bop sound.

It took some time for Blakey's enterprise to harden into a tradition. The 1956 sessions collected on *The Jazz Messengers* (Columbia) are evidence of a band trying to find a clear direction. By this time, alto saxophonist Jackie McLean and trumpeters Bill Hardman and Donald Byrd had become members of an evolving front line that, over the next couple of years, included tenor saxophonist Johnny Griffin, a small man with a huge, agile sound. The recorded highlight of these years was the 1957 album *Art Blakey's Jazz Messengers With Thelonious Monk* (Atlantic), in which the drummer recaptures much of the magic of those late 1940s and early 1950s Blue Note sessions with Monk.

Four Philadelphia-born musicians—trumpeter Lee Morgan, tenor saxophonist Benny Golson, pianist Bobby Timmons, and bassist Jymie Merritt—came to the Messengers in 1958, giving coherence and shape to Blakey's band. Morgan and Golson were veterans of Dizzy Gillespie's big band and also worked together on Morgan's first three Blue Note albums. Pianist Timmons brought with him some of the same R&B/funk-influenced stylings as Silver, but with a lighter touch.

This edition of the Messengers recorded one of Blakey's landmark albums, *Moanin'* (Blue Note), in 1958. The album provided an occasion for, among other things, the first recorded versions of three tunes, "Blues March," "Along Came Betty," and the title track, that became fixtures in the Messengers' songbook—and classic compositions in the modern jazz repertoire. "Moanin' " was written by Timmons, and its call-and-response melody is regarded as an exemplar of hard bop's "down home" personality. Golson wrote "Blues March" and "Along Came Betty," and their melodies are as simple and "soulful" as that of "Moanin'." One is also aware, especially in "Betty," of a moodier, more astringent approach to harmony and rhythm than is found on "Moanin' "—which suggested early on in hard bop's history that the genre, however tightly it clung to rhythm and blues, was flexible enough to allow composers like Golson room for their own idiosyncracies to flourish.

Golson's year with the Messengers was long enough to help establish a paradigm for future Blakey bands. The saxophonist's warm, clipped playing offered a dramatic contrast to Morgan's slash-and-burn dynamics. This play of constrasting personalities was to be a hallmark of Blakey's most distinctive editions of the Messengers through the 1980s. By 1960 Golson's place in the group's front line would be taken by a Newark-bred saxophonist-composer named Wayne Shorter. For the succeeding four years, Shorter, who was also the group's musicial director, built upon Golson's legacy to expand the conceptual range of hard bop without straying too far from the genre's thickly layered sound and heavy beat. Shorter's playing was even moodier and darker than Golson's, and the titles of his compositions for Blakey ("The Midgets," "The Chess Players," "Ping Pong," "Children of the Night") suggest an imagination as richly enigmatic as Monk's. Moreover, the contrast between Shorter's ruminations and Morgan's bravado made for compelling tension in such 1960–61 Messenger albums as *The Big Beat*, *A Night in Tunisia*, and *The Freedom Rider* (all on Blue Note).

Morgan left the Messengers in 1961, and it is possible to imagine

Messengers devotees worrying at the time that he had taken the group's fire and dynamism with him. But Freddie Hubbard, Morgan's replacement in the Messengers' trumpet chair, shared the latter's agility and drive as a soloist. Pianist Cedar Walton replaced Timmons, and trombonist Curtis Fuller added another layer of sound to the front line of Hubbard and Shorter, who was still musical director. Their 1961 album, *Mosaic* (Blue Note), is a showcase for compositions by Shorter ("Children of the Night"), Hubbard ("Crisis"), Walton ("Mosaic"), and Fuller ("Arabia").

By the mid-1960s Blakey's Jazz Messengers had become established as a dynasty cum finishing school for the music's finest, toughest players. The turnover would remain steady over the remaining two decades of the Messengers under Blakey's leadership. (He died in 1990, just five days after his seventy-first birthday.) Blakey gave each member of his glittering alumni list the chance to both test and find himself. Some critics may argue that Blakey's Messengers, in concept, standardized small-group performance so consummately that it became impossible to imagine any departure from its model. Others contend that this model permits all who follow it to do whatever they want.

Right Coast, Left Coast

Philadelphia, which gave Blakey his 1958 Messengers, is often regarded as a "city of neighborhoods." In similar fashion, hard bop is regarded as an idiom of cities, with different regions providing enough musicians to embody a sound, a school of playing. Besides Golson, Morgan, Timmons, and Clifford Brown, saxophonists John Coltrane and Jimmy Heath, drummers Philly Joe Jones, bassists Reggie Workman and Percy Heath, drummer Albert "Tootie" Heath, and pianist McCoy Tyner were only a few players who grew up, musically or otherwise, in Philadelphia. A similar ferment could be found in Detroit, whose contributions to hard bop included bassists Paul Chambers and Doug Watkins, trombonists Curtis Fuller and Frank Rosolino, drummers Louis Hayes and Elvin Jones, trumpeters Donald Byrd, Thad Jones, and Marcus Belgrave, guitarist Kenny Burrell, singers Sheila Jordan and Betty Carter, and pianists Hank Jones, Tommy Flanagan, Roland Hanna, and Barry Harris.

One region of the United States not often associated with hard bop is the West Coast. Indeed the words *West Coast* are often used to define a whole idiom of jazz music widely assumed to be "softer" than hard bop in its rhythmic and melodic attack. Such a polarized viewpoint has been taken as conventional wisdom for so long that it has all but obscured the presence in hard bop of such strong Los Angeles–based voices as Curtis Counce, Carl Perkins, and Harold Land, who remains better known for his work with the Brown-Roach ensembles than for such albums as *Harold in the Land of Jazz* (Contemporary/OJC, 1958) and *The Fox* (Contemporary/OJC, 1959).

Both those recordings give prominence to the dry, sinewy lyricism Land exhibited in his work with an ensemble led by bassist Curtis Counce, a onetime member of the Stan Kenton orchestra, who formed his quintet of Land, trumpeter Jack Sheldon, pianist Carl Perkins, and drummer Frank Butler in the mid-1950s. The group's airtight rhythms and aggressive horn playing made it, in Ted Gioia's words, "an East Coast band in spirit if not in geography." (1992, 318). Yet they seldom performed far from Southern California, which Land and others blame for the group's lack of recognition compared with other hard-bop groups of the era. *You Get More Bounce* (Contemporary/OJC, 1956) and *Landslide* (Contemporary/OJC, 1957) display the best music of this underrated group. Sheldon, better known as a "cool school" player before and after his association with Counce, is bright and dynamic, an agile foil for Land's broad-shouldered soloing. Perkins turned what has often been called a "crablike" attack on the piano into artful, idiosyncratic percussiveness. Counce and Butler were a strong tandem, but it is the drummer's powerful imaginative soloing on "A Drum's Conversation" from Counce's *Sonority* (Contemporary/OJC, 1956, 1958) that gives this group a distinctive presence among hard-bop units crowded at opposite ends of the continent.

Counce's quintet encountered some turnover in 1958. Gerald Wilson, better known as an arranger and big band leader, replaced Sheldon, and Perkins left to rejoin alto saxophonist Art Pepper, himself no slouch as a hard-bopper, as proven by such albums as *Art Pepper Meets the Rhythm Section* (Contemporary/OJC, 1957). Perkins died in March 1958 of ailments related to alcoholism. The Curtis Counce group went through several variations, most of them featuring pianist Elmo Hope, before the bassist's death of a heart attack in 1963.

It's Got to Be Funky

The liner notes to Horace Silver's *Serenade to a Soul Sister* (Blue Note) include the pianist's "guidelines to musical composition: a.) Melodic Beauty, b.) Meaningful Simplicity, c.) Harmonic Beauty, d.) Rhythm, e.) Environmental, Heredity, Regional and Spiritual Influences."

Many have interpeted the fifth guideline as an elaborate definition of what came to be known as the "funky" essence of Silver's music given its suggestion of African-American strains of blues and gospel. One also hears throughout Silver's music a brash, affectionate mockery reminiscent of late-'40s R&B, especially in such tunes as "Sister Sadie" from *Blowin' the Blues Away* (Blue Note, 1959).

Silver became closely identified with "funk," but he cannot be solely defined by it. As the title of his 1958 album, *Further Explorations by the Horace Silver Quintet* (Blue Note), implies, Silver had always been interested in testing and expanding his principles without straying from his music's melodic and rhythmic accessibility. The album, whose quintet features trumpeter Art Farmer and tenor saxophonist Clifford Jordan in the front line, includes such Silver compositions as "Pyramid," "Moon Rays," and "Safari," which all combine the warmth and ingenuity that Silver sustained through more than twenty more albums recorded under his leadership for Blue Note.

Besides the aforementioned albums, one can also cite *The Tokyo Blues* (Blue Note, 1962) and *The Jody Grind* (Blue Note, 1966) for their exemplary displays of Silver's mastery of thematic development within tight grooves. *Song for My Father* (Blue Note, 1964) is considered Silver's peak achievement and, perhaps, his most popular, given the title track's commercial success. Both *Song* and *Cape Verdean Blues* (Blue Note, 1965) carried Silver's music beyond the "funk bag" he had helped create by exploring the African-Iberian rhythms linked to his Cape Verdean roots.

Other musicians would likewise take up R&B-gospel motifs while maintaining their connections with bebop and swing. As a result, many of the tunes closely associated with what became known as "soul jazz" became as much a part of the African-American community's soundtrack as the burgeoning black pop music put out from the late 1950s through the 1960s. The names of Wes Montgomery, Jimmy Smith, and Julian "Cannonball" Adderley, for instance, were as recognizable on a corner jukebox in a black neighborhood as Ray Charles, James Brown, and Smokey Robinson.

A self-taught guitarist from Indianapolis, Montgomery apprenticed (like many others in hard bop) with Lionel Hampton's band in the late 1940s and spent most the 1950s working in his hometown's nightclub circuit. After performing and recording in groups with his brothers Monk (on bass) and Buddy (on piano and vibes), Montgomery organized his own trio and began recording under his own name in 1959 for Riverside. The following year, *The Incredible Jazz Guitar of Wes Montgomery* (Riverside/OJC, 1960) was recorded and released to critical acclaim. Using what became the most celebrated thumb in jazz guitar, Montgomery deployed a velvety attack and liberated the rest of his fingers to play the unison octaves and parallel chords that gave distinction and influence to his style. He even paid tribute to the digit in a tune called "The Thumb," which can be found on the 1966 album *Tequila* (Verve), one of the heavily orchestrated albums produced late in the guitarist's life that have drawn fire from critics and historians for being too commercial. In spite (or because?) of the pop luster of such covers as "Goin' Out of My Head," "California Dreamin'," or "A Day in the Life," Montgomery, who died at forty-three in 1968, remains the most influential guitarist in jazz after Charlie Christian.

The influence of organist Jimmy Smith, a frequent recording partner with Montgomery during the late 1960s, is just as vast and enduring. Though he was not the first player to bring the electronic organ to jazz (Fats Waller and Count Basie, among others, had preceded him), Smith gave the instrument the expressive power that Coleman Hawkins and Charlie Parker had given their respective saxophones. Inspired by such blues-based organists as Wild Bill Davis and Bill Doggett, Smith, trained as a pianist, took up the Hammond B-3 organ in the early 1950s when he was in his twenties. By 1955 he was leading a trio that included a guitar and a trap set. Two years later, he appeared at the Newport Jazz Festival, where he was launched to international fame.

Smith's deployment of "walking" bass lines through his organ's pedals and his percussive left-handed chords provided the legs for his style, while his wildly aggressive right hand would summon colorful narrative phrasing. Smith's Hammond was a down-and-dirty orchestra in itself. Yet his recordings often profited from brassy ensembles of varied sizes. The title track of *The Sermon* (Blue Note, 1958) is an extended blues jam loosely based on "Walkin'." During the 1960s, Smith also played in big-band sessions arranged by Lalo Schifrin (*The Cat*, Verve, 1964) and Oliver Nelson (*Bashin', The Unpredictable Jimmy Smith*, Verve, 1962). But it is in the smaller ensembles, including those with Montgomery, that Smith's dramatics can best be savored. Just the titles of Smith's albums, from *Back at the Chicken Shack* (Blue Note, 1960) and *Midnight Special* (Blue Note, 1960) through *Got My Mojo Workin'* (Verve, 1966) all the way to *Damn!* (Verve, 1995), evoke the unabashed, rough-edged aura of the blues. Generations of organists, notably Jack McDuff, Jimmy McGriff, and Richard "Groove" Holmes, followed his lead and shared his popularity.

Julian Edwin Adderley, whose nickname "Cannonball" was a childhood corruption of cannibal, describing his large appetite, first came into prominence shortly after Charlie Parker's death in 1955 when he was dubbed "the new Bird." Within a decade, this perception would alter somewhat as Adderley became widely known for wry, crowd-pleasing "down home" jazz closer in spirit to Louis Jordan, though Adderley's bop credentials remained solid until his death in 1975 from a stroke.

The Florida-born-and-bred altoist had spent most of his early career teaching and leading a high school band. He came to New York in the mid-1950s to play with his cornetist brother Nat. Over the next five years, Adderley would play in various groups; some were co-led with Nat, others led by Miles Davis, who would guest star on one of the saxophonist's noteworthy albums, *Somethin' Else!* (Blue Note, 1958). After leaving Davis's band in 1959, Adderley formed a quintet with Nat that played hard-rocking, blues-infused jazz. The pianists would change (from ex-Messenger Bobby Timmons to Barry Harris to Victor Feldman to Joe Zawinul), but the rhythm section of bassist Sam Jones and drummer Louis Hayes would remain stalwart throughout much of the 1960s. The band became known for such tunes as Timmons's "Dat Dere" and Nat's "Work Song," both found on *Them Dirty Blues* (Riverside/OJC, 1960), and also for "Sack o' Woe," which was performed at the band's live *At the Lighthouse* (Riverside/OJC, 1960). The Adderleys enjoyed steady success up to the release, in 1966, of *Mercy, Mercy, Mercy! Live at "The Club"* (Capitol), whose title track, written by Zawinul, became a pop phenomenon, coming perilously close to the Top Ten on the pop charts.

The Blue-and-White Label

The preeminence of hard bop in the jazz mainstream from the late 1950s to the mid-1960s was such that it was a staple of just about every major record label in jazz music. But even the most casual listener knows that if hard bop had a home base, it was Blue Note Records, founded in 1939 by a blues-loving German expatriate named Alfred Lion. The label's golden age—between 1955 and 1967—coincided roughly with hard bop's own. Almost every artist associated with hard bop recorded for Blue Note; even such major figures of the period as Miles Davis, Sonny Rollins, and John Coltrane were nourished by hard bop's elemental synthesis of blues, swing, and bop.

Coltrane, for instance, recorded only once for Blue Note. Yet there are some who claim that *Blue Train* (Blue Note, 1957) outshines the many albums the tenor saxophonist had recorded during the late 1950s for Prestige.

Sonny Rollins had played with both Miles Davis and Clifford Brown by the time he joined Blue Note in December 1956. He had by then also established his reputation as a great improviser with such albums as *Saxophone Colossus* (Prestige, 1956). The five albums he recorded through 1957 for Blue Note—including *Sonny Rollins, Vols. 1 and 2*; *Newk's Time*; and *A Night at the Village Vanguard, Vols. 1 and 2*, are regarded as quintessential hard bop for their aggressive dynamics and deep-bottomed "soulfulness." In these and such varied recordings as *Way Out West* (Contemporary, 1957), *The Freedom Suite* (Riverside, 1958), and *The Bridge* (RCA, 1961), Rollins's style, though more complex in execution than most other hard-bop players of the era, was, along with Coltrane's and Davis's, an influence, an example, a grail for others to follow.

Dexter Gordon was another major tenor player who found a nexus to the hard-bop movement through his association with Blue Note. A swashbuckling bebop innovator in the late 1940s, Gordon spent most of the 1950s in and out of prison for drug offenses. In May 1961, a year after his release for the second of two jail terms he served in the previous decade, Gordon cut his first album with Blue Note, *Doin' Alright*. Thus began a four-year association with the label that many critics consider to be his professional peak, an assertion backed by the rich inventiveness found in Gordon's playing on such albums as *Go!* (Blue Note, 1962), *A Swingin' Affair* (Blue Note, 1962), *Our Man in Paris* (Blue Note, 1963), and *Gettin' Around* (Blue Note, 1965).

With dominant figures like these on the scene, it is not difficult to see in retrospect how the surplus of tenor saxophonists who flourished during hard bop's heyday could be relatively or unfairly neglected. Among those who recorded for Blue Note who fit this category, Tina Brooks and Hank Mobley may offer the most poignant examples. Mobley, among the first of the Jazz Messengers, was also one of the busiest members of the Blue Note stable. His lean, taut approach lacked Gordon's flamboyance or Rollins's intricacy. But he was melodically inventive enough to find inspiration in a variety of settings, whether "soul jazz" or basic bop. The most adventurous of his many albums may well have been *No Room for Squares* (Blue Note, 1963), on which he played modal jazz with both the dashing ex-Messenger Lee Morgan and the idiosyncratic pianist Andrew Hill. With hard bop's decline in the early 1970s, Mobley fell into a troubled eclipse himself. Health problems forced him into retirement for most of the years leading to his death in 1986.

In contrast to Mobley, Brooks was practically forgotten when he died in 1974. Yet in recent years, his plaintive tone and sinuous phrasing have come to be regarded as among the most imaginative and inspired products of the hard bop era. Like Mobley, Brooks played on countless Blue Note sessions led by such artists as Jimmy Smith *(The Sermon)* and alto saxophonist Jackie McLean *(Jackie's Bag,* Blue Note, 1959). *True Blue* (Blue Note, 1960), the only Brooks-led album released in his lifetime, offers the listener both the blues-oriented basics of hard bop and the wounded, passionate voice of Brooks himself—evidence enough of hard bop's capacity to contain as many sensibilities and moods as jazz music permits.

If voices like Brooks's became lost over time, it may be in part because, by the early sixties, hard bop was perceived as falling into a kind of lethargy relieved only by the innovations made by (and fresh talent found within) bands led by Silver, Blakey, and others. Though "soul jazz" remained commercially vital—thanks to the presence of such Blue Note fixtures as tenor saxophionist Stanley Turrentine and guitarist Grant Green—the label's music began to absorb some of the innovations made outside hard bop's parameters by Miles Davis's modal experiments and the emergent "free jazz" movement personified by Ornette Coleman.

Jackie McLean, who had recorded with Davis, Rollins, and Blakey, among others, was one of the first Blue Note artists to make use of what was being called in the early sixties "the new thing." The alto saxophonist released three albums in those years whose titles, *Let Freedom Ring* (Blue Note, 1962), *One Step Beyond* (Blue Note, 1963), and *Destination Out* (Blue Note, 1963), proclaim his impulse to move away from pure bop changes and toward a more adventurous relationship with harmony and rhythm. Soon Blue Note's reputation was enhanced as a home office for musicians able to play both "outside" and "inside" conventional jazz settings. A quirky yet seductive impressionism was the hallmark of such 1960s Blue Note stars as saxophonists Joe Henderson *(Inner Urge,* 1964) and Wayne Shorter *(Speak No Evil,* 1964), pianists Herbie Hancock *(Maiden Voyage,* 1965) and Andrew Hill *(Point of Departure,* 1964), organist Larry Young *(Unity,* 1965), and McLean's erstwhile bandmates Grachan Moncur III *(Evolution,* 1963) and Bobby Hutcherson *(Dialogue,* 1965).

If there was a prototypical Blue Note artist of this fertile period, it may have been Lee Morgan, whose career had stalled for a while after leaving the Jazz Messengers in 1961, mainly because of heroin addiction. He returned to Blakey's band in 1964, but not before recording (in December 1963) one of Blue Note's most popular albums, *The Sidewinder*. The hip-shaking title tune was exactly the kind of soul jazz standard that could hold its own with any pop tune making its way up the charts. His next album, *Search for the New Land* (Blue Note, 1964), was one of the few Morgan albums released through the rest of the decade that departed from the groove-heavy pattern set by *Sidewinder*'s success. *Search*'s title track was darker and more thematically adventurous than the previous album's. But for the most part, Morgan's subsequent Blue Note albums from 1964 to 1967 (*Tom Cat, The Rumproller, Cornbread, The Gigolo, Delightfulee*, and others) carried the same slick veneer as *Sidewinder*. Morgan's playing throughout is bright, bold, and relentlessly aggressive enough to occasionally carry such efforts beyond mere formulaic repetition.

Still, like many hard boppers who began their careers with their genre in the mid-1950s, Morgan found himself at a crossroads in the early 1970s. Unwilling to leave the United States for greater opportunities for club dates overseas or to cast his lot with jazz-rock fusion, Morgan had become an outspoken polemicist for the kind of acoustic jazz that was losing its primacy even in the black communities that helped nurture it. His death, at thirty-three, in 1972 from gunshots fired by a jealous woman in a New York nightclub is seen by many as emblematic as the end of what had started eighteen years before with Blakey, Silver, Brown, and others. But as its revival a decade later would prove, hard bop remains a wellspring of inspiration for younger musicians and a touchstone for listeners captivated enough with its boldness and energy to seek out and embrace the whole of jazz music.

Miles Davis

Bob Belden

Few musicians of our time have had such an important and influential impact on jazz as Miles Davis. His lyrical tone on trumpet and the sound of his groups are instantly recognizable; many of the themes written for his bands have become jazz standards and are consciously imitated by musicians today. Davis was able to imprint his sound and style on the tributaries of jazz and pop: bebop, hard bop, cool, funky, avant-garde, fusion, R&B, soul, dance, and rap. He developed three highly lyric qualities on the trumpet: a noble, New Orleans–based sound, an operatic approach, and a plaintive style. Davis considered himself a modernist, and this view was reflected in his never-ending quest for change. His bands became a pool for up-and-coming talent: John Coltrane, Cannonball Adderley, Bill and Gil Evans, George Coleman, Chick Corea, Herbie Hancock, Wayne Shorter, John McLaughlin, Keith Jarrett, Dave Liebman, Mike Stern, Marcus Miller, and John Scofield all became important contributors to jazz as a result of Davis's touch.

Miles Davis was born in Alton, Illinois, on May 26, 1926. He was raised in East St. Louis, Illinois, an integrated suburban community. His father, Miles Davis II, was a local oral surgeon and farmer; his

389

Miles Davis. Photo: Lee Tanner. Courtesy of the Institute of Jazz Studies, Rutgers University.

mother, Cleota Henry, was a housewife. The Davis family (there were two other children, Dorothy and Vernon) lived in relative comfort, even during the Depression years. Young Miles was first encouraged by his mother to play the violin, but his father bought him a trumpet. He received early instruction from Elwood Buchanan, a local trumpet teacher who encouraged Davis to develop a straight, vibratoless tone, in sharp contrast to the wide-vibrato approach popular in the day (Armstrong, James, Eldridge). His first steady job was with Eddie Randle's Blue Devils, a local dance band. When Billy Eckstine came through East St. Louis with Dizzy Gillespie and Charlie Parker, Davis was intent on heading to New York with the band. He applied to the Juilliard School of Music and was accepted; by September 1944 he was living in Manhattan.

Davis never applied himself to the curriculum at Juilliard. Eventually, the lure of the New York jazz scene led him to drop out of school. He connected with Charlie Parker, and soon they were rooming together. Parker took Davis around with him everywhere. By the winter of 1945, Davis was a member of Parker's quintet. Playing night after night with Parker was a significant experience for Davis, and the lessons in the jazz life were to stay with him for the rest of his life.

Stylistically, Davis had grown from a young disciple of Gillespie to a man searching for his own voice. His first recording session was for Savoy Records (April 24, 1945) and was with the Herbie Fields Band that featured the blues singer Rubberlegs Williams. His next foray into the studio was with Parker's quintet (also for Savoy, November 26, 1945). The hallmarks of Davis's early style were Parker's sense of time, some obvious Gillespie-isms (relying on bebop as a prime harmonic language), and an almost pensive approach to playing phrases. His phrasing was intensely precise within the pulse of the rhythm section, but at the same time his phrases were relatively laid-back; with his pure tone, this gave the listener a detached, laconic feeling.

By 1947 Davis had recorded with a host of artists (including Earl Coleman, Illinois Jacquet, and one of his early employers, Coleman Hawkins). With Parker's quintet, he made some classic sides (with Max Roach as the drummer) for Dial and Savoy. Davis's first original composition ("Donna Lee") was recorded in May 1947 for Savoy ("Cheryl" and "Chasin' the Bird" are from the same session). An August 1947 Savoy session, his first as a leader, produced "Little Willie Leaps" and "Sippin' at Bells."

By December 1948 Davis had ended his sideman relationship with Parker. Still looking for his own sound, he met regularly at Gil Evans's basement apartment on West 55th Street with Gerry Mulligan and a few other simpatico musicians. (Davis had been a fan of the Claude Thornhill Orchestra; Thornhill, who enjoyed the newer, exotic sounds, had hired creative arrangers, among them Mulligan and Evans. After leaving Thornhill, they headed for "the Street" and connected with Davis.)

This "brain trust" pooled their talents, worked out the instrumentation, and secured a job at the Royal Roost under Davis's leadership in September 1948, with the arrangers getting marquee credit. The group employed players (Lee Konitz, Mulligan, and Roach) and arrangers (Mulligan, Evans, John Lewis, and Johnny Carisi) on the cutting edge of the jazz scene.

A recording contract from Capitol Records followed, and the nonet went into the studio in January 1949 and cut four titles. Two more sessions followed in April 1949 and March 1950, but the music was not a commercial success, although some bandleaders and arrangers were attracted to the sound of the nonet (among them Woody Herman, Shorty Rogers, and J. J. Johnson). When the three sessions were compiled and released as *The Birth of the Cool*, mainstream jazz musicians took notice. The music became the inspiration for the West Coast–based "cool school," which shared with the Davis nonet a detached, detailed approach, a clarity of ensemble, a light feeling, smooth articulation, and counterpoint.

After performing at the Paris Jazz Festival (May 1949), Davis found work in the United States hard to get. He became addicted to heroin, and his career began to be somewhat erratic. The years from 1950 to 1954 are considered to be Davis's dark period, a time when the ravages of addiction drove him to near obscurity. Still, after sessions with Sarah Vaughan for Columbia (May 1950), he signed a recording contract with Prestige Records and an exclusive deal to appear as a featured artist at the jazz club Birdland. In May 1952 he recorded for Blue Note, and these recordings are more reflective of his musical state of mind than the Prestige sessions. During 1953 he recorded three sessions for Prestige and one for Blue Note in April, which produced a few tracks that even Davis liked including, "Tempus Fugit" and "Kelo." The Blue Note sessions were eventually released on LP as *Miles Davis, Volumes 1 and 2.* He moved to Detroit for a time and worked at the Bluebird bar with many of the young local musicians such as Tommy Flanagan, Elvin Jones, Barry Harris, Thad

Jones, and Kenny Burrell. Sometime during this period, Davis managed to kick his drug habit, and by 1954 he had moved back to New York.

Davis entered the studio one more time for Blue Note, in March 1954, with a new rhythm section: Horace Silver, Percy Heath, and Art Blakey. This session hints at a new direction for Davis: hard bop. With J. J. Johnson, Lucky Thompson, Silver, Heath, and Kenny Clarke for Prestige on April 29, he created a succinct and definitive example of this new sound (released as *Walkin'*). He pared down his approach to soloing, losing some of the frantic excesses of bebop phrasing. His playing was relaxed and confident, reflecting a respect for the earlier trumpet styles of Armstrong, Eldridge, and Henry "Red" Allen. "Walkin'" and "Blue 'n' Boogie" place Davis in the center of the new direction; his solo on "Walkin'" was his most original in concept and execution up to that time. On December 24, Davis led a band of the top musicians who were championing this new sound: Thelonious Monk, Milt Jackson, Heath, and Clarke. The albums *Bags' Groove* and *Miles Davis and the Modern Jazz Giants* further defined the new sound of Davis and his inner circle.

By early 1955, Davis had connected with drummer Philly Joe Jones, and they started to form a band. On Jones's recommendation, Davis hired pianist Red Garland and bassist Oscar Pettiford, and the foursome recorded an album for Prestige (*The Musings of Miles*). Paul Chambers (a prodigy from Detroit) eventually became the regular bassist.

Davis had a core group, but to obtain steady work, he needed a catalyst, something that would push him further into the jazz public's mind. As if taken from the page of a novel, a single shot at the Newport Jazz Festival in July 1955 reinvigorated his career. Davis played a set as an unannounced guest with an ad hoc group made up of Mulligan, Zoot Sims, Monk, Heath and, Connie Kay. Davis's performance on Monk's "'Round About Midnight" created such a sensation that George Avakian, a producer for Columbia Records, ran up to Davis after the set had ended and made him an offer to record for Columbia. A deal was made that allowed Davis to record for Columbia before his contract expired with Prestige, and Davis and his new quintet—now including a tenor saxophonist from Philadelphia, John Coltrane—went into the Columbia studio on October 27, 1955. The music recorded on this session was released erratically over four different albums: *'Round About Midnight, Facets, Jazz Omnibus,* and *Miles 1958*. The group returned to the studio for Prestige in November 1955 and recorded the album *The New Miles Davis Quintet.*

In May 1956 Davis and the quintet recorded fourteen tracks for Prestige. During June they recorded three titles for Columbia for the *'Round About Midnight* album, which was completed in October. Also in October, as a featured soloist for Columbia with a large ensemble assembled by Gunther Schuller and John Lewis, Davis recorded *Three Little Feelings* and *Poem for Brass*, released on *Music for Brass.* Three days later, Davis finished his obligations to Prestige, which released the quintet's results over five LPs: *Workin', Steamin', Cookin', Relaxin',* and *Miles Davis and the Modern Jazz Giants.*

Davis had discovered the intimate nature of the Harmon mute, which produced a whisper-like sound when played softly into a microphone; in the studio, the addition of reverb to the Harmon sound further enhanced the personal nature of Davis's tone. Coltrane's style had fused Parker and Dexter Gordon, and his choice of harmony would soon become deeply personalized. As a whole, the band had a hard swinging approach and a propulsive drive, and the beat was so pronounced and relaxed that the listener was drawn into the feel of the music. The model for Davis's rhythm section, whose players were in total sync with one another, was the Ahmad Jamal Trio: the Jamal sound was light but swinging, and Jamal's left-hand comping was appropriated by Red Garland. Davis recorded many popular songs associated with Jamal's group ("Surrey With the Fringe on Top" and "All of You" being two examples). The many freelance recordings made by the rhythm section demonstrated the style's popularity among musicians, and steady work in clubs provided the proof of Davis's success with the general public.

In November 1956, Davis traveled to Europe to perform as a single (Lester Young was on the same tour). By May 1957, Davis had begun a project for Columbia that established his importance as a voice in jazz. The album, *Miles Ahead*, featured arrangements and two original compositions by Gil Evans, and it had an instant effect on the music community. Davis's pure tone and Evans's soft-focus orchestrations were merged into a seamless suite. Evans seemed to find a heroic quality in Davis's sound, and by bringing out the dramatic qualities of this tone (often underpinning Davis with French horn, woodwinds, and double reeds) he was able to personalize the music in a way that had been rare in jazz. In December Davis was asked by director Louis Malle to improvise to his current film *L'Ascenseur pour l'échafaud;* it was the first such use of jazz music in film.

Davis returned to the States and re-formed his quintet with altoist Julian "Cannonball" Adderley, Tommy Flanagan, Paul Chambers, and Art Taylor. In early 1958 Coltrane, Jones, and Garland rejoined the band, and Davis had his first sextet. The Columbia album *Milestones*, recorded in April 1958, marked its debut and was the first recording of Davis's new direction: on the title track, the group improvises on scales instead of chords. Soon Bill Evans and Jimmy Cobb joined the sextet, replacing Garland and Jones, respectively. Evans had a profound effect on Davis and brought a sophisticated harmonic approach to the group. This band debuted in the studio in May 1958; music from this session was released on the *Jazz Track* album (along with the music from the Malle film). Columbia also recorded the group on July 4 at the Newport Jazz Festival and on September 9 at the Plaza Hotel but did not release the music until 1963 (*Miles and Monk at Newport*) and 1973 (*Jazz at the Plaza*) respectively.

In August 1958 Davis and Gil Evans were brought back into the studio to record the music from the Gershwin opera *Porgy and Bess*. Evans's arrangement of "Summertime" utilizes the same triadic background pattern as "Milestones," and Davis further embraces the scalar approach on "I Loves You, Porgy" and "Prayer." Getting deeper into the simplicity of scales, Davis began to pare down his style even further; he was starting to play fewer notes and less complex patterns.

In March and April 1959, Davis was in the studio with the sextet. (Wynton Kelly was now the regular pianist; Bill Evans was also invited to the session.) The results of these two sessions are considered a landmark in jazz history. *Kind of Blue* is a near-perfect album. Each composition is original in concept and style, with "So What," "All Blues," and "Flamenco Sketches" reflecting the new scalar approach. ("Flamenco Sketches" is actually five scales that the musicians improvise over.) The shifting form of "Blue in Green" anticipates the "contract/expand" style of Davis's mid-sixties quintet, and "Freddie Freeloader" is a straight-ahead swinger. When Adderley left the band, Davis did not hire a replacement; he still had Coltrane. Kelly, Chambers, and Cobb had become a stellar rhythm section and developed a rapport that allowed them to transcend their traditional role.

In November 1959 Columbia had Davis back in the studio with Evans. *Sketches of Spain* took five sessions to complete (the last was in March 1960), and the music created was again a beautiful showcase for the talents of Davis and Evans, with Davis "singing" his parts above the exotic texture of the orchestra. The highlight of the album is a rendition of the second movement of Rodrigo's *Concierto de*

Aranjuez, orchestrated for winds, brass, percussion, and Davis. This recording was popular with both musicians and the general public and was awarded a Grammy in 1961.

After the March sessions, the quintet was off to Europe, where it received mixed reviews. Coltrane's playing by now was harmonically dense and his solos long, and when the band returned Europe in April, he left. Davis hired Sonny Stitt, a bebopper immersed in the language of Parker, but Stitt's straight-ahead style did not fit into the quintet. Hank Mobley, a highly melodic swinger, joined up, and the band started playing medium tempos. The ongoing Kelly-Chambers-Cobb team could be compared to the Silver-Heath-Blakey rhythm team Davis was so fond of in the mid-fifties. The Columbia albums *Someday My Prince Will Come* (March 1961) and *Friday and Saturday Night at the Blackhawk* (April 1961) capture the essence of this quintet; "No Blues" and "Teo" (recorded on both albums) are prime examples. This Davis group had a relaxed approach to the time feel and gave an unhurried atmosphere to a performance.

In May 1961 Davis's quintet and the Evans Orchestra shared a public stage for the first time at Carnegie Hall: the results were later released by Columbia as *Miles Davis at Carnegie Hall*. In 1962, to capitalize on the current bossa nova trend, Davis and the Evans Orchestra were back in the studio to record the album *Quiet Nights*. It was considered less than a success by fans and critics, but "Song No. 2" is a marvelous performance.

Two sextet sessions with Bob Dorough and featuring arrangements by Evans were recorded for Columbia in August 1962 (with Wayne Shorter making his studio debut with Davis). Mobley had quit, and George Coleman was hired; Chambers left, and his replacement was Ron Carter. Cobb agreed to stay on until Davis found a drummer. During the winter of 1962, Davis and Philly Joe Jones auditioned drummers. When Davis heard a seventeen-year-old from Boston named Tony Williams, he knew he had found the right guy.

On April 16 and 17, 1963, in the Columbia Hollywood studios, a transitional quintet recorded seven tracks: "Joshua," "So Near, So Far," "Seven Steps to Heaven," and four standards. When Davis returned to New York, he had to hire a new pianist, because Victor Feldman had refused to leave the studios in Los Angeles. Both Williams and Carter recommended Herbie Hancock. On May 14, 1963, the new Davis quintet entered Columbia's New York studio to finish the album started in Los Angeles. They re-recorded "So Near, So Far," "Joshua," and "Seven Steps to Heaven" and coupled them with three standards from the earlier April sessions. Released as *Seven Steps to Heaven*, the juxtaposition of these two sessions is clear evidence of Davis's upcoming change in direction.

The new quintet (Coleman, Hancock, Carter, and Williams) began to work, both in concert halls and in clubs (with a no-alcohol policy because of Williams's age). Steady employment and the leader's "practice on the bandstand" philosophy led these musicians, like all of Davis's sidemen, into exploring form and pulse. The group would twist the form to suit their needs, and Hancock and Carter developed a singular harmonic canvas that shifted with the form. The band could play as hot as the Garland-Chambers-Jones rhythm team, which gave the up-tempo performances a unique edge. The quintet was taped live in July 1963 by the French national radio network, and five tracks were released by Columbia as *Miles in Europe*. The album received a five-star review from *Down Beat* magazine, and even Davis confessed that he found the music inspiring. Davis was particularly happy with Williams, whose pulse and drive pushed the band to a higher level of performance.

In the fall of 1963, Davis and Gil Evans were involved in composing incidental music for Peter Barnes's play *The Time of the Barracudas*. Recorded at Columbia's Hollywood studio in October 1963, the music utilizes Hancock, Carter, and Williams with a small wind and brass ensemble and is primarily short cues. A twelve-minute suite was released in 1996 and is included as bonus material on the *Quiet Nights* CD.

Columbia arranged to record a concert that the Davis quintet was giving on February 12, 1964, at Philharmonic Hall in New York City. The entire concert was released (but not in concert order) over two albums, *My Funny Valentine* and *Four and More*. Davis's performances on "My Funny Valentine" and "Stella by Starlight" are stunning, demonstrating a fresh approach to interpreting ballads. The rhythm section pulls and pushes Davis to improvise, and any note Davis plays, Hancock and Carter accent and voice accordingly. The improvisational concepts used by the rhythm section were moving forward into the modern way of thinking: open forms, harmony by implication, and nonlinear directions in melodic motion. Hancock, Carter, and Williams were young and adventurous, and Davis gave them more freedom to search.

In the spring of 1964, Coleman left the quintet and Bostonian Sam Rivers joined (again on the recommendation of Williams). Rivers was considered avant-garde in some music circles, and his style, like Stitt's a few years earlier, didn't jell with the sound Davis wanted. This version of Davis's quintet was recorded live on July 14, 1964, by Columbia's Japanese affiliate, and five tracks were released as *Miles in Tokyo*. When Davis discovered that Wayne Shorter had left Art Blakey, he immediately offered Shorter the job; Shorter accepted, bringing to the band his unique talents as a composer and arranger, as well as a probing, individual sense of the dramatic as a soloist.

The quintet, now complete, headed off to Europe in the fall of 1964, and Columbia's German affiliate recorded the September 25 concert and released it as *Miles in Berlin*. The performances on this disc indicated a new direction for Davis. His lines had become looser and cliché free. He seemed to be a little more relaxed and would often just play "in a direction" rather than take a predictable "play the changes" approach. This gave him leeway to direct the band with his choice of notes. He would often use his higher range for dramatic effect.

In the United States, the quintet worked sporadically, as jazz clubs began to close in the face of the rock revolution. After a two-week stint in San Francisco, the quintet recorded the *ESP* album in Columbia's Hollywood studio on January 20–22, 1965. The album is a departure from Davis's previous recordings (excepting *Kind of Blue*): all of the music is composed by members of the group, and the forms and harmonies of the compositions shift away from eight- and twelve-bar forms. "ESP" is an angular sixteen-measure piece, with an extensive use of the perfect fourth interval in the melody. Many of the group's compositions would be similarly constructed.

As soon as the group began to build some momentum, Davis required hip surgery. This situation kept him from working until late November 1965. On the nights of December 22 and 23, Columbia recorded the quintet in a Chicago club. *Miles Davis: The Complete Live at the Plugged Nickel* captured the band heading into unknown territory. Davis's sound was weakened by his recovery, but he was following the lead of his sidemen as never before. Shorter, Hancock, Carter, and Williams had grown in Davis's absence, and they brought all of their musical discoveries into the band. Shorter was developing a futuristic linear approach that defied analysis, and Hancock was taking the art of accompaniment to a higher level. Williams could now keep a smooth, tight groove underneath the soloist or explode in a flurry of sound and rhythm. By the time they returned to Columbia's New York studio (October 24–25, 1966), the group was in terrific form. *Miles Smiles* is a strong representation of the quintet at high speed, like a supercharged Tristano-Konitz-Marsh group.

Hancock's decision to "not play" creates a wide-open sound, so that the interaction is primarily among Davis, Shorter, and Williams, with Carter providing a counterpoint to the soloist on "Delores," "Orbits," and "Gingerbread Boy." The minor-blues "Footprints" became a concert favorite. However, as Davis began to follow a more abstract path with his music, record sales declined.

On May 5, 1967, after finishing a West Coast tour, Davis recorded one track, "Limbo," in Hollywood; it would be released in 1981 on the *Directions* album. Buster Williams was the bassist. Back in New York, Davis entered the Columbia studios (with Carter back on bass) eight times between May 16 and July 19. Three albums were released from these sessions: *Sorcerer, Nefertiti,* and *Water Babies.* Form and mood were now the focus of the music, mostly composed by Shorter. "Nefertiti" shows the quintet improvising on the melody and letting Williams display his aggressive style throughout. Davis's playing over this music has all the romantic elements of his earlier styles, but his melodic shapes are unique. The scalar approach has been modified, and intervals (like half-step chromatic motions) have become part of his language.

The Davis quintet toured Europe in the fall of 1967 and returned to the studio in December. The songs "Circle in the Round" and "Water on the Pond" signaled yet another new approach to Davis's music: ostinatos and drones, rock rhythms, complex bass lines doubled with a now-added guitar, and electric keyboards. By the spring of 1968, Davis had been in the studio twelve times (once with the Gil Evans Orchestra), and Columbia eventually released five albums from these sessions: *Miles in the Sky, Directions, Circle in the Round, Water Babies,* and *Filles de Kilimanjaro.* By the fall of 1968, both Hancock and Carter had left the group and been replaced by Chick Corea and Dave Holland. In September, this group finished the *Filles de Kilimanjaro* album. Its unique compositions such as "Frelon Brun," "Petits Machins," "Tout de Suite," and "Mademoiselle Mabry" touch the furthest reaches of jazz at the time.

The group now began to work not only in jazz clubs but at rock-oriented clubs and festivals, with Corea on the Fender Rhodes electric piano. Davis began collaborating with Joe Zawinul, and by February 18 and 20, 1969, this partnership had produced the *In a Silent Way* album, a collection of melodies and grooves that were assembled by producer Teo Macero from parts of performances into an album that created a mood and feeling in tune with the late 1960s. By March 1969 Jack DeJohnette had joined the group, replacing Tony Williams.

During three days in August 1969 with the help of Macero, Davis created a highly influential album that became the Rosetta stone for the jazz-fusion movement. Released in April 1970 as *Bitches Brew*, it changed jazz forever. Critics and fans now had a clear marker to show them what direction jazz was capable of heading in at the time, and several major bands had roots in these sessions: Weather Report, Herbie Hancock's Sextet, Return to Forever, and the Mahavishnu Orchestra. "Bitches Brew" and "Pharoah's Dance" are heavily edited collections of grooves. "Spanish Key" and "Sanctuary" retain some of the "live" sound of the band, and "Miles Runs the Voodoo Down" is reworked from live gigs into a deeper funky feeling. After this seminal album, Davis would document his bands and ideas in the studio less frequently.

A soundtrack to a boxing documentary, *Jack Johnson*, pushed Davis more into the rock world, with hard-edged grooves and a significant amount of editing. *Black Beauty* and *Live at Fillmore* captured the group live. In March 1970 Shorter left; he was replaced by Steve Grossman and later Gary Bartz. Davis added percussionist Airto Moreira to the band, and Keith Jarrett joined in May, giving Davis two incredible keyboard players. By August 1970 Corea and Holland had left the band to form the group Circle, and in early 1971 DeJohnette left. The album *Live/Evil*, recorded during this time of transition, mixed studio and live tracks but also signaled an end to the "jazz" period of Davis's recording career. He would soon hire R&B and funk players to contrast with the few jazz musicians who would remain.

Davis returned to the studio in June 1972 to record the *On the Corner* album. This recording is filled with postproduction techniques, massive overdubbing and echo, and a clap track. The music sounds like a cross between Sly Stone and Karlheinz Stockhausen. By this time, the Davis group consisted of Dave Liebman on saxes and flute, Pete Cosey and Reggie Lucas on guitar, Michael Henderson on electric bass, Al Foster on drums, and Mtume and Don Alias on percussion. The group did not perform music that resembled straight-ahead jazz in any way; the Davis sound during this time was characterized by long grooves ("Black Satin") and short melodic phrases. Twenty- to forty-minute vamps were not uncommon. Davis wanted to create and sustain a mood, and his band responded sympathetically.

This group stayed together until early 1976 (with Sonny Fortune replacing Liebman in 1974) and recorded the albums *In Concert, Dark Magus, Get Up With It* (which included the period masterpiece "He Loved Him Madly"), *Agharta*, and *Pangaea*. Their music was moody and dense and left many listeners at the time confused. Its emphasis was not on improvisation but on sustaining a mood or a feeling. Although Liebman or Fortune would often create spontaneous backgrounds that retained some jazz sensibility, Davis was heavily into the sonic possibilities of the wah-wah pedal and large amps.

Davis had all but lost his jazz audience and had never gotten over to the black mass audience he so longed for. Health problems led him to "retire" from recording and performing in 1976, and his hiatus lasted (except for a 1978 session with Larry Coryell) until 1980. His nephew Vincent Wilburn had formed an R&B band in Chicago and landed a Columbia recording contract. Davis was brought in as a producer, and soon he was inspired to go back into the studio. At first he used his nephew's band, but eventually, with the help of Liebman, he put together a new group: Bill Evans on reeds, Mike Stern on guitar, Marcus Miller on bass, Al Foster on drums, and Mino Cinelu on percussion. This new group appears on part of *The Man With the Horn*, where their performance on the track "Ursula" hints only so briefly at 4/4 jazz. As Davis's first new release since 1976, the album was greeted with mixed reactions, but Davis quickly became a festival attraction (and would remain one until his death), and his concerts sold out throughout the world.

Columbia quickly recorded his new group live (*We Want Miles*) and in the studio (*Star People*), and for the next few years Davis released albums on a regular schedule. In 1984 he had a hit single with a cover of Cyndi Lauper's "Time After Time." Columbia released *You're Under Arrest* in 1985 but kept his last major orchestral/acoustic work *Aura* (a 1985 collaboration with Palle Mikkelborg) unreleased for four years. Davis left Columbia in 1985 after recording for the label for thirty years. He still chose to play over long grooves, but the sound of the band was much clearer. There was a sparseness that distinguished this group from the 1972–76 band, and also much less mystery and more predictability.

When Davis signed with Warner Bros. Records, he entered his final recording phase. He had assembled a band that was more influenced by the rock singer-composer Prince than by any previous Davis band. The first project recorded for the new label touched on the idea of another great collaboration. *Tutu*, released in 1986, was composed and arranged by Marcus Miller and produced by Tommy LiPuma. Miller captured the essence of Davis as no one since Evans had. The team of Davis, Miller, and LiPuma did two more albums together, *Amandla* and the soundtrack *Siesta*. All three recordings echo the influence of the Davis-Evans collaborations; "Tutu," a beautiful song, sounds like it was written just for Miles. A collection of performances by Davis's working bands compiled from "board tapes" made during the eighties and nineties was released posthumously as *Live Around the World* by Warner Bros. in 1996; it featured Kenny Garrett and Rick Margitza on reeds, Adam Holzman, Robert Irving III, Deron Johnson, and Kei Akagi on keyboards, Foley on guitar, Richard Patterson and Benny Rietveld on bass, and Ricky Wellman on drums. Davis reconnected with Michel Legrand for the 1991 soundtrack album *Dingo*. (Davis also played a role in the film.) The last official album Davis was involved in was an experiment with hip-hop and rap music with Kool-Moe-B; released in 1992 as *Doo-Bop*, the recording actually sampled Davis's solos from 1985 and incorporated them into the hip-hop mix.

In July 1991, at the Montreux Jazz Festival, with a fifty-two-piece orchestra, Davis performed music from his three classic collaborations with Evans. A few days later, in Paris, Davis was honored by the French government and participated in a concert that reunited many of his sidemen, including Jackie McLean, Corea, Hancock, Foster, Zawinul, and Shorter. Upon his return from Europe in September, Davis became ill and entered the St. John's Hospital and Health Care Center in Santa Monica, California. On September 28, Miles Davis passed away. He was buried with his trumpets at the Woodlawn Cemetery in the Bronx, New York.

The Davis legacy is one that satisfies both the avid fan and the dedicated musician, but his influence goes beyond the world of music. With his gravel-toned voice, his eye for musical and social fashion, and his candid views on many subjects, he was a man whose talent and taste went beyond the musical world. Davis's music connects the swing era to the hip-hop and rap world, and his innovations and groundbreaking actions have inspired and influenced countless composers, arrangers, instrumentalists, and critics. The legacy of Miles Davis will continue to be held in high regard by musicians and fans all over the world.

Big Bands and Jazz Composing and Arranging After World War II

Doug Ramsey

When American servicemen left to fight World War II, the swing era was full of vigor. When they came home, it was dying. Jazz was no longer the nation's popular music, no longer mainly for dancing. Bebop was beginning to inform the music even of leaders who predated it. Yes, the swing era—that unprecedented congruence of quality and popularity—died a slow postwar death, but the big bands did not die with it.

Except for those maintained as museum pieces, big bands changed. The intricacies, rhythmic urgencies, and humor of bop were in the air. Even before the war ended, they insinuated themselves into the bands of Earl Hines, Cootie Williams, and Billy Eckstine. Soon, swing leaders like Benny Goodman, Duke Ellington, Harry James, Artie Shaw, Boyd Raeburn, Ray McKinley, Stan Kenton, Charlie Barnet, Woody Herman, and Count Basie found themselves hosts to an infectious new strain of jazz. Some embraced it, at least briefly (Herman, Raeburn, Shaw, McKinley, Kenton). Some absorbed and transformed it (Ellington, James, Barnet). Goodman tried bebop for a while and dropped it. Basie tolerated it. The tendency was away from dancers and toward listeners. You could dance, rapidly, to Goodman's

Dizzy Gillespie Orchestra, RCA Victor Studios, New York, August 22, 1947. Left to right: Milt Jackson (hidden), vibraphone; Raymond Orr, trumpet; Cecil Payne, baritone sax; Elmon Wright, trumpet; Bill Shepherd, trombone; James Moody, tenor sax; Dave Burns, trumpet; Howard Johnson, alto sax; Taswell Baird, trombone; Matthew McKay, trumpet; John Brown, alto sax; John Collins (hidden), guitar; John Lewis (hidden), piano; Joe Gayles, tenor sax; Ray Brown, bass; Gillespie, trumpet. Courtesy Frank Driggs Collection.

"Undercurrent Blues" (Capitol), but your terpsichorean concentration would be disturbed by the adventurism of Chico O'Farrill's arrangement and shattered by Doug Mettome's perfect bop trumpet solo. Dancing to Eddie Sauter's "Idiot's Delight" (RCA Victor, reissued on Smithsonian) for the Ray McKinley band would be all but impossible unless your dance were choreographed by Martha Graham.

Composers and arrangers who wrote for big bands from the mid-1940s on included a number who immersed themselves not only in the jazz tradition but in Stravinsky, Bartók, Ravel, and Debussy. The influence of modern European music affected the work of George Handy, Eddie Sauter, Billy Strayhorn, George Russell, Johnny Richards, Bill Holman, and Bill Russo, among others. Their sophisticated arrangements complemented the increased complexity of the art of jazz improvisation. Charlie Parker, Dizzy Gillespie, and Bud Powell took the solo to new levels. Their standards placed demands on musicians and created challenges for listeners. More than ever, jazz was a soloist's art. Under the cover of war and a two-year musicians' union recording ban, it had gone through a period of intense development. For the soldiers, sailors, and marines coming home, the music must have been shocking or, if they had big ears, exhilarating. To search for a parallel in classical music, you might imagine going to sleep to Brahms and awakening to hear, for the first time, Stravinsky.

Bop's harmonic intricacies changed jazz, but the music's fundamental characteristic remained, for coursing through it in the mid-forties was the rhythmic pulse that distinguishes jazz from other music and gave the swing era its name. The Count Basie band of the late thirties and early forties was the embodiment of swing. Centered in the rhythm section of Basie at the piano, guitarist Freddie Green, bassist Walter Page, and drummer Jo Jones, its irresistible impetus set a standard that has applied in jazz ever since. Whatever their other attributes, to one degree or another most of the big bands that followed aspired to Basie's quality of swing.

Woody Herman's band observed the Basie imperative, incorporated the new wave of bebop harmonic change and classical influences, and was one of the few to reach America's warriors. Herman, a leader since 1936, had begun remaking his band in 1943, bringing together by the end of 1944 a remarkable contingent of musicians that included drummer Dave Tough, trombonist Bill Harris, tenor saxophonist Flip Phillips, pianist and arranger Ralph Burns, trumpeter and arranger Neal Hefti, and the ebullient bassist Chubby Jackson. He reached an audience essential to the band's success by getting around the recording ban slapped on by James Petrillo, president of the American Federation of Musicians, in a dispute over pay for juke-box and radio play of records. Months before the ban ended, Herman made V-discs, recordings distributed only to the troops.

People in the service got a preview of the exciting Herman First Herd in pieces like "Apple Honey," "Northwest Passage," and "Caldonia." When they got home in 1945, they wanted more. The Herd was ready for them. With Jackson as head cheerleader and talent scout, Herman had attracted some of the most formidable young musicians in the country, gifted in technique and expression. "Apple Honey," "Bijou," "Your Father's Moustache," and "Blowin' Up a Storm" were performances of pulse-racing excitement that made the band—as trombonist Milt Bernhart puts it—"killers of the mid-'40s, the most thrilling bunch of musicians ever assembled." The band's popular success was reflected in sales of its Columbia records and its own sponsored network radio program. Its triumph was never to be repeated by any postwar big band, including Herman's Second Herd. That 1947–49 group, the so-called Four Brothers band, was a collection of brilliant musicians that did not capture the public's imagination in the way the First Herd did. Among the stars of the band were saxophonists Stan Getz, Zoot Sims, Al Cohn, and Serge Chaloff, trumpeters Shorty Rogers and Red Rodney, pianist Lou Levy, and trombonist Harris. In 1995 composer-arranger Johnny Mandel called the Second Herd "the best white band that ever played music." Herman continued to lead successful bands until a few months before his death in 1987.

Had it not been for the recording ban, Billy Eckstine's might have been the first big bop band to come to significant public attention. Organized in 1944 by Dizzy Gillespie and Budd Johnson, with adventuresome arrangements by Gillespie, Johnson, and Gerry Valentine, the band had superb musicianship and Eckstine's charisma as leader and singer. Sidemen included Charlie Parker, Miles Davis, Fats Navarro, Art Blakey, Gene Ammons, and Dexter Gordon. The girl singer was young Sarah Vaughan. Remembered as astonishing in live performance, after the Petrillo ban the Eckstine band was poorly recorded by small companies with little distribution. In 1947 Eckstine gave it up.

Boyd Raeburn never achieved commercial success either, but he was as important as Eckstine and Herman in putting into big band action the lessons of bebop. Raeburn debuted in the Chicago area in 1933, when he was twenty, at the helm of an ordinary dance band.

By 1944 he was catching up to the new music. Gillespie sat in with the band on several occasions. One of its recordings introduced his "Interlude," later called "A Night in Tunisia" (Jewell), with Dizzy as soloist. It was one more instance of Gillespie's effect as a catalyst in the transition from swing to bop. Raeburn attracted some of the best of the young bop musicians, among them Benny Harris, Earl Swope, Hal McKusick, Al Cohn, Oscar Pettiford, Shelly Manne, Lucky Thompson, and Serge Chaloff. One of the band's enthusiastic backers was Duke Ellington, who offered moral and financial support.

Composer-arranger George Handy introduced daring and density inspired in part by modern classical composers but mainly growing out of his own fertile creative impulse. Beginning late in 1945, Handy's arrangements made the Raeburn band an ever more adventurous outpost of the new music. Johnny Richards succeeded Handy in 1946. He was a fine arranger, sometimes an inspired one, but he lacked Handy's incandescent brilliance. Mired in drink and drugs, Handy never followed through on the promise of his writing for the Raeburn band. His breathtakingly difficult and very funny "The Bloos" for Norman Granz's *The Jazz Scene* (Verve) album of 1949 was his last masterpiece.

As early as 1942, Gillespie was paving the way for big band bop with arrangements like "Down Under" (Decca) for Herman. He created his big band model for Eckstine, then left in 1945 to form his own band. It lasted only a few months. Gillespie assembled a large group again in 1946 and this time kept it going for four years. He employed the veteran drummer Kenny Clarke and emerging stars like alto saxophonst Sonny Stitt, bassist Ray Brown, vibraharpist Milt Jackson, pianist John Lewis, and conga drummer Chano Pozo. Pozo helped Gillespie to establish an Afro-Cuban strain that has enriched jazz ever since. In addition to his own arrangements, Gillespie used Lewis, Tadd Dameron, and Walter Fuller to translate to sixteen pieces the blend of tumult and discipline that he and Parker pioneered in bop combos. Gillespie fared better than Eckstine in the studios, but recordings of the band (RCA, Prestige) give only glimpses of the excitement it generated. Gillespie's next big band, in the 1950s, was another important talent incubator. It developed trumpeter Lee Morgan, pianist Wynton Kelly, tenor saxophonist–composer Benny Golson, alto saxophonists Ernie Henry and Phil Woods, drummer Charli Persip, and arranger Melba Liston. With it, Gillespie toured parts of Asia, the Middle East, Eastern Europe, and South America under the auspices of the U.S. State Department.

Claude Thornhill was respected and successful even before he formed his first band in 1939. He was musical director for the Skinnay Ennis band and arranged the hit recording of "Loch Lomond" (Vocalion) for Maxine Sullivan. A pianist, Thornhill thought that a big band could reflect his concern with tone and touch. Once his organization got rolling, he proved his thesis with recordings for Columbia of "Snowfall," "Where or When," and other ballad arrangements distinguished by tonal depth and careful attention to dynamics, hardly hallmarks of most bands in the late thirties and early forties. He carried those qualities into up-tempo pieces as well. His 1941 "Portrait of a Guinea Farm" was a musicians' favorite for years. The next year, the flag-waving "Buster's Last Stand" introduced the work of arranger Gil Evans. After three years in the Navy, Thornhill emerged in 1946 to reestablish the band with many of his original sidemen and Evans, who contributed arrangements that captivated both laymen and musicians. Evans accommodated the urgencies of bebop to Thornhill's mandate for rich textures and dynamics, without compromising either. A young trumpet player named Miles Davis was especially taken with the Thornhill-Evans sound. Later, in two periods of close collaboration, Evans and Davis extended Thornhill's concepts and produced some of the most influential music of the twentieth century. As for Thornhill, both the ethereal and swinging aspects of his band continued until 1948 with fine musicians like saxophonist Lee Konitz, trumpeter Red Rodney, bassist Joe Shulman, drummer Billy Exiner, and singer Fran Warren, whose "A Sunday Kind of Love" with Thornhill made her famous. According to big band historian George Simon, Thelonious Monk said Thornhill's was "the only really good big band I've heard in years." Thornhill's bands of the fifties and sixties were not successes.

Following the war, most of the bands that dominated popular music before 1941 stayed in business in a declining market, some with more success than others. With dancing on the downswing, listeners did not take up the economic slack. Veterans raising families and buying houses did not have budgets for much live entertainment. Even in a recessionary period it became increasingly expensive to transport, board, and feed fifteen or sixteen musicians. The musicians' union introduced another recording ban in 1948, and in that year television sets began to move into American homes in numbers that decreased the sizes of audiences in clubs and concert halls. Additionally, as Gene Lees pointed out in his essay "Pavilion in the Rain," the automobile was driving out public transportation. As streetcar lines and trolleys disappeared, it became difficult or impossible for those without cars to reach the large suburban or country halls where big bands so often played. Nonetheless, Ellington, Basie, Shaw, Barnet, Goodman, and James held on, and Kenton was able to increase his audience.

In the immediate postwar period, Ellington's popularity was high. He was riding on the immense success and quality of the music of his great bands of the early forties. For a variety of reasons, however, the music he produced in 1945 and 1946 was not at that level, at least in part because he had lost so many musicians who inspired him to write for their unique talents. Cootie Williams, Ben Webster, and Barney Bigard were long gone. Saxophonist Otto Hardwicke and cornetist Rex Stewart left. The incomparable trombonist Tricky Sam Nanton died. Ellington was recycling his previous music, and many of his new pieces for recording were lightweight. Exceptions like "The Clothed Woman," "Air-conditioned Jungle," and a reworking of "Take the 'A' Train" with singer Betty Roché were few. In 1949 Juan Tizol and Fred Guy moved on. In 1951 Johnny Hodges left to form his own band and did not return until four years later. Hodges was Ellington's greatest loss since the death of Jimmy Blanton. Ellington continued until 1950 the series of annual Carnegie Hall concerts that introduced *Black, Brown and Beige* (Prestige) in 1943. Other extended works, including *Liberian Suite* (Prestige), debuted at Carnegie. The long-playing record's emergence in the 1950s encouraged further long-form works by Ellington, among them *A Tone Parallel to Harlem, Such Sweet Thunder, Suite Thursday*, and *The Far East Suite* (RCA). He remained the standard of excellence to which all jazz composers and arrangers were compared, even in periods when his band's performance was uninspired.

Ellington never joined the bop movement, although bebop had transformed jazz. He and Billy Strayhorn occasionally bowed in its direction in their writing or on rare occasions when he used arrangements from others, notably Gerald Wilson's reworking of "Perdido" in 1960. His later bands included soloists like Clark Terry, Willie Cook, and Paul Gonsalves who incorporated massive bop influences, but their work was in his context, never vice versa. Ellington's genius demanded that his own creativity, not the image of others', direct his music. Until his death in 1974, he maintained his band as a reflection of that genius. All of the Ellington recordings mentioned are on Columbia unless otherwise noted.

At its best, Basie's band of 1937–41, sometimes called his Old

Testament band, was the epitome, the essence, of loose, loping, re-laxed swing. Its spirit came from Basie and the so-called All-American rhythm section, but also from the camaraderie and wit of Lester Young, Dicky Wells, Harry Edison, Buck Clayton, and its other horn men. It was rooted in the blues, and many of its best arrangements were created *en banc* as head arrangements. Over a period of years, the band transmuted into the New Testament version, called by some with a smile and some with a sneer a "swing machine." Slowly, some of Basie's laid-back quality gave way to the discipline of formal ar-rangements, brassier brass, louder drumming, greater technique. The swing never stopped. The band never lost its blues heart. But the music that always demanded foot tapping and head bobbing became less Kansas City home-made, more New York machine-tooled. Per-haps the watershed recording, after which the transition became a divide, was "Rambo" (Columbia), arranged by and starring as soloist in 1946 the young bop trombonist J. J. Johnson. Johnson's virtuosity is unquestionable, his arrangement ingenious. But they are distinct and far removed from Dicky Wells in "Dickie's [*sic*] Dream" or Lester Young in "Pound Cake" (both Columbia). The old rhythm section ethos is mostly intact, but it is in a wrestling match with the ar-rangement and the soloist. Through the forties and into the early fifties, the Basie band tended toward dryness, even abrasiveness. Eco-nomics forced Basie to cut back to a combo for a couple of years. After he regrouped in 1951, arrangers like Frank Foster, Neal Hefti, and Ernie Wilkins helped lead him to an approach based on smooth-ness and bottom-to-top power. Foster's "Blues in Hoss' Flat" (Rou-lette) is a prime example of the style. Quincy Jones, Billy Byers, and Sammy Nestico built on that tradition. In Basie's later years, the style jelled. Although there were often good soloists—including saxophon-ists Foster and Frank Wess, trumpeter Joe Newman, cornetist Thad Jones, trombonist Al Grey, and singer Joe Williams—the ensemble was the thing. It became a magnificent set piece, perfectly preserved and swinging in place.

There was a postwar slump in his popularity, and Harry James nearly gave up. He disbanded in 1946, then a few months later re-grouped. Rejuvenated, he never returned to the schmaltz that made him rich in the forties. Until shortly before he died in 1983 he led a band with spirit and swing akin to that of the Basie band he ad-mired, using arrangements by members of Basie's corps of arrangers, including Neal Hefti, Thad Jones, and Ernie Wilkins. Some of those arrangements had substantial elements of bop. His trumpet skills and musicianship as great as ever, James proved himself one of the few swing era soloists able to negotiate bebop's harmonic challenges. His improvisation in 1967 on Jones's "That's Thad" (Dot, reissued on Smithsonian) is impressive evidence of his undiminished ability and his band's drive.

Following his Navy service, Artie Shaw reorganized in 1944 and at the end of the war was leading a band with a phenomenal roster of instrumental and arranging talent. His clarinet playing was inspired. Shaw's example and leadership and the atmosphere of the band stimulated fellow trumpeter Roy Eldridge, the former Barnet pianist Dodo Marmarosa, and guitarist Barney Kessel. They, bassist Morris Rayman, and drummer Lou Fromm were also in Shaw's celebrated Gramercy Five, which, despite its name, was a sextet. Eddie Sauter contributed brilliant work to this edition of the Shaw band. His arrangements on "Summertime" and "The Maid With the Flaccid Air," considered experimental at the time, are remarkable for their undated inventiveness. The band's Bluebird and Musicraft recordings also contain superior work by Ray Conniff, Buster Harding, and Jimmy Mundy. Conniff, a swing trombonist featured in Shaw's prewar band, was an arranger with his ear to the ground. The 1944–45 band was not a bop organization, but Conniff hinted at the dialect in his "Lucky Number" (Bluebird). At the end of 1946, Shaw broke up the band in order to study music and concentrate on classical performance. He regrouped in late 1949, when the big band business was at its nadir, filling the band with beboppers. Among them were Zoot Sims, Al Cohn, Herbie Steward, Jimmy Raney, and Don Fagerquist. Shaw and Conniff wrote arrangements. He got others from Cohn, Johnny Mandel, George Russell, Tadd Dameron, and Gene Roland—among the most accomplished of the new writers. The band lasted three months. Shaw stopped playing in 1954. In 1983 he organized a big band that still tours occasionally under the leadership of clarinetist Dick Johnson, but Shaw has refused all pleas that he again take up his instrument.

Like Ellington's, Benny Goodman's stored momentum kept him popular after the war. His book continued to have superb arrangements by Eddie Sauter, Fletcher Henderson, Mel Powell, and others, but the quality of his band declined. Although future stars, including Stan Getz, Zoot Sims, and Kai Winding, passed through Goodman's outfit, it became increasingly difficult for him to attract and hold the best of the new generation of musicians. An exciting improviser, but never profound in the harmonic sense, Goodman was uncomfortable with bop. Yet, he admired some bop players and in 1948 experimented with the new idiom in a sextet including tenor saxophonist Wardell Gray and trumpeter Fats Navarro. The next year, continuing the sextet as a nucleus, he formed a big band centered in bebop. It had brilliant soloists, but Goodman never adapted to bop. The organization lasted less than a year.

Charlie Barnet was devoted to Ellington and Basie, but as early as 1943 he demonstrated his openness to new ideas with "The Moose" (Decca), Ralph Burns's adventurous setting for the virtuosity of pianist Dodo Marmarosa. The ideas percolating through jazz from bebop intrigued Barnet. In contrast to Goodman, he accepted them enthusiastically and applied them to his own playing, but the bop band he established in 1949 lasted no longer than Goodman's. His *Big Band 1967* (Creative World, reissued on Mobile Fidelity) was the last recording not only of Barnet but of alto saxophonist Willie Smith. With arrangements by Billy Byers and Bill Holman, it was one of Barnet's best latter-day albums.

Just as often as Stan Kenton's jazz instincts were overridden by his dedication to weight and volume, his importance is underestimated. Beginning in 1945, when he made Pete Rugolo his chief arranger, Kenton's band provided a workshop and outlet for some of the music's most inventive writers and best players. Anita O'Day, Art Pepper, Conte Candoli, Lee Konitz, Shelly Manne, Maynard Ferguson, Kai Winding, and Zoot Sims were among the soloists who developed or were featured with Kenton. Although Rugolo was capable of bombast that met Kenton's specifications, he also produced arrangements of sensitivity and complexity that reflected his apprenticeship with Darius Milhaud. Kenton encouraged Bob Graettinger, Shorty Rogers, Gerry Mulligan, Bill Russo, Bill Holman, and Johnny Richards, among others. The broad range represented by those composer-arrangers—from Holman's and Mulligan's centrism to Graettinger's monumental density—resulted over the years in a repertoire whose richness was exceeded only by Ellington's. The band's Capitol recordings include Graettinger's *City of Glass*, Richards's *Cuban Fire*, and the influential *Contemporary Concepts* album. Many of the best works of the Kenton band of the fifties are reissued in *Stan Kenton: The Holman and Russo Charts* (Mosaic).

In a survey chapter, it is impossible to do justice to all of the big bands and arrangers who have made substantial contributions in the past fifty-five years. Among the full-time bands that cannot be overlooked are those of Gene Krupa and the gifted co-leaders Eddie Sauter and Bill Finegan. In an important sense, although the drummer was its focus and it had gifted soloists like Roy Eldridge, Red Rodney, Don Fagerquist, and Frank Rosolino, Krupa's was an arrangers' band. George Williams, and especially Gerry Mulligan, made it a modern outfit with which to reckon. Even Mulligan's more conservative 1946–47 scores for Krupa, like "Disc Jockey Jump" (Columbia), were at the leading edge of jazz writing and had significant influence on developing arrangers, including Bill Holman.

Their 1952 novelty hit "Doodletown Fifers" (RCA) led to a five-year life for the Sauter-Finegan Orchestra, during which the leaders created a book of arrangements still admired for their depth, colors, textures, and humor. Their book encompassed *concertante* pieces but also full-out jazz arrangements such as "The Loop" and the moody ballad "Nina Never Knew," with a classic vocal by Joe Mooney. Despite his brilliant twenty-year history, some of Sauter's most impressive writing was still ahead of him in scores supporting Stan Getz, the album *Focus* (Verve), and the sound track of the Arthur Penn motion picture *Mickey One* (Verve).

Mulligan was one of a group of young writers and players who in the late 1940s assembled in the Manhattan basement room of Gil Evans, their guru, to exchange ideas. Like Miles Davis, Mulligan was enchanted with Evans's work for Claude Thornhill. Evans and Mulligan wrote for Davis's nine-piece group, as did John Lewis and Johnny Carisi, with the Thornhill sound as their basic model. The band's 1949 and 1950 records, later collected as *The Birth of the Cool* (Capitol), became one of the most influential bodies of music in jazz. Their concepts led to the Evans-Davis collaborations that resulted in *Miles Ahead, Porgy and Bess,* and *Sketches of Spain* (Columbia), Mulligan's 1953 *Tentette* (Capitol), and his Concert Jazz Band (Verve, Eurojazz).

In addition to Mulligan, contributors to the CJB's book included seasoned writers like Bob Brookmeyer, Bill Holman, George Russell, Johnny Mandel, and Al Cohn. As Bill Kirchner emphasized in his notes for *Big Band Renaissance* (Smithsonian), the arranging surprise of the Mulligan concert band was Gary McFarland. Twenty-seven years old and new in New York in 1960, McFarland took to Mulligan his pieces "Weep" and "Chuggin'." Mulligan and his musicians embraced those ingenious arrangements, which marked the beginning of an important career that ended when McFarland died in 1971. His reworking of the score of *How to Succeed in Business Without Really Trying* (Verve) was a masterpiece. It has been reissued in a compact disc with

Brookmeyer's *Gloomy Sunday and Other Bright Moments*, another high point of the yeasty New York jazz scene of the early 1960s.

Brookmeyer combines the technical skills of a classical writer with the risk-taking and humor that characterize his virtuoso valve trombone improvisations. His arrangements for Mulligan, his own studio recordings, and the Thad Jones–Mel Lewis Jazz Orchestra set standards for other arrangers and composers. Brookmeyer is in a modern jazz arranging elite with Evans, Mulligan, Holman, Cohn, Thad Jones, Mandel, Russell, Billy Byers, Quincy Jones, Oliver Nelson, Manny Albam, and Gerald Wilson. Some of his works of the 1980s and 1990s seem closer to the modern European classical avant-garde than to mainstream jazz, but in "Celebration" (Challenge), his 1994 tribute to Mulligan, he clearly demonstrates his mastery of his native idiom.

Albam's suite *The Blues Is Everybody's Business* (Coral) and three works of George Russell must be mentioned among the composing and arranging highlights of the second half of the twentieth century. Russell had a profound impact on big band music in the 1960s. Convinced that jazz had to grow on its own terms, from within, Russell developed a pantonal system of composition and improvisation that concentrated on chromaticism. His celebrated *All About Rosie* of 1957 (Columbia) was an early big band expression of Russell's Lydian Concept of Tonal Organization. Two later recordings, *New York, N.Y* (1958) and *Jazz in the Space Age* (1960), contained some of the most adventurous writing of the second half of the century, with studio bands that included soloists of the stature of John Coltrane, Bill Evans, Bob Brookmeyer, and Art Farmer.

Charles Mingus's writing for big bands was eccentric, unmistakably personal, and often viscerally exciting. Sloppy and unfinished though it is, his *Epitaph* (Columbia) has brilliant moments. His 1957 "Revelations" (Columbia) has nothing but.

Through the fifties, particularly after Bill Haley, Elvis Presley, and the advent of rock-and-roll in 1955, the few remaining working big bands struggled to stay alive. By the time the Beatles hit in 1964, of the classic big bands only Ellington, Herman, Basie, Kenton, and James were able to maintain full-time schedules. Increasingly, big band music became the territory of arrangers, not leaders. In Los Angeles and New York, the centers of jazz, part-time bands developed as outlets for players and writers. In Boston, Herb Pomeroy's band fulfilled that function, and in Washington, D.C., in the fifties, there was THE Orchestra, led by Joe Timer and Willis Conover.

Four important bands that managed varying degrees of employment were led by Maynard Ferguson, Buddy Rich, Terry Gibbs, and Don Ellis. Ferguson, Rich, and Gibbs stayed within the modern mainstream. Ellis roamed through the challenging territory of polyphony and of time signatures as unorthodox as 13/8 and 33/8.

Gil Evans, regarded by many as the most gifted of all jazz arrangers but Ellington, never had his own full-time band. For three decades, he did his magical work with specially chosen musicians in studios or concert halls or with his once-a-week band at a New York nightclub. The evidence of his genius with shimmering vertical harmonies, moving lines, and mysterious voicings is in a body of recordings in addition to the collaborations with Davis. Some of the essential ones: *Gil Evans and Ten* (Prestige), *New Bottle, Old Wine* and *Great Jazz Standards* (Pacific Jazz), *The Individualism of Gil Evans* (Verve), *Out of the Cool* (Impulse), and *Where Flamingos Fly* (Artists House, reissued on A&M). Evans's encounters with rock music, including his album of Jimi Hendrix tunes (RCA), are highly regarded by a few musicians and critics but seem to this one insubstantial compared with the work mentioned above.

With Evans in the pantheon of modern arrangers, but with a linear style quite different from Evans's vertical one, is Bill Holman. Holman wrote notable music for virtually every first-rank big band except Ellington's. Kenton, Basie, Herman, Barnet, Shaw, Mulligan, Buddy Rich, and Maynard Ferguson all sought him out. Rarely, in the fifties and sixties, he assembled bands of his own for recording. *In a Jazz Orbit* (Andex, reissued on V.S.O.P.) is one of his best from the fifties. In the eighties and nineties he has maintained a Los Angeles band of talented and fiercely loyal sidemen and a rigorous rehearsal schedule. Holman's *A View From the Side* and *Brilliant Corners: The Music of Thelonious Monk* (JVC) contain examples of his masterly ability to weave simple linear ideas into complex tapestries of harmonic depth, hung on compelling rhythmic frameworks.

The Thad Jones–Mel Lewis Jazz Orchestra was a part-time band that developed into an institution and a pervasive influence because it had great players, a spirited collective personality, and writing by Jones. He was a trumpet, cornet, and flugelhorn artist with an ear for harmony that led him to distinctiveness as a soloist and a composer-arranger. Almost from the moment it debuted at New York's Village Vanguard on a Monday night in February 1966, the Jones-Lewis band was the talk of the jazz world. A generation of aspiring jazz writers found new heights to try for when they heard

Jones arrangements like "Cherry Juice" (A&M Horizon), "A Child Is Born," and "A-That's Freedom" and Brookmeyer's arrangements on "ABC Blues" and Fats Waller's "Willow Tree" (all Solid State, reissued on Mosaic). Many of the big bands that followed after the deaths of the leaders (Jones in 1986, Lewis in 1990) emulated Jones-Lewis and used its aesthetic for their own departures. The Vanguard Jazz Orchestra continues to this day. In a 1997 album, *Lickety Split* (New World Records), its pianist, Jim McNeely, demonstrates in a stunningly personal way that Thad Jones's arranging and composing legacy is a force in music as the century ends.

Three of the best part-time bands are led by Ed Palermo, John Fedchock, and Maria Schneider. Schneider sharpened her talent in studies with Brookmeyer and Evans. She shows promise of approaching and perhaps matching their achievements. Her first compact disc, *Evanescence* (Enja), was one of the most important arranger debuts in years. Trumpeters Wynton Marsalis and Jon Faddis direct the Lincoln Center Jazz Orchestra and the Carnegie Hall Jazz Band, respectively. In Washington, D.C., the respected composer-arranger David Baker guides another important repertory group, the Smithsonian Jazz Masterworks Orchestra. The pianist Toshiko Akiyoshi has written music of substance for many years for a band co-led by her husband Lew Tabackin. Sun Ra, his quirky vibrance, and his Solar Arkestra are gone, but Muhal Richard Abrams's and Carla Bley's bands scout the far fringes of jazz.

In Los Angeles, the veterans Gerald Wilson, Bob Florence, and Tom Talbert continue to turn out stimulating work and manage to maintain bands to play and record it. Fine bands in other parts of the United States include Bill Russo's Chicago Jazz Ensemble and a scattering of groups in New Orleans, Seattle, Columbus, Cleveland, Dallas, and other cities. Bands in the U.S. military—the Air Force's Airmen of Note, the Navy Commodores—often produce surprisingly good, decidedly unmilitary, music. Toronto boasts a superior big band headed by a gifted writer, Rob McConnell. In Europe, Holland's Metropole Orchestra, although it exists at state expense to play all kinds of music, does impressive jazz work. State radio orchestras in Germany and Scandinavia often commission American composer-arrangers including Holman, Brookmeyer, and the increasingly impressive Alan Broadbent. Other European bands that have made an international impression are the Vienna Art Orchestra, the Kenny Clarke–Francy Boland Big Band (a 1961–73 all-star ensemble of Europeans and American expatriates), and those led by Ted Heath, John Dankworth, George Gruntz, and Willem Breuker.

Without question, the big band is alive. It is unlikely ever again to dominate popular music, but its future as a medium for serious artistic effort seems assured.

It is unfortunate that space in this brief overview of big bands since World War II does not allow examination of many that deserve it, including those of Neal Hefti, Chubby Jackson, Quincy Jones, Duke Pearson, Roy Porter, Frank Capp–Nat Pierce, Louie Bellson, Benny Carter, Tom Pierson, Doc Severinsen's Tonight Show Band, Jeff Hamilton–John Clayton, Billy May, Bill Potts, Bob Belden, Clare Fischer, Gustav Brom, and Johnny Richards. The reader is encouraged to seek out their recordings.

Thelonious Monk and Charles Mingus

Brian Priestley

A s Scott DeVeaux has pointed out, much of what became bebop evolved from the private jam sessions of the 1930s. Hence the prevalence in the bop era of the theme-solo-solo-solo-theme format, which also came to dominate not only the Chicago-style wing of the traditional revival but, in due course, the 1950s and 1960s swing-mainstream revival. Because of the huge influence of bebop, many comparative subtleties that were part of the fabric of prebop music seemed for a while all but lost.

Bebop made considerable demands on performers' rhythmic, melodic, and harmonic virtuosity and, in the hands of its leading figures, brought these to a new peak of development. But many of the boppers themselves, having conquered its challenges, demonstrated a certain dissatisfaction with its limitations. Charlie Parker in the 1950s espoused first strings and then a woodwind-and-vocal ensemble, and also expressed a desire to study modern "classical" composition, because of his stated feeling that he had achieved everything he could within the bebop style.

In the case of Dizzy Gillespie, his restlessness was perhaps mixed with nostalgia for certain aspects of the swing era big band setting in which he made his debut a full decade before the successful completion of the bebop "revolution." His own classic compositions of the mid-1940s, including those on which he collaborated with Parker, frequently contained complex introductions and codas, while his big band originals also sported written backgrounds for soloists and textural contrasts from one section to another within a single piece. Although Gillespie later capitalized on the combination of bop with Afro-Caribbean musics, he still maintained this type of structural interest, even when the material itself was comparatively slight.

Two key musicians of the same generation, as well as showing the influence of the swing era and even earlier styles, had a significant effect on what came after the heyday of bebop. However, possibly because Thelonious Monk and Charles Mingus both played rhythm-section instruments, neither was widely recognized as either an important bandleader or an influential composer until a dozen years after Gillespie. Indeed, despite what differentiates them, Monk and Mingus have many things in common, some of which it may be useful to summarize.

Monk was born in the same month as Gillespie and, though much more active in small groups, had short big band stints with Cootie Williams, Lucky Millinder, Andy Kirk, and with Gillespie; before this, he had considerable experience playing gospel music in his formative years. Mingus, nearly five years younger than Dizzy and two years younger than Parker, was profoundly influenced by gospel (though he never played it professionally) and worked briefly in the bands of Louis Armstrong, Lionel Hampton, and Duke Ellington. In addition, both musicians were great admirers of Duke's best work.

Perhaps thanks to the example of Ellington, Monk and Mingus each made his reputation in the late 1950s by playing largely their own works, when it was still more common to include a number of popular standards. Each of them had a performing style on his own instrument that was to some extent at odds with the accepted approach of the day and became an essential ingredient of their composing style. They were each notoriously intolerant of sidemen who found either the music or the personality of its composer difficult to handle, and, though both had a well-developed sense of humor readily discernible in their creations, both suffered periods of severe depression.

Of course, there are also significant differences, which should be noted here. At the personal level Monk was taciturn, except with very close friends (and sometimes even with them). Mingus, on the other

Thelonious Monk, Bee Hive, Chicago, 1955. Photo: Frank Malcolm. Courtesy Frank Driggs Collection.

hand, was a living definition of volubility, expressing his opinions about everything to anyone who would listen. This contrast too is reflected in their music, for Monk's impressive dedication to the fine detail of his idiosyncratic method was at first perceived as a form of tunnel vision, until it became evident that the method had a wider relevance. Initial perceptions of Mingus were rather that he worked in a number of different styles, and it was only gradually realized that the input of Ellington, bebop, swing, gospel, and other elements had been transformed by Mingus into a new and influential dialect.

Although born in North Carolina, Thelonious Monk was brought up in New York from the age of five, living in the San Juan Hill area, where Lincoln Center now stands. The first highlight of his playing career was touring nationally with the show of a singing evangelist, which, among other things, enabled him to meet in Kansas City pianist-composer Mary Lou Williams, who later became a mentor to him. He was then probably in his late teens, and we have no indication of how he sounded playing gospel music (except to note that he later recorded two well-known hymns in a fairly conventional interpretation). By this time, however, he had already accompanied his mother's singing in church and played small local jazz gigs, as well as spending much time admiring and hanging out with leading pianists of the poststride school, including Art Tatum.

When in late 1940 Monk began a couple of years in the house quartet at Minton's Playhouse, he was stimulated by the group's leader, drummer Kenny Clarke, and began to refine his style. Through the Monday "celebrity nights" he met many famous musicians and some ambitious young experimentalists, such as Gillespie, Parker, and Charlie Christian. Although contemporary live recordings of both Gillespie and Parker were done at Monroe's Uptown House without Monk, he is heard (distantly but recognizably) with Christian and (more audibly) on tracks with trumpeter Joe Guy and others. In 1944 he worked in the band of Coleman Hawkins, whose recording "Flyin' Hawk" (Joe Davis/Prestige) shows that Monk was already utterly individual and explains why Hawkins had to field criticism for employing such an "incompetent" pianist.

Although Monk was by this time a mentor to the young Bud Powell, his own style differed considerably from bebop. His improvisation was certainly linear but quite terse and riff-oriented, with unexpected silences and rhythmic displacement of repeated phrases. He frequently simulated the tonal distortions possible on a horn by sounding two notes simultaneously (either a third apart or a semitone, in the manner of blues pianists), but he also made allusions to the whole-tone scale and other more angular note choices. Some of this quirky mixture recalled the pianism of Duke Ellington—a link acknowledged by both parties—and it carried over into Monk's early compositions. "Epistrophy," cowritten with Kenny Clarke, and "'Round Midnight" were already documented by Cootie Williams's band, while the next couple of years saw the premieres of "Hackensack" (aka "Rifftide"), "Stuffy" (a.k.a. "Stuffy Turkey"), and "I Mean You"—all recorded by Hawkins after Monk left his group—along with "52nd Street Theme" as done by Gillespie and "Off Minor" by Powell.

The enthusiasm of the Blue Note record company finally led to Monk making three sessions under his own leadership in the fall of 1947, although slow sales meant that release of the material was spread over several years. In these sessions, with a sextet, a trio, and a quintet (all including the exemplary Art Blakey on drums), Monk demonstrates further developments in his playing. His extended solo on the up-tempo "Thelonious" (Blue Note) includes an allusion to the stride-piano style, by then seen as old-fashioned even by swing musicians but used uninhibitedly and creatively by Monk, especially in ballads such as "Ruby, My Dear." The exposition of the latter also employs chordal fill-in phrases that illustrate how the orchestral conception of his arrangements differs from his more linear improvisation, as does Monk's own first recording of "'Round Midnight," arranged so that his piano takes the lead with alto and trumpet being largely accompanimental.

The thematic phrase of "Humph" is built on the whole-tone scale, yet the way the same phrase is reused in the bridge (an idea typical of many Monk pieces) is redolent of the call-and-response of swing and even gospel. Then again, the main use of the phrase in the A sections is underpinned by a rapid movement through the key-cycle popularized by Tatum and by saxist Don Byas, for instance on Gillespie's recording of "52nd Street Theme." (First put on disc in a version of "I Got Rhythm" by the obscure pianist Garnet Clark, it was a concept Monk returned to on later records such as "Rhythm-a-Ning" but which was incorporated in the Gershwin song "Nice Work if You Can Get It"—a number already performed by Monk at Minton's as well as for Blue Note.) A comparably rapid but chromatic chord movement is heard in the bridge of "Well You Needn't," which, following the example of a 1954 cover version by Miles Davis, is usually played incorrectly.

There is much more of interest in the 1947 recordings, and two succeeding sessions are especially valuable for the leader's accompaniments. These were fairly conventional in 1944, but now, with the vibraphone of Milt Jackson a featured front-line instrument, Monk gets an equally ringing tone from sparse chords dropped in the most unexpected places. "Misterioso" from 1948 and 1951's "Straight No Chaser" (both Blue Note) gain much of their spice from the percussive interplay between Jackson and Monk and represent the latter's first recorded playing on the blues sequence. In addition, the first session's version of "I Mean You" has the pianist using a glissando on the black notes, an effect he favored at the time and later sometimes replaced by using his right forearm on the keys. The same piece includes a written introduction reused as an interlude and a coda, where it is treated as a three-and-a-half-bar phrase, while the 1951 "Criss Cross" is built on examples of Monk's use of rhythmic displacement—not only in its opening phrase but in the eight-bar bridge, which is heard as 3+3+2.

The month after the "Straight No Chaser"/"Criss Cross" session, Monk and Bud Powell had a run-in with narcotics agents, following which Monk served a two-month sentence and found himself banned from performing in New York clubs. Work had never been plentiful; now, despite invitations to perform in Paris in 1954 and Chicago in 1955, it became virtually nonexistent. But, thanks to his single-mindedness and the practical support of his mother and his wife Nellie, he continued to compose and make recordings, winning a three-year contract with Prestige, then moving to the even newer Riverside company. The latter's commitment to the long-playing album, and their canny packaging of Monk's supposedly "difficult" music, worked in happy combination with his public unavailabilty to garner considerable interest when he returned to nightclub work in 1957.

In the first half of the 1950s he had rehearsed and recorded with the young Sonny Rollins, when the latter was beginning to make a reputation in Miles Davis's band, and now he formed a quartet including John Coltrane, of whom the same was true. The impact of live performances by this group was compared by fellow musicians to that of Parker and Gillespie twelve years earlier, yet Monk was already an established force and Coltrane still discovering himself. The stark contrast between them is illustrated by the most striking of their few recordings together, "Trinkle Tinkle," heard on both Jazzland/OJC (studio version) and Blue Note (live). The pianist had a self-contained style based on detailed examination and weighing of minute musical elements—a significant influence on Rollins—while the effusive Trane made vastly different use of the implication of Monk's methods.

When the tenor player rejoined Davis, his intensity was emulated more entertainingly by Johnny Griffin, who was replaced the following year by Charlie Rouse. Rouse had recorded with pianist-composer Tadd Dameron in the late 1940s, and his more succinct style initially seemed well suited to Monk's music but, in a working relationship of some eleven years, proved severely limited by Rouse's imagination. Monk himself went from strength to strength as an improviser during this period, but, like the diminishing quality of his bass and drum accompanists, his compositional output became sparse. Some of the few new items premiered in the 1960s are laconic to the point of parody, such as "Bright Mississippi" or "Oska T," while only "Raise Four" and "Green Chimneys" (all Columbia) are worthy of mention alongside the early works.

This lessening of creativity, as Monk moved toward his half century, served as a prelude to his withdrawal into depression during the late 1960s and early 1970s, coinciding with the music industry's infatuation with the "rock explosion." Aside from two 1971–72 international tours with an all-star assemblage containing Gillespie and Blakey, which led to a Monk retrospective recorded in London, he hardly performed at all during the last decade of his life. Living under the financial and emotional protection of the Baroness Pannonica (Nica) de Koenigswarter, he evaded the fate of many players of his and earlier generations—that of going through the motions in public as often as possible, because of never having earned enough to retire.

In retrospect, a few works of the 1950s have multinoted themes that illustrate how close Monk was to bebop, yet how far from it: "Trinkle Tinkle" (first recorded in 1952 in a trio performance for Prestige/OJC), "Four in One," and "Skippy" (both Blue Note), which use space far less than other Monk tunes. "Four in One" bases its A section on the chords of "Please Don't Talk About Me When I'm Gone," while "Skippy" relies on a fast-moving "Humph"-like sequence actually derived from the pianist's reharmonization of "Tea for Two" (only later recorded on Riverside/OJC). Conversely, his continued reference to the directness of the blues tradition is heard on the popular "Blue Monk" (Prestige/OJC), "Blues Five Spot," and the unaccompanied "Functional" (both Riverside/OJC).

Monk's underlying simplicity, even when seemingly off-center, was one of the main inspirations for the eventual reaction against bebop. The most dramatic illustration is perhaps "Friday the 13th" (Prestige/OJC), a theme and countermelody occupying a mere four bars over a chordal vamp repeating every two bars. Similarly, such numbers as "Little Rootie Tootie" and "Locomotive" have A sections (nominally based on "I Got Rhythm") which actually imply a complete absence of chordal movement for eight bars, as do the B sections of "Monk's Dream" and "We See." It is perhaps no coincidence that Miles Davis's first piece of which the same could be said, the 1954 "Swing Spring," was prepared for his one record session with Monk at the piano (all five tracks are on Prestige/OJC).

Another aspect of Monk's eventual influence is the seeming freedom of several themes from the metrical regularity of earlier music, with the exception of folk-blues. "Criss Cross" has already been mentioned, while "Trinkle Tinkle" has a theme that is complete after six bars followed by a drum break which, in the Prestige/OJC version, fills the remaining two bars of the A section—while, for the two versions with Coltrane, it is only a bar and a half. The normal AABA chorus structure of "Comin' on the Hudson" (Riverside/OJC) has sections of five bars, five, three and a half, and five respectively.

Something similar is true of the remarkable "Brilliant Corners" (Riverside/OJC), with its chorus structure of A(8 bars)/B(7)/A1(7); additionally, it has alternate choruses at twice the tempo, an innovation maintained throughout the solos and rarely attempted by anyone subsequently. (The pianist Bill Evans did so, in his own and the Miles Davis recordings of "Blue in Green," which both have sections at twice the opening tempo and then four times the opening tempo.) The implied metric freedom of thematic material was surely an inspiration to Ornette Coleman, who like Miles was a self-confessed admirer of Monk. "Brilliant Corners" also necessitates that the sidemen should bear in mind the theme as a base for their improvisation, rather than merely running the chord changes. This practice, common in early jazz, was considered highly desirable by Monk, with an influence first on Sonny Rollins, later on Ornette, and also on much more recent generations.

Many of the same developments in jazz of the 1950s and 1960s were equally affected by the work of Charles Mingus, despite the fact that his background differed from Monk's and his own music was equally individualistic. Born on an army base in Arizona, Mingus was brought up from only a few months later in the Watts section of Los Angeles.

After an unsuccessful attempt to learn the trombone and more fruitful lessons on the cello, he was already aware of Ellington, swing, gospel, and some European art music by the time he switched to the double-bass in his mid-teens. This was done in order to take part in his school jazz band, with the encouragement of fellow pupils Britt Woodman (a future Ellingtonian) and Buddy Collette (later to work with Chico Hamilton).

Work at a professional level soon followed with ex-Ellingtonian Barney Bigard and with Louis Armstrong's band, while Mingus also rubbed shoulders with boppers-to-be such as Art Pepper and Dexter Gordon. However, there was something of a cultural time lag between the East Coast and the West, so that the first records of Gillespie and Parker and the visiting musicians themselves arrived in Los Angeles like a bolt of thunder in late 1945. Mingus had been involved meanwhile in composing and recording several would-be popular songs, but, enthused by the new music, he formed an idealistic cooperative group with Woodman, Collette, and others, which failed to get a record deal.

In 1947 Mingus made his first impact on the national scene when he joined the touring band of Lionel Hampton, making some bop-influenced small-group tracks and being spotlighted on a self-composed big band piece, "Mingus Fingers" (Decca/GRP). Inspired by Ellington bassist Jimmy Blanton, Mingus already has impressive facility, alternating seamlessly between improvisation and rhythm playing, making confident forays into the upper register, and even including a brief passage played *arco* (with the bow). A riposte to Dizzy Gillespie and Oscar Pettiford's "One Bass Hit" (recorded by Gillespie's big band as a feature for Ray Brown), Mingus's composition is surprisingly adventurous. The very first bars feature clarinet and flute, the brass occasionally use plunger mutes, and there are passages that lean toward atonality. In addition, the thirty-two-bar chorus structure is broken up by no fewer than three interludes with no harmonic movement but with repeated bass figures.

Mingus's bass work subsequently continued to expand its virtuosic tendencies, especially in improvisation uninhibited by the underlying chord structures. His exposed playing in the 1950–51 Red Norvo trio (led by Norvo on vibes with Tal Farlow on guitar) soon earned him a wider reputation and led indirectly to his settling in New York at age twenty-nine. Brief associations with groups led by Miles Davis, Stan Getz, Duke Ellington, Art Tatum, Bud Powell, Lennie Tristano, and Charlie Parker completed his exposure to the whole history of

jazz thus far, and a potent symbol of peer acceptance was his performance (much of it overdubbed, due to the limitations of live recording in 1953) with the so-called Quintet of the Year—completed by
Parker, Gillespie, Powell, and Max Roach—on *Jazz at Massey Hall*
(Debut/OJC).

Mingus contracted the personnel on behalf of the concert orga-
nizers, arranged for its recording, and issued it on the small label he
directed with Roach and coadministered with his second wife, Celia.
This came into being because of the founders' problems in finding
anyone willing to document their compositions. (A minor exception
was Miles Davis, who recorded Mingus's "Smooch" [Prestige/OJC]
with the composer at the piano.) Ironically, it was eventually his work
for other labels that finally crystallized Mingus's revolutionary ideas,
especially "Pithecanthropus Erectus" (Atlantic) in 1956. Just as the
jazz world was accepting Parker's death the previous year, this piece
went crashing beyond bebop's boundaries. It incorporated extended
passages based on a single scale (or "mode"), sudden changes of volume and of rhythmic feel, unaccustomed vocalization of the horn-
players' tones, and collective improvisations unpredetermined as to
length and only terminated on cue.

It is often said that the free jazz of the 1960s actually starts here.
In particular the emotional climate was, for the time, unexpected and
violent and was symbolic of Mingus's reaction to the burgeoning civil
rights movement. Titles referring to this explicitly or obliquely—
"Haitian Fight Song" (Atlantic 1957), "Fables of Faubus" (Columbia
1959; Candid 1960), and "Prayer for Passive Resistance" (Mercury
1960)—are also pieces that work resoundingly well as music. Mingus
was equally successful in commenting on such other problems of
American society as the space race and the nuclear arsenal, commem-
orating cherished performers such as Parker, Gillespie, Ellington, and
Jelly Roll Morton, and graphically evoking Mexican music and gospel
in "Ysabel's Table Dance" (RCA Victor) and "Wednesday Night
Prayer Meeting" (Atlantic).

By the second half of the 1950s Mingus was regularly leading his
own group, the Jazz Workshop, and a frequently changing cast of
sidemen were putting his methods into practice. They were expected
to bear in mind the composer's thematic ideas when soloing (as with
Monk), and the complex rhythmic hurdles of pieces such as "Pithecanthropus," "Haitian," and "Faubus" ensured that they could hardly
forget. In addition, the horn players had to improvise collectively in
a way unheard of beyond New Orleans and Dixieland, and indeed to

play their written parts without notated guidelines, for Mingus discovered that performances were more idiomatic and more compelling when material was learned by ear—usually from dictation at the piano. (Another parallel with Monk is that, while the latter gave his sidemen written parts, these were frequently so difficult that they often ended up learning them aurally.)

Mingus's sidemen were under more pressure and therefore played with more individuality than in conventional ensembles, and the resultant self-realization of such players as Jackie McLean, Jimmy Knepper, John Handy, Booker Ervin, Eric Dolphy, and Roland Kirk exemplifies this. The Mingus "sound" was always a compound of idiosyncratic contributions rather than a mere idea in the writer's head. The unacademic harmonization of themes such as "Nostalgia in Times Square" (United Artists/Blue Note), "My Jelly Roll Soul" (Atlantic), "Better Git It in Your Soul" (Columbia), or "Wham Bam Thank You Ma'am" (Atlantic) reveals the method whereby the frontline players had to find their own parts. "Self-Portrait in Three Colors" (Columbia) gains much of its effect from the personalization of the composed countermelodies played by first Knepper and then Ervin, while the semi-improvised pyramid structures of, for example, "E's Flat, Ah's Flat Too" and "Moanin'" (both from *Blues and Roots*, Atlantic) make the actual "composition" a collective effort.

This was a severe shock to the system, at a time when Dave Brubeck and John Lewis were seeking respectability while younger musicians such as Donald Byrd and Quincy Jones were undertaking formal studies in Paris. Mingus's own first visits to Europe were for a brief appearance in 1960 and a longer tour in 1964; both of them involved Dolphy, one of his most distinctive interpreters, but his personnel and his fortunes continued to fluctuate. The most continuous musical relationship was with drummer Dannie Richmond, who regularly seconded Mingus from 1956 to 1970 and again from 1973 to 1978. Richmond's largely self-taught playing was in almost telepathic communication, not only with the leader's bass but with the complexity and simplicity of his writing. The alternation between 4/4 and 6/4 in "Dizzy Moods" (RCA Victor) and similar rhythmic changes are convincing because of Richmond's energy and commitment, while the many multisection pieces such as "West Coast Ghost" (Bethlehem) are directed as much by the drums as by the leader.

As a result, there is never any uncertainty in the execution of numbers with unconventional section lengths: for instance, the aforementioned "Fables of Faubus," which has sections of nineteen bars

and eighteen bars, and "Self-Portrait in Three Colors," which alternates between six bars (one of these in 2/4) and nine bars. Among
_____ "Orange Was the Color of Her Dress" (Charles
_____ nds like a blues but isn't quite,
_____ —if one discounts the expanded
_____ anges—actually fits the framework
_____ ic structure of "What Love" (Can-
_____ gh based on the Cole Porter stan-
_____ Love?," alternating choruses are in
_____ associated with Ornette Coleman's
_____ many varied details in the work of
_____ th the free-tempo and the in-tempo

_____ the first half of the 1960s, and some
_____ r suffered like Monk's in the second
_____ clinical depression and breakdown
_____ comeback was given a boost by the
_____ version of the autobiography he had
_____ 1950s, published as *Beneath the Un-*
_____ wife, Sue, the return of Richmond
_____ ment of younger players like saxists
_____ gave Mingus new inspiration that
_____ mpelling works as "Sue's Changes"
_____ (both Atlantic). The latter, taped in
_____ r, the last of his recordings on which
_____ y, and the following fall he was di-
_____ Gehrig's disease (amyotrophic lateral

Mingus's passing started the positive
reevaluation of his influence. It is interesting to note, however, that
his compositional methods were most easily applied to six- or seven-
piece groups (i.e., with three to four horns, as on *Mingus Ah Um*),
and their successful application to the nine-piece band of *Blues and
Roots* was at the time a most unlikely achievement. By comparison,
on the rare occasions when finances and circumstances enabled Mingus to expand his regular small groups to full big band format (twelve
horns or more), he usually reverted to more conventional methods of
sectional writing learned in his youth.

This applies to the most famous example, his *Epitaph* suite (best
known in the posthumous realization by Gunther Schuller on Columbia, but partially recorded by Mingus himself at his 1962 Town Hall

Concert for United Artists/Blue Note). Indeed, this incorporates a few pieces written as early as the late 1940s, such as "The Soul," originally done for the Lionel Hampton band. On such occasions Mingus often involved other arrangers, which risked diluting the original conception further, though Sy Johnson deserves praise for his big band adaptations of "Don't Be Afraid, the Clown's Afraid Too" and "The Shoes of the Fisherman's Wife" (both on *Let My Children Hear Music*, Columbia). Similarly, Jaki Byard's nine-horn orchestration of the previous three-horn composition "Meditations on Integration" comes off splendidly in its live Monterey Festival performance (Charles Mingus Enterprises/Prestige).

However, the most remarkable project for a medium-sized band (in this case, with seven horns) is the 1963 suite *Black Saint & The Sinner Lady* (Impulse). Significantly, the recording was preceded by three weeks of nightly appearances with the same lineup and is an outgrowth of the abovementioned Town Hall Concert; the ensemble writing of *Epitaph*'s "Ballad (In Other Words, I Am Three)" recurs in *Black Saint*, for instance, at 1'12" into the fourth movement. This unique album-length composition combines Mingus's influences and ensemble techniques into a convincing whole which, despite its expansive and even sprawling surface, belies an underlying control not easily achieved, even in the recording studio. Liberal use of tape editing and overdubbing (all planned in Mingus's mind, according to the producer), and the excellent contributions he drew from soloists not often associated with him, namely saxist Charlie Mariano and ex-Ellington trombonist Quentin Jackson, are finally less impressive than the variety and unity of the whole.

By contrast, Monk's only noteworthy work with larger groups, in his 1959 Town Hall and 1963 Lincoln Center concerts, consists of his usual repertoire rearranged by Hall Overton. Despite his intelligent orchestration of the composer's keyboard voicings (and the transcription of his recorded improvisation on "Little Rootie Tootie" and "Four in One"), these illustrate all too clearly that the only expansion of his material envisaged by Monk was to extend the list of soloists on each piece. If he had other ambitions, there is no evidence of them in either his published output or his extremely rare public pronouncements. It may be for this reason that many commentators prefer his three-minute works intended for 78 rpm records—up to and including his sessions of 1952—since the artificial constraint ensures a compression that seems appropriate to Monk's overall approach. Also, it has to be said that he evinced little interest in textural variety, employing different instruments interchangeably on the same parts, and indeed so did Mingus in his small groups.

In each case, necessity was the mother of some extremely demanding music for the horn players, since Mingus as well as Monk tended to conceive his melodies first of all in terms of the keyboard. Interestingly, the same has sometimes been alleged of Ellington, but, if anyone followed him in creating music with individual performers in mind, or in allowing the sidemen's revisions or spontaneous thoughts to influence the final form of a composition, it was Mingus. On this level, while both of them were extremely significant in resurrecting certain traditional practices that had been ignored, Monk's main contribution to the future was in encouraging the use of thematic motives in improvisation. He also inspired a small, select school of pianist-composers, whereas Mingus's effect on subsequent players is more wide-ranging. They are inspired by the openness of Mingus's sound and the concentration of Monk's mind.

The existence of repertory groups playing the music of these two—the T. S. Monk Band led by Thelonious's drummer son, T.S., and the Mingus Big Band supervised by Sue Mingus—provides a final parallel. For, while such ventures lack the authentic stamp of the composers' instrumental contributions, their body of work is too vital to remain restricted to the original versions. Any player or listener who has experienced the perennial fascination of Monk's intricately crafted detail, or Mingus's compelling emotional landscape, will not begrudge others the possibility of coming to this music in the flesh. Nor will they neglect the continued study of the masters' recordings.

John Coltrane

Lewis Porter

One of the major musicians of the twentieth century, John Coltrane reshaped the way jazz is perceived. A tenor and soprano saxophonist and a significant composer, he demonstrated how world music, classical music, and classical theory could all be incorporated into powerful blues-based jazz.

He was born John William Coltrane in Hamlet, North Carolina, on September 23, 1926. Both of his parents came from literate families in North Carolina, descended from former slaves and named for the former slaveowners. Coltrane's mother was musical—she sang and also played piano—and his father, John Robert Coltrane, played violin, ukulele, and possibly clarinet.

Probably beginning in the fall of 1939, Coltrane received his first instrumental training playing alto horn in a community band. He soon switched to the clarinet. When he joined the high school band the next year, young Coltrane, inspired by tenor saxophonist Lester Young, took up the alto saxophone. It appears that he also did some singing in school groups.

John's father died on January 2, 1939, of stomach cancer, a common ailment at that time (and unrelated to liver cancer). In order to get work, John's mother moved near relations in Atlantic City, New Jersey, probably during his senior year, 1942–43. John lived alone with boarders in High Point until his graduation from high school (which ended at eleventh grade). In June 1943 he moved to Philadelphia and found a factory job.

Probably in 1944 and continuing for about a year, Coltrane began taking saxophone lessons and theory classes. Early in 1945 he began practicing with tenor saxophonist Benny Golson. Alto saxophonist Johnny Hodges was his idol until June 5, 1945, when he and Golson went to see Dizzy Gillespie perform with Charlie Parker; from that point he emulated Parker.

Coltrane was in the Navy from August 6, 1945, through August 11, 1946. After going through training, he was sent to Pearl Harbor, Oahu, Hawaii, where he played saxophone and clarinet in a band known as the Melody Masters. He first recorded July 13, 1946, in an impromptu session, not for release, with a small group of musicians from the segregated white band including drummer Joe Theimer (a.k.a. Timer). The eight titles—one of which, "Hot House," is now issued (Rhino)—included a number of recent Parker tunes. One can hear that Coltrane at nineteen had good dexterity but was clearly not familiar with all the chord changes.

After the Navy, Coltrane probably resumed saxophone lessons, but his primary focus beginning probably in the fall of 1946 and continuing until somewhere between 1950 and 1952 was at the Granoff Studios, where his veteran's benefits paid for his tuition. There he studied on and off, when he was in town, with Dennis Sandole. He also began picking up steady freelance work alongside pianist Ray Bryant, Golson, and others.

He called his "first professional job" the tour with Joe Webb from September 1946 in Philadelphia through the end of the year. He then joined the band of King Kolax from February 1947 through about April. From about May 1947 through the end of 1948, Coltrane freelanced around Philadelphia, often with saxophonist Jimmy Heath's big band.

By 1948, Coltrane was drinking heavily, smoking perhaps as much as two packs of cigarettes a day, and using heroin. These habits caused him to be professionally inconsistent and were probably a major factor in his obscurity over the next seven years. Though everyone recognized him as a fine musician and took notice of his incessant practicing, no one could have predicted that he would become a major force in musical history.

John Coltrane. Courtesy of the Institute of Jazz Studies, Rutgers University.

He first played tenor professionally while touring on one-nighters with Eddie "Cleanhead" Vinson from November 20, 1948, through April or May 1949. His inspirations on tenor included Lester Young, Young's disciple Jimmy Oliver (a Philadelphia legend), Coleman Hawkins, Dexter Gordon, Wardell Gray, and Sonny Stitt. He once said he liked Stitt best, but many hear the Gordon influence strongest.

From September 16, 1949, he played lead alto in Dizzy Gillespie's big band, but he kept his now preferred tenor around and used it on recordings with singer Billy Valentine. Gillespie's band went out of business after June 20, 1950; when he reformed with a small group around August 1950 he retained Coltrane on tenor. Gillespie took the group into a studio in Detroit on March 1, 1951. Coltrane's solo on the blues "We Love to Boogie" (DeeGee/Savoy) was the only work of his available to the general public until he joined Miles Davis late in 1955. On that recording, he plays with passion and has clearly come far since his Navy days. With Gillespie he also learned about sophisticated harmonies, Latin music, and vamps. He began seeking out any and all method books, even the piano books of Hanon and Czerny. This was the beginning of his arrival at a novel approach.

By early April 1951, he was back in Philadelphia, freelancing and playing in a group named the Dizzy Gillespie Alumni led by Heath. In January 1952 he recorded with the Gay Crosse group in Philadelphia and perhaps in Nashville as well. He continued to study and practice relentlessly, saw Sandole for lessons on a regular basis, and got together with fellow musicians, including a legendary pianist and theorist named Hasaan Ibn Ali, to exchange ideas.

Coltrane toured with Earl Bostic from April 1 through early December of 1952. Bostic was a virtuoso alto saxophonist, and Coltrane said, "He showed me a lot of things on my horn." During 1953 it seems that he freelanced around home. In late 1953 or March 1954 he joined his early idol Johnny Hodges. Though he did not solo on the studio recordings, a live recording of the band (Enigma) shows Coltrane much changed since his Gillespie days, more fleet, lighter in tone, more rhythmically varied. Though he does not sound like Hodges or Bostic, he learned a lot about saxophone playing itself during those tours.

He must have left Hodges around the beginning of September 1954, because he was gigging afterward in Philadelphia. In September 1955 Coltrane was working at Spider Kelly's in Philadelphia with organist Jimmy Smith when two major events changed his life: he married for the first time, and he was "discovered" by Miles Davis.

On September 27, 1955, in Baltimore he began his first engagement with Davis. Perhaps bolstered by his new security, he was joined by Naima (née Juanita) Austin, and they married there on October 3. Naima was a single mother with a daughter, Syeeda (or Saeeda).

Coltrane began to record prolifically with Davis for Prestige and Columbia and as a sideman with others, mostly on Prestige. Among his reviewers, a pattern was soon apparent that was to remain true to the end of his life: he was mostly praised, though sometimes with reservations, while a minority violently dismissed his work. In either case, it was clear that he had developed a distinctive style.

Even though they were recorded during the same time period, the Prestige and Columbia recordings differ from each other considerably. Prestige encouraged musicians to record one take of each number and to get through as much material as possible at each session. Recording for Columbia was more formal. Each number was recorded for as many takes as needed to get it right, and splicing was used to combine the best moments from different takes. (On the later sessions, as the Davis band became more experienced, less splicing was necessary, and by the *Kind of Blue* album in 1959 there was virtually none.)

Davis's first Columbia album was '*Round About Midnight*, a title that Dizzy Gillespie and others, but not the composer, had sometimes used for Thelonious Monk's " 'Round Midnight." The title piece was recorded on September 10, 1956, in a smoky, evocative Gil Evans arrangement that became a jukebox hit in black neighborhoods in its 45 rpm release. Davis's solo is hushed and confidential, enhanced by his sizzling Harmon-mute sound. After an interlude, Coltrane solos with a double-time feeling in the rhythm section; the chords go by just as slow as for Davis, but the drums and bass accent in between the beats behind Coltrane to give it more motion. Coltrane's solo is exotic, daring. It has a soulful sound and unusual ornaments. It is a mixture of balladic paraphrase—that is, using notes of Monk's theme—and technical passages. It was one of his first recordings to attract widespread attention.

But his alcohol and drug addictions continued to interfere with his performance. When Davis fired him after an engagement that ended on April 28, 1957, because of his unreliability, he finally rid himself of the heroin habit by quitting "cold turkey" during a week in May when he was leading a quartet in Philadelphia. He would later refer to this experience in the liner notes to his album *A Love Supreme* in this way: "During the year 1957, I experienced, by the grace of God, a spiritual awakening which was to lead me to a richer, fuller, more productive life." He planned to continue leading his own group and did so for a few gigs, and cut his first record as a leader on May 31.

During this time period he began his next significant association, one with Thelonious Monk. He had first recorded with him on April 16 and now began visiting him and playing with him informally on an occasional basis. He began working on multiphonics, the playing of several notes at once; he said that Monk "just looked at my horn and 'felt' the mechanics of what had to be done to get this effect," but that he learned the specifics of it from John Glenn, a local Philadelphia player.

Monk asked Coltrane to join his group at the Five Spot from July 18 or 19 through New Year's Eve, 1957 (with a few weeks off and a few nights when Monk was not present). The engagement was critical for both of them, and Coltrane's playing drew raves from most. In addition, Coltrane's album *Blue Train* (Blue Note) was recorded on September 15, 1957. It was the best display of Coltrane's talents as a player and composer to date; all but one of the five tunes were his. Composing was a major preoccupation for him and something he took as seriously as his performing.

At the end of the Monk engagement, in early January 1958, Davis rehired Coltrane. It was a very different Coltrane, one who played with uninhibited emotion, impressive authority, and dazzling virtuosity. Listening to any of the recordings (his own for Prestige, Davis's for Columbia) made in 1958, one can hear the transformation in his playing. First and foremost is the sheer speed, the blinding flurries of notes that Ira Gitler had dubbed "sheets of sound." Harmonically, Coltrane's runs were adventurous; he would superimpose or stack up chords. Miles Davis explained it this way: "What he does, for example, is to play five notes of a chord and then keep changing it around, trying to see how many different ways it can sound. It's like explaining something five different ways. And that sound of his is connected with what he's doing with chords at any given time."

Coltrane, who was notoriously self-critical and also refreshingly honest even in the media, acknowledged that his playing of this time was complex rhythmically. "I found there were a certain number of chord progressions to play in a given time, and sometimes what I played didn't work out in eighth notes, sixteenth notes, or triplets. I had to put the notes in uneven groups like fives and sevens in order to get them all in...I want to be more flexible where rhythm is concerned. I feel I have to study rhythm some more." By 1959 he was using the sheets of sound more sparingly.

During the spring of 1959, he was involved in what have become two of the most famous jazz albums ever made, representing two very different approaches: Davis's *Kind of Blue* (Columbia) and his own *Giant Steps*. The latter was his first album as a leader for Atlantic. This time, all seven compositions were his own, and he was the only wind player. His writing and playing throughout were remarkable, but it was the title piece that knocked the jazz world on its ear. "Giant Steps" represents the culmination of Coltrane's developing interest in third-related chord movement, which means that the keys change rapidly, and he played it at a murderous tempo. He made a thorough study of the possibilities of third relations, and he employed them on a number of pieces during 1959 and 1960, notably "Countdown," "Exotica," "Satellite" (a variation on "How High the Moon"), "26-2" (based on Charlie Parker's "Confirmation"), and his influential arrangements of "But Not for Me" and "Body and Soul" (all Atlantic/Rhino).

Giant Steps also included four tributes to family and friends: "Naima" (a serene, exotic tribute to his wife), "Cousin Mary," "Syeeda's Song Flute," and "Mr. P. C." (for bassist Paul Chambers). Around this time he also wrote "Like Sonny" (Atlantic/Rhino; other version on Roulette) for Rollins; later (1962, Impulse) he wrote "Tunji" for percussionist Michael Olatunji.

As important as "Giant Steps" was, from 1960 onward Coltrane consistently referred to it as a passing phase, a period when he was obsessed with chords, something he had grown out of. In his own groups, and in his composing, "modal" pieces would predominate. For at the same time that Coltrane was developing his "Giant Steps" chordal concepts, Miles Davis had become interested in doing away with chord progressions. In 1958 Davis, with his pianist Bill Evans and the unrelated Gil Evans and also inspired by George Russell, had begun to experiment with the use of modes (i.e., medieval church scales). Davis was playing modes other than major and minor, the most common in Western music, and was working with simplified chord sequences—in a way, quite the opposite of "Giant Steps"—so that one could stay on one mode for as long as sixteen measures at a time.

Though not the first album to employ this approach, *Kind of Blue* was the one that popularized what became known as "modal jazz." On "So What," a Davis piece with a Gil Evans–written introduction, Coltrane created a tightly unified solo notable both for the abstract quality of its melodic motives and for the way he develops each of them. He was clearly liberated by the slow harmonic movement. By being able to spend so much time on each chord and mode, he was allowed to grow in his ability to develop musical ideas while improvising. It also allowed him to concentrate on rhythm, which he had said he wanted to do.

Coltrane had for some time wanted to lead his own group—he did so periodically between gigs with Davis—and in late July 1959 he quit Davis. He was persuaded to return in mid-August but left for good after Davis's tour of Europe in March and April 1960.

On April 16, 1960, Coltrane led a group at Town Hall, Manhattan, on a bill with Dizzy Gillespie and others, and May 3 he began a two-month engagement at the Jazz Gallery. Apparently he had wanted to hire McCoy Tyner on piano, Art Davis on bass, and Elvin Jones on drums; but none of them was available, so he opened with Steve Kuhn on piano, Steve Davis on bass, and Pete Sims "LaRoca" on drums. Tyner joined in about a month, and Jones in late September, while the group was touring nationally. The bass chair changed around—Reggie Workman played for most of 1961, sometimes in tandem with Art Davis—and finally went to Jimmy Garrison at the end of 1961.

Coltrane had purchased a soprano saxophone around February 1, 1959, and tried it out that week on a gig at the Sutherland Hotel in Chicago. He began using it regularly in May 1960; his recording of "My Favorite Things" (Atlantic/Rhino) that October reestablished the soprano, rarely used in modern jazz, as a favored jazz instrument. His arranging concept was equally brilliant as his playing; essentially he took one chorus of the song and extended it vastly with long vamp sections. That same week he recorded all the material that would eventually become *Coltrane Plays the Blues* and *Coltrane's Sound*. He signed with the Impulse record label in April 1961. (All of the remaining albums mentioned are on Impulse except as noted.)

He was increasingly popular. *Down Beat* honored him as Jazzman of the Year in its review of the year 1961. In both the magazine's International Critics Poll and Readers Poll that year, he won for best tenor saxophonist and for miscellaneous instrument (soprano saxophone); the critics also voted his the new star combo. But his detractors grew louder with the addition of Eric Dolphy to the group for most of 1961. A majority of English critics (though not all) lambasted him on his first European tour that November. Coincidentally, the November 23 issue of *Down Beat* contained a scathing review from John Tynan, who spoke of "musical nonsense currently being peddled in the name of jazz . . . a horrifying demonstration of what appears to be a growing anti-jazz trend." Coltrane and Dolphy responded with an article in *Down Beat* published April 12, 1962.

Coltrane also considered expanding his group to a sextet with the addition of guitarist Wes Montgomery. They performed together in California in September 1961 and again in 1962. But neither Montgomery nor Dolphy stayed, and Coltrane's best-known quartet—with Tyner, Garrison, and Jones—remained intact from April 1962 through the fall of 1965, except for some absences of Jones.

By this time his repertory was dominated by the blues and his modal pieces, as he had realized that he could play through his complex harmonic ideas while the rhythm section supported him with more open, modal backgrounds. He became deeply involved in motivic improvisation and with building a sense of structure throughout each solo. His solo on "Equinox," from *Coltrane's Sound* (Atlantic), provides a good illustration of how concise his improvising became in the 1960s. His detractors were so busy noticing how many notes he played that they failed to grasp how sensibly he was using all these notes. Coltrane develops his solo on "Equinox" out of just a few motives, beginning with a repeated-note idea. The power, the concentration, and the depth of blues feeling are gripping. He played long solos, but there was good reason for this seemingly inordinate length. He was concerned with following his compositional ideas of the moment and preferred not to try to curtail, edit, or predetermine this process.

He moved further and further into a self-reliant sound world, a world that by the 1960s had less and less in common with the music that he started with: the music of Lester Young and Charlie Parker. For one thing, Coltrane was never partial to quoting—that is, to making musical references to famous solos or songs. What's more, he developed a vocabulary of licks, or formulas, that are in many cases not traceable to his predecessors. One way that Coltrane developed this unique sound world was by bringing into his music—and, through his influence, into all of jazz and beyond—an eclectic collection of method books, exercises, and scales from around the world. Yet Coltrane's music was always focused because he anchored all these sources in the deep soulful sound of the blues, particularly the blues in minor keys.

Coltrane's sound world with his quartet was built around little fourth-based motives such as the chant from *A Love Supreme* (which fills a fourth), or Tyner's tendency to use stacked fourths as the basis of his piano chording, rather than the arpeggios of major chords that are such a critical part of most jazz—and Western music generally. This gives his music a serious, rather abstract sound, and it probably contributes to the spiritual element in his music. His tunes became more and more spare, until, with "Dear Lord" and "Love" in 1965, a few well-chosen scale tones would suffice. The way he builds his solos by developing short ideas at length, repeating them in different registers and building up to higher and higher notes, makes him a preacher on the saxophone. He does this most clearly on a slow out-of-tempo piece such as "Psalm," as we'll see. But as German jazz educator Gerhard Putschögl has pointed out, Coltrane builds his solos the same way even when working with the rhythm section at a medium or fast tempo. And because those little fourths are a basis of the blues, his music is simultaneously drenched in blues feeling. That mixture of intense blues and spiritual fervor gives his music astounding power.

Jazz historian Dan Morgenstern recalls a typical evening at the Half Note around 1964 or 1965: "The intensity that was generated was absolutely unbelievable. I can still feel it, and it was unlike any other feeling within the music we call jazz. It carried you away. If you let yourself be carried by it, it was an absolutely ecstatic feeling. And I think that kind of ecstasy was something that Coltrane was looking for in his music."

Just as "My Favorite Things" was a soprano feature, "Impressions" became his tenor theme song. This is based on the same AABA structure and D Dorian mode (E flat for the bridge) as "So What," but the A section (main) melody was derived from Morton Gould's "Pavanne" [*sic*] and the B section was taken from yet another "Pavane," Maurice Ravel's *Pavane pour une infante défunte* (or from the popular song that was based on it, "The Lamp Is Low"). Far from indicating any paucity of inspiration on Coltrane's part, this is a characteristic example of his remarkable breadth of interests and his ability to apply these diverse sources to jazz.

He was among the first to play what is now called "world music." For some years Coltrane had been exposed to the music of other cultures—India, parts of Africa, Latin America—through Dennis Sandole, Gillespie, Yusef Lateef, and others. He must have also learned about Middle Eastern music from Ahmed Abdul-Malik, the bassist during most of his Monk engagement, and John invited him to play the tamboura (not the oud) on "India" at the Village Vanguard in November 1961. He arranged to meet Ravi Shankar in New

York in December 1961, the first of a handful of informal lessons. He even named his second son Ravi.

He based some of his pieces on the sources he found. His "Spiritual" is a melody for "Nobody Knows de Trouble I See" from James Weldon Johnson's *Book of American Negro Spirituals*. "Olé" was based on a song known as "Venga Vallejo" or as "El Vito." The notes to *Africa/Brass* state that "he listened to many African records for rhythmic inspiration. One had a bass line like a chant, and the group used it, working it into different tunes."

"India" appears to be based on a recorded Vedic chant (that is, with a text coming from the Vedas, religious books of the 1500s) that was issued on a Folkways LP at the time. "I like Ravi Shankar very much," he told French writers Jean Clouzet and Michel Delorme in 1962. "What brings me closest to Ravi is the modal aspect of his art. Currently, at the particular stage I find myself in, I seem to be going through a modal phase. . . . There's a lot of modal music that is played every day throughout the world. It's particularly evident in Africa, but if you look at Spain or Scotland, India or China, you'll discover this again in each case. . . . It's this universal aspect of music that interests me and attracts me; that's what I'm aiming for."

It wasn't only the sound of world music that attracted him; Coltrane was interested in all kinds of religion and in all kinds of mysticism. He knew that in some folk cultures, music was held to have mystical powers, and he hoped to get in touch with some of those capacities. He told Nat Hentoff, "I've already been looking into those approaches to music—as in India—in which particular sounds and scales are intended to produce specific emotional meanings."

His mystical, spiritual interests are explicit in *A Love Supreme*, his best-known and still best-selling album, recorded in December 1964. Its four sections—"Acknowledgement," "Resolution," "Pursuance," and "Psalm"—suggest a kind of pilgrim's progress, in which the pilgrim acknowledges the divine, resolves to pursue it, searches, and, eventually, celebrates what has been attained in song. Virtually the whole piece is based on the little "A Love Supreme" motive chanted by Coltrane (overdubbed as two voices) at the end of Part One. Perhaps most striking is the way he incorporates his poem, which appears in the liner, into Part Four. His saxophone solo is a wordless "recitation" of the words of the poem, beginning with the title, "A Love Supreme."

Eventually Coltrane accepted the diversity of human belief as representing different ways of recognizing one God. The titles of Coltrane's last compositions suggest a mixture of religious influences. Only "The Father and the Son and the Holy Ghost" is specifically Christian. Others, such as "Dear Lord" and *Meditations*, are more general, while "Om" suggests Eastern beliefs. He is quoted on the back of *Meditations* saying, "I believe in all religions." He made a special study of Indian Buddhism, but he also was interested in what Sonny Rollins had to say about the Rosicrucians. And he found Einstein's profound mixture of science and mysticism especially inspiring. "My goal," he said,

is to live the truly religious life and express it in my music. If you live it, when you play there's no problem because the music is just part of the whole thing. To be a musician is really something. It goes very, very deep. My music is the spiritual expression of what I am—my faith, my knowledge, my being.... When you begin to see the possibilities of music, you desire to do something really good for people, to help humanity free itself from its hangups. I think music can make the world better and, if I'm qualified, I want to do it. I'd like to point out to people the divine in a musical language that transcends words. I want to speak to their souls.

Coltrane never saw himself as a guru of any sort; he was too modest for that, and too self-critical. He always felt that he could be better and could do better, and he was always pushing himself, always searching for new things. In 1965 he said, "I don't know if you can ever be a complete musician. I'm not. But I don't think I'll know what's missing from my playing until I find it."

A Love Supreme was voted album of the year by both *Down Beat* and *Jazz* in 1965, and *Down Beat* readers also named Coltrane Jazzman of the Year, and best tenor saxophonist and elected him to the magazine's Hall of Fame. But he continued to excite controversy. He was enamored of Ornette Coleman and the so-called avant-garde. Coltrane talked quite a bit about music with Coleman, and they reportedly discussed putting a group together but never did. Coltrane helped to arrange recording sessions at Impulse for Archie Shepp and others, and he was always generous about letting these younger players sit in with his group at performances. On June 28, 1965, he gathered eleven musicians together for a recording session that produced one of his most awesome, and daunting, recordings, *Ascension*. Besides his regular quartet, and bassist Art Davis, he used trumpeters Freddie

Hubbard and Dewey Johnson, alto saxophonists Marion Brown and John Tchicai, and tenor saxophonists Shepp and Pharoah Sanders.

By September, Sanders was a regular member of Coltrane's group. On October 1, 1965, they recorded "Om," which opens with the chanting of words from the Bhagavad-Gita. Coltrane's work, disturbing to some, revelatory to as many more, continued to have profound musical substance, and his own solos were as tightly organized as ever.

He was playing in free time, without the bass walking, and decided to try out two drummers on a regular basis; beginning at the Village Gate in Manhattan in November 1965, he hired Rashied Ali as a second drummer. However, this prompted the departure of Tyner by the end of 1965. Jones left soon after. Jimmy Garrison stayed with Coltrane through the summer of 1966 (though he returned for recording sessions) along with Sanders, Rashied Ali, and pianist Alice McLeod Coltrane (his second wife).

In his last two years, Coltrane did away with rehearsed material almost completely in order to devote himself purely to the manipulation of abstract motivic ideas. His last works are, on one level, about form, just as they are concerned with metaphysical and philosophical concepts on another level. He also came upon a richer tone, with fuller vibrato, than he had ever used before.

The barrage of sound presented by Coltrane's last works may, unfortunately, conceal from many listeners the magnificent power of his playing. What seems to be chaotic is just the opposite. Coltrane managed to create long solos that flowed seamlessly from theme to improvisation—which is just what he said he wanted. And the improvisations were devoted relentlessly to the exploration of abstract motivic ideas. (The posthumous release *Interstellar Space* is the perfect place to hear this because it consists entirely of duets with drums.)

In the fall of 1966, Coltrane began to cut back on touring (even Sanders began to lead his own band) and made plans to stay around New York, probably as much for family reasons as for health reasons. (He was not yet aware of any serious illness.) He had begun to take control of his own business affairs. He had arranged for his own label imprint and was planning some self-produced concerts jointly with Olatunji; they already had reserved January 14, 1968, at Lincoln Center's Philharmonic Hall. He spoke of opening a space in New Jersey or in Greenwich Village where rehearsals and performances would be open informally to the public for a nominal charge. By the spring of 1967, he was reportedly planning on performing less often or even taking a break altogether, while he concentrated on producing younger artists and possibly doing some teaching.

But by the spring of 1967, Coltrane's health was failing. On April 23, he appeared in a benefit concert for and at the new Olatunji Center of African Culture on East 125th Street. His final performance was in Baltimore on May 7. He died in a hospital in Huntington, Long Island, New York, of liver cancer on July 17, two months before what would have been his forty-first birthday. The cause has never been definitively found, but it was apparently not related to the drugs and alcohol he ingested as a youth, though it might have been a long-term effect of a dirty needle causing hepatitis.

A funeral service was held on July 21, 1967, at St. Peter's Church in Manhattan. A thousand people attended. A longtime friend, composer Cal Massey, read the poem "A Love Supreme." The quartets of Ornette Coleman and Albert Ayler performed one number each.

Historical markers have been raised in Hamlet and High Point. His cousin Mary still lives on North 33rd Street in Philadelphia in a house he bought in 1952; it is now the base of the John W. Coltrane Cultural Society. A Christian church in San Francisco centers its ritual on the album and poem *A Love Supreme*.

Coltrane's impact was profound and nearly all-pervasive, not only musically but as part of jazz culture. Everyone who plays jazz since has had to contend, in some way, with his legacy, and the naysayers have dwindled to a few. Many musicians are influenced directly by the notes he played and by his approaches to composition; an equal number are inspired by his approach to the profession, by the seriousness and nobility that he brought to his work. Without intending to, and with utmost humility, he redefined what it means to be a jazz musician.

The Avant-Garde, 1949–1967

Lawrence Kart

Reacting to the music of alto saxophonist Ornette Coleman, who had arrived on the national scene less than a year before, composer George Russell explained in the course of a June 1960 dialogue with critic Martin Williams that "if there weren't new things happening in jazz since Charlie Parker, jazz wouldn't be ready to accept Ornette. ... The way has been paved and the ear prepared by rather startling, though isolated, developments in jazz since the forties."

Russell knew what he was talking about, for he himself had created some of those pre-Coleman "new things." And when he went on to say that he believed jazz was "ready to accept other innovators as convincing as [Coleman]," he knew that at least two of them, pianist Cecil Taylor and alto saxophonist–bass clarinetist–flautist Eric Dolphy, were already hard at work.

But perhaps, in 1960, only a prophet could have foreseen the advent of a figure as iconoclastic as tenor saxophonist Albert Ayler or have anticipated all the places tenor and soprano saxophonist John Coltrane was going to take his own music in the seven years that remained before his death. And few listeners then would even have been aware of such innovators as Jamaican alto saxophonist Joe Harriott and clarinetist Joe Maneri, pianist Hasaan Ibn Ali, and tenor

446

saxophonist Fred Anderson, whose work was going to remain relatively obscure because of accidents of geography, temperament, and the like.

Russell's focus in that dialogue was on specific musical issues, especially on the "war on the chord" that he felt had been going on in jazz since the bop era and that Coleman had taken up in his own way, liberating himself "from tonal centers," as Russell put it, in order "to sing his own song . . . without having to meet the deadline of any particular chord." But while it is to specific musical issues that we must always return, labels and the attitudes they represent also are part of the story.

However haphazardly the term *avant-garde* might have been applied to this music—the "new thing" was its other early name, "free jazz" would come a bit later on—something more than labeling was involved. The artistic avant-garde is a relatively modern phenomenon (as critic Renato Poggioli pointed out in his study *The Theory of the Avant-Garde*, it reaches back no further than 1880s France). The term itself was borrowed from radical politics, which had borrowed it from the military, so it should come as no surprise that ideology and attitudes can play a major role both in the making of an avant-garde work and in our ability to recognize that we are in the presence of such a thing.

One need only think of the way John Cage's notorious silent piano piece *4'33"* depends for its effect on our sense of what normally occurs when a person sits down at a piano in a concert hall to realize that *4'33"* links two avant-garde traits—antagonism (a negative reaction to the traditional) and nihilism (destructive labor)—and slyly puts them to work. (Poggioli identifies the other traits of the avant-garde as Agonism, an air of passionate, hyperbolic struggle; Futurism, the quest for the new as an absolute; Alienation, profound doubt about one's relation to society as a whole and to the audience in particular; and Experimentalism, new techniques as a means of more than technical transformation, the work as a transcendental laboratory or proving ground.)

Not every figure in the jazz avant-garde exhibits all of those traits, but they all exhibit some of them. For example, the very titles of Sun Ra's recordings and compositions ("Outer Nothingness," "We Travel the Space Ways," "Other Planes of There," etc.) proclaim his music's personal blend of Futurism and Alienation, while Agonism takes on exceptionally vivid form in the works of John Coltrane and Albert Ayler.

In a 1965 interview, Ayler stated, "music has changed so much

Ornette Coleman. Courtesy of the Institute of Jazz Studies, Rutgers University.

from when Ornette Coleman started playing around the beat. [Coleman's music is] neo-avant-garde music and this beat will be eliminated." He surrounded those remarks with a host of well-worn avant-garde gestures ("[O]ur music is pure art.... I'm not trying to entertain people, I'm playing the truth for those who can listen.... [R]eal beauty [is] beyond most people, it's only for the select few")—all of which suggest that eliminating the beat was a more than purely musical choice for him. But Ayler and others did make that choice, and the music they went on to create in nonmetrical frameworks would have specific and not wholly foreseeable *musical* consequences.

Looking through the jazz past for music that paved the way for Coleman et al., one can find instances of George Russell's "startling ... isolated, developments" long before the 1940s. It is their isolation, though, and their intent to startle, that is the point. Pieces like Don Redman's "Chant of the Weed" (Vocalion/Decca, 1931), Coleman Hawkins's "Queer Notions," recorded by the Fletcher Henderson Orchestra (Vocalion/Columbia, 1933), and Arthur Schutt's "Delirium," recorded by the Charleston Chasers (Columbia, 1927) are, as composer-critic Gunther Schuller put it, acts of "conscious modernity"—exotic exceptions to a norm that is, in effect, being reinforced.

Intimations of a more forthright jazz avant-gardism emerge in the 1940s in the simultaneously anguished and exuberant virtuosity of the bebop masters (alto saxophonist Charlie Parker, trumpeter Dizzy Gillespie, pianist Bud Powell) and in the logic with which composer-pianist Thelonious Monk built oblique but coherent structures out of seeming fragments of musical discourse. Perhaps even more significant to the development of the nascent jazz avant-garde were such orchestral works as George Handy's "Dalvatore Sally" and "Forgetful," recorded by the Boyd Raeburn Orchestra (Jewell/Savoy, 1945–46), Bob Graettinger's "Thermopylae" (1947) and *City of Glass* (1948, revised version 1951), written for the Stan Kenton Orchestra (Capitol), George Russell's "A Bird in Igor's Yard" (Capitol, 1949), written for the Buddy DeFranco Orchestra, and Charles Mingus's "Half-Mast Inhibition" (Mercury, written in the mid-1940s, recorded in 1960).

Not all of these works were successful ("Half-Mast Inhibition" is a near-chaotic soufflé), but in all of them modern (or modernistic) techniques are being handled by young composers who not only had a taste for the hyperbolic but also found themselves writing for large virtuoso ensembles that could, so to speak, realize their wildest dreams. The angular, harmonically wayward vocal line of "Forgetful" (suavely sung by David Allyn) speaks of fraught, esoteric emotions that the piece presents as an inescapable reality; the grinding dissonances of "Thermopylae" and *City of Glass* seemingly have "roots in some unseen dimension," as critic Max Harrison put it, while the goal is an agonized transcendence.

The alienation that Graettinger's works express is built into the music, which alienates itself from at least one familiar jazz trait; marked by immense rhythmic tension, this music does not (and does not mean to) swing. The bursts of driving 4/4 time in "Dance Before the Mirror" from *City of Glass* and "A Trumpet" from Graettinger's *This Modern World* (Capitol, 1953) are quotes from another, more visceral language spoken in another, more optimistic world, and are there to be cut short and abandoned.

The music of the men who gathered around pianist Lennie Tristano in the mid-1940s has been regarded as crucial to the development of the jazz avant-garde because "Intuition" and "Digression" (Capitol, 1949)—recorded by an ensemble that included saxophonists Lee Konitz and Warne Marsh and guitarist Billy Bauer—are reputed to be the first "free" (that is, totally improvised) jazz performances. But the link between those haunting works and most post-Coleman music seems tenuous; challenging to create, the Tristano ensemble's free pieces finally sound very Tristano-like—just as the free improvisation "Abstract No. 1" (Contemporary/OJC) that trumpeter Shorty Rogers, saxophonist-clarinetist Jimmy Giuffre, and drummer Shelly Manne recorded in 1954 resembles the music that Rogers and especially Giuffre would produce in more structured contexts.

The deeper significance of the Tristano-ites lies in two directions: first, that Tristano transforms jazz's historical self-consciousness into a rationale for making a new kind of music; second, that he and his disciples have crucial things to say about jazz rhythm.

By the end of the 1930s, jazz certainly was aware that it had a history—the New Orleans revival of that time would have been inconceivable otherwise—but even in the 1920s, it would seem, a sense of the music's past was a good part of what works such as Duke Ellington's "Black and Tan Fantasy" and "Creole Rhapsody" and Jelly Roll Morton's "Dead Man Blues" were about.

In any case, the Tristano school was not just a gathering of like-minded talents but a school almost literally—one whose "curriculum" (solos by Louis Armstrong, Lester Young, Roy Eldridge, Charlie Parker, Charlie Christian, and other chosen masters were sung, memorized, and analyzed) traced a particular historical and critical line in order to give rise to a new one. That it managed to do so (Konitz and Marsh, while owing great debts to Tristano, also proved to be quite individual masters) suggests that historical self-consciousness in jazz had become a potentially vital source of creativity.

Tristano's rhythmic approach involved superimposing layers of polyrhythms onto the 4/4 pulse in order to free up the placing of accents and generate microsubdivisions of the beat—as though the goal were to travel by other means to the place where Charlie Parker's music lived. That Tristano had to get there is evident from the passion of such improvisations as "Line-Up" (Atlantic/Mosaic, 1955) and "C-Minor Complex" (Atlantic/Mosaic, 1960); he knew (as the rest of jazz would come to know) that Parker's virtuosity had brought jazz rhythm to a state of near-crisis.

However "swing" is defined, it would seem that up to and including Parker, jazz's rhythmic language depended on the presence of relatively stable metrical frameworks—ones in which rhythmic events could be shaped by, as Igor Stravinsky put it, "the fruitful convention of the bar." But in Parker's music, the ability to make meaningful microsubdivisions of the beat within such frameworks may have reached a kind of physical or perceptual barrier. In any case, nearly five decades after his death (a very long time for an art such as jazz), that barrier arguably remains unbreached—by John Coltrane, by Ornette Coleman, by anybody. New metrical frameworks, looser metrical frameworks, no metrical frameworks—the issues were in the air.

One hallmark of the pre-Coleman jazz avant-garde was an overt, technically sophisticated experimentalism. Such composers as George Russell, John Carisi, Duane Tatro, Gil Melle, Teddy Charles, Jimmy Giuffre, Teo Macero, and Charles Mingus were well aware of this century's developments in modern classical composition and eager to sort out which aspects of Stravinsky, Schoenberg, Bartók, et al. might bear fruit in a jazz context. One thinks in particular of Carisi's "Lestorian Mode" (Savoy, 1950) and "Moon Taj" (Impulse, 1961); of the remarkably varied moods of Russell's *Jazz Workshop* album (RCA, 1956) and of his bristlingly compact "Lydian M-1" (Atlantic, 1956) and more expansive *All About Rosie* (Columbia, 1957) and "Chromatic Universe" (Decca, 1960), on most of which his writing stirred striking solo responses from pianist Bill Evans; of the way Tatro's "Minor Incident" (Contemporary/OJC, 1955), with its solemn central horn call, consumes all it proposes with a passionate puritanism; of those stark yet delicate Melle pieces whose moods are exemplified by the title of one of his albums, *Primitive Modern* (Prestige/OJC, 1956); and of the restless harmonic ingenuity of Charles's "Green Blues" (Atlantic, 1956).

To say that this music would be overtaken by history is in one sense a simple fact. And much the same fate would await such different but not totally dissimilar figures of the 1960s as pianist Andrew Hill, trombonist Grachan Moncur III, saxophonist Sam Rivers, and perhaps even trumpeters Booker Little and Eric Dolphy. At moments of peak expressionistic fervor, the music of those latter artists was avant-garde–like; one thinks, in particular, of Dolphy's performances with Mingus on "What Love," "Folk Forms No. 1," and "Stormy Weather" (all Candid/Mosaic, 1960) and of his own best album, *Out to Lunch* (Blue Note, 1964). Yet this music's air of experimentation rests upon implicitly conservative, "extending the boundaries" premises. Witness Dolphy's statement that "I play notes that would not ordinarily be said to be in a given key, but I hear them as proper." For the rhythmic and harmonic fluidities of a Hill or a Rivers to work, the underlying musical language must be stable enough to accept the weight of their typically oblique inventions, and soon that stability would be gone.

The fate of an artist within an art is to some extent a matter of historical position; George Russell's music, for instance, began to alter (and perhaps not for the better) when it became clear that while players like Dolphy could inhabit his structures, they were not going to be crucially inspired by them, as Bill Evans had been before. Yet history's verdict does not erase aesthetic value; the best music of Russell, Tatro, Charles, Melle, and their colleagues survives, as does that of their mid-1960s near-counterparts.

Ornette Coleman's "daring simplifications" (the term is Max Harrison's) would seem to come from a different world from that of all the avant-garde jazz that preceded them; and in one sense that is true. Coleman was a native of Fort Worth, Texas, and his early music sounds as though the techniques of Charlie Parker were being read backwards until they trailed away into the jazz, folk, and popular music pasts of the American Southwest—from the loping swing of guitarist Charlie Christian and Bob Wills's Texas Playboys back to blues singers like Blind Lemon Jefferson. Coleman made pitch flexible and speech-like (you can, he famously said, play flat in tune and sharp in tune), while the irregular length and shape of his phrases, and their relation to his no less plastic sense of harmonic rhythm, had an air of raw, homemade freedom that seemed to violate jazz's norms of craft professionalism.

Much has been, and should be, made of Coleman's initial misunderstanding of a basic musical fact: when he acquired his first alto saxophone at age fourteen or fifteen and taught himself to play by ear, he thought that "the first seven letters of the alphabet were the first seven letters of music, ABCDEFG." (The alto saxophone is a transposing instrument; C on the piano is A on the alto, a major sixth higher than concert pitch, and Coleman did not realize this when he started playing the alto.) But the tension between what Coleman "knew" (all the things that his ear was telling him in unique, homemade detail) and what he didn't know (standard musical terminology) proved to be immensely fruitful.

Having separated the names of pitches and their meanings (to him) allowed Coleman to enter a vividly personal world of harmonic relativism, though this relativism was not the "loosening" it might have seemed. Harmony for Coleman remained an area of major potential meaning, and for that reason, his music should not be thought of as modal in the sense that *modality* was used to describe the music that Miles Davis and Bill Evans began to make in the late 1950s and early 1960s.

For those men, and the host of musicians they influenced, modal procedures served to protect a potentially fragile lyrical growth. Witness Davis's remark, "When you go that way [curtail chordal change and increase its ambiguity] you can go on forever ... [and] do more with the [melodic] line." But Coleman's appetite for cadence often was as vigorous as his melodic gift; he and his partners did not need to curtail cadential harmonic events but rather to be cadential when and where they wanted to be.

Coleman's body of work from 1959 to 1967 is large, despite periods when he withdrew from the scene because of dissatisfaction with the business side of the music business, and quite varied—the southwestern lope of "Ramblin'," the keening cries of "Lonely Woman," the threatened wholeness of "Peace," the astonishing one-off group composition "Beauty Is a Rare Thing," the epic compendium that is his "Cross Breeding" solo, and so forth (Atlantic, 1959–61)—all of this in the company of some remarkable partners and peers: trumpeter Don Cherry, bassists Charlie Haden, Scott LaFaro, Jimmy Garrison, and David Izenzon, and drummers Billy Higgins, Ed Blackwell, and Charles Moffett.

That the members of Coleman's rhythm sections were expected to be full partners in his music was evident from the first. The speechlike phrases of "Lonely Woman," for one, are inseparable from Haden's thrummed-out ostinato; and the continuing dramatic interaction between Coleman and Haden on this piece is all the more satisfying because one feels certain that neither man is merely playing a part. Even more striking, because the interaction takes place on a deeper level, is the way Haden's bowed arabesques and the lines traced by Blackwell's tom-toms crucially shape the remarkable and largely spontaneous "Beauty Is a Rare Thing."

Coleman's own rhythm is, in one sense, less complex than Parker's—as is the rhythmic sense of every post-Parker jazz musician, if one is speaking of rhythmic events that take place within a metrical framework. "Ornette Coleman's playing seemed very different when I began listening to him," said trumpeter Doc Cheatham, "but I finally figured out that what he was doing was playing a lot of old swing patterns and putting them in different places than we did, phrasing them differently within the beat." Against that, one should place Coleman's own remark, overheard by Martin Williams at a 1961 rehearsal: "I wish it were possible to maintain the swing without making an obvious beat. I confess I don't know how to do that." There is, however, another way to look at this situation, and it was up to pianist Cecil Taylor to propose it.

Pre-Coleman jazz was marked by a steady increase in harmonic complexity. And this took place against the backdrop of this century's Western concert music, in which an increase in harmonic complexity had led not only to a radical loosening of tonal function but also to Arnold Schoenberg's invention or discovery of a way of organizing music that did not depend on tonal function at all. Thus such early Taylor recordings as *Jazz Advance* (Transition/Blue Note, 1955) and *Looking Ahead!* (Contemporary/OJC, 1958) led composer-critic Gunther Schuller to conclude that the high level of dissonance in Taylor's music meant that his work must be related to that of the "minority of jazz composer-performers" whose music "often spills over into areas so removed from any center of tonal gravity that it can be thought of as 'atonal.'"

But while dissonance for Taylor would come to play almost no tonally functional role, that was not because he had a need to stretch or weaken tonal functions. Rather, what he seems to have been trying to do was collapse all elements onto the level of melodicized rhythm—into a series of leaps, attacks, and their resulting, accumulating shapes in which dissonance plays an accent, dynamics, or attack role more than a harmonic one. That is, in any chord or cluster that Taylor strikes, the degree of dissonance essentially serves to alter one's sense of the force with which the blow has been struck and the obliqueness with which the blow has been delivered—the resulting control over rhythmic detail being, at best, near-microscopic.

Taylor's early partner, bassist Buell Neidlinger, has said that despite its apparently formidable level of complexity, he found from the first that Taylor's music "was *clear*. I could *see* it as well as *feel* it." Consider, for instance, the accelerating burst of notes with which Taylor emerges from the ensemble on "Mixed" (Impulse, 1961). While the passage does not take place within the boundaries of the piece's already loose metrical framework, except in the sense that Taylor's outburst and the framework coexist, the melodic-rhythmic shape of that outburst is so far from amorphous as to be almost tangible. It is as though Taylor's gestures are being traced across the musical equivalent of a nonillusionistic painting, one whose sense of surface and space those gestures in turn create.

Taylor still reserves the right to make harmony do some work on the level of local expectations, but it is the skein of melodicized beats that usually tells the story—its "collapsing of elements" principle as evident as the weather. (On the other hand, few kinds of music are more frustrating if the listener cannot bring to it the hands-off attentiveness it requires.) Indeed, Taylor's musical language can be alarmingly (or thrillingly) unencoded; as the poet Frank O'Hara wrote of the "things" in Jackson Pollock's work: "They were left intact, and given back. Paint is paint, shells and wire are shells and wire, glass is glass, canvas is canvas.... [O]ne is present at the problem and at the solution simultaneously."

A father figure to much of the avant-garde, John Coltrane, like Moses, was not destined to enter the promised land. There were, in the latter portion of Coltrane's career, at least two dramatic turning points: first, his shift from the dense "sheets of sound" harmonic patterning of "Giant Steps" (Atlantic, 1959) to the agonized, harmonically stripped down expressionism that would be exemplified by "Chasin' the Trane" (Impulse, 1961); and second, his abandonment of meter, which began in 1965 and continued to his death in 1967. Both of those developments were startling, and both arose because the relationship between foreground and background in Coltrane's music was an uncommonly uneasy one—so much so that it seemed at times as though he wished to erase the line between foreground and background and fuse all elements into one. That is certainly what happens on "Giant Steps": to negotiate at speed the harmonic obstacle course that Coltrane devised for himself is to find that many melodic and rhythmic choices have almost been predetermined—which may be why, as Ekkehard Jost has pointed out, "some melodic patterns in the first chorus [of Coltrane's "Giant Steps" solo] appear note for note later on." On "Chasin' the Trane," the uneasy background/foreground turbulence yields a very different-sounding yet finally similar result. On "Blue Train" (Blue Note, 1957), Coltrane had invented a corruscatingly brilliant, "foreground" solo against a spare blues backdrop; on "Chasin' the Trane," against an even more stripped-down blues framework, he plays a long expressionistic solo of such narrow melodic scope that pitches seem to have become almost irrelevant—the goal, in the face of Elvin Jones's galvanic drums, again being to virtually merge with an extravagant background rather than to differentiate oneself from it. In 1961 Coltrane said, "I admit I don't love the beat in the strict sense, but at this phase I feel I need the beat somewhere." By 1965 it had become clear, in the words of his biographer Lewis Porter, that Coltrane "no longer wanted to swing" but rather to play over "a general churning pulse of fast or slow." Here, too, the example of Charlie Parker may have been crucial. While Coltrane was regarded by his peers as perhaps the most *forcefully* swinging soloist of his time, he could not, within a metrical framework, approach Parker's dauntingly transcendent rhythmic acuity.

The music of Sun Ra has been described as enigmatic and ambiguous; the same could be said of the music of Albert Ayler. And the careers of both men have a somewhat similar, odd shape in relation to those of most other major figures in the jazz avant-garde.

There can be little doubt that Ayler, before his death in 1970 at age thirty-four, had largely forsaken the disruptive and eruptive musical vision that he had realized with striking power on such albums as *Spiritual Unity* (ESP, 1964), *Ghosts* (Debut, 1964), and *Bells* (ESP, 1965) and had instead begun to traffic, on albums like *New Grass* (Impulse, 1968), in a music of love-beads and peace-sign banality.

By the same token, Sun Ra's bold athematic structures of the mid-1960s—"The Magic City" (Saturn, 1965), "Other Planes of There" (Saturn, 1966), and "Outer Nothingness" (ESP, 1965)—are never more than a few steps removed from what Terry Martin has called a "comic strip futurism," which in turn is crucial to the air of the alienated prophet that bound to Sun Ra the very musicians who would realize his ideas with a dedication that only a community of true believers could have supplied. And Sun Ra, like Ayler, eventually would step back from, though not entirely renounce, his most striking music—offering up stage shows of surrealistic vaudeville and shaky re-creations of Fletcher Henderson arrangements. (Sun Ra had played piano in Henderson's band in 1946–47; the late-1940s stage shows at Chicago's Club DeLisa for which Sun Ra wrote arrangements are the source, reflected in a funhouse mirror, for his band's costumed theatrics.)

Listening to Ayler's music, one can understand why critics as astute as Martin Williams ("Does Albert Ayler attempt to make music from only a negative premise?") and André Hodeir ("[a] facile . . . search for paroxysmic expression") had the responses to it they did. Once the bugle-call, march, or hymn themes have been stated, one is in a world where, as Ayler himself said, Ornette Coleman's music sounds "neo-avant-garde," where the tempered scale and meter have been jettisoned, the range of dynamics is without precedent, at least in nonelectronic music, and the persona of the improviser seems to veer between delirium and bathos.

Yet there is Max Harrison's estimate that Ayler's notes "follow a real, if unfamiliar, logic," Terry Martin's detection, "despite the arhythmic atmosphere," of a "complex division of the beat," and this writer's belief—having heard Ayler "live" under optimal conditions (with trombonist Roswell Rudd and alto saxophonist John Tchicai) in 1964—that his music's ability to overwhelm, its rhetoric of sheer scale, had a more than subjective basis. In particular—and this trait, striking in performance, seems evident on record only at odd moments on several tracks on *Ghosts*—Ayler's unprecedented range of volume seemed not just a matter of dynamics but the dawn of a language of timbres, a possibility that would echo in the work of such post-Ayler figures as saxophonists Evan Parker and Roscoe Mitchell.

At the time, this writer and some others felt that the past, present, and future of the jazz avant-garde had been encapsulated in *Sound* (Delmark, 1966), the first album made under the leadership of Roscoe Mitchell, later one of the founders of the Art Ensemble of Chicago. Much that has happened since has confirmed that view (mostly, in Mitchell's case, the music he would make under his own name, especially the solo and saxophone-quartet versions of "Nonaah," "L-R-G," and "The Maze" [Nessa, 1976–78]). And to that music and the early work of other figures who were part of the remarkable Chicago avant-garde nexus (pianist Muhal Richard Abrams, saxophonists Joseph Jarman and Anthony Braxton, trumpeter Leo Smith, et al.), I would now emphatically add the work of England's Spontaneous Music Ensemble.

Sound contained a piece titled "Ornette," but the offhand savagery of its theme statement and of Mitchell's solo were far from Coleman-like. A practicing postmodernist before the fact and without the b.s., Mitchell presents us with a frenzy that is at once real and an object; "I'm looking at someone," his solo seems to say, "who happens to be me and is possessed." "The Little Suite," also from *Sound,* not only gives us those fierce multiple viewpoints, now cloaked in a vivid orchestral fabric, but also builds into the performance a serio-comic historical self-awareness—as though Mitchell had picked the lock of the imaginary museum and begun to jitterbug with the artifacts.

That Mitchell is such an inherently thoughtful artist brings us both to the music of the SME and its related figures and to a series of questions that many musicians and listeners must have been asking themselves during this period: What in the jazz avant-garde is the relationship between "heat" and creativity? Is this music inherently hyperbolic, alive only when it is poised on the brink of frenzy? Or does it have room for artists of cooler temperament who may wish to push toward extremes without dramatizing their intent or immolating themselves in the process?

Soprano saxophonist Steve Lacy said of the response of European musicians when he toured Europe in the mid-1960s that "it was as if some of them had been waiting for someone to thrust this music upon them." Surely, some thrusting could have been done in return by the musicians (trumpeter Kenny Wheeler, trombonist Paul Rutherford, saxophonists Evan Parker and Trevor Watts, guitarist Derek Bailey, bassists Dave Holland and Barry Guy, and drummer John Stevens) who recorded under the SME aegis the soundtrack for a film titled *Withdrawal* (Emanem, 1966–67) and the album *Karobyin* (Island/Chronoscope, 1968). Collectively created by artists of reflective as well as explosive temperament, those distinctive works also made it clear that the jazz avant-garde no longer would be, if it ever had been, a matter of one dominant style or set of techniques.

"You have improvised music," Evan Parker has said, "where it's pretty clear what kinds of things can happen and why and when. And then you have improvised music where the fact that there's an understanding [among the musicians] is clear, but quite how it works is moved to a level of mystery again."

Pianists of the 1960s and 1970s

Bob Blumenthal

Boundaries can be deceptive things, especially when it comes to a topic as rich as "jazz pianists of the sixties and seventies." The borders of our subject are marked off clearly enough, yet they take in many more players than one might intially imagine. After all, the entire history of jazz piano was still being practiced by its originators during the twenty years in question, often in close proximity to each other. I recall hearing Willie "the Lion" Smith and Jaki Byard at the same club within a week in 1971 and considering the juxtaposition atypical yet hardly unique. When festival producer George Wein organized a concert for the White House in 1978, he was able to include Eubie Blake, Teddy Wilson, Mary Lou Williams, Dick Hyman, McCoy Tyner, Herbie Hancock, Chick Corea, and Cecil Taylor on the same bill. There is probably no other score of years during which the complete evolution of a single instrument has been displayed as comprehensively or as well.

Since many of the veterans were not simply surviving but thriving, and since several of the period's dominant stylists were players who emerged in the previous decade and were just hitting their stride, the standards against which emerging talents were measured during the

Bill Evans. Courtesy of Frank Driggs Collection.

sixties and seventies were particularly high. At the same time, trends such as the popularity of the Hammond B-3 organ in the early sixties, the introduction of electric pianos and synthesizers by decade's end, and the elimination of keyboards by the majority of avant-garde bands throughout the period created several new pianoless ensembles. These were the years when it became common to speak of "acoustic" pianos, and when many pianists settled for portable electric alternatives out of nothing so much as frustration with the inferior instruments they encountered on the road.

By the end of the seventies, jazz piano encompassed an even more elaborate tapestry of styles and stylists than it had twenty years earlier. A handful of essential new voices had emerged and blossomed into influences for a broader pool of players, while the music of giants from previous decades took on added relevance. What resulted remains a grand legacy that resists being graphed according to sequential changes in technique or shifts in public taste. The era is best appreciated by considering several generations of musicians who made the sixties and seventies the piano's golden jazz age.

The Classic Stylists

Nothing indicates the multigenerational riches of the period as clearly as the resurgence of Earl Hines. In 1960 it appeared that Hines's greatest years were behind him. His triumphs with Louis Armstrong and his own Grand Terrace Orchestra were now part of history, with the future holding out a series of demeaning dixieland jobs. Yet Hines rallied in 1964 at a now-legendary New York concert documented on *The Real Earl Hines* (Contact) that found his technique more aggressive, his ideas more abstract, and his emotions more charged than ever. He then embarked on a recording binge that lasted throughout the period and is highlighted by two live *Grand Reunion* volumes (Limelight) that place him in the feisty company of Roy Eldridge and Coleman Hawkins, and such classic solo collections as *Spontaneous Explorations* (Red Baron) and the series of *Quintessential Recording Sessions* (Chiaroscuro) that reprise his earliest solo efforts. As a result, Hines dominated the piano category of jazz critics' polls for much of the period.

It was a creative time for several of his contemporaries as well. Duke Ellington produced his best piano-and-orchestra recital, *Piano in the Background* (Columbia), dipped his toes in the avant-garde with Charles Mingus and Max Roach on *Money Jungle* (Blue Note), and concluded his career with intimate performances like the duet *This*

One's for Blanton (Pablo) with bassist Ray Brown. The perpetually self-effacing Count Basie placed more attention on his own playing with a series of small-group albums for Pablo beginning in 1973, including the trio effort For the First Time and the unlikely yet charming series of Satch and Josh encounters with Oscar Peterson. One of the surviving stride masters compiled a delightful illustrated oral history on The Memoirs of Willie the Lion Smith (RCA Victor) and taped stunning duets with Don Ewell on Grand Piano (Sackville). Emerging from an obscurity even deeper than Hines's, Jay McShann returned as a paragon of Kansas City piano (and blues singing) in the seventies with a string of rafter-shaking albums including Crazy Legs and Friday Strut (Sackville) with Buddy Tate and The Last of the Blue Devils (Atlantic). Mary Lou Williams was also rediscovered in the seventies after years of inactivity and recorded the forward-looking trio collection Zoning (Smithsonian/Folkways) as well as Embraced (Pablo Live), a less successful live encounter with Cecil Taylor. Dick Wellstood and His Famous Orchestra (Chiaroscuro) found the young classicist in eloquent duet with Kenny Davern, while Art Hodes and Teddy Wilson also continued to soldier on.

Modernists in Maturity

The popular modern pianists of 1960 proved to be a resilient bunch over the next two decades. A few, like Red Garland and George Shearing, lost their hold on the public, and André Previn (a momentary audience favorite for his jazz versions of Broadway shows) shifted his attention to classical music. The seminal Bud Powell and his childhood friend Elmo Hope each succumbed to societal forces and personal demons after returning to New York for a brief moment of resurgence. Yet the more common experience for the reigning pianists of 1960 was to sustain the quality of their music with little evolution in their concepts. Ray Bryant, Hank Jones, Billy Taylor (the last with an increased profile after leading the band on David Frost's television show), and, until their deaths, Sonny Clark, Wynton Kelly, and Erroll Garner were consistent in their approach and collectively helped to define the amorphous notion of the modern mainstream. Several of their contemporaries survived these decades with significant changes in their performing situations if not their styles, often dictated by economic rather than aesthetic considerations.

Oscar Peterson may have experienced the easiest transition. Over this twenty-year span, he was the most consistently popular jazz pianist with the general public and the obvious inheritor of Art Tatum's mantle as the instrument's reigning virtuoso. Peterson also entered the sixties leading his greatest trio, featuring bassist Ray Brown and drummer Ed Thigpen; the group made its definitive recordings in 1961 on a series of live albums now collected as *The London House Sessions* (Verve). Yet the commercial dominance of rock in the late sixties made it difficult for even Peterson to sustain a working band and a recording presence in the United States. He taped solo albums and uncommon pairings like a series of duets with trumpet players and the aforementioned encounters with Basie. Once his manager, Norman Granz, returned to the record business with the Pablo label in 1973, Peterson again became jazz's most prolifically documented pianist; but the era of the Oscar Peterson trio with fixed personnel was over.

Road weariness and changes in the music business caught up with other audience favorites as well. Dave Brubeck, who entered the sixties at a commercial peak with the million-selling single "Take Five" and continued to press his experiments with time signatures, disbanded his signature quartet with Paul Desmond in 1967 and played out the period with a series of similarly designed units, the most notable of which had Gerry Mulligan in the saxophone chair. John Lewis sustained the profile of the Modern Jazz Quartet as a premier concert attraction until 1974, when the group temporarily disbanded and Lewis turned much of his attention to teaching. The classic Ahmad Jamal trio was dissolved in 1962, and the group Jamal led for much of the next decade, heard to best advantage on *The Awakening* (Impulse) from 1970, found the pianist in a decidedly more assertive voice. After dabbling with electric piano, he was taken out of the limelight by the economic woes that permeated jazz in the seventies.

Horace Silver was a lesser presence as well by 1980, although in his case an arthritic condition was a contributing factor. Yet Silver sustained his early success better than most, thanks to the prominence of what became identified as soul jazz and the consistent quality of his quintet music. Japanese strains merged with the already prevalent Latin and gospel touches in Silver's writing in the early sixties; and after disbanding his classic quintet with trumpeter Blue Mitchell and tenor saxophonist Junior Cook, heard to excellent advantage on the 1963 album *Silver's Serenade* (Blue Note), Silver turned right around and released his greatest hit, *Song for My Father* (Blue Note). New stars including Joe Henderson, Woody Shaw, and the Brecker Brothers kept the Silver band in the forefront well into the seventies; and the public's taste for funky piano jazz, which momentarily created an opening for the talented Bobby Timmons and brought more lasting success to Les McCann and Ramsey Lewis, ensured that Silver's brittle, sanctified inventions would continue to be heard.

And then there was Thelonious Monk. Listeners already won over to his writing, playing, and quartets by 1960 could argue that Monk offered nothing new during the remainder of his career; but the general public needed time to catch up. Monk found unexpected success and prominence (including a 1964 cover story in *Time* magazine) throughout the sixties, and his new recording affiliation with Columbia produced such worthy albums as *Criss-Cross* and *Big Band and Quartet in Concert*. He also toured with a Giants of Jazz unit including Dizzy Gillespie, Sonny Stitt, and Art Blakey in 1971–72 before withdrawing from active performing. Two students of Monk's dissonant, rhythmically charged, and sonically rich approach were far less successful in America and expatriated after recording seminal works: Mal Waldron, who cut his masterpiece *The Quest* in 1961 and moved to Germany four years later, and Randy Weston, who followed such early-sixties triumphs of African-inflected jazz as *Uhuru Afrika* (Roulette) and *African Cookbook* (Atlantic/Koch Jazz) with a move to Morocco in 1968.

Other modern pianists suffered in domestic obscurity despite continuing to create important music. The innovative Lennie Tristano devoted most of his final years to teaching, although he did release an exceptional solo album in 1961, *The New Tristano* (Atlantic), that marked significant growth in both his technical and expressive capacity. The dazzling Phineas Newborn Jr., while hampered by mental problems throughout the period, produced an intermittent series of trio recordings on Contemporary (of which the initial *A World of Piano!* is the best) that also revealed a new emotional commitment. Hampton Hawes, who completed his drug-related incarceration in 1963, continued to play with exemplary intensity and feeling until his death fifteen years later without attracting more than passing attention. Jimmy Rowles somehow managed to buck the trends, emerging in the late seventies from decades of little-noticed work to attain hidden-treasure status by displaying his quietly subversive style and voluminous repertoire in collaborations with saxophonists including Stan Getz on *The Peacocks* (Columbia) and Zoot Sims on *If I'm Lucky* (Pablo).

Postmodern Fountainheads

This wealth of piano greats collectively provided the foundation from which new piano voices emerged. Those with the greatest influence and originality had surfaced by 1970, and most of them could claim affiliation at one point or another with Miles Davis, suggesting just how crucial the trumpeter's taste proved to be in the piano's evolution. It was Davis who made electric pianos acceptable in the jazz world by incorporating their sound into his quintet beginning in 1968, and Davis who replaced keyboards with guitars in his group in 1973, two gestures that proved to be accurate barometers of the piano's short-term health.

Prior to the sixties, Davis's endorsement had done much to further the reputations of Ahmad Jamal (who never worked with the trumpeter), Red Garland, and Wynton Kelly; but the most important pianist to receive the Davis imprimatur had been Bill Evans. It might be argued that the hallmarks of the Evans style—the intimate touch and lucid lyricism, the harmonic inversions that produced such striking voicings, the subtly propulsive rhythmic shifts, the command of modal rather than chordal improvising, even the collective balance of his trio concept—had already emerged in the fifties. After all, *Portrait in Jazz* (Riverside/OJC), the first recording by the classic Evans trio with bassist Scott LaFaro and drummer Paul Motian, was taped at the end of 1959. Yet the sixties were the period when Evans came into his own and became the most influential jazz pianist since Bud Powell.

It appeared at first that the era would be dominated by the original Evans trio, in which the audacious bass lines of LaFaro achieved an unprecedented prominence and Motian's floating rhythms further blurred the traditional distinction between soloist and accompanist. The group made great strides during its brief existence and was captured in brilliant voice on what proved to be its final appearance on the Riverside/OJC albums *Sunday at the Village Vanguard* and *Waltz for Debby*. Then LaFaro was killed in a highway accident in July 1961, and Evans, already burdened by heroin addiction, retreated into one of the debilitating periods that would mark the final two decades of his life.

He emerged a year later to organize another trio, and until his death in 1980 Evans further refined his probing yet lyrical approach. There were a few experiments with solo and multitracked playing like the beautiful *Conversations With Myself* (Verve) in 1963, occasional studio projects with horn soloists, and even an odd turn to the electric keyboard; yet trio playing was Evans's strength, and he pursued it with unflagging intensity up to the very end. From the numerous examples of his work in these years, *At the Montreux Jazz Festival* (Verve, 1968, with Eddie Gomez and Jack DeJohnette) and

Highlights From Turn Out the Stars (Warner Bros., 1980, with Marc Johnson and Joe LaBarbera) offer excellent perspectives on his influential style.

Of the many pianists whose work reflected the Evans influence, a short list would have to include Clare Fischer, Don Friedman, Steve Kuhn, Andy LaVerne, Mike Nock, and Denny Zeitlin.

The growing fascination with modal improvisation led pianists to both Evans and the period's other most influential new pianist, McCoy Tyner. While he never worked with Miles Davis, Tyner did support John Coltrane in the saxophonist's epochal quartet from 1960–1965, and it was there that Tyner brought his flurries of pentatonic scales and pendular left-hand punctuations to bear on Coltrane's increasingly expressionistic compositions. Tyner finally struck out on his own in 1966, after Coltrane had dispensed with fixed rhythms and key centers; but by this time the pianist had added his stamp to a host of classic Coltrane performances, including the Impulse! albums *Impressions, John Coltrane and Johnny Hartman, Crescent*, and *A Love Supreme*.

Impulse was also the label where Tyner launched his own solo career, although he did not truly come into his own until moving to Blue Note and recording *The Real McCoy* in 1967. That album, which found Tyner extending his Coltrane experience while retaining ties to postbop conventions, includes the best example of his talents as a composer. Other excellent albums such as *Extensions* followed, even as the rise of rock and fusion put Tyner's acoustic, edge-of-avant-garde approach in great commercial peril. Yet he survived throughout the seventies as an acoustic bellwether, refusing to adopt electric keyboards and recording a succession of popular albums for Milestone, including sessions for combo (*Sahara*), solo recitals (*Echoes of a Friend*), and even a collection with strings (*Fly Like the Wind*).

Among the younger players who were touched by Tyner, Alice Coltrane, Stanley Cowell, John Hicks, Harold Mabern, and Lonnie Liston Smith were among the most widely recorded.

For sheer versatility, however, both Evans and Tyner were eclipsed by Herbie Hancock, whose evolution might stand as a summary for the entire period. Hancock first emerged with trumpeter Donald Byrd in 1961 as a modernist who combined touches of soul, Evans-like introspection, and harmonic experimentation in a generally modern-mainstream style. If his funky composition "Watermelon Man" from his first Blue Note album, *Takin' Off*, was widely popular, Hancock could also turn around and challenge his listeners. This became even clearer when Miles Davis hired Hancock in 1963, which brought the pianist into nightly contact with bassist Ron Carter and drummer Tony Williams. The daring and range of this unit's work is best appreciated by hearing them with Davis (on the excellent 1966 Columbia disc *Miles Smiles*, for example) and operating under Hancock's name on Blue Note in the evocative *Empyrean Isles* (1964) and *Maiden Voyage* (1965).

When Davis prevailed upon Hancock to use the electric piano in 1968, a major shift in keyboard playing and jazz in general was launched. The tingling, switched-on sound that Hancock obtained on the Davis album *Filles de Kilimanjaro* (1968) and elsewhere pointed jazz in the direction of rock, an avenue the pianist explored more extensively after forming his own sextet in 1968. A second synthesizer player, Patrick Gleeson, was even added to obtain more dense electronic textures. Some bracing music resulted, particularly on the extended 1970 and 1972 performances included on *Mwandishi* (Warner Bros.); but the experimental edge of this music proved to be commercial poison. So Hancock reorganized his band in 1973, and on the new unit's debut album, *Headhunters* (Columbia), he blended layered keyboards and funk rhythms into a winning pop formula. From there, Hancock worked both sides of the street, returning to acoustic piano in reunions of his Davis associates under the name V.S.O.P., then delving further into electric funk in what proved to be his ongoing fascination with new keyboard technology.

Hancock's influence would spread quickly, and continues to spread. It was felt most directly among those pianists who followed him in the Miles Davis band. Each worked exclusively on electric keyboards with the trumpeter, and each became a significant stylist in his own right.

Chick Corea shared a bit of Hancock's funky background through his work with Blue Mitchell and added a strong affinity for Latin music nurtured during time as a sideman with Willie Bobo and Herbie Mann. In addition, Corea revealed an appreciation for European composers and freer forms of improvisation, especially on his excellent 1968 trio album *Now He Sings, Now He Sobs* (Blue Note). These interests were placed on hold while Corea worked with Miles Davis in 1968–70, then briefly reemerged when Corea and bassist Dave Holland jointly left Davis to pursue the avant-garde in the cooperative quartet Circle.

Even as Circle released some of the era's most persuasively interactive free music on *Paris Concert* (ECM, 1971), Corea was retrenching into more accessible approaches. Like Hancock, for the remainder of the decade he sustained both an acoustic and electric direction in his music. His embrace of unaccompanied playing on two excellent volumes of *Piano Improvisations* (ECM, 1971) was the first indication that solo piano performance would become fashionable, while his duet work with vibist Gary Burton on *Crystal Silence* (ECM) in the following year introduced a partnership that has been sustained for nearly three decades.

Corea also returned to the electric piano for a brief 1972 stand accompanying Stan Getz, after which he took his partners in the Getz rhythm section and formed Return to Forever. The first addition of RTF featured Brazilians Airto Moreira and Flora Purim and presented a distinctly samba-oriented view of fusion; but this band was short-lived. With only bassist Stanley Clarke remaining, Corea retooled RTF to reflect the overtly technical and guitar-centered sound of John McLaughlin's Mahavishnu Orchestra, albeit with Corea's more lyrical profile peeking through the compositions. Yet even as fusion made Corea a star, he kept his acoustic facilities limber, and even mixed idioms on projects like his 1976 *My Spanish Heart* (Polydor).

Two more Miles Davis keyboard players made a major impact in the 1970s, although one—Joe Zawinul—had virtually given up playing acoustically by the time he began collaborating with the trumpeter in 1969. Zawinul was the true electric piano pioneer; he had played a Wurlitzer on a Jazzmobile truck while with Cannonball Adderley's band, an experience that inspired Zawinul to compose the crossover hit "Mercy, Mercy, Mercy." His efforts with Davis and Weather Report fall outside the context of this essay, though his success with ever more elaborate synthesizers could not help but be noticed by anyone who played a piano.

In contrast, Keith Jarrett put electric keyboards aside after his 1970 tenure with Davis and became the most vocal champion of acoustic playing. Drawing upon his prodigious technique and a musical knowledge that managed to simultaneously embrace gospel music, Bill Evans, European classical composers, and Ornette Coleman, Jarrett became the dominant new piano voice of the 1970s. His extended solo concert improvisations became an international rage after being documented on *The Köln Concert* (ECM, 1975); his more swing-oriented quartet music was performed by two bands, an American quartet heard on Impulse (*Treasure Island*, 1973) and a European counterpart that recorded different original music for ECM (*Belong-*

ing, 1974); and his symphonic compositions also began to be played and documented. Jarrett was often overindulgent and pompous, especially in his solo concerts; but there were undeniable stretches of brilliance in even his most tedious marathons, and his music reached a huge number of jazz and nonjazz listeners alike.

Freer Frontiers

While the majority of improvising pianists in the 1960s and 1970s were formed by the Evans/Tyner/Hancock extension of the jazz keyboard continuum, a whole new world of music was opening to those who dared move beyond fixed harmonies, fixed rhythms, and fixed intonation. As a rule, efforts in this freer realm tended to have greater success (especially in the use of space and control of dynamics) when the piano was omitted, which produced a smaller number of influential pianists. Then again, many critical components of what was initially called the "new thing" spring from the work of one dominant pianist, Cecil Taylor.

Taylor is another carryover from the fifties, where his complex harmonies, ferocious keyboard attack, and mobile sound clusters had begun to chip at the wall of postbop convention. It was not until 1961, however, with the tracks that he recorded for initial release under the sponsorship of Gil Evans (they are now included on the Impulse anthology *Mixed*) that he began to move away from fixed swing rhythms and symmetrical phrase construction. In live recordings made in Denmark a year later, Taylor had reduced his working Unit to its basic components of Jimmy Lyons's alto sax, the drums of Sunny Murray, and Taylor's own piano, which stirred the music into a kinetic stew at the constant edge of overboil. As the decade progressed, Taylor returned to a larger sound canvas, with more horns to state the knotty melodic cells that triggered the improvisations and two bass players working in distinct textural areas. The 1966 recording *Unit Structures* (Blue Note) is the masterpiece of this period, though even in this septet it is Taylor's piano that constantly dictates direction.

The uncompromising nature of Taylor's music, magnified by the excessive length of his Unit's improvisations, severely limited his performing opportunities, so for economic as much as aesthetic reasons Taylor also began to work as a solo performer. This move placed his superhuman stamina and passionate attack on direct display, even as it omitted the charged interaction at the heart of his concept—and it did move some listeners to give Taylor a second listen when he began releasing albums again in the seventies. *Silent Tongues* (Freedom), his live solo recording from the 1974 Montreux Jazz Festival, was his most visible album of the decade, and is frequently cited as an entry point into Taylor's music; but his self-produced *Spring of Two Blue-Js* (Unit Core) from the previous year is more comprehensive with its side each of solo and quartet music, and the 1978 *3 Phasis* (New World) reveals just how powerful Taylor's extended band creations (this time by a sextet) remained at decade's end.

There were other pianists who participated in jazz's musical liberation movement, to be sure. Several, like Germany's Joachim Kuhn and Alexander von Schlippenbach and Holland's Misha Mengelberg, worked in the company of European improvisers with less attachment to swing, the blues, and popular song forms than the typical American musician, who tended to retain at least echoes of more conventional styles. Muhal Richard Abrams, Dave Burrell, and Horace Tapscott are surely examples of experimenters who frequently exposed their roots, especially Abrams in his neglected masterpiece from 1975 *Sightsong* (Black Saint). This is not to deny the greater formal ambitions of these pianists, or such younger players who followed as Anthony Davis, who took a more organized approach to improvising on albums like *Of Blues and Dreams* (Sackville, 1978) that made the term *free* seem a true misnomer. Then there was Sun Ra, who had been working with odd electric keyboards, walls of percussion, and collective improvisation in the fifties, and who found time at the head of his Arkestra to create everything from interplanetary chaos on *The Magic City* (Evidence, 1965) to cosmic funk on *Space Is the Place* (Impulse, 1972), with stops along the way for Fletcher Henderson and Ellington covers on *Sunrise in Different Dimensions* (hatART, 1980).

The less bombastic approach of Paul Bley, drawn from the blues-based melodic freedom of Ornette Coleman and extending the ensemble alchemy of Bill Evans, can be seen as the period's true alternative free approach to the Taylor standard. Bley was a bebop stylist who gained liberating notions while working with Coleman, George Russell, and—during a critical period in 1961–62—clarinetist Jimmy Giuffre. It was in the Giuffre 3 with bassist Steve Swallow that Bley first confronted free collective improvisation from melodic fragments, and he extended this approach into a trio that pushed the Evans/LaFaro/Motian model of interaction to its formal limits while retaining the texture and weight of more conventional piano/bass/drum units. Bley also dabbled in synthesizers and acoustic solo playing, even returning to chord changes when circumstances called for it, and assembled one of the period's largest discographies, of which the trio *Closer* (ESP, 1965) and solo *Open, to Love* (ECM, 1972) are among his most memorable efforts.

Neglected Masters

Every period has its overlooked geniuses who created brilliant original music yet made little impact on fellow musicians or the public at large. Of the many who might wear this dubious mantle from the sixties and seventies, Jaki Byard and Andrew Hill were the most potentially productive. They won polls in the "deserving wider recognition" categories and had many of their efforts hailed by critics, yet this was hardly enough to sustain performing careers. By 1980 each was a peripheral presence on the jazz scene.

Byard, who was nearly forty when he recorded his first albums in the early sixties, may have simply known too much music. He had made it a point to learn several instruments and recorded on saxophone and guitar as well as piano; and at the keyboard, he could shift from ragtime to no time in the course of a single piece with a bit of Erroll Garner mimicry along the way. Some of Byard's most famous work was as a sideman, with Charles Mingus (on the 1963 Impulse album *The Black Saint and the Sinner Lady*) and such Mingus alumni as Booker Ervin (*The Freedom Book*, Prestige, 1963) and Roland Kirk (*Rip, Rig and Panic*, Limelight, 1965); but his own multifaceted playing and writing made such Prestige trio and quintet albums as *Out Front!* (1964) and *Freedom Together!* (1966) and the Muse solo recital *Empirical* (1972) stunning—if eccentric—tours de force.

Andrew Hill pursued a more single-minded course, one that extended the harmonic richness of Monk in compositions with more asymmetrical structures and improvisations where an expansive keyboard technique enhanced his polychordal and polyrhythmic conception. Hill recorded a number of Blue Note albums during the 1963–65 period, and they suggested a way of opening up jazz through an exploration of complex chorus structures rather than the obliteration of formal signposts. Of these, *Black Fire* and *Point of Departure* feature the richest ensembles and the boldest writing. These concepts proved no more commercially viable than Cecil Taylor's—less, actually, without the revolutionary promise that Taylor's music conveyed. By 1970 Hill had become an itinerant sage, working outside the major jazz markets and occasionally resurfacing with recordings on foreign labels; and this sporadic profile remains his lot to this day.

There were other jazz pianists of great promise who showed early brilliance yet were sidetracked into other, more commercial directions. Roger Kellaway, who appeared at the same time as Hancook, showed similar signs of encompassing technique and stylistic scope. He recorded as a jazz pianist less frequently as the era progressed, though; and, despite the memorable jazz-classical fusion of his cello quartet, turned his attention toward the studio existence that rewarded him more lucratively for creations like the end theme of the TV series *All in the Family*.

A period so rich in piano talent inevitably left some great players by the wayside, only to find them emerging as significant figures in the ensuing decades. Consider, for instance, some of the most heralded players of recent years, who were active in the sixties and seventies yet essentially were footnotes to the general keyboard activity:

Dave McKenna, now hailed as a solo master from the premodern end of the spectrum, who spent most of the period in question living and playing on Cape Cod, and who did not launch the recording career with Concord Records that would make him a keyboard titan.

Tommy Flanagan, who created at least one classic recording in these years, *Eclypso* (Enja, 1977), yet was known in 1980 primarily for his long service supporting Ella Fitzgerald rather than as the jazz world's definitive trio pianist.

Kenny Barron, sideman of choice for Dizzy Gillespie, Freddie Hubbard, Yusef Lateef, Ron Carter, and many others, yet with only a handful of albums under his own name at the end of this active twenty-year period (including the 1973 *Sunset to Dawn*, reissued on the 32 Jazz album *Soft Spoken Here*).

Abdullah Ibrahim, a.k.a. Dollar Brand, the South African native whom Duke Ellington discovered in 1963, and whose early solo recitals such as *African Piano* (Japo, 1969) may have provided a model for Keith Jarrett, yet was more of a political curiosity than a musical force until he formed his septet Ekaya in 1982.

Don Pullen, a knuckles-and-elbows avant-gardist, whose mid-sixties duo *Nommo* (SPR) with drummer Milford Graves pushed the piano to its limits, yet who spent much of the period playing organ behind singers until a term with Charles Mingus in 1973–75 provided the impetus for co-leading an exceptional quartet with tenor saxophonist George Adams that debuted with *Don't Lose Control* (Soul Note) in 1979.

They too were pianists of the sixties and seventies—although few noticed until the eighties.

Jazz Singing Since the 1940s

Will Friedwald

Singing is the key area in which jazz interacts with the bigger, broader world of popular culture just beyond its boundaries. Although not a hyphenated term, *jazz singing* is in fact a hyphenated concept. In its narrowest definition, the phrase refers only to vocalists who do exactly what musicians do: improvise choruses of wordless melody on top of chord changes. At its broadest, the term stretches to the furthest reaches of classic American pop. This was particularly true in the '30s and '40s, when the swing era was so embedded in the collective mindset that even pop stars like Perry Como and Dinah Shore recorded credible jazz performances. Similarly, without exception, all of the major figures of jazz singing, from Louis Armstrong to Billie Holiday, Ella Fitzgerald, Sarah Vaughan, Anita O'Day, Dinah Washington, and Mel Tormé, also have at least one foot in pop. Even Betty Carter, who was as "pure" a jazz singer as it's possible to be, had a firm footing in standard song form and the popular repertoire.

For most of his career, the late Johnny Hartman worked with jazz musicians and in jazz clubs but insisted that he was not a "jazz singer"; "I'm an all-around singer," he would say. He thought that the jazz classification pigeonholed and therefore limited him. On the

Nat King Cole. Courtesy of the Institute of Jazz Studies, Rutgers University.

other hand, Tony Bennett was first heard of as a pop headliner who had to fight hard to earn the right to be included in the jazz community. He went out of his way to share his stage with Count Basie and Duke Ellington and show that his capacity for swing was second to none. Even so, the *New York Times* balked when Bennett, in a duo concert with Bill Evans, opened the Newport Jazz Festival in 1976.

Jazz singing proper begins with Louis Armstrong, and it is impossible to miss the influence of Armstrong on Bennett. What Miles Davis once said about Armstrong's trumpet playing ("You really can't play anything that Louis hasn't played, I mean, even modern") applies no less to singing. In the late '20s and '30s, Armstrong's influence on his colleagues—Ethel Waters, Bing Crosby, Billie Holiday, Ella Fitzgerald, Leo Watson—was deep and profound. No less remarkable is that this lineage of influence has never stopped; it is equally apparent in such postwar giants as Frank Sinatra, Anita O'Day, Billy Eckstine, Tony Bennett, Betty Carter, Peggy Lee, and Mel Tormé. None of them sounds like any of the others, yet they all sound a little bit like Louis Armstrong. They could not be considered part of the jazz experience unless they did.

In the postwar years, singers refined Armstrong's innovations and personalized them to a remarkable degree, but still virtually everything they did was traceable back to Pops. It might even be argued that singers stayed closer to Louis's legacy than instrumentalists: it was easier to hear the Louis lineage in major pop stars like Sinatra and Bennett than in jazz giants like Sonny Rollins or Clifford Brown.

If Armstrong was the unassuming genius who launched the phenomenon, Frank Sinatra was vocal music's Manhattan Project, the irresistible force that forever delineates the prewar and postwar periods. By now some readers are rankling at the inclusion of Sinatra in a jazz discussion, the same folks who write to *Down Beat* aghast whenever that leading journal of the jazz world puts Old Blue Eyes on its cover. Yet whether one personally considers Sinatra a jazz vocalist (on certain records, like *Songs for Swingin' Lovers*, on Capitol Records, and *Sinatra-Basie*, on Reprise, it's particularly hard to deny) or not is immaterial. No other artist has had such a widespread and lasting effect on everyone who sings the Great American Songbook, whether in a jazzy way or not, as Sinatra, who must be considered by far the most influential of Armstrong's torchbearers.

While bebop was the major musical revolution of the postwar years, the big economic and cultural upset of the same period was the decline of the big bands and conquest of the crooners, a movement precipitated by Sinatra. In 1942 the Hoboken-born vocalist graduated from Tommy Dorsey's band (empowered with a few hit records and phrasing techniques informed by the master trombonist himself) and in the process inspired an avalanche of former bandsingers to go solo. Sinatra upped the ante for popular music via his heightened sensitivity and his jazz-derived sense of rhythm. Although Sinatra never limited himself exclusively to jazz, his love of Armstrong and the big band ideal of the swinging beat—in either love songs or up-tempo numbers—are the foundation elements of his music. Long before Ella Fitzgerald's milestone *Song Book* albums (most on the Verve label), Sinatra was the first mainstream artist to concentrate on classic songs—the works of Cole Porter, George Gershwin, etc. His expressivity and depth (inspired to a degree by both Crosby and Holiday) directly made the careers of most subsequent pop and jazz singers possible, beginning with Eckstine and Nat Cole and even continuing into the current era.

Perhaps the most remarkable thing about pop singing in the Sinatra age was that so much of it was jazz. Ten years earlier, when Crosby was the dominant influence, that could have been said about a lot of the popular big bands of the '30s, but not star singers in general, who were still sounding like operetta tenors. By the postwar years, most male singers were a hybrid blend of Crosby's deep, rich sound tempered with Sinatra's heightened sensitivity. That applied to a lot of the white singers like Dick Haymes and Johnny Desmond who liberated themselves from the bands that spawned them, and also to black singers, who were, for the first time in pop history, being permitted to sing love songs.

Nat "King" Cole liked to claim that his whole singing career was an accident. Like the story of Louis Armstrong allegedly dropping the music to "Heebie Jeebies" and being forced to invent scat singing then and there, Cole's press agents liked to tell people that the King was a piano player who casually began vocalizing at the insistence of a persistent drunk. Cole's piano skills were so prodigious that he became, and could have remained, a major star without ever opening his mouth; it's one of American music's great ironies that the pop star who ended his career with "Rambling Rose" and "Those Lazy, Hazy, Crazy Days of Summer" began as a pianist worthy of mention in the same breath as Earl Hines, Teddy Wilson, and Bud Powell. On his earliest recordings with his soon-to-be famous King Cole Trio, Cole sings only intermittently, somewhat roughly, and strictly as a side dish. Yet by the time of his breakthrough vocal hits a decade later, such as "The Christmas Song" and "Nature Boy" (both on Capitol Records), his vocal instrument had developed into one of the smoothest sounds in pop. Like Sinatra, he had a capacity rare in pop for catching every beat of the pulse with his voice, and he was as hard a swinger, vocally, as his material allowed him to be. Some would say Cole's taste in songs wasn't as rarefied as Sinatra's; others would diplomatically claim it was simply more eclectic, an attribute which allowed him to have hits in the vein of country music and quasi-rock at the end of his short life.

Cole had a longer career as a hitmaker than Billy Eckstine; Cole kept landing hits until his death at forty-seven in 1965, whereas Eckstine had not been on the charts for almost a decade by then. Yet there were far more singers at the time who patterned themselves after Eckstine, and the most celebrated of his disciples was Sarah Vaughan, whom he referred to as his "little sister." They weren't exactly male and female equivalents of each other; Vaughan tended to play around with her melodies more, which allowed her to conform to a more conventional definition of the term *jazz singer* (although as Eckstine's classic version of "Body and Soul" shows, he could be just as jazzy as Vaughan).

But where it mattered, Eckstine and Vaughan were two peas in a pod: both got their start with pianist Earl Hines and had a deep technical knowledge of music (Eckstine played all the valve instruments, particularly trumpet, and Vaughan, piano). Both used their rich voices and rarefied sensibilities to incorporate the enhanced harmonic palette of modern jazz into love songs. While Eckstine (who vies with Nat Cole for the title of first black "crossover" star) only occasionally ventured beyond ballads, Vaughan worked in all manner of tempos. She was perhaps the most playful of jazz singers, using an endless array of rhythmic and tonal inventions to make even her distortions sound beautiful.

As mentioned above, high tenors—like Andy Kirk's Pha Terrell and Jimmie Lunceford's Dan Grissom—tended to predominate in the '30s, even among black bands and even after Bing Crosby. The success of Eckstine led to a reaffirmation of Crosby's discovery that the low notes were where the money was. After the success of "Mr. B," suddenly all the black singers were baritones or lower: particularly Al Hibbler, Duke Ellington's longest-lasting male singer, who combined Eckstine's harmonic richness with a surrealist's sense of distortion. Where Hibbler was more scabrous than Eckstine, Johnny Hartman was even smoother: his earliest sides show the young Chicagoan varying between Sinatra-style ultra-legato lines and Eckstinian sonic depth. Hartman's two masterpiece recordings, the 1956 *Songs From the Heart* (with trumpeter Howard McGhee, on Bethlehem) and the 1963 *John Coltrane and Johnny Hartman* (Impulse), brought jazz balladeering to new levels, each contrasting Hartman's rich voice and sensitive phrasing with a single master horn soloist and obbligatist.

In a sense, it was ironic that bebop's greatest contribution to vocal music was a clique of crooners who sang love songs with an expanded harmonic sense. Still, there were bebop singers who sounded more like what you would expect a bop singer to sound like, starting with Ella Fitzgerald and Anita O'Day. Although there had been a few established jazz stars who at least dabbled in the new music, like Benny Goodman and Coleman Hawkins, Fitzgerald, who had started her career at the birth of the swing era with Chick Webb's band, became bop's most essential spokeswoman.

As early as the end of the '30s, Fitzgerald had established herself as the greatest of all scat singers after Armstrong; a decade later she used the possibilities of the new music to elevate her vocal improvisations to an even higher plateau. She was, after all, roughly the same age as Dizzy Gillespie and the other founding fathers of the modern jazz movement, which exploded in the mid-'40s. With a musical mind as keen as Fitzgerald's, it was inevitable that she too would respond to the new harmonic and rhythmic challenges poised by bebop. Indeed, as the star of Jazz at the Philharmonic, the music's leading touring package, she would spend most of the '50s and '60s traveling with the essential players of both the swing and bop persuasions. And what she did for scat (most incredibly on her all-scat masterpiece, *Lullabies of Birdland*, Decca), she did even more fully for the songbook, recording a series of single-composer collection albums (starting officially with *The Cole Porter Song Book*, Verve) that were second only to Sinatra's legacy in establishing the canon of essential American songs.

Two years younger than Fitzgerald, Anita O'Day also found herself assigned to several camps. Like Fitzgerald and virtually every other vocalist of the era, she started as a swing band singer (in her case, with Gene Krupa and Stan Kenton); by the '50s, she was collaborating with many leading lights of the West Coast "cool school." Yet though she did much to help create the vocal subdivision of this latter genre, Anita O'Day is essentially a bebopper at heart. Her swingingly staccato style and clipped, vibratoless phrases are the very stuff that bop is made of. Also like Fitzgerald, O'Day is one of the most eminently listenable of all scat singers; though she lacks Fitzgerald's over-powering, superhuman virtuosity, O'Day scats with a unique dramatic flair and is never less than mesmerizing. Though described as "cool" because of her vibratoless tone, O'Day's singing is nevertheless emotionally rich, ranging from the jubilation of up-tempos like "Them There Eyes" and "Johnny One Note" to melancholy moods like "Angel Eyes" and her own "Waiter, Make Mine Blues" (all on Verve). All types of songs benefit from O'Day's commanding way with a melody, which she unceasingly plays with, speeds up, slows down, and rearranges in the hippest imaginable fashion.

O'Day ended up as the center of a movement: though she only sang a short while with Stan Kenton's orchestra, O'Day nonetheless established the vocal sound of that formidable aggregation. Subsequent singers with Kenton, most notably June Christy and Chris Connor, had to at least start their careers by adopting O'Day's distinctive sound. Christy is most celebrated as a dramatist, not for the musical drama of scat but the lyrical drama of words; in such classic albums as *Something Cool* and *The Misty Miss Christy* (both on Capitol) Christy reveals herself to be one of jazz's most accomplished storytellers.

Jeri Southern also belongs in this category, even though she never worked with Kenton; indeed, only her comparatively lesser recordings even employ a big band. Using small-group settings often centered around her own piano, Southern was a first-class cool-school vocalist of the most intimate kind. Helen Merrill, who made her premiere recordings with her first husband, clarinet Aaron Sachs, in Earl Hines's band in 1954, is certainly the most productive student of the cool school in later decades. From her early albums with Gil Evans and Clifford Brown (EmArcy) to more recent outings with Wayne Shorter (Polygram), Merrill's artistry is about casting a sonic spell. It's pure sound that matters, even more than the accompaniment or the material.

The one major singer who consciously sought to use the cool sound in his work, however, was Mel Tormé, and even he objected to the term itself. Torme too had swing roots, not only with the big bands of Artie Shaw and Chico Marx, but with his own innovative vocal group, the Mel-Tones. But Tormé was inspired by the sound of the Miles Davis Nonet and the Gerry Mulligan Tentet, the two celebrated mini big bands that had set off the cool reaction to bop's heat. He and West Coast arranger Marty Paich put together a ten-piece unit patterned after both the Davis and Mulligan bands. In a masterful series of sets like *Mel Tormé and The Marty Paich Dektette* (Bethlehem) and *Mel Tormé Swings Shubert Alley* (Verve), Tormé and Paich brilliantly recast familiar show tunes into fresh, exciting new forms.

If cool singing was born in deliberate reaction to bop, it's difficult to say whether modern jazz had any influence at all on the blues revival of the postwar years (it more likely was the other way around, since the blues were an integral part of bop). Singer and saxist Louis Jordan was at the center of so many movements (as was the only slightly less bluesy trumpeter Louis Prima), primarily swing, blues, and novelty pop. The latter, surprisingly, would soon establish itself as the dominant mode of postwar popular music, as record buyers made hits out of one goofy novelty after another—a trend that continued unabated into the 1960s. Jordan was a blues-based entertainer who infiltrated the white mainstream with comedy songs, whereas Dinah Washington and Joe Williams achieved only slightly lesser popular success with "serious" blues.

There are no better examples of the multigeneric montage that is jazz singing than Washington and Williams. Like virtually every vocalist in this period, both started in big bands; in fact, both were part of Lionel Hampton's orchestra circa 1943, although Williams did not earn national attention until his mid-'50s tenure with Count Basie. Both essentially came out of the blues, theirs being an idiom related equally to the Bessie Smith, the Robert Johnson, and the Louis Jordan definitions of that form. Yet both had the flexibility and swing of genuine, post–Louis Armstrong jazz singing, and both were comfortable in the world of straight-down-the-middle pop. Williams in particular had the ability to switch in half a heartbeat between material by Harry Warren and Bill Withers, doing equal justice to the idioms of both. With her intense, searing sound and irresistible beat, it was inevitable that Washington would break out of the "race records" market to be heard by the bigger white audience beyond.

There were other first-class singers who dwelt on the boundaries between blues and jazz singing, like Etta Jones, Ernie Andrews, and Little Jimmy Scott; all had something unique to offer, but clearly Williams and Washington were the ones to beat in this cross-genre area. Yet where other artists crossed genre lines, Ray Charles very nearly trampled them to death. Indeed, the one consistent factor of the incredibly diverse career of this brilliant singer, pianist, and bandleader has been his ability to take entire traditions in his stride. Although he too, like Washington, first rose to fame by courtesy of the rhythm-and-blues (or black) market, Charles began his career under the more mainstream jazz-and-pop influence of Nat Cole. With his raspy voice and passionate delivery, Charles rose to the top of the "race" charts by reinfusing black pop with an extra heavy dose of gospel (via his Georgia-born church roots and his choirlike vocal group, the Raelettes) and jazz (with his remarkable band, boasting such star saxists as Fathead Newman and Hank Crawford), laying the foundation for a sound that later became known as "soul." By the early '60s, the Ray Charles juggernaut was branching to take on Tin Pan Alley (his "Come Rain or Come Shine" on Atlantic and "Georgia on My Mind" on ABC-Paramount are second to none) and the great songwriters of Nashville as well.

The Vocalese movement was deeply rooted in both the big band tradition and the blues. Indeed, Jon Hendricks, the genre's leading poet, has spent just as much of his career writing in blues contexts. As distinct from its usage in classical music (e.g., Rachmaninoff's "*Vocalise*), *vocalese* in jazz terms connotates the act of singing words to an instrumental jazz solo. There are examples of the form going at least as far back as Bee Palmer in 1929 and Marion Harris in 1934 (who both sang words to the classic Frank Trumbauer–Bix Beider-becke recording "Singin' the Blues"), but vocalese would not catch on until the arrival of Eddie Jefferson and King Pleasure (real name Clarence Beeks) in the early '50s. The breakthrough record was "Moody's Mood for Love," a lyricization of alto saxist James Moody's treatment of the standard "I'm in the Mood for Love." Sung by Plea-sure and supposedly written by Jefferson, the disc was a chart hit that inspired a flurry of vocalese activity, the most durable of which was by the trio of Lambert, Hendricks and Ross.

With the exception of Mel Tormé's short-lived unit, the innovative Mel-Tones, there had been no vocal group that truly captured the sound and fury of what jazz was all about since the Boswell Sisters and the early incarnation of the Mills Brothers, twenty years earlier (although it should be noted that both the Hi-Los and the Four Freshmen did unique and worthwhile things with harmony, winning many converts in the jazz audience). Lambert, Hendricks and Ross provided the perfect combination of elements necessary to revitalize both the jazz vocal group and the vocalese genre. Dave Lambert came out of the big band tradition (specifically, Gene Krupa's orchestra) and helped create the kind of loosely arranged harmonies that made LH&R sound so hip and swinging. Jon Hendricks, jazz's greatest lyricist, was steeped in both bebop and blues. Annie Ross shared all of these backgrounds and also brought the group the theatrical flair and vocal muscle that it needed. Concentrating mainly on jazz compositions associated with Count Basie and Horace Silver, LH&R became, for a few brief years, exactly what the title of their best album proclaimed: *The Hottest New Group in Jazz* (Columbia).

Annie Ross, who was born and lived many of her post-LH&R years in England, is also remarkable in that she is by far the most compelling jazz singer to come from shores beyond the North American continent. Both Ross and her British colleague, Cleo Laine (who has spent the larger part of her jazz career working with her husband, saxist, composer, and bandleader John Dankworth), have oftimes ventured beyond jazz into cabaret and musical comedy; the classically concerned Laine has also explored such fields as Shakespeare and Schoenberg. Just as northern Europe produced players who conceived their own approach to the cool school of Gerry Mulligan and Chet Baker, Sweden, Holland, Norway, and other locales sired such smokey-voiced sirens as Karin Krog, the more traditional Alice Babs, whose career in classical music, pop, and jazz was climaxed by a collaboration with Duke Ellington, and Rita Reys, who very nearly reaches the heights of June Christy and Chris Connor. Like their American counterparts, such Eurojazz "avant-gardists" as Tiziana Ghiglioni (Italy), Valentina Ponomareva (Russia), Maggie Nicols, Kate Westbrook, and Norma Winstone (all England) have all experimented with forms ranging from the purely improvised to the completely composed. What is ultimately surprising about European jazz is not how many great singers have originated in far-flung lands but how few: certainly they have not produced any heavyweight vocal figures on the level of Tubby Hayes, Lars Gullin, Martial Solal, or Toshiko Akiyoshi. The situation may be changing, however, in that there are probably more major vocalists outside of America now than ever before. Among the best are Claire Martin (England), Denise Jannah (Holland), and Jeri Brown (Canada).

Vocalese, the form that Annie Ross helped elevate into a high art, is notable in another respect: it may be the last thing to happen to the development of jazz singing that could be called a "movement." During the war, virtually all American "sonic culture" was closely integrated into the musical entertainment unit known as the big band, which incorporated show music, blues, pure jazz, novelties, and the best singing; there were even country-western big bands. Leaders as disparate as Kay Kyser and Johnny Otis viewed their orchestras as vaudeville that you could dance to. As late as the '50s, jazz, show music, and pop were all closely intertwined, but within a decade these individual strains had gone their separate ways. Since the 1960s, jazz singing has itself been too far away from the income-producing pop mainstream to afford such luxuries as a movement or a trend.

Virtually every major singer, with very few exceptions, to emerge before 1960 came out of the big band experience. Annie Ross and Ernestine Anderson were latter-day vocalists with Lionel Hampton (after Williams, Washington, Little Jimmy Scott, Jackie Paris, Betty Carter, and others) who became stars. Likewise, Nancy Wilson cut her teeth on the blues-driven unit of Rusty Bryant (not big, but still part of the band tradition), and Carmen McRae, who had been older than most of her fellow chanteuses at the time she achieved national attention, sang with Mercer Ellington. Even Tony Bennett, back in 1946, gave his first important performances with the Army-operated swing band that had succeeded Glenn Miller's famous Army Air Force orchestra.

Perhaps the most visible sign that jazz and entertainment were going in different directions was the decline of the singing musician. In the band era, virtually every trumpeter who led his own group on 52nd Street or on the jukeboxes stepped up to the microphone to sing the blues and what they then called "rhythm songs." Where the hornmen of the '30s, from Roy Eldridge to Red Allen to Hot Lips Page, had turned to vocalizing as a way of reaching outward to an audience, paradoxically, the major singing musicians to establish themselves in the '50s and beyond tended to be the most introverted players around. Concentrating on feeling rather than technique, Chet Baker (whose emotional range was as vast as that of his trumpet and throat were limited), Blossom Dearie (with her endearing, babylike voice), and Shirley Horn (whose entrancingly slow phrasing never fails to hypnotize a crowd) all employed a minimalist technique and fundamentally small vocal instruments.

Even if the echoes and the influence of the bands had faded by the age of the Beatles, one aspect of that heritage remained no less true then than it does today: the best vocalists still inevitably worked with the best musicians. Thus, even though it would be inappropriate (or anachronistic) to describe Cassandra Wilson as the "canary" with Steve Coleman or Henry Threadgill or refer to Abbey Lincoln as the "girl singer" with Max Roach, the dynamics between jazz instrumentalists and vocalists are still all-important.

Tony Bennett is especially significant in that he may be the last major figure to stand at the exact midpoint between pop and jazz. Paying homage to Louis Armstrong and Miles Davis on one side and Judy Garland and Jimmy Durante on the other, Bennett is a dynamic, swinging amalgam of both traditions who constantly shows how the two legacies are intertwined. He has recorded pop novelties and jazz standards; he has sung with contemporary poppers like k. d. lang and Elvis Costello and with Bill Evans, Ellington, and Basie.

Bennett's approximate female contemporary (in career if not in age or in sound) is Carmen McRae, who in the mid-'50s established herself as the last great diva of jazz singing in the lineage that extends from Bessie Smith to Billie Holiday to Ella Fitzgerald to Sarah Vaughan to Dinah Washington. An arresting stylist, McRae was at once stunningly musical and dramatically lyrical. McRae's sound was biting, sharp, and amazingly clear, full of pure jazz variations and brilliant paraphrases that never undercut her masterful interpretive style.

Yet McRae was merely the most remarkable of a generation of terrific female singers who all seemed to be reaching their zenith in the '50s. Benny Goodman veteran Peggy Lee, though denied a place in many jazz reference works, remains an arresting jazz stylist whose swing, subtlety, and empathy for the blues were never compromised by her popular success. Rosemary Clooney, like Tony Bennett, came out of the stable of novelty hitmakers shepherded by pop Svengali Mitch Miller; it was through sheer determination that she was able to establish her jazz credentials (being the first guest vocalist to cut an entire album with Duke Ellington). When Clooney came back to the scene in the '70s, with a prolific series of (mostly Song Book) albums for Concord, she was solidly on the jazz circuit. Likewise, Abbey Lincoln, Ernestine Anderson, and Nancy Wilson (at least in the '60s, when she was singing quality material in a high style that made her the equal of her primary influence, Little Jimmy Scott) all have a commanding tone and an unwavering command of the beat.

In the '40s and '50s, the advanced romanticism of Eckstine and Vaughan, the cool, composition-oriented style of Mel Tormé and June Christy, the blues-based populism of Joe Williams and Dinah Washington, and the vocalese of Lambert, Hendricks and Ross all existed roughly simultaneously. If the last forty years have been marked by any trend, it is that jazz singers, as a whole, tend to specialize less.

Jazz singers in the bebop era leaned no less heavily on traditional ballads than did their swing forebears. In a parallel phenomenon, singers who allied themselves with what is loosely known as the "avant-garde" jazz movement of the '60s did not necessarily do what instrumentalists of that era did, although there are some vocalists who produced what can be described as extemporaneous, completely "free" sounds. Most of the time, the experimentally oriented singers of that period worked more in the artistic and literary tradition of the avant-garde. Singers like Jeanne Lee and Sheila Jordan can do lyrics or wordless sounds, their own compositions or standards, and like all of the artists in this area, they sure as hell don't sound like anybody else.

Both Betty Carter (that is, before her untimely passing in October 1998) and Mark Murphy would probably balk if you labeled them, for all their relentless experimentation, as avant-gardists. They are probably better described as swinging eclectics, and as such are perhaps the most influential vocal artists of the last few decades. Both are jazz composer-performers, in the tradition of, say, Benny Golson or Wayne Shorter, whose instrument happens to be their voice; in the work of Carter and Murphy we find the most dogmatic, idiosyncratically individualistic approach—or rather, collection of approaches—to singing jazz imaginable.

In many ways, Carter is a mass of contradictions. At face value, her music bespeaks total freedom. She has committed to record scat solos of over twenty minutes in length, and yet, at that same time, she is probably the most carefully controlled and meticulously rehearsed performer in jazz. Even when it sounds like she's going off the deep end, a closer listen reveals that Carter knows exactly where she's going at all times. Though her music may be said to be "about" improvisation at its purest, she has also established herself, like Abbey Lincoln, as one of the more gifted songwriters and composers of recent decades. Particularly well represented on live albums like *Live at the Village Vanguard* and *The Audience With Betty Carter* (both Verve), Carter at times leads the listener to believe that her music is totally freeform and far out. But often only a song or two later, she will switch to using the most basic of 1920s pop tunes as a starting point.

Both Murphy and Carter encourage the use of a wide range of techniques and rhythms, including scat, bossa nova, original compositions (comparatively rare in this music, which has produced only a handful of singer-songwriters), playful sonic distortions, and, in Murphy's case, even poetry recitations. (A pair of two-CD collections, *Stolen and Other Moments* and *Jazz Standards*, both on 32 Jazz, do an admirable job of sampling Murphy's eclectic canon.) It should also be noted that Murphy teaches directly as well as by example, giving clinics and classes almost as frequently as he makes club appearances and concerts. Careerwise, both are examples of the old adage about things coming to those who wait, as each has had to endure many decades of working on the fringe before attracting the attention of major labels and mass media. In recent months, Murphy's performances have even drawn praise from purveyors of hip-hop and acid jazz.

It would be hard to find worthwhile contemporary vocalists who have not learned from Murphy and Carter. Generally there are more men who sound like the former and women who sound like the latter, but these lessons are far from gender specific. For decades, there was a dearth of new male jazz singers on the scene, yet several important artists have emerged in the mid- to late '90s. The two who have made it to major label status are Kevin Mahogany and Kurt Elling, while Allan Harris remains not far behind in this respect. While Elling, who studied directly with Murphy, is not surprisingly the most Murphy-esque, all three are inherently eclectic. Mahogany comes out of a deep-voiced baritone tradition that allows him to sing both ballads and blues meaningfully, yet he is also a convincing scat singer. No less an improviser, Elling can also evoke the young Sinatra with "Polka Dots and Moonbeams" and has imaginatively revived the long-dormant tradition of vocalese (a genre primarily explored in the '80s and '90s, oddly, by the pop quartet Manhattan Transfer).

Still, the leading lights in jazz singing at the millennium may well be Cassandra Wilson, Dianne Reeves, and Dee Dee Bridgewater (with Jeanie Bryson and Kendra Shank winning honors as rising young talents), who are eclecticism personified. All three draw from across the whole of the jazz and pop tradition, from the show tunes canonized by Fitzgerald and Sinatra to the blues of Robert Johnson, as well as pop-rock hits that have never been performed with such musicality. From the beginning, Reeves and Bridgewater have always been very outgoing entertainers who have known exactly how to handle an audience. As years go by it becomes clearer and clearer that Reeves has much of musical substance to offer as well. Although Bridgewater, after a promising start in the early '70s, was briefly waylaid by pop and fusion, the '90s have witnessed her triumphant return to the straight and narrow.

By contrast, Wilson can be downright cryptic, often seeming (especially in her early years) like she had something to say but was afraid to come out of her shell and say it. The big audience, however, was waiting for her to make that breakthrough. Like the great ladies of the Holiday-Fitzgerald-Vaughan line, Wilson is one of the few musicians under fifty, on any instrument, to have concocted an immediately identifiable sound of her own, one rooted in folk and blues traditions as much as in jazz. As Reeves has pointed out, both ladies were deeply influenced by the folk-blues-pop singer Nina Simone, yet both are considerably more expressive and dynamic than the generally monotonal Simone. With her original compositions and her unique, poetic perspective, Wilson is altogether a formidable package.

Indeed, there may well have been a time, from the late '60s to the early '80s, when rock's inundation ensured that no new jazz or traditional pop singers were appearing. Thankfully, that is no longer the case. Singers in all manner of jazz genres are proliferating, from jazz-related cabaret stylists to the rhythmically driven singer-instrumentalists of the neo-swing/jump movement; from nonverbal, experimental scatters to strict revivalists. It's hard to think of any time since the '50s when there has been so much jazz vocal activity. It's still going stronger than ever. All we have to do is open up our ears and listen.

Jazz Since 1968

Peter Keepnews

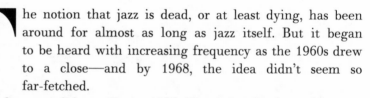

T he notion that jazz is dead, or at least dying, has been around for almost as long as jazz itself. But it began to be heard with increasing frequency as the 1960s drew to a close—and by 1968, the idea didn't seem so far-fetched.

Jazz, of course, did not die in 1968. Three decades later, in terms of objective criteria like audience size and institutional support if not necessarily in terms of more subjective ones like artistic quality, it is not just alive but healthy. But the past three decades have been a strange, unpredictable, and often contentious time for the music— and the question of how well jazz fared in those years largely depends on how one chooses to define the word *jazz*.

By 1968 it had been roughly a decade since Ornette Coleman, Cecil Taylor, and other advocates of what was variously called "the new thing," "free jazz," or simply the avant-garde first challenged the notion that jazz had to contain such supposedly fundamental elements as a steady rhythmic pulse and regularly repeating chord patterns. Their rebellion caused a deep schism in the jazz community and even spurred debate over whether their music deserved to be called jazz. In terms of jazz's continued relevance in a changing world, this schism could hardly have happened at a less opportune time.

Rock-and-roll had evolved into a serious and often adventurous form of music called just plain rock. Listeners who a few years earlier might have gravitated toward jazz had by the late sixties discovered in the music of the Beatles, Bob Dylan, Jimi Hendrix, and others not just the visceral excitement that had always been at the heart of rock-and-roll but also a considerable degree of musical sophistication—as well as lyrics that, in one way or another, addressed the growing, if vaguely defined, sense that the old social and political order was crumbling and some sort of utopian revolution was in the air.

It was hard for jazz, a primarily instrumental music with roots stretching back to the early days of the century, to compete with a music that literally spoke to its listeners about the concerns and emotions of the moment. And the jazz world, torn by internal warfare that reflected a serious identity crisis, was unable to present a unified front in the face of such competition.

At a time when "Don't trust anybody over thirty" was a popular slogan and people on both sides of the generation gap were terrified of seeming unhip, practitioners of older styles of jazz saw their audiences drop precipitously. Exponents of free jazz fared no better; if anything, the average avant-gardist had even more trouble finding an audience than his more tradition-oriented counterparts in those years, at least in the United States. (Europe and Japan were far more receptive to all varieties of jazz, and many American musicians settled overseas, some permanently, throughout the sixties and seventies.)

This was the fragile state in which jazz found itself as the sixties ended: drowned out by sounds that were seemingly more relevant to young people's lives; plagued by dissension in the ranks; its new breed making abstract and difficult music that few people wanted to hear while its old guard made time-tested music that fewer and fewer people cared about.

And yet, in ways no one could have predicted, things were already beginning to change.

One of those ways involved a new approach (or, to be more accurate, variety of approaches) that came to be known first as jazz-rock and eventually as fusion. Although critics and historians have tended to dismiss it as a movement dictated by business rather than artistic considerations, the truth is that both factors were involved.

Certainly many jazz musicians, in adopting some of the trappings of rock, both musical (electric keyboards and basses, heavy backbeats and ostinatos) and extramusical (long hair, hippie clothing), were pursuing a strategy of "if you can't beat 'em, join 'em." And certainly, at a time when the commercial prospects for records that adhered to

The Art Ensemble of Chicago. Left to right: Lester Bowie, Don Moye, Malachi Favors Magoustous, Roscoe Mitchell, Joseph Jarman. Photo: Guida Harari. Courtesy of the Institute of Jazz Studies, Rutgers University.

a traditional jazz aesthetic were dwindling, many record companies encouraged this strategy. But the move to fuse jazz with elements of rock, soul, and other musical styles had artistic motivations as well.

Miles Davis's 1969 recording *Bitches Brew* (Columbia) was the first fusion album to sell in significant quantities and introduced the veteran trumpeter to a vast new audience. Many of Davis's former sidemen—among them keyboardists Herbie Hancock, Chick Corea, and Josef Zawinul, saxophonist Wayne Shorter, and drummer Tony Williams—went on to lead successful fusion bands of their own. But it seems reasonable to conclude that not just Davis but many other musicians in the first fusion generation were motivated at least as much by artistic curiosity as they were by the desire for a hit album. After all, the thick textures and impressionistic improvisations of *Bitches Brew* might not have added up to jazz as most people understood the word, but they hardly added up to rock or soul in any conventional sense either. The same can be said for such other early fusion albums as *Weather Report* (Columbia), by the band of the same name co-led by Shorter and Zawinul, and the Tony Williams Lifetime's *Emergency!* (Polydor/Verve).

But if much early fusion seemed intent on breaking musical molds, by the middle seventies the jazz-rock-soul synthesis had largely degenerated into a commercially malleable formula. Some jazz musicians who chose to go this route studiously avoided the word *jazz*. The Jazz Crusaders changed their name to the Crusaders in 1971 to reflect their evolution from hard bop to a kind of instrumental rhythm-and-blues with a slight jazz tinge. Herbie Hancock, whose extremely successful 1973 album *Head Hunters* (Columbia) melded jazz solos with hard-edged funk accompaniment, began dividing his time between acoustic jazz projects and electrified, groove-oriented albums that in his own view had nothing to do with jazz.

The record industry, however, classified this emerging genre of jazz-tinged pop music as jazz, and its success contributed to the misleading claim that jazz was undergoing a commercial renaissance. In fact jazz in the more serious sense remained commercially marginal in the seventies. However, the views of some present-day revisionist historians notwithstanding, those years were far from artistically barren.

Many young jazz musicians were striving to find a niche for themselves that drew on tradition without being shackled to it, while steering clear of the twin extremes of the avant-garde and fusion. And as a significant portion of the audience cautiously grew more open-minded, at least a few musicians with strong individual styles, who did not fit comfortably in any category other than the vague "acoustic jazz," were able to attract a following.

Pianist McCoy Tyner, whose career had foundered after he left John Coltrane's group in 1965, established himself as a leader on albums like *Sahara* and *Fly Like the Wind* (Milestone), displaying a musical vision that layered an emotional intensity reminiscent of free jazz on top of a pounding rhythmic pulse. Saxophonist-flutist Rahsaan Roland Kirk, whose approach straddled all styles and eras of jazz, commanded attention with albums like *Blacknuss* (Atlantic/32 Jazz) and *Bright Moments* (Atlantic/Rhino) and with performances that were compellingly flamboyant and eccentric. By the end of the decade, even some older musicians whose styles had remained fundamentally unchanged were once again working regularly, in some cases more regularly than they had in years.

Other musicians were finding inspiration in unlikely places—of which the unlikeliest, and one of the most important, was West Germany, where a young recording engineer and classically trained bassist named Manfred Eicher began a record company called ECM in 1969. At first devoted largely to the avant-garde, ECM gradually developed a unique aesthetic built around, as Eicher himself put it, "quiet music." Using a meticulous approach to recording that captured overtones and other subtle aural nuances, Eicher specialized in a kind of chamber jazz. Many of his recordings dispensed with drums, and a number featured instrumental duets or unaccompanied solo performances. A series of totally improvised solo concert recordings (notably the multidisc set *The Köln Concert*) by pianist Keith Jarrett—who had played in one of Miles Davis's first electric bands, but who abandoned electric keyboards in the early seventies and even proselytized against their use in jazz—achieved unexpected sales success, focusing new attention on the art of unembellished improvisation in general and on the low-key ECM approach in particular.

ECM had its share of critics. Many of them, sounding a variation on what had by this time become a familiar theme, argued that what the company was offering simply wasn't jazz (too cerebral, insufficient rhythmic drive, too "European"). Perhaps the most accurate way to characterize the label's output—which was never as monolithic as its critics claimed—is as a variation on fusion. It tended to be played on acoustic instruments and to eschew the more bombastic qualities of jazz-rock, but it contained elements from enough other sources, including folk and chamber music, to throw its pure-jazz pedigree into question.

In any event, by the late seventies, when ECM was enjoying its greatest success, such distinctions had become so slippery as to be almost meaningless. Eicher himself, in a 1979 interview, argued that the music he recorded was "rooted in jazz" but conceded that "the jazz movements were so different over the last twenty years" that it was "hard to pin it down to one expression which is jazz."

Indeed, thanks in large part to Eicher's efforts, it was no longer even possible to characterize jazz as a strictly American music. Many of the musicians he recorded—including saxophonist Jan Garbarek, bassist Eberhard Weber, and guitarist Terje Rypdal—were European, and their mastery of the jazz idiom was indicative of a new phenomenon.

There had been non-American jazz musicians before, of course, but with a handful of exceptions they had not been of the first rank and had not attracted a following outside their own turf. The seventies saw a dramatic improvement in the quality of jazz being made in other countries—not just in Europe but in Japan, Brazil, South Africa, and elsewhere. Many of the new non-American artists, particularly Brazilians like percussionist Airto Moreira and composer-keyboardist Hermeto Pascoal, incorporated so many elements from their own cultures into their music that when they collaborated with American musicians the result, inevitably, was a further blurring of the line between what was and wasn't jazz.

Perhaps most surprisingly, the middle and late seventies saw an upturn in the fortunes of two forms of jazz that up until then had stood far outside the commercial mainstream: the avant-garde, whose practitioners had maintained their enthusiasm and sense of adventure even though their audience had remained small; and bebop, which had once seemed revolutionary but in the view of many musicians and listeners had been obsolete, or at least irrelevant, for a decade or more.

The jazz avant-garde had lacked a forceful and charismatic leader since John Coltrane's death in 1967, and it had been further demoralized in 1970 when saxophonist Albert Ayler, one of the most adventurous and influential adherents of free jazz, was found dead under mysterious circumstances at the age of thirty-four. But by the end of the seventies the movement had been revitalized by an infusion of both musical daring and pure showmanship, thanks largely to two groups: the Art Ensemble of Chicago, formed in 1969, and the World Saxophone Quartet, formed in 1976.

Both groups devoted considerable attention to group dynamics and compositional form, in contrast to the stereotype (which in the past had often, if not always, proved to be accurate) of free jazz as a music literally free of structure and boundaries. And they both presented their music not with the intense seriousness that had come to be identified with the avant-garde but with a bracing sense of theatricality and even playfulness.

The Art Ensemble, like many other groups and musicians who emerged in this period, was an offshoot of the Chicago musicians' cooperative known as the Association for the Advancement of Creative Musicians. Muhal Richard Abrams, who founded the AACM in 1965 and served as a mentor to a generation of avant-gardists, was a talented pianist and composer whose best recordings, among them *Levels and Degrees of Light* (Delmark) and *The Hearinga Suite* (Black Saint), manage a graceful balancing act between ensemble writing and unfettered improvisation.

The Art Ensemble of Chicago, consisting of saxophonists Joseph Jarman and Roscoe Mitchell, trumpeter Lester Bowie, bassist Malachi Favors Magoustous, and drummer Famoudou Don Moye, learned much from Abrams. But their approach probably owed even more to the otherworldly showmanship of the pianist-composer-bandleader Sun Ra, who had been a fixture on the Chicago scene for years and served as a kind of spiritual godfather to the AACM. Taking its cue from Sun Ra, the group enlivened its performances with costumes, makeup, poetry recitations, and even the occasional comedy routine.

If the Art Ensemble's music was sometimes in danger of getting lost in the shuffle, it was powerful enough to withstand the onslaught, and it was varied enough to hold audiences' attention. (Jarman, Mitchell, and Bowie were all prolific composers, and all three recorded several albums as leaders in addition to their work with the Art Ensemble.) Indeed, with its mixture of free improvisation and complex composition, seasoned with an overlay of African and other influences, the Art Ensemble's music arguably merited the label "fusion" as much as anyone else's did—although the group itself preferred "great black music." (And as if to suggest that categories are meaningless anyway, in the late seventies and early eighties the Art Ensemble made a series of outstanding albums, including *Nice Guys* and *Urban Bushmen*, for ECM Records, supposedly the most "European" of all jazz labels.)

Other graduates of the AACM were less theatrical in their approach but just as adventurous, and also managed to find an audience. Two of the more uncompromising Chicagoans, saxophonist-composers Henry Threadgill and Anthony Braxton, were even briefly signed to a large pop-oriented record company, Arista.

Threadgill led a trio, Air, which in 1980 released an album, *Air Lore* (Arista), devoted to the compositions of Scott Joplin and Jelly Roll Morton, anticipating by a few years the fascination with history and tradition that would come to dominate jazz—although, in contrast to what eventually became the standard approach to the jazz canon, he used these decades-old themes as springboards for highly personal and idiosyncratic improvisation. Following the demise of Air, Threadgill went on to lead a larger group, Very Very Circus, and to experiment with compositional form on albums like *Too Much Sugar for a Dime* (Axiom).

Braxton's unique take on jazz was often quite austere and at times seemed to emphasize structure and texture to the virtual exclusion of improvisation. (Some listeners found his music dauntingly unemotional, and it almost goes without saying that some of his detractors said it was not jazz.) But he was unquestionably ambitious: his output ranges from *For Alto* (Delmark), an extended recital of unaccompanied improvisation, to exercises in writing for large ensembles like *Creative Orchestra Music* and the remarkable *For Four Orchestras* (Arista). And as if to confront the skeptics on their own turf, he has occasionally recorded albums like *In the Tradition* (Inner City) on which both repertoire and instrumentation are defiantly conventional.

These and other musicians from the Chicago school proved that it was possible to make a living, if not necessarily to get rich, by playing a form of jazz that mixed complex structure with free improvisation. The World Saxophone Quartet (Hamiet Bluiett, Julius Hemphill, Oliver Lake, and David Murray) followed that basic formula and, by developing a euphonious ensemble sound and presenting its music in a way that entertained without pandering, emerged as the closest thing to a mainstream success the jazz avant-garde had seen since John Coltrane.

The members of the quartet all had separate solo careers, most notably tenor saxophonist Murray: with a style whose antecedents ranged from Duke Ellington's onetime star soloist Ben Webster to Albert Ayler, Murray blossomed, in performance and on such albums as *Ming* (Black Saint) and *Ballads* (DIW), into one of the most distinctive (and prolific) jazz musicians of the eighties and nineties. But it was as a unit that the four musicians found their largest audience, and arguably the most effective outlet for their compositions as well. Alto and soprano saxophonist Hemphill's departure for health reasons in 1990 (he died five years later), and the group's inability to find a satisfactory permanent replacement, fatally crippled the World Saxophone Quartet's development. But their legacy, as documented on

Steppin' (Black Saint), *Dances and Ballads* (Elektra Musician), and other albums, is formidable.

The resurgence of the avant-garde was one of the more unexpected jazz events of the seventies. But is was not as unexpected as the hoopla surrounding Dexter Gordon's return to the United States.

Gordon had been the most influential tenor saxophonist to emerge in the bebop era, but in 1962 he had moved to Europe, like many other musicians of his generation, largely because he was unable to make a decent living at home. He played the occasional return engagement, but not until triumphant New York nightclub appearances in 1976 and 1977, followed by the live album *Homecoming* (Columbia) and a successful tour, did he begin receiving significant attention in his native land.

Gordon's comeback was in some ways an isolated phenomenon. It was attributable in part to his personal magnetism as a performer (he would later turn to movie acting and win an Academy Award nomination in 1987 for playing an aging jazz saxophonist in the film *'Round Midnight*) and in part to an aggressive marketing and publicity campaign waged on his behalf by CBS Records, which signed him to a long-term contract largely because its president was a jazz fan.

But it wasn't *entirely* isolated: Gordon's return to the scene also satisified an unspoken and maybe even unconscious desire on the part of many jazz fans. Not just charismatic but tirelessly inventive, he was a bona fide star who remained committed to the old verities of chord-based improvisation and the steady, infectious, layered four-four time feel of bebop. And unlike many of his contemporaries, he had neither stagnated nor compromised over the years.

It would be an exaggeration to say that Gordon's comeback spearheaded a full-fledged bebop revival. But it did help revive the careers of a few other important musicians of his generation, like his fellow saxophonists Johnny Griffin and James Moody, who had been living overseas or otherwise out of the public eye for years. And, more significant, it provided encouragement to a growing number of musicians in their twenties and thirties, like the saxophonists Ricky Ford and Richie Cole and the trumpet virtuoso Jon Faddis, who saw bebop not as a relic of an earlier time but as a living music that allowed them room to make their own personal statements.

Faddis, who was born in 1953 and joined the big band of Thad Jones and Mel Lewis in 1972, was a seeming anomaly in that he modeled his playing directly (some would say slavishly) on that of

Dizzy Gillespie, one of the icons of the bebop era. In the seventies there were various stylistic options available to jazz trumpeters, ranging from the uncompromising avant-garde approach of Lester Bowie to the slick commercialism of Freddie Hubbard to the not-quite-bebop, not-quite-free path followed by Woody Shaw and many other adventurous young players. The signs were far from clear at the time, but musicians like Faddis—and like saxophonist Scott Hamilton and cornetist Warren Vaché, who modeled their styles on instrumentalists of the swing era—represented the first stirrings of a new jazz trend: a youth movement based less on a quest for new means of expression than on an eagerness to mine the music's past for inspiration. The man who would ultimately be credited with spearheading this trend was trumpeter Wynton Marsalis, but in truth the seeds were already planted several years before Marsalis's career began.

Appropriately enough, Wynton Marsalis was introduced to the jazz world, along with his saxophonist brother Branford, by the great drummer Art Blakey. Blakey's band, the Jazz Messengers, had carried the torch for the sophisticated but viscerally exciting variant of bebop known as hard bop since the middle fifties, along the way serving as a valuable training ground for numerous young musicians. Blakey had managed to keep his band together through good times and bad, and he had never had trouble finding sidemen. But it is worth noting that by the time he hired the Marsalis brothers, he had begun looking rather far afield: the man Wynton Marsalis replaced as the band's trumpeter, Valery Ponomarev, was born in Russia.

At first Marsalis attracted attention, in performance with Blakey and on recordings like *Album of the Year* (Timeless), primarily because of his command of the trumpet—which would have been impressive under any circumstances, but was all the more impressive because he was only eighteen when he joined the Jazz Messengers in 1980. After he followed in Dexter Gordon's footsteps by signing with CBS Records, he attracted further attention by insisting on making an album devoid of electric instrumentation and other commercial trappings.

That was an unusual and even risky move for a young jazz musician on a major label at the time, and according to Marsalis himself it was not what CBS initially had in mind. But by the time his first album, produced by Herbie Hancock and titled simply *Wynton Marsalis* (Columbia), was released in 1982, the company was ready to promote it aggressively. Marsalis's subsequent success has often been attributed to record-company clout, but it is important to note that he gave the company a lot to work with. He was not just talented but young, good-looking, well-dressed, articulate, and classically trained. (He recorded both jazz and classical albums for CBS, and in 1984 he became the first musician to win Grammy Awards in both categories.) He also proved willing and even eager to serve as an advocate for what had come to be called "straight-ahead" jazz.

Older musicians and fans were heartened by Marsalis's seriousness of purpose and dedication to the jazz tradition—a dedication that, at least on his early albums, was mixed with a sense of adventure and a willingness to experiment that kept things from getting too stiflingly reverent. But at first his advocacy seemed to exist in a kind of vacuum, and it hardly seemed inevitable that he would emerge as the leader of a full-fledged movement.

By the end of the eighties, however, such a movement was in full force, and Marsalis's position as its leader was beyond dispute. Numerous young musicians had chosen to follow a path similar to his, seeking inspiration in a vocabulary that predated (or ignored) the avant-garde, fusion, and virtually every other development of the preceding two decades. Record companies, even major labels like RCA and Atlantic that had paid hardly any attention to acoustic jazz since the late sixties, now saw it as a marketable commodity—as long as it was played by young and good-looking musicians—and had begun looking for Wynton Marsalises of their own.

The record companies' emphasis on youth often meant that promising but still-developing musicians got pushed into the spotlight prematurely, while serious and talented musicians who were older than forty—or whose styles contained avant-garde elements, or who were otherwise deemed insufficiently marketable—continued to scuffle. And while the so-called young lions who followed in Marsalis's wake were for the most part both talented and knowledgeable, their almost obsessive focus on jazz's past led many people to dismiss them as "neoconservatives" who were not making any significant contribution to the music's future.

Such a judgment is somewhat harsh. At the very least, such Marsalis disciples as pianist Marcus Roberts, on albums like *Deep in the Shed* (RCA Novus), and trumpeter Terence Blanchard, in his scores for a number of Spike Lee's films, displayed an impressive flair for composition. But as improvising musicians, the first wave of young lions often seemed restricted by the notion that jazz was an easily defined discipline with a specific set of rules that had to be followed, rather than an ever-evolving art form built on risk-taking.

In 1990 Wynton Marsalis was the focus of a cover story in *Time* magazine, portentously entitled "The New Jazz Age," which proclaimed that straight-ahead jazz, after having "almost died in the 1970's," was being revitalized by "a whole generation of prodigiously talented young musicians" that was "going back to the roots." Marsalis was the first jazz musician to make *Time*'s cover since Thelonious Monk in 1964—although it had only been thirteen years since a national newsmagazine, in this case *Newsweek*, last ran a cover story announcing that jazz was back.

Marsalis was at the center of another major development a year later, when New York's Lincoln Center for the Performing Arts became the first organization of its kind to establish a full-time jazz department and appointed him artistic director. Jazz at Lincoln Center maintained a full-time big band on its payroll and specialized in presenting what it deemed to be classic works of the jazz canon, with an emphasis on Duke Ellington. It also provided Marsalis with a forum for his own compositions, most of which revealed a pronounced Ellington influence. (In 1997 he became the first jazz composer to win the Pulitzer Prize, for his oratorio *Blood on the Fields*. Ellington himself had been recommended for a Pulitzer thirty-two years earlier, but he was denied the prize. He finally received a special Pulitzer for his body of work in 1999, on the occasion of his centennial.) And, to the dismay of many musicians and critics who favored a more open-minded approach, Marsalis used his Lincoln Center pulpit to make rather autocratic proclamations about what did or didn't deserve to be called jazz.

He acknowledged that his approach was conservative, but he defended his conservatism as a necessary first step toward moving jazz to the next level. "If you're going to be forward-looking," he said in 1991, "you have to look back on what somebody like Duke Ellington was doing and really learn about it. And then, eventually, you can begin to address the modern world."

In the nineties, a new crop of young musicians did indeed take tentative steps toward a jazz that addressed the modern world, or at least displayed more sparks of individuality (and, occasionally, idiosyncrasy) than had been typical of the first post-Marsalis wave. But even the more talented of these younger lions tended to be more conservative than the typical young jazz musician of two decades earlier, and the record companies tended to encourage this conservatism.

Saxophonist Joshua Redman offers a telling example. Barely out of his teens when he broke onto the New York scene, Redman—who, like Wynton and Branford Marsalis, was the son of a professional jazz musician—dazzled listeners with remarkable technique, boundless energy, and a style that, while not entirely original, was recognizably his own and refreshingly edgy. Signed to Warner Bros. Records, he released several impressive albums, including *Joshua Redman* and *Wish*, and attracted a large following.

But by the end of the decade it had become difficult to say whether Redman's success was a positive sign for jazz or simply a triumph of marketing: at the same time that he was receiving massive promotional support, including a tie-in with a clothing designer that was unprecedented for jazz, his music seemed to be growing less challenging, and his ingratiating and showboating stage persona sometimes seemed to be at war with his sounder musical instincts.

A number of other talented young musicians who paid homage to jazz history while cautiously searching for ways to advance it were also the beneficiaries of major-label largess. Trumpeters Roy Hargrove and Nicholas Payton, saxophonist James Carter, pianists Brad Mehldau and Jacky Terrasson, and bassist Christian McBride were among the new generation of straight-ahead musicians who provided some hope for the music's future—even if they fell short of the kind of breakout success Redman achieved, perhaps because they lacked his marketable looks and stage presence.

And in this relatively jazz-friendly climate, even a handful of underappreciated veteran musicians like tenor saxophonist Joe Henderson and pianist Tommy Flanagan—as well as a select few gifted players who were less than veterans but too old to qualify as young lions, notably tenor saxophonist Joe Lovano and trumpeter-flugelhornist Tom Harrell—saw their careers rejuvenated by the record industry's renewed interest in what *Billboard* magazine, in establishing a new sales chart to document its fortunes, dubbed "traditional jazz." (The more overtly commercial type of jazz-oriented instrumental music, dubbed "contemporary jazz" by *Billboard*, continued to sell in far greater quantities, although by now it could be said to constitute a totally separate genre.)

If the "traditional jazz" musicians who seemed more concerned with polishing their craft and honoring tradition than with taking chances got most of the media attention, they were far from the whole story. The avant-garde, while not exactly thriving, remained active, even if by the nineties it had become harder than ever to say exactly what *avant-garde* meant.

An open-ended approach to both composition and improvisation that might, for lack of a better term, be called the "anything goes" or "cut and paste" school grew up around iconoclastic eccentrics like alto saxophonist John Zorn (who has recorded the music of both Ornette Coleman and the Italian film composer Ennio Morricone) and clarinetist Don Byron (whose repertoire includes free jazz, klezmer music, the compositions of Duke Ellington, and the music of the seventies funk band Mandrill).

Young musicians like saxophonists Steve Coleman and Greg Osby and pianist Geri Allen devoted great energy and resourcefulness to crafting a kind of contemporary, cutting-edge variation of fusion that grafted essentially free improvisation onto a foundation built on elements of funk and even hip-hop.

Attempts at a fusion of jazz and hip-hop, rap, and other more commercial forms were also intermittently mounted from the other side of the divide, with limited success. More successful, surprisingly, was the so-called swing revival—although the music being played by the self-styled swing bands of the late nineties was closer in both sound and spirit to the jump blues played by bands like Louis Jordan's Tympani Five in the forties and fifties than to the music of the actual swing era.

Clearly, the jazz world at the turn of the millennium is a crowded place, with room for a variety of approaches covering the gamut from tradition at all costs to newness for its own sake—even if the degree to which the historically oriented approach has come to dominate both the discourse and the marketplace has led some alarmists to fear for the music's future. But whatever one thinks about the current state of the art, and however one chooses to define the word, it cannot be denied that jazz of one form or another is being performed, recorded, studied, taught, supported, and appreciated, not just in the United States but all over the world.

It certainly can be (and has been) argued that the music is no longer moving forward in any meaningful way; it can also be argued that it has become fragmented beyond recognition. Still, three decades after even some of its more optimistic proponents were ready to write its obituary, the mere fact that jazz is still around—let alone being subsidized by foundations, taught at universities, and for that matter used in television commercials—must be considered an impressive accomplishment, and a testimony to the music's enduring power.

Fusion

Bill Milkowski

Although fusion music was not the first hybrid form in the history of jazz, it was certainly the most notorious. A by-product of strange bedfellows, it brought together the seemingly disparate worlds of rock and jazz into a volatile marriage that was reviled by older jazz purists (who smugly referred to it as "con-fusion") and revered by a younger generation that easily related to its throbbing high energy.

In its earliest incarnation, fusion music was raw and full of abandon, an iron fist upside the head of jazz complacency. A renegade movement fueled by the spirit of search and risk, it provided a bridge for both listener and player between the explosive bombast of Jimi Hendrix and Cream on the one hand and the probing, heightened improvisations of John Coltrane and Pharoah Sanders on the other. It ambitiously melded instrumental virtuosity on the level of Charlie Parker and Dizzy Gillespie with the sheer decibels of the Who and the psychedelia of the post–*Sergeant Pepper's* Beatles, turning a generation of die-hard rockers on to jazz in the process.

While Miles Davis's *Bitches Brew* (Columbia, recorded Aug. 19–21, 1969) is generally cited as the galvanizing statement in fusion, it was hardly the first recording to combine a jazzy sensibility with rock intensity. That notion had been bubbling up for some time before. The fuse for this explosive movement was lit as early as 1965, when jazz-trained hippies in Greenwich Village began picking up on the energy of rock music and boldly blending both aesthetics at nightclubs like Café Au Go Go, the Scene, and the Gaslight.

As pioneering guitarist Larry Coryell (dubbed "the Godfather of Fusion" by his own disciple Al Di Meola) once put it: "We were in the middle of a world cultural revolution. Everybody was dropping acid and the prevailing attitude was, 'Let's do something different.' We loved Wes but we also loved Bob Dylan. We loved Coltrane but we also dug the Beatles. We loved Miles but we also loved the Rolling Stones."

Coryell had come to town from Seattle, intent on becoming the next Wes Montgomery. He soon found himself splitting his time between two gigs to satisfy separate musical urges. His jazzier swinging side was played out in the context of the Chico Hamilton Quartet while his more raucous, experimental side was channeled through Free Spirits, an adventurous fusion band he formed with bassist Chris Hills, drummer Bob Moses, rhythm guitarist Chip Baker, and tenor saxophonist Jim Pepper. In 1966 Coryell recorded *The Dealer* (Impulse) as a member of the Chico Hamilton Quartet. That same year, Free Spirits released its seminal jazz-rock statement, *Out of Sight and Sound* (ABC). Coryell would go on to blaze the fusion trail with the Gary Burton Quartet (*Duster*, RCA, 1967, and *Lofty Fake Anagram*, RCA, 1968).

Jeremy and the Satyrs was another band tapping into a bold new spirit of experimentation that was in the air around Greenwich Village during those counterculture years. Led by flutist Jeremy Steig and featuring drummer Donald McDonald, bassist Eddie Gomez, pianist Warren Bernhardt, guitarist Adrian Guillery, and a young vibist named Mike Mainieri, Jeremy and the Satyrs reached across the jazz-rock divide with its own take on the emerging new music.

Simultaneously on the West Coast, saxophonist Charles Lloyd began mixing rock rhythms with jazz improvisation in a quartet he formed with three unknowns: drummer Jack DeJohnette, bassist Ron McClure, and pianist Keith Jarrett. They received enthusiastic reviews at the Monterey Jazz Festival in September of 1966, which led to an appearance at the Fillmore Auditorium in San Francisco, the top rock emporium in the world. Their *Love-In* (Atlantic), recorded live in early 1967 at the Fillmore, became a phenomenal seller in the jazz field and beyond.

Weather Report in the late 1970s. Left to right: Wayne Shorter, Josef Zawinul, Peter Erskine, Jaco Pastorius, Bobby Thomas Jr. Courtesy Frank Driggs Collection.

Frank Zappa's contribution to this cross-fertilization process that was occurring between rock and jazz in 1966 cannot be overstated. On his first album—the highly experimental underground classic *Freak Out!* (Verve, released in July of 1966)—Zappa listed the names of jazz greats Cecil Taylor, Roland Kirk, Eric Dolphy, and Charles Mingus along with pop singers Joan Baez and Bob Dylan, bluesmen Howlin' Wolf and Muddy Waters, and iconoclastic composers Edgard Varèse and Karlheinz Stockhausen as important influences on his music. During an extended engagement with his Mothers of Invention at New York's Garrick Theater in 1967, Zappa invited Jimi Hendrix—fresh from his smashing (literally) success at the Monterey Pop Festival and the release of his stateside debut, *Are You Experienced?* (Reprise)—to sit in with the band one night. The results were, by all accounts, exhilarating and deafening.

Volume was a key component of the early fusion movement and part of the new vocabulary that jazzers were becoming acquainted with. Propelled by sheer decibels and a blistering intensity, this adventurous new music was tempered by a sophisticated sense of harmony and theory that went well beyond the scope of most rock musicians of the day.

The year 1967 was pivotal for the courtship of rock and jazz. In its July issue that year, the staunch jazz publication *Down Beat* announced that it would expand its coverage to encompass rock. Eddie Harris bridged the gap by introducing the electric tenor saxophone on *The Tender Storm* (Atlantic). Jimi Hendrix melded electronic feedback to Mitch Mitchell's swinging ride cymbal work on "Third Stone from the Sun," arguably Jimi's "jazziest" tune and a centerpiece on his subversive debut, *Are You Experienced?* Earlier that year, Hendrix had jammed with Rahsaan Roland Kirk at Ronnie Scott's nightclub in London. Back in the States, Roger McGuinn had John Coltrane's "sheets of sound" in mind when he recorded his droning guitar parts to the Byrds' "Eight Miles High," while Lou Reed had Ornette Coleman in mind when he cut his avant-punk guitar solo to "I Heard Her Call My Name" from the Velvet Underground's *White Light/White Heat* (Verve). Detroit's notorious proto-punk band MC5 began using feedback as a musical tool and loudness as an aesthetic unit in its long, extended improvisations inspired by the avant-garde jazz movement.

Clearly, the two worlds were on a collision course.

Things started to coalesce in 1968. On a May 17 session for *Miles in the Sky*, Miles Davis stuck one toe into the electronic pool by having Herbie Hancock play electric piano on a rocky vamp called "Stuff." He took the full plunge on *Filles de Kilimanjaro,* recorded in June and September of that year, in which both Herbie and Chick Corea played spikey electric piano. It is somehow revealing that "Mademoiselle Mabry," named for Davis's second wife, Betty Mabry, is based on a motif from Hendrix's "The Wind Cries Mary" from *Are You Experienced?* As Davis noted in his autobiography: "The music I was really listening to in 1968 was James Brown, Jimi Hendrix and a new group, Sly and the Family Stone."

For the February 18, 1969, session that produced *In a Silent Way,* Miles recruited British guitarist John McLaughlin, a phenomenal technician who played with scorching intensity on the instrument. McLaughlin had previously played in the United Kingdom with Alexis Korner and Graham Bond before recording his own debut as a leader, *Extrapolation* (Polydor, 1969). This guitar innovator would figure prominently in the direction of the early fusion movement, not only with Miles Davis but also with Tony Williams Lifetime and later with his own highly influential Mahavishnu Orchestra.

Williams had left the Miles Davis quintet in February of 1969 to form Lifetime. He had joined Davis in 1963 at the ripe old age of seventeen and made huge contributions to a string of important recordings with Davis's second classic quintet (featuring pianist Herbie Hancock, saxophonist Wayne Shorter, and bassist Ron Carter). His revolutionary approach to the kit, combining uncanny rhythmic invention with unprecedented power, changed the face of jazz drumming. Williams's departure from such a celebrated gig was bewildering at the time. His eventual formation of a raucous power trio was even more shocking. As he recalled in a 1992 interview, "I got into Jimi Hendrix and Cream back then, and that was some of the stuff that influenced me when I decided to leave Miles. I wanted to create a different atmosphere from the one I had been in. So I said, 'What better way to do it than to go electric? Organ, guitar and drums, but do it in a real aggressive manner with a lot of rock 'n' roll kind of feeling, energy, power... BAM!!' "

With Williams on drums, McLaughlin on guitar, and Larry Young on organ, the band joined rock's ear-splitting energy with jazz's spontaneity; a kind of cross between the hip Hammond B-3 organ trios of Williams's youth in Boston and the thrashing jam-oriented rock bands of the day like Cream and MC5. Their best moments can be heard on 1969's *Emergency!* (Polydor, recorded May 26 and 28, 1969) and the 1970 follow-up *Turn It Over* (Polydor). Both albums have been compiled along with material from 1971's *Ego* and 1973's *The Old Bum's Rush* on the Verve two-CD set, *Spectrum: The Anthology.*

While McLaughlin's ferocious guitar work in Lifetime deftly connected the worlds of Jimi Hendrix and John Coltrane, organist Young provided another link to the Hendrix mystique. Two weeks prior to the *Emergency!* session he had jammed with Jimi in the studio (documented on the posthumously-released *Nine to the Universe* [Warner Bros.]). Three months after Lifetime's landmark *Emergency!* sessions, Miles Davis would record the influential *Bitches Brew.* With McLaughlin again providing that all-important connection to the rock world via the electric guitar, this adventurous double album brought rock listeners into jazz in unprecedented numbers while also setting a new standard for jazz exploration. Several of the sidemen on this historically important session went on to form influential groups of their own, including keyboardist Joe Zawinul and saxophonist Wayne Shorter (who formed Weather Report in 1971), keyboardist Chick Corea (who formed Return to Forever in 1971), and guitarist McLaughlin (who formed the Mahavishnu Orchestra in 1971).

Three other early entrants into the fusion fray were the Fourth Way, co-led by pianist Mike Nock and violinist Michael White, Mike Mainieri's White Elephant, and Dreams, a jazz-rock outfit formed in 1969 and featuring trumpeter Randy Brecker, his younger brother Michael on tenor sax, Barry Rogers on trombone, Billy Cobham on drums, and John Abercrombie on guitar. Dreams released two adventurous crossover albums on Columbia before disbanding in 1972. In 1974, after a stint on the front line with Horace Silver, Randy and Michael would form the Brecker Brothers, which became one of the more commercially successful jazz-rock-funk bands of the 1970s. (They would reunite in 1992 for *Return of the Brecker Brothers* on GRP and its 1994 follow-up for the label, *Out of the Loop.*)

With the release of Miles Davis's *Jack Johnson* (Columbia, 1970), the fusion floodgates had opened wide. McLaughlin's sledgehammer guitar work on "Right Off," a tune recorded just two months after Hendrix's death, has all the angry proto-punk appeal of the Who. The guitarist's own album that year, *Devotion,* featuring Jimi's Band of Gypsies drummer Buddy Miles and Lifetime's Larry Young, is a frighteningly intense cauldron of rock backbeats, grooving bass lines, and bubbling Hammond B-3 organ with tons of distortion-laced guitar that foreshadowed McLaughlin's later work in the Mahavishnu Orchestra. McLaughlin also acquitted himself with savage abandon that year on Carla Bley's magnum opus, *Escalator Over the Hill*

(Watt), and on Miles Davis's electrified *Live-Evil.* Regarding this volatile period, Davis wrote in his autobiography: "By now I was using the wah-wah on my trumpet all the time so I could get closer to that voice Jimi [Hendrix] had when he used a wah-wah on his guitar."

The early 1970s saw the formation of Miles alumni bands like Weather Report, the Mahavishnu Orchestra, Return to Forever, and funk-fusion pioneers Headhunters, led by Herbie Hancock. These potent groups, along with Larry Coryell's Eleventh House, set the pace in fusion through the first half of the decade. Their playing was marked by a high degree of complex interplay and discipline and underscored by a sense of jazzy abandon in the solos. All but one would eventually disband by 1976. Only Weather Report would continue to prosper into the '80s, though Corea would re-emerge in the mid-'80s with his Elektric Band.

A separate and similarly influential fusion movement—an amalgam of the United Kingdom's progressive rock movement and America's own fusion scene—was developing simultaneously overseas in the early '70s. Among the top U.K. bands in this genre were Soft Machine (featuring guitar hero Allan Holdsworth), Brand X (cofounded by bassist Percy Jones and guitarist John Goodsall with, alternately, Phil Collins, Kenwood Dennard, and Mike Clark on drums), Bruford (led by former Yes-King Crimson drummer Bill Bruford and featuring Holdsworth and bassist Jeff Berlin), and Ian Carr's Nucleus. Other entrants into the Euro-fusion movement included Klaus Doldinger's Passport (Germany), Magma (France), violinist Michal Urbaniak (Poland), and a whole slew of accomplished fusion guitarists including Karl Ratzer (Austria), Volker Kriegel (Germany), Jan Akkermann (Holland), Janne Shaffer (Sweden), Jukka Tolonen (Finland), and Terje Rypdal (Norway). In Japan, guitarists Kazumi Watanabe and Ryo Kawasaki (who was recruited in 1974 by Gil Evans to play on a project of Jimi Hendrix music) had also been significantly affected by the early fusion movement.

Miles Davis continued to embrace electronics with a vengeance just before going into a self-imposed retirement in 1975. His explosive live albums *Agharta* and *Pangaea,* documenting separate concerts in Japan on February 1, 1975, feature his wicked wah-wah trumpet in a dense whirlwind of percussive, throbbing sound that predates the current jungle or drum-and-bass movement by two decades. This provocative electric band included two and sometimes three guitarists all flailing away with a vengeance.

The fusion movement had become codified and diluted by the late

'70s. Groups and individuals like the Crusaders, Chuck Mangione, Bob James, Ramsey Lewis, Grover Washington Jr., Spyro Gyra, and Jeff Lorber Fusion began smoothing off the rough edges, producing a more palatable strain of pop-jazz that paved the way for the commercially successful New Adult Contemporary movement of the '90s. Perhaps the leading light of this new softer approach to fusion was guitarist George Benson, whose breakthrough album, *Breezin'* (Warner Bros., 1976), sold in unprecedented numbers.

Meanwhile, Weather Report prevailed with its own provocative approach. A cult favorite in the early '70s, the groundbreaking band became phenomenally popular with the addition of electric bass guitarist Jaco Pastorius in 1976. A revolutionary player with a natural flair for showmanship, Pastorius came to embody the idea of fusion itself by effortlessly referencing everything from Hendrix's "Purple Haze" and "Third Stone From the Sun" to Coltrane's "Giant Steps" and Duke Ellington's "Satin Doll," Charlie Parker's "Donna Lee," Wilson Pickett's "Funky Broadway," and the Beatles' "Blackbird." Crowds flocked to witness his onstage antics with Weather Report while marveling at his sheer technical facility. After leaving Weather Report in 1982, Pastorius would continue to produce innovative fusion music throughout his solo career. His volatile composition "Crisis" from *Word of Mouth* (Warner Bros., 1982), for instance, is a brilliant blending of rock bombast and the tumult of free jazz with a touch of Stravinsky's more dissonant abstractions added to the mix.

Another innovator, former Gary Burton guitarist Pat Metheny, put his imprint on the genre in the mid-'70s with a style that managed to be both accessible and highly personal. His debut, *Bright Size Life* (ECM, 1975), was a breath of fresh air on the jazz scene that featured inspired interplay with Pastorius and drummer Bob Moses. But it was the widespread popularity of subsequent albums, particularly *American Garage* (ECM, 1979), that earned Metheny the status of a pop star. He continued to expand his audience through the '80s and '90s while also undertaking movie soundtracks and ambitious side projects with such artists as Ornette Coleman, Derek Bailey, Herbie Hancock, Dewey Redman, Michael Brecker, and Roy Haynes.

By the mid-'80s, a new generation of musicians began taking its cues more from the radio-friendly aesthetic of Steely Dan than the raucous expressions of Hendrix and Coltrane. This trend toward tidiness was typified by such successful acts as Kenny G, Yellowjackets, the Rippingtons, and Lee Ritenour. Meanwhile, a few fusion renegades persisted, notably drummer and Ornette Coleman disciple

Ronald Shannon Jackson, whose Decoding Society accounted for some of the most fiercely defiant and provocative sounds of the decade, and Herbie Hancock, who scored a massive radioplay hit in 1983 with "Rock-It" (*Future Shock*, Columbia), a kind of techno updating of his funk-fusion anthem from the previous decade, "Chameleon" (from *Headhunters*, Columbia, 1973).

Though this more hardcore approach to fusion was subverted in the '90s by a kinder, gentler strain alternately known as "smooth jazz," "happy jazz," "hot tub jazz," or "fuzak," there were some notable exceptions. The late avant-garde guitar pioneer Sonny Sharrock (who participated, uncredited, in Miles Davis's seminal *Jack Johnson* session) teamed up with jazz legends Pharoah Sanders, Elvin Jones, and bassist Charnett Moffett on the Bill Laswell–produced *Ask the Ages* (Axiom, 1991), a defiant fusion gem in an age of smooth jazz; Tony Williams (in one of his last recordings) participated in a ferociously uncompromising fusion project entitled *Arc of the Testimony* (Axiom, 1997) under the collective name Arcana, which teamed him with bassist-producer Bill Laswell, saxophonist Pharoah Sanders, and electric guitar shredder Buckethead; electric bass guitarist Jonas Hellborg (formerly of the mid-'80s edition of the Mahavishnu Orchestra) captured the spirit of search and rebellion in a string of three fiercely uncompromising collaborations with '90s guitar hero Shawn Lane and thunderous drummer Jeff Sipe; drummer Dennis Chambers (P-Funk, John Scofield, Brecker Brothers) joined forces in 1997 with rock bass virtuoso Billy Sheehan (David Lee Roth band, Mr. Big) and Hammond B-3 organist John Novello to form Niacin, a power organ trio harkening back to the high-energy jams of Tony Williams Lifetime.

That same over-the-top electrified attitude is being conveyed by new bands on the scene like Screaming Headless Torsos, Full Metal Revolutionary Ensemble, Brave New World (led by keyboardist and former Miles Davis sideman Adam Holzman), and the improvising power trio Harriett Tubman (featuring electric bass guitarist Melvin Gibbs, drummer J. T. Lewis, and guitarist Brandon Ross). Drummer-composer Bobby Previte is keeping the renegade spirit of fusion alive with two bands, the organ-fueled quintet Latin for Travelers and his larger ensemble, the Horse, which specializes in the music from *Bitches Brew* as well as early Lifetime and Weather Report material.

Charter members of the mid-'80s M-BASE collective—saxophonists Steve Coleman and Greg Osby and trumpeter Graham Haynes—continue to explore new modes of expression with their respective cutting-edge groups that draw on elements of rock, funk, hip-hop, and trance music. Harmolodic guitarist James Blood Ulmer is still full of subversive surprises, whether in the context of the Music Revelation Ensemble, Third Rail (with Bill Laswell, Zigaboo Modeliste, and Bernie Worrell), or his own stripped-down trio with drummer Warren Benbrow and violinist Charles Burnham.

Meanwhile, reissues of classic fusion recordings continue to flood the market, triggering a renewed interest in these renegade sounds by a generation of listeners who were too young to catch them the first time around. Several jam-oriented alternative rock bands, including Primus, Phish, Aquarian Rescue Unit, and Fiji Mariners, have pushed the envelope in concert while the adventurous instrumental organ trio Medeski, Martin, and Wood has provided these same young fans an organic bridge into jazz with their groove-heavy improvisations.

Sensing a resurgence in a more aggressive brand of instrumental music, drummer Steve Smith (Journey, Vital Information, Steps Ahead) has joined forces with heavy metal maven Mark Varney (head of the Bay Area–based Shrapnel Records) to form Tone Center, a label devoted strictly to documenting and promulgating fusion music. Their first batch of releases features Smith in an explosive trio format with Tribal Tech guitarist Scott Henderson and electric bassist extraordinaire Victor Wooten (Béla Fleck and the Flecktones) on *Vital Tech Tones*, with guitarist Frank Gambale (Chick Corea Elektric Band) and electric bassist Stu Hamm (Joe Satriani Band) on *Show Me What You Can Do*, and with fusion guitar pioneer Larry Coryell and keyboardist Tom Coster (Santana, Vital Information) in a raucous, ripping B-3 organ trio affair entitled *Cause and Effect*.

A few other old-guard fusioneers have also returned to the fold with recent fusion offerings. Guitarist John Abercrombie participated in a Hendrix-inspired organ trio project with B-3 legend Lonnie Smith and drummer Marvin "Smitty" Smith (*Purple Haze*, MusicMasters, 1996). Weather Report cofounder Joe Zawinul is still going strong with his crack pancultural outfit, the Zawinul Syndicate (*World Tour*, Zebra, 1998). And Herbie Hancock recently toured on the strength of a twenty-five-year reunion project (*Return of the Headhunters*, Verve, 1998).

Proving once again the truth of the adage: what goes around comes around.

Jazz Repertory

Jeffrey Sultanof

The phrase *jazz repertory* has many definitions and dimensions. Perhaps the most basic definition is: the study, preservation, and performance of the many diverse musical styles in jazz. In recent years, the phrase most often applies to big bands and jazz ensembles performing classic and new music written for reeds, brass, and rhythm section in various sizes and combinations.

In a sense, the small-group jazz repertoire movement began in the late 1930s. There had always been a core of traditional jazz fans and artists during the big band era, but a national focus on older styles was evident from new recordings made in the late '30s by Jelly Roll Morton, the Original Dixieland Jazz Band, Sidney Bechet, et al. The rediscovery of trumpeter Bunk Johnson prompted new activity in older styles by such ensembles as those led by Lu Watters and Turk Murphy. Younger musicians such as Bob Wilber and Kenny Davern felt more sympathy with the music of an earlier era. Wilber even studied with his hero, Sidney Bechet, and became his protégé.

Further interest in older styles of jazz was prompted by the publication of *They All Played Ragtime,* written by Rudi Blesh and Harriet Janis. Blesh's own record label, Circle, concentrated on ragtime and older jazz styles. Admittedly, much of the interest and recordings of these styles was centered more on its novelty value (Lou Busch and Knuckles O'Toole [Dick Hyman]), but many worthwhile recordings by such artists as Dick Cary, Dick Wellstood, and Ralph Sutton gave new life to early jazz styles.

The late '50s saw the first small ensemble to perform music encompassing the earliest to the most contemporary styles of jazz: the Bobby Hackett ensemble, a band that could play dixieland classics and more up-to-date (for the period) jazz tunes. Given the fact that most ensembles still specialize in one particular era of music, it is rather amazing that this ensemble remains so little known.

Study and performance of more traditional styles of jazz can be found in the activities of such musicians as Bob Wilber, James Dapogny, Dan Barrett, and Randy Sandke. Sandke and Dapogny in particular have made major strides in this area. Dapogny edited an edition of Jelly Roll Morton compositions (G. Schirmer). Sandke has rediscovered and performed Louis Armstrong compositions the master never recorded himself. Even though many of the musicians listed above specialize in the music of particular eras, Hyman and Sandke have shown that they can play many different musical styles, from dixieland to modal and aleatoric jazz.

With regard to more modern styles, small groups that have been assembled to re-create and celebrate the music of particular innovators are Supersax (the music and solos of Charlie Parker—five saxophones and rhythm), Dave Pell's Prez Conference (the music and solos of Lester Young—four saxophones and rhythm), and the Tony Rizzi Ensemble (the music and solos of Charlie Christian—five guitars and rhythm). Other notable repertory small groups include Marty Grosz's Sounds of Swing, Bob Wilber and Kenny Davern's Soprano Summit, and Wilber's Bechet Legacy.

Excluding so-called ghost bands, which exist to perpetuate the music of a leader who has passed away, the first real jazz repertory big band was the Bob Crosby Orchestra of the late '30s. With musical directors Bob Haggart, Matty Matlock, and Deane Kincaide, the band featured an older, more New Orleans style of jazz, playing and recording such evergreens as "Muskrat Ramble," "Beale Street Blues," "Sugar Foot Strut," and "Panama." It also played the pop hits of the day in a two-beat style. The full orchestra and the Bobcats, the small group within the band, had a strong following and recorded prolifically for Decca Records. Crosby's postwar forays into bandleading were more modern in nature, but the Bobcats remained a New Orleans–style group.

The idea of studying and re-creating the music of vintage big

Benny Carter with the American Jazz Orchestra in rehearsal at Cooper Union, New York, 1987. Left to right: Carter, alto sax; Ron Carter, bass; Dick Katz, piano; Remo Palmier, guitar; Lew Tabackin, tenor sax; John Purcell, alto sax; Bill Easley, alto sax. Photo: Ed Berger.

bands began to take shape in the late 1960s. This writer wrote an article in 1972 (never published) about playing this music in concert and wondered if the music existed and where it was. The repertory band movement caught fire soon after, with several ensembles appearing and individuals actively transcribing, studying, and performing music from many periods of the big band. The New McKinney's Cotton Pickers began in 1972, when Dave Hutson, an alto saxophonist and disc jockey from Detroit, interviewed the original McKinney banjoist, Dave Wilborn, on the radio. That interview led to Wilborn's active participation in the new orchestra, which went on to record three LPs and tour Europe.

In 1973 two important ensembles were created in New York. Chuck Israels, former bassist with Bill Evans and teaching at Brooklyn College at the time, believed that an ensemble should be created that would not only perform the big band music of the past but also commission and play new music. He received grants from the New York State Council on the Arts and the National Endowment for the Arts. The National Jazz Ensemble gave its first concert in July of 1973. In its four-year existence, it gave many concerts in New York and other parts of the United States and made two albums. Its repertoire ranged from Duke Ellington transcriptions by David Berger to arrangements written by Israels of pieces by Bix Beiderbecke and Charles Mingus to new music by several writers.

The other ensemble was masterminded by Newport Jazz Festival creator George Wein. Entitled the New York Jazz Repertory Ensemble, this ambitious undertaking was announced to the press on July 2, 1973. There were several concerts in the first year, spearheaded by four musical directors representing jazz past and present: Stanley Cowell, Gil Evans, Sy Oliver, and Billy Taylor. This ensemble was also funded by the New York State Council on the Arts, as well as the NEA and the Carnegie Hall Corporation. The first year of the ensemble's existence was only partially successful, with losses of over forty thousand dollars. The key problem was that individual concerts were made up of both older and newer styles of jazz; most often the newer music was programmed after intermission, and members of the audience did not return after the break. Having four musical directors was abandoned in 1974. For the second year, only one style or theme would be presented per concert, and a planning committee made up of Stanley Dance, Dick Hyman, Joe Newman, Jimmy Owens, and Bob Wilber designed the concert series. This plan existed until the ensemble played its last concert in 1975.

Even though its life was short, the New York Jazz Repertory Ensemble pointed the way to later, more successful jazz repertory orchestras. Its concert programming included the small ensemble music of King Oliver and Jelly Roll Morton, the big bands of Jimmie Lunceford and Count Basie, the small-group and big band music of George Russell, the music of Bix Beiderbecke, musically directed by Richard Sudhalter, a concert of the music of John Coltrane, musically directed by tenor saxophonist and Coltrane scholar Andrew White, and commissioned works by such composers as Charles Tolliver. Perhaps the high point of the ensemble's existence, however, was Dick Hyman's presentation of the music of Louis Armstrong. This presentation toured the world and was recorded and issued by Atlantic on LP.

Writer-historian Martin Williams produced a series of historical jazz concerts at the Smithsonian in the mid-'70s, which included an Ellington concert featuring *Symphony in Black*.

Another important leader of vintage big band music in the 1970s was bass saxophonist–bassist Vince Giordano. Giordano had been a student of the legendary Jean Goldkette/Paul Whiteman arranger Bill Challis, and met and played with many of the musicians active in the '20s jazz scene. He collected published arrangements from the '20s and '30s and organized his own bands by 1976. More often than not, Giordano's bands were made up of both young and older musicians who had an interest in playing these styles. By 1981 Vince Giordano's New Orleans Nighthawks had a regular engagement at the Red Blazer Too in New York City and also played at the swank Café Carlyle, as well as parties and dances. The library contained over thirty thousand arrangements. The band was inactive for a number of years until Giordano re-formed it in 1999.

Starting in this era, ensembles were organized to focus on particular big band styles or books. The bands most often featured were those of Count Basie (the music of Thad Jones, Frank Foster, Neal Hefti, Sam Nestico), Stan Kenton (the Kenton book was the first important library to be made available to musicians and educators; new editions of compositions and arrangements are available from Bob Curnow's company, Sierra Music), Thad Jones and Mel Lewis, Duke Ellington, Buddy Rich, and Woody Herman. Many of the pieces from the books of these bands were being published by such companies as Kendor Music, Hal Leonard, Lifeline Press, Jenson Publications, and Warner Bros. Publications. Other music circulated among collectors. In 1979 and 1980, the Mike Crotty band, based in Washington, D.C., gave two concerts of the music of the Boyd Raeburn ensemble of 1944–48. The book was rediscovered by Crotty band manager Bill Schremp in a basement in Long Island. In its time, the music was considered quite advanced, but the modern performances of this still provocative-sounding music by George Williams, Johnny Mandel, Milt Kleeb, Ed Finckel, Johnny Richards, and particularly George Handy were well received. Schremp marketed some of this music, but few copies of the publications were sold.

One important band formed to perform the music of a single big band book was the ensemble begun by Harvey Estrin in 1976 playing the music of the Sauter-Finegan Orchestra. Estrin's orchestra was made up of the best of the younger generation of instrumentalists just starting as professional musicians in the New York area, most of whom had never even heard of the band, let alone heard the music. The book was eagerly embraced by the musicians and audiences alike; after twenty-odd years, the music was still fresh and challenging, one of the unique big band libraries of any era. Both Eddie Sauter and Bill Finegan attended rehearsals, coached, advised, and generally had a wonderful time. The ensemble was active for several years. Alas, it never recorded professionally.

The United Kingdom was also full of activity in the '70s. One of the most important ensembles was led by cornetist-trumpeter-author Richard Sudhalter. He obtained over two hundred arrangements from the Paul Whiteman library housed at Williams College in Massachusetts and organized the New Paul Whiteman Orchestra. The orchestra featured Sudhalter playing the parts originally written for Bix Beiderbecke, while saxophonist–sound engineer John R. T. Davies played the Frank Trumbauer parts. The band gave several well-received concerts during 1974–75, broadcast over BBC radio, and was profiled on BBC television. One of the concerts was recorded by the band's bassist, Peter Ind, and was later issued on his Wave label in England and on Monmouth Evergreen in the United States. One of the members of this ensemble, Keith Nichols, later formed the Midnight Follies Orchestra.

The '80s brought several new ensembles. On May 12, 1986, the American Jazz Orchestra, masterminded by writer-historian Gary Giddins and pianist-composer John Lewis, gave its first concert in the Great Hall of Cooper Union in New York. Tenor saxophonist Loren Schoenberg later became co–musical director. The ensemble had an extensive board of trustees, including Benny Goodman, Benny Carter, Thad Jones, Muhal Richard Abrams, Albert Murray, and George

Wein. The AJO performed both music from the past and scores especially commissioned from Abrams, Carter, Bob Brookmeyer, Sy Oliver, Henry Threadgill, Gerald Wilson, and David Murray. It was forced to cease operation in 1992.

The ensembles discussed below are still going strong at this writing. Formed in 1988, the Lincoln Center Jazz Orchestra has been quite successful under the direction of Wynton Marsalis. Even though the ensemble plays a wide range of classic and new music, it is mainly known for its performances of the music of Duke Ellington (most often transcribed by David Berger) and of Marsalis himself. The Smithsonian Jazz Masterworks Orchestra began giving concerts in 1991 under the direction of its musical directors Gunther Schuller and David Baker. (When Schuller was affiliated with the New England Conservatory of Music, he organized and conducted ensembles devoted to *The Red Back Book* of Scott Joplin and his own transcriptions of the music of Duke Ellington.) The U.S. government gave the Smithsonian $242,000 to found the orchestra and to fund transcription and preservation of the classic jazz repertoire. The ensemble has given many free concerts at its home base in Washington, D.C. The Carnegie Hall Jazz Band, directed by trumpeter Jon Faddis, is the brainchild of George Wein. Founded in December of 1991, the ensemble's purpose is to "[showcase] classic tunes in refreshingly novel forms as well as many new works." All of these ensembles have toured widely and recorded CDs.

On the West Coast, Mark Masters has led his Jazz Composers Orchestra since the early '80s. While he concentrates on the repertoire and arrangers of the Stan Kenton band, he has also performed the music of other composers such as Ornette Coleman and Jimmy Knepper. Masters is known particularly for giving outstanding concerts of the difficult music of Robert Graettinger. The ensemble has recorded three CDs.

The Chicago Jazz Ensemble, with distinguished composer William Russo as its musical director, was founded in 1965 to perform Russo's compositions, although it also gave performances of Duke Ellington's First Concert of Sacred Music; this ensemble disbanded in 1968. Upon its reorganization in 1991, the ensemble gave concerts featuring the music of Ellington, Billy Strayhorn, and music from the books of Stan Kenton and Count Basie. In 1995 it gave the first complete live performance of Gil Evans's *Sketches of Spain*, originally written for Miles Davis. The ensemble is in residence at Columbia College and has recorded two CDs.

In Holland, the Ebony Band specializes in "concert jazz," performing the music of the Stan Kenton Innovations Orchestra, John Carisi, and George Handy. They have recorded two CDs.

On another level, conductor-historian Maurice Peress has presented re-creations of two important concerts involving large ensembles and jazz. In 1988 he toured widely with the original 1924 Paul Whiteman Aeolian Hall concert, which introduced George Gershwin's *Rhapsody in Blue,* and in 1989 he researched and musical-directed a re-creation of the 1912 concert of James Reese Europe's Clef Club Orchestra. Both concerts were critically well received.

From the very beginning of the jazz repertory movement, several issues arose with regard to source material and performance issues. Some leaders feel that compositions and arrangements should be performed exactly as recorded, and recorded solos should be reproduced in concert. Others feel that older big band music should not be locked in a time capsule and that solos should be original. This difference in attitude and philosophy is also reflected in the publication of this music. The Classic Edition publications of David Berger's Ellington transcriptions have rhythm parts that are basically guides, as are Walter van de Leur's editions of Billy Strayhorn's compositions; the Smithsonian's own publications have all solos and rhythm parts totally written out.

It has been noted that many of the important works of the big band era exist in stock arrangements. The term *stock arrangement* was first used in music publishing circles as early as the nineteenth century. During the big band era, stock arrangements were, more often than not, issued by publishers and provided free to bandleaders so the publisher's songs would be played. In the cases where stock arrangements were issued that reflected a hit record by a particular band, often the arrangement was orchestrationally altered or musically simplified to make it playable by most bands. The stock arrangement of Artie Shaw's hit version of "Begin the Beguine," for example, has saxophone parts that are different from the original so that Artie Shaw's clarinet solo could be incorporated into the section proper. In addition, the recorded arrangement is in the key of D; the stock arrangement is in the key of C. For this reason, stock arrangements must be carefully scrutinized before they can be deemed authentic. Many need extensive audio checking and major surgery before they are ready for use. A full score must be prepared, not only to do this work more effectively but to root out note, rhythmic, and dynamic errors.

One of the most important pieces of advice is also the most obvious:

try as much as possible to ascertain whether the original arrangement exists in a collection or library. There are at least three known transcriptions of "King Porter Stomp" where the original score and parts are now housed, at the Benny Goodman Collection at Yale University. Yale even has a complete listing of the collection that is available for purchase.

The Smithsonian Institution and the Library of Congress continue to acquire important collections; among the most notable libraries these organizations now house are those of Duke Ellington, Charlie Barnet, Gerald Wilson, and Gerry Mulligan. In addition, both are dedicated to making the music available to those organizations who wish to perform it. In many other cases, however, the music is spread far and wide. A partial list of such collections follows:

Louis Armstrong: Queens College, Flushing, New York
Les Brown, Larry Clinton, Bob Crosby: University of Wyoming, Laramie
Benny Goodman: New York Public Library; Yale University, New Haven, Connecticut
Harry James: University of Wyoming, Laramie
Stan Kenton: University of North Texas, Denton
Red Nichols: University of Oregon, Eugene
Red Norvo: Yale University
Boyd Raeburn: Institute of Jazz Studies, Rutgers University, Newark, New Jersey; Tulane University, New Orleans
Artie Shaw: Mugar Memorial Library, Boston University

Composer-historian Andrew Homzy has been assembling a master list of compositions, arrangements, and transcriptions of such big band material. Over a thousand pages in length, it is still quite a few years away from completion at this writing, particularly due to new donations of such material in the recent past.

In essence, the chances of obtaining usable material for a wide-ranging concert of big band music are erratic at best. With further research and the efforts of current and future historians of the jazz ensemble past and present, this will most certainly change in the years to come. However, as with film, much material is still is in private hands and has not gotten into active circulation. Given the nature of the paper the music is written on (much of this paper, manufactured and printed during World War II, is highly acidic and unstable), it is essential to photocopy, recopy by hand or computer, and otherwise preserve what remains of the known big band libraries and published arrangements before it is too late.

The state of the jazz repertory movement is also dependent on the current audience for such music. This is best illustrated by the experiences of the New York Jazz Repertory Company and the American Jazz Orchestra. One of the main reasons for the dissolution of these ensembles may be seen in the great popularity of the Basie, Ellington, Goodman, and Lunceford concerts and the lack of interest in the concerts featuring more modern big band music. Jazz repertory, in the main, is still supported by audiences sixty and older, who listen to this music as a nostalgic experience. Perhaps it is true that a well-rounded jazz repertory, representing music from all eras of the jazz ensemble, is several years away from full acceptance. We must remember that there was relatively little interest in the music of Bach after his death until Felix Mendelssohn began performing it in the mid-nineteenth century.

Jazz repertory represents an important direction and challenge for the future: to acknowledge the creative gifts of the men and women who created ensemble music for listening and dancing, and to prepare usable performance materials so that ensembles can easily play and study it. Just imagine if materials from the baroque and classical eras of music had been allowed to collect dust in attics or languish in special collections in colleges and archives without editing and publication; by this time, they would probably have ceased to exist. We are only now accepting that the music of the big band is unique and warrants saving, not just in terms of American cultural history but of world music as well. It is imperative that this work continue for the sake of indigenous American music. Perhaps wide interest in this music is still several years away; yet the time to save it is now.

Latin Jazz

Gene Santoro

I n the beginning there was the beat, and it was manifold.

Most jazz critics and historians rely on the all-purpose term *swing*, whose virtue resides at least partly in its evocative vagueness. But Jelly Roll Morton was more precise and expansive. While he was taking credit for jazz's birth and development in his N'Awlins hometown, he famously noted "the Spanish Tinge," which he deemed central to the nascent sound of surprise. Many since have paid lip service to Morton's assertion, but only a few, like John Storm Roberts, have seriously pursued its implications.

If the New World has been this century's major source of popular music, it is due largely to the rich social and cultural mixtures that historically horrific situations like slavery and conquest left as their loamy residue. In the United States, the collisions of African and European sensibilities, musical forms, instruments, and techniques yielded work songs, minstrel shows, blues, jazz, gospel, and rock. Brazil boasts hybrids like samba, bossa nova, and tropicalia. From Jamaican reggae to Trinidadian calypso, the Caribbean teems with offshoots of the same roots.

But dolly the camera back a minute. The Mediterranean cultures that colonized Latin America were already Afro-European hybrids. Witness political history like Hannibal's conquest of Italy and Islamic rule over Iberia, and cultural history like the Arab- and African-influenced arts, philosophy, and sciences of medieval and Renaissance southern Europe. So when they clambered ashore with African slaves and overwhelmed Caribbean peoples, the Latin colonizers deposited a historical palimpsest. No wonder that what unfolded in the New World was what evolutionists and biologists call parallel development.

For instance, it's impossible to tell the story of Cuban or U.S. music without constantly referring from one to the other. In the nineteenth century, Cuba was an epicenter of the New World's cultural matrix. For four hundreds years after the conquistadors, the island was aswirl with Mediterranean dances (the contradanse, the quadrille, etc.) alongside beats brought by the West and Central African slaves working the sugar plantations. Underlying their buoyant polyrhythms was *clave*, the two-bar pattern with a three-against-two beat that American rocker Bo Diddley gave his name to.

By the 1930s, clave became the basis for Latin, or Afro-Cuban, jazz. And like clockwork, every generation since has triggered a renaissance of clave's jazzy offshoots, from rumba to mambo to salsa. But Morton's observation depicts clave as critical to jazz's birth and early development as well.

Historically and culturally, New Orleans is a Caribbean city attached to the Mississippi Delta. Through its port, trade and immigration washed people and their cultural baggage from across the region, with its indigenous Indians and imported black slaves ruled by the same Spanish and French who first ruled New Orleans. Congo Square, in the city's center, was the site of Sunday slave gatherings and music-making forbidden elsewhere in the United States. Free blacks and Creoles were often educated and well off. The Haitian slave revolt of 1791 inspired "uptown" blacks, but Creoles were part of the "downtown" cultural elite—until the 1894 passage of Louisiana's race codes pushed them resentfully across the racial divide. The elements that created early jazz were mingling.

Culturally, the Crescent City's daily rhythms pulsed with mestizo ideas. European high and middle culture often involved whites, Creoles, and free blacks. Down-home blues were a-borning uptown. For the 1884 World's Exposition, a sixty-plus–member Mexican military band performed Mozart, "Dixie," and Sousa, thrilling audiences and selling piles of sheet music. Mexican and Cuban sounds filled the Hispanic parts of the French Quarter. And Mardi Gras parades and funeral processions featured highly eclectic marching bands.

Composer Louis Gottschalk went to Havana in 1854 and returned

Machito Orchestra, December 1955: Mario Bauza, trumpet and arranger (fourth from right); Doc Cheatham, trumpet (far right). Courtesy Frank Driggs Collection.

with Cuban-inflected pieces that became popular. The Tio family, famed clarinetists who taught many early Crescent City jazzers, were among the city's Mexican early-jazz pioneers, though they have often been labeled Creole. The confusion was understandable. Lots of Creole musicians had their sort of formal training—some from Lorenzo Tio Jr.

A Creole himself, Morton exemplified the Big Easy's stylistic and ethnic interactivity. "We had Spanish, we had colored, we had white," he said of prewar New Orleans pianists. He combined all three strains personally and musically. But though he arranged the Cuban hit "La Paloma" into what he called "ragtime tango," his jazz's Spanish Tinge was more spice than entree. And that's mostly how it stayed until the early bebop era.

While early jazz flowered in turn-of-the-century New Orleans, Havana was full of *son*, improvised vocals with guitar backing, the blues in clave. Adding brass to its bands (again thanks to the influence of military marching outfits), son moved from the country to town, where it flourished in segregated black neighborhoods. (George Gershwin befriended the great sonero and Septeto Nacionál leader Ignacio Pineiro and lifted one of his melodies for "Cuban Overture.") Outstanding examples are collected on *Cuban Counterpoint: The History of Son Montuno* (Rounder).

Meanwhile *charanga*, performed by ballroom groups deemphasizing percussion and replacing the son septet's horns with flutes and violin, was wealthy white Havana's dance music. Built on *danzón*, a syncopated Creole version of the eighteenth-century French contradanse invented in late 1800s Oriente province—Cuba's most "African" region—charanga aspired to elegance: white-gloved bands would allude to Liszt in their music.

By the late 1920s, Cuban emigration to New York had spawned El Barrio—the East Harlem enclave that houses many Latinos today. El Barrio was soon a market. U.S. record companies, which started signing Cuban son conjuntos earlier that decade, stepped up recording Latin sounds to sell both there and throughout Latin America. As important, El Barrio provided a base for the growing network of Cuban and jazz musicians. Cuban flautist Alberto Socarras, for instance, did session work for Columbia, performed in Benny Carter's jazz band, and led his own orchestra, which blended Cuban, jazz, and classical idioms.

From the turn-of-the-century cakewalk on, American music history can be viewed as a series of successive dance crazes, often based on imported rhythms. So it happened that in late 1930 "El Manicero" (The Peanut Vendor) launched the rumba in the United States. An outgrowth of son, rumba kicked the Argentine tango (the previous Latin dance craze) out of its way to introduce Cuban rhythms to a mass American audience. Dom Aspiazú, whose hit it was, took up residence at the New York Palace—the first lengthy engagement a Cuban band had outside El Barrio. A year later, manufacturers like Gretsch advertised "rumba instruments." Bandleaders like Desi Arnaz and Xavier Cugat waxed hits doing the conga, rumba's more commercial, less subtle cousin. (Outstanding examples are gathered on *A Carnival of Cuban Music* [Rounder].)

While conga lines stretched across America's dance floors, the late 1930s brought *conjuntos* into vogue in Havana. Derived from black carnival parade bands in roughly the same ways that New Orleans jazz bands had evolved four decades earlier, conjuntos consisted of one or two vocalists, two or three trumpets, a bass, various drums, and a piano. Adding the conga drum, which offered a looser, improvisatory commentary on the underlying clave and deepened the fierce rhythmic and thematic crosstalk, is attributed to Arsenio Rodriguez, a blind guitar-playing sonero. Along with multi-instrumentalist Mario Bauza and vocalist Machito, Rodriguez and bassist Israel "Cachao" Lopez, who forged elements of early mambo for a famous 1930s Havana charanga, were precursors of what would, at the war's end, become mambo mania.

When Oscar Hijuelos was looking for an overarching metaphor reflecting the deep intimacies and inevitable frictions between Cuban and American culture, he didn't pull mambo out of a hat. Mambo yearns to carry that symbolic weight. A descendant of Congolese cult-music, born in Cuba, raised in New York, mambo circled back to its birthplace via the Mexican-based dance band of Cuban-born Perez Prado, its most successful popularizer.

As a teenaged veteran of Romeu's orchestra, Mario Bauza emigrated from Havana to Harlem's Sugar Hill; soon he was playing with Noble Sissle, Chick Webb, Fletcher Henderson, Don Redman, and Cab Calloway. Calloway, thanks to Bauza, hired a horn player named Dizzy Gillespie and incorporated Latinisms into his band. Around the same time, Duke Ellington made Puerto Rican trombonist Juan Tizol's "Caravan" a hit. Latin spices were again bubbling in jazz. But modern Latin jazz developed from the marriage of mambo and bebop, thanks to Bauza and his circle.

By 1937 Bauza had been musical director for Webb's big band—where he had helped persuade Webb to hire a young vocalist named Ella Fitzgerald—for four years, when he wrote his brother-in-law Frank Grillo to "come and starve with me." Grillo, known as Machito, apprenticed with Pineiro in Havana, but New York was, as jazzers said, "the big apple." So there he went, and the duo founded the Afro-Cubans, a seminal band that overrode musical and racial barriers by mingling Cubans, Puerto Ricans, and Americans.

The genius of Machito's Afro-Cubans lay in recognizing the affinity between swing era jazz and their own traditions. Radically different though the two idioms' rhythms were, they shared other aspects: both were fundamentally about dancing to singing and improvised solos over cyclic backing riffs. (Machito was one of the most powerful soneros of the tradition, silky smooth and able to improvise verbally and rhythmically with jazz-level skills while wielding his maracas.) But Afro-Cuban jazz, or Cubop, as the captivating hybrid was called, presented rhythmic difficulties to American jazzers; clave's precise organization of the beats threw musicians used to playing in 4/4, or common, time. From the other side, big band ensemble playing was much more precisely charted than *orquestra típica* parts. Then too, the convoluted melodies and harmonies boppers like Charlie Parker and Gillespie used were far removed from mambo's improvising section, montuno, simple repeated figures over two or three chords.

As Amiri Baraka noted in *Blues People*, bebop represented jazz as a self-conscious art form—a sharp break with the music's history of the streets and bordellos, bars, and dance halls. He also noted that, contrary to widespread belief, many fans danced to it. This helps explain why Gillespie, who loved dancing to Latin music, felt drawn to mesh clave into the loose, fractured beats powering bop. The Palladium, the "Temple of Mambo" on Broadway and 53rd Street, attracted high-voltage fans like Gillespie, Marlene Dietrich, Jackson Pollock, Allen Ginsberg, and Marlon Brando (who sometimes sat in on bongos) to its dance contests. Jazzers working down the street at Birdland and the Royal Roost ran up in between sets to check out the Cuboppers, and the Latin musicians returned the favor. (*Mucho Macho Machito* [Pablo] collects seminal Machito collaborations.)

Some formal differences between bebop and mambo were bridged by tunes like the Afro-Cubans' 1940s hit "Tanga." The title—"marijuana" in an African dialect—underscored how Gillespie once described Cuban-American musical collaborations: "We both speak African." "Manteca" teamed Gillespie's blistering trumpet with Chano

Pozo's fiery conga improvisations. The Cuban was trained in Abakwa—a cult with roots in Nigeria. Onstage, the hard-living, showstopping Pozo stripped to the waist to show off his oiled torso, sing, dance, and play simultaneously—often in different meters.

By the late 1940s, Cuboppers were experimenting with extended forms like *Afro-Cuban Suite,* written by Gillespie and Pozo. George Russell, an advanced composer and theorist, penned "Cubana Be" and "Cubana Bop" for them. In September 1947 Gillespie's big band appeared at Carnegie Hall, featuring Pozo, and the latest Spanish Tinge's role in the bop era was clinched. (*The Complete RCA Victor Recordings, 1937–1949* captures Gillespie's early Cubop outings.)

It probably helped that Gillespie played trumpet. Cuban, like American, military bands had featured cornets. The trumpet thus became a staple in the Cuban-blues septetos, commenting and rippling with flourishes in the fanfare fashion that still identifies many Cuban hornmen. In fact, Gillespie's frenetic lines might well have sounded less "strange" to Cubans than to American audiences and swing era jazzmen. In turn, he became a model who transformed the sound of Cuban trumpeters ever after.

Gillespie was among the most successful Americans trying to forge modern Latin jazz, but he was far from alone. Bauza, Machito's musical director, suggested they feature special guests, like Buddy Rich, Herbie Mann, Johnny Griffin, and Curtis Fuller, as well as Gillespie and Parker. Between 1948 and 1952, Norman Granz—the man who broke the audience color bar in Los Angeles, holding benefit concerts after the notorious 1940s anti-Latino "zoot suit" police riots—recorded Parker hitching his mercurial alto to Latin beats. The results, collected on *South of the Border* (Verve), demonstrate Bird's remarkable rhythmic agility, his deft sense of how to remain himself yet play in clave.

All too few of his disciples could, but trumpeter Fats Navarro forged an interesting alliance with Chano Pozo. Born in heavily Hispanic Key West, Navarro was black, Chinese, and Cuban. With Pozo, he cuts tunes like "Lady Bird" and "Jahbero" that seamlessly melded bop's in-the-moment arcana with mambo's buoyantly structured propulsion. Along with Gillespie, Navarro prefigured jazz trumpeters, from Doc Cheatham to Jack Walrath, who steadily doubled in Latin music.

As Gillespie and Pozo debuted at Town Hall, Stan Kenton recorded "El Manicero." He had already waxed "Machito," using the bandleader's percussionists. Soon he hired Laurindo Almeida and explored Brazilian styles. In 1945 Woody Herman cut "Bijou," a rumba with jazz solos.

Latin musicians were eager to cross over into jazz—and mainstream American culture. Machito's band, for instance, played with Dexter Gordon, Stan Getz, and Zoot Sims while nurturing talent like Chico O'Farrill.

Born in Havana, O'Farrill went to a Georgia military school, where he became a big band fan and learned the trumpet. Back in Havana, he studied composition and led a swaggering outfit. In New York in 1948, he penned music for Benny Goodman and Kenton. But it was his work with Machito and Gillespie that made his mark. *Afro-Cuban Jazz Suite* was the first important extended work in a truly Cubop idiom, and it led O'Farrill into a landmark series of recordings (for Granz) collected as *Cuban Blues: Chico O'Farrill Sessions* (Verve).

O'Farrill wasn't alone. As Cubop and mambo heated up the postwar jazz world, the next generation emerged from Afro-Cuban big bands. Top-drawer outfits like Marcelino Guerra's and Jose Curbelo's incubated future leaders like Tito Rodriguez and Tito Puente alongside vets like Pozo. In a short time the two Titos would join Machito as New York's Mambo Kings.

Mambo took the entire U.S. pop world by storm. The same year Gillespie and Pozo played Town Hall, Bing Crosby recorded "Quizas Quizas Quizas." Rosemary Clooney and Ruth Brown also sang hit mambos. Nat King Cole went to Cuba to cut *Rumba à la King,* with Cuban trumpeter Chocolate Armenteros. In New Orleans, Professor Longhair, Fats Domino, and James Booker transmuted the latest Spanish Tinge into rock-and-roll.

The Cubop fires of rediscovery burned hot and fast. By the time *I Love Lucy,* in which Arnaz played a Copacabana bandleader, ruled the airwaves, its audience was peaking. As was its revolutionary force: like bebop, Cubop had mingled so much it had become a language with many dialects—Latin jazz.

In 1953 British-born, classically trained pianist George Shearing formed a Latin-jazz quartet with Willie Bobo, Cal Tjader, Mongo Santamaria, and Armando Peraza. Shearing was a huge star, but on *Latin Escapade* (Capitol) he served up a period piece of cocktail music, boleros, and mambos. Still, despite Herbie Mann's charanga-inflected outings, Sonny Rollins's calypso annexations, and the mambos undergirding the work of Horace Silver and Art Blakey's Jazz

Messengers, for most American jazzers of this period, the Spanish Tinge reverted to a seasoning.

For Latin jazzers, though, the 1950s were glory days. Puente and Rodriguez both started bands in 1947. From then on, they shared with Bauza and Machito the creative shaping of New York mambo. Puente, a New York Puerto Rican multi-instrumentalist, wrote fluent but edgy charts that reflected his hometown's high-strung vitality and pace—and became an institution, after more than a hundred albums. A driving force behind the birth of salsa, Puente's 1950s big bands included Santamaria, Bobo, Johnny Pacheco, and Ray Barretto and lofted hits like "Abaniquito," which led RCA to sign him. Rodriguez, born in Puerto Rico, was an improvising sonero with less highly wired arrangements; he toured hotspots like Miami, Las Vegas, and L.A. When the Palladium went all-mambo in 1953, its three steady head-liners were Machito, Puente, and Rodriguez.

Like many after the 1959 Cuban revolutions, singer Celia Cruz left Havana, where she was a star, for New York, where she hooked up with Pacheco and Puente. The Puente-Cruz partnership endures on-stage and in the movie version of *The Mambo Kings Play Songs of Love*. A dazzling improviser and flamboyant performer, the contralto-voiced Cruz was later dubbed "the Queen of Salsa."

For late-1950s crossover audiences were leaving the thrills of Cubop for less tumultuous cha-cha-chas. Percussionists Ray Barretto and Candido lent rhythmic perfume to countless recordings that are not really Latin jazz. The new format's creative heat had dissipated. And so O'Farrill moved to Mexico City, not to return until 1965, when he became musical director for a TV series, *Festival of the Lively Arts*, and wrote for Count Basie, Machito, Gillespie, and newcomer Gato Barbieri.

In culture, innovation and expansion usually lead to consolidation and retrenchment, and the 1950s mambo explosion was no exception. Even as mambo held sway, classic charanga, Creolized eighteenth-century French dances, was being revived and remapped by Pacheco and the Joe Cuba Sextet and attracting the post-Castro exodus of hundreds of thousands of Cubans to the United States. Postwar eco-nomics doomed not just the swing bands but the big Cubop outfits, spurring a return to small groups. And so Latin jazz combos replaced the traditional violin with a trombone, as on albums by Santamaria (*Afro-Roots* [Prestige]) and Cal Tjader (*Latino* [Fantasy]).

The Havana-born Santamaria, who had traded violin for percussion as a student, was a veteran of his hometown's Tropicana club, Perez Prado's big band, and groups led by Puente and Tjader. In 1959 his soaring hit "Afro-Blue" inspired covers by Gillespie and John Coltrane. Three years later, he led a gig at a Bronx Cuban club, where Herbie Hancock showed the band a new blues. "Watermelon Man" made Hancock and Santamaria stars.

The U.S. charts saw lots of Latinized hits in this era, as the *bugalú* (adapted by jazzers and soulsters) and other Cuban dance rhythms cycled into American music. By 1966 the charanga-meets-salsa of the Joe Cuba Sextet hit with a million-seller, "Bang Bang." Shortly after, Santana made Tito Puente's "Oye Como Va" a counterculture staple.

From this stew emerged 1970s New York salsa. Central figures like Ruben Blades and Willie Colon have suggested salsa was a pan-Latin musical language, a way to communicate and conserve and adapt diverse cultures within a shared musical frame. Originally used by Cuban musicians the way jazzers use swing, salsa was the tag for a fusion of son vocals, jazz improvisation and voicings, Cuban rhythms, and, by the 1980s, rock chord sequences and electronic instruments.

It figures: the 1960s were the heyday of cultural eclecticism. The time's mix-and-match aesthetic ran like a figure in the carpet through American society. And like pop, Latin jazz offered something the period's avant-jazzers couldn't: dance-floor rhythms. One young saxist, Gato Barbieri, unleashed Coltrane-esque sheets of sound over his native Argentine beats. (He scored big with his 1972 award-winning *Last Tango in Paris* soundtrack.)

Enter the Palmieri brothers, Charlie and Eddie. Charlie, the elder, played mesmerizing piano where percussion met Liszt. A sideman with Puente and Rodriguez, he became music director for the Alegre All-Stars, a record-label house band that led other Latin labels like Fania (which produced Colon and Blades) to follow suit. The result: more job opportunities for Latin-jazz musicians, and a wider public. In 1961 younger brother Eddie started La Perfecta, which inspired the likes of Herbie Mann with its flute-plus-trombones lineup. After dabbling in bugalú, he studied arranging and expanded his palette to include Monk, R&B, rock, and salsa—all threaded with jazz improvisation and modal solos. By the 1990s, he led a formidable young group, caught on *Arete* (RMM).

Jazzers usually brand the 1970s with a bum rap. Sure, lots of overblown fusion records and ill-advised commercial pop-crossovers swamped the market. But for Latin jazz, growth and development combined with a return to Afro-Cuban roots. One flowering was Irakere, the crack outfit that—in a Cuban parallel to Art Blakey's Jazz Messengers—served for twenty-five years as a Latin jazz tutorial for musicians and audiences alike.

Under its musical director, brilliant pianist Jesus "Chucho" Valdes, Irakere trained modern Afro-Cuban musicians like saxist Paquito D'Rivera and trumpeter Arturo Sandoval. As crucial, it reexamined source material from Cuban folk songs (which thread through Latin jazz history); its probing improvisation incorporated postbop ideas with astounding, crowd-pleasing fluency. *The Best of Irakere* (Columbia) demonstrates why and how the band became a legend, as does Valdes's U.S. debut, *Bele Bele en La Habana* (Blue Note).

D'Rivera was inspired by Gillespie. So when he defected in the early 1980s (Sandoval followed a few years later), he joined the trumpeter's United Nation orchestra. He also cut *Live at Keystone Korner* (Columbia), where his audacious solos and inventive beats bypassed the period's stale arguments between jazz avant-gardists and neoconservatives.

In New York, Fania Records, directed by Johnny Pacheco, responded to Charlie Palmieri's challenges with the cutting edge of salsa, including New Yorican sounds. Trombonist Colon hired Puerto Rican cuatro picker Yomo Toro, covered Brazilian tunes, and backed singers like Celia Cruz—facets collected on *Grandes Exitos de Willie Colon* (Fania). In the later 1970s, his partnership with Blades produced pointed political tunes with dance beats that became salsa standards. Blades later recorded the breakthrough album *Buscando America* (Elektra) and, now a movie star and politician, narrowly missed winning Panama's presidency.

In Havana, Los Van Van mixed trombones and violins with synthesizers, a hyped-up clave, call-and-response vocals, and jazz solos on *Songo* (Mango). Los Van Van vets Jose Luis Cortes and vocalist Isaac Delgado lead NG La Banda, which rides taut, whipsaw rhythms and ensemble work behind Delgado's snaky yet effortless vocals.

As I write this, jazz is in the midst of one of its periodic Latin renaissances.

The Gonzalez brothers, Jerry and Andy, were born in the Apple, grads of the high school in *Fame*, and leaders of the Fort Apache band, which ironically took the cops' name for the bombed-out South Bronx precinct that was home to many Latinos. Andy is the sturdy, imperturbable bassist, while his younger brother doubles on percussion and trumpet, which he wields with an attack that mingles Gillespie's with Miles Davis's. Gonzalez, too, was a Gillespie protégé, and it shows on albums like *Rumba Para Monk* (Sunnyside).

From Havana comes Gonzalo Rubalcaba, with awesome technical expertise. Like Chucho Valdes, Rubalcaba is a second-generation Cuban pianist; their fathers were classically trained stars, and both studied in the island's best conservatories. At thirty-five, Rubalcaba still slips into the macho athleticism of much Cuban music, where fifty-seven-year-old Valdes has transmuted that totally into art. But Rubalcaba has grown by playing with American jazzers like Charlie Haden and Jack DeJohnette, with whom he recorded *The Blessing* (Blue Note).

One of Gillespie's last disciples is pianist Danilo Perez, whose *PanaMonk* (Impulse!) marked him as a key talent. Another late Gillespie-ite, saxist David Sanchez, combines compositional sophistication with a burly tone and bebop chops on albums like *Street Scenes* (Columbia).

And Latin jazz, once again, is not just for Latin musicians. Trumpeter Roy Hargrove went to Cuba to study the music and cut the outstanding *Habana* (Verve). Altoist Steve Coleman also made the trek, with more avantist results on *The Sign and the Seal* (RCA).

It's just the beginning. As relations between Cuba and the United States are normalized, and the island's pent-up performers cross into the adopted land where 30 percent of Cubans live, the only sure thing is that Latin jazz will yield more fireworks.

Jazz in Europe: The Real World Music . . . or the Full Circle

Mike Zwerin

When you date the arrival of jazz in Europe depends on what you mean by *jazz* and how you define *arrive*.

To begin with, it grew out of a combination of European and African influences, harmony and rhythm respectively. Appropriate instruments (brass saxhorns as well as saxophones) were invented in the nineteenth century by the Belgian Adolphe Sax. About half of the roots can be considered European. It was brewed in America by African Americans, and it matured in mixed blood there. Eventually, it came full circle and bounced back to Europe full of vim and vigor. So where are we, and what next?

Americans taught the Europeans how to play it. Once they learned, they distilled and added to it until they felt that they no longer needed Americans hanging around taking their gigs. From the reverse angle, Americans no longer particularly wanted to hang around Europe either. As Europe grew richer it became more expensive; there were more taxes, and they were harder to avoid. And the home playing field began to level out for African Americans.

Players preferred not to uproot their families and make their children learn French or Swedish or whatever. Plenty of good European work remained but, with cheaper and more frequent transatlantic flights, Americans could commute to five or six tours a year. So why move?

The saying goes, "There is only one inch of difference between New York and Paris, but it's the inch I live in." Paris functions; public transportation works, you don't need a car, and you can still walk for hours and not see anything seriously ugly. The intercity trains are fast, clean, inexpensive, and on time in Europe in general, and the cities are closer together; touring is more efficient and comfortable. Europeans consider jazz musicians to be artists, and even poor artists earn respect over here if they are honest and happy. That's good for at least half an inch right there.

Dutch residence, a French agent, a Swedish wife, a Swiss record company, Spanish tags on the car, plenty of gigs in Germany—it was tailor-made. The bureaucratic confusion such a lifestyle left in its wake made it possible for a musician to live in a cool Left Bank hotel on a tourist visa for months and even years and still get paid in tax-free cash. It was kind of like the Wild West. The IRS, the CIA, and other such acronyms were not yet alphabetizing this particular frontier.

All of that has been changing. Bob Dylan sang: "To live outside the law you must be honest." A certain outlaw mentality went with playing music the establishment did not approve of, but jazz is now heard in prestigious law-abiding venues as much as in smoky cellars. With the end of the "Evil Empire" and of empires in general, there were more immigrants in Western European countries—foreigners of any kind not so welcome anymore. What's more, with the coming of the Euro we will all soon be on the same computer. An honest life "outside the law" will become harder still.

One of the first important European classical musicians to appreciate the strength and beauty of American jazz and its impact on European composers such as Darius Milhaud and Igor Stravinsky was the highly respected classical music teacher, philosopher, conductress, and composer Nadia Boulanger. Later, she taught Quincy Jones and Astor Piazzolla as well as Roy Harris and Marc Blitzstein and too many other major twentieth-century classical composers to name. In 1928 Boulanger talked about the "coming-of-age of an American music that was not imitation French music nor revamped Russian music nor diluted German music; but music that is distinguishable as American and represents the American mind and the American soul . . . the music born of jazz."

It is possible to go back a decade earlier, but at that time the roots

Django Reinhardt, c. 1947. Photo: William P. Gottlieb. From the Library of Congress Collection.

were only implied. They were unsturdy and suspect and became evident only in retrospect. During World War I, black U.S. Army regiment bands like Lieutenant Will Vodery's, which somebody described as the "jazziest, craziest" outfit in France, were stationed in Europe. James Reese Europe's Hellfighters were called the "best damn brass band in the U.S. Army." And then there was Lieutenant Tim Brymn's Seventy Black Devils. The Devils played for the peace conference in Versailles.

These were good bands with muscle and great musicians, but they were basically brass bands; they were loud and unsubtle, and there was little or no improvisation. Jazz it was not. If what they played can be called jazz, well then, so can, say, Kenny G.

Jazz is not something that comes by default. Just because it is instrumental does not make it jazz. The most original, durable, and serious improvisers have always looked on jazz as a kind of religion, a cosmic expression of the human spirit stressing spiritual purity and freedom. Jazz is "as serious as your life," as the writer Valerie Wilmer said. It is not made by insensitive people of dubious intent living on the outskirts who claim to be downtown.

The real thing began to cross the Atlantic after World War I. It was not easy for those pioneers—changing cultures and languages, leaving friends and family behind. But once here, they liked it. It felt good to be appreciated, and they told the others and came back.

Trumpeters Bill Coleman and Arthur Briggs and the soprano saxophonist Sidney Bechet went back and forth, gradually integrating into French society. Milton "Mezz" Mezzrow got hooked on French racetracks and Left Bank cellars. Coleman Hawkins traveled far and wide and became a Continental hero.

One of the most important twentieth-century international cultural migrations was under way. It can be compared to German directors and composers moving to Hollywood in the early days of film. Condescended to back home, African-American jazzmen found that they were artists over here and that their color was more of an advantage than a handicap.

After playing with Willie Lewis in Paris, Benny Carter was hired as staff arranger for the Henry Hall BBC dance orchestra in London. This meant big-time money and a degree of acceptance by the white media unheard of even for such a talented black man back home. He spent several years traveling through Scandinavia, the Netherlands, and France before sailing to New York on the SS *Ile de France* in 1938. War clouds were gathering.

Thanks to a large degree to the late Charles Delaunay, Sidney Bechet became a star in France. Delaunay produced Bechet's recordings for Vogue Records after the war, and Bechet's hits "Petite Fleur" and "Les Oignons," a jazz version of a New Orleans Creole folk song, sold millions of copies. Vogue was called "the house that Bechet built." A square in the Riviera town of Antibes was named after Bechet, and his statue was put in it. It's still there.

Before the war, Delaunay had founded the Hot Club de France, a combination musicians' association, bar, booking agency, and fan club where members could sit and discuss and drink coffee and spirits and listen to or partake in the jam sessions. He started the magazine *Jazz Hot* in 1934, just four months after the first issue of the first American jazz magazine, *Down Beat*. Son of the celebrated painters Sonia and Robert Delaunay, Charles grew up with people like Nijinsky and Stravinsky passing through his living room.

Along with Nadia Boulanger, Delaunay illustrates the high social and intellectual level jazz occupied in France, and Europe in general. The Belgian writer Robert Goffin wrote one of the first books about jazz in any language (in French) in the 1930s. (France later gave the Legion d'Honneur, its most prestigious civilian medal, to Miles Davis.)

Delaunay's friend and colleague the critic and writer Hugues Panassié was called "the Pope of Montauban," referring to the southwestern French town to which he retreated during World War II. (The two of them also wrote books about jazz in French in the 1930s.) Panassié was surrounded by disciples who took his judgments as gospel. The influential French novelist Boris Vian, also one of the best jazz critics ever in any language, was much cooler than either Pope. Because yes, dear reader, there were two Popes. Vian thought they were both totally out to lunch, and he called Panassié "the clown of Montauban."

In 1947 came what is described, in all seriousness, as "the Schism." They took jazz seriously in France, a Catholic country. In the Catholic Church, *Schism* was the term applied to the period in the Middle Ages when the church was divided and there were two Popes, one in Rome and one in Avignon. It was a very great Schism indeed.

The great jazz Schism was caused by the arrival of a record with a red label called "Salt Peanuts." Hot Club members were proud to be among the first to hear new American jazz recordings. This was the first time they had heard Charlie Parker and Dizzy Gillespie and bebop. The members could not decide if bebop was good or bad, but they formed a line up the stairs to Delaunay's office in the Hot Club building on Rue Chaptal to hear it.

When Django Reinhardt first heard "Salt Peanuts" on the record with the red label, he shook his head with disbelief and said: "They play so fast. I don't know if I can keep up with them." The Gypsy guitarist Reinhardt, who could play pretty fast himself, is the only non-American worthy of being in the pantheon of jazz greats who left their imprint on the music, changed it, made it richer. His Gypsy/jazz synthesis extended the boundaries. But World War II had isolated him from important cultural events. By the time it was over he felt as though he had lost a step. If he is not now as well known as Louis Armstrong or Duke Ellington, this is to a large degree due to being born and working in Europe, speaking French, and not being familiar with African-American history and culture.

Austrian-born Joe Zawinul, cofounder of Weather Report and composer of the song "Birdland," has said that to be authentic all foreign-born jazz musicians have to "pass through Brooklyn sooner or later." By this metaphor, he meant that it was essential for foreigners like himself to assimilate the culture native to the music, which was, after all, called "America's native art form." In a manner of speaking, Django carried Brooklyn around with him. He had an authenticity all his own.

By the age of fourteen, he was accompanying accordionists, fiddlers, and xylophone players in restaurants and theaters. A faded photo reveals that he resembled an oriental prince by the age of eighteen. He spent a lot of time in billiard parlors and practiced walking like the movie star George Raft. Playing the guitar came so easy to him, he considered getting paid for it almost like stealing. The young Django had no bank account; there was usually a thick wad of cash in his pocket. Barely able to write his own name, he avoided taking the Paris metro because he could not read station names. The poet Jean Cocteau called him a "proud hunted beast."

Just before Django was to leave for London to join Jack Hylton, a popular British bandleader who played "symphonic jazz" in the style of Paul Whiteman, his caravan caught fire. The pinky and ring fingers of his fretboard hand were permanently paralyzed by the burns. So much for his first big break.

He learned how to play the guitar all over again by busking in cafés on the French Riviera. Dragging his two crippled fingers along the strings, he invented unorthodox voicings and played octaves using his thumb. Later, when they became aware of each other, Django said he was only copying his "brother" Charlie Christian. Christian said he was copying Django.

Django grew from a cult hero to a star when he formed the Quintet of the Hot Club de France with the violinist Stephane Grappelli. Much later, Grappelli joked: "We were the first rock 'n' roll band in the world. I don't know anybody who had three guitars before we did." Despite the absence of a drummer, the three Gypsy guitarists (including Django's brother Joseph) comped so hard that Grappelli was pushed to swing very hard indeed. He quickly became one of the most influential jazz violinists in history. (He outlived Django by over forty years, continuing to play his butt off and win polls well into his eighties.)

As the Nazis occupied Europe, people were humming Django's hit song "Nuages" (Clouds). Posters with his image on them were on the walls of Paris. He had top billing in lavish nightclub revues, ate in the best Italian restaurants, checked into the Ritz Hotel. You did not have to be a jazz fan to love Django. He was freedom and joy personified. Even the Germans loved him. They kept inviting him to tour Germany, something he dearly wanted to avoid. Gypsies were being sent to concentration camps. He kept raising his price.

Although German soldiers attended his concerts, Django was never accused of collaboration. He was viewed as running a good hustle. A Gypsy jazz musician was a double outlaw. Josef Goebbels knew instinctively that jazz was subversive. He spoke out against it and banned it. It has been said that "the enemy of my enemy is my friend." And so the music picked up a lot of fans who would not otherwise have been interested. They were attracted by its outlaw side.

Finally the pressure became too great and Django tried to escape across the border to Switzerland. He was caught, arrested, and delivered to the local German commanding officer. "My dear Django," the officer said. "Please do not try to do this again or I will have to arrest you." Another fan.

More Americans came after the war. Kenny "Klook" Clarke was sick and tired of being tired and sick in New York. He was under great pressure, working day and night, making plenty of money playing the drums everywhere with everybody, but his lifestyle left life wanting. He knew something was seriously wrong when he found himself hiding inside his apartment pretending he wasn't there as Miles Davis knocked and knocked on his door begging him to accept a record date.

"I just wanted some peace and quiet," Klook said, explaining why he packed up and left for Europe.

Ben Webster also left, eventually moving into Mrs. Hartlooper's apartment in Amsterdam. A jolly grandmotherly type, she cooked and sewed for him and even gave him financial advice. One reason Webster moved to Amsterdam was that his good friend Don Byas, another legendary tenorman, had already moved there. Byas was beginning to speak English with a Dutch accent.

Like Kenny Clarke, Byas had been winning American jazz polls. He did very well in Europe at first. After a while, however, he found that he wasn't "exotic" any more. He came to be considered a "local." His price went down. Locals tend to take locals for granted. At the same time, living abroad, he was forgotten in the United States.

Klook handled both the "local" and the "forgotten" problems by moving around a lot—from Brussels to London to Copenhagen. Living in Paris, a big cosmopolitan city with plenty of recording studios, helped. For a while he was just about the only world-class drummer in Europe. And he co-led, with the Belgian pianist-arranger Francy Boland, one of the best big bands in history (unknown and underrated in the United States, of course).

The pianist Kenny Drew settled in Copenhagen, married an SAS stewardess, became an entrepreneur, and built up a successful recording and music publishing company. Tenorman Brew Moore also moved to Copenhagen. Once when somebody remarked that he was looking good, he replied: "If this is good, what did I look like the last time you saw me?"

Some Europeans copied American mistakes as well as attributes. They accepted the risks as well as the rewards of the lifestyle and they died young. Swedish baritone saxophonist Lars Gullin was a prime motivating force behind the popularity of Swedish jazz in the 1950s. The trombonist Åke Persson, who also died ahead of his time, and who played with the Clarke/Boland big band, was an unfortunate casualty in the fast lane. Stan Hasselgard would possibly have been a star international clarinetist if not for his premature death in a car crash. The late trumpeter Rolf Ericson was a star, although he struggled. The Swedish film *Sven Klang's Quintet,* one of the best jazz movies ever made, is about both the ups and the downs of some of these talented, tragic people in those days.

In the 1960s composer George Russell, living and working in Oslo, was promoting the prowess of a teenaged Norwegian saxophonist named Jan Garbarek. Garbarek later became one of the best and most successful Europeans. In the 1970s Dane Palle Mikkelborg sat next to the monster Woody Shaw recording "The Trumpet Machine" by the Swiss composer, arranger, and bandleader George Gruntz in a studio in the Black Forest. And what a trumpet machine it was! Jon Faddis was on his other side, and Canadian-cum-Brit Kenny Wheeler and the Swiss Franco Ambrosetti were further down the line. Still further down, an octave down, I was playing the bass trumpet. (During the 1970s Mikkelborg directed the renowned Danish Radio Big Band.)

Perhaps the biggest single event in the development of young European talent was a contest in 1966 in Vienna under the direction of the Austrian pianist Friedrich Gulda. Judges included Cannonball Adderley, Joe Zawinul, and Art Farmer. Some of the winners whose successful international careers can be traced back to this contest were Joachim Kuhn, an East German pianist who defected and eventually became Ornette Coleman's duo partner, the "bad Czech" bassist George Mraz, and Polish trumpeter Tomasz Stanko.

Flash forward. The 1980s. Meet the Parisian resident trombonist and ex–Los Angelino Glenn Ferris. One of the best trombonists on the planet, Ferris is forgotten in America and "local" in Paris—the worst of both worlds. He does well, however, disappearing into well-paid but low-profile work in Germany, Switzerland, and Scandinavia.

The presence of Webster and Byas in Amsterdam helped give birth to a vibrant Dutch scene that began to reach its potential after the 1968 student demonstrations. The cooperative called BIM, the Dutch acronym for improvising musicians, set up a subsidy system. Willem Breuker's successful big band combined theatricality with improvisation. Han Bennink the percussionist, the pianist Misha Mengelberg, and the cellist Ernst Rejsiger are three more world-class improvisers who came out of BIM.

Great Britain is jazzistically rich but suffers from cultural schizophrenia caused by its "special relationship" with the United States. It cannot make up its mind whether or not it is part of Europe. The sensitive reedman John Surman lives in Kent (near the Channel) whence he can commute easily to work on the Continent. Yorkshireman John McLaughlin lives in Monaco. Bassist Dave Holland left his island to play with Miles Davis and now resides in New York State. The late tenorman Ronnie Scott (who also was with Clarke/Boland) is possibly the best-known English jazz name, having run his famous eponymous jazz club. Cleo Laine and John Dankworth, singer and composer-arranger-bandleader respectively, may be even better known than Scott. Generally speaking, British jazz musicians are well known for not being very well known anywhere else. Drummer Tony

Oxley, Gordon Beck the pianist (with Phil Woods and Helen Merrill), arranger and bandleader Gail Thompson, and trumpeter Harry Beckett deserve more appreciation.

Germany has given birth to some important jazz players, thanks to a large degree to the fact that it is the third largest economy in the world; there is lots of well-paid work there. But here too the players tend to stay at home. Major trombone player Albert Mangelsdorff can play two notes and sometimes three at the same time more readily than he gets on a transatlantic flight. He has an amazingly authentic and swinging blues feeling. He is a hero in Germany, a footnote in America. And once more we are reminded of Joachim Kuhn, who was part of a swinging Euro-trio with Daniel Humair, the fine product of the rich Swiss military drumming tradition, and the late great French bassist Jean-François Jenny-Clark. Being so admirably international and playing so very well together did not, however, gain them a reputation in the United States.

An essential and fascinating historical perspective of European jazz is often overlooked. It thrived under two totalitarian systems, one after the other: the Nazis followed by the Eastern European Communist regimes. It can be argued, and some historians have done so, that these two back-to-back dictatorships—from roughly 1933 to 1989, more than half the music's life span—constituted a kind of golden age of jazz.

For once in its life it was politically important. Like rock in the 1960s, it had mass appeal. Great numbers of people listened to jazz for what it represented and symbolized as much as, or more than, for the music itself. It was about freedom.

Jazz music never meant more in the lives of so many ordinary people. It was never so pertinent, never as universal. Repressed people want freedom. By definition, jazz is about as good an artistic expression of freedom as can be found. You cannot censor improvisation. Jazz is, or ought to be, based on the principle that it is never the same twice. Nobody knows exactly what's going to happen next. In addition to the looseness of swing, the creative process involved in making jazz is in itself democratic. Freedom of speech is at the core of it. Free and uncensored conversation. Everybody having their say.

Under the Nazis, the French changed the titles—"St. Louis Blues" became "La Tristesse de Saint Louis," "Sweet Sue" was called "Ma Chére Suzanne"—and they called it French folklore and went on playing that "decadent Judeo capitalist" a.k.a. "plutocratic capitalist" (both Nazi terms) music. The fact that the Germans did not know that Artie Shaw's real name was Arshawsky and that he was Jewish and so let his records be played was cause for rejoicing in certain underground circles.

Two decades later, members of the Moscow Jazz Club welcomed the Earl "Fatha" Hines band at the airport when it arrived in Moscow on a U.S. State Department cultural exchange tour. That night they staged a party in a club. The commissars did not know exactly what to do about jazz. It confused them, put them off balance. The Czech "Jazz Section," which did not actually have very much to do with jazz (the word just sounds free, so it became a kind of code word for freedom), played a big part in their country's cultural and even political resistance.

With the help of the Polish Jazz Society, Poland produced world-class players like the pianist Adam Makowicz. Krzysztof Komeda composed jazz-influenced soundtracks for films like *Knife in the Water* and *Rosemary's Baby* by his friend Roman Polanski. The Poles learned how to suck money from the socialist system to pay their musicians to attack it. This produced some passionate music. After the coming of the free market, however, they were lucky to get a gig playing on a Norwegian cruise boat. Polish jazz dried up along with the socialist system. It was no longer a symbol or a metaphor for anything. It was just another commodity.

During a meeting in the Aquarium jazz club in central Warsaw in 1989, delegates from several Eastern European countries gathered to discuss the new situation. Tomasz Tluczkiewicz, president of the Polish Jazz Society, said: "We jazz people in Poland have been ahead of our time. The Polish Jazz Society was a creative invention put into operation to accommodate the jazz scene with the so-called socialist system. So in the past, jazz life in Poland has been richer than in neighboring countries. But now, in a market economy, we have only bad news ahead of us."

A Hungarian musician named Janos came to the microphone and clearly pronounced final punctuation on the end of an era. "I am not a Communist," he said. "I am not a socialist. I am a saxophonist."

Since then, the big European festivals have continued to grow in both size and number. They resist hiring Europeans because they don't draw as well as Americans. (There are something like 250 jazz festivals a year in France alone.) And America does not import Europeans for the same reason.

Europeans are becoming more respectable, if not more marketable.

Jazz has become the true world music. It influences almost every other music, and is influenced in return. However, the concept of jazz as solely American music is "history," as Americans use that word. Washed up, yesterday's news. Historically, America remains the inventor. It is certainly still the only jazz superpower. But its days of sole dominion are history. New ideas also come from other places now.

To conclude, the geographical orientation of the music has changed. Its posture, so to speak, has changed. Instead of a few geniuses in very few places, we now find competent players everywhere. Jazz is still music for intellectuals, minority music, not for everyone; but more people in more places than ever are dealing with it, and it gives them a great deal of joy.

Its posture has become horizontal—like a thick coat of bright paint or a lush lawn. It was once vertical, with so many towering peaks— graceful soaring spires named Pops, Prez, Bird, Duke, Monk, Trane, Miles, and Ornette. There is a lack of height now; jazz is hugging the ground. Not because it is sick or tired or dying but because it is flourishing in a new way. It is covering more and more ground. Who knows to where it will overflow next? Where will it plant roots next?

"Americans still have trouble appreciating the music they invented and sent out into the world," says Didier Levallet, the leader of the Orchestre National de Jazz (ONJ). "You can imagine how much trouble they have accepting French jazz." An ironic smile accompanies his gross understatement.

Paris is the jazz capital of Europe. The Art Ensemble of Chicago was in residence for several years at the American Center in Montparnasse. With his French and French-resident band, soprano saxophonist Steve Lacy has lived in Paris for thirty years; he is called a guru, and his influence abounds. Tenorman Archie Shepp and trumpeter Don Cherry both spent a lot of time moving in and out of Paris. Saxman Johnny Griffin lives in a chateau near Poitiers. The late Dexter Gordon was awarded a Chevalier de L'Ordre des Arts et Des Lettres (something comparable to a Pulitzer Prize) by Minister of Culture Jack Lang after "Long-Tall" was nominated for an Oscar for playing Dale Turner in Bertrand Tavernier's film 'Round Midnight, about American jazzmen in Paris.

The ONJ is subsidized by the French state to prove how good the French are at playing music invented in America. Bizarre. It is well known that the French consider the Americans cultural imperialists.

The orchestra's very existence illustrates the fact that the Americans no longer enjoy a monopoly. In 1998 the ONJ performed in the Ukraine, Finland, Lithuania, Britain, Spain, Turkey, Portugal, and France. A musician in Kiev told Levallet: "I would like to live my life the way your orchestra sounds." France being considered the image of where "America's only native art form" lives is one weird stop indeed on the new horizontal circuit.

Pierre Michelot was the bassist with the Miles Davis band that recorded the soundtrack for Louis Malle's classic film *Elevator to the Guillotine* and included the grotesquely underrated Franco-American Barney Wilen on tenor saxophone. American bass players will tell you that Michelot was among the very best in the world. Henri Texier, now more active than ever, played the bass with Phil Woods's seminal band the European Rhythm Machine (it also included Humair and Gruntz). Pianist Martial Solal and violinist Jean-Luc Ponty have been two of Europe's best known jazz musicians for decades, while the late pianist Michel Petrucciani, a very small man with a very large heart, defies description and classification but proves our point with an exclamation.

The French scene overflows south of the Alps. Enrico Rava has been called, with only a slight edge of irony, the "Godfather of Italian Jazz." The self-taught Rava, who speaks French and works mostly in France, learned a lot about playing the trumpet from Chet Baker when the latter lived in Turin for a few months. After assimilating the influence of Baker and other Americans (Rava lived in New York for some years), he began to translate it into his own experience.

He recorded arias from Puccini's opera *Tosca.* He and the French accordionist with an Italian name, Richard Galliano, have presented a program of Nino Rota songs from Federico Fellini movies. Rava has recorded his version of arias from *Carmen* and performed them in China, Canada, France, and Italy. He has not played in America for years. So what? Jazz music has provided him with a lifestyle that includes a home overlooking the Mediterranean on the Italian Riviera. There's that inch of difference again.

The list of European names gets longer with each passing year. Ferenc Snetberger, Antonello Salis, Paul Rutherford, Paolo Fresu, Niels Lan Doky, Bobo Stenson, Dominique Pifarely, Roy Ben Sira, Anouar Brahem, Renaud Garcia-Fons, Han Bennink, Philip Catherine, Miroslav Tadic, Louis Sclavis. . . . You may never have heard of many of them, but they have European reputations. Some of them are from the Middle East, North Africa, and beyond. So it goes with "America's only native art form."

Multi-reedman Michel Portal is a leading exponent of a style of music described by the oversimplified, often pejorative soundbite *Eurojazz*. A ballpark category, from left field to begin with, just about meaningless, it is applied to describe music made in almost any nation in the world except the United States. "Eurojazz" festivals feature Brazilians (Egberto Gismonti), Argentines (Gato Barbieri), Indians (Trilok Gurtu), and even Australians (James Morrison).

The term *Eurojazz* implies music with more European influence than African; an absence of swing. Portal is one of Europe's most honored classical clarinetists, playing Mozart and Stockhausen as well as jazz, and he explains it: "We never really learned jazz over here in France. All I could do was imagine it. It is impossible to learn something just by imagining it."

Currently some 40 percent of the students at the Berklee College of Music in Boston are of foreign origin. Gary Burton (the vibraphonist, also Berklee's dean of curriculum) has performed and recorded the *tango nuevo* with the late Argentine composer Astor Piazzolla. Piazzolla, remember, studied composition with Nadia Boulanger, whom we have also already met. It all comes full circle.

One thing is sure. More Europeans are playing, teaching and listening to jazz than ever. All ages, colors, nationalities and both sexes. The internationalization of jazz is picking up speed. Just about every young musician just about everywhere in Europe plays or would like to play jazz.

Jazz and Brazilian Music

Stephanie L. Stein Crease

I n 1959 the release of the Brazilian film *Black Orpheus* introduced the musical bounty of Brazil to international audiences.
The award-winning film presented many viewers with their
first glimpse of the authentic music and culture of Brazil, one
of the largest and most populous countries in the world. In
the film, the Greek myth about the lovers Orpheus and Eurydice is
played out in Rio de Janeiro during *carnaval*. Exotic percussion instruments and the call-and-response singing typical of Rio's *escolas
de samba* fill the soundtrack, interspersed with melodies played by
solo guitar and compositions by Antonio Carlos Jobim and Luiz Bonfa,
then young musicians in Rio's artistic community. Their music combined the textures and rhythms of Brazil with elements from American jazz, classical and twentieth-century composition, and even Hollywood film music. These elements fused into the style that would
soon have an enormous influence on jazz and popular music around
the world: the *bossa nova*, literally, "new beat."

The bossa nova was typically played with a slow samba rhythm
and performed in a light, unaccented manner, comparable to the "cool
jazz" popular in the United States during the 1950s. It was a modern
distillation of the major influences—African, Portuguese, European—

that have given Brazilian music a sound and cadence all its own. The bossa was also a catalyst for forging a connection with American jazz.

Brazilian music is distinctly different from that of other countries in the Western Hemisphere that also have strong ties with American jazz, and where an African cultural presence was equally profound. The differences are striking. Brazilian music is, for the most part, performed with a less aggressive percussive attack than Cuban music or the rich Latin-based hybrids that became the basis for New York–style salsa. The result is a more laid-back feel; Brazilian rhythms often have a loping quality even when played at a fast tempo. Brazilian influences on American jazz have been more intermittent than those of Cuba or Puerto Rico for various reasons: the far larger Hispanic-speaking population in the States, the Caribbean's closer proximity, and a longer history of Latin musicians working in jazz centers like New York. Nonetheless, the overall impact of Brazilian music on jazz—and vice versa—has been strong and enduring.

At the core of all Brazilian music is its rhythm—or rather, its rhythms: subtle and varied traditional rhythms, with a built-in weave of polyrhythms and syncopation. And at the core of these rhythms is the African connection, the legacy of Brazil's slave trade, the jewel bought at such a great price.

The African Connection

Slavery in Brazil continued longer than in any other country in the Western Hemisphere, from the arrival of the first slaves from Africa in 1538 until the abolition of slavery in 1888. Portugal had already been active in the international slave trade for a century when it started colonizing Brazil in 1532; by midcentury, Brazil's quickly expanding sugar plantations were demanding large-scale importation of slaves. The slaves brought rituals from many parts of Africa in which music and dance were of utmost significance; this legacy has stretched into the twentieth century via *candomble* and other widely practiced pantheistic Afro-Brazilian religions, whose deities (*orixas*) are summoned by music and dance.

Over the centuries, accents, phrasing and the secularization of African rituals evolved into music, dances, and rhythms that were unique to Brazil, some of which became the basis for urban popular styles. The far larger influx of African slaves in Brazil, and the more tolerant Portuguese attitudes toward racial mixing and African tribal customs, meant that Brazilian music remained close to its African sources. Many African musical elements have persisted in Brazil's

Stan Getz and João Gilberto. Courtesy Frank Driggs Collection.

contemporary music: distinctive rhythmic patterns, inherent poly-rhythms, the use of call and response, and improvisation. Above all, Brazilian music, like African, is the lifeblood of the culture.

In Brazil, as in the United States, the musical traditions of the slaves were influenced by those of the slaveowners; in Brazil's case, the Portuguese colonists and ruling class. Portuguese musical culture included a lyric song tradition that expressed itself in the Brazilian *modinha*, a very popular song style of the 1700s that figured largely in the evolution of a recognizable Brazilian music. The Portuguese also had an affinity for complex rhythms, which as Ricardo Pessanha and Chris McGowan point out in *The Brazilian Sound* (new ed., 1998), meshed well with the music the Africans brought to Brazil. Musical instruments like the *violão*, a large six-stringed guitar, and the *cavaquinho*, a small four-stringed guitar, are now as emblematic of Brazilian music as certain percussion instruments. The Portuguese flair for improvisation was exemplified by song "contests" like the *desafio*, which was rooted in the troubadour tradition, in which the participants would challenge each other improvisationally. The pageantry of the Catholic *autos* (religious-dramatic presentations), Portuguese street celebrations with costumes and parades, and Afro-Brazilian celebrations eventually culminated in *carnaval*.

Detailed records made by the French Jesuit Jean de Léry in 1557 revealed a rich musical culture among the coastal Indians, who played conch horns and percussion instruments and were accomplished singers. And in "grim reminder of cannibalistic practices," as David P. Appleby points out in his book *The Music of Brazil* (1983), they also used instruments made from human bones. But many of the Indians perished from diseases brought by the Europeans, while others fled Portuguese domination to the jungle. Those that survived were so successfully recultured by the Jesuits that few traces of the native musical culture have remained.

The Emergence of Popular Styles

During the nineteenth century, the African, Portuguese, and European influences and performance practices coalesced into a musical language that was Brazil's own. This language served as the precursor for both the twentieth-century nationalist movement in music, exemplified by the work of composer Heitor Villa Lobos, and popular urban styles like the samba. One crucial factor in the emergence of this language was the gradual liberation of Brazil's musical elite from the sway of Europe. Another was the high level of musicianship in mulatto and black communities, which sprang up and expanded quickly in Rio and other large cities after emancipation.

The story of the *lundu*, a sexy dance that arrived with the slaves from Angola, illustrates Brazil's multifaceted musical fusion. The *lundu* was originally a circle song/dance, which included the *umbigada*, the touching of navels by couples that initiates the dance. By the early 1800s, the *lundu*'s erotic elements were tamed, and it was danced in the salons of Rio and other large cities; by the mid-1800s the term *lundu* applied to both instrumental pieces and songs, was played to a double-time 2/4 rhythm, and had a call-and-response song structure. In this form the much-transformed *lundu* was an ancestor of the samba.

By the 1870s what might be called the "Afro-Brazil-ation" of European dances such as the schottische, polka, and mazurka crystallized in the *choro*, an instrumental style that emerged in Rio but became Brazil's reigning popular music style through the 1920s. The word *choro*, which literally means "to weep" (many *choros* had lament-like melodies), applied both to the style itself and the ensembles that performed it. Most of the early *choro* musicians were amateurs who played the European dances in vogue by ear, injecting them with Afro-Brazilian rhythms. The music flourished in Rio between 1870 and 1919; hundreds of *choro* groups roved from party to party all night, playing for food and drinks. Like the later samba—or the blues—*choros* could run the gamut from slow to fast, and happy to sad; the style's key elements were improvisation and a virtuosic reach. *Choros* laid the groundwork for the eventual growth of Brazilian jazz.

One of the most prominent early *choro* musicians was Antonio da Silva Callado, a virtuoso flutist and gifted improviser. His group, the Choro Carioca, which included flute, two *violãos*, and *cavaquinho*, was the most famous early *choro* ensemble; it was widely imitated and popularized the style.

Pixinguinha is considered the greatest *choro* musician of them all. He was a prolific composer and virtuoso flutist, and his skill as an arranger helped further the development of Brazilian instrumental music. His group was the first to incorporate the greater use of percussion instruments in the *choro* setting. He and his musicians formalized the sambas they had been playing in jam sessions, combining elements from *choro*, *maxixe*, and *marchas* (other popular dance/musical forms in the early twentieth century); all three shared a fast 2/4 tempo. As such, Pixinguinha is a founding father of the samba, imbuing the new style with a song structure and defining roles for various instruments. *Pixinguinha* (Blue Jackel, 1998) features Paulo Moura, a latter-day *choro* musician and highly regarded jazz musician in Brazil, playing classic *choro* compositions.

Samba

During the 1920s, the urban samba began to rival the *choro* and supplanted *marchas* as the dominant style for *carnaval*. Brazil's quickly expanding radio media and recording industry helped it along, and sambas were heard everywhere—whether it was carnival season or not. Today samba is still the best known and most widely played form of Brazilian music.

Samba is an all-inclusive musical form, and its origins are diffuse. Though it surfaced in Rio in the first decade of the twentieth century, it sprang from black folk traditions, and was transformed by everyone—the newly urban blacks, white bourgeois musicians, and a generation of songwriters like Ary Barroso and Dorival Caymmi, whose work comprised samba's golden age during the 1930s. From its early years, there were several kinds of samba: the *samba de asfalto*, a "samba song," with string accompaniment; the *samba cançao*, a slower, more sentimental form of samba song; and the *samba de morro*, which came from Rio's hillside slums and was characterized by its call-and-response singing and large battery of percussion instruments (*batucada*). These basic types have melded together over the decades.

Popular music was also an important ingredient. As John Storm Roberts has pointed out in *The Latin Tinge* (1979), the popular samba singers of the 1940s were as indebted to American popular singers like the Andrews Sisters as they were to Brazilian traditions. This contributed to the somewhat bland international pop style of the 1940s and 1950s. This tendency gave rise to a predictable counter-reaction; in the 1960s and 1970s a new generation of *sambaistas*, including Paulinho da Viola, Beth Carvalho, Alcione, and Martinho da Vila, became prominent, restoring the samba's earthy sensibility and folkloric heritage.

The Brazilian Crossover

Starting in the 1920s, the samba, along with other Latin dance-based styles, had begun to stream into American popular music and Broadway shows. The flow increased markedly over the years and was often accompanied by stereotypic gestures, costumes, and gimmickry. In this way, Brazilian music entered the American mainstream. *Flying Down to Rio*, the 1933 movie, included Vincent Youmans's "Carioca," the first samba-based number to become a hit in the United States. In 1939 the Broadway musical revue *On the Streets of Paris* included "South American Way," a song-and-dance number that made Carmen Miranda a star in North America. Another standout in 1939 was the U.S. release of the song "Aquarelo do Brazil" (commonly known as "Brazil") by Ary Barroso, one of the most enduring of all Latin standards. At the end of the 1930s Artie Shaw recorded two versions of "Carioca," laying the groundwork for further crossover in the 1940s. Two Walt Disney films also helped introduce the samba to a wide American audience: *Saludos Amigos* (1943), in which Carmen Miranda's sister sang "Brazil" and "Tico Tico"; and *Three Caballeros* with Bing Crosby singing "Bahia."

The result of these crossovers was a homogenizing of several Brazilian and Latin musical elements. The tango, rhumba, mambo, cha-cha, samba, and bossa nova all became fads for varying periods of time. The cost of their sweeping popularity, as John Storm Roberts put it, was that it gave rise to some "fairly frivolous and nonsensical spinoffs" that obscured the music's importance and dignity.

The Bossa Nova

Jazz provided the arena in which that dignity was recovered. In Brazilian music, the bossa nova was the link for the jazz connection and, though it emerged decades after the samba, gave many American jazz musicians their introduction to the older form. The bossa also awakened musical curiosity among jazz musicians about Brazilian music in general.

The bossa nova was a soft, pared-down version of the samba. It was usually played by small combos, the distilled samba rhythm transferred to trap drums. Non-Brazilian musicians could play it far more easily than the samba: its more "minimalist" approach to the rhythm was easier to learn, and the sophisticated chords and harmonic progressions favored by Jobim, Bonfa, and João Gilberto, et al., had roots in American jazz. The guitar—long a pillar of Brazilian music—was key to the development of the bossa nova. When played by a guitarist-singer like Gilberto, the style spoke elegantly for itself. Eventually it had an enormous impact in Brazil: its sophisticated contemporary sound contrasted not only with full-fledged sambas but also with the prevalent international pop style.

Jobim and Bonfa were at the forefront of the largely white middle-class crowd of musicians and friends whose work informally gave rise to the new style. Jobim was a singer, guitarist, pianist, and arranger, but his greatest impact was as a composer. Songs like "Desafinado," "Corcovado," and "One Note Samba" brought him international renown and have been recorded by an impressive array of vocalists and jazz musicians. One of Jobim's most significant songwriting partners was the lyricist Vinicius de Moraes, an established writer, poet, and diplomat. Jobim first collaborated with Moraes on his play *Orfeu da Conceiçaõ* (a great success in Rio, and the inspiration for the film *Black Orpheus*); their most famous songs include "Chega de Saudade (No More Blues)," "A Felicidade," "The Girl From Ipanema," and "Insensatez."

João Gilberto, a guitarist, composer, and singer, experimented with combining elements from samba and "cool" jazz as a young musician. His efforts went largely unnoticed until he became one of Jobim's many collaborators in the early 1950s. At the time, Jobim's guitar style—intimate and ingeniously imitative of samba's percussion parts—was completely innovative. In 1958 Jobim and Gilberto made their first single with "Chega de Saudade" and Gilberto's "Bim Bom." The record was a hit and led to Gilberto's first album in 1959; these were the first bossa recordings in Brazil.

In the early 1950s Luiz Bonfa wrote several songs that presaged the bossa, but like Jobim's, Bonfa's international career took off with the film *Black Orpheus*. In addition to his work as a composer, Bonfa was a masterful guitarist with a subtle grasp of harmony. Other prominent bossa guitarists are Baden Powell, Bola Sete, Roberto Menescal, Carlos Lyra, and Oscar Castro-Neves. In the States, the Brazilian guitarist Laurindo Almeida played in a style that also prefigured the bossa nova but had a different rhythmic base. In 1953 Almeida recorded *Laurindo Almeida Quartet Featuring Bud Shank* (Pacific Jazz; reissued in 1961 as *Brazilliance*, World Pacific), with Shank on flute. The first Brazilian jazz album, it was very well received by other jazz musicians.

The American jazz guitarist Charlie Byrd first heard the bossa nova while visiting Brazil in 1961 and introduced it to other jazz musicians, notably the tenor saxophonist Stan Getz. In 1962 Byrd and Getz recorded *Jazz Samba* (Verve), which included several songs from Gilberto's first album. It was a tremendous success and effectively started the bossa trend in the States. Getz's cool lyrical style was a perfect fit for the bossa.

The bossa wave hit hard, and for the first time since the Big Band years, jazz and popular music overlapped. "The Girl From Ipanema," recorded for *Getz/Gilberto* (Verve), the 1963 album by Getz and João and Astrud Gilberto (then a nonprofessional singer who was coaxed into recording the song in English on the spot), was one of the biggest jazz-pop hits of all time. The record inspired hundreds of imitations and countless bossa spin-offs, like Elvis Presley's "Bossa Nova Baby."

In 1964 the Beatles suddenly monopolized the pop music charts, but the bossa fad was also finally abating. The bossa nova itself remained: songs by Jobim, Gilberto, Bonfa, and others quickly entered the jazz repertoire and have remained there. Herbie Mann, Kenny Dorham, and Paul Winter were very involved with bossa in the 1960s, and an array of jazz musicians and vocalists recorded bossa tunes, some even composing their own or devoting whole albums to the style: Cannonball Adderley, Coleman Hawkins, Dizzy Gillespie, Ella Fitzgerald, Frank Sinatra, and Lalo Schifrin were just a few. More recently, Joe Henderson, Joanne Brackeen, Toots Thielemans, the Brazilian jazz pianist Eliane Elias, Mark Murphy, and the late Sarah Vaughan have explored this now classic style.

The bossa has left a far more substantial legacy than anyone—in the midst of the fad—would have thought. Artists such as Jobim, Bonfa, and both Gilbertos have had sustained international careers. The mastery of the bossa guitarists revived the use of the acoustic guitar in jazz and inspired a new generation of Brazilian guitarists, such as Toninho Horta and Romero Lubambo. The bossa also opened up further exploration of all kinds of Brazilian music by jazz musicians. During the 1960s in Brazil, the bossa nova engendered MPB, the *musica popular brasileira* (Brazilian popular music), which at the time referred to the music of several emerging artists. Singers like Gal Costa and the late Elis Regina (both nationally treasured performers) and singer/songwriters, notably Milton Nascimento, Gilberto Gil, Caetano Veloso, Chico Barque, Ivan Lins, and later Djavan, produced music that could hardly be categorized and did not need to be; rock-and-roll, jazz, Brazilian rhythms, and the use of electronic instruments were all intertwined, held together with strong melodies and poetic lyrics. Under the loose banner of MBP, they and other contemporary Brazilian musicians have created global music that has managed to keep its Brazilian essence.

The Jazz Connection

The bossa nova's tremendous popularity led to an increased intermingling of Brazilian musicians and jazz musicians; by the late 1960s several Brazilian musicians came to work or live in the United States. Among them were the drummer-percussionist Airto Moreira and his wife, the vocalist Flora Purim. Airto was for a time one of the most influential Brazilian musicians in the United States. In Brazil, early in his career, he worked with Hermeto Pascoal, one of Brazil's most inventive instrumental musicians. While working with Miles Davis (Airto appears on *At Fillmore* and *Live-Evil* [Columbia/Sony, 1970]), word of the percussionist's artistry—as an impressionistic colorist rather than timekeeper—spread quickly. He almost single-handedly revolutionized the role of percussion in jazz and popular music; with his influence, the *agogô*, *cuica*, *berimbau*, and rain sticks became part of the palette underlying many jazz and pop records from the early 1970s onwards.

Flora Purim, who also worked with Pascoal, was known for her fantastic range (which covered five octaves) and her risk-taking scat singing. Her work with Stan Getz and Gil Evans helped establish her career in the States; by the early 1970s she was a founding member of Chick Corea's Return to Forever, one of the most widely appealing jazz fusion groups of the 1970s.

Other Brazilians who came to the United States and were very active in the jazz world in the 1960s and 1970s are drummers Edison Machado and Don Um Romão, multi-instrumentalist Sivuca, trumpeter Claudio Roditi, trombonist Raoul de Souza, and percussionist Guilherme Franco.

Brazil, meanwhile, has its own vital jazz community, and the prolific composer and multi-instrumentalist Hermeto Pascoal is one of its most prominent members with an international following. Gil Evans and Miles Davis were both admirers of his work; he played piano and contributed two compositions for Davis's *Live-Evil* album. *Brazil, Universo* (Som da Gente, 1989) is a great example of Pascoal's wildly creative style.

Composer-guitarist-pianist Egberto Gismonti and percussionist Nana Vasconcelos, like Hermeto, have been more closely aligned with jazz than anything else; their music also defies ready categorization. *Dança das Cabeças* (ECM, 1977), a very successful duo recording by Gismonti and Vasconcelos, illustrates their impressionistic approach to sound and texture. Over the years their collaborations with jazz musicians such as Don Cherry, Charlie Haden, and Pat Metheny have been similar in sport to Wayne Shorter's work with Brazilian musicians on *Native Dancer* (Columbia/Sony, 1975): instead of exploring a particular style (e.g., samba or bossa), these recordings are examples of individualistic musicians seeking each other out to explore new possibilities. Percussionist Cyro Baptista is another such collaborator;

he has worked with musicians as diverse as the jazz artist Cassandra Wilson, the pop star Paul Simon, and the classical flutist Paula Robison. Meanwhile, other Brazilian musicians are known for their work in a contemporary mainstream jazz context; among them are guitarist Romero Lubambo (who has worked with Tom Harrell and Phil Woods), the vocalists Leni Andrade and Tania Maria, the pianist Eliane Elias, and the electric bassist Sergio Brandão.

The history of the presence of Brazilian music in American jazz has been a complex interaction in this century. The common pulse, naturally, is the rhythmic and musical legacy of Africa. But it is the samba and the bossa nova that have been the widest conduits for the intermingling of jazz and Brazilian music. These styles have helped further the slow and steady musical give-and-take that has taken place over decades. Various trends, techniques, use of instruments, and individual musicians have continued to keep the cross-currents flowing back and forth across the equator and around the globe.

Jazz in Africa: The Ins and Outs

Howard Mandel

Jazz in Africa has always been a question of: going *to* or coming *from?*

Self-perpetuating myth and twenty-first-century common sense suggest that jazz—arguably the most modern of the world's musics—must indeed have started with seeds from Africa, come to the Americas long before even the birth of the blues out of which jazz sprang. But simultaneously, jazz is acknowledged as first and foremost native to the United States, restlessly spreading up from New Orleans to Kansas City, St. Louis, California, Chicago, Texas, Seattle, New York, Europe by World War I, and ever-further outposts fast in the Jazz Age, via increasing wide-roaming musicians and/or newly burgeoning electronic media.

By the first view, the jazz art is based on some innate talents, carried in genes that must have passed through a particular continent at some unspecified point in time. By the second, jazz may certainly take root and thrive in Africa, as it has elsewhere—and the qualities it probably adapted from and certainly shares with traditional African musics (including its emphasis on rhythm, spontaneous creativity, group interplay, multilayered activity, and cyclical form) have been acknowledged as vital since American jazz's start.

Abdullah Ibrahim (Dollar Brand), 1976. Photo: Sulaiman Ellison. Courtesy of the Institute of Jazz Studies, Rutgers University.

But hardly anyone in or out of Africa disputes that jazz was initially imported there. And the identification of Africa as jazz's source, discussed in penetrating length by Norman C. Weinstein in *A Night in Tunisia: Imaginings of Africa in Jazz*, would appear to be ideological wish fulfillment, rather than musicological history. From all we know, there should be no confusion: jazz *didn't* originate in Africa, and its specific practices (as opposed to its overall imagery and symbolic value) haven't penetrated to the point of domination there, even after eighty years of exposure.

Before venturing any further: what "jazz" are we speaking of here, what Africa and what America? Let's call "jazz" a mutable musical form (to account for its substyles and continuing evolution) that blends in various ratios such identifiable ingredients as swing feel, blues and pop song content, instrumental "vocalization," solo and group improvisation, and social functionality, depending on the interests and intents of its purveyors. Such jazz serves as a means of expression and entertainment for its listeners as well as its players. At its best, this jazz can be either a self-conscious or an inspired effort, or both.

"America," for our purposes, refers not only to the most cosmopolitan centers of all fifty states, but also to the Caribbean, to Central and South America, and to Canada, to the borderless contemporary urban world, and to seemingly unlimited millennial cyberspheres. "Africa," on the other hand, is a distinct and tradition-bearing though enormous land, comprising many peoples and ways of life. It divides uneasily along east/west, north/south meridians, for a start.

Employing these definitions, "jazz in Africa" might be a category big enough to embrace everything it ought to. It may include the late '20s syncopations of the West African Instrumental Quintet, a string band, and the swing band covers and *marabi* and *mbaquanga* fusions of bands such as the Jazz Maniacs, the Merry Blackbirds, the Jazz Revelers, and the Harlem Swingsters, which performed in township halls starting in the '30s. It can encompass post–World War II "high life" like that popularized by Ghanian trumpeter-saxophonist E. T. Mensah and his Tempos, the sweet pennywhistle tunes of South Africa *kwela* street musicians, and South African *isicathamiya* choirs (Ladysmith Black Mambazo is the best known) inspired by "American minstrelsy, spirituals, missionary hymnody, Tin Pan Alley and Hollywood tap-dance ... as well as Zulu traditional idioms" (according to Christopher Ballantine in *Marabi Nights: Early South African Jazz and Vaudeville*).

Congolese rumba groups such as African Jazz, led by Joseph Kabasele in the '60s, OK Jazz, led by guitarist Franco, and Afrisa International, led by Tabu Ley Rochereau; Afro-Parisian productions of the '80s and '90s featuring West Africans King Sunny Adé, Chief Ebenezer Obey, Ray Lema, Youssu N'Dour, Ishmael Lo, Habib Koité, and Salif Keita (who collaborated with Viennese-born, Weather Report—famed composer-keyboardist Joe Zawinul); the fierce political rants of Nigerian singer-songwriter-bandleader-saxophonist Fela Anikulapo-Kuti (who welcomed such sitters-in as American vibist Roy Ayers, trumpeter Lester Bowie, and British drummer Ginger Baker, famed for his stint in the psychedelic blues rock trio Cream)—all may fairly be claimed as representing "jazz in Africa," in those terms' broadest sense. And this list scants investigation of Tanzania's Juwata Jazz and Vijana Jazz bands, Kenya's Shirati Jazz and Kapere Jazz Band, Uganda's AFRIGO band, or any music of Angola, Ethiopia, Madagascar (where hard-to-categorize American guitarists Henry Kaiser and David Lindley mounted an expedition to "discover" and record a slew of open-minded local virtuosos), and the entire North African range, Egypt included.

Jazz purists might hasten to insist that "jazz in Africa" be more rigidly defined. They would surely allow *in* the music of composer-pianist-bandleader Abdullah Ibrahim, known as Dollar Brand back in '59 when he organized Masekela, Jonas Gwangwa, and Kippie Moeketsi into Cape Town's Jazz Epistles and hosted jam sessions that gave impetus to white South African pianist Chris McGregor, whose interracial Blue Notes and Brotherhood of Breath were invaluable politically as well as musically.

That McGregor's brethren are jazz folk is beyond dispute: alto saxophonist Dudu Pukwana, trumpeter Mongezi Feza, bassist Johnny Dyani, and drummer Louis Moholo all had international careers in which they played and recorded with star American and European jazzers in jazz clubs and jazz festivals. Of course, they had to go into exile in London and Denmark to do so.

Similarly, percussionists Babatunde Olatunji, Mor Thiam, and Paco Serry, the Mandinka griot Jali Foday Musa Fuso, and most recently the electric bassist—vocalist Richard Bona of Cameroon have infused projects by Don Cherry, Bill Laswell, Don Pullen, the World Saxophone Quartet, and Zawinul, among others, with true African sounds. These projects, however, are jazz *out* of Africa.

The question becomes: where do purists draw the line? Should we disqualify as "jazz" all the African music that partakes (as much West

African music does) of the Latin (read: Caribbean) tinge that Jelly Roll Morton said was essential to the jazz he "invented"? Do we toss out international pop instrumental hits like trumpeter Masekela's "Grazin' in the Grass" and Cameroonian saxophonist Manu Dibango's "Soul Makossa"? Discredit the links between Cape Verdean vocalist Cesaria Evora and jazz diva Billie Holiday? Deny the ties between the American Boswell and Andrews Sisters and the Skylarks, from which Miriam Makeba emerged?

To dismiss such horn-heavy, improv-inclusive, jazz-celebrating groups as Dexter Johnson's Super Star de Dakar and Cardinal Rex Lawson and His Mayor's Band of Nigeria as nonjazz, or relegate them to the catch-all "Afro pop," is akin to casting quasi-swing/R&B combos like Louis Jordan's Tympani Five and Latin dance orchestras like Perez Prado's, and maybe Paul Whiteman's Orchestra or Red Nichols's Five Pennies, out of the jazz fold because they're compromised by commercialism. Still, it's a fair question: just because jazz exerts an influence, is the result necessarily "jazz"?

Equally puzzling: dare we think of the Master Musicians of Joujouka as a jazz-graced ensemble because Ornette Coleman jammed with them, as did the Klezmatics? What about the Taureg musicians who appeared with Archie Shepp in the 1969 Pan-African Festival in Algeria? The Gnawa musicians of Morocco introduced to the West by Randy Weston? Or Cheik Tidiane-Seck, whose 1995 album with jazz pianist Hank Jones, *Sarala*, is one of the most sprightly of all African-American jazz collaborations?

The mutual attraction of jazz and African musicians, and musics, is long-standing and irrevocable. Ballantine, in *Marabi Nights*, reports that touring American minstrel shows and jubilee singers reached South Africa as early as 1848; he claims that "during the early decades of this century...the black jazzing subculture in South Africa was inventing, developing and perfecting styles of music, musical performance and dance without which many of the South African musics so revered today would never have come about." John Storm Roberts writes in his lamentably hard-to-find volume *Black Music of Two Worlds* that the Lagos Police Band was listening to Duke Ellington records in the early 1930s.

The occurrence of African music in America is invoked in the opening of the seminal history *Jazzmen* (1939), which describes gatherings of slaves for recreational purposes in early nineteenth-century central New Orleans: "The Negroes...still speak of the place as Congo Square.... A century ago, slaves met there every Saturday and

Sunday night to perform the tribal and sexual dances which they had brought with them from the Congo. . . . That the Negroes had not forgotten their dances, even after years of repression and exile from their native Africa, is attested by descriptive accounts of the times."

Okay: black Americans have not forgotten or rejected the culture of their African origins, hundreds of years past though they may be. And there is jazz in Africa—which Abdullah Ibrahim once called a "jazz-crazy black country." Some American-born jazz musicians have sought their musical roots in Africa: Edmond Hall, Louis Armstrong's clarinetist during Pops's historic 1956 visit to Ghana (but whose attempt to resettle there didn't take); Darius Brubeck (who, as associate professor at the University of Natal in Durban, initiated the first jazz studies course offered by an African institution of higher education); and saxophonist René McLean. Prejazz conditions, such as the availability of brass instruments and drums and increased urbanization, were similar in Africa and America at the turn of the last century. Similar doesn't mean the same, though, and historical, social, economic, and racial differences of the sort that exist between the United States and Africa count for quite a lot.

So we can call all this music "jazz," but understand there are many varieties.

Traveling in West Africa in the winter of 1981, I lucked into meeting the Gambian band Ifan Bondi just as it was about to play its weekly gig at a resort on the outskirts of Banjur that catered to Norwegian tourists. The tall, blond crowd at the open-air bar overlooking the stage had come from watching the television show *Roots* in the hotel's lobby. A few days later I attended another Ifan Bondi concert, in a tavern crowded with the band's homeboys (few women hung out in bars in prominently Muslim West Africa), where the drinking and stag dancing were wild. The band seemed typical of its place and time, though I was no expert: its success with the Norwegians and Africans alike was based on its modal melodies, implacable rhythms, strong male voices, subtle guitar, bass, and keyboard interactions, and feel-good vibe. Most of its songs were sung in Wolof and (I was told) derived from traditional riffs, but the arrangements were flexible, opening for instrumental breaks, and glossily electric.

Ifan Bondi rewarded attentive listening and was good for dancing. Its music pulsed with its setting—ocean, shore, jungle, dance hall. If it embodied an indigenous West African style, it was closer to Afro-Cuban and Caribbean musics—with their stop-time fanfares, two-chord vamps, and claves—than to anything U.S.-"American" or "jazz." Not that Ifan Bondi claimed to play jazz. The band's members simply said they respected what they'd encountered of jazz, and knew some names: Coltrane, Miles Davis, Mingus, Monk, Armstrong.

On that same trip I heard Frank Foster's fine postbop quintet play a couple of times for the *gentil membres* of Senegal's Club Med and once in a free concert in a public gathering place for the good people of greater Dakar, who were polite, perhaps appreciative, but not demonstrably moved. These listening experiences still color my perspective on jazz *in* and *of* Africa, which was confirmed by a casual comment made to me by Ifan Bondi's manager, a Gambian culture vulture named Oko Drameh.

Drameh was probably thirty, with a large, dramatic face and dreadlocks. He wore jeans and a loose West African–style dashiki; on the long, thick fingers of his hands were several silver rings decorated with animal totems, including a duck-billed platypus. He was a dealmaking, trend-setting radio deejay who, besides managing Ifan Bondi, had a financial stake in the popular Mobile Disco, an easily transportable two-turntable setup that was rented out, in the care of a trusted record-spinner, for weekend dances.

We'd been drinking beer and chatting about music—jazz, blues, and Ifan Bondi—in the two-room stucco hut he'd painted top-to-bottom with stark black and white phantasms, images of ghosts emerging from leafy thickets. It was sunset, the peanut dust of the region was palpable in the sticky, hot air, and as we sauntered down a dirt path of the compound he lived in on the outskirts of town, Oko Drameh turned to me and offhandedly delivered the bottom line.

"My village," he said, "isn't really much like New Orleans."

Jazz in Japan

Kiyoshi Koyama

The history of jazz in Japan has an age of imitation in its beginning. The oldest jazz record in Japan, "Walla Walla" (Nitto/King), was recorded in 1925 by the Nitto Jazz Band, whose members are now unknown. From this incunabulum to "Blues Suite No. 3" (Victor), recorded in 1962 by the Hideo Shiraki Quintet, almost all of the jazz in Japan was more or less imitative of the jazz heard on records. The performance of the Nitto Jazz Band was clearly a copy of the idea heard in "Livery Stable Blues" by the Original Dixieland Jazz Band, featuring mimics of animal bleats. "Blues Suite No. 3" was nothing more than another version of "Señor Blues," recorded by Horace Silver in the 1950s.

In the 1950s, two exceptions to this rule of imitation were two very talented pianists, Shotaro Moriyasu and Toshiko Akiyoshi. Moriyasu was one of the pioneers of modern jazz in Japan; he interpreted the concept of bebop and put it into practice. With his rich knowledge of music, utmost skill, and natural but still perfect talent, Moriyasu had a great impact on the younger generation, but tragically, he killed himself at the age of thirty-one in September 1955, a few months after his idol Charlie Parker died. Moriyasu did not leave any official recordings in his too-brief life, but there was a legendary all-night jam session at Mocambo, a nightclub in Yokohama, that he participated in with Akiyoshi, the American pianist Hampton Hawes (then stationed in Japan), alto saxophonist Sadao Watanabe, tenor saxophonist Akira Miyazawa, and others. The performance, which took place on July 27, 1954, was recorded by Kiyoshi Iwami (the Japanese counterpart of Jerry Newman, who documented embryonic bebop sessions in Harlem during the early 1940s) and is now available as a three-CD set, *The Historic Mocambo Session '54: Shotaro Moriyasu/Toshiko Akiyoshi* (Polydor). We can hear their passionate and untiring devotion in trying to cast off the imitative age.

Toshiko Akiyoshi had made her first official recording six months earlier. Oscar Peterson, who was in Japan as part of Jazz at the Philharmonic, discovered Toshiko and introduced her to Norman Granz, who recorded her for his Norgran label. Toshiko is literally Japan's "First Woman in Jazz." She was the first Japanese musician who was recognized by an American producer and who recorded with famous American musicians. Three years later, Toshiko went to the States to study at the Berklee School of Music in Boston. She then became the first Japanese musician to have a significant career in America. Since the late '50s, she has been a notable pianist, composer-arranger, and leader (since 1973) of her own big band in Los Angeles and New York.

American Jazz Rush

In prewar days, only a few American jazz musicians visited Japan, and of all of the overseas jazz artists who did, vocalist Midge Williams was the only one who left behind some recordings. She came to Japan in December 1933 and performed at the Imperial Hotel and a dance hall, Florida, with Roger Segure as her accompanist. She also recorded five titles with Japanese musicians for Nippon Columbia in February 1934; we can still listen to three of them—"Dinah," "St. Louis Blues," and "Lazy Bones"—on *Japanese Jazz Songs: Prewar Edition* (Nippon Columbia). These are the historic first recordings of Japanese jazz musicians with American artists. Costarring were popular Japanese musicians who were active in the front lines before and after World War II, such as Fumio Nanri (who was called "the Japanese Louis Armstrong") on trumpet and Takashi Tsunoda, an avant-garde courier who during the 1950s pursued Charlie Christian's legacy, on guitar.

The end of World War II brought novel culture from the United States, the victor nation, to Japan, and music was the entertainment

Toshiko Akiyoshi, Concord Jazz Festival, 1977. Photo: John F. Howard. Courtesy of the Institute of Jazz Studies, Rutgers University.

that Japanese people jumped at first. During wartime, jazz had been considered to be hostile music and was banned, but now people could enjoy it freely. Radio programs of the Far East Network, intended for the American occupation forces, aired the latest popular music and jazz to people in Japan, too. The first American jazz group to come to Japan in the postwar era was the Gene Krupa Trio in 1952. Victor Records in Japan welcomed the Krupa Trio to their studio and had them play "Moon on the Ruined Castle," a popular Japanese song composed by Rentaro Taki, and "Badger's Party," a well-known Japanese nursery rhyme; these recordings, hurriedly released, accelerated the popularity of jazz. In 1953 Norman Granz's Jazz at the Philharmonic and Louis Armstrong's All Stars followed. JATP consisted of fourteen great musicians, including Charlie Shavers, Roy Eldridge, Benny Carter, Ben Webster, Oscar Peterson, Ray Brown, and Ella Fitzgerald.

These visits by American jazz musicians became landmark events for Japanese jazz, and consequently, George Kawaguchi formed the Big Four, modeled after saxophonist Charlie Ventura's Big Four. The group had Kawaguchi (then twenty-four years old) on drums, Hidehiko Matsumoto (twenty-seven) on tenor saxophone, Hachidai Nakamura (twenty-two) on piano, and Mitsuru Ono (twenty-four) on bass; all of them were named Number One in their respective categories in the *Swing Journal* (Japan's leading jazz magazine, first issued in 1947) readers' poll. (Kawaguchi himself was already a star player in Japan; he was voted Number One drummer six years in a row from 1951 to 1956). Moreover, since these four had been heard regularly on a Wednesday-night radio program starting in January 1953, their showpieces such as "Drum Boogie" and "Flying Home" were already known to many people. The Big Four had their debut concerts in a large theater, Nichigeki, in Yurakucho, Tokyo, for eight days starting on May 1, 1953. They were so popular that all of the seats (for three concerts a day) were filled. Kawaguchi says about those days: "That youthful, sparky energy of the Big Four . . . and the full-hearted, dashy image of us . . . , that's what beguiled and aroused the sympathy of young people all over Japan, I think. We were coming out of the dark postwar period, and young people were beginning to openly enjoy the joys of peace and freedom. They were on the edge of exploding their heated energy of youth toward something . . . , and that's when the Big Four entered the stage."

The Big Four was named the Number One combo in the 1954 *Swing Journal* poll, and it created an all-time jazz boom in Japan during the postwar period, but the group itself was short-lived; their live recordings from 1953–54 are compiled on *The Legendary Japanese Jazz Scene, Volume 1: George Kawaguchi and the Big Four* (King). Other combos very popular in those days were Shin Watanabe's Six Joes (modeled after the George Shearing Quintet) and tenor saxophonist Teruo Yoda's Six Lemons. At this time, Japanese jazz won popularity on a national scale comparable to the swing craze in 1930s America. But in the late 1950s the young generation came to prefer "rockabilly" (a combination of rock-and-roll and hillbilly), and jazz fell into disfavor. The double album, *Jazz in Japan, 1947–1962* (Victor) is a collection of typical recordings by popular bands during the boom.

Between 1957 and 1960, the only American jazz musicians we welcomed were Benny Goodman (1957), Jack Teagarden (1959), and Helen Merrill (1960). But in 1961, when Art Blakey and the Jazz Messengers and the Modern Jazz Quartet arrived one after another and both achieved dazzling success, things changed dramatically. Blakey's was the first top-notch modern jazz group to visit Japan. The Jazz Messengers, at the bare mention of their appearance in the Tokyo area, attracted some thirty thousand people to their eleven concerts (matinees included) from January 2 to 6 and 13 to 15 at Sankei Hall. (This theater no longer exists.) Youthful performances by Messengers Wayne Shorter and Lee Morgan raised a storm of excitement in Japanese jazz fans. (In the audience was a world-renowned contemporary composer, Toru Takemitsu.)

Many popular American musicians followed as though an invisible dam between the two countries had broken. In 1962 we welcomed Horace Silver, Chris Connor, Frank Sinatra, Machito's Orchestra, the Golden Gate Quartet, and the Delta River Boys; in 1963, Thelonious Monk, Sonny Rollins, Count Basie, and seventeen other groups. In July 1964 Japan held its first international jazz festival, the World Jazz Festival, which included Miles Davis, J. J. Johnson, Carmen McRae, and many others. That same year, almost forty groups visited Japan, including Duke Ellington, George Lewis and his New Orleans All-Stars, Gerry Mulligan, Ella Fitzgerald, and Louis Armstrong. At the peak in 1978, we were visited by as many as sixty groups. In addition, vast numbers of American jazz records—many of which were unavailable in their home country—were released in Japan.

In 1977 an outdoor jazz event, Live Under the Sky (Tokyo, 1977–90), started with Herbie Hancock's V.S.O.P. Quintet as its main guest; its success prompted other big international jazz events in Japan. In the 1980s we had the Aurex Jazz Festival (Tokyo, 1980–84), the New-port Jazz Festival in Madarao (Nagano, 1982–94), the Mount Fuji Jazz Festival with Blue Note (Yamanashi, 1986–95), and others. These events drew audiences of tens of thousands, which led jazz events from concert halls to large-scale outdoor festivals. In the late 1990s we had several international jazz festivals: the Ocean Blue Jazz Festival in Hitachinaka, the Newport Jazz Festival in Madarao (jump-started after a four-year interval), the Monterey Jazz Festival in Noto, and the Fujitsu Concord Jazz Festival in Japan. Local festivals with Japanese jazz artists were also thriving, drawing audiences of almost four hundred thousand people for about fifty festivals during July and August.

Takayanagi, Sadao, Hino, Kikuchi: Founders of Japanese Jazz

With the increase in overseas jazz musicians visiting Japan, Japanese jazz players were slowly being driven out of jobs. On the other hand, ambitious players in Japan were highly motivated by the latest jazz brought to them in person. In 1961 Masayuki Takayanagi (guitar) and Hideto Kanai (piano) organized other new-blood jazz players—Terumasa Hino (trumpet), Masabumi Kikuchi (piano), Yosuke Ya-mashita (piano), and Masahiko Togashi (drums)—to found Jazz Academy (later renamed New Century Music Lab). Their aim was to present creative jazz, and they appeared regularly at a *chansons* café, Ginparis (a live-music spot where people gathered mostly to hear French *songs* played and sung by Japanese artists). In the 1960s Tak-ayanagi was in the limelight for his experimental activities through Jazz Academy, and in the 1970s and 1980s he pursued radical free improvisation while also playing Lee Konitz's "Subconscious-Lee" in a Billy Bauer–ish way with his great guitar technique. He appeared to cheering crowds at the International New Jazz Festival Moers 1980 in Germany. Today's Japanese jazz leaders, such as Hino, Kikuchi, and Yamashita, were all inspired by Takayanagi; he could be com-pared to Lennie Tristano in the United States. In the album *Ginparis Session* (Three Blind Mice) (TBM/DIW), released in the 1970s, we can hear vivid performances by these creative young musicians from 1963.

Apart from the Jazz Academy, other musicians began studying in the United States. In 1962 Sadao Watanabe went to Boston to study at the Berklee School of Music. Bassist Yasuo Arakawa followed in 1965, pianist-composer Masahiko Sato in 1966, and Masabumi

Kikuchi in 1968. After three and a half years of study, as well as work with drummer Chico Hamilton and composer-vibraphonist Gary McFarland, Sadao Watanabe returned to Japan. His homecoming made 1966 a happy year for Japanese jazz—the first in ten years. Ardent musicians gathered around Sadao to learn the music theory he had studied at Berklee. Some jazz spots opened that were intended only for Japanese jazz, such as Pit-Inn or Taro in Shinjuku, Tokyo. Pit-Inn is the Japanese counterpart of New York's Village Vanguard, and after more than thirty years, it is still loved by fans.

At the end of 1966, Takt, the first record label devoted only to Japanese jazz, recorded its first album, Sadao's *Jazz and Bossa*. At a time when jazz was thought of as America's specialty, the idea of releasing albums only by Japanese musicians seemed rash. In fact, of the 380 jazz albums released by Japanese record companies in 1967, only eleven were by Japanese artists, and seven of those were released by Takt. Contrary to expectations, when *Jazz and Bossa* was released in February 1967, it hit the best-seller list, and the label took off wonderfully. Supported by Sadao's popularity, Takt in the next few years recorded new players and groups such as Terumasa Hino, the Hino-Kikuchi Quintet, George Ohtsuka, and Motohiko Hino. The important role that this label played in furthering Japanese jazz in the 1960s could never be overestimated.

In the 1968 *Swing Journal* poll, Sadao Watanabe was named Number One not only as Jazzman of the Year and for Record of the Year (two categories that were established for the time that year) but also for combo, alto sax, miscellaneous instrument (flute), and composer. This made him a sextuple poll winner, and nobody has ever been able to best this achievement. For more than thirty years, Sadao has played an important role in fostering young jazz players in Japan and popularizing jazz among the Japanese public.

Terumasa Hino first went to Germany in 1965 to play at the Berlin Jazz Festival as a member of the Hideo Shiraki Quintet. (Drummer Shiraki's group was named Number One combo in the *Swing Journal* readers' poll for eight years in a row from 1958; they were the first Japanese jazz group to launch out on an overseas expedition.) Joachim E. Berendt, producer of the festival, said admiringly that he had no idea Japan had such a wonderful trumpeter. Hino left Shiraki and in January 1968 started a quintet with co-leader Masabumi Kikuchi. This unit caught on because of Kikuchi's electric piano, as well as his compositions and arrangements, and Hino's improvising, but it ended only nine months later when Kikuchi left for the United States to study at Berklee. Hino rode on a wave of popularity in 1970 when his live album *Hi-Nology* (Takt/Nippon Columbia) became a huge seller. Hino was now another leader in Japan along the lines of Sadao Watanabe. In 1975 the trumpeter moved to New York and, as is widely known, has been active in the front lines till today.

Recent Developments

In the 1970s and 1980s many fusion groups were formed in Japan, as in other countries, that featured synthesizers and electric bass. Sadao Watanabe and Terumasa Hino did so and reached larger markets. Other popular groups in this field were Native Son (early 1980s), led by the stellar tenor saxophonist Kousuke Mine; Kylyn Band (1970s) and the Mobo Club Band (1980s), both led by an ace guitarist, Kazumi Watanabe; and T-Square, which is still popular. Meanwhile, Masahiko Togashi, Yosuke Yamashita, and Masahiko Sato have been questing for the jazz that they believe in. Their contributions to jazz in Japan will be remembered for a long time.

A self-taught drummer and composer, Togashi is a musical near-genius who has had a variety of experience from bebop to experimental jazz. He has been awarded the Jazz of Japan award (critics' choice) nine times. Among the awards were those in 1969 for the bold free-jazz album *We Now Create*, in 1975 for *Spiritual Nature* (East Wind), in 1980 for the duo *Kizashi* (Next Wave) with Yosuke Yamashita, and in 1991 for *Plays Bebop, Volume 1* (Polydor) by his latest group, J. J. Spirits, (J. J. stands for Japanese Jazz), with Sato, Kousuke Mine, and a leading Japanese bassist, Nobuyoshi Ino. Since an accident in 1970, Togashi has been a paraplegic; he devised a unique drumset that enables him to play in a wheelchair.

One of our most interesting recent developments has been the use of Japanese traditional music as a basis for improvisation. Pianist-composer Masahiko Sato assembled Japanese musicians such as Kousuke Mine and Kazutoki Umezu, and international artists such as Americans Wayne Shorter and Ray Anderson and Brazilian Nana Vasconcelos, in an ambitious attempt to transmit new possibilities of jazz from a rather closed Japanese jazz circle to the outside world. This experiment, which Sato calls Randooga (an anagram of *garandoo*, Japanese for "empty inside") was unveiled onstage at Live Under the Sky in July 1990. Tunes such as "Well Digger's Song," "Tanokuro-Bushi," and "Sutemaru"—with motifs from traditional Japanese folk songs—were recorded live and released on *Masahiko Sato: Randooga* (Epic Sony). This album received the Jazz of Japan award in 1990.

Sato has continued his efforts to improvise music with Mine and

Umezu and Japanese traditional koto players, as well as Korean saxophonist Kan Tae Hwan. In Randooga's second album, *Kam-Nabi* (Nippon Crown, 1992), Sato took up "Tuva-Lak," with a motif from a traditional melody passed from ancient times among the Tuba tribe, a nomadic people living near the Mongolian border in Russia, and "Field Song of Kyeshon," based on a melody of the Kyeshon region of northeast India. His brave idea of combining jazz with Asian music seems to have no boundaries.

Yosuke Yamashita, who since 1980 has often been named Number One pianist, is a cult figure in Japan, often compared to Cecil Taylor in the United States. With his rich talent in literature, he has published several essay collections and has been popular among university students since the 1970s. Yamashita says that the catharsis that jazz extemporization can give both to players and audiences can be compared to the exhilaration of sports. This unique methodology swept away the "abstrusity" of free jazz and has been enthusiastically supported. Yamashita formed the New York Trio with bassist Cecil McBee and drummer Pheeroan akLaff in 1988 and has toured Europe and appeared regularly at Sweet Basil in New York, all of which makes him one of the most widely known Japanese jazz musicians overseas. His *Kurdish Dance* (Verve), recorded with American tenor saxophonist Joe Lovano, received the Jazz of Japan award in 1992.

During the 1990s, several young powers began to assert themselves in Japan. Some of the musicians who had studied at Berklee (pianists Makoto Ozone and Junko Onishi and drummer Masahiko Osaka) returned to Japan to start active careers. In 1998 Ozone received his first Jazz of Japan award for *The Trio* (Verve), and Onishi's *Wow* (Somethin' Else) received the same award in 1993. Osaka, who toured with trombonist Delfeayo Marsalis while still at Berklee, returned to Japan in 1990 and formed a quintet with a very talented trumpeter, Tomonao Hara. They were invited to perform in concert at the Kennedy Center for *East Meets West: Japanese Jazz Jam* with Toshiko Akiyoshi in 1997.

We have many gifted young artists in Japan now, such as alto saxophonist Jo Yamada, pianist Yutaka Shiina, vocalist Keiko Lee, and violinist Naoko Terai, to name only a few, but it is still unknown whether younger generations can fully bloom out of the rich soil cultivated for a long time by Toshiko Akiyoshi, Sadao Watanabe, Masahiko Togashi, Masahiko Sato, and others. And only time will tell if we will ever have another Toshiko, or an even greater Toshiko, in the future of jazz in Japan.

Jazz in Canada and Australia

Terry Martin

So near, so far"—or is it rather "Too near, too far": the polar situations of would-be jazz musicians in Canada and Australia. In considering their situations we immediately face the question of individual voice versus local dialect. Can we speak of shared musical attributes that could define a Canadian or Australian jazz sound? And how can the individual voices that will generate the dialect form in the first place?

Canadian jazz historian Mark Miller poses the "so near" syndrome. Not only is the north-of-border jazzman likely to be well informed of the latest developments to the south by the availability of recordings and by the relative ease of experiencing the U.S. jazz scene in the flesh. Canada is also only a slight northerly swing in any tour of the States. A successful Canadian musician is likely to be subsumed readily into the American or international jazz network, ceasing to be generally recognized as Canadian; witness the notable examples of composer-arranger Gil Evans, pianists Oscar Peterson and Paul Bley, and trumpeters Maynard Ferguson and Kenny Wheeler. That the emigration of future jazzmen of note from Canada began early is illustrated by the example of pianist Tiny Parham, who recorded in Chicago in the 1920s. Recent examples of Canadians now prominently

New Zealand pianist Mike Nock. Courtesy of the Institute of Jazz Studies, Rutgers University.

associated with the U.S. scene include pianist Renée Rosnes and vocalist-pianist Diana Krall.

The growth of an indigenous jazz milieu was slow in both Canada and Australia, although the isolation of the latter makes this more apparent. Behind the glaring cultural light of the U.S. jazz scene some early pockets of unique creativity are apparent to the north; most notable among these is the 1940s piano scene in the St. Henry neighborhood of Montreal that included, among other mentors, Harold "Steep" Wade. A particularly energetic fusion of Teddy Wilson, Art Tatum, and Nat Cole with boogie-woogie seems to have occurred at the Café St.-Michel during this period, giving rise to Oscar Peterson, Milt Sealey, and Oliver Jones—a tradition carried on by Jean Beaudet.

It was in the very nature of the music that the development of free jazz took place in relative isolation during the '60s. The most prominent Canadian of the new music, Paul Bley, had left Montreal during the previous decade to begin associations with Charles Mingus and Ornette Coleman that would make him a leader on the international scene. But nevertheless, lurking in Bley's discrete spacy style there perhaps lingers a link to the laconic approaches of other Canadian jazzmen. John Norris, founding editor of the excellent *Coda* jazz magazine, has suggested that there is a "prairie" aspect to the work of some Canadian musicians. While that characterization scarcely suits the stay-at-home fireplug trumpeter Herbie Spanier, there is a distinct reticence in the work of famous expatriate Kenny Wheeler, whose intelligent music easily slides into the ECM Records mold; but one also must remember Wheeler's significant role in one of Anthony Braxton's more notable groups.

Sonny Greenwich, who also made an early impression on the international scene performing with U.S. artists by way of a novel adaptation of some aspects of Coltrane to the guitar, appears to have to withdrawn north, there to concentrate on the more philosophical traits admired in the master saxophonist. Nonetheless, Greenwich belongs with that remarkably diverse group of significant Canadian jazz guitarists that embraces the swing styles of Oliver Gannon and Ed Bickert, the stylistic crossover of Lenny Breau, the personalized and urgent modernism of Nelson Symonds, and the edgy avant-garde realms of Rene Lussier.

The so-called mainstream (a chameleon term at best) has existed in Canada jazz at least since the swing era. For example, anyone who appreciates the neo–Zoot Sims tenor stylings of, say, Scott Hamilton should give the recordings of Fraser MacPherson an attentive ear; similarly, the Johnny Hodges–touched soprano saxophone of the ex-Scot Jim Galloway may appeal. More contemporary stylists like pianist Bernie Senensky and bassist-pianist Don Thompson are well respected by their U.S. peers, and saxophonists P. J. Perry, Dave Turner, and Mike Murley can match most of their stateside counterparts. More generally known, the big band of valve-trombonist–composer–arranger Rob McConnell continues along established lines, which serves to throw into relief the more idiosyncratic big band ventures of clarinetist Phil Nimmons, one of the few to write music specifically related to the country. Other orchestras are at work attempting to update big band jazz: the Vancouver Ensemble of Jazz Improvisation and the Neufeld-Occhipinti Orchestra.

Orchestras still serve as a reservoir and training pool for jazz soloists, many of whom make up the small groups of the current postbop-derived mainstream. As in Australia, the younger Canadians have been influenced by a very different type of popular music than that heard by their jazz models and are open to the in-pourings of "world music." The growing influence of world music is apparent in the well-known Cuban connection music of soprano saxophonist–flutist Jane Bunnett, as well as that of pianist D. D. Jackson.

Following the departure of Paul Bley, the free jazz styles appear to have had a number of separate new beginnings in the provinces. In Vancouver in the 1960s, the late pianist-artist Al Neil made a largely singular effort to create an avant-garde; woefully unrepresented on record, Neil is in urgent need of rediscovery. In the 1970s, Toronto musician-artist-filmmaker Michael Snow (director of the legendary avant-garde jazz film *New York Eye and Ear Control*) formed the Canadian Creative Music Collective (CCMC) along with percussionist Larry Dubin and saxophonist–jazz journalist Bill Smith, among others, perhaps with an eye to Chicago's Association for the Advancement of Creative Musicians (AACM). More recently, on the West Coast the avant-garde stream has been carried forward by the intense pianist Paul Plimley, frequently in the company of the virtuoso bassist Lisle Ellis and the classically trained clarinetist François Houle. In the east during the 1980s, l'Ensemble de musique improvisee de Montreal (EMIM) formed a rallying point for the more experimental music of saxophonist Jean Derome, guitarist Lussier, and their fellow explorers. It is clear that a number of these players do not necessarily consider themselves "jazz musicians" in the conventional sense, and perhaps more wish to be regarded as members of the international improvisers' community. The bold programming of the Vancouver and Victoriaville festivals, which shames most jazz festivals elsewhere, has reinforced this attitude by providing opportunities for the local artists to interact with musicians from around the world—opportunities their peers in Australia cannot hope to find on their parched home turf.

Meanwhile, at the other pole, the "too far" Australians have faced a crisis of identity of a different, more existential nature, one born of cultural displacement and isolation for the European-derived majority of the inhabitants. Aficionados and budding musicians have historically felt themselves to be jazz-starved: few overseas recordings available, few peers, and, because of the great distance and small population, extremely few visiting artists. While Australia has provided no "names" to the international jazz community that match Evans, Ferguson, and Peterson, the "too far" effect may have provided the opportunity for the gestation of a local "color" that can shade Australian jazz artists of diverse styles.

As described in Andrew Bisset's groundbreaking *Black Roots, White Flowers* (1979), exemplars of black prejazz music had performed on the vaudeville circuit in Australia in the early 1900s; groups such as the Fisk Jubilee Singers were seemingly well received, perhaps touching a spark of solidarity with the "common-folk" aspects of the growing Australian "identity." Increasingly attentive to the latest international fads, the press noted the New York performances of the Original Dixieland Jazz Band, whose records began appearing in Australian catalogs in 1920. At this time, local musicians began an attempt to reproduce what some perceived as the "antics" of American hot dance music; their publicity material aped the famous photographs of the ODJB et al. As elsewhere outside its birthplace, nascent jazz elements were nurtured by dance orchestras, as individual musicians became increasingly aware of the peculiar virtuosity that was part and parcel of the liberated emotional expressivity of the great American players, black and white, even if only at second hand by way of the more widely distributed white dance orchestras.

In 1928 the first black jazz band to tour Australia, Sonny Clay's Colored Idea, apparently caused some concern among the conservative establishment, while cruelly demonstrating the expressive deficiencies of the local aspirants. Until the Second World War forced greater international contact and grim awareness on the larger Australian public, jazz was largely under the wing of the more successful dance orchestras. Notable among these was Frank Coughlan's Trocadero

Orchestra; Coughlan himself was a more than competent trumpeter-trombonist and had a sense of the real thing.

The war brought greater cultural contact with Americans, black and white, and increased the availability of recordings by the true originators of the music; V-discs were treasure. In the immediate postwar period, a peculiar conjunction of embryonic modernism, Marxism, and traditional jazz gave birth to what are plausibly the first Australian accents in the jazz language. (This convergence is celebrated in Dave Dallwitz's 1976 *Ern Malley Suite*.) Seemingly simultaneously and independently, musicians in the southern arc of the continent (Melbourne, Hobart, and Adelaide) took spirit from the great Chicago recordings of the '20s to generate a style that, while sharing some aspects with the slightly earlier revivalists in the United States, had in its prime a joy of liberation and swing all of its own. Notables included Melbourne's Graeme Bell, Tony Newstead, and, later, the bands of Frank Johnson and Len Barnard (featuring the brilliant early Louis-influenced work of Bob Barnard), Tom Pickering and Ian Pearce in Hobart, and the Southern Jazz Group in Adelaide. Outside of the international center of Sydney, these homegrown vintages provided inspiration for a few truly unique voices, including multi-instrumentalist Ade Monsbourgh, probably the most generally admired "individual" of Australian traditional jazz.

The realization of common interests in this cluster of states led to the First Australian Jazz Convention in Melbourne in 1946; locals argue that this is the longest continuously running jazz festival in the world. A spin-off of the convention was the journey of pianist Graeme Bell's band to the 1947 World Youth Festival in Prague; the unaffected spirit and individuality of the band, which included the wonderful lead playing of Roger Bell, as well as brass and reed player Monsbourgh, would spark the popular revival of traditional jazz styles in continental Europe and Britain. Aspirants to earlier jazz styles are advised to seek out the Australian traditional jazz recordings of the '50s, as well as some later incarnations, being particularly cautioned to open their ears to the Dallwitz tribute to mock-poet "Ern Malley" as an idiosyncratic example of a historic style made new.

During the late '40s and early '50s American soloists ventured to play with local bands, leaving little obvious trace, though some excellent recordings of ex-Ellington cornetist Rex Stewart with the Bell band survive; this tour would have a profound influence on the individualistic trumpet of Keith Hounslow. Later visits by the Louis Armstrong All Stars, the Dave Brubeck Quartet, and the Oscar Peterson Trio would leave indelible marks, the latter two in particular molding the embryonic local modern scene. Given the hermetic tendencies of bebop and the small audience for jazz of any kind, modernism seems to have had a particularly difficult time in Australia. Again, small groups of musicians struggled in isolation to evoke the sounds heard in the trickle of recordings from the United States. Among others, altoist Frank Smith, reportedly much admired by Benny Carter, strove to transform a fundamental swing style into the new form. The lamentably few examples of Smith's art available whet the appetite for more by this artist, who died in 1973. More widely known and with some international recognition is flute and reed player Don Burrows, who as the country's figurehead modern jazz virtuoso has covered many bases, somewhat diffusing the artistic impact of his work.

The tardiness in responding to the challenge of bebop may be partially responsible for the relative lack of contributions by Australians to the international jazz scene in comparison to those by Canadian expatriates. The Australian Jazz Quartet (including tenor saxophonist–bassoonist Errol Buddle and vibraphonist Jack Brokensha) had a brief period of recognition in the States in the mid-'50s, clearly drawing on the well-crafted examples of the Modern Jazz Quartet and Brubeck. Originally inspired by the Peterson trio, the New Zealand transplant Mike Nock formed a piano trio that captured some of the drive and popularity of the model. Nock is one of the Antipodeans who works liberally around the world; as current director of the Naxos jazz program, he appears to be committed to furthering the recognition of musicians not directly placed in the publicity centers. Multibrass virtuoso James Morrison has also been notable on the American scene in the last decade. Morrison seems likely to inherit the public mantle of "the Australian jazz musician" from Don Burrows, with the associated positives and negatives.

If the arrival of bebop down under was delayed, then similar factors conspired to limit the development of free jazz styles. From the laboratory of the '60s, two quite different altoists stand out: the well-trained studio musician Charlie Munro and the self-invented Bernie McGann. Since the '60s various tides have swept in sundry influences on the local scene. The hard core of energy music can be found in the '70s recordings of pianist Serge Ermoll's Free Kata (featuring the fire breathing tenor of Eddie Bronson and the innovative drums of Lou Burdett). The oddly coupled influences of the Chicago AACM with Miles Davis's fusion extravaganzas have also left their marks on the younger generation. These diverse influences, coupled with European modernism, were furthered by pianist Roger Frampton and others, leading to current groups such as the Australian Art Orchestra, under pianist Paul Grabowsky, drummer John Pochee's Ten-Part Invention, and saxophonist Sandy (Sandra) Evans's Clarion Fracture Zone. The more extreme improvisational musics suffer acutely from the inherent small audience. The iconoclastic violinist-improviser Jon Rose, for some time an Australian resident, has moved his field of operations to the greener pastures of Europe.

In parallel with the more conservative drift of the international jazz scene, saxophonist Dale Barlow, an Art Blakey Jazz Messengers alumnus, serves as a reference point in a burgeoning crowd of neo-boppers. Players growing up hearing, without much choice, the ubiquitous rock, as well as early fusion, are carrying these influences into more centrally jazz contexts, and a few, such as saxophonists Evans and Mark Simmonds, and trumpeter Scott Tinkler, appear to have picked up a local tang to their musics along the way.

One final aspect of the Australian jazz scene is a rather unique version of creative eclecticism, by which some "musos" assume the traditional "ocker" stance and thumb their noses at stylistic boundaries. Perhaps not so unusual for the young postmodernist, but somewhat surprising in an older musician such as the late John Sangster, who began in the 1940s playing traditional cornet and then drums with the Bell band, engaged as jack-of-all-percussion in early essays at free jazz, and wrote a ten-LP tribute to the worlds of J.R.R. Tolkien that encompasses almost every style of jazz one can conceive.

For the younger musician, the contemporary scene retains a disparate mix of styles, whose players must perforce, because of the small size of the jazz community, interact with each other to a degree unnecessary in the American or international jazz worlds. In the absence of major contributors to the ultimate evolution of jazz, it is the discovery of some individual—occasionally eccentric—voices, and some collective spirits, perhaps sharing a distinctive accent, that justifies attention to the Australian jazz scene.

The Clarinet in Jazz

Michael Ullman

The first jazz record, the Original Dixieland Jazz Band's "Livery Stable Blues," announced in 1917 a new kind of music but also, startlingly, a new kind of clarinet playing, heard in the forthright, repeated squeal, a high E flat, by clarinetist Larry Shields. Shields's thin, abrasive tone sounds like a wild cry as it carries above the rest of the band. On the "Dixieland Jass Band One-Step," he flings out high notes before him, letting them sag in pitch in a manner that might have been plaintive but for the insistently upbeat style of the band. His two-bar breaks include the whinnying sounds and brash glissandos heard repeatedly in early jazz. Those high notes, pushed out dramatically, are inevitable if he is going to be heard, but his vibrato-laden tone is not. It is indicative of a New Orleans style of clarinet playing, which frequently took the instrument's sound in a direction radically different from the classical tradition.

That tradition began with the clarinet's invention in 1700. The crucial modification of the single-reed instrument known as the chalumeau, the clarinet's predecessor, was the addition of the register key, which extended the clarinet's range while making a sometimes obvious break in sound between the lower, so-called chalumeau range

Benny Goodman, Hotel Pennsylvania, 1937. Courtesy Frank Driggs Collection.

and its upper regions. One productive way of looking at the history of jazz clarinet playing is to consider the attitude of the players toward this register break—and toward the various sounds the clarinet can make. Many New Orleans clarinetists exploited it, alternating choruses or phrases in the deep, woody, chalumeau register with aggressive high sounds in the upper registers. To the classical listener, this division can sound like incapacity. The distinguished critic Gunther Schuller lists (in *Early Jazz*) "the pronounced register break" heard in the playing of the great Johnny Dodds as one of "his problems," whether it came from planning, "reed problems," or "acoustical conditions." The decision clarinetists must make is whether to exploit, overcome, or ignore the register break, and whether to exploit or restrict the clarinet's various sound possibilities. Some jazz players, beginning perhaps with Jimmie Noone, would have agreed with Schuller. These clarinetists developed a fluency, ease, and consistency of tone that reflected classical training. Buddy DeFranco, who became the preeminent clarinetist in the postwar bebop era, notes that "the thrust of my early playing was technical—pure and simple technique. ... I considered the idea of a legitimate clarinet tone the best thing to use. ... I didn't use much vibrato."

New Orleans players did. Before there was jazz, there were brass bands in New Orleans, and small bands that played for dancing and partying. Some commentators, including New Orleans players, believed that with the advent of jazz and blues, "ratty music," the standards of instrumental playing degenerated. Clearly, clarinetists stopped trying for a legitimate tone. Bechet comments in his *Treat It Gentle* on the older-style clarinetist George Baquet: "What he played, it wasn't really Jazz ... he stuck real close to the line in a way. He played things ... straight out how it was written. ... There wasn't none of these growls and buzzes which is a part of ragtime music, which is a way the musicianer has of replacing different feelings he finds inside the music and inside himself." Called "the first hot clarinet," New Orleans clarinetist Lorenzo Tio Jr. advised: "You must handle your tone. Happen sometime you can put some *whining* in the blowing of your instrument. There are a whole lot of sounds you can shove in—such as *crying*—everywhere you get the chance. ... Don't play like you're at no funeral."

Of course, playing at funerals was exactly what brass bands had been doing in New Orleans, and eventually jazz changed the style with which they did so. At some point the brass bands developed the distinctly nonclassical sound we can hear in revivalist recordings. In

Brass Bands and New Orleans Jazz, William Schafer talks of the "characteristic outdoor-playing style that utilized a hoarse and 'crying' tone, wide vibrato, and a peculiar instrumental attack not heard in jazz and dance bands." William Russell describes the sound of Alphonse Picou on the high-pitched E-flat clarinet: "Picou's part could always be heard above the band, usually he played rather staccato, and alternated between a couple notes and also repeated notes." In his re-creations of clarinet playing in brass bands, New Orleans clarinetist George Lewis, playing E-flat clarinet in 1945 with veteran trumpet player Bunk Johnson (American Music) plays a style distinguished by bits of melody, decorative arpeggios, and high held notes with a pronounced vibrato. On the hymns played by John Casimir with the Young Tuxedo Jazz Band, Casimir plays melody on E-flat clarinet with a striking, even shocking, pinched wail and a persistent, unchanging vibrato (Atlantic/Mosaic).

The first generations of New Orleans clarinetists and their followers, including Dodds, Omer Simeon, and Albert Nicholas, favored the Albert system clarinet rather than the Boehm system that has become the standard. Barney Bigard called the Albert system with its large bore, relatively large tone-holes, and few keys "the real McCoy." It was in several ways preferable. In his *The Clarinet,* British expert Geoffrey Randall notes: "The intonation and tone of these instruments were very fine—they have in fact never been surpassed—and were, generally speaking, much superior to those of the contemporary Boehm." Each note on the Albert system clarinet "should be available with near-perfect tuning," according to Colin Lawson in his *Clarinet.* But the Boehm system has more keys and allows more fluency. Almost inevitably, musicians interested in fluid, chromatic passages ended up with the Boehm system instrument, particularly as the rough-and-ready clarinet style often heard in the twenties gave way to the elegance of Goodman and Shaw.

In *Early Jazz,* Gunther Schuller has observed that "the first generation of important jazz clarinetists came from New Orleans." These include Jimmie Noone, Johnny Dodds, Larry Shields, Leon Roppolo, Barney Bigard, and, preeminently, Sidney Bechet. There were important but less celebrated figures as well, including Lorenzo Tio Jr., who taught Bigard and Bechet. (Bechet also studied with George Baquet, who was born in 1883 and recorded in 1929 with Jelly Roll Morton. Baquet's stuttering, chalumeau-register solo can be heard on Morton's "Burning the Iceberg" [Bluebird/BMG].) Tio sounds wild on the midtempo "Sud Bustin' Blues," a 1923 recording with Armand

Piron (Jazz Archives). In the ensemble we hear him growling low notes or wailing above, often playing with pinched notes, in a novelty sound reminiscent of the ODJB. Tio treats the upper and lower registers virtually independently, a New Orleans tradition that we can also hear in the 1928 recording "Ideas" by Sidney Arodin with Monk Hazel. Arodin plays rapid staccato passages, takes his first break low down, and then plays high over the ensemble. We don't hear the slithering chromatic passages of swing clarinetists here. Nevertheless, this roughness wasn't inevitable for New Orleans clarinetists, as witness the elegant, fluent solos on "Waffle Man's Call," by the obscure Charlie Scaglioni with Johnny Bayersdorffer and His Jazzola Novelty (Jazz Archives).

But variations of the style we first heard on the ODJB recordings are common, even with distinguished jazz groups such as the Friars Society Orchestra and the New Orleans Rhythm Kings, whose records were made in 1922 and 1923. Featuring clarinetist Leon Roppolo, both groups sounded more relaxed, more gently swinging, than did the ODJB. On "Wolverine Blues" Roppolo takes a central solo that begins in the upper range. It includes held notes with the expanded New Orleans vibrato and climactic high notes with an attenuated bleat. Roppolo shifts dramatically to the chalumeau register to finish with a dark, woody sound. He keeps the two ranges separate while staying out of the range of the lead trumpet, decorating the lead's lines, filling in the gaps, and pushing along the rhythm. On "That's a Plenty," he mimics the trumpet lead, playing when Paul Mares does and breathing when Mares does. He reminds us that the clarinet was sometimes used in New Orleans as a second lead instrument, often to spell a cornetist with a tired lip.

Although both were overshadowed in jazz history by the flamboyant Sidney Bechet, perhaps the quintessential New Orleans–bred clarinetists were the great Johnny Dodds and Omer Simeon, who is best known for his twenties recordings with Jelly Roll Morton. Morton had featured another clarinetist—Volly De Faut—who splits his choruses on the 1925 "Wolverine Blues" between upper and lower registers in the expected style, and he would employ Barney Bigard and Darnell Howard as well, but Simeon made the biggest impact with Morton. We can hear Simeon's ripping up-tempo breaks and joyful ensemble playing on "Black Bottom Stomp," which has a chalumeau solo in midarrangement. His wailing breaks on "Smoke-House Blues" remain fine examples of the tradition (BMG/Bluebird).

Dodds, who first became widely known through his recordings with

King Oliver, had a powerful, throbbing sound. As we hear at the beginning of the 1923 Oliver "Canal St. Blues," he was a sagacious, exciting ensemble player. The strongly swinging opening chorus depends on the lead playing of Oliver and Louis Armstrong, but also on the beautifully tactful fills and filigree of Dodds, whose arpeggios and held notes never seem like mere decoration. His simplest figures have a distinguishing thrust. His solo, whose first chorus circles around a simple sagging note repeated, is a highlight of the record. As Schuller has suggested, Dodds played as if he thought of the clarinet as split between registers. He could make the split work sublimely, as on the Louis Armstrong recording "S.O.L. Blues" (Columbia). He plays a bittersweet chorus in midrange, but his climactic statement is all chalumeau, a deeply affecting, woody chorus that would have been hard for anyone but Armstrong to top. Under the influence of Armstrong, he started to play longer, more vocal lines, without ever totally abandoning his original style.

Dodds was born in 1892, but his first instrumental hero was evidently the precocious, largely self-taught Sidney Bechet, who was five years younger. Bechet was an imperious man who admitted to growing up in a New Orleans clarinet tradition but diffident about admitting he had teachers. He went beyond them all. Bechet became more famous as a soprano saxophonist, but he started on the clarinet. He developed an unparalleled sound, deep, woody, and broad in the chalumeau range, expansive, even rhapsodic above. He maintained the wide New Orleans vibrato but developed a virtuosic technique. On clarinet, he would devote whole choruses, especially on blues, to the chalumeau range. His was an impetuous, flamboyant music. His performances on clarinet include his accompaniment to Eva Taylor on "Oh Daddy Blues" in 1923, the 1932 "Sweetie Dear," and later masterpieces such as "Blue Horizon," a slow blues which he begins with casually descending phrases and builds with majestic intensity. One should also listen to his duets with another New Orleans clarinetist, Albert Nicholas, especially "Weary Way Blues," with its graceful interweaving of the two improvised clarinet parts (Blue Note).

If Bechet had few early imitators, it may be because jazz history led the clarinet in the thirties towards a less vibrato-laden sound. Not everyone followed the trend. The white Chicagoan Frank Teschemacher was bowled over by the likes of Roppolo and Dodds. Teschemacher developed a dramatic if awkwardly passionate style. Saxophonist Bud Freeman said of him, with gentle irony, that "Tesch soon mastered the technique of playing the clarinet, but he never let the technique master him." It's unclear that he even tried. He was an audacious musician, with a shrill piping sound, who took the most innocent phrases in unexpected directions. His solo on the 1927 "China Boy" (Time/Life) moves in fits and starts and yet somehow maintains a forward motion, finding an unlikely resting place after a group of staccato notes on an extended squeal. Artie Shaw spoke of Teschemacher's "deliberately fumbling way," which "in its own grotesque way . . . made a kind of musical sense." Even if he hadn't died in a car accident in 1932, Teschemacher clearly wasn't going to influence the swing era players.

A more suggestive player was the eccentric, sad-faced Pee Wee Russell, whose typical choruses, even when he was playing with the upbeat Eddie Condon dixieland groups, stand out for their odd growls, flutters, and even half-swallowed notes. Even his earliest solos, as on "Honolulu Blues," with Miff Mole in 1927, are surprisingly poignant. His greatest work came later, as in his touching, and unforgettably tender, reworking of "Embraceable You" in 1938 (Commodore). Or one can listen to his growling, chattering playing on "Take Me to the Land of Jazz" from 1944. He achieves real pathos in his various versions of "I'd Climb the Highest Mountain" (Impulse). Perhaps in deference to his long-standing originality and emphasis on shades of tone, Russell was later hailed, in a way that must have puzzled him, as an avant-garde figure. Everyone sensed that Russell, whether due to his personality or style, stood outside the jazz mainstream.

Not so the New Orleans–born Jimmie Noone, from whom Russell learned the fluttering trill both used regularly in their solos. Noone performed with the Freddie Keppard band from New Orleans as early as 1914 and traveled to Chicago with King Oliver, with whom he recorded in 1923. On "Play That Thing" (Classics), Noone shows that he was an excellent ensemble player and that he had as much control of the range of the clarinet as Bechet. Initially he did not try to expand the New Orleans tradition. He treated the register break with respect, playing a chorus of blues in the chalumeau register in "Play That Thing" before moving upward. It's in the last choruses of the ensemble that we hear him moving fluently up and down the range of the clarinet.

In 1928 Noone made a series of important recordings with an innovative small group that featured pianist Earl Hines. He had smoothed out his technique. He played swinging eight-note lines but was just as distinguished playing slow ballad-like numbers or weaving sinuously around the alto saxophone of Joe Poston. Noone's graceful duet with Poston on "Four or Five Times" follows the vocal: we hear a sweetly lyrical entrance and follow him dipping into his warm chalumeau as Poston plays the melody. Then Noone plays a stuttering downward figure only to resolve it in a sweeping, beautifully executed arpeggio. Noone's fluttering trills and circular patterns suggest experience with classical technique.

Early jazz arrangers exploited the particular qualities of jazz clarinet playing. Don Redman's busy arrangements for Fletcher Henderson feature clarinet trios, sometimes only for short breaks, or to help state the melody in a shrill, vibrant way, as on "Go Long Mule" (1924). On "Copenhagen," Buster Bailey is joined on clarinet by Redman himself and by Coleman Hawkins. The clarinet trio is used at first playing four bars of melody down low, but later the trio plays an entire twelve-bar chorus of blues. Redman was just as likely to pitch the clarinets up high and let them wail in a shrill, tense fashion that was one of the most distinct sounds of the era.

Duke Ellington admired unreservedly the passion and commitment of Sidney Bechet and hired Bechet to join his Washingtonians in 1924. Ellington remained loyal to the clarinet. In 1928 Ellington hired New Orleans native Barney Bigard, saying that he particularly appreciated the woody tone of Bigard's Albert system clarinet and adding: "He was invaluable for putting the filigree work into an arrangement." Bigard can sound frilly, but Ellington used him perfectly, whether by having him play arpeggios behind Cootie Williams on "Paducah" or using his smoky, mysterious tone on "Mood Indigo." Bigard's playing had at times a noodling quality: his fluency, and perhaps his pat accenting, could sound weightless. Ellington exploited what sounds like a weakness, strikingly on "Charlie the Chulo," a 1940 piece which begins with Bigard playing around in the low register (BMG/Victor).

By the end of the twenties, clarinetists were doubling in reed sections of big bands, where their ability to play saxophones was as least as important as their ability to solo on clarinet. The large New Orleans vibrato would not fit snugly in a reed section, and the new arrangements demanded skilled, fluent readers. By the time the recording industry was recovering from the Depression, the young virtuoso Benny Goodman was ready to emerge from the studio work in which he did his apprenticeship, bringing with him a new standard of virtuosity.

It would be difficult to overestimate his influence—and that of Artie Shaw—on the history of jazz clarinet playing. The swing era made New Orleans–based music seem old hat. The clarinetists who would emerge in the thirties would typically play Boehm system clarinets with a less exotic tone than the New Orleans players and their protégés. As always, there were exceptions. Bob Crosby used the hot New Orleans sound of Irving Fazola to re-create the sound of a bygone era in his spirited band. (Fazola's warm tone can be heard briefly on Billie Holiday's "A Fine Romance.") Clarinetists became leaders: the clarinet was used to ride over the ensemble of a big band. In Goodman's hands, it was a virtuoso instrument. Goodman extended its range, as on his famous Carnegie Hall solo on "Sing Sing Sing." He sounded cool, contained even as he was playing a solo on "It Had to Be You." There he uses a beautifully controlled terminal vibrato, rising gracefully into the higher register. He could keep his poise even while floating above the band in a climactic final chorus, while paraphrasing exquisitely the melody of "Body and Soul," and while playing a rushed, expectant first chorus on the trio version of "After You've Gone" (BMG/Bluebird). Goodman also kept his technique— and swing—intact over a long career: his 1958 "The World Is Waiting for the Sunrise," recorded live in Brussels, is as exciting as his thirties recordings (Columbia).

Artie Shaw had a fruitier sound but comparable control. His hits were mostly unexpected: they included "Frenesi," hardly a typical jazz piece, his threatening theme song "Nightmare," and "Begin the Beguine," the wonderfully wrought long-form Cole Porter composition. Shaw could play more convincingly higher in the clarinet's range than anyone before him, and yet, with his liquid tone, he never sounded obsessed with technique. He rarely swung Goodman style. Although he could be conventionally exciting when pushed by a Buddy Rich or Dave Tough, his best solos are artful variations on midtempo pieces. The divine elegance of Artie Shaw's "Star Dust," the seeming simplicity and suavity of his "Begin the Beguine," may have been difficult to duplicate, but reed players tried. There were clarinetist leaders less well known than Shaw or Goodman such as Woody Herman, whose clarinet playing, especially on blues, remains underrated, and eventually Jerry Wald.

Jimmy Dorsey's technical accomplishments on both clarinet and alto saxophone perhaps exceeded his forcefulness as an improviser, but he was influential on, among others, Charlie Parker. One can hear his liquid, rounded tone and his fluent phrases with their almost flippant grace notes on the 1938 "I Can't Face the Music." The controlled rush upward of his phrase on "I Cried for You" during the same year is as impressive as is the ability to move gracefully all over the clarinet on the up-tempo "I Got Rhythm." Yet his playing always sounds unsurprising as well as cleanly accomplished.

Buster Bailey's playing is similar. Bailey played with Fletcher Henderson beginning in 1924 and in the mid-thirties could be heard with the Mills Blue Rhythm Band. His greatest impact came from his years with bassist John Kirby's sextet, 1937–46. Bailey sounded more comfortable in this restrained ensemble, playing sweetly voiced classically derived numbers, than with Henderson. The sextet opposed his clarinet to the hotter trumpet of Charlie Shavers. The basis of Kirby's appeal was in the lyrical decorousness of his arrangements, the band's air of distinction, and light swing. There was also their humor, as we hear on "I Love You Truly." One can exaggerate its coolness: the band's repertoire included eccentrically named virtuoso numbers such as "Rehearsin' for a Nervous Breakdown," but also suavely swinging pieces such as "Paper Moon." Bailey's clarinet did sound more technically accomplished than revelatory.

Lester Young's clarinet playing was another thing entirely. He did not seem to take it seriously. He avoided virtuosic displays, yet became one of the clarinet's most expressive players. He played clarinet on the 1938 "I Want a Little Girl" and "Pagin' the Devil" only because producer Milt Gabler asked him to. Yet his vulnerable tone, his beautifully directed solos and fetchingly modest ensemble work, seemed to suggest a new direction for the clarinet. Years later, Jimmy Giuffre would follow Young's lead.

There seems to be no inevitable reason for the decline of the clarinet in the bebop era: after the war, Goodman was still playing brilliantly, Herman had emerged, and Ellington still regularly featured clarinetists, including eventually the distinguished Jimmy Hamilton. (Hamilton was featured on many Ellington pieces: I'd particularly recommend his playing, and that of his sectionmate Russell Procope, on *Tout Suite*.) Younger players such as Sam Most, Tony Scott, and Buddy DeFranco were playing on 52nd Street, and the New Orleans stalwart Edmond Hall was making his own recordings. The stress on small bands didn't necessarily doom the clarinet: Armstrong went back to a New Orleans–style group that featured Barney Bigard. With hindsight, one can deduce reasons for the instrument's relative eclipse, beginning with the fact that Charlie Parker was a saxophonist, and every young player wanted to be like Parker. Rhythm and blues became a force in the mid-forties: it was the honking, wailing saxophone of men like Louis Jordan that was favored. Parker preferred difficult lines with a minimum of arrangement. A saxophone and a trumpet can play "Ornithology" and "Anthropology" in unison with some balance. In the same circumstance, the clarinet sounds thin.

The popular dominance of Goodman and Shaw might have made the instrument seem simultaneously intimidating and old hat. Their smooth techniques seemed to define the instrument, but bebop rewarded angularity and unexpected accents. Benny Goodman could put a rasp into his tone, but by the early forties the effect sounded artificial. Unlike Edmond Hall or the revivified Sidney Bechet, the new clarinetists were playing with a contained sound. Compared to Parker, to say nothing of Louis Jordan, they sounded distant. Was it a mistake for clarinetists to have purified their tones?

We have relatively few examples of bebop clarinet playing, and the leading lights of the forties were not clarinetists. Clarinetists recorded—Tony Scott led a 1944 date with Dizzy Gillespie, Ben Webster, and Sarah Vaughan! On Scott's bopping "Ten Lessons With Timothy," Scott adds a burr, a hint of a growl à la Goodman, in the last bars of his solo. He seems to be reaching for notes to extend the chords, straining for the boppish quality that doesn't yet come naturally. Perhaps it never did. Scott made several successful recordings, including his *Music for Zen Meditation* (Verve) in another genre entirely. John LaPorta can be heard with Charlie Parker on a live "Hot House," but this excellent musician sounds exposed and unsure in this dynamite company. A young Swedish Goodman acolyte, Stan Hasselgard, demonstrated briefly that he was moving toward bop. He died prematurely in 1948, leaving behind a handful of promising recordings. His promise may have been partially fulfilled by another Swedish clarinetist, Putte Wickman, whose early recordings include swing numbers, "Liza" and "Blue Skies," but also newer-style pieces such as "Boppin' at the Dodge." A 1988 duet recording with bassist Red Mitchell finds Wickman playing a slyly oblique "Sweet Georgia Brown," in which he never quite states the melody and, with a pure tone and smooth technique, plays often pianissimo choruses with boppish note choices, all in an informal, conversational style (Dragon).

The dominant figure in this shrinking world of postwar clarinet playing is nonetheless Buddy DeFranco. DeFranco had no intention of being revolutionary: he made a recording of Shaw and Goodman favorites, and he opined that Shaw's "Star Dust" was the greatest clarinet solo on record. DeFranco took the high-flying solo on Tommy Dorsey's "Opus No. 1" (BMG/Bluebird). His early recordings, such as the 1945 "Serenade to a Pair of Nylons," are in the tradition of

Artie Shaw's Gramercy Five—except for the choice of notes. By 1945 DeFranco was already modernist, if not entirely in his accenting. In 1949 DeFranco sounds completely up-to-date on George Russell's experimental "A Bird in Igor's Yard." By the mid-fifties, he was making his most distinctive records, including the ones featuring pianist Sonny Clark. This quartet attacks "Now's the Time" on a run, with DeFranco playing with his typical bright fluency and billowing beat (Mosaic). On ballads, DeFranco is a decorative but not meretricious player. He adds a series of grace notes to the swiftest passages: he also bends and inflects his held notes tastefully.

DeFranco, whose own career has been checkered, did not bring back the clarinet. The instrument was virtually sidelined in bebop's heroic era, but Parker's innovations had an interesting, delayed effect, as his influence prompted experimentation of all kinds. In the late forties and fifties, first Lennie Tristano and then others (including Charles Mingus featuring John LaPorta) tried out free improvisations, and some arrangers worked with new instruments, French horns, flutes—and in some cases, clarinets. As "cool" became a label for a style of progressive jazz, the clarinet found a place again with the soft-spoken Jimmy Giuffre.

Texas-born reed player Giuffre plays mostly in the midrange of the clarinet in a cleanly articulated murmur. He rebelled against the fast-moving chord changes of bop—he called them "vertical prisons"—and against "the insistent pounding of the rhythm section." Swing was an effect, not an absolute end, with Giuffre, as we hear on the 1956 "Two Kinds of Blues," which he introduces with a subdued call on the clarinet. The piece begins with a slow, out-of-tempo, conversation between clarinet and guitar, then moves into a gently swinging middle section: eschewing the wild accents of bop and the thrusting virtuosity of swing era clarinet, Giuffre creates a new, folksy, unimposing image of the instrument (*The Jimmy Giuffre Clarinet*, Atlantic). Giuffre was interested in sonorities. He arranged "The Sheepherder" as a trio for his own B-flat clarinet, for alto clarinet, and for bass clarinet. The clarinetist Perry Robinson, who played a restrained, folksy kind of free jazz, was influenced by Giuffre's approach.

The bass clarinet had been used in jazz before, by Harry Carney in the Ellington band, for instance. In 1964 Buddy DeFranco recorded *Blues Bag* on bass clarinet. In the fifties and sixties, Eric Dolphy made it one of his specialties. If Giuffre was willing to remain a "tangent" of jazz, Dolphy extended its mainstream with his angular, postbop phrasing, his odd choices of notes, his habit of entering a solo from an unexpected place harmonically. He was fluent without ever seeming smooth. He featured the bass clarinet on a repeatedly recorded, tour-de-force solo version of "God Bless the Child," on which he alternates a swirling arpeggiated pattern with fragments of Billie Holiday's melody. The angularity broke away from Parker: it also seemed to fit the clarinet (Prestige).

Anthony Braxton thought so: his style is a development in angularity out of Dolphy, as well as a reaction against the unparalleled intensity of Coltrane. In Chicago in the late sixties, musicians such as Roscoe Mitchell, Joseph Jarman, and Braxton were investigating sonorities through a wide variety of reed instruments. Clarinets became part of the mix again, perhaps especially because they were not seen as bop instruments or part of the newer music defined by Coltrane. Braxton used the clarinet in a way that brings out once again its register break, its spiky contrasts. He also introduced occasional solos on the contrabass clarinet, an instrument whose subterranean rumbles seem unlikely to catch on elsewhere (Arista).

Avant-garde music avoids smoothly flowing melodies: as Stravinsky demonstrated in his three solo pieces for clarinet, the clarinet is an excellent vehicle for reproducing the jagged edges of contemporary compositions. When Jimmy Giuffre made a "free jazz" recording, his *Free Fall* (Columbia), he changed his restrained style: "Propulsion" opens with a sweeping phrase across the registers, and much of his ensuing improvisation features large skips in pitch. German clarinetist Rolf Kuhn demonstrated similar daring in his *Impressions of New York* (Impulse). Today, clarinetist Don Byron seems to have two techniques to go along with two sides of his repertoire: when he is re-creating the music of John Kirby or Raymond Scott, he plays with a controlled tone and keeps his fingers close to the keys in the prescribed classical manner. Improvising freely, his fingers flap and he allows a certain wildness of tone to enter his playing. Byron, who grew up in Brooklyn, has said that his choice of the clarinet was considered eccentric among jazz fans in his neighborhood. The clarinet has not made it all the way back into the mainstream.

It is not forgotten, however. The success of the World Saxophone Quartet may have spurred the eighties performances of Clarinet Summit, a four-clarinet group that matched Ellington stalwart Jimmy Hamilton with younger players David Murray, John Carter, and Alvin Batiste. Later, John Carter made an enormous contribution with his suites (including *Castles of Ghana* and his solo clarinet work *A Suite of Early American Folk Pieces,* both on Gramavision). The musical possibilities suggested by the World Saxophone Quartet underlie the Trio de Clarinettes, led by French clarinetist Louis Sclavis, whose sometimes free, sometimes composed, and often lyrical work can be heard on *Green Dolphy Street* (Enja).

The clarinet is represented in virtually every style. Bob Wilber still performs the Bechet repertoire. New Orleans–based Alvin Batiste performs a mixture of musics, including down-home blues, on his Albert system clarinet, as does Dr. Michael White, also of New Orleans. Kenny Davern and Ron Odrich do their part to sustain the clarinet in mainstream jazz. Eddie Daniels was first heard as a tenor saxophonist who doubled on clarinet. He subsequently made a series of brilliant, boppish recordings that showed his fluency, control, and inventiveness, as on *To Bird With Love* (GRP). In the sixties, British clarinetist Tony Coe was frequently heard with the Kenny Clarke–Francy Boland Big Band: he is alternately fluent and deliberately awkward on "Fellini 712," as if he wants to avoid the Goodman effect (MPS).

Boppers Phil Woods and Paquito D'Rivera double on clarinet, D'Rivera particularly to bring out aspects of his Cuban heritage of music. Avant-garde player Marty Ehrlich performs on B-flat and bass clarinets and also writes for multiple clarinets. Whereas Braxton and in his own way Byron appreciate the wildness the instrument can introduce, Ehrlich emphasizes its classical, restrained sound. The blend of the clarinet sound with strings is at the core of his ensemble, Dark Woods. He exploits different techniques in different pieces: we hear his beautifully controlled arpeggiated patterns on his "Thickets" (New World). Don Byron's influence is felt in various attempts to bring back the particularly exotic, flamboyant clarinet playing of the klezmer tradition. If no one today is particularly exploiting the sweet reasonableness, the gentle romance, that is one of the clarinet's possibilities, the instrument's unique variety of sounds, its ability to be hot or cool, to sound controlled or wild, smooth or spiky, will ensure its use among the adventurers of jazz.

The Saxophone in Jazz

Don Heckman

Adolphe Sax was, by every indication, a dreamer. And an ambitious one, at that. But it's doubtful that the Belgian musician-inventor, even in his most visionary fantasies, ever imagined the impact that his most successful invention—the saxophone—would have upon the world. Ironically, the instrument's birth was almost accidental. It happened in 1841, when Sax was developing a family of valved brass that he called "Saxhorns"—similar to today's tubas, flugelhorns, and baritone horns.

Sometime during the working process, Sax experimentally attached a bass clarinet mouthpiece (and reed) to an ophicleide, a brass instrument with keys instead of valves. Intrigued by the results, he explored further and, in 1842, produced a bass saxophone in the key of C. On February 3, 1844, it was heard for the first time in concert in a demonstration with a chamber wind ensemble. The performer was Sax, and the performance was impressive.

He patented his invention and quickly signed an exclusive contract with the French army to supply saxhorns and saxophones for their various bands. By 1846 he had produced an entire family of saxophones—seven in F and C, and seven in E flat and B flat. Interestingly,

Benny Carter, c. 1941. Courtesy Frank Driggs Collection.

surviving instruments from the mid-1800s reveal a device remarkably similar to contemporary saxophones—a tribute to Sax's genius in creating an instrument that, from its very inception, has had virtually limitless potential for expressive use.

What does all this have to do with the saxophone in jazz? Quite a bit, actually, on several counts. The blended parentage of the saxophone—a brass instrument on one side, a reed instrument on the other—resulted in a musical machine with unusually broad possibilities. Capable of sounding with the declamatory bravura of the brass family, it also could be subdued to the subtle tonal gradations of the woodwind instruments.

Its relatively late arrival—compared to the other instruments of jazz—meant that it had few definitive classical references. Saxophone virtuosi did indeed arrive on the scene, and the instrument began to find a position in the classical repertoire: orchestrally, for example, in the alto saxophone solo in Bizet's score for the opera *L'Arlesienne*, in Richard Strauss's *Domestic Symphony*—which includes a saxophone quartet—and works by Berlioz, Meyerbeer, Massenet, Saint-Saëns, and others, and in solo compositions such as Claude Debussy's *Rhapsody* for alto saxophone and chamber orchestra, as well as works by Ibert, Milhaud, and Villa-Lobos. But it never became either visible or weighty enough in the classical literature for a specific sound and technique to be become dominant. Even today, young jazz saxophonists, unlike clarinet, trumpet, and trombone players, rarely have their early training framed within a large body of classical music references.

This is not to say that there was a complete absence of stylistic parameters. The saxophone's initial star soloists, nearly all French, played with a clear, focused sound and a virtuosic technique that reached up into the altissimo register, an octave and more above the standard key range. But the saxophone sounds first heard in this country were generally associated with the then hugely popular music of concert and military bands—among them the bands led by Patrick Gilmore and, especially, John Philip Sousa.

Almost simultaneously, the saxophone became a prime element in vaudeville novelty acts. There were saxophone ensembles of every stripe, from clown groups to all-female aggregations, the Saxophone Highlanders, and—the most famous vaudeville saxophone act—the Six Brown Brothers. Combining the instrument's inherent tonal flexibility with its rapid-fire technical potential, acts such as these soon established the saxophone's capacity to create sounds and methods reaching past the narrow outlines of the French classical style.

This capacity to speak in so many voices, as well as the relative ease with which the fundamentals of the instrument could be learned, led to the widespread popularity (primarily due to the amazing virtuosity of vaudeville performer Rudy Wiedoeft) in the 1920s of the C-melody saxophone. Because of its pitch, one whole tone above the more standard B-flat tenor saxophone, the C-melody instrument could read from piano sheet music, creating a potential for easygoing, living room saxophone and piano duets. How popular was it? Here's one example: the Buescher Company—with Conn and Martin the most important of the early U.S. saxophone manufacturers—generated a sales campaign that proclaimed that instrument purchasers would experience "Popularity Plus! The glad hand of welcome everywhere!"

Although it may not have seemed so at the time, the combination of flexible tonal resources, a fairly short learning curve, and the lack of any particularly influential role model made the saxophone an unusually appropriate instrument for jazz. It could sing with vocal suppleness, suddenly shift timbres, and sound different when played by different performers—all qualities that served well the sense of individualism that would become such a critical factor in the art of jazz.

Despite this, however, the saxophone was not immediately embraced by the early practitioners of jazz. The reason, one suspects, is that, in early New Orleans jazz groups, both the instrumentation and the roles played by individual instruments evolved from the structure of nineteenth-century band music. The strong-voiced trumpet played the lead; the clarinet contributed harmony, a counterline, or a melodic ornamentation; the trombone played another counterline, one that provided harmonic and rhythmic support; the tuba and drums added a foundation of metric rhythm.

Saxophones periodically found their way into this fairly well defined musical formation (by 1919, clarinetist Larry Shields occasionally played alto saxophone with the Original Dixieland Jazz Band). And various-sized saxophone ensembles—ranging from Paul Whiteman's two-altos section of the early twenties to the more standard trio of saxophones (sometimes two altos and tenor; sometimes alto, tenor, and baritone)—became a regular element in the dance bands of the time. By mid-decade, doubling was rampant, and many saxophone sections featured catalogs of saxophone and woodwind instruments, with players seated behind banks of soprano, alto, tenor, baritone, and bass saxophones, clarinets, flutes, and oboes.

It remained for soprano saxophonist (and clarinetist) Sidney Bechet to break the instrument out of its still indistinct jazz state and establish it as one of the primary entries in the pantheon of jazz voices. His playing, along with that of tenor saxophonist Coleman Hawkins, paved the way for the instrument—in its various forms—to surface as the music's standard bearer for innovation and change.

The Manifestations of the Beast

The use of the saxophone in jazz has been almost completely limited to four instruments: the B-flat soprano, the E-flat alto, the B-flat tenor, and the E-flat baritone. In its brief season of prominence, the C-melody saxophone—essentially a slightly higher-sounding tenor—had a vital, if not generally acknowledged, influence through the playing of Frankie Trumbauer.

Among the other configurations, the large, unwieldy bass saxophone in B flat experienced a flurry of activity in the twenties and thirties, principally in the work of Adrian Rollini. In the forties it was effectively used by Joe Rushton and, especially, Charlie Ventura. More recently, its elephantine sound has been present in the work of Scott Robinson (who also plays the contrabass saxophone), the players of the Art Ensemble of Chicago, and Los Angeles's Vinny Golia.

At the north end of the spectrum, the high sopranino in E flat (pitched an octave above the alto) has popped up occasionally in the hands of avant-gardists such as Anthony Braxton and Joseph Jarman and of Japanese saxophonist Sadao Watanabe, as well as in the large-group arrangements of orchestrators such as John Clayton.

And Rahsaan Roland Kirk has to be credited with adding such oddities as the manzello, the saxello, and the stritch to the battery of jazz saxophones. The manzello (so named by Kirk) is one of his modifications of the saxello, a variant on the soprano produced in the twenties by King Instruments. The stritch is a Kirk adaptation of a straight E-flat alto produced by Buescher.

Finally, there is one of the most unusual saxophone manifestations ever to make its way into jazz (or any other kind of music)—the slide saxophone, a kind of hybrid amalgamation of the saxophone and the trombone. Its key exponent was Snub Mosely, who played the awkward device with intonation that can most charitably be described as shaky.

Given this array of instrumental resources, it is not surprising that the history of the saxophone in jazz encompasses such a startling assortment of styles, attitudes, and sheer aural inventiveness. A brief list of the key names responsible for the creation of that assortment has to include soprano saxophonists Bechet, Steve Lacy, and John Coltrane; alto saxophonists Johnny Hodges, Benny Carter, Charlie Parker, Lee Konitz, Eric Dolphy, Ornette Coleman, Hank Crawford, and David Sanborn; tenor saxophonists Coleman Hawkins, Lester Young, Stan Getz, Sonny Rollins, John Coltrane, Wayne Shorter, and Michael Brecker; and baritone saxophonists Harry Carney, Serge Chaloff, Pepper Adams, and Gerry Mulligan.

But the manner in which that history has unfolded—like all histories—is filled with unexpected starts and stops, twists and turns. Here are a few of the key points and passages.

Coming in by the Back Door

As noted above, the saxophone was not often heard in the early New Orleans ensembles that defined the first jazz bands. Its pathway into jazz, in fact, was circuitous.

The route led through the dance bands that were arriving in the early years of the century. When Ferde Grofé, among others, began to write arrangements in the mid-teens for the Art Hickman Orchestra in San Francisco, he used the two-saxophone section as a harmonized unit to intersperse between solos and to counter the trumpet and trombone sections. A few years later, when Grofé moved on to the Paul Whiteman Orchestra, the sounds that emerged—usually called symphonic jazz, but closer to the "sweet" sounds of society dance orchestras—were widely examined, producing a powerful impact upon such young bandleaders as Fletcher Henderson, Duke Ellington, Jean Goldkette, et al. By the mid-twenties, Don Redman (also a fine alto saxophonist) was expanding the role of the saxophone section for Henderson and McKinney's Cotton Pickers.

The music that resulted from the interplay between sections of saxophones, trumpets, trombones, and rhythm was enormously varied, even if one only considers the diversity between, say, the Ellington, Henderson, and Count Basie orchestras. As a framework, it was sturdy, versatile, and useful—so useful that it has remained an essential aspect of big jazz bands into the present. Its success positioned the saxophone within jazz in a fashion that had never happened in New Orleans–style instrumentation. And it opened the portal for the arrival of innovative players and, through them, the debut of the saxophone as a major jazz voice.

Of course, this meant that the saxophone had to step out of the ensemble and take its place as a solo instrument. And, in that sense, it was subject to the same developmental process that affected the other jazz instruments.

Melody or Harmony: Vertical or Linear

Improvisation doesn't just appear. It has to begin someplace. And in the very earliest years of jazz (and, to some extent, into the present), there was no consensus of where that starting place should be. The legendary trumpeter Buddy Bolden, whose late nineteenth-century group is thought by many to be the first jazz band, reportedly (no one knows for sure, since there are no surviving recordings of his work) improvised via the use of melodic ornamentation. That is, he played traditional or popular melodies, paraphrasing and decorating them with personalized twists and turns rather than inventing new melodies over the fundamental harmonies.

By the early twenties, improvisation based upon newly created melodies rather than paraphrase built upon the underlying chords of a theme began to appear. And the arrival of trumpeter Louis Armstrong in the early years of the decade, first with Henderson, later with his own Hot Fives, provided a firm stamp of authority to this style of improvising.

But the paraphrasing, melodic improvisational style never quite disappeared. It was simply transformed. Instead of decorating and ornamenting existing melodies, it became adaptive, assimilating the notion of chordal-based improvisation, while retaining a melodic flow, floating over the harmonies instead of specifically outlining them.

Blues and the City

There was another pivotal feature present in these two streams of improvisation. The vertically oriented, chordal style tended to have urban roots and was identified with the technically sophisticated players centered around New York City. The linear approach, with its blues resonances, was more connected to the loosely swinging, blues-derived styles that emerged from Kansas City and the Midwest in the twenties and thirties. These parallel approaches to improvisation vitally impacted the saxophone in jazz. And the division between the two approaches can be seen—sometimes prominently, sometimes in a more subliminal fashion—throughout the music's changing stylistic eras.

Saxophonist Coleman Hawkins, arguably one of the instrument's handful of seminal progenitors, can best be delineated as a vertical player. His revered version of "Body and Soul" (1939), as well as his much earlier reworking of "One Hour" (1929), established, for many musicians of the period, an irresistible, harmonically lush, baroque-like method of architectonic improvising.

But Hawkins must also be given credit for getting the whole

process of jazz saxophone off the ground in the first place. His initial recordings with the Henderson orchestra are almost comedic sounding (he reportedly found them repugnant in retrospect), filled with slap-tonguing and herky-jerky lines. That he was able, within a few years, to produce a solo of the quality of "One Hour" is testimony to an uncommon musical imagination (and, perhaps, to the effect Louis Armstrong was having upon the musicians of the twenties).

Hawkins very quickly became one of the most imitated performers in jazz, with players such as Chu Berry, Herschel Evans, Vido Musso, Ike Quebec, Al Sears, Buddy Tate, Flip Phillips, and dozens of others following wholeheartedly—in their own unique ways—in his footsteps. Ben Webster, with a musical mind of his own, took what he could use from the Hawkins legacy and adjusted it to his own lush and breathy sound; Bud Freeman combined elements of Hawkins with the brisk precision of the Chicago players affected by Bix Beiderbecke; and Don Byas bridged the gap between Hawkins and the bebop ingredients that were interfacing in the early forties.

Lester "Pres" Young took a different turn in the path. Touring with bands such as Walter Page's Blue Devils, Bennie Moten, and others, his playing evolved from the laid-back, blues-based swing of the ensembles that worked out of Kansas City. Building solos from long, lean lines and repeated, rifflike motivic fragments, his method was procedural and linear rather than vertical and architectonic. He started out as an alto player and identified Trumbauer and (amazingly) Jimmy Dorsey as influences, and, at least in one sense, there is a similarity of timbre—a focused, classical sound in which vibrato is minimized.

"Trumbauer was my idol," he once told the late Leonard Feather, former jazz critic of the *Los Angeles Times*. "I tried to get the sound of a C-melody sax on a tenor; that's why I don't sound like other people. Trumbauer always told a little story, and I liked the way he slurred the notes."

Maybe so, but the feeling of flow, the stunning capacity to superimpose invented melodies, constructed from often extremely basic thematic segments (clearly present in early solos such as "Lady Be Good," from 1936), was very much a product of Young's own creativity. Jazz historian Gunther Schuller put it precisely right when he described Young's soloing as "a minimum of activity with a maximum of expression."

But Young's method was not especially honored in the pre–World War II years, when Hawkins's reign was virtually unquestioned. When Young briefly replaced Hawkins in the Henderson orchestra in 1934, he was derided by the other musicians, and Henderson eventually was obliged to fire him. Two years later, he was one of the factors in the success of the Basie orchestra, but his principal influence upon other saxophonists would have to wait until the forties.

The two stylistic streams that were so clearly represented by Hawkins and Young were less apparent in the prewar alto saxophonists. Jimmy Dorsey and Frankie Trumbauer (who, as noted, also played C-melody saxophone) were among the instrument's first prominent soloists. Dorsey's technique was an extension of the fast-fingered showboating of the prejazz saxophone soloists; his solos were filled with rapid runs, multiphonics, and high harmonics. Trumbauer played longer, leaner lines, more vocally expressive than Dorsey's, and ultimately influential upon a number of players, including Young.

The most influential prewar alto saxophone sound was initiated by Johnny Hodges with a style that was rich with elegant, sometimes florid lines, filled with bent notes and glissandos, expressed with a strikingly lush, vocalized sound. He was copied from the moment he joined the Ellington orchestra in 1928, his musical aura resonating through the work of musicians such as Hilton Jefferson, Willie Smith, Russell Procope, Toots Mondello, Woody Herman, and nearly every lead alto saxophonist in the country.

As a matter of fact, it is probably important to note the importance of section playing for saxophonists. Prior to World War II, players generally made their livings playing in sections, and the sound of a saxophone section was set by the lead altoist. What that meant for the other musicians in the section was that they were expected to adjust their sound and their phrasing to synchronize with the lead alto's phrasing, timbre, and rhythmic accents. In that sense, the saxophone section was dissimilar from the trumpet and trombone sections, its differing gradations of the same basic instrument not unlike the grouping of violinlike instruments in the string quartet.

With Hodges as the prototype of choice for most alto players, his style was hard to avoid. Even Benny Carter, a major artist with a distinctive methodology of his own, was impacted to some extent by Hodges. Granting that connection, however, Carter's cooler, less rhapsodic, more gently swinging playing contrasted with Hodges in a fashion not unlike the way Young countered Hawkins.

The Wheel Turns
The advent of Charlie "Bird" Parker in the forties was, by any estimation, a watershed event in jazz history—for the music overall, and

specifically for saxophonists. All saxophonists, that is, since the force of his music was irrepressible, changing players of his own generation and dramatically inspiring generations of players well into the present.

Parker's first recordings with Jay McShann's orchestra are tinged with references to Lester Young and Buster Smith. But they also are quintessentially Parker, solidly assembled using two of the four elemental aspects of his style: a passion for the blues and for melodies shaped by motivic phrases. So innovative and so original were his choruses on "Hootie Blues," "Swingmatism," "The Jumpin' Blues," and "Sepian Bounce" that today they have an almost eerie effect, as though a player from the future had been transported back into the swing surroundings of the McShann aggregation.

The other two elements? The first was Parker's harmonic vision, which opened up basic chord patterns with extensions into the upper partials of the harmonies, as well as adding chromatic passing chords and chord substitutions. Parker described the process by which he first became aware of this potential in a 1949 *Down Beat* article by Michael Levin and John S. Wilson. "I kept thinking there's bound to be something else," he noted, while recounting a 1939 jam session in which he was playing "Cherokee." "I could hear it sometimes, but I couldn't play it." Then, as Levin and Wilson explain, he "suddenly found that by using higher intervals of a chord as a melody line and backing them with appropriately related [chord] changes he could play this thing he'd been 'hearing.' "

The final element in the composite of the Parker style was his perception of rhythm—a sense of time that made a subtle, but crucial transformation of swing era articulation into a more even phrasing approach that became fundamental to bebop and most other postwar forms of jazz.

The outcome of all this, essentially, was a mingling of the two stylistic streams typified by the playing of Hawkins and Young. Parker co-opted the Young method, with its blues allusions, cool sound, understated but propulsive rhythm, and melodic orientation. But he coupled it with the Hawkins harmonic sophistication, with its rich lexicon of altered chords, chromatic changes, and upper-harmony improvising.

The impact upon the saxophonists of jazz was electric. And the legion of Parker acolytes grew rapidly. Some were Parker wannabes, some were Parker clones, some were simply admirers and devotees. All were affected by his extraordinary leap. Like Bach, he summed up the history of the music that preceded him and recast it into his own creative image.

The net result was that, in the decade after the end of World War II, it was difficult to find a saxophonist who was not powerfully influenced by either Parker or Young, or, more commonly, by both. The names are not difficult to recall: Sonny Stitt, Phil Woods, Lou Donaldson, Gigi Gryce, Jackie McLean, Frank Morgan, Charlie Mariano, Cannonball Adderley, Bud Shank, Sonny Criss, and literally dozens of others, among the alto players. And the Parker impact didn't stop there. Tenor players were equally affected (some, in part, by the few recordings Parker did on tenor). Listen to Eddie "Lockjaw" Davis, Don Byas, Dexter Gordon, Wardell Gray, Teddy Edwards, Lucky Thompson, Sonny Stitt (on tenor), Frank Foster, Harold Land, Gene Ammons, James Moody, and Paul Gonsalves, and the Parker/Young echoes are easy to hear.

But the stylistic stream in jazz saxophone playing has never been content to remain merged into a single flow, nor has it coursed at a steady rate. And, despite the eminence of Parker, the Young current found a channel of its own in the forties and fifties. It was apparent fairly early in the work of Gordon, Gray, Budd Johnson, and Paul Quinichette (so similar to Young that he was known as the "Vice-Pres").

The real force of Young's influence first came to the attention of the wider jazz audience with the Woody Herman Four Brothers Band of the late forties. Stan Getz's Young-inspired solo on "Early Autumn" touched listeners outside the jazz arena. And the other tenors in the band—Zoot Sims, Al Cohn, Jimmy Giuffre, Herbie Steward (and, later, Ammons)—emulated Young with the same intensity with which other saxophonists were examining Parker.

Equally significant, Giuffre's "Four Brothers" and Ralph Burns's "Early Autumn" brought a new saxophone section sound—one based upon the combination of three tenor saxophones and one baritone saxophone. It was a combination that never would have worked with players possessing the big, wide-vibrato sound of Hawkins. But with each of the Herman saxophonists using cool-toned, relatively vibratoless Young timbres, the smooth, grainy sound that emerged was so effective that it ruled the Herman book for years to come. Less obviously, it colored saxophone section playing in general, with a Four Brothers–like sound turning up in other bands—Stan Kenton, Buddy Rich, Maynard Ferguson—in which lead alto players in traditional two-alto, two-tenor, and baritone sections adopted a comparably cool and tenorlike tone. (The Basie and Ellington orchestras, their identities already well established, stuck with the more sumptuous textures of the prewar, Hodges-led section style.)

The Herman group, an important saxophone incubator, also provided visibility for Serge Chaloff, one of the first baritone saxophonists to demonstrate that the intricate workings of bebop could be executed on a bigger, more cumbersome instrument. Prior to Chaloff, the baritone had largely been dominated by Harry Carney's pioneering use of the instrument with the Duke Ellington Orchestra. First Ellington, then Billy Strayhorn, recognizing that the baritone—in Carney's hands—had enormous potential for both anchoring the saxophone section harmonies and providing a timbral quality that enriched the sound of the entire orchestra, continually cast it prominently in their compositions and arrangements. The impact of Carney's work upon both the saxophone sections of the swing era and the playing of individual baritone saxophonists was pervasive.

Chaloff was joined, in his quest to take the baritone beyond the orbit of Harry Carney, by Gerry Mulligan. Although he, too, was a bebopper, Mulligan reached into New Orleans jazz, into Carney and Young, to produce a style that would penetrate the West Coast cool jazz of the fifties. By the late fifties, Detroit's Pepper Adams added the final piece to the postwar baritone saxophone style with a rich, intense, hard-driving approach that blended dark, Carney-like textures with the aggressive rhythms and crisp articulation of hard bop. Other baritone players followed, among them Sahib Shihab, Leo Parker, Nick Brignola, Ronnie Cuber, Gary Smulyan, Charles Davis, and Cecil Payne, as well as Sweden's Lars Gullin, Scotland's Joe Temperley, and England's John Surman and Ronnie Ross. Avant-garde practitioners of the instrument include Pat Patrick and Hamiet Bluiett.

Nor was the soprano saxophone completely shut out from the revolutionary innovations precipitated by Parker, Young, and bebop. Dominated for decades by Bechet and, to a somewhat lesser extent, by Hodges, who played in a Bechet-influenced style until he abandoned the instrument in 1940, the soprano made a major transition in the fifties. Steve Lacy, originally motivated by Bechet's music, and a strong New Orleans player, shifted to contemporary jazz, revealing an articulate style tinged with traces of Young. Eclectic to the core, he moved on to a fascination with Thelonious Monk, participation in the avant-garde music of the sixties, and—into the present—a continually probing vision of improvisation. After John Coltrane embraced the instrument in 1960, fully revealing its expressive potential, it became a prime voice for many of the younger players arriving on the scene. One of the most important was Wayne Shorter, who used the soprano prominently in the electric Miles Davis groups of the late sixties, with Weather Report in the seventies, and in a series of impressive duo performances with Herbie Hancock in the nineties.

The work of Lacy, Coltrane, and Shorter served as a watershed for the soprano, with dozens of talented players taking on an instrument often described as difficult to play in tune—an unjust and inaccurate criticism. Among the prominent players: Bob Wilber, who moved easily between a Bechet-influenced traditionalism and a more contemporary approach, Dave Liebman, Canada's Jane Bunnett, Gerry Niewood, Jane Ira Bloom, Roscoe Mitchell, Julius Hemphill, Joseph Jarman, Norway's Jan Garbarek, England's Evan Parker, and crossover artists Grover Washington Jr., George Howard, Ronnie Laws, and Kenny G.

Young's influence continued to be present—if in a more subtle fashion—in the playing of alto saxophonists Art Pepper, Lee Konitz, and Paul Desmond. Each played with a loose-loping phrasing directly descended from Young, as are their melodically oriented improvisations. And Konitz deserves special mention for maintaining a determinedly independent sound and method (encouraged by longtime associate Lennie Tristano) and doing original, envelope-stretching playing during a period when it was nearly impossible for young alto saxophonists to elude the Parker musical persona.

Another Turn of the Wheel

The Parker stream, occasionally mixing and blending with the current from Young, dominated the saxophone world until another division took place, this one recalling—at least for a while—the Hawkins/Young polarity. In the late fifties, two voices rose above the chorus of Parker/Young disciples with calls for a different direction. And, in doing so, they once again created a division in the flow of jazz saxophone history.

Both Sonny Rollins and John Coltrane began as Parker apostles (and each played alto before switching to tenor). Rollins was one of a number of tenors—Benny Golson, Johnny Griffin, Hank Mobley, Gene Ammons—who, while paying allegiance to Parker and Young, retained some of the gruff, thick-toned qualities of Hawkins. These somewhat edgy qualities, combined with a resurgent interest in the blues and gospel music that resulted in a subgenre known as soul jazz, energized bebop with a new adjective and a new, aggressive style; it was called hard bop.

Rollins's path was more individualistic. Blessed with a rich, meaty sound and a stunning harmonic imagination, he used bop as a starting point, then added the buoyant rhythms of the West Indies, an encyclopedic knowledge of classic pop songs, and a whimsical sense of humor.

Coltrane, more introverted, passionately resolved to enlarge his improvisational frontiers, took a route similar to that chosen by Parker when he moved into the upper partials of harmony. Coltrane expanded the concept even more, scouring every possible chordal variant, pushing the limits of the tenor saxophone as he did so.

By 1960 the two players were the dominant voices on the jazz saxophone. But the decade brought others to the plate—most notably alto saxophonist Ornette Coleman, whose arrival in New York City in late 1959 triggered an inordinately fertile, if exceedingly chaotic, interval for jazz and the saxophone. Rollins took a hiatus to consider his options; Coltrane navigated from harmonic improvising through modal playing and into his own grappling with the free playing espoused by Coleman.

At the same time, musicians such as multi-instrumentalist Eric Dolphy, tenor saxophonists Archie Shepp and Albert Ayler, and Chicago avant-gardists including Roscoe Mitchell were also exploring the horizons of free jazz, Wayne Shorter was making a more structured but no less resourceful exploration with Miles Davis, and Rahsaan Roland Kirk was surreptitiously using circuslike multi-instrument playing to foment his own version of an improvisational revolution.

Beyond the U.S. borders, jazz saxophonists—dating back as far as the twenties and thirties via the playing of French artists André Ekyan and Alix Combelle—continued to proliferate. Among the prominent players arriving in the fifties and sixties (in addition to Surman, Ross, Watanabe, and others mentioned above) were England's Danny Moss, Tubby Hayes and Tony Coe, France's Barney Wilen, Belgium's Bobby Jaspar, and the USSR's Vladimir Chekasin and Gennady Gol'shteyn.

It was a heady time for jazz, and for the jazz saxophone. At the other end of the decade, however, lay a very different period. Artists such as Shorter, Charles Lloyd, Joe Henderson, and others carried the Coltrane legacy forward after his death. And Rollins continued—as he did into the nineties—to be a major presence in jazz, neither his imagination nor his vitality dimmed by age.

But electric jazz loomed ahead. Shorter made the best of it with Weather Report, and players such as Michael Brecker, Dave Liebman, and Bill Evans kept the jazz fires burning within the ostinato rhythms and the instrumental high voltage. And a further split in the stream of the jazz saxophone took place with the emergence of smooth jazz, jazz/funk, and all the other variants that really described a kind of pop instrumental music.

Its connection with the mainstream of jazz was intermittent. David Sanborn, Brecker, and Hank Crawford were particularly influential; their distillation of blues and bop elements, combined with an extensive use of the altissimo register and a flexible approach to tone reproduction affected virtually every young player who arrived on the scene after the seventies. In the hands of players such as Sanborn, Brecker, Crawford, Grover Washington Jr., Eddie Harris, and Ronnie Laws, the music's jazz qualities remained strong, even though they strayed far from the Hawkins/Young/Parker axis, their primary association with tradition connecting via John Coltrane. In the hands of players such as Kenny G, Richard Elliot, and Dave Koz, however, a similar sound and style was channeled instead into the tributary of instrumental pop music.

The diminished mainstream that managed to make its way through the seventies and eighties finally began to increase in intensity again in the late eighties and nineties, especially in the playing of the so-called Young Lions. Their work represented a neoclassical fascination with the past as jazz players—urged on by the leadership of Wynton Marsalis—rigorously revisited the music of the forties and fifties.

The most visible saxophonists of the decade—Branford Marsalis, Joshua Redman, Steve Coleman, Greg Osby, Joe Lovano, James Carter—all performed at a superior level of competence, drawing inspiration from Hawkins, Young, Parker, Rollins, and Coltrane in varying composites. Yet none, as yet, has disclosed the urgent drive, the passionate spark of originality, that has been at the heart of all the great creative jazz saxophonists.

What's next? One thing's for sure. It will be hard to top a century as creatively robust as the twentieth was for the jazz saxophone. The route from Adolph Sax's nineteenth-century invention through the slap-tonguing, vaudeville music of this century's early years to the virtuosic, musically sophisticated playing that was being done at the close of the century is comparable in spirit to the journey between the first flight of the Wrights and the voyages of today's space shuttle.

And the journey doesn't end there. With the world rapidly shrinking, with jazz pouring across national and stylistic borders, the jazz saxophone will once again—as it has so often in the past—play a prominent role as the music expands from its American-century roots into its global future.

The Trumpet in Jazz

Randy Sandke

etal trumpets were known in Egypt as far back as the second millennium B.C., but it wasn't until the early nineteenth century that the valved instrument, capable of playing a full chromatic scale, was invented. The cornet, a descendent of the military bugle, developed around the same time. Trumpets and cornets are made of brass and share the same range and technique, differing only in the diameter of their tubing: trumpets have a uniformly cylindrical bore until the flare of the bell, whereas cornets have a constantly expanding "conical" bore. This produces a generally brighter, more penetrating tone on the trumpet and a darker, more rounded tone on the cornet.

Toward the latter half of the nineteenth century the trumpet was the preferred instrument of symphony orchestras, where it played and continues to play a largely subservient role, while the cornet became the leading voice in wind bands. As such, the cornet developed more quickly as a solo instrument, capable of dazzling agility and expressiveness. This was the golden age of the cornet virtuoso as personified by J. B. Arban (author of the method book brass players still cut their teeth on) and Herbert L. Clarke, soloist of the Sousa band.

Clifford Brown, 1953. Photo: Ross Burdick. Courtesy Frank Driggs Collection.

It is against this backdrop that jazz began in New Orleans, a town awash in brass bands and cheap marching band instruments, many left over from the Civil War. And so it was that the first major voice of jazz was a cornetist, the legendary Buddy Bolden.

Whether or not Bolden was the lone genius who single-handedly melded the vocal blues style with the instrumental marching band tradition, ragtime, Creole French and Spanish music, and African-derived rhythms, or whether he was simply the most celebrated exponent of a developing regional style, will remain a mystery. Either way, his influence was profound and indisputable. His brand of extemporized, driving, and heartfelt music became the rage in New Orleans in the years surrounding the turn of the century. Unfortunately Bolden's career was cut short in 1907 when he suffered a mental breakdown.

It is the cornetists of the succeeding generation that we first hear on recordings: players such as Oscar Celestin, Sam Morgan, Freddie Keppard, and Nick LaRocca. Celestin and Morgan stayed in New Orleans and did not record until 1925 and 1927 respectively. Both players share a keen blues sensibility, displayed in the application of vocal techniques to the horn: bending blue notes, growling, creating moaning "wa-wa" effects with a mute, a pronounced vibrato, along with the relaxed rhythmic feel of the blues. The connection between blues singing and early jazz is vividly shown on Sam Morgan's "Short Dress Gal" (Columbia/Jazz Oracle), in which the cornetist sings and plays in a style virtually identical to Mississippi Delta blues.

By contrast, Freddie Keppard and Nick LaRocca exhibit more of a ragtime-military style, playing in short, clipped notes and preferring the sound of the open horn. Keppard was offered the chance to record as early as 1916, but he turned it down because, according to Sidney Bechet, he didn't like seeing the music he loved turned into a business. The distinction of making the first jazz record fell to LaRocca and the Original Dixieland Jazz Band in 1917. It proved to be a smash hit, outselling all previous Victor releases including those of Caruso and Sousa, and did much to stir a national awareness of the new music from New Orleans.

By far the most important of the cornetists of the post-Bolden era was Joseph "King" Oliver. Oliver, like Celestin and Morgan, had a deep affinity for the blues, with all the "singing" inflections that went with it. Like them, he also recorded relatively late in his career, beginning in 1923 at the age of thirty-seven. The records he made, with his Creole Jazz Band, have been beloved by collectors ever since and for many represent the apex of the relaxed but forceful New Orleans style. They also mark the debut of the dynamic twenty-one-year old Louis Armstrong.

Almost from the start Oliver was overshadowed by his protégé, but Armstrong always acknowledged his debt to "Papa Joe." This is clearly shown on Armstrong's famous 1928 recording of "Muggles" (OKeh/Columbia) in which he quotes the first half-chorus of his mentor's solo on "Jazzin' Babies Blues" (OKeh/King Jazz) from 1923. Oliver's direct descendants were Tommy Ladnier and the white Chicago cornetist Muggsy Spanier, whose middle-register styles were preferred by Sidney Bechet over the more assertive Armstrong. Louis couldn't help but dominate every musical situation he encountered, and eventually the jazz world itself.

In 1924, after leaving Oliver's band in Chicago, Armstrong arrived in New York to join the Fletcher Henderson Orchestra. His fame began to spread far and wide after he returned to Chicago the following year and began a series of recordings under his own name: the famous Hot Five and Hot Seven sessions. These were to produce masterpiece after masterpiece, ever expanding the depth and scope of the jazz solo.

The originality of Armstrong's style resulted from a mixture of his own creative genius with an almost childlike openness to any other kind of music that caught his fancy. In 1917 he purchased his first phonograph and began buying opera records by Caruso, Galli-Curci, and others. The drama and grandeur of this music are clearly evident in Armstrong's mature style, somehow managing to complement his deep grounding in the blues. Armstrong already understood harmony and voice-leading from singing in a vocal quartet in the streets of New Orleans as a youngster. The now forgotten commercial trumpeter B. A. Rolfe inspired Louis to explore the upper register of the trumpet. By 1930 Armstrong extended the usable range of the trumpet from the customary upper limit of high C (trumpet key) up a fourth to F.

Armstrong switched from the cornet to the more brilliant-sounding trumpet sometime in the mid-twenties (it was unclear even in Armstrong's recollection exactly what year it was), effectively ending the cornet's dominance in jazz. His technique was largely self-taught; even the way he held the instrument was unique. Armstrong wrapped his right thumb over the first valve casing with his fingers lying flat across the valves, much as blues guitarists extend their thumb over the fingerboard in order to bend strings, contrary to standard technique. He sacrificed a bit of dexterity, but his unique grip allowed him to invent the seamless half-valve gliss. It also gave him his signature vibrato and "shake," the point at which vibrato turns into a trill. All of these innovations would be mere tricks had not Armstrong's unfailing musicality put them to such great effect.

Armstrong's rhythmic freedom, including his use of half-time and double-time figures, had an enormous impact on the musicians of his time. His classical sense of phrasing and proportion within a solo would eventually give way to "notier" styles of a later generation, but his basic sense of swing became the lingua franca of jazz.

The only other player in the twenties to offer a significant jazz style that departed from Armstrong's was the cornetist Bix Beiderbecke. The two were friends and mutual fans, and both took up the idea of a "correlated" solo made up of interlocking phrases, each an answer to the one preceding. However, the results were vastly different, as can be heard on Bix's 1924 recording of "Flock o' Blues" (Gennett/Bix Records) and Louis's "Carolina Stomp" (Columbia/King Jazz) made a year later with Henderson (which, despite the different titles, are in fact the same tune).

Bix, whose premature death resulted in a recording career lasting only six years, was a sensitive, introverted man, burdened by unresolved psychological conflicts and an addiction to alcohol. His music is subtle and complex, at once fiery and delicate but above all lyrical. His moving solo on "Singin' the Blues" (OKeh/Columbia/Bix Records) has been credited as the first recorded example of the jazz ballad. Like Armstrong, Beiderbecke was a self-taught musician whose unorthodox technique only helped to enhance his unique approach. Bix was also a pianist possessing an intimate knowledge of harmony and a taste for the impressionists, which gave his playing a quality of refinement and sophistication.

Of the many cornet stylists of the twenties, Joe Smith, a featured soloist of the Fletcher Henderson Orchestra and Bessie Smith's favorite accompanist, had one of the loveliest sounds. His limpid tone provides an effective contrast to Smith's earthy voice on the latter's recording of "Weeping Willow Blues" (Columbia). He was essentially a romantic player, but ill-health forced him to retire before the lush ballad became popular in jazz. Echoes of Joe Smith can be heard in the work of Charlie Shavers, as on the 1941 recording of "What Is This Thing Called Love?" (HMV/Bluebird) with Bechet.

The most prolific cornetist in the recording studios of the period was Red Nichols. He possessed a distinctive sound and a flawless execution, but his rhythmic approach was rooted in the commercial music of the day, unlike the pacesetters Beiderbecke and Armstrong. During the first years of the Depression he employed a band on radio and recordings that became a kind of preschool of swing for Benny Goodman, Jimmy Dorsey, Glenn Miller, Jack and Charlie Teagarden, and Gene Krupa. Together they made such forward-looking recordings as Miller's arrangement of "Shimme-Sha Wabble" (Brunswick/Jazz Archives).

Duke Ellington and his organization spawned a dynasty of trumpet stylists from the late twenties on. His first discovery was Bubber Miley, whom Ellington encouraged to develop a "growl" style, which combined flutter tonguing, or a rasp in the throat, with the use of a plunger mute. None of this was new to jazz: King Oliver had achieved similar effects using a doorknob or small straight mute, but the combination of Miley's reliance on the technique and Ellington's evocative writing added a new dimension to the music. Miley and Ellington collaborated on many compositions, including "Black and Tan Fantasy" (Victor/Classics), which did much to establish the unique Ellington sound.

When Miley left the band in 1929 he was replaced by Cootie Williams, who further elaborated the growl style and become a wizard of muted effects. He also possessed a singing open horn, and Ellington was fond of showing off both facets of Cootie's playing, as in "Echoes of Harlem" (Brunswick/Classics) and "Concerto for Cootie" (Victor/Bluebird), later retitled "Do Nothin' Till You Hear From Me."

In 1934, Cootie Williams was joined in Ellington's trumpet section by cornetist Rex Stewart, who had apprenticed with Fletcher Henderson. His distinctive contribution to the trumpet vocabulary was a half-valve, almost talking style that Ellington exploited on such features as "Boy Meets Horn" (Brunswick/Columbia). Stewart also invokes a roaring "Menelik (the Lion of Judah)" (HMV/Bluebird) with the aid of pedal tones.

The trumpeter who first formulated the "streamlined" swing style that was to dominate the thirties was Henry "Red" Allen, specifically the Red Allen of the hugely influential Fletcher Henderson recordings of 1933–34 such as "King Porter Stomp" (Vocalion/GRP) and "Down South Camp Meeting" (Decca/GRP). Originally from New Orleans and a singer as well as trumpeter, Allen was brought to New York in 1929 by Victor Records to compete with the enormous success of Louis Armstrong on the OKeh label. At the same time, and for the same reason, Brunswick signed the quirky and sometimes brilliant Jabbo Smith, but mass appeal was to elude them both. Later, up through the 1960s, Allen developed a highly personal and almost uncategorizable style, but it was his work with Henderson that set the tone for the leading lights of the decade: Harry James of the Benny Goodman band, Buck Clayton and Harry "Sweets" Edison of the Count Basie band, and Bunny Berigan, notably with Goodman, Tommy Dorsey, and his own big band.

The font from which all these trumpeters ultimately flowed was still Louis Armstrong. Swing music was the rock-and-roll of its day, with all the attendant frenzy and hype, and these players exhibited the showy, quicksilver fieriness that their screaming fans demanded. Louis was the first to inspire this kind of adulation, meeting the challenge head on as early as 1931 with such potboilers as "Shine" (OKeh/Columbia). But the role of "trumpet star" as sideman was a new phenomenon, and it required an aggressive style, bursting forth in a sudden explosion of energy.

Harry James combined a prodigious technique (he was probably the most accomplished technician to appear on the jazz scene up to this time) with an unabashedly sentimental ballad style, making him one of the most popular trumpeters of his day. His talents are well demonstrated in his famous solo on "Sing Sing Sing" (Columbia) from Goodman's 1938 Carnegie Hall concert. (The solo's one-chord structure makes it an early example of modal playing.)

It is a wonder that Buck Clayton and Sweets Edison were able to sound incendiary and relaxed at the same time, probably owing to the influence of Lester Young, the "teacher" of the Basie band. Both would go on through long careers developing this new hot and cool attitude in their own distinctive ways, and both were also revered vocal accompanists: Buck by Billie Holiday, and Sweets by Nat King Cole, Ella Fitzgerald, and Frank Sinatra.

Bunny Berigan was able to shine in the sideman role, as on Tommy Dorsey's "Marie" (Victor/BMG), and he could also sustain a moving performance through an entire tune, as on his own "I Can't Get Started" (Victor/Classics). On the latter Berigan explores the entire range of the trumpet from low F sharp to the F above high C, all the time maintaining a warm, glowing sound.

Benny Carter, though best known as a saxophonist, contributed one of the most harmonically astute trumpet solos of the swing era. In his rendition of "More Than You Know" (Vocalion/Classics) from 1939, every chordal nuance is deftly defined, and his command of the trumpet is uncanny. As a composer-arranger Carter led the way for other trumpeter-writers such as Sy Oliver, Neal Hefti, Gerald Wilson, and Quincy Jones.

The man who rivaled the dexterity and technical brilliance of James and the passion of Armstrong was Roy Eldridge. In 1936 he took over Red Allen's chair in the Fletcher Henderson band and contributed an impressive solo on "Christopher Columbus" (Vocalion/Classics) that commences on the E flat above high C. From the late thirties into the forties Eldridge alternated leading his own band with duties as featured soloist with Gene Krupa and Artie Shaw. On his own recording of "After You've Gone" (Decca/GRP) he explores the full compass of the trumpet up to the A above high C with lightning speed and flexibility. "Body and Soul" (Decca/GRP) displays his romantic side along with a penchant for odd harmonic turns of phrase.

Dizzy Gillespie came up in the big band era, replacing his idol, Roy Eldridge, in the Teddy Hill band before joining Cab Calloway and Billy Eckstine. During the war years he and a coterie of other iconoclasts such as Charlie Parker and Thelonious Monk developed the new "bebop" style. Their innovations were regarded as so radical that a line in the sand has been drawn ever after between "modern" and "traditional" jazz. After a half century of hindsight it is perhaps easier to recognize more similarities than differences in the various movements in jazz, but there is no disputing that bebop represented startling new harmonic and rhythmic challenges for players and listeners alike.

The harmonic vocabulary of jazz expanded, and horn players, like Gillespie, now needed a working knowledge of keyboard harmony. (Dizzy sat in on piano on Charlie Parker's first date as a leader in 1945.) Gillespie could match Eldridge's range and command of the instrument, adding a new suppleness of rhythm, daringly asymmetrical phrases, and complex chromatically embellished runs executed at breakneck speed. Gone were the ripe, singing vibratos of the swing era and in was a drier, more hard-edged sound.

The epochal association of Gillespie and Charlie Parker began in 1943 when both were members of Earl Hines's big band. In 1945 they recorded together for the first time. Within a period of three months they laid down the conerstone of bop repertoire with such classics as "Hot House," "Shaw 'Nuff," "Groovin' High," and "Salt Peanuts" (Guild/Prestige). The next year Gillespie formed a big band, which remained active until 1949. This band popularized Gillespie's unique synthesis of Afro-Cuban music and jazz with the compositions "Manteca" and "Cuban Be–Cubana Bop" (Victor/Bluebird), though Dizzy's fascination with Latin rhythms was already evident in "A Night in Tunisia" from 1942.

Widespread public acclaim caught up with Gillespie in the fifties. In 1956 he was selected by the U.S. State Department as the first jazz musician to tour as a cultural ambassador, first to the Near and Middle East, and later to South America. In Brazil he discovered the samba, and it too became a staple of the Gillespie repertoire. In Argentina he met pianist Lalo Schifrin, who became a regular member of Dizzy's touring quintet, and in 1960 he commissioned Schifrin to write *Gillespiana* (Verve). Dizzy continued to tour and record for the next three decades; his long and fruitful career ended only months before his death in 1993.

Fats Navarro was Dizzy's equal in technique, possessing a fuller, more radiant tone but a more conjunct, less dramatic approach. His recording career lasted a scant five years (he died of tuberculosis at the age of twenty-six), but it was enough to establish him as one of the great modern trumpeters. Navarro and Howard McGhee, another pioneer of bebop, can be heard sparring together on their 1948 recording of "Double Talk" (Blue Note).

A tragic early death seemed to befall many of the brightest trumpet stars of the modern era. Clifford Brown rose to prominence in a band led by drummer Art Blakey and later one he co-led with Max Roach. Brown had studied mathematics in college and applied the same diligence and determination to his study of music. His manner of articulation was highly original, and he possessed a luminous sound and keen melodic gifts. His solos are full of logic and intensity; his death in a car accident at the age of twenty-five was a severe loss for jazz.

Another brilliant player who had even less chance to reach his full potential was Booker Little. Little was a restless and adventuresome spirit who found a soulmate in saxophonist Eric Dolphy. Together they recorded at the Five Spot (Prestige) in New York only three months before Little succumbed to uremia at the age of twenty-three. In the last two years of his life he recorded four fine albums as a leader, which reveal him as a highly original player and writer, just on the threshold of achieving full maturity.

The new harmonic and rhythmic ideas of modern jazz led to an exploration of extremes: extremes in tempo, range, and dexterity. In this crucible the trumpet lost some of its influence to the less demanding and in some ways more flexible saxophone. It is within this context that Miles Davis stands out as such a revelation and a reminder that the less tangible elements of music are as important as advances in technique, however revolutionary.

Davis began his career at the age of nineteen with the unenviable task of following Gillespie into Charlie Parker's quintet. He realized early on that he could not rival Dizzy and Bird in virtuosity and needed to find his own direction. What he found was in some ways a throwback to the melodic styles of the twenties, but filtered through the harmonic and rhythmic revolutions of his own time. The result was a highly individual style in which elliptical phrases are punctuated by dramatic silence; what is implied seems almost as important as what is stated.

He was the first trumpeter to exploit the new intimacy that the microphone afforded, playing into it as if whispering into a lover's ear. The microphone also allowed him to explore the expressive potential of the Harmon mute.

Davis refined his personal brand of minimalism in a variety of settings: the "Birth of the Cool" nonet; the classic 1955–57 "neobop" quintet with John Coltrane; the 1958–59 "modal" sextet with Coltrane, Cannonball Adderley, and Bill Evans; the Gil Evans orchestral collaborations; and the groundbreaking Herbie Hancock–Wayne Shorter quintet of the sixties. In this last group Davis found colleagues who shared his vision of pushing standard jazz forms to the limits of comprehension. Since Davis was an avocational painter, it is not far-fetched to point out a similarity between him and Picasso: both flirted with total freedom yet never completely surrendered to it.

There were a host of other notable modernists, each with an identifiable sound and point of view. Chet Baker came to prominence in the early fifties as a member of Gerry Mulligan's quartet, which quickly established them both as leading exponents of the West Coast school. Like Bix, he was an often understated "poet" of the horn and unfortunately, similarly self-destructive. Other notable West Coast trumpet stylists include Don Fagerquist, Conte Candoli, and Jack Sheldon.

Art Farmer was a fluid and thoughtful player who, like Miles, applied a melodic inclination to the advanced harmonies of bop. Joe Wilder, in addition to being a graceful and sensitive jazz soloist, was one of the first African-American musicians to work in symphony orchestras, Broadway pit bands, and recording studios. Johnny Coles's bare but evocative style was a favorite of Gil Evans, who used it to advantage on such recordings as *Great Jazz Standards* (Pacific Jazz) and *Out of the Cool* (Impulse).

Clark Terry, a stalwart of the studios as both sideman and leader, combines a technical brilliance with a wailing blues feel in a highly original way. Terry grew up in St. Louis and was an early influence on a teenaged Miles Davis. Both of them, along with Shorty Rogers on the West Coast, helped popularize the flugelhorn. Terry and Clifford Brown were among the first to adapt the double-tongue (or "doodle-tongue") articulation to jazz.

Through the big band era to the present day the usable range of the trumpet has increased ever upward. Section leaders such as Paul Webster of Jimmie Lunceford's band, Snooky Young of Lunceford and Basie (and later the *Tonight Show* band), Cat Anderson with Duke Ellington, and Ernie Royal of Basie and numerous studio recordings encouraged composers and arrangers to exploit their high-note capabilities. Maynard Ferguson, with Stan Kenton and later with his own big bands, did the most to develop a whole style around his phenomenal range, which extended to an F above double high C.

The various bands led by drummer Art Blakey established the most significant trumpet dynasty in modern jazz. His first unit featured Kenny Dorham, whose harmonic inventiveness influenced sax and trumpet players alike. Dorham was followed by Clifford Brown. Later groups included Lee Morgan, a soulful player of great wit, and Freddie Hubbard, who went on to become one of the major voices in jazz of the sixties and seventies. Hubbard displays a warm and vibrant tone as big as the great swing players' yet with a thoroughly modern conception. He is a prodigious technician, and his solos, on both ballads and up-tempo numbers, are full of passion and fire.

Pianist Horace Silver led a series of quintets starting in the early fifties that provided an important showcase for a succession of trumpeters. Many became closely identified with one or more of Silver's compositions: Kenny Dorham with "Doodlin'" and "The Preacher," Donald Byrd with "Señor Blues," Blue Mitchell with "Peace" and "Sister Sadie," and Carmell Jones with "Song for My Father" (all recorded for the Blue Note label).

The free jazz movement owes its genesis largely to the music of Ornette Coleman. On Coleman's seminal recordings he was accompanied by cornetist Don Cherry, who exerted a great influence in his own right. Both led the way in abandoning standard jazz forms (the tyranny of the repeating chorus) and replacing them with open-ended melodic improvisations free to digress in any direction at any moment, but often highly motivic. Cherry integrates solos with written music very successfully in his own composition "Complete Communion" (Blue Note), recorded in 1965. The most notable trumpeter to follow Cherry's lead is Lester Bowie of the Art Ensemble of Chicago and later his own bands, including Brass Fantasy.

John Coltrane left another rich and varied legacy to jazz, and Woody Shaw was the first trumpeter to systematically explore many of the saxophonist's harmonic innovations. Specifically these ideas involved superimposing distantly related chords or cycles of chords over an underlying harmonic pedal point. To spell all this out required an even busier style than bebop, and beats became divided and redivided, often in irregular groups of fives, sevens, nines, etc. Shaw, like Coltrane, was a master at "laying it down" as well as "taking it out," constantly playing one off against the other.

The cornet had never entirely disappeared from jazz. Bobby Hackett was something of an anachronism even in the late thirties when he made his first recordings. He has largely been associated with the neodixieland movement centered around guitarist Eddie Condon, along with fellow cornetists Jimmy McPartland and Wild Bill Davison. But Hackett produced much timeless music that is rich in melodic invention tempered with a thorough harmonic understanding that came from his years as a guitarist (he played both instruments in Glenn Miller's band).

Another cornetist who initially followed along similar lines but developed one of the most fluent and personal styles in jazz is Ruby Braff. Braff's conservatism has left him often overlooked, but he has decisively shown that one can be creative and original while playing within older jazz styles. This lesson was not lost on Warren Vaché, who carries on today in a similar vein yet with a totally distinctive voice.

Modernists did not entirely ignore the cornet either. Nat Adderley (brother of Cannonball) and Thad Jones (brother of Hank and Elvin) had exuberant styles that were not as idiomatic to the instrument as Hackett's or Braff's. Adderley is perhaps the only cornetist who ever favored the upper register of the horn. Jones was an adventurer who liked odd and jagged intervals, which he explored further in his very influential writing, first for Basie and then the Thad Jones–Mel Lewis big band. The cornet is represented more recently in the work of Olu Dara and Graham Haynes.

In the late sixties and on into the seventies, rock threatened to push jazz off the cultural map. Many of the best musicians of the time sought to combine the sophistication of jazz with the raw power of rock. Miles Davis was one of the first to explore this new territory in his 1969 album, *Bitches Brew* (Columbia). He also began applying some of the new electronic effects developed for the guitar to the trumpet, including echo devices and the wah-wah pedal (which ironically was originally inspired by the plunger-muted trumpet).

Randy Brecker took these new developments a step further in his work with the Brecker Brothers band (Arista/One Way) in the mid-seventies. He developed a technique of combining the natural sound of the trumpet with a full panoply of electronic devices such as pitch-shifters, phasers, compressors, etc., effectively utilizing these new timbres over intricate funk rhythms. Throughout his career Brecker has also remained connected to the modern mainstream tradition, as has his contemporary, Tom Harrell. Harrell's consistently fluent and tasteful playing can be heard on recordings with Bill Evans, with Phil Woods, and several under his own name.

Don Ellis was a rare combination of trumpeter, composer, and visionary in the sixties to mid-seventies. He had worked and recorded with George Russell and Maynard Ferguson before founding his own big band. It featured an unorthodox instrumentation (two drum sets and three basses) and was largely devoted to Ellis's explorations of unusual time signatures. He was fond of meters in five, seven, and nine, as well as such exotic combinations as 27/16. He was a fiery soloist, playing on a custom-built four-valve trumpet (the fourth valve enabling him to play quarter tones).

The eighties dawned with the arrival of another Blakey discovery, Wynton Marsalis, who almost overnight achieved a celebrity status unprecedented in the jazz world. By 1982 he had a contract with Columbia, and in 1983 and again in 1984 he won Grammy Awards in both classical and jazz categories. By dint of his classical training he set a new technical standard for the jazz trumpet, and his devotion to acoustic jazz sparked a whole rebirth in interest. In 1987 he was appointed artistic director of Jazz at Lincoln Center in New York, and in 1997 he received the Pulitzer Prize for his composition *Blood on the Fields*. In all his creative work, as performer, composer, band leader, and concert producer, Marsalis seems less concerned with exploring new territory than with summing up the jazz tradition as he sees it (which includes just about everything except fusion and the avant-garde).

Wynton Marsalis has helped nurture the careers of many of the best of the new trumpeters around today, such as his fellow Blakey alumnus Terence Blanchard, who is a formidable technician and powerful voice in his own right. Other more recent arrivals on the scene include the spirited Roy Hargrove, Nicholas Payton, who has a deep respect and understanding of the trumpet tradition going back to Armstrong, and Ryan Kysor, 1990 winner of the prestigious Thelonious Monk competition.

Other young trumpeters have struck out on their own course, but inspired by specific role models. One of the first was Jon Faddis, the disciple and practically adopted son of Dizzy Gillespie. Faddis has become the premier high-note soloist of today, and in 1992 he was named artistic director of the Carnegie Hall Jazz Band. Wallace Roney follows the lead of Miles Davis, and Tim Hagans continues to expand upon the Woody Shaw legacy.

One of the most fascinating amalgamation of styles to appear in recent years is that of Dave Douglas. In his work with John Zorn and his own various groups, Douglas combines a brilliant technique with Don Cherry's freedom and sonic range and Louis Armstrong's openness to all forms of music.

Today the jazz trumpet tradition has spread throughout the globe via international schools and festivals and the ubiquitous availability of recorded jazz. Over the years many American trumpeters, such as Bill Coleman, Benny Bailey, and Art Farmer, have taken up residence in foreign countries. Virtually every American jazz musician active over the last fifty years has made numerous trips overseas and, indeed, depends on such exposure for a livelihood. The inevitable result of all this close contact is that world-class players have cropped up almost everywhere. A small sampling might include Terumasa Hino from Japan, James Morrison from Australia, Kenny Wheeler from Canada (though now living in England), Till Brönner from Germany, Franco Ambrosetti from Switzerland, Enrico Rava from Italy, and Brazil's Claudio Roditi, Cuba's Arturo Sandoval, Viet Nam's Cuong Vu, and Russia's Valery Ponomarev (the last four currently living in the United States). Many of these players draw upon their native musical backgrounds to further extend the boundaries of jazz.

Nor is jazz the exclusive province of men, as such accomplished female players as Stacy Rowles and Ingrid Jensen make abundantly clear.

Obviously there is no lack of talent on the jazz scene today. However, the climate of conservatism that has dominated the jazz world since the eighties seems at odds with further artistic development and renewal. Critical and commercial rewards have gone most often to those comfortable working within the established tradition, and the importance of forging a unique identity and blazing new trails (formerly the prerequisites of becoming a "jazz star") is now often overlooked.

Some believe that an exhaustion of musical resources accounts for this trend, but I strongly disagree. I believe that jazz is increasingly driven by marketing rather than musical interests, and it is always easier to sell a known quantity than an unknown. Art grows in even the most hostile environments but for now, commerce seems to be calling the tune.

The Trombone in Jazz

Gunther Schuller

The trombone is the only instrument in the Western music tradition that is virtually unchanged in its basic construction (shape and size) and technical function since its first appearance in the late fifteenth century. All other instruments—whether the violin, the organ, or even the trumpet—have experienced important changes or physical additions (such as valves on trumpets). Although a valve trombone was developed eventually in the early nineteenth century, it never replaced in classical music or in jazz the so-called slide trombone, the instrument with which this article will be primarily concerned.

Thus, given the trombone's stable and venerable history, it is somewhat ironic that it was originally developed as an offshoot of the Renaissance slide trumpet, in use in late medieval music, extending the brass family's registral range to the tenor and baritone regions. Moreover, from its very beginnings the trombone, with its inherent agility of movement and potential freedom from fixed pitches (a limitation, for example, for valved or keyed instruments), was considered no less versatile than a violin or cornetto. This goes a long way toward explaining the instrument's central and consistent place in the music literature of the last five hundred years.

This intrinsic versatility also accounts for the prominent role the trombone has played in jazz from its inception and even in its prehistory, rivaled only by the trumpet and possibly the clarinet. Late nineteenth-century ragtime ensembles, the concert bands prevalent all over the United States and the Americas, and especially the brass and parade bands so popular in New Orleans around the turn of the century all featured the trombone in a variety of musical functions, ranging from soloistic to accompanimental, from individual to ensemble roles. Thus it cannot come as a surprise that in the earliest manifestation of jazz (i.e., the New Orleans collective ensemble style) the trombone was a preeminent, indispensable member of the so-called three-instrument front line: cornet (or trumpet), clarinet, and trombone. In that typical formation the three instruments were assigned quite specific roles, with the trombone providing commentary asides, countermelodies, and harmonic fill-ins to the main tune played by the cornet and the clarinet's high-register obbligatos, in general providing a link between the melodic/thematic material and the rhythm section, even occasionally and intermittently participating in both areas. Much of the earliest "jazz" in the first two decades of the century—before it had even acquired the name *jazz* and before the advent of jazz recordings in 1917—was played outdoors, at picnics, church functions, fraternity dances, or funeral processions and on advertising wagons, with the trombonist usually positioned at the back of the wagon so that he could freely manipulate his five-foot-long slide. This type of playing acquired the name *tailgate*. It featured a copious use of glissandos, a sliding effect endemic to the slide trombone and not particularily practical on other wind instruments; it later became an overused cliché in dixieland bands and the 1940s New Orleans revival.

In the earliest decades of the century, the musician who contributed most to the evolution of the trombone in jazz was Kid Ory. An early specialist in the tailgate style, he developed stylistically along with the advances in jazz in the 1920s, working effectively with such jazz greats as Louis Armstrong (Hot Five) and Jelly Roll Morton (Red Hot Peppers). A fine example of his playing can be heard on "Ory's Creole Trombone/Society Blues," recorded in 1922 in Los Angeles as Ory's Sunshine Orchestra (incidentally the first black New Orleans–style jazz band to be recorded).

Two other fine early trombonists were George Brunis (originally Brunies) and Jim Robinson. Brunis came to prominence in the early 1920s with the excellent New Orleans Rhythm Kings and later was

Jack Teagarden, 1941. Courtesy Frank Driggs Collection.

an important participant in the New Orleans revival and popular at Eddie Condon's famous New York club. Robinson's work can best be heard on Sam Morgan's superb 1927 recordings made in New Orleans. He also worked with Bunk Johnson's band in the mid-1940s and acquired considerable national fame in the 1970s with the New Orleans–based Preservation Hall Band.

These musicians were essentially self-taught and initially non- or semiprofessional, playing in simple, relatively crude personal styles. But under the influence of a number of dramatic developments in jazz in the 1920s, musicians—trombonists, of course, included—began to rise to new challenges. It was during the early 1920s that jazz developed into the major dance and entertainment music of the country and became a viable profession in music (even for blacks); the initial small groups in jazz (quintets, sextets, septets) expanded to ten- and twelve-piece orchestras; composers and arrangers gradually created even more sophisticated performance demands (both in terms of solo improvisations and ensemble work); and, even more compelling, major innovative virtuosos, such as trumpeters Armstrong, King Oliver, and Jabbo Smith and trombonists Jack Teagarden and Miff Mole, challenged the whole field to reach out to new technical and creative heights.

Mole in particular represented an astonishing advance in trombone playing, technically and conceptually. His virtually complete mastery of the instrument can be ascribed in large part to the fact that he became primarily involved in his younger years in New York with high-level dance and show bands (e.g., Jimmy Durante, band tours on the Orpheum theater circuit, Earl Carroll's *Vanities* revues) as well as doing much freelance radio and studio work. By the time he joined Red Nichols's Five Pennies in 1926, Mole had acquired an astounding technical fluency on the instrument, easily encompassing its entire range, enabling him to realize instantaneously any musical idea that came to his mind. Mole was also one of the first trombonists to eschew the old tailgate mannerisms, developing instead a highly flexible and precisely executed style that, with its unusual twists and turns and speed, anticipated much of the technical dexterity of the bop era.

Jack Teagarden also brought a whole new level of musical sophistication and expressivity to trombone playing. He started playing the instrument at age ten, working at first with small bands in the Southwest (Oklahoma and Texas, including the legendary Peck Kelley's Bad Boys). By 1927 Teagarden had moved to New York, where he made his first recordings, amazing his fellow musicians with his technical versatility, original ideas, and profoundly moving ways of playing the blues. Teagarden had a very easy, secure high register, and as a consequence was one of the first trombonists to develop an abundance of "unorthodox" alternate slide positions, playing mostly on the upper partials of the harmonic series and thus rarely having to resort to the lower (fifth to seventh) positions. Since many of these alternate positions are impure in intonation, it is remarkable how in tune Teagarden's playing was for that time. He had also developed an astonishingly easy lip trill—a sine qua non for today's trombonists, but still a great rarity in the 1920s—and was constantly experimenting with novel sonorities, produced by, for example, playing with a water glass held over the bell of his horn, or removing the bell altogether.

Teagarden was unique among trombonists in playing with a laidback, "lazy" style, which many observers called a "Texas drawl." He also had quite a reputation as a singer, particularly of the blues, again in a superbly relaxed manner. Teagarden's essentially vocal, lyric trombone style, using lots of what brass players call "soft tonguing," has its parallel in the "slurred speech" approach—almost to the point of mushiness—in his singing. Of the hundreds of outstanding recordings Teagarden made in his busy career, one must mention at least the early "Strut Miss Lizzie" (1930, Brunswick, with Irving Mills's Hotsy Totsy Gang), the middle-period "I Gotta Right to Sing the Blues" (1933, with Benny Goodman), and the late "Lover" (1950, Jump, with Charlie LaVere's band). All are fine examples of Teagarden's remarkably wide-ranging lyrical and technical abilities.

Teagarden's major New York rival was Jimmy Harrison, a first-rate soloist evolving basically out of the midwestern brass-playing tradition, and also much influenced by Armstrong and Tommy Ladnier (King Oliver's most loyal disciple). Harrison's style, in contrast to Teagarden's essentially vocal approach, is characterized by a driving rhythmic intensity, with a potent brassy sound and hard-tonguing, blistering attacks, crackling slurs, and the habitual use of a strong terminal vibrato (as developed originally by Armstrong). Although Harrison worked often with Fletcher Henderson's seminal band, his best recorded solos can be heard on "Walk That Thing" (1928, Bluebird with Charlie Johnson), "Dee Blues," and "Bugle Call Rag" (both 1930, Columbia, Benny Carter's Chocolate Dandies). "Dee Blues" is a simple, perfectly constructed twelve-bar blues; the latter, a major musical statement in a beautifully relaxed swing, epitomizes what used to be called a "hot trombone." If Harrison's playing, seen and heard in its totality, was ultimately somewhat inconsistent, we must remember that he led a rather erratic personal and professional life, playing with many (perhaps too many) different orchestras, and died very young, at age thirty, never quite fulfilling his real potential.

The 1920s saw a number of other outstanding trombone players come to the fore, among them Claude Jones, Vic Dickenson, J. C. Higginbotham, Benny Morton, Dicky Wells, Sandy Williams, Trummy Young, Tommy Dorsey, Glenn Miller, and, last but not least, the three remarkable players associated with Duke Ellington's orchestra: "Tricky Sam" Nanton, Juan Tizol, and Lawrence Brown. Although most of these players were not major innovators, technically and creatively, they did build in various personal ways on the advances of their immediate brass-playing predecessors.

Claude Jones, a great admirer of Miff Mole, developed a similarly punchy, agile style, full of exuberant leaping figures, and was quite at ease in the trombone's high register. His exciting work can be heard to good effect on trumpeter John Nesbitt's remarkable charts for "Put It There" and "Stop Kidding" (both Victor, with the 1928 McKinney's Cotton Pickers) and on Fletcher Henderson's 1930 "Chinatown, My Chinatown" (Columbia, again Nesbitt's arrangement). Years later, after a long stint with Cab Calloway, Jones played valve trombone with Duke Ellington, replacing Juan Tizol in that important chair.

J. C. Higginbotham, Benny Morton, and Sandy Williams all contributed significant solo work with many of the major orchestras of the late 1920s and 1930s (Fletcher Henderson, Horace Henderson, Chick Webb, Luis Russell). All three were greatly inspired by Jimmy Harrison. Their strongly swinging efforts can be sampled on Henderson's 1932 "New King Porter Stomp" (Columbia, both Williams and Higginbotham) and on the same orchestra's 1931 "Sugar Foot Stomp" (Brunswick), a brilliant and wonderfully varied solo by Morton, part of it set over four bars of stop-time on which five 3/4 measures are overlayed on the underlying 4/4 meter. But perhaps Higginbotham's most personal and inspired playing occurred on his 1930 "Higginbotham Blues" and a series of profoundly moving and poignant blues recordings in 1939 for the Blue Note label.

Sandy Williams was a particularly versatile player who enjoyed adjusting his work to whatever prevailing style a given band espoused, whether quirkily "boppish" (as on Jelly Roll Morton's "Fickle Fay Creep," Victor) or in warmly expressive, wailing, blues-ish microtones (Roy Eldridge's "Fish Market," Decca) or robustly swinging (on Chick Webb's "Stompin' at the Savoy" and "Blue Minor," Decca).

It must be counted as a serious loss to jazz that Williams, suffering from poor health since the 1950s, was forced to abandon music altogether in his forties, working for several decades as an elevator operator.

Two of the most inventive and adventurous players of the 1930s were Vic Dickenson and Dicky Wells. Both worked with fine bands, such as Benny Carter's and Count Basie's. Wells, indeed, was a mainstay in the Count's orchestra for twelve years, contributing strongly to the freewheeling, open-ended, spontaneous feel and powerful swing of the early "classic" Basie band. Both Dickenson and Wells also had in common a healthy sense of humor, which they were frequently able to reflect in their solos: Wells at times ribald and off-the-wall, full of well-placed glissandos, rips, and smears (so unique to the trombone); Dickenson more subdued, sly, and witty, at times even sardonic and world-weary. On the other hand, Wells is at his most soulful and elegant in a masterful obbligato solo on Tab Smith and Jimmy Rushing's superb "Harvard Blues" (Columbia, with Basie, 1940). The best of Dickenson can be heard on his wonderful 1953 septet recordings for the Vanguard label, during a period when he was living and working in Boston, playing also with the great blues trumpeter Frankie Newton (performances that were unfortunately never recorded).

Trummy Young is best remembered for his flamboyant work with the Earl Hines and Jimmie Lunceford orchestras. Although he became more popular with the latter band for his comedic talent and novelty vocals, he was nevertheless an impressive new, brashly confident voice on the trombone, displaying a lithe tone (perfect for his ballad work) and a spectacularly easy high register. Young loved to move far into the trumpet range—hear his repeated dead-sure high notes on the Lunceford band's 1938 Decca recording of "Margie" (including, for the time, an unheard-of high F sharp)—and was an early expert with high-range rips and smears, which, however, later often became self-indulgent mannerisms.

Although Tommy Dorsey initially aspired to be a "true" jazz trombonist, he is ultimately remembered as the supreme ballad player of the 1930s and 1940s. His early years with the Scranton Sirens and the Goldkette and Whiteman orchestras led to his becoming one of the most sought-after studio and Broadway pit orchestra players. But it was when he formed his own band in 1935 that he began to feature his balladic stylizations, starting with his world-famous "I'm Getting Sentimental Over You" (Victor). With his mastery of a smoothly elegant and seemingly effortless singing style (which he virtually invented on the trombone), aided and abetted by flawless breath control, he was the envy of almost all other trombonists, even of those who, by virtue of a wholly different embouchure, lung capacity, and musical background, knew that they could never hope to emulate this master "balladeer." Dorsey, of course, also became famous as a bandleader; but as far as real jazz is concerned his orchestra did not come into its own until trumpeter Sy Oliver took over the arranging reins in 1939, turning it virtually overnight into one of the most exciting swing bands of the era.

Dorsey's fellow trombonist friend and sometime rival, Glenn Miller, deserves mention here only as one of the most commercially successful bandleaders (between 1939 and 1942) of all time—this after years of struggle in New York as an arranger-composer and studio and pit band player. As a trombonist he was proficient but not in any sense outstanding or original, although he did learn to perfect himself in the Dorsey ballad style, which he often featured leading his orchestra's three- and four-part trombone section.

No account of jazz trombone developments in the swing era can be considered factual and faithful without citing the work of three players who for a while comprised what is perhaps the most remarkable trombone section in the whole history of jazz, those players obviously being "Tricky Sam" Nanton, Juan Tizol, and Lawrence Brown of Duke Ellington's orchestra. What is so remarkable about this threesome is that, although no more individualistic and stylistically dissimilar trombonists can be found in all of jazz, when they played in ensemble, which they did continually, they instantly blended into a beautifully voiced and balanced trio.

Nanton, the first of the three to join Ellington's orchestra, became the first great trombone exponent of the "plunger and growl" style, which he inherited from his trumpet mate Bubber Miley—a style of playing that was uniquely identified with the young Ellington orchestra and became its "jungle-style" signature trademark. Nanton rarely played in any other fashion (except in ensemble situations), primarily because he was, especially at first, in most trombonistic respects a rather limited player. He had a coarse, blustery tone, not much technical (slide) agility, and a limited range—in practical terms not more than an octave and a half, but fortunately located firmly and securely in the trombone's upper register. With these finite resources Nanton could nonetheless produce one exciting solo after another, hardly ever missing a note, cleverly exploiting the special acoustical phenomenon that makes playing with pixie and plunger possible, even to the point of virtually talking—wah-wah, ya-ya—on his trombone. Despite its rough-hewn quality, or perhaps because of it, Nanton's playing exuded at once a primal intensity and an inner beauty that made his solos haunting experiences. Because he was very secretive about of his distinct abilities with the plunger and the precise techniques involved, it was several decades before other trombonists were able to emulate Nanton's idiom. Of the dozens of fine Nanton solos one might single out, perhaps most outstanding are his three separate forays on the 1930 "Old Man Blues" (OKeh, first version), "Ko-Ko" (Victor, 1940), and "C-Jam Blues" (Victor, 1942).

Juan Tizol came from an entirely different world of trombone playing, specifically the Italian parade or concert band tradition, which had settled in Central and South America during the nineteenth century, including in Tizol's homeland, Puerto Rico. In this tradition not only was the valve trombone preferred to the slide version, but the instruments had relatively narrow bores and a smallish bell, producing a light, lithe, agile sound, and were always played with a rather quick vibrato. Ellington did not use Tizol as a major soloist but rather exploited the valve trombone's special tone color and trumpet-like nimbleness, often in harmonic ensemble with the saxophones ("Azure," Brunswick, 1937; "Sepia Panorama," Victor, 1940), occasionally in rapid-fire running passages (as on the lively "Dinah," Victor, 1932) and perky zigzag, leaping two-octave passages ("Battle of Swing," Brunswick, 1938). Ellington even wrote special lines for Tizol that could only be played on the valve trombone, for example, the twelve-bar main theme of "Ko-Ko," which, with its half-step move from low B flat to C flat, cannot be rendered swiftly and cleanly enough on a slide trombone.

Lawrence Brown, one of the very greatest artists on the trombone in all of jazz—or any music, for that matter—was not only another highly distinctive voice in the Ellington trombone section, entirely different from his two partners, but beyond that so versatile that, as occasion demanded it, he could be three trombone players rolled into one. First, he was the section's superb lead trombone, with a beautiful expressive tone, a splendid, easy high register, and excellent dynamic control. Second, he was one of the trombone's supreme lyric, melodic soloists, perhaps the best in jazz with the possible exception of Dorsey. Among the abundance of sublime solo statements by Brown, one must single out "Sheik of Araby," "Slippery Horn" (both Brunswick, 1932),

"Delta Serenade" (Victor, 1934), "Blue Light" (Columbia, 1938), and "All Too Soon" (Victor, 1940). Third, he could play as "hot" and blistering a jazz solo as anyone; witness, for example, his solo near the end of "Main Stem" (Victor, 1942). He could play one- or two-octave glissandos, supposedly "impossible" on the trombone, which still baffle players today sixty years later. He was without question the most versatile all-around trombonist of his time.

Given the distinctive individualism of Ellington's three trombonists, it is miraculous how they could blend chameleon-like into a single symbiotic sonority, where the separate parts are so well alloyed as to be no longer distinguishable, whether in the dazzling hoquet virtuosity of "Braggin' in Brass" (Brunswick, 1938) or such exquisite three-part ensembles as can be heard on "Dusk" (Victor, 1940) and "Carnegie Blues" (Victor, 1944). Their technical achievements aside, Nanton, Tizol, and Brown can be considered, each in his way, as among the very few true poets on their instrument.

Another remarkable trombone section, totally different from Ellington's was that of Stan Kenton's orchestra. Beginning in the mid-1940s, its style initiated and set by Kai Winding, it revolutionized trombone playing stylistically, especially in terms of sound (brassier, more prominent in the ensemble) and type of vibrato (slower, and mostly lack thereof), as well as by adding the "new sound" of a bass trombone (Bart Varsalona, later George Roberts). The Kenton trombone section's influence was enormous and pervasive, and continues to this day. Although the section's personnel changed often over the decades, it retained an astonishing stylistic consistency, not only because such stalwarts as Milt Bernhart and Bob Fitzpatrick held long tenures in the orchestra, but because incoming players, such as Bob Burgess and Frank Rosolino and a host of others, were expected to fit into the by-then-famous Kenton brass sound.

In the transitional period during the first half of the 1940s when swing gave way to bebop (or bop), a relatively modest number of trombonists were able to progress with the times. For these were confusing years for many musicians, as the relative comfort and economic security of the swing era appeared to be threatened by the greater musical and technical demands the new artistic directions began to impose. Also, the leaders of the bop revolution were mainly saxophonists (Parker, Young), trumpet players (Gillespie, Navarro), and pianists (Monk, Powell, Tristano, Marmarosa)—not trombonists. Yet some of the young players in their twenties and early thirties—Jack Jenney, Murray McEachern, Will Bradley, Buddy Morrow, Eddie

Bert, Fred Beckett, and especially Bill Harris—were listening closely, eager to join the battle between new and old on the side of the new. Bradley, Jenney, and Morrow, though already technically at ease with the increased virtuoso demands, for various reasons drifted more toward the commercial safety of balladry (à la Dorsey), while McEachern, Beckett, Bert, and, above all, Harris strove to emulate on their valveless instruments—a daunting task, to be sure—what their young trumpet-playing colleagues (like Gillespie) had already achieved. Jenney and Beckett died young (at age thirty-five and twenty-nine respectively), their musical ambitions partially unrealized, but with Jenney contributing, when he was with Artie Shaw, one of the all-time finest trombone solos on the 1940 *Star Dust* (Victor). His playing is inspired, elegant, and full-toned; boasting a magnificent octave leap to high F, then the Mount Everest of the trombone's upper range. Bert and Harris (the former with Red Norvo's crackerjack 1941–42 orchestra; the latter with Woody Herman's First Herd, starting in 1944), successfully made the transition to the sleek, fast-moving lines and more complex harmonic demands of proto-bop. Harris especially combined complete command of his instrument with a wild creative imagination, boundless driving energy, and a quirky, often sardonic sense of humor. A good sampling of his playing would have to include "Apple Honey," "Fan It," "Bijou," and "Goosey Gander," all with Herman (Columbia).

But the biggest breakthrough on the trombone toward full membership in the bop fraternity was accomplished by J. J. Johnson, who essentially proved convincingly that anything Gillespie could do on the trumpet could now also be matched on the trombone. Johnson is regarded as the true founder of the modern school of jazz trombone, developing astounding (for the time) speed and agility on the instrument, and thus becoming a charter member of the bop evolution/revolution. These outstanding qualities, as well as his solid, full, rich, centered tone, can be happily savored on "The Champ" (DeeGee, with Dizzy Gillespie) and "Jay and Kai" (Columbia, 1955).

Johnson spawned a host of followers, foremost among them Jimmy Cleveland, whose speed and dexterity on the trombone were even more dazzling than J. J.'s (which led to him being called "the Snake"), the Danish-born player Kai Winding (with whom J. J. teamed up in a highly successful two-trombone duo) in the 1950s, the Swedish trombonist Åke Persson, and young turks like Frank Rosolino, Frank Rehak, Urbie Green, and Jimmy Knepper. All were spectacular technicians, easily expanding the range of the trombone to the trumpet's

(!) upper register (high B flat and C), and with their new-won technical wizardry capable of playing things that a few years earlier could have only been played on a trumpet, or a flute or violin. Knepper in particular carved out a remarkably successful career in New York, both as a much sought-after, highly individual freelance studio and session player—possessing superior reading skills and the ability to play in a variety of jazz styles—and, most important, as Charles Mingus's favorite trombonist, which led to a long-term association with the great composer-bassist.

Urbie Green, for several years a mainstay of Woody Herman's orchestra, settled in New York in the mid-1950s and became, even more than Knepper, the central figure in that city's freelance jazz recording scene. Gifted with a truly spectacular, dead-sure technique, incredible speed, and a rich, perfectly centered warm tone, his playing could encompass the complete range of musical expression, from the suavest elegance to the most exuberantly lusty drama. If a personal note be permitted, this author as a fellow brassplayer (hornist) found his eyes filled with tears of joy and admiration on many an occasion listening to Green.

In that same generation of white post-J. J. trombonists, the black wing of boppers was represented by many superb players, such as Britt Woodman, Al Grey, Benny Powell, Slide Hampton, and Curtis Fuller, all except Grey still in varying degrees active today. Working mostly as sidemen in such orchestras as Gillespie's, Basie's, Hampton's, and Ellington's, although in varying degrees influenced by J. J. Johnson, they each in their individual ways have carried forward the basic mainstream trombone tradition of, say, Harrison and Teagarden, but richly inflected with the stylistic essentials of bop and modern jazz.

Since the arrival by 1960 of the so-called avant-garde of Ornette Coleman, Eric Dolphy, John Coltrane, Cecil Taylor, and "free jazz," a number of trombonists have contributed compellingly to that musical arena: Roswell Rudd, Julian Priester, Grachan Moncur III, Eje Thelin, Paul Rutherford, Gary Valente, and Frank Lacy. Their "unorthodox" exploits include experimenting with microtones, multiphonics, and new sonorities.

However, the ultimate master of such new trombonistic developments is the German Albert Mangelsdorff. First heard in the United States during the 1958 Newport Jazz Festival as a member of the talent-studded European International Youth Band, Mangelsdorff became one of the major innovative jazz artists of the European scene, working as the leader of numerous small groups as well as a freelancer in concerts, opera, radio, and television. In the early 1970s he began a career as an unaccompanied soloist. In his wholly individual "free jazz" style, he has in effect reinvented the trombone, creating an extensive, unprecedented repertory of fresh ideas, techniques, sounds, and effects unique to the instrument. His unaccompanied playing is superbly represented on *Trombirds* (MPS, 1972) and *Purity* (Mood, 1989), while his more "orthodox" work can be heard to fine advantage on *Animal Dance* (Atlantic, 1962, with John Lewis) and *Albert Mangelsdorff and His Friends* (MPS, 1969).

Another player who occupies a rather exceptional position in the trombone world is Bob Brookmeyer, the major performer for many years on the valve trombone and a gifted all-around musician—composer, arranger, pianist. He acquired almost instant fame in the West Coast jazz scene as a member of Gerry Mulligan's highly successful pianoless quartet (replacing Chet Baker). Subsequently he solidified his niche as the world's preeminent valve trombonist in various stints with Bill Evans, Clark Terry, and the Thad Jones–Mel Lewis Orchestra. Brookmeyer's playing, for all its modernity, also reaches back creatively to the earlier blues and swing traditions. His fine work can be heard on numerous recordings, especially *Mel Lewis: Live at the Village Vanguard* (Gryphon/DCC, 1980) and *The Blues Hot and Cool* (Verve, 1960).

Among present-day trombonists who continue the legacy of, say, Urbie Green, Rosolino, and Knepper, many are active mostly as freelancers in Los Angeles and New York. Mention must be made of some of the more outstandingly versatile players, such as Carl Fontana, Wayne Andre, Bill Watrous, Steve Turre, Jim Pugh, Jiggs Whigham, Ed Neumeister, Robin Eubanks, Ray Anderson, Art Baron, Conrad Herwig, and Rick Stepton.

In today's highly eclectic jazz scene (worldwide), where hardly any rules of behavior exist and an excess of "freedom" has led to much self-indulgence, thousands of "Sunday" composers, and a widespread "anything goes" attitude, it is hard to foresee where jazz and the trombone in jazz will go. Certainly, today there is a consistent emphasis on the highest technical standards and a growing shift to more written-out compositions, as differentiated from improvisation. No grand stylistic breakthroughs or compelling leaders—in the sense of an Armstrong or a Parker or a Coleman—have appeared on the horizon. Moreover, what few new innovative seeds are being sown have emanated from trumpet players (Douglas), multi-instrumentalists

(Braxton), even string players (Feldman)—not trombonists (except for Mangelsdorff). While we hopefully await any new developments, it may be sufficient to note that all musical and technical advances on the trombone have come in the last seventy years from jazz players, ultimately greatly influencing their classical colleagues and thus vastly enriching the trombone's universe.

The Electric Guitar and
Vibraphone in Jazz: Batteries
Not Included

Neil Tesser

In 1950 the recordings of the George Shearing Quintet began to capture the attention of not only the demimonde of jazz hipsters but the larger sphere of American pop music as well. A British pianist raised on swing, Shearing now became a leading popularizer of bebop: his group hammered home bop's angular intervals and tense chords, yet softened the blow with plush harmonization and cushiony textures.

But the "Shearing sound" relied as much on his then-unique combination of electric guitar and vibraphone, which replaced the standard-issue bebop horns—and which makes his band a perfect starting point for this discussion. What's more, the band achieved its success in the early 1950s, the very middle of a century dominated by the spread of electricity to every aspect of our lives—and without electrical amplification, we'd have heard little from either the guitar *or* the vibes in jazz, since neither instrument on its own can generate enough dynamic force to challenge the presence of trumpets, saxophones, piano, and drums.

Still, amplification alone would not have equipped these instruments for jazz's rigorous demands of expression and improvisation. Their success depends at least as much on *sustain* as it does on *volume*.

Electricity allows Milt Jackson or John McLaughlin to play a note that rings and carries, without having to execute a percussion roll (in the first case) or a banjo strum (in the second). Electricity thus affects *phrasing* as well as *dynamics* in these two instruments.

Before amplification, the guitar had relatively little impact on jazz, with a dozen or so important exceptions. Two banjoists turned guitarists, Lonnie Johnson and Johnny St. Cyr, both recorded with Louis Armstrong; "Hotter Than That," by Armstrong's Hot Seven, provides a solid example of Johnson's blues-based, single-note improvising. Another single-note specialist, Teddy Bunn, worked as a first-call substitute in Duke Ellington's band of the late 1920s before his clarion melodies became the lead voice of a Washington, D.C., band called the Spirits of Rhythm in the 1930s. Ellington's regular guitarist, Fred Guy, played an integral role in the band's rhythm section in the 1920s and 1930s and remained with the band until 1949; the other noteworthy acoustic guitarist of the big band era, Freddie Green, made his full chords and unwavering beat a signature of the Count Basie orchestra from 1937 until his death fifty years later.

The most influential early guitarist—and the instrument's first jazz virtuoso—was Eddie Lang. He effortlessly balanced lustrous single-note lines with "rhythm playing" (percussive chording), and he also had a command of the blues that few other white musicians could match. He died at thirty, but his work with violinist Joe Venuti produced perhaps the most admired chamber jazz of the traditional era, as heard on *Joe Venuti and Eddie Lang, 1926–1933* (ABC).

Lang inspired several slightly younger guitarists, principally Carl Kress and George Van Eps, who began to exploit the flexible tonality unique to string instruments. By retuning the strings—and in the case of Van Eps, by adding a new string entirely, bringing the total to seven—these players expanded the guitar's expressive capabilities. Van Eps arrived at an unusually pianistic approach, while others emphasized aggressive chording; the duets recorded by Kress and another ex-banjoist, Dick McDonough, remain shining examples of the acoustic guitar's jazz capabilities. (You can hear Lang, Kress, and McDonough on *Pioneers of Jazz Guitar, 1927–1938*, from Challenge Records.)

Acoustic jazz guitar reached an apotheosis with Django Reinhardt (whose French-made guitar had an extra internal sound chamber, which helped boost the volume). Reinhardt founded his vibrant melodies upon fervid folk rhythms and unexpected chord voicings,

Charlie Christian. Photo: Charles B. Nadell. Courtesy Frank Driggs Collection.

inventions of necessity: a fire that damaged two fingers on his left (chord-making) hand forced him to reimagine his approach to harmony. Reinhardt belied the then prevalent opinion that "Europeans can't play jazz"; tapping his experiences as a minority "outsider" (he was a Gypsy), he achieved an emotional power commensurate with that of jazz's African-American inventors, and his finger-picking technique continued to stun jazz and even rock guitarists into the 1960s. *Souvenirs* (London) remains the best single-disc collection of his work with the Quintette du Hot Club de France, costarring Reinhardt's brilliant alter ego, violinist Stephane Grappelli.

What we now think of as the jazz electric guitar—a hollow-bodied instrument that sends an amplified signal to an external speaker—didn't appear until the late 1930s. But the ES150 then introduced by the Gibson Company was hardly the first wedding of guitar and electronics. Its immediate predecessor, a steel-string instrument called "the Frying Pan" (because of its round body and cast-aluminum construction), dated to 1931; even earlier, in 1923, Gibson produced an electrostatic pickup that captured vibrations coming off the soundboard. But not until the mid-1930s—when Gibson and others began fitting Spanish-style guitars with electro*magnetic* pickups, to amplify the strings themselves—did jazz guitarists have what they needed. In 1937 Eddie Durham recorded the first electric-guitar solo, a few bars on a Count Basie side called "Time Out" (Decca); by the late 1940s, even Reinhardt had switched to electric guitar. Subsequent refinements by guitarist Les Paul and inventor Leo Fender in the 1950s helped the instrument achieve its current stature and versatility.

Still, it took a scrawny young man from an Oklahoma City slum to show the world what the electric guitar could really do. As a boy, Charlie Christian couldn't afford even a cheap acoustic guitar, so he made his own, using a cigar box for the body. By 1937 he'd acquired his first amplified guitar and met Durham, a pivotal influence; two years later, at the age of twenty-three, he joined Benny Goodman's band and acquired a national audience for his effervescent, explosive style, which could match most horn players' for expressive virtuosity. Three years later, he was dead of tuberculosis.

History would remember Christian if he had only pioneered the electric guitar as a full-fledged jazz instrument. But he also played a vital role in the development of bebop: indeed, no musician better represents the transition of swing to bop than Christian, who would often finish a Goodman engagement in New York, pack his guitar, and head uptown for Minton's Playhouse in Harlem, joining with Gillespie and Monk in the late-night jam sessions where bop evolved. Christian's vivid, much admired chromaticism left its mark in the imaginative chord colors that would distinguish the new idiom. You can find a poorly recorded document of these sessions on *Live at Minton's* (Jazz Anthology); Christian's studio work, much of it with Goodman, is available on *The Genius of the Electric Guitar* (Columbia).

After Christian's death, the mantle fell to Oscar Moore, who might well have worn it even had Christian lived: as guitarist in the hugely popular Nat King Cole Trio, Moore had a wide audience. Cole's trio excluded drums, forcing its members to share the rhythmic duties; it thus gave Moore a dream showcase for his inventive accompaniments as well as his voluptuous melodic work. The King Cole Trio's "Body and Soul," "What Is This Thing Called Love?," and "Honeysuckle Rose" display his consummate skill; these tracks, along with several starring Moore's replacement, Irving Ashby, fill *Best of the Nat King Cole Trio—Instrumental* (Capitol).

In the 1940s, Cole's trio did more than anyone else to spotlight the electrified guitar, making the piano-bass-guitar trio a viable jazz unit that successors such as Art Tatum, Oscar Peterson, and Ahmad Jamal would later exploit. (For one of the liveliest examples of the Christian-Moore style, hear Cole's memorable "duel" with Les Paul on the track "Blues," from *Jazz at the Philharmonic: The First Concert* on Verve.) Meanwhile, a white Chicagoan named George Barnes—who like Christian had been influenced by both country music and blues—emerged as one of the most remarkable single-string players. Barnes leaned toward a modified version of country swing, which by the 1950s had fallen completely out of favor, and this perhaps explains why historians often ignore him. None of his vintage work exists on CD; *Gems* (Concord), featuring Joe Venuti, was recorded two years before his death.

Despite a few bona fide bebop pickers—particularly Barney Kessel, who recorded with Parker and planted the seeds for such players as Herb Ellis and Charlie Byrd—the electric guitar didn't fully blossom until jazz's second golden age, the 1950s. Technological improvements allowed guitarists to manipulate the tone and create a variety of timbral identities, so the instrument could easily span the divide between cool jazz and hard bop. And following the example of Christian, guitarists focused on elaborate single-note lines rather than chords, aligning themselves with the front-line hornmen instead of rhythm-section accompanists.

Tal Farlow, Jimmy Raney, and Johnny Smith used a softer tone and less pronounced attack to mold the guitar into a cool-jazz voice: Smith became a household name for his romantic balladry on *Moonlight in Vermont* (Roulette), while Raney's work with Stan Getz (*Stan Getz Plays*, Verve), builds upon the unruffled interplay that marked Billy Bauer's work in the Lennie Tristano Sextet of the 1940s. This style—with emotionalism present but constrained, and always secondary to more cerebral concerns—enlisted its strongest disciple in Jim Hall, whose guitar replaced the piano in Sonny Rollins's quartet of the early 1960s. Hall's work with the harmonically mercurial Rollins showed his supple command of subtle chord variations; while only a few bands had previously replaced the piano with guitar, Hall's success made this format increasingly prevalent in modern jazz.

Also in the 1950s, two midwesterners created a hard-bop guitar persona that had a major impact on the instrument's history. Detroit's Kenny Burrell displayed an exceptionally mellow tone and relaxed solo style that could (and did) complement John Coltrane, but his blues phrasing was earthy enough to support the sanctified funk that soon typified hard bop. Good examples include *All Night Long* (Fantasy) and Burrell's collaborations with organist Jimmy Smith from the 1960s (*Organ Grinder Swing*, Verve) through the 1990s (*The Master*, Blue Note). In Indianapolis, Wes Montgomery was dazzling audiences with a deep swing that gave his melodies unusual propulsion. Montgomery was the first guitarist to improvise in octaves, a then startling and still effective technique, as heard on the album considered his masterpiece, *The Incredible Jazz Guitar* (Riverside/OJC). He later garnered pop success with heavily produced arrangements for horns and strings on a series of Verve albums that were both a response to and a catalyst for the growing popularity of jazz guitar. Burrell and Montgomery paved the way for their contemporary Grant Green, whose soulful tone and ringing lyricism distilled the bluesy essence of 1960s hard bop; *The Best of Grant Green, Volume 1* (Blue Note) combines tracks from six of his best albums. Green's powerful stylings resulted in his performing as sideman and leader on nineteen different Blue Note sessions—in 1961 alone.

The guitar's prominence in organ trios and on "funky jazz" records constitutes one of two vectors in establishing the instrument as a mainstay of modern jazz; the other was the popularity of rock music, in which the guitar replaced horns and often piano as the voice of choice. It's no surprise that the spread of jazz guitar paralleled the rise of rock. "Funky jazz" had dipped deep into the blues, a guitar-driven music and the primary precursor of rock-and-roll. As rock ascended in the 1960s, the guitar came to dominate American music; as rock and jazz converged, the guitar symbolized the evolving musical fusion.

In 1966 vibist Gary Burton—no stranger to the sound of guitar and vibes, having played in the George Shearing Quintet—formed a quartet with guitarist Larry Coryell; shortly later, the proto-fusion band Soft Machine followed Burton's example by using the guitar in place of a horn. In 1968 no less a jazz icon than Miles Davis released the first of his albums to incorporate electric guitar: *Miles in the Sky* (Columbia) with guest George Benson, the successor to Wes Montgomery and Grant Green. When Davis expanded his band to create the fusion milestone *Bitches Brew* (Columbia), he hired a young British rock-and-blues aficionado, John McLaughlin—the first great jazz-rock guitarist, influenced as much by Jimi Hendrix as by John Coltrane. Other recommendations of McLaughlin's playing include *Emergency* (Verve), led by drummer Tony Williams, and *The Inner Mounting Flame* (Columbia) by McLaughlin's own quintet, the Mahavishnu Orchestra.

McLaughlin's music emblematizes the identity of electric guitar in mainstream jazz of the late twentieth century: a slashing, dynamic, high-energy, and ultimately romantic role, subject to a wide variety of interpretations. Larry Coryell came close to matching McLaughlin in sheer virtuosity—especially with his own fusion band, the Eleventh House—and a slew of trigger-happy guitarists followed in their wake. But at the same time, guitarist Ralph Towner grabbed ears with his highly charged *acoustic* playing in the band Oregon, using spectacular finger-picking technique to create brittle and shimmering textures, best heard on Towner's *Solo Concert* (ECM) from 1979.

Since then a steady stream of electric-guitar romanticism has flowed forth from the combined source of McLaughlin and Towner. A contemporary, John Abercrombie, uses reverberation to create a dreamy, sated sound for his discursive solos, heard to advantage on his early *Timeless* and his later *Gateway* (both on ECM). John Scofield's rugged, rawboned sound fits his trademark blend of hard bop, fusion, electric blues, and the rock music he grew up on in the 1960s; but his gift for intrepid, sharply chiseled improvisations has made him a favorite of jazz purists as well as fusioneers through such albums as *Meant to Be* and *Hand Jive* (his collaboration with Eddie Harris), both on Blue Note.

Bill Frisell and Pat Metheny each utilize the guitar's country-music heritage in different ways. Frisell draws a gauzy tone from the instrument and in the 1990s has gained success exploring an unlikely source of inspiration: antique folk music, played with the string-band instrumentation and unhurried pace of nineteenth-century America. Metheny at first used his flawless, globular tone and a rich if mostly diatonic melodicism to echo his Midwest upbringing. But since then, he has incorporated the influences of other guitar-based musics—soft rock, acid rock, and Brazilian tropicalia, on the ECM albums *Offramp* and *Project X* (with free-jazz pioneer Ornette Coleman) and the Geffen album *Still Life (Talking)*—to become the predominant jazz guitarist of the last quarter century.

Metheny's *outré* work with Coleman presaged another collaboration guaranteed to give most of his fans fits; in 1996, on the triple album *The Sign of 4* (Knitting Factory), Metheny hooked up with Derek Bailey, whose use of the electric guitar in free-jazz experiments of the 1960s remains among the most adventurous and abstract music ever produced on the instrument. The potential for such techniques as distortion and electronic manipulation has made the guitar an important player in the jazz avant-garde from the 1970s to the present, particularly in the music of Sonny Sharrock, who merged free jazz and fusion, first with Miles Davis and later in the quartet Last Exit, with German saxist Peter Brötzmann.

A few guitarists, most notably Arto Lindsay, have undertaken radical retunings of the instrument—recalling the 1920s finagling of Carl Kress and George Van Eps—to paint often bizarre soundscapes. Another guitarist aware of the past, James Emery, shuns the electric instrument altogether, using deceptively fragile single-note picking on driving avant-garde solos, both in the String Trio of New York and his own groups, such as the sextet heard on *Spectral Domains* (Enja). The finest free-music guitarist of the 1990s, Joe Morris, makes full use of the electric guitar's expressive gamut without resorting to gimmicks, and his busy solos have grace as well as power; his trio disc *Antennae* (Aum Fidelity) is an excellent introduction to his work.

While merely adopting the guitar (by plying it with ample amounts of juice), the twentieth century actually gave birth to the vibraphone, an instrument fundamentally different from the mallet instruments it is based on, the xylophone and marimba. A prototype called the "steel marimba" first appeared in 1916, but the vibraphone stems from the mid-1920s; the name refers to the vibrato produced by the small rotating blades placed above each of the resonating tubes. These blades alter the air column within each tube, causing slight variations in the pitch, and are driven by an electric motor, the speed of which controls the speed of the vibrato. This makes the vibraphone much more than an "amplified xylophone"; the infusion of electricity creates an instrument with an expressive technique (vibrato) unattainable on its acoustic predecessors.

But the cool metallic sound of the vibraphone, while distinct and refreshing, has never exerted the cyclonic impact of the guitar, and it has drawn relatively few adherents. Remarkably, until the death of Red Norvo and Milt Jackson in 1999, every one of the instrument's main movers and shakers was still alive and kicking, and you could count them on both hands with fingers to spare.

Red Norvo improvised on the nonelectric xylophone with enough skill and imagination to transcend its limitations before switching to the vibraphone in the 1940s. To hear Norvo's evolution as a mallet player, listen first to his 1930s recordings on *Dance of the Octopus* (Hep), then to his modernistic 1950s tracks on *The Red Norvo Trio* (Savoy). The protean bandleader Adrian Rollini, best known for his work on the bass sax, unveiled the first full-fledged vibraphone style in the early 1930s, heard on several tracks that appear on his *Bouncin' in Rhythm* (Topaz) and on "Vibraphonia," recorded with Joe Venuti's Blue Five in 1933.

The most influential early mallet man, Lionel Hampton, started as a drummer and became a vibist almost by accident: according to jazz lore, he spotted the instrument in a recording studio and just began "fooling around" with it. But by the time Benny Goodman tapped him to join his trio—thus creating the famed Goodman Quartet of the mid-1930s—Hampton had become one of the era's prime "hot" jazz soloists. His ebullient playing featured a fast vibrato and melodic vitality, but his percolating technique left no doubt that he played a *percussion* instrument; examples abound on Goodman's *Avalon—The Small Groups, Volume 2* (RCA) and on *Lionel Hampton Greatest Hits* (RCA), which features a who's who of swing era soloists. For all that, Hampton achieved the greatest success with his always exciting big bands. Not even his own vaunted showmanship—reflected in often silly stagecraft and faddish costumery—could obscure the musical mettle of the best Hampton bands, such as the mid-1940s orchestra heard on *Midnight Sun* (GRP/Decca).

The first stylistic advance after Norvo and Hampton, and the most important single innovation in the instrument's history, came from bebop vibist Milt Jackson. Jackson slowed the vibrato and, more important, scaled back the percussive attack and on-the-beat phrasing that often made the vibes sound cartoonish; instead he offered a flowing, relaxed style that took its cue from contemporaneous hornmen rather than pianists and drummers. His lines breathed, lyrically and almost vocally; they sometimes whispered and even sighed. His immaculately balanced improvisations make him one of the great modern soloists on *any* instrument, as you can hear from his own discs—such as *Opus de Jazz* (Savoy) and *Very Tall* (Verve)—and those of the Modern Jazz Quartet, the iconic chamber-jazz band he fronted for more than four decades (*Pyramid* or *The Comedy*, both on Atlantic).

While every vibist after Jackson incorporated his breakthrough, a handful went further and built upon it. Terry Gibbs fused Jackson's vocabulary with Hampton's antic fire to make blistering bop on the West Coast; Teddy Charles sought more experimental textures in recordings with Charles Mingus's Jazz Workshop and under his own name; and Cal Tjader turned his attention toward Afro-Cuban jazz, where he vied with the Latin bandleader (and sometime vibist) Tito Puente for top honors. But not until the mid-1960s, with the arrival of Bobby Hutcherson and Gary Burton, was the bar raised for jazz vibists.

Hutcherson attracted attention on the 1964 albums *Out to Lunch* (by Eric Dolphy) and *Judgment* (Andrew Hill), both on Blue Note, which brought the vibes to the left bank of the jazz mainstream. A little earlier, Walt Dickerson had attempted to translate the furious energy and angular ideas of John Coltrane to the vibes, and Lem Winchester had begun to explore the shimmering, "spacey" textures the instrument can produce. But neither of them displayed the exacting technique or emotional range of Hutcherson, who transferred Jackson's loquacious cool to the progressive modernism of the 1960s. The albums *Dialogue* and *Stick-Up* reveal this side of Hutcherson's music, while the early 1970s *San Francisco* (all on Blue Note) shows his move toward a more populist lyricism.

Gary Burton ignored the bluesy, boppish aspect of Jackson's playing in creating the most original vibes style since the 1940s. His technique extends beyond his dizzying melodic spins and rhythmic subdivisions: controlling two or even three mallets in each hand allows him to play full chords with a truly pianistic approach, and in fact he has performed without accompaniment in the manner of a solo pianist. (In the 1970s he also discovered a method of bending notes on the instrument, previously considered impossible.) Burton's work bridges an enormous stylistic range. It includes his pioneering fusion band of the 1960s (combining jazz with rock and country), heard on *Lofty*

Fake Anagram (RCA); his recording of *A Genuine Tong Funeral* (RCA), Carla Bley's jazz "opera without words"; his leadership of the "new cool school" in the 1970s, heard on *Dreams So Real* (ECM); his ongoing (since 1973) duet partnership with pianist Chick Corea; and his work with Astor Piazzolla's conjunto on *The New Tango* (Atlantic).

In the 1960s Karl Berger and Gunter Hampel, two German vibists (and influential teachers) living in the United States, emphasized free improvising and avant-garde textures; at the same time, Roy Ayers made effective use of the vibes in soul-jazz and even disco settings. But from the 1970s on, most younger vibraphonists have either emulated Hutcherson or found ways to combine his and Burton's styles; these include Monte Croft, Jay Hoggard, Joe Locke, Bill Ware, and, most recently, young Stefon Harris. In the 1980s two vibists influenced primarily by Burton, David Friedman and Dave Samuels (better known for his work in the pop fusion band Spyro Gyra), formed a unique quartet called Double Image, in which each of them played both vibes and marimba (the nonelectric cousin of the xylophone on which wooden tone bars produce a mellow, folksy sound).

Despite the appeal of the Shearing Quintet and the success of Burton's bands, the distinctive twined sound of electric guitar and vibes has appeared rarely in jazz. The first recordings to make prominent use of both instruments came in 1939 and 1940, when Benny Goodman added Charlie Christian to the small band featuring Lionel Hampton. In the 1950s, Red Norvo led a drummerless and pianoless trio that starred guitarist Tal Farlow (later replaced by Jimmy Raney), and Wes Montgomery featured his brother Buddy on vibes in the family trio's early recordings (1958). And in the late 1990s guitarist Charlie Hunter—renowned for simultaneously improvising guitar and bass lines, each on a separate amplifier channel—led a guitar-vibes-drums trio called Pound For Pound.

Pound for pound, no jazz instruments have been more profoundly affected by twentieth-century technology than the guitar and vibraphone.

Miscellaneous Instruments in Jazz

Christopher Washburne

M usicians create jazz in innumerable ways, and at times have defied orthodoxy by developing their voices on instruments that have not attained a prominent role in jazz. This brief discussion serves as an introduction to a number of pioneering musicians. The instruments discussed range from those that were first introduced as novelties and have grown to be widely accepted as viable jazz voices (flute, organ, and Latin percussion) to others that played an integral role in early jazz styles although their subsequent roles have faded or significantly changed (violin, banjo, tuba, and euphonium) to those that have remained on the fringes (cello, French horn, oboe, English horn, bassoon, accordion, and harmonica) and to others that have remained novelties since their introduction (kazoo, bagpipes, harp, and jazz whistlers).

The flute was used only sporadically in early jazz styles; its popularity, however, has steadily grown throughout this century. Wayman Carver, who performed with Benny Carter and Chick Webb, is known as the first jazz flautist. In 1933 he recorded one of the earliest flute solos on Carter's "Devil's Holiday" (Columbia). Webb's 1937 recording of "I Got Rhythm" (Decca) is particularly representative of

Joe Venuti on violin. Courtesy of the Institute of Jazz Studies, Rutgers University.

Carver's work. It was not until the 1950s that the flute's use became widespread, due in part to the interest of several saxophonists—known as "doublers," for their ability to play a variety of woodwind instruments—to play jazz on the instrument. The doublers active in the 1950s who became noted as accomplished flautists include Frank Wess, James Moody, Yusef Lateef, Buddy Collette, and Bud Shank. Wess, a saxophonist with the Count Basie orchestra (1953–64), was one of the first popularizers of the instrument. His warm, breathy, rich sound and virtuosic ability are heard on the 1955 Basie recording "Midgets" (Verve). James Moody's approach to flute soloing favored a beautiful clear tone and cleanly executed virtuosic melodic lines. One of his most remarkable solos is heard on his recording of "Cherokee" (Milestone). Lateef explored more unconventional approaches to playing the instrument and popularized the multiphonic technique of simultaneously singing and playing. A good example is heard on Lateef's 1957 recording of "Take the 'A' Train" on *The Sounds of Yusef Lateef* (Prestige), where he alternates between playing a conventional bop solo and multiphonics. In 1958 Buddy Collette was the first to record all the instruments of the modern flute family (piccolo, flute, alto, and bass), on *Buddy Collette's Swinging Shepherds* (EmArcy). Bud Shank was an important figure in West Coast jazz of the 1950s, playing with Howard Rumsey's Lighthouse All-Stars. His 1954 recording with Laurindo Almeida, *Brazilliance* (World Pacific), captures his soloing style.

Other notable doublers include Eric Dolphy, Rahsaan Roland Kirk, Joe Farrell, and Lew Tabackin. Dolphy played flute in modern and free jazz settings. His work with Chico Hamilton on the 1958 recording *Gongs East* (Warner Bros.) showcases his expressive soloing style. Roland Kirk explored more unconventional playing styles utilizing multiphonics and circular breathing extensively. In addition to playing the modern flute, Kirk performed on a variety of wooden and ethnic flutes. His 1964 all-flute album *I Talk With the Spirits* (Limelight/Verve) showcases his abilities. Joe Farrell was a member of Chick Corea's Return to Forever, a group that fused Brazilian and Latin musics with contemporary jazz. Their 1972 recording *Return to Forever* (ECM) includes several extended flute solos, capturing Farrell's light, clear, and vibratoless tone. Lew Tabackin has been a featured soloist with the Toshiko Akiyoshi Big Band and his own groups since the 1970s.

Musicians who are known primarily as flautists include Sam Most, Herbie Mann, Hubert Laws, Jeremy Steig, and James Newton. Most's first recording as a bandleader (1953), *The Sam Most Sextet* (Prestige), firmly established him as the first bop flautist. Herbie Mann was the first jazz musician to establish his career performing only on flute. Although versatile in many jazz styles, it was with his jazz-rock playing and his explorations into Latin music styles in the 1960s and 1970s, well represented on his 1968 recording *Memphis Underground* (Atlantic), that he attained his greatest popularity. Hubert Laws also plays flute exclusively and is accomplished in both the jazz and classical styles. His 1964 recording *The Laws of Jazz* (Atlantic) demonstrates his large and refined tone and impeccable intonation. Jeremy Steig was active in jazz-rock and other modern jazz settings. He favored an approach to soloing that often included the use of vocalizations; his work on Bill Evans's 1969 recording *What's New* (Verve) is illustrative of this. James Newton, inspired by Eric Dolphy, has been active in avant-garde and other settings since the late 1970s; his 1981 album *Axum* (ECM) is a good introduction to his work.

The pipe organ was first introduced to jazz by pianist Fats Waller. Waller used instruments that were installed in theaters by the Wurlitzer Company to accompany silent films. His most notable performances are his collaborations with Fletcher Henderson's band, such as the 1926 "The Chant" (Columbia). Pianist Count Basie, who studied organ technique with Waller, often performed with his band at theaters that housed pipe organs. His 1939 recording of "Live and Love Tonight" (Ajax) provides a good example of his playing style. Other noteworthy recordings using pipe organs are Fred van Hove's free jazz performance on his 1979 recording *Church Organ* (FMP) and pianist Dick Hyman's 1976 recording *Fats Waller's Heavenly Jive* (Chiaroscuro).

The inability to transport pipe organs to locations where jazz is typically performed has limited its use. In response the Hammond Company developed the portable B-3 electric organ in 1935. Both Waller and Basie adopted this new instrument. The most influential performer and technical pioneer of the B-3 is Jimmy Smith. Forming his own group in the 1950s, he adapted bebop keyboard technique on the instrument as well as developing the use of the foot pedals to play bass lines. By omitting a bass player, he established a new instrumental configuration known as the organ trio (organ, drums, and saxophone or guitar). His 1956 recording *New Sounds on the Organ* (Blue Note) provides an example of his bluesy and exciting playing. Jack McDuff, Jimmy McGriff, Bill Doggett, Don Patterson, Shirley Scott, Groove Holmes, and Charles Earland were influenced by his style and often performed with organ trios. Other significant players include Wild Bill Davis and Larry Young. Davis, a player steeped in the blues tradition, was active from the 1940s; his recording with Duke Ellington, *New Orleans Suite* (Atlantic), captures his soulful soloing style. Larry Young, known as the "Coltrane of the organ" because of his modal and chromatic soloing approach, can be heard on his recording *Unity* (Blue Note).

With the growing popularity of electric pianos and synthesizers, the 1970s saw a decline in younger players using the B-3. However, in the 1990s several players—including Dan Wall, Larry Goldings, John Medeski, Joey DeFrancesco, and Barbara Dennerlein—have renewed its presence and sought innovative uses for the B-3 in modern jazz settings.

Latin percussion first appeared on jazz recordings as an ancillary novelty where the players were rarely given credit. For instance, on the first jazz recording to use Latin percussion (castanets and claves), Louis Armstrong's 1930 version of "Peanut Vendor" (OKeh), no performance credits are provided. The first Latin percussion solo occurs on Cab Calloway's 1940 recording "Goin' Conga" (OKeh). Again credits are omitted; however, Mario Bauza claimed that he played maracas and Allejandro Rodriguez played the bongo solo.

Since the mid-1940s percussionists have played a significantly larger role, especially in Latin jazz. The collaboration between Dizzy Gillespie and Cuban conga player Chano Pozo in 1946–48 was integral in establishing the conga drum's use in jazz settings. Further, their compositional collaborations resulted in several Latin jazz standards, such as "Manteca" and "Tin Tin Deo." Their 1947 milestone recording of George Russell's "Cubano Be–Cubano Bop" (Victor) features solos by Pozo. New York–born Sabú Martinez worked with both Dizzy Gillespie, after Pozo's premature death in 1948, and Art Blakey throughout the 1950s. His 1957 recording with Blakey, *Orgy in Rhythm* (Blue Note), captures his style. Cuban conguero Candido Camero was a pioneer in developing the simultaneous playing of multiple drums (before him, conga players used only one drum). This extended the ability of players to play melodies and provided more timbral options. After performing with Gillespie and Stan Kenton, he formed his own band and became the first of many conga-playing bandleaders. Other conguero/bandleaders include Mongo Santamaria, Ray Barretto, and Willie Bobo (William Correa). Santamaria's 1959 recording *Afro Roots* (Prestige) demonstrates his desire to combine traditional Afro-Cuban rhythms with jazz and his strong sense of groove. His composition "Afro Blue" has become a jazz standard. Nuyorican Ray Barretto was one of the first players to develop the technique of playing with a swung eighth-note feel. This enabled him to record with many jazz players, such as Cannonball Adderley, Kenny Burrell, and Freddie Hubbard. Nuyorican Willie Bobo performed on both congas and bongos. As a leader, he combined elements of Latin dance music, soul, and jazz. His 1966 release *Bobo Motion* (Verve) is representative of his style. Another conguero worthy of note is Cuban Carlos "Patato" Valdez, who worked with Herbie Mann from 1959 to 1972. Mann's 1963 recording *Live at Newport* (Atlantic) demonstrates Patato's expressively melodic approach to soloing. The younger generation of percussionists has been led by the Puerto Rican conga player Giovanni Hidalgo, who is renowned for his extremely rapid hand technique that has set new standards of virtuosity for conga soloing. Puerto Rican Richie Flores, who performs with Eddie Palmieri, has also adapted Hildalgo's style.

Bandleader, timbale player, and vibraphonist Tito Puente played a large role in Latin jazz, making over a hundred recordings and employing many prominent jazz musicians. His 1957 recording *Night Beat* (RCA) demonstrates his melodic soloing ability on timbales and his adeptness at combining and balancing big band jazz with Latin rhythms and performance practices, yielding Latin jazz at its best.

After the bossa nova craze of the 1960s the use of Brazilian percussionists in jazz groups became popular. Influential Brazilian percussionists include Airto Moreira, Dom Um Romao, Guillermo Franco, and Cafe. After moving to New York in 1970, Moreira became one of the most well known percussionists in jazz, working with Miles Davis and Weather Report. His work on Weather Report's 1971 debut album (Columbia) demonstrates his pioneering work that uses a wide range of instruments for timbral enhancement and to intensify grooves. Dom Um Romao eventually replaced Moreira in Weather Report. He can be heard on their 1971–72 recording *I Sing the Body Electric* (Columbia). Guillermo Franco is the leader of his own New York–based samba group, Pe De Boi. He also can be heard on Keith Jarrett's 1974 recording *Treasure Island* (Impulse). Cafe leads the next generation of percussionists and has worked in a wide array of jazz settings.

The earliest use of the violin as a solo instrument in jazz stems from its prominent role in ragtime ensembles. The recording entitled *The New Orleans Ragtime Orchestra* (Arhoolie) provides some characteristic examples. Early jazz ensembles in New Orleans, such as A. J. Piron's Band, continued the practice and occasionally featured the violin. However, it was the talents of four gifted violinists—Joe Venuti, Stephane Grappelli, Stuff Smith, and Eddie South—that firmly established the violin as a solo instrument in jazz. Venuti is viewed as the pioneer in jazz violin soloing, and his duet records with guitarist Eddie Lang (1926–28) were influential, inspiring Grappelli's collaborative work with Django Reinhardt. The 1928 recording *Doin' Things/Wild Cats* (Victor) captures the intimate style of the Venuti/Lang duo. French violinist Stephane Grappelli was a member of the popular band Quintette du Hot Club de France (formed in 1934). His long, active career included numerous recordings, two of which distinctly illustrate his beautiful clear tone and fluid harmonic language that is rooted in the swing tradition. They include his 1966 release *Violin Summit* (Saba) and his 1969 recording with George Shearing, *I Remember Django* (Black Lion). Eddie South was classically trained and was known for his impeccable swing-feel technique, agility at fast tempos, and dark tone. His 1937 recording *Eddie's Blues/Sweet Georgia Brown* (Swing) is representative of his playing style. Stuff Smith was comparatively more adventurous harmonically and in his playing technique, which favored a rough, vibratoless tone. The performance on his 1957 recording *Have Violin, Will Swing* (Verve) captures his venturesome approach. In the 1930s he was the first to amplify his violin, enabling his sound to project over large ensembles. This became a standard practice, allowing violinists to perform in a wide variety of jazz settings.

Michel Warlop, Ray Nance, and Svend Asmussen were three other important players working during the swing era. Warlop, a Frenchman, was as accomplished as Grappelli and South and performed in a violin trio with them in 1937. Nance performed with Duke Ellington as a violinist, trumpeter, and vocalist, appearing on numerous recordings. His work on the 1942 recording of "Moon Mist" (Victor) and the 1958 release of "Come Sunday" (Columbia) is particularly notable. Danish violinist Asmussen worked mainly in Europe; his 1965 recording *Evergreens* (Odeon) demonstrates his fluid swing style.

Players active in modern jazz, free jazz, jazz-rock, and other contemporary styles include Joe Kennedy, Leroy Jenkins, Jean-Luc Ponty, Michal Urbaniak, and Zbigniew Seifert. Joe Kennedy's work with Ahmad Jamal is outstanding and can be heard on the 1960 recording *Listen to the Ahmad Jamal Quintet* (Argo). Leroy Jenkins, who was a member of the AACM in Chicago, is most noted for his use of extended techniques, borrowed from contemporary classical music practices, in his improvisations, and for exploring the use of longer compositional forms in free jazz improvisation. French violinist Jean-Luc Ponty was a pioneer in the use of the electric violin, experimenting with electronic effects and at times performing on five- and six-string violins that extend the lower range of the instrument. His efforts popularized the violin's use in jazz-rock and fusion styles. Although competent in styles ranging from bop to fusion, as a leader he favors the jazz-rock style, playing with a bluesy, lyrical, and vibratoless tone. His 1975 recording *Upon the Wings of Music* (Atlantic) highlights his virtuosic improvisatory abilities. Like Ponty, Polish violinist Michal Urbaniak plays the electric violin with added strings and effects. He has also experimented with the violectra, an electric bowed string instrument that sounds one octave lower than the violin. His 1974 recording *Atma* (Columbia) combines jazz-rock with elements of Polish folk music. Another Polish violinist, Zbigniew Seifert, was active in the free jazz, modal, and jazz-rock scenes, and his 1976 Coltrane-esque album *Man of the Light* (MPS) captures his contemporary soloing approach. Other violinists of note include Billy Bang (William Walker), a student of Leroy Jenkins and active since the 1970s, playing free jazz and leading the String Trio of New York; John Blake, whose 1987 recording *Adventure of the Heart* (Gramavision) demonstrates his contemporary approach that combines pop and jazz styles with bluesy soloing; and Mark Feldman and Regina Carter, who lead the youngest generation of jazz violinists.

The banjo was used in ragtime, early blues, and New Orleans jazz styles, and it still remains an integral part of the rhythm section in dixieland. The first notable and influential jazz soloist was Johnny St. Cyr, who played with Louis Armstrong's Hot Five and Hot Seven, as well as with Jelly Roll Morton. His 1926 recording with Morton of "The Chant" (Victor) is representative of both his melodic approach to soloing and the rhythmic drive and chordal support he used in his accompanying. Other prominent players in New Orleans and dixieland styles included Emanuel Sayles, Bill Johnson, and John Marrero. With the advent of the big band era of the 1930s, the use of the guitar became standardized, replacing the banjo in its rhythm-section role. With the exception of a brief period of renewed interest in traditional jazz styles in the 1940s, the banjo has not played a significant role in jazz since the 1920s. Players specializing in traditional jazz styles and active since the 1940s include Danny Barker, George Guesnon, and Lawrence Marrero, brother of John. Béla Fleck is perhaps the only significant player who has played the banjo in a modern jazz setting, specializing in fusion and jazz-rock styles. On his 1991 recording *The Flight of the Cosmic Hippo* (Warner) he plays both banjo and electric banjo, inventively improvising in a modern jazz language.

Since the beginning of jazz, tubas have often been employed in rhythm sections in place of the string bass. Tubas are still frequently used in dixieland jazz styles. In the 1930s the use of the string bass became standardized, replacing tubas in their rhythm section role. In the late 1940s bandleader Claude Thornhill began experimenting with the tuba in a more melodic role as part of the brass section, exploiting its tone color for orchestral blending. Bill Barber, who played with Thornhill and the Miles Davis nonet, was one of the first tubists to record in a modern jazz setting. Don Butterfield, known for his trumpet-like technique, played with Sonny Rollins, Bill Evans, and Charles Mingus. After working for Thornhill, arranger and bandleader Gil Evans continued incorporating the tuba in his projects, including his influential collaborations with Miles Davis (1948–68). His efforts renewed the use of the tuba in jazz and provided an outlet for several virtuosic jazz improvisers. Bassist and tubist Red Callender also contributed to the tuba's revival in jazz groups. *Callender Speaks Low* (Crown) demonstrates his lyrical approach that favors the middle and lower registers. Baritone saxophonist, pennywhistler, and tubist Howard Johnson is known for his extended range and virtuosic soloing ability. His solo on Gil Evans's arrangement of "Voodoo Chile" on *Gil Evans Plays Hendrix* (RCA) demonstrates both his remarkable range and virtuosic soloing ability. In 1966 he formed Substructure, a group that featured four tubas and folksinger Taj Mahal. This group eventually led to the formation of Gravity, which includes eight tubas and euphoniums with rhythm. Their 1996 recording *Gravity!!!* (Verve) features solos by Johnson as well as by Dave Bargeron. Bob Stewart, another member of Gravity, has recorded both as a leader and as a sideman with Lester Bowie and Carla Bley. He is known for his heavy grooves and accomplished soloing ability, both of which are well represented on his own group's 1996 recording *Then and Now* (Postcards). A good example of his free jazz playing is captured on Arthur Blythe's 1977 *The Grip* (India Navigator). Other players of note include Joe Daley and Marcus Rojas.

The euphonium, or baritone horn, was frequently used throughout the 1800s in prejazz styles, such as New Orleans brass bands. Stemming from that tradition, it was included in early parade jazz bands.

However, with a few notable exceptions, its use as a solo instrument in jazz is rare. Kiane Zawadi (Bernard McKinney), best known for his bop soloing ability on the euphonium, recorded with Freddie Hubbard in 1961 on *Ready for Freddie* (Blue Note), and his solo on "Arietis" exemplifies his style. The most expressive of euphonium players was Rich Matteson. He was a virtuosic tuba player as well and was known for his beautiful full sound and hard-swinging bop improvising style on both instruments. A good example of his tuba playing can be heard on Louis Armstrong's 1960 *Great Alternatives* (Chiaroscuro). His impeccable tone and virtuosic valve technique are well represented on his own recording *Easy Street* (Four Leaf). Dave Bargeron's euphonium solo on Gravity's "'Way' Cross Georgia" (Verve) demonstrates his remarkable range and lyric improvisational approach. This cut also includes one of the few jazz pennywhistle solos, played by the group's leader, Howard Johnson. Gus Mancuso is another accomplished euphonium soloist.

Bassists who doubled on cello were some of the first players to introduce the instrument in jazz. Its higher register and easier technical demands made it attractive for bassists who wanted to play fast bop solos. The earliest examples include Oscar Pettiford, Sam Jones, and Ray Brown. Pettiford, one of the first to play jazz on the cello, developed a fluid bop pizzicato soloing style, which can be heard on his 1954 recording *Basically Duke* (Bethlehem). Sam Jones also used a pizzicato soloing style, but with a heavier bluesy feel. The playing on his 1961 recording "The Chant" (Riverside) is representative of his work. The differences in bridge structure and tuning—the bass is tuned in fourths and the cello in fifths—discouraged some bassists from playing the cello. In response, Ray Brown, who plays cello on his 1960 recording *Jazz Cello* (Verve), assisted in the development of a hybrid instrument that combined the features of both the cello and bass, including a modified bridge and basslike machine-head tuning. This led to the development of the piccolo bass, which is used extensively by Ron Carter. On his 1977 recording *Piccolo* (Milestone) he performs solely on the instrument, playing both arco and pizzicato solos and using the instrument as the lead melodic and solo voice.

Those players who primarily play cello include Calo Scott, Fred Katz, Nathan Gershman, David Darling, and Abdul Wadud (Ronald DeVaughn). Scott was one of the first jazz cellists; he began working with Gerry Mulligan in the late 1950s. His most impressive playing can be heard on Charlie Rouse's 1974 recording *Two Is One* (Strata-East). Chico Hamilton's quintet featured the cello and provided a creative outlet for cellists to explore improvisatory possibilities in a West Coast jazz setting. Two gifted cellists, Fred Katz and Nathan Gershman, were regular members of that band. Katz plays on the 1955 recording *The Chico Hamilton Quintet With Buddy Colette* (Pacific Jazz) and Gershman on the 1958 release *Gongs East* (Warner Bros.). David Darling performed with the Paul Winter Consort and can heard on the 1971 recording *Icarus* (Epic). He explored the use of a solid-body, eight-string electric cello of his own design, and both his conventional and electric cello playing are well represented on his 1979 recording *Journal October* (ECM). Abdul Wadud performed extensively with Julius Hemphill and Arther Blythe. He is credited with extending both jazz arco and pizzicato technique and developing the instrument's accompanying role. His 1977 recording with Blythe, *The Grip* (India Navigation), demonstrates his inventive soloing style and sensitive accompanying technique. Other notable cellists include Doug Watkins, David Eyges, Erik Friedlander, Akua Dixon, and Diedre Murray.

Beginning in the early 1940s, the option of adding French horns to the standard big band instrumentation was established by both Glenn Miller and Claude Thornhill. Both bands included horn players as regular performing members. Addison "Junior" Collins was one of the first jazz horn pioneers, performing with Glenn Miller's Army Air Force Band, Thornhill, and the Miles Davis nonet. Collins plays a lyrical solo on Miller's version of "Songs My Mother Taught Me" (Phontastic). Gil Evans also included French horn in his own groups. Although the original horn players in Evans's groups were not known as accomplished jazz improvisers, their prominent role in his ensembles led the way for future players to explore more improvisatory roles. John Graas, who performed with Thornhill, and Willie Ruff were two important players who worked with Evans. Julius Watkins, one of the most active horn soloists, was known for his fluent bop improvising. He recorded and performed with Thelonious Monk, Sonny Rollins, Quincy Jones, Charles Mingus, and Oscar Pettiford. As a leader of Jazz Modes, his bop quintet (1956–59), he recorded *Jazzville* (Dawn), which serves as a good representation of his work. John Clark, who performed with Gil Evans throughout the 1980s, is representative of the later generation of Evans's horn players. He is an accomplished jazz soloist, and his own recording, *I Will* (Postcards), demonstrates his modern soloing style that includes both a modal and chromatic approach. Another fluent improviser is Tom Varner. His solo on his own 1985 recording of "What Is This Thing Called First

Strike Capability" (New Note) demonstrates how Varner has been able to adapt bop valve technique and the modern jazz vocabulary onto the instrument. The 1990s saw a proliferation of gifted soloists, including Alex Brofsky, Vincent Chancey, Arkady Shilkloper, and Rick Todd.

The oboe and English horn were first used as jazz solo instruments in the 1950s and were played mostly by saxophonists. Tenor saxophonist Bob Cooper was active as a leader and a sideman in the West Coast jazz scene throughout the 1950s, playing oboe with Stan Kenton, Howard Rumsey's Lighthouse All-Stars, and his own groups. Yusef Lateef, a tenor saxophonist who frequently doubled on a variety of woodwind instruments, developed a bluesy and soulful oboe-playing style, using a wide vibrato that is well represented on "In the Evening" on *The Complete Yusef Lateef* (Atlantic). Marshall Allen and Makanda Ken McIntyre, two saxophonists active in the free jazz scene of the 1960s, both performed on oboe. Allen can be heard on Sun Ra's 1963 recording of "Thither and Yon" on *Cosmic Tones for Mental Therapy* (Saturn) and on *Other Planes of There* (Evidence). McIntyre plays oboe on Cecil Taylor's 1966 recording *Unit Structures* (Blue Note). What differentiates Paul McCandless from other jazz oboists is that he is primarily known for his virtuosic oboe and English horn playing. He is a founding member and featured soloist in the group Oregon (1970). Oregon's 1976 recording *Together* (Vanguard) and his 1979 recording *All the Mornings Bring* (Elektra) demonstrates his creative improvising abilities on both oboe and English horn, drawing upon a variety of sources including classical music, modal and free jazz, and ethnic influences. Other notable performers include Joe Farrell, who played oboe on *The Joe Farrell Quartet* (CBS), and Joseph Celli, a free jazz improviser who performs on both Western and non-Western oboes (especially the Korean piri).

The bassoon's earliest appearance in jazz was in the 1920s; like the oboe, it was primarily played by saxophonists. At first, it was employed to enhance orchestral colors in written parts. Paul Whiteman's 1928 recording of "Sweet Sue" (Columbia) is one of the earliest recorded examples of the bassoon used in this way. One of the earliest solos was played by saxophonist Frank Trumbauer on the 1929 recording of "Runnin' Ragged," also known as "Bamboozlin' the Bassoon" (OKeh), by Joe Venuti's Blue Four. However, its use quickly faded and was not renewed until the late 1950s with the advent of the cool and West Coast jazz styles. At that time, arrangers sought a larger palette of instrumental colors to draw upon and turned to the bassoon primarily for part writing. Gil Evans's 1957 recording *Gil Evans and 10* (Prestige/OJC) provides one example. It was not until the 1960s that several jazz soloists emerged. Illinois Jacquet, after a long and well-established career as a saxophonist, began playing bassoon in 1965. His 1969 recording of " 'Round Midnight" (Prestige) demonstrates how he transferred his rich saxophone sound to the bassoon. Yusef Lateef plays bassoon solos on his 1963 recording *Jazz 'Round the World* (Impulse). And saxophonist Frank Tiberi, who performed with Woody Herman, distinguished himself as an exceptional jazz bassoonist. His 1979 recording *Woody and Friends* (Concord) is representative of his work. More recently, Michael Rabinowitz has taken jazz bassoon soloing entirely to a new level. His 1996 release *Gabrielle's Balloon* (Jazz Focus) shows his ability to use the bassoon as an effectively expressive voice in a modern jazz setting. Other notable players include Ray Pizzi, based in Los Angeles, and Errol Buddle, who played with the Australian Jazz Quartet.

The accordion has for many years remained on the fringes of jazz, never becoming a prominent solo voice. Nonetheless, there have been some exceptionally gifted accordion soloists. One of the earliest examples is pianist Buster Moten, brother of Bennie, who played with his brother's band. He solos on "Moten Blues" (Victor), recorded in 1929. Charles Melrose provides another early jazz accordion example with his solo on the 1930 Cellar Boys recording of "Wailing Blues/Barrel House Stomp" (Vocalion). Duke Ellington wrote and recorded "Accordion Joe" (MCA/Classic), which features Joe Cornell, in 1930.

The next generation of accordion players was led by Joe Mooney, who had a swing quartet and was active in the 1940s playing in the 52nd Street clubs. His 1946 rendition of "September Song" (Decca) displays his tasteful approach to jazz interpretation and arranging as he accompanies himself singing. Swedish pianist Bengt Hallberg is particularly adept at playing in the swing jazz style and can be heard on *Hallberg's Hot Accordion* (Phontastic). Bop accordionists include Art Van Damme, the Dutch Mat Mathews, George Shearing, Alice Hall, and Leon Sash. Van Damme's solos are hard-swinging and virtuosic with a fluid bop improvisatory style that favors single-line soloing. His 1970 recording *Blue World* (Pausa-MPS) is representative of his playing style. Mathews's 1953 recording *Mat Mathews Quintet* (Brunswick) captures a virtuosic playing style that is not as hard-swinging as Van Damme's and favors chordal improvisation versus the single-line approach. Although best known as a pianist, George

Shearing is also an accomplished accordionist. His recording "Cherokee/Four Bars Short" (Discovery) displays that he has transferred his imaginative and refined musical approach on piano onto the accordion. Leon Sash can be heard on his recording *I Remember Newport* (Delmark). Few recordings exist of Alice Hall, but her rendition of "What Is This Thing Called Love?" on the *Planet Squeezebox* compilation (Ellipsis Arts) attests to her knowledge of the jazz vocabulary and inventive soloing style. Eddie Monteiro performs in modern jazz settings and is most noted for his duo work with singer Nancy Marano. He frequently sings along with his accordion solos, an expressive technique that can be heard on Marano and Monteiro's 1993 recording *Double Standards* (Denon). He has also experimented with electronic effects and a MIDI-controlled (musical instrument digital interface) accordion on *A Perfect Match* (Denon). Other accordionists of note include Tommy Gumina, Gil Goldstein, and Frank Morocco.

Although the harmonica plays a prominent role in blues traditions, its use in jazz groups has been limited. Larry Adler, Buddy Lucas, and Toots Thielemans are a few notable exceptions. In 1936 London-based Larry Adler recorded with Django Reinhardt (Disques Swing), making him one of the first harmonica players to record with a jazz group. He also worked with Duke Ellington, Stephane Grappelli, and John Kirby during a long and illustrious career that has extended over sixty years. Buddy Lucas recorded with the Thad Jones–Mel Lewis Orchestra in the mid-1970s. Belgian multi-instrumentalist Toots Thielemans's ability as an improviser on the harmonica is unsurpassed. After emigrating to the United States in 1951, he performed with Benny Goodman, Quincy Jones, Oscar Peterson, and many others. His composition "Bluesette" (ABC Paramount) has become a jazz standard. More recently, the German Hendrik Meurkens has been acclaimed for similar fluency.

The kazoo and comb-and-tissue were occasionally played in the bands of the 1920s; however, they have remained dormant since that time. Red Mackenzie—singer, comb-and-tissue player, and talent scout—was an important figure in the 1920s. His most representative recording on comb-and-tissue is the Mound City Blue Blowers' 1929 recording of "Hello Lola" (Victor) where he expressively mimics a muted trumpet, incorporating growls, slides, and trills. Bandmate Dick Slevin played kazoo, and both can be heard on the 1924 recording of "San" (Brunswick/Retrieval).

The bagpipes have remained outside of the jazz tradition with the exception of Rufus Harley, who was active throughout the 1960s and

1970s. His 1966 recording of "Scotch and Soda" (Atlantic) is representative of his improvising style.

Though the harp has been used frequently in jazz orchestral recordings, there have been only a handful of improvising jazz harpists. Among them are Casper Reardon, Adele Girard (both active in the 1930s), and, more recently, Corky Hale, Dorothy Ashby, David Snell, and Alice Coltrane (better known as a pianist).

Jazz whistling has remained a novelty, yet some remarkable solos have been captured on jazz recordings. One of the earliest whistling solos was performed by pianist Meade Lux Lewis in 1937 on "Whistlin' Blues" (Victor). He whistles an expressively bluesy solo filled with glisses and a wide vibrato while accompanying himself on the piano. The most famous whistling cut is "Big Noise From Winnetka" (Jazz Archives/EPM Musique), recorded in 1938 by drummer Ray Bauduc and bassist Bob Haggart, who does the whistling. In this duo performance Haggart whistles the melody with a breathy tone, then plays an extended bass solo with Bauduc accompanying. Toots Thielemans often whistles along with his guitar melodies in unison or one octave above; his live recording of "Bluesette" on *Toots Thielemans Live* (Inner City Records) provides an example. Pianist Tania Maria also employs this technique, doubling her melodies by whistling. Ron McCroby, who prefers to be called a puccolist, is one of the few jazz musicians who performs solely as a whistler. His solo on "Cherokee" (Concord) demonstrates his knowledge of the bop vocabulary and his ability to execute virtuosic improvisations.

The Bass in Jazz

Bill Crow

The string bass has been called the "heartbeat of jazz" for good reason. It provides a deep pulse, sometimes felt as much as it is heard, giving the music both a harmonic and a rhythmic foundation. As in many other forms of music, the role of the bass in jazz is mainly supportive. Bass players certainly have developed marvelous techniques for soloing, especially in recent years. But a bassist doesn't have to be a great soloist to be in demand. The main thing other jazz musicians want from a bass player is "good notes," bass notes that thread through the harmony in an interesting way, and "good time," a steady rhythmic feeling that helps bring the music to life.

Bass notes are stepping-stones for the rest of the band. They form a path that provides support and direction. To be able to consistently select good notes and drop them into exactly the right places in the music, a bass player needs a strong sense of harmony and rhythm and an empathetic connection with the other members of the rhythm section. In small groups, the bassist chooses his line as the music goes along. Even when playing written music in larger ensembles, jazz bass players usually recompose their lines, using what the arranger has written as a guide but relying on their experience and their "sixth sense" to choose the particular notes and figures to be played.

String basses have been used in jazz rhythm sections since the music began. Photos of Buddy Bolden's band in New Orleans show Jimmy Johnson playing the string bass. Another Johnson, Bill, played string bass and banjo with King Oliver. String basses were even added to brass bands on occasion, though those groups more usually used what was called the brass bass or bass horn, which included helicons, sousaphones, and tubas of several different sizes. Brass basses have louder voices than string basses and are easier to play while marching, and so they were preferred for band concerts, parades, and other outdoor work. And at first the brass bass was more often used on jazz records, because string basses did not reproduce well on early acoustic recording equipment (Louis Armstrong, "Wild Man Blues" [Columbia])

The string bass has two advantages over the brass bass, which eventually made it the instrument of choice in jazz and swing bands: its tone quality blends more easily with other instruments in all combinations, and it can be played continuously. Since playing a brass bass requires great lungfuls of air, bass lines are most comfortably played on them at two beats to the 4/4 measure, with the rests between beats allowing space for breathing. Few tuba players are comfortable playing the continuous 4/4 bass lines that became the standard style in jazz, especially during the swing and bebop eras. A string bass player can play connected 4/4 lines all night long at any tempo without being concerned about running out of breath.

A third bass instrument, the bass saxophone, has fallen out of general use today except in some groups that play the early traditional repertoire. It is a bulky instrument that is difficult to keep in proper alignment because of the size and weight of its keys, rods, and pads. But during the 1920s and early 1930s, Adrian Rollini made recordings with Bix Beiderbecke, Joe Venuti, and Red Nichols using a bass saxophone on which he played imaginative bass lines that had a strong influence on the conception of many string bass players of the day (Rollini with Beiderbecke, "At the Jazz Band Ball" [OKeh/CBS]).

Jazz bass lines are a natural outgrowth of bass parts in traditional European songs, dance tunes, marches, etc. In New Orleans and elsewhere in America, as African and Spanish rhythms were added to these forms, the phrasing of the bass notes became more syncopated. The practice of placing bass notes directly on the first and third beats of a measure was altered by prejazz bassists, both brass and string, who displaced certain strong beats by playing them a bit sooner than expected and adding accents and double beats in a way that made parade and dance music more exciting (Young Tuxedo Brass Band,

Charles Mingus, Hammerveld Jazz Festival, Roermond, Holland, 1973. Courtesy of the Institute of Jazz Studies, Rutgers University.

Jazz Begins [Atlantic]). These inventions were adopted by string bass players in early jazz bands.

Sometimes, bassists had to improvise their instruments as well as their music. A usable bass could be constructed from a washtub, a short pole, and a length of twine. The twine was knotted between one end of the pole and a hole in the center of the washtub's bottom. Using the edge of the upturned tub as a fulcrum for the bottom of the pole, the bass player could stretch the twine tighter for high notes and looser for low ones, with the washtub acting as a resonating chamber to amplify the sound.

Pops Foster, one of the early New Orleans jazz bassists, tells in his autobiography how he learned to play on a homemade two-string bass made from a barrel and a two-by-four, with strings twisted from twine. Later he played a cello that was set up and tuned like a bass, and then, in 1906, he finally got a real string bass, which he played with a powerful resonance. A self-taught musician, Pops never learned the classic German fingering system used by teacher-trained bassists. He discovered that firm pressure on the strings with the left hand produced the strongest tone, and he used whatever grips he could devise for strength. He wasn't looking for fast technique as much as penetrating sound (Foster with Louis Armstrong, "Jubilee," [Decca]).

Early bassists in dance bands and road shows, following orchestral tradition, played their bass notes mostly with the bow. During plucked passages the bow remained held in the right hand. Foster and Bill Johnson were among the earliest players who chose to pluck the bass most of the time. They laid the bow down and invented ways of pulling more sound from the instrument, sometimes swinging the entire forearm with a hooking motion, more often using the right thumb as a fulcrum against the side of the fingerboard as an aid to pulling the string strongly with the forefinger. Bassists who could make each note ring until the next one began were said to have a "long sound."

At first, bass players would play on the first and third beats of each measure, using mostly roots and fifths of the chords. Some began to add decorative notes to this pattern, following the beat of the drummers. When the music changed in a way that inspired bassists to play four beats to a measure, most of them began by playing pairs of roots and fifths, but soon they began moving up and down the scale or through the chord. This sort of steplike motion, called "walking," was also developed by stride piano players in their left-hand patterns

(Israel Crosby with Edmond Hall, "Profoundly Blue" [Blue Note]; James P. Johnson, "Mule Walk" [Columbia]).

Walter Page played both brass and string basses around the Southwest, and in 1925 he organized a musically influential band called the Blue Devils. Later, he was much imitated in his walking bass style when he recorded with Count Basie's band. Drummer Jo Jones credited Page with the invention of Basie's famous rhythm section sound. Jo's light cymbal and bass-drum beats, Page's strong walking bass, Freddie Green's steady guitar chording, and Basie's sparse, bright piano figures created a sound that was admired and emulated by many other bands (Page with Count Basie, "Swingin' at the Daisy Chain" [Decca/HEP]).

As bass players walked more varied lines, pianists avoided conflict by playing fewer bass notes. Many of them developed a "comping" style on piano that fed the band chords played with both hands. The "stride" left hand with which solo pianists carried the bass line became less common in swing rhythm sections and disappeared entirely in bebop piano playing (Nat Cole-Lester-Young, Red Callender Trio, "Body and Soul" [Aladdin], Bud Powell with Charlie Parker, "Donna Lee" [Savoy]).

Until the 1950s, bass strings were made of gut, with the lower two strings wound with fine wire. Gut produced a warm sound but wore out quickly with use. When played vigorously, gut strings vibrate in a wide arc. Jazz bass players used high bridges that kept the strings nearly an inch above the lower end of the fingerboard to prevent them from bouncing noisily against the ebony. This high action and the string tension it created made rapid passages difficult to play but gave the instrument a powerful voice.

Instead of trying to avoid string noise, some bassists snapped the strings directly at the fingerboard when plucking them, giving each note a loud click that projected well. A multiple click could be produced by slapping the strings against the fingerboard with the palm of the right hand. Some slap techniques included double and triple slaps as the strings were grasped and plucked, making a lively tap-dancing sound along with the bass line. Milt Hinton is one of the last masters of the slap technique and has recorded several good examples of it. When asked how he learned to play that way, he said, "When I was coming up, if they gave you a solo and you *didn't* play that way, it was a long time before they gave you another solo!" (Milt Hinton, *Old Man Time*, "Slap Happy" [Chiaroscuro]).

Bassists of the thirties like Hinton, Wellman Braud, Beverly Peer,

Bob Haggart, Billy Taylor Sr., and especially Israel Crosby continued to develop the walking bass style and were sometimes featured on solos (Hinton with Cab Calloway, "Ratamacue" [Vocalion/CBS]; Braud with Duke Ellington, "Mood Indigo" [Brunswick]; Peer with Chick Webb, "Clap Hands! Here Comes Charlie" [Decca]; Haggart with Bob Crosby, "Big Noise From Winnetka" [Decca]; Taylor as leader, "Carney-val in Rhythm" [Keynote]; Crosby with Teddy Wilson, "Christopher Columbus" [Brunswick/CBS]).

Had Israel Crosby received the presentation and major-label record distribution that Duke Ellington gave Jimmy Blanton, he might have been a primary influence in jazz bass playing during the late 1930s. He had a big, warm sound and virtuoso technique, and he played imaginative figures with perfect time. But Ellington hired Blanton, a spectacular musician, and Blanton set the standard for bass playing during the short time he played with Duke before his death from tuberculosis in 1942. Crosby was highly respected in every group he played with, but he had to wait until 1954 for national recognition, when he recorded and performed extensively with Ahmad Jamal.

Blanton played so well that Ellington hired him as soon as he first heard him, even though he already had a bass player, Billy Taylor. The two bassists played side by side with Duke until Taylor finally resigned in disgust. "I'm not going to stand up there next to that young boy playing all that bass and be embarrassed," he said. Blanton's agile technique, rich sound, good intonation and infectious swing sparked the Ellington band during two of its most fruitful recording years (Ellington, "Plucked Again" [Columbia]; Ellington, "Jack the Bear" [RCA]).

Though tuberculosis ended his life at the age of twenty-three, Blanton's playing remained the ideal for most jazz bassists for decades after his death. His style was carried forward and expanded upon in the work of Oscar Pettiford, Red Callender, Slam Stewart, George Duvivier, Ray Brown, Wilbur Ware and many others (Pettiford with Lucky Thompson, "Tricrotism" [ABC]; Callender with Lester Young, "Tea for Two" [Aladdin]; *Slam Stewart* [Savoy]; Duvivier with Shelly Manne, *The Sicks of Us* [Impulse]; Brown, *Bass Hit* [Verve]; Ware, *The Chicago Sound* [Riverside]).

The 1920s through the early 1950s were the years of heavy physical labor for bass players. It took stamina to play the instrument, to make a sound that could be heard through the rest of the band, and to do it for long hours, night after night. Blisters could develop, and adhesive tape was only a temporary aid. It protected the fingers but made an unsatisfying sound on the strings. Bass players preferred to develop thick calluses on their fingertips, which they carefully protected from harm.

Finger and hand strength was important in producing a big sound, but it was also good to have an instrument with a clear tone that projected well. Good string basses are hand-carved from various woods: maple for the back and sides, ebony for the fingerboard, and spruce for the top plate, which resonates with the vibrations sent to it from the strings via the maple bridge. The sound of each instrument is determined by the age and character of the wood and by the skill of the bass maker. A bass player may spend years searching for an instrument that will produce the specific sound he wants to hear.

During the big band era, a few companies here and in Europe produced string basses made of plywood. Some are still made today, mostly for students. Plywood basses do not usually resonate as well as carved instruments, but they have the advantage of being less expensive and less fragile. Chubby Jackson, while he was Woody Herman's star bassist, developed a signature line of plywood basses made by the Kay Company, some of them fitted with a fifth string. In order to get more big band punch in the high register, Chubby used his fifth string as a high C, rather than the low-C tuning used by most other five-string bass players (Jackson with Woody Herman, "Apple Honey" [Columbia]). Some manufacturers have made basses of aluminum and of plastic, but maple, spruce, and ebony remain the materials of choice for a good sounding string bass.

With the development of electrical amplification in the 1930s, bassists hoped to find a better way to make themselves heard. Guitarists Eddie Durham, Charlie Christian, and Les Paul popularized a method of amplifying guitars for solo use, and magnetic pickups for the string bass soon appeared on the market, but none of them reproduced the sound of a bass the way bass players wanted to hear it. Wellman Braud used a primitive bass amplifier with Duke Ellington for a while but gave it up. Some of the Latin bands found that the DeArmond bass pickup was useful in making Latin bass lines heard through the roar of timbales, conga drums, and bongos but it produced a sound that was too boomy to support the 4/4 bass lines used in swing bands, and the amplifiers that were available then did not reproduce the lowest bass notes very well.

In 1950 in New York, Everett Hull mounted a small microphonic pickup inside a bass on the upper end of the adjustable peg on which the instrument rested; he named his product Ampeg. In order to get a truer bass sound he also developed an amplifier with larger transformers and speaker magnets that could more faithfully reproduce low notes. His pickup wasn't popular with bass players, but his Ampeg amplifier was an instant hit.

The Ampeg amplifier appeared at the same time that Leo Fender in California invented the Fender bass, which was quickly adopted as the bass instrument of choice by rock-and-roll bands. Some big jazz bands also tried it, notably Lionel Hampton, who featured Monk Montgomery playing the prototype of the Fender Precision Bass in 1950 (*Lionel Hampton and His Paris All Stars* [Clef/Verve]). But at that time, most bandleaders preferred the sound of the string bass.

For a while, drummers had taken their cue from Sid Catlett, Jo Jones, Dave Tough, Kenny Clarke, Roy Haynes, and Max Roach and learned to swing with a light touch, giving unamplified basses and pianos a chance to be heard. But the influence of louder drummers like Buddy Rich, Art Blakey, Philly Joe Jones, Elvin Jones, and Tony Williams gradually raised the general volume level of drumming so that the bass really began to need amplification. The development and refinement of the transducer pickup for the bass in the mid-1950s finally made good sound quality possible, allowing bassists, when they wished, to play lighter and faster while letting their amplifiers do the work of producing volume.

In the bebop era, bassists like Pettiford, Brown, Curley Russell, Tommy Potter, Teddy Kotick, Nelson Boyd, Arnold Fishkin, Clyde Lombardi, and Percy Heath developed bass lines to fit modern harmonies. They were also learning to play at the fast tempos favored by Charlie Parker and Dizzy Gillespie. Drummers, finding it difficult to swing while playing four beats to a measure on the bass drum at those tempos, began to leave the steady pulse to the bass player, saving the bass drum for accents.

Charles Mingus added other devices to his walking line, such as ostinatos, pedal point lines, double stops, and sudden tempo changes; later he was influential as a bandleader and composer. But it was Oscar Pettiford and Ray Brown who set the standard for bebop bass players. Both could swing powerfully with a rich tone and good intonation, and both had a command of their instrument that allowed them to solo well in all keys. Pettiford went on to lead several interesting groups of his own, and Brown for many years anchored the musically demanding Oscar Peterson Trio (Russell with Charlie Parker, "KoKo" [Savoy]; Potter with Charlie Parker, "Passport" and "Visa" [Verve]; Kotick with Charlie Parker, "Au Privave" [Verve];

Boyd with Miles Davis, "Half Nelson" [Savoy]; Fishkin with Lennie Tristano, "Subconscious-Lee" [Prestige]; Lombardi with Eddie Bert, *Let's Dig Bert* [TransWorld]; Heath with Charlie Parker, "Chi Chi" [Clef/Verve]; Mingus, *Pithecanthropus Erectus* [Atlantic]; *Oscar Pettiford, Volume 2* [Bethlehem]; Brown with Oscar Peterson, *The Trio* [Verve]).

In small groups, a bass player would be given more solo space for variety, or to rest the horn players' lips. Solos were no longer reserved just for the virtuosi. It became expected of every bass player to be able to take a chorus now and then. Instead of plucking or slapping, Slam Stewart bowed his solos and sang the same notes he was bowing an octave higher, using a nasal vocal sound that emulated the growl effects used by brass players. Later, Major Holley perfected a similar style, but he sang in a voice pitched nearly an octave lower than Slam's (Stewart with Lester Young, "Just You, Just Me" [Keynote/Fontana]; Stewart and Holley, *Shut Yo' Mouth* [Delos]).

On orders from his doctor, Red Mitchell spent a year away from smoke-filled jazz clubs in 1951 because of a lung infection. During that time, while playing at home, he developed a new solo technique on the bass. He lowered his action and played softer, and found that he was able to articulate more rapidly, initiating some notes by plucking the strings with fingers of his left hand, and getting more speed by plucking lightly with two alternating fingers of his right hand. He could play faster passages with this technique, and he could also play his melodic ideas with a more legato, less percussive style. Mitchell's new way of playing recorded well, but it was not as successful when he finally returned to nightclub work. The lower volume and less percussive attack did not ring through the sound of a large group, and even when he played with trios and quartets, it was difficult to hear him in noisy rooms. He was at his best in quiet concert halls. Later, flexible steel strings and amplification gave Red (and other bass players) the necessary control of sound and volume (Mitchell with Bob Brookmeyer, "Liberty Bell" and "Doe Eyes" [Pacific Jazz]; Red Mitchell–Harold Land Quintet, "Hear Ye" [Atlantic]).

Mitchell made another innovation in 1966. Orchestral bassists are often required to modify their instruments so that they can play down to a low C, an octave below the cello's lowest note. This usually is done by adding an extension to the top of the fingerboard to lengthen the E string. Red, doing studio work in Hollywood, kept getting requests for the low C, but didn't want his favorite bass to have to undergo the necessary carpentry. Instead, he retuned his E string to low C and refingered everything else on that string. He wasn't happy with the looseness of the low string in that new tuning, so he decided to start with the low C and retune the whole instrument in fifths, like a cello (C-G-D-A). Basses are usually tuned in fourths (E-A-D-G) because the fingering distance between half-steps in the lower positions is very wide.

Playing a bass tuned in fifths requires more left-hand shifting than with the standard tuning. Of course, it also requires a complete relearning of the fingering system. When asked how long it took to make the switch, Red said, "I practiced hard all one weekend, went back to work on Monday and made a lot of mistakes." Mitchell continued to play on fifth-tuned basses for the rest of his life (Mitchell with Roger Kellaway, *Alone Together* [Dragon]).

Trying to find a more facile solo voice, some jazz bassists experimented with playing the cello as an adjunct to the bass. Most of them tuned the instrument in fourths like a bass, as did Oscar Pettiford. Harry Babasin, Ray Brown, Doug Watkins, Sam Jones, and Ron Carter all played the cello on occasion, and Brown, Carter, and Stanley Clarke have also played the piccolo bass, a smaller bass that usually has a higher tuning than the standard instrument. In his own groups, Carter sometimes plays the piccolo bass as a solo instrument, with another bassist with a standard instrument in his rhythm section (Pettiford, *Cello Again* [Savoy]; Babasin with Dodo Marmarosa, "Bopmatism" and "Tradewinds" [Dial]; Brown, *Jazz Cello* [Verve]; Watkins, *Doug at Large* [New Jazz]; Jones, *Cello Again* [Xanadu]; Carter, *Piccolo* [Milestone]).

During the early 1950s, experiments were made with plastics in an effort to improve bass strings. One string maker wrapped gut strings with thin plastic ribbon, which provided a surface that frayed less and still kept the sound of the gut. Another made strings made entirely of plastic; they were durable, but they had a rubbery feel, and their smooth surface did not respond well to bowing. The revolution came when steel strings for the bass were perfected.

Bassists in classical orchestras first experimented with the steel strings that were being developed in Germany and Austria in the late 1940s, and jazz players gradually followed their example. The first steel strings on the market were made of thin stainless-steel wire, much like piano strings. They had a brilliant sound, were easy to bow, and were very durable, but their lack of flexibility was a serious problem. In certain seasons, as the wood in a bass changed with the weather, the tension of steel strings would increase, making it difficult to press them to the fingerboard. Steel was very hard on fingers that were accustomed to gut strings. String makers eventually learned to twist string cores of fine wire and nylon thread and wrap them with a thin steel ribbon or wire to make strings that are more flexible.

Steel strings speak louder than gut with less plucking and bowing effort, and they do not vibrate in such a wide arc, so the bridge can be kept lower, moving the playing action much closer to the fingerboard. Faster fingering is possible on strings that don't have to move so far. Bass repairmen invented adjustable bridges and redesigned fingerboard shapes to accommodate the lower steel-string action.

Liberated from the physical work of playing with high action, jazz bassists rapidly expanded their technique during the 1950s and 1960s. Extending a concept begun by Red Mitchell and Charles Mingus, Scott LaFaro developed a rapid fingering and plucking system, and found the perfect place to use it when he joined the Bill Evans Trio in 1959, with Paul Motian on drums. Together, the three musicians invented a style of jazz in which no one was required to spell out the tempo with an explicit beat. This gave LaFaro the freedom to invent a new kind of "conversational" bass accompaniment, made up of short melodic figures and phrases rather than of a steady pulsing line. Like Blanton, LaFaro died (in an auto accident) only two years after becoming a major influence in jazz, but his recordings continue to inspire jazz bass players (LaFaro with Bill Evans Trio, *Waltz for Debby* [Riverside/OJC]).

As recordings spread jazz around the world, foreign audiences clamored for live concerts by American jazz musicians. By the 1930s they had begun to travel long distances to reach their new audiences. Before long, good local jazz musicians were cropping up all over the world. France's Pierre Michelot, England's John Hawksworth and Peter Ind, and Indonesia's Eddie de Haas were bassists who came to the attention of American listeners by the 1950s, and later bassists like Don Thompson from Canada, Niels-Henning Ørsted Pedersen from Denmark, George Mraz and Miroslav Vitous from Czechoslovakia, Eberhard Weber from Germany, and David Holland from England established themselves firmly in the jazz world.

Many bassists have continued to develop the Blanton legacy. Musicians like Wendell Marshall, Jimmy Woode, Major Holley, Aaron Bell, Earl May, John Simmons, Joe Benjamin, Joe Mondragon, Al Hall, Paul Chambers, Sam Jones, Henry Grimes, Eugene Wright, Ben Tucker, Eddie Calhoun, Eddie Jones, John Ore, Leroy Vinnegar, Jimmy Garrison, Curtis Counce, Reggie Workman, Andy Simpkins, and Christian McBride have expanded on the principles that Blanton established, their central concern being with the power of the bass to swing the band.

Others like Monk Montgomery, Bob Cranshaw, and Steve Swallow continued in that tradition while transferring it to the fender bass. (The word *fender* is used here to represent the genre of guitar-like electric basses, not as a brand name.) Other fender bassists, notably Jaco Pastorius and Stanley Clarke, played the instrument in a virtuoso style that related more to the jazz guitar (Montgomery with the Mastersounds, "Stompin' at the Savoy" [Jazz West Coast]; Cranshaw with Sonny Rollins, *The Reel Life* [Milestone]; Swallow with Carla Bley, "Social Studies" [Watt]; Pastorius, "Donna Lee" [Epic]; Stanley Clarke and the Jazz Explosion, *This Is Jazz #41* [Sony/Epic Legacy]).

After pioneer work done by Mingus, Mitchell, and LaFaro, many bassists developed techniques using the higher register of the bass, in what is called the thumb position, where the left thumb is brought from behind the neck of the bass up onto the fingerboard to be used with the other fingers of the left hand in stopping the strings. Since the strings are much shorter in this register, the voice of the bass is less deep, but it is possible to play very rapid passages in this position because the notes are closer together at the upper end of the fingerboard. Richard Davis, Art Davis, Eddie Gomez, Dave Holland, Michael Moore, Rufus Reid, Niels-Henning Ørsted Pedersen, George Mraz, and Lynn Seaton are notable among many bassists who have mastered the thumb position (Richard Davis, *Fancy Free* [Galaxy]; Art Davis, *Live!* [AKM]; Gomez with Bill Evans, *Intuition* [Fantasy]; Holland, *Emerald Tears* [ECM]; Moore with Roger Kellaway and Gene Bertoncini, *Roger Kellaway Meets the Duo* [Chiaroscuro]; Reid, Tana-Reid, *Back to Front* [Evidence]; Ørsted Pedersen with Kenny Drew, *Looking at Bird* [Steeplechase]; Mraz with Tommy Flanagan, *Jazz Poet* [Timeless]; Seaton with John Fedchock, *New York Big Band*, "Blues du Jour" [Reservoir]).

When Ornette Coleman brought a group to the Five Spot in New York in the fall of 1959 playing what came to be called "free jazz," a new role was created for the bass player. Since the collective group improvisations did not follow a preset harmonic structure, the bassist, Charlie Haden, played a sort of intuitive counterpoint that complemented the explorations of the other musicians. Haden uses a full sound and a percussive attack, sometimes strumming across all four strings in a chordal style. His work with Paul Bley and with Coleman set the style for the genre, and he worked in the same vein with Denny Zeitlin, Keith Jarrett, and Archie Shepp, as well as with groups of his own (Haden with Coleman, *The Shape of Jazz to Come* [Atlantic]).

As Walter Page with Count Basie, Jimmy Blanton with Duke Ellington, Ray Brown with Oscar Peterson, Charles Mingus with his own groups, and Scott LaFaro with Bill Evans created milestones in the development of jazz bass playing, so did Ron Carter with the 1960s edition of the Miles Davis Quintet. Miles's earlier rhythm sections, in which Paul Chambers's supple straight-ahead playing came directly out of the Blanton-Pettiford-Brown tradition, had tremendous impact on other jazz musicians (Chambers with the Miles Davis Quintet, "Cookin'" [Prestige]). But with his new quintet, Miles combined Carter, drummer Tony Williams, pianist Herbie Hancock, and tenor saxophonist Wayne Shorter and stepped into a new realm of group improvisation in which the bass, piano, and drums created harmonic and rhythmic forms that shifted quickly with the mood and instinct of the musicians. Carter, with good intonation and sound quality and an excellent command of his instrument, used his ability to listen and respond to the other members of the group at an instantaneous, almost mind-reading level to help Miles turn improvised jazz in a new direction (Carter with Miles Davis, *Highlights From the Plugged Nickel* [Columbia]).

With the divergence of jazz forms and styles that has come about since the innovations of Ornette Coleman, Paul Bley, Jimmy Giuffre, John Coltrane, and Cecil Taylor, the bass player's role as he moves from group to group has become more varied than ever. In some musical situations he is expected to anchor the time, and in others he is encouraged to avoid playing a steady pulse. He may be expected to spell out the basic chord changes, or he may be asked to wander "freely." (*He* is used only as a language convenience . . . many women are playing jazz bass nowadays.)

During first hundred years of jazz, the general level of musicianship among bassists has grown tremendously. Skills that were considered a distant goal by the average bass player in the 1940s are expected today of every advanced student of the string bass. Among the new generation, it is interesting to note that some bassists remain devoted to the Blanton-Pettiford-Brown tradition, some have branched out from the Mitchell-Mingus-LaFaro-Haden beginnings into even more advanced forms, and others are re-creating the music that was played in the 1920s and 1930s by bassists like Page, Hinton, and Crosby. A number of these last have brought the string bass full circle, going back to using gut strings played without amplification. Together, they are all carrying forward a marvelously rich tradition of bass playing.

Jazz Drumming

Burt Korall

The drummer, a primary supportive-interactive-inspirational source in jazz, is a product of an ever-evolving musical tradition. Like all jazz musicians, the keeper of the rhythmic flame has melded elements out of our own culture and those of Africa and Europe. Drummers have expanded their vision and reinvented themselves as jazz has developed and diversified. However, the soulful energy and time, always the drummer's responsibility, remains alive at the music's core—in one form or another.

Jazz rhythm owes an ongoing debt to black music and musicians. Though deeply responsive to black life, the music covers a wider arc and, as performed through history, exemplifies democracy in action. Seemingly disparate elements mingle and compatibly blend.

Our jazz tale focuses on unusually gifted drummers—those who originated techniques and concepts and avoided the commonplace. The story begins in New Orleans, a port city notable for the mix of black, brown, and beige, of Spanish and French cultural influences. The definition of a melting pot, it was a logical place for jazz to take form.

Musicians, black, white, and Creole, shaped the music—neither

Max Roach, Massey Hall, Toronto, 1953. Courtesy Frank Driggs Collection.

haphazardly nor with great deliberation—in the years following emancipation. Progressively a compatible blend of musical elements came into full view. Jazz-impelled brass bands, with a march-rhythm foundation, performed for parades in the open air, utilizing three percussionists: a bass drummer, a snare drummer, and a cymbal player. Smaller versions of these bands played all over New Orleans for a variety of functions: funerals, park concerts, dances with just one drummer. Toward the end of World War I, a number of jazz musicians, some of whom had already played elsewhere, filtered into other cities, notably Chicago.

Jazz and a component thereof—ragtime, which was born in the Midwest—had reached into a variety of cities and countries earlier than you might suspect. Drummers playing in the syncopated ragtime style effectively brought into play European military/march technique, particularly on the snare drum.

James Lent, an American in England, with the London Regimental Band in 1904, and the energetic, unyieldingly pulsating Charlie Johnson, one of four black Americans comprising the Versatile Four in London in 1916, have left behind unusually well recorded, potent examples of their work, documented in *Anthology of Jazz Drumming, Volume 1* (Masters of Jazz). The *Anthology* also includes the surprising Buddy Gilmore, recorded in New York in 1914, with the influential James Reese Europe and his Society Orchestra. A technically adept drummer, he dashes around the set on "Castle Hill Rag," building to a convincing, climactic solo, during which he concentrates on single strokes—provocatively accented—and one basic motif. It is quite evident that the variegated, highly rhythmic patterns of tap dancing had a more than passing influence on Gilmore—as on other drummers through history.

Jazz drums became a noted presence in New York in 1917 when Tony Spargo, a talented percussionist, came to town from New Orleans with the Original Dixieland Jazz Band. A white novelty-dance unit, it enjoyed success at Reisenweber's and was recorded. Though not an innovator, Spargo opened the way for others.

There seems little doubt, considering existing evidence, that Baby Dodds was the most important New Orleans jazz drummer. He studied the instrument and could read music. By today's standards, Dodds was not a great technician, but certainly he was a memorable *musician*. He could play simply and in a sophisticated manner as well. But no matter where he took the music—often he dealt with polyrhythms—he maintained his musical balance, never obscuring or losing hold of the pulsation that he felt was so crucial to jazz. His time, the way he used elements of the set, his sensitivity to the details and overall form of a piece of music, and his press roll endeared him to musicians. On a live Folkways recording, done at New York's Town Hall in 1946, Dodds is heard with the clarity lacking on his recordings with King Oliver, Sidney Bechet, Louis Armstrong, Jelly Roll Morton, and others. You realize how well he developed material and made music work.

Zutty Singleton, another innovator from Louisiana, was one of the first to effectively use brushes and added a sock cymbal, a forerunner to the hi-hat, to his set. He also brought to the fore a manner of soloing that closely followed the form of the music. A straight and simple stylist, he was notable for his warmth and natural sense of swing. The march rhythms and syncopations of New Orleans were in his blood. But he could and did play all kinds of jazz, adapting, taking cues from the music and the players, never sounding intimidated, out of place, or "old." His versatility is well documented on *Louis Armstrong Volume 4: Armstrong and Earl Hines* (Columbia Jazz Masterpieces), *Roy Eldridge—Little Jazz* (Columbia Jazz Masterpieces), *Fats Waller and His Rhythm—The Last Years (1940–43)* (Bluebird), and sessions with Slim Gailliard in the 1940s, including Dizzy Gillespie and Charlie Parker.

Brilliant from childhood, Vic Berton had the sort of ability that made him a factor in music of every sort. But Louis Armstrong and other jazz musicians never forgot what he could do in a jazz context. Recordings with Red Nichols's Five Pennies and Nichols groups under a variety of names, done in the 1920s and re-released by Columbia and Brunswick, including "Boneyard Shuffle" and "Mean Dog Blues," helped establish Berton's jazz credentials. He developed new techniques and equipment that would make the drummer's job easier, including a forerunner of the hi-hat, an L-shaped rod on which to mount a cymbal on the bass drum, and pedal timpani that he would use on some of his best jazz recordings. Berton's admirable facility served the music. Very skillful in the playing, accenting, and manipulation of triplets, he was a relaxed, swinging, free ensemble player and soloist—yet very much in control.

Ben Pollack, a drum star and bandleader in the 1920s and beyond, was responsible for a number of drum innovations. Ray McKinley, the excellent drummer and personable bandleader, told me that "Ben used the set as an orchestra of instruments. Everything he did fed the pulse of the band. He was the first drummer I ever heard play the dotted eighth and sixteenth rhythm, with a stick and a brush, splitting the rhythm up between the snare and bass drum. He was a pioneer who did several things first."

The Pollack 1926 performance of "High Society," as a sideman with trumpeter Sharky Bonano and His Sharks, illustrates what made him a major drummer. Bringing unusual spirit to a New Orleans–oriented small band, Pollack combines cogently phrased rolls over strong four-beat bass drumming and makes things happen. Originally recorded for Vocalion, this Pollack performance most recently reappeared in a Columbia LP collection, *The Sound of New Orleans.*

As jazz and drummers moved from one growth level to another, new and better equipment paralleled, even anticipated, developments. Through the 1920s various forms of the "low boy," a two-cymbal contrivance, operated by the left foot—if you were right-handed—appeared and were used. By 1929 four drum companies were advertising the hi-hat, a taller version of the "low boy." To operate it in an optimum manner, the drummer had to develop a form of "independence," freeing his foot and hands and moving off the snare.

The kit itself began to take form in the late 1890s when New Orleans's Dee Chandler, who drummed with Buddy Bolden and the John Robichaux Orchestra, invented a primitive wooden bass drum pedal. This was a key step forward.

In the 1920s and into the next decade, George Stafford, the drummer with Harlem's Charlie Johnson band, and Kaiser Marshall and Walter Johnson with the Fletcher Henderson band contributed in a major way to the evolutionary process of both the drums and jazz. They played time in a deft, economic manner—most of the time on the hi-hat. Rhythm-section unity and a clear-cut thrust emerged.

Coming to New York with the Basie band in 1936, Jo Jones tied it all in a neat package. He played in a smooth, poised, responsive, relaxed, linear style, given unmistakable identity by his singing/swinging, unparalleled hi-hat work. "Papa Jo" brought to jazz time an inner excitement, a subtlety, and a sense of possibility it never had before. Though not a virtuoso, Jones spontaneously devised fitting, telling fills and breaks that were an indisputable asset to the music. His recordings with Basie—most of which are available on Columbia—make his case.

Chick Webb, the heroic, chronically ill, hunchback genius, who led one of Harlem's most popular bands, defined the swing style for drums. Like Jo Jones, Webb was a sparkplug—a section man who tied in with the bass, piano, and guitar. He used the whole set for timekeeping but gave the bass drum and hi-hat precedence. A stunning soloist, Webb was viewed by other drummers as God-like but puzzling. Repeatedly they tried to unravel what he played. The little drummer was fast; his ideas tumbled one over the other, feeding the music and propelling it. But drummers walked away, shaking their heads. Totally untutored, Webb could execute almost anything he thought of or remembered. A major influence on Gene Krupa, Buddy Rich, and a host of others with roots in the explosive swing period, he was a victim of imperfect recordings and broadcasts. Some indication of his hypnotizing talent is accessible to you on *Spinnin' the Webb: Chick Webb and His Orchestra* (Decca Jazz/GRP).

Undoubtedly, Gene Krupa did more to popularize drums and drumming than almost anyone else. A gentleman of all gentlemen, he was an uncommonly talented, innovative musician who—in the parlance of vaudeville—knew how "to hold his spot." The magnetic Krupa shot to unbelievable fame with the Benny Goodman band (1935–38). "That Ace Drummer Man," with his glittering white-pearl set, not only embodied the period but gave drums, drum solos, and jazz performances on the instrument a legitimacy they never had before. A dedicated student, Krupa took the raw materials—the twenty-six drum rudiments—and experimented, striving tirelessly to make them work as well in jazz as they did in other forms of music. He succeeded, and his supportive playing and rudimentary solos pulsated, establishing a key truth for drummers: that formal materials can be made to work and work well in an informal context.

Krupa's work reflects the influence of his "first major mentor and teacher" Baby Dodds, his obsession with Chick Webb, and, later, an interest in Max Roach. His best performances combine taste, skill, and power, an identifiable sound on the instrument, and the capacity to make music come alive and mean something. Try "Swingtime in the Rockies" and "I'm a Ding Dong Daddy From Dumas"—with the Goodman big band and small group, respectively (on RCA Victor), and a variety of things with his own band—e.g., well-regulated performances of arrangements and compositions by Gerry Mulligan, George Williams, and Ed Finckel, which are available on Columbia. Though Krupa did not invent a new jazz drum style, he put a highly discernible mark on what already existed, often making it more polished and accessible to the public.

Buddy Rich had a freakish talent. A drumming, dancing child star—Traps, the Drum Wonder—in the 1920s, he found jazz and it soon discovered him early in the next decade. Bandleaders—Artie

Shaw, Tommy Dorsey, Les Brown, Benny Goodman, Harry James, Count Basie, Woody Herman—and a variety of top jazz soloists, including Lester Young, Charlie Parker, Dizzy Gillespie, and Art Tatum, hired him for what he could bring to their music.

The super drummer headed his own big bands and small groups beginning in 1945. He ultimately made peace with progress, leading adventurous bands, mirroring contemporary trends in jazz and popular music. Did Buddy Rich change things? Yes and no. He played the hell out of a variety of styles, summed up jazz history on the instrument, and made the listener aware of what was possible. But he did not make a revolution or prepare the way for one.

Dave Tough, Sidney "Big Sid" Catlett, and Rossiere "Shadow" Wilson did.

The brilliant Tough was plagued by inconsistencies and difficulties. His great gift for music constantly was at war with that which would stifle it—epilepsy and drink. But an extraordinary pulse resided within him. When he played, Tough energized and elevated music in an almost unbelievable manner. In and out of things in the 1920s, he spent time in Europe in the latter part of the decade. Then he all but disappeared, reemerging in New York in 1935. Tough joined Tommy Dorsey's band in 1936, then Benny Goodman, Artie Shaw, Charlie Spivak, and Jack Teagarden, among others, over the next few years.

Tough set an example on the hi-hat and cymbals, intensifying the pulse by leaving the hi-hat partially open, playing for sound and time, increasing the width and depth of the beat. He began using cymbals, particularly a large, battered Chinese, as time vehicles. Where others made accents on the snare, Tough would hit fast-speaking cymbals instead. His well-tuned bass drum was perfect for rhythm and sharply rendered detonations under ensembles.

Though virtually without technical resources, Tough fully established his updated manner of dealing with the drums and cymbals in the Woody Herman First Herd in 1944–45. Don Lamond, who would bring a highly original, modern drum style to the Herman band two years later, replaced him. Tough died after a fall in Newark. Was it liquor or epilepsy? No one knows for sure. Only one thing is certain: it was a tragedy.

Catlett, a completely engaging artist, had an ageless quality to his drumming that erased the line separating then and now. He could play with anyone, ranging from Louis Armstrong to Dizzy Gillespie and Charlie Parker. Drummers who changed the course of drumming in the 1940s to accommodate bebop looked to Catlett and, of course, Jo Jones. Both had outlined a more flexible manner of playing, with cymbals and rhythmic counterpoint on the snare and bass drum more of a factor, particularly as the tempos rose. Listen to Catlett on the Keynote sides with Lester Young, the Gillespie/Parker recordings—"Shaw 'Nuff," "Salt Peanuts," "Lover Man," and "Hot House" (now available on Prestige), on which he replaced Stan Levey—and his performances with Armstrong in big and small bands (Decca) and with Benny Goodman and Fletcher Henderson (Columbia).

Shadow Wilson, a shadowy figure indeed except to an ever-narrowing circle of musicians and critics, was a troubled, luminous messenger of drum modernism. But for all of his problems with drugs, he was one of the most creative drummers of all. After he came to New York in 1939, he drummed with a wide variety of bands and groups. He was part of the modern experiments in the Earl Hines band in 1943. Billy Eckstine built his band around him in 1944. "Shadow was perfect for the new music," the singer declared. The drummer made the first Eckstine records but was drafted, and Art Blakey got his opportunity.

Wilson, who replaced Jo Jones with Basie (1944–46 and 1948), had great impact on late-night network Basie broadcasts from New York's Hotel Lincoln and on the band's Columbia records. He played patterns and fills and the sort of cymbal-propelled time that would become common in jazz. Recordings with Illinois Jacquet, Tadd Dameron, Erroll Garner, Thelonious Monk, and the Oscar Pettiford big band also tell us how potent he could be. Wilson's impossibly perfect, double-time, climactic two-bar turnaround on the Basie Columbia recording of Jimmy Mundy's "Queer Street" is his masterpiece.

Kenny Clarke was working on new ways and means for drums as far back as 1935, with Lonnie Simmons's band in Greenwich Village. He further developed his ideas with the Edgar Hayes band, with Claude Hopkins, and certainly with the Teddy Hill band, where he was encouraged by Dizzy Gillespie. Clarke started played time on his top cymbal, rather than on the hi-hat or snare drum, using the snare and bass drum for color and accents. This manner of performance gave the music a more linear feeling and also made it easier for the drummer to deal with fast tempos. "Klook," as he came to be known, wanted drums to be more expressive and musical. By the time he began working as musical director at Minton's in Harlem in 1941, with Thelonious Monk and other venturesome musicians, the essentials of his style were in place: the crisp, light drum sound and the techniques that were the result of his snare-drum training and the music itself.

A rare accompanist, with few equals as a "time" player, he was the very essence of discretion and buoyant swing and made a virtue of simplicity, whether working with Louis Armstrong, Sidney Bechet, Count Basie, or Dizzy Gillespie. The link between Jones and Catlett and Max Roach, Clarke made his reputation in America, then spent his middle and late years living in Paris, performing and teaching throughout Europe and North Africa, less encumbered by matters of race. Recordings with the Dizzy Gillespie small and big bands and Tadd Dameron in the 1940s, with Miles Davis in the early 1950s, with the Modern Jazz Quartet before he left for France in 1956, and with the Clarke-Boland Big Band later provide a good introduction to his work.

When Max Roach's first records with Charlie Parker were released by Savoy in 1945, drummers experienced awe and puzzlement and even fear. Stan Levey, one of the most impressive and naturally accommodating drummers in the modern style, was stunned when he first heard Roach at the Onyx Club in New York in 1944: "The way he broke things up between his hands and feet confused me at first. But I came to realize that, because of him, drumming no longer was just *time*, it was *music*."

Roach had the unparalleled ability to "hear" and understand and deal with this new, demanding, fragmented music. To listen to him on records, over the years, is a lesson in ambition. The Parker records, plus those with his own groups, large and small, define a love of craft and a deepening of the drummer's art. Roach brought boldness of vision to drums and challenges to jazz; not the least of these was playing in time signatures other than 4/4 and 2/4 and making them swing.

Art Blakey, a volcanic performer and bandleader, moved to the center of things with the Billy Eckstine band (1944–47). Inspired by Chick Webb and coached by Dizzy Gillespie, as were many drummers, Blakey brought techniques to jazz drumming that raised the music's level of interest and intensity. Diverse patterns on a cymbal or cymbals, spirited closing of the hi-hat on the two and four, in 4/4 time, coupled with cross-rhythms on the snare and/or tomtoms and explosive footwork made his performances readily identifiable. His recordings with the Eckstine band, various editions of his band—the Jazz Messengers—and with groups headed by Thelonious Monk, Miles Davis, and others continue to be informing and exciting long after the fact.

Shelly Manne, like Blakey, learned by playing. He stimulated and brought a sense of security and relaxation to bands of all kinds. Dave Tough and Jo Jones, his idols and mentors, taught him by example. His subtle tendencies, however, went out the window, for the most part, during his association with various editions of the gymnastic Stan Kenton band in the 1940s and early 1950s. But this musical relationship made him a star and opened the way to an enormously successful career as a group leader and super studio musician in Hollywood.

A drummer who preferred a supportive role to solos, he played exciting time, aptly decorated, making his performances generally stimulating. Manne could play any kind of music. Try the Capitol recordings with Kenton, particularly with the Innovations Orchestra, and his albums on Contemporary: *Swing Sounds,* featuring his group, the Men, and including his striking solo work on Bud Powell's "Un Poco Loco"; *The Three and the Two*—free and abstract playing in the company of Shorty Rogers, Jimmy Giuffre, and Russ Freeman; and five intensely pulsating small-group CDs recorded live in 1959 at the Blackhawk in San Francisco.

Philly Joe Jones, who integrated key modern drum styles into something very much his own, made his name with the Miles Davis group in the 1950s. Tony Williams insisted that *Milestones,* a Davis set on Columbia, featuring Jones, was "the perfect jazz drumming record." Don Lamond speaks reverently of what Jones played on "Billy Boy," on the same recording, citing his exchanges with pianist Red Garland. Jones credited Cozy Cole for his early technical development. Subsequently Philly Joe made rudiments work very well in the modern context, developing variations, compressed versions, and extensions of them that were adopted by others.

Just about everyone of consequence worked and recorded with Jones. His recording with Tadd Dameron (Riverside) and his own album dedicated to the work of the pioneering jazz composer and arranger, *Dameronia—To Tadd With Love* (Uptown), are definitive examples of his "sound," taste, time, and individuality. Jones did so many things well. Certainly his brush work was exemplary. But longtime drug addiction worked against him, making financial security and continuing creativity and development all but impossible.

In the midst of all the creative turbulence of bebop, there were drummers innovating within the swing style, integrating modern elements for color and relevance. One of the most important was Norman "Tiny" Kahn. He never made a noise or wrote a note that intruded on the forward motion of the music. Essentially a self-trained drummer and writer, he composed and arranged and played for the Henry Jerome, Georgie Auld, Boyd Raeburn, Charlie Barnet, Chubby Jackson, Stan Getz, and Elliot Lawrence bands and CBS Radio, among others. At the time of his sudden death from a heart attack—at twenty-nine in 1953—he was at a point when his worth was being widely discovered. Oh, what he might have become!

Mel Lewis had much in common with Kahn. A spare, telling player, whose time feeling was relaxed yet firm, he played with a variety of big bands—Boyd Raeburn, Tex Beneke, Ray Anthony, Gerald Wilson, Stan Kenton and Terry Gibbs—and small groups. But the excellent orchestra that he co-led with Thad Jones, then headed alone, allowed his considerable talent to grow as never before. His recordings, with Kenton (Capitol), Gibbs (Contemporary), and on his own (multiple labels), are quite uplifting.

The drummers in the bebop generation not only made musical and rhythmic changes, they altered and added to the drum set. The hi-hat cymbals grew in size, as did the cymbals for crash and time purposes. The bass drum diminished in size. Roy Haynes and Max Roach introduced a shallow snare drum because of its responsiveness and crackling sound. Louie Bellson, one of our most masterful drummers, designed and used a set that had two bass drums and additional tomtoms. This was but the beginning of a major equipment revolution.

Roy Haynes tied bebop to the future. One of our most imaginative, adventurous, and rhythmically fluent drummers, he had to wait for the music and the critics to catch up to him. Only in recent years has he received what long has been due him. A professional as a teenager, he played every style, on his home ground in Boston, before coming to New York with the Luis Russell big band in 1945. His talent was immediately understood by Lester Young and Charlie Parker, who hired and admired him.

Haynes plays *ideas* and follows through on them, rather than exclusively concentrating on "ding, ding-a-ding." A dense, less linear player than his great inspiration, Jo Jones, he has amplified the drummer's role and speaks the language of the contemporary player, as Papa did. There are so many records that tell you what Roy Haynes can do. The Parker and Coltrane things are an excellent start. *Now He Sings, Now He Sobs* (Blue Note), a now-famous CD with Chick Corea, captures Haynes's time-impelled, contributive performances on their highest level of creativity.

When Elvin Jones came to New York from Detroit in the 1950s, he experienced more than a little rejection. Trumpeter Donald Byrd remembers: "I used Elvin and many musicians complained: 'Why do you want *that* drummer? He plays weird time and the accents fall in the wrong places.'" What was so objectionable? Moving into odd-meter figures; his underlying triplet, 12/8 rhythmic feeling where others moved along in stricter 4/4; a very busy left hand; and "unwieldy" ideas some musicians insisted only masked the time.

Michael James, a British critic, said Jones was "contemptuous" of the soloist. On the contrary, Jones directly involves himself with the music and the soloist ... but on more than one level. He plays what he feels and what, in his view, the music asks for: it could be closing the hi-hat on two and four or one and three, or all four beats; moving the tempo up or down; or soloing at great length ... until he's through. Certainly whatever he plays is "on the tune" and guided by time and pulsation. "The time is always there," says saxophonist Pat LaBarbera. "Elvin doesn't give you all of it. He makes you rely on yourself."

Jones found the John Coltrane quartet the ideal context. The musicians worked one against the other in an acutely reactive way. The innovative saxophonist, an excellent, goading foil, was particularly taken with Jones's ability to juggle rhythms and keep everything fresh. If asked for a definitive introduction to Jones's work, I would recommend the Coltrane records (Impulse). They speak volumes.

Tony Williams joined Miles Davis at seventeen, following years of preparation. He started drumming in 1954 at age eight. He worked his way through the contemporary drum styles of Max Roach, Roy Haynes, Art Blakey, Louis Hayes, and Philly Joe Jones, studying and analyzing them, practicing until he mastered what he couldn't play.

Williams made a revolution with the Miles Davis band, using the drum set, his hi-hat, and cymbals in very personal ways to project his thoughts and view of time. He interacted in the purest sense with his colleagues, mingling provocative coloration and inventive rhythmic commentary into what often seemed overly tumultuous. But there was beauty, flawless presentation, and consistent relevancy in what he played. Like Elvin Jones, Williams elevated the drummer to a position of equality in the jazz group by liberating his conception and the drum set itself.

Williams's Davis years (1963–69)—and the recordings (Columbia)—were his most memorable. Over time, he continued on his creative course. One of the first to be involved in the "fusion" of seemingly disparate musical elements in his group, Lifetime, he kept trying things: avant-garde jazz; rock music; returning to the mainstream; writing songs, jazz, and so-called "serious" compositions. He always studied—theory, arranging, composition, languages, drums/percussion—whatever he felt was necessary. And so many things were necessary to him. Then, suddenly, he was gone, with so much yet to do.

Some drummers have taken the "advanced" free/color abstractions of Pete La Roca Sims, and Elvin Jones and Tony Williams, almost beyond the realm of time and pulsation. Sunny Murray, Rashied Ali, Andrew Cyrille Beaver Harris, Milford Graves, and later Pheeroan akLaff and Ronald Shannon Jackson involved themselves in this sort of experimental work, trying to find their own answers.

Jack DeJohnette, one of the most influential present-day drummers, like Jones and Williams, seldom states time as directly as many of his antecedents. Working with and against the band and the players, he moves rhythms around the set, suggesting pulsation and the character of a piece in his responses to the music. Most jazz devotees initially became aware of DeJohnette in the 1960s or early 1970s when he worked and recorded with Charles Lloyd, Bill Evans, and Miles Davis. Subsequently, his activities—and certainly his recordings—italicized his need to experience new music and summon untapped feelings and responses. DeJohnette plays on a "large" set—snare, bass drum (he has tried two), six tomtoms, a hi-hat, and five cymbals—and sometimes incorporates electronics. He has learned from Jo Jones, Max Roach, and Philly Joe Jones; he also speaks fondly of Vernel Fournier and Paul Motian, but insists he adapted what he liked about Elvin Jones and Tony Williams and came up with Jack DeJohnette.

In the 1970s and beyond, increasingly large drum sets, and seemingly countless cymbals, taxed reality. But Billy Cobham has made all this equipment—the triple bass drums, all the pedals, multiple tomtoms and cymbals, and electronic connections—work for him. His recordings with John McLaughlin's Mahavishnu Orchestra, with Miles Davis, and on his own, indicate his great facility, interest in various sorts of music, and the need to project whatever is possible on his instrument. As far back as the 1970s, he insisted that the era of the timekeeper was over, that the drummer had to assume a new, more forceful role and be ready to move in any direction. And he has.

Steve Gadd, a prodigy, became a first-call New York studio

drummer in the 1970s and has done countless sessions, most of them in the pop, rock, R&B, and funk areas. Gadd plays jazz with precision, swing, care, and love. (His best jazz recordings have been made with pianist Chick Corea.) Take a look at his video, *Steve Gadd Live at Pas* (CPP Media/Warner Bros.) His talent is unmistakable.

Other drummers on the contemporary scene who are interesting to listen to and think about include the ever-improving Peter Erskine, a student of the instrument whose experience is all over the place—Stan Kenton to Weather Report to John Abercrombie and his own groups; Terry Clarke, a quietly effective small-group accompanist and superb big band drummer who immediately translates drum parts into music; Jeff Hamilton—effective in just about any musical situation; Cindy Blackman, a stylistic descendant of Art Blakey and Tony Williams, who burns brightly; the increasingly provocative Adam Nussbaum and Ralph Peterson; Danny Gottlieb, a well-trained, wide-ranging performer; Kenny Washington, the most historically informed and valid of the younger drummers; Lewis Nash, versatile, well grounded, spontaneous—one of the best young drummers; Dave Weckl, admired by many for his technical wizardry; Paul Motian, a veteran, who remains a factor because he can play relevantly with anyone; Joey Baron, another player with know-how, emerging out of wide-ranging experience, who is open and often quite surprising; Dennis Chambers, a stunning technician with striking coordination, who effectively calls on a variety of rhythms and feelings characteristic of jazz and of other idioms; and Bill Stewart, an imaginative, responsive player who shapes and accents the rhythmic line his own way. Lest we forget: the talented, increasingly mature Marvin "Smitty" Smith, Jeff Watts, and John Riley.

Lest we forget, indeed—other notable contributors—some departed, others still with us: Stan Levey, an influential bebop pioneer who brought uplift and invention to bands headed by Bird and Dizzy, Woody Herman and Stan Kenton, and to countless West Coast recording sessions; the earthy Bernard Purdie; Ike Day, the legendary modern-jazz innovator from Chicago; Sonny Greer, Louie Bellson, and Sam Woodyard, the best of the Duke Ellington drummers; the dedicated and accomplished Cozy Cole; Joe Morello, the gifted drummer and teacher, warmly remembered for his work with Dave Brubeck; versatile Ed Shaughnessy, an early bebopper, who has applied what he knows and feels in contexts ranging from avant-garde jazz to network television; the never intrusive, always swinging Jimmy Crawford; the quietly sensitive Vernel Fournier and Connie Kay; the deeply rooted, multifunctional Ed Blackwell, Billy Higgins, and Billy Hart; Grady Tate, the very essence of finesse and style; singularly authoritative and swinging big band drummers Jack Sperling, Sonny Igoe, Butch Miles, Charli Persip, Gus Johnson, Sonny Payne, Dick Shanahan, Alvin Stoller, Jake Hanna, and Nick Ceroli; Frank Butler, Ben Riley, Jimmy Cobb, and Arthur Taylor, evocative, modern time players; Louis Hayes, a creative modernist who has been heard with Horace Silver, Julian "Cannonball" Adderley, Oscar Peterson, and his own bands; Danny Richmond, Charles Mingus's source of multilevel pulsation and color; Ed Thigpen, Chico Hamilton, and Frank Isola—excellent brush players who carry on a lost art; Joe Chambers, an experienced drummer of strength and sensitivity; the unusual Don Moye; the always swinging Osie Johnson and Al Foster; and such European drummers as Phil Seamen, Daniel Humair, Allan Ganley, Kenny Clare, Tony Oxley, Han Bennink, Alex Riel, and Jon Christensen.

The future? *Modern Drummer* editorial director Bill Miller says this generation is starting to go back to less ornate drum sets, reverting to the virtues of simplicity. What will happen with the music? Only one thing is certain: it will tell drummers what to do. Always has.

Jazz and Dance

Robert P. Crease

I n the beginning, the word *jazz* was not a noun naming a musical genre but probably an adjective describing a certain quality of movement and behavior: spirited, improvised, often sensual, and with a quirky rhythm. By the end of the second decade of this century the term was applied to both a kind of music and a kind of dancing. In the supplements to the *Oxford English Dictionary* (in the 1970s, when *jazz* and other slang terms were first admitted), the first definition of *jazz* is "a kind of ragtime dance." Jazz dance and music are so intertwined that the origins and early history of each would be unthinkable without the other. How did they evolve together, foster each other, and even depend on each other for several decades? Why did the music and the dance eventually go separate ways? What are the long-range effects and implications of these developments?

Jazz dance referred initially to several mostly syncopated popular dances, influenced by African-American traditions, which had originated in the southern United States. In *Steppin' on the Blues*, dance scholar Jacqui Malone lists some hallmarks of these early dances— "improvisation and spontaneity, propulsive rhythm, call-and-response patterns, self-expression, elegance, and control"—and approvingly cites novelist Zora Neale Hurston's description of African-American dancing as characterized by "compelling insinuation" and "dynamic suggestion." Antecedents to these dances can be found in the 1890s, when the first generation of jazz artists was in its infancy. In New Orleans, for instance, new dance styles began to appear along with new music styles at local dances—often unruly environments, readily accessible to African Americans, in which experimentation in both music and dance was encouraged and rewarded. Charles "Buddy" Bolden, for instance—the greatest legend in the prehistory of jazz—was a dance musician, and if he played for listeners at picnics or carnivals, the music spilling from his trumpet was still dance music. Meanwhile, the spread of ragtime music was also allied with dancing. "Virtually all ragtime, including 'classic' ragtime," writes music historian Thornton Hagert, "seems to have been strongly influenced by the prevailing fashion in dance music." Ragtime dancers favored in particular the two-step, a version of the polka that left out the initial hop and whose basic foot pattern was step-together-step.

The symbiosis of jazz dancing and music continued after the turn of the century, when several new sexy dances appeared, including the turkey trot, black bottom, and Texas Tommy. Some persisted for a time on their own, while key moves of others were incorporated into more flexible dances like the one-step. By the end of the first decade of the century, such dances were denounced as scandalously vulgar and erotic by civil and religious leaders, who also condemned dance halls as centers of sin and sex. Yet people continued to frequent them, keeping the musicians in business. In his autobiography, *Jazz*, Paul Whiteman (soon publicized as the "King of Jazz") relates that, after arriving in San Francisco in 1911, he—like myriads of others—heard his first jazz in a dance hall dive, a "smoke-hazed, beer-fumed" room on the Barbary Coast. The music, he wrote, was "rhythmic, catching as the small-pox and spirit-lifting. . . . It made me want to dance."

In 1913 a society dance craze, the celebrity figures of which were Vernon and Irene Castle (accompanied by James Reese Europe's orchestra), began to sweep across all social strata. The craze revolved around an offspring of ragtime dancing called the fox-trot, which was not especially a jazz dance. Still, the craze did much to lay the groundwork for the subsequent development of jazz music and dance. Dance halls were rescued from their seedy reputation and became respectable places to visit, while the insatiable demand for dance music encouraged the formation of stable, professional bands with regular personnel. "Without this wide public enthusiasm for the foxtrot,"

Dancers, Savoy Ballroom, Harlem, New York, 1940s. Courtesy Frank Driggs Collection.

writes Albert McCarthy in *The Dance Band Era*, "the history of dance music, and indeed of jazz, would have been profoundly altered."

Meanwhile, an important change was taking place in popular dancing. Until then, the appeal of popular dances usually lay in their steps, gestures, or occasionally (as with the waltz and polka) in the thrill generated by the movement; in the second decade of the century, some popular dances arose that were captivating because of their rhythms. The result transformed popular dancing and paved the way for *jazz* dancing. Jazz dancing and jazz music were continuing to develop in contexts—picnics and nightclubs, riverboats and brothels, weddings and funerals—where they did not command the center of attention before a quiet and respectful audience but were related elements of a larger social event. Music and dance made common cultural cause. Did the music make you feel like throwing yourself bodily into it? If it didn't, you were probably either confused or a stuffed shirt; you didn't "get" it. When the Original Dixieland Jazz Band opened at New York's Reisenweber's Restaurant in 1917, the clientele at first sat stunned and puzzled and had to be told that what they were hearing was dancing music; within two weeks, even the New Yorkers had caught on.

The next decade, the 1920s, witnessed key developments in the interaction between jazz dance and music. One was a concert put on by Paul Whiteman at New York's Aeolian Hall in 1924, meant to show the "advance" that jazz music had made from its "raucous" early days to the "melodious" forms of the present, and the concert culminated with the debut of *Rhapsody in Blue*, with composer George Gershwin at the piano. This concert aimed to promote the idea that jazz had superseded its origins as dancing music and needed to be concertized to take its rightful place as a musical art form.

But the momentum clearly lay with dancing jazz rather than concertizing it. A growing number of dance bands began to value what jazz historian James T. Maher calls the "tactile bond" between musicians and dancers. In a cross-country tour around 1922, bandleader Art Landry would spend the first set mingling with dancers on the floor to pick up the local tempo. In 1924 Fletcher Henderson's orchestra opened at the Roseland Ballroom, helping to make it the most famous ballroom in New York City. The growing enthusiasm for dancing led to a dramatic increase in the openings of ballrooms, some of which would become key venues for jazz in the next decade; e.g., the Palomar Ballroom in Los Angeles (1925) and the Savoy Ballroom in New York City (1926).

The 1920s also saw jazz dancing establish itself onstage. Until then, jazz-style dancing rarely appeared in shows (an exception being *Dark-town Follies*, 1913). But the unexpected smash success of the revue *Shuffle Along*, which toured the country after opening in New York City in 1921, firmly established a place for it. The first all-black show on Broadway, *Shuffle Along* showcased a spectrum of jazz dancing, from soft shoe and tap to acrobatic dancing, and introduced many jazz dancers (including an attention-getting chorus girl named Josephine Baker).

Tap dancing began to flourish; many of its key figures, including legendary dancer Bill Robinson, choreographer Buddy Bradley, and innovators like James Barton, John Bubbles, and Frank Condos, first came to general attention in the 1920s. And of the more social jazz dances, the 1920s witnessed the popular Charleston and the birth of the lindy hop.

The Charleston was a thoroughly syncopated dance. While the fox-trot's beat was on one and three, the Charleston's was generally slightly *before* the one and three. This brought the dancer into an entirely different relation with the beat, forcing the entire body to carry it rather than just the feet. The Charleston followed a trajectory typical of popular dances. It had low-class origins (in the southern United States around the turn of the century) and reached other regions through ports and urban areas. It was rejected as ugly and vulgar by professional dance instructors and was condemned by civil, intellectual, and religious leaders as either the cause or symptom of a cultural decline. Called a "dance of death," it was blamed for several catastrophes, including the collapse of the Pickwick Club in Boston (1924), which killed forty-four, injured scores more, and provoked calls that the Charleston be banned from public dance halls. Yet it spread like wildfire, guaranteeing a continued demand for musicians who could play the music, and showed up onstage (in the all-black show *Runnin' Wild* in 1923, whose hit song was James P. Johnson's "Charleston"). Eventually it was reluctantly accepted by professional instructors who promoted a cleaned-up version for the ballroom floor.

Far more influential and longer-lasting was the lindy hop, which originated in Harlem about 1927 (later, it was also called jitterbug or swing). While the rhythm of the Charleston usually anticipated the one and three, the rhythm of the lindy moved into the offbeats— the two and four. This went hand in hand with the emerging swing musical style, which was moving to a greater rhythmic fluidity; the rhythmic anticipation of the offbeat generated a much more propulsive feel in both the music and the dance. The lindy's basic footwork is a two-bar (eight-count) basic step rather than the one-bar basic characteristic of many other dances, which allowed movements to be more elaborately phrased. The lindy carried the rhythmic unity in the overall body motion, so that even the feet could improvise, opening up more expressive possibilities. And while in most couple dances the partners held each other so closely that they generally had to mirror each other's steps lest they tread on each other's feet, the lindy involved a "breakaway" in which the partners stepped back at arm's length or separated from each other entirely. The breakaway was an extraordinary development; it gave each partner a new measure of freedom and turned the basic recurring footwork pattern into a flexible structure on which to improvise. *Hop* was a dance term dating back to the previous century; Charles Lindbergh's nickname became attached after the aviator "hopped" the Atlantic solo in May 1927 to become a folk hero overnight. The lindy was associated in particular with the Savoy Ballroom in New York City, which was already becoming a hothouse for the development of both jazz music and dance. This was due to the quality of the bands (both black and white) that played there and to the musically demanding, and integrated, audience that came to dance on its block-long floor. The Savoy patrons, wrote jazz historian Marshall Stearns, were the 'hippest' dance audience in the world, and to perform there was the acid test of a true dance band."

The lindy first appears on film in *After Seben* (1929), in a scene in which one of the lindy's originators, George "Shorty" Snowden, performs with a partner to music provided by the (off-camera) Chick Webb Orchestra; in it, the dance still shares a certain choppiness with its ancestor, the Charleston. Snowden put together a group of three couples that danced in talent contests and Harlem nightclubs and in 1934 landed a job outside Harlem, performing exhibitions for Whiteman at the Paramount. Snowden's rival, Herbert White, an ex-prizefighter who worked as a bouncer at the Savoy, organized his own set of dancers called Whitey's Lindy Hoppers, which soon dominated show-business jobs for lindy hoppers. White's most creative dancer, Frankie Manning, helped the group to fashion a smoother and more fluid crouched-down swing style of lindy hopping. Manning also contributed several exciting choreographic innovations such as ensemble dancing, where several couples dance the same steps simultaneously, and "air steps," where one partner flips another in acrobatic-type moves. While air steps were rarely done in social dancing, they soon became a symbol of the lindy/jitterbug itself.

By the mid-1930s, at the beginning of the swing era, the term *jazz dance* loosely covered many different kinds of dancing. It covered some dances done socially by amateurs (e.g., the Charleston and lindy) and stage versions of the same done by professionals. It covered tap dancers from elegant Fred Astaire to "class acts" like Charles "Honi" Coles and Charles "Cholly" Atkins to "flash acts" like the Nicholas Brothers. It covered utter singularities, such as Earl "Snake Hips" Tucker, whose act was one long sexually suggestive performance. These jazz dances shared many common rhythms and a movement vocabulary constantly fed by new steps. They were often done in exhibitionist situations like challenges, cutting contests, or occasions where performers were asked to "shine." A give-and-take existed among all these forms.

The crystallization of the swing era gave a boost to all these dances. For a few years, jazz music and dance were America's choice in popular culture. The music was based on popular song forms—usually nothing more than what would fit on the three-minute 78 rpm records—but a dancer could experience this as a powerful force. The lindy, says Stearns, is "choreographed swing music." The swing era had both an experiential and a cultural dimension, as traced by Lewis A. Erenberg in *Swingin' the Dream: Big Band Jazz and the Rebirth of American Culture* and David W. Stowe in *Swing Changes: Big Band Jazz in New Deal America*. Experientially, "jazz bore the spontaneous, improvisatory energy of this one realm and freedom and expressed the body as a natural and divine feature of human existence," Erenberg writes. "On the dance floor, amid a crowd of other people, ecstasy and personal freedom could be asserted against the depersonalized and restrictive modern world." Culturally, "the jitterbug represented both the emotional loosening of American musical culture and its democratization. . . . In swing, personal liberation and the revitalization of democratic culture went together."

The swing era, however, involved not a single culture but many—in different regions, and of different classes and ethnic lines—with different relations to the music and dance. There were also subcultures like the "alligators," who liked to stand in front of the bandstand just to listen, though they were often dispersed by bouncers. Another subculture was the "jitterbugs," who embraced the dance in an aggressive and extreme way. Their exhibitionistic antics—which could include jumping onstage, dancing in strange places, and clapping out of time—could often disrupt performers and other dancers. It is confusing that the word *jitterbug* can refer both to a dance (which for all practical purposes is the lindy) and to a member of this subculture, but the two meanings are different.

Attempts to concertize the music continued, though with music critics rather than musicians usually in the lead. "Don't Spit on the Jitterbug—Educate Him!" editorialized *Down Beat* in 1937, claiming that jitterbugs were merely in "an elementary stage" of music appreciation. But the momentum still lay with the dancers, and the periodic upsurge of new dance forms and fads—peckin', truckin', big apple, shag—added to their movement vocabulary. The dance became still more fluid, as can be seen by comparing the film clips of Whitey's Lindy Hoppers in the Marx Brothers' *A Day at the Races* (MGM, 1937) and then four years later in *Hellzapoppin'* (1941), which is one of the hottest dance sequences on film. The dance audience also had a major impact on the music; the dance called for rhythmic steadiness but infectious performances. And as philosopher Roger Scrutin argues in *An Aesthetics of Music,* one key ingredient of a vital musical culture is the existence of an educated and attentive audience. In the swing era, the dancers provided that audience, one that was demanding and at times unforgiving.

During World War II, the lindy's fortunes crested when U.S. GIs took it all over the world, making it a kind of universal dance. But important changes were afoot. During the swing era, much of the fluidity that had existed between different jazz dance traditions, and between the dance and the music, was lost in the growing commercialization of the big band business and of show business generally. In the 1943 film *Stormy Weather,* for instance, the place where one would have expected a lindy-hop scene was occupied by the Katherine Dunham dancers, heralding a new professionalization in jazz dance choreography and a new degree of separation between vernacular and theatrical jazz dance forms.

The future belonged to the alligators. After World War II, the jazz dancing and music cultures separated. Many big bands broke up, defeated by escalating costs, changing tastes, and dwindling audiences. Big bands that survived found themselves playing more and more in concert halls. The new jazz style—bebop, whose landmark was not a dance hall but a nightclub named Minton's—was a musician's music. The bop revolution, wrote dancer Rusty Frank, "affected anybody who had anything to do with dance." Bop's asymmetrical melodies and elliptical accents were harder to dance to than the more predictable phrasing of riff-based swing compositions. Dizzy Gillespie once complained about those who said that bebop was undanceable: "I could dance my ass off to it.... Jazz should be danceable.... [I]t should always be rhythmic enough to make you wanna move. When you get away from that movement, you get away from the whole idea." No doubt. One can dance to bebop in the sense that one can dance to Beethoven's Seventh Symphony—if you choreograph to it or freely improvise. But youths whose idea of a good time was to fling oneself bodily into live music with peers sought out other kinds of sounds: rhythm-and-blues, rock-and-roll, Latin music. Bop was also a watershed for tap dancers. Some, like Pete Nugent (who tried to dance to bebop while touring with Billy Eckstine's 1944 band), found themselves so unable to adapt that they soon hung up their shoes forever. Others, like Baby Laurence and Teddy Hale, managed to adapt well. And a new generation of tap dancers, which included Brenda Bufalino, grew up on the bop rhythms.

This development is so significant that Maher speaks of jazz history "A.M." and "P.M.": "ante-Minton's" and "post-Minton's." Loss of the dance audience was keenly felt by some jazz fans. Jitterbugs were "a precious nuisance but, brother, we certainly could use them or a reasonable facsimile of the same today," *Down Beat* editorialized in 1948, in a turnaround. "At least they meant chips at the box office." Two years later, *Down Beat* put out a special "Everybody Dance" issue, whose articles had titles like "Dance Music, Not Bop, Is Our Bread, Butter," and which optimistically proclaimed that "the dance band business is on the upbeat as never before." In vain. Ballrooms continued to be torn down or converted to supermarkets, movie theaters, bowling alleys, roller-skating rinks, and restaurants.

With jazz music no longer for dancers only, regional descendents of swing dancing began to appear, such as the Carolina shag, which adapted lindy style to rhythm and blues-influenced "beach music"; the imperial style in St. Louis, which retained elements of the Charleston; and the whip and push in Texas. In the mid-1950s, Marshall Stearns teamed up with two former members of Whitey's Lindy Hoppers, Leon James and Al Minns, in an attempt to form a dance company, American Jazz Dancers, to preserve jazz dance traditions. Calling for "a return to the folk roots of the jazz dance," Stearns protested against what was then called "jazz dance" on the Broadway stage: the mixture of jazz, ballet, and acrobatics, with an emphasis on exhibitionism and sexy body movements. But even when Stearns's lecture-demonstrations were enthusiastically received at the Newport Jazz Festival, they seemed like history—ancient history. However, the book he authored with his wife Jean, *Jazz Dance* (1968), remains the single best source on all varieties of early jazz dancing, though the chapters on the lindy are weakened by overreliance on the sometimes self-aggrandizing accounts of James and Minns.

Contemporary jazz dancing falls into two main categories. "Classic jazz dance" draws heavily on social dances like the lindy or is characterized by a heavy reliance on improvisation like tap. Such dancing has been featured in musicals like *Black and Blue,* whose Tony Award–winning choreographers are some of the great names in classic jazz dance: Cholly Atkins, Henry LeTang, Frankie Manning, and Fayard Nicholas. "Modern jazz dance," by contrast, consists of more recent forms of dancing for the stage. It grew out of the continuing assimilation, reinterpretation, and adaptation of jazz dance traditions by Broadway and modern dance choreographers, and its practitioners are more indebted to Broadway or modern ballet than to vernacular traditions.

Today, the jazz musical experience is ensconced in the concert hall, nightclub, or listening room. Jazz dance is equally professionalized and confined to the stage (though a recent swing dance resurgence, in which Frankie Manning has played a key role, has revived swing dancing to live music, mainly "jump" bands). Histories, with a few exceptions, take this separated condition for granted and depict the origin of jazz solely as a history of music—relating the swing era, for instance, mainly as a history of bands, of their recordings and innovations, and of the personalities and rivalries of their leaders.

This is not only bad history, it distorts the meaning of the music. Albert Murray, Jacqui Malone, and others have emphasized that the participatory experience of music in jazz dancing is one of the most enduring and significant elements of the African-American arts legacy. In the United States, where awareness of African-American influences on the arts was at first suppressed, efforts are being made to recognize and honor them. It is therefore a cruel irony to see such swing era classics as Basie arrangements of "Jumpin' at the Woodside" or "One O'Clock Jump" celebrated through performances in concert halls, where the opportunity for this participatory experience is, once again, stifled. The interaction of the music and the dance, and the consequences of their separation, is the single most important still-untold story in the history of jazz.

Jazz and Film and Television

Chuck Berg

J azz and film, both artistic children of the twentieth century, are arguably America's greatest gifts to world culture. Born and nurtured at the fringes of proper society, each has risen to attain respectability. After decades of being shunned by Eurocentric guardians of high culture, jazz and film are now deemed subjects worthy of serious study. With film screenings and jazz concerts at the White House and formal recognitions by Congress, these two prototypically American arts, with their melting-pot parentage and kinetic New World dynamism, speak passionately of diverse peoples seeking their destinies as individuals as well as groups. Indeed, when future historians look back to identify the mainsprings that drove the past millennium's last centenary, jazz and movies will undoubtedly top the list of those phenomena best capturing the artistic and cultural vigor that was "the American Century."

Although jazz and film (and film's electronic offspring, television and video) have traveled along mostly parallel and therefore separate tracks, there are intersections where the two have met head on. These junctures are the subject of this essay. In mapping these crossroads, a largely chronological approach is employed. Still, as the intertwined tale of jazz and film unfolds, several recurring topics should be noted.

The first, "jazz on film," focuses largely on portrayals of jazz musicians, actual and fictional, and varying depictions of the jazz life. "Jazz in film," the second, concerns the use of jazz as an element in scoring narrative features, cartoons, and experimental films. The third, "jazz and television," examines how jazz has been presented on TV as a marquee event and as an element of scoring. The fourth, "documenting jazz," spotlights jazz documentaries, educational programs, and instructional videos.

Jazz in the Silent Film

Jazz and film first met in the cramped and smoke-filled nickelodeons that served America's urban working class during the first decade of the twentieth century. Sitting beneath celluloid ribbons of dreams, movie pianists riffed and ragged through the standard tunes of the day. Occasionally such improvised pastiches helped underscore the story. Mostly, however, these medleys served to fill the aural voice of the "silent" film theater while simultaneously covering up such distracting noises as the clattering of the projector and off-color wisecracks. As the need for dramatically apt background music became apparent, ragtime passages came to be associated with nightclub and party scenes. Recognizing ragtime's power to indicate such specific times and places, Erno Rapee, author of the comprehensive handbook for silent era musicians, *Encyclopedia of Music for Pictures* (1925), included sixty-two "Rags."

As post–World War I America kicked up its heels during the twenties, jazz became a resonant metaphor for an affluent era that boldly proclaimed itself "the Jazz Age." Hollywood, now the film capital of the world, picked up the beat and dramatized the jazz life in over sixty films. In *The Girl With a Jazz Heart* (1921), *The House That Jazz Built* (1921), and *Children of Jazz* (1923), the twenties' version of the jazz life was generally portrayed as the reckless pursuit of hedonistic thrills among the well-to-do. There were also films such as *Syncopating Sue* (1926) that dealt with the lives of jazz-oriented musicians. For these, as well as the obligatory cabaret scenes in jazz-life movies, musicians in orchestra pits offered up appropriate jazz-inflected arrangements.

Jazz Meets the Sound Film

In 1927 the movies entered a brave new world with the electrifying appearance of the singing and talking Al Jolson. Indeed, it was Jolson's "jazz" singer that signaled the silent era's coda. Although not

Original LP cover for the soundtrack to the motion picture '*Round Midnight*, produced by Herbie Hancock, 1986. Original LP cover for the first *Peter Gunn* soundtrack album, with music from the TV show composed and conducted by Henry Mancini. Both, courtesy of the Institute of Jazz Studies, Rutgers University.

the first sound film, it was *The Jazz Singer* (1927) that captured the public's imagination, thereby triggering the film industry's rush to sound. With the transition to "talkies" completed by 1930, jazz and the movies entered into a new era. Left behind were thousands of theater musicians who lost their jobs accompanying silent films. On the other hand, filmmakers rejoiced. With the new synchronized sound technology, what was heard by movie patrons was no longer the domain of theater managers. Now, directors had the technological means to control and choreograph sounds as well as images.

Thanks to Dudley Murphy, an enterprising young director fresh from the avant-garde scene in Paris, the new sound film was put to almost immediate jazz use in two enduring classics lensed in New York City during the glory days of the Harlem Renaissance. In *St. Louis Blues* (1929), we meet blues diva Bessie Smith in her only appearance on film, in a thinly dramatized yet moving version of the W. C. Handy standard that also included members of Fletcher Henderson's band and pianist James P. Johnson. For Murphy's *Black and Tan* (1929), which marked Duke Ellington's cinematic debut, Ellington's fabled Cotton Club Orchestra was featured along with the Hall Johnson Choir and chanteuse Fredi Washington in a program that included the melancholy title tune as well as "The Duke Steps Out," "Black Beauty," and "Cotton Club Stomp."

In Hollywood, jazz and film initially met in the form of the band short. While catering to the desires of music fans to see as well as hear favorite performers, the film studios, because of their increasing tie-ins with recording, radio, and music publishing, saw shorts as effective means of simultaneously promoting several related products. In this prototype of today's multipronged promotional paradigm, band shorts (forerunners of music videos), records, sheet music, and broadcasts helped publicize and therefore sell one another. During the swing era, there were shorts by popular white bands such as those led by Jimmy Dorsey, Woody Herman, and Artie Shaw. There also were shorts devoted to prominent black bands, including those of Duke Ellington, Cab Calloway, and Benny Carter. Usually, a short allowed enough screen time for several numbers. In a 1934 Vitaphone short spotlighting Don Redman, for example, audiences heard "Yeah Man," "Ill Wind," "Nagasaki," and "Why Should I Be Tall?"

A second avenue of jazz exposure during the thirties was the Hollywood feature film. Noting the success of the band shorts and the public's seemingly insatiable appetite for swing, directors jammed bands into as many productions as possible. Thus, when Benny Goodman caught fire in the mid-thirties, he and his band were whisked away to *The Big Broadcast of 1937* (1936) and *Hollywood Hotel* (1937).

In big-budget features, the essentially no-frills documenting approach of the shorts was expanded as Hollywood "jazzed up" the jazz. In *Ball of Fire* (1941), for instance, Gene Krupa's drums are replaced by a pair of matchsticks and a matchbox. In *Las Vegas Nights* (1941), Tommy Dorsey's band is served up with the sweetening of a hundred and one strings. In contrast, feature films with black musicians were often more faithful to the music since the performances were designed as self-contained attractions with virtually no dramatic links to the principal characters or plots. In this way, studios could avoid the "hazards" of dealing with integration while simultaneously capitalizing on black performers' popularity. The strategy also allowed southern theater operators to easily excise such interludes if deemed too "controversial." Consequently, Cab Calloway's turn in W. C. Fields's *International House* (1934) and that of Duke Ellington in Mae West's *Belle of the Nineties* (1934) were not always seen by white audiences in the South. In spite of these censorial problems, appearances by self-assured artists like Ellington and Calloway helped alter, albeit slightly, the then prevailing stereotypes of blacks, to cite the title of film historian Donald Bogle's groundbreaking book, as *Toms, Coons, Mulattoes, Mammies, and Bucks* (1974).

The thirties also witnessed the first couplings of jazz and animation. One ploy, similar in appeal to the band shorts and interludes, relied on the celebrity of popular musicians. Louis Armstrong and cartoon superstar Betty Boop, for instance, were teamed in 1932 for animator Max Fleischer's *I'll Be Glad When You're Dead You Rascal You.* Although now valuable for documenting Armstrong's performance style of the period, *I'll Be Glad* reverted to the racial cliché of black buck (a cartoon version of Armstrong) in hot pursuit of chaste maiden (Boop). Fleischer also introduced Boop to Cab Calloway in *Minnie the Moocher* (1932) and to Don Redman in *I Heard* (1933).

Even when music and musicians were not integral parts of cartoon story lines, jazz still figured in their soundtracks. Here, musical conventions from both silent film and vaudeville practices were employed. For blurry-eyed drunks there was a bluesy slide trombone, for sultry temptresses a red hot trumpet, and for gala nightclub scenes a stomping swing band. On the production side, small groups of versatile studio musicians adept at improvisation proved more flexible for pinpoint "Mickey Mouse" synchronization than the full-blown symphonic orchestras generally used for scoring feature films during the thirties and forties. Using smaller ensembles also helped keep music costs in line.

In addition to the story cartoons of Disney and the major studios, jazz and animation became fused in various experimental contexts. German animator Oskar Fischinger was among the first to explore these possibilities. In *Study No. 5* (1930), Fischinger's dancelike figures are matched to a jazz treatment of "I've Never Seen a Smile Like Yours." Fischinger's experiments are also significant for their influence on Walt Disney's conceptualizing of *Fantasia* (1940). In the forties, Fischinger's work and that of New Zealander Len Lye inspired a string of brilliant painting-on-film abstractions by the Canadian Norman McLaren. Two of these used prominent jazz pianists, Albert Ammons for *Boogie Doodle* (1948) and Oscar Peterson for *Begone Dull Care* (1949). In another notable series, Hungarian filmmaker George Pal sometimes set his animated Puppetoons to jazz. Charlie Barnet and Peggy Lee, for example, are heard in *Jasper's in a Jam* (1946), while Duke Ellington backdrops a bevy of dancing perfume bottles in *Date With Duke* (1947).

Jazz has also been an important element in impressionistic film studies of the urban landscape. D. A. Pennybaker's *Daybreak Express* (1953), a lyrical ride along New York's long gone Third Avenue el, is propelled by Duke Ellington's driving composition. A similar city symphony–like work is Shirley Clarke's *Bridges Go Round* (1958), in which Teo Macero's jazzy colors mesh with Clarke's visual permutations of New York's celebrated East River spans. Clarke and Macero also collaborated on *Skyscraper* (1959), an inspired hymn to Manhattan's skyline.

Back on the Hollywood front, musical shorts and feature film interludes continued to be popular. There were, however, several new wrinkles. In 1940 coin-operated jukebox machines using rear projection were introduced to public places such as bars and train stations. Sensing the competition, theater exhibitors exerted enough muscle to eventually muzzle the threat. Still, hundreds of now invaluable performances survive the soundies' run from 1940 to 1946. In one of these three-minute films, *Ain't Misbehavin'* (1941), Thomas "Fats" Waller breezes through his mischievous composition to the delight of a group of enthused onlookers. A decade later, five-minute made-for-television shorts were produced by Snader Telescriptions to fill gaps in early television programming schedules.

During the war years of the forties, big bands enlivened backstage and variety formats designed to boost morale and give the boys "over there" a taste of home. While Glenn Miller cheered up *Orchestra Wives* (1942) and Jimmy Dorsey anchored *The Fleet's In* (1942), Harry James put his *Best Foot Forward* (1943). Soon, Hollywood reasoned that if one band was good for the box office, two or more would be even better. The strategy resulted in all-star revues like *Stage Door Canteen* (1943), which featured Count Basie and Benny Goodman, and *Jam Session* (1944), which brought to the fore Charlie Barnet and the inimitable Louis Armstrong.

Armstrong, whose gravelly voice and ebullient trumpeting conveyed a palpable warmth that made him one of the world's best-loved jazz musicians, was featured in a score of Hollywood films. Between cameos in *Pennies From Heaven* (1936) and *Hello, Dolly!* (1969), Hollywood's favorite jazzman showed up in biopics like *The Glenn Miller Story* (1953), in fictive jazz features such as *Paris Blues* (1961), and in speaking as well as musical roles in *High Society* (1956) and *A Man Called Adam* (1966). Armstrong also appeared in the groundbreaking *Cabin in the Sky* (1943), MGM's all-black musical starring Ethel Waters, Lena Horne, and Duke Ellington's Orchestra. Following MGM's lead, Twentieth Century–Fox lensed the plot-thin but musically rich *Stormy Weather* (1943), an all-black showcase with Lena Horne, Cab Calloway, and Fats Waller.

By the end of the war, big band interludes had just about run their course. Yes, there was *New Orleans* (1947), notable for its segments devoted to Woody Herman's and Louis Armstrong's bands, and Billie Holiday in her only feature film role singing "Do You Know What It Means to Miss New Orleans?" This, though, was an exception. Nonetheless, big bands, or at least their leaders, were kept in public view through the genre of the biopic. Leading the way were *The Fabulous Dorseys* (1947), *The Glenn Miller Story* (1953), *The Benny Goodman Story* (1955), *The Gene Krupa Story* (1959), and *The Five Pennies* (1959), a limning of cornetist Red Nichols's life tailored as a star vehicle for actor Danny Kaye. Like most Hollywood biopics, the line between fact and fiction often blurred beyond recognition. In *The Benny Goodman Story*, for instance, we witness the clarinetist (played by Steve Allen) struggling to compose Edgar Sampson's "Don't Be That Way." More problematic, especially for jazz fans, was the often condescending attitude taken toward jazz musicians and their music. In the Goodman biography, the clarinetist proves himself equal to the woman he loves only after a bravura performance of

Mozart's *Clarinet Concerto*. Reenforcing the "serious" music yardstick are the patronizing lines of dialogue given to Teddy Wilson and Gene Krupa, who play themselves. After Goodman's triumph with Mozart, Wilson opines, "I guess I'll have to learn some long-hair lingo." Krupa replies, "Yeah, he's a mean man with the licorice stick." *Lady Sings the Blues* (1972), in which Diana Ross impersonates Billie Holiday, and *Bird* (1988), Clint Eastwood's tribute to bebop icon Charlie Parker, provoked similar complaints. As with earlier biopics, there were grumbles about the melodramatic fabrications. Other barbs were directed to the darkish portrayals of the jazz life.

From the standpoint of the jazz connoisseur, such laments are on target. However, they miss the larger point that Hollywood is in business to produce mass entertainment, not history. Still, biopics, even with their limitations, have had a salutary impact. Indeed, many new fans have been attracted to jazz precisely because of Hollywood's dramatically charged and largely sympathetic portrayals of jazz stars. In fact, releases of jazz biopics have almost always been accompanied by brisk-selling soundtrack albums and appreciable upturns in sales of reissued and inventory titles by those musicians given the Hollywood treatment.

A related group of postwar films featured fictional jazz musicians. The first of these was *Young Man With a Horn* (1949), a melodramatic makeover of Bix Beiderbecke's life story starring Kirk Douglas. Jack Webb's *Pete Kelly's Blues* (1955), an engagingly gritty story of a twenties cornetist struggling against a gang of racketeers, was bolstered by the singing presence of Ella Fitzgerald and Peggy Lee and the taut arrangements of Matty Matlock's Dixielanders. Less successful dramatically was Martin Ritt's *Paris Blues* (1961). Burdened by platitudinous dialogues on race between a white trombonist (Paul Newman) and black tenor saxophonist (Sidney Poitier), *Paris Blues* was redeemed mainly through Duke Ellington's apt underscoring and several rousing cameos by Louis Armstrong. *A Man Called Adam* (1966), another melodramatic attempt to deal with race through the prism of jazz, remains of interest because of Benny Carter's incisive score, the presence of the ubiquitous Armstrong, and the on-screen appearance of musicians Billy Kyle, Buster Bailey, Tyree Glenn, Jo Jones, and Frank Wess.

Bertrand Tavernier's *'Round Midnight* (1986), in which jazz legend Dexter Gordon plays expatriate tenor saxophonist Dale Turner, is perhaps the most satisfying jazz film yet made, largely because its jazz roles were played by actual musicians. It was also a personal triumph for Gordon, who was nominated for a Best Actor Oscar. Similarly outstanding because of its realistic portrayal of working musicians and the personal struggle of trying to balance art (jazz) against commerce (cocktail music) is *The Fabulous Baker Boys* (1989), with Jeff and Beau Bridges playing the lounge pianists alluded to in the title. Greatly anticipated by jazz fans because of its prerelease hype as the first serious jazz film by a black director, Spike Lee's *Mo' Better Blues* (1990), with its jazz-cum-rap score and sprawling story, proved a disappointment. Robert Altman's *Kansas City* (1996), in large part a reverie on growing up during the thirties when the midwestern metropolis was the "Paris of the Plains," included several extended jams featuring nineties newcomers Joshua Redman, James Carter, Geri Allen, and Kevin Mahogany. Altman became so taken with the filming of his all-star musicians that he wound up with enough jam-session material to produce an hour-long public television special, *Robert Altman's Jazz '34: Remembrances of Kansas City* (1996).

The most bitingly pessimistic of jazz fiction films is Shirley Clarke's adaptation of Jack Gelber's play *The Connection* (1961). An uncompromising view of the claustrophobic and paranoid world of heroin addicts, Clarke's unflinching exposé includes extended bop-based improvisations by Freddie Redd, Jackie McLean, Michael Mattos, and Larry Ritchie. Another independently produced dramatization of jazz musicians was John Cassavetes's *Too Late Blues* (1962). A study of the fragile interpersonal relationships among members of a jazz combo, the film boasts a score by David Raksin of "Laura" fame and performances by Benny Carter, Jimmy Rowles, Red Mitchell, and Shelly Manne. Raksin's score is particularly significant because the vocabulary of jazz was called upon to shade dramatic moments in which music itself was not an actual part of the scene.

Jazz in Movie and Television Soundtracks

In the thirties and forties, jazz was seldom heard in the background of feature films. This was, after all, the golden age of the Hollywood factory system in which each studio had its own music department replete with conductors, composers, arrangers, and musicians. It was also the era of the large-scale orchestral score. Composers like Max Steiner, Miklos Rosza, Dmitri Tiomkin, Franz Waxman, Bronislau Kaper, and Erich Wolfgang Korngold, schooled in and inspired by the European symphonic tradition, set the standard. It was not until the fifties that jazz-influenced underscoring emerged as a viable alternative to the symphonic score.

Why jazz in the fifties? First, jazz itself had undergone a major revolution. Stifled by the highly arranged big band format with its infrequent opportunities for improvisation, adventurous musicians began explorations during the forties that culminated in what became known as bebop. A player's music, rather than arranger's, bebop, or bop, swept away big bands in favor of small groups, which allowed innovators like Charlie Parker and Dizzy Gillespie the range to probe new melodic, harmonic, and rhythmic frontiers.

The sophistication of bop, and the "progressive jazz" that followed in the fifties, helped legitimize jazz in the view of the establishment as a valid artistic medium. The music's new complexity appealed to artists, intellectuals, and others who could identify with the sacrifices made by jazz musicians on behalf of idealistic aesthetic principles. For the mass audience, swing had been utilized mostly for dancing. Bop, in contrast, was something for intense listening and contemplation. So in the fifties, as swing lost its legions to rock and pop, bop and progressive found a small but devoted as well as articulate and influential audience.

The new seriousness in jazz interacted with the evolution of film scoring in several ways. In contrast to the previous generation of conservatory-trained composers, the new wave of up-and-coming film scorers had received much of their training and professional experience in jazz. Among this new breed were Henry Mancini, Quincy Jones, Oliver Nelson, Johnny Mandel, and Lalo Schifrin. Also significant was jazz's newly recognized complexity. With novel sounds of surprise derived from unexpected shifts in melody, harmony, rhythm, meter, timbre, and instrumentation, bop and progressive offered a palette of colors more varied than that of the typical big bands of the thirties and forties.

The Supreme Court also had a hand in setting the stage for jazz. In the Paramount case (1948), the Court ruled that the studios' control of production, distribution, and exhibition was a monopolistic arrangement in restraint of trade. To remedy the situation, the Court ordered the studios to divest themselves of their theaters. This, coupled with the competition for audiences from television, brought the studios to the brink of fiscal disaster. Among their responses to the crisis was the wholesale dismissal of contract personnel. Of these, studio musicians were among the hardest hit. Another casualty of these upheavals was the disruption of the nearly three-decade tradition of the symphonic score. Now, full orchestral battalions were called out only for epics and other prestige pictures. For more tightly budgeted productions, new musical means were sought. The fashionably chic and compact jazz combo was one obvious solution.

Another factor favoring jazz was the maturing "adult" nature of movie content. In the fifties and sixties, society's outcasts were given increased screen attention. Set in the margins of the American mainstream, these nocturnal dramas were heavily populated by alcoholics, junkies, prostitutes, criminals, and other misfits. In this nightmarish urban cosmos, bars and clubs and the musicians who played in them were key elements in a verisimilitude constructed from popularly held, and too often accurate, negative stereotypes.

Otto Preminger's *The Man With the Golden Arm* (1955) epitomized fifties realism and provided composer Elmer Bernstein a perfect opportunity to map the parameters of the new jazz-inflected dramatic score. The story concerns a former junkie, Frankie (Frank Sinatra), who faces the combined problems of keeping straight, dealing with a manipulative wife, and attempting a career as a jazz drummer. While setting mood and establishing atmosphere, Bernstein's music functions at deeper dramatic levels. Indeed, the music is a gauge to the trajectory of Frankie's career and state of mind. In one climactic scene, a band lets Frankie sit in. With Shelly Manne's brushes in hand, the hypertense Frankie, back on heroin, fails to hold the tempo. Here, the dramatic arena is the bandstand. Unlike most source music, used primarily for ambience, Frankie's botched performance is a pivotal moment serving to reveal character and propel plot. Where source music is not involved, Bernstein's jazz-nuanced textures provide a cohesive backdrop that effectively tracks and amplifies the narrative's dramatic unfolding. Although quickly attaining landmark status, the score provoked second thoughts even from its composer, who lamented its impact in sealing associations between jazz and cinematic sleaze.

Such problems notwithstanding, jazz-oriented scores were often effective. Alex North's Bourbon Street–flavored backing for Elia Kazan's *A Streetcar Named Desire* (1951) successfully evoked New Orleans and the tempestuous relationship between Marlon Brando's Stanley and Vivien Leigh's Blanche. Leith Stevens's underlining of Laslo Benedek's *The Wild One* (1953) pointed up tensions between rival biker gangs and the townspeople they threaten. Other noteworthy efforts of the period include Elmer Bernstein's score for Alexander MacKendrick's *Sweet Smell of Success* (1957), which also featured on-screen appearances by Chico Hamilton's quintet; Johnny Mandel's emotionally wrenching orchestral jazz for *I Want to Live* (1958); and Duke Ellington's roiling undercurrents for Otto Preminger's *Anatomy of a Murder* (1959). Off the well-beaten Hollywood path was Marcel Camus's French-Italian-Brazilian production of *Black Orpheus* (1959), which by winning an Oscar as Best Foreign Film helped catapult the bossa nova and Brazilian composers Luiz Bonfa and Antonio Carlos Jobim to international fame.

The trend toward jazz was further accelerated by the pioneering television work of Henry Mancini. Restricted to an ensemble of eleven musicians for Blake Edwards's *Peter Gunn* (1958–61), Mancini made the limitation a virtue and established the percussion section as an important new source of dramatic embellishment. In breaking with past conventions, Mancini sought new dramatic-musical configurations through intimate passages featuring flutes, vibes, and guitar. In another Blake Edwards–produced TV detective drama, *Mr. Lucky* (1959–60), Mancini repeated the successful formula he had honed for *Peter Gunn*. Moving to the big screen, Mancini scored big with his dynamic Latin-laced backdrop for Orson Welles's *Touch of Evil* (1958) and his sax-savvy evocation of Edwards's *The Pink Panther* (1964). For Bruce Geller's action-adventure TV hit, *Mission Impossible* (1966–73), Lalo Schifrin built dramatic suspense with tightly sprung scores melding exotic flutes, stinging brass, and taut percussion effects.

In the sixties, in contrast to heavily orchestrated movie jazz scores like those of Bernstein, there were efforts to maximize jazz's improvisatory dimension. One of the first such efforts was Shirley Clarke's *The Cool World* (1963), in which trumpeter Dizzy Gillespie sails above a provocative score by Mal Waldron. In Arthur Penn's enigmatic *Mickey One* (1965), the inner angst of Warren Beatty's tormented character is expressed by the evocative flights of tenor saxophonist Stan Getz set atop edgy arrangements by Eddie Sauter. For Lewis Gilbert's *Alfie* (1966), tenor titan Sonny Rollins, augmented by British tenorist Tubby Hayes, embodies the bravado of Michael Caine's swaggering protagonist. The significant aspect of these scores is the wide latitude given the improvisers. In each, Gillespie, Getz, and Rollins display the kind of virtuoso musicianship that secured their places in the pantheon of modern jazz.

By the seventies, the use of background jazz in films had peaked. True, there was the galvanizing tenor saxophone of Gato Barbieri for Bernardo Bertolucci's *Last Tango in Paris* (1973), the resurrected rags of Scott Joplin in George Roy Hill's *The Sting* (1974), and the haunting Bernard Herrmann anthem for Martin Scorsese's *Taxi Driver* (1976). Other forces, however, had been at work. On one hand, the relentless quest for pop themes kept producers busy surveying the *Billboard* charts hoping to make a lucky Top Forty connection. This, coupled with box office demographics showing the bulk of filmgoers falling into the mid-teen to mid-twenties age range, led to endless pastiches cobbled together from rock-and-roll oldies and current pop hits. On the other hand, the equally relentless search for new sounds provoked a surge in scores employing ever expanding batteries of electronically modulated sounds. So, ironically, the qualities found novel and commercially exploitable in jazz during the fifties and sixties—the potential of a hit single or album like those derived from *Peter Gunn*; the economy and flexibility of a small ensemble of improvising musicians; the uniqueness of a lexicon of previously untapped materials—were, in the seventies, found largely in rock and electronics. Also, with the megasuccess of George Lucas's *Star Wars* (1977), and its sweeping melodramatic score by John Williams, the large-scale symphonic backdrop successfully reasserted itself as the preferred accompaniment for big-budget blockbusters.

As we enter a new millennium—with the exception of a handful of directors such as Clint Eastwood, Robert Altman, and Woody Allen, all devoted jazz fans—Hollywood's new generation of filmmakers shows little appreciation of jazz. Perhaps, if jazz enlarges its hold on the general public, Hollywood will sit up and take notice. Until then, jazz-inflected scoring seems likely to be used mainly as an indicator of specifically jazz-evoked times and places of the past, and as a musical condiment for a dash of the exotic.

Documenting and Teaching Jazz

The impulse to document jazz, as suggested above, can be partially seen in the band shorts of the thirties and biopics of the fifties. However palpable such documentary urges might have been, they were secondary to the primary motive of producing commercially successful entertainments. In contrast to Hollywood producers, documentarians, like dedicated historians, are driven to get the facts straight. The overarching goal is to put the creators of jazz at the center of the frame.

The first notable jazz documentary was Gjon Mili's *Jammin' the Blues* (1944), which combined the talents of icons Lester Young, Harry Edison, and Jo Jones with atmospheric high-contrast lighting and fluid camera movements reminiscent of German expressionism. Bert Stern's *Jazz on a Summer's Day* (1960) captured a parade of all-stars set against the sunny milieu of the 1958 Newport Jazz Festival. In contrast to these poeticized works are the intensely focused portraits of individual jazz personalities such as the gritty *Mingus* (1968), Thomas Reichman's probing examination of bassist-composer Charles Mingus caught in a moment of crisis; Gary Giddins and Kendrick Simmons's *Celebrating Bird: The Triumph of Charlie Parker* (1987), a revealing look at the bebop pioneer compiled from interviews, rare footage of Parker playing alto, and brisk montages of record jackets and headlines; and *Thelonious Monk: Straight No Chaser* (1989), Charlotte Zwerin and Bruce Ricker's loving tribute to the idiosyncratic pianist.

Another documentary mode has involved the more or less direct recording of jazz musicians in action. The approach, now sometimes called performance video, had its origins in television. Among the first such TV ventures were *Art Ford's Jazz Party* (1958) and Ralph J. Gleason's *Jazz Casual* series (1960–68). Other examples of the music-first format include the Steve Allen–produced *Jazz Scene, U.S.A.* (1963), hosted by Oscar Brown Jr., and *Jazz at the Smithsonian* (1982–83). The tradition has most recently been carried on by Wynton Marsalis's *Jazz from Lincoln Center* series of the nineties.

In television's early days, jazz occasionally took center stage in stand-alone specials such as Robert Herridge's *The Sound of Jazz* (1957), an informal studio summit that has been repeatedly excerpted by documentarians looking for telling footage of stars such as Billie Holiday, Count Basie, and Thelonious Monk. Herridge was also responsible for the seminal *The Sound of Miles Davis* (1959) and *Jazz from Studio 61* (1959). There were also prime-time specials such as *Texaco's Swing Into Spring* (1957), headlined by Benny Goodman and Ella Fitzgerald. Since the sixties, however, jazz on the major commercial networks has been limited almost solely to a background role in dramas with an occasional cameo appearance on entertainment programs such as the sitcom *The Cosby Show* (1984–92).

Related to the documentary are those programs devoted to jazz education. Leonard Bernstein was the form's most influential practitioner. His first venture into unraveling the wonders of improvisation, *The World of Jazz* (1955), was illustrated by variations on "Sweet Sue" and a performance of Bernstein's *Prelude, Fugue and Riffs*, written for and featuring clarinetist Benny Goodman. In *Jazz in Serious Music* (1959), Bernstein used excerpts from Copland, Mahler, Satie, and Stravinsky to demonstrate jazz's influence on modern classical music For his *Young People's Concerts* (1958–72) with the New York Philharmonic, Bernstein presented *Jazz in the Concert Hall* (1964), a meditation on the merging of jazz and classical. Broadcast nationally by CBS, these programs had tremendous reach. Given Bernstein's high ethos in classical circles and his telegenic personality, the programs also did much to legitimize jazz as a serious art form for the general public.

The paradigm established by Bernstein was successfully revived in the nineties by Wynton Marsalis. In *Marsalis on Music* (1995), for example, the trumpeter collaborates with Seiji Ozawa, Yo-Yo Ma, the Tanglewood Music Center Orchestra, and Marsalis's Septet to map the common ground shared by both jazz and classical. For *Uptown Blues—Ellington at 100* (1999), a part of the *Live from Lincoln Center* series, Edvard Grieg's *Peer Gynt Suite* is rendered in its original form by Kurt Masur and the New York Philharmonic, and then in its Ellington–Billy Strayhorn reincarnation by Marsalis and the Lincoln Center Jazz Orchestra. Pianist Billy Taylor, in a contrasting role, has brought a number of jazz talents to national attention through his appearances as a commentator since the early eighties for *CBS Sunday Morning*.

If the future of jazz in Hollywood seems limited, its prospects on cable and video and on the Internet appear bright. Hollywood jazz features of the past, from *The Glenn Miller Story* to *The Man With the Golden Arm*, are in constant rotation on cable movie channels such as American Movie Classics. And with video cassette players in most homes and schools, instructional tapes such as *Live in New York City, the Abercrombie/Erskine/Mintzer/Patitucci Band: A Concert/Clinic* (1999) allow aspiring players to take teachers home. Even on late-night television, in a tradition initiated by Steve Allen and embellished by Johnny Carson, there are still snippets of jazz coming in and out of the commercial breaks.

Also heartening is the reissue of classic jazz tracks such as Duke Ellington's 1961 score for *Paris Blues* (1997) and Gato Barbieri's 1972 improvisations in *Last Tango in Paris* (1998). And equally compelling is the contemporary cine-inflected work of bassist Charlie Haden's Quartet West and trumpeter Terence Blanchard's Jazz in Film. Ironically, given jazz's humble beginnings a century ago, the gauzy improvisations now used regularly to sell upscale cars and other luxury goods in TV ads represents yet another significant link between jazz and film.

As to the future, the niche services being created by the communications revolution bode well for jazz fans. Indeed, it is not hard to imagine a day in the not too distant future when any of the titles mentioned above—feature films, documentaries, or soundtrack recordings—will be immediately at hand to dial up or download from the ever expanding and ubiquitous Web.

Jazz Clubs

Vincent Pelote

Between the years 1890 and 1920 a great social upheaval took place in American culture. The old American ethic of hard work and emotional constraint was replaced with a new outlook that stressed pleasure and self-expression. This shift led to the development of new institutions such as dance halls, cabarets, ritzy restaurants, and theaters. Less elegant forms of the aforementioned had already existed in New York's unsavory tenderloin districts, the bohemian areas of San Francisco's Barbary Coast, and black ghettos. Around the turn of the century, the white middle class adopted these institutions, imbued them with respectability, and integrated them into the mainstream of American culture. The nightclub grew out of these early dance halls and cabarets.

Nightclubs proliferated after World War I, taking the place of the larger, less intimate music halls. The lineage of the nightclub in America can be traced to the nineteenth-century, European-inspired cabarets. These large establishments, which were particularly prevalent in New York, featured elaborate entertainment with music. The nightclub as we recognize it today, with its atmosphere of intimacy, developed in the speakeasies that came to fruition during Prohibition.

Speakeasies were illegal saloons that lacked the huge bars, elaborately decorated mirrors, large rooms, and many tables that were the standard for other saloons. This allowed easy escape from raids by law enforcement officials. As the popularity of the speakeasies grew, food, entertainment, and dancing were introduced. The entertainment could be anything from performances by a single pianist and vocalist, or a four- or five-piece jazz band, to huge, elaborately staged productions featuring singers, chorus lines, comedians, and large jazz orchestras. These clubs were generally run by bootleggers, who either distilled or smuggled the liquor that was served. Since not all nightclubs featured jazz, discussion here will be limited to those establishments that had a strict jazz policy.

Prohibition helped to spread jazz. People who frequented speakeasies considered jazz the perfect musical backdrop to their activities. When Prohibition was repealed in 1933, many of the speakeasies and nightclubs that had sprung up during the previous decade continued, with new ones as legitimate establishments opening along the way. As the popularity of jazz declined after World War II, so did jazz clubs, for a number of reasons including economic factors, the availability of recordings, and competition from other forms of entertainment (especially television). The fact that modern jazz was suited more for listening than for dancing may have also contributed to the clubs' decline. While jazz clubs still exist, especially in major cities like New York, Chicago, and Los Angeles, their numbers pale in comparison to those of the 1920s, '30s, and '40s.

New Orleans

New Orleans, considered the "birthplace of jazz," had an "uptown" and a "downtown." Uptown was generally westward from Canal Street. Names like Buddy Bolden and King Oliver were associated with the rough type of jazz that flourished in this part of the city. Downtown, below Canal Street (including the French Quarter and Storyville), gave rise to a more genteel style of jazz ("Creole style") mainly associated with Armand J. Piron, John Robichaux, and Alphonse Picou. Storyville (with its celebrated brothels) was not the place to hear jazz music in New Orleans, contrary to popular belief. The myth has been perpetuated for too long that jazz was a product of the red light district. Actually, some of the music's brightest stars never even played in Storyville. The district never employed more than a few musicians on any given night, even during Mardi Gras. By the time Storyville came into existence (1897) there were

52nd Street, 1948. Photo: William P. Gottlieb. From the Library of Congress Collection.

hundreds of musicians who had already been playing jazz for more than a decade.

Some of the earliest jazz was performed in halls like the Masonic Hall, the Funky Butt Hall, and Artisan Hall. The legendary Buddy Bolden played in both the Masonic Hall and the Funky Butt Hall, while a young Sidney Bechet played at the Artisan Hall. The Fewclothes Cabaret opened in 1902 and was owned by George Foycault. Big Eye Louis Nelson, Freddie Keppard, King Oliver, Baby Dodds, and Sidney Bechet were just some of the future legends who performed there. The Cadillac Club featured trumpeter Willie Hightower and his American Stars (1914–15). The Bienville Roof Gardens, located on the roof of the Bienville Hotel, featured a popular orchestra in the late 1920s led by Monk Hazel. The Gypsy Tea Room was advertised in the 1930s as "the largest nightclub of the South" and featured Kid Rena and his band (1936). The Famous Door (an important club for dixieland) and the El Morocco were among the well-known later jazz clubs in New Orleans.

Jazz still flourishes in New Orleans today, though mainly as a tourist attraction. Preservation Hall, home of the world-renowned Preservation Hall Jazz Band, opened in 1961 and is still a popular tourist spot. Clarinetist Pete Fountain has a jazz club in the Hilton Hotel, and trumpeter Al Hirt plays regularly at Patout's. The "young lions" who emerged from New Orleans, such as Wynton and Branford Marsalis and Nicholas Payton, had little to do with the Bourbon Street scene. When they are in town, they can usually be found at clubs where more modern jazz is featured, such as Snug Harbor or the Funky Butt.

New York

New York may not be able to claim fame as the birthplace of jazz, but it definitely has been and continues to be the place where the best musicians come to prove themselves. Jazz clubs have dotted Manhattan from Greenwich Village to Harlem. One of the earliest clubs in Harlem was Smalls' Paradise, founded in 1925 by Ed Smalls. It was the home in the '20s and '30s of Charlie Johnson's Paradise Orchestra and stayed in business into the 1950s. The Cotton Club is probably the most famous of Harlem clubs; its heyday was re-created in a 1984 movie by Francis Ford Coppola. Known for its elaborate floor shows (heavily laced with bogus "jungle" motifs), for years it served as the home base for Duke Ellington and His Famous Orchestra and later Cab Calloway's orchestra. The Cotton Club, like a number of establishments at that time, hired black entertainment but had an exclusively white clientele. Connie's Inn, opened by Connie and George Immerman in 1923, offered the Cotton Club stiff competition for audiences and performers. In 1919 the Roseland Ballroom opened on Broadway and served as the home for Fletcher Henderson and his orchestra until 1942. Harlem's Savoy Ballroom, known as "the Home of Happy Feet," was where many of the jazz dance crazes of the 1920s and 1930s originated. The resident big band was led by drummer Chick Webb, and it would regularly (and successfully) engage visiting bands in musical "battles" during the swing era.

Probably the most famous stretch of clubs was found on the legendary 52nd Street (a.k.a. "the Street," "Swing Street," or "Swing Alley"). The clubs on that block between Fifth and Sixth Avenues have attained legendary status. During Prohibition, 52nd Street had a larger concentration of speakeasies than any other neighborhood, and many of these became nightclubs after Repeal. Three major styles of jazz are associated with 52nd Street: dixieland, small-combo swing, and bebop. In the mid-1940s it was possible to hear all three styles in a single night. The names of musicians who played on 52nd Street reads like a veritable who's who of jazz and includes Art Tatum, Billie Holiday, Coleman Hawkins, Hot Lips Page, Roy Eldridge, Teddy Wilson, Fats Waller, Erroll Garner, John Kirby, Slim [Gaillard] & Slam [Stewart], Stuff Smith, Leo Watson, Sidney Bechet, Dizzy Gillespie, Charlie Parker, and a host of others.

The jam session and the practice of "sitting in" are also associated with 52nd Street and have added to its fame. Jam sessions, informal gatherings held by and for musicians, allowed participants to "stretch out" musically in ways that were not possible on their regular jobs and to try out and exchange ideas. Originally jam sessions were semiprivate affairs, but someone had the idea of organized sessions for the entertainment of the public. This idea did not originate on 52nd Street. Ralph Berton, the sometime disc jockey brother of drummer Vic, claims to have organized jam sessions downtown at Nick's before any club on 52nd Street held them. (Even before Berton, Harry Lim, the Javanese jazz critic, conducted successful jams in the Panther Room at Chicago's Hotel Sherman.) Sitting in did not originate on 52nd Street, either, but became one of its hallmarks. It was not uncommon for musicians whose gigs had ended earlier in the evening or who were between sets to sit in with a group at another club for the sheer joy of playing.

The best known of the 52nd Street clubs were the Onyx, the Famous Door, the Hickory House (located between Sixth and Seventh Avenues), Kelly's Stable, the Yacht Club, Jimmy Ryan's, the Three Deuces, and the Spotlite. The Onyx, formerly a speakeasy, opened as a legitimate club in 1934. Owned by Joe Helbock, it was closed by a fire in February 1935 but reopened in July of that same year. The club's resident featured attraction was violinist Stuff Smith and his swinging group. When Smith left for Hollywood, he was replaced by bassist John Kirby and his group. One of the few big bands to play 52nd Street, Jimmy Mundy's Orchestra, played the Onyx in 1939. In 1944 Dizzy Gillespie brought into the Onyx a group co-led with Oscar Pettiford that has been regarded as the first bop combo to appear in a club. Count Basie's Orchestra had an important residency at the Famous Door in 1938. New Orleans trumpeter Louis Prima, with a small band featuring Pee Wee Russell, was the popular opening attraction at the Famous Door. Both Teddy Wilson and Joe Bushkin did stints as intermission pianists at this club, originally owned by a consortium of jazz-minded studio musicians. Red Norvo followed Prima at the Famous Door with a group that didn't play dixieland and had no piano or drums.

The Hickory House, cofounded by John Popkin and Jack Goldman, was one of the earliest clubs on 52nd Street to feature jazz. Though first known for the small-group swing sounds of Wingy Manone and Joe Marsala, the Hickory House later became a haven for outstanding pianists, among them Joe Bushkin, Hazel Scott, Mary Lou Williams, Billy Taylor, and Marian McPartland. The bastion of dixieland jazz was Jimmy Ryan's, owned by ex-hoofer Ryan and his partner Matty Walsh. Milt Gabler of Commodore Records introduced and organized the very popular Sunday jam sessions at Ryan's, the last club to feature jazz on the original block. It moved to 54th Street in 1962. Kelly's Stable, owned by Ralph Watkins, was where Nat King Cole first sang in public. Besides featuring such talents as Stuff Smith, the Spirits of Rhythm, Slim and Slam, Coleman Hawkins, and Art Tatum, Kelly's also had organized jam sessions. Singer Billy Eckstine made his New York debut at the Yacht Club, and Fats Waller played there often. In 1944, when the Gillespie-Pettiford group at the Onyx broke up, Dizzy formed a new group with Budd Johnson and opened at the Yacht Club. The Three Deuces, run by Sammy Kay and Irving Alexander, was also hospitable to bop. Both Gillespie and Charlie Parker played there, as did nonboppers Erroll Garner, Eddie Heywood, and Johnny Guarnieri. The short-lived Spotlite existed for only two years (1944–46) and mainly featured practitioners of the new music, though it also booked 52nd Street stalwarts Harry "the Hipster" Gibson and Billie Holiday. Both Parker and Gillespie led groups there.

Traditional jazz flourished in two Greenwich Village clubs, Nick's (1936–63) and Eddie Condon's (1945–85). (The last editions of Condon's were located in midtown.) Also in "the Village," in January 1939, Barney Josephson opened Café Society (he later opened another one on 58th Street). In this club, known for its liberal policies, blacks and whites mixed freely. Billie Holiday had one of her most important engagements here.

Two great Harlem clubs, Minton's Playhouse and Monroe's Uptown House, will forever be linked to the development of modern jazz. Minton's Playhouse, located in the Hotel Cecil, has been called the "incubator of bop." The club was owned by former saxophonist Henry Minton, who hired former saxophonist and bandleader Teddy Hill as manager. Minton and Hill wanted to provide musicians with a place to jam and hang out on 118th Street. Hill hired a house band led by drummer Kenny Clarke and Joe Guy that included young Thelonious Monk on piano. The jam sessions, attended by such greats as Dizzy Gillespie, Charlie Christian, Lester Young, Ben Webster, and many others, are credited with much of the experimentation that eventually led to the birth of modern jazz. Monroe's Uptown House, owned by ex-hoofer Clark Monroe, had a house band, led by pianist Al Tinney, which at various times included drummer Max Roach and trumpeter George Treadwell. Like Minton's, Monroe's was a place where musicians could come after their regular gigs and jam. Many of the players who frequented Minton's were regulars at Monroe's as well, although Charlie Parker, who was often at Monroe's, never played at Minton's.

Two Broadway venues that opened in the '40s, and where bop could be frequently heard, were the Royal Roost and Birdland (named for Charlie "Bird" Parker). Birdland was one of the most famous New York City jazz spots of the 1950s. Charlie Parker, Lester Young, Count Basie, and Miles Davis were among the jazz greats who performed here. Birdland closed in the 1960s, but a number of attempts have been made over the years to open a club using that famous name. As of this writing a Birdland currently resides on West 44th Street.

Originally located on the edge of the Bowery, the Five Spot, where many major events took place, was opened by Joe and Iggy Termini in the mid-1950s. Ornette Coleman, Cecil Taylor, and Thelonious Monk all had important residencies here. The Half Note originally opened in Greenwich Village in 1957 (moving uptown in 1972) and quickly became established as a center for contemporary styles of jazz. Prominent musicians who performed there include Charles Mingus, Lennie Tristano, John Coltrane, Al Cohn and Zoot Sims, and Wes Montgomery with the Wynton Kelly Trio.

The oldest surviving New York jazz club, the Village Vanguard, was opened at its current location (178 Seventh Avenue) in 1935 by Max Gordon. It wasn't until the mid-1950s that the basement locale became mainly known as a jazz club. Since that time, some of the greatest names in the history of jazz have performed at the Village Vanguard including Dizzy Gillespie, Sonny Rollins, Miles Davis, and Gerry Mulligan. John Coltrane performed there often and recorded some of his best albums at the club. The Thad Jones–Mel Lewis Orchestra (from 1979 the Mel Lewis Orchestra; now the Vanguard Jazz Orchestra) has been a regular Monday night feature from February 1966 to the present. Besides the Village Vanguard (and the aforementioned Birdland), other current well-known jazz establishments in Manhattan include the Blue Note, Iridium, and the Knitting Factory.

Chicago

Chicago in the 1920s was a major jazz center. Chicagoans listened and/or danced to jazz in a variety of settings, including jazz clubs, dance halls, and theaters. While an unusually large number of music establishments could be found on Chicago's South Side, with its large African-American population, one could hear jazz all over the Windy City.

One of the most important South Side clubs before 1910 was the Pekin Inn. It was the first to employ musicians who were closely associated with ragtime and prejazz popular music. Joe Jordan, Tony Jackson, and Wilbur Sweatman performed there. In 1917 the Athenia Café hired the Louisiana Five, a New Orleans band led by drummer Anton Lada, for a six-month engagement. It was one of the earliest residencies by a jazz-oriented unit in Chicago. The Lincoln Gardens was a dance hall where King Oliver's Creole Jazz Band held forth from 1922 to 1924. The Dreamland Ballroom was home for Doc Cook's Orchestra (with Freddie Keppard and Jimmie Noone) for six years from 1922. The Vendome Theater was home to Erskine Tate's Orchestra (1919–28), which featured Louis Armstrong in 1926. The Sunset Café, one of the most popular South Side clubs, was known as a "black and tan" because it catered to both white and black patrons. Carroll Dickerson's band had a long residency here and included in its ranks both Louis Armstrong and Earl Hines. Close to the Sunset was the Apex Club, where clarinetist Jimmie Noone with his unique small band was a regular attraction from 1926 until the spring of 1928, when the club closed.

Both Fletcher Henderson's and Benny Goodman's orchestras had stays at the Congress Hotel, Henderson in 1927 with regular broadcasts over station KYW and Goodman famously in 1936. The Grand Terrace (like New York's Cotton Club) featured elaborate floor shows with music. Earl Hines and his orchestra were in residence here from 1928 to 1938. Chicago's Three Deuces was noted for a long residency by Roy Eldridge, starting in 1936. During this time the club, located in the Loop, enjoyed tremendous popularity. Art Tatum played piano in the Swing Room, a small room downstairs from the main club. Others who played there include Zutty Singleton, Art Hodes, Jimmy McPartland, Baby Dodds (the house drummer from 1936 to 1939), and Johnny Dodds. The Bee Hive Club opened in 1948 and at first featured older performers like Bertha "Chippie" Hill, Art Hodes, and Baby Dodds. Lester Young played here in 1949, and it was the scene of Charlie Parker's last Chicago engagement. (In the 1970s a double-LP set was issued of 1955 broadcasts from the Bee Hive featuring the Clifford Brown–Max Roach Quintet.) The Blue Note Club flourished in the 1940s and early 1950s. It was operated by Frank Holzfiend; among the musicians who led resident bands were Muggsy Spanier (1947), Paul Mares (1948), and Sidney Bechet (during an American tour in 1951). Count Basie considered the Blue Note his home base in Chicago and played there regularly from 1949 to 1958.

The Jazz Showcase, run by Joe Segal, has been presenting the best in jazz talent since the late 1940s. The club has had a number of locations through the years including, roughly, a twenty-year stay at the Blackstone Hotel (from the 1970s). As of this writing, the Jazz Showcase resides at 59 West Grand Avenue.

Kansas City

In the opening pages of this essay it was mentioned that the precursors to the early jazz clubs were illegal speakeasies that sprang up during Prohibition. Nowhere was this as true as in Kansas City. Once the notorious political boss Tom Pendergast took control of the city it was pretty much "anything goes." Illegal merchandising of beer and alcohol went unchecked. Gangster-run saloons and cabarets proliferated at an increasing rate until Kansas City boasted the largest concentration in America, and, naturally, entertainment was needed for all of these clubs. Also, the black district offered major potential for profitable enterprises, and nightclubs were quickly and inexpensively opened there. There was plenty of work for musicians, plenty of booze, and the clubs stayed open as long as they desired (some never closed). No wonder Kansas City was called a "wide open town." Jam sessions and sitting in were two specialties of the Kansas City jazz scene, where the longest jam sessions in history took place almost nightly. Nowhere were jam sessions taken as seriously as in Kansas City, and for some musicians, jamming practically became a way of life. The competition was said to be so fierce that the "cutting contest," where one musician tried to outplay the other, became quite commonplace.

During the Pendergast years, it has been estimated that between two hundred and five hundred nightclubs were in existence. Of these, there were approximately thirty leading clubs where jazz was performed. The Reno Club has to be considered the "queen of Kansas City jazz clubs." Run by "Papa Sol" Epstein, a member of the Pendergast syndicate, it catered to both blacks and whites. Unfortunately, racial mixing was discouraged. There were separate bars, separate sections of tables and booths, and separate dance floors. Its reputation was built on the fact that the customers got a lot of entertainment for their money, including a good band and an elaborate floor show. The Reno Club will forever be remembered for the jam session in which drummer Jo Jones tossed his cymbal to show his displeasure at the young Charlie Parker's musical ineptness. It was also at the Reno that John Hammond discovered Count Basie in 1936 via a broadcast on W9XBY, an experimental shortwave radio station. The Sunset Club was the earliest and most popular place to jam. The club was white-owned but managed by a black man named Piney Brown, who became known throughout the Southwest as a special friend to musicians and a patron of jazz. Its house band included Baby Lovett on drums and Pete Johnson on piano, with Joe Turner tending bar and singing the blues. The Sunset was especially favored by saxophonists, among them Lester Young, Herschel Evans, Buster Smith, Ben Webster, Dick Wilson, and Charlie Parker. The Subway Club was also managed by Piney Brown. It was located in a basement and set up for jam sessions. Musicians were given all the food and liquor they wanted. The jam sessions at the Subway Club were very popular with such out-of-town jazzmen as Benny Goodman, Gene Krupa, Harry James, the Dorsey brothers, Roy Eldridge, and Chu Berry.

Los Angeles

Contrary to certain opinions, Los Angeles's Central Avenue was not just the West Coast's answer to New York's 52nd Street. By the 1920s, 40 percent of the black population in L.A. lived within a few blocks on either side of Central Avenue between 11th Street and 42nd Street. Businesses, residences, social clubs, restaurants, and nightclubs were in abundance on this stretch.

The Cadillac Café has the distinction of being one of the first venues in L.A. to present jazz music. Jelly Roll Morton performed there in 1917. The Club Alabam was known as the Apex Club when it was founded by drummer and bandleader Curtis Mosby in the 1920s. It was the focal point of the jazz scene in L.A. in the 1930s and 1940s. Two doors away from Club Alabam was the Down Beat Club. It was here that Howard McGhee presented his pioneering bop band, the first modern jazz ensemble on the West Coast. Charles Mingus and Buddy Collette premiered their short-lived group the Stars of Swing here. The Casa Blanca, a celebrated after-hours joint, was owned and managed by guitarist Stanley Morgan. Charlie Parker performed there frequently, and occasionally Morgan would bring his fourteen-year-old son, Frank, down to the club to play.

While Central Avenue's importance to the L.A. jazz scene is indisputable, clubs located in other areas were as important. Billy Berg's Swing Club on Vine Street in Hollywood was one such. Berg presented swing and bop, and one of the first groups to play there was led by Lester and Lee Young (1941). Benny Carter's Orchestra was the first big band that Berg engaged in 1943. Charlie Parker and Dizzy Gillespie had their most important gig here when they came to the West Coast in late 1945.

The Lighthouse Café started presenting jazz in 1949 at the suggestion of bassist Howard Rumsey. In 1951 he formed the Lighthouse All-Stars, who played there regularly and made a number of "live" albums at the club. Rumsey eventually became manager and part owner of the Lighthouse and helped turn it into the leading nightclub for West Coast jazz during the 1950s, '60s, and early '70s; Art Pepper, Shorty Rogers, and Jimmy Giuffre were among the important musicians who appeared. The Halg was another club for West Coast jazz; Red Norvo, Gerry Mulligan's famous quartet, Laurindo Almeida, and Bud Shank were among those who performed here during the 1950s.

In 1960 drummer Shelly Manne opened Shelly's Manne-Hole, and for slightly over a decade it was an important club to hear jazz; Manne's own group appeared there regularly.

Jazz Clubs Abroad

Because of the worldwide popularity of American jazz, clubs that present the music can be found in almost every country. Many of these countries have a long and rich history of jazz, and to list the many jazz clubs that have come and gone over the years would be impossible here. Instead, honorable mention will be made of some of the famous jazz clubs that have played a major part in the music's progression.

Possibly the most important club in England is Ronnie Scott's in London. It was founded by tenor saxophonist Ronnie Scott in 1959 and is still going strong at this writing. American stars, including Sarah Vaughan, Count Basie, Ben Webster, Buddy Rich, Don Byas, Wes Montgomery, and many others, have performed here. Ronnie Scott's also has an excellent track record of promoting British musicians and has been a frequent recording location.

Today, Paris has excellent places to hear jazz like the Sunset and Petit Opportun, but during the 1930s the city boasted some of the finest clubs in the world. Best known of these was Bricktop's, run by the American entertainer Ada Smith (a.k.a. "Bricktop"). Les Ambassadeurs and the Embassy Club were two other important venues for jazz. Two well-known clubs during the 1950s and 1960s were the Blue Note and Club Saint-Germain. Lester Young played his final engagements at the former, and Django Reinhardt, Stephane Grappelli, Miles Davis, and Kenny Clarke performed at the latter.

The foremost jazz club in Scandinavia, Denmark's Montmartre, presented both Scandinavian and foreign musicians. Niels-Henning Ørsted Pedersen and other Danish musicians got their starts there, and long residencies were enjoyed by Dexter Gordon, Kenny Drew, Stan Getz, Horace Parlan, Thad Jones, and many others. A number of memorable recordings and broadcasts originated from the Montmartre. Bud Powell and Ornette Coleman were among the American stars to play Stockholm's Golden Circle.

Japan has embraced jazz with a gusto unlike any other country's. American musicians still marvel at the large and appreciative crowds that routinely attend their performances. Jazz clubs can be found in many parts of Japan from Aichi to Toyama, but the largest number of clubs is, naturally, in Tokyo. Alfee, Blues Alley, Cygnus, Diamond Club, Satin Doll, Sonoka, and Valentine are some of Tokyo's finest venues for jazz at this writing. The Blue Note International Franchise, besides having a New York locale, also operates Blue Note clubs in Tokyo, Osaka, and Fukuoka.

Jazz and American Literature

Gerald Early

Doubtless, the most famous American novel about a jazz musician, and arguably the most seminal, in part, because it was the first and most commercially and critically successful novel about jazz, is Dorothy Baker's *Young Man With a Horn*, published in 1938. It certainly established or intensified a number of conventions about jazz musicians as they have come to be portrayed in popular and literary culture, two most especially. First, the novel gives us the highly romantic image of the jazz musician as brooding, self-destructive, antidomestic genius, without formal training, dedicated only to the sound that he hears in his head. Second, *Young Man With a Horn* gives us the charismatic white jazz musician as a kind of political and moral innocent—combining Billy Budd and Huckleberry Finn—drawn to blacks, the authentic source of jazz, in a quest for artistic purity as only blacks can embody as against the white world's superficiality, bourgeois respectability, and commercialism.

Baker was born Dorothy Dodd in Missoula, Montana, in April 1907. *Young Man With a Horn*, her first novel, was an immediate success. Published in May 1938, when Baker was thirty-one, it was certified a best-seller by a *Life* magazine article on swing music in the August 8 issue—a good portion of which was devoted to jazz—of the same year. The author makes clear in a prefatory note that "[the] inspiration for the writing of this book had been the music, but not the life, of a great musician, Leon (Bix) Beiderbecke."

It is unclear whether Baker was a fan of jazz or of Beiderbecke or if she was simply struck by him as a subject for a novel after reading Otis Ferguson's July 1936 *New Republic* essay entitled "Young Man With a Horn," which described Beiderbecke's music as well as provided the bare bones of the Beiderbecke myth. Ferguson was a much-admired jazz, literary, and film critic of the 1930s who was killed by an explosion on a merchant ship in 1943. Baker had written that Hemingway and Ferguson were her two biggest influences, and it is clear that she took both the title and subject of her novel from Ferguson's essay, with his permission.

Beiderbecke would make a good subject for a novel because he so personified the very conventions that have become a virtual stereotype of the obsessed artist: he was considered a genius musician by his fellows, although he had little formal training as either a cornetist or a pianist, a point that Ferguson makes much of noting: "For his talent there were no conservatories to get stuffy in"; he cared about nothing but music and never really outgrew his provincial Iowa background; he mightily resisted commercialism, despite the fact that he played with Paul Whiteman, one of the most commercially successful American bandleaders in history; he died at the age of twenty-eight from alcoholism. In short, he was a wondrous combination of Keats, Stephen Foster, and F. Scott Fitzgerald. Rick Martin, Baker's hero, is a perfect embodiment of this type of tragic artist.

Martin, an anonymous boy growing up in Los Angeles with his uncle and aunt, is essentially a feckless character, uninterested in school or in much of anything until he discovers a piano in a mission. But Martin has also a fey quality; he is special in his own indolent, aimless way, possibly because he becomes so driven about music, while so careless about everything else. The contrast makes him seem more compelling than he truly is. At the mission, he works hard to teach himself to play by learning hymns, an ironic contrast to the "devil's music" that he is destined to master. He loses access to the mission piano and eventually winds up working in a bowling alley, where he becomes friendly with a fellow worker, Smoke Jordan, a black boy who is also a drummer. Through Smoke, Martin is introduced to the world of black jazz in Los Angeles and to alcohol, which will ultimately be Martin's undoing. Martin masters black jazz,

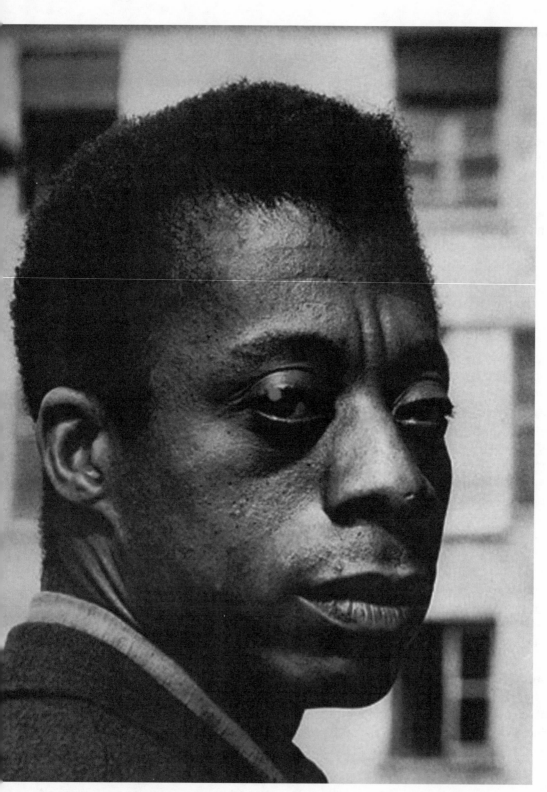

James Baldwin. Photo © Bettmann/CORBIS.

learning piano from Jeff Williams and trumpet from Art Hazzard (art hazard or hazardous art?), working ceaselessly: "He'd sit at the Cotton Club piano and practice until his fingernails ached from being sent the wrong way, and he'd play the trumpet until his lip crumpled up on him and shook miserably in the face of further discipline." Martin then becomes a professional musician in the white world, eventually joining the highly successful Lee Valentine band and then Phil Morrison's. (These are clearly fictionalized version of Jean Goldkette and Paul Whiteman, whose bands Beiderbecke played with.) There follows an unhappy marriage to an artistically inclined woman named Amy, and a slow decline caused by drinking and the frustration of being unable to play what he hears in his head. When he leaves Morrison's band, his drinking becomes uncontrollable. He goes downhill quickly and dies.

The popularity of the novel probably has much to do with (1) the popularity of swing music in particular and jazz in general in 1938 and its growing status as a music worthy of being considered an artform; (2) the cult surrounding Bix Beiderbecke, who had died seven years earlier, becoming the first tragic hero of jazz, signaling a change in how musicians of popular music were being seen by the American public, more as misunderstood, charismatic artists, less as freakish or degenerate or tasteless entertainers; (3) and the fact, finally, that Beiderbecke was white but played like a Negro or with Negro soul. The novel is also well written and tightly controlled; while it is romantic, it is never sentimental. The narrator's views about music-making are hard-edged and realistic; the relationship between Martin and the black musicians is drawn with great sensitivity. There is no attempt to be either archly hip or patronizingly racist with the black characters in their speech or action. An interesting complement to Baker's novel in its depiction of black jazz musicians is Eudora Welty's short story "Powerhouse," written a few years later in 1941, which tells the story of a Fats Waller–type pianist during an intermission in his show, how he gets along with his musicians, the tension between his public persona and his private character.

If *Young Man With a Horn* is the definitive American jazz novel, then James Baldwin's "Sonny's Blues," published in *Partisan Review* in 1957, is, without question, the most famous jazz short story, having been anthologized more than any other jazz short story or, indeed, any other piece of fiction by Baldwin. (For instance, "Sonny's Blues" is the only Baldwin fiction in *The Norton Anthology of African-American Literature*.) Only a handful of Baldwin's essays enjoy the same high literary regard as "Sonny's Blues." Baldwin, born in New York City in 1924 and reared in Harlem, left the United States for France in 1948, six years after graduating from high school. He returned to the United States in 1957, the same year that "Sonny's Blues" was published. He was, by that time, one of the most celebrated black writers in the United States. It is unclear how much of a jazz fan Baldwin was; he certainly knew a number of jazz musicians and particularly was good friends with trumpeter Miles Davis. In "Prince and Powers," he talked about how jazz might remotely approximate the "creative interdependence" that exists between the African artist and his audience, but he went on to speak of "the ghastly isolation of the jazz musician" and "the neurotic intensity of his listeners." It is a certainty that Baldwin knew a great deal less about the techniques and history of jazz than his contemporary Ralph Ellison.

"Sonny's Blues" makes use of several of the conventions about the jazz musician that Baker employed in *Young Man With a Horn.* But there are important differences between *Young Man With a Horn* and "Sonny's Blues." Baldwin's story is about the relationship between two African-American brothers, one a public school math teacher and the other a jazz pianist. Because his hero is black, the entire social implications of jazz's relationship to race is changed. Baldwin's story is not concerned with jazz as an expression, in its purest form, of racial egalitarianism. Whites do not figure importantly in the story. Sonny's downfall is heroin, not alcohol. Jazz musicians of Sonny's generation were attracted to heroin as an expression of both art and rage.

When Sonny finally confesses to his brother that he wants to be a jazz musician, his brother responds, "You mean—like Louis Armstrong?" Sonny rejoins, "No. I'm not talking about none of that old-time, down home crap." Sonny goes on to describe his admiration for Charlie Parker, aspects of whose lifestyle he is clearly trying to emulate. His brother, permitting Baldwin to show the generational and philosophical division between the two men, has never heard of Parker. The exchange suggests not only the artistic but the political implications of jazz styles among its black players, a dimension touched upon much more simplistically in *Young Man With a Horn,* where blacks are a homogenous group and whites bow to their "natural" ability to play jazz. Baldwin is more concerned with what it costs a black person to be an artist in a racist society.

It must be noted as well that Sonny rejects the idea of playing classical music ("That isn't what interests me," he says), for much the same reason that Oceola Jones rejects classical music for the blues in Langston Hughes's deft 1934 story about black art and white patronage entitled "The Blues I'm Playing." For Sonny, jazz is his tradition, as blues are Oceola's tradition. (A striking counterpoint to "The Blues I'm Playing" is Dorothy Baker's "The Jazz Sonata" [1937], about a concert pianist who is helped to prepare for a classical concert by a jazz pianist.) Many critics consider Baldwin's story to be the finest American jazz fiction ever written. It is, without doubt, his best short story.

Around these two epoch-making pieces of jazz fiction are clusters of other works of considerable artistic and cultural importance that deal with jazz or have a jazz-related theme. Critics such as Nathan Huggins and Harold Cruse have complained about the inability of literary figures of the Harlem Renaissance to appreciate jazz, in part because they were elitist. This is generally true but not entirely so. Alain Locke, one of the main leaders of the Harlem Renaissance, wrote about jazz fairly perceptively in the 1930s. Amateur historian J. A. Rogers's essay "Jazz at Home," which appeared in the 1925 anthology *The New Negro*, was also knowledgeable and insightful.

Claude McKay's 1929 novel *Banjo* is about a black southern musician of the same name and his picaresque adventures on the waterfront of Marseilles, largely existing among lowlife characters. There are several musical scenes in the novel, with Banjo and other musicians performing in clubs for wildly dancing and usually wildly appreciative audiences. (At the time *Banjo* was published, one could still find the banjo in jazz bands, as Duke Ellington's Brunswick recordings of the late 1920s show, although it was not as prominent as it had been in the 1910s and earlier.) While there may be something stereotypical and even distasteful for some in this formulation by McKay (Negroes with happy feet, as it were), it must be said that Czech-born Josef Skvorecky makes similar associations with jazz in his fictional works "The Bass Saxophone," "Emoke," and "Eine Kleine JazzMusik," all published in 1977, where jazz is portrayed as distinctly opposed to the reactionary, kitsch-oriented sensibilities of repressive, fascist politics.

In several Harlem Renaissance novels, including Carl Van Vechten's *Nigger Heaven*, Nella Larsen's *Quicksand* and *Passing*, Claude McKay's *Home to Harlem*, Wallace Thurman's *Infants of the Spring* and *The Black the Berry*, and Jean Toomer's *Cane*, jazz playing or jazz musicians are featured in a scene, sometimes very briefly, often associated with some form of sensuality or emotional freedom. Indeed, Zora Neale Hurston wrote a short parody of this literary characterization of jazz in her 1928 essay "How It Feels to Be Colored Me," in which she described her atavistic response to a jazz orchestra: "I dance wildly inside myself; I yell within, I whoop; I shake my assegai above my head, I hurl it true to the mark yeeeeooww! I am in the jungle and living in a jungle way.... I want to slaughter something." Roentgenologist Rudoph Fisher's short story "Common Meter" (1930), about a battle of two jazz dance bands as their leaders fight over a girl, is both a humorous and insightful look at the world of black jazz musicians and Harlem.

Probably a more important Harlem Renaissance work in its portrayal of the musician is James Weldon Johnson's *The Autobiography of an Ex-Colored Man* originally published in 1912 and republished in 1927. Johnson, field secretary of the NAACP during the 1920s, had been U.S. consul to Venezuela and Nicaragua and, along with his brother, Rosamond, and Bob Cole, a composer of musical comedies at the turn of the century. *The Autobiography of an Ex-Colored Man*, about a light-skinned black man who ultimately decides to pass for white, is about jazz's precursor, ragtime. The nameless narrator-hero, a musician and composer, decides to make ragtime an "elevated" art form, espousing Johnson's own view about this music (not dissimilar to Antonin Dvořák's views of black music when he visited this country in 1892; several black musicians Johnson knew well, like Will Marion Cook and Harry T. Burleigh, studied under Dvořák). There are several long passages in the book about the nature and future of ragtime, which is generally associated with the black sporting world. But Johnson's view about this music is decidedly more complex than Paul Laurence Dunbar's in his novel *The Sport of the Gods* (1902), where ragtime, as literary jazz depictions sometimes were in the 1920s, is associated with the northern city and a southern, small-town character's moral downfall and sexual degeneracy.

During the 1920s, when jazz was a revolutionary new music, despised by many, loved by others, probably the most influential white literary voice was F. Scott Fitzgerald, the man who named the era the Jazz Age, although he was not a big fan of music and did not care for jazz. Fitzgerald grew up during the ragtime era and was very influenced by it as a revolt against Victorianism. He became a big-time writer just as jazz emerged in American popular culture as a music associated not only with blacks and black culture but with the rebellion of white youth. Fitzgerald saw himself as the writer of the youth culture of the period. Jazz was instrumental in how that culture saw itself. Fitzgerald wrote this, rather strangely, about jazz: "The word *jazz* in its progress toward respectability has meant first sex, then dancing, then music. It is associated with a state of nervous stimulation, not unlike that of big cities behind the lines of a war." It is difficult to tell from Fitzgerald's passage whether jazz causes the nervous stimulation or is caused by it. Jazz certainly represents an extreme in emotional expression to Fitzgerald, yet it also symbolizes bourgeois progress: human expression moving from sex to art, from act to the sublimation of the act.

There are a couple of important jazz references in *The Great Gatsby* (1925), Fitzgerald's greatest novel, including an orchestra at Gatsby's house playing "Vladimir Tostoff's 'Jazz History of the World.'" This is a clear reference to the symphonic jazz movement and an attempt to give jazz a European facade, especially as the orchestra described in the novel so closely resembles in makeup Paul Whiteman's band, the leading orchestra in the symphonic jazz movement. Fitzgerald's view of jazz was not dissimilar to that of McKay, Rogers, or other Harlem Renaissance blacks, and his view proved to have long-lasting influence.

Most of the important jazz fiction has been written since World War II, as jazz has attracted more literary types. The most important novels and short stories about jazz musicians include John A. Williams's *Night Song* (1961), about a character based on Charlie Parker; William Melvin Kelley's *A Drop of Patience,* about a blind black jazz musician who has a breakdown as a result of being jilted by his white lover; Michael Ondaatje's *Coming Through Slaughter* (1976), a fictional account of the life of Buddy Bolden; John Clellon Holmes's *The Horn* (1958), a story about a declining saxophonist's attempt to reclaim past glory; Frank Conroy's *Body and Soul* (1993), a coming-of-age, rags-to-riches story about a pianist who plays both classical and jazz music; and Amiri Baraka's (LeRoi Jones) "The Screamers" (1963), about a honking saxophonist of the Illinois Jacquet–Eddie "Lockjaw" Davis variety who leads black club patrons into the street, where they start a riot (very much in keeping with Baraka's views about the connection between jazz and revolutionary politics, and the general view, established by Fitzgerald, that jazz is an art form that opposes societal repression).

In recent years, jazz mysteries have begun to appear. Bill Moody has written a series of novels around a detective character named Evan Horne, a former jazz pianist unable to play because of a freakish car accident that severed tendons in his arm. It is only his musical knowledge that separates this character from the standard noir-type detective, but it is an interesting distinction. Among Horne's adventures has been solving the mystery surrounding the death of tenor saxist Wardell Gray (*Death of a Tenor Man*, 1995). Harper Barnes wrote a mystery about the death of Bennie Moten called *Blue Monday* (1989) with a good deal of Kansas City jazz ambience.

Among the most recent jazz novels is Bart Schneider's *Blue Bossa* (1998), a finely written account about jazz trumpeter Ronnie Reboulet (Chet Baker) trying to make a comeback, his daughter, Rae, an aspiring singer, and her biracial son. Other noteworthy novels featuring jazz are Warren Miller's coming-of-age novel about a Harlem boy, *The Cool World* (1961) (made into a film with a soundtrack by Dizzy Gillespie), and Rafi Zabor's highly acclaimed *The Bear Comes Home* (1998).

Jazz has also influenced literature aesthetically. Some writers have tried to write novels that are not necessarily about jazz musicians but show the influence of jazz as a form, as a way of organizing imaginative concepts. Probably the two most famous "jazz" novels, works supposedly shaped like jazz improvisations, are, first, Ralph Ellison's *Invisible Man* (1952), about a nameless narrator who travels from the South to the North, from innocence to experience, through a number of ideologies and identities. The novel makes important references to Louis Armstrong and several allusions to jazz but is not, in any way, about music. Ellison wrote several essays about jazz; particularly impressive are those about growing up with jazz in Oklahoma, featured in his collections *Shadow and Act* (1964) and *Going to the Territory* (1986). Second is Jack Kerouac's *On the Road* (1957), also an odyssey novel, about two friends traveling across country by car. There are several references to jazz musicians and jazz in the novel, but it is, like *Invisible Man*, not about jazz or music making. It is interesting to note that James Baldwin, in his essay "The Black Boy Looks at the White Boy" (1961), explicitly articulates his dislike of the portrayal of blacks and the Negro mystique in *On the Road.*

Jazz as a literary aesthetic has had a bigger impact on poetry than on prose. Many poets have written poems dedicated to or about specific jazz musicians. (More poems have been written about tenor saxophonist John Coltrane than any other jazz musician, possibly because of his spiritual and philosophical pretensions and because he emerged as a major force in jazz at the time of the civil rights and black power movements, which had intensified a quest among black writers and intellectuals for a black aesthetic that combined spirituality and political protest, which Coltrane seemed, for some, to embody.) But many more poets have been influenced by jazz as an aesthetic expression, as a source of inspiration, as a way of shaping a poem.

The most famous poet to use jazz as an aesthetic was, without question, Langston Hughes, the only Harlem Renaissance writer with an undying and deep passion for jazz. He recorded poetry with jazz musicians and even wrote a children's book about jazz. Not only did Hughes write about jazz musicians in such poems as "Song for Billie Holiday," "Jazzonia," and "Flattened Fifths," but he also evoked a jazz mood or celebrated the jazz aesthetic through sound in such poems as "Jam Session" and through a sense of hipness in poems like "Motto."

Vachel Lindsay, Hart Crane, and Carl Sandburg (who was a considerable influence on Hughes) also wrote poems that not only specifically mentioned jazz but seemed, in trying to capture something of urban life, to try to catch the spirit of jazz as a new aesthetic. Sandburg, for instance, seemed clearly to be doing this in "Jazz Fantasia" (1920). Much of this poetry saw jazz in much the same light as Fitzgerald—liberatory, often hedonistic—and usually black jazz musicians were depicted in a racist manner, as primitives or worse. Hughes partook of some of this romanticism of jazz and the jazz musician, but despite the seeming simplicity of his work, his jazz poetry offered a far more complex and appreciative view of jazz and black jazz musicians than virtually any by the white poets.

Jazz poetry became a major mode or subgenre after World War II, with the emergence of the Beat movement, an intellectual and literary counterculture group that closely identified with the lifestyle and aesthetics of the jazz musician, especially the black jazz musician. Allen Ginsburg's poetry, blatantly influenced by Walt Whitman's, was also much shaped by jazz. Ginsburg even thought of himself as blowing solos when he was reading his work, and felt he had to breathe as if he were a jazz horn player. Gregory Corso, Jack Kerouac, and Lawrence Ferlinghetti were all major Beat poets who experimented with jazz. Both Kerouac and Ferlinghetti recorded and read publicly with jazz musicians, as did Ginsburg. Ted Joans was a minor Beat poet, an African American, who made his reputation writing jazz poetry.

Possibly the most remarkable, though not necessarily most talented, poet to emerge from the Beats was LeRoi Jones, who changed his name to Amiri Baraka in the middle 1960s. Baraka, an African

American from Newark, born in 1934, had a deep love of jazz. He wrote liner notes and reviews in the 1950s; he also wrote a book about black music, *Blues People* (1963), and produced a compilation of his pieces on avant-garde or new wave jazz, *Black Music* (1967). Among his most noted jazz and jazz-influenced poems are "Black Dada Nihilismus" (1964), which he recorded with the New York Art Quartet (Roswell Rudd, John Tchicai, Lewis Worrell, Milford Graves), "Symphony Sid" (1961), *Am/Trak* (1979), and *In the Tradition* (1982). He was a highly influential poet in the mid-1960s when he helped launch the black arts movement.

From the black arts movement emerged poetry groups like the Last Poets and the young poet-singer Gil Scott-Heron, both of whom refined the methods of chanting poetry to jazz music started by the Beats and were also seminal figures in the formation of rap. The emergence of rap and hip-hop has intensified the connection between orality, jazz, and poetry; the idea of improvisation and spontaneity, of reading poetry aloud, of performing poetry in much the way a jazz musician performs a concert or a set, has become of central importance for many. Essentially, the associations made with jazz fifty years ago are still being made today: the jazz musician as martyr, the jazz musician as genius, the jazz musician as symbol of integrity in a corrupt, commercialized world. Michael Harper also appeared in the wake of Baraka, although he is a quite distinct voice. Harper has built his reputation on writing jazz poetry. He has probably been a bigger influence on younger poets today who want to write jazz poetry than Baraka. Among the most recent poets on the scene today whose work is closely associated with jazz are Nathaniel Mackey, Quincy Troupe, Yusef Komunyakaa, Hayden Carruth, and Al Young. The jazz musicians most commonly written about are Miles Davis, Thelonious Monk, John Coltrane, Charlie Parker, and Billie Holiday.

Jazz Criticism

Ron Welburn

Jazz criticism is a significant branch of music criticism. It began as a journalistic phenomenon, a new literature for a new music in a new century. In the United States, the home of jazz, those who wrote about it contributed to the making of this fresh and distinct form of journalism about a stimulating indigenous musical form. Jazz criticism defines and explains jazz's evolving styles and plays a controversial role as liaison between performer, performance interpretation, and listener tastes. It reflects the intense debates about the music it describes, and occasionally it has antagonized the public's preferences for dancing, listening, and appreciating the art of jazz. In the 1930s the jazz critic emerged as both a studious listener and an irritant to musicians and fans. As jazz aficionados developed their own publications, jazz writing found an identity as a viable and informative prose form, and how it developed reflects how criticism for a cultural genre evolves.

Jazz criticism is as phenomenal as film criticism and has no other kindred precedent. The emergence of a serious critical journalism for lowly jazz was heretical to followers of classical music. But jazz criticism persisted to create for its writers a forum in which observations and assessments of jazz, profile features of its musicians, and historical

Marshall Stearns. Courtesy of the Institute of Jazz Studies, Rutgers University.

chronologies and evaluations became standard elements. Jazz criticism can be appreciated as having three major historical concentrations: (1) jazz writing as social literature; (2) jazz as the basis for a new symphonic art music reflecting musical nationalism; and (3) jazz criticism as the evaluative literature of live and recorded performance, as feature articles about performers, and as essays on topical areas related to jazz's aesthetic fundamentals and pedagogy. However, simply viewing these three approaches as a progression ignores the co-existence of social and evaluative criticism.

Between 1900 and 1930, most writing about jazz blamed syncopated dance music for threatening the mores of American youth and for posing a serious danger to the survival of Western civilization. Not up to the level of critical writing that followed, this literature reported the need for social restrictions, attacked the character of jazz, its musicians, and its devotees, and expressed admonitions about the fate of society. Defenders of jazz celebrated its quintessential modernism and its national character. The civil rights movement helped renew the social literature of jazz by emphasizing African-American awareness issues.

Orchestra leader James Reese Europe played a significant role in jazz criticism's development by describing jazz in one of its early forms. The success of the Clef Club Orchestra in 1913 and the return from the war of the Harlem "Hellfighters" Orchestra in 1919 prompted interviews with him. Although Europe, like an increasing number of later musicians, benefited from an amanuensis, his quoted descriptions are early examples of journalistic jazz critical response. Newspapers otherwise reported on jazz and nightlife in their "sporting" pages; in fact, reporter "Scoop" Gleeson in 1913 may have been the first to render the word *jazz* as slang in the *San Francisco Call-Bulletin* while discussing baseball. Besides newspapers, periodicals catering to all manner of professional and cultural tastes reported what someone had to say about jazz and its sordid influence.

Writing seriously about jazz in the twenties meant discussing the "modernist" work of academic composers like John Alden Carpenter's *Krazy Kat*, Zez Confrey's piano exercise "Kitten on the Keys," Czech composer Ernest Krenek's light opera *Jonny spielt auf*, and George Gershwin's *An American in Paris*. At the height of the debates on jazz and public mores, both American and visiting European critics responded to the Aeolian Hall concert of February 12, 1924, when orchestra leader Paul Whiteman gave a program that exhibited jazz's lowly origins but culminated in a new work, Gershwin's *Rhapsody in Blue.* This classical work with evocations from African-American folk music reflected Whiteman's desire "to make a lady out of jazz," and, like James Reese Europe before him, he was sought after for his observations and definitions, eventually publishing *Jazz* (1926), with Mary Margaret McBride. Other early jazz books, Henry O. Osgood's *So This Is Jazz* and Alfred Frankenstein's *Syncopating Saxophones* (both 1926), profiled "jazz composers" like the above. Gilbert Seldes's widely read "Toujours Jazz" (1923), Don Knowlton's "The Anatomy of Jazz" (1925), writings by B. H. Haggin, and Roger Pryor Dodge's "Negro Jazz" were distinguished essays about what for many listeners seemed like a momentary trend. Seldes, editor of *The Seven Lively Arts* (1923), was recognized as a lonely defender of small-group jazz who believed the focus on symphonic jazz to be excessive. As other writers were practicing the jazz essay, they seemed ignorant of the essence of jazz performed by blacks, missing altogether the performances of King Oliver, Louis Armstrong, Fletcher Henderson, Jelly Roll Morton, and Duke Ellington. Not until 1933 did a lengthy appreciation of Ellington appear, by Wilder Hobson for *Esquire.*

Europeans also contributed substantially to the development of jazz criticism. In England the magazines *The Gramophone* and *Melody Maker* began printing reviews of recordings in the middle twenties, followed in Holland by *De Jazzwereld* in 1930 and *Jazz-Tango-Dancing* in 1932. John Hammond recalled *Aux Frontières du Jazz* (1932) as a major book by the Belgian lawyer Robert Goffin; but it was never translated from the French. *Le Jazz Hot* (1934) by Hugues Panassié did appear in English, as *Hot Jazz* (1936). Despite possessing flawed musicological assumptions, *Hot Jazz* upheld Armstrong and Ellington as seminal jazz figures and established Panassié as among the most perceptive of jazz historians. In later decades England's Max Harrison and Germany's Joachim Berendt demonstrated cogent historical knowledge about major developments in jazz, and Chris Goddard in *Jazz Away From Home* (1979) chronicled the effect early visiting American musicians had on Europe's jazz and jazz journalism. American and British critics contributed to jazz periodicals in postwar Eastern Europe. Harry Lim's *Swing Magazine* prevailed briefly in Java from 1938 to 1939, and postwar Japan's *Swing Journal* remains an awesome advertising medium. But few jazz critics from Asia, Africa, and South America are known in the West other than as magazine correspondents.

Those writers who championed symphonic jazz served as the catalysts for the emergence of the collegiate jazz follower, as new writers appeared who enjoyed the earlier jazz the record companies began reissuing. At the end of the 1920s, these young writers began asserting a place in cultural journalism. A range of subgenres became evident, from brief tabloid-like descriptions of where and when bands performed and their impact on audiences, to analytical discussions of recordings, to attempts to develop a historiography of jazz. In the thirties, reportage dominated all published jazz writing; yet, while an evaluative criticism was maturing, writers displayed two preferences: performance evaluations, usually of records, and the history-informed feature essay. By the fifties, most writers supplied both as magazine needs dictated.

Jazz musicians have had a tenuous, often stormy relationship with jazz critics, some of whom are musically illiterate. Also, record collector-critics in the thirties irritated musicians by barraging them with questions about recording personnel. This circumstance was the by-product of two developments in the recording industry. Early jazz musicians had no idea their recordings would be deemed historically important and become the subject of persistent inquiries from young critics. Details like the changing personnel of bands or dates of recordings little impressed them. But this interest in details led to the scholarly phenomenon of the jazz discography. Meanwhile, jazz musicians did not appreciate critics whose comments emblazoned headlines in the trade magazines, such as that directed at one vocalist: "Martha Tilton Stinks!" But where Count Basie agreed with one critic's opinion about a sloppy band performance, bandleader and composer Benny Carter on the other hand quipped about critics in 1937 in *Metronome*: "They sing not, neither do they play, hence forget them or forgive them . . . for they do not what they know."

Although most commentators acknowledged the African-American roots of jazz, few African Americans wrote about it with critical depth. Those who did, like musician Dave Peyton in the *Chicago Defender* (1927–38) and Lucien White in the *New York Age* (1913–27), discussed jazz on a social and audience level. Blacks took literally the meaning of *criticism*, preferring not to, as they saw it, put down their own. One black journalist in the 1980s disdainfully recalled Frank Marshall Davis, whose analytical record reviews were syndicated in the thirties through the Associated Negro Press, as a "stylist." White writers have dominated jazz critical journalism. In the thirties, their direct or implied comparative descriptions of white and black stylists juxtaposed images like "exquisite" or "dulcet" with the sexual or the exotic. Wilder Hobson, for example, who was sympathetic to Louis

Armstrong and Duke Ellington, stated in *The Musical Record* in 1933 that the late Bix Beiderbecke could have smoothed out the rough edges of black jazz. Such an attitude has changed. Since the late fifties a few blacks have gained some visibility and respect as critics, among them Barbara Gardner (a pioneer modernist on race and gender levels), Amiri Baraka (né LeRoi Jones), a. b. spellman [*sic*], Bill Quinn, trumpeters Rex Stewart and Kenny Dorham, and Phyl Garland, followed by Willard Jenkins and Stanley Crouch. Also, there are salsa historian Max Salazar and part-black/Native Americans Herb Boyd, Hugh Wyatt, and Ron Welburn.

The first stage of the template for jazz criticism occurred in 1927 when a young R. D. Darrell, who reviewed classical recordings for *Phonograph Monthly Magazine*, reviewed (as "Rufus") Duke Ellington's "Black and Tan Fantasy," praising its "amazing eccentric instrumental effects." To follow were equally perceptive analyses of newer Ellington releases like "Black Beauty" (1928), where he mentioned the "curiously twisted and wry trumpet passages" by Bubber Miley. Finding that Ellington's music bore a striking resemblance to some characteristics of classical harmony and color, Darrell asserted not what Ellington meant in any larger historical and aesthetic context, but what struck him as a listener about the quality of individual Ellington performances. Unwittingly, Darrell's Ellington reviews elevated the orchestra leader to a significant catalytic position in the early development of a true jazz criticism. He became the first important record reviewer in American jazz criticism, establishing the economical style of the record review genre. While later American jazz magazines would permit longer reviews from their writers, beginning in the 1960s *Coda: Canada's Jazz Magazine* and some European magazines published lengthy descriptions of recordings and live performances in which writers extemporized (sometimes in a pyrotechnical style) by sharing experiences and insights germane to the music.

Jazz writers found a few nonmusic publications occasionally sympathetic to their interests. These include newspapers and magazines for sophisticated readers like *Esquire* and *Fortune*. But selected music and recordings magazines and, of course, the jazz magazines themselves, represent a phenomenal development that has undergone great changes in characteristics and purpose. The key jazz periodicals actually stem from the phenomenon of recorded music and its sales. As early as 1913, a British trade magazine, *Talking Machine News*, began publishing one-sentence descriptions of recorded rags. As recording technology and playback equipment improved, *The Gramophone* (1923) and *Melody Maker* (1926), also British periodicals, led with jazz commentary, followed by Darrell's Boston-based publication. In France, Hugues Panassié's *Jazz-Hot* was an influential magazine in the years surrounding World War II. *American Music Lover* continued Darrell's periodical, and Enzo Archetti began writing for it in 1935. Archetti's "Defense of Ellington" used *Reminiscing in Tempo* to insist that important recorded jazz be given descriptive analysis qualitatively equal to that accorded classical music recordings. Although an important figure in the formulation of criteria for jazz criticism, Archetti remains the most obscure jazz critic of his era. Another major figure who seldom wrote in the "jazz press" was John Hammond. Under the name "Henry Johnson," Hammond's essays in the leftist journal *New Masses* about blues singers and jazz musicians, their recordings, and the way companies mistreated them contributed to his being remembered as the most influential jazz writer of the thirties.

Metronome, begun in 1892 as a parlor music periodical, completed a ten-year transition in 1935 to become a magazine for dance and radio studio musicians. Drummer George T. Simon, using a pseudonym to evaluate records in his "DISCussions" column, was the first practicing swing musician to write about jazz with authority, writing candidly perceptive reviews about the appeal of orchestra arrangements to dancers. In *Simon Says* (1971), his compilation of twenty years at *Metronome,* he admitted, however, favoring many white bands over good black ones. Indeed, *Metronome* and other swing publications during the thirties and forties rarely portrayed black musicians on their covers. In 1934 *Down Beat* magazine was established in Chicago. Despite having important jazz writers early in their careers like Marshall Stearns and Helen Oakley (Dance), *Down Beat*'s editors encouraged gossip, "cheesecake" photos on its covers, and provocative headlines. Female singers were referred to as "chirpers" or "warblers," and black musicians and patrons as "jigs." Stearns's "History of Jazz Music" series that began in June 1936 sparked letters from Nick LaRocca of the Original Dixieland Jazz Band, claiming that they, not blacks, invented jazz. Other vendettas followed. *Down Beat*'s writers widened a schism between themselves and the musicians they purportedly served. In a column begun in 1938, "Critics in the Doghouse," musicians could self-evaluate and explain their music and its appeal. Two "watchdog" critics at *Down Beat* were the garrulous George Frazier and the erudite Paul Eduard Miller.

Metronome's demise in 1961 left *Down Beat* as America's only mass-circulated jazz magazine. Several distinguished writers continued writing for it. John S. Wilson, Martin Williams, Nat Hentoff, Don DeMicheal, Dan Morgenstern, John A. Tynan, Gene Lees, Ira Gitler, and Pete Welding elevated its stature as a popular jazz periodical. Each new generation of critics responds to what it perceives to be a media neglect of jazz, and most begin writing for short-lived organs. Bob Blumenthal, Scott Yanow, John Corbett, Patricia Myers, and Bill Shoemaker are among the post-1970 critics who exhibit both an acumen about jazz's history and a sense of their responsibilities to music and readership.

Most swing magazines of the thirties were short-lived and featured no sophisticated criticism. But two appeared at the end of the thirties issued by different record stores. Charles E. Smith and others founded the *H.R.S. Society Rag*, and Stephen Smith started *Jazz Information*. Critic Russell Sanjek remembered their mutual antagonism as "a Montague-Capulet situation" over jazz preferences. Ralph Gleason, later an editor at *Down Beat*, demonstrated sober judgments; William Russell managed to write for both. Later writers avoided such internecine strife. Whitney Balliett's *New Yorker* essays set a high standard for jazz prose; and in the *Village Voice* Gary Giddins explores a range of historical styles.

The jazz discography, spawned by record collectors, is now indispensable for jazz critics. Under the aegis of the magazine *Jazz-Hot*, Charles Delaunay compiled the first edition of *Hot discographie* in 1936. Some jazz fans' demand for specific details about recordings appeared to be insatiable. Investigative work began when record company errors left contacting either the companies themselves or the musicians as the only recourse for corrections. Recording companies cooperated by giving Delaunay matrix numbers and recording dates, and he corresponded with musicians, met them and critics visiting France, and proceeded to set up, for its time, a useful classification system. Despite the German occupation, Delaunay updated *Hot discographie* in 1943; he did not visit the United States until 1946. Of later discographies, Brian Rust's *Jazz Records A–Z, 1897–1942* has been a model for multivolume efforts by Jorgen Jepsen, who sought to update Rust's work from 1942 to the 1960s, Walter Bruyninckx, and Tom Lord, the first major American discographer. Individual musicians' discographies and solographies have been published alone and as addenda to biographies. *Studies in Jazz Discography* (1971) confirmed a scholarly place for this research tool.

Autobiographies and biographies constitute another important facet of jazz criticism. Louis Armstrong's *Swing That Music* (1936), graciously praised many fellow musicians, and Benny Goodman's *The Kingdom of Swing* (1939) contained several anecdotes. Both books provided glimpses of the social influences affecting their authors and raised questions about reliability. Better critical biographies on them would appear later, but through 1958 few jazz biographies or memoirs in book form appeared. European writers produced a number of lengthy jazz musician profiles during the fifties and sixties. As for latter day American efforts, three Charlie Parker biographies, by Robert Reisner (1962), Ross Russell (1972), and Carl Woideck (1996), exemplify differing yet sympathetic approaches to bebop's foremost genius. Dizzy Gillespie's *To Be or Not to Bop* (1979) is an authoritative personal narrative, as is Miles Davis's colorful *Autobiography* (1989). The jazz biography demands shrewd investigative skills to verify itineraries, travel experiences, changes of fellow bandsmen, and motivations for innumerable choices in a life in music.

The jazz history generates as much interest as biographies. The late thirties saw three serious critical histories appear: Winthrop Sargeant's *Jazz Hot and Hybrid* (1938), Wilder Hobson's *American Jazz Music* (1939), and a collection of essays on jazz historical topics, *Jazzmen*, edited by Frederic Ramsey and Charles Edward Smith (1939). Sargeant reiterated the ordinary complaints critics had about effete jazz, but his best chapter deals with the act of improvisation and the importance of rhythm that distinguish jazz. Critic Otis Ferguson considered Hobson's book a jazz primer but admonished him for too little independent thinking. In contrast to Sargeant's, Hobson's book has a record-review prose quality. *Jazzmen* remains an admired critical history, including essays by Ferguson, Hobson, Roger Pryor Dodge, William Russell, and black cartoonist E. Simms Campbell. Its methodology incorporated field study and interviews, along with verification of statements, anecdotes, and recordings. It covered New Orleans jazz, blues, collecting, and New York jazz with class, yet some reviewers found it to be formless and disconcertingly arranged.

These books affirmed the arrival of a sympathetic body of jazz critical literature, one offering jazz followers something more than just its recordings as historical documents. Some years elapsed before significant critical histories and musicological studies appeared. In *Shining Trumpets* (1946), Rudi Blesh virtually ignored post-traditional styles. His disinclination revealed a schism in jazz loyalties and definitions, with *The Record Changer*, a collector's magazine, defending the conservative position against the brash bebop musicians and fans who contemptuously regarded traditional jazz devotees as "moldy figs." But in the fifties Blesh, Barry Ulanov, Marshall Stearns, André Hodeir, and Leonard Feather published highly respectable jazz histories. *Hear Me Talkin' to Ya: The Story of Jazz by the Men Who Made It* (1955), edited by Nat Shapiro and Nat Hentoff, featured a unique oral history approach. Hentoff then coedited with Albert McCarthy *Jazz: New Perspectives on the History of Jazz by Twelve of the World's Foremost Jazz Critics and Scholars* (1959), a compilation that secured for jazz writing a literary sophistication, and he wrote *The Jazz Life* (1961), a social history of modernists. Leonard Feather compiled five editions of *The Encyclopedia of Jazz*; in England, *Jazz—The Rough Guide* (1995) continued Feather's practice of the short critical profile. Other major works include Martin William's essays in *The Jazz Tradition* (1970); two outstanding musicological studies by Gunther Schuller, *Early Jazz* and *The Swing Era*; and *The New Grove Dictionary of Jazz*. Spellman and Barry McRae of England brought early attention to musicians in the nascent avant-garde. Since the seventies a new school of jazz critical historians has been concentrating on particular periods. Some were motivated by Martin Williams's *Jazz Masters* series from Macmillan Press, itself inspired by *Jazz: The Transition Years, 1940–1960* by John S. Wilson. John Litweiler and Michael J. Budds probed the decade of the sixties, and Graham Lock has taken a postmodernist approach to saxophonist-composer Anthony Braxton. Scott DeVeaux's *The Birth of Bebop* (1997) is indispensable reading.

Today's jazz critics are less brash than the young writers who made the 1930s the decade of the jazz critic. The earlier writers hesitated to call themselves "critics," but they were opinionated college graduates, often Ivy Leaguers, who collected records, patronized nightclubs, and wrote well enough for specialized and sophisticated magazines about what was still considered a popular and novel music. They came of age at a propitious time in American music culture, filling, as it were, a journalistic vacuum. Many pursued their craft, blithely neglecting the need to establish criteria for their critical opinions; and although such criteria emerged unwittingly from their writings, some mature writers in the later thirties began formulating what the jazz critic should know and how to communicate it to readers. Darrell, Archetti, Hammond, and Simon applied classical music journalism's techniques to this new prose. George Frazier's claim in 1936 that jazz criticism "should send you!" was resisted by critics like Paul

Eduard Miller and France's Panassié, who then began to identify their own criteria for jazz criticism. Miller opposed tabloidism and believed jazz was ready for serious intellectual criteria; Panassié recommended keener listening habits for comparing and contrasting styles, "broad views" to reconcile misapprehensions, being musically trained, and writing well and logically. In 1947 Stanley Dance felt that the critic's first duty was to serve as liaison between musicians and the public. Standards for assessment must stem from being adaptable to experiences and focusing on content more than style.

Dodge's essay "Consider the Critics," in *Jazzmen* evaluated writers and their responsibility. With *A Critic Looks at Jazz* (1946), Ernest Borneman developed an ideology of jazz criticism around "standards of opinion" held by everyone involved in the jazz profession. S. Raich's *Criticisms of Jazz: Fundamental Standards of Art Criticism,* published in Spain in a trilingual edition (1958), voiced a psychological approach to critical journalism. *The Jazz Review* (1958–61) offered scholarly criticism continued by *The Journal of Jazz Studies* (1972–84).

Finally, writers versed in theory and musicology have produced exceptional texts. In *Down Beat* saxophonist Don Heckman described elements of the "new music"; in biweekly columns Bill Mathieu illustrated modal improvising and chordal suspension; and in the seventies William Fowler offered comprehensive lessons in jazz theory. Their writings, and books by George Russell, William Russo, Gunther Schuller, John Mehegan, Mark Gridley, and Paul Berliner, remain indispensable references for jazz critics.

Jazz produced a critical journalism that serves as its interpretative companion in an uneasy relationship. It is perhaps significant that jazz criticism both reflects and helps clarify how people everywhere respond to American culture and its most resilient indigenous art.

Jazz Education

Charles Beale

Jazz education is concerned specifically with learning to play jazz and with teaching students and others to be jazz musicians. This essay looks at the gradual emergence of jazz education as its own discipline and discusses common issues faced by jazz students and educators, including repertoire, learning style, ethnicity, and what jazz education is trying to achieve. It argues that jazz has many facets, some of which seem to appear more often in education than others. And it suggests that jazz education has a crucial role to play in the future of the jazz tradition.

A comprehensive history of jazz education around the world has yet to be written, and what follows cannot be more than a thumbnail sketch. Material is scarce, and we rely, particularly for the early years, on personal accounts and oral histories stored in jazz archives, such as the Institute of Jazz Studies at Rutgers, the Hogan Jazz Archive at Tulane, and the archive at Darmstadt, in Germany.

Early players came from a wide range of musical backgrounds and trainings. Two patterns of learning jazz remain constant throughout the first half of the century. Some musicians had fewer lessons and learned more by experience, while others went through a formal training more influenced by classical music. At one end of the scale was the more formal training of, for example, the Creole-French Tio family of New Orleans, and in particular clarinetist Lorenzo Tio Jr., who taught Barney Bigard, Albert Nicholas, Johnny Dodds, and Jimmie Noone for a time in the 1920s. This style of training originated in the opera orchestras and the other concert and marching bands prevalent in New Orleans as jazz was emerging. At the other end was the early experience of players like Louis Armstrong, who were primarily self-taught and learned often by ear, sitting in at local honky-tonks and other venues where jazz developed. From a later generation, Miles Davis, for example, started playing the trumpet in his St. Louis grade school and continued regular lessons, even enrolling at the Juilliard School in New York in 1944, while Dizzy Gillespie and Thelonious Monk, by contrast, were primarily self-taught.

The unhelpful, perhaps racist stereotype of the intuitively gifted and untrained jazz musician has persisted, and this has led to a long-standing if increasingly outdated debate as to how far jazz *can* be formally taught as opposed to caught. Formal training, it is argued, goes against the free and personal spirit of the music: Thelonious Monk's touch would perhaps never have sounded as distinctive as it did if he had been formally "taught" the piano. Likewise, it is argued that the hundreds of students graduating from university jazz courses in recent years sound too similar to each other because they have all been through the same system. Yet it is now recognized that formal, classroom-based education was a significant element in the musical experience of many jazz musicians of all generations, and that it can save students time and focus them on key concepts and skills efficiently.

In the earlier part of the century, apprenticeships as sidemen allowed musicians to learn to play in jam sessions and big bands. In jam sessions, learning tended to be slower, based more on the ear than on written music, more on the lived experience of the music than on abstract facts and concepts. This approach, favoring practice over theory, remains a guiding principle across jazz education today, because it forces learners and players to re-create and embellish the tradition interactively in a long game of jazz Chinese Whispers.

Apprenticeship often also involves the learner in working with key mentors rather than teachers. Armstrong had King Oliver, for example. Mentors are sometimes just friends with big record collections or musicians seen in brief but crucial encounters where advice is given. They may also be older, more experienced players in a band who guide the learner's developing practice. At the top level, mentors

Bassist Reggie Workman with jazz students at the New School University, New York, late 1990s. Courtesy of the New School University.

who have guided sidemen in the past include Art Blakey, Miles Davis, Woody Herman, and Buddy Rich. All brought on generations of international stars in their late teens and twenties, by working with them, nurturing and challenging them on the road. Blakey's Jazz Messengers is perhaps the most famous and long-standing band of this kind, including as members at different times Wayne Shorter, Keith Jarrett, and Wynton Marsalis.

Learning from notated transcriptions of solos and directly off records is another approach established early in the history of jazz education. Transcriptions of Louis Armstrong solos, for example, were first published in *50 Hot Choruses for Cornet* and *125 Jazz Breaks for Cornet* in 1927, and jazz enthusiasts have learned the melodic and rhythmic vocabularies of their heroes like this ever since then. Direct imitation of recordings is established as a vital means of learning important and often unnotatable elements of jazz style, including feel, phrasing, internal dynamics, and sound.

From 1950 onward, jazz education began to change. As jazz became less commercially successful, many bands of apprentices run by key guru figures were forced out of business. The widespread culture of jam sessions, rehearsals, and gigs, which had provided a training ground for Gillespie between 1937 and 1941, for example, began to lose the depth and variety it had when much of the mainstream repertoire was first invented. Formal courses and workshops and classes in jazz appreciation run by musicians and college lecturers began to supersede such learning. A broader jazz education emerged, whose aim was not only to train new jazz musicians but also to build an audience and raise the profile of jazz for a wider public of amateurs.

In the 1950s and 1960s, too, came the first few big American university jazz courses, including those at the University of North Texas at Denton and the Berklee College of Music. Key educators such as Jerry Coker, David Baker, and Jamey Aebersold laid the groundwork for current educational practice. The need to justify jazz education as worthy of institutional and cultural attention led to a clear, if in retrospect slightly limited, definition of a single jazz style and related set of skills. The first round of textbooks and other resources was characterized by an emphasis on strict formalization and structure, on the definition of levels, and on establishing a relatively narrow core repertoire broadly around bebop and hard bop, via, for example, the early Aebersold books. In this clarification process, harmonic structures also became codified, and progressions such as the twelve-bar blues and II-V-I were defined as the easiest and most common, as indeed they were at the time.

Small and big band arrangements became divided into Initial, Intermediate, and Advanced and were often for all manner of instrumental combinations. Often "harder" arrangements were seen as involving playing higher, faster, and with more complex ensemble textures. Small-band repertoire focused around "classic" tunes from the 1950s and 1960s by Herbie Hancock and Miles Davis like "Cantaloupe Island," "So What," and "Milestones," and at higher levels around the bebop standards.

For many, bebop, perhaps the most complex and virtuosic jazz style, which emerged in the late 1930s and 1940s, remains the basis of jazz education, along with, to a lesser extent, the early Armstrong Hot Fives and Hot Sevens albums from the late 1920s. Dave Liebman, for example, a highly influential player and educator who has written key books and gives frequent clinics internationally, calls bebop the "callisthenics" of jazz improvisation. Bebop vocabulary gives students the flexibility to work in other styles in a coherent and harmonically sophisticated way and an insight into jazz processes at the highest level; it was perhaps the apogee of jazz's early development as an art form, in his view.

Opponents argue that bebop, however important "in itself," has lost its audience and is simply too specialized to be useful for many students. It makes technical and interpretational demands beyond those that the mass of students can fulfill, and it can be socially exclusive, competitive, emotionally narrow, and sometimes even racially divisive. Uncontextualized, they argue, it can give students a single vocabulary that only works over some tunes and works less well over more recent improvisation structures. It was in any case only a single element in a complex stylistic dialectic of the time, which continued with the spacious textures and sonorities of cool jazz and the more blues-based hard bop.

This first bebop-related flowering of jazz education established important and influential norms. The tunes, arrangements, and later tape and CD "music minus one"–style accompaniments from this era are still a key part of the world jazz education repertoire over thirty years later. For some, this has tended to codify jazz education and slant the players it produces toward the mainstream styles and tunes of the United States and toward tunes that are deemed educationally useful as well as those that remain musically significant. Learners today are now faced in these materials with a set of specialized educational models and improvising methods deemed valuable "in themselves," as happened in classical music with Bach chorales. More formal methods have also sometimes led to current musicians becoming "star" bandleaders and getting record deals before they are ready. Because they lack gigging experience and that crucial worldly wisdom that can only be gained on the road, they find it harder to control the musical and personal aspects of their careers.

Around 1950, then, jazz and jazz education began to part company. Jazz moved on, adapting to its recent lack of commercial success by growing away from its roots and becoming more varied, specialized, and fragmented. Since the 1950s, it has broken more stylistic boundaries, developing fertile links with the musics of Latin America, India, South Africa, and many other non-Western cultures and folk musics. European jazz has established its own character. At the same time, it has been subject to interaction with popular musics of many styles. More intriguingly, some players, such as Keith Jarrett, Chick Corea, and Jan Garbarek, are beginning to perform classical pieces in jazz recitals and improvise on "classical" ideas in related styles.

The majority of educators seem to have chosen not to use these developments as the core of their teaching except at the most "advanced" levels, arguing that the U.S. "tradition" should be the basis of the jazz learner's experience early on. A minority have responded by creating courses in jazz and popular music, jazz and light music, jazz and studio music, or jazz and contemporary musics. They also argue that musicians leaving jazz college often end up making a living in the world of popular musics, so a knowledge of relevant popular styles, session-musician culture, and music technology is just as important to the working jazz musician as being able to play Charlie Parker solos in twelve keys.

In recent times, a glance at the jazz education magazines like *Jazz Educators Journal* reveals a burgeoning industry where respected world-class jazz players like Kenny Barron and Billy Taylor earn much of their bread and keep the music alive by touring, organizing clinics, and selling their wares. As arts funding came under pressure in the 1980s and 1990s, more and more respected players entered the university systems of their respective countries as professors, workshop leaders, or researchers, rather than choosing the harder and less secure life on the road.

Formal courses are increasingly being offered in a range of countries across the United States, Eastern and Western Europe, and places as far in distance from the roots of the music as South Africa. Some universities, including the New School in New York and the Amsterdam School of the Arts, offer whole under- or postgraduate degrees in jazz, while literally hundreds of others offer modules, pathways, or other components in jazz studies alongside studies in popular musics or classical music. Conservatory style training in jazz, focused on performing and instrumental skills, sits alongside more academic courses specializing in the history, analysis, and cultures of jazz.

A rich variety of academic routes now exists, even for postgraduate students. In the master's program in jazz musicology of Rutgers University, jazz is studied primarily through its history and analysis, while the more ethnomusicological approaches and research methods of the University of Chicago or Goldsmiths, University of London, see jazz as interacting with other musics and cultural contexts to a greater extent and acknowledge insights from critical theory and postmodernism. Others again emphasize pure performing. Learned academic journals including *ARJS* (*Annual Review of Jazz Studies*), *Jazz Research Papers*, and *Jazz Forschung* now sit alongside performers' magazines like *Down Beat* and *Jazz Journal* on the library shelves.

At high school level and below, jazz education appears patchy and lacks continuity. Welcome periods of intense national funding for particular jazz initiatives and related educational projects for musicians in schools are often followed by long periods of inactivity, when exciting work begun is not followed through. In some schools in the United States and Europe, the whole music curriculum is structured around jazz, while in others no music is offered at all or the approach is purely that of the Western classical canon. In schools, jazz often counts as a popular or alternative music in the context of a general ideological battle with classical music. Recent research has shown that high school music departments favoring the development of multicultural understandings or study of the black communities of the world often tend to do more jazz.

The status of jazz within music education remains a source of potential conflict. Discrimination against jazz in more conservative institutions is seen by some as reflecting racism within establishment musical cultures and by others as reflecting a perception of a lack of complexity or artistic value within the music. The field is filling up with committed teachers, many of whom also play, often working in their own schools and colleges but communicating relatively little with each other. Many still feel embattled, either because they are working in departments dominated by other styles, or because they feel they have become small cogs in the huge bureaucratic and often uncreative machines that are large university music faculties.

In U.S. high schools, the big band tradition thrives, albeit often using pastiche core repertoire of varying degrees of musical and educational worth; for some students, this is their only direct experience of the music. The many competitions in the United States keep levels of discipline and of technical and instrumental skill high but tend to cultivate improvisation skills less. Typical of the growing specialization of jazz education is the ever-enlarging range of school-level big band material sold that requires little or no improvising. While there are precedents for this in the tradition from Jelly Roll Morton to Duke Ellington and Gil Evans, such pieces and training styles do not bode well for the future creative development of the music. In the United Kingdom, new national jazz syllabuses from the Associated Board of the Royal Schools of Music are establishing pioneering improvisation-based assessment jazz schemes from beginner to high school level.

At the same time, some jazz education still takes place in the informal sector, through community or regional small and big band organizations, summer schools, one-off workshops, jam sessions, and competitions. Here musicians who would fail to flourish in more formal settings are able to cut their teeth. Levels are variable, and the approach tends to be more empowering for learners and less prescriptive and institutionalized.

What is jazz, then, as jazz educators project it, and what are the skills they foster? Some elements are relatively easy to identify: clearly a jazz musician must know how to play an instrument, how to write or arrange in common and more personal styles, and how to improvise over a groove. They must be able to hear as a jazz musician, know what to look for when listening to jazz, and know how to speak the language and behave like a jazz musician in the music and around it.

Jazz also involves a particular way of interacting with a musical starting point. It is the art of personalizing and inflecting a given tune by embellishing, reharmonizing, and generally transcending the material in a flexible and open formal structure. Recent research also indicates that at the center of all jazz education should be the way musicians work together in groups. Seen in this light, jazz is not a musical vocabulary as much as a set of musical conventions for interacting with other musicians. The musician learns expected ways to listen closely, to respond positively and with projection as a soloist, to accompany others sensitively, and how to take risks as a leader or support others cooperatively.

To summarize, educators maintain a delicate balance between two contradictory views within jazz. One asserts that learning to re-create the rich traditions of the past is important. This involves an understanding not only of the musical processes but also of the historical context of racial conflict, relative poverty, bohemian excess, and sheer hard work that gave rise to them. Listeners expect to hear the tradition in the melodic fragments or inflections of a player's improvising, and to hear too a historical and emotional understanding of what ideas like the "blues" meant to musicians and listeners of the time. A jazz education that fails to do this will seem superficial and patronizing to some of the African-American communities from which it sprang.

The opposite movement in jazz education asserts that such tunes and the sometimes tragic and emotionally rich contexts that gave them meaning are in the past now. If jazz is to survive, jazz education must nurture that "ache" all jazz musicians feel that the music should be contemporary, always moving on and breaking new boundaries. It emphasizes the now, the personal, creative, and searching elements of jazz.

The best educators manage to combine the two. They embed the apprentice jazz musician's understanding of the past within the overarching aim to develop the inner musician, to enable the learner to find his or her own voice. By analyzing the best work of past and present musicians, sometimes memorizing whole solos by rote, players learn what works and become more flexible in their playing. Above all they aim eventually to develop and define their own personal direction.

As jazz education becomes fully established, it must adjust to pressures from educational institutions that require it to be predicated on clear definitions of aims and objectives, repertoire, instrumentation, and teaching methods. Clear and objectively verifiable standards are needed on which evaluation of learners can be based, qualifications can be issued, and state funds claimed.

Yet the style seems to be moving in the direction of increasing fluidity and plurality. Many of the answers to questions first asked in the 1950s seem no longer as secure as they once were. Should the newer jazz styles be taught in a particular order, and why are they less important than the older ones? Should they be taught in the same order, regardless of the country in which the learning is taking place? Is there more than one conception of "easy" and "hard" in jazz improvising, and how should it be assessed? Are rock grooves "easier" than swing for students of certain musical backgrounds? At what stage of students' development should they be able to decide their own direction? These are complex issues, involving a two-way relationship between jazz and jazz education. Future research is needed to establish how educators on the ground are responding to changes in the idiom itself and how jazz education is beginning to affect jazz performing.

While jazz players jealously guard what they see as a creative plurality of practice in jazz performance, the danger remains, then, that jazz education will continue to be dominated by narrower, less creative, and therefore less stylish ways of working. Certainly a new jazz education for the many is developing that ensures academic credentials for its musicians and a future audience for the music. But might its very consistency and rigor fail to generate those special individuals on whom the future strength of the tradition depends, and even inhibit them? Western classical music, for example, has suffered from a museum culture that has marginalized it from the musical lives of many of its students.

Jazz is accepted now, both as one of several significant world musics of the twentieth century and also as big business for universities and schools. Like classical music, the financial and cultural health of jazz and of its mortgage-paying and increasingly middle-class musicians is now sustained as much by educational activity as by performing. Jazz education must provide the foundation on which a future world jazz tradition will be built, and the image of jazz it communicates to its students will become ever more influential.

The challenge, then, for jazz educators is to develop ways of teaching and learning that reflect the richness, variety, immediacy, and dynamic growth of the style without codifying it, putting it in an educational box and suffocating it. Above all, learners of jazz need to study in an environment where the several musical languages and traditions of past jazz are given their due, but equally where a future jazz can grow and flourish, whatever its direction.

Recorded Jazz

Dan Morgenstern

J azz and the phonograph were made for each other. Without the medium of recording, a music so defined by spontaneity of invention, individuality of instrumental sound, and rhythmic complexity that defies musical notation could not have been so rapidly or widely disseminated, nor lent itself so readily to rehearing, studying, and copying. Without recordings, jazz might have remained a temporary regional phenomenon.

Yet the ideal union between two near-contemporaneous artistic and technical inventions took time to be consummated. The fledgling record industry saw jazz as strictly a salable new kind of dance music and had not the slightest awareness of or interest in its potential as art. (Nor, admittedly, did all but a handful of its practitioners.)

The first genuine jazz captured by a recording device was played by the Original Dixieland Jazz Band in the New York studio of Columbia Records on January 30, 1917. Just two weeks earlier, these five young white New Orleans musicians had opened at a midtown Manhattan spot for dining and dancing, creating more of a stir than during an entire previous year in Chicago. But when Columbia's managers heard the sounds they had recorded, they cried "cacophony" and shelved the masters. Less than a month later, the band recorded two numbers for Victor, which promptly issued them. "Livery Stable Blues" and "Original Dixieland Jass [*sic*] Band One-Step" became one of the best-selling records of its day.

It may be an irony of history that the first jazz band to record should have been white, but this was not the result of racism. In 1913 and 1914 Victor had issued four twelve-inch discs by James Reese Europe's Society Orchestra, then the rage of dancing New York. The music was ragtime, not jazz, as was that recorded by the black clarinetist Wilbur Sweatman in 1916. In the summer of 1917, Columbia recorded three productive sessions with W. C. Handy's Memphis Orchestra (also still playing ragtime) and followed up by signing Sweatman, now leading an ODJB-styled band, which made some thirty sides for the label over the next few years. A similar number was recorded by Europe's erstwhile associate Ford Dabney in 1919, when Europe himself made his final records, directing the civilian version of the army band with which he had scored such resounding successes in France. Several of these were considerably more jazz-influenced than his earlier discs, and all were more interesting than the repetitious, military-band–styled Dabneys.

The ODJB continued to make records, some of the best during a year-long stay in England in 1919–20 for the British branch of Columbia, but a session by a band that included Sidney Bechet made in London around the same time was never issued. A white New Orleans group led by clarinetist Alcide Nunez, the Louisiana Five, recorded prolifically in New York at the turn of the decade, while trombonist Tom Brown, first to bring jazz to Chicago from New Orleans, was busy in the New York studios, recording mainly with groups directed by Harry Yerkes. And the New Orleans Creole clarinetist Achille Bacquet (brother of George) worked and recorded in New York at this time with Jimmy Durante's New Orleans Jazz Band, passing for white.

By far the most prolific and durable of the ODJB-styled recording bands was the Original Memphis Five (four from Brooklyn, one from Long Island), co-led by cornetist Phil Napoleon and pianist Frank Signorelli and often including the fine trombonist Miff Mole. Between 1922 and 1931 they made hundreds of sides for dozens of labels under a variety of pseudonyms—a common practice in the industry during the 1920s, when masters were routinely leased nonexclusively.

Another feature of the record business in this period was the existence of special ethnic series catering to every conceivable nationality. Arabic, Danish, Greek, Irish, Polish, Italian, Yiddish, and

Original LP cover for *Ellington at Newport*. Recorded in performance at the Newport Jazz Festival, Newport, R.I., July 7, 1956. Courtesy of the Institute of Jazz Studies, Rutgers University. Original LP cover for *Sonny Rollins, Volume 2*. Courtesy of Blue Note Records.

Hebrew records were sold in the appropriate neighborhoods or available on special order. There was also an "old time" series, later renamed "hillbilly," for what would later (and more flatteringly) become country music. Thus it was only logical that African-American music should be added to the list, once demand became demonstrable. The enterprising songwriter, music publisher, and sometime vocalist and pianist Perry Bradford accomplished this, first persuading OKeh Records to allow a black singer, Mamie Smith, to record his "Crazy Blues," and then promoting the record assiduously in Harlem. Within less than a month of its release in September 1920, it had sold more than seventy-five thousand copies.

Smith now began to record regularly, accompanied by her Jazz Hounds, a touring band that then included the Memphis-born cornetist Johnny Dunn. (The band's instrumental from January 1921 of the standard-to-be "Royal Garden Blues" has been proposed as the first genuine jazz recording by a black ensemble.) Later in 1921, OKeh introduced its "race" series of blues, gospel, and jazz aimed at black customers. ("The race" was then the preferred term for African-Americans, consistently used by the black press, public spokespeople, and advertisers, and is mistakenly perceived by later generations as pejorative.) Other labels soon followed suit, and 1921 also saw the debut of the first black-owned record label, Black Swan. Its major discovery was singer Ethel Waters, and Fletcher Henderson made his first records for it, but it was short-lived. Meanwhile Columbia had signed Johnny Dunn, whose clever use of muted effects and showmanship made him a popular attraction. His replacement in the Jazz Hounds was Bubber Miley, another master of mutes, and a teenaged tenor saxophonist Mamie Smith had picked up in Kansas City named Coleman Hawkins made his recording debut with the Hounds in 1922.

Solo piano recorded well in the acoustic mode. Two great stride pianists, James P. Johnson (who had been cutting piano rolls since 1917) and his protégé Fats Waller, made solos for OKeh in 1922. The label's race series was now in the good hands of the New Orleans–born pianist-songwriter-publisher Clarence Williams, who also had considerable influence at Columbia (the two labels would come under joint ownership in 1926). He first brought the great Bessie Smith to OKeh, then, when they declined her services, placed her with Columbia. Though her first record was a "cover" of an already established song, "Downhearted Blues," recorded by its composer, Alberta Hunter, and other singers, Bessie's version sold more than three hundred thousand copies. She became Columbia's most consistent seller, billed as "the Empress of the Blues."

Smith's debut came in early 1923, a watershed year for the recording of important black jazz and blues artists. Jelly Roll Morton, Sidney Bechet, King Oliver's Creole Jazz Band, and Ma Rainey now became able to reach a wider audience. Oliver's band included a young cornetist from New Orleans named Louis Armstrong and made its (and his) first records for a small label, Gennett, located in Richmond, Indiana, which for a decade would produce an extraordinary amount of notable jazz and blues records. The best white jazz band in Chicago, the New Orleans Rhythm Kings, had recorded for Gennett in the summer of 1922, and about a year later, they were joined in the label's studio (a rickety barnlike structure adjacent to a railroad siding and thus subject to sudden interruptions) by Jelly Roll Morton for the first deliberately integrated record date in the United States. (The first such event occurred in England in May 1921: the American clarinetist Edmund Jenkins recorded with a band led by the soon-to-be-famous Jack Hylton.) And in early 1924 a band from Indiana, the Wolverines, with twenty-year-old Bix Beiderbecke on cornet, made their first session for Gennett.

Bechet's debut inaugurated a long and distinguished series of records issued as by the Clarence Williams Blue Five, though it was often more than a quintet. In 1925, while Armstrong was in New York with Fletcher Henderson's band, Williams paired him with Bechet, and the results, notably on "Cake Walking Babies From Home," were spectacular. The cornetist also accompanied several blues singers, including Bessie Smith and Ma Rainey (the latter for Paramount, an important blues label that also recorded jazz and was headquartered in Wisconsin), and made many sides with Henderson. If he was less prominently featured than one might expect, there were such exceptions as the 1925 "Sugar Foot Stomp," one of the first great jazz records made by the newly introduced electrical process, which much improved sound quality, if not consistently so from the start. (The acoustic method lingered on for a while, like silent films after sound had come in, but by the end of 1927, it was gone for good.)

The new technology worked particularly well for large ensembles, and Henderson's was by no means the only big jazz band now sounding better on discs. Duke Ellington first recorded in late 1924 at the helm of a sextet. Two years later he had ten pieces and was in the process of becoming the first jazz artist to realize that the medium of recording was fundamentally different from live performance. In the mid-1920s recordings of popular music still ran a distant second to sheet music sales as a source of income for publishers, and many performers also saw them mainly as an extension of song-plugging and a tool for promoting in-person appearances. (This attitude explains to a degree why so many artists accepted relatively low fees for making records.) Not so Ellington, who soon made himself the master of the three-minute musical gem and paid close attention to the proper placement of players in the studio and to the special tonal characteristics of that new contraption, the microphone.

Armstrong, who late in 1925 began the extraordinary series of Hot Five and Hot Seven recordings for OKeh in Chicago, now became the first jazz artist to demonstrate the true power of the phonograph record. Musicians throughout the United States and abroad (his records were soon issued in Europe; the record business was international) learned Armstrong solos by heart, and his way of phrasing a melody or parsing the rhythm caught on with arrangers as well as instrumentalists.

But perhaps the single most influential record in this period was made by an ad hoc recording unit, drawn mainly from the ranks of the Jean Goldkette band, under the leadership of C-melody saxophonist Frank Trumbauer and featuring solos by himself and Bix Beiderbecke. The profound impact of "Singin' the Blues" on musicians black and white was due to the quality and length of the two solos (both complete choruses), the relaxed tempo (slower than customary for the tune, a standard in the repertory of jazz and dance bands), and the fact that neither soloist stated the melody—for 1927, this was extended improvisation.

The Goldkette band was subject to a very different kind of musical power: that vested in recording directors (now called A&R men). Famed for its jazz soloists and the fine "hot" numbers featuring them, the band was prevented from recording all but two of these by Victor's Eddie King, who disliked jazz but favored the treacly vocalizing practiced by singers of the pre–Bing Crosby era that mars so many 1920s band records.

(It stands to reason that recorded jazz of any era can only reflect a minute fraction of the music actually performed; aside from many deserving players and bands who never entered a studio, those who did record were not always captured at their best. Since it is inevitable that our picture of the music's history is so strongly colored by what exists on record, this should be kept in mind.)

The opposite of the Goldkette situation applied to the New

York–based musicians who often recorded under the leadership of cornetist Red Nichols, a very successful record and radio studio player and contractor. (Radio's role in the dissemination of all kinds of music grew as the decade moved on, and almost all that music was made live; the disc jockey was a 1930s phenomenon.) Under a variety of band names, famously as Red Nichols and his Five Pennies, these gifted instrumentalists, including many bandleaders-to-be, between 1926 and 1932 made records of jazz played for its own sake, often quite experimental in nature. These records were very influential among musicians. (A special offshoot of this jazz branch was the charming chamber music of violinist Joe Venuti and guitarist Eddie Lang.)

Chicago was a comparable recording nexus of black talent. Transplanted New Orleans players ruled the studio roost. Clarinetists Johnny Dodds and Jimmie Noone recorded frequently in a variety of settings, Dodds in a mostly traditional idiom, Noone more contemporary, his popular Apex Club Band featuring a front line of clarinet and alto sax, with Earl Hines at the piano. Jelly Roll Morton never led a band in public in Chicago, but his carefully rehearsed and handpicked Red Hot Peppers made a brilliant series of discs for Victor that can be considered the artistic apotheosis of New Orleans style. His later New York–based groups were less successful, musically and commercially.

While recording activity was centered on New York and Chicago (and late in the decade in Los Angeles as well), several labels regularly sent mobile recording units on field trips to capture local talent, primarily to stimulate regional sales, but also in hopes of unearthing acts of national potential. Cities visited included New Orleans (Columbia's 1927 trips preserved the unique Sam Morgan band, and there were other fine catches); Kansas City (OKeh got hold of Bennie Moten early on; his later Victors were made in Chicago or Camden, while Brunswick caught Andy Kirk's fledgling Clouds of Joy); Dallas, Houston, and San Antonio (with a good yield of Texas blues and territory bands, but Alphonse Trent's, the state's best, recorded for Gennett in Indiana); St. Louis (another jazz center, where OKeh and Vocalion documented such riverboat-associated bands as Charlie Creath's and Dewey Jackson's); and the blues centers Atlanta and Memphis (the latter the source of the intriguingly archaic sounds of Williamson's Beale Street Folic Orchestra on Victor, a label that also ventured to Savannah and even Seattle).

All told, an amazing (and amazingly varied) amount of music was captured by recording devices during the first dozen years of jazz recording, even pipe organ solos by Fats Waller, who managed to make the monster swing in Victor's Camden studios.

On Black Thursday, when the stock market first began to crumble, an unknown band from the Midwest, managed by the Goldkette Office and called the Casa Loma Orchestra, recorded its first of many sides for OKeh in New York. With its well-tooled section work and riff-laden hot arrangements and romantic ballads, it would pave the way for the swing era, an event also forecast by Ellington's "It Don't Mean a Thing If It Ain't Got That Swing," introduced in 1932. Between those dates, the Great Depression cut deeply into the record business, sending annual sales from more than a hundred million units to a rock-bottom ten. Race records were among the worst-hit markets—even the great Bessie Smith stopped making records in 1931. Yet Armstrong and Ellington (not confined to the race lists) and newcomer Cab Calloway, who had replaced Ellington at the Cotton Club and also was managed by the shrewd music publisher and recording director Irving Mills, all continued to record with surprising frequency.

In 1932 a new chapter in the story of jazz on records began when John Hammond became active as a producer. Motivated solely by a commitment to the music and its makers, regardless of race, modified only by strong personal preferences, he was young (twenty-one) and fearless (his mother was a Vanderbilt, and he was not beholden to any employers). Hammond had been writing about American jazz for Britain's *Melody Maker* and now started to produce records for Columbia's London-based branch (they were soon also issued in the United States). His talent roster included Benny Carter (in small group and big band settings, the marvelous young pianist Teddy Wilson involved in both), Fletcher Henderson ("Talk of the Town" featured Coleman Hawkins's longest recorded solo to date), a Joe Venuti–led all-star group, and Benny Goodman with Jack Teagarden (and in 1933 with an unknown teenaged singer named Billie Holiday). By 1934 Goodman was leading his first big band and recording with it, Hammond serving as his adviser.

These names would loom large during the swing years just around the corner, helping to revive the record business, slowly but surely. And a new element now came into play: the jazz record collector. Opera, and to a lesser degree instrumental classical music, had long since attracted dedicated listeners who sought out favorite performers and performances deleted from active record catalogs. Such seekers after "collector's items" were still rare in jazz during the 1920s, though there was a nucleus of knowledgeable collectors at Princeton University. In Europe, affiliated labels issued U.S. masters, including items culled from the race lists, which gave local fanciers easier access than their American counterparts, who had to visit stores in black neighborhoods or special-order the discs. By 1930 the eighteen-year-old Frenchman Hugues Panassié was already writing surprisingly astute record reviews for the short-lived *Revue du Jazz* and the longer-lasting *Jazz Tango Dancing*. And in New York City, a young record store manager began to stock cutout jazz and blues items, catering to a small but growing clientele of collectors, among them musicians, songwriters, and journalists from the staff of nearby Time, Inc. This was Milt Gabler, his store was the Commodore Music Shop, and one of his best customers was John Hammond. Soon, Gabler was ordering custom pressings (minimum order three hundred) of deleted material from the American Record Company, which had gobbled up a host of bankrupt or near-bankrupt labels during the early Depression days (Columbia, OKeh, Brunswick, and Perfect among them) for release on his own white-label Commodores.

Meanwhile, the accelerating popularity of swing, spurred by Benny Goodman, prompted a steady flow of new releases, mostly by big bands but also by small groups. These might be working units, such as bassist John Kirby's "biggest little band in the land," a versatile sextet, or ad hoc all-star studio gatherings, such as the splendid series for Brunswick under the leadership of Teddy Wilson, produced by Hammond, and for Victor, headed up by Lionel Hampton. Wilson's records often had vocals by Billie Holiday, who also recorded under her own name for Vocalion; the difference was that with Wilson, she would sing one chorus, framed by instrumental work, while on her own records, the players got the middle passages. Hampton handled his own vocals, as did the popular and prolific Armstrong-inspired New Orleans trumpeters Wingy Manone (on Victor's thirty-five-cent Bluebird label) and Louis Prima (Brunswick).

But the most prolific and popular singing instrumentalist was the irrepressible Fats Waller, who between 1934 and 1942 made more than three hundred sides for Victor and Bluebird with his six-piece Rhythm, not counting piano solos and occasional big band ventures. Discs like Waller's were prime fodder for the by now ubiquitous jukeboxes, a boon to the record industry and a thorn in the side of the musicians' union, since no royalties were derived from this kind of public performance. The rapidly growing popularity of the disc jockey was also viewed as a threat to live music on radio, though there was as yet no shortage of that, not least in the form of "remotes" from ballrooms and nightclubs all over the land, carrying the sounds of swing.

By the later 1930s the record industry, dominated by RCA Victor, ARC, and the upstart Decca—founded in 1934 and, unlike the competition, retailing all its popular output, even by such top performers as Crosby and Armstrong, at thirty-five rather than seventy-five cents per disc (three for a dollar)—was still under the considerable influence of the music publishers. They wanted quick recordings of the songs, mostly ephemeral, issuing forth in a steady stream from Tin Pan Alley. No big band recorded more of these than Tommy Dorsey's, led by a man with publishing interests. But Dorsey's biggest hits of the decade, "Marie" and "Song of India," were sparked by the trumpet solos of Bunny Berigan, who had also lit up Goodman's seminal 1935 "King Porter Stomp." Inevitably, Berigan wound up as leader of his own band, and with it he recorded one of the swing era's most enduring works, "I Can't Get Started." All these bands recorded for Victor, and so, by 1938, did an ambitious young clarinetist named Artie Shaw. He had just switched from ARC's Vocalion label to Victor's Bluebird imprint when he struck gold with an instrumental version of Cole Porter's "Begin the Beguine," a song neither new nor popular. Its stunning success was yet another demonstration of the phonograph's power; in its wake, Shaw became Goodman's chief rival in the swing sweepstakes. The Goodman band never had a comparable hit record, though "Sing, Sing, Sing" sold well for a twelve-inch record. That size was still rare for jazz, but Berigan's "I Can't Get Started" also was of that diameter.

Both discs were part of Victor's somewhat pretentiously named *A Symposium of Swing*, an album set of four twelve-inchers, to which Decca responded with *Five Feet of Swing*, going Victor one disc better. The usual jazz album contained four to six ten-inch discs. Victor led off in the genre in 1936 with a *Bix Beiderbecke Memorial Album* that set high standards. It contained several so-called alternate takes. Routinely, more than one version of a selection would be recorded, sometimes at a single session, sometimes at different dates; one was chosen for release, but others might be saved as "safeties." In the case of significant soloists, such alternative versions might be quite different and of great interest to specialists and collectors. The Beiderbecke album also came with a booklet of excellent annotations by the pioneer discographer Warren Scholl. Subsequent Victor albums were mainly compilations of hits until the label launched its *Hot Jazz Classics* series in the 1940s. Decca was more enterprising with its anthologies of white and "colored" jazz, instrumental surveys such as *Sliphorn* (trombonists), *Blackstick* (clarinetists), *Saxophobia* (tenor saxists), and *Drummer Boy*. And Decca's 1939 *Chicago Jazz* was an innovation: the first jazz album of newly recorded material, produced and conceived by nineteen-year-old George Avakian, who would become a notable record producer. Columbia, though in financial doldrums, was persuaded by Hammond to issue a Bessie Smith memorial album in 1938.

A year before, Hugues Panassié and his coeditor at the French magazine *Jazz Hot*, Charles Delaunay, who in 1936 had published his unprecedented *Hot Discography* (a slightly earlier British book, *Rhythm on Records*, was not a proper discography since it omitted exact recording dates, complete personnel listings, matrix numbers, and original issue), launched the world's first record label exclusively dedicated to jazz. Called Swing, it made an auspicious debut with a session starring Coleman Hawkins and Benny Carter, joined by leading French practitioners such as Django Reinhardt and Stephane Grappelli (on piano) and another American in Paris, drummer Tommy Benford.

Meanwhile Milt Gabler had continued his reissue program, now on the UHCA label (the initials stood for United Hot Clubs of America, patterned on the Hot Club de France, best remembered for the sponsorship of a quintet that bore its name and starred Reinhardt and Grappelli), but he had long wanted to record freshly minted jazz of the kind closest to his heart. In early 1938 his Commodore label made its debut as the first American jazz label, with a session under Eddie Condon's leadership, featuring Bud Freeman, Pee Wee Russell, Jess Stacy, and newcomer Bobby Hackett in a latter-day Chicago-style setting. Shortly after the first Commodore release, Gabler's friendly rival Steve Smith, who ran the Hot Record Shop and its Hot Record Society reissue label, launched HRS Originals with a session led by Pee Wee Russell, but now in the company of James P. Johnson, a couple of Count Basie sidemen, and drummer Zutty Singleton.

The Basie band, one of Hammond's happiest discoveries, had first been heard by the jazz proselytizer on his powerful car radio, broadcasting on a shortwave station from Kansas City, where he promptly caught them in person. He meant to sign them to Vocalion, an ARC label, but Decca's Jack Kapp jumped in with a contract. Hammond did manage a preview, recording a small Basie group including the leader and Lester Young, billing it as "Smith-Jones, Inc." (Smith and Jones were on trumpet and drums.) But he had to wait two years to produce records by his favorite band.

The existence of an independent jazz label like Commodore made it possible to record, when Hammond's bosses turned down the idea, some of the finest small-group swing music of the decade, a kind of follow-up to the Smith-Jones date, which had introduced Lester Young to records. Now another Basie spinoff, this time without the leader, or any piano, but with two guitars—one electric—and Young doubling clarinet (Gabler's idea), recorded for Commodore as the Kansas City Six some jazz gems that have seldom been out of circulation since. The label also played a key role in Billie Holiday's career. She was still contracted to Vocalion, now owned by CBS, and Hammond was still her producer, but they were most reluctant to let the singer record a very unusual song recently added to her repertory at Café Society, the country's only nightclub catering to integrated audiences. This was "Strange Fruit," which dealt in unsparing terms with lynching. Holiday approached Gabler, long her friend, who persuaded Hammond to loan the singer to Commodore for one date. As it turned out, the controversial song's flip side, a blues, "Fine and Mellow," concocted by Holiday and Gabler for the occasion, became the label's first modest hit.

Under new ownership, the Columbia label once again became a major player in the record business. In 1939 Hammond helped to lure Goodman away from Victor, where the clarinetist's trio and quartet records had become catalog staples. With Lionel Hampton as the sole holdover, he now formed a sextet including yet another Hammond find (with help from Mary Lou Williams), the electric guitarist Charlie Christian, who, not least due to his Goodman Sextet records, would change the role of the guitar in jazz (and popular music) forever. Another youngster had a similar effect on his chosen instrument, the bass. This was Jimmy Blanton, whose 1939 arrival in the Ellington band coincided with a new creative peak in Ellington's career and a fruitful new association with Victor (whose engineers were still the best). The unprecedented Ellington-Blanton duets launched the bass as a solo voice in jazz.

Simultaneous with such new developments, the rediscovery of jazz's past continued apace. Hugues Panassié, visiting the United States, was invited to supervise sessions for Victor's Bluebird label and enlisted his friend and mentor, the clarinetist Mezz Mezzrow, to assist him. The results, while uneven, helped to launch Sidney Bechet to his first fame in his homeland and gave New Orleans trumpeter Tommy Ladnier his last chances to record. "Revolutionary Blues," featuring these two, announced what would become the New Orleans revival movement. Jelly Roll Morton, aided by Alan Lomax's documentary recording project for the Library of Congress in 1938 (not issued until nine years later, on critic Rudi Blesh's small Circle label), was recorded solo in Washington, D.C., by the Jazz Man label, formed by Neshui Ertegun, son of the Turkish ambassador to the United States, and subsequently brought to New York to record for Bluebird with a band including Bechet and other veterans from Morton's hometown. The year 1939 also saw the publication of *Jazzmen*, an influential book that became the sacred text of the revival, soon further spurred by the discovery in New Iberia, Louisiana, of the legendary trumpeter Bunk Johnson, rumored to have taught young Louis Armstrong.

Johnson did not record until 1942, but in 1940 music by a band made up of New Orleans elders, led by trumpeter Kid Rena and performing in a pre-Oliver Creole Jazz Band style, was issued on the Delta label. This had appeal to the still limited circle of serious collectors and students of jazz history. Considerably more resonant was the not-so-archeological music recorded for Bluebird by the short-lived but excellent Muggsy Spanier Ragtimers. Small independent jazz labels now began to proliferate. Some, like Solo Art, dedicated exclusively to blues and boogie-woogie piano, did not last, but others, like Blue Note, which also began life as a boogie-woogie piano label, survived the century. By 1942 the list included Bob Thiele's Signature, Collector's Item, and the aforementioned Jazz Man, now relocated to California and introducing Lu Watters's Yerba Buena Jazz Band, a bunch of obscure San Franciscans attempting to copy classic Oliver and Morton—two cornets, banjo, brass bass, and all.

On the swing front, such Kansas City–based bands as Harlan Leonard's Rockets (with a young arranger named Tadd Dameron) and Jay McShann's (with a young altoist named Charlie Parker), recording for Bluebird and Decca respectively, were pointing in new directions, as were the remarkable Art Tatum (prolific on Decca since 1934) and fellow pianist (and singer) Nat King Cole, at the helm of a swinging trio (at first on Decca's "Sepia Series" race list, then signed by Capitol, a label formed in 1942 by a Los Angeles triumvirate including songwriter Johnny Mercer and record store owner Glenn Wallichs. Since 1938 Decca also had been the home of Louis Jordan's Tympany Five, a hip little band that godfathered rhythm-and-blues and by the early 1940s had "crossed over" to the general catalog. And it is impossible to ignore the effect of an instrumental record that became an unexpected hit and reestablished Coleman Hawkins as the rightful king of the tenor saxophone shortly after his return from Europe in 1939. "Body and Soul" remains a jazz landmark, its two choruses of improvisation (the melody stated only in two opening bars) a lesson in solo construction—a kind of successor to "Singin' the Blues."

But there was trouble ahead for the record business. Effective August 1, 1942, the mercurial president of the American Federation of Musicians, James Caesar Petrillo, ordered a ban on all recording by instrumentalists, the labels having failed to agree to a demand for royalties to musicians for broadcast and jukebox play. Changes wrought by World War II, such as the shortage of shellac and the effects of the draft, were already a burden on the music industry, and the ban had a profound impact on jazz. Without new instrumental records, the singers, already growing in popularity, might not have prospered with such rapidity, though Frank Sinatra would undoubtedly still have made his impact. In any event, a ray of jazz recording light emanated from the V-disc program of special records made solely for distribution to the Armed Forces, with union dispensation and a surprisingly high percentage of jazz, most of it produced by jazz critic George T. Simon. A bit later on, transcription sessions made for radio use only were permitted by the union and also yielded a fair amount of jazz. (Decades later, the release of music from broadcasts made for the Armed Forces, notably the Jubilee series aimed at black troops, added to the slender record of jazz made during the ban.)

It took more than two years to fully rescind the ban. Decca was first among the majors to settle, late in 1943, but Victor and Columbia held out longer. In the interim, independent labels sprang up all over the land, making their own deals with the union and issuing country music, gospel, rhythm-and-blues—and jazz. These upstarts, and the older independents, would document new trends in jazz well before the majors came on board. Among the first was Savoy, located in Newark, New Jersey, and, like Commodore and HRS, the offspring of a retail store dealing in radio parts, used records, and other "dry goods." After an inauspicious debut, Teddy Reig, an enterprising habitué of 52nd Street and the Harlem jazz scene, was hired as producer, adding to Savoy's roster such budding stars as Erroll Garner, Don Byas, and above all Charlie Parker, who made his first leader's date for the label. Parker's earlier discs with Dizzy Gillespie had been made first for Guild, then for the older independent that gobbled it up, Musicraft, which also launched Sarah Vaughan; the producer here was veteran Albert Marx, first to record Art Tatum in 1933. Musicraft also recorded Gillespie's big band, later signed by Victor, but the trumpeter's first own date was made for another Newark-based label, Manor. The two fathers of bebop also recorded for Continental, not a jazz-only label but also the home of such established artists as Mary Lou Williams, Hot Lips Page, and Slam Stewart.

Williams did most of her sessions for Moe Asch's Asch and Disc labels, later to become Folkways Records. The first of Norman Granz's Jazz at the Philharmonic live concert recordings appeared on Asch and Disc; it was an influential innovation in jazz recording and, with its twelve-inch album releases, a prelude to the long-playing record. Behind many of the small-label modern jazz sessions was the enter-prising critic, broadcaster, concert producer, and prolific songwriter Leonard Feather, who had been producing dates of his own since 1937, beginning in his native England. An early booster of bebop, he was responsible for getting the new sounds through Victor's door. That label also recorded the annual Metronome All Star dates, spon-sored by and featuring the poll winners of *Metronome* magazine, second only to *Down Beat* among jazz periodicals. Other jazz names on Victor included Coleman Hawkins, the most bop-friendly among established stars, who also recorded modern sessions for Capitol, Joe Davis, Sonora, and Apollo—the latter yet another record store–asso-ciated label, this with the Rainbow Music Shop in Harlem.

Capitol was for more than two decades the home of Stan Kenton, whose self-styled "progressive jazz" had a big following that enabled the pianist-arranger-bandleader to include in his voluminous recorded output much music of a highly experimental nature. Another big band leader to find success in the postwar era was Woody Herman, long a Decca artist with his Band That Plays the Blues, but then leader of his First Herd on Columbia, the more boppish Second Herd on Capitol, and several more to follow. Many other leaders disbanded in the mid-1940s, at least temporarily, as television and the growth of suburbs cut into nightlife and jazz was replaced as the number one dance music by rhythm-and-blues and then rock-and-roll.

By 1946 Charlie Parker was recording for still another label spawned by a record store, Ross Russell's Dial, based in Los Angeles. Dial also signed a former Savoy artist, Dexter Gordon, whose double-sided 78 "tenor battle" with Wardell Gray, "The Chase," transcended bop and appealed to the same listeners who responded so well to Hampton and Basie alumnus Illinois Jacquet, the tenor sparkplug of early Jazz at the Philharmonic.

Parker's marvelous quintet recordings for Dial (and Savoy, to fulfill old contracts), with Miles Davis on trumpet and Max Roach on drums, became bebop classics, but Parker's biggest sales resulted from his somewhat later sessions with strings, produced by Norman Granz and distributed by Mercury, like Capitol a new label with major ambitions. Chicago based, Mercury at first recorded blues and boogie woogie, in the process discovering tenorman Gene Ammons, the son of famed boogie-woogie pianist Albert. The son would score his biggest hits with a new jazz label, Prestige, also a record store offshoot, founded in New York by Bob Weinstock. Mercury soon spawned EmArcy as a jazz subsidiary, with Bob Shad as producer. This brings us to the dawn of the LP era, which began in 1948 and would profoundly change the nature of jazz recording.

The LP, introduced in a ten-inch format, was initially perceived primarily as a boon to classical music, since long works could now be recorded (or remastered) without the annoying pauses or cuts mandated by 78s. For jazz and popular music, the LP was seen mainly as a compact compilation medium, in the image of the 78 album. This format had become increasingly popular for jazz reissues (including unreleased masters and alternate takes) during the recording ban, but lingered on beyond it. Columbia led in this field, but Victor as well as Decca and its subsidiaries also had been active, and now these labels all converted them to LP, sometimes adding material.

It was one of the new independent jazz labels that pointed the way to creative use of the new technology. Prestige included an eight-minute excursion by tenorman Zoot Sims, "Zoot Blows the Blues," as a track on an LP—a prelude to the "blowing sessions" the label would soon specialize in. This formula called for gathering a bunch of compatible horn players, bringing them together with a strong rhythm section, and maximizing studio time to generate several lengthy, jam session–like pieces, sometimes taking up an entire side of an LP (the soon-prevailing twelve-inch format included). Columbia also launched a series of studio jam sessions under the leadership of ex-Basie trumpeter-arranger Buck Clayton, produced by George Avakian with Hammond. Blue Note, which gradually had moved from revivalist jazz to swing, now entered the modern field with a coup, courageously and successfully recording pianist-composer Thelonious Monk in his debut as a leader. Excepting a lingering loyalty to Sidney Bechet, greatly admired by the label's founder, Alfred Lion, and his partner, Francis Wolff, Blue Note now became fully focused on modern jazz; loyalty to favorite artists remained a label characteristic, most fully expressed in more than two decades of association with Horace

Silver, one of the founders of the hard-bop style that Blue Note mined with great success.

Monk would find this kind of affiliation, after a brief Prestige interlude that followed his Blue Note period, with the third of the "big three" jazz independents, Riverside. Founded by Bill Grauer and Orrin Keepnews, it began as a reissue operation, having obtained rights to the classic Gennett and Paramount catalogs, and then joined the modern sweepstakes. Keepnews nurtured Monk, played an essential role in the career of a very different pianist, Bill Evans, and became the legendary guitarist Wes Montgomery's first and best producer. He was aided in the latter coup by Riverside's leading seller, altoist Cannonball Adderley, whose quintet specialized in hard bop, and whose role as highly valued informal artistic adviser reflected a unique relationship between producer and artist. The veteran tenorman Ike Quebec played a similar role as talent scout and facilitator at Blue Note. This kind of involvement by musicians in the recording process had begun with Eddie Condon and Milt Gabler and became more direct with pianist Art Hodes's Jazz Record, Mezz Mezzrow's King Jazz, and bassist Al Hall's Wax, all short-lived. The longest-lasting and most visible of musician-owned (or operated) labels was Charles Mingus's Debut (1952–57), entering auspiciously with the famous Massey Hall concert LPs, starring Parker, Gillespie, and Bud Powell, and living up to its name by introducing a number of artists.

Prestige's leading players were Miles Davis and Sonny Rollins. The trumpeter was lured away by Columbia's Avakian in 1955, and the tenorman (after fruitful Blue Note and Riverside albums) was signed by the selfsame Avakian, by now with Victor, to what was claimed to be the most lucrative contract offered a jazz artist. It is safe to assume, however, that Davis's two-decade-long association with Columbia, resulting in such landmarks as *Kind of Blue, Sketches of Spain*, and *Bitches Brew*, yielded much more. Teo Macero produced the latter two LPs and also worked with Monk when the pianist came to Columbia in 1962. Columbia was most committed to jazz of the majors, not least due to the unusually enlightened presidency of Goddard Lieberson (and later, and more briefly, Bruce Lundvall), but also thanks to the resounding success of Dave Brubeck, brought to the label by Avakian after the pianist's quartet had proven its appeal with a California independent, Fantasy. The fortunes of the California-based jazz labels were not at all limited to so-called West Coast jazz. With Richard Bock in the producer's chair, Pacific Jazz developed such leading West Coast lights as Gerry Mulligan and Chet Baker but also nurtured Gerald Wilson's big band and much else. The most consistently interesting Californian label was Lester Koenig's Contemporary, put on a solid business footing by the unanticipated and huge (for jazz) sales of its jazz version of the score from *My Fair Lady*, performed by André Previn, piano, Leroy Vinnegar, bass, and Shelly Manne, drums. It spawned a long-lived genre: jazz versions of Broadway musicals. Koenig, unlike other producers also a first-rate engineer, was guided by excellent and wide-ranging taste. His sizable catalog included much of Art Pepper's best work, a pair of superb Sonny Rollins LPs, Ornette Coleman's first studio recordings, and most of Phineas Newborn Jr.'s output. He also tended to traditional style on his Good Time Jazz label, much of it supervised by Neshui Ertegun, who subsequently took charge of the Atlantic label's jazz wing.

Atlantic, like Contemporary, mirrored its producer's tastes. Ertegun's commitment to the Modern Jazz Quartet (and other John Lewis ventures) lasted for twenty-five years. He had a fruitful association with Coleman, worked patiently with Charles Mingus, and presented Ray Charles in jazz settings. And he took risks with trumpeter Tony Fruscella and the gifted vibist-composer Teddy Charles that paid off artistically if not commercially. Some of Mingus's most politically outspoken work was done for Candid, aptly named but short-lived, which also brought out the most agit-prop of civil rights–related jazz pieces, Max Roach's *Freedom Now* suite, and some striking early Cecil Taylor (who had also recorded for Contemporary). Writer Nat Hentoff was Candid's producer, but it was a subsidiary of Cadence Records, home of the popular singer Andy Williams, who years later acquired and reissued much of the Candid catalog on his Barnaby label.

No jazz label was more prolific or prolix than Norman Granz's Verve (which absorbed its antecedents, Clef and Norgran), or less tied to the bottom line. His multiple Jazz at the Philharmonic releases included the first jazz LPs to be marketed in boxed sets, and he commissioned fine cover art, notably from David Stone Martin. Some of his ventures, such as the Ella Fitzgerald *Song Book* series, were commercial successes (and prime examples of how intelligent record production and packaging and promotion can boost an artist's career) while others were not, among them several first-rate LPs featuring the altoist Lee Konitz and those starring veteran jazz violinist Stuff Smith. But Granz recorded who and what he liked—no one more frequently than the pianist he had first brought from Montreal to

Carnegie Hall, Oscar Peterson. Granz's loyalty to great jazz figures no longer in their prime (Lester Young and Billie Holiday, and later Coleman Hawkins) has no parallel. Possibly his crowning achievement was his Art Tatum project, which over the last four years of the great pianist's life yielded more than a dozen solo piano albums as well as great encounters with peers Benny Carter, Roy Eldridge (a special Granz favorite), Ben Webster, Lionel Hampton, Buddy DeFranco, and Buddy Rich. Granz sold Verve in 1961 but returned to the fray in 1973 with Pablo, for which he bought back his Tatum masters, re-signed Fitzgerald, Peterson, and Eldridge, and continued to behave more like a patron of the arts than a businessman.

Duke Ellington was among Granz's Verve and Pablo artists but enjoyed his longest LP-era relationship with Columbia. Among the first established recording artists to grasp the potential of the new medium, he was now able to comfortably record a long work like *Harlem*, combining it with an extended version of "Take the 'A' Train" in an LP he called *Ellington Uptown*, and giving similar expanded treatment to such staples as "Mood Indigo" and "Solitude" for *Masterpieces by Ellington*. By the mid-1950s, when stereo recording had arrived, Ellington was specializing in suites, a genre well suited to the LP. He continued in this vein, including his term with Frank Sinatra's Reprise label, until the sunset of his half-century recording career, when the Sacred Concerts (all three on record) had become his main pursuit. A Columbia LP that played a pivotal role in Ellington's later career was also one of the best-known samples of yet another LP genre, the live recording. This was *Ellington at Newport*, recorded at the 1956 festival, which, when reissued in expanded form on CD in 1999, turned out to have been only partially "live." But there is no doubting the authenticity of another live Columbia LP that had a most positive effect on an artist's career, Erroll Garner's *Concert by the Sea*, an album with great initial success and longevity. The pianist had been recording for all comers, but once he had entered the major leagues, he became the first jazz artist to exercise complete artistic control over his product, à la Horowitz.

These were festival and concert recordings, but perhaps the most significant live LPs were those that captured music made in nightclubs. New York's Village Vanguard is primary among these venues, the site of classic performances by various Bill Evans trios (notably the first, on Riverside), by Sonny Rollins in a very different trio format (Blue Note), and by the John Coltrane Quartet and Quintet, caught in the act on the Impulse label in 1961, near the beginning of the influential saxophonist's lengthy relationship with veteran producer Bob Thiele. As the decade moved on and rock music came to dominate the record business, Coltrane was among the few jazz performers to still enjoy a solid contract and steady sales. He was even able to bring out the unique *Ascension*, a continuous spontaneously improvised ensemble performance stretching over an entire LP (and unintentionally issued in two versions).

There was, however, another saxophonist whose recording fortunes were not ill affected by the 1960s. This was Stan Getz, once cited by Coltrane as a favorite and among the Verve artists held over after the label's sale to MGM. The new producer, Creed Taylor (incidentally the man who had signed Coltrane to Impulse), got off to a good start with Getz by way of the unusual *Focus* LP, a work for strings and rhythm section ingeniously conceived by Eddie Sauter to provide a backdrop for the saxophonist's improvised solo part. This was an artistic triumph for Getz, but his next venture would make him one of the most commercially successful of all jazz musicians. At the behest of guitarist Charlie Byrd, Getz joined him in a program of recent Brazilian tunes in a style known in its homeland as bossa nova. While the LP was issued as *Jazz Samba*, it put bossa nova on the musical map to stay and also spun off a single (the 45 rpm configuration had long since replaced 78 for such discs) that would become the only jazz instrumental of the decade to place in the trade magazine charts, "Desafinado." (Getz and the bossa nova gave birth to an even bigger hit, "The Girl From Ipanema," but this had a vocal by Astrud Gilberto.)

Taylor eventually left Verve to start his own CTI label, which employed effective packaging and marketing to gain a goodly share of what remained of the jazz record market by the 1970s. Its leading artists included trumpeter Freddie Hubbard, flutist Hubert Laws, and tenorman Stanley Turrentine, all engaged by Taylor in accommodations with rock, while another three-letter label, the German-based ECM, nurtured such newcomers as keyboard players and composers Chick Corea and Keith Jarrett and later came to specialize in so-called world music. Other European labels would make significant jazz contributions, among them the Danish SteepleChase, Italian Black Saint/Soul Note, Danish Storyville, the German Enja, the Swiss Hat Hut, and the Dutch Criss Cross. Without these labels, many gifted musicians would have gone unrepresented on records. An American label that consistently attended to deserving jazz and blues artists was the Chicago-based Delmark, founded by Bob Koester, with his record store as the base of operations; it was first to record the music of the city's 1960s avant-garde, including several members of the Art Ensemble of Chicago and Anthony Braxton in his recording debut.

The last years of the LP exhibited the sort of gigantism associated with an earlier vanishing species, the dinosaurs. ECM presented a ten-LP box, *The Sun Bear Concerts*, of Keith Jarrett solo concert performances in Japan—a haven for jazz in the lean years. But it was reissues that weighed in heaviest, as with *The Complete Keynote Recordings*, twenty-one LPs celebrating an independent jazz label of the 1940s, produced by a jazz expert from Java, Harry Lim. The reissue set was lovingly produced by one of Japan's foremost jazz authorities, Kiyoshi Koyama, whose penchant for large-scale projects earned him the nickname of "Boxman."

A pioneering and still-unique multi-LP project (still available in a five-CD format) was *The Smithsonian Collection of Classic Jazz* (Smithsonian Collection of Recordings), released in 1973 and revised in 1987. This collection, selected and annotated by critic Martin Williams, has not been without its detractors, but it still stands as the best anthology of recorded jazz history.

When the CD was introduced, forecasters anticipated a decade-long coexistence with the LP, but the handy new format established itself in half that time. "Vinyl," as the LP is called in the CD era, survives in occasional limited editions aimed at collectors and audiophiles (in 1999, the Japanese branch of Blue Note issued two dozen ten-inch LPs in exact replications) and at second hand in a lively international collectors' market. The LP's reign was shorter than the 78's, and at the turn of the century it seems certain that the days of the CD are numbered. The format, however, has long since made its mark on jazz. With disc duration averaging an hour, it confronted the artist with the very real problem of how to sustain sufficient listener interest, notably when he or she is expected to record with some frequency. A result has been the proliferation of original compositions, many of which are neither. Another, since CDs are much easier than LPs to store, carry, and even produce, is an abundance of self-produced records. There are very many small labels as well, usually specializing in niche markets.

And there is a cornucopia of reissues, some approaching the scope (if nowhere near the heft) of the latter-day LP boxes. These include the eighteen-CD Bill Evans box and the sixteen-CD Ella Fitzgerald *Song Book* set, both on Verve, and an eighteen-CD Nat King Cole box issued by Mosaic, a mail-order label specializing in complete sets of various kinds, licensed for limited editions from the record companies created in the mergers of the last three decades of the century that now control the bulk of the recorded legacy of jazz. A notable and happy exception is Fantasy Records, which thanks to the success of the rock band Creedence Clearwater Revival was able to acquire in turn Prestige, Riverside, Milestone, Contemporary, Pablo, and some smaller labels, and is keeping a commendably large percentage of its huge catalog in circulation.

At the turn of the century, the amount and variety of recorded jazz readily available, now also via Internet, is staggering. It encompasses almost everything of significance from every era, and in constantly improving sound quality. There are of course regrettable gaps at any given moment, and every connoisseur has favorites that remain unreissued. But when one considers such vintage 1999 bonanzas as *The Complete Duke Ellington on RCA Victor* (twenty-four CDs with extensive annotation) from the perspective of more than fifty years of listening to and acquiring jazz records, the advantages of the present are undeniable.

Jazz Improvisation and Concepts of Virtuosity

David Demsey

Improvisation is at the very center of the jazz experience. In many ways, improvisation gives jazz a unique place in Western music. While other musical genres share similarities with jazz in terms of form, harmony, melodic line, instrumentation, or even the concept of swing, no musical situation is more singularly thrilling, joyful, and sometimes terrifying for a performer as walking onto a jazz stage and literally not knowing what is about to happen musically.

What Improvisation Is Not: Two Misconceptions

There are two common misconceptions about jazz improvisation, held as often by nonjazz musicians as by the general public. One is that it simply involves "playing whatever comes to mind" or "being spontaneous." This idea is naturally drawn from dictionary definitions of the term, which commonly contain words such as *offhand* or *spur of the moment*. In truth, the performance of an improvised jazz solo is similar to the delivery of a concise, eloquent answer to a question in conversation. The spoken response requires knowledge of the issue at hand, a powerful vocabulary, and a quick mind; improvisation requires the same tools. Dizzy Gillespie often said that he disliked the term *serious music* as a comparison to jazz, because jazz performers were the most serious musicians he knew. A jazz improviser must have a working knowledge of harmony, an innate feel for form and melodic line, a strong technique, a quick, relaxed mind, and a deep sense of history.

A second misconception is that jazz improvisation is created by divine intervention. This idea is perhaps drawn from some jazz artists who have fostered the image that they are struck onstage by a bolt of creativity that wrenches the music from them. In reality, the notes of an improvised jazz solo are no more spontaneously created than are the words of a spoken language. At this most integral level, sentences have been spoken before, in some form; individual words have been enunciated countless times until they roll smoothly off the tongue. In musical terms, melodic ideas are repeated and replayed for years until they become the individual vocabulary of a soloist; difficult chord progressions and awkward keys are endlessly practiced until they are mentally familiar and fall easily under the hands. In a great soloist's repertoire, every tune is like a familiar subject of conversation: although fresh ideas are always emerging, the language used to communicate them has a consistency for each individual.

What Improvisation Is: Elements of an Improvised Solo

If an improvised jazz solo is not simply unfettered freedom, and if it is not a form of otherworldly communication, then what is involved in this creative process? From a player's perspective, an improvised solo is made up of several elements.

The first of these are form and harmony, which are of nearly singular importance as a coherent vocabulary emerges in the early stages of an improviser's development. As the improviser matures and this vocabulary becomes second nature, the process moves to the same subconscious level as adult speech. Jazz musicians do not need the melody of a standard tune to recognize it; they are equally familiar with its form and underlying harmony. An experienced jazz player would need only the chords or even just the bass line of the opening seconds of "All the Things You Are" to be instantly in familiar surroundings. This skill, akin to recognizing any of Beethoven's symphonies by hearing only the cello or bass parts, is born of necessity: improvised jazz is cyclic. Improvisations generally occur over the repetitions, or choruses, of a song's chord sequence. An internalized sense of this repeating form, created by the unique harmonic nooks and crannies of each tune, lets jazz performers keep their bearings.

Coleman Hawkins in the 1960s. Photo: Lee Tanner. Courtesy of the Institute of Jazz Studies, Rutgers University.

Another element of improvisation is the melody, the tune's most recognizable feature, which is joined inexorably with its harmony. A tune's melody is its main identity, far more accessible than its abstract chord sequence. Many jazz musicians hasten to add that it is also the original improvisation, performed by the composer using a pen as an instrument. Improvisers keep the melody in their mind's ear as a reference point as they glide through the harmonies; they may refer to it in brief, coded bits during their solos as a marker of the form. In rare instances when Sonny Rollins gives workshops on improvisation, he inevitably asks students if they know the lyrics of the tune they are studying. Rollins not only knows the published lyrics to the tunes in his repertoire, as do many great soloists; he has said that he often mentally applies instantaneous lyrics to his improvised melodies as they emerge from his saxophone.

Another crucial element of improvisation is the establishment of strong voice-leading. This is the ability of any compelling melody, improvised or composed, to imply an interconnected line of sound that moves smoothly from one chord to the next. An example is the opening phrase of Vincent Youmans's "Tea for Two," which can be sung as a sustained, chorale-like descending line by omitting its bouncing rhythms. In the opening of "My Funny Valentine," Richard Rodgers creates two simultaneous melodies in counterpoint as the descending bass line interacts with the vocal line. Every standard tune has intriguing voice-leading opportunities such as these, some more hidden than others. The improviser is challenged to find and use them during a solo to create a unified statement. Although this part of the improvised vocabulary is difficult to hear, it is this subtle element that ties together the jazz dialects of the different style periods. Why, when we listen to a solo by Louis Armstrong or Charlie Parker or John Coltrane, do we seem to know what they are going to play next? Why does a great improvised solo line just seem to "work"? One clear answer, I believe, lies in strong voice-leading, which occurs with stunning consistency throughout the solos of the great improvisers. Aurally memorable notes of one gesture are invariably picked up and answered by the next gesture—an implied line different from the tune's original melody, but no less important.

Finally, and truly the most crucial elements, are rhythm and time. When John Philip Sousa said in the early days of jazz that the art form would "endure as long as people hear it with their feet instead of their brains," he predated by decades Duke Ellington's famous "It Don't Mean a Thing . . ." song title on the same subject. In musicians' terms, cascades of strange notes are excusable if a soloist is rhythmically interesting and the pulse is solid, but four hours of harmonic perfection will fall on deaf ears if solos are rhythmically drab or the time is inconsistent. The concepts of "swinging" and playing with "good time" are elusive not only because they differ with each player. Rhythm occurs in real time, in contrast to harmony and melody, which retain their identity when slowed to a crawl or isolated for analysis.

While the craft of improvisation can be described in the above categories of harmony and form, melody, voice-leading, and time and rhythm, it is the true art of improvisation that holds its magic. This artistry is as difficult to articulate for improvisers themselves as for the lay listener because the art and magic of improvisation are unique for each individual performer. When the two aspects of improvisation—the art and the craft—come together, the actual act of creation occurs.

How does this process work, as an idea that darts instantly from the mind's musical imagination to the ear, then through the voice or instrument? Again, the answer is as different from one soloist to another as each human voice is unique. This is especially true for the jazz masters, those individuals whose musical voices have been so strong and convincing that they have shaped the very language of jazz. By highlighting some of these individuals, we can discern the "ground rules" that formed their musical performances. The traits that mark their singular styles give a clearer picture of the act of improvisation.

The First Great Soloist: Louis Armstrong

Louis Armstrong is considered by most to be the first great influential jazz soloist. Armstrong's soaring solos established his style in the twenties as the moving force in jazz. He was able to rise above his sometimes lackluster accompaniments and was a powerful influence on nearly every musician who heard him. His creative process demonstrates the central role of the ear in building an improvised melody line. For example, Armstrong's work on the 1927 "Hotter Than That" (OKeh/Columbia) is one of a number of his recordings that involve his improvised scat singing as well as trumpet playing. When Armstrong scatted, he sang the same long, interconnected lines he played on the trumpet, using many of the same melodic ideas. His musical language would have emerged from any instrument he happened to choose, not just from the trumpet with which we are so familiar.

Although not a songwriter per se, Armstrong was the supreme melodist. The spontaneously created melodies he improvised on a tune were as strong and memorable as the original, as naturally inspired and brilliantly structured as any notated composition.

Two Tenors: Coleman Hawkins and Lester Young

Tenor saxophonist Coleman Hawkins gained prominence in the thirties and was the most powerful improviser after Armstrong. Just as Armstrong was a melodist, Hawkins was a harmonic virtuoso. Using a huge, broad sound and wide vibrato, he was keenly adept at outlining harmonies as though he were attempting to create three or four simultaneous melodies. Not satisfied to improvise upon the basic harmonies of standard tunes, Hawkins systematically inserted passing chords between the existing harmonies, substituting alternate chords at moments of tension and release. Hawkins's landmark 1939 version of "Body and Soul" (Bluebird) is an example of this that has been studied, imitated, and internalized by generations of jazz musicians. In the performance, actually an impromptu afterthought to an otherwise long-forgotten recording session, Hawkins begins with a nod to the original melody. By the second phrase, he is creating his own improvised composition, sliding substitutions and additional chords between the original harmonies as he builds to a huge climax over two choruses. Hawkins's sound and harmonic approach directly influenced great tenor players of the fifties, including Sonny Rollins, Dexter Gordon, and John Coltrane.

Just a month before the "Body and Soul" session, tenor saxophonist Lester Young recorded "Lester Leaps In" (Vocalion) as a soloist with Count Basie's Kansas City Seven. Young's improvisation on this "I Got Rhythm"–based tune was as influential as Hawkins's recording, for contrasting reasons. While Hawkins dug into the chord changes, extracting every possible harmonic nuance, Young danced across the harmony, ignoring the passing details in favor of a simpler vocabulary. He toyed with the rhythm of the chords' occurrence, forecasting the sound of an upcoming chord before it happened or hanging on to a harmony after the chord progression had moved on. The most dramatic contrasts between Hawkins and Young came in their sounds and rhythmic approaches. While Hawkins played powerfully and landed on each beat, Young used a light, airy, vibratoless sound and played with more even, smooth phrasing, which directly inspired a legion of later tenor players, including Zoot Sims, Al Cohn, Stan Getz, Flip Phillips, and Paul Quinichette.

Bebop: Charlie Parker, Dizzy Gillespie, and Thelonious Monk

The most heralded players in the next generation were those who founded the musical movement now known as bebop. In the forties, Charlie Parker, Dizzy Gillespie, Thelonious Monk, and others combined Young's smoother swing approach with Hawkins's penchant for substitute chords to achieve a more modern sound, often taken at blistering tempos. The bebop era is considered by most jazz performers and educators to be the "common practice" period in the history of jazz. Just as music students learn European classical music by studying the compositions of Bach, Mozart, and Beethoven, most agree that bebop was central to the development of modern jazz.

Charlie Parker was widely recognized by his peers as the genius who could actually execute all of bebop's complex concepts, having the incredible instrumental virtuosity to match his mental acuity. In a radio interview with saxophonist Paul Desmond, Parker described how he had discovered his harmonic concept after becoming frustrated at playing over the chords of "Cherokee." By "using the higher intervals of a chord as a melody line" he could play what he had been hearing all along. It was a seminal moment for him, and for all of jazz. His improvisational style grew to embody all that had gone before him. His musical ideas had the inspired freshness and exuberance of Armstrong. His harmonic ingenuity took Hawkins's ideas to a startlingly complex level. His sense of time grew from Lester Young's sailing swing and lit the afterburners. Parker's influence on improvisation is unparalleled.

Another, less recognized pioneer of the bebop era was pianist Thelonious Monk. While Monk had a deep understanding of bebop harmonic and rhythmic concepts—and some assert that he was the musical mentor of Parker and Gillespie—his playing style was the antithesis of theirs. He developed what might best be called a nontechnique at the piano, using his fingers flat on the keys to intentionally strike clusters and blur his faster runs. While Parker's solos (and even the melodies of his compositions) sounded unmelodic to some, as though he couldn't wait to burst through the constraints of the melody with his own ideas, Monk often referred to the melody constantly throughout his improvisations. He, too, toyed with the rhythmic structure, but his playfulness was almost childlike in its simplicity while deadly serious in its conviction.

The Birth of the Modern Era: Miles Davis and John Coltrane

The two improvisational styles that are arguably most influential in modern jazz are those of Miles Davis and John Coltrane. These two careers share an unusual characteristic: both men evolved through several conceptual approaches, each spawning a number of important players.

Miles Davis developed his trumpet style during, or perhaps more accurately because of, his early experience as a sideman with Charlie Parker. Handed the role of following Parker's virtuosic, lightning-fast solos night after night, Davis became Parker's more laid-back foil rather than taking on the impossible task of competing with him. As Davis formed his own groups in the mid-fifties backed by high-energy players like Coltrane and drummer Philly Joe Jones, he retained this level of controlled virtuosity, swinging magnificently yet with a firm hold on the reins. His style was codified with the recording of the 1949–50 *Birth of the Cool* album (Capitol) with arrangements by Gerry Mulligan, Gil Evans, John Lewis, and Johnny Carisi, influencing an entire "cool" school of super-controlled improvisers, which included Gerry Mulligan, Stan Getz, Lee Konitz, and others. Remarkably, Davis managed to retain his own instantly recognizable trumpet sound as he built and rebuilt his bands over the next three decades, launching the careers of players who would shape sixties, seventies, and eighties jazz. These included Coltrane and Julian "Cannonball" Adderley; a landmark group with Wayne Shorter, Herbie Hancock, Ron Carter, and Tony Williams; freer experiments with Chick Corea, Keith Jarrett, and John McLaughlin; and funk-oriented groups featuring drummer Al Foster, alto saxophonist Kenny Garrett, and guitarists John Scofield and Mike Stern in the last part of his life. While Davis's improvisational style remained constant, his evolving concepts of ensemble interplay and rhythmic function had a huge effect upon the development of jazz.

By contrast, the various stages of John Coltrane's meteoric career had much to do with the dramatic, even musically violent, changes that repeatedly transformed his improvisational voice. Early in his career, as a Dizzy Gillespie sideman, he was a swinging, bebop-oriented player who sounded more like Dexter Gordon and Lester Young than he did the Coltrane that most listeners recognize. After he joined Davis's band, then formed his own groups in the late fifties, he experimented with sweeping, out-of-meter phrases dubbed by Ira Gitler "sheets of sound," techniques of thirds-related substitute harmony that were new to jazz, and a more intense sound. It is amazing that, even as Coltrane was recording *Giant Steps* (Atlantic), his first album of only his own compositions, using the most densely packed chords yet heard in jazz, he was simultaneously recording the historic *Kind of Blue* (Columbia) as a member of Davis's sextet, with modal compositions having the least possible number of chord changes—all within a period of under two months in 1959! In the sixties, Coltrane himself eschewed his densely chordal approach and moved to more open compositions, which allowed him to adapt a freer, seemingly dissonant harmonic approach. In fact, what sounded like dissonance was Coltrane superimposing the same types of reharmonizations he had devised earlier, but now over a static bass line. In the later stages of his career, starting with the 1964 album *A Love Supreme* (Impulse), Coltrane became less concerned with harmony. Instead, he developed motivic ideas to increase and maintain energy in unity with his immensely powerful rhythm section of McCoy Tyner, Jimmy Garrison, and Elvin Jones on a series of remarkable spiritual statements. Each of the stages of Coltrane's career had powerful influences over a legion of players. Wayne Shorter, David Liebman, Freddie Hubbard, Woody Shaw, Michael Brecker, and Joe Lovano were influenced by earlier Coltrane recordings; Liebman, Pharoah Sanders, Albert Ayler, and others were followers of Coltrane's later playing.

Concepts of Freedom: Cecil Taylor and Ornette Coleman

Two of the most influential figures in the movement toward freer jazz improvisation in the sixties were Cecil Taylor and Ornette Coleman. They used very different processes to achieve the same goal of freedom in harmony, form, and texture. Their approaches cause the listener to use a different set of ground rules and adopt different values in understanding and analyzing their music.

Pianist Cecil Taylor was influenced by the textural concepts of Dave Brubeck, Lennie Tristano, and later Duke Ellington and Thelonious Monk, but he employed their language in a much different, more dissonant manner. Although his earlier playing featured single-line melodies, albeit applied over unconventional chord voicings, his later performances employ note clusters and huge glissandos produced with his palms, elbows, and fists to create an unceasingly energetic, violent style. This approach perhaps owes more to avant-garde "classical" music than to the jazz tradition, with its abandonment of traditional jazz form, harmony, or textures. Although this concept may appear random and unstructured, analysis of his music shows a surprising level of underlying formal and textural structure. Taylor's unwavering musical approach is as controversial today as when he first gained recognition in the sixties.

Saxophonist Ornette Coleman's musical theories and language may be the source of as much controversy as Taylor's, but his musical process is very different. Coleman burst on the scene with an engagement at New York's Five Spot in 1959 and influenced Coltrane's later playing as he recorded albums like *The Shape of Jazz to Come* (Atlantic) with his quartet and the collective free improvisation of *Free Jazz* (Atlantic). Like Taylor, Coleman often dispenses with harmonic, formal, and metric conventions. However, he does so in a deceptively simple manner that recalls blues and field hollers—the very origins of jazz—in an almost folklike approach that features his crying sound and microtonal pitch placement. Since much of his concept centers on collective improvisation, understanding of his improvisations can best be gained in terms of his entire group's output, rather than Coleman's in isolation.

Creation of a Personal Improvisational Language: The Work Ethic

The crucial factor that ties together the careers of the great improvisers throughout the history of jazz is often forgotten by their audiences: they all possessed an unmatched work ethic. Any discussion of improvisation, from a musician's point of view, must include this subject lest the wrong impression be created that a great improviser simply "has a natural gift."

John Coltrane's legendary practice habits, for example, serve as inspiration for jazz musicians. By numerous accounts, he was nothing short of an obsessive practicer, slipping offstage into the dressing room after an exhausting forty-minute solo to practice while his fellow band members soloed onstage, or keeping a host waiting at the dinner table for three hours while he practiced scale studies.

Seemingly extemporaneous solos heard in performance are actually the tip of the musical iceberg, the result of countless hours of daily practice for years, to the point where the music becomes the primary language, spoken dialect the second. Many top-level soloists can reflect upon a time in their lives when they gave birth to their improvisational vocabulary by doing literally nothing but practicing, sleeping, and eating over a period of months or years. Charlie Parker told Paul Desmond that he developed his concepts as he practiced eleven to fifteen hours a day over a period of three or four years.

It is in the solitude of the practice room—the "woodshed"—where, for the most inexperienced student and the legendary jazz master alike, the basic elements of form and harmony are ingrained, new melodies or voice-leading pathways are learned, and experiments are made in rhythmic manipulation. In the end, it is this constant state of learning, expanding, and practicing that achieves art and beauty.

Selected Bibliography

Aebersold, Jamey. *The II V7 I Progression: A New Approach to Jazz Improvisation*. New Albany, Ind.: Aebersold, 1974.

Allen, Walter C., and Brian A. L. Rust, revised by Laurie Wright. *King Oliver*. Chigwell, Essex: Storyville Publications, 1987.

Anderson, Gene. "The Genesis of King Oliver's Creole Jazz Band." *American Music* 12 (Fall 1994): 283–303.

Appleby, David P. *The Music of Brazil*. Austin: Univ. of Texas Press, 1983.

Armstrong, Louis. *Satchmo: My Life in New Orleans*. New York: Prentice-Hall, 1954; rpt. New York: Da Capo Press, 1986.

———. *Swing That Music*. New York and London: Longmans-Green, 1936; rpt. New York: Da Capo Press, 1993.

Arom, Simha. *African Polyphony and Polyrhythm: Musical Structure and Methodology*. Trans. from French by Martin Thom, Barbara Tuckett, and Raymond Boyd. Cambridge: Cambridge Univ. Press, 1991.

Badger, Reid. *A Life in Ragtime: A Biography of James Reese Europe*. New York: Oxford Univ. Press, 1995.

Baker, David. *Jazz Improvisation: A Comprehensive Method for All*. Bloomington, Ind.: Frangipani Press, 1983; Alfred Publishing, 1987.

———. *Jazz Styles and Analysis: Trombone—A History of the Jazz Trombone via Recorded Solos*. Chicago: Down Beat Music Workshop Publications, 1973.

———. *J. J. Johnson: Jazz Monograph Series*. New York: Shattinger International Music, 1979.

Baker, Dorothy. *Young Man With a Horn*. Boston: Houghton Mifflin, 1938.

Ballantine, Christopher. *Marabi Nights: Early South African Jazz and Vaudeville*. Johannesburg: Ravan Press, 1993.

Balliett, Whitney. *American Musicians II: Seventy-one Portraits in Jazz*. New York: Oxford Univ. Press, 1996.

———. *American Singers*. New York: Oxford Univ. Press, 1988.

———. *The Sound of Surprise*. New York: Dutton, 1959.

Baraka, Amiri (né LeRoi Jones). *Black Music*. New York: William Morrow, 1967.

———. *Blues People*. New York: William Morrow, 1963.

Basie, Count, and Albert Murray. *Good Morning, Blues: The Autobiography of Count Basie*. New York: Donald I. Fine, 1985.

Batchelor, Christian. *This Thing Called Swing: A Study of Swing Music and the Lindy Hop, the Original Swing Dance*. London: Original Lindy Hop Collection, 1997.

Beale, Charles. *Jazz Piano From Scratch*. London: ABRSM Publishing, 1998.

Bebbington, W., ed. *The Oxford Companion to Australian Music*. Melbourne: Oxford Univ. Press, 1997.

Bebey, Francis. *African Music: A People's Art*. Trans. Josephine Bennett. Brooklyn: Lawrence Hill Books, 1975.

Bechet, Sidney. *Treat It Gentle*. New York: Hill & Wang, 1960.

Bell, Graeme, with discography by Jack Mitchell. *Graeme Bell, Australian Jazzman*. Frenchs Forest, New South Wales: Child, 1988.

Berendt, Joachim E. *Das Jazz Buch*. Frankfurt, Germany: M. Fischer Buchere, 1953; rev. 1959; trans. and rev. 1962, 1982.

Berg, Charles Merrell. "Cinema Sings the Blues." *Cinema Journal* 17, no. 2 (Spring 1978): 1–12.

Berger, Morroe, Edward Berger, and James Patrick. *Benny Carter: A Life in American Music*. Metuchen, N.J.: Scarecrow Press, 1982.

Bergreen, Laurence. *Louis Armstrong: An Extravagant Life*. New York: Broadway Books, 1997.

Berlin, Edward A. *King of Ragtime: Scott Joplin and His Era*. New York: Oxford Univ. Press, 1994.

———. *Ragtime: A Musical and Cultural History*. Berkeley: Univ. of California Press, 1980.

Berliner, Paul F. *Thinking in Jazz: The Infinite Art of Improvisation*. Chicago: Univ. of Chicago Press, 1994.

Berrett, Joshua, ed. *The Louis Armstrong Companion*. New York: Schirmer Books, 1999.

Berton, Ralph. *Remembering Bix: A Memoir of the Jazz Age*. New York: Harper & Row, 1974.

Bethell, Tom. *George Lewis: A Jazzman From New Orleans*. Berkeley: Univ. of California Press, 1977.

Bird, Christiane. *The Jazz and Blues Lover's Guide to the U.S.* New York: Addison-Wesley, 1994.

Bissett, Andrew. *Black Roots, White Flowers: A History of Jazz in Australia*. Australian Broadcasting Corporation, 1979; rev. 1987.

Blades, James. *Percussion Instruments and Their History*. New York: Praeger, 1970.

Blesh, Rudi. *Shining Trumpets: A History of Jazz*. New York: Knopf, 1946.

Blesh, Rudi, and Harriet Janis. *They All Played Ragtime*. New York: Knopf, 1950; 4th ed. (rev.), Oak, 1971.

Bodichon, Barbara Leigh Smith. *An American Diary, 1857–8*. London: Routledge and Kegan Paul, 1972.

Borneman, Ernest. *A Critic Looks at Jazz*. London: Jazz Music Books, 1946.

Bowdich, T. Edward. *Mission From Cape Coast Castle to Ashantee*. 1819; London: Frank Cass, 1966.

Bregman, Robert M., Leonard Bukowski, and Norman Saks. *The Charlie Parker Discography*. Redwood, N.Y.: Cadence, 1993.

Brown, Scott E., and Robert Hilbert. *James P. Johnson: A Case of Mistaken Identity*. Metuchen, N.J.: Scarecrow Press. 1986.

Browning, Barbara. *Samba: Resistance in Motion*. Bloomington: Indiana Univ. Press, 1995.

Brunn, H. O. *The Story of the Original Dixieland Jazz Band*. Baton Rouge: Louisiana State Univ. Press, 1960.

Büchmann-Møller, Frank. *You Just Fight for Your Life/You Got to Be Original, Man*. New York: Praeger, 1990.

Budds, Michael. *Jazz in the Sixties: The Expansion of Musical Resources and Techniques*. Iowa City: Univ. of Iowa Press, 1978.

Buerkle, Jack V., and Danny Barker. *Bourbon Street Black: The New Orleans Black Jazzman*. New York: Oxford Univ. Press, 1973.

Bushell, Garvin. *Jazz From the Beginning*. Ann Arbor: Univ. of Michigan Press, 1988.

Carmichael, Hoagy. *The Stardust Road*. New York: Rinehart, 1946; rpt. New York: Da Capo Press, 1999.

Carr, Ian. *Miles Davis: A Biography*. New York: William Morrow, 1982.

Carr, Ian, Digby Fairweather, and Brian Priestley. *Jazz: The Essential Companion*. Englewood Cliffs, N.J.: Prentice-Hall, 1988.

———. *Jazz: The Rough Guide*. London: Rough Guides, 1995.

Chamberlain, Dorothy, and Robert Wilson, eds. *The Otis Ferguson Reader*. Highland Park, Ill.: December Press, 1982.

Chambers, Jack. *Milestones: The Music and Times of Miles Davis*. New York: William Morrow, 1983, 1985; rpt. New York: Da Capo Press, 1998.

Charters, Samuel B., and Leonard Kunstadt. *Jazz: A History of the New York Scene*. Garden City, N.Y.: Doubleday, 1962; rpt. New York: Da Capo Press, 1981.

Cheatham, Adolphus "Doc." *I Guess I'll Get the Papers and Go Home*. London: Cassell, 1995.

Chernoff, John Miller. *African Rhythm and African Sensibility: Aesthetics and Social Action in African Musical Idioms*. Chicago and London: Univ. of Chicago Press, 1979.

Chilton, John. *Billie's Blues: The Billie Holiday Story, 1933–1959*. New York: Stein & Day, 1975.

———. *Sidney Bechet: The Wizard of Jazz*. London: Macmillan, 1987.

———. *The Song of the Hawk: The Life and Recordings of Coleman Hawkins*. Ann Arbor: University of Michigan Press, 1990.

Clare, John. *Bodgie Dada and the Cult of Cool*. Univ. of New South Wales, 1995.

Clarke, Donald, ed. *The Penguin Encyclopedia of Popular Music*. New York: Viking Press, 1989.

Clayton, Buck, with Nancy Miller Elliott. *Buck Clayton's Jazz World*. New York: Oxford Univ. Press, 1987.

Clear, Rebecca D. *Jazz on Film and Video in the Library of Congress, Motion Picture, Broadcasting and Recorded Sound Division*. 1993.

Coan, Carl. *John Coltrane Solos*. Milwaukee: Hal Leonard, 1995.

Coker, Jerry. *The Teaching of Jazz*. Rottenburg, Germany: Advance Music, 1989.

Collier, James Lincoln. *The Making of Jazz: A Comprehensive History*. Boston: Houghton Mifflin, 1978.

Collins, John. *E. T. Mensah, King of Highlife*. London: Off the Record Press, 1986.

Coltrane, John. *The Music of John Coltrane*. Milwaukee: Hal Leonard, 1991.

Condon, Eddie, and Hank O'Neal. *The Eddie Condon Scrapbook of Jazz*. New York: Galahad Books, 1973.

Condon, Eddie, and Richard Gehman, eds. *Eddie Condon's Treasury of Jazz*. New York: Dial, 1956.

Condon, Eddie, and Thomas Sugrue. *We Called It Music: A Generation of Jazz*. New York: Henry Holt, 1947.

Cook, Richard, and Brian Morton. *The Penguin Guide to Jazz*. New York: Penguin, 1996.

Crowther, Bruce, and Mike Pinfold. *Singing Jazz*. San Francisco: Miller Freeman, 1997.

Dahl, Linda. *Stormy Weather: The Music and Lives of a Century of Jazzwomen*. New York: Proscenium Publishers, 1984.

Dahlhaus, Carl. *Studies on the Origin of Harmonic Tonality*. Trans. Robert O. Gjerdingen. Princeton: Princeton Univ. Press, 1990.

Dance, Stanley. *The World of Duke Ellington*. New York: Charles Scribner's Sons, 1970; rpt. New York: Da Capo Press, 1981.

Dauer, A. M. *Jazz, die magische Musik: Ein Leitfaden durch den Jazz*. Bremen, Germany, 1961.

Davis, Miles, with Quincy Troupe. *Miles: The Autobiography*. New York: Simon & Schuster, 1989.

DeJohnette, Jack, and Charlie Perry. *The Art of Modern Jazz Drumming*. Long Island, N.Y.: Drum Center Publications, 1981.

Delaunay, Charles. *Hot Discography*. Trans. Ian Munro Smyth. Paris: Hot Jazz, 1936.

Demsey, David. *John Coltrane Plays "Giant Steps."* Milwaukee: Hal Leonard, 1997.

DeVeaux, Scott. *The Birth of Bebop: A Social and Musical History*. Berkeley: Univ. of California Press, 1997.

Dodds, Baby, as told to Larry Gara. *The Baby Dodds Story*. Rev. ed. Baton Rouge: Louisiana State Univ. Press, 1992.

Driggs, Frank, and Harris Lewine. *Black Beauty, White Heat: A Pictorial History of Classic Jazz, 1920–1950*. New York: William Morrow, 1982.

Dupuis, Robert. *Bunny Berigan: Elusive Legend of Jazz*. Baton Rouge: Louisiana State Univ. Press, 1993.

Ellington, Duke. *Music Is My Mistress*. Garden City, N.Y.: Doubleday, 1973; rpt. New York: Da Capo Press, 1976.

Ellington, Mercer [Duke] with Stanley Dance. *Duke Ellington in Person: An Intimate Memoir*. Boston: Houghton Mifflin, 1978; rpt. New York: Da Capo Press, 1979.

Ellison, Ralph. "The Golden Age, Time Past." In *Shadow and Act*. New York: Random House, 1964.

Emery, Lynne Fauley. *Black Dance: From 1619 to Today*. Princeton: Princeton Book Company, 1988.

Erenberg, Lewis A. *Swingin' the Dream: Big Band Jazz and the Rebirth of American Culture*. Chicago: Univ. of Chicago Press, 1998.

Erlewine, Michael, Vladimir Bogdanov, Chris Woodstra, Stephen Thomas Erlewine, and Scott Yanow, eds. *All Music Guide to Jazz*. 3d. ed. San Francisco: Miller Freeman, 1998.

Evans, Philip R., and Linda K. Evans. *Bix: The Leon Bix Beiderbecke Story*. Bakersfield, Calif.: Prelike Press, 1998.

Feather, Leonard. *The Book of Jazz From Then Till Now*. New York: Horizon Press, 1957, 1965.

———. *Inside Bebop*. New York: J. J. Robbins, 1949; rpt. 1977 as *Inside Jazz*.

———. *The Jazz Years: Earwitness to an Era*. New York: Da Capo Press, 1987.

Feather, Leonard, and Ira Gitler. *The Biographical Encyclopedia of Jazz*. New York: Oxford Univ. Press, 1999.

Fidelman, Geoffrey Mark. *First Lady of Song, Ella Fitzgerald: for the Record*. Secaucus, N.J.: Birch Lane Press, 1994.

Floyd, Samuel A. Jr. *The Power of Black Music: Interpreting Its History From Africa to the United States*. New York: Oxford Univ. Press, 1995.

Fountain, Charles. *Another Man's Poison: The Life and Writing of Columnist George Frazier*. Chester, Conn.: Globe Pequot Press, 1984.

Fox, Ted. *In the Groove: The People Behind the Music*. New York: St. Martin's Press, 1986.

Francis, A. *Jazz*. Paris rpt. 1958. English tran. by Martin Williams. New York: Grove Press, 1960; New York: Da Capo Press, 1976.

Frank, Rusty E. *Tap!* New York: Da Capo Press, 1994.

Friedwald, Will. *Jazz Singing: America's Great Voices From Bessie Smith to Bebop and Beyond*. New York: Charles Scribner's Sons, 1990.

———. *Sinatra! The Song Is You, a Singer's Art*. New York: Da Capo Press, 1997.

Fujioka, Yasuhiro, with Lewis Porter and Yoh-Ichi Hamada. *John Coltrane: A Discography and Musical Biography*. Lanham, Md.: Scarecrow Press, 1995.

Gabbard, Krin. *Jammin' at the Margins: Jazz and the American Cinema*. Chicago: Univ. of Chicago Press, 1996.

———. *Jazz Among the Discourses*. Durham, N.C.: Duke Univ. Press, 1995.

———, ed. *Representing Jazz*. Durham, N.C.: Duke Univ. Press, 1995.

Giddins, Gary. *Celebrating Bird: The Triumph of Charlie Parker*. New York: William Morrow, 1987.

———. *Satchmo*. Garden City, N.Y.: Doubleday, 1988.

———. *Visions of Jazz: The First Century*. New York: Oxford Univ. Press, 1998.

Gillespie, Dizzy, and Al Fraser. *To Be or Not to Bop: Memoirs by Dizzy Gillespie*. Garden City, N.Y.: Doubleday, 1979; rpt. New York: Da Capo Press, 1985.

Gioia, Ted. *The History of Jazz*. New York: Oxford Univ. Press, 1997.

———. *The Imperfect Art: Reflections on Jazz and Modern Culture*. New York: Oxford Univ. Press, 1988.

———. *West Coast Jazz: Modern Jazz in California*. New York: Oxford Univ. Press, 1992.

Gitler, Ira. *Swing to Bop: An Oral History of the Transition in Jazz in the 1940s*. New York: Oxford Univ. Press, 1985.

Gleason, Ralph J. *Celebrating the Duke and Louis, Bessie, Billie, Bird, Carmen, Miles, Dizzy and Other Heroes*. Boston: Little, Brown, in association with Atlantic Monthly Press, 1975.

Goddard, Chris. *Jazz Away From Home*. New York: Paddington Press, 1979.

Goffin, Robert. *Aux Frontières du Jazz*. Paris: Ed. du Sagittaire, 1932.

Goggin, Jim. *Turk Murphy: Just for the Record*. San Francisco: Traditional Jazz Foundation, 1982.

Goggin, Jim, and Peter Clute. *The Great Jazz Revival*. San Rafael, Calif.: Donna Ewald, 1994.

Goldsmith, Peter. *Making People's Music: Moe Asch and Folkways Records*. Washington, D.C.: Smithsonian Institution Press, 1998.

Gonzáles-Wippler, Migene. *Tales of the Orishas*. New York: Original Publications, 1985.

Gordon, Robert. *Jazz West Coast: The Los Angeles Scene of the 1950s*. London and New York: Quartet Books, 1986.

Gourse, Leslie. *Louis's Children*. New York: Quill, 1984.

————. *Sassy: The Life of Sarah Vaughan*. New York: Charles Scribner's Sons, 1993.

————, ed. *The Ella Fitzgerald Companion: Seven Decades of Commentary*. New York: Schirmer Books, 1998.

Green, Benny. *The Reluctant Art*. New York: Horizon, 1963.

Gridley, Mark C. *Jazz Styles: History and Analysis*. Englewood Cliffs, N.J.: Prentice-Hall, 1978, 1985, 1988, 1991, 1996, 1997, 1999.

Gushee, Lawrence. "The Nineteenth-Century Origins of Jazz." *Black Music Research Journal* 14 (Spring 1994): 1.

————. "A Preliminary Chronology of the Early Career of Ferd 'Jelly Roll' Morton." *American Music* 3 (Winter 1985): 389–412.

Hadlock, Richard. *Jazz Masters of the Twenties*. New York: Macmillan, 1965.

Hajdu, David. *Lush Life: A Biography of Billy Strayhorn*. New York: Farrar, Straus & Giroux, 1996.

Hammond, John, with Irving Townsend. *John Hammond on Record: An Autobiography*. New York: Summit Books, 1977.

Handy, W. C. *Father of the Blues*. 1941; rpt. New York: Da Capo Press, 1991.

Hardy, Phil, and Dave Laing. *The Da Capo Companion to Popular Music*. New York: Da Capo, 1995.

Harrison, Max. *A Jazz Retrospect*. Boston: Crescendo, 1976; rpt. London: Quartet Books, 1991.

Haskins, James. *Black Dance in America*. New York: HarperCollins, 1990.

Hasse, John Edward. *Beyond Category: The Life and Genius of Duke Ellington*. New York: Simon & Schuster, 1993.

————. *Ragtime: Its History, Composers, and Music*. New York: Schirmer, 1985.

Hennessey, Mike. *Klook: The Story of Kenny Clarke*. London: Quartet Books, 1990.

Hennessey, Thomas J. *From Jazz to Swing: African-American Musicians and Their Music, 1890–1935*. Detroit: Wayne State Univ. Press, 1994.

Hentoff, Nat. *The Jazz Life*. 1961; rpt. New York: Da Capo Press, 1978.

Hentoff, Nat, and Albert J. McCarthy, eds. *Jazz: New Perspectives on the History of Jazz by Twelve of the World's Foremost Jazz Critics and Scholars*. New York: Rinehart, 1959.

Herder, Johann Gottfried von. *Auszug aus einem Briefwechsel über Ossian und die Lieder alter Völker* (1773). In *Herders Werke*, 5 vols., 2:193–234. Berlin and Weimar: Aufbau-Verlag, 1969.

Hitchcock, Wiley H., and Stanley Sadie, eds. *The New Grove Dictionary of American Music*. London: Macmillan, 1986.

Hobson, Wilder. *American Jazz Music*. New York: Norton, 1939; revised 1941.

Hodeir, André. *Jazz: Its Evolution and Essence*. Rev. ed. Trans. David Noakes. New York: Grove Press, 1956, 1979.

————. *The Worlds of Jazz*. New York: Grove Press, 1972.

Holiday, Billie, with William Dufty. *Lady Sings the Blues*. New York: Doubleday, 1956.

Holtje, Steve, and Nancy Ann Lee, eds. *MusicHound Jazz: The Essential Album Guide*. Detroit: Visible Ink, 1998.

James, Burnett. *Billie Holiday*. Spellmount, N.Y.: Hippocrene Books, 1984.

————. *Bix Beiderbecke*. London: Cassell, 1959.

Jasen, David A., and Trebor Tichenor. *Rags and Ragtime*. New York: Seabury, 1978.

Jepsen, Jorgen Grunnet, and Karl Emil Knudsen, eds. *Jazz Records: 1942–1962*. Holte, Denmark: Knudson, 1964.

Johnson, Bruce. *The Oxford Companion to Australian Jazz*. Melbourne: Oxford Univ. Press, 1987.

Jones, A. M. *Studies in African Music*. 2 vols. London: Oxford Univ. Press, 1959.

Jones, Cliff. *J. C. Higginbotham*. London: Discographical Society, 1944.

Jones, Max, and John Chilton. *Louis: The Louis Armstrong Story*. Boston and Toronto: Little, Brown, 1971; rpt. New York: Da Capo Press, 1994.

Jost, Ekkehard. *Europas Jazz, 1960–1980*. Frankfurt, Germany, 1987.

———. *Free Jazz*. New York: Da Capo Press, 1994.

Kebede, Ashenafi. *Roots of Black Music*. Englewood Cliffs, N.J.: Prentice-Hall, 1982.

Keepnews, Orrin, and Bill Grauer Jr. *A Pictorial History of Jazz: People and Places From New Orleans to Modern Jazz*. New York: Crown Publishers, 1956.

Kenney, William Howard. *Chicago Jazz: A Cultural History, 1904–1930*. New York: Oxford Univ. Press, 1993.

Kernfeld, Barry, ed. *The New Grove Dictionary of Jazz*. New York: Grove, 1988.

Kinzer, Charles E. "The Tios of New Orleans and Their Pedagogical Influence on the Early Jazz Clarinet Style." *Black Music Research Journal* 16, no. 2 (Fall 1996).

Kirchner, Bill, ed. *A Miles Davis Reader*. Washington, D.C.: Smithsonian Institution Press, 1997.

Koch, Lawrence O. *Yardbird Suite: A Compendium of the Music and Life of Charlie Parker*. Bowling Green, Ohio: Bowling Green Univ. Popular Press, 1988.

Korall, Burt. *Drummin' Men*. New York: Schirmer Books, 1990.

Lange, Horst Heinz. *Jazz in Deutschland: Die Deutsche Jazz-Chronik, 1900–1960*. Berlin, 1966.

Lees, Gene. *Singers and the Song II*. New York: Oxford Univ. Press, 1998.

Liebman, Dave. *Self-Portrait of a Jazz Artist: Musical Thoughts and Realities*. Rottenburg, Germany: Advance Music, 1988.

Lindemeyer, Paul. *Celebrating the Saxophone*. New York: Hearst Books, 1996.

Litchfield, Jack. *The Canadian Jazz Discography, 1916–1980*. Toronto: Univ. of Toronto Press, 1982.

Litweiler, John. *The Freedom Principle: Jazz After 1958*. New York: William Morrow, 1984.

———. *Ornette Coleman: A Harmolodic Life*. New York: Da Capo Press, 1994.

Lock, Graham. *Forces in Motion: Anthony Braxton and the Meta-Reality of Creative Music, Interviews and Tour Notes*. London: Quartet Books, 1985.

Lomax, Alan. *Mister Jelly Roll: The Fortunes of Jelly Roll Morton, New Orleans Creole and "Inventor of Jazz."* New York: Pantheon Books, 1950; 3d ed., Berkeley: Univ. of California Press, 1993.

Lyttelton, Humphrey. *I Play as I Please*. London: MacGibbon & Kee, 1954.

———. *Second Chorus*. London: MacGibbon & Kee, 1959.

McCarthy, Albert. *Big Band Jazz*. London: Barrie & Jenkins, 1974.

———. *The Dance Band Era: The Dancing Decades from Ragtime to Swing, 1910–1950*. London: Spring Books, 1971.

McGowan, Chris, and Ricardo Pessanha. *The Brazilian Sound*. New ed. Philadelphia: Temple Univ. Press, 1998.

McGregor, Maxine. *Chris McGregor and the Brotherhood of Breath: My Life With a South African Jazz Pioneer*. Flint, Mich.: Bamberger Books, 1995.

Machlin, Paul S. *Stride: The Music of Fats Waller*. Boston: Twayne, 1985.

Marquis, Donald. *In Search of Buddy Bolden*. New York: Da Capo Press, 1978.

Martin, Henry. *Charlie Parker and Thematic Improvisation*. Lanham, Md.: Scarecrow Press, 1996.

———. *Enjoying Jazz*. New York: Schirmer Books, 1986.

Meeker, David. *Jazz in the Movies: A Guide to Jazz Musicians, 1917–1977*. New Rochelle, N.Y.: Arlington House, 1977.

Melly, George. *Owning-Up*. London: Weidenfeld & Nicolson, 1965.

Mezzrow, Mezz, and Bernard Wolfe. *Really the Blues*. New York: Random House, 1946.

Miller, Marc H., ed. *Louis Armstrong: A Cultural Legacy*. Seattle: Univ. of Washington Press, 1994.

Miller, Mark. *Boogie Pete and the Senator—Canadian Musicians in Jazz: The Eighties*. Toronto: Nightwood Editions, 1987.

———. *Jazz in Canada: Fourteen Lives*. Toronto: Univ. of Toronto Press, 1982.

———. *Such Melodious Racket: The Lost History of Jazz in Canada*. Toronto: Mercury Press, 1997.

———. jazz ed.; *Encyclopedia of Music in Canada*. Ed. H. Kallman, G. Potvin, and K. Winters. Toronto: Univ. of Toronto Press, 1992.

Miller, Nonna, and Evette Jensen. *Swingin' at the Savoy: The Memoir of a Jazz Dancer*. Philadelphia: Temple Univ. Press, 1996.

Mitchell, Jack. *Australian Jazz on Record 1925–1980*. Canberra: AGPS Press, 1988.

Monson, Ingrid. *Saying Something: Jazz Improvisation and Interaction*. Chicago and London: Univ. of Chicago Press, 1996.

Morgenstern, Dan. *Jazz People*. New York: Harry N. Abrams, 1976.

Morris, Roland L. *Wait Until Dark: Jazz and the Underworld, 1880–1940*. Bowling Green, Ohio: Bowling Green Univ. Popular Press, 1980.

Murray, Albert. *The Hero and the Blues*. Columbia: Univ. of Missouri Press, 1973.

————. *Stompin' the Blues*. New York: McGraw-Hill, 1976.

Nabe, Marc-Edouard. *L'âme de Billie Holiday*. Paris: Editions Denoel, 1986.

Newberger, Eli H. "Archetypes and Antecedents of Piano Blues and Boogie Woogie Style." *Journal of Jazz Studies* 4, no. 1. (Fall 1976): 84–109.

————. "The Development of New Orleans and Stride Piano Styles." *Journal of Jazz Studies* 4, no. 2, (Spring–Summer 1977): 43–71.

————. "Refinement of Melody and Accompaniment in the Evolution of Swing Piano Style." *Annual Review of Jazz Studies* 1 (1982): 85–109.

————. "The Transition From Ragtime to Improvised Piano Style." *Journal of Jazz Studies* 3, no. 2 (Spring 1976): 3–18.

Newton, Francis. *The Jazz Scene*. London: MacGibbon & Kee, 1959.

Nicholson, Stuart. *Billie Holiday*. Boston: Northeastern Univ. Press, 1995.

————. *Ella Fitzgerald: A Biography of the First Lady of Jazz*. New York: Macmillan, 1993.

Nisenson, Eric. *'Round About Midnight: A Portrait of Miles Davis*. New York: Dial Press, 1982; rpt. New York: Da Capo Press, 1996.

Nketia, J. H. Kwabena. *Drumming in Akan Communities*. New York: Thomas Nelson & Sons, 1963.

————. *The Music of Africa*. New York: Norton, 1974.

Oliver, Paul. *Savannah Syncopators: African Retentions in the Blues*. New York: Stein & Day, 1970.

O'Meally, Robert, with Linda Lipnack Kuehl. *Lady Day: The Many Faces of Billie Holiday*. New York: Arcade, 1991.

Osgood, Henry O. *So This Is Jazz*. Boston: Little, Brown, 1926.

Owens, Thomas. *Bebop: The Music and the Players*. New York: Oxford Univ. Press, 1995.

Panassié, Hugues. *Hot Jazz*. Trans. Lyle Dowling and Eleanor Dowling. New York: M. Witmark & Sons, 1936.

————. *The Real Jazz*. New York: Smith & Durrell, 1942.

Patrick, James. "Al Tinney, Monroe's Uptown House, and the Emergence of Modern Jazz in Harlem." *Annual Review of Jazz Studies* 2 (1983): 150–79.

Pearson, Nathan W., Jr. *Goin' to Kansas City*. Chicago: Univ. of Illinois Press, 1987.

Peretti, Burton W. *The Creation of Jazz: Music, Race, and Culture in Urban America*. Urbana and Chicago: Univ. of Illinois Press, 1992.

Perrone, Charles. *Masters of Contemporary Brazilian Song: MPB, 1965–1985*. Austin: Univ. of Texas Press, 1989.

Peterson, Bernard L., Jr. *A Century of Musicals in Black and White*. Westport, Conn.: Greenwood Press, 1993.

Placksin, Sally. *American Women in Jazz, 1900 to the Present: Their Words, Lives, and Music*. New York: Wideview Books, 1982.

Pleasants, Henry. *Death of a Music? The Decline of the European Tradition and the Rise of Jazz*. London: Victor Gollancz, 1961.

————. *The Great American Popular Singers*. New York: Simon & Schuster, 1974.

————. *Serious Music and All That Jazz! An Adventure in Music Criticism*. New York: Simon & Schuster, 1969.

Poggioli, Renato. *The Theory of the Avant-Garde*. Cambridge, Mass.: Belknap Press of Harvard Univ. Press, 1968.

Porter, Lewis. *John Coltrane: His Life and Music*. Ann Arbor: Univ. of Michigan Press, 1998.

————. *A Lester Young Reader*. Washington, D.C.: Smithsonian Institution Press, 1991.

Porter, Lewis, Michael Ullman, and Edward Hazell. *Jazz From Its Origins to the Present*. Englewood Cliffs, N.J.: Prentice-Hall, 1993.

Priestley, Brian. *Jazz on Record: A History*. New York: Billboard Books, 1991.

Raich, S. *Criticisms of Jazz: Fundamental Standards of Art Criticism*. Barcelona: Casa Provincial de Caridad, 1958.

Ramsey, Frederic, Jr., and Charles Edward Smith, eds. *Jazzmen: The Story of Hot Jazz Told in the Lives of the Men Who Created It*. New York: Harcourt, Brace, 1939, 1977.

Read, Oliver, and Walter L. Welch. *From Tinfoil to Stereo*. Indianapolis: H. W. Sams, 1976.

Reig, Teddy, with Edward Berger. *Reminiscing in Tempo: The Life and Times of a Jazz Hustler*. Metuchen, N.J.: Scarecrow Press, 1990.

Riis, Thomas. *Just Before Jazz*. Washington, D.C.: Smithsonian Institution Press, 1989.

Riley, John. *The Art of Bop Drumming*. New York: Manhattan Music, 1994.

———. *Beyond Bop and Drumming*. New York: Manhattan Music, 1997.

Roberts, John Storm. *Black Music of Two Worlds*. New York: William Morrow, 1974.

———. *The Latin Tinge: The Impact of Latin American Music on the United States*. New York: Oxford Uiv.n Press, 1979.

Rose, Al, and Edmond Souchon. *New Orleans Jazz: A Family Album*. Baton Rouge: Louisiana State Univ. Press, 1984.

Rosenthal, David H. *Hard Bop: Jazz and Black Music, 1955–1965*. New York: Oxford Univ. Press, 1992.

Russell, Bill, Barry Martyn, and Mike Hazeldine, eds. *New Orleans Style*. New Orleans: Jazzology Press, 1994.

Russell, Ross. *Jazz Style in Kansas City and the Southwest*. Berkeley: Univ. of California Press, 1971.

Russo, William. *Composing for the Jazz Orchestra*. Chicago: Univ. of Chicago Press, 1961.

Rust, Brian. *Jazz Records, 1897–1942*. 4th ed. New Rochelle, N.Y.: Arlington House, 1978.

Sanjek, Russell. *Pennies From Heaven: The American Popular Music Business in the Twentieth Century*. Updated by David Sanjek. New York: Da Capo Press, 1996.

Santoro, Gene. "La Cucaracha: A Survey of Cuban Music." In *Stir It Up*. New York: Oxford Univ. Press, 1997.

Sargeant, Winthrop. *Jazz, Hot and Hybrid*. New York: Dutton, 1938, 1946; rpt. New York: Da Capo Press, 1975.

Schafer, William J. *Brass Bands and New Orleans Jazz*. Baton Rouge: Louisiana State Univ. Press, 1977.

Schafer, William J., and Johannes Riedel. *The Art of Ragtime: Form and Meaning of an Original Black American Art*. Baton Rouge: Louisiana State Univ. Press, 1973.

Schreiner, Claus. *Musica Brasileira*. New York and London: Marion Boyars, 1993.

Schuller, Gunther. *Early Jazz: Its Roots and Musical Development*. New York: Oxford Univ. Press, 1968.

———. *The Swing Era: The Development of Jazz, 1930–1945*. New York: Oxford Univ. Press, 1989.

Self, Len, and Gus Kuhlman. *Lee Wiley: A Bio-Discography*. Brunswick, N.J.: Self-published, 1997.

Shapiro, Nat, and Nat Hentoff, eds. *Hear Me Talkin' to Ya: The Story of Jazz by the Men Who Made It*. New York: Rinehart, 1955; Dover, 1966.

———. *The Jazz Makers*. New York: Grove Press, 1957.

Shaw, Arnold. *The Street That Never Slept: New York's Fabled 52nd Street*. New York: Coward, McCann & Geoghegan, 1971.

Shipton, Alyn. *Fats Waller: His Life and Times*. New York: Universe Books, 1988.

Simon, George T. *The Big Bands*. 4th ed. New York: Schirmer Books, 1987.

———. *Simon Says: The Sights and Sounds of the Swing Era. 1935–1955*. New Rochelle, N.Y.: Arlington House, 1971.

Small, Christopher. *Music of the Common Tongue: Survival and Celebration in AfroAmerican Music*. London: Calder and New York: Riverrun Press, 1987.

Smith, Willie "the Lion." *Music on My Mind*. New York: Doubleday, 1964.

Southern, Eileen. *The Music of Black Americans: A History*. 3d. ed. New York: Norton, 1997.

Spellman, A. B. *Black Music: Four Lives*. New York: Shocken Books, 1970.

Stapleton, Chris, and Chris May. *African All-Stars: The Pop Music of a Continent*. London: Quartet Books, 1987.

Stearns, Marshall. *The Story of Jazz*. New York: Oxford Univ. Press, 1956.

Stearns, Marshall, and Jean Stearns. *Jazz Dance*. New York: Macmillan, 1968.

Steinel, Mike. *Building a Jazz Vocabulary: A Resource for Learning Jazz Improvisation*. Milwaukee: Hal Leonard, 1995.

Stewart, Milton L. "Earl Hines's 'Trumpet' Piano Style: The Influence of Louis Armstrong." *Annual Review of Jazz Studies* 4 (1988): 189–95.

Stewart, Rex. *Boy Meets Horn*. Ed. Claire P. Gordon. Ann Arbor: Univ. of Michigan Press, 1991.

———. *Jazz Masters of the Thirties*. New York: Macmillan, 1972; rpt. New York: Da Capo Press, 1982.

Stoddard, Tom. *The Autobiography of Pops Foster, New Orleans Jazzman*. Berkeley: Univ. of California Press, 1971.

Stowe, David W. *Swing Changes: Big Band Jazz in New Deal America*. Cambridge, Mass.: Harvard Univ. Press, 1994.

Stratemann, Klaus. *Duke Ellington Day by Day and Film by Film*. Copenhagen: JazzMedia Aps, 1992.

———. *Louis Armstrong on the Screen*. Copenhagen: JazzMedia Aps, 1996.

Stroman, Scott, and Richard Michael. *Creative Jazz Education*. London: Stainer & Bell, 1990.

Stuckey, Sterling. *Slave Culture: Nationalist Theory and the Foundations of Black America*. New York: Oxford Univ. Press, 1987.

Studies in Jazz Discography. New Brunswick, N.J.: Institute of Jazz Studies, Univ. Extension Division, Rutgers Univ., 1971.

Sudhalter, Richard M. *Lost Chords: White Musicians and Their Contribution to Jazz, 1915–1945*. New York: Oxford Univ. Press, 1999.

Sudhalter, Richard M., with Philip R. Evans and William Dean-Myatt. *Bix: Man and Legend*. New Rochelle, N.Y.: Arlington House, 1974.

Taylor, Billy. *Jazz Piano: History and Development*. Dubuque, Iowa: Wm. C. Brown, 1982.

Tesser, Neil. *The Playboy Guide to Jazz*. New York: Plume, 1998.

Timner, W. E. *Ellingtonia: The Recorded Music of Duke Ellington and His Sidemen*. 4th ed. Lanham, Md.: Scarecrow Press, 1996.

Tirro, Frank. *Jazz: A History*. New York: Norton, 1977.

Toledano, Ralph de. *Frontiers of Jazz*. New York: Durrell, 1947.

Tormé, Mel. *My Singing Teachers*. New York: Oxford Univ. Press, 1994.

Tucker, Mark. *The Duke Ellington Reader*. New York: Oxford Univ. Press, 1993.

———. *Ellington: The Early Years*. Urbana and Chicago: Univ. of Illinois Press, 1991.

Tyrmand, L. *On the Side of Jazz*. Kraków, Poland, 1957.

Ulanov, Barry. *Duke Ellington*. New York: Creative Age Press, 1946; rpt. New York: Da Capo Press, 1975.

———. *A History of Jazz in America*. New York: Viking Press, 1952.

Vail, Ken. *Bird's Diary: The Life of Charlie Parker, 1945–1955*. Chessington, Surrey: Castle Communications, 1996.

———. *Lady Day's Diary: The Life of Billie Holiday, 1937–1959*. Chessington, Surrey: Castle Communications, 1996.

Varnedde, Kirk, and Adam Gopnik. *High and Low: Modern Art, Popular Culture*. New York: Museum of Modern Art, 1990.

Walker, Leo. *The Big Band Almanac*. New York: Da Capo Press, 1989.

Wareing, Charles, and George Garlick. *Bugles for Beiderbecke*. London: Sidgwick & Jackson, 1958.

Washburne, Christopher. "The Clave of Jazz: A Caribbean Contribution to the Rhythmic Foundation of an African-American Music." *Black Music Research Journal* 17, no. 1 (Spring 1997).

Waters, Howard J., Jr. *Jack Teagarden's Music: His Career and Recordings*. Stanhope, N.J.: W. C. Allen, 1960.

Weinstein, Norman C. *A Night in Tunisia: Imaginings of Africa In Jazz*. New York: Limelight Editions, 1994.

Wilber, Bob. *Music Was Not Enough*. New York: Oxford Univ. Press, 1988.

Wildman, Joan M. "The Function of the Left Hand in the Evolution of Jazz Piano." *Journal of Jazz Studies* 5, no. 2 (Spring-Summer 1979): 23–59.

Williams, Martin. *The Art of Jazz: Essays in the Nature and Development of Jazz*. New York: Oxford Univ. Press, 1959.

———. *Jazz Changes*. New York: Oxford Univ. Press, 1992.

———. *Jazz Heritage*. New York: Oxford Univ. Press, 1985.

———. *Jazz Masters of New Orleans*. New York: Macmillan, 1967.

———. *Jazz Panorama: From the Pages of Jazz Review*. New York: Crowell-Collier, 1962; rpt. New York: Da Capo Press, 1979.

———. *The Jazz Tradition*. New and rev. ed. New York: Oxford Univ. Press, 1983.

Wilson, John S. *Jazz: The Transition Years, 1940–1960*. New York: Appleton-Century-Crofts, 1966.

Wilson, Richard Guy, Dianne H. Pilgrim, and Dickran Tashjian. *The Machine Age in America, 1918–1941*. New York: Harry N. Abrams, 1986.

Woideck, Carl. *Charlie Parker: His Music and Life*. Ann Arbor: Univ. of Michigan Press, 1996.

———. *The Charlie Parker Companion: Six Decades of Commentary*. New York: Schirmer Books, 1998.

———. *The John Coltrane Companion: Five Decades of Commentary*. New York: Schirmer Books, 1998.

World Music: The Rough Guide. London: Rough Guides, 1994.

Yurochko, Bob. *A Short History of Jazz*. Chicago: Nelson/Hall Publishers, 1993.

Zahan, Dominique. *The Religion, Spirituality, and Thought of Traditional Africa*. Trans. of *Religion, spiritualité, et pensée africaines*. Chicago: Univ. of Chicago Press, 1979.

Index of Names and Subjects

Baraka, Amiri, 527, 741, 743–44, 750

Barbarin, Paul (1899–1969), 93, 156, 271

Barber, Bill (John William) (b. 1920), 661

Barber, Chris (b. 1930), 5, 313

Barbieri, Gato (b. 1934), 530, 531, 547, 717–18, 720

Barbour, Dave (1912–1965), 229, 231

Barefield, Eddie (1909–1991), 273

Bargeron, Dave (b. 1942), 661, 662

Bargy, Roy, 31, 126, 130

Barker, Danny (1909–1994), 83, 660

Barlow, Dale (b. 1959), 582

Barnaby label, 783

Barnard, Bob, 315, 580

Barnard, Len, 580

Barnes, George (1921–1977), 646

Barnes, Harper, 742

Barnes, Peter, 397

Barnet, Charlie (1913–1991), 285, 289–90, 403, 409, 411, 412, 415, 520, 691, 711, 712

Baron, Art, 640

Baron, Joey (b. 1955), 694

Barons of Rhythm, 70

Barque, Chico, 556

Barrett, Dan (b. 1955), 513

Barretto, Ray (b. 1929), 530, 657, 658

Barris, Harry, 161

Barron, Kenny (b. 1943), 472, 761

Barroso, Ary, 553, 554

Bartók, Béla, 281, 317, 346, 405, 451

Barton, James, 700

Bartz, Gary (b. 1940), 400

Basie, William "Count" (1904–1984), 61, 70–71, 139, 145, 170–71, 193, 196, 197, 198, 201, 212, 214, 217, 229, 233, 247, 251, 258, 259, 273, 282, 284–85, 289, 290, 360, 365, 370, 375, 384, 403, 405, 409–10, 412, 414, 415, 462, 475, 480, 482, 484, 516, 518, 521, 530, 570, 602, 605, 608, 619, 623, 624, 634, 639, 643, 645, 655, 656, 672, 680, 685, 687, 688, 689, 705, 712, 719, 727, 728, 730, 731, 733, 749, 776–77, 793. *See also specific musician or recording*

"Basing," 14

Bass, 293, 384, 661, 662, **668–80**, 674, 777. *See also specific musician*

Bassoon, 664–65

Batiste, Alvin (b. 1932), 595, 596

Battle, Edgar (1907–1977), 282

Battles, jazz. *See* Cutting contests; Duels; Jam sessions

Batucada (percussion instruments), 553

Bauduc, Ray (1906–1988), 667

Bauer, Billy (b. 1915), 450, 571, 647

Bauza, Mario (1911–1993), 526–27, 528, 530, 657

Bayersdorffer, Johnny, 587

Bayes, Nora, 223

BBC Orchestra, 537

BBC radio/television, 517, 537

"Beach music," 704

Beale Street Folic Orchestra (Williamson band), 772

Beatles, 120, 140, 289, 313, 341, 414, 483, 489, 502, 503, 509, 556

Beat movement, 743–44

Beatty, Warren, 717

Beaudet, Jean, 577

Bebey, Francis, 9, 11, 12

Bebop: and arranging and composing for big bands, 284; and Australian jazz, 581; and avant-garde music, 449; and big bands after World War II, 403; and blues, 300; as central to development of modern jazz, 794; characteristics of, 293; as "commercial" entertainment, 301–2; and cool jazz, 336, 340; and dance, 703–4; emergence of, 22–23, 176, **292–305**, 351, 362; and films and TV, 715; first use of term, 292; and improvisation, 293, 303, 794; influence and dominance of, 418; initial reactions to, 316–17; and instruments, 217, 293, 592, 593, 596, 604, 608, 610, 620, 637, 638, 645, 650–51, 662, 664, 665, 672, 675–76, 688, 691; and jam sessions, 293, 295–97, 299, 300, 302, 303, 304, 567, 646; and Japanese jazz, 566; and JATP, 219; and jazz clubs, 726, 727, 728, 732; and jazz criticism, 754; and jazz education, 760; and jazz in Europe, 538; and jazz since 1968, 493, 496; and jazz singing, 228, 234, 475–76, 478–79, 481, 484; and Latin music, 526, 527–28; and New Orleans revival, 310, 315; in New York City, 75; and nightclubs, 302; and pianists, 173, 363, 370; popularity of, 228, 642; and race, 298–99, 301–3; and radio, 302; and recording industry, 299, 302–3, 304, 780, 781; revival of, 496; and rhythm, 293; and rhythm-and-blues, 75; role models for, 216; and roots of jazz, 22–23; and small-group jazz, 298–99, 303; and soloists, 216, 217, 293, 303; songs as precursors of, 250; standardizing, **379–81**; and swing, 293, 295, 296; traditionalists' feud with, 117. *See also specific musician or band/ orchestra*

Bechet, Sidney (1897–1959), 20, 24, 25, 47, 67–68, 88, 89–90, 91, 92, 93–94, 96–97, 99–101, 106, 109, 110, 115, 151, 155, 210, 258, 309, 311, 312, 313, 343, 346, 512, 537, 538, 585, 586–87, 588, 589, 590, 593, 596, 600–601, 602, 608, 609, 615, 616, 617, 684, 689, 725, 726, 730, 767, 770, 777–78, 781, 617. *See also specific recording*

Beckett, Fred (1917–1946), 638

Beckett, Harry, 543

Beck, Gordon (b. 1936), 543

Bee, David, 283

Bee Hive Club (Chicago), 730

Beeks, Clarence. *See* Pleasure, King

Beethoven, Ludwig von, 17, 28, 317, 704, 789, 794

Beggar's Holiday (musical), 144

Begone Dull Care (film), 711

The Beiderbecke Affair (TV film), 131

The Beiderbecke Connection (TV film), 131

Beiderbecke, (Leon) Bix (1903–1931), 22, 105, **122–31**, 151, 153, 156, 157, 158, 161–62, 175, 193, 199, 209, 210, 232, 233, 251, 256–57, 305, 307, 310, 333, 345, 346, 351, 481, 515, 516, 517, 604, 617, 618, 622, 669, 713, 734–35, 737, 750, 770, 771. *See also specific person or recording*

The Beiderbecke Tapes (TV film), 131

Béla Fleck and the Flecktones, 511

Belden, Bob (b. 1956), 389, 417

Bel Geddes, Norman, 212

Belgium: Armstrong in, 115, 116

Belgrave, Marcus (b. 1936), 381

Bell, Aaron (b. 1922), 678

Bell band, 582

Belle of the Nineties (film), 710

Bell, Graeme (b. 1914), 309, 311, 580

Bell, Roger, 309, 580

Bells (instrument), 10, 12

Bellson, Louis (b. 1924), 417, 691, 694

Belmont Theater (New York City), 85–86

Benbow, William, 93

Benbrow, Warren, 511

Benedek, Laslo, 716

Benedetti, Dean, 327

Beneke, Gordon "Tex" (1914–2000), 289, 691

Benford, Tommy (1905–1994), 184, 776

Benjamin, Joe (1919–1974), 243–44, 678

Benjamin, Rick, 265

Bennett, Tony (b. 1926), 261, 475, 483–84

Bennink, Han (b. 1942), 542, 546, 695

The Benny Goodman Story (film), 712

Benson, George (b. 1943), 509, 648

Benson Orchestra (Chicago), 157

Berendt, Joachim E., 572, 748

Berg, Billy, 302, 732

Berger, David (b. 1949), 515, 518, 519

Berger, Karl (b. 1935), 652

Berger, Kenny, 177

Bonfa, Luiz, 548, 554, 555, 556, 717
Bongos, 658
Boogie Doodle (film), 711
Boogie-woogie, 71–72, 169–70, 173, 174, 175, 362, 577, 778
Booker, James, 529
Booking agencies, 272
Borneman, Ernest, 755
Bossa nova, 132, 140, 341, 485, 522, 548–49, **554–56**, 558, 658, 785. *See also specific musician or band/ orchestra*
Bostic, Earl (1913–1965), 435
Boston, Massachusetts: dance catastrophe in, 700; part- time bands in, 414
Boston Pops Orchestra, 37
Boston University: collections at, 520
Boswell, Connee (Connie) (1907– 1976), 224–25, 233, 239
Boswell, Martha, 224
Boswell, Vet, 224
Boswell Sisters, 220–21, 224–25, 481, 563
Boulanger, Nadia, 535, 538, 547
Boulez, Pierre, 348
Bowdich, T. Edward, 9
Bowie, Lester (1941–1999), 494, 497, 562, 624, 661
Boyd, Herb, 750
Boyd, Nelson (1928-d?), 675, 676
Boyer, Richard O., 138
Boyette, Lippy, 61
Boy-next-door legend, 253
Brackeen, Joanne (b. 1938), 556
Braddock Hotel (New York City), 241
Bradford, Perry "Mule" (1895– 1970), 78, 769
Bradley, Buddy, 700
Bradley, Will (1912–1989): 637, 638
Braff, Ruby (b. 1927), 121, 624
Brahem, Anouar, 546
Brancusi, Constantin, 212
Brandâo, Sergio, 558
Brandeis University Festival of the Arts, 354
Brando, Marlon, 527, 716
Brand X (Jones-Goodsall band), 508
Brass bands, 23, 24, 25, 27, 48, 51– 52, 268, 525, 537, 585- 86, 615, 629, 661–62, 683
Brass Fantasy (Bowie band), 624
Brass instruments/players, 69, 75, 102. *See also specific musician or instrument*
Braud, Wellman (1891–1966), 99, 307, 672–73, 674
Brave New World (Holzman band), 510
Braxton, Anthony (b. 1945), 457, 494, 495, 577, 595, 596, 601, 640, 754, 786
Brazil, 493, 522, 529, **548–58**, 621, 649, 655, 658
Breau, Lenny (1941–1984), 577
Brecker, Michael (b. 1949), 463, 507, 509, 510, 602, 611, 796

Brecker, Randy (b. 1945), 463, 507, 510, 625
Brecker Brothers band, 507, 625
Breuker, Willem (b. 1944), 417, 542
Brick House (New Orleans), 103
Bricktop's (Paris), 733
Bridges, Beau, 714
Bridges Go Round (film), 711
Bridges, Jeff, 714
Bridgewater, Dee Dee (b. 1950), 486
Briggs, Arthur, 537
Briggs, Bunny, 140
Brignola, Nick (b. 1936), 608
Broadbent, Alan (b. 1947), 416
Broadway. *See* Musical theater; *specific musical*
Brodsky, Irving, 269
Brofsky, Alex, 664
Brokensha, Jack (b. 1926), 581
Brom, Gustav, 417
Brönner, Till, 626
Bronson, Eddie, 581
Brookmeyer, Bob (b. 1929), 337, 356, 413, 414, 416, 518, 640, 676
Brooks, Garth, 263
Brooks, Russell, 61
Brooks, Tina (1932–1974), 386, 387
Brothels/bordellos, 42, 48, 88, 246
Brotherhood of Breath (McGregor band), 562
Brothers, Thomas, 15–16
Brötzmann, Peter (b. 1941), 649
Brown, Charles, 74
Brown, Cleo (1909–1995), 232
Brown, Clifford (1930–1956), 244, 376, 377–79, 381, 382, 386, 388, 475, 479, 621, 623, 730,
Brown, James, 76, 383, 506
Brown, Jeri, 482
Brown, Lawrence (1907–1988), 137, 138, 139, 213, 633, 635, 636–37
Brown, Les (b. 1912), 520, 687
Brown, Marion (b. 1935), 444
Brown, Oscar, Jr. (b. 1926), 719
Brown, Pete (1906–1963), 217
Brown, Piney, 731
Brown, Ray (b. 1926), 240, 257, 407, 426, 462, 463, 569, 662, 673, 675, 676, 677, 680
Brown, Ray Jr., 240
Brown, Ruth (b. 1928), 529
Brown, Steve (1890–1965), 128, 151, 159, 273, 275
Brown, Tom, 43, 267, 767
Brown, Walter, 72
Brubeck, Dave (b. 1920), 120, 140, 251, 262, 337, 338–39, 340, 353, 355, 365, 366–67, 428, 463, 580, 581, 694, 782, 796
Bruce & Bruce Stock Company, 91
Bruford, Bill, 508
Brunis, George (1902–1974), 151, 210, 308, 310, 629, 631
Bruns, Ralph, 607
Brunswick Records, 772, 774. *See also specific artist or recording*
Brussels, Belgium: Goodman in, 591
Bruyninckx, Walter, 752

Bryant, Ray (b. 1931), 369, 433, 462
Bryant, Rusty (1929–1991), 483
Brymn, Tim, 537
Bryson, Jeanie (b. 1958), 486
Bubbles, John, 700
Buchanan, Elwood, 391
Buckethead (guitarist), 510
Buckner, Milt (1915–1977), 75, 361
Budapest String Quartet, 346
Buddle, Errol (b. 1928), 581, 665
Budds, Michael, 754
Buescher Company, 600, 601
Bufalino, Brenda, 704
Bugalu, 531
Bunch, John (b. 1921), 371
Bunnett, Jane (b. 1956), 578, 609
Bunn, Teddy (1909–1978), 643
Bunny hug, 35, 58
Burdett, Lou, 581
Burgess, Bob, 637
Burke, Raymond (1904–1986), 314
Burleigh, Harry T., 740
Burnham, Charles, 511
Burns, Ralph (b. 1922), 228, 251, 258, 285, 290, 351, 352, 405, 412
Burrell, Dave (b. 1940), 470
Burrell, Kenny (b. 1931), 146, 381, 393, 647, 658
Burr, Henry, 109
Burrows, Don (B. 1928), 581
Burton, Gary (b. 1943), 355–56, 468, 503, 509, 547, 648, 651–52
Busch, Lou, 513
Bushell, Garvin (1902–1991), 61, 313
Bushkin, Joe (b. 1916), 228, 359, 727
Butler, Billy (1924–1991), 75
Butler, Frank (1928–1984), 382, 695
Butterfield, Billy (1917–1988), 28, 287, 314
Butterfield, Don (b. 1923), 661
Byard, Jaki (1922–1999), 372, 430, 459, 471
Byas, Don (1912–1972), 71, 187, 203, 216, 284, 299, 422, 541, 542, 604, 607, 733, 779
Byers, Billy (1927–1996), 410, 412, 414
Byrd, Charlie (1925–1999), 555, 646, 785
Byrd, Donald (b. 1932), 379, 381, 428, 466, 623, 692
Byrds, 505
Byron, Don (b. 1958), 501, 595, 596

Cabaret cards, 248, 323
Cabarets, 261–62, 722. *See also specific cabaret*
Cabin in the Sky (film), 712
Caceres, Ernie (1911–1971), 289
Cadence Records, 783
Cadillac Café (Los Angeles), 732
Cadillac Club (New Orleans), 725
Café Au Go Go (New York City), 503
Cafe (Brazilian percussionist), 658
Café Carlyle (New York City), 516

Davis, Miles (1926–1991), 102, 125,
209, 258, 259, 295, 301, 304, 328,
329, 335–336, 339, 340, 341, 345,
350, 367, 369, 370, 377, 387, **389–
402**, 408, 413, 415, 422, 435–36,
438–39, 453, 465, 467, 468, 475,
479, 480, 484, 491, 492, 502–3,
505–6, 507, 508, 510, 518, 533,
538, 557, 565, 570, 581–82, 609,
610, 622, 623, 625, 626, 648, 649,
658, 661, 663, 676, 680, 689, 690,
692, 693, 719, 728, 729, 733, 738,
744, 753, 757, 760, 759, 781, 782,
795–96. *See also specific musician
or recording*
Davis, Miles II, 389
Davison, Wild Bill (1906–1989),
210, 286, 312, 624
Davis, Richard (b. 1930), 243–44,
679
Davis, Steve (1929–1987), 439
Davis, Vernon, 391
Davis, Walter Jr. (1932–1990), 363
Davis, Wild Bill (b. 1918), 75, 384,
657
Dawn Club (San Francisco), 313
Dawn, Dolly, 228
A Day at the Races (film), 703
Daybreak Express (film), 711
Day, Doris, 122, 241
Day, Ike, 694
Dean-Myatt, William, 123
Dearie, Blossom (b. 1926), 228, 483
Debussy, Claude, 17, 22, 126, 159,
345, 347, 405, 599
Debut label, 378, 782. *See also
specific artist*
Decca Records: and ban on
recording industry, 299, 316, 779;
founding of, 72, 116, 775; LPs at,
781; and New Orleans revival,
311; and race, 72, 74, 249, 778;
and soloists of 1930s and 1940s,
209; and swing, 775, 776. *See
also musician or recording*
Decoding Society (Jackson group),
510
De Falla, Manuel, 350
De Faut, Voltaire "Volly" (1904–
1973), 96, 587
DeFrancesco, Joey (b. 1971), 657
DeFranco, Buddy (b. 1923), 176,
376, 449, 585, 592, 593–94, 784
De Haas, Eddie (b. 1930), 678
De Jazzwereld magazine, 748
DeJohnette, Jack (b. 1942), 399,
400, 465, 503, 533, 693
Delaunay, Charles, 100, 101, 307,
310, 538, 752, 776
Delaunay, Sonia, 538
De Léry, Jean, 551
Delgado, Isaac, 532
Delmark label, 785–86
Delmark Records, 785–86
Delorme, Michel, 442
Delta River Boys, 570
DeMicheal, Don (1928–1982), 752
De Moraes, Vinicius, 555
Denmark: Armstrong in, 115–16;

Hawkins in, 183; jazz clubs in,
733; Snow in, 231
Dennard, Kenwood (b. 1956), 508
Dennerlein, Barbara (b. 1964), 657
De Pachmann, Vladimir, 61
de Paris, Sidney (1905–1967), 154
de Paris, Wilbur (1900–1973), 312–
13
Deppe, Lois, 171, 172
Derome, Jean, 578
Desmond, Johnny, 476
Desmond, Paul (1924–1977), 337,
338–39, 340, 353, 366, 463, 609,
794, 797
De Souza, Raoul, 557
Detroit, Michigan: blacks in, 301;
Davis in, 392; hard bop in, 381;
and pianists in 1940s and 1950s,
364
"Detroit School," 363
DeVaughn, Ronald. *See* Wadud,
Abdul
DeVeaux, Scott, 186, 292, 418, 754
DeViese, Elinore. *See* Holiday, Billie
Devol, Frank, 241
Dexter, Dave, 209
Diaghilev, Sergei, 19–20
Dial Records, 303. *See also specific
artist or recording*
Diamond Club (Tokyo), 733
Dibango, Manu, 563
Dickenson, Vic (1906–1984), 24,
284, 314, 633, 634
Dickerson, Carroll (1895–1957),
110, 153, 729–30
Dickerson, Walt (b. 1931), 651
Diddley, Bo, 523
Dietrich, Marlene, 527
Di Meola, Al (b. 1954), 503
Dingo (film), 402
Disc Jockey (film), 244
Disc jockeys, 772, 774–75
Discography, 749, 752, 776
Disc Records, 780
Disney Studios, 120, 140, 554, 711
Dixieland, 129, 209, 210, 286, 310,
513, 629, 660, 661, 726, 727. *See
also* New Orleans jazz
Dixielanders (George Webb band),
313
Dixielanders (Matlock band), 713
Dixie Syncopators (Oliver band),
96, 98
Dixon, Akua, 663
Dixon, Charlie (1898–1940), 286,
289
Dixon, George, 195
Dixon, Lawrence, 283
Dizzy Gillespie Alumni (Heath
band), 435
Djavan, 556
Doctorow, E. L., 31
Dodds, Warren "Baby" (1898–
1959), 46, 94, 95, 106, 109, 110,
152, 311, 683–84, 686, 725, 730
Dodds, Jimmy, 106
Dodds, Johnny (1892–1940), 25, 92,
94, 95, 100, 109, 152, 307, 311,
585, 586, 587–88, 757, 772

Dodge, Roger Pryor, 748, 753, 755
Dodworth, Allen, 265
Dodworth, Charles, 265
Dodworth, Harvey, 265
Dodworth, Thomas, 265
Doggett, Bill (1916–1996), 75, 76,
241, 384, 656
Doky, Niels Lan (b. 1963), 546
Doldinger, Klaus (b. 1936), 508
Dolphy, Eric (1928–1964), 182, 337,
428, 439, 440, 446, 452, 505, 594–
95, 602, 610, 621, 639, 651, 655,
656
Dominique, Natty (1896–1982), 89,
96, 152
Domino, Fats, 114, 529
Donahue, Sam (1918–1974), 200
Donaldson, Lou (b. 1926), 76, 376,
378, 607
Donaldson, Walter (1893–1947),
129
Donegan, Lonnie, 313
"Doodle-tongue," 623
Dorham, Kenny (1924–1972), 319,
377, 379, 556, 623, 750
Dorough, Bob (b. 1923), 396
Dorsey, Frank, 476
Dorsey, Jimmy (1904–1957), 158,
160, 161, 216, 217, 223, 224, 225,
233, 275–76, 279, 282, 314, 317,
591–92, 604, 605, 618, 709, 712,
731
Dorsey, Tommy (1905–1956), 81,
157, 160, 161, 173, 209, 213, 214,
216, 223, 224, 225, 233, 269, 272,
275–76, 279, 282, 308, 350, 351,
359, 476, 593, 619, 633, 634–35,
636, 638, 687, 710, 712, 731, 775.
See also specific recording
Double Image (Samuels group), 652
Douglas, Aaron, 146
Douglas, Dave (b. 1963), 626
Douglas Gilmore Theater
(Baltimore), 81
Douglas, Kirk, 122, 257, 713
Dove, Billie, 246
Dowell, Edgar, 61
Down Beat Club (Los Angeles), 732
Down Beat magazine: and Coltrane,
439–40, 443; and dance, 702, 703,
704; and dance/concert music
debate, 703; Davis reviews in,
397; first issue of, 538; Fitzgerald
notices in, 238; founding of, 751;
and Hackett (Bobby), 210; Hall
of Fame, 335, 443; and Jazz at
the Philharmonic, 219; and jazz
criticism, 751–52, 755; and jazz
education, 762; as leading jazz
magazine, 780; on Parker, 320,
606; and race issues, 298; rock
covered by, 505; and vocalists,
475; Wilson (Teddy) award from,
174
Drameh, Oko, 565
Dreamland Ballroom/Cafè
(Chicago), 92, 109, 152, 729
Dreamland Band, 94
Dreams (jazz-rock band), 507

Graas, John (1924–1962), 663
Grabowsky, Paul, 582
Grace Cathedral (San Francisco), 140
Grace, Teddy, 231
Gracia, Russ, 241
Graettinger, Bob (1923–1957), 352, 412, 449, 450, 518
Grainger, Percy, 347
Grainger, Porter, 84
Gramercy Five (Shaw band), 217, 360, 365, 411, 594
Grammy Awards, 245, 396, 498, 625
The Gramophone magazine, 748, 751
Grand Terrace (Chicago), 231, 730
Grand Terrace Orchestra, 461
Grand Theater (Chicago), 51
Granoff Studios, 433
Grant, Stephen, 315
Granz, Norman, 119, 176, 187, 188, 204, 218–19, 239, 240, 249, 259, 322, 366, 407, 463, 528, 529, 567, 569, 780, 781, 783–84. *See also* Jazz at the Philharmonic; *specific musician*
Grappelli, Stephane (1908–1997), 184, 350, 366, 540, 645, 659, 666, 733, 776
Grauer, Bill, 782
Graves, Milford (b. 1941), 472, 693, 744
Gravity (group), 661, 662
Gray, Jerry (1915–1976), 285, 288
Graystone Ballroom (Detroit), 127, 156, 268, 273
Gray, Wardell (1921–1955), 216, 284, 326, 412, 435, 607, 742, 780
Great Britain, **542–43**; and Australian jazz, 580; Beiderbecke films shown in, 131; dance orchestras in, 265; fusion in, 508; jazz clubs in, 733; jazz criticism in, 748; and jazz education, 763; and New Orleans revival, 311, 313; racial integration of bands in, 770; radio broadcasts in, 200; recording industry in, 780; repertory movement in, 517. *See also specific musician or group*
Great Day (musical), 111–12, 161
A Great Day in Harlem (film), 190
Great Depression, 70, 98, 115, 130, 162, 255, 275, 773, 774. *See also specific musician or band*
The Great Gatsby (Fitzgerald novel), 741
Green, Abel, 273–74
Green, Benny (1923–77), 242
Green, Charlie "Big" (1900–1936), 69, 84, 107
Greene, Freddie, 71, 198, 284
Green, Freddie (1911–1987), 212, 360, 405, 643, 672
Green, Grant (1931–1979), 76, 387, 647, 648
Green, Hazel, 81
Green, Johnny (1908–1989), 250

Green, Juanita, 87
Green, Lil (1919–1954), 229
Green, Silas, 81
Green, Urbie (b. 1926), 638, 639, 640
Greenwich, Sonny (b. 1936), 577
Greenwich Village: jazz clubs in, 728–29
Greer, William "Sonny" (1895–1982), 136, 138, 212, 230, 694
Gretsch Manufacturing Company, 526
Grey, Al (1925–2000), 410, 639
Gridley, Mark, 755
Grieg, Edvard, 144, 350, 720
Griffin, Johnny (b. 1928), 379, 424, 496, 528, 545, 609
Grillo, Frank. *See* Machito
Grimes, Henry (b. 1935), 188, 678
Grimes, Tiny (1916–1989), 302, 321, 359
Grissom, Dan, 477
Grofé, Ferde, 57, 155, 268–69, 270, 275, 348, 349, 602
Grossman, Steve (b. 1951), 400
Grosz, Marty (b. 1930), 513
Grove (Ambassador Hotel, Los Angeles), 242
Gruntz, George (b. 1932), 417, 542, 546
Gryce, George "Gigi" (1925–1983), 378, 607
Guarnieri, Johnny (1917–1985), 203, 351, 359–60, 727
Guerin, Art, 269
Guerra, Marcelino, 529
Guesnon, George, 660
Guillery, Adrian, 503
Guitar, 72, 75, 551, 554, 555, 556, 625, **642–49**, 651–52, 660, 672, 674, 777
Gulda, Friedrich (b. 1930), 354, 542
Gullin, Lars (1928–76), 482, 541, 608
Gumina, Tommy (b. 1931), 666
Gurtu, Trilok (b. 1951), 547
Gushee, Lawrence, 42, 43
Guy, Barry, 458
Guy, Fred (1899–1971), 409, 643
Guy, Joe (1920–1962), 248, 421, 728
Gwangwa, Jonas, 562
Gypsy Tea Room (New Orleans), 725
Gyra, Spyro, 509, 652

Hackett, Bobby (1915–1976), 173, 289, 308, 513, 624, 776
Hackett, Buddy, 210, 228
Haden, Charlie (b. 1937), 453, 454, 533, 557, 679, 680, 720
Hadlock, Richard, 305
Hagans, Tim (b. 1954), 626
Hager, Fred, 78, 81–82
Hagert, Thornton, 697
Haggart, Bob (1914–1998), 287, 314, 513, 667, 673
Haggin, B. H., 748

Haig, Al (1924–1982), 322, 362–63, 364
Hale, Corky (b. 1931), 667
Hale, Teddy, 704
Haley, Bill, 414
Half Note (New York City), 441, 728–29
The Halg (Los Angeles), 732
Hall, Adelaide (1901–1993), 154, 272
Hall, Al (1915–1988), 678, 782
Hall, Alice, 665, 666
Hall, Edmond (1901–1967), 216, 314, 564, 592, 593, 672
Hall, Everett, 674–75
Hall, George, 228
Hall, Henry, 537
Hall, Jim (b. 1930), 647
Hall Johnson Choir, 709
Hallberg, Bengt (b. 1932), 665
Hallett, Mal, 231
Hambone Kelly's (San Francisco restaurant), 313
Hambone pat, 13
Hamilton, Chico (b. 1921), 336, 426, 503, 572, 655, 662–63, 695, 717
Hamilton, Even, 336–37
Hamilton, Jeff (b. 1953), 417, 694
Hamilton, Jimmy (1917–1994), 133, 139, 592, 595
Hamilton, Scott (b. 1954), 497, 577
Hamlisch, Marvin, 37–38
Hamm, Stu, 511
Hammerstein, Oscar, 254
Hammond Five (Hardman band), 193
Hammond, John, 71, 86, 87, 100, 170, 196–97, 198, 201, 229, 246, 247, 731, 748, 751, 754, 773, 774, 776–77, 781
Hampel, Gunter (b. 1937), 652
Hampton, Lionel (b. 1908), 72–73, 87, 114, 173, 213, 215, 216, 218, 233, 251, 361, 367, 375, 378, 383, 419, 426, 430, 480, 483, 639, 650, 651, 652, 675, 774, 777, 784. *See also specific recording*
Hampton, Locksley "Slide" (b. 1932), 639
Hancock, Herbie (b. 1940), 389, 387, 396–97, 398, 399, 400, 402, 459, 466–67, 469, 491, 497, 505, 506, 508, 509, 510, 511, 531, 570, 609, 622, 680, 760, 795
Handy, George (1920–1997), 352, 405, 407, 449, 517, 519
Handy, John (b. 1933), 428
Handy, William Christopher (1873–1958), 45, 52, 58, 65, 67, 68, 86, 709, 767
Hanna, Jake (b. 1931), 695
Hanna, Sir Roland (b. 1932), 363, 371, 381
Hanshaw, Annette, 220, 224, 233
"Happy jazz," 510
Hara, Tomonao (b. 1966), 574

Instrumental jazz: as heir to ragtime, 55
Instrumentalists: and classical music, 343–46; and jazz singing since 1940s, 483
Instruments: and bebop, 293; and blues, 69, 72; and cool jazz, 335; in dance bands, 273; electronic, 217–18, 531; and fusion, 77; and jazz in Europe, 554; and Latin music, 551, 552–53, 556, 656, 657–58; miscellaneous, **653–67**; and New Orleans jazz, 658–59; and origins of jazz, 10, 11–12, 13, 14, 20, 24, 46, 49; purpose of, 11–12; and soul jazz, 75. *See also specific instrument or artist*
International House (film), 710
International New Jazz Festival Moers (Germany, 1980), 571
Invisible Man (Ellison book), 112, 742
Irakere (band), 532
Iridium (New York City), 729
Irving, Robert III, 402
Irwin, May, 34
Isham, John, 56
Isola, Frank, 695
Israels, Chuck (b. 1936), 515
Italy: Armstrong in, 116, 120; band traditions in, 636
Iwami, Kiyoshi, 567
Izenzon, David (1932–1979), 453

J. J. Spirits (Japanese Jazz), 573
Jack Johnson (documentary), 400
Jack, Sam T., 56
Jackson, Bullmoose, 74
Jackson, Chubby (b. 1918), 302, 405, 406, 417, 674, 691
Jackson, Cliff (1902–1970), 61
Jackson, D. D., 578
Jackson, Dewey (b. 1900), 772
Jackson, Mahalia, 241
Jackson, Milt (1923–1999), 339, 393, 407, 423, 643, 650–51
Jackson, Quentin (1909–1970), 430
Jackson, Ronald Shannon (b. 1940), 510, 693
Jackson, Tony (1876–1921), 42, 729
Jackson, Willis "Gator" (1928–1987), 76
Jacobson, Bud, 153
Jacquet, Illinois (b. 1922), 71, 73, 74, 200, 216, 219, 375, 391, 665, 688, 741, 780
Jam Session (film), 712
Jam sessions: and arranging and composing, 269; and bebop, 293, 295–97, 299, 300, 302, 303, 304, 567, 646; and cool jazz, 333; and electric guitar, 646; Goodman-Young, 198; and jazz clubs, 726, 727, 728, 731; and jazz education, 763; and jazz singing between blues and bebop, 234; and musicians's union, 299; and New Orleans revival, 307; public, 299; and recording industry, 780, 781;

and soloists of 1930s and 1940s, 218–19. *See also* "Cutting contests"; *specific musician*
Jamal, Ahmad (b. 1930), 362, 367, 369, 394, 463, 465, 646, 659, 673
James, Bob (b. 1939), 509
James, Harry (1916–1983), 207, 216, 228, 349, 351, 391, 403, 409, 410–11, 414, 520, 619, 620, 687, 712, 731
James, Leon, 704
James, Michael, 692
Jammin' the Blues (documentary film), 203–4, 718
Janis, Harriet, 37, 311, 512
Jannah, Denise, 482
Janos (Hungarian musician), 544
Japan, 314, 489, 493, 508, **566–74**, 733, 748, 786. *See also specific musician or group*
Jarman, Joseph (b. 1937), 457, 494, 595, 601, 609
Jarrett, Keith (b. 1945), 346, 355, 389, 400, 468–69, 492, 503, 658, 679, 759, 761, 785, 786, 795
Jaspar, Bobby (1926–1963), 610
Jasper's in a Jam (film), 711
Java: jazz criticism in, 748
Jazz: African roots of, **7–16**, 20, 24, 26, 27; bebop- traditionalist feud in, 117; decline of, 723; definitions/characteristics of, 3–5, 42–44, 220, 488, 561, 696, 741; documenting and teaching, 718–21; *A Drum Is a Woman* as history of, 139; early origins of, **39–52**; European roots of, 15, **17–28**; as fine-art form, 27–28; as hybrid, 27–28; myths about, 41–42; purists and progressive debate about, 310; schism about, 488–89; seriousness of, 537; since 1968, **488–501**; as slang term, 747; and social and economic development, 44–46
Jazz Academy, 571
Jazz Age, 19, 36, 68, 69, 89, 91, 132, **148–62**, **163–76**, 559, 740–41
"Jazz at Home" (Rogers essay), 739
Jazz at Lincoln Center (New York City), 499, 625
Jazz at the Philharmonic (JATP), 187, 204–5, 219, 239, 240, 249, 258, 478, 567, 569, 780, 783
Jazz at the Smithsonian (documentary film), 719
Jazz Casual (documentary film), 719
Jazz and Classical Music Society, 353
Jazz clubs. *See* Clubs, jazz; 52nd Street; *specific club*
Jazz Composers Orchestra, 518
Jazz in the Concert Hall (documentary film), 720
Jazz Crusaders, 491
Jazz Educators Journal, 761
Jazz Epistles, 562

Jazz Explosion, 679
Jazz in Film project, 720
Jazz from Lincoln Center (documentary film), 719
Jazz from Studio 61 (TV special), 719
Jazz Gallery (New York City), 439
Jazz Hounds, 769
Jazz Information magazine, 752
Jazz magazine, 443
Jazz Man label, 778
Jazz Maniacs, 561
The Jazz Messengers (Blakey band), 376, 377, **379–81**, 386, 388, 497, 529–30, 532, 570, 582, 689, 759
Jazz Modes (Pettiford band), 663
Jazz Record label, 782
Jazz Records A-Z (Rust), 752
Jazz Revelers, 561
The Jazz Review magazine, 755
Jazz Scene, U.S.A. (documentary film), 719
Jazz in Serious Music (documentary film), 719–20
Jazz Showcase (Chicago), 730
The Jazz Singer (film), 709
Jazz singing: and avant-garde music, 482, 485; and bebop, 475–76, 478–79, 481, 484; and big bands, 483; and blues, 68, 480–81, 484, 486, 487; between blues and bebop, **220- 34**; and composing, 485°d cool jazz, 478, 479–80, 482, 484; decline of, 483; and definition of jazz singer, 477; and Europe, 482; and improvisation, 473, 478, 485; and instrumentalists, 483; and musicals, 486; since 1940s, **473–87**; and pop, 485, 486; and race, 480; and ragtime, 34; and rhythm-and-blues, 74, 75, 481; and roots of jazz, 11–12, 16; and soul jazz, 76; and swing, 473; and vocalese, 232, 481, 482–83, 484, 486. *See also* Vocalists. *specific vocalist*
"The Jazz Sonata" (Baker short story), 739
Jazz studies, 307, 564, **756–65**
Jazz on a Summer's Day (documentary film), 719
Jazz Workshop (Mingus), 427, 651
Jazz-Hot magazine, 538, 751, 752, 776
Jazz-rock, 489, 491, 591, 660, 661
Jazz-Tango Dancing magazine, 748, 774
Jazzmen (Ramsey and Smith), 99, 100, 310, 311, 563–64, 753, 755, 778
Jefferson, Blind Lemon, 68, 452
Jefferson, Eddie (1918–1979), 232, 481
Jefferson, Hilton (1903–1968), 217, 291, 605
Jenkins, Edmund, 770
Jenkins, Gordon, 241
Jenkins, Leroy (b. 1932), 659–60

Jenkins, Willard, 750
Jenney, Jack (1910–1945), 288, 637, 638
Jennings, Bill, 75
Jennings, Waylon, 263
Jenny-Clark, Jean-François, 543
Jensen, Ingrid, 626
Jenson Publications, 516
Jepsen, Jorgen, 752
Jeremy and the Satyrs, 503
Jerome, Henry, 301–2, 691
Jerry's (Harlem club), 154
Jewell label, 74
Jimmy Ryan's (New York City), 313, 727
Jimmy's Chicken Shack (Harlem), 296
Jitterbug, 703, 704. *See also* Lindy hop
Joans, Ted, 743
Jobim, Antonio Carlos (1927–1994), 548, 554–55, 556, 717
Joe Davis Records, 187, 780
John Kirby Sextet, 214, 231, 350, 359
John Stark & Sons, 32, 33
John W. Coltrane Cultural Society, 445
Johnson, Bill (1872–1972), 92, 94, 267, 660, 669, 671
Johnson, Budd (1910–1984), 115, 186, 190, 200, 242, 281, 283, 284, 299, 607, 727
Johnson, Buddy (1915–1977), 72, 73, 406
Johnson, Charles L., 33
Johnson, Charlie (1891–1959), 154, 246, 271, 279, 632, 683, 685, 725
Johnson, Deron, 402
Johnson, Dewey, 444
Johnson, Dexter, 563
Johnson, Dick (b. 1925), 411
Johnson, Ella, 73
Johnson, Francis (1792–1844), 265
Johnson, Frank, 580
Johnson, Gus (b. 1913), 695
Johnson, Henry. *See* Hammond, John
Johnson, Howard (b. 1941), 661, 662
Johnson, J. C., 223
Johnson, J. J. (b. 1924), 187, 219, 340, 353, 354, 377, 378, 392, 393, 410, 570, 638, 639
Johnson, J. Rosamond, 56
Johnson, Jack, 507, 510
Johnson, James P. (1891–1955), 31, 43, 51, 60, 61–62, 63, 69, 84, 136, 154, 165–67, 168, 169, 170, 176, 182, 255, 309, 345, 350, 672, 700, 709, 769, 776
Johnson, James Weldon, 35, 56–57, 189, 442, 740
Johnson, Jimmy, 253, 669
Johnson, Keg (1908–1967), 115
Johnson, Lonnie (1889–1970), 158, 161, 643
Johnson, Marc (b. 1953), 466
Johnson, Margaret, 111

Johnson, Marge, 246
Johnson, Osie (1923–1966), 695
Johnson, Pete (1904–1967), 71, 731
Johnson, Robert (1911–1938), 480, 486
Johnson, Rosamond, 35
Johnson, Sy (b. 1930), 430
Johnson, Walter (1904–1977), 212, 685
Johnson, Will, 79
Johnson, William "Bunk" (1879–1949), 50, 259, 311, 312, 313, 314, 512, 586, 631, 778
Jolson, Al, 220, 233, 707
Jones, A. M., 20
Jones, Carmell (1936–1996), 623
Jones, Clarence M., 51
Jones, Claude (1901–1962), 156, 157, 633
Jones, David, 105
Jones, Eddie (1929–1997), 678
Jones, Elvin (b. 1927), 381, 392, 395, 439, 440, 444, 456, 510, 624, 675, 692, 693, 796
Jones, Etta, 76, 480
Jones, Hank (b. 1918), 219, 362, 363, 364, 381, 462, 563, 624
Jones, Herbie, 240
Jones, Isham (1894–1956), 268, 272
Jones, Jimmy (1918–1982), 241, 243, 244, 367–68
Jones, Jo (1911–1985), 70, 189, 193, 195, 197, 199, 212, 360, 405, 672, 675, 685, 688, 689, 691, 693, 713, 718, 731
Jones, Jonah (1909–2000), 291
Jones, LeRoi. *See* Baraka, Amiri
Jones, Maggie, 108
Jones, Oliver (b. 1934), 577
Jones, Percy, 508
Jones, Philly Joe (1923–1985), 381, 393, 396, 675, 690, 692, 693, 795
Jones, Quincy (b. 1933), 71, 245, 410, 414, 417, 428, 535, 620, 663, 666, 715
Jones, Richard M. (1892–1945), 109, 311
Jones, Sam (1924–1981), 385, 662, 677, 678
Jones, Thad (1923–1986), 71, 188, 284, 284, 381, 392–93, 397, 410, 411, 414, 415–16, 496–97, 516, 517, 624, 640, 666, 691, 729, 733
Joplin, Janis, 87, 341
Joplin, Scott (1868–1917), 31, 32–33, 36–38, 45, 51, 61, 255, 311, 348, 371, 495, 518, 717–18
Jordan, Clifford (1931–1993), 383
Jordan, Irving "Duke" (b. 1922), 322, 364
Jordan, Joe, 729
Jordan, Louis (1908–1975), 74, 232, 375, 385, 480, 501, 563, 592, 593, 778
Jordan, Paul, 351
Jordan, Sheila (b. 1929), 381, 485
Jordan, Taft (1915–1981), 213–14, 286
Joseph, Willie, 61

Josephson, Barney, 247, 728
Jost, Ekkehard, 456
The Journal of Jazz Studies, 755
Journals: and jazz education, 762. *See also specific journal*
Juba pat, 12–14, 16
Jubilee Records, 74
Juilliard School of Music, 345, 391
Jump for Joy (revue), 137, 144
Jump music, 77, 375, 501, 705
Jungles (Harlem club district), 62
Jupiter (San Francisco club), 93
Just Jazz concert (Los Angeles, 1949), 244
Juwata Jazz Band, 562

Kabasele, Joseph, 562
Kahn, Roger Wolfe, 158
Kahn, Tiny (Norman) (1924–1953), 301, 690–91
Kaiser, Henry, 562
Kalban, Bernard, 37
Kaminsky, Max (1908–1994), 210, 282, 289, 308, 310
Kanai, Hideto, 571
Kane, Helen, 159, 224
Kangaroo hop, 35
Kansas City, 69–72, 251, 603, 604, 730–31, 742, 778. *See also specific musician or club*
Kansas City (film), 714
Kansas City Five/Six/Seven (Basie Band), 193, 199, 201, 217, 257, 777, 793
Kaper, Bronislau, 258, 714
Kapere Jazz Band, 562
Kapp, Jack, 72, 776
Kart, Lawrence, 446
Katz, Dick (b. 1924), 6, 189, 357
Katz, Fred (b. 1919), 662, 663
Kawaguchi, George, 569–70
Kawasaki, Ryo (b. 1947), 508
Kay, Connie (1927–1994), 339, 393, 694
Kay, Sammy, 727
Kaye, Danny, 712
Kay Company, 674
Kazan, Elia, 716
Kazoo, 666
Kebede, Ashenafi, 12
Keep Shufflin' (musical), 165
Keepnews, Orrin (b. 1923), 782
Keepnews, Peter, 488
Keita, Salif, 562
Kell, Reginald, 346
Kellaway, Roger (b. 1939), 355, 472, 677, 679
Kelley, John "Peck" (1898–1980), 631
Kelley, William Melvin, 741
Kelly, Pete, 229, 240, 713
Kelly, Spider, 435
Kelly, Wynton (1931–1971), 188, 368, 395, 396, 407, 462, 465, 729
Kelly's Stable (New York City), 183, 184, 185, 186, 201, 727
Kendor Music Company, 516
Kennedy Center for the Performing Arts (Washington, D.C.), 574

Lewis, George (1900–1968), 311, 313, 314, 570, 586

Lewis, J. T., 510

Lewis, John (b. 1920), 204, 250, 251, 262, 263, 335, 339, 353, 355, 360, 365, 378, 392, 394, 407, 413, 428, 463, 517, 640, 783, 795

Lewis, Meade Lux (1905–1964), 71, 170, 667

Lewis, Mel (1929–1990), 414, 415–16, 496–97, 516, 624, 640, 666, 691, 729

Lewis, Ramsey (b. 1935), 76, 464, 509

Lewis, Ted (1892–1971), 268, 269

Lewis, Willie (1905–1971), 283, 537

Library of Congress, 25, 26, 50, 99, 107, 241, 520, 778

Lieberson, Goddard, 782

Liebman, Dave (b. 1946), 389, 400, 401, 609, 611, 760, 796

Life magazine: and New Orleans revival, 308

Lifeline Press, 516

Lifetime (Tony Williams band), 491, 506–7, 510, 693

Liggins, Joe, 73

Lighthouse All-Stars (Rumsey band), 378, 655, 664, 732

Lighthouse (Hermosa Beach, California, club), 337, 732

Lim, Harry, 726, 748, 786

Lincoln, Abbey (b. 1930), 189, 483, 484, 485

Lincoln Center Jazz Orchestra, 416, 518, 720

Lincoln Center for the Performing Arts (New York), 263, 430, 444, 499. *See also* Jazz at Lincoln Center

Lincoln Gardens (Chicago), 94, 106, 153, 729

Lincoln Theater (New York City), 154

Lincoln Theater (Pittsburgh), 83

Lindbergh, Charles, 701

Lindley, David, 562

Lindsay, Arto, 649

Lindsay, Vachel, 743

Lindy hop, 700–701, 702, 703, 705

Lins, Ivan, 556

Lion, Alfred, 385, 781

The Lion King (film/musical), 263

Lipman, Joe (b. 1915), 276, 289

LiPuma, Tommy, 401

Liston, Melba (1926–1999), 407

Literature: and jazz, **734–44**. *See also specific author or work*

Little, Booker (1938–1961), 188, 452, 621

Little Club (New York City), 270

Litweiler, John, 754

Live from Lincoln Center (TV series), 720

Live in New York City, the Abercrombie/Erskine/Mintzer/ Patitucci Band: A Concert/Clinic (instruction tape), 720

Live Under the Sky (Tokyo, 1977–90), 570, 573

Livingston, Joseph Anthony "Fud" (1906–1957), 158, 269, 345

Lloyd, Charles (b. 1938), 503, 610, 693

Lo, Ishmael, 562

Local 208 (Chicago union), 51

Lock, Graham, 754

Locke, Alain, 739

Locke, Eddie (b. 1930), 188

Locke, Joe (b. 1959), 652

Lockridge, Richard, 85

Lodge, Henry, 33

Loewy, Raymond, 212

Lomax, Alan, 10–11, 15, 50, 99, 778

Lombardi, Clyde, 675, 676

Lombardo, Guy, 159, 161, 275

London, England. *See* Great Britain

London, Julie, 234

London Regimental Band, 683

Longhair, Professor, 529

Longshaw, Fred, 84

Lopez, Israel "Cachao," 526

Lopez, Vincent, 269, 272, 274

Lorber, Jeff, 509

Lord, Tom, 752

Los Angeles, California: blacks in, 73, 301, 732; and blues, 76; hard bop in, 382; jazz clubs in, 723, **732**; Just Jazz concert in, 244; modern jazz in, 336; and New Orleans revival, 313; part-time bands in, 414; recording industry in, 772. *See also specific musician or band*

Louisiana Five (Lada band), 729, 767

Louisiana Five (Nunez band), 767

Lovano, Joe (B. 1952), 500, 574, 611, 796

Love, Earl, 81

Lovett, Baby, 731

Lowe, Sam, 285

LP records, 781–86

Lubambo, Romero (b. 1955), 556, 558

Lucas, Buddy, 666

Lucas, George, 718

Lucas, Reggie, 400

Lucas, Sam, 55

Lunceford, Jimmie (1902–1947), 22, 72, 254, 274, 276, 279, 280, 281–82, 284, 285, 288, 365, 376, 477, 516, 521, 623, 634

Lundu (African dance), 552

Lundvall, Bruce, 782

Lussier, Rene, 577, 578

Lutcher, Nellie, 232

Luter, Claude, 312

Lye, Len, 711

Lyons, Jimmy (1932–1986), 469

Lyra, Carlos, 555

Lytell, Jimmy (1904–1972), 157

Lyttleton, Humphrey (b. 1921), 312, 313

M-BASE collective, 510–11

Ma, Yo-Yo, 348, 720

Mabern, Harold (b. 1936), 466

Mabry, Betty, 506

McBee, Cecil (b. 1935), 574

McBride, Christian (b. 1972), 500, 678

McBride, Mary Margaret, 748

McCain, David W., 231

McCandless, Paul (b. 1947), 664

McCann, Les (b. 1935), 76, 464

McCarthy, Albert, 699, 754

McClure, Ron (b. 1941), 503

McConnell, Rob (b. 1935), 416, 578

McConville, Leo, 130

McCormack, John, 109, 345

McCroby, Ron, 667

McDonald, Donald, 503

McDonough, Dick (1904–1938), 643

McDonough, John, 206

McDowell, Edward, 126

McDuff, Brother Jack (b. 1926), 76, 384, 656

McEachern, Murray (1915–1982), 637, 638

Macero, Teo (b. 1925), 354, 399, 451, 711, 782

McFarland, Gary (1933–1971), 354, 413–14, 572

McGann, Bernie, 581

McGarity, Lou (1917–1971), 314

McGhee, Howard (1918–1987), 187, 285, 287, 297, 300, 303, 478, 621, 732

McGoon, Earthquake, 314

McGowan, Chris, 551

McGregor, Chris (b. 1936), 562

McGriff, Jimmy (b. 1936), 76, 384, 656

McGuinn, Roger, 505

Machado, Edison, 557

Machito (1912–1984), 526, 527, 528, 529, 530, 570

McHugh, Jimmy (1894–1969), 113, 155

McIntyre, Makanda Ken (b. 1931), 664

McKay, Claude, 739, 741

McKay, Louis, 248

MacKendrick, Alexander, 716–17

McKendrick, "Little Mike," 97

McKenna, Dave (b. 1930), 368–69, 472

Mackenzie, Red (1899–1948), 233, 666

Mackey, Nathaniel, 744

McKinley, Ray (1910–1995), 352, 405, 684–85

McKinney, Bernard. *See* Zawadi, Kiane

McKinney, William (1895–1969), 156, 270, 273, 279, 283, 287, 515, 602, 633

McKusick, Hal (b. 1924), 407

McLaren, Norman, 711

McLaughlin, John (b. 1942), 389, 468, 506, 507, 542, 643, 648, 693, 795

McLean, Jackie (b. 1931), 379, 387, 402, 428, 607, 714

McLean, René (b. 1946), 564

McLean, Richard "Abba Labba," 165

McMillan, Allan, 87

McNair, Sylvia, 348

Milhaud, Darius, 338, 347, 353, 366, 412, 535, 599
Mili, Gjon, 718
Milkowski, Bill, 502
Miller, Bill, 309, 695
Miller, Eddie (1911–1991), 287, 289, 308
Miller, Glenn (1904–1944), 161, 162, 256, 274, 285, 288, 289, 256, 269, 351, 483, 618, 624, 633, 635, 663, 712, 720
Miller, Johnnie, 152
Miller, Marcus (b. 1959), 389, 401
Miller, Mark, 575
Miller, Mitch, 484
Miller, Paul Eduard, 751, 754–55
Miller, Punch (1894–1971), 152
Miller, Warren, 742
Millinder, Lucky (1900–1966), 72, 73, 297, 419
Mills, Florence, 154, 223
Mills, Irving, 136, 271, 279–80, 632, 773
Mills Brothers, 221, 225, 481
Mills Music catalog, 37
Milton, Roy, 73
Mimimalist music, 341
Mine, Kosuke (b. 1944), 573–74
Mingus Big Band, 431
Mingus, Charles (1922–1979), 139, 175, 341, 353–54, 370, 378, 414, **419, 421, 425–31**, 449, 451, 452, 461, 471, 472, 505, 515, 565, 577, 594, 639, 651, 661, 663, 675, 676, 678, 679, 680, 695, 719, 729, 732, 782, 783
Mingus (documentary film), 719
Mingus, Sue, 429, 431
Minnie the Moocher (film), 710
Minns, Al, 704
Minstrel shows, 55, 78, 194, 220, 522, 563
Minton, Henry, 728
Minton's Playhouse (New York City), 186, 293, 295, 296, 297, 299, 300, 421, 422, 646, 688, 703, 728
Miranda, Carmen, 554
Mission Impossible (TV program), 717
Mississippi blues, 64, 65, 615
Mississippi Days (musical), 85
Mississippi river boats, 105, 772
Mitchell, George (1899–1972), 97
Mitchell, Mitch, 505
Mitchell, Red (1927–1992), 593, 676–77, 678, 679, 680, 714
Mitchell, Richard "Blue" (1930–1979), 463, 467, 623
Mitchell, Roscoe (b. 1940), 457, 458, 494, 595, 609, 610
Miyazawa, Akira, 567
Mo' Better Blues (film), 714
Mobile Disco, 565
Mobley, Hank (1930–1986), 377, 379, 386–87, 396, 609
Mobo Club Band, 573
Mocambo (Yokohama nightclub), 567

Modal music, 19
Modeliste, Zigaboo, 511
Modern jazz: bebop as central to development of, 794; and bebop-traditionalists feud, 117; birth of, **795–96**; and Blue Note label, 781–82; and blues, 76, 77; and composing and arranging for big bands, 290; development of, 375; first recordings of, 316; and miscellaneous instruments, 661, 664; and rhythm and blues, 75; rise of, 117
Modern Jazz Quartet (MJQ), 250, 335, 339–40, 341, 353, 354, 365, 463, 570, 581, 651, 689, 783
Modern Jazz Society, 353
Modern Records, 73–74
Moeketsi, Kippie, 562
Moffett, Charles (1929–1997), 453
Moffett, Charnett (b. 1967), 510
Moholo, Louis, 562
Mole, Irving "Miff" (1898–1961), 24, 157–58, 160, 161, 589, 631, 633, 767
Moncur, Grachan (b. 1915), 226
Moncur, Grachan III (b. 1937), 387, 452, 639
Mondello, Toots, 605
Mondragon, Joe (b. 1920), 678
Monk, Gertie, 61
Monk, Susie, 61
Monk, T. S. (b. 1949), 431
Monk, Thelonious (1917–1982), 173, 186, 187, 188, 189, 201, 203, 209, 234, 251, 258, 291, 292, 295, 298, 299, 300, 337, 353, 360, 361, 362, 364, 368, 369, 371, 376–77, 379, 380, 393, 395, 408, **419, 421–25**, 427, 428, 429, 430, **431**, 436, 437, 441, 449, 464, 471, 499, 531, 565, 570, 608, 620, 637, 646, 663, 688, 689, 719, 728, 744, 757, 781, 782, 794, 796. *See also specific recording*
Monogram Theater (Chicago), 51
Monroe, Clark, 248, 728
Monroe, Jimmy, 248
Monroe's Uptown House (Harlem), 186, 248, 295, 297, 300, 421, 728
Monsbourgh, Ade, 309, 580
Monteiro, Eddie (b. 1948), 666
Monterey Jazz Festivals, 120, 139, 261, 430, 503, 571
Montgomery, Charles "Buddy" (b. 1930), 383, 652
Montgomery, John "Wes" (1925–1968), 76, 383–84, 440, 503, 647, 648, 652, 729, 733, 782
Montgomery, William "Monk" (1921–1982), 383, 675, 679
Montmartre (Denmark), 733
Montreux Jazz Festival, 402, 470
Moody, Bill, 741–42
Moody, James (b. 1925), 481, 496, 607, 655
Mooney, Hal, 242, 244
Mooney, Joe (1911–1975), 413, 665
Moore, Johnny, 74

Moore, Michael (b. 1945), 679
Moore, Milton "Brew" (1924–1973), 541
Moore, Monette, 246
Moore, Oscar (1916–1981), 646
Morath, Max, 6, 29
Morehouse, Chauncey (1902–1980), 128
Moreira, Airto (b. 1941), 400, 468, 493, 556–57, 658
Morello, Joe (b. 1928), 339, 694
Morgan, Frank (b. 1933), 607, 732
Morgan, Ike, 50
Morgan, Lee (1938–1972), 379–81, 388, 407, 570, 623
Morgan, Les, 387
Morgan, Richard, 86, 87
Morgan, Sam, 49–50, 615, 631, 772
Morgan, Stanley, 732
Morgenstern, Dan, 102, 185, 377, 441, 752
Moriyasu, Shotaro, 566–67
Morocco, Frank, 666
Morricone, Ennio, 501
Morris, Audrey, 228
Morris, Joe (b. 1958), 649
Morrison, James (b. 1962), 547, 581, 626
Morrow, Buddy (b. 1919), 637, 638
Morrow, George (1925–1992), 378
Morton, Benny (1907–1985), 102, 155, 157, 314, 633
Morton, Fred, 89
Morton, Harrison, 155
Morton, Ferdinand "Jelly Roll" (1885–1941), 23, 24, 25–26, 27, 42, 43, 44, 46, 47, 48, 50, 67, 88, 89, 91, 93, 95–96, 97–98, 99, 101, 149, 151, 152–53, 171–72, 251, 307, 309, 310, 312, 313, 315, 345, 427, 450, 495, 512, 513, 516, 522, 523, 525, 563, 586, 587, 629, 633, 660, 684, 732, 748, 763, 770, 772, 778. *See also specific recording*
Mosaic Records, 786–87
Mosby, Curtis, 732
Moscow Jazz Club, 544
Mosely, Snub (1905–1981), 601
Moses, Bob (b. 1948), 455, 503, 509
Moss, Danny (b. 1927), 610
Most, Sam (b. 1930), 592, 655–56
Moten, Bennie (1894–1935), 70, 170, 171, 194, 211, 215, 273, 274, 279, 280, 283, 604, 742, 772
Moten, Buster, 665
Mothers of Invention, 505
Motian, Paul (b. 1931), 188, 465, 470, 678, 693, 694
"Mouldy figs," 117, 310
Mouldy figs, 754
Mound City Blue Blowers, 182, 666
Mount Fuji Jazz Festival with Blue Note (Japan, 1986–95), 571
Moura, Paulo, 553
Moye, Famoudou Don (b. 1946), 494, 695
Mozart Clarinet Quintet, 346

New York Art Quartet, 744

New York City: bebop in, 75, 293, 295, 298–99; black musicians in, 35, 50–51, 53–63, 298–99; black theater in, 50, 53–54; blues in, 68, 69; cabarets in, 261–62; Cuban immigration to, 525; dance orchestras in, 265; and dissemination of jazz, 49, 50; drumming in, 683; El Barrio of, 525, 526; Fifteenth Regiment Band in, 59; 52nd Street in, 186, 187, 218, 298, 299, 300, 302, 304, 308, 314, 726–27; film in, 709; hot music in, 151, 153–54, 155, 156, 158, 161; jazz clubs in, 722, 723, 725–29; and New Orleans revival, 308, 311, 314; part-time bands in, 414; pianists in, 163, 165; ragtime in, 35, 36, 37, 55, 56–57, 58, 60–61; and roots of jazz, 41, 50–51, 52, 53–63; during World War II, 75. *See also* Harlem; Musical theater; *specific musician or club*

New York Eye and Ear Control (film), 578

New York Jazz Repertory Ensemble, 515, 516, 521

New York Philharmonic Orchestra, 720

New York Public Library: collections at, 520

New York State Council on the Arts, 515

New York Times, 148, 475

New York Trio (Yamashita group), 574

New Yorker magazine, 138, 752

Newark, New Jersey, 62, 83

Newborn, Phineas Jr. (1931–1989), 369, 464, 783

Newman, David "Fathead" (b. 1933), 481

Newman, Jerry, 297, 567

Newman, Joe (1922–1992), 410, 515

Newman, Paul, 713

Newport Jazz Festival in Madarao (Japan), 571

Newport Jazz Festivals, 139, 229, 261, 384, 393, 395, 475, 515, 639, 704, 719, 784

Newstead, Tony, 580

Newsweek magazine, 499

Newton, Frankie (1906–1954), 86, 232, 634

Newton, James (b. 1953), 655, 656

NG La Banda (Delgado band), 532

Niacin (Novello band), 510

Nice, France: jazz festival (1948) at, 118

Nichigeki (Tokyo theater), 569

Nicholas, Albert (1900–1973), 99, 155, 271, 309, 586, 588, 757

Nicholas, Fayard, 705

Nicholas Brothers, 702

Nichols, Herbie (1919–1963), 368, 371

Nichols, Ernest Loring "Red" (1905–

1965), 127, 151, 157–58, 160, 161, 224, 269, 563, 345, 351, 520, 617–18, 631, 669, 684, 712, 772

Nichols, Keith, 515, 517

Nicholson, Stuart, 237, 238, 245

Nick's (New York City), 308, 728

Nicols, Maggie, 482

Niewood, Gerry (b. 1943), 609

Nigeria, 369, 562

Nightclubs, 261, 302, 703, 705, 722, 723, 731, 732, 775, 777, 784–85. *See also* Cabarets; Clubs, jazz; *specific club*

Nimmons, Phil, 578

"91" Theater (Atlanta), 81

1920s. *See* Jazz Age

Nitto Jazz Band, 566

Nketia, J. H. Kwabena, 10, 12

Noble, Ray (1903–1978), 258

Nock, Mike (b. 1940), 466, 507, 581

Noone, Jimmie (1895–1944), 25, 152, 210, 225, 307, 311, 585, 586, 589–90, 729, 730, 757, 772

Norgran Records, 783

Norman, Fred, 289

Norris, John, 577

North, Alex, 716

Norvo, Red (Kenneth Norville) (1908–1999), 160, 218, 226, 227, 281, 285, 288, 303, 351, 352, 426, 638, 650, 652, 727, 732

Novello, John, 510

Nugent, Pete, 704

Nunez, Alcide (1884–1934), 767

Nussbaum, Adam (b. 1955), 694

Oakley, Helen, 751

Obey, Ebenezer, 562

Oboe, 664

O'Brien, Floyd (1904–1968), 287

Ocean Blue Jazz Festival (Japan), 571

Octoroons (Isham company), 56

O'Day, Anita (b. 1919), 234, 412, 473, 475, 478–79

Odrich, Ron, 596

O'Farrill, Chico (b. 1921), 405, 529, 530

Ogerman, Claus (b. 1930), 355

O'Hara, Frank, 455

Ohtsuka, George, 572

OK Jazz Band, 562

OKeh Records, 45, 78, 108, 112, 152, 769, 772, 774. *See also specific musician, band, or song/album*

Olatunji, Babatunde, 444, 562

Olatunji, Michael, 438

Olatunji Center of African Culture, 445

Oliver, Jimmy, 435

Oliver, Joseph "King" (1885–1938), 27, 41, 44, 67, 88, 91–92, 93–95, 96, 97, 98–99, 101, 105, 106–7, 111, 120, 135, 152, 153, 181, 194, 268, 281, 285, 288, 307, 308, 309, 310, 311, 312, 516, 587–88, 589, 590, 615–16, 618, 631, 632, 669,

684, 723, 725, 729, 748, 757, 770, 778

Oliver, Sy (1910–1988), 84, 273, 282, 515, 518, 620, 635

Olympia Band (Piron band), 92, 268

On Green Dolphin Street (film), 258

On with the Show (film/musical), 223

On the Streets of Paris (musical), 554

Ondaatje, Michael, 741

Onishi, Junko (b. 1967), 574

Ono, Mitsuru, 569

Onward Brass Band, 91

Onyx Club (New York City), 203, 299, 300, 689, 726, 727

Opera, 23, 24–25, 253, 343, 345, 616

Oral history, 754

The Orchestra, 414

Orchestra U.S.A., 355

Orchestra Wives (film), 712

Orchestre National de Jazz (ONJ), 545–56

Ore, John (b. 1933), 678

Oregon (Towner group), 664

Orfeu da Conceiçaô (play), 555

Organ, 75–77, 167, 584–85, 461, 506, 507, 510, 511, **656–57**

Organized crime, 45, 70, 116

Original Creole Orchestra (Bill Johnson band), 267

Original Dixieland Jazz Band (ODJB), 39, 41, 42, 48, 49, 50, 67, 91, 109, 114–15, 126, 127, 148, 149, 151, 210, 251, 258, 267, 305, 308, 309, 310, 311, 313, 512, 566, 579, 587, 600, 615, 683, 699, 766; and clarinet, 587, 751, 766–67

Original Jazz Hounds, 180

Original Memphis Five, 157, 767

Orpheum theater circuit, 631

Orpheum Theater (Newark, New Jersey), 83

Ørsted Pedersen, Niels-Henning (b. 1946), 678, 679, 733

Ory, Edward "Kid" (1886–1973), 47, 82, 91, 92–93, 96, 97, 99, 105, 109, 110, 152, 210, 307, 313, 629

Osaka, Masahiko (b. 1966), 314, 574

Osby, Greg (b. 1960), 501, 510, 611

Oscar Awards, 714, 717

Osgood, Henry O., 748

Otis, Johnny (b. 1921), 73, 482–83

O'Toole, Knuckles, 513

"Out-chorus," 303–4

Overton, Hall (1920–1972), 430

Owens, Jimmy (b. 1943), 515

Owens, Thomas, 324, 330

Oxley, Tony (b. 1938), 542–43, 695

The Oyster Man (musical), 56

Ozawa, Seiji, 720

Ozone, Makoto (b. 1961), 574

P-Funk, 510

Pablo Records, 463, 784, 787

Rainbow and Stars (New York City cabaret), 261–62

Rainey, Gertrude "Ma" (1886–1939), 68, 78, 81, 83, 108, 770

Raksin, David, 262, 714

Ramblers (Dutch group), 183, 184

Ramblers Inn (New York State), 269

Ramirez, Ram (1913–1994), 372

Rampal, Jean-Pierre, 548

Ramsey, Doug, 403

Ramsey, Frederic (b. 1921), 99, 311, 753

Randall, Geoffrey, 586

Randle, Eddie, 391

Randooga experiment, 573, 574

Raney, Jimmy (1927–1995), 258, 340, 411, 647, 652

Rank, Bill (1904–1979), 129, 160

Rap music, 402, 501, 744

Rapee, Erno, 707

Rattles, 15

"Ratty music," 585

Ratzer, Karl, 508

Rava, Enrico (b. 1939), 546, 626

Ravel, Maurice, 22, 126, 345, 347, 405, 441

Rayman, Morris, 411

Razaf, Andy, 112, 223, 230, 251

RCA Victor Records, 97, 307, 309, 498, 775. *See also* Victor Records; *specific musician, band/orchestra, or recording*

Reardon, Casper (1907–1941), 667

The Record Changer magazine, 102, 753–54

Recording industry, **766–87**; and age of artist, 498; and arranging and composing for big bands, 272; ban during World War II in, 72, 73, 138, 299, 316, 321, 405, 406, 779; and bebop, 299, 302–3, 304, 780, 781; black-owned businesses in, 45, 769; and blues, 67–68, 69, 78, 770, 772, 778; and boogie-woogie, 71, 778; and CDs, 786–87; and Chicago jazz, 51; and classical/concert music, 773; Columbia as dominant in, 777; and early modern jazz, 316; in Europe, 774, 785; and first jazz records, 39–40; in Great Depression, 115, 130, 255, 275, 773, 774; and hard bop, 782; and hot music, 149–50, 152, 156–57; and improvisation, 779; and instruments, 618–19, 769, 777; and jam sessions, 780, 781; in Japan, 786; and jazz criticism, 749, 750–51; and jazz since 1968, 491, 497–98; and Latin music, 525, 553, 785; LP-era in, 781–86; and musicals, 783; musicians' involvement in, 782; and New Orleans black bands, 67–68; and New Orleans revival, 307, 778; and nightclub recordings, 784–85; and origins of jazz, 45, 49; and payola, 260; post-World War II

ban in, 408; and race, 45, 74, 78, 81, 108, 116, 159, 249, 303, 480, 767, 769, 770, 773, 774, 778, 779; and radio, 772, 774–75, 779; and ragtime, 767; RCA Victor domination of, 775; reissues by, 209, 786–87; and rhythm-and-blues, 74; search for talent by, 772; and sheet music, 771; and soloists of 1930s and 1940s, 209; and songs, 255, 260; and swing, 773, 774–75, 776; and Tin Pan Alley, 775; and world music, 785. *See also specific musician, band/ orchestra, label, or song/album*

The Red Back Book (Joplin), 37, 312, 518

Red Blazer Too (New York City), 516

Red Hot Peppers (Morton band), 67, 96, 97–98, 149, 151, 152–53, 251, 629, 772

The Red Moon (musical), 56, 57

Red Onion Jazz Babies, 109

Red Pennies. *See* Nichols, Red: bands and orchestras of

Redd, Freddie (b. 1928), 714

Redman, Dewey (b. 1931), 509

Redman, Don (1900–1964), 107, 108, 110, 128, 155, 156, 181, 254, 270, 273, 274, 275, 280, 283, 285, 287, 289, 291, 449, 526, 590, 602, 709, 710

Redman, Joshua (b. 1969), 499–500, 611, 714

Reed, Lou, 505

Reed, Waymon (1940–1982), 244

Reeds, 15. *See also specific instrument*

Reeves, Dianne (b. 1956), 486, 487

Reggae, 522

Regina, Elis, 556

Rehak, Frank (1926–1987), 638

Reichman, Thomas, 719

Reid, Rufus (b. 1944), 679

Reig, Teddy, 779

Reinhardt, Django (1910–1953), 116, 184, 350, 539–40, 643–44, 645, 659, 666, 733, 776

Reinhardt, Joseph, 540

Reisenweber's Café/Paradise Room (New York), 148, 149, 267, 683, 699

Reisman, Leo, 227

Reisner, Robert, 753

Rejsiger, Ernst, 542

Reliance bands (Laine's bands), 95

Rena, Kid (1898–1949), 311, 725, 778

Reno Club (Kansas City), 70, 197, 731

Repertory, jazz, **512–21**

Reprise label, 784

Return to Forever (Corea group), 400, 468, 507, 508, 557, 655

Revue du Jazz (journal), 774

Reys, Rita (b. 1924), 482

Rhapsody in Black (musical), 231

Rhythm: and arranging and

composing for big bands, 284; and bebop, 293; and dance, 699; and drums/drumming, 681; in Europe, 183; of Hawkins, 182–83; and improvisation, 182, 792, 794; and jazz criticism, 753; and Latin music, 527, 531, 548–49, 551, 552, 558; and roots/origins of jazz, 10, 11, 12, 13–14, 16, 19–20, 23, 24, 46, 49, 50, 61; and songs, 483; of Young, 193. *See also* Rhythm-and-blues; Rhythm section

Rhythm-and-blues: arrangers for, 74; and blues in jazz, 74– 77; and cool jazz, 338; and dance, 704; development of, 375; early recordings of, 74; and funk, 383; and hard bop, 375–76, 380; and instruments, 375, 592; and jazz since 1968, 491; and jazz singing, 229, 481; and race, 301; revival of, 77; vocalists for, 74, 75. *See also specific musician or recording*

Rhythm Boys (Whiteman band), 225, 233

Rhythm section: All-American, 410; and avant-garde music, 453–54; and banjo, 660; of Basie, 405, 410, 672; and bass, 672; of Coleman, 453–54; Coltrane, 440, 441, 796; of Davis, 394, 395, 397; of Ellington, 643; and guitar, 643, 646; and third stream, 354; and tuba, 661

Rhythmakers, 162

Rich, Bernard "Buddy" (1917–1987), 204, 212, 288, 362, 415, 516, 528, 591, 607, 675, 686–87, 733, 759, 784

Richards, Johnny (1911–1968), 405, 407, 412, 417, 517

Richmond, Dannie (1935–1988), 428, 429, 695

Ricker, Bruce, 719

Riddle, Nelson (1921–1985), 241

Ride 'Em Cowboy (film), 240

Riel, Alex (b. 1940), 695

Rietveld, Benny, 402

Riffs: and arranging and composing for big bands, 270; and bebop, 300, 303; and hard bop, 377; and Latin music, 527; and Morton, 98; and New Orleans jazz, 98; and Parker style, 326; and pianists, 169, 171; and ragtime, 33; and roots of jazz, 10, 14, 16; and soloists, 211, 214, 216; of Young (Lester), 199

Rifkin, Joshua, 37

Riis, Thomas L., 53

Riley, Ben (1933), 695

Riley, John (b. 1954), 694

Riley, Mike (1904–1987), 308

Ring shout, 13

Rinker, Paul, 225

Rippingtons (fusion band), 509

Ritchie, Larry, 714

Ritenour, Lee (b. 1952), 509

Ritt, Martin, 139

Rivers, Sam (b. 1923), 397–98, 452
Riverside Records, 76, 782, 787. *See also specific artist or recording*
Rizzi, Tony (b. 1923), 513
Roach, Max (b. 1924), 139, 187, 189, 203, 242, 299, 300, 303, 322, 377, 378–79, 382, 391, 392, 427, 461, 483, 621, 675, 686, 689, 691, 692, 693, 728, 730, 781, 783
Robbins, Jack, 125
Robert Altman's Jazz '34: Remembrances of Kansas City (TV special), 714
Roberts, Charles Luckeyeth "Lucky" (1887–1968), 36, 51, 60, 61, 62–63, 154, 165
Roberts, George, 637
Roberts, John Storm, 24, 522, 553, 554, 563
Roberts, Marcus (b. 1963), 498
Robertson, Zue (1891–1943), 96
Robeson, Paul, 247
Robichaux, John (1886–1939), 48, 57, 685, 723
Robinson, Bill "Bojangles," 154, 700
Robinson, Jim (1925–1976), 311, 314, 629, 631
Robinson, Perry (b. 1938), 594
Robinson, Prince (1902–1960), 156
Robinson, Scott (b. 1959), 601
Robinson, Smokey, 383
Robison, Paula, 558
Roché, Betty (1918–1999), 229–30, 409
Rochereau, Tabu Ley, 562
Rock, 77, 132, 260, 489, 491, **502– 11**, 522, 531, 624–25. *See also specific musician or band/ orchestra*
Rockabilly, 570
Rock-and-roll, 71, 414, 489, 529, 556, 619, 647–48, 675, 704
Rockets (Leonard band), 778
Rockland Palace (New York City), 97
Rockwell, Tommy, 116, 128
Rockwell-O'Keefe booking agency, 116, 272
Rodgers, Gene (1910–1987), 185
Rodgers, Jimmie, 114
Rodgers, Richard (1902–1979), 228, 240, 261, 262, 791
Roditi, Claudio (b. 1946), 557, 626
Rodney, Red (1927–1994), 406, 408, 413
Rodrigo, Joaquin, 350, 395
Rodriguez, Allejandro, 657
Rodriguez, Arsenio, 526
Rodriguez, Tito, 529, 530, 531
Rogers, Alex, 35
Rogers, Barry, 507
Rogers, J. A., 739
Rogers, Milton "Shorty" (1924– 1994), 258, 337–38, 352, 370, 392, 406, 412, 450, 623, 689, 732
Rojas, Marcus, 661
Roland, Gene (1921–1982), 411
Rolfe, B. A., 616
Rolling Stones, 503

Rollini, Adrian (1904–1956), 129, 157, 158, 161, 269, 601, 650, 669
Rollins, Theodore Walter "Sonny" (b. 1930), 189, 190, 205, 258, 363, 379, 386, 387, 423, 424, 425, 475, 570, 602, 609–10, 647, 661, 663, 679, 717, 729, 782, 783, 784, 791, 793. *See also specific recording*
Romeu's orchestra, 526
Roney, Wallace (b. 1960), 626
Rongetti, Nick, 308, 310
Ronnie Scott's club (London), 542, 733
Roosevelt Theater (Cincinnati), 83
Roppolo, Leon (1902–1943), 25, 95, 151–52, 308, 586, 587, 588
Rose, Jon, 582
Rose, Wally, 37, 309
Roseland Ballroom (New York City), 107, 108, 128, 155, 159, 181, 268, 270, 273, 699, 726
Rosemary's Baby (film), 544
Rosenthal, David H., 373
Rosnes, Renée (b. 1962), 577
Rosolino, Frank (1926–1978), 381, 413, 637, 638, 640
Ross, Annie (b. 1930), 120, 232, 481, 482, 483, 484
Ross, Brandon, 510
Ross, Diana, 713
Ross, Ronnie (1933–1991), 608, 610
Rosza, Miklos, 714
Rota, Nino, 546
Roth, David Lee, 510
Rouse, Charlie (1924–1988), 189, 424, 662
Rowles, Jimmy (1918–1996), 241, 245, 249, 370, 464, 714
Rowles, Stacy (b. 1955), 626
Roxy Theatre (New York City), 161
Royal, Ernie (1921–1983), 623
Royal Gardens (Chicago), 92, 93
Royal Roost (New York City), 392, 527, 728
Rubalcaba, Gonzalo (b. 1963), 533
Rubin, Vera, 10
Rudd, Roswell (b. 1935), 457, 639, 744
Ruff, Willie (b. 1931), 663
Ruffin, Rebecca, 320
Rufus Rastus (musical), 35, 87
Rugolo, Pete (b. 1915), 351, 412
Rumba, 24, 523, 526, 529, 554, 562
Rumsey, Howard (b. 1917), 378, 655, 664, 732
Runnin' Wild (musical), 165, 700
Rushing, Jimmy (1903–1972), 70, 199, 229, 233–34, 273, 634
Rushton, Joe (1907–1974), 601
Russell, Bill, 311, 314
Russell, Charles "Pee Wee" (1906– 1969), 161, 162, 190, 210, 228, 308, 310, 589, 727, 776
Russell, Dillon "Curley" (1920– 1986), 376, 322, 675
Russell, George (b. 1923), 351, 354, 355, 405, 411, 413, 414, 438, 446,

447, 449, 451, 452, 470, 516, 528, 541, 594, 625, 657, 755
Russell, Luis (1902–1963), 155–56, 271, 279, 283, 288, 307, 633, 691
Russell, Ross, 753, 780
Russell, William, 99, 586, 752, 753
Russia, 119, 482
Russo, Bill (b. 1928), 354, 405, 412, 416, 518, 755
Rust, Brian, 752
Rutgers University, Institute of Jazz Studies, 520, 756, 762
Rutherford, Paul, 458, 546, 639
Ryan, Jimmy, 313, 727
Ryker, Doc, 128
Rypdal, Terje (b. 1947), 493, 508

Saarinen, Eero, 213
Sachs, Aaron (b. 1923), 479
Saddler, Frank, 268
St. Cyr, Johnny (1890–1966), 97, 106, 109, 643, 660
St. Francis Hotel (San Francisco), 268
St. Louis Blues (film), 86, 240, 709
St. Louis, Missouri, 32, 99, 156, 301, 704, 772
Salazar, Max, 750
Salis, Antonello, 546
Salle Pleyel concerts: of Armstrong, 116
Salle Productions, 243
Salsa, 523, 530, 531, 532, 549
Saludos Amigos (film), 554
Samba, 522, 548–49, 552, **553**, 554, 558
Sampson, Edgar (1907–1973), 285, 286, 712
Samuels, Dave (b. 1948), 652
San Francisco, California: Barbary Coast in, 697, 722; jazz clubs in, 697, 722; Morton in, 93; New Orleans jazz in, 602; and New Orleans revival, 313, 314
Sanborn, David (b. 1945), 602, 611
Sanchez, David (b. 1968), 533
Sandburg, Carl, 743
Sanders, Pharoah (b. 1940), 444, 502, 510, 796
Sandke, Randy (b. 1949), 6, 125, 131, 513
Sandole, Dennis, 433, 435, 441
Sandoval, Arturo (b. 1949), 532, 626
The Sandpiper (film), 262
Sangster, John (b. 1928), 582
Sanjek, Russell, 752
Sankei Hall (Japan), 570
Santamaria, Mongo (b. 1922), 529, 530–31, 657–58
Santana, 511, 531
Santoro, Gene, 522
Saratoga Club (New York City), 155
Sargeant, Winthrop, 753
Sash, Leon, 665, 666
Satchmo the Great (documentary), 118
Satie, Erik, 347, 719–20
Satin Doll (Tokyo), 733

Teagarden, Charlie (1913–1984), 160, 618

Teagarden, Jack (1905–1964), 67, 118, 157, 159, 160, 161, 210–11, 218, 220, 223, 232–33, 269, 314, 570, 618, 631–32, 639, 687, 773

Television, 240, 260, 408, **714–21**

Temperley, Joe (b. 1929), 608

Tempo Club (New York City), 57, 267

Ten-Part Invention (Pochee group), 582

Tent show bands, 51–52, 267

Terai, Naoko, 574

Termini, Iggy, 728

Termini, Joe, 728

Terrasson, Jacky (b. 1965), 500

Terrell, Pha, 477

Territory bands, 272–73, 284, 772

Terry, Clark (b. 1920), 138, 409, 623, 640

Teschemacher, Frank (1906–1932), 153, 162, 286, 307, 588–89

Texaco's Swing Into Spring (TV special), 719

Texas: dance in, 704

Texas blues, 772

Texas dime store circuit, 91

"Texas draw" style, 632

Texas Playboys (Wills band), 452

Texas Tommy dance, 697

Texier, Henri (b. 1945), 546

Thacker, Eric, 110

Tharpe, Sister Rosetta (1921–1973), 72

THE Orchestra (Timer-Conover band), 414

Theatre Owner's Booking Association (TOBA), 82, 85, 86

Theatrical industry: and origins of jazz, 44

Theimer, Joe (Joe Timer) (1923–1955), 414, 433

Thelin, Eje (1938–1990), 639

Thelonious Monk: Straight No Chaser (documentary film), 719

Thelonious Monk competition, 626

Thiam, Mor, 562

Thiele, Bob, 778, 785

Thielemans, Jean "Toots" (b. 1922), 556, 666, 667

Thigpen, Ed (b. 1930), 257, 463, 695

Third Rail (fusion band), 511

Third stream, 335, 353–56

This Is Jazz (radio show), 311

This and That (revue), 63

Thomas, George "Fathead," 156

Thomas, Kid (1896–1987), 314

Thomas, Michael Tilson, 245

Thomas, Walter "Foots" (1907–1981), 290

Thompson, Sir Charles (b. 1918), 75, 370

Thompson, Creighton, 39

Thompson, Don (b. 1940), 578, 678

Thompson, E. E., 59

Thompson, Eli "Lucky" (b. 1924), 71, 301, 377, 393, 407, 607, 673

Thompson, Gail, 543

Thornhill, Claude (1909–1965), 230, 335, 350, 392, 408, 413, 661, 663

Thornton, Argonne (Sadik Hakim) (1922–1983), 364

Threadgill, Henry (b. 1944), 483, 494, 495, 518

Three Blazers (Johnny Moore band), 74

Three Caballeros (film), 554

Three Deuces (Chicago), 730

Three Deuces (New York City), 302, 727

Three Sounds (trio), 76

The Threepenny Opera (musical), 118

369th Infantry Regiment, 59

Thurman, Wallace, 739

Tiberi, Frank (b. 1928), 665

"Ticklers," 163, 165, 175

Tidiane-Seck, Cheik, 563

Tilton, Martha, 749

The Time of the Barracudas (play), 397

Time magazine, 139, 336, 367, 464, 499

Time-lines, 10, 13, 14, 15

Timer, Joe (Joe Theimer) (1923–1955), 414, 433

Timmons, Bobby (1935–1974), 371, 380, 381, 385, 464

Timms, Jonathan. *See* Abdul-Malik, Ahmed

Tin Pan Alley: and African jazz, 561; and Bessie Smith, 87; and Ellington, 133; and influences on Parker, 317; and jazz singing, 220, 232, 481; and radio/television, 255, 260; and ragtime, 36; and recording industry, 775; and roots/origins of jazz, 45, 60

Tinkler, Scott, 582

Tinney, Al, 728

Tio, Lorenzo Jr. (1893–1933), 525, 585, 586, 757

Tio, Louis "Papa," 89

Tio family, 525, 757

Tiomkin, Dmitri, 714

Tippett, Sir Michael, 347

Tizol, Juan (1900–1984), 133, 258, 326–27, 409, 526, 633, 635, 636, 637

Tjader, Cal (1925–1982), 529, 530, 531, 651

Tluczkiewicz, Tomasz, 544

Todd, Rick, 664

Togashi, Masahiko (b. 1940), 573, 574

Tokyo, Japan. *See* Japan

Tolkien, J.R.R., 582

Tolliver, Charles (b. 1942), 516

Tolliver's Circus and Musical Extravaganza, 68

Tolonen, Jukka, 508

Tom Brown's White Band From Dixieland, 152

Tonal system, 19, 20, 21–22, 23, 26, 28, 46

Tone Center label, 511

Tonight Show Band (Severinsen band), 417, 623

Tony Awards, 223, 705

Too Late Blues (film), 714

Toomer, Jean, 739

Tormé, Mel (1925–1999), 473, 475, 479–80, 481, 484

Toro, Yomo, 532

Touch of Evil (film), 717

Tough, Dave (1908–1948), 153, 210, 212, 282, 288, 304, 316- 17, 405, 591, 675, 687, 689

Town Hall concerts (New York City), 204, 211, 228, 429–30, 439, 528, 529, 684

Towner, Ralph (b. 1940), 648

Treadwell, George (1919–1967), 242–43, 244, 728

Treemonisha (opera), 33, 37, 348

Trent, Alphonso (1905–1959), 273, 772

Trent, Jo, 135

Trianon Ballroom (Chicago), 268

Triangle (instrument), 13

Trio de Clarinettes (Sclavis group), 596

A Trip to Coontown (musical), 56

Tristano, Lennie (1919–1978), 219, 258, 340, 353, 365, 367, 398–99, 426, 450, 451, 464, 571, 594, 609, 637, 647, 676, 729, 796

Trocadero Orchestra (Coughlan group), 579–80

Trombone, 14, 24, 49, 213, 530, 600, **628–41**. *See also specific musician*

Tropicalia, 522

Tropicana (Havana club), 531

Troupe, Quincy, 744

Trumbauer, Frank (1901–1956), 127–28, 129, 156–57, 158, 159, 160, 180, 181, 193, 194, 232, 233, 256–58, 273, 275, 333, 517, 601, 604, 605, 664, 771

Trumpet, 14, 24, 69, 167, 213, 375, 528, 600, **613–27**. *See also specific musician*

Tsunoda, Takashi, 567

Tuba, 14, 600, 661

Tuba tribe, 574

Tubman, Harriett, 510

Tucker, Ben (b. 1930), 678

Tucker, Bobby (b. 1923), 249

Tucker, Earl "Snake Hips," 702

Tucker, Mark, 132

Tucker, Sophie, 223, 246

Tulane University, 91, 92, 520, 756

Tunstall, Fred, 61

Turkey trot, 35, 36, 58, 697

Turner, Dale, 545, 713

Turner, Dave, 578

Turner, Joe (1907–1990), 61

Turner, Joe (1911–1985), 71, 731

Turney, Joe, 64

Turney, Pete, 64

Turre, Steve (b. 1949), 640

Turrentine, Stanley (b. 1934), 387, 785

111, 161, 220, 221, 223–24, 226, 228, 229, 231, 233, 246, 475, 712, 769

Waters, Muddy, 68, 505

Watkins, Doug (1934–1962), 379, 381, 663, 677

Watkins, Julius (1921–1977), 663

Watkins, Ralph, 727

Watrous, Bill (b. 1939), 640

Watson, Leo (1898–1950), 221, 234, 475, 726

Watters, Lu (1911–1989), 309, 311–12, 313, 512, 778

Watts, Jeff (b. 1960), 694

Watts, Trevor, 458

Wax label, 782

Waxman, Franz, 714

Weather Report, 132, 400, 468, 507, 508, 509, 510, 511, 539, 562, 609, 611, 658, 694

Webb, George, 311, 313

Webb, Jack, 713

Webb, Joe, 433

Webb, William "Chick" (1902–1939), 72, 212, 238–39, 241, 242, 243, 279, 285, 286, 375, 478, 526, 527, 633, 653, 655, 673, 683, 685–86, 689, 701, 726

Weber, Eberhard (b. 1940), 493, 678

Webster, Ben (1909–1973), 137, 173,176, 196, 210, 215, 216, 219, 229, 247, 259, 409, 495, 541, 542, 569, 593, 604, 728, 731, 733, 784

Webster, Paul (1909–1966), 623

Weck, Dave, 694

Weeks, Anson, 272

Weill, Kurt (1900–1950), 347

Wein, George (b. 1925), 459, 515, 517–18

Weinstein, Norman C., 561

Weinstock, Bob, 781

Weiss, Helen, 131

Welburn, Ron, 750

Welding, Pete, 752

Welles, Orson, 717

Wellman, Ricky, 402

Wellman, Wilburn, 402

Wells, Dicky (1909–1985), 71, 213, 283, 410, 633, 634

Wells, John "Preacher," 244

Wellstood, Dick (1927–1987), 312, 371, 461, 513

Welty, Eudora, 737

Wenrich, Percy, 33

Werley, Pete, 81

Wess, Frank (b. 1922), 410, 655, 713

West Africa, 562–63, 564–65

West African Instrumental Quintet, 561

West Coast: and blues, 76; concert music on, 352–53; fusion on, 503; and hard bop, 381–82; and New Orleans revival, 309, 313; and origins of jazz, 41; territory bands on, 273. See also California; Los Angeles, California; San Francisco, California; West Coast jazz

West Coast jazz, **332–42**, 370, 392,

478, 479, 608, 622, 640, 655, 663, 664, 732. See also Cool jazz

West Indies music, 610

West, Mae, 710

West Side Story (musical), 259, 349

Westbrook, Kate, 482

Westminster Abbey (London): Ellington at, 140

Weston, Paul, 282

Weston, Randy (b. 1926), 146, 369, 464, 563

Wettling, George (1907–1968), 288, 308

Wexler, Jerry, 74

Wheeler, Kenny (b. 1930), 458, 542, 575, 577, 626

Whetsol, Arthur (1905–1940), 136

Whigham, Jiggs (b. 1943), 640

Whipper, Leigh, 81

Whistling, 667

White, Andrew (b. 1942), 516

White Elephant (Mainieri band), 507

White, Harry (1898–1962), 290

White, Herbert, 701

White, Lucien, 749

White, Michael (b. 1933), 507

White, Dr. Michael, 596

White House (Washington, D.C.), 245, 459, 706

Whiteman, Paul (1890–1967), 22, 24, 59, 126, 129–30, 131, 158, 160, 161, 193–94, 209, 210, 225, 228, 233, 257, 268–70, 272, 274–75, 279, 281, 286, 288, 345, 348–49, 351, 516, 517, 519, 539, 563, 600, 602, 664, 697, 699, 701, 735, 741, 745–46, 747–48. See also specific musician or recording

Whiteman, Walt, 743

Whitey's Lindy Hoppers, 701, 703, 704

Who, 502, 507

Whyte, Zach, 273

Wickman, Putte (b. 1924), 593

Wiedoeft, Rudy, 317, 600

Wiggin, John, 130

Wiggins, Fred, 151

Wilber, Bob (b. 1928), 131, 312, 315, 512, 513, 515, 596, 609

Wilborn, Dave, 515

Wilburn, Vincent, 401

Wilcox, Eddie (Edwin) (1907–1968), 282

Wilcox, Spiegel (1903–1999), 128

Wild, Herb, 130

The Wild One (film), 716

Wildcats (Wilber band), 312

Wilder, Alec (1907–1980), 144, 259–60, 349

Wilder, Joe (b. 1922), 622

Wilen, Barney (1937–1996), 546, 610

Wiley, Lee (1915–1975), 220, 221, 227–28, 233

Wilkins, Ernie (1919–1999), 71, 244, 410

Willard, Patricia, 235

William Morris Agency, 184

Williams, Andy, 783

Williams, Bert, 35, 56

Williams, Charles "Buster" (b. 1942), 399

Williams, Charles "Cootie" 1910–1985), 69, 136, 137, 139, 214–15, 232, 291, 298, 403, 409, 419, 422, 590, 618

Williams, Clarence (1893–1965), 45, 91, 92, 96–97, 108–9, 143, 151, 155, 290, 769, 770

Williams, Claude, 70

Williams, Corky, 61

Williams, Elmer, 286

Williams, George, 413, 517, 686

Williams, Henry "Rubberlegs" (1907–1962), 303, 391

Williams, Joe (1918–1999), 71, 229, 410, 480, 484

Williams, John: *Star Wars* score by, 718

Williams, John A., 741

Williams, Martin, 146, 326, 446, 454, 457, 516, 752, 754, 786

Williams, Mary Lou (1910–1981), 140, 170, **172–73**, 190, 200, 285, 287, 296, 360–61, 376, 421, 459, 462, 727, 777, 780

Williams, Midge (1908–1940s), 567

Williams, Sandy (1906–1991), 286, 633–34

Williams, Tony (1945–1997), 396, 397, 398, 399, 467, 491, 506–7, 510, 648, 675, 680, 690, 692–93, 694, 795

Williams College: Whiteman collection at, 517

Wills, Bob, 452

Wilmer, Valerie, 537

Wilson, Cassandra (b. 1955), 483, 486–87, 558

Wilson, Dick (1911–1941), 287, 731

Wilson, Edith, 112

Wilson, Gerald (b. 1918), 202, 240, 241, 242, 382, 409, 414, 416, 518, 520, 620, 691, 783

Wilson, Jack "the Bear," 61

Wilson, John S., 606, 752, 754

Wilson, Nancy (b. 1937), 483, 484

Wilson, Olly, 12

Wilson, Quinn, 283

Wilson, Rossiere "Shadow" (1919–1959), 687, 688

Wilson, Teddy (1912–1986), 115, 173–74, 175, 193, 198, 204, 214, 215, 218, 226, 246, 247, 254, 257, 259, 302, 303, 345, 357, 359, 360, 361, 362, 363, 364, 367, 459, 462, 476, 577, 673, 713, 726, 727, 773, 774. See also specific recording

Winchester, Lem (1928–1961), 651

Windhurst, Johnny (1926–1981), 312

Winding, Kai (1922–1983), 411, 412, 637, 638

Winsted's Broadway Rastus, 87

Winstone, Norma (b. 1941), 482

Winter Garden (New Orleans), 92

Winter, Paul, 556, 663

Withdrawal (film), 458

Withers, Bill, 480

Wodehouse, P. G., 268

Index of Songs and Recordings

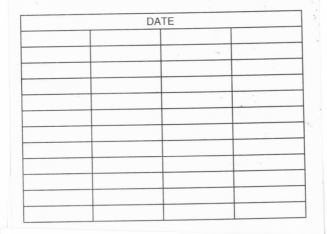